# Sources of East Asian Tradition

## VOLUME 1

INTRODUCTION TO ASIAN CIVILIZATIONS

*Introduction to Asian Civilizations*

Wm. Theodore de Bary, General Editor

*Sources of Japanese Tradition*
(1958; vol. 1, 2nd ed., 2001; vol. 2, 2nd ed., 2005; vol. 2, 2nd ed., abr., 2006)

*Sources of Indian Tradition*
(1958; 2nd ed., 1988)

*Sources of Chinese Tradition*
(1960; vol. 1, 2nd ed., 1999; vol. 2, 2nd ed., 2000)

*Sources of Korean Tradition*
(vol. 1, 1997; vol. 2, 2001)

*Sources of East Asian Tradition*
(vols. 1 and 2, 2008)

# Sources of East Asian Tradition

## VOLUME 1: PREMODERN ASIA

*Edited by Wm. Theodore de Bary*

WITH THE COLLABORATION OF

Irene Bloom

Yongho Ch'oe

Carol Gluck

Peter H. Lee

Donald Keene

Richard Lufrano

George Tanabe

Paul Varley

Burton Watson

COLUMBIA UNIVERSITY PRESS
NEW YORK

Columbia University Press
*Publishers Since 1893*
New York   Chichester, West Sussex

Library of Congress Cataloging-in-Publication Data
Sources of East Asian tradition / edited by Wm. Theodore de Bary with the collaboration of
Irene Bloom . . . [et al.].
        v. cm.—(Introduction to Asian civilizations)
    Contents: v. 1. Premodern Asia
            v. 2. The modern period
    ISBN 978-0-231-14304-2 (vol. 1 cloth : alk. paper)
    ISBN 978-0-231-14305-9 (vol. 1 paper : alk. paper)
    ISBN 978-0-231-14322-6 (vol. 2 cloth : alk. paper)
    ISBN 978-0-231-14323-3 (vol. 2 paper : alk. paper)
    1. East Asia—Civilization—Sources.   I. De Bary, William Theodore, 1919–
DS509.3.S677    2008
950—dc22                                                    2007028403
∞

Columbia University Press books are printed on permanent and durable acid-free paper.
Printed in the United States of America
c 10 9 8 7 6 5 4 3 2 1
p 10 9 8

# CONTENTS

# PREFACE

As a theater of cultural exchange, East Asia has been a reality since prehistoric times and, at least for the Koreans and Japanese, a political and economic fact of life throughout history. Recently, a growing interdependence — including economic, political, and military involvements among the people of East Asia — has spread even into the sphere of popular culture. What remains for us to recognize more fully now is the need in education to understand better the deeper cultural commonalities that link China, Korea, and Japan, which may also afford us some shared ground on which to evaluate cultural differences.

Each of the countries on the rim of Asia cherishes its own autonomy, but each also recognizes that in today's world independence can be preserved only in association with its neighbors and with some degree of mutual support. The Taiwanese, for instance, cannot assert their own autonomy (whatever form that might take) if they see their identity — their cultural roots — as simply Chinese and not shared to some degree with other East Asian, or even Western, countries.

If, however, none of the major Asian traditions (for example, Confucianism, Buddhism) can be appreciated today simply as products of one particular culture, they are still particular enough so that no one can be taken for the whole. To regard any single culture or tradition as representing "the East," Asia, or East Asia can be just as misleading and, at worst, productive of a misbegotten "inevitable clash of civilizations" (as, say, between "China and the West").

Nevertheless, for all of us, learning has to start somewhere. Even though no one can say definitively what the starting point should be for anyone else, at some stage in the process, comparison comes into play. It is the purpose of *Sources of East Asian Tradition* to help readers make some of those comparative judgments in an Asian context before they are tempted to make direct, often simplistic, comparisons with their own culture.

To start the process with source readings assumes that it is best done by looking first at what each of these traditions has had to say for itself, insofar as original texts in translation can serve this need. Better to work inductively from the established artifacts ratified by each tradition itself—what has survived the scrutiny and contestation of sustained discourse over time—than to proceed from some preconceived modern or postmodern theory. Granted that this notion itself is "theory," it at least tries to show respect for what others have thought about themselves before forming one's own judgment.

To compress six volumes of *Sources* (Chinese, Korean, and Japanese) into two, "Premodern" and "Modern," naturally runs the risk of gross oversimplification; however, we trust that readers aware of this danger will check the original *Sources* for fuller treatments of the topics dealt with in these books.

WM. THEODORE DE BARY

# ACKNOWLEDGMENTS

Since *Sources of East Asian Tradition* draws largely on the previously published *Sources of Chinese, Korean,* and *Japanese Traditions,* it is appropriate to acknowledge this as one more stage in a process that has depended on the accumulated wisdom and generous cooperation of many scholars over the years. So ambitious a project could not have been conceived or brought to its first stage of completion in 1958 to 1960 had it not been for the collaboration of Ryusaku Tsunoda, who initiated Japanese studies at Columbia in the 1930s, and Wing-tsit Chan, who pioneered in the teaching of Chinese philosophy at the University of Hawaii and Dartmouth and Chatham Colleges. Among the many others who have contributed (and are mentioned more in particular elsewhere in this volume), some whose larger editorial as well as scholarly contributions should be acknowledged here are Irene Bloom, Yongho Ch'oe, Carol Gluck, Peter H. Lee, Donald Keene, Richard Lufrano, George Tanabe, Paul Varley, and Burton Watson.

Throughout the long history of this project, two other persons who have rendered outstanding service in the publication process are Miwa Kai, former curator of the Japanese Collection at Columbia, and my secretary for more than eighteen years, Marianna Stiles. More recently, the process has been facilitated by David Nee, carrying on with the work once done by his mother, Brett de Bary Nee, in the 1950s. As a family project, it almost goes without saying, its most enduring supporter over the fifty-eight years of its life has been my wife, Fanny Brett de Bary.

WM. THEODORE DE BARY

PART I

# Traditional China

*Edited by*
**Wm. Theodore de Bary**

WITH THE COLLABORATION OF

*Irene Bloom*
*Wing-tsit Chan*
*Ron Guey Chu*
*David N. Keightley*
*Richard John Lynn*
*Sarah Queen*
*Harold Roth*
*Nathan Sivin*
*Daniel Stevenson*
*Franciscus Verellen*
*Burton Watson*
*Philip B. Yampolsky*
*Chün-fang Yü*

# EXPLANATORY NOTE

The sources of translations given at the end of each selection are rendered as concisely as possible; full bibliographical data can be obtained from the list of sources at the end of the book. Unless otherwise indicated, the author of the text is the writer whose name precedes the selection; the initials following each selection are those of the translator, as indicated in the table of contents. Excerpts that have been taken from existing translations have sometimes been adapted or edited in the interests of uniformity with the book as a whole.

In translating Chinese terms it is rarely possible to find an exact or full equivalent in Western languages. In view of this difficulty, some scholars consider the path of strict virtue to lie in reproducing the romanized form of the word rather than some mere approximation of it. This may do for those already familiar with the original language but not for readers who have difficulty coping with many foreign names and terms all at once, especially if they are encountering for the first time several Asian traditions in succession and several different (and often confusing) romanization systems. Consequently, we have felt obliged to give a rendering in English wherever possible, and some explanation where it is not possible. Although this policy may not satisfy the purist (for whom only a reading of the text in the original would really suffice), it does face, directly if not perfectly, what these terms can mean in another language instead of leaving the meaning altogether obscure behind the veil of romanization.

Given the need to translate, we have tried to be consistent, but often it is not possible to provide a single rendering of terms so broad in meaning as to function in different senses in different contexts. Therefore, at the point of first appearance we insert the romanized Chinese word in parentheses following the translation, and if another rendering has to be given later for the same word in Chinese, we insert the romanized form again. At the end of part I is a glossary of key terms listed in romanized Chinese (*pinyin* and Wade-Giles), with alternate renderings in English; from this the reader can approximate the range of meanings that cluster around such pivotal terms.

Chinese words and names are rendered according to the *pinyin* system of romanization. For readers unfamiliar with *pinyin*, it is useful to know that the consonants *q* and *x* are to be read as *ch* and *hs*, respectively. The Wade-Giles romanization is also given for names and terms already well known in that form, as are the renderings preferred by important modern figures and in common use (such as Sun Yatsen). A comparative table of *pinyin* and Wade-Giles romanizations may be found at the end of part I. Indic words appearing in the chapters on Buddhism as technical terms or titles in italics follow the standard systems of transliteration.

Chinese names are rendered in their Chinese order, with the family name first and the personal name last. Chinese names are romanized in the *pinyin* system, except for persons known to have preferred Wade-Giles or an alternative spelling, in which case that preference is honored both in the text and in the bibliography. Dates given after personal names are those of birth and death; in the case of rulers, their reign dates are preceded by "r." An approximation of the active lifespan of persons whose exact dates of birth and death are not known is indicated by "fl." (*floruit*). Generally the name by which a person was most commonly known in Chinese tradition is the one used in the text. Since this book is intended for the general reader rather than the specialist, we have not burdened the text with a list of the alternate names or titles that usually accompany biographical reference to a scholar in Chinese or Japanese historical works.

Titles of collections frequently cited are abbreviated as follows:

BNB     *Bonaben ershisi shi*. 820 ce. Shanghai: Commercial Press, 1930–1937.

DZ      [*Zhengtong*] *Daozang*. 1,120 vols. Taipei: Yiwen yinshu guan, 1962.

GXJC    *Guoxue jiben congshu*. Shanghai: Commercial Press, 1932?–1939?

SBBY    *Sibu beiyao*. 537 titles in 1,372 ce. Shanghai: Zhonghua shuju, 1927–1935.

SBCK    *Sibu congkan*. 1st ser. 323 titles in 2,102 ce. Shanghai: Commercial Press, 1920–1922, reprint 1929. 3d ser. Shanghai: Commercial Press, 1935.

SKQS    [*Wenyuan ge*] *Siku quanshu*. 1,500 vols. Taibei: Taiwan shangwu yinshu guan, 1983–1986.

TD      *Taishō* [*shinshū*] *daizōkyō*. Ed. Takakusu Junjirō and Watanabe Kaigyoku. 85 vols. Tokyo: Taishō issai-kyō kankō-kai, 1914–1922.

ZZ      [*Dai-Nihon*] *zoku zōkyō*. 750 vols. Kyoto: Zōkyō shoin, 1905–1912.

ZZMJ    *Zhongguo zixue mingzhu jicheng*. Taibei, 1977.

# CONTRIBUTORS

The translators' initials follow each selection.

| | |
|-----|-----|
| AD | Albert Dien |
| BW | Burton Watson |
| CFY | Chün-fang Yü |
| CH | Charles Hartman |
| CO | Charles D. Orzech |
| CS | Conrad Schirokauer |
| deB | Wm. Theodore de Bary |
| DNK | David N. Keightley |
| DS | Daniel Stevenson |
| DSN | David S. Nivison |
| DWYK | Daniel W. Y. Kwok |
| EF | Edward Farmer |
| GT | George Tanabe |
| HR | Harold Roth |
| IB | Irene Bloom |
| JHS | Joanna Handlin Smith |
| JM | John T. Meskill |
| KS | Kidder Smith |
| LH | Leon Hurvitz |
| MG | Marie Guarino |

| | |
|---|---|
| NS | Nathan Sivin |
| PY | Philip B. Yampolsky |
| RGC | Ron Guey Chu |
| RJL | Richard John Lynn |
| SQ | Sarah Queen |
| TGF | T. Griffith Foulk |
| THT | Tsai Heing-ting |
| TK | Theresa Kelleher |
| TW | Tu Weiming |
| WTC | Wing-tsit Chan |

# CHRONOLOGY

*Prehistory and Early History*
(Pre-Zhou dates and entries are traditional; modern dating in parentheses)

| B.C.E. | Dynasty | | |
|---|---|---|---|
| 2852 | | | Fu Xi, inventor of writing, nets and snares, hunting and fishing |
| 2737 | Culture heroes | | Shen Nong, inventor of agriculture, commerce, |
| 2697 | | | Yellow Emperor |
| 2357 | Sage kings | | Yao |
| | | | Shun |
| | | | Yu, virtuous founder of dynasty |
| 1818 | Xia | | Jie, degenerate terminator of dynasty |
| 1766 | Shang or Yin | | King Tang, virtuous founder of dynasty |
| [c. 1300] | | | [Beginning of archaeological evidence] |
| 1154 | | | Zhou, degenerate terminator of dynasty |
| Three Dynasties | Zhou | | King Wen, virtuous founder of dynasty |
| 1122 (1045/1040?) | | | King Wu, virtuous founder of dynasty |
| | | | King Cheng, virtuous founder of dynasty |

|  |  |  |
|---|---|---|
| 771 { | Western Zhou |  |
|  | Eastern Zhou |  |
| 722–479 |  | Spring and Autumn period |
| 551–479 |  | Confucius |
| 479–221 |  | Warring States period (479–221) |
| 6th to 3d centuries |  | Period of the "hundred schools" of thought: Confucius, Mozi, Mencius, Laozi (?), Zhuangzi, Terminologists, Shang Yang, Xunzi, Sunzi, Han Fei |
| 4th to 3d centuries |  | Extensive wall-building and waterworks by Qin and other states |
| 249 |  | Lü Buwei, prime minister of Qin |
| 221–207 | Qin | The First Emperor; Li Si, prime minister |
| 214 |  | The Great Wall "completed" |
| 202–9 C.E. | Former Han dynasty |  |
| 202–195 | Reign of Han Gaozu |  |
| 170 | Lu Jia (?–170), advisor to Han Gaozu |  |
| 188–180 | Reign of Empress Lü |  |
| 180–157 | Reign of Emperor Wen |  |
| 201–168? | Jia Yi, poet, essayist, and advisor to Emperor Wen |  |
| 178 | Memorial on encouragement of agriculture by Chao Cuo |  |
| 141–87 | Reign of Emperor Wu |  |
| 136 | Doctors for the Five Classics appointed |  |
| 124 | Increased use of examinations in recruitment of officials |  |
| 122 | Death of Liu An, patron of compilers of *Huainanzi* |  |
| c. 120 | Employment of Legalist-minded officials to manage fiscal operations of the state. State monopoly of production of iron and salt; debased coinage and commercial taxes; expansion of empire |  |
| 115 | Campaigns into western regions |  |
| 195?–105? | Dong Zhongshu, leading Confucian philosopher and advisor to Emperor Wu |  |
| 108 | Chinese administration in north Korea |  |
| 101 | Conquest of states of Tarim basin |  |
| 145?–86? | Sima Qian, author of *Records of the Grand Historian* |  |
| 81 | Debates on Salt and Iron |  |
| C.E. |  |  |
| 1 | Wang Mang regent |  |
| 9–23 | Xin dynasty, established by usurper Wang Mang |  |
| 25–220 | Latter Han dynasty |  |
| 32–92 | Ban Gu, principal compiler of the *History of the Former Han* |  |
| c. 65 | First reference to Buddhism in China |  |

| | |
|---|---|
| 684–705 | Reign of Empress ("Emperor") Wu |
| 7th century | Civil service examinations further developed; adoption of system of land nationalization and apportionment according to family size |
| 712 | Fazang (643–712), third patriarch and systematizer of teachings of the Flower Garland (Huayan) school of Buddhism |
| 713 | Huineng (638–713), sixth patriarch of Chan Buddhism |
| 713–756 | Reign of Tang Emperor Xuanzong |
| 721 | Liu Zhiji (661–721), author of the *Understanding of History* (*Shitong*) |
| 755–763 | An Lushan Rebellion |
| 762 | Li Bo (701–762), poet of High Tang |
| 770 | Du Fu (712–770), poet of High Tang |
| 780 | Adoption of Twice-a-Year Tax of Yang Yan (727–781) |
| 801 | *Comprehensive Statutes* (*Tongdian*) by Du You (735–812) |
| 814 | Baizhang Huaihai (720–824), reputed author of first Chan monastic rules |
| 819 | Liu Zongyuan (773–819), poet, essayist, official; defender of centralized government |
| 824 | Han Yu (768–824), poet, essayist, civil servant; critic of Buddhism and Daoism; supporter of strong, centralized monarchy |
| 845 | Official repression of Buddhism under Emperor Wuzong (r. 841–845) |
| 867 | Linji Yixuan (d. 867), founder of Linji school of Chan Buddhism |
| 869 | Dongshan Liangjie (807–869), founder of Caodong sect of Chan Buddhism |
| 901 | Caoshan Benji (840–901), follower of Liangjie in the Caodong tradition |
| 907–960 | Five Dynasties period: disunion after fall of Tang |
| 932 | First printing of Nine Classics begun |
| 933 | Du Guangting (850–933), scholar and court Daoist |
| 960–1279 | Song dynasty |
| 960–1126 | Northern Song period |
| 972 | Printing of Buddhist canon begun |
| 11th century | Period of Confucian revival |
| 1019 | Daoist canon (*Daozang*) printed under state sponsorship |
| 1023–1063 | Reign of Emperor Renzong; reform program of Fan Zhongyan |
| 1063–1135 | Yuanwu Keqin, Chan master whose lectures are collected in the *Blue Cliff Records* (*Biyanlu*) of 1128 |
| 1068–1085 | Reign of Emperor Shenzong; Wang Anshi and his New Measures: state marketing, Ever-Normal Granary, crop loans, militia system, local service exemption, "square-fields" system |
| 1086 | Sima Guang prime minister; author of *Comprehensive Mirror in Aid of Government* (*Zizhi tongjian*) |

| | |
|---|---|
| 1098 | Fan Zuyu (1041–1098): Lectures from the Classics Mat |
| 1112–1170 | Wang Zhe, founder of the Quanzhen tradition of Daoism |
| 1126 | Beginning of Southern Song period; Jurchen invade north China, establishing Jin dynasty in north and forcing Song to move south |
| 1127–1279 | Southern Song period |
| 1162 | *Comprehensive Treatises* (*Tongzhi*) by Zheng Qiao (1104–1162) |
| 1193 | Lu Jiuyuan (Xiangshan, 1139–1193); the universal mind and the mind as principle |
| 1194 | Chen Liang (1143–1194); "utilitarian" Confucianism |
| 1200 | Zhu Xi (1130–1200); the Neo-Confucian synthesis; philosophy of principle and material-force, the mind of the Way and the human mind, the nature endowed by Heaven and the physical nature; community granaries and community compact; education for "the governance of men" |
| 1227 | Mongols' destruction of Xixia; death of Chinggis Khaghan |
| 1229 | Printing of the *Extended Meaning of the Great Learning* (*Daxue yanyi*) by Zhen Dexiu (1178–1235) |
| 1260–1368 | Yuan (Mongol) dynasty; defeat of the Song, 1279 |
| 1281 | Xu Heng (1209–1281), transmitter of Neo-Confucianism to Emperor Shizu (Khubilai Khaghan, r. 1260–1294) |
| 1313 | Adoption by Mongol government of civil service examinations based on Confucian classics |
| 1324? | Ma Duanlin (1254–1324?), compiler of *Wenxian tongkao* |
| 1368–1644 | Ming dynasty |
| 1368–1398 | Reign of Ming Taizu, first emperor of the Ming; the Great Ming Code, the Great Ming Commandments; reestablishment of the examination system; abolition of prime ministership; Sacred Edict; deepening of autocracy |
| 1402 | Yongle usurpation; accession of Chengzu (r. 1402–1424) |
| 1402 | Martyrdom of Fang Xiaoru (1357–1402) |
| 1406–1421 | Mongolian campaigns; intervention in Annam; maritime expeditions of Zheng He |
| 1417 | Zhu Xi's commentaries on the classics and other Neo-Confucian writings published under authority of the Yongle emperor; edited by Hu Guang (1370–1418) |
| 1529 | Wang Yangming (1472–1529); the unity of knowledge and action; extension of innate knowledge |
| 1541 | Wang Gen (1483–1541); follower of Wang Yangming, left-wing Taizhou school |
| 1547 | Luo Qinshun (1465–1547); the philosophy of *qi*; critic of subjectivism of Wang Yangming thought |
| 1567 | Chen Jian (1497–1567), scholar and historian, critic of Wang Yangming school |

1583          Wang Ji (1498–1583); follower of Wang Yangming; believed human mind to be beyond good and evil; faith in innate knowledge

1602          Matteo Ricci established in Peking

1602          Li Zhi (1527–1602); individualism, subjectivism, non-conformism

1604          Neo-orthodox Donglin Academy founded, Gu Xiancheng (1550–1612) principal founder; criticism of corruption at Ming court

1618          Lü Kun (1536–1618); compassion for common people; dedication to humanitarian service

1644          Fall of the Ming to internal revolt and invading Manchu forces

1645          Suicide of Liu Zongzhou (1578–1645)

## Chapter 1

## THE ORACLE-BONE INSCRIPTIONS OF THE
## LATE SHANG DYNASTY

## THE SHANG DYNASTY

Traditional accounts of early China present the Shang as the second historical dynasty (ca. 1554–1045/1040 B.C.E.),[1] succeeding to the Xia and succeeded by the Zhou (1045/1040–256 B.C.E.). Because no written records of the Xia have yet been discovered, the Shang, with its inscriptions on oracle bones and bronze vessels, may currently be regarded as China's first historical dynasty. Archaeology now reveals that other incipient Bronze Age states were emerging from the chiefdom stage toward the end of the second millennium B.C.E. It was the Shang, however, that literati of the Zhou and Han (206 B.C.E.–220 C.E.) came to regard as one of the dynastic models upon which later versions of the Chinese polity were founded. Modern research generally confirms that judgment. The oracle-bone inscriptions indicate the degree to which the Late Shang kings and their diviners articulated many of the concerns

---

1. The traditional dating of the Shang and Zhou dynasties has been revised in recent years on the basis of modern studies of archaeological and astronomical evidence. Chinese historians once dated the Shang dynasty from the eighteenth century to the late twelfth century B.C.E.; the revised dating places Shang rule slightly later on the time line, from the sixteenth century to the middle of the eleventh century B.C.E. Experts still disagree about the precise dating of the Zhou conquest, some favoring 1045 and others 1040 B.C.E.

that were to be central to the classical Chinese tradition. In many cases they appear to have provided solutions that proved seminal.

Approximately 150,000 fragments of inscribed Shang oracle bones have now been recovered from near Anyang, in the northern Henan panhandle. This was evidently the site of a major cult center where the Late Shang (ca. 1200–1045 B.C.E.) worshiped their ancestors and buried their last nine kings in large cruciform pit burials in the royal cemetery situated at Xibeigang. The inscriptions, written in an early Chinese script that scholars have been laboring to decipher since the importance of the oracle bones was first recognized a century ago, reveal the existence of an incipient state whose elites dominated a highly stratified society and whose king was able to exercise sovereignty as he issued orders to the officers and populations of various territories under his control. Benefiting from highly developed craft specialization and relying upon an administrative hierarchy, the king and his supporters extracted the agricultural surplus from the dependent peasants and mobilized them for large public works and for warfare.

The dynasty was centered on the royal lineage in which the title of king (*wang*; the graph—i.e., Chinese character—represented the frontal view of a "big man") was often passed from brother to brother before descending to the next generation, though increasingly toward the end of the dynasty, it was passed directly from father to son. Various other powerful groups were attached to this lineage by ties of kinship, real or fictive, and by political interest. Assisted by a core of officers at the capital, the king was able to mobilize his laborers and foot soldiers in groups of thousands, direct them in the construction of royal tombs, send his armies into battle against numerous regional powers on the periphery of the Shang homeland, and, like the rest of the Shang elite, enjoy the products of a sophisticated bronze-casting industry of almost industrial proportions, whose most important products were thousands of glistening ritual bronze vessels. The living used these bronzes in their sacrifices to the ancestors and then placed them in burials, evidently in the belief that the dead could thereby continue to perform cultic practices in the next world, still participating in what may be regarded as "a great chain of ancestral being."

The cult offerings to the ancestors involved the shedding of much blood—of both animal victims and human captives. That a Shang king, when he died, was buried with numerous retainers from all levels of society who accompanied him in death indicates the degree to which the fate of the living was tied to that of their rulers and the degree to which status in this life was continued into the next. Such ties of hierarchical dependency—sanctified by religious belief and reinforced by, as they reinforced, political linkages—were among the great emotional resources of the evolving state, in which religion and kin were inseparable from secular and political activities.

# THE ORACLE-BONE INSCRIPTIONS

Although archaeological discoveries are now suggesting the existence of written characters scratched on Neolithic pots as early as 3000 B.C.E., the earliest corpus of Chinese writing consists of the oracle-bone inscriptions of the Late Shang. These inscriptions record the pyromantic divinations performed at the court of the last nine Shang kings. In this kind of divination, the king or his diviners would address an oral "charge," such as "We will receive millet harvest,"[2] to a specially prepared turtle plastron or cattle scapula while applying a hot poker or brand to produce a series of heat cracks in the shell or bone. They then interpreted these cracks as auspicious or inauspicious, and the king would deliver a prognostication, such as "Auspicious. We will receive harvest."[3] After the divination had taken place, engravers carved the subject of the charge, and (sometimes) the king's forecast, and (less frequently) the result, into the surface of the shell or bone—hence the modern Chinese term *jiaguwen*, "writings on shell and bone." The diviners themselves—whose names, like Chu, Gu, Bin, Que, and Xing, appear in the inscriptions translated below—were apparently members of groups capable of casting their own ritual bronzes, groups whose social and political power was at the service of the king.

Because the twenty-first Shang king, Wu Ding (fl. 1200–1181 B.C.E.), in particular, divined about a wide range of matters—including sacrifices and rituals, divine assistance or approval, requests to ancestral or Nature Powers, sickness, childbirth, the good fortune of the night, the day, or the coming ten-day week, disaster, distress, trouble, dreams, troop mobilizations, military campaigns, meteorological and celestial phenomena, agriculture, settlement building, administrative orders, hunting expeditions and excursions—the inscriptions, carved on bones that the king himself must frequently have seen and handled, provide us with a direct and vivid sense of his daily activities and his religious beliefs.

Many of the divination charges were about what the king should do; he sought the guidance of the cracks in making up his mind. In other cases, the king informed the bone or shell of his intended plans, seeking spiritual reassurance and validation. Many of these charges may be regarded as wishful predictions, demonstrating that Shang divination served as a form of royal prayer, conjuration, and legitimation. In yet other cases the king sought to discover the symbolic, spiritual meaning of events—such as crop failures, illnesses, and dreams—that had already happened. In all these instances, the Shang diviners were searching for hidden meanings—in the cracks themselves and also in

---

2. *HJ* 9950 front. *HJ* is an abbreviation for the standard collection of oracle-bone rubbings; Guo and Hu, *Jiaguwen heji* (hereafter *HJ*).

3. *HJ* 9950 back.

the mundane but spiritually charged phenomena of their daily lives. Because the inscriptions document the king's continual attempts to contact the spiritual Powers that shaped his universe, they throw much light on the concerns of the Shang elite at a time when the earliest Chinese state was being created. The sample inscriptions translated below will indicate how the Shang diviners worked.[4]

## THE HIGH GOD (DI) AND OTHER POWERS

The Shang kings lived in a world that was dominated by a complex pantheon of Powers that included: Di, the High God; Nature Powers, like the (Yellow) River, the Mountain, and Ri, the Sun; Former Lords, like Wang Hai, who were apparently ex-humans whom the cultists now associated with the dynasty; predynastic ancestors, like Shang Jia; dynastic ancestors, whose cult started with Da Yi and ended with the deceased father of the reigning king; and the dynastic ancestresses, the consorts of those kings on the main line of descent, who likewise received cult in the order of their husbands' accession. The worship of the nondynastic Powers, whether natural or human (a distinction that was not sharp), strengthened the king's position by enlarging the scope of his influence in the spiritual world. Such worship may be regarded as a form of "spiritual imperialism" in which the powers worshiped by local populations were co-opted into the Shang pantheon, frequently being placed in the shadowy, and relatively "empty," predynastic space in the ritual genealogy before the time of Da Yi, the founder. The jurisdictional distinctions within the pantheon, particularly those between the Nature Powers, Former Lords, and Predynastic Ancestors at the head of the hierarchy, were by no means rigid; the Shang ritualists conceived of these Powers as sharing many essential features, applying names like High Ancestor to some of them.

The original meaning of the word *di*, the name or title by which the Shang kings addressed their High God and, occasionally, their royal ancestors, remains hard to determine. It is equally hard to determine if the Shang kings regarded Di as their distant ancestor, but the lack of cult addressed to Di suggests that the ancestral tie, if it ever existed, had been greatly muted. If Di had once been an ancestor, the Late Shang kings treated him with uncharacteristic parsimony. The contrast with the generous way in which the kings treated their ancestors is so notable that it implies a difference in kind.

---

4. As with all texts, the meaning of particular divinations needs to be considered in context; other inscriptions on the same bone or shell or about the same topic on another bone or shell, for example, may sometimes provide more information than the brief presentation of one divination by itself can do.

Di's jurisdictions were not always exclusive. The ancestors and Nature Powers could, like Di, also affect harvest, weather, campaigns, and the king's health.[5] It is clear, however, that Di stood at the peak of the ultra-human, ultra-natural hierarchy, giving orders, which no ancestor could do, to the various natural phenomena and responding to the intercessions of the Shang ancestors who were acting on behalf of their living descendants below. That Di was virtually the only Power who could directly order (*ling*) rain or thunder, as well as the only Power who had the winds under his control, sets him apart from all the other Powers, natural, predynastic, or ancestral. His ability to act in this commanding way helps to establish his unique role as the sky god of the Shang pantheon, foreshadowing the role of Heaven in the Zhou period that followed.

Although Di's wishes were not easy to divine, his approval was important to the Shang:

1A.   Crack-making on *renzi* (day 49), Zheng divined: "If we build a settlement, Di will not obstruct (but) approve." Third moon.

1B.   Crack-making on *guichou* (day 50), Zheng divined: "If we do not build a settlement, Di will approve."[6]

2A.   Crack-making on *xinchou* (day 38), Que divined: "Di approves the king (doing something?)."

2B.   Divined: "Di does not approve the king (doing something?)."[7]

Di was also a provider of rain. The king evidently took pride in his ability to forecast Di's meteorological intentions:

3A.   Crack-making on *wuzi* (day 25). Que divined: "Di, when it comes to the fourth moon, will order the rain."

3B.   Divined: "Di will not, when it comes to the present fourth moon, order the rain."

3C.   (Prognostication:) The king read the cracks and said: "On the *ding*-day (e.g., *dingyou* [day 34]) it will rain; if not, it will be a *xin*-day (e.g., *xinchou* [day 38] (that it rains)."

3D.   (Verification:) "(After) ten days, on *dingyou* (day 34), it really did rain."[8]

And, like the ancestors, Di was also capable of causing harm to the Shang:

4A.   Divined: "It is Di who is harming our harvest." Second moon.

4B.   Divined: "It is not Di who is harming our harvest."[9]

---

5. As, for example, in 8A–B, 11, and 12.
6. *HJ* 14206.
7. *HJ* 14198.
8. *HJ* 14138.
9. *HJ* 10124 front.

Di's role as a sender of difficulties, moreover, was not limited to the floods, droughts, and crop failures of the natural world; he could also, on occasion, stimulate an enemy attack:

5. [Divined:] "The Fang (enemy) are harming and attacking (us); it is Di who orders (them) to make disaster for us." Third moon.[10]

6A. Divined: "(Because) the Fang are harming and attacking (us, we) will raise men."

6B. Divined: "It is not Di who orders (the Fang) to make disaster for us."[11]

Di was in part a god of battle. Some twenty divinations end with the incantatory formula "Di will confer assistance on us," and, when the context was specified, Di's assistance always involved warfare, as in:

7. Crack-making on *jiachen* (day 41), Zheng divined: "If we attack the Mafang (another enemy group), Di will confer assistance on us." First moon.[12]

Di's great distance from the Shang, evident in the lack of cult and in his readiness to order enemy attacks (as in 5 and 6A–B) suggests that Di was accessible to various groups, Shang and non-Shang, and probably enigmatic to all. Di at best was an uncertain ally. The Shang prayed for his assistance (as in 7) but divined no ritual or sacrificial procedures for obtaining it in a routine, institutionalized way. After the reign of Wu Ding, in fact, they ceased to divine about Di's assistance at all. Di, in short, does not appear to have been a Jehovah-like figure, watching over his chosen Shang people. That the divination inscriptions record virtually no cult to Di was perhaps because his allegiance was so uncertain that no attempt to influence his intentions was worth pursuing or, at least, divining. The Shang placated their ancestors through the offering of cult; it was evidently the ancestors who were expected to intercede with Di.

Harm might also come from the Nature Powers.

8A. Crack-making on *bingwu* (day 43) divined: "It is the Mountain Power that is harming the rain."

8B. "It is the (Yellow) River Power that is harming the rain."[13]

One of the most common of all Shang divinations, in fact, involved the apotropaic conjuration, divined on the last day of the Shang week, that "in the next ten days (i.e., the next week), there will be no disasters." It was the king's constant concern to

---

10. *HJ* 39912.

11. *HJ* 6746.

12. *HJ* 6664 front.

13. *Tunnan* 2438.

forestall harm and disasters of various types by identifying and mollifying the Powers that might be causing them. The king was particularly exposed to harm (frequently conceived in terms of bad weather) when he left the confines of the cult center on campaign or hunt, as the following conjurations suggest:

9.   "On the present *xin*-day, if the king hunts, the whole day (he) will have no disasters and it will not rain."[14]

10.   "If the king goes to hunt, the whole day he will not encounter the Great Winds."[15]

Other inscriptions reveal that the Winds were not simply meteorological phenomena but were conceived as Powers of great spiritual significance. It is evident, indeed, that the Shang kings lived in and traveled through a landscape that was pregnant with spiritual meaning. They offered cult and prayer to a variety of these non-Shang Powers:

11.   Crack-making on *renwu* (day 19): "To the (Yellow) River Power (we) pray for rain and offer a holocaust."[16]

12.   Crack-making on *xinwei* (day 8): "To the Mountain Power, (we) pray for rain."[17]

The considerable overlap in the jurisdictions of the ancestors and other Powers where the weather and harvests were concerned suggests, in fact, that the Shang had not yet developed orderly and consistent religious explanations for such large and strategically capricious phenomena.

## DIVINATION AND LEGITIMATION

The power of the Shang elites depended, in part, upon their control of superior armaments like bronze dagger-axes and horse-and-chariot teams, but the true authority of the dynasty—like that of the Neolithic chieftains who had preceded them—was psychological. Their material power had to be sanctified and legitimated. Much of the elites' legitimacy derived from their ability—through divination—to define, explain, and control reality, a reality that, in a Bronze Age theocracy, was primarily conceived in religious and familial terms.

The virtual absence of divinatory records that clearly contradict the king's forecasts suggests that the process of divination and record-keeping was generally designed to

---

14. *HJ* 29093.
15. *HJ* 29234.
16. *HJ* 12853.
17. *HJ* 34916.

validate the king's powers as a seer or spiritual intermediary who could forecast and perhaps influence the future, as in:

13A.   Crack-making on *jimao* (day 16), Que divined: "It will not rain."
13B.   Crack-making on *jimao*, Que divined: "It will rain." (Prognostication:) The king read the cracks (and said): "If it rains, it will be on a *ren*-day." (Verification:) On *renwu* (day 19), it really did rain.[18]

In this case, the king had forecast rain on a *ren*-day, and the record proved that he had been right. Verifications, in fact, frequently confirmed royal prognostications where divinations about the weather were concerned, as already seen in 3C–D.

Wu Ding, moreover, appears to have validated his role as prognosticator and king by anticipating impending trouble:

14.   Crack-making on *guisi* (day 30), Que divined: "In the (next) ten days there will be no disasters." (Prognostication:) The king read the cracks and said: "There will be calamities; there will be (someone) bringing alarming news." (Verification:) When it came to the fifth day, *dingyou* (day 34), there really was (someone) bringing alarming news from the west. Zhi Guo reported and said: "The Tufang have attacked in our eastern borders and have seized two settlements. The Gongfang likewise invaded the fields of our western borders."[19]

The king's forecast of calamities had been confirmed by events. This inscription, furthermore, like many others from the reign of Wu Ding, has certain striking features—the large, bold calligraphy, the use of red pigment to beautify the inscribed characters, and the inscribing of the charge, prognostication, and verification as a single continuous unit—which suggest that such validating records had been made for display. Perhaps they were intended to impress the king's supporters.

## THE LEGACY OF SHANG

There can be little doubt that the cultural assumptions of the Late Shang prepared the way for many of the more elaborate articulations of Zhou and later times. The divinatory impulse itself, for example, which sought to uncover the hidden meanings of events, may be regarded as ancestral to the "new text" (*jinwen*) interpretations of the Han,[20] whose political history, like that of the Zhou, was marked by an enduring concern with divination and portents. The

---

18. *HJ* 902 front.
19. *HJ* 6057 front.
20. See chap. 10.

rigid scheduling of the cult to the ancestors, the use of a limited number of day-name categories to classify them, and the willingness to give them ordinal temple names, such as "fourth Ancestor Ding," all indicate a preference in the religious world for the kind of orderly and impersonal arrangements that can be associated with the development of the imperial bureaucracy in Zhou and Han.

The Shang king's concern for good harvests and rainfall[21] was also continued in a variety of Zhou and Han rituals, such as the ploughing of the sacred field at the start of the agricultural year (referred to in the *Classic of Odes* and the *Record of Rites*), all of which assumed the ruler's responsibility for encouraging Heaven's benevolence toward the state and its people.

And, not least, the Zhou conception of a supreme being, *Tian* (Heaven), presiding over the universe,[22] was analogous to the Shang conception of Di, who not only stood above the ancestors and Nature Powers but might on occasion command other groups to attack the Shang[23] in a way that appears, at least in its mechanism, to have anticipated the Zhou "Mandate of Heaven."

[DNK]

---

21. As in 3A–D and 4A–B.
22. See chap. 2.
23. As in 6B; see also 3A–B for another instance in which Di issues commands.

*Chapter 2*

## CLASSICAL SOURCES OF CHINESE TRADITION

The classics of almost every major tradition have at some point in their history invited close scrutiny and intense debate, with those who have valued them disagreeing over such issues as dating, authenticity, authorship, and stratification (the layers of the text as it was built up over time). This has been particularly true of the most ancient Chinese texts—and not only in the light of modern critical scholarship. From early times to the present day, the Chinese classics have been carefully studied, deeply mined, and extensively compared.

We turn then to a body of literature traditionally accepted by the Chinese as a heritage of these ancient times, the Confucian classics. According to the order in which they are customarily discussed in later times, the first of these is the *Classic of Changes* (*Yijing*). As we have seen, the people of the Shang dynasty had practiced divination by means of cattle scapulas and turtle plastrons. Toward the end of the Shang another method of divination was coming into use based on sixty-four hexagrams (six-line symbolic diagrams) that were consulted through the casting of milfoil stalks. The *Classic of Changes* consists of a short text giving clues to the interpretation of the results of this type of divination, followed by a number of appendices or "wings," which elaborate upon the metaphysical significance of the interpretations. The basic text is attributed to very ancient times, while Confucius was traditionally supposed to have provided the "wings." Because the *Classic of Changes* came into existence over time and was later compiled and assumed its special importance in the tradition during the Former Han period (second and first centuries B.C.E.), it is discussed in chapter 10.

The second classic is the *Classic of Documents* or *Classic of History* (*Shujing*, also known as the *Shangshu*). This work consists of announcements, counsels, speeches, or similar oral reports said to have been made by various rulers and their ministers from the times of the sage rulers Yao and Shun down to the early Zhou period. Several hundred years ago, scholars in China established that many parts of the *Shujing* (though not the parts represented here) were later forgeries, probably of the fourth century c.e. Still, most Chinese have until recent times accepted this classic as providing accurate descriptions of the people and society of ancient China. Moreover, the collection of texts was traditionally believed to have been edited by Confucius, who was thought to have written a short introduction to each document explaining the circumstances of its composition.

The third classic is the *Classic of Odes* or *Classic of Poetry* (*Shijing*), an anthology of some three hundred poems dating mostly from early Zhou times. Some of these are folk songs from the various feudal states, while others are songs used by the aristocracy in their sacrificial ceremonies or at banquets and other functions. One section doubtfully purports to include ceremonial songs of the earlier Shang period. Confucius is supposed to have selected and edited these poems from a larger body of material, and, though this tradition is open to question, there seems no reason to doubt the authenticity of the songs themselves.

The fourth classic, the *Rites*, is actually a collection of texts, the most famous of which is the *Record of Rites* (*Liji*). These texts cover a vast range of subjects from the broadest philosophical pronouncements to the most minute rules for the conduct of everyday life. It is uncertain when the collections assumed their present form, though the texts themselves appear to date from middle or late Zhou times down to early Han. Again, Confucius is often credited with having been the compiler and editor of some of these texts.

The fifth of the classics, the *Spring and Autumn Annals* (*Chunqiu*), is a laconic chronicle of events in or affecting the state of Lu in the years from 722 to 481 b.c.e. Lu was the native state of Confucius, and it has been asserted that Confucius himself compiled the *Annals* from earlier records existing in the archives of Lu. Because the text of the *Annals* is so spare, a number of commentaries have been appended to explain the background and significance of the events referred to in the basic text. Of these, the most important are the *Zuo Commentary* (*Zuozhuan*), the *Gongyang*, and the *Guliang* commentaries. The exact dating of these commentaries is still a matter of controversy, though they were all apparently in existence by early Han times. It is in the light of these three commentaries that the *Spring and Autumn Annals* has traditionally been read and interpreted.

These works make up the Five Confucian Classics. A sixth, the "Music," is often mentioned in early writing. Whether there was ever a separate text on music we do not know. No such separate work exists today, though an essay on music is found in the *Record of Rites*.

All of these texts, with the exception of the *Record of Rites* and the *Spring and Autumn Annals*, with its three commentaries, purport to date from pre-Confucian times and to represent the earliest literature of the Chinese people, although modern scholarship in some cases denies such claims. In every case Confucius himself is assigned a personal role as transmitter, editor, and even commentator. From the time in the first century B.C.E. when Confucianism gained general acceptance, the Five Classics became for the educated class the chief object of study; they were regarded by many not only as the final authority on questions of ancient history and practice but also as the embodiment of the moral law of Confucius and his predecessors and the source of all wisdom and right knowledge.

Let us note now a few of the terms and concepts that seem to be of greatest importance in this body of ancient literature. As we have seen in the discussion of the religious culture of the Shang, the inscriptions on the oracle bones and shells contain frequent references to a deity called Di—God—or, much more rarely, Shangdi—the High God. There are many references also to Ancestral Powers and Nature Powers, such as the Yellow River, other rivers and streams, and sacred mountains. The practice of sacrifice to ancestors, especially on the part of the Shang king, was central to religious life and, as we shall see, was to remain an important part of the political and religious culture of the Zhou.

At some point, certainly no later than the early Zhou period, a second concept, that of *Tian*—Heaven or Nature—began to appear alongside that of Di—or God. Moreover, Di is often referred to in Zhou sources as Shangdi—the High God. Just how the three terms were understood in the early Zhou is less than clear, but it appears that, over time, the term *di* would come to be used increasingly to refer not to a supreme deity, as in the Shang, but to the supreme ruler of human society, the emperor, while the word *tian*, or "Heaven," would more often be employed to denote the power that governed all creation. As the term is used in Zhou texts, *Heaven* seems to represent a more universalized concept—a cosmic moral order, and a being or power, possessing intelligence and will, that impartially guided the destinies of human beings.

After the leaders of the Zhou lineage had overthrown the Shang dynasty and set up their own rule, around 1045/1040 B.C.E., they issued a number of proclamations, preserved in the *Classic of Documents*, explaining to the defeated Shang people why they should submit to their conquerors. In their arguments the Zhou rulers appealed to a concept called *tianming*, or the Mandate of Heaven. Heaven, they said, charged certain good men with rulership over the lineages of the world, and the heirs of these men might continue to exercise the Heaven-sanctioned power for as long as they carried out their religious and administrative duties with piety, rightness, and wisdom. But if the worth of the ruling family declined, if the rulers turned their backs upon the spirits and abandoned the virtuous ways that had originally marked them as worthy of the mandate to rule, then Heaven might discard them and elect a new family or lineage to be the destined rulers of the world. Thus the Zhou rulers explained the change of dynasties not as an action by which a strong state overthrew a weak one but as a Heaven-directed process by which a new group of wise and virtuous leaders was commissioned to take up the moral mandate forfeited by an older group whose wickedness and corruption had disqualified them as rulers.

The following, then, are among the basic beliefs that emerge in the Chinese literature of the Zhou period: a belief in a supreme deity or moral force that ruled the world and took an interest in the affairs of mankind; a belief in the existence and power of ancestral spirits who had to be served and placated with sacrifices; and a belief in the celestial sanction of the political order and the grave responsibility of the ruler to fulfill his moral duties to Heaven and to his people. The more purely religious belief in the existence and power of intervention of the spirits is probably older, going back at least to the Shang, and continued to be of importance in Chinese religious life, while reverence for the spirits of ancestors also continued to be a vital factor in the Chinese family system. But the concept of the moral responsibilities of the ruler, and the way in which the ruler should discharge these responsibilities so as not to lose the favor and protection of Heaven, became a major concern of Chinese thinkers.

## The *Classic of Documents*

### THE "CANON OF YAO" AND THE "CANON OF SHUN"

These texts, which appear at the beginning of this classic, purport to relate the events and pronouncements of the sage kings Yao and Shun, said to have reigned around the twenty-second century, who stand as the founding fathers and exemplars of Chinese civilization.

In this ideal conception, with the ruler personifying civil and familial virtue rather than military domination, his gentle charisma radiates out to successive degrees of kinship, so that all humankind is harmonized in one loving family. The core value here—that of personal virtue—is underscored by Yao's passing over his own son to find a successor in Shun, himself the embodiment of modesty and filial duty.

Examining into antiquity, we find that the Emperor Yao was called Fangxun. He was reverent, intelligent, accomplished, sincere, and mild. He was sincerely respectful and capable of modesty. His light covered the four extremities of the empire and extended to Heaven above and the Earth below. He was able to make bright his great virtue and bring affection to the nine branches of the family. When the nine branches of the family had become harmonious, he distinguished and honored the hundred clans. When the hundred clans had become illustrious, he harmonized the myriad states. The numerous people were amply nourished and prosperous and became harmonious. Then he charged Xi and He with reverence to follow August Heaven and calculate and delineate the sun, the moon, and the other heavenly bodies, and respectfully to give the people the seasons. . . . The emperor said, "Ah, you Xi and He, the year has three hundred and sixty-six days, and by means of an intercalary month you must fix the four seasons and complete the year. If you earnestly regulate all the functionaries, the achievements will all be glorious." The emperor said, "Who will carefully attend to this? I will raise him up and employ him." Fang Qi said, "Your heir-son Zhu is enlightened." The emperor said, "Alas, he is deceitful and quarrelsome; will he do?" . . . The emperor said, "Promote someone who is already illustrious, or raise up someone who is humble and of low status." They all said to the emperor, "There is an unmarried man in a low position called Shun of Yu." The emperor said, "Yes, I have heard of him. What is he like?" The Chief said, "He is the son of a blind man. His father is stupid, his mother is deceitful, his half brother Xiang is arrogant. Yet he has been able to live in harmony with them and to be splendidly filial. He has controlled himself and has not come to wickedness." The emperor said, "I will try him; I will wive him and observe his behavior toward my two daughters." . . .

The emperor said, "Come, you Shun, in the affairs on which you have been consulted, I have examined your words; your words have been accomplished and capable of yielding fine results for three years; do you ascend to the imperial throne."

[From "Yaodian," "Shundian," *Shujing*; BW]

## SHAO ANNOUNCEMENT

The "Shao Announcement" (*Shaogao*) purports to record the occasion of the founding of a new Zhou capital near the Luo River, an event that occurred during the reign of King Cheng. King Cheng was at this time still young, and his uncles, the Duke of Shao and the Duke of Zhou, served as his chief advisers.

The interest of the declaration lies in its powerful articulation of the concept of the Mandate of Heaven (*tianming*) as a doctrine of political legitimization and its assertion of a concomitant responsibility on the part of the ruler to listen to wise counsel and to benefit the people.

He [the Duke of Zhou] said,

"I salute with joined hands and bow my head to the ground, in respect for you, king-favored duke. And in a [formal] announcement I declare [this] to [you] Yin peoples and to your managers of affairs.

"Ah! August Heaven, High God, has changed his principal son and has revoked the Mandate of this great state of Yin. When a king receives the Mandate, without limit is the grace thereof, but also without limit is the anxiety of it. Ah! How can he fail to be reverently careful!

"Heaven has rejected and ended the Mandate of this great state of Yin. Thus, although Yin has many former wise kings in Heaven, when their successor kings and successor people undertook their Mandate, in the end wise and good men lived in misery. Knowing that they must care for and sustain their wives and children, they then called out in anguish to Heaven and fled to places where they could not be caught. . . .

"Look at the former peoples of ancient times, the Xia. Heaven guided, indulged, and cherished them, so that they would strive to understand what Heaven favors, but by this time they have let their Mandate fall to the ground. Now look at the Yin; Heaven guided them, stayed near them, nourished them, so that they would strive to comprehend what Heaven favors; but now they have let their Mandate fall to the ground.

"Now a young son succeeds to the throne; let him not, then, neglect the aged and experienced. Not only do they comprehend the virtue of our men of old—nay, more, they are sometimes able to comprehend counsels that come from Heaven. . . .

"Let the king reverently function in his position; he cannot but be reverently careful of his virtue. . . .

"Dwelling in this new city, now let the king just earnestly have reverent care for his virtue. If it is virtue that the king uses, he may pray Heaven for an enduring Mandate. As he functions as king, let him not, because the common people stray and do what is wrong, then presume to govern them by harsh capital punishments; in this way he will achieve much. In being king, let him take his position in the primacy of virtue. The little people will then pattern themselves on him throughout the world; the king will then become illustrious."

[From "Shaogao," *Shujing*; DSN]

## The *Classic of Odes*

### FROM THE GREATER ODES

This ode celebrates the virtues of King Wen, founder of the Zhou, as successor to the Shang rulers who failed to fulfill their moral responsibility. Heaven's Mandate or charge is no less real and compelling for being intangible (i.e., spiritual, moral values not reducible to words), and his successors can take King Wen as an example to live up to.

## King Wen (Ode 235)

**1**

> King Wen is on high,
> Oh, he shines in Heaven!
> Zhou is an old people,
> but its Mandate is new.

The leaders of Zhou became illustrious,
was not God's Mandate timely given?
King Wen ascends and descends
on the left and right of God.

### 4

August was King Wen,
continuously bright and reverent.
Great, indeed, was the Mandate of Heaven.
There were Shang's grandsons and sons,
Shang's grandsons and sons.
Was their number not a hundred thousand?
But the High God gave his Mandate,
and they bowed down to Zhou.

### 7

The Mandate is not easy to keep;
may it not end in your persons.
Display and make bright your good fame,
and consider what Yin had received from Heaven.
The doings of high Heaven
have no sound, no smell.
Make King Wen your pattern,
and all the states will trust in you.

[From "Wenwang" *Da ya, Shijing;* BW]

# Chapter 3

## CONFUCIUS AND THE ANALECTS

Kong Qiu (551–479 B.C.E.) was known among his contemporaries as Kongzi or Master Kong. Among some later followers he was honored as Kong Fuzi — "our Master Kong," which became the basis for "Confucius," the Latinized form that has been widely used in the West. It is also common in the West to acknowledge the importance of Confucius in the later history of China and of East Asia by designating the tradition of thought and practice with which he was associated as Confucianism. In the languages of East Asia, however, this tradition has often been identified with a scholarly group known as *ru*. *Ru* means "soft," "gentle," "enduring," and, sometimes, "weak." Very likely the term *ru* — evoking a commitment to learning, refinement, cultural accomplishments, and the practice of rites and music — came to be applied to persons whose notion of virtue had more to do with decorous conduct than with martial prowess. Confucius did not think of himself as the founder of this tradition but as one who hoped to keep it alive in the world. His followers were, from early times, identified as *ru*.

Early sources suggest that Confucius was born in the feudal state of Lu in eastern China into a family of the lower ranks of the nobility, one that was probably in straitened circumstances. It is clear that by the middle of the sixth century the Zhou dynasty, whose founders he honored, was in an advanced state of decline, having lost much of its real power and authority some two centuries earlier. Warfare was endemic, as the rulers of contending states vied for territory and power. Uncertainty surrounded the future of those states, and, in the eyes of many, shrouded the fate of civilization itself. Confucius emerged as one of a number of scholars who responded to an apparent crisis of civilization. He traveled from one feudal state to another, seeking an audience with various rulers and hoping to be employed by one capable of sharing his vision. He put forward the perspective of the *ru*—his purpose having been to promote the style and manners of the noble person (*junzi*) and the efficacy of moral force or virtue (*de*), rather than violence and coercion, as a strategy for rulers. Toward the end of his life, disappointed but evidently unembittered by his failure to gain an influential political office, he continued in the role of a teacher to promote these same causes. Over a period of centuries, the significance of Confucius as a teacher would become apparent, and within a century or so he would acquire the reputation of a sage. In subsequent centuries his example would be woven into the fabric of an entire culture as perhaps its most persistent pattern.

The *Analects* is the single most important source for understanding the thought of Confucius and the traditions to which he subscribed. It is clearly, however, not a work that he himself wrote. The English word *analects* (from the Greek *analekta*) means "a selection," while the Chinese title *Lunyu* may be translated as "conversations." This selection of conversations was compiled by later followers, themselves apparently representing different points of view. Some evidently contributed to the written record a century or more after Confucius's lifetime. The twenty short chapters or books of the *Analects* contain, among other things, recollections of conversations that transpired among Confucius and his disciples or between Confucius and rulers of several of the feudal states that he visited during the peripatetic phase of his teaching career. There are also descriptions of the man, brief but often telling vignettes of the way he appeared to those most intimately acquainted with him.

Most of the conversations recollected in the *Analects* focus on the practicalities of interpersonal relationships, personal cultivation in the context of those relationships, and the relationship of personal cultivation on the part of rulers and ministers to the conduct of government. In many exchanges Confucius speaks about the conduct and the dispositions of the *junzi*—a term commonly translated as "gentleman," "superior man," or "noble person." Originally, the meaning of the term *junzi* was "son of a lord," but the descriptions of the *junzi* found in the *Analects* suggest something different. Here the *junzi* is less the noble man whose nobility derives from inherited *social* nobility than the noble person whose nobility derives from personal commitment and a developed *moral* power (*de*). Still, a careful reader of the *Analects* may discover a kind of tension in the text's references to the *junzi*. On the one hand, the term seems to have a far more egalitarian implication than it could have had in earlier usage, since in the Confucian perspective anyone could become a *junzi*. On the other hand, it is clear that one who aspired to become a *junzi* faced stringent moral requirements that applied no less to attitude and motivation than to behavior. The term *de*, which in earlier sources conveyed a sense of charismatic power or force, almost magical in character, here takes on the meaning of "virtue," though without necessarily shedding its former associations.

Among the kinds of conduct that Confucius associated with moral nobility, and evidently expected of the *junzi*, perhaps the three most important were filial devotion (*xiao*), humaneness (*ren*), and ritual decorum (*li*). The moral vocabulary of Confucius is by no means exhausted in these three, but these are central, expressing in three distinct modes the Confucian awareness of and concern with human interrelatedness. Close attention to each of them as they occur in the selections that follow should make clear that what Western readers may be inclined to encounter as ideas are, from the perspective of Confucius and his followers, also feelings and practices—understood to have a bearing on what a human being will be like as a person, within as well as without. Embedded in these thoughts are not simply behavioral rules or standards but expectations about what the practitioner of these virtues should be like as a cultivated human being.

Each of these three practices—filiality, humaneness, and ritual decorum—figures into Confucius's views on government as well. Inasmuch as he sees governance as modeled on the family, he understands the practice of filial devotion to have a bearing on the stability of society as a whole. He is convinced that filial devotion practiced within one's family has ramifications in a far wider sphere. Humaneness, associated with fellow feeling,[1] is bound up with reciprocity. From a Confucian perspective, perhaps the most important capacity that a ruler can have is the capacity for recognizing that he must treat the people as he himself would want to be treated in their position.[2] Ritual, which affords an ideal means for ordering one's personal life, also represents the ideal mode of governance because the rites are the vehicle through which the ruler expresses his own virtue or moral power and also encourages a sense of dignity and responsiveness among the people.

The concept of the Mandate of Heaven (or "what Heaven ordains," *tianming*) that had emerged in the early Zhou period, with a largely political significance,[3] finds its way into his reflections on his own life, suggesting that the ordered process that prevails in the wider world is found to operate in an individual life as well (*Analects* 2:4). And while it appears to be just that—an order, rather than a deity—it is a beneficent presence, to which Confucius feels personally responsible, as well as a source of life, support, and even a certain austere comfort. He recognizes that it will not always be given to human beings to understand Heaven's functioning, an insight that shows up in his conversations and observations in a distinctive and often poignant interplay of confidence and resignation. There can be no expectation that the reward for right conduct or punishment for its opposite will be immediately apparent within the lifetime

---

1. In other translations *ren* is rendered as "Goodness," "benevolence," "kindness," "supreme virtue," and so on, but the graph for *ren* refers to humankind, not abstract ideas of "Goodness" (Waley) or benevolence (literally, "goodwill").

2. See, for example, 12:2 and 12:22.

3. See chap. 2.

of particular individuals: Heaven's ordinations are apparently expressed within a longer and larger frame. Still, he seems to believe that human beings have a home in the natural order and some assurance of the ultimate significance, and even resonance, of moral action. There is something remarkably subtle about this view and something immensely powerful as well, a subtlety and a power that seem to have inhered as much in the personality as in the ideas of this very worldly teacher.

## Selections from the *Analects*

There are enough differences in the way Confucius' teaching is described in the twenty chapters of the received text of the *Analects* to suggest that there must have been multiple recorders or compilers, and it seems clear that these chapters must have been incorporated into the text at different times. Without attempting to reconstruct the historical strata of the work, we offer the following selections in an order that follows the arrangement of the received text as it has been known over the course of centuries to readers in China and in East Asia as a whole.

1:1 The Master said, "To learn, and at due times to practice what one has learned, is that not also a pleasure? To have friends come from afar, is that not also a joy? To go unrecognized, yet without being embittered, is that not also to be a noble person?"

1:2 Master You [You Ruo] said, "Among those who are filial toward their parents and fraternal toward their brothers, those who are inclined to offend against their superiors are few indeed. Among those who are disinclined to offend against their superiors, there have never been any who are yet inclined to create disorder. The noble person concerns himself with the root; when the root is established, the Way is born. Being filial and fraternal — is this not the root of humaneness?"

1:3 The Master said, "Those who are clever in their words and pretentious in their appearance, yet are humane, are few indeed."

1:4 Zengzi[4] said, "Each day I examine myself on three things: In planning on behalf of others, have I failed to be loyal? When dealing with friends, have I failed to be trustworthy? On receiving what has been transmitted, have I failed to practice it?"

1:5 The Master said, "In ruling a state of a thousand chariots, one is reverent in the handling of affairs and shows himself to be trustworthy. One is economical in expenditures, loves the people, and uses them only at the proper season."

---

4. Zengzi was one of the most important of Confucius' followers. He is quoted numerous times in the *Analects* and is Confucius' sole interlocutor in the *Classic of Filial Piety* (see chap. 10).

1:6 The Master said, "A young man is to be filial within his family and respectful outside it. He is to be earnest and faithful, overflowing in his love for living beings and intimate with those who are humane. If after such practice he has strength to spare, he may use it in the study of culture."

1:7 Zixia said, "One who esteems the worthy and has little regard for sexual attraction, who in serving his parents is able to summon up his entire strength, who in serving his ruler is able to exert himself with utmost devotion, who in interacting with friends shows himself trustworthy in his words—though it may be said of him that he has not studied, I would definitely call him learned."

1:8 The Master said, "If the noble person is not serious,[5] he will not inspire awe, nor will his learning be sound. One should abide in loyalty and trustworthiness and should have no friends who are not his equal.[6] If one has faults, one should not be afraid to change."

1:11 The Master said, "When a person's father is alive, observe his intentions. After his father is no more, observe his actions. If for three years he does not change his father's ways, he is worthy to be called filial."

1:14 The Master said, "The noble person who seeks neither satiety in his food nor comfort in his dwelling, who is diligent in his undertakings and careful in his speech, who goes together with those who possess the Way in order to be corrected by them—he is worthy to be called a lover of learning."

1:16 The Master said, "One should not grieve that one is unrecognized by others; rather, one should grieve that one fails to recognize others."

2:1 The Master said, "One who governs through virtue may be compared to the polestar, which occupies its place while the host of other stars pay homage to it."

2:3 The Master said, "Lead them by means of regulations and keep order among them through punishments, and the people will evade them and will lack any sense of shame.[7] Lead them through moral force (*de*) and keep order among them through rites (*li*), and they will have a sense of shame and will also correct themselves."

*The following passage might be described as the world's shortest autobiography, in which Confucius describes, with exquisite brevity, his maturation throughout the course of his life.*

2:4 The Master said, "At fifteen, my heart was set upon learning; at thirty, I had become established; at forty, I was no longer perplexed; at fifty, I knew

---

5. Literally, "heavy" or "weighty."

6. I.e., in moral terms.

7. Or, as Arthur Waley interprets it, "self-respect."

what is ordained by Heaven;[8] at sixty, I obeyed; at seventy, I could follow my heart's desires without transgressing the line."

2:5 Meng Yi Zi asked about being filial. The Master said, "Let there be no discord." When Fan Chi was driving him, the Master told him, "Mengsun asked me about being filial and I said, 'Let there be no discord.'" Fan Chi said, "What did you mean by that?" The Master said, "When one's parents are alive, one serves them in accordance with the rites; when they are dead, one buries them in accordance with the rites and sacrifices to them in accordance with the rites."

2:6 Meng Wu Bo asked about being filial. The Master said, "One's parents' only concern should be lest one become ill."

2:11 The Master said, "One who reanimates the old so as to understand the new may become a teacher."

2:12 The Master said, "The noble person is not a tool."[9]

2:14 The Master said, "The noble person is inclusive, not exclusive; the small person is exclusive, not inclusive."

2:15 The Master said, "To learn without thinking is unavailing; to think without learning is dangerous."

2:17 The Master said, "You,[10] shall I teach you what knowledge is? When you know something, to know that you know it. When you do not know, to know that you do not know it. This is knowledge."

2:21 Someone said to Confucius, "Why does the Master not take part in government?" The Master said, "What do the *Documents* say about being filial? 'Be filial. Just being filial and friendly toward one's brothers has its effect on government.'[11] Why should one have to take part in government?"

4:1 It is humaneness that brings beauty to one's surroundings. Should one not make the choice to abide in humaneness, how could one become known?

4:2 The Master said, "One who is not humane is able neither to abide for long in hardship nor to abide for long in joy. The humane find peace in humaneness; the knowing derive profit from humaneness."

4:5 The Master said, "Wealth and honor are what people desire, but one should not abide in them if it cannot be done in accordance with the Way. Poverty and lowliness are what people dislike, but one should not avoid them if it cannot be done in accordance with the Way. If the noble person rejects humaneness, how can he fulfill that name? The noble person does not abandon

---

8. In Chinese, *tianming*, also translated in other contexts as the Mandate of Heaven. See pp. 25–26 (*Classic of Documents*).

9. Unlike a tool, a noble person is thought neither to have just one particular function nor to be merely a tool of others.

10. Zhong You, also known as Zilu, was known especially for his impetuousness.

11. *Classic of Documents*, "Jun Chen." Legge, *The Chinese Classics* 3:535.

humaneness for so much as the space of a meal. Even when hard-pressed he is bound to it, bound to it even in time of danger."

4:15 The Master said, "Shen! In my Way there is one thing that runs throughout." Zengzi said, "Yes." When the Master had gone out the disciples asked, "What did he mean?" Zengzi said, "The Master's Way is loyalty and reciprocity, that is all."

4:16 The Master said, "The noble person is concerned with rightness; the small person is concerned with profit."

6:2 Duke Ai asked who among the disciples loved learning. Confucius replied, "There was Yan Hui. He loved learning. He did not transfer his anger, nor did he repeat a mistake. Unfortunately, his allotted span was short, and he died. Now that he is gone I have not heard of one who loves learning."

6:9 The Master said, "How excellent was Hui! Having just a single bowl of food and a single ladle of drink, and living in a narrow lane—others could not have endured such hardship, while Hui's joy was unaltered. How excellent was Hui!"

6:20 Fan Chi asked about wisdom. The Master said, "Devote yourself to what must rightly be done for the people; respect spiritual beings, while keeping at a distance from them. This may be called wisdom." He asked about humaneness. The Master said, "One who is humane first does what is difficult and only thereafter concerns himself with success. This may be called humaneness."

6:28 Zigong said, "What would you say of someone who broadly benefited the people and was able to help everyone? Could he be called humane?" The Master said, "How would this be a matter of humaneness? Surely he would have to be a sage? Even Yao and Shun were concerned about such things. As for humaneness—you want to establish yourself; then help others to establish themselves. You want to develop yourself; then help others to develop themselves. Being able to recognize oneself in others, one is on the way to being humane."[12]

7:1 The Master said, "I transmit but do not create. In believing in and loving the ancients, I dare to compare myself with our old Peng."[13]

7:7 The Master said, "From one who brought only a bundle of dried meat[14] on up, I have never declined to give instruction to anyone."

7:8 The Master said, "To one who is not eager I do not reveal anything, nor do I explain anything to one who is not communicative. If I raise one corner for someone and he cannot come back with the other three, I do not go on."

---

12. Literally, "The ability to take what is near and grasp the analogy may be called the direction of humaneness."

13. The identity of "our old Peng" is unclear, but he is usually taken to be the Chinese counterpart to Methuselah.

14. Dried meat, or other food, was offered as a present for teachers. Here it suggests the least one might offer.

7:15 The Master said, "Having coarse rice to eat, water to drink, a bent arm for a pillow—joy lies in the midst of this as well. Wealth and honor that are not rightfully gained are to me as floating clouds."

7:19 The Master said, "I am not one who was born with knowledge; I am one who loves the past and is diligent in seeking it."

7:21 The Master said, "Walking along with three people, my teacher is sure to be among them. I choose what is good in them and follow it and what is not good and change it."

7:29 The Master said, "Is humaneness far away? If I want to be humane, then humaneness is here."

7:37 The Master was mild and yet strict, dignified and yet not severe, courteous and yet at ease.

8:7 Zengzi said, "The man of service[15] cannot but be stout-hearted and resolute. His burden is heavy, and his way is long. Humaneness is the burden that he takes upon himself. Is it not heavy? Only in death does his way come to an end. Is it not long?"

9:4 Four things the Master eschewed: he had no preconceptions, no prejudices, no obduracy, and no egotism.

9:10 Yan Yuan, sighing deeply, said, "I look up to it and it is higher still; I delve into it and it is harder yet. I look for it in front, and suddenly it is behind. The Master skillfully leads a person step by step. He has broadened me with culture and restrained me with ritual. . . ."

9:17 The Master said, "I have never seen anyone who loved virtue (de) as much as he loved beauty (se)."

9:25 The Master said, "The Three Armies can be deprived of their commander, but even a common person cannot be deprived of his will."

11:8 When Yan Yuan died, the Master said, "Alas, Heaven is destroying me! Heaven is destroying me!"

11:11 Jilu asked about serving spiritual beings. The Master said, "Before you have learned to serve human beings, how can you serve spirits?" "I venture to ask about death." "When you do not yet know life, how can you know about death?"

12:1 Yan Yuan asked about humaneness. The Master said, "Through mastering oneself and returning to ritual one becomes humane. If for a single day one can master oneself and return to ritual, the whole world will return to humaneness. Does the practice of humaneness come from oneself or from others?" Yan Yuan said, "May I ask about the specifics of this?" The Master said, "Look

---

15. Or officer.

at nothing contrary to ritual; listen to nothing contrary to ritual; say nothing contrary to ritual; do nothing contrary to ritual." . . .

12:2 Zhonggong [Ran Yong] asked about humaneness. The Master said, "When going abroad, treat everyone as if you were receiving a great guest; when employing the people, do so as if assisting in a great sacrifice. What you do not want for yourself, do not do to others. There should be no resentment in the state, and no resentment in the family." . . .

12:5 Sima Niu, grievingly, said, "Other men all have brothers; I alone have none."[16] Zixia said, "Shang[17] has heard this: Death and life are ordained; wealth and honor depend on Heaven. If the noble person is reverent, unfailingly courteous toward others, and observant of the rites, then all within the four seas are his brothers. Why should he be distressed at having no brothers?"

12:7 Zigong asked about government. The Master said, "Sufficient food, sufficient military force, the people's trust." Zigong said, "If one had, unavoidably, to dispense with one of these three, which of them should go first?" The Master said, "Get rid of the military." Zigong said, "If one had, unavoidably, to dispense with one of the remaining two, which should go first?" The Master said, "Dispense with the food. Since ancient times there has always been death, but if people don't trust it a state cannot stand."

12:11 Duke Jing of Qi asked Confucius about government. Confucius replied, "Let the ruler be a ruler; the minister, a minister; the father, a father; the son, a son." "Excellent," said the duke. "Truly, if the ruler is not a ruler, the subject is not a subject, the father is not a father, and the son is not a son, though I have grain, will I get to eat it?"

12:19 Ji Kang Zi asked Confucius about government, saying, "How would it be if one killed those who do not possess the Way in order to benefit those who do possess it?" Confucius replied, "Sir, in conducting your government, why use killing? If you, sir, want goodness, the people will be good. The virtue of the noble person is like the wind, and the virtue of small people is like grass. When the wind blows over the grass, the grass must bend."

12:22 Fan Chi asked about humaneness. The Master said, "It is loving people." He asked about wisdom. The Master said, "It is knowing people." When Fan Chi did not understand, the Master said, "Raise up the upright, put them over the crooked, and you should be able to cause the crooked to become upright." . . .

13:3 Zilu said, "The ruler of Wei has been waiting for the Master to administer his government. What should come first?" The Master said, "What is necessary is the rectification of names. . . . If names are not rectified, then language

---

16. It was not that he actually had no brothers but that he was worried about his elder brother, Huan Tui, who was an enemy of Confucius.

17. Referring to himself.

will not be appropriate, and if language is not appropriate, affairs will not be successfully carried out. . . . Therefore the names used by the noble person must be appropriate for speech, and his speech must be appropriate for action. In regard to language, the noble person allows no carelessness, that is all."

13:9 When the Master went to Wei, Ran You served as his driver. The Master said, "How numerous the people are!" Ran You said, "Since they are already numerous, what more should be done for them?" He said, "Enrich them." Ran You said, "And when they have been enriched, what more can be done for them?" He replied, "Teach them."

13:16 The Duke of She asked about government. The Master said, "Those who are nearby should be pleased, and those who are far off should be attracted."

13:18 The Duke of She told Confucius, "In our part of the country there is one Upright Gong. His father stole a sheep, and the son bore witness against him." Confucius said, "In our part of the country, the upright are different from that. A father is sheltered by his son, and a son is sheltered by his father. Uprightness lies in this."

13:21 The Master said, "Since I cannot get those who follow the middle way to associate with, I must accept the madly ardent and the cautiously restrained. The madly ardent go forward and seize their opportunities, while the cautiously restrained have things that they will not do."

13:23 The Master said, "The noble person is conciliatory but not conformist; the small person is conformist but not conciliatory."

13:30 The Master said, "To lead the people to war without having taught them is to throw them away."

14:18 Zigong said, "Surely Guan Zhong[18] was not humane? When Duke Huan killed his brother, Jiu, Guan Zhong was unable to die with Jiu and even became prime minister to Duke Huan." The Master said, "Guan Zhong became prime minister to Duke Huan and made him hegemon among the lords, uniting and reforming all-under-Heaven. Down to the present day the common people continue to receive benefits from this. Had it not been for Guan Zhong we would be wearing our hair unbound and folding our robes to the left.[19] How can this be compared to the ordinary fidelity of the common man and woman who might commit suicide in a ditch without anyone's knowing of it?"

14:23 Zilu asked how to serve a ruler. The Master said, "You may not deceive him, but you may stand up to him."

14:25 The Master said, "In ancient times learning was for the sake of oneself, whereas now learning is for the sake of others."[20]

---

18. Guan Zhong was a Legalist minister famous for his service to the hegemon, Duke Huan of Qi. Some of the statements attributed to Confucius in the *Analects* are critical of Guan Zhong, and others, like the one that follows here, are laudatory, perhaps suggesting different views among the compilers of the text.

19. In the style common among the non-Chinese tribes.

20. I.e., in order to gain their approval rather than for the full development of the self.

14:37 The Master said, "There is no one who knows me." Zigong said, "How could it be that no one knows you?" The Master said, "I bear neither a grievance against Heaven nor a grudge against men. And as learning here below penetrates to what is above, it must be Heaven that knows me!"

15:2 The Master said, "Zi, do you think of me as one who learns many things and remembers them all?" He replied, "Yes. But perhaps this is not so?" The Master said, "It is not. With me there is the one that runs throughout it all."[21]

15:3 The Master said, "You, those who understand virtue (*de*) are few indeed."

15:8 The Master said, "It does not happen that the dedicated officer and the humane person seek life if it means harming their humaneness. It does happen that they sacrifice their lives so as to complete their humaneness."

15:18 The Master said, "The noble person is anxious about his own lack of ability, not about the failure of others to recognize him."

15:23 Zigong asked, "Is there one word that one can act upon throughout the course of one's life?" The Master said, "Reciprocity (*shu*)—what you would not want for yourself, do not do to others."

15:30 The Master said, "I have spent an entire day without eating, and an entire night without sleeping, so as to think. It was of no use. It is better to learn."

15:35 The Master said, "In the matter of humaneness, one should not defer even to one's teacher."

15:38 The Master said, "In education there should be no class distinctions."

16:8 Confucius said, "The noble person has three objects of awe: he is in awe of the ordinances of Heaven (*tianming*);[22] he is in awe of the great man; and he is in awe of the words of the sage. The small man, not knowing the ordinances of Heaven, is not in awe of them; he is disrespectful toward great men; and he ridicules the words of the sages."

17:2 The Master said, "By nature close together; through practice set apart."[23]

17:9 The Master said, "Little ones, why does none of you study the Odes? The Odes may be used for stimulation, for contemplation, and for sociability. Through them you are able to express your grievances. At home they may be used to serve your parents and, abroad, to serve your ruler. Through them you may gain broad acquaintance with the names of birds and animals, plants and trees."

---

21. This is sometimes translated as "With me, there is one thread that runs right through it." The image conveyed by the verb *guan* is that of cowrie shells threaded on a single string.

22. Also translated as the "Mandate of Heaven."

23. This simple observation attributed to Confucius was agreed upon as the essential truth with regard to human nature and racial difference by a group of international experts in the UNESCO "Statement on Race" published in July 1950.

17:21 Zai Wo inquired about the three years of mourning,[24] saying that one year was quite long enough. . . . The Master said, "If you were to eat good food and wear fine clothing, would you feel at ease?" "I would feel at ease." "If you would be at ease, then do it. But the noble person, throughout the period of mourning, derives no pleasure from the food that he eats, no joy from the music that he hears, and no comfort from his dwelling. Thus he does not do it. But now you would feel at ease, and so you may do it." After Wo went out the Master said, "How inhuman[25] Yu [Zai Wo] is! Only when a child is three years old does it leave its parents' arms. The three years' mourning is the universal mourning everywhere under Heaven. And Yu—was he not the darling of his father and mother for three years?"

17:25 Women and servants are most difficult to nurture. If one is close to them, they lose their reserve, while if one is distant, they feel resentful.

18:6 Chang Ju and Jie Ni were working together tilling the fields. Confucius passed by them and sent Zilu to inquire about the ford. . . .

Zilu then inquired of Jie Ni. Jie Ni said, "Who are you, sir?" "Zhong You." "The follower of Kong Qiu of Lu?" "Yes." "A rushing torrent—such is the world. And who can change it? Rather than follow a scholar who withdraws from particular men, would it not be better to follow one who withdraws from the world?" He went on covering seed without stopping.

Zilu went and told the Master, who sighed and said, "I cannot herd together with the birds and beasts. If I do not walk together with other human beings, with whom shall I associate? If the Way prevailed in the world, [I] Qiu would not be trying to change it."

19:1 Zizhang said, "The scholar who, perceiving danger, is prepared to sacrifice his life;[26] who, seeing the possibility for gain, thinks of rightness; who, in sacrificing, thinks of reverence; who, in mourning, thinks of grief; is worthy of approval."

19:6 Zixia said, "In broadly learning, in being genuinely dedicated, in earnestly inquiring, in reflecting on things at hand—humaneness lies right here."

20:3 The Master said, "Without knowing what is ordained [by Heaven], one has no way to become a noble person. Without knowing the rites, one has no way to take one's stand. Without knowing words, one has no way to know other people."

[IB]

---

24. This passage implies that the ritual prescription for mourning for parents specified a period of three years, or, more precisely, twenty-five months—one month into the third year.

25. Literally, "not humane."

26. Literally, "to fulfill the ordinance (of Heaven)."

*Chapter 4*

## MOZI: UTILITY, UNIFORMITY, AND UNIVERSAL LOVE

The Warring States period (479–221 B.C.E.) in ancient China witnessed a remarkable proliferation of philosophical schools—often referred to as the "hundred schools of thought." Among the "hundred philosophers" of ancient China, Mozi had a place of special importance. When Mencius, the first great follower of Confucius, felt called upon to defend and revitalize Confucianism in the fourth century B.C.E., he singled out the philosophy of Mozi as being among its most dangerous rivals. Although Mohism did not hold this strong position for long, its founder and his teachings were extremely influential in later Chinese thought. Today they serve as a reminder that the eventual supremacy of Confucian ideas and values was not achieved simply by default or intellectual inertia but was won in a difficult struggle with worthy opponents.

Mo Di, who became known as Mozi, or Master Mo, apparently lived during the period of about a century between the death of Confucius and the birth of Mencius. The name Mo was in all likelihood not a surname: it has been thought by some to have denoted a form of punishment, indicating that the man known as Mo Di may have come from a class of prisoners or slaves. However that may be, the Mohist school came to be associated with the interests and energies of artisans, merchants, and small-property owners, and the text attributed to Mozi often characterizes the Confucians as pretentious aristocrats who stand very much on their own dignity and on ceremony, suggesting perhaps a degree of plebeian hostility on the part of Mozi's followers. Mozi was, however, well educated in the classics and may even have followed the Confucian school himself until he took up a position of strong opposition on certain fundamental points. Thus he condemned what he viewed as the skepticism of many Confucians in regard to Heaven and spiritual beings, their tendency toward fatalism, and their preoccupation with ritual. These criticisms may perhaps be understood as testimony to the direction in which Confucius's thought was being taken by his immediate followers.

Some of Mozi's most striking arguments are political in nature and reveal a characteristic blend of populism and authoritarianism. To illustrate this blend, we offer excerpts from one of a set of three chapters of the *Mozi*, "Honoring the Worthy"—in which Mozi argues that government positions should be filled by the most qualified individuals—and two of a set of three chapters, "Identifying with the Superior"—in which he insists on the need for uniformity of thought, based on an elaborate form of thought control, to achieve social order.

Mozi's most characteristic doctrine comes close to asserting that "all human beings are equal before God." Believing in Heaven as an active power manifesting love for all, he urged that all people follow Heaven in this by practicing universal love. But this has nothing to do with love between persons or human affectivity. His standard of action is strictly based on utility: love for all human beings is demonstrated by satisfying their immediate material needs and by abandoning all forms of activity and expense that do not contribute to the feeding, clothing, and housing of the people. For this reason Mozi condemned ritual and music, extravagant entertainment, and, above all, offensive warfare. Moreover, to concentrate human energies on the achievement of social goals, Mozi believed, unity of thought and action was necessary, with the people obeying their leaders and the leaders following the will of Heaven.

What we know of Mozi's career shows him to be a rigorist who set the most exacting standards for himself and his followers. In trying to gain acceptance for his principles, he drove himself tirelessly and unmercifully. Unlike the Confucians, who offered advice only when treated respectfully by a ruler and assured of his honorable intentions, Mozi was ready to preach his gospel to anyone who would listen. At times, upon hearing of the plans of a state to make war, he would hasten to dissuade the ruler from perpetrating such an outrage. On one of these peace missions, it is said, he walked ten days and ten nights, tearing off pieces of his garments to bind up his sore feet as he went. Often Mozi and his followers, failing in their efforts at conciliation, would rush to aid in the defense of the state attacked, gaining a reputation for their skill in siege operations. In this way they became a tightly knit and highly disciplined group, leading an ascetic life and, even after Mozi's death, obediently following the directions of their "elders."

Some of the chapters of the *Mozi* are believed to represent the views of his later followers, whose utilitarian aims inevitably led them into the study of more basic questions of both a philosophical and a technical character. Thus, for instance, their evangelistic approach and readiness to discuss or debate with anyone may explain why the later Mohist canon is so much concerned with logic and dialectics. Yet even in the portions believed to represent Mozi's original teaching, there is a laborious, even tedious attention to step-by-step argumentation. For this reason, perhaps, Mozi has been much less admired for his literary style, or even for his ideas, than for the nobility of spirit that he revealed in his life of service to others.

## Selections from the *Mozi*

### SECTION 9: HONORING THE WORTHY (PART 2)

Mozi said, "In caring for the people, presiding over the altars of the soil and grain, and ordering the state, the ruler and high officials these days strive for stability and seek to avoid any error. But why do they fail to perceive that honoring the worthy is the foundation of government?. . .

"The sage kings of ancient times took great pains to honor the worthy and employ the capable, showing no special consideration for their own kin, no partiality for the eminent and rich, no favoritism for the good-looking and attractive. They promoted the worthy to high places, enriched and honored them, and made them heads of government; the unworthy they demoted and rejected, reduced to poverty and humble station, and condemned to penal servitude. Thus the people, encouraged by the hope of reward and awed by the fear of punishment, led each other on to become worthy, so that worthy persons increased in number and the unworthy became few. This is what is called advancing the worthy. And when this had been done, the sage kings listened to the words of the worthy, watched their actions, observed their abilities, and on this basis carefully assigned them to office. This is called employing the capable. . . .

"When a worthy man is given the task of ordering the state, he appears at court early and retires late, listens to lawsuits, and attends to the affairs of government. As a result, the state is well ordered and the laws and punishments are justly administered. When a worthy man heads a government bureau, he goes to bed late and gets up early, collecting taxes on the barriers and markets and on the resources of the hills, forests, lakes, and fish weirs, so that the treasury will be full. As a result the treasury is full and no source of revenue is neglected. When a worthy man governs an outlying district, he leaves his house early and returns late, plowing and sowing seed, planting trees, and gathering vegetables and grain. As a result there will be plenty of vegetables and grain and the people will have enough to eat. When the state is well ordered, the laws and punishments will be justly administered, and when the treasury is full, the people will be well off. The rulers will thus be supplied with wine and millet to use in their sacrifices to Heaven and the spirits, with hides and currency to use in their intercourse with the feudal lords of neighboring states, and with the means to feed the hungry and give rest to the weary within their realm, to nourish their subjects, and to attract virtuous persons from all over the world. Then Heaven and the spirits will send down riches, the other feudal lords will become their allies, the people of their own realm will feel affection for them, and the worthy will come forward to serve them. Thus all that they plan for they will achieve, and all that they undertake will be brought to a successful conclusion. If they stay within their realm, their position will be secure, and if they venture forth to punish an enemy, they will be victorious. . . .

"But if one knows only the policy to be adopted, but does not know what means to use in carrying it out, then he cannot be sure of success in government. Therefore three principles should be established. What are the three principles? They are that if the titles and positions of worthy men are not exalted enough, then the people will not respect such men; if their stipends are not generous, then the people will not have confidence in them; and if their orders are not enforced, then the people will not stand in awe of them. . . .

"All of this comes about as a result of understanding petty affairs but failing to understand important ones. Now the rulers and high officials know that if they cannot cut a suit of clothes for themselves, they must employ the services of a skilled tailor, and if they cannot slaughter an ox or a sheep for themselves, they must employ the services of a skilled butcher. In these two instances the rulers are perfectly aware of the need to honor the worthy and employ the capable to get things done. And yet when they see the state in confusion and their altars of soil and grain in danger, they do not know enough to employ capable men to correct the situation. Instead they employ their relatives, or men who happen to be rich and eminent or pleasant-featured and attractive. . . . If men such as these are given the task of ordering the state, then this is simply to entrust the state to men who are neither wise nor intelligent, and anyone knows that this will lead to ruin."

[*Mozi jicheng* 2:5a–6b, 8a–9b; adapted from Watson, *Mo Tzu*, pp. 22–24, 26–28]

## SECTION 11: IDENTIFYING WITH THE SUPERIOR (PART 1)

Mozi said, "In ancient times, when humankind was first born and before there were any laws or government, it may be said that each person's view of things was different. One person had one view, two persons had two views, ten persons had ten views—the more persons, the more views. Moreover, each person believed that his own views were correct and disapproved of those of others, so that people spent their time condemning one another. . . . Those with strength to spare refused to help out others, those with surplus wealth would let it rot before they would share it, and those with beneficial doctrines to teach would keep them secret and refuse to impart them. The world was as chaotic as if it were inhabited by birds and beasts alone.

"To anyone who examined the cause, it was obvious that this chaos came about because of the absence of rulers and leaders. Therefore the most worthy and able man in the world was selected and set up as the Son of Heaven.[1] After the Son of Heaven had been set up, because his strength alone was insufficient, other worthy and able men were selected from throughout the world and installed as his three high ministers. . . . After the feudal lords and chiefs had been set up and because their strength alone was insufficient, worthy and able men were chosen from the various states to act as their officials.

"When all these officials had been installed, the Son of Heaven proclaimed the principle of his rule to the people of the world, saying, 'Upon hearing of good or evil, one shall report it to one's superior. What the superior considers right all shall consider right; what the superior considers wrong all shall consider wrong. If the superior commits any fault, his subordinates shall remonstrate with him; if his subordinates do good, the superior shall recommend them. To identify oneself with one's superior and not to form cliques on the lower levels—such conduct as this shall be rewarded by those above and praised by those below.'

"The head of each local community was the most humane man in the community, and when he took office, he proclaimed to the people of the community the principle of his rule, saying, 'Upon hearing of good or evil, you shall report it to the town head. What the town head considers to be right all shall consider right; what the town head considers wrong all shall consider wrong. Leave your evil words and imitate the good words of the town head; leave your evil actions and imitate the good actions of the town head!' As long as this command was heeded, how could there be any disorder in the township?. . ."

*In closing, Mozi makes the point that the people must ultimately identify with Heaven itself, though how they are to do this is not specified.*

"If we examine the reason why the world was well ordered, we find that it was simply that the Son of Heaven was able to unify the standards of judgment throughout the world, and this resulted in order. . . .

"But although all the people in the world may identify themselves with the Son of Heaven, if they do not also identify themselves with Heaven itself, then calamities will never cease. . . ."

[*Mozi jicheng* 3:1a–2b, 3a; adapted from Watson, *Mo Tzu*, pp. 34–36, 37]

---

1. It is not clear who does the selecting. In the original, the sentence is in the active mood but with no subject expressed, a construction that is perfectly permissible in Chinese but that must be rendered into English in the passive unless the translator chooses to supply a subject. If pressed, Mozi, like the Confucians, would no doubt say that Heaven, expressing its will through some human or natural agency, did in fact select the Son of Heaven.

## SECTION 16: UNIVERSAL LOVE (PART 3)

Mozi said, "It is the business of the humane person to try to promote what is beneficial to the world and to eliminate what is harmful. Now at the present time, what brings the greatest harm to the world? Great states attacking small ones, great families overthrowing small ones, the strong oppressing the weak, the many harrying the few, the cunning deceiving the stupid, the eminent lording it over the humble—these are harmful to the world. . . .

"When we inquire into the cause of these various harms, what do we find has produced them? Do they come about from loving others and trying to benefit them? Surely not! They come rather from hating others and trying to injure them. And when we set out to classify and describe those who hate and injure others, shall we say that their actions are motivated by universality or partiality? Surely we must answer, by partiality, and it is this partiality in their dealings with one another that gives rise to all the great harms in the world. . . ."

Mozi said, "Partiality should be replaced by universality. But how can partiality be replaced by universality? If men were to regard the states of others as they regard their own, then who would raise up his state to attack the state of another? It would be like attacking his own. If men were to regard the cities of others as they regard their own, then who would raise up his city to attack the city of another? It would be like attacking his own. If men were to regard the families of others as they regard their own, then who would raise up his family to overthrow that of another? . . .

"When we set out to classify and describe those persons who love others and benefit others, shall we say that their actions are motivated by partiality or by universality? Surely we must answer, by universality, and it is this universality in their dealings with one another that gives rise to all the great benefits in the world. . . ."

Mozi said, "Let us examine for a moment the way in which a filial son plans for the welfare of his parents. When a filial son plans for his parents, does he wish others to love and benefit them, or does he wish others to hate and injure them? It stands to reason that he wishes others to love and benefit his parents. Now if I am a filial son, how do I go about accomplishing this? Do I first make it a point to love and benefit other men's parents, so that they in return will love and benefit my parents? Or do I first make it a point to hate and injure other men's parents, so that they in return will love and benefit my parents? Obviously, I must first make it a point to love and benefit other men's parents, so that they in return will love and benefit my parents. . . .

"Now universal love and mutual benefit are both profitable and easy beyond all measure. The only trouble, as I see it, is that no ruler takes any delight in them. . . ."

[*Mozi jicheng* 4:10b–11b, 12b–14a, 15a–b, 18a–b, 20a;
adapted from Watson, *Mo Tzu*, pp. 39–42, 44, 46–47, 49]

## SECTION 26: THE WILL OF HEAVEN (PART 1)

Mozi said, "The gentlemen of the world today understand small matters but not large ones. How do we know this? We know it from the way they conduct themselves at home. If at home a man commits some offense against the head of the family, he may still run away and hide at a neighbor's house. And yet his parents, brothers, and friends will all join in warning and admonishing him, saying, 'You must be more cautious! You must be more circumspect! When you are living at home, how can it be right for you to offend the head of the family?'

"This is true not only of a man who lives at home but of a man who lives in a state as well. . . .

". . . And yet with regard to Heaven the gentlemen of the world for some reason do not know enough to warn and admonish each other. Thus I know that the gentlemen of the world understand small matters but not large ones.

"Now what does Heaven desire and what does it hate? Heaven desires rightness and hates what is not right. . . .

"How do I know that Heaven desires rightness and hates what is not right? In the world, where there is rightness there is life; where there is no rightness there is death. Where there is rightness there is wealth; where there is no rightness there is poverty. Where there is rightness there is order; where there is no rightness there is disorder. Now Heaven desires life and hates death, desires wealth and hates poverty, desires order and hates disorder. So I know that Heaven desires rightness and hates what is not right.

"Moreover, rightness is what is right. Subordinates do not decide what is right for their superiors; it is the superiors who decide what is right for their subordinates. Therefore the common people devote their strength to carrying out their tasks, but they cannot decide for themselves what is right. . . .

". . . Now the books of the gentlemen of the world are too numerous to be listed, and their sayings too many to be examined in full. In the higher circles the gentlemen lecture to the feudal lords, and in lower circles they expound to men of honor. And yet on matters of humaneness and rightness they are far apart. How do I know? Because I measure them by the clearest standard in the world [i.e., the intent of Heaven]."

[*Mozi jicheng* 7:1a–3a, 4a–b, 5a; adapted from Watson, *Mo Tzu*, pp. 78–80, 81–83]

## SECTION 27: THE WILL OF HEAVEN (PART 2)

Mozi said, "The intent of Heaven does not desire that large states attack small ones, that large families overthrow small ones, that the strong oppress the weak, the cunning deceive the stupid, or the eminent lord it over the humble. This is what Heaven does *not* desire. But this is not all. It desires that among men those who have strength will work for others, those who understand the Way will teach others, and those who possess wealth will share it with others. It also desires that those above will diligently attend to matters of government, and those below will diligently carry out their tasks. . . ."

[*Mozi jicheng* 7:6b; adapted from Watson, *Mo Tzu*, pp. 85–86]

## SECTION 39: AGAINST CONFUCIANS (PART 2)[2]

"The Confucians say, 'There are degrees to be observed in treating relatives as relatives, and gradations to be observed in honoring the worthy.'[3] They prescribe differences to be observed between close and distant relatives and between the honored and the humble. . . .

"When a Confucian takes a wife, he goes to fetch her in person. Wearing a formal black robe, he acts as his own coachman, holding the reins and handing her the cord by which to pull herself up into the carriage, as though he were escorting an honored parent. The wedding ceremonies are conducted with as much solemnity as the sacrifices to the ancestors. High and low are turned upside down, and parents are disregarded and scorned. Parents are brought down to the level of the wife, and the wife is exalted at the expense of service to the parents. How can such conduct be called filial?. . .

"In addition, the Confucians believe firmly in the existence of fate and propound their doctrine, saying, 'Long life or early death, wealth or poverty, safety or danger, order or disorder are all decreed by the ordinance of Heaven[4] and cannot be modified. Failure and success, rewards and punishments, good fortune and bad, are all fixed. Human wisdom and strength can do nothing.' If the various officials believe such ideas, they will be lax in their duties; and if the common people believe them, they will neglect their tasks. . . .

"Moreover, the Confucians corrupt men with their elaborate and showy rites and music and deceive parents with lengthy mournings and hypocritical grief. They propound fatalism, ignore poverty, and behave with the greatest arrogance. . . .

"The Confucians say, 'The noble person must use ancient speech and wear ancient dress before he can be considered humane.' But we answer, 'The so-called ancient speech and dress were all modern once, and if at that time the men of antiquity used such speech and wore such dress, then they must not have been noble persons. Must we then wear the dress of those who were not noble persons and use their speech before we can be considered humane?'"

[*Mozi jicheng* 9:16a–18b, 19b–20a; adapted from Watson, *Mo Tzu*, pp. 124–28]

---

2. This chapter, while numbered part 2 in the *Mozi* text, is actually the only surviving chapter of this pair, part 1 having been lost.

3. The *Mean*, a section of the Confucian *Record of Rites*, contains a passage much like this: "Humaneness is what it means to be human, and being affectionate toward one's kin is the greatest part of it. Rightness is doing what is right, and honoring the worthy is the greatest part of it. The diminishing degree of affection due to one's kin and the different gradations of honor owed to the worthy are born of ritual" (*Zhong yong* 20:5). See chap. 10.

4. The Chinese term is *tianming*, elsewhere translated as the "Mandate of Heaven."

# Chapter 5

## THE WAY OF *LAOZI* AND *ZHUANGZI*

Next to Confucianism, the most important and influential native philosophy of the Chinese has undoubtedly been Daoism. In many ways the doctrines of Confucianism and Daoism complement each other, running side by side like two powerful streams through all later Chinese thought and literature. To the solemn gravity and burden of social responsibility of Confucianism, Daoism opposes a flight from respectability and the conventional duties of society; in place of the Confucian concern for things worldly and human, it holds out a vision of other, transcendental worlds of the spirit. As the two streams of thought developed in later times, Confucianism has often been understood to represent the mind of the Chinese scholar in his office or study, concerned with matters of family and society, while Daoism represents the same individual in a private chamber or mountain retreat, often seeking surcease from the cares of official life.

## METAPHYSICS AND GOVERNMENT IN THE *LAOZI*

The term *Daoist*—the school or family of the Dao—did not enter the Chinese vocabulary until the Han dynasty, around the second century B.C.E. In earlier periods this current of thought was referred to as "the teachings of the Yellow Emperor and Laozi" (Huang-Lao, in Chinese) and, later, of "the teachings of Laozi and Zhuangzi." Though the Yellow Emperor is a legendary figure, we do possess two books attributed to Laozi and Zhuangzi.

The name Laozi simply means "the old master." Who the philosopher known as Laozi was, when he lived, and what his connection was with the text that has come down to us, are questions that have been debated for centuries. There have also been lively controversies about when the text was compiled and whether it actually appeared any earlier than the third century B.C.E. Contemporary scholars are generally inclined to agree that the book known as the *Laozi* or *Daodejing* was likely the work of more than one author, writing over a period of time, and that it contains different textual strata. Still, the compiler or compilers of the work seem to have had a rather consistent integrative vision, and despite—or perhaps because of—its brevity the document that has come down to us is one of the most provocative and inspired works in all Chinese literature.

In a sense the *Laozi*, like so many of the works of this period of political chaos and intellectual ferment, proposes a philosophy of government and a way of life for the ruling class, probably the only people who were capable of reading it. Yet its point of view and approach to the problems of government are vastly broader than this statement might suggest. The teaching of the *Laozi* is based on a great underlying principle, the Way, or Dao (from which the later name of the school derives), which is the source of all being, the governor of all life, human and natural, and the basic, undivided unity in which all the contradictions and distinctions of existence are ultimately resolved. Much of the book deals with the nature and workings of this first principle, while admitting that it must remain essentially indescribable and can be known only through a kind of mysterious intuition. The way of life that accords with this basic Dao is marked by an impulse toward acceptance and yielding, an absence of strife and coercion, and a manner of action that is completely spontaneous, effortless, and inexhaustible. This approach to action is often expressed in terms of "doing nothing"—or doing nothing that is unnatural or out of keeping with the Way (*wuwei*).

In the human sphere the *Laozi* describes the perfect individual, the sage, who comprehends the Dao and whose life and actions are ordered in accordance with it. It is clear that the sage is conceived of as the ideal ruler, for the *Laozi* gives definite instructions as to how the sage's government is to be conducted. The sage is to refrain from meddling in the lives of the people, give up warfare and luxurious living, and guide the people back to a state of innocence, simplicity, and harmony with the Dao. This is a state thought to have existed in the most ancient times, before civilization appeared to arouse the material desires of the people and impel them to strife and warfare, and before morality was invented to divert their minds from simple goodness and to beguile them with vain distinctions.

But such is the vagueness and ambiguity of the *Laozi* text and the subtlety of its thought that it may yield different interpretations and be approached on very different levels. At times in Chinese history, notably at the beginning of the Han dynasty, a political interpretation of the text has been highlighted and attempts have been made to translate the doctrines of the *Laozi* into action through government policies embodying an extreme laissez-faire attitude. But the teachings of the *Laozi* may also be understood as the philosophy of the recluse, the person of superior wisdom and insight who, instead of taking part in society, chooses to retire from public life to perfect a personal purity and intelligence and to seek harmony with the world of nature. It is this interpretation of the *Laozi* that has often prevailed in later Chinese thought.

The style of the *Laozi* is quite unlike that of the works of other schools. The text appears to be a combination of very old adages or cryptic sayings, often in rhyme, extended passages of poetry, and sections of prose interpretation and commentary. There is extensive use of parallel construction and balanced phrases; the statements are laconic and often paradoxical, intended not to convince the mind by reasoning but to startle and capture it through poetic vision. Among the prominent images are those of water—symbol of a humble, self-effacing force that is in the end all-powerful—and the female and the mother—symbol of passivity and creativity. This symbolism—and the paradoxical and poetic view of life that it suggests—has won for the work a popularity and influence that have endured through the centuries. These same appealing qualities have made it the Chinese work most often translated into foreign languages.

### FROM THE *DAODEJING*

#### 1

The Way that can be spoken of is not the constant Way;
The name that can be named is not the constant name.
The nameless is the beginning of Heaven and Earth;
The named is the mother of all things.
Thus be constantly without desire,
so as to observe its subtlety,
And constantly have desire,
so as to observe its outcome.
These two have the same origin,
But are named differently.
Both may be called mysterious.
Mysterious and still more mysterious,
The gateway of all subtleties!

#### 2

When everyone in the world knows beauty as beauty,
ugliness appears.
When everyone knows good as good,
not-good arrives.
Therefore being and non-being give birth to one another;
Difficult and easy give completion to one another;

Long and short form[1] one another;
High and low fill[2] one another;
Sound and voice harmonize with one another;
Ahead and behind follow after one another.
Therefore the sage accomplishes things by doing nothing (*wuwei*),
Furthering a teaching that is without words.
All things arise, and he does not leave them.
He gives them life but without possessing them.
He acts but without relying on his own ability.
He succeeds but without dwelling on his success.
And because he does not dwell on it, it does not leave him.

3

Do not exalt the worthy,
and the people will not compete.
Do not value goods that are hard to come by,
and the people will not steal.
Do not display objects of desire,
and the people's minds will not be disturbed.
Therefore the ordering of the sage
empties their minds,
fills their bellies,
weakens their ambitions,
strengthens their bones.
He always causes the people to be without knowledge,
without desire,
And causes the wise ones not to dare to act.
He does nothing (*wuwei*), and there is nothing that is
not brought to order.

4

The Way is empty.
It may be used without ever being exhausted.
Fathomless, it seems to be the ancestor of all things.
Blunting the sharpness,
Untying the tangles,

---

1. Reading *xing* with the Mawangdui texts rather than *qiao* with the text of the third-century commentator, Wang Bi.
2. Reading *ying* with the Mawangdui texts rather than *qing* with the Wang Bi text.

Subduing the light.
Merging with the dust.
Profound, it appears to exist forever.
Whose child it is I do not know.
It seems to have existed before the Lord.


5


Heaven and Earth are not humane,
Regarding all things as straw dogs.[3]
The sage is not humane,
Regarding the people as straw dogs.
Between Heaven and Earth—how like a bellows!
Vacuous but inexhaustible,
Moving and producing ever more.
An excess of words ends in impoverishment.
It is better to hold to the center.


6


The spirit of the valley does not die.
It is called the mysterious female.
The gate of the mysterious female
Is called the root of Heaven and Earth.
Being continuous, it is as if it existed always.
Being used, it is still not exhausted.


10


In preserving the soul and embracing the One,
can you avoid departing from them?
In concentrating your $qi$[4] and arriving at utmost weakness,
can you be like an infant?
In cleansing and purifying your profound insight,
can you be without fault?
In loving the people and governing the state,
can you be without knowledge?

---

3. Straw dogs were used for sacrifices in ancient China. After they had been used, they were thrown away and there was no sentimental attachment to them.

4. *Qi* is a fundamental concept in Chinese thought. Its sense depends on the context, but among the most frequently encountered translations are "vital energy," "vital force," "material-force," and "breath."

In the opening and closing of the gates of Heaven,
can you play the role of the female?
In understanding all within the four reaches,
can you do nothing (*wuwei*)?
Give life to things, rear them,
Give them life but without possessing them,
Act but without relying on your own ability,
Lead them but without ruling them—
This is called profound virtue.

### 11

Thirty spokes conjoin in one hub;
there being nothing in between,
the cart is useful.
Clay is molded to form a vessel;
there being nothing inside,
the vessel is useful.
Doors and windows are carved out to make a room:
there being nothing within,
the room is useful.
Thus, with something one gets advantage,
While with nothing one gets usefulness.

### 12

The five colors cause a person's eyes to go blind,
The five tones cause a person's ears to go deaf.
The five flavors cause a person's palate to be spoiled.
Racing and hunting cause a person's mind to run wild.
Goods that are hard to come by impede a person's actions.
This is why the sage concerns himself with the belly,
not the eye.
And why he rejects the one and chooses the other.

### 17

The highest is one whose existence no one knows,
The next is one who is loved and admired,
The next, one who is feared,
And the next, one who is hated.

When his faith in them is not sufficient,
They will have no faith in him.
Anxiously, he values his words,
Fulfills his tasks, completes his work.
The people all say,
"And with us, it happened naturally."

## 18

When the great Way declined,
There were humaneness and rightness.
When intelligence and wisdom emerged,
There was great artifice.
When the six relations[5] were no longer harmonious,
There were filial children.
When the realm fell into disorder,
There were loyal ministers.

## 19

Do away with sageliness, discard knowledge,
And the people will benefit a hundredfold.
Do away with humaneness, discard rightness,
And the people will once more be filial and loving,
Dispense with cleverness, discard profit,
And there will be no more bandits and thieves.
These three, to be regarded as ornaments, are insufficient.
Therefore let the people have something to cling to:
Manifest plainness,
Embrace uncarved wood,
Diminish selfishness,
Reduce desires.

## 28

Knowing the male, but keeping to the female,
One may become a ravine to the world.
Becoming a ravine to the world,
The constant virtue does not depart;

---

5. The six relations are those between parent and child, older and younger brother, husband and wife.

One returns to the state of infancy.
Knowing the white, but keeping to the black,
One may become a model for the world.
Becoming a model for the world,
The constant virtue does not deviate;
One returns to the limitless (*wuji*).
Knowing honor but keeping to lowliness,
One may become a valley to the world.
Becoming a valley to the world,
The constant virtue will be sufficient;
One returns to uncarved wood.
When the uncarved wood is broken up, it becomes vessels.
The sage, using them, becomes head of the officials.
Great carving does not rend asunder.

## 37

The Way is constant: by doing nothing,
nothing is left undone.
If lords and kings can hold to it, all things will,
of themselves, be transformed.
If, as they are transformed, desires arise,
I suppress them by means of the nameless uncarved wood.
From the nameless uncarved wood comes absence of desire,
Through not desiring one becomes tranquil,
And the empire, of itself, becomes settled.

## 38

. . . [A]fter the Way was lost there was virtue,
After virtue was lost there was humaneness,
After humaneness was lost there was rightness,
And after rightness was lost there was ritual propriety.
Now ritual is the wearing thin of fidelity and trustworthiness
and the beginning of chaos.

. . . . . . . . . . . . . . . . . . . . . .

## 39

. . . . . . . . . . . . . . . . . . . . . . . . . . . . . . . . . . . . . .

. . . [W]hat is honored is rooted in the humble;
And what is exalted is founded in the lowly.

This is why lords and kings refer to themselves
as the orphaned, the lonely ones, the unfortunate.
Is this not taking humility as the root?

. . . . . . . . . . . . . . . . . . . . . . . . . . . . .


## 43

What is softest in the world
Overcomes what is hardest in the world.
No-thing penetrates where there is no space.
Thus I know that in doing nothing there is advantage.
The wordless teaching and the advantage of doing nothing—
there are few in the world who understand them.


## 48

Devotion to learning means increasing day by day;
Devotion to the Way means decreasing day by day.

. . . . . . . . . . . . . . . . . . . . . . . . . . . . . . . . . . . .


## 56

Those who know do not speak;
Those who speak do not know.
Close the openings;
Shut the gates.
Untie the tangles;
Subdue the light.
Merge with the dust:
This is called the mysterious merging.

. . . . . . . . . . . . . . . . . . . . . . . . . . . .


## 57

. . . . . . . . . . . . . . . . . . . . . . . . . . . . . . . . .

The more prohibitions there are in the world,
The poorer are the people.
The more sharp weapons the people have,
The more disorder is fomented in the family and state.
The more adroit and clever men are,
The more deceptive things are brought forth.

The more laws and ordinances are promulgated,
The more thieves and robbers there are.
Therefore the sage says:
I do nothing (*wuwei*),
And the people are transformed by themselves.

. . . . . . . . . . . . . . . . . . . . . . . . . . . . . . . . . .

## 60

Governing a large state is like cooking a small fish.
By using the Way to manage the empire,
Spiritual forces lose their potency.
Not that they lose their potency,
But that their potency does not harm people.

. . . . . . . . . . . . . . . . . . . . . . . . . . . . . . . . . .

## 61

A large state is the effluence of a river,
Confluence of the world,
Female of the world.
Through stillness the female always overcomes the male.
Through stillness she submits.
Thus, by submitting, a large state wins a small one,
And a small state, by submitting to a large state,
wins the large state.
Thus one submits in order to win.

. . . . . . . . . . . . . . . . . . . . . . . . . . . .

## 65

Of old, those who were good at practicing the Way
Sought not to illuminate the people but to keep them ignorant.
The people become difficult to govern
as their knowledge increases.
Therefore one who governs a state through wisdom
is the robber of the state.
One who does not govern the state through wisdom
is the blessing of the state.
Knowing these two things one is also a standard and a guide;
Always knowing the standard and the guide is called
mysterious virtue.

Mysterious virtue is deep and far-reaching:
With it, all things revert [to their true reality],[6]
And then reach great harmony.

## 66

What enables the great rivers and seas to be king
over all the valley streams
Is that they are good at staying below them,
And thus can be kings over the valley streams.
Therefore if one wants to be above the people,
One must, in using words, remain below them.

. . . . . . . . . . . . . . . . . . . . . . . . . . . . . . . . . .

## 67

. . . . . . . . . . . . . . . . . . . . . . . . . . . . . .

I have three treasures to hold and to keep:
The first is compassion.
The second is frugality.
The third is not daring to be first in the world.

. . . . . . . . . . . . . . . . . . . . . . . . . . . . . . . . .

Now if one abandons compassion so as to be courageous,
If one abandons frugality so as to be broad-minded,
If one abandons being last so as to be first,
This is death.

. . . . . . . . . . .

## 80

Let the state be small and the people be few.
There may be ten or even a hundred times as many implements,
But they should not be used.

. . . . . . . . . . . . . . . . . . . . . . .

Though they have boats and carriages, none shall ride in them.
Though they have armor and weapons, none shall display them.

. . . . . . . . . . . . . . . . . . . . . . . . . . . . . . . . . . . . . . . . .

Let them savor their food and find beauty in their clothing,
peace in their dwellings, and joy in their customs.

---

6. Following the interpretation of Wang Bi.

Though neighboring states are within sight of one another,
And the sound of cocks and dogs is audible
from one to the other,
People will reach old age and death
and yet not visit one another.[7]

[From *Laozi* (*SBBY*); IB]

# TRANSFORMATION AND TRANSCENDENCE IN THE *ZHUANGZI*

In Zhuang Zhou—or Zhuangzi—we encounter a true intellectual and spiritual genius, one of the most philosophically challenging and verbally adept contributors to the early Chinese tradition and also one of its wittiest and most intriguing personalities. Zhuangzi probes philosophical depths in ways that are often unsettling and even unnerving; simultaneously he achieves literary heights that are literally breathtaking. While the *Daodejing* offers its sententious wisdom in the form of a kind of gnomic poetry, the text that bears Zhuangzi's name is a linguistically flamboyant tour de force, opening with a dazzling flight of the spirit and closing, thirty-three chapters later, with a comprehensive and remarkably sober survey of the world of thought in the late Warring States period. In between there are conversations, often highly fanciful, between real or, more often, imaginary people, along with anecdotes, parables, meditations, and poems. The characters that inhabit the pages of the *Zhuangzi* include craftsmen, cripples, a slyly reconstructed Confucius, and a talking tree—among a host of others.

While it is now generally accepted that the author and teacher known as Laozi, "the old master," was not actually a single person, Zhuang Zhou, though biographical detail concerning his life is scant, has been recognized as a distinct individual. The Han dynasty historian Sima Qian (145?–86? B.C.E.) records that he was a native of a place called Meng, where he once served as "an official in the lacquer garden," and that he lived during the times of King Hui of Liang (370–319 B.C.E.) and King Xuan of Qi (319–301 B.C.E.). The location of Meng is still uncertain, but it may well have been in the feudal state of Song, where hundreds of years earlier the vestiges of the Shang royal family had been enfeoffed. The years of Zhuang Zhou's life are also not reliably known, but if Sima Qian's chronology is even approximately correct, Zhuang Zhou would have been a contemporary of Mencius.

Following the fourth-century commentator Guo Xiang (d. 312 C.E.), scholars generally attribute to this presumably historical Zhuang Zhou the first seven

---

7. According to the commentary by Wang Bi, this is because there is nothing they want to acquire.

chapters of the *Zhuangzi*, which have become known as the Inner Chapters. All of the selections that follow below derive from these seven chapters.

### FROM CHAPTER 1, "FREE AND EASY WANDERING"

In the bald and barren north, there is a dark sea, the Lake of Heaven. In it is a fish that is several thousand *li* across, and no one knows how long. His name is Kun. There is also a bird there, named Peng, with a back like Mount Tai and wings like clouds filling the sky. He beats the whirlwind, leaps into the air, and rises up ninety thousand *li*, cutting through the clouds and mist, shouldering the blue sky, and then he turns his eyes south and prepares to journey to the southern darkness.

The little quail laughs at him, saying, "Where does he think *he's* going? I give a great leap and fly up, but I never get more than ten or twelve yards before I come down fluttering among the weeds and brambles. And that's the best kind of flying anyway! Where does he think *he's* going?" Such is the difference between big and little.

Therefore a man who has wisdom enough to fill one office effectively, good conduct enough to impress one community, virtue enough to please one ruler, or talent enough to be called into service in one state, has the same kind of self-pride as these little creatures. Song Rongzi[8] would certainly burst out laughing at such a man. The whole world could praise Song Rongzi and it wouldn't make him exert himself; the whole world could condemn him and it wouldn't make him mope. He drew a clear line between the internal and the external, and recognized the boundaries of true glory and disgrace. But that was all. As far as the world went, he didn't fret and worry, but there was still ground he left unturned.

Liezi[9] could ride the wind and go soaring around with cool and breezy skill, but after fifteen days he came back to earth. As far as the search for good fortune went, he didn't fret and worry. He escaped the trouble of walking, but he still had to depend on something to get around. If he had only mounted on the truth of Heaven and Earth, ridden the changes of the six breaths, and thus wandered through the boundless, then what would he have had to depend on?

Therefore I say, the Perfect Man has no self; the Holy Man has no merit; the Sage has no fame. [pp. 29–32]

Huizi said to Zhuangzi, "I have a big tree of the kind men call *shu*. Its trunk is too gnarled and bumpy to apply a measuring line to, its branches too bent and

---

8. Referred to elsewhere in the literature of the period as Song Jian or Song Keng. According to chapter 33 of the *Zhuangzi*, he taught a doctrine of social harmony, frugality, pacifism, and the rejection of conventional standards of honor and disgrace.

9. Lie Yukou, a Daoist sage frequently mentioned in the *Zhuangzi*. The *Liezi*, a work attributed to him, is of uncertain date and did not reach its present form until the second or third century C.E.

twisty to match up to a compass or a square. You could stand it by the road and no carpenter would look at it twice. Your words, too, are big and useless, and so everyone alike spurns them!"

Zhuangzi said, "Maybe you've never seen a wildcat or a weasel. It crouches down and hides, watching for something to come along. It leaps and races east and west, not hesitating to go high or low—until it falls into the trap and dies in the net. Then again there's the yak, big as a cloud covering the sky. It certainly knows how to be big, but it doesn't know how to catch rats. Now you have this big tree and you're distressed because it's useless. Why don't you plant it in Not-Even-Anything Village, or the field of Broad-and-Boundless, relax and do nothing by its side, or lie down for free and easy sleep under it? Axes will never shorten its life, nothing can ever harm it. If there's no use for it, how can it come to grief or pain?" [p. 35]

> [*Zhuangzi* (SBBY) 1:1a–5b, 9a–b;
> adapted from Watson, *Chuang Tzu*, pp. 29–32, 35]

### FROM CHAPTER 2, "THE SORTING WHICH EVENS THINGS OUT"

This chapter is considered the most philosophically significant in the *Zhuangzi*, dealing as it does with matters of knowledge and language, life and death, dream and reality. In the following passage Zhuangzi starts from a quotation or provisional formulation of his own. His theme is the mind or heart, the organ of thought. Should it be allowed to take charge of our lives? Isn't it merely one of many organs, each with its own functions within an order that comes from beyond us, from the Way?

"Without an Other there is no Self, without Self no choosing one thing rather than another."

This is somewhere near it, but we do not know in whose service they are being employed. It seems that there is something genuinely in command, and that the only trouble is we cannot find a sign of it. That as "Way" it can be walked is true enough, but we do not see its shape; it has identity but no shape. Of the hundred joints, nine openings, six viscera all present and complete, which should I recognize as more kin to me than another? Are you people pleased with them all? Rather, you have a favorite organ among them. On your assumption, does it have the rest of them as its vassals and concubines? Are its vassals and concubines inadequate to rule each other? Isn't it rather that they take turns as each other's lord and vassals? Or rather than that, they have a genuine lord present in them. If we seek without success to grasp what its identity might be, that never either adds to nor detracts from its genuineness. [p. 51]

Once we have received the completed body we are aware of it all the time we await extinction. Is it not sad how we and other things go on stroking or jostling each other, in a race ahead like a gallop which nothing can stop? How can we fail to regret that we labor all our lives without seeing success, wear ourselves out with toil in ignorance of where we shall end? What use is it for man to say that he will not die, since when the body dissolves the heart dissolves with it? How can we not call this our supreme regret? Is man's life really as stupid as this? Or is it that I am the only stupid one, and there are others not so stupid? But if you go by the completed heart and take it as your authority, who is without such an authority? Why should it be only the man who knows how things alternate and whose heart approves his own judgments who has such an authority? . . . [p. 52]

*The following passage refers to conventions of disputation or argument that were current in Zhuangzi's time. In disputation, if an object fits the name "ox," one affirms with the demonstrative word shi "[That] is it"; if it is something other than an ox one denies with a fei "[That] is not." Here Zhuangzi tries to discredit disputation by the objection that at any moment of change both alternatives will be admissible. He appeals to a paradox of Hui Shi, "The sun is simultaneously at noon and declining, a thing is simultaneously alive and dead," and generalizes to the conclusion that any statement will remain inadmissible at the very moment when it has just become admissible. It was also recognized in current disputation (as practiced by followers of Mozi) that one can say both "Y is long" (in relation to X) and "Y is short" (in relation to Z) and that even with words such as black and white, which are not comparative, one has to decide whether to "go by" (yin) the black parts or the white when deeming someone a "black man." Zhuangzi sees it as the lesson of disputation that one is entitled to affirm or deny anything of anything. He thinks of Confucians and Mohists who stick rigidly to their affirmations and denials as lighting up little areas of life and leaving the rest in darkness; the illumination of the sage is a vision that brings everything to light.*

Saying is not blowing breath, saying says something; the only trouble is that what it says is never fixed. Do we really say something? Or have we never said anything? If you think it different from the twitter of fledglings, is there proof of the distinction? Or isn't there any proof? By what is the Way hidden, that there should be a genuine or a false? By what is saying darkened, that sometimes "That's it" and sometimes "That's not"? Wherever we walk, how can the Way be absent? Whatever the standpoint, how can saying be unallowable? The Way is hidden by formation of the lesser, saying is darkened by its foliage and flowers. And so we have the "That's it, that's not" of Confucians and Mohists, by which what is *it* for one of them for the other is not, what is *not* for one of them for the other is. If you wish to affirm what they deny and deny what they affirm, the best means is Illumination. [p. 52]

*In the following exchange Gaptooth is pressing for an admission that there must be something that is knowable. Wang Ni denies it, perhaps because there could be no independent viewpoint from which to judge a universally shared opinion. Then at least one knows what one does not know. But that is another contradiction, or so Zhuangzi thinks. Then one knows that no one knows anything—another contradiction.*

Gaptooth put a question to Wang Ni.

"Would you *know* something of which all things agreed 'That's it'?"

"How would I know that?"

"Would you know what you did not know?"

"How would I know that?"

"Then does no thing know anything?"

"How would I know that? However, let me try to say it—'How do I know that what I call knowing is not ignorance? How do I know that what I call ignorance is not knowing?'" . . .

[Gaptooth said,] "If you do not know benefit from harm, would you deny that the utmost man knows benefit from harm?"

[Wang Ni replied,] "The utmost man is daemonic.[10] When the wide woodlands blaze, they cannot sear him, when the Yellow River and the Han freeze they cannot chill him, when swift thunderbolts smash the mountains and whirlwinds shake the seas they cannot startle him. A man like that yokes the clouds to his chariot, rides the sun and the moon, and roams beyond the four seas; death and life alter nothing in himself, still less the principles of benefit and harm!" [p. 58]

[Changwuzi said,] "How do I know that to take pleasure in life is not a delusion? How do I know that we who hate death are not exiles since childhood who have forgotten the way home? Lady Li was the daughter of a frontier guard at Ai. When the kingdom of Jin first took her the tears stained her dress; only when she came to the palace and shared the king's square couch and ate the flesh of hay-fed and grain-fed beasts did she begin to regret her tears. How do I know that the dead do not regret that ever they had an urge to life? Who banquets in a dream, at dawn wails and weeps; who wails and weeps in a dream, at dawn goes out to hunt. While we dream we do not know that we are dreaming, and in the middle of a dream interpret a dream within it; not until we wake do we know that we were dreaming. Only at the ultimate awakening shall we know that this is the ultimate dream. Yet fools think they are awake, so confident that they know what they are, princes, herdsmen, incorrigible! You and Confucius are both dreams, and I who call you a dream am also a dream. This saying of his, the name for it is 'a flight into the extraordinary'; if it happens once in ten thousand ages that a great sage knows its explanation it will have happened as though between morning and evening." [pp. 59–60]

[*Zhuangzi* (SBBY) 1:10a–15a, 15b–17b, 20a–23b;
adapted from Graham, *Chuang-tzu*, pp. 51–52, 58–60]

Once Zhuang Zhou dreamed he was a butterfly. A butterfly fluttering happily around—was he revealing what he himself meant to be? He knew nothing of Zhou. All at once awakening, there suddenly he was—Zhou. But he didn't know

---

10. Or spiritual, *shen.*

if he was Zhou having dreamed he was a butterfly or a butterfly dreaming he was Zhou. Between Zhou and the butterfly there must surely be some distinction. This is known as the transformation of things.

[From *Zhuangzi* (SBBY) 1:25b; IB]

### FROM CHAPTER 3, "THE SECRET OF CARING FOR LIFE"

Your life has a limit but knowledge has none. If you use what is limited to pursue what has no limit, you will be in danger. If you understand this and still strive for knowledge, you will be in danger for certain! If you do good, stay away from fame. If you do evil, stay away from punishments. Follow the middle, go by what is constant, and you can stay in one piece, keep yourself alive, look after your parents, and live out your years.

Cook Ding was cutting up an ox for Lord Wenhui. At every touch of his hand, every heave of his shoulder, every move of his feet, every thrust of his knee — zip, zoop! He slithered the knife along with a zing, and all was in perfect rhythm. . . .

"Ah, this is marvelous!" said Lord Wenhui. "Imagine skill reaching such heights!"

Cook Ding laid down his knife and replied, "What I care about is the Way, which goes beyond skill. When I first began cutting up oxen, all I could see was the ox itself. After three years I no longer saw the whole ox. And now — now I go at it by spirit and don't look with my eyes. Perception and understanding have come to a stop and spirit moves where it wants. I go along with the natural makeup, strike in the big hollows, guide the knife through the big openings, and follow things as they are. So I never touch the smallest ligament or tendon, much less a main joint.

"A good cook changes his knife once a year — because he cuts. A mediocre cook changes his knife once a month — because he hacks. I've had this knife of mine for nineteen years and I've cut up thousands of oxen with it, and yet the blade is as good as though it had just come from the grindstone. There are spaces between the joints, and the blade of the knife has really no thickness. If you insert what has no thickness into such spaces, then there's plenty of room — more than enough for the blade to play about it. That's why after nineteen years the blade of my knife is still as good as when it first came from the grindstone.

"However, whenever I come to a complicated place, I size up the difficulties, tell myself to watch out and be careful, keep my eyes on what I'm doing, work very slowly, and move the knife with the greatest subtlety, until — flop! the whole thing comes apart like a clod of earth crumbling to the ground. I stand there holding the knife and look all around me, completely satisfied and reluctant to move on, and then I wipe off the knife and put it away."

"Excellent!" said Lord Wenhui. "I have heard the words of Cook Ding and learned how to care for life!" . . . [pp. 50–51]

[From *Zhuangzi* (SBBY) 2:1a–4a; Watson, *Chuang Tzu*, pp. 50–51]

## FROM CHAPTER 4, "IN THE WORLD OF MEN"

This chapter of the *Zhuangzi* opens with an exchange between Confucius and his favorite disciple, Yan Hui—an exchange concocted, of course, by Zhuangzi. Zhuangzi imagines Yan Hui requesting permission to journey to the state of Wei and contemplating what he might do to exert a positive influence over the young ruler of that state. Confucius is skeptical about Yan Hui's chances for success and points out that rulers motivated by concerns for fame or gain are likely to be intractable. After repeatedly cautioning Yan Hui, he asks to hear the disciple's plan.

Yan Hui said, "If I am grave and empty-hearted, diligent and of one mind, won't that do?"

"Goodness, how could *that* do? You may put on a fine outward show and seem very impressive, but you can't avoid having an uncertain look on your face, any more than an ordinary man can. And then you try to gauge this man's feelings and seek to influence his mind. But with him, what is called "the virtue that advances a little each day" would not succeed, much less a great display of virtue! He will stick fast to his position and never be converted. Though he may make outward signs of agreement, inwardly he will not give it a thought! How could such an approach succeed?"

"Well, then, suppose I am inwardly direct, outwardly compliant, and do my work through the examples of antiquity? By being inwardly direct, I can be the companion of Heaven. Being a companion of Heaven, I know that the Son of Heaven and I are equally the sons of Heaven. Then why would I use my words to try to get men to praise me, or try to get them not to praise me? A man like this, people call The Child. This is what I mean by being a companion of Heaven.

"By being outwardly compliant, I can be a companion of men. Lifting up the tablet, kneeling, bowing, crouching down—this is the etiquette of a minister. Everybody does it, so why shouldn't I? If I do what other people do, they can hardly criticize me. This is what I mean by being a companion of men.

"By doing my work through the examples of antiquity, I can be the companion of ancient times. Though my words may in fact be lessons and reproaches, they belong to ancient times and not to me. In this way, though I may be blunt, I cannot be blamed. This is what I mean by being a companion of antiquity. If I go about it in this way, will it do?"

Confucius said, "Goodness, how could *that* do? You have too many policies and plans and you haven't seen what is needed. You will probably get off without incurring any blame, yes. But that will be as far as it goes. How do you think you can actually convert him? You are still making the mind[11] your teacher."

Yan Hui said, "I have nothing more to offer. May I ask the proper way?"

---

11. Not the natural or "given" mind but the mind that makes artificial distinctions.

"You must fast!" said Confucius. "I will tell you what that means. Do you think that it is easy to do anything while you have [a mind]? If you do, Bright Heaven will not sanction you."

Yan Hui said, "My family is poor. I haven't drunk wine or eaten any strong foods for several months. So can I be considered as having fasted?"

"That is the fasting one does before a sacrifice, not the fasting of the mind."

"May I ask what the fasting of the mind is?"

Confucius said, "Make your will one! Don't listen with your ears, listen with your mind. No, don't listen with your mind, listen with your spirit.[12] Listening stops with the ears, the mind stops with recognition, but spirit is empty and waits on all things. The Way gathers in emptiness alone. Emptiness is the fasting of the mind." [pp. 56–58]

> [*Zhuangzi* (SBBY) 2:6a–8a, 12a–13a;
> adapted from Watson, *Chuang Tzu*, pp. 56–58]

### FROM CHAPTER 6, "THE GREAT AND VENERABLE TEACHER"

Nanbo Zikui said to the Woman Crookback, "You are old in years and yet your complexion is that of a child. Why is this?"

"I have heard the Way!"

"Can the Way be learned?" asked Nanbo Zikui.

"Goodness, how could that be? Anyway, you aren't the man to do it. Now there's Buliang Yi—he has the talent of a sage but not the Way of a sage, whereas I have the Way of a sage but not the talent of a sage. I thought I would try to reach him and see if I could get anywhere near to making him a sage. It's easier to explain the Way of a sage to someone who has the talent of a sage, you know. So I began explaining and kept at him for three days, and after that he was able to put the world outside himself. When he had put the world outside himself, I kept at him for seven days more, and after that he was able to put things outside himself. When he had put things outside himself, I kept at him for nine days more, and after that he was able to put life outside himself. After he had put life outside himself, he was able to achieve the brightness of dawn, and when he had achieved the brightness of dawn, he could see his own aloneness. After he had managed to see his own aloneness, he could do away with past and present, and after he had done away with past and present, he was able to enter where there is no life and death. That which kills life does not die; that which gives life to life does not live.[13] This is the kind of thing it is: there's nothing it doesn't send off, nothing it doesn't welcome, nothing it doesn't destroy, nothing it doesn't

---

12. Literally, with your *qi*, material-force or vital energy.

13. I.e., that which transcends the categories of life and death can never be said to have lived or died; only that which recognizes the existence of such categories is subject to them.

complete. It's name is Peace-in-Strife. After the strife, it attains completion. . . ." [pp. 82–83]

Yan Hui said, "I'm improving!"

Confucius said, "What do you mean by that?"

"I've forgotten humaneness and rightness."

"That's good. But you still haven't got it."

Another day, the two met again, and Yan Hui said, "I'm improving!"

"What do you mean by that?"

"I've forgotten rites and music."

"That's good. But you still haven't got it."

Another day, the two met again, and Yan Hui said, "I'm improving!"

"What do you mean by that?"

"I can sit down and forget everything."

Confucius looked very startled and said, "What do you mean, sit down and forget everything?"

Yan Hui said, "I smash up my limbs and body, drive out perception and intellect, cast off form, do away with understanding, and make myself identical with the Great Thoroughfare. This is what I mean by sitting down and forgetting everything."

Confucius said, "If you're identical with it, you must have no more likes! If you've been transformed, you must have no more constancy! So you really are a worthy man after all![14] With your permission, I'd like to become your follower." [pp. 90–91]

> [From *Zhuangzi* (SBBY) 3:7a–10a, 14a–b;
> Watson, *Chuang Tzu*, pp. 82–83, 90–91]

## FROM CHAPTER 7, "FIT FOR EMPERORS AND KINGS"

The sovereign of the Southern Sea is called Impatient; the sovereign of the Northern Sea is called Impulsive; the sovereign of the center of the world is called the Primal Whole (*hundun*). Impatient and Impulsive met from time to time in the territory of the Primal Whole, and the latter treated them well. Impatient and Impulsive discussed together how they could repay his kindness. They said, "All men have seven holes in their bodies for seeing, hearing, eating, and breathing. Our friend here has none of these, Let us try to bore some holes for him." Each day they bored one hole. On the seventh day the Primal Whole died.

> [From *Zhuangzi* (SBBY) 3:19a–b; deB]

---

14. *Zhuangzi* may have intended a humorous reference to the words of Confucius in *Analects* 6:9: "The Master said, 'What a worthy man was Hui!'"

*Chapter 6*

## THE EVOLUTION OF THE CONFUCIAN
## TRADITION IN ANTIQUITY

In the two and a half centuries following the death of Confucius, the Chinese world changed enormously. During the lifetime of Confucius, China was still nominally ruled by the Zhou dynasty, though in fact the Zhou had lost virtually all of its actual power some three hundred years earlier, with real, if always uncertain, power having passed by the eighth century B.C.E. into the hands of the wayward rulers of contending feudal states. A certain tension seems to come through at various points in the Confucian *Analects* surrounding the status and prerogatives of the feudal lords who exercised power within the states but were nonetheless judged by Confucius to be deficient when it came to their claims to legitimacy. Several statements attributed to Confucius seem to imply that the prerogatives of the Zhou house should not have been usurped. Nonetheless, Confucius's recorders seem to have sensed in him—or attributed to him—an uncertainty about the future political order and, with it, a tendency to think of the Zhou more in terms of the nobility of its ancient culture than in terms of any possible restoration of its power.

Mencius (385?–312? B.C.E.), the first great successor to Confucius, held out even less hope for the future of the House of Zhou, or such is the implication of questions that are raised repeatedly, if often indirectly, in the Mencian conversations: who might be capable of uniting "all under Heaven," and by what means? The same questions occupied Xunzi (310?–219? B.C.E.), the third major figure in the early Confucian tradition, who returns to them repeatedly in his own reflections on government. By the closing years of Xunzi's lifetime, these questions would be at least partially resolved. When in 221 B.C.E. the feudal state of Qin conquered the last of the remaining feudal states, uniting China for the first time under a single ruler, the feudal order would finally be destroyed, and in its place a new empire would be established. That the empire would be founded on force was apparent; that the empire could be maintained and stabilized through force was not. Some of the long-standing questions about governance would persist and become ever more closely intertwined with questions about culture and history.

In fact, long before the Qin conquest and the founding of the empire, questions had begun to arise about the nature and the hold of the past—how it should be understood and in what respects it should be honored in changing circumstances. These may, in fact, have been the most persistent and pervasive questions to be pondered and debated at the time, not only among Confucians but among other thinkers of the Warring States period (479–221 B.C.E.) as well. For Confucians, the most urgent questions focused on the survival of moral attitudes and ritual forms that had been associated with the older feudal order. What was the role of courtesy and ritual, honor and fidelity, in a world marked by increasing social mobility, ever greater uncertainty about established social relationships, and escalating violence?

It was typical of Confucians to recognize civilization as both an ongoing process and an inheritance from the past, but was the cumulative achievement of "the ancients" to be preserved in the fullness of its form and detail or was their record of accomplishment to be treasured more for the noble and inspiring personal models that they provided for later generations following in a common cause? In either case, how much was to be preserved in the name of civilization as a legacy from the past, and how much was susceptible to change in defense of larger human purposes?

In this chapter we present excerpts from three of the most important texts of the Confucian tradition in ancient China. Each of them addressed these questions, though in different ways. The *Mencius* and the *Xunzi* may be described as philosophical works—quite different from each other in both form and content, yet similar in the sense that they reflect on matters of governance and personal cultivation and, like virtually all Confucian works, assume a direct relationship between the two. The *Zuozhuan*—or *Zuo's Commentary*—is China's oldest narrative history. It is not, perhaps, a Confucian work in the same sense that the *Mencius* and the *Xunzi* are, but at many points it vividly illustrates a similar alertness to the connection between the moral dispositions of individuals and the dynamics of their lives and political careers. Moreover, from very early times the *Zuozhuan*, traditionally believed to be a commentary on the classic known as the *Spring and Autumn Annals*, was itself accorded the status of a Confucian classic, whereas the *Mencius* was so honored only much later, in the twelfth century, and the *Xunzi*, for complex reasons, not at all. Each of these texts provides a fascinating perspective on changes in values in the time of Confucius and in the subsequent Warring States period, while together they suggest the variety and complexity to be found within the Confucian tradition as it evolved in ancient China.

# MENCIUS

Meng Ke — or Mencius, as he is known to readers of English translations — lived in the fourth century B.C.E., more than a century after the time of Confucius. Confucius, who in his own lifetime had enjoyed only the most qualified success, had by Mencius's time acquired the reputation of a sage. Mencius acknowledged him as such and seems to have shared his most cherished values, though not without transforming many of them. The Warring States period witnessed a process of consolidation in which larger and more powerful feudal states swallowed up smaller and weaker ones. A concomitant of this development was a change in the character of warfare, which now became more brutal, with large conscript armies pitted against each other in battles that typically took a terrible toll in human lives. During these uncertain times Mencius traveled from one feudal state to another, speaking to rulers about government, deploring the effects of warfare on the people, and pleading the case for the practicality of humaneness. His response to the political situation was determined, yet subtle: he reaffirmed a profound Confucian confidence in the efficacy of morality but was resigned to the possibility that he himself might not figure into, or even personally witness, the restoration of a moral order.

The *Mencius* is a record of conversations between Mencius and rulers of the contending feudal states, disciples, and philosophical adversaries. It also includes pronouncements by Mencius on a variety of subjects, especially government and human nature. We find in it not an authorial presence providing form, structure, and coherence to the work but rather a more disparate, even fragmented collection of exchanges that occurred at various times and places and were recorded after the fact. Many of these exchanges take the form of arguments. While maintaining that he was disinclined to argument, he insists that his career as a controversialist has been forced upon him — that he is compelled to dispute with rulers and scholars who fail to understand the legacy of civilization and, underlying it, the human potential for goodness.

In the selections that follow, some of the most prominent Mencian attitudes and themes emerge. A recurrent theme — one that echoes and reechoes in virtually all later Confucian discourse — is the idea that what ultimately matters in human interactions is the motivation of the actors and their capacity for mutual respect and regard based on recognition of a common humanity. Mencius both recalls and enlarges the Confucian idea of *ren*, or humaneness. Alongside it he places the complementary principle of *yi*, or rightness, a complex idea of what is right in particular situations as individuals perform their distinct roles and confront the different circumstances of their lives.

Mencius appeals to rulers to draw on humaneness in their conduct of affairs of state rather than doubting their own capacity for compassion and to recognize the claims of rightness rather than succumbing to the expedient. He is direct to the point of acerbity in criticizing rulers for their role in instigating warfare, devout in deploring war's pernicious effects on the lives of the common people. Perhaps influenced by his adversaries, the Mohists and the Legalists, he displays a keen awareness that human beings have certain basic needs—food, clothing, shelter, and education—and that these must be met if their very existence as human beings is to be possible. War inevitably interferes with the satisfaction of these basic human needs, he observes, as does overindulgence on the part of rulers.

Mencius's discussions of matters of state draw on historical memory—or recreations of history. He seems to reclaim, in memory, the moral aura of a time before the beginning of the dynastic system, when rulers were selected on the morally compelling basis of merit rather than the less reliable basis of heredity. Much that he has to say about the ancient sage kings Yao, Shun, and Yu has to do with the moral authority that they wielded by virtue of their having gained the empire through the will of Heaven as signaled in the willingness of the people. Mindful of the potent idea of the Mandate of Heaven that he believed derived from the early Zhou, Mencius maintains that Heaven oversees a kind of overarching moral order in which it is given to rulers to rule for the sake of the common people, with the object of achieving their well-being and prosperity.

At many points in these conversations the reader will find evidence of Mencius's psychologically rich conception of human moral potential. One notable instance may be found in his discussion of the varieties of courage and of the cultivation of the "vast, flowing $qi$"—a psychophysical energy or vitality within the individual that he seems to find directly related to moral effort. Most famous are his discussions of the "four beginnings"—natural tendencies within all human beings that, he believes, can be cultivated and developed into the capacities for humaneness, rightness, propriety, and wisdom. This idea of a natural human tendency toward sympathetic responsiveness to others is, in fact, one of Mencius's most important contributions to the later history of Chinese thought.

It is clear from Mencius's arguments that many in his own time held different views of human nature, discounting his optimism, questioning his confidence in a moral potential inherent in each person, doubting his affirmation of the human capacity for perfectibility through self-cultivation. Some who followed Mencius, including such eminent Confucians as Xunzi, also challenged his views. Still, a survey of the long history of Confucian thought confirms that Mencius was the single most influential contributor to a view of human nature that would ultimately become dominant, not only in China but also in the rest of Confucianized East Asia, and not only in the thought of an intellectual and social elite but in the value system of an entire culture.

## Selections from the *Mencius*

1A:1 Mencius saw King Hui of Liang.

The king said, "So venerable an elder, having come a thousand *li*, and not considering that too far, must surely have some means to profit our state?"

Mencius replied, "Why must the king speak of profit? There are humaneness and rightness, that is all. If the king says, 'How can I profit my state?' the officers will say, 'How can I profit my house?' and the gentlemen and the common people will say, 'How can I profit my person?' Those above and those below will be competing with one another for profit, and the state will be imperiled. One who would murder the ruler of a state with ten thousand chariots would have to be from a house of a thousand chariots; one who would murder the ruler of a state of a thousand chariots would have to be from a house of a hundred chariots. A share of a thousand out of ten thousand or a hundred out of a thousand is hardly negligible; yet when rightness is subordinated to profit the urge to lay claim to more becomes irresistible. It has never happened that one given to humaneness abandons his parents, or that one given to rightness subordinates the interests of his lord. The king should speak of humaneness and rightness. Why is it necessary to speak of profit?"

1A:2 Mencius saw King Hui of Liang. As he stood overlooking a pond, watching the geese and the deer, the king asked, "Do the worthy also enjoy such things?"

Mencius replied, "Being worthy, they enjoy these things. Were they not worthy, although they might have such things, they would find no enjoyment in them. . . .

"King Wen used the strength of the people to build his tower and his pond, and the people found their delight and their joy in it. They called his tower the spirit tower and his pond the spirit pond and found joy in his having deer, and birds, and turtles. The ancients shared their joys with the people and it was this that enabled them to feel joy." . . .

1A:5 King Hui of Liang said, "No state in the empire was stronger than Jin [or Liang], as the venerable elder is aware. But when it came to this solitary man, we were defeated by Qi in the east, and my eldest son died there. In the west seven hundred *li* were lost to Qin, while in the south we were humiliated by Chu. This solitary man, having incurred such shame, wishes, for the sake of the departed, to expunge it. How may this be done?"

Mencius replied, "With a territory of so much as one hundred *li*, one can become a king. If the king bestows humane government on the people, reduces punishments, and lightens taxes, causing the plowing to be deep and the weeding thorough, the strong will be able to use their leisure time to cultivate filiality and brotherliness. Within the home they will serve their fathers and brothers, and outside they will serve their elders and superiors. They can then be made to take up sticks and overcome the strong armor and the sharp weapons of Qin and Chu." . . .

1A:7 King Xuan of Qi asked, "Would it be possible to hear about the affairs of Huan of Qi and Wen of Jin?"[1]

Mencius replied, "The followers of Confucius would not speak of the affairs of Huan and Wen, and thus nothing about them has been transmitted to later generations. Not having heard, and having nothing to say on that matter, how would it be if the minister were to speak of kingship?"

The king said, "What must one's virtue be like in order to become a king?"

Mencius said, "One who protects the people becomes a king, and no one is able to stop him."

"Could someone like this solitary man protect the people?"

"He could."

"How do you know that I could?"

"The minister heard Hu He say that, while the king was seated in the upper part of the hall, someone led an ox through the lower part. Upon seeing this, the king asked where the ox was going and was told that it was being taken to serve as a blood sacrifice in the consecration of a bell. The king said, 'Spare it. I cannot bear its trembling, like one who, though blameless, is being led to the execution ground.' Asked whether in that case the consecration of the bell should be dispensed with, the king said, 'How can it be dispensed with? Substitute a sheep instead.' Did this actually happen?"

"It did."

Mencius said, "With such a mind one has enough to become a king. Though the people all thought that it was because the king grudged the ox, the minister certainly knows that it was because the king could not bear to see its suffering."

The king said, "That is so. The people must truly have thought this, but, although the state of Qi is small and narrow, how could I grudge a single ox? It was because I could not bear its trembling, like one who, though blameless, was being led to the execution ground, that I had a sheep substituted instead."

Mencius said, "The king should not think it strange that the people assumed that he grudged the ox. How could they know why he substituted the smaller thing for the larger one? Had the king been grieving over its being led, blameless, to the execution ground, then what was there to choose between an ox and a sheep?"

The king smiled and said, "What kind of mind was this, after all? It was not that I grudged the expense, and yet I did exchange the ox for a sheep. No wonder the people said that I grudged it."

---

1. Duke Huan of Qi (r. 685–643 B.C.E.), one of the most powerful feudal lords of the seventh century, was considered the first of the "Five Hegemons," and Duke Wen of Jin (r. 636–628 B.C.E.) was considered the second. Mencius's statement in the ensuing passage that he has "heard nothing about" these hegemons is not to be taken literally. The reputation of neither ruler was entirely negative, but Mencius is making the point here that he prefers to talk about morally legitimate kings (*wang*) rather than "hegemons" (*ba*), whose claim to rule was believed by most Confucians to be more ambiguous, morally speaking.

Mencius said, "There is no harm in this. This was after all the working of humaneness—a matter of having seen the ox but not the sheep. This is the way of the noble person in regard to animals: if he sees them alive, then he cannot bear to see them die, and if he hears their cries, then he cannot bear to eat their flesh. And so the noble person stays far away from the kitchen."

The king was pleased and said, "When the Ode says, 'What other people have in their minds, I measure by reflection,'[2] it is speaking about the Master. When I tried it, going back and seeking my motive, I was unable to grasp my own mind. Yet when the Master spoke of it, my mind experienced a kind of stirring. How is it that this mind of mine accords with that of a king?"

Mencius replied, "Suppose someone were to report to the king, saying, 'My strength, while sufficient to lift a hundred *jun*, is not sufficient to lift a feather. My sight, while sufficient to scrutinize the tip of an autumn hair, is not sufficient to see a cartload of firewood.' Would the king accept this?"

"No," he said.

"Then what is there so different about the case of kindness sufficient to extend to animals yet without its benefits reaching the people? Not lifting a feather is the result of not exerting one's strength to do so; not seeing a cartload of firewood is the result of not employing his eyesight on it. That the people are not protected is because one does not exercise kindness toward them. Therefore, that the king is not kingly is because he does not do it; it is not because he is unable to do it."

The king asked, "How can one distinguish between 'not doing something' and 'being unable to do it'?"

Mencius said, "If it were a matter of taking Mount Tai under your arm and jumping over the North Sea with it, and one were to tell people, 'I am unable to do it,' this would truly be a case of being unable to do it. If it is a matter of breaking off a branch of a tree at the request of an elder, and one tells people, 'I am unable to do it,' this is a case of not doing it rather than a case of being unable to do it. And so the king's failure to be a king is not in the category of taking Mount Tai under one's arm and jumping over the North Sea with it; his failure to be a king is in the category of not breaking off a branch for an elder. By treating the elders in one's own family as elders should be treated and extending this to the elders of other families, and by treating the young of one's own family as the young ought to be treated and extending this to the young of other people's families, the empire can be turned around on the palm of one's hand. The Ode says,

> He set an example for his wife;
> It extended to his brothers,
> And from there to the family of the state.[3]

---

2. Ode 198. Translation adapted from Legge, *The Chinese Classics*, 4:342.
3. Ode 240.

"This speaks of taking this mind and extending it to others, that is all. Thus if one extends his kindness it will be enough to protect all within the four seas, whereas if one fails to extend it, he will have no way to protect his wife and children. The fact that the ancients so greatly surpassed others was nothing other than this: that they were good at extending what they did. . . ."

The king said, "I am unintelligent and have been unable to progress this far. I should like the Master to assist my will and be clear in giving me instruction, so that, while I am not clever, I may endeavor to carry it out."

"It is only a gentleman who will be able to have a constant mind despite being without a constant means of livelihood. The people, lacking a constant means of livelihood, will lack constant minds, and when they lack constant minds there is no dissoluteness, depravity, deviance, or excess to which they will not succumb. If, once they have sunk into crime, one responds by subjecting them to punishment—this is to entrap the people. With a person of humanity in a position of authority, how could the entrapment of the people be allowed to occur? Therefore an enlightened ruler will regulate the people's livelihood so as to ensure that, above, they have enough to serve their parents and, below, they have enough to support their wives and children. In years of prosperity they always have enough to eat; in years of dearth they are able to escape starvation. Only then does he urge the people toward goodness; accordingly, they find it easy to comply.

"At present, the regulation of the people's livelihood is such that, above, they do not have enough to serve their parents and, below, they do not have enough to support wives and children. Even in years of prosperity their lives are bitter, while in years of dearth they are unable to escape starvation. Under these circumstances they only try to save themselves from death, fearful that they will not succeed. How could they spare the time for the practice of rites and rightness?"

"If the king wishes to put this into practice, he should return to the root of the matter. Let mulberry trees be planted around households of five *mu*, and people of fifty will be able to be clothed in silk. In the raising of chickens, pigs, dogs, and swine, do not neglect the appropriate breeding times, and people of seventy will be able to eat meat. With fields of a hundred *mu*, do not interfere with the appropriate seasons of cultivation, and families with eight mouths to feed will be able to avoid hunger. Attend carefully to the education provided in the schools, which should include instruction in the duty of filial and fraternal devotion, and gray-haired people will not be seen carrying burdens on the roads. It has never happened that people of seventy have worn silk and eaten meat, and the black-haired people have been neither hungry nor cold, without the ruler having been a true king."

## THE DUTY OF MINISTERS TO REPROVE A RULER

In the following exchanges Mencius goes so far as to remind King Xuan of Qi that a ruler risks being deposed for crimes against humanity. This very forceful assertion, sometimes understood in our own time as implying a "right of revolution," actually involves no notion of either "rights" or "revolution" per se, having been advanced by Mencius centuries before the idea of rights was conceived anywhere in the world. In another conversation with King Xuan (translated in 5B:9) Mencius says that before the situation in a state reaches the point at which the ruler must be deposed, his ministers should remonstrate with him, quit his court if not listened to, and then have ministers of the royal blood depose him as a last resort. Thus Mencius's main emphasis is on the need for remonstrance and reproof, lest the situation in a state come to violence.

1B:6 Mencius said to King Xuan of Qi, "Suppose that one of the king's subjects entrusted his wife and children to his friend and journeyed to Chu. On returning he found that he had allowed his wife and children to be hungry and cold. What should he do?"

The king said, "Renounce him."

"Suppose the chief criminal judge could not control the officers. What should he do?"

The king said, "Get rid of him."

"Suppose that within the four borders of the state there is no proper government?"

The king looked left and right and spoke of other things.

1B:8 King Xuan of Qi asked, "Is it true that Tang banished Jie and King Wu assaulted Zhou?"[4]

Mencius replied, "This is contained in the records."[5]

"For a minister to slay his ruler—can this be countenanced?"

"One who despoils humaneness is called a thief; one who despoils rightness is called a robber. Someone who is a robber and a thief is called a mere fellow. I have heard of the punishment of the fellow Zhou but never of the slaying of a ruler."

2A:2 Gongsun Chou asked, "If the Master were appointed to be a high officer and prime minister of Qi, and were able to put the Way into practice, it would hardly be surprising if the ruler were to become leader of the feudal lords or even king. Were this to occur, would your mind be moved or not?"

Mencius said, "No, since I was forty my mind has been unmoved."

"In that case the Master far surpasses Meng Bin."

"This is not difficult. Gaozi attained an unmoved mind before I did."

"Is there a way to attain an unmoved mind?"

---

4. According to tradition, Tang, as the first ruler of the Shang dynasty, was responsible for ousting the depraved Jie, the last ruler of the Xia dynasty. King Wu, as one of the founders of the Zhou dynasty, is credited with deposing the wicked Zhou, the last ruler of the Shang.

5. Tang's ousting of Jie is recorded in the *Classic of Documents*, "The Announcement of Zhonghui" and "The Announcement of Tang," and King Wu's removal of Zhou in the *Classic of Documents*, "The Great Declaration" and "The Successful Completion of the War."

"There is. Bogong Yu's way of nourishing his valor was neither to shrink from blows nor to avert his gaze. He thought that merely to be jostled by someone was like being flogged in the marketplace. What he would not accept from a poor fellow in coarse clothing he would not accept from a lord with ten thousand chariots, and he would cut down the lord with ten thousand chariots as soon as he would the poor man, coarsely clad. He was unawed by any of the several lords, and if an insult came his way he would invariably return it.

"Meng Shishe's way of nourishing his valor is expressed in his saying, 'I regard defeat just as I do victory. To advance only after having assessed the strength of the enemy, to engage only after having calculated the prospects for victory—this is to be intimidated by the opposing force. How can I be certain of victory? I can only be fearless, that is all.'

"Meng Shishe resembled Zengzi, while Bogong Yu resembled Zixia. I do not know which kind of valor should be considered superior, but Meng Shishe kept hold of what is essential. Formerly, Zengzi said to Zixiang, 'Does the Master[6] love valor? I once heard this account of great valor from the Master:[7] "If, on examining myself, I find that I am not upright, I must be in fear of even a poor fellow in coarse clothing. If, on examining myself, I find that I am upright, I may proceed against thousands and tens of thousands."' So Meng Shishe's keeping hold of his *qi* was, after all, not comparable to Zengzi's keeping hold of what is essential." . . .

". . . The will is the leader of the *qi*, and it is *qi* that fills the body. When the will goes forward the *qi* follows it. Therefore I say, maintain the will and do no violence to the *qi*."

"Since you say, 'When the will goes forward the *qi* follows it,' why is it that you also say, 'Maintain the will and do no violence to the *qi*'?"

"If the will is unified it moves the *qi*, whereas if the *qi* is unified it moves the will. Now when a person stumbles or runs, it is the *qi* that acts, but it also moves the mind."

"May I presume to ask the Master in what he excels?"

"I understand words. I am good at nourishing my vast, flowing *qi*."

"May I presume to ask what is meant by 'vast, flowing *qi*'?"

"It is difficult to speak of it. This is *qi*: it is consummately great and consummately strong. If one nourishes it with uprightness and does not injure it, it will fill the space between Heaven and Earth. This is *qi*: it is the companion of rightness and the Way, in the absence of which it starves. It is born from an accumulation of rightness rather than appropriated through an isolated display. If one's actions cause the mind to be disquieted, it starves. I therefore said that Gaozi did not understand rightness because he regarded it as external.

---

6. That is, Zixiang.

7. That is, Confucius.

"Always be doing something, but without fixation, with a mind inclined neither to forget nor to help things grow. One should not be like the man of Song. There was a man of Song who, worried that his seedlings were not growing, pulled them up. Having done so, he returned home wearily, telling people, 'I am tired today—I have been helping the seedlings to grow.' When his sons rushed out to have a look, they found the seedlings were all withered. There are few in the world who do not try to help the seedlings to grow. Those who believe that there is no benefit in it neglect them and do not weed the seedlings. Those bent on helping them grow pull them up, which is not only of no benefit, but, on the contrary, causes them injury." . . .

2A:3 Mencius said, "One who, supported by force, fakes being humane is a hegemon, and a hegemon has to have a large state. One who out of virtue practices humaneness is a king, and a king does not need anything large. Tang did it with only seventy *li*, and King Wen did it with a hundred.

"When one uses force to make people submit, they do not submit in their hearts but only because their strength is insufficient. When one uses virtue to make people submit, they are pleased to the depths of their hearts, and they sincerely submit. So it was with the seventy disciples who submitted to Confucius. The Ode says,

> From the west, and from the east,
> From the south and from the north,
> No one thought of not submitting.[8]

This is what was meant."

2A:6 "All human beings have a mind that cannot bear to see the sufferings of others. The ancient kings had a commiserating mind and, accordingly, a commiserating government. Having a commiserating mind, and effecting a commiserating government, governing the world was like turning something around on the palm of the hand.

"Here is why I say that all human beings have a mind that commiserates with others. Now,[9] if anyone were suddenly to see a child about to fall into a well, his mind would always be filled with alarm, distress, pity, and compassion. That he would react accordingly is not because he would use the opportunity to ingratiate himself with the child's parents, nor because he would seek commendation from neighbors and friends, nor because he would hate the adverse reputation. From this it may be seen that one who lacks a mind that feels pity and compassion would not be human; one who lacks a mind that feels shame

---

8. Ode 244.

9. At the beginning of the passage Mencius recalls that the ancient kings had this "mind that cannot bear to see the sufferings of others." Here he affirms that people of the present also have it.

and aversion would not be human; one who lacks a mind that feels modesty and compliance would not be human; and one who lacks a mind that knows right and wrong would not be human.

"The mind's feeling of pity and compassion is the beginning of humaneness (*ren*); the mind's feeling of shame and aversion is the beginning of rightness (*yi*); the mind's feeling of modesty and compliance is the beginning of propriety; and the mind's sense of right and wrong is the beginning of wisdom.

"Human beings have these four beginnings just as they have four limbs. For one to have these four beginnings and yet to say of oneself that one is unable to fulfill them is to injure oneself, while to say that one's ruler is unable to fulfill them is to injure one's ruler. . . ."

## THE WELL-FIELD SYSTEM OF LANDHOLDING

The following conversation between Mencius, a ruler, and one of his ministers offers another illustration of Mencius's concern for the responsibility of the state to help the people meet their basic needs for material livelihood. It also illustrates a typically Confucian style of argument. In his discussion of the well-field system Mencius harks back to a time in the past when, according to tradition, landholding among the common people had been generally equal and village life had been cooperative. Whether the well-field system actually pertained in the past, as Mencius claims, or represented an idealization that gained reality through a process of re-creation of the historical past, his recalling it suggests that equality of landholding and mutual cooperation among the people represented themes of considerable antiquity and moral resonance. Many later Confucians would follow Mencius in identifying with these themes. Their defense against recurring charges of impracticality rested in the claim that the principles and measures they advocated had been implemented by sage rulers in the historical past and had formed the basis for civilized life.

3A:3 Duke Wen of Teng asked about governing the state. Mencius replied, "The people's business may not be delayed. The Ode says,

> In the morning gather the grasses,
> In the evening twist the ropes;
> Be quick to climb to the housetop,
> Begin to sow the hundred grains.[10]

"The Way of the people is this: that when they have a constant livelihood, they will have constant minds, but when they lack a constant livelihood, they will lack constant minds. When they lack constant minds there is no dissoluteness,

---

10. Ode 154.

depravity, deviance, or excess to which they will not succumb. If, once they have sunk into crime, one responds by subjecting them to punishment—this is to entrap the people. When a humane man is in authority, how could the entrapment of the people be allowed to occur? Therefore an exemplary ruler must be respectful, frugal, and reverent toward his subjects, and must take from the people only in accordance with the regulations. . . .”

The duke sent Bi Zhan to inquire about the well-field system. Mencius said, “Since the Master's lord intends to practice humane government, and the Master has been selected by him for employment, he must put forth great effort. Now humane government must begin with the setting of boundaries. If the boundaries are not set correctly, the division of the land into well-fields will not be equal and the grain allowances for official emoluments will not be equitable. . . . Now while the territory of Teng is narrow and small, it has both noblemen and country people. Without noblemen, there would be no one to rule the country people, and without the country people there would be no one to feed the noblemen. Please allow that in the countryside one square of land out of nine should be used for mutual aid. In the capital the people should assess themselves with a tax amounting to one part in ten. From the highest officers on down everyone must have a *gui* field,[11] and that *gui* field should be fifty *mu*. Remaining males should have twenty-five *mu*. Neither at the occasion of a death nor of a change of residence should people leave the village. When those in a village who hold land in the same well-field befriend one another in their going out and their coming in, assist one another in their protection and defense, and sustain one another through illness and distress, the hundred surnames will live together in affection and harmony. A square *li* constitutes a well-field, and the well-field contains 900 *mu*. The central plot among them is a public field, and eight families each have private holdings of a hundred *mu*. Together they cultivate the public field, and only when the public work is done do they dare attend to their private work, this being what distinguishes the country people. This is the general outline; the elaboration of it will be up to the ruler and to the Master.”

3A:4 [Mencius said,] “. . . There are the affairs of the great man, and the affairs of the small man. In the case of any individual person, the things that the craftsmen make are available to him; if each person had to make everything he needed for his own use, the world would be full of people chasing after one another on the roads. Therefore it is said, ‘Some labor with their minds, while others labor with their strength. Those who labor with their minds govern others, while those who labor with their strength are governed by others. Those who are governed by others support them; those who govern others are supported by them.’ The rightness of this is universally acknowledged in the world. . . .

---

11. Officials received a *gui* field, the income from which was to be used to support the conduct of sacrifices.

"Hou Ji taught the people to sow and to reap and to cultivate the five grains. When the grains ripened, the people had their nourishment. It is the way of human beings that when they have sufficient food, warm clothing, and comfortable dwellings, they will, without education, come close to the birds and beasts. It was the part of the sage to grieve anxiously over this. He caused Xie to be Minister of Education and to teach people about human relations: that between parents and children there is affection; between ruler and minister, rightness; between husband and wife, separate functions; between elder and younger, proper order; and between friends, trust. . . .

"To share one's wealth with others is called kindness. To teach others to be good is called loyalty. To find the right man for the empire is called humaneness. Thus to give the empire to someone is easy, whereas to find the right man for the empire is difficult. Confucius said, 'Great indeed was Yao as a ruler. Only Heaven is great, and yet Yao patterned himself after Heaven. How vast, how magnificent! The people could find no name for it. What a ruler was Shun! How lofty, how majestic! He possessed the empire as if it were nothing to him.' As Yao and Shun ruled the empire, it could not have been done without their fully devoting their minds to it, but they did not devote themselves to tilling the fields." . . .

## MENCIUS' ARGUMENTS WITH YANG ZHU AND MOZI

Philosophically speaking, Mencius identifies as his primary antagonists the adherents of the schools of Yang Zhu and Mozi. Yang Zhu, sometimes characterized as an individualist, evidently defended the individual's withdrawal from public life or from official service in the interests of self-preservation. Mozi, as we have seen, espoused a morality predicated on the idea that a very practical sort of wisdom based on a self-regarding calculation of personal advantage should prompt everyone to adopt the imperative of universal love, or love without discrimination. Such love, which was to be extended to everyone equally and to be received from everyone equally, without regard to the primacy of family bonds, put morality at a remove from the familial context that Mencius recognized as its natural source and matrix. For him, Yang Zhu's idea entailed the denial of one's ruler and Mozi's, denial of one's parents. His own morality, by contrast, was based on a conception of the subtlety and richness of the human moral sense, with its roots in the deepest dimensions of biological and psychic life and its ramifications in the whole of human experience.

3B:9 Gongduzi said, "Outsiders all say that the Master is fond of argument. I venture to ask why?"

Mencius said, "How should I be fond of argument? I am compelled to do it. A long time has passed since the world was born, and periods of order have alternated with periods of chaos. In the time of Yao the waters overflowed their channels, inundating the Middle Kingdom; snakes and dragons dwelled in it, depriving the people of a settled life. . . .

"The overflowing waters refers to the waters of the deluge. Shun caused Yu to control them, and Yu dug out the earth so that the water would flow to the sea. . . . Once the dangers had been removed, and the birds and beasts that had injured people had disappeared, the people got the level ground and could dwell in it.

"Once Yao and Shun were no more, the Way of the sages declined, and oppressive rulers arose one after another. . . .

". . . Deviant speech and oppressive actions again became prevalent. There were cases of ministers murdering their rulers, of sons murdering their parents. Confucius was afraid, and he made the *Spring and Autumn Annals*. The *Spring and Autumn* is concerned with the affairs of the Son of Heaven, and thus Confucius said, 'It is by the *Spring and Autumn* alone that I will be known, and for it alone that I will be condemned.'

"Once again sages and kings do not appear, the lords become arbitrary and intemperate, and unemployed scholars indulge in uninhibited discussion. The words of Yang Zhu and Mo Di overflow the world; the world's words all go back if not to Yang then to Mo. Yang holds for egoism, which involves denial of one's sovereign; Mo holds for universal love, which entails denial of one's parents. To deny one's parents or to deny one's sovereign is to be an animal. . . . If the way of Yang and Mo is not stopped, and the way of Confucius is not made known, the people will be deceived by these deviant views, and the path of humaneness and rightness will be blocked. When the path of humaneness and rightness is blocked, animals are led to eat humans, and then humans come to eat one another. I am fearful about this and defend the way of the former sage by resisting Yang and Mo and banishing their licentious words. Those who espouse deviant views must be prevented from putting them into effect, for what is effected in the mind causes harm in affairs, and what is effected in affairs causes harm to government. . . .

"As the Duke of Zhou would have chastised those who denied fathers and rulers, I too want to correct people's minds, to stop deviant speech, to resist distorted actions, to banish licentious words, and so to carry on the work of the three Sages. In what way am I fond of argument? I am compelled to do it. Whoever can resist Yang and Mo with words is a follower of the sage."

4A:1 Mencius said, "If one had the clarity of Li Lou and the skill of Gongshuzi, but lacked the compass and square, one would not be able to form squares and circles. If one had the keen ear of Music Master Kuang, but lacked the six pitch pipes, one would not be able to adjust the five notes correctly. If one had the Way of Yao and Shun, but lacked humane government, one would not be able to rule the world. Though he may have a humane heart and a reputation for humaneness, one from whom the people receive no benefits will not serve as a model for later generations because he does not practice the Way of the former kings. Therefore it is said, 'Goodness alone does not suffice for the conduct of government; Laws alone do not implement themselves.' . . .

"To be indifferent is to be remiss. Serving the ruler without rightness, advancing and withdrawing without regard to rites, and maligning the Way through one's words—this is like being remiss. Therefore it is said, 'Charging one's ruler with what is difficult is called showing respect for him. Exposing goodness while foreclosing on evil is called being reverent toward him. Saying that he is "unable to do it" is called stealing from him.' "[12]

4A:4 Mencius said, "If one loves others yet they are not affectionate, he should turn within and examine his own humaneness; if one rules others yet they are not well governed he should examine his own wisdom; if one behaves decorously toward others yet they do not respond, he should examine his own reverence. Whenever one acts to no avail one should turn within and examine oneself. When one has made one's own person correct, the rest of the world will follow. . . ."

4A:5 Mencius said, "Among the people there is the common saying, 'The empire, the state, the family.' The empire has its basis in the state; the state has its basis in the family, and the family has its basis in oneself."

4A:10 Mencius said, "With those who do violence to themselves, one cannot speak, nor can one interact with those who throw themselves away. To deny decorum and rightness in one's speech is what is called 'doing violence to one-self.' To say, 'I am unable to abide in humaneness or follow rightness' is what is called 'throwing oneself away.' . . ."

4A:19 Mencius said, "Of all forms of service, which is the greatest? It is serving one's parents. Of all kinds of vigilance, which is the greatest? It is vigilance over one's own person. I have heard of those who by not losing their own persons have been able to serve their parents, but I have not heard of those who, having lost their own persons, have been able to serve their parents. There are many services one must perform, but the serving of one's parents is the root of all of them. There are many kinds of vigilance that one must exercise, but vigilance over one's own person is the root of all of them. . . ."

4A:26 Mencius said, "There are three things that are unfilial, and the greatest of them is to have no posterity. The reason that Shun married without informing his parents was out of concern that he might have no posterity. The noble person considers that it was as if he had informed them."

4A:27 Mencius said, "The reality of humaneness is serving one's parents; the reality of rightness is following one's elder brother; the reality of wisdom is knowing these two things and not departing from them; the reality of ritual propriety is regulating and adorning these two; the reality of music is in taking joy in these two. When there is joy, they grow; when they grow, how can they be stopped? When they come to the point where they cannot be stopped, then, without one's realizing it, the feet begin to dance and the hands to move."

---

12. See 1A:7, where Mencius makes the distinction between "not doing" something and "being unable" to do it. See also 2A:6.

4B:3 Mencius said to King Xuan of Qi, "When the ruler regards his ministers as his hands and feet, the ministers regard the ruler as their stomachs and hearts. When the ruler regards his ministers as dogs and horses, the ministers regard the ruler as just another person. When the ruler regards his ministers as dirt and grass, the ministers regard the ruler as a bandit and an enemy." . . .

4B:12 Mencius said, "The great person is one who does not lose the child's mind."

4B:14 Mencius said, "The noble person delves into it deeply according to the Way, wishing to get it for himself. As he gets it for himself, he abides in it calmly; abiding in it calmly, he trusts in it deeply; trusting in it deeply, he draws on its source, which he finds both at his left and at his right. This is why the noble person wishes to get it for himself."

4B:28 Mencius said, "That whereby the noble person differs from others is that he preserves his mind. The noble person preserves his mind through humaneness, preserves his mind through courtesy. One who is humane loves other people; one who possesses courtesy respects other people. One who loves other people is always loved by them; one who respects other people is always respected by them. . . ."

5A:5 [Mencius said,] "The Son of Heaven can present a man to Heaven, but he cannot cause Heaven to give him the realm. The lords can present a man to the Son of Heaven, but they cannot cause the Son of Heaven to make him a feudal lord. A great officer can present a man to the lords, but he cannot cause the lords to make him a great officer. Yao presented Shun to Heaven, and it was Heaven that accepted him. He displayed him to the people, and the people accepted him. This is why I said that, 'Heaven does not speak.' This was manifested simply through his actions and his conduct of affairs."

[Wan Zhang said,] "I venture to ask how it was that Yao presented him to Heaven and Heaven accepted him, and he showed him to the people and the people accepted him?"

"He caused him to preside over the sacrifices, and the hundred spirits enjoyed them. This shows that Heaven accepted him. He put him in charge of affairs, affairs were well ordered, and the hundred surnames were at peace. This shows that the people accepted him. . . ."

5B:2 Bogong Qi asked, "How were the ranks of nobility and the emoluments arranged by the house of Zhou?"

Mencius said, "The details of it cannot be heard, as the several lords, disliking them as having been damaging to themselves, did away entirely with the records. Yet the essentials of it I have heard. The Son of Heaven represented one rank; the dukes one rank; the marquises, one rank; the earls, one rank; the viscounts and the barons shared one rank. Altogether there were five levels. The ruler represented one rank; the chief ministers, one rank; the great officers, one rank; the scholars of the highest grade, one rank; the scholars of the middle grade, one rank; the scholars of the lower grade, one rank. Altogether there were six levels. The land allotted to the Son of Heaven was a thousand *li* square; the land allotted to the dukes and marquises was in all cases a hundred *li*; to the earls and viscounts, seventy *li*; to the barons, fifty *li*. Altogether there were four levels. One who could not have fifty *li* could not have access to the Son of Heaven but, being attached to one of the marquises, was called a 'dependent.'

"The chief ministers of the Son of Heaven received land equivalent to that of the marquises; the great officers received land equivalent to that of the earls; a scholar of the first rank received land equivalent to that of a viscount or a baron. In a great state in which the territory was a hundred *li* square, the ruler had an emolument ten times that of the chief minister; the chief minister, an emolument four times that of the great officers; a great officer, twice that of a scholar of the highest grade; a scholar of the highest grade, twice that of a scholar of the middle grade; a scholar of the middle grade, twice that of a scholar of the lower grade; a scholar of the lower grade, the same emolument as an ordinary person serving in an official position, an emolument sufficient to compensate for what would have been earned tilling the fields.

"In a state of the next size, with a territory equal to seventy *li*, the ruler would have ten times the emolument of the chief minister; a chief minister three times that of a great officer; a great officer, twice that of a scholar of the highest grade; a scholar of the highest grade, twice that of a scholar of the middle grade; a scholar of the middle grade, twice that of a scholar of the lower grade; a scholar of the lower grade, the same emolument as an ordinary person serving in an official position, an emolument sufficient to compensate for what would have been earned tilling the fields.

"In a small state, with a territory equal to fifty *li*, the ruler would have an emolument ten times that of the chief minister; a chief minister, twice that of a great officer; a great officer, twice that of a scholar of the highest rank; a scholar of the highest rank, twice that of a scholar of the middle rank; a scholar of the middle rank, twice that of a scholar of the lower rank; a scholar of the lower grade, the same emolument as an ordinary person serving in an official position, an emolument sufficient to compensate for what he would have earned tilling the fields.

"As to the tillers of the fields, each received a hundred *mu*. With an allotment of a hundred *mu*, the most capable tillers could feed nine people; the next level, eight; the next level, seven; the next level, six; and the lowest level, five. The emoluments of ordinary people serving in office were adjusted according to this."

5B:9 King Xuan of Qi asked about high ministers.

Mencius said, "Which high ministers is the king asking about?"

The king said, "Are the ministers not the same?"

"They are not the same. There are ministers who are from the royal line and ministers who are of other surnames."

The king said, "May I inquire about those who are of the royal line?"

"If the ruler has great faults, they should remonstrate with him. If, after they have done so repeatedly, he does not listen, they should depose him."

The king suddenly changed countenance.

"The king should not misunderstand. He inquired of his minister, and his minister dares not respond except truthfully."

The king's countenance became composed once again, and he then inquired about high ministers of a different surname.

"If the ruler has faults, they should remonstrate with him. If they do so repeatedly, and he does not listen, they should leave."

6A:1 Gaozi said, "The nature is like willow wood; rightness is like cups and bowls. To make humaneness and rightness out of human nature is like making cups and bowls out of the willow wood."

Mencius said, "Are you able to make cups and bowls while following the nature of the willow wood? You must do violence to the willow wood before you can make cups and bowls. If you must do violence to the willow wood in order to make cups and bowls, must you also do violence to a human being in order to make humaneness and rightness? The effect of your words will be to cause everyone in the world to think of humaneness and rightness as misfortunes."

6A:2 Gaozi said, "The nature is like swirling water. Open a passage for it in the east, and it will flow east; open a passage for it in the west, and it will flow west. Human nature does not distinguish between good and not-good any more than water distinguishes between east and west."

Mencius said, "It is true that water does not distinguish between east and west, but does it fail to distinguish between up and down? The goodness of human nature is like the downward course of water. There is no human being lacking in the tendency to do good, just as there is no water lacking in the tendency to flow downward. Now by striking water and splashing it, you may cause it to go over your head, and by damming and channeling it, you can force it to flow uphill. But is this the nature of water? It is the force that makes this happen. While people can be made to do what is not good, what happens to their nature is like this."

6A:6 Gongduzi said, "Gaozi says that the nature is neither good nor not-good. Others say that the nature can be made to be good or not-good, which is why during the reigns of Kings Wen and Wu the people were inclined to goodness, whereas under the reigns of You and Li, the people were inclined to violence. Still others say that the natures of some are good and the natures of others are not-good, which is why when Yao was the ruler there could be Xiang,[13] while

---

13. According to this view of human nature, which is obviously not that of Mencius, the fact that a violent man like Xiang could have lived during the reign of the sage king Yao is evidence that people differ widely in their natures. Xiang was the depraved brother of Yao's exemplary successor, Shun.

with a father like Gusou there could be Shun,[14] and with Zhou[15] as the son of their elder brother as well as their ruler there could be Qi, the Viscount of Wei, and Prince Bigan. Now you say that the nature is good. Does this mean that these others are all wrong?"

Mencius said, "As far as the natural tendencies are concerned, it is possible for one to do good; this is what I mean by being good. If one does what is not good, that is not the fault of one's capacities. The mind of pity and commiseration is possessed by all human beings; the mind of shame and aversion is possessed by all human beings; the mind of respectfulness and reverence is possessed by all human beings; and the mind that knows right and wrong is possessed by all human beings. The mind of pity and commiseration is humaneness; the mind of shame and dislike is rightness; the mind of reverence and respect is decorum; and the mind that knows right and wrong is wisdom. Humaneness, rightness, decorum, and wisdom are not infused into us from without. We definitely possess them. It is just that we do not think about it, that is all. Therefore it is said, 'Seek and you will get it; let go and you will lose it.'[16] . . ."

6A:7 Mencius said, "In years of abundance, most of the young people have the wherewithal to be good, while in years of adversity, most of them become violent. This is not a matter of a difference in the capacities sent down by Heaven, but rather of what overwhelms their minds.

"Now let barley be sown and covered with earth. The ground being the same, and the time of planting also the same, it grows rapidly, and in due course of time it all ripens. Though there may be differences in the yield, this is because the fertility of the soil, the nourishment of the rain and the dew, and the human effort invested have been incommensurate." . . .

6A:8 Mencius said, "The trees on Ox Mountain were once beautiful. But being situated on the outskirts of a large state, the trees are hewn down by axes. Could they remain beautiful? Given the air of the day and the night, and the moisture of the rain and the dew, they do not fail to put forth new buds and shoots, but then cattle and sheep also come to graze. This accounts for the barren appearance of the mountain. Seeing this barrenness, people suppose that the mountain was never wooded. But how could this be the nature of the mountain? So it is also with what is preserved in a human being: could it be that anyone should lack the mind of humaneness and rightness? If one lets go of the innate good mind, this is like taking an axe to a tree; being hewn down day after day, can it remain beautiful? Given the rest that one gets in the day and the night, and the effect of the calm morning $qi$, one's likes and dislikes will still resemble

---

14. Gusou, also known as the blind man, was the paradigm of the cruel father, to whom Shun remained nonetheless filial and devoted.

15. Zhou was universally believed to have been a monstrous tyrant. His elder brother, Qi, and his uncle, Bigan, attempted, with notable lack of success, to counsel him.

16. See also the statement attributed to Confucius at the end of *Mencius* 6A:8.

those of other people, but barely so. One becomes fettered and destroyed by what one does during the day, and if this fettering occurs repeatedly, the effect of the night *qi* will no longer be enough to allow him to preserve his mind, and he will be at scant remove from the animals. Seeing this, one might suppose that he never had the capacity for goodness. But can this be a human being's natural tendency? Thus, given nourishment, there is nothing that will not grow; lacking nourishment, there is nothing that will not be destroyed. Confucius said, 'Hold on and you preserve it; let go and you lose it. There is no appointed time for its going out and coming in, and no one knows its direction.' In saying this, was he not speaking of the mind?"

6A:10 Mencius said, "I desire fish, and I also desire bear's paws. If I cannot have both of them, I will give up fish and take bear's paws. I desire life, and I also desire rightness. If I cannot have both of them, I will give up life and take rightness. It is true that I desire life, but there is something I desire more than life, and therefore I will not do something dishonorable in order to hold on to it. I detest death, but there is something I detest more than death, and therefore there are some dangers I may not avoid. If among a person's desires there were none greater than life, then why should he not do anything necessary in order to cling to life? If among the things he detested there were none greater than death, why should he not do whatever he had to in order to avoid danger? There is a means by which one may preserve life, and yet he does not employ it; there is a means by which one may avoid danger, and yet he does not adopt it.

"Thus there are things that we desire more than life, and things that we detest more than death. It is not only exemplary persons who have this mind; all human beings have it. It is only that the exemplary ones are able to avoid losing it, that is all." . . .

6A:11 Mencius said, "Humaneness is the human mind. Rightness is the human path. To quit the path and not follow it, to abandon this mind and not know enough to seek it, is indeed lamentable. If a man has chickens and dogs, and they are lost, he knows enough to seek them. But when he has lost his mind, he does not know enough to seek it. The way of learning is none other than this: to seek for the lost mind."

6A:15 Gongduzi asked, "All are equally persons, and yet some are great persons and others are small persons—why is this?"

Mencius said, "Those who follow the part of themselves that is great become great persons, while those who follow the part of themselves that is small become small persons."

[Gongduzi] said, "Since all are equally persons, why is it that some follow the part of themselves that is great, while others follow the part of themselves that is small?"

Mencius said, "The faculties of seeing and hearing do not think and are obscured by things. When one thing comes into contact with another, they are led away. The faculty of the mind is to think. By thinking, one gets it; by not thinking, one fails to get it. This is what Heaven has given to us. When we first establish the greater part of ourselves, then the smaller part is unable to steal it away. It is simply this that makes the great person."

6A:16 Mencius said, "There is the nobility of Heaven and the nobility of man. Humaneness, rightness, loyalty, and truthfulness—and taking pleasure in doing good, without ever wearying of it—this is the nobility of Heaven. The ranks of duke, minister, or high official—this is the nobility of man. Men of antiquity cultivated the nobility of Heaven and the nobility of man followed after it. Men of the present day cultivate Heavenly nobility out of a desire for the nobility of man, and, once having obtained the nobility of man, they cast away the nobility of Heaven. Their delusion is extreme, and, in the end, they must lose everything."

6A:19 Mencius said, "The five kinds of grain are the finest of all seeds. But if they are not mature, they are not even as good as the tares or weeds. With humaneness too, ripeness is everything."

6B:2 Cao Jiao asked, "Is it true that all human beings are capable of becoming a Yao or a Shun?"

Mencius said, "It is true."

"I have heard that King Wen was ten feet tall, while Tang was nine feet tall. I am nine feet four inches tall,[17] and yet all I can do is eat millet. What shall I do to become a Yao or a Shun?"

"What is there to do but just to do it? Here we have a man who is not strong enough to lift a chicken; he is a man who lacks strength. If he now says that he can lift a hundred *jun*, he is a man of strength, for by lifting Wu Huo's burden one becomes Wu Huo. Why should a person make a calamity of what he has not yet mastered? It is just that he has not done it. To walk slowly behind an elder brother is called fraternal; to walk quickly ahead of an elder brother is called unfraternal. Is there anyone who is unable to walk slowly? It is just that he does not do it. The Way of Yao and Shun was that of filial and fraternal duty, that is all. By wearing the clothes of Yao, speaking the words of Yao, and performing the actions of Yao, you become Yao. By wearing the clothes of Jie, speaking the words of Jie, and performing the actions of Jie, you become Jie." . . .

6B:15 Mencius said, ". . . When Heaven intends to confer on a person a great responsibility it first visits his mind and will with suffering, toils his sinews and bones, subjects his body to hunger, exposes him to poverty, and confounds his projects. Through this, his mind is stimulated, his nature strengthened, and his inadequacies repaired. People commonly err, but later they are able to reform; their minds are troubled and their thoughts perplexed, but then they become capable of acting. This becomes evident in their expressions, emerges in their voices, and, finally, they understand.

---

17. Obviously, the Chinese foot was considerably shorter than the Western measurement.

"Thus in the absence of law-abiding families and worthy counselors within and hostile states and external challenges without, a state will often perish. From this we may know that out of sorrow and calamity life is born, while from comfort and joy comes death."

7A:4 Mencius said, "All the ten thousand things are complete in me. To turn within to examine oneself and find that one is sincere—there is no greater joy than this. To dedicate oneself in all earnestness to reciprocity—there can be no closer approach to humaneness."

7A:15 Mencius said, "What people are able to do without having learned it is original, good ability. What they know without having to think about it is original, good knowledge. There are no young children who do not know to love their parents, and there are none who, as they grow older, do not know to respect their older brothers. To be affectionate toward those close to one—this is humaneness. To have respect for elders—this is rightness. It is just this that is shared by everyone in the world."

7B:14 Mencius said, "The people are of greatest importance, the altars of the soil are next, and the ruler is of least importance. This is why one who gains the allegiance of the peasants will become the Son of Heaven, and one who gains the allegiance of the Son of Heaven will become one of the several lords, and one who gains the allegiance of the several lords will become a great officer. When one of the lords endangers the altars of the soil and grain, he is replaced. . . ."

7B:35 Mencius said, "To nourish the mind, there is nothing better than making the desires few. Here is a man whose desires are few; although there may be certain instances in which he is unable to preserve his mind, they will be few. Here is a man whose desires are many; although there may be instances in which he is able to preserve his mind, they will be few."

7B:37 Wan Zhang asked, "When Confucius was in Chen he said, 'Would it not be better to return home? The scholars of my school are madly ardent and impetuous. Intent on going forward and seizing their opportunity, they do not forget their origins.'[18] Since Confucius was in Chen, why should he have been thinking about the mad scholars of Lu?"

Mencius said, "Since Confucius did not get those who followed the middle way, he had to accept the madly ardent and the cautiously restrained.[19] The ardent go forward and seize their opportunities; the restrained have things that they will not do. Confucius would have preferred those who followed the middle way but, since he could not be sure of getting them, he thought in terms of the next best."

---

18. Cf. *Analects* 5:21.
19. Cf. *Analects* 13:21.

"I venture to ask what they were like—those who were called the 'madly ardent'?"

"Those whom Confucius called 'madly ardent' were such persons as Qin Zhang, Zeng Xi, and Mu Pi."

"Why were they called 'madly ardent'?"

"Their resolution led them to ostentatious invocations of 'The ancients! The ancients!' But, impartially assessed, their actions did not measure up to their words. When even the 'madly ardent' could not be found, Confucius wanted to get scholars who would not deign to involve themselves with anything impure. These were the cautiously restrained, and they were his next choice."

"Confucius said, 'When people pass my door without entering my house, it is only in the case of the village paragon that I feel no regret. The village paragon is the thief of virtue.' What sort of person was this that he could be referred to as a 'village paragon'?"

"He is the sort of person who might say, 'Why are you so ostentatious? Your words are not supported by your actions, nor are your actions supported by your words, yet you invoke "the ancients! the ancients!" Why are you so self-possessed, so cold? We are born into this world and must be of this world. It is quite enough simply to be good.' Eunuch-like, he ingratiates himself with a whole generation—such is the village paragon." . . .

"Confucius said, 'I dislike something that appears to be what in reality it is not; I dislike the weed for fear it will be confused with the grain; I dislike flattery for fear it may be confused with rightness; I dislike verbal facility for fear it may be confused with faithfulness; I dislike the music of Zheng for fear it be confused with authentic music; I dislike violet for fear it may be confused with vermilion; I dislike the village paragon lest his qualities be confused for virtue.' . . ."

[From *Mencius*, in *Shisan jing zhushu*; IB]

# XUNZI

Xun Kuang or Xun Qing, better known as Xunzi, or Master Xun, was born about 310 B.C.E. He lived a very long life, during which he may have witnessed the final demise of the Zhou dynasty, which Mencius had anticipated but had not lived to see. In all probability, he was still alive in 219 B.C.E., and perhaps for several years thereafter, which would mean that he endured through not only the final conquest in 221 B.C.E. by the state of Qin of all of the surviving feudal states but also through at least the initial stages of the formation under the Qin dynasty (221–207 B.C.E.) of the first unified empire. The wars leading up to this conquest in the late third century were almost indescribably brutal, and the intrigues surrounding them often intensely bitter. Xunzi was not only aware of many of these events but personally involved in some of them. It is hardly surprising, then, that he held views of society, government, education, and especially of human nature that contrasted with those of Mencius. His view of the world was darker than that of Mencius, and the remedies he advocated for its troubles were more cautious and complex.

The differences between Mencius and Xunzi have often been explained in terms of these momentous changes that were under way in the Chinese world between the fourth and third centuries. Still, Xunzi's thought cannot be reduced to an inevitable or predictable reaction to the troubling political situation in the waning years of the Zhou, nor can it be understood simply as a repudiation of a lofty and expansive Mencian optimism in favor of a cramped and pervasive pessimism. Xunzi was sober, even somber, when it came to his assessment of the basic nature of human beings—their original disposition—and he explicitly challenged Mencius's positive conception of human nature as fundamentally good. At the same time he reaffirmed certain shared and enduring Confucian values, above all the devotion to learning, culture, and the possibility of human perfectibility—all the more remarkable an affirmation in light of his personal experience of what must sometimes have seemed an almost limitless human capacity for violence, treachery, and self-aggrandizement.

The aspects of the Confucian inheritance that Xunzi was apparently inclined, both by personal temperament and intellectual disposition, to emphasize were the commitment to order and hierarchy and the highly formalistic mode of personal cultivation and community organization associated with ritual. In these commitments he was firmly grounded in the earlier tradition associated with the *ru* or ritualists, in ideas and values that were, in a sense, Confucian bedrock. At the same time he involved himself with great intellectual fervor and, evidently without temperamental reluctance, in contemporary intellectual debates. Many of his most distinctive ideas, particularly those having to do with government, education, and the relation of the human world to Heaven or the natural order, seem to have been articulated in the course of these debates, not only with Mohists and Daoists, but also with adherents of the school that later became known as Legalism, or the School of Law.

Xunzi began his scholarly career at the Jixia Academy in the feudal state of Qi, an academy long famous as a gathering place for scholars of virtually every school or filiation of thought current at the time. In a time marked by contention among the so-called hundred schools of thought and in a place where lively and serious controversies among scholars were actively encouraged, Xunzi seems to have encountered and become engaged with some of the outstanding thinkers and most of the leading ideas and teachings of his day. After Qi became engulfed in political crisis around 284 B.C.E., Xunzi departed for the state of Chu, only to return some years later to Qi and to a restored Jixia Academy, apparently becoming its leading figure. But though he spent altogether well over twenty years of his life in the role of an academician, Xunzi was by no means cut off from the major political events of the third century. In the mid-260s he traveled to the state of Qin, where he had the opportunity to observe firsthand its highly authoritarian form of government and its relentless rise to military prominence. Later, during a stay in his native state of Zhao, then menaced by Qin, he had further occasion to reflect on the implications of Qin's Legalist policies and offensive strategies and on the prospect of its conquest of the empire. The closing years of Xunzi's life were spent in Lanling, in southern Shandong, where he was employed for several extended periods as a magistrate, yet always simultaneously engaged as a teacher. His students included Han Fei and Li Si, who would become leading figures in the Legalist school and in the state of Qin, as well as several Confucian scholars who would assume an extremely influential role in the intellectual life of the ensuing Han dynasty.

The work that bears Xunzi's name, having been compiled and edited more than a century after his time, has not come down to us in its original form. Whatever the interventions of the first-century compiler of the text may have entailed, however, the basic form of the work was probably not significantly altered. As the selections that follow will indicate, Xunzi's work is distinguished from the *Analects* and the *Mencius* by the fact that it is not a record of conversations but a work composed primarily of essays. Unlike the relatively fragmentary form of the Confucian or Mencian conversations, reconstructed after the fact, these essays by Xunzi seem to involve his sustained reflections on topics of particular concern to him—including learning, self-cultivation, government, military affairs, Heaven or Nature, ritual, language, and human nature. In the selections presented here we encounter a powerful intellect arguing, often eloquently and always strenuously, for values and views that, for him, were essential to the cultivation of the individual as well as the preservation of civilization in a world where its survival must have seemed by no means assured.

## Selections from the *Xunzi*

### CHAPTER 1: ENCOURAGING LEARNING

Xunzi is known as a scholar of highly refined intelligence and powerful intellect. Though Mencius personally valued and publicly promoted learning, one does not find in his conversations and pronouncements the self-conscious sense of intellectuality that is everywhere present in the writing of Xunzi. It is noteworthy, however, that in this opening chapter Xunzi seems to be arguing more against a laissez-faire Daoism than against Mencius. Thus, deeply concerned with finding accessible models and promoting learning that is relevant to the present, he makes a strong case for the value of *personal* association with a teacher and of *personal* involvement in ritual practice as against a bookish or antiquarian absorption in the past. Although Xunzi is best known for his chapter "Human Nature as Evil," this chapter speaks of human beings as perfectible.

The noble person says: Learning must never cease. Blue comes from the indigo plant, yet it is bluer than indigo. Ice is made from water, yet it is colder than water. Wood as straight as a plumb line may be bent into a wheel that is as round as if it were drawn with a compass, and, even after the wood has dried, it will not straighten out again because this is the way it has been bent. Thus wood marked by the plumb line will become straight, and metal that is put to the whetstone will become sharp. The noble person who studies widely and examines himself each day will become clear in his knowing and faultless in his conduct.

Therefore if you do not climb a high mountain, you will not know the height of Heaven; if you do not look down into a deep valley, you will not know the depth of the earth; and if you do not hear the words handed down from the ancient kings, you will not know the greatness of learning and inquiry. . . .

Once I spent an entire day in thought, but it was not as good as a moment of study. Once I stood on tiptoe to gaze into the distance, but it was not as good as climbing to a high place to get a broad view. . . . By borrowing a horse and carriage you will not improve your feet, but you can cover a thousand *li*. By borrowing a boat and paddles you will not improve your ability in water, but you can cross rivers and seas. The noble person is by birth no different from others, but he is good at borrowing from external things.

. . . If raspberry vines grow in the midst of hemp, they will stand up straight without being staked; if white sand is mixed with mud, it too will turn black. If the root of the orchid and the rhizome of the valerian are soaked in the water used to wash rice,[20] the noble person will not go near them, and the commoner will not wear them—not because their substance is not beautiful but because of what they have been soaked in. Therefore the noble person will choose with care the place where he will reside, and will be accompanied by scholars when he travels. In this way he avoids depravity and meanness and approaches centrality and correctness.

. . . Accumulate goodness to create virtue, and spiritual clarity will naturally be acquired; there the mind of the sage will be fully realized. . . .

If you start carving, and then give up, you cannot even cut through a piece of rotten wood; but if you persist without stopping, you can carve and inlay metal or stone. . . . Crabs have six legs and two pincers, but unless they can find an empty hole dug by a snake or a water serpent, they have no place to lodge. This is because they allow their minds to go off in all directions. Thus if there is no dark and dogged will, there will be no bright and shining clarity; if there is no dull and determined effort, there will be no brilliant and glorious achievement. One who travels two roads at once will arrive nowhere; one who serves two masters will please neither. . . .

---

20. Following the reconstruction proposed by Knoblock in *Xunzi*, vol. 1, pp. 137, 268–269.

The learning of the noble person enters his ear, is stored in his mind, spreads through his four limbs, and is made visible in his activity and his tranquillity. In his smallest word, in his slightest movement, in everything, he may be taken as a model and a standard. The learning of the lesser man enters his ear and comes out his mouth. With only four inches between ear and mouth, how can he possess it long enough to beautify a seven-foot body? In antiquity learning was carried on for the sake of one's self; today learning is carried on for the sake of others.[21] The learning of the noble person is for the sake of beautifying himself; the learning of the lesser man is offering bird and beast [to win attention from others]. . . .

In learning nothing works so well as to be near a person of learning. The Rites and the "Music" provide models but no explanations. The Odes and the Documents are devoted to antiquity and lack immediacy. The Spring and Autumn Annals is laconic and not readily accessible. But following alongside a person of learning and repeating the explanations of the noble person bring one honor everywhere and allow one comprehensive knowledge of the world. Therefore it is said that "In learning nothing works so well as to be near a person of learning."

In the course of learning there is nothing more expedient than to devote yourself to a person of learning, and next to this is to pay homage to the rites. If you can neither devote yourself to a person of learning nor pay homage to the rites, how will you do anything more than learn randomly or passively follow the Odes and the Documents? In this case you will never to the end of your days escape from being merely a vulgar scholar. . . .

The noble person knows that what is not complete or what is not pure is unworthy to be called beautiful. Therefore he recites and reiterates so as to integrate it, reflects and ponders so as to comprehend it, determines his associations so that he may dwell in it, and eliminates what is harmful in order to preserve and nourish it. . . . [H]is mind will benefit more from it than from possession of the world.[22] Therefore he cannot be subverted by power or profit, nor swayed by the masses and multitudes, nor unsettled by the whole world. He follows this in life; he follows it in death—this is what is called holding firm to inner power. He who holds firm to inner power is able to order himself; being able to order himself, he can then respond to others. He who is able to order himself and respond to others is called the complete man. Heaven manifests itself in its brightness; Earth manifests itself in its breadth; the noble person values his completeness.

[From "Quanxue," *Xunzi yinde*, 1–2; IB]

---

21. Quoting *Analects* 14:25. A similar idea is found in *Mencius* 4B:14. The idea is that learning is properly dedicated to self-improvement but often distorted in the interests of impressing others.

22. Knoblock reads this, alternatively, to mean, "his mind benefits from possessing all that is in the world" (*Xunzi*, vol. 1, p. 142).

## CHAPTER 2: CULTIVATING ONESELF

. . . [T]hose who have good reason to find fault with me are my teachers; those who have good reason to find me praiseworthy are my friends; and those who flatter me do me injury.[23]

Therefore the noble person honors his teachers, feels affection for his friends, but hates those who do him injury. Being untiring in his love of the good, he accepts criticism and is able to take warning from it. . . .

The proper way to regulate the *qi* and cultivate the mind: With a temperament that is too strong and vigorous, soften it with balance and harmony. With an intellect that is too penetrating and deep, unify it with mildness and geniality. Given courage and daring that are too violent and fierce, be guided by obedience to the Way. Given a mind that is too quick and speech that is too glib, regulate them through activity and repose. What has become narrow and constrained, broaden with liberality and magnanimity. What has become base and low due to greed for gain, raise up with high resolve. . . . Of all the ways to regulate the *qi* and cultivate the mind, none is more direct than to follow ritual, none more essential than to find a teacher, none more spiritual than to love one thing alone. This is what is called the method of regulating the *qi* and cultivating the mind. . . .

Ritual is the means by which one's person is rectified; the teacher is the means by which ritual is rectified. Without ritual, how can you rectify yourself? Without a teacher, how can you know which ritual is correct? By behaving according to ritual, your emotions will find peace in ritual. . . . Not to approve of a teacher and a guide, preferring to do everything your own way, is like relying on a blind man trying to distinguish colors or a deaf man, tones. . . .

[From "Xiushen," *Xunzi yinde*, 3–5; IB]

## CHAPTER 9: THE REGULATIONS OF THE KING

The following selection reveals several of the characteristic features of Xunzi's political thought, including his concern with ranks and social distinctions and with what in modern parlance might be called the management of human resources. In a sense he may be described as a realist in politics. Whereas Mencius refused to talk about a lord-protector or hegemon, being willing only to talk about the ideal way of a true king, Xunzi undertakes to describe the different styles of government suitable to a "man who understands force," a lord-protector, and a true king. At the same time it is clear that he, no less than Mencius, believes that the humaneness and rightness of the true king give him an unassailable authority and an ability to compel the allegiance of others.

---

23. Literally, "play the thief toward me." Mencius uses the same image; see *Mencius* 2A:6, 4A:1, 6A:1, etc.

In the final passage in this selection Xunzi speaks of the noble person "providing the patterns for Heaven and Earth" and "forming a triad with Heaven and Earth," a theme he takes up again in his chapter "A Discussion of Heaven."

Even before social distinctions have been fixed, there will still be [such basic distinctions as] the one between the left and the right ancestors in the mortuary temple.[24] Although they may be descendants of kings, dukes, men of service, or grand officers, if they are unable to adhere to the rites and to moral principles, they should be consigned to the ranks of the commoners. Although they may be the descendants of commoners, if they have acquired culture and learning, are upright in their personal conduct, and are able to adhere to the rites and moral principles, they should be assigned to the ranks of prime minister, men of service, or high court officials. . . .

Where ranks in society are equal, there will not be proper distinctions; where power is equally distributed, there will be no unity; when the masses are on the same level, it will be impossible to employ them. That there is Heaven and there is Earth shows that there are differences of higher and lower, but it is only after an enlightened king is established that the state is managed on the basis of regulations. . . . The former kings abhorred chaos, and therefore they established rites and morality so as to bring about ranks. They created sufficient distinctions between rich and poor, eminent and humble, such that it was possible to bring people together and supervise them. . . .

One who understands the way to use force does not rely upon force. Rather, he considers how to utilize the king's mandate in order to perfect his strength and consolidate his inner power. . . .

The lord-protector is not like this. He opens up wilderness lands for cultivation, fills the granaries and storehouses, and makes provision for necessities. He is careful in recruiting and selecting officials, employing scholars of talent and ability and thereafter gradually bestowing rewards and commendation in order to encourage them or strictly applying penalties and punishments in order to correct them. He preserves those faced with destruction and sustains those threatened with extinction; he protects the weak and prohibits aggression. If he is not minded to annex the territories of his neighbors, then the several lords will draw close to him. . . . Therefore he makes clear through his actions that he does not intend to annex their territories, and he inspires confidence in them through his way of treating them as friends and equals. If there is no true king in the world, he will always be victorious. This is the way of one who understands how to be a lord-protector. . . .

---

24. The mortuary temple of the founder of a noble family occupied the central position, with the temples of his descendants in the second, fourth, and sixth generations arranged to the left and called *zhao*, and those of descendants in the third, fifth, and seventh generations arranged to the right and called *mu*. Here Xunzi refers to the kind of distinction that, to him, seems prior to other social arrangements.

A true king is not like this. His humaneness is the loftiest in the world, his rightness is the loftiest in the world, and his authority is the loftiest in the world. . . . With an authority that cannot be opposed and a way that compels the allegiance of others, he gains victory without battle and attains his objectives without attack. Without his wearing out his arms and men, the whole world submits to him. This is the way of one who understands how to be a king. . . .

On the model of a king: He fixes the several rates of taxation, regulates affairs, and utilizes the myriad things in order to nourish the myriad people. From the product of the fields, the tax rate is one part in ten. At the barriers and in the marketplaces, goods are inspected, but no tax is imposed. The mountains and forests, marshes and weirs, are closed or opened according to the season, but taxes are not levied. Land is inspected for its quality, and taxes are differentially assessed. The distance over which goods must be transported is taken into account in fixing tribute payments. The circulation of resources and grain is unimpeded, allowing them to be offered and exchanged so that "all within the four seas are like one family." Therefore those who are close do not hide their abilities, and those who are distant do not resent their labors. Nowhere in the state, in however secluded or remote a place, are there any who do not hasten to serve him or who do not find peace and joy in him. This is called being a leader of the people. This is the model of a king. . . .

. . . Heaven and Earth are the beginning of life; rites and rightness are the beginning of order; and the noble person is the beginning of rites and rightness. . . .

[From "Wangzhi," *Xunzi yinde*, 25–28; IB]

## CHAPTER 17: A DISCUSSION OF HEAVEN

In translating this selection we have in most instances retained the translation "Heaven" for the Chinese word *tian*, even while recognizing that at many points we would come much closer to Xunzi's understanding of the concept were we to render it as "Nature." Actually neither "Heaven" nor "Nature" fully expresses the meaning of *tian*, which has a variety of senses, including the sky, weather, the natural order, and also a moral order. Uses of the word also varied over time and among different filiations or schools of thought. From at least as far back as the early Zhou period, when the idea of the Mandate of Heaven assumed such powerful political and moral significance, the relation of the human world to Heaven or the natural order was a central concern of Chinese thought. Over the course of centuries a number of crucial issues arose, including how *tian* should be conceptualized, how it might intervene in human affairs, and how its imperative or will might be discovered.

Here Xunzi represents *tian* as a natural order, operating according to unchanging principles, not intervening in extraordinary ways in human affairs but, rather, providing the context within which all living things exist. Against those, like Zhuangzi, who seemed to overemphasize the natural order and deemphasize the role of the human, Xunzi reverses the argument: Heaven, Earth, and human beings exist in a relationship of complementarity; human beings should neither encroach on the work of Heaven nor neglect their own. Against believers in a variety of superstitions that depicted unusual events as signs or portents indicating intervention by Heaven in the human sphere, he makes a similar point: human beings must recognize that they themselves are in control of their own affairs. Heaven's ways, being constant, do not vary in accordance with changes in human government, so that what matters in ensuring human prosperity and well-being is human effort. Xunzi's assertion that in recognizing the complementary relationship among the three spheres human beings are able to "form a triad with Heaven and Earth" became one of the seminal ideas in Confucian cosmological and ethical thought.

The processes of Heaven are constant, neither prevailing because of Yao nor perishing because of Jie. Respond to them with order, and good fortune will result; respond to them with chaos, and misfortune will result. If you strengthen what is basic and are frugal in your expenditures, then Heaven cannot make you poor. If you nourish and provide for the people, acting in accordance with the seasons, then Heaven cannot cause you to be ill. . . . If you turn your back on the Way and behave recklessly, then Heaven cannot bestow good fortune on you. . . . You should not blame Heaven; it is a matter of the way you have followed. Therefore if you can distinguish between the natural and the human you deserve to be called a perfect man.

. . . Heaven has its seasons; Earth has its resources; man has his government. For this reason it is said that they may form a triad. If one abandons that which allows him to form a triad, yet longs for the triad, he is deluded. . . .

When the work of Heaven has been established and the achievements of Heaven brought to completion, the form is made whole, and the spirit is born. The love and hate, delight and anger, sorrow and joy that are stored there are called Heaven-endowed (or natural) feelings. Ears, eyes, nose, mouth, and body each have perceptions that do not share the same competencies, and these are called Heaven-endowed (or natural) faculties. The mind-and-heart dwells in the vacuity at the center and governs the five faculties, and thus it is called the Heavenly (or natural) lord. . . .

Are order and chaos determined by Heaven? I say, the sun and moon, the stars and constellations revolved in the same way in the time of Yu and in the time of Jie. Yu achieved order thereby; Jie brought disorder. Order and chaos are not determined by Heaven. Are they determined by the seasons? . . .

. . . Heaven has its constant Way; Earth has its constant measurements; the noble person has his constant substance. The noble person follows what is constant; the petty person calculates his achievements. . . .

. . . Because the noble person cherishes what is within his competence and does not long for what is within the competence of Heaven, he goes forward day by day. Because the lesser person sets aside what is within his competence and longs for what is within the competence of Heaven, he goes backward day by day. . . .

. . . Eclipses of the sun or the moon, the untimely coming of wind or rain, the appearance of strange stars—there has never been an age when such events have not occurred. If the one above is enlightened, and his government is just, then even if such events occur simultaneously, no harm will come of it. . . .

When such events do occur, the ones to be feared are human portents. When the plowing is poorly done so that the crops suffer, when the weeding is badly done so that the harvest fails; when the government is reckless and the people are lost; when the fields are neglected and the crops badly tended; when grain is sold dear and the people are starving; when there are people dying on the roads—these are what is called human portents. . . . The explanation for their occurance may be found close by; the injury they cause is most grievous. . . .

Therefore if you set aside what belongs to the human and contemplate what belongs to Heaven, you miss the genuine realities of all things.

[From "Luntian," *Xunzi yinde*, 62–64; IB]

### CHAPTER 19: A DISCUSSION OF RITES

Ritual is at the heart of Xunzi's version of Confucian thought. The following selection affords an illustration of how his highly practical orientation and his aesthetic concerns are blended.

What is the origin of rites? I reply, human beings are born with desires, and when they do not achieve their desires, they cannot but seek the means to do so. If their seeking knows no limit or degree, they cannot but contend with one another. With contention comes chaos, and with chaos comes exhaustion. The ancient kings hated chaos and therefore established rites and rightness in order to limit it, to nurture people's desires, and to give them a means of satisfaction. They saw to it that desires did not exhaust material things and that material things did not fall short of desires. Thus both desires and things were supported and satisfied, and this was the origin of rites. . . .

Rites have three roots. Heaven and Earth are the root of life, the ancestors are the root of the human species, and rulers and teachers are the root of order. If there were no Heaven and Earth, how could there be life? If there were no ancestors, how could there be begetting? If there were no rulers and teachers, how could there be order? If even one of these were lacking, human beings would have no peace. Thus rites serve Heaven above and Earth below; they honor ancestors; they exalt rulers and teachers. These are the three roots of rites. . . .

Rites always begin in coarseness, are completed in forms, and end in joy. Thus in their most perfected state both emotion and the forms are fully realized; in the next state, emotions and forms prevail by turns; and in the lowest state, everything returns to emotion and reverts to a great unity. . . .

The principle of the rites is truly deep. Discriminations of hard and white, same and different,[25] enter there and drown. The principle of the rites is truly great. Crass and vulgar theories on wielding authority and exerting control enter there and perish. The principle of the rites is truly lofty. Contumelious arrogance, haughty disdain, and the contempt for common customs that presumes one's own superiority to ordinary people[26] enter there and are brought low. . . .

Rites are most strict in the ordering of birth and death. Birth is the beginning of a human being; death is his end. When both beginning and end are good, the human way is complete. Therefore the noble person is reverential toward the beginning and watchful over the end, so that beginning and end are as one. This is the way of the noble person; this is the refinement of rites and rightness. . . .

Because the rites of the dead can be performed only once for each individual, and never again, they provide the final occasion at which the subject may express the utmost respect for his ruler, and the son may express the utmost respect for his parents. . . .

Rites contract what is too long and expand what is too short, reducing excesses and repairing deficiencies, pervading the forms of love and reverence and enlivening the beauties of right conduct. Therefore, while refined beauty and coarse ugliness, joyful music and mournful weeping, calm contentment and anxious grief are opposites, rites bring them together and make use of them. . . .

It is always true that rites, when they serve the living, are an adornment to joy, and when they serve the dead, an adornment to grief. In sacrifices they are an adornment to reverence, and in military affairs, an adornment to authority. This was the same for the rites of the hundred kings; it is what unites antiquity and the present. The source for this we do not know. . . .

Sacrificial rites give expression to the feelings of remembrance and longing for the dead. There inevitably come times when one is overwhelmed by emotions of grief and loss, and a loyal minister or a filial son finds that, even while others are given to the enjoyment of congenial company, these sorrowful emotions arrive. If when they come to him, and he is greatly moved, he nonetheless represses them, his feelings of remembrance and longing will be thwarted and unfulfilled. . . .

[From "Lilun," *Xunzi yinde*, 70–75; IB]


## CHAPTER 23: HUMAN NATURE AS EVIL

Human nature is evil; its goodness derives from conscious activity. Now it is human nature to be born with a fondness for profit. Indulging this, contention

---

25. Referring to the Mohist logicians and to the dialecticians such as Hui Shi and Gongsun Long.

26. Possibly referring to the followers of Prince Mou of Wei, a contemporary of Xunzi's known for his hedonism.

and strife arise, and the sense of modesty and yielding with which one was born disappears. One is born with feelings of envy and hate, and, by indulging these, one is led into banditry and theft, so that the sense of loyalty and good faith with which he was born disappears. One is born with the desires of the ears and eyes and with a fondness for beautiful sights and sounds, and, by indulging these, one is led to licentiousness and chaos, so that the sense of ritual, rightness, refinement, and principle with which one was born is lost. Hence, following human nature and indulging human emotions will inevitably lead to contention and strife, causing one to rebel against one's proper duty, reduce principle to chaos, and revert to violence. Therefore one must be transformed by the example of a teacher and guided by the way of ritual and rightness before one will attain modesty and yielding, accord with refinement and ritual, and return to order. From this perspective it is apparent that human nature is evil and that its goodness is the result of conscious activity. . . .

Mencius said, The fact that human beings learn shows that their nature is good. I say this is not so; this comes of his having neither understood human nature nor perceived the distinction between the nature and conscious activity. The nature is what is given by Heaven: one cannot learn it; one cannot acquire it by effort. Ritual and rightness are created by sages: people learn them and are capable, through effort, of bringing them to completion. What cannot be learned or acquired by effort but is within us is called the nature. What can be learned and, through effort, brought to completion is called conscious activity. . . .

Mencius said, Now, human nature is good, and [when it is not] this is always a result of having lost or destroyed one's nature. I say that he was mistaken to take such a view. Now, it is human nature that, as soon as a person is born, he departs from his original substance[27] and from his natural disposition, so that he must inevitably lose and destroy them. Seen in this way, it is apparent that human nature is evil. . . .

. . . For a son to yield to his father and a younger brother to yield to his elder brother, or for a son to work on behalf of his father and a younger brother to work on behalf of his elder brother—these two acts are contrary to the nature and counter to the emotions, and yet they represent the way of filial devotion and the refinement and principle that are associated with ritual and rightness. Hence, to follow the emotional nature would mean that there would be no courtesy or humility; courtesy and humility run counter to the emotional nature. From this perspective it is apparent that human nature is evil, and that goodness is the result of conscious activity. . . .

When a person desires to do good he always does so because his nature is evil. A person who is shallow aspires to depth; one who is ugly aspires to beauty; one who is narrow aspires to breadth; one who is poor aspires to wealth; one

---

27. The word Xunzi uses here is *pu*, a term that occurs frequently in the *Daodejing* and is often translated in that context as "the uncarved block."

who is humble aspires to esteem. Whatever one lacks in oneself he must seek outside. . . . One can see from this that the reason human beings desire to do good is that their nature is evil. . . .

. . . Now since human nature is evil, people must await ordering by the sage kings and transformation through ritual and rightness, and only then do they attain order and accord with goodness. . . .

"The man in the street can become a Yu."[28] What does this mean? I reply, What made the sage emperor Yu a Yu was the fact that he practiced humaneness and rightness and took uprightness as his standard. This being so, humaneness, rightness, and proper standards must be based upon principles that can be known and practiced. Any man in the street has the natural endowment needed to understand humaneness, rightness, proper standards, and uprightness and the ability to practice humaneness, rightness, proper standards, and uprightness. Therefore it is clear that he can become a Yu.

[From "Xing'e," *Xunzi yinde*, 86–89; IB]

# THE *ZUOZHUAN*

There are many mysteries surrounding the text of the *Zuozhuan*, including its authorship and its original form. *Zuozhuan* or *Zuoshi zhuan* means "The Commentary of Mr. Zuo," and this Mr. Zuo has often been identified as Zuo Qiuming or Zuoqiu Ming, allegedly a contemporary of Confucius. Actually, however, the identity of the author is unknown. A traditional view of the *Zuozhuan* is that it was written as a commentary on the *Spring and Autumn Annals* (*Qunqiu*). While this is possible, it seems more likely in the case of the *Zuozhuan* that it was originally an independent work that was later broken up and attached to the text of the *Annals*. However the work came into being, it has become part of the Confucian canon and has survived as a masterpiece of Chinese prose and one of the most important historical works in a tradition in which the art of history would assume central and abiding importance.

### SELECTION FROM THE *ZUOZHUAN*

In the following passage Duke Dao of Jin discusses with Shi Kuang, or Music Master Kuang, the forced abdication of Duke Xian, ruler of the neighboring state of Wei. Duke Xian had been driven out of his domain in 559 B.C.E. as a result of his own misrule. Shi Kuang uses the opportunity to speak of the love and concern of Heaven for the common people and to underscore the responsibility of a ruler to devote himself

---

28. This was apparently an old saying. Cf. *Mencius* 6B:2: "Cao Jiao asked, 'Is it true that all human beings are capable of becoming a Yao or a Shun?' Mencius said, 'It is true.' "

to their well-being and, especially, to heed the remonstrations of his ministers. In this case, however, all levels of society, down to the very lowest, are seen as participating in the process of admonition. Particularly striking is the inclusion of artisans, blind musicians, merchants, and commoners in this picture of a participatory process that does not restrict the counseling function only to the elite.

## Duke Xiang, 14th year (559 B.C.E.)

Shi Kuang was attending the ruler of Jin. The latter said, "The people of Wei have driven out their ruler—what a terrible thing!"

Shi Kuang replied, "Perhaps it was the ruler himself who did terrible things. When a good ruler goes about rewarding good and punishing excess, he nourishes his people as if they were his children, shelters them like Heaven, accommodates them like the Earth. And when the people serve their ruler, they love him as they do their parents, look up to him like the sun and moon, revere him like the all-seeing spirits, fear him like thunder. How could they drive him out? . . .

"Heaven gave birth to the people and set up rulers to superintend and shepherd them and see to it that they do not lose their true nature as human beings. And because there are rulers, it provided helpers for them who would teach and protect them and see that they do not overstep the bounds. Hence the Son of Heaven has his chief officers, the feudal lords have their ministers, the ministers set up their collateral houses, gentlemen have their friends and companions, and the commoners, artisans, merchants, lackeys, shepherds, and grooms all have their relatives and close associates who help and assist them. If one does good they praise him, if he errs they correct him, if he is in distress they rescue him, if he is lost they restore him. . . .

"Thus from the sovereign on down, each has his father or elder brother, his son or younger brother to assist and scrutinize his ways of management. The historians compile their documents, the blind musicians compose poems, the musicians chant admonitions and remonstrances, the high officials deliver words of correction, the gentlemen pass along remarks, the commoners criticize, the merchants voice their opinions in the market, and the hundred artisans contribute through their skills. . . .

"Heaven's love for the people is very great. Would it then allow one man to preside over them in an arrogant and willful manner, indulging his excesses and casting aside the nature Heaven and Earth allotted them? Surely it would not!"

[Adapted from Watson, *The Tso chuan*, pp. xv–xvi]

*Chapter 7*

## LEGALISTS AND MILITARISTS

"Legalism" (*fajia*) is a name that came to be applied to a set of ideas and practices associated with the rise of the Chinese imperial bureaucratic state in the third and second centuries B.C.E. The key term in this name, *fa*, refers to several ways in which state power could be organized and exercised: through laws and punishments, administrative and military systems, policy planning, statecraft, or methods of personnel management. Although comparatively late in developing a systematic doctrine, the Legalists—as they would become known—while not actually a formal school, had unquestionably the greatest influence of any upon the political life of the time. Typically proponents of these ideas were practicing statesmen more concerned with immediate problems and specific mechanisms of control than with theories of government. Indeed, some of them were strongly anti-intellectual and evidenced a special hostility toward the "vain" talk of philosophers.

In its earliest form, "Legalism" was probably the outgrowth of a need for more rational organization of society and resources so as to strengthen a state against its rivals. This was to be accomplished by concentrating power in the hands of a single ruler and by adopting governmental institutions that afforded greater centralized control. Guan Zhong in the seventh century, for example, worked to make Qi the strongest state of his time by increasing the power of the ruler, but at the same time he upheld many of the traditional moral virtues and accepted the old enfeoffment system.

As the struggle among the Warring States became more intense, however, technicians of power came forward who put the state and its interests ahead of all human and moral concerns—who, in fact, glorified power for its own sake and looked upon human beings as having no worth apart from their possible use to the state. Men like Shang Yang (d. 338 B.C.E.) completely rejected the traditional virtues of humanity and rightness that the Confucians had urged upon rulers, denying that such lofty ideas had any practical relationship to the harsh realities of political life. They openly advocated war as a means of strengthening the power of the ruler, expanding the state, and making the people strong, disciplined, and submissive. They conceived of a political order in which all old feudal divisions of power would be swept away and all authority would reside in one central administration headed by an absolute monarch. The state would be ordered by a set of laws that would be administered with complete regularity and impartiality. Severe punishments would restrain any violations, while generous rewards would encourage what was beneficial to the strength and well-being of the state. Agriculture, as the basis of the economy, would be promoted intensively, while commerce and intellectual endeavor, regarded as nonessential and diversionary, were to be severely restricted. The people would live frugal and obedient lives devoted to the interests of the state in peace and war. These ideas were put into actual practice by the rulers of the state of Qin.

In their complete rejection of traditional ethical values, in their emphasis upon government by law rather than by personal example, and in their scorn for the ideals drawn from the past, the Legalists represent the antithesis of Confucian thinking. On the other hand, the Legalists obviously learned something from both the Mohists and the Daoists. Mozi's stress on uniform standards and on the mobilization of society for the achievement of utilitarian ends is strongly echoed in the totalitarian aims of the Legalists, although they obviously had no use for his doctrine of universal love or his condemnation of offensive warfare. Laozi's idea of nonassertion (*wuwei*) as a way of government is applied to the Legalists' own conception of the ideal ruler, who takes no direct part in the government but simply presides as a semi-divine figurehead while the elaborate legal machinery of government functions of its own accord, obviating the need for the ruler's direct intervention. Having so regulated the lives of his people that there is no longer any possibility of disorder or need for improvement or guidance, the ruler may retire to dwell, as Han Fei (d. 233 B.C.E.) says, "in the midst of his deep palace," far removed from the eyes of the populace, enjoying the luxuries and sensual delights appropriate to his exalted position.

With the final unification of China by the First Emperor of the Qin, it looked as if the harsh policies of Shang Yang and Han Fei had won out over the other schools of political thought. The proponents of "Legalism" were now in a position of power from which, by repressive measures, they could at last deal the death blow to their rivals.

## THE *GUANZI*

The text titled *Guanzi* (Master Guan), attributed to the seventh-century statesman Guan Zhong, but actually of much later date, contains an unsystematic mix of pronouncements concerning governmental administration, political economy, and public morality. Much of it is Confucian in tone, but more attention is given to practical, organizational matters and economic problems of the kind with which the Legalists were identified. Thus, out of its heterogeneous contents, the *Guanzi* often served as the earliest reference to such recurring issues and practices as collective responsibility for law and order in the local community, the analysis of supply and demand in the market, the use of "Ever-Normal Granaries" to maintain food stocks and price stability, and so on. Such systems became perennial features of Chinese government in later times. The following passage illustrates how traditional virtues (usually thought to be Confucian) were to be promoted and enforced by local systems of collective responsibility. This general model was adopted, in variant forms and with somewhat different degrees of social pressure and legal enforcement, in most imperial dynasties. The statesman Shang Yang (represented in the second selection in these readings) was also closely identified with this system.

All special cases of filial piety and respect for elders, loyalty and faithfulness, worthiness and goodness, or refinement and talent on the part of the sons, younger brothers, male or female slaves, and retainers or guests of the head of a household shall be reported accordingly by the leaders of the groups of ten or five [families] to the clan elder of the circuit. The clan elder shall report them to the village commandant, who in turn shall report them to the subdistrict prefect. He shall summarize them for the district governor, who will record them for the chief justice.

In all cases where the participants in a crime are members of a household, collective responsibility shall extend to the head of the household. If the participants include the heads of households, collective responsibility shall extend to the leaders of the groups of ten and five. If the participants include these leaders, collective responsibility shall extend to the clan elder of the circuit. If the participants include clan elders, collective responsibility shall extend to the village commandant. If the participants include village commandants, collective responsibility shall extend to the subdistrict prefect. If the participants include subdistrict prefects, collective responsibility shall extend to the district governor. If the participants include district governors, collective responsibility extends to the chief justice.

Reports shall be made once every three months, summaries once every six, and permanent records once every twelve. Whenever the worthy are promoted, they shall not be allowed to exceed their proper rank. When the able are employed, they shall not be allowed to hold more than one office at a time. When punishments are imposed, they shall not be applied to the guilty person alone. When rewards are granted, they shall not be bestowed merely on the person credited with the achievement.

[*Guanzi* (GXJC), p. 13; trans. adapted from Rickett, *Guanzi*, pp. 104–105]

## THE BOOK OF LORD SHANG

Credit for the rise to power of the state of Qin in the fourth century B.C.E. is usually assigned to the innovative methods of Gongsun Yang or Shang Yang (d. 338 B.C.E.), who was prime minister of Qin in the middle of the fourth century. The *Book of Lord Shang* (*Shangjun shu*), though of later date and uncertain provenance, contains a variety of materials representative of the ideas and policies for which he became well known, especially the need for strong and decisive leadership, state domination over the people, and reliance on strict laws, including generous rewards and harsh punishments rather than on traditional fiduciary relations and family ethics. Shang Yang also advocated concentration of the people's energies on agriculture and war and suppression of political parties, particularly targeting Confucian scholars who raised troublesome political issues.

## Reform of the Law

Duke Xiao [of Qin] discussed his policy. The three Great Officers, Gongsun Yang (Shang Yang), Gan Long, and Du Zhi, were in attendance on the ruler. Their thoughts dwelt on the vicissitudes of the world's affairs; they discussed the principles of rectifying the law, and they sought for the way of directing the people. The ruler said, "Not to forget, at his succession, the tutelary spirits of the soil and of grain, is the way of a ruler; to shape the laws and to see to it that an intelligent ruler reigns are the tasks of a minister. I intend, now, to alter the laws, so as to obtain orderly government, and to reform the rites, so as to teach the people, but I am afraid that all-under-Heaven will criticize me."

Gongsun Yang said, "I have heard it said, that he who hesitates in action does not accomplish anything, and that he who hesitates in affairs gains no merit. Let your highness settle your thoughts quickly about altering the laws and perhaps not heed the criticism of all-under-Heaven. . . ." [pp. 167–169]

## Agriculture and War

The means whereby a ruler of men encourages the people are office and rank; the means whereby a country is made prosperous are agriculture and war. Now those who seek office and rank do not do so by means of agriculture and war but by artful words and empty doctrines. That is called "wearying the people." The country of those who weary their people will certainly have no strength. . . . [p. 185]

The way to organize a state well is, even though the granaries are filled, not to be negligent in agriculture, and even though the state is large and its population numerous, to have no license of speech. [This being so,] the people will be simple and have concentration. . . . [pp. 186–187]

The way to administer a state well is for the laws regulating officials to be clear; one does not rely on men to be intelligent and thoughtful. The ruler makes the people single-minded so they will not scheme for selfish profit. Then the strength of the state will be consolidated, and a state whose strength has been consolidated is powerful, but a country that loves talking is dismembered. . . . [p. 188]

The people will love their ruler and obey his commandments, even to death, if they are engaged in farming morning and evening; but they will be of no use if they see that glib-tongued, itinerant scholars succeed in being honored in serving the prince, that merchants succeed in enriching their families, and that artisans have plenty to live upon. If the people see both the comfort and the advantage of these three walks of life, then they will indubitably shun agriculture; shunning agriculture, they will care little for their homes; caring little for their homes, they will certainly not fight and defend them for the ruler's sake. . . . [pp. 192–193]

## Discussing the People

In this passage, the disparagement of "virtue" refers to the traditional Confucian family ethic, seen here as prejudicial to the workings of an impersonal bureaucratic rationality. The virtue that Shang Yang favors, as in the final paragraph, is directed toward service of the state.

Sophistry and cleverness are an aid to lawlessness; rites and music are symptoms of dissipation and license; kindness and humaneness are the mother of transgressions; employment and promotion are opportunities for the rapacity of the wicked. If lawlessness is aided, it becomes current; if there are symptoms of dissipation and license, they will become the practice. . . . [pp. 206–207]

If virtuous officials are employed, the people will love their own relatives, but if wicked officials are employed, the people will love the statutes. To agree with and to respond to others is what the virtuous do; to differ from and to spy upon others is what the wicked do. If the virtuous are placed in prominent positions, transgressions will remain hidden; but if the wicked are employed, crimes will be punished. In the former case the people will be stronger than the law; in the latter, the law will be stronger than the people. . . . [p. 207]

If the people are poor, they are weak; if the state is rich, they are licentious, and consequently there will be parasites and parasites will bring weakness. Therefore, the poor should be benefited with rewards, so that they become rich, and the rich should be injured by punishments, so that they become poor. The important thing in undertaking the administration of a state is to make the rich poor and the poor rich. If that is effected, the state will be strong. . . . [p. 210]

## Making Orders Strict

The six parasites are: rites and music, odes and history, cultivation and goodness, filial devotion and brotherly love, sincerity and trustworthiness, uprightness and integrity, humaneness and rightness, criticism of the army and being ashamed of fighting. . . .[1] [p. 256]

In applying punishments, light offenses should be punished heavily; if light offenses do not appear, heavy offenses will not come. This is said to be abolishing penalties by means of penalties, and if penalties are abolished, affairs will succeed. . . . [p. 258]

## Rewards and Punishments

Punishments should know no degree or grade, but from ministers of state and generals down to great officers and ordinary folk, whoever does not obey the king's commands, violates the interdicts of the state, or rebels against the statutes fixed by the ruler should be guilty of death and should not be pardoned. . . . [I]f among the officials who have to maintain the law and to uphold an office, there are those who do not carry out the king's law, they are guilty of death and should not be pardoned, but their punishment should be extended to their family for three generations. . . . [pp. 278–279]

## Weakening the People

A weak people means a strong state and a strong state means a weak people. Therefore, a state that has the right way is concerned with weakening the people. If they are simple they become strong, and if they are licentious they become weak. Being weak, they are law-abiding; being licentious, they let their ambition go too far; being weak, they are serviceable, but if they let their ambition go too far, they will become strong. . . . [p. 303]

[*Shangzi* (SBCK), chaps. 1–5; trans. adapted from Duyvendak,
*Lord Shang*, pp. 167–303]

---

1. There is obviously a textual problem here: the "six parasites" actually involve sixteen items. Despite the problem of numbering, the list is significant and suggestive.

### THE *HAN FEIZI*

Han Fei (d. 233 B.C.E.) was said to have been a student of Xunzi but turned away from the latter's emphasis on Confucian self-cultivation and practice of rites to become a synthesizer of several strains of Daoist and Legalist thought. This synthesis involved a Daoist-type mystique of the ruler, now envisioned as presiding over a perfectly defined system of laws and institutions, using techniques of statecraft developed by another Legalist thinker, Shen Buhai (d. 337 B.C.E.). For a time Han Fei enjoyed the favor of the Qin state, but he eventually met a violent death through the machinations of the prime minister of the Qin, Li Si (d. 208 B.C.E.), a former fellow student under Xunzi. A quarter century later, Li Si himself met a similar fate.

It is ironic that these prime spokesmen for Legalist "realism," should have shown such an idealistic faith in the rational uses of power yet in the end suffered a quixotic martyrdom—both of them meeting untimely deaths as the result of power struggles from which they could not extricate themselves.

## Chapter 49: The Five Vermin

Past and present have different customs; new and old adopt different measures. To try to use the ways of a generous and lenient government to rule the people of a critical age is like trying to drive a runaway horse without using reins or whip. This is the misfortune that ignorance invites.

Now the Confucians and the Mohists all praise the ancient kings for their universal love of the world, saying that they looked after the people as parents look after a beloved child. And how do they prove this contention? They say, "Whenever the minister of justice administered some punishment, the ruler would purposely cancel all musical performances; and whenever the ruler learned that the death sentence had been passed on someone, he would shed tears." For this reason they praise the ancient kings.

Now if ruler and subject must become like father and son before there can be order, then we must suppose that there is no such thing as an unruly father or son. Among human affections none takes priority over the love of parents for their children. But though all parents may show love for their children, the children are not always well behaved. . . . And if such love cannot prevent children from becoming unruly, then how can it bring the people to order? . . . [pp. 101–102]

Now here is a young man of bad character. His parents rail at him, but he does not reform; the neighbors scold, but he is unmoved; his teachers instruct him, but he refuses to change his ways. Thus, although three fine influences are brought to bear on him—the love of his parents, the efforts of the neighbors, the wisdom of his teachers—yet he remains unmoved and refuses to change so much as a hair on his shin. But let the district magistrate send out the government soldiers to enforce the law and search for evildoers, and then he is filled with terror, reforms his conduct, and changes his ways. . . .

The best rewards are those that are generous and predictable, so that the people may profit by them. The best penalties are those that are severe and inescapable, so that the people will fear them. The best laws are those that are uniform and inflexible, so that the people can understand them. . . . [pp. 103–104]

Hardly ten men of true integrity and good faith can be found today, and yet the offices of the state number in the hundreds. If they must be filled by men of integrity and good faith, then there will never be enough men to go around; and if the offices are left unfilled, then those whose business it is to govern will dwindle in numbers while disorderly men increase. Therefore the way of the enlightened ruler is to unify the laws instead of seeking for wise men, to lay down firm policies instead of longing for men of good faith. Hence his laws never fail him, and there is no felony or deceit among his officials. . . . [pp. 108–109]

Farming requires a lot of hard work, but people will do it because they say, "This way we can get rich." War is a dangerous undertaking, but people will take part in it because they say, "This way we can become eminent." Now if men who devote themselves to literature or study the art of persuasive speaking are able to get the fruits of wealth without the hard work of the farmer and can gain the advantages of eminence without the danger of battle, then who will not take up such pursuits? . . .

Therefore, in the state of an enlightened ruler there are no books written on bamboo slips; law supplies the only instruction. There are no sermons on the former kings; the officials serve as the only teachers. There are no fierce feuds of private swordsmen; cutting off the heads of the enemy is the only deed of valor. Hence, when the people of such a state make a speech, they say nothing that is in contradiction to the law; when they act, it is in some way that will bring useful results; and when they do brave deeds, they do them in the army. Therefore, in times of peace the state is rich, and in times of trouble its armies are strong. . . . [pp. 110–111]

These are the customs of a disordered state: Its scholars praise the ways of the former kings and imitate their humaneness and rightness, put on a fair appearance and speak in elegant phrases, thus casting doubt upon the laws of the time and causing the ruler to be of two minds. Its speechmakers propound false schemes and borrow influence from abroad, furthering their private interests and forgetting the welfare of the state's altars of the soil and grain. Its swordsmen gather bands of followers about them and perform deeds of honor, making a fine name for themselves and violating the prohibitions of the five government bureaus. Those of its people who are worried about military service flock to the gates of private individuals and pour out their wealth in bribes to influential men who will plead for them, in this way escaping the hardship of battle. Its merchants and artisans spend their time making articles of no practical use and gathering stores of luxury goods, accumulating riches, waiting for the best time to sell, and exploiting the farmers.

These five groups are the vermin of the state. If the rulers do not wipe out such vermin, and in their place encourage men of integrity and public spirit, then they should not be surprised, when they look about the area within the four seas, to see states perish and ruling houses wane and die. . . . [pp. 116–117]

## Chapter 50: Eminence in Learning

When the scholars of today discuss good government, many of them say, "Give land to the poor and the destitute, so that those who have no means of livelihood may be provided for." Now, if men start out with equal opportunities and yet there are a few who, without the help of unusually good harvests or outside income, are able to keep themselves well supplied, it must be due either to hard work or to frugal living. If men start out with equal opportunities and yet there are a few who, without having suffered from some calamity like famine or sickness, still sink into poverty and destitution, it must be due either to laziness or to extravagant living. The lazy and extravagant grow poor; the diligent and frugal get rich. Now if the ruler levies money from the rich in order to give alms to the poor, he is robbing the diligent and frugal and indulging the lazy and extravagant. If he expects by such a means to induce the people to work industriously and spend with caution, he will be disappointed. . . . [pp. 120–121]

Then there are other men who collect books, study rhetoric, gather bands of disciples, and devote themselves to literature, learning, and debate. The rulers of the time are sure to treat them with respect, saying, "It is the way of the former kings to honor worthy men." The farmers are the ones who must pay taxes to the officials, and yet the ruler patronizes scholars—thus the farmer's taxes grow heavier and heavier, while the scholars enjoy increasing reward. If the ruler hopes, in spite of this, that the people will work industriously and spend little time talking, he will be disappointed. . . . [pp. 121–122]

When a sage rules the state, he does not depend on people's doing good of themselves; he sees to it that they are not allowed to do what is bad. If he depends on people's doing good of themselves, then within his borders he can count fewer than ten instances of success. But if he sees to it that they are not allowed to do what is bad, then the whole state can be brought to a uniform level of order. Those who rule must employ measures that will be effective with the majority and discard those that will be effective with only a few. Therefore they devote themselves not to virtue but to law. . . . [p. 125]

When the Confucians of the present time counsel rulers, they do not praise those measures that will bring order today, but talk only of the achievements of the men who brought order in the past. They do not investigate matters of bureaucratic system or law, or examine the realities of villainy and evil, but spend all their time telling tales of the distant past and praising the achievements of the former kings. . . . No ruler with proper standards will tolerate them. Therefore the enlightened ruler works with facts and discards useless theories. He does not talk about deeds of humaneness and rightness, and he does not listen to the words of scholars. . . .

... The reason you cannot rely on the wisdom of the people is that they have the minds of little children. If the child's head is not shaved, its sores will spread; and if its boil is not lanced, it will become sicker than ever. But when it is having its head shaved or its boil lanced, someone must hold it while the loving mother performs the operation, and it yells and screams incessantly, for it does not understand that the little pain it suffers now will bring great benefit later. [pp. 127–129]

[From *Han Feizi* (SBCK), chaps. 49, 50; Watson, *Han Fei Tzu*, pp. 97–129]


## LI SI: LEGALIST THEORIES IN PRACTICE

The feudal state of Qin, utilizing Legalist practices of strong centralization of power, regimentation of its people, and aggressive warfare, had built itself up to a position of formidable strength in the late years of the Zhou dynasty. Finally, under the vigorous leadership of King Cheng, it succeeded in swallowing up the last of its rivals and uniting all of China under its rule. In 221 B.C.E. King Cheng assumed the title of Qin Shihuangdi, the First Exalted Emperor of the Qin.

He had been aided in his efforts toward unification by a group of astute and ruthless statesmen identified with Legalist doctrines, the most important of whom was Li Si, who became prime minister of the new empire. Thus, for the first time, one of the schools of classical thought had its teachings adopted as the official doctrine of a regime ruling all of China.

At Li Si's urging the First Emperor carried out a series of sweeping changes and innovations that, in the course of a few years, radically affected the entire structure of Chinese life and society. One of these was the complete abolition of all feudal ranks and privileges and the disarmament of all private individuals. The entire area of China was brought under the direct control of the central court through an administrative system of prefectures and counties. With this unification of the nation came measures for the standardization of weights, measures, and writing script, the destruction of all feudal barriers between districts, and the construction of better roads and communications. Wars were undertaken to subdue neighboring peoples and expand the borders of the nation, great masses of people were forcibly moved to new areas for purposes of defense or resettlement, and labor gangs were set to work constructing the Great Wall out of smaller defensive walls of the old feudal states.

The First Emperor of the Qin was a man of extraordinary vision and demonic energy. He worked tirelessly to build up the power and prestige of his regime, directing campaigns, constructing defenses, erecting magnificent palaces for himself and his court, and traveling on extensive tours of inspection throughout his realm. With the aid of Li Si and a few other trusted advisers he managed to carry out his drastic measures and hold down the ever-growing threat of revolt among his subjects. Never before had China been so vast and powerful.

For a while it seemed that Legalism as a theory of government had achieved incontrovertible success. But with the death of this dictatorial emperor the weakness in the Legalist system became apparent. The emperor had ruled from behind the scenes, remaining aloof from his people and ministers. This placed enormous power in the hands of a few trusted officials and eunuchs who were allowed access to him. On his death a struggle for power broke out. Li Si and the powerful eunuch Zhao Gao, by concealing the death of the emperor and forging orders in his name, succeeded in destroying their rivals and seizing actual control of the government. The Second Emperor became a helpless puppet, cut off in the depths of the palace from all contact with or information about the outside world. Then Zhao Gao turned on Li Si and destroyed him and his family, using against him the very Legalist methods that Li Si had employed. Popular revolts broke out all over the nation as the people grew increasingly restless under the burden of taxation and oppression. But all news of the seriousness of the situation was kept from the court by officials who had learned to fear the consequences of speaking out. The government was paralyzed by the force of its own autocratic laws. In the end the Second Emperor was forced to commit suicide, Zhao Gao was murdered, and the last ruler of the Qin submitted meekly to the leader of a popular revolt. In 207, less than fifteen years after its glorious establishment, the new dynasty had come to a violent and ignoble end.

The Qin, though short-lived, had a profound effect upon the course of Chinese history. The measures for unification, standardization, and centralization of power, coercive though they were, destroyed for all time the old enfeoffment system and gave to the Chinese people a new sense of unity and identity. The destruction of the old feudal states, the shifts of population, and the wars and uprisings that accompanied the downfall of the dynasty wiped out the old aristocracy of Zhou times and opened the way for new leaders and new families to rise to power. Nevertheless, the spectacular failure of the Legalists to stamp out rival schools of thought, to suppress criticism by police control, and to rule the people by exacting laws and harsh penalties discredited Legalist policies for centuries to come. Later regimes might in fact make use of Legalist ideas and methods in their administrations, but never again did they dare openly to espouse the hated philosophy of the Qin. The First Emperor and his advisers became the symbols of evil and oppression in Chinese history.

## MEMORIAL ON THE ABOLITION OF THE ENFEOFFMENT SYSTEM

The foregoing view of the First Emperor and Li Si is reflected in the following memorials as recorded by Sima Qian, the foremost historian of early China. That Sima Qian's record represents a Han view of the Qin past is significant.

Numerous were the sons, younger brothers, and other members of the royal family that were enfeoffed by King Wen and King Wu at the founding of the

Zhou dynasty. But as time passed, these relatives became estranged and alienated one from another; they attacked each other as if they were enemies. Eventually the feudal lords started wars and sent punitive expeditions against one another, and the king could do nothing to stop them. Now, owing to the divine intelligence of Your Majesty, all the land within the seas is unified and it has been divided into commanderies and prefectures. . . . To institute an enfeoffed nobility again would not be advantageous.

[From *Shiji* (BNB) 6:12b; BW]

## MEMORIAL ON THE BURNING OF BOOKS

Among the most infamous acts of the First Exalted Emperor of the Qin were the "burning of books," ordered in 213 B.C.E., and the "execution of scholars," ordered in 212. The first was an effort to achieve thought control through destroying all literature except the *Classic of Changes*, the royal archives of the Qin house, and books on technical subjects, such as medicine, agriculture, and forestry. The measure was aimed particularly at the *Classic of Documents* and the *Classic of Odes*. The execution of some 460 scholars in the following year[2] was an attempt to eliminate opposition to the emperor by ruthlessly destroying all potentially "subversive" elements.

In earlier times the empire disintegrated and fell into disorder, and no one was capable of unifying it. Thereupon the various feudal lords rose to power. In their discourses they all praised the past in order to disparage the present and embellished empty words to confuse the truth. Everyone cherished his own favorite school of learning and criticized what had been instituted by the authorities. But at present Your Majesty possesses a unified empire, has regulated the distinctions of black and white, and has firmly established for yourself a position of sole supremacy. And yet these independent schools, joining with each other, criticize the codes of laws and instructions. Hearing of the promulgation of a decree, they criticize it, each from the standpoint of his own school. At home they disapprove of it in their hearts; going out they criticize it in the thoroughfare. They seek a reputation by discrediting their sovereign; they appear superior by expressing contrary views, and they lead the lowly multitude in the spreading of slander. If such license is not prohibited, the sovereign power will decline above and partisan factions will form below. It would be well to prohibit this.

Your servant suggests that all books in the imperial archives, save the memoirs of Qin, be burned. All persons in the empire, except members of the Academy of Learned Scholars, in possession of the *Classic of Odes*, the *Classic of Documents*, and discourses of the hundred philosophers should take them to

---

2. Traditionally referred to as "the burial of the scholars," on the view that the scholars were actually buried alive, though it is not certain that they met their end in this way.

the local governors and have them indiscriminately burned. Those who dare to talk to each other about the *Odes* and *Documents* should be executed and their bodies exposed in the marketplace. Anyone referring to the past to criticize the present should, together with all members of his family, be put to death. . . .

[From *Shiji* (BNB) 87:6b–7a; BW]

## MEMORIAL ON EXERCISING HEAVY CENSURE

The worthy ruler should be one able to fulfill his kingly duties and employ the technique of censure.[3] Visited with censure, the ministers dare not but exert their ability to the utmost in devotion to their ruler. When the relative positions between minister and ruler are thus defined unmistakably, and the relative duties between superior and inferior are made clear, then none in the empire, whether worthy or unworthy, will dare do otherwise than exert his strength and fulfill his duties in devotion to the ruler. Thus the ruler will by himself control the empire and will not be controlled by anyone. Then he can enjoy himself to the utmost. How can a talented and intelligent ruler afford not to pay attention to this point?

Hence, Shen Buhai[4] has said, "To possess the empire and yet not be able to indulge one's own desires is called making shackles out of the empire." The reason is that a ruler who is unable to employ censure must instead labor himself for the welfare of the people as did Yao and Yu. Thus it may be said that he makes shackles for himself. Now, if a ruler will not practice the intelligent methods of Shen Buhai and Han Feizi, or apply the system of censure in order to utilize the empire for his own pleasure, but on the contrary purposelessly tortures his body and wastes his mind in devotion to the people—then he becomes the slave of the common people instead of the domesticator of the empire. . . .

. . . If, now, a ruler does not busy himself with what prevents rebellion, but instead engages in the same practices by which the affectionate mother spoils her children, indeed he has not understood the principles of the sages. When one fails to practice the statecraft of the sages, what else does he do except make himself the slave of the empire? Is this not a pity? . . .

The intelligent ruler is one able . . . to exercise alone the craft of the ruler, whereby he keeps his obedient ministers under control and his clear laws in effect. Therefore his person becomes exalted and his power great. All talented rulers should be able to oppose the world and suppress established usage,

---

3. The Chinese term rendered as "censure" here may be more literally translated as "inspection and punishment." To relieve the awkwardness from the repeated use of this cumbersome expression, we have adopted "censure" as a more convenient, though less exact, equivalent throughout the memorial.

4. A Legalist philosopher, d. 337 B.C.E.

destroying what they hate and establishing what they desire. Thus they may occupy a position of honor and power while they live and receive posthumous titles that bespeak their ability and intelligence after they die. So, the intelligent ruler acts on his decisions by himself, and none of the authority lies with his ministers. . . .

[From *Shiji* (BNB) 87:15a–18a; BW]

## THE MILITARY TEXTS: THE *SUNZI*

War brings change. And endemic warfare in the fifth, fourth, and third centuries B.C.E. altered Chinese tradition. Not only were all of the central states consumed by Qin, but as battles increased in size, severity, and consequence, the lives of peasant, townsperson, and functionary were forced into new patterns. State power was centralized and extended, conscripting farmers for violent acts far from home. Huge armies demanded a multitude of standardized weapons, elaborate transportation systems, and the effective extraction and management of wealth. Ruthless warfare brought ruin or reward. In these processes social values changed profoundly.

According to the idealized code of warfare of Shang and Western Zhou times, combat was viewed as an aristocratic affair, governed by complex protocols that may be aptly compared to the chivalry of European knighthood. Battle was to be between individuals, on horseback in Europe, in chariots in China. Honor required fair treatment of one's enemy, and insult to honor required vengeance. Oaths of men and nations were sealed in blood.

Remnants of these values could still be discerned in the Spring and Autumn period (771–479). The state of Song, seat of the deposed Shang kings, was weak. Yet in 638 its duke felt compelled to fight a much stronger state. When the duke's forces were outnumbered at the battle, his minister of war urged him to attack the enemy while they were still fording a river and again before they had drawn up ranks after crossing. The duke twice refused; he was wounded, his army routed. In defense the *Zuozhuan* put these words into his mouth: "The noble person (*junzi*) does not inflict a second wound. He does not capture those with graying hair. Of old, when campaigning one did not obstruct those in a defile. Though I am but the remnant of a destroyed state, I will not drum to attack when they have not drawn up ranks" (Duke Xi, 22d year).

In a chivalric world of interstate negotiations, the duke's sense of honor might once have possessed considerable functionality. Now, however, such honor was "but the remnant of a destroyed state." Instead of supporting this moribund value system, his minister of war retorted, "My lord does not know battle. If the mighty enemy is in a defile or with his ranks not drawn up, this is Heaven assisting us." Whether his invocation of Heaven was cynical or devout, the minister's message is clear: warfare is not about virtue, it is about taking advantage of fleeting opportunities. By the middle of the Warring States period, when huge, recurrent battles engulfed the populace in unprecedented acts of destruction, warfare was about creating those conditions of advantage by any means, even those conventionally considered immoral. The *Sunzi* puts it bluntly: "The military is a way (*dao*) of deception." In this Warring States world no political or social thinker could ignore the military. Most masters (*zi*) were political thinkers. Some were moralists, some simply administrators, but their texts treated military matters as an aspect of governance.

According to his biography in the *Records of the Grand Historian*, Sunzi, or Master Sun, was a contemporary of Confucius who served the state of Wu in its battles with rival states in the late Spring and Autumn period. There is, however, no historical evidence for this patriarch of East Asian strategy in any records before the third century B.C.E., and the text that bears his name was probably compiled from oral traditions in the second half of the fourth century B.C.E.

"One hundred victories in one hundred battles is not skillful. Subduing the other's military without battle is skillful" (chap. 3). Warfare is destructive, of life, property, and value systems. Whether one's goal is conquest or defense, it is generally preferable to win without expending resources. This does not mean, of course, that the *Sunzi* is pacifist, or reluctant to engage. It does, however, imply the next epigram: "What is meant by skilled is to be victorious over the easily defeated" (chap. 4). Great generals of the past were not those who charged uphill against overwhelming odds. On the contrary, they chose to fight when they knew in advance that they could easily win—thus they were "victorious over those who were already defeated." For "the victorious military is first victorious and after that does battle."

How is this done? "Knowing the other and knowing oneself, in one hundred battles no danger" (chap. 3). The general wins through knowledge, not prowess. Sun Bin, reputed grandson of Sunzi, is the best exemplar of this. Punished by having his legs chopped off at the knees, he was unable even to walk to the battlefield—yet he was still revered as a legendary strategist.

For the *Sunzi* knowledge must comprehend everything pertinent to war—terrain, morale, logistics, spies, weather, economics, psychology, and so on. These factors are related to each other in discernible yet shifting ways. Their relationship is discussed as the term *shi*, which refers both to the power inherent in a particular arrangement of elements and to its developmental tendency—the potential to change in definite directions. The *Sunzi* compares the power of *shi* to rocks atop a mountain. At rest, they are a form of potential energy. When released, they cascade down with overwhelming natural force. "Thus the *shi* of one skilled at setting people to battle is like rolling round rocks from a mountain one thousand *ren* high" (chap. 5). The good general can both recognize and create *shi*. But configurations always change, and once enacted, a strategy loses its power of surprise. Thus, "do not repeat the means of victory, but respond to form from the inexhaustible" (chap. 6).

Deception and strategic mutability lead to a particular kind of indirect approach in which the general ideally achieves victory without either expending his own resources or utterly destroying those of the enemy. The essence of this approach lies first in comprehensively conceiving the elements that constitute warfare and then identifying an action that is easy to accomplish (because it engenders no opposition) and effective (because it fundamentally rearranges the configuration of forces to the general's advantage).

The intellectual world of the Warring States period was characterized not only by bitter debate but also by the broad sharing of ideas; through both of these means the *Sunzi* is conceptually related to many of its contemporaries. One of its more unexpected kinships is with the *Laozi*, which also eschews conventional morality, emphasizes reversal, and views all things in terms of their relationships.

The *Sunzi* has been the most influential strategy text in East Asia. Its earliest surviving commentary comes from the hand of the great general Cao Cao (155–220 C.E.), who participated in the overthrow of the Han dynasty in the early third century. Canonized as the first of the *Seven Military Classics* (*Wujing qishu*) in early Song times, it is read today in the military academies of the People's Republic, the Republic of China, Japan, and the United States.

SELECTIONS FROM THE *SUNZI*

## Deception and Reversal

The *Sunzi* has been consistently reviled by Confucians for advocating deception. As we shall see, however, the *Sunzi* is concerned with deception as entirely situation-oriented: it depends for its effectiveness on the accurate reading of present conditions, which by their nature cannot be entirely foreseen.

The military is a way (*dao*) of deception.
>   Thus when able, manifest inability. When active, manifest inactivity.
>   When near, manifest as far. When far, manifest as near.
>   When he seeks advantage, lure him.
>   When he is in chaos, take him.
>   When he is substantial, prepare against him.
>   When he is strong, avoid him.
>   Attack where he is unprepared. Emerge where he does not expect.
>   These are the victories of the military lineage. They cannot be transmitted in advance. [chap. 1]

## On Victory

In general, the method of employing the military—
>   Taking a state whole is superior. Destroying it is inferior to this.
>   Taking a division whole is superior. Destroying it is inferior to this. . . .

Therefore, one hundred victories in one hundred battles is not skillful. Subduing the other's military without battle is skillful. . . .

Knowing victory has five aspects.
Knowing when one can and cannot do battle is victory.
Discerning the use of the many and the few is victory.
Superior and inferior desiring the same is victory.
Using preparation to await the unprepared is victory.
The general being capable and the ruler not interfering is victory.
These five are a way (*dao*) of knowing victory. . . . [chap. 3]

In the past the skillful first made themselves invincible to await the enemy's vincibility.
Invincibility lies in oneself. Vincibility lies in the enemy. . . .
Invincibility is defense. Vincibility is attack.
Defend and one has a surplus. Attack and one is insufficient. . . .

Victory in battle that all-under-Heaven calls skilled is not skilled. . . .
What is meant by skilled is to be victorious over the easily defeated. Thus the battles of the skilled are without extraordinary victory, without reputation for wisdom, and without merit for courage. . . .
Therefore, the victorious military is first victorious and after that does battle. The defeated military first does battle and after that seeks victory. [chap. 4]

## The Orthodox and the Extraordinary

This is the most famous pair of terms in the *Sunzi*. The orthodox, or *zheng*, refers to military action that is conventionally correct—for example, that one should not fight with one's back to water, as that leaves no route for retreat. It is military operations by the book, and as such it constitutes an indispensable part of any military action. But to obtain victory the *Sunzi* advocates "the extraordinary"—or, literally, "the strange" (*qi*)—that which the enemy does not expect. From the interplay of these two elements emerges an unending series of strategies.

Note that what is at first extraordinary immediately loses its surprise value. Eventually it may even turn into orthodoxy. Thus in certain circumstances it may be more extraordinary to do that which is normally considered orthodox. What is most striking about the pair, then, is that the label *extraordinary* or *orthodox* is applied to strategies not according to some assessment of their intrinsic nature but rather in light of the enemy's expectations. In this sense strategy is a matter of perception.

This long selection, which probably contains two or more passages that were originally separate, also introduces the term *shi*. In the Warring States administrative texts later grouped under the heading "Legalism," *shi* comes to mean the power that the ruler has by virtue of sitting on the throne—in other words, the authority of his position. It is thus relational but static. In the *Sunzi*, however, this power also has a dynamic aspect. It is something that one develops or cultivates and then releases at the right moment. Here the central images of *shi* are the crossbow that has been drawn and rocks that are poised to roll down a mile-high mountain. This aspect of *shi* is best rendered "potential energy."

In general when in battle:
Use the orthodox to engage. Use the extraordinary to attain victory. . . .
. . . The *shi* of battle do not exceed the extraordinary and the orthodox, yet all their variations cannot be exhausted.

The extraordinary and orthodox circle and give birth to each other, like a circle without beginning. Who is able to exhaust it?

The rush of water, to the point of tossing rocks about: this is *shi*. The strike of a hawk at the killing snap: this is the node.

Therefore, one skilled at battle: his *shi* is steep, his node is short.

*Shi* is like drawing the crossbow. The node is like pulling the trigger. [chap. 5]


## Order

The passages assembled here address the common military problem of chaos, cowardice, and weakness. Normally one wishes to create their opposites—order, bravery, and strength—but to attempt to do so, the text suggests, merely continues a slide around the continuum from negative to positive and back to negative—since "chaos is born from order." Instead, the *Sunzi* recommends stepping out of this polarity and using impersonal forces such as *shi* that will bring about the desired behavior on the soldiers' part. In this instance no attempt is made to discipline human beings or improve their nature.

The subsequent section makes a more precise recommendation: place your troops in an environmental configuration where their natural responses will be what you want, where it will be a matter of "rolling round rocks from a mountain one thousand *ren* high."

One who uses *shi* sets people to battle as if rolling trees and rocks. As for the nature of trees and rocks: When still, they are at rest. When agitated, they move. When square, they stop. When round, they go.

Thus the *shi* of one skilled at setting people to battle is like rolling round rocks from a mountain one thousand *ren* high. This is *shi*. [chap. 5]


## Form and Formlessness

Beginning with a loose collection of materials, this section then turns to the complex question of *form* (*xing*), a term whose meaning ranges from the most concrete issues of military drill to the most abstract sense of formlessness. Like water, the skillful general has no predetermined form. Thus he can transform endlessly, spiritlike. He may even act like the cosmos itself.

One who takes position first at the battleground and awaits the enemy is at ease. One who takes position later at the battleground and hastens to do battle is at labor.

Thus one skilled at battle summons others and is not summoned by them. . . .

Thus with one skilled at attack the enemy does not know where to defend. With one skilled at defense the enemy does not know where to attack. . . .

The ultimate in giving form to the military is to arrive at formlessness. When one is formless, deep spies cannot catch a glimpse and the wise cannot strategize.

Rely on form to bring about victory over the multitude, and the multitude cannot understand. People all know the form by which I am victorious, but no one knows how I determine form.

Do not repeat the means of victory, but respond to form from the inexhaustible.

Now, the form of the military is like water. Water in its movement avoids the high and hastens to the low. The military in its victory avoids the solid and strikes the empty.

Thus water determines its movement in accordance with the earth. The military determines victory in accordance with the enemy. . . . [chap. 6]

## Invading Enemy Territory

This passage provides a final example of how the general relies on *shi*—the dynamic configuration of things—to attain the result he seeks. Here his troops are deep in enemy territory, fearing for their lives. He does not attempt to alter their state of mind but rather uses it to make them invincible.

In general, the way (*dao*) of being an invader:

Enter deeply and one is concentrated. The defenders do not subdue one. Plunder rich countryside. The army has enough to eat.

> Carefully nourish and do not work them.
> Consolidate *qi* and accumulate strength.
> Move the army and appraise one's strategies.
> Be unfathomable.

Throw them where they cannot leave. Facing death they will not be routed. Officers and men facing death, how could one not gain their utmost strength?

> When military officers are sinking, they do not fear.
> Where they cannot leave, they stand firm.
> When they enter deep, they hold tightly.
> Where they cannot leave, they fight.

Therefore, they are

> Unregulated yet disciplined,
> Unsought yet obtained,
> Without covenant yet in kinship,
> Without orders yet trusting.

Prohibit omens, remove doubts, and even death seems no disaster. . . . [chap. 11]

[From Yang, *Sunzi huijian*, pp. 1–9, 12–15, 33–35, 45–55, 62–76, 84–89, 161–169; KS]

*Chapter 8*

## THE HAN REACTION TO QIN ABSOLUTISM

Though China witnessed periods of imperial splendor under several dynasties, the Qin (221–207 B.C.E.) and Han (202 B.C.E.–220 C.E.) clearly represent the original "imperial age," because in these years the basic pattern for succeeding empires was laid out. The rule of the Qin was short-lived but marked a great turning point in Chinese history. For the first time the country was brought under a single unified administration, a centralized state wielding unprecedented power, controlling vast resources, and displaying a magnificence that inspired both awe and dread among its subjects. Achieved after years of steady, systematic conquest, this empire nevertheless proved an unexpected graveyard for the grandiose ambitions of its masters.

Yet when the Qin suddenly collapsed, it left to the House of Han an important legacy: the idea of empire and the governmental structure to embody it. For almost four centuries under the Han the implications of this great fact were to work their way out in all aspects of Chinese life, not least in the intellectual sphere. It is with this long period of consolidation and coordination that we shall be chiefly concerned here. In several fundamental respects it shaped the intellectual and institutional traditions of China until modern times, and not of China only but of much of East Asia as well.

The downfall of the Qin, more dramatic and sudden even than its rise, had a profound effect upon the thinking of the Chinese. It proved to their satisfaction that terror and strength alone could never rule the world. But the men who wrested from the Qin the vast empire it had created were not bent simply on restoring the old order of things.

The aristocratic families of the older feudal states of Zhou, which had bitterly resisted the expansion of Qin, had been seriously weakened by the steps the conqueror later took to prevent them from again threatening his power. The opposition that eventually proved fatal to the Qin dynasty, therefore, came not from the ranks of the old aristocracy but from the common people. Chen She, who led the first major revolt against Qin rule, was a day laborer in the fields. Liu Ji, the man who finally set up the Han dynasty after destroying both the Qin and rival rebel factions, was likewise of humble origin, as were most of his comrades who fought with him to victory.

As commoners under the Qin, these men knew firsthand the suffering that its harsh rule had brought to the people. They were quick to abolish its more offensive laws and institutions, while leaving intact much of the rest of its elaborate machinery of government. Under their leadership the new regime of the Han was marked by plebeian heartiness and vigor, simplicity and frugality in government, and abhorrence of the Legalist doctrines of the hated Qin.

The early years of the Han were marked by a long, slow struggle to recover for the empire the advantages of the harsh unification effected by the Qin and to establish them firmly in the pattern of Chinese society. The Qin had abolished the enfeoffment system in one sweeping stroke, yet it arose again among the followers and family of the founder of the Han, whose successors had set about quietly and patiently whittling away at feudal rights and holdings until they were finally and for all time reduced to an empty formality. The great web of central government, held together by the terror of Qin's laws and the personal power of its First Emperor, had quickly disintegrated with the fall of the dynasty. The Han worked gradually to build it up again, unifying, organizing, and standardizing the vast area brought under its control. This effort at standardization extended even to the systematizing of thought in which, again, the Han succeeded in accomplishing, by gradual and peaceful means, what the violent proscriptions of the Qin had failed to secure.

## JIA YI: "THE FAULTS OF QIN"

The following excerpt is from the celebrated essay "The Faults of Qin" ("Guo Qin lun"), by the Han poet and statesman Jia Yi (201–168? B.C.E.). Jia Yi, employing the florid style popular at this time, reviews the history of Qin and analyzes the causes of its precipitous downfall. Note, however, that he finds fault not with the Qin state itself but primarily with the failings of the founder of the empire and his heir, the Second Emperor, who squandered the magnificent achievements of their forebears.

Duke Xiao of Qin, sequestered in the natural stronghold of Yaohan and based in the land of Yongzhou,[1] with his ministers in proper array, eyed the House of Zhou with the thought of rolling up the empire like a mat, enveloping the entire universe, pocketing all within the Four Seas, and swallowing up everything in all Eight Directions. At the time he was counseled by Lord Shang,[2] who aided him in establishing laws, encouraging agriculture and weaving, preparing the tools of war for defense and offense, and negotiating alliances far and near so that the other feudal lords fell into strife with one another. . . .

[Later] when the First Emperor ascended [the throne] he flourished and furthered the accomplishments of the six generations before him. Brandishing his long whip, he drove the world before him; destroying the feudal lords, he swallowed up the domains of the two Zhou dynasties. He reached the pinnacle of power and ordered all in the Six Directions, whipping the rest of the world into submission and thus spreading his might through the Four Seas. . . . With the empire thus pacified, the First Emperor believed that, with the capital secure within the pass and prosperous cities stretching for ten thousand *li*, he had indeed created an imperial structure to be enjoyed by his royal descendants for ten thousand generations to come.

Even after the death of the First Emperor, his reputation continued to sway the people. Chen She was a man who grew up in humble circumstances in a hut with broken pots for windows and ropes as door hinges and was a mere hired field hand and roving conscript of mediocre talent. He could neither equal the worth of Confucius and Mozi nor match the wealth of Tao Zhu or Yi Dun, yet, even stumbling as he did amidst the ranks of common soldiers and shuffling through the fields, he called forth a tired motley crowd and led a mob of several hundred to turn upon the Qin. . . .

During that time, the world saw many men of prescience and far-reaching vision. The reason for their not showing deep loyalty by helping to correct evils [at court] lay in the Qin's excesses in proscribing contrary opinions. Often before upright words could even be uttered, the body had met death. Thoughtful people of the empire would only listen and incline their ears, standing with one foot on the other, not daring to offer their services while keeping their mouths shut in silence. The three sovereigns lost the proper way while loyal officials offered no remonstrance and advisers no plans. With the realm in chaos and unworthy officials not reporting troubles to their superiors, was this not a tragedy?

[From *Xinshu*, "Guo Qin lun" (*SBCK* 1:1a–8b); DWYK]

---

1. Yaohan refers to the mountain pass linking Mount Yao and the Hangu Pass in present-day He'nan, near Tongguan in Shaanxi province. Yongzhou was one of nine provinces occupied by the Qin, consisting of most of present-day Shaanxi and portions of Gansu and Qinghai.

2. See chap. 7.

### THE REBELLION OF CHEN SHE AND WU GUANG

This description of the beginning of the first major revolt against the Qin dynasty is taken from the biographies of its leaders, Chen She and Wu Guang, in the *Records of the Grand Historian* (*Shiji*) and the *History of the Former Han* (*Hanshu*).

During the first year of the Second Emperor of Qin (209 B.C.E.), in the seventh month, an order came for a force of nine hundred men from the poor side of the town to be sent to garrison Yuyang. Chen She and Wu Guang were among those whose turn it was to go, and they were appointed heads of the levy of men. When the group had gone as far as Daze County, they encountered such heavy rain that the road became impassable. It was apparent that the men would be unable to reach the appointed place, an offense punishable by death. Chen She and Wu Guang accordingly began to plot together. "As things stand, we face death whether we stay or run away," they said, "while if we were to start a revolt we would likewise face death. Since we must die in any case, would it not be better to die fighting for the sake of a state?" . . .

Wu Guang had always been kind to others and many of the soldiers would do anything for him. When the officer in command was drunk, Wu Guang made a point of openly announcing several times that he was going to run away. In this way Wu Guang hoped to arouse the commander's anger, get him to punish him, and so stir up the men's ire and resentment. As Wu Guang had expected, the commander began to beat him, when the commander's sword slipped out of its scabbard. Wu Guang sprang up, seized the sword, and killed the commander. Chen She rushed to his assistance, and they proceeded to kill the other two commanding officers as well. Then they called together all the men of the group and announced: "Because of the rain we encountered, we cannot reach our rendezvous on time. And anyone who misses a rendezvous has his head cut off! Even if you should somehow escape with your heads, six or seven out of every ten of you are bound to die in the course of garrison duty. Now, my brave fellows, if you are unwilling to die, we have nothing more to say. But if you would risk death, then let us risk it for the sake of fame and glory! Kings and nobles, generals and ministers—such men are made, not born!" The men of the garrison all replied, "We'll do whatever you say!"

[From *Shiji* (BNB) 48:1a–3a; BW]

### THE RISE OF LIU BANG, FOUNDER OF THE HAN

Liu Bang, like Chen She, was a man of humble birth who formed a small band of adventurers and opposed Qin rule. When his forces grew to a sizable army, he entered into an agreement with other rebel groups that the one who first reached the capital area of Qin, Guanzhong or the land "within the Pass," should become its ruler. In 207 B.C.E. Liu Bang succeeded in fighting his way to the capital city of Xianyang, and the Qin dynasty came to an end. At this time he issued his famous three-article code (ten characters in Chinese) to replace the elaborate legal code of Qin. Though when the dynasty got on its feet a more elaborate set of laws had to be worked out, this three-article code has often been held up as an example of the simplicity and leniency of early Han government. The translations are from the biography of Liu Bang, the "Annals of Emperor Gaozu" (his posthumous title) in the *Records of the Grand Historian*. Liu Bang's various titles have been omitted for the sake of clarity.

In the tenth month of the first year of Han (November–December 207 B.C.E.) Liu Bang finally succeeded in reaching Bashang [near the capital] ahead of the other leaders. . . . He sealed up the storehouses containing Qin's treasures and wealth and returned to camp at Bashang. There he summoned all the distinguished and powerful men of the districts and addressed them, saying, "Gentlemen, for a long time you have suffered beneath the harsh laws of Qin. . . . I hereby promise you a code of laws consisting of three articles only: he who kills anyone shall suffer death; he who wounds another or steals shall be punished according to the gravity of the offense; for the rest I hereby abolish all laws of Qin. Let the officials and people remain undisturbed as before. I have come only to save you from further harm, not to exploit or tyrannize over you. Therefore do not be afraid! . . .

[From *Shiji* (BNB) 8:15a–16b; BW]

## LIU BANG BECOMES THE FIRST EMPEROR
## OF THE HAN DYNASTY

To ensure the loyalty of his comrades and supporters, Liu Bang was obliged to hand out titles and fiefs to them as his conquests advanced. In 202 B.C.E., when his final success seemed assured, they in turn urged him to assume the old Qin title of Exalted Emperor, arguing that if he failed to do so their own titles would lack authority. Like Caesar he modestly declined three times before accepting.

In the first month [of 202 B.C.E.] the various nobles and generals all joined in begging Liu Bang to take the title of Exalted Emperor (*huangdi*), but he replied, "I have heard that the position of emperor may go only to a worthy man. It cannot be claimed by empty words and vain talk. I do not dare to accept the position of emperor."

His followers all replied, "Our great king has risen from the humblest beginnings to punish the wicked and violent and bring peace to all within the four seas. To those who have achieved merit he has accordingly parceled out land and enfeoffed them as kings and marquises. If our king does not assume the supreme title, then all our titles as well will be called into doubt. On pain of death we urge our request!"

[From *Shiji* (BNB) 8:28b; BW]

# Chapter 9

## SYNCRETIC VISIONS OF STATE, SOCIETY, AND COSMOS

During the period of intense conflict in the late fourth and third centuries B.C.E., one independent kingdom after another fell to the overwhelming military power of the Qin state, which, as we have seen, conquered all others and unified China under a single emperor in 221 B.C.E. This was a chaotic period for everyone, including the intellectuals who scrambled for patronage at the various local courts and attempted to develop philosophies that would be effective in combating tyranny and governing the state.

In this period we see the rise of highly politicized syncretisms, founded on the cosmological ideas of many thinkers and on the self-cultivation theories of the *Laozi* and *Zhuangzi* and that extended them, often in a quite specific manner, to the problems of government. Sometimes called "Huang-Lao," after the Yellow Emperor and Laozi, these new doctrines integrated relevant ideas from several philosophical lineages, such as the Confucian, Mohist, and Legalist, and synthesized them within a Daoist framework. By the first part of the Han dynasty, this syncretic form became so dominant that the famous historian Sima Tan believed that it defined the essence of Daoism. It even received imperial sanction for several decades until the ascent to power of Emperor Wu in 141 B.C.E.

We include in this chapter selections from a number of texts that span more than a century from about 250 B.C.E.

Taken individually, these texts represent the work of many authors who did not belong to a single philosophical lineage. Taken together, they exhibit so many striking similarities in philosophical outlook that they can fairly be viewed as representing stages of syncretism, influenced in varying degrees by the *Laozi* and *Zhuangzi*, that were a dominant intellectual influence in this period and beyond.

Perhaps the predominant theme in these texts is that of the spiritual self-perfection of the ruler. Human society must be governed by an individual who has attained profound integration through techniques of "inner cultivation" and who has gained the gnostic vision of the unifying power of the Way that enables him to govern effectively. Living in a holistic universe governed by resonances between macrocosm and microcosm, a universe of which human societies were perceived to be integral parts, subject to its laws, such a sage king perceived these fundamental patterns of Heaven and Earth and established a government based upon them. This governing framework having been constructed, the sage king would be able to govern through nonaction, that is, without interfering with natural processes. By delegating responsibilities to his subordinates and cultivating clarity of mind he could respond spontaneously and harmoniously to any situation that arose.

## THE THEORETICAL BASIS OF THE IMPERIAL INSTITUTION

### The *Springs and Autumns of Mr. Lü* (*Lüshi chunqiu*)

Lü Buwei, after whom the text is named, was not a typical intellectual. His official biography explains that he began as "a big merchant of Yangdi who traveled back and forth, buying cheap and selling dear, until his family had stored up a thousand in gold." But he used his wealth to become councilor-in-chief of Qin and the greatest patron of learning in his time.

The book is oriented toward control of a large state with an active officialdom whose knowledge and capacities make up for the ruler's inevitable limits and who, unlike him, must be subject to restraint and correction. The good social order is patterned on Nature. The state's dynamism is that of Nature's cyclic processes. The demarcation of sky and earth, moral and hierarchic as much as spatial, dictates the separation of ruler and officials. The monarch's responsibility is self-cultivation, which puts him in touch with the order of Heaven-and-Earth. His commands must be obeyed. At the same time, his mystical link to the cosmic flow is essential to overcome his own arbitrariness and selfishness. Administration is not his business, but that of the bureaucrats. He is unable to act except through them. Their inner lives, unlike that of the monarch, are of no concern to Lü so long as they are upright and keep within the strict limits of their posts. These restrictions separate officials from each other as surely as from the sovereign.

## THE ROUND WAY

The following excerpt is perhaps the most eloquent expression in Chinese—among a great many—of the notion that the state is a microcosm, a miniature replica of the universe.

The opening of this chapter explains why one speaks of the Way of Heaven as round and that of Earth as square. This contrast came to stand for the overarching magnanimity of Heaven as distinct from the boundedness of Earth. Heaven and round became the yang in relation to the yin of Earth and squareness. By calling on these yin-yang correspondences Lü implies that ruler and subordinates are inherently complementary, not antagonistic, opposites. Yang is creative, yin receptive, and neither can be realized except by interaction with the other.

But as this symbolism separated Heaven and Earth, they were reunited by the mediation of man, above all of the emperor.

The Way of Heaven is round; the way of Earth is square. The sage kings took this as their model, basing on it [the distinction between] above and below. How do we explain the roundness of Heaven? The essential *qi* alternately moves up and down,[1] completing a cycle and beginning again, delayed by nothing; that is why we speak of the way of Heaven as round. How do we explain the squareness of Earth? The ten thousand things are distinct in category and shape. Each has its separate responsibility [as an official does], and cannot carry out that of another; that is why one speaks of the way of Earth as square. When the ruler grasps the round and his ministers keep to the square, so that round and square are not interchanged, his state prospers. . . .

The One is most exalted of all. No one knows its source. No one knows its incipient form (*duan*). No one knows its beginning. No one knows its end. Still the myriad things take it as their progenitor. The sage kings took it as their model in order to perfect their natures, to settle their vital forces, and to form their commands.

A command issues from the ruler's mouth. Those in official positions receive it and carry it out, never resting day and night. . . .

When the Former Kings appointed high officials, they insisted that they be upright [literally, "square and correct"], in order to keep their responsibilities definite, so that [the ruler] would not be obstructed by those below. Yao and Shun were worthy rulers. They took worthies as their successors. . . . Nowadays the rulers of men insist merely that the succession not be lost, so that they can bestow [the kingdom] on their own sons and grandsons. When they appoint high officials they cannot demand that they be upright, for their own selfish desires have thrown [the state] into chaos. Why is that so? Because their desires extend so much further than their awareness.

[From *Lüshi chunqiu jiao shi* 3:5, pp. 171–173; NS]

---

1. This refers to the movements of the energies that correspond to the seasons.

## The *Huang-Lao Silk Manuscripts* (*Huang-Lao boshu*)

During the first six decades of the Han dynasty, a philosophy called Huang-Lao, named after the mythical Yellow Emperor Huangdi and the sage Laozi, was the predominant influence at the imperial court. It seems to have completely disappeared, however, after the ascendancy of Confucianism under Emperor Wu (r. 141–87 B.C.E.) beginning in 136 B.C.E. Known from terse references in historical writings, it was said to advocate a central government controlled by a ruler who had achieved profound states of tranquillity and who governed by taking no intentional action (*wuwei*), concepts found in the *Daodejing*.[2]

In 1973 a major cache of texts was discovered at a tomb excavation near the village of Mawangdui, close to the present-day city of Changsha in Hunan province. Among the silk scrolls unearthed at this tomb, which had been closed in 168 B.C.E., were two manuscripts of the *Daodejing* and four texts of varying lengths that were attached to one of them. The four texts, titled *Normative Standards* (*Jingfa*), *Sixteen Canons* (*Shiliu jing*), *Collected Sayings* (*Cheng*), and *The Source That Is the Way* (*Daoyuan*), are of widely varying lengths: the first contains 5,000 characters divided among nine distinct essays, while the last is a complete essay a mere 464 characters in length. Here we translate and analyze two essays from the first text.

There is as yet no scholarly consensus on the date and compilation of these four texts, but one would not go wrong in thinking of these texts as compilations that were written down between the middle of the third century and 200 B.C.E.

The philosophy found in the texts, particularly the two that follow, can best be described as a syncretism that is grounded in a cosmology of the Way and an ethos of self-cultivation that fully embraces relevant concepts from the Daoists, Mohists, Legalists, Terminologists,[3] and Naturalists.[4]

### BOOK 1: NORMATIVE STANDARDS (*JINGFA*), PART 1

The first selection is an essay titled "The Standards of the Way," which begins *Normative Standards*. It speaks of the Way as the ultimate source of all things within the cosmos but focuses on the standards it generates that serve as models for human behavior at both the societal and the individual levels. In order to act in harmony with this Way (and hence to succeed in every undertaking), the ruler must know

---

2. See chap. 5.

3. The Terminologists (School of Names) (*ming jiao*) were concerned with the correspondence of names and reality.

4. Or the yin-yang school.

its relevant standards in a particular situation and set his state on the right course by bringing his behavior and that of his people in line with these cosmic patterns. The sage king is able to do this because of the attainment of a profound level of self-cultivation that confers the ability to "look at and know," that is, spontaneously and accurately to assess the details and underlying pattern of any situation that presents itself.

## The Standards of the Way (*Daofa*)

### I

The Way generates standards. Standards serve as marking cords to demarcate success and failure and are what clarify the crooked and the straight.

Therefore, those who hold fast to the Way generate standards and do not dare to violate them; having established standards, they do not dare to discard them. . . .

### II

Empty and Formless:
Its core is impenetrably dark.
It is where all living things are generated. . . .

### III

The Way to look at and know
Is simply to be empty and to have nothing.

When you are empty and have nothing, even if an autumn hair comes into view, it will inevitably have its own form and name.[5] When forms and names are established, then distinctions [such as] black and white are already there.[6]

---

5. The inherent form and name of a thing will be obvious when the sage does not impose preexisting categories upon it. The autumn hair is a common metaphor in early Chinese philosophical texts for something that is extremely fine because the hair grown by animals in the fall was said to be this way.

6. Sages who empty their minds of everything can directly perceive the inherent identity and shape of each thing and of each human endeavor and instantly know the appropriate name that corresponds to this form. Once these are established for the sage, life is extremely clear-cut and unambiguous, literally "black and white."

Therefore, when those who hold fast to the Way observe all-under-Heaven:

> They cling to nothing.
> They settle in nothing.
> They do nothing.
> They are partial to nothing. . . .

## IV

Those who are unbiased are lucid; the completely lucid are efficacious.

Those who are completely on the right course are tranquil; the completely tranquil are sagely.

Those who are impartial are wise; the completely wise are the norms of all-under-Heaven. . . .

## V

The Way of responding to transformations is to balance them out fairly and nothing more. When unimportant and important have not been evaluated, this is called "losing the Way."

> Heaven and Earth have their constant regularities;
> All people have their constant endeavors;
> The noble and base have their constant positions;
> Shepherding the ministers has its constant Way;
> Employing the people has its constant measures. . . .
>
> [From *Mawangdui Hanmu boshu*, pp. 43–44]

### NORMATIVE STANDARDS (JINGFA), PART 5

The two sections of this essay that are translated here deal with concrete examples of the kind of cosmic patterns and their human parallels spoken of in a more general fashion above. They also give a more detailed presentation of what it means to comply with or deviate from these underlying patterns and the consequences of the latter—which are dire indeed.

## The Four Measures (*Sidu*)

### I

When ruler and ministers change places,
We call this deviant.

When the worthy and the unworthy are established on a par,
We call this chaotic.
When activity and tranquillity are not timely,
We call this deviant.
When generating and killing do not correspond [to cosmic patterns],
We call this cruel.
With deviance, you lose the foundation.
With chaos, you lose the organization.
With deviance, you lose the Heavenly [correspondences].
With cruelty, you lose human beings. . . .

When ruler and ministers are in their corresponding positions,
We call this quiescence.
When worthy and unworthy are in their corresponding positions,
We call this being on the right course.
When activity and quiescence align with [the patterns of] Heaven and Earth,
We call this civility (*wen*).
When punishments and (prohibitions)[7] are seasonally corresponding,
We call this martiality (*wu*).

With quiescence there is security.
With being on the right course there is order.
With civility there is lucidity.
With martiality there is strength.
With security you attain the foundation.
With order you attain [the allegiance of] human beings.
With lucidity you attain the Heavenly.
With strength you act majestically. . . .

## II[8]

. . .

The periodic movements of the sun, moon, stars, and planets,
The limits of the four seasons,
The [sequential] positions of activity and quiescence,
The [relative] locations of inner and outer:
These are the Norms of Heaven.

---

7. Here we conjecturally restore an illegible graph to *jin* (prohibitions), following Chen
Guying, *Huangdi sijing jinzhu jinyi*, p. 156.
8. This passage begins from page 51, line 14 of the Wenwu edition.

That high and low do not obscure their forms;
That beautiful and ugly do not conceal their true characters:
These are the Norms of Earth.

That ruler and minister do not lose their [relative] positions,
That scholars do not lose their places [in government],
To employ the capable and not exceed their strengths,
To discard the partial and establish the unbiased:
These are the Norms of human beings. . . .

### III

. . .

If you wield the martial sword
And then use civility to follow in its wake,
Then you will achieve success.

The one who uses two parts civility
And one part martiality
Is the king.

[From *Mawangdui Hanmu boshu*, pp. 51–52]

## The *Guanzi*

### TECHNIQUES OF THE MIND, I (*XINSHU, SHANG*)

The *Guanzi*, a collection of essays mainly devoted to social and political philosophy (see chapter 7), is traditionally ascribed to the statesman Guan Zhong, who lived in the seventh century B.C.E. The text actually originated in the state of Qi in the mid-fourth century B.C.E. and was augmented for some two centuries or more, probably reaching final form early in the first century B.C.E. While it later came to be known as a Legalist work, it was initially classified as "Daoist" in the bibliographical section of the *History of the Former Han*.

"Techniques of the Mind, I" is devoted to demonstrating how its prescribed methods of self-cultivation, limiting lusts and desires, emptying the mind of thoughts and precedents, and developing a profound tranquillity give the ruler the means to respond spontaneously and harmoniously to any situation that may arise.

### I

The position of the mind in the body
[Is analogous to] the position of the ruler [in the state].

The functioning of the nine apertures
[Is analogous to] the responsibilities of the officials.

> When the mind keeps to its Way,
> The nine apertures will comply with their inherent guiding principles.[9]
> When lusts and desires fill the mind to overflowing,
> The eyes do not see colors, the ears do not hear sounds.
> When the one above departs from the Way,[10]
> The ones below will lose sight of their tasks.

Therefore we say, "The techniques of the mind are to take no action and yet control the apertures."[11] [13:1a]

## II

> Things inherently have forms; forms inherently have names. . . .

The unspoken words [of the sage] are [spontaneously] responsive. To be responsive is to take others just as they are. Take control of their names; pay attention to how they develop.[12] This is the Way to be responsive.[13]

The Way of doing nothing is to adapt to [other things]. Adapting means that nothing is added to them and nothing is subtracted from them. To make the name by adapting to the form, this is the technique of adaptation.[14] Names are what the sage makes use of to sort out all living things. [13:4a]

---

9. This means that the sense organs will function properly and spontaneously if the mind does not interfere with them. This occurs because each has an inherent pattern of activity that derives from its individual characteristics and its relation to the whole body. In translating texts of this period, the term *li*—which we will encounter again in later texts as "principle"—is more often translated as "patterns" or "inherent patterns." In English, however, "patterns" may have a stronger determinative force than does *li*. If a pattern is understood as a regular form or order (e.g., a behavioral pattern), this might suggest that things or activities must conform to it exactly, with little room for individual variation. By contrast, *li* admits of freedom within structure; the *li* guide the spontaneous responses that develop from the natures of things.

10. Deleting *gu yue* (therefore it says) at the start of the sentence, following many scholars.

11. Moving this sentence here following Guo Moruo from a position in the Comment section (just before the final line), to which it was erroneously displaced.

12. Deleting *ying* (respond) as an erroneous insertion, following Wang Yinzhi.

13. Reading *zhi* (it, of, this) as *zi* (this), following many scholars.

14. Responsiveness refers to the sage's ability spontaneously to perceive things "just as they are" and, without any forethought, to react to them in a completely appropriate and harmonious manner. Adaptation refers to the sage's ability to go along with other things and not force them into a predetermined mold. These are cardinal qualities of the Daoist sage in this text and other related ones that some believe are part of the Huang-Lao tradition.

## III

Most people can be executed because they dislike death.
They can be harmed because they like profit.
But noble persons are neither enticed by likes
Nor oppressed by dislikes.
Calm and tranquil, they take no action,
And they discard wisdom and precedent.
Their responses are not contrived.
Their movements are not chosen.
The mistake lies in intervening directly oneself.
The fault lies in altering and transforming things.
Therefore the ruler who has the Way:
At rest, seems to be without knowledge,
In response to things, seems to fit together with them.
This is the Way of stillness and adaptation.
[13:2a]

## IV

What is empty and Formless, we call the Way.[15]
What transforms and nurtures the myriad things, we call Inner Power.

What is involved in the interactions between ruler and official, father and son, and among all human beings, we call rightness (yi).

That there are levels of ascending and descending, bowing and ceding, honoring and humbling, and that there is the reality of familiarity and distance—this we call rites (li).[16]

That things both small and great are subjected to a uniform way of execution and extermination, prohibition and punishment—this we call laws (fa). [13:1b][17]

[From Guanzi (SBCK) 13:1a–4a; HR]

## The Syncretist Chapters of the Zhuangzi

The seven "inner chapters" of the Zhuangzi were transmitted—probably among the followers of their putative author, Zhuang Zhou—for almost two centuries into the early Han dynasty, when a number of chapters were added to the core

---

15. Emending wu (nothing) to er (and), following Wang Niansun.
16. Emending zhi (possessive particle) to you (there is, there are), following Ding Shihan.
17. Emending wei (not yet) to da (great), following Guo Moruo.

text, including a final group advocating a syncretism similar to the other sources in this chapter.

## THE WORLD OF THOUGHT (*TIANXIA*)

The following selection is drawn from the final chapter of the *Zhuangzi*, known as "The World of Thought" (*Tianxia*). This is, again, a later addition to the text, reflecting syncretic tendencies of the Qin-Han period. It assumes, like most early Chinese thinkers, including Zhuangzi, that the Way existed in its fullness and wholeness in primordial antiquity but later somehow became fragmented. In the lofty perspective of this chapter, each of the schools of late Zhou thought is seen as serving its own distinct, relative function but not as embracing the whole. The author includes characterizations of leading thinkers (among them Confucians, Mohists, Legalists, Daoists, and Logicians), the succinct descriptions of which became famous for their aptness in distilling the essence of each school. The excerpt that follows focuses on characterizations of the Mohists and the Daoists—and, most tellingly, of Zhuangzi himself.

To make Heaven his source, Virtue his root, and the Way his Gate, revealing himself through change and transformation—one who does this is called a sage.

To make humaneness his standard of kindness, rightness his model of reason, rites his guide to conduct, and music his source of harmony, serene in mercy and humaneness—one who does this is called a Noble Person. . . .

How thorough were the men of ancient times!—companions of holiness and enlightenment, pure as Heaven and Earth, caretakers of the ten thousand things, harmonizers of the world, their bounty extended to the hundred clans. . . .

The wisdom that was embodied in their policies and regulations is in many cases still reflected in the old laws and records of the historians, handed down over the ages. As to that which is recorded in the *Classic of Odes* and *Classic of Documents*, the *Rites* and the "Music," there are many gentlemen of Zou and Lu,[18] scholars of sash and official rank, who have an understanding of it. The *Classic of Odes* describes aspirations; the *Classic of Documents* describes events; the *Rites* speaks of conduct; the "Music" speaks of harmony; the *Classic of Changes* describes the yin and yang; the *Spring and Autumn Annals* describes titles and functions. . . .

To teach no extravagance to later ages, to leave the ten thousand things unadorned, to shun any glorification of rules and regulations, instead applying ink and measuring line to the correction of one's own conduct, thus aiding the world in time of crisis—there were those in ancient times who believed that the

---

18. Zou and Lu were the native states of Mencius and Confucius, respectively.

"art of the Way" lay in these things. Mo Di (Mozi) and Qin Guli[19] heard of their views and delighted in them, but they followed them to excess and were too assiduous in applying them to themselves.

Mozi wrote a piece "Against Music" and another titled "Moderation in Expenditure," declaring there was to be no singing in life, no mourning in death. With a boundless love and a desire to ensure universal benefit, he condemned warfare, and there was no place in his teachings for anger. Again, he was fond of learning and broad in knowledge, and in this respect did not differ from others. His views, however, were not always in accordance with those of the former kings, for he denounced the rites and music of antiquity. . . .

Men want to sing and he says, "No singing!"; they want to wail and he says, "No wailing!"—one wonders if he is in fact human at all. A life that is all toil, a death shoddily disposed of—it is a way that goes too much against us. To make men anxious, to make them sorrowful—such practices are hard to carry out, and I fear they cannot be regarded as the Way of the Sage. They are contrary to the hearts of the world, and the world cannot endure them. Though Mozi himself may be capable of such endurance, how can the rest of the world do likewise? Departing so far from the ways of the world, they must be far removed indeed from those of the true king. . . .

To regard the source as pure and the things that emerge from it as coarse, to look upon accumulation as insufficiency; dwelling alone, peaceful and placid, in spiritual brightness—there were those in ancient times who believed that "the art of the Way" lay in these things. The Barrier Keeper Yin[20] and Lao Dan (Laozi) heard of their views and delighted in them. They expounded them in terms of constant nothingness and headed their doctrine with the concept of the Great Unity. Gentle weakness and humble self-effacement are its outer marks; emptiness, void, and the noninjury of the ten thousand things are its essence. . . .

Lao Dan said, "Know the male but cling to the female; become the ravine of the world. Know the pure but cling to dishonor; become the valley of the world."[21] Others all grasp what is in front; he alone grasped what is behind. He said, "Take to yourself the filth of the world." Others all grasp what is full; he alone grasped what is empty. He never stored away—therefore he had more than enough; he had heaps and heaps of more than enough! In his movement he was easygoing and did not wear himself out. Dwelling in inaction, he scoffed at skill. Others all seek good fortune; he alone kept himself whole by becoming twisted. He said, "Let us somehow or other avoid incurring blame!" He took profundity to be the root and frugality to be the guideline. He said,

---

19. A leading disciple of Mozi.

20. Legend has it that when Laozi was leaving China he was asked by Barrier Keeper Yin for some written exposition of his teachings and produced the *Daodejing* as a result.

21. Cf. *Daodejing* 28.

"What is brittle will be broken, what is sharp will be blunted." He was always generous and permissive with things and inflicted no pain on others—this may be called the highest achievement. . . .

Blank, boundless, and without form; transforming, changing, never constant: are we dead? are we alive? do we stand side by side with Heaven and Earth? do we move in the company of spiritual brightness? absentminded, where are we going? forgetful, where are we headed for? The ten thousand things ranged all around us, not one of them is worthy to be singled out as our destination—there were those in ancient times who believed that the "art of the Way" lay in these things. Zhuang Zhou (Zhuangzi) heard of their views and delighted in them. He expounded them in odd and outlandish terms, in brash and bombastic language, in unbound and unbordered phrases, abandoning himself to the times without partisanship, not looking at things from one angle only. . . . He came and went alone with the pure spirit of Heaven and Earth, yet he did not view the ten thousand things with arrogant eyes. He did not scold over "right" and "wrong" but lived with the age and its vulgarity. . . .

Above he wandered with the Creator; below he made friends with those who have gotten outside of life and death, who know nothing of beginning or end. . . .

[*Zhuangzi*, chap. 33; adapted from Watson, *Chuang Tzu*, pp. 362–367, 371–374]

## The *Huainanzi* on Rulership

The *Huainanzi* is a work of twenty-one essays that was composed by a group of scholars and adepts working at the court of Liu An, first king of Huainan, under the king's direction. Presented by Liu to his nephew, the powerful Han emperor Wu, on a court visit in 139 B.C.E., this work was intended to be a compendium of all the knowledge the Daoist sage ruler needed in order to govern effectively. Thus its topics run a wide gamut from cosmology and astrology to inner cultivation, government, and political thought.

### HUAINANZI 9, THE TECHNIQUES OF RULERSHIP (*ZHUSHU*)

The techniques of the ruler are to
Keep to effortless actions
And practice wordless teachings.
Clear and quiescent, he does not act,
Once he acts, he is not agitated.[22]
Adapting and complying, he entrusts his subordinates.
Holding them to account, he does not labor.

---

22. Reading *du* (standard) as *dong* (to act), after Wang Shumin. Lau, *Concordance*, p. 67.

Therefore, although his mind knows the principles, he permits the imperial tutors to explain the Way to him.[23]

Although his mouth is able to speak, he permits his diplomats to announce the ceremonial words.

Although his feet are able to walk, he permits his ministers to lead the way.

Although his ears are able to hear, he permits his administrators to propose their own strategies.[24] . . .

## HUAINANZI 14, INQUIRING WORDS (QUANYAN)

Zhan He said:[25]

"I have never heard of the ruler's [inner] person (*shen*) being well ordered and the state being chaotic.

I have never heard of the ruler's [inner] person being chaotic and the state being well-ordered." . . .

When you get to the source of the Decree of Heaven, then you are not deluded by bad or good fortune.

When you master the techniques of the mind, then you are not led astray by pleasure and anger.[26]

When you make likes and dislikes comply with inherent patterns, then you do not crave what is useless.

When you accord with your true responses and innate nature, then desires do not exceed their appropriate limits.

When you are not deluded by bad or good fortune, then in activity and quiescence you will comply with inherent patterns.

When you are not led astray by pleasure and anger, then rewards and punishments will not affect you.

When you do not crave what is useless, then you will not allow desires to interfere with your innate nature.[27]

When desires do not exceed their limits, then you understand what is sufficient to nourish your innate nature.

---

23. Reading *dao* (to guide) as *Dao* (the Way), after the *Qunshu zhiyao*. Lau, *Concordance*, p. 67.

24. Reading *jian* (to admonish) as *mou* (strategy), the variant given in the Kao You commentary. Lau, *Concordance*, p. 67.

25. Zhan He is the late Warring States Daoist teacher who appears in *Han Feizi* 20 and *Liezi* 5. The eminent Chinese scholar Ch'ien Mu identified him with the Zhanzi in *Zhuangzi*, chapter 28, gave his dates as 350–270 B.C.E., and suggested that he was perhaps the first Huang-Lao teacher. See Ch'ien, *Hsien Ch'in chu-tzu hsin-nien*, pp. 223–226, 448.

26. Reading *wang* (to forget) as *wang* (to be led astray) after the Daoist Canon edition. Lau, *Concordance*, p. 133.

27. Deleting *yong* (utility), after Wang Niansun. Lau, *Concordance*, p. 133.

Of these four [principles]:
Do not seek them externally,
Do not borrow them from others;
Return to the self and they will be attained.

The following selection has been described as resembling a Daoist version of the *Great Learning*, a major Confucian text translated in chapter 10.

The foundation of governing lies is making the people content.[28]
The foundation of making the people content lies in giving them sufficient use [of their time for farming].
The foundation of giving them sufficient use lies in not stealing their time [for state endeavors].
The foundation of not stealing their time lies in restricting the state's endeavors.
The foundation of restricting the state's endeavors lies in limiting the desires [of the ruler].
The foundation of limiting the desires [of the ruler] lies in his returning to his innate nature.
The foundation of returning to one's innate nature lies in removing what fills the mind.
When one removes what fills the mind, one is empty.
When one is empty, one experiences equanimity.
Equanimity is the simplicity of the Way.
Emptiness is the abode of the Way. . . .

[From Lau, *Concordance*, pp. 4, 67, 133; HR]

## THE MEDICAL MICROCOSM

The new universal order of the Han was configured as a microcosm, a small model of Nature. As such it was aligned with another miniature counterpart of Nature, namely, the human body. Thus, the ruler should regulate his officers just as an individual must control his limbs if he is to live a normal life. Han thinkers often speak of the healthy body as in harmony with Nature, opening itself to illness if it does not maintain that concord.

Medicine gradually separated from philosophy between the third and first centuries B.C.E. as physicians worked out detailed and comprehensive doctrines to put in order their experience of the body, health, and illness, and to pass on their understanding to their pupils. Three books that carry the main title *Inner Canon of the Yellow Emperor*—namely, the *Basic Questions* (*Huangdi neijing suwen*),

---

28. Deleting *wu* (to endeavor), after Lau, *Concordance*, p. 133.

its companion, the *Divine Pivot* (*Huangdi neijing ling shu*), and an overlapping compilation, the *Grand Basis* (*Huangdi neijing taisu*)—are the main surviving documents of several great medical syntheses of the Han period.[29]

The Han medical masters greatly elaborated the idea of cosmos and body as interacting organisms. This was, of course, not the only way to make sense of human suffering and healing, but it seemed a desirable one because by the first century the parallel had already become a staple of philosophers. We find it in many important writings, and, as political ideology, it was one of the consequential ideas of its time.

We can see a reflection of the latter in the form of the *Inner Canon*. Four fifths of the chapters (*pian*) in the two books are in the form of a dialogue between the Yellow Emperor and one of his ministers. In all except a few, the Yellow Emperor is asking the questions one would expect of a disciple when he is being prepared to receive a text from his teacher. The minister is at the same time a master initiating his disciple and a sage adviser counseling his sovereign. This form reflects that of the Huang-Lao texts associated with the Yellow Emperor that were so influential in earlier Han thought. Like the others, it mirrors the political ideals of the elite in its master image of the emperor as a man of knowledge concerned not with running a government but with embodying the link between the cosmic order and the individual. This image is so pervasive that in a passage on the correspondence of acupuncture points to compass points and yin-yang orientations, the body described is that of "the sage enthroned facing south," that is, the emperor.[30]

This may seem an odd affiliation between politics, philosophy, and medicine, but such clear-cut modern distinctions are of little use in making sense of ancient culture. In the last three centuries B.C.E., as we have seen, there was no boundary between philosophy and political thought. The physicians were defining their own domain of learning out of general philosophy, but at the same time they were contributing to it. Among other things, the *Divine Pivot* and the *Basic Questions* set out what may be the first theory that fully integrates the two major concepts of Chinese abstract reasoning: yin/yang, and the Five Phases (*wuxing*).[31] To form an overview of Han thought about Nature, society, and humanity, the *Inner Canon* is essential reading.

---

29. The current versions of the first two were edited in 762 C.E. and further revised in the eleventh century; the third was compiled between 666 and 683 C.E. The content of all three is close to early quotations of the Han *Inner Canon*, but the arrangement is different. No one of the three is consistently more reliable than the others. The original *Inner Canon* assembled writings of several medical traditions, the earliest of which may have been first set down in the third century. There is thus a great deal of inconsistency, which can be resolved only by examining the constituent writings individually.

30. *Suwen* 6:2; *Taisu* 5:13.

31. This judgment depends on uncertain dating of the two books and of other writings. If, as some scholars believe, the *Inner Canon* is from the first century C.E., priority would go to Yang Xiong's *Supreme Mystery* (*Taixuan*) (4? B.C.E.). The approach of the latter is very different.

THE *DIVINE PIVOT*[32]

The Yellow Emperor inquired of Bogao, "I would like to hear how the limbs and joints of the body correspond to sky and earth."

Bogao replied, "The sky is round, the earth rectangular;[33] the heads of human beings are round and their feet rectangular to correspond. In the sky there are the sun and moon; human beings have two eyes. On earth there are the nine provinces; human beings have nine orifices.[34] In the sky there are wind and rain; human beings have their joy and anger. In the sky there are thunder and lightning; human beings have their sounds and speech. In the sky there are the four seasons; human beings have their four extremities. In the sky there are the Five Sounds; human beings have their five yin visceral systems.[35] In the sky there are the Six Pitches; human beings have their six yang visceral systems. In the sky there are winter and summer; human beings have their chills and fevers. In the sky there are the ten-day 'weeks'; human beings have ten fingers on their hands. In the sky there are the twelve double-hours; human beings have ten toes on their feet, and the stalk and the hanging ones complete the correspondence.[36] Women lack these two members, so they are able to carry the human form [of the fetus]. In the sky there are yin and yang; human beings are husband and wife.

"In the year there are 365 days; human beings have 365 joints. On the earth there are high mountains; human beings have shoulders and knees. On the earth there are deep valleys; human beings have armpits and hollows in back of their knees.[37] On the earth there are twelve cardinal watercourses; human beings have twelve cardinal circulation tracts.[38] In the earth there are

---

32. Probably first century B.C.E. The version in the *Divine Pivot* (*Ling shu*) has been collated with the partial text in the *Grand Basis* (*Huangdi neijing taisu*, 666–683 C.E., 5:1–12), which corresponds to the translation from "in the sky there are yin and yang" to the end. Parallels in the *Basic Questions* (*Huangdi neijing suwen*) have also been consulted. For the *Taisu*, the photographic reproduction in *Tōyō igaku zempon sōsho*, vols. 1–3, was used, and for *Suwen* and *Ling shu*, the *Huangdi neijing zhangju suoyin* edition.

33. It is clear from some of the correspondences that follow that "sky" is used, as often happens, to stand for "sky and earth," or Nature generally.

34. The nine provinces are a legendary system often mentioned in cosmology. The orifices are ears, eyes, mouth, nostrils, and the urethral and anal openings.

35. The Five Sounds are the musical modes. In the Han there are various counts of the systems of bodily functions associated with the viscera; this one refers to the yin systems, which like the Five Sounds correspond numerologically to the Five Phases. The next sentence cites their yang counterparts.

36. I.e., the penis and testicles.

37. The basis of these associations is prominent convex shapes for the yang features and concavities for the yin.

38. This set of correspondences is greatly elaborated in *Taisu*, 5:25–40, with a parallel passage in *Ling shu* 12.

veins of water; human beings have defensive *qi*.[39] In the earth there are wild grasses; human beings have body hair. On the earth there are daylight and darkness; human beings have their [times for] lying down and getting up. In the sky there are stars set out in constellations; human beings have their teeth. On the earth there are little hills; human beings have their minor joints. On the earth there are boulders on the mountains; human beings have their prominent bones. On the earth there are groves and forests; human beings have their sinews.[40] On the earth there are towns and villages in which people gather; human beings have their bulges of [thickened] flesh. In the year there are twelve months; human beings have their twelve major joints. On the earth there are seasons when no vegetation grows; some human beings are childless. These are the correspondences between human beings and sky and earth. . . ."

The Yellow Emperor asked, "I have heard that Heaven is yang and Earth yin, that the sun is yang and the moon yin. How is this matched in human beings?"

Qibo said, "From the waist up is Heaven; from the waist down is Earth; thus Heaven is yang and Earth yin. The twelve cardinal circulation tracts connected with the feet correspond to the twelve months. The moon is engendered from water. Thus what is below is yin. The ten fingers of the hand correspond to the ten days of the week. The sun is engendered from fire. Thus what is above is yang."[41]

The Yellow Emperor said, "How are they matched in the circulation vessels?"

Qibo said, "The third [astronomical month], the first civil month, engenders yang, and is in charge of the immature yang [circulation vessel] of the left foot.[42] The eighth [astronomical month], the sixth civil month, is in charge of

---

39. Defensive *qi* (*weiqi*) flows round the perimeter of the body and protects it from invasion. *Taisu*, p. 3, instead of "veins of water" (*zhuanmai*), has two characters, the first of which is only partly legible; the compound may be "the *qi* of rain" (*yuqi*).

40. The sinews (*jin, jinmo*) are the muscles, ligaments, and other fibrous tissues that operate the locomotive system of the body. This association refers to their gathered fibers.

41. In ancient China days were grouped into tens to determine days of rest for civil servants. The point of this reply is that yin, water, and the moon correspond, and are complementary to yang, fire, and the sun.

42. Though this varied from state to state, in the Zhou system the first lunar month was the one that contained the winter solstice. New Year's Day thus fell at the end of November or in December. The Qin and its successors, with some minor divergences, called the solstitial month the eleventh, which put the civil new year in late January or February, as is still the case. But astronomers continued to use the Zhou standard, just as in the time of Copernicus astronomers were still using the ancient Egyptian calendar. A given astronomical month fell two months earlier than the civil month with the same number. *Zhu*, "is in charge of," connotes bureaucratic responsibility. This "authority" determines in which circulation branch the vital substances concentrate at a given time, an important datum in therapy.

the immature yang [circulation vessel] of the right foot. . . ." [The enumeration continues for the twelve months and the twelve circulation branches connected with the feet.]

"The first day [of the ten-day week] is in charge of the immature yang vessels of the left hand. The sixth day is in charge of the immature yang vessels of the right hand." [The enumeration continues for the ten days and ten of the twelve circulation branches connected with the hands. Qibo then itemizes the subdivisions of yin and yang and warns against using acupuncture on the circulation branches in which human *qi* is concentrated in each season.]

The Yellow Emperor said, "According to the Five Phases, the eastern quarter, the first two of the ten stems [used to count days in the week], and the phase Wood rule over spring. Spring [is associated with] the color of the blue sky and governs the liver functions. The liver functions are those of the attenuated yin tracts connected with the feet. But now you claim that the first stem [corresponds to] the immature yang tract connected with the left hand, which does not tally with these regular relationships. Why is that?"

Qibo said, "These are the yin and yang [correspondences] of Heaven and Earth, not the sequential changes of the four seasons and the Five Phases. Now yin and yang are names without physical form [i.e., abstractions, not concrete things]. They can be enumerated ten ways, separated a hundred ways, distributed a thousand ways, deduced a myriad ways' refers to this."[43]

[From *Huangdi neijing ling shu* 71:2, 41; NS]

## A SYNCRETIST PERSPECTIVE ON THE SIX SCHOOLS

*Records of the Grand Historian*, completed by Sima Qian in about 100 B.C.E., contains a seminal essay on early Chinese thought written by his father, Sima Tan, who began the compilation of this text. In it he provides a brief assessment of each of six early philosophical traditions and attaches to them the suffix of *jia* (family), which has been taken to mean "school" but which is probably closer to the notion of "lineage." Sometimes in the West *jia* has been translated by the suffix -*ism*—hence, "Confucianism," Daoism," "Legalism," and so on. These terms refer, however, not to monolithic schools but to evolving traditions of practice and philosophy handed down by lineages of masters and disciples.

---

43. Quotation from an unidentified book. The *Inner Canon* often quotes its predecessors, and sometimes names them. The main point of Qibo's reply is that because yin and yang and the Five Phases are concepts, they can be interpreted on many levels. In this instance, Qibo claims he had been talking about their spatial meanings in the circulation system, not their meanings in time sequences. He reminds his monarch that the two need not correspond in detail.

Sima Tan was a follower of Huang-Lao thought, and he assesses the relative merits of the five other lineages in order to establish the superiority of his own. In the process he provides a picture of how this major early Han intellectual tradition conceived of itself. The essay also clearly demonstrates that early Han Daoism was thoroughly syncretic in nature and adopted elements from other schools.

## SIMA TAN: "ON THE SIX LINEAGES OF THOUGHT"

The *Great Commentary* to the *Classic of Changes* says: "All-under-Heaven share the same goal, yet there are a hundred ways of thinking about it; they return to the same home, yet follow different pathways there." The Naturalists (*yin yang jia*), Confucians, Mohists, Terminologists (*ming jia*), Legalists, and Daoists all strive to create order [in the world]. It is just that, in the different routes they follow and in what they say, some are more perceptive than others.

I once observed that the techniques of the Naturalists magnify the importance of omens and proliferate avoidances and taboos, causing people to feel constrained and to fear many things. Nonetheless, one cannot fault the way they set out in order the grand compliances of the four seasons.

The Confucians are erudite yet lack the essentials. They labor much yet achieve little. This is why their doctrines are difficult to follow completely. Nonetheless, one cannot detract from the way they set out in order the various rituals between ruler and minister and father and son and enumerate the various distinctions between husband and wife and elder and younger.

The Mohists are frugal and difficult to follow. This is why it is not possible fully to conform to their doctrines. Nonetheless, one cannot disregard the way they strengthen the foundation [agriculture] and economize expenditures.

The Legalists are harsh and lacking in compassion. Nonetheless, one cannot improve upon the way they rectify the distinctions between ruler and minister and superior and subordinate.

The Terminologists cause people to be strict [with words], yet they outdo themselves and lose sight of the truth. Nonetheless, one cannot disregard the way they rectify names and their realities.

The Daoists enable the numinous essence within people to be concentrated and unified. They move in unison with the Formless and provide adequately for all living things. In deriving their techniques, they follow the grand compliances of the Naturalists, select the best of the Confucians and Mohists, and extract the essentials of the Terminologists and Legalists. . . .

The Confucians are not like this. They maintain that the ruler is the exemplar for all-under-Heaven. For them, the ruler guides and the officials harmonize with him; the ruler initiates and the officials follow. Proceeding in this manner, the ruler labors hard and the officials sit idle.

The essentials of the Great Way are simply a matter of discarding strength and avarice and casting aside perception and intellect. One relinquishes these and relies on the techniques [of self-cultivation]. When the numen (*shen*, "spirit") is used excessively it becomes depleted; when the physical form labors excessively it becomes worn out. It is unheard of for one whose physical form and numen are agitated and disturbed to hope to attain the longevity of Heaven and Earth.

[From *Shiji* (*BNB*) 130:3a–6b; HR, SQ]

# Chapter 10

## THE IMPERIAL ORDER AND HAN SYNTHESES

With the expanding horizons of the Han empire came a broadening of intellectual interest in questions of cosmology and the natural order, accompanied by a conviction of the sort expressed in the *Mean* (22) that the person who is perfectly sincere can "assist in the transforming and nourishing powers of Heaven and Earth; being able to assist in the transforming and nourishing powers of Heaven and Earth, he can form a triad with Heaven and Earth."[1]

This concept that Heaven, Earth, and humankind can form a triad is basic in Han thought. It was first of all the duty of human beings to observe and comprehend the order presided over by Heaven in both a religious and a physical sense. Equally strong is the conviction, hardly to be wondered at in an agricultural society, that human beings, and especially the government, must attend to concerns of the earth, particularly to matters of irrigation, land usage, and flood control. Han thinkers stressed, as had Mencius earlier, that economic welfare is the basis of popular morality. The scholar or sage might deliberately choose to remain poor if riches could be his only by resorting to unworthy means. The masses, however, could not be expected to adhere to such a high standard. They naturally desire material well-being. If it cannot be acquired by just means, they will seek it by any means available. If a poor man steals, it is because he is unable to make a living honestly. Therefore the course of profit and the course of virtue

---

1. See pp. 181–84.

must be made identical, so that the people's needs can be met by proper means. Accordingly, the ruler bears a responsibility to provide for both the material welfare and the moral instruction of the people, thereby "transforming" them and enabling them to form a harmonious triad with Heaven and Earth.

Confucianism talks a great deal about this duty of the government to transform or bring to completion the nature of the people—in other words, to civilize them. The first step in the process is to provide peace and prosperity. The second step is moral training or education, done mainly through rites (which include everything from the most solemn religious ceremonies to the simplest daily courtesies), music (instrumental music, song, and mimic dance), and literature. Rites and music can be appreciated, and even learned to some extent, by all men, but literate discourse, being a long and difficult study, can be mastered only by the intelligent and the leisured. The final product of such study is the sage, whose learning is confirmed in the most refined moral sense. Ideally, he should become emperor, but in practice, since the Confucians generally eschewed any struggle for power, the dynastic principle of hereditary rulership was accepted, and the sage or scholar was expected to take up a position as adviser to the emperor or participant in government service, working through the established machinery of government, which has total responsibility for the economic, social, and spiritual welfare of the empire.

During the Han period the social conscience of the Confucians, and their scholarly qualifications, brought them in increasing numbers into the new officialdom that replaced the feudal aristocracy of Zhou times. Reconciling themselves to the new imperial system and its bureaucratic structures, they succeeded in having a state college and system of competitive examinations set up, which, at least in normal times, assured a dominant position for scholars in the civil bureaucracy.

## GUIDELINES FOR HAN RULERS

The following selections are from two early Han figures, Lu Jia (d. 170 B.C.E.) and Jia Yi (201–168? B.C.E.). The former advised the dynasty's founder, Liu Bang, later known by the title Han Gaozu (or High Ancestor of the Han, r. 206–195 B.C.E.), while the latter counseled Emperor Wen (r. 180–157 B.C.E.). Lu Jia advised on how the Qin failed and the Han could benefit from that lesson. Jia Yi, after experiencing some twenty years of ruthless court politics surrounding Han Gaozu's widow, the Empress Lü, which saw a return to "feudal" practices of enfeoffing the princes, advised Emperor Wen on imperial dignity, strength, and moral scope. Both scholars addressed central questions concerning the nature of power and authority and involved themselves in critiques of its use and abuse. In so doing, they not only helped define Han Confucianism but stood in a line of Confucian tradition that, out of its humane concern with moral issues, was to show a capacity for regeneration, growth, and expansion over the course of centuries to come.

## LU JIA: THE NATURAL ORDER AND THE HUMAN ORDER

The following selections from Lu Jia come from the first two chapters of his *New Discourses* (*Xinyu*), a work of twelve chapters responding to Han Gaozu's charge to offer a discourse on "why the Qin failed and the Han succeeded, and also on the merits of rulers throughout history." Both cosmological and practical aspects of imperial rule can be found in these passages.

What is in Heaven can be discerned; what is on Earth can be measured. What is in the material world can be ordered; what is in the human world can be contemplated. . . . [The Earth] maintains all things and sustains the species. It establishes all living beings, keeping their essences while exhibiting their forms. . . .

For these reasons, those who know Heaven raise their heads and observe the patterns of Heaven, and those who know Earth bend their heads and study the principles of Earth. All species that walk and breathe, those that fly and crawl, those on land or on sea, and deep-rooted plants with leafy crowns, all will be peaceful of mind and calm of nature; all will be brought to completion when Heaven and Earth interact, and the vital energies (*qi*) resonate with each other.

The former sage [Fu Xi] thus raised his head and observed the patterns of Heaven and looked down and studied the principles of Earth, charting the cosmos[2] and setting the human way. Thus enlightened, the people came to know filiality between parent and child, rightness between ruler and minister, the proprieties of husband and wife,[3] and the order between elder and younger. Henceforth the offices of state were established and the kingly way arose. . . .

When the people only feared the laws, they could not know rites and rightness. Thus the middle sages [Emperor Wen of Zhou and the Duke of Zhou] set up various levels of schools (*xu* and *xiang*) and academies (*piyong*),[4] so as to rectify the principles governing superior and inferior and make manifest rites between parent and child, as well as bonds between ruler and minister. This way, the strong would not oppress the weak, the many would not victimize the one, while greed and avarice would be replaced by pure and refined conduct.

When rites and rightness were not practiced and regulations and disciplines were not maintained, succeeding generations became weak and decadent. Thus the later sage [Confucius] defined the Five Classics[5] and taught the Six

---

2. Literally, *qian* and *kun*. Legend has it that Fu Xi, having observed Heaven and Earth, devised the Eight Trigrams, of which *qian* and *kun* were the two most important diagrams. *Qian* represents Heaven and all yang-related things, and *kun* represents earth and all yin-related things. See pp. 170–73.

3. Literally, the separate functions of husband and wife.

4. *Xu* were village schools; *xiang* were local schools; *piyong* were high academies established by kings.

5. Lu Jia was the first to refer to the Five Classics as consisting of the *Classic of Odes*, the *Classic of Documents*, the *Classic of Rites* (at first referring to the *Yili*, later replaced by the *Liji*), the *Classic of Changes*, and the *Spring and Autumn Annals*.

Arts,[6] following the principles of Heaven and Earth, all the while exhaustively pursuing the minutest ways of things and events. Studying human sentiments and establishing the basis, he ordered interpersonal relationships. Basing himself on the principles of Heaven and Earth, he edited and revised the classics to be passed on to future generations, benefiting even the world of birds and beasts. . . .

Later generations became self-indulgent and wicked, made still worse by the music of the states of Zheng and Wei.[7] The people forsook what is basic[8] and pursued what is secondary.[9] . . .

Donkeys and mules, camels, rhinoceroses and elephants, along with tortoise-shells, amber and coral, kingfisher feathers, pearls and jades, are all found either on mountains or in water. They are found in their habitats, pure and clear, damp and moistened as the case may be. . . . They await their usefulness and their nature being turned into useful implements. Thus it is said that the sage brought them to fulfillment. . . .

Now actions that do not combine humaneness and rightness are doomed to failure; structures that forsake a firm foundation for a high perch are certain to topple. Thus the sage uses the classics and the arts to prevent disorder, as the craftsman uses the plumb line to correct crookedness.

. . . The sovereign rules over a good government with humaneness; the ministers conduct orderly affairs in keeping with rightness. The people of the realm respect each other through humaneness, and the officials of the court discourse with each other on the basis of rightness. . . . The yang energy is born of humaneness, and the yin rhythm is set by rightness. The "call of the deer"[10] is humane in its thoughtfulness for companionship; the "call of the osprey"[11] is correct in its expression of propriety. The *Spring and Autumn Annals* makes denunciations and condemnations in the name of humaneness and rightness, and the *Odes* uses humaneness and rightness to preserve or discard. Heaven and Earth are harmonized by humaneness; the Eight Trigrams are interrelated through rightness. The *Documents* traces the nine family relationships through humaneness. Between sovereign and ministers, loyalty is governed by rightness.

---

6. There are two versions of the Six Arts: as the Six Classics, with that of Music added to the above five; and as the six arts or skills of ritual observance, musical performance, archery, charioteering, calligraphy, and mathematics. Ordinarily, the reference is to the first meaning, but here it refers to the second, as it would be redundant following the mention of the Five Classics.

7. Two states known for their licentious music.

8. I.e., agriculture.

9. I.e., commerce.

10. A reference to Ode 161 in the *Classic of Odes*. The deer, when foraging for grass and feed, will call for their companions to come and share the food. The sound of the deer is thus taken to express humaneness or fellow-feeling.

11. A reference to Ode 1 in the *Classic of Odes*. The osprey were reportedly often seen in pairs of female and male and were known for their distinct mating calls.

The *Rites* tells of ritual decorum governed by humaneness and of music informed by humaneness. . . .

. . . The *Guliang Commentary to the Spring and Autumn Annals* states, "Humaneness is there to regulate family relations; rightness is there to benefit parents and elders. If for ten thousand ages there were no disorder, it would be because of the rule of humaneness and rightness."

[From Lu Jia, *Xinyu*, "Daoji" (*Zhongguo zixue mingzhu jicheng*) 1:189–198; DWYK]

## Be Current and Relevant

Those skilled in speaking of antiquity see its reflection in the present, and those skilled in speaking of distant affairs measure them against those close by. . . .

The Way is never far from us, so there is no need to go to remote antiquity to find it. One needs only to discern essential and consequential matters. The *Spring and Autumn Annals* does not mention the Five Emperors and the Three Rulers[12] but narrates the minor accomplishments of Duke Huan of Qi and Duke Wen of Jin and describes the political conduct of the twelve dukes of Lu. From their deeds, the standards of success and failure are obvious. What need is there to go back to the Three Rulers? By the same token, the deeds of the ancients are similar to those of the present. . . .

Thus while nature abides with humankind, vital force (*qi*) reaches Heaven. Whether the matter be minute or huge, by learning here below we may penetrate to what is above.[13] . . . Those who are concerned with the branches must mind the roots; those who want to see proper images in the mirror must first correct their own countenance. When the roots are nurtured, the branches and leaves flourish; when one's intentions and vital force are in balance, the Way is unswerving.[14] . . .

[From *Xinyu*, "Shushi" (*Zhongguo zixue mingzhu jicheng* ed.) 2:199–206; DWYK]

### JIA YI: THE PRIMACY OF THE PEOPLE (*MINBEN*)

Jia Yi's contributions to early Han thought are in the elegance, range, and pertinence of his ideas. His major work, the *New Writings* (*Xinshu*), is composed of three kinds of materials: his seminal writings, his advice at the court of Emperor Wen, and his counsels to Prince Liang in Changsha, where he served as assistant grand tutor

---

12. According to Sima Qian in his *Records of the Grand Historian* (see chap. 12), the five emperors were the Yellow Emperor, Zhuan Xu, Ku, Yao, and Shun; the three rulers were Yu of Xia, Tang of Shang, and Wu of Zhou.

13. Alludes to *Analects* 14:37. See chap. 3.

14. Alludes to *Daodejing* 4. See chap. 5, where the phrase is differently translated.

before dying there at the age of thirty-three. This material is organized into fifty-eight chapters ranging over fifty subjects, including how to handle princes, manage vassals, centralize royal authority, exercise powers of coinage, employ the right talents, interpret yin-yang and the Five Phases (*wuxing*) in the moral and social makeup of the prince, provide prenatal care of the royal heir, and, of course, analyze the faults of Qin ("Guo Qin lun").[15]

It is said that in government, the people are in every way the root (base) [*ben*].[16] . . . For the state, the ruler, and the officials, the people constitute the root. . . . For the state, the ruler, and the officials all depend on the people for their mandate. The life or death of the state depend on the people, the vision or blindness of the ruler depends on them, and whether officials are respected or not depends on them. This is why the people are in every way the mandate. . . .

Still further it is said that the people are the power on which the state, the ruler, and the officials all depend for their power. If victory is won, it is because the people want to be victorious. . . . Disaster and fortune, as we see, are determined not in Heaven but by the officers (*shi*) and the people. . . .

. . . The ruler is honorable only because the officers and people honor him. This is true honor. The ruler prospers only because the people are pleased to cause him to do so. This is true prosperity. . . .

Thus the people are the root of [dynastic] longevity, never to be taken lightly. . . . Moreover, the people have great strength and cannot be opposed. Oh, be warned, in any opposition to the people, the people will win.

[From *Xinshu*, "Dazheng" (*SBCK*) 9:541–549; DWYK]

## DONG ZHONGSHU

When the Han dynasty established an imperial system of government that was to persist until 1911, Confucian scholars of that day, among them Dong Zhongshu (195?–105? B.C.E.), articulated a vision of an omnipotent but disciplined sovereign, who sought to align the population with the norms of Heaven and Earth, based on the advice and counsel of scholar-officials versed in the classical traditions of antiquity. This ideal of the ruler as high priest and fount of wisdom contained within it basic patterns and tensions that came to define the relationship between the state and intellectual, center and periphery, power and authority, and politics and culture for centuries to come.

---

15. As seen in chap. 8.

16. *Ben-mo* is a dichotomy expressing Chinese estimations of value, priority, or sequence. Thus *ben* (originally the root or trunk of the tree) is the base or fundamental value, and *mo* (the branches of the tree) is the subordinate means or secondary, often nonessential, value. The former is associated here with the honest occupations of plowing and weaving and the latter with business activities that are thought to distort human nature through utilitarian calculations.

Confucian scholars were deeply engaged in the politics of their day. They sought to gain political power by influencing the policies and practices emanating from the emperor based on their textual interpretations. At the same time, they endeavored to maintain an independent and critical voice based on the authority and prestige they derived from their mastery of the Confucian texts. To what extent would cultural endeavors restrain politics or be restrained by them? To what extent would other centers of regional power rival or reinforce the emperor's court in either literary prowess or military power? These unresolved tensions reemerged in every dynasty to follow. Moreover, some scholars would argue that, even after the abolition of imperial government in 1911 and the Communist revolution of 1949, many of these issues continue to shape the political culture of contemporary China.

Like his predecessors Lu Jia and Jia Yi, Dong Zhongshu sought to develop a rationale and a model of rulership appropriate to the new circumstances of the unified state. He vied for political influence and competed for literary patronage with devotees of esoteric learning and popular lore as diverse as the different areas over which the Han rulers now claimed sovereignty. Chief among them were the followers of Huang-Lao (the Yellow Emperor and Laozi),[17] whose techniques and texts were favored by Emperor Jing (r. 157–141 B.C.E.), and the doctors, diviners, and magicians known collectively as *fangshi* (masters of technical methods or technicians), who bedazzled his successor, Emperor Wu (r. 141–87 B.C.E.) with their elixirs of immortality. The confluence of local cultural traditions at the Han court also gave rise to the cross-fertilization of philosophical ideas, cosmological principles, and political techniques among advocates of these various traditions. As they evolved in the pluralistic intellectual atmosphere, shifting political alliances, and changing imperial patronage of the Former Han, traditions—master-disciple lineages centering on a text or corpus of texts that transmitted a set of doctrines and techniques—were neither impermeable nor immune to other intellectual trends at court. Thus Dong Zhongshu's contributions to the Han ideal of rulership involved both the rejection and the absorption of ideas, principles, and techniques from other traditions. Nor were they unaffected by the personalities and proclivities of the successive Han emperors, empresses, and empress dowagers whose varying receptivity toward Confucian scholars often determined the critical difference between Confucian principle and practice.

Relying on two attitudes that characterized the Confucian scholar, a respect for the past and a veneration for the writings of Confucius, Dong hoped to reform imperial sovereignty by re-creating both history and text. Following his predecessors Lu Jia and Jia Yi, he also sought to discredit the Qin dynasty. The demonic character of the dynasty was a prominent theme in his writings

17. See chap. 9.

and came to define traditional historiography for centuries to follow. This interpretation of the Qin provided an intellectual rationale for discrediting the political and religious framework of imperial sovereignty that had developed under the earlier regime.

It was through his interpretations of the Confucian texts that Dong delineated his program for renewed kingship. This was particularly true of the *Spring and Autumn Annals* (*Chunqiu*) and the accompanying *Gongyang Commentary* (*Gongyang zhuan*), Dong Zhongshu's special focus of inquiry. He believed the *Spring and Autumn Annals* could resolve Qin excesses and endeavored to explicate how and why the text was relevant, indeed indispensable, to the creation of an alternative social, political, and religious culture for the Han. Consequently, Dong Zhongshu and his disciples read into the *Spring and Autumn Annals* a particular vision of history and ascribed to the text new modes of legal, ritual, and cosmological authority that were relevant to their reformist goals. His persuasive interpretations, among other factors, enabled Dong Zhongshu and other reformist scholars under Emperor Wu to end state support for the teaching of non-Confucian texts and to establish a text-based ideology represented in the first Confucian canon. Thenceforth, the Confucian canon played a prominent role in the doctrinal and political life of the traditional state. The designation in 136 B.C.E. of official posts known as the "Erudites of the Five Classics" and the establishment in 124 B.C.E. of the Imperial College, where these texts were taught as a basic prerequisite for training in the polity, were the institutional expressions of this canonization.

Although traditionally ascribed to Dong Zhongshu, the *Luxuriant Gems of the Spring and Autumn Annals* (*Chunqiu fanlu*) is most likely the product of an anonymous compiler who lived sometime between the third and sixth centuries. The text is best understood as an anthology: a collection of materials authored by Dong Zhongshu and records of his doctrinal expositions to different audiences in diverse venues. But it also contains other writings, probably by his disciples and critics. The translations that follow from the *Luxuriant Gems of the Spring and Autumn Annals* represent what are generally accepted to be the original teachings of this Han master. The final selection is from "Deciding Court Cases According to the *Spring and Autumn Annals*," another work of Dong's.

## Luxuriant Gems of the Spring and Autumn Annals (Chunqiu fanlu)

### DERIVING POLITICAL NORMS FROM MICROCOSMIC AND MACROCOSMIC MODELS

Like other intellectuals of the late Warring States and Han periods, Dong sought to legitimate his views of government based on natural models derived, on the one hand, from the macrocosm of Heaven and Earth and, on the other, from the microcosm of the human body. In the first essay, Dong correlates the conduct of the ruler with Heaven and that of the minister with Earth. In the second essay, he correlates techniques to regulate and nourish the body with those meant to order and vitalize the state. Thus, while striving to secure exclusive patronage for the Confucian canon, Dong endeavored to synthesize many intellectual trends that had historically stood beyond the purview of the Confucian tradition.

### THE CONDUCT OF HEAVEN AND EARTH

The conduct of Heaven and Earth is beautiful. For this reason Heaven holds its place high and sends down its manifestations; conceals its form and reveals its light; arranges the stars and accumulates vital essence; relies on yin and yang and sends down frost and dew. Heaven holds a high position and so is honored. It sends down its manifestations and so is humane. It conceals its form and so is numinous. It reveals its light and so is brilliant. It orders and arranges the stars and so there is mutual succession. It accumulates vital essence and so endures. It relies on yin and yang and so completes the year. It sends down frost and dew and so brings life and death.

The norms of the people's ruler are derived from and modeled on Heaven. Therefore he values ranks and so is honored. He subjugates other states and so is humane. He resides in a hidden place and does not reveal his form and so is numinous. He appoints the worthy and employs the capable, observes and listens to the four corners of his realm, and so is brilliant. He confers office according to capability, distinguishing the worthy and stupid, and so there is mutual succession. He induces worthy men to draw near and establishes them as his legs and arms and so endures. He investigates the true nature of the ministers' achievements, ranks and orders them as the worst and the best, and so completes his age. He promotes those who possess merit and demotes those who lack merit and so rewards and punishes. . . .

The norms of the people's ministers are derived from and modeled on Earth. Therefore from morning to evening they advance and retreat, taking up various tasks and responding to various inquiries, and so serve the honored [ruler]. They provide food and drink, attend to him in sickness and illness, and so provide nourishment [to the ruler]. They entrust and sacrifice their lives and serve without thoughts of usurpation and so are loyal. They expose their ignorance, manifest their true feelings, do not gloss over their mistakes, and so are trustworthy. They maintain proper conduct even when facing death, do not covet life, and so relieve others in distress. . . .

For this reason Earth manifests its principles and acts as the mother of all living things. The minister manifests his duties and acts as the counselor of a single state. The mother must be trustworthy. The counselor must be loyal. . . .

[From *Chunqiu fanlu yizheng* 17:9b–12b; SQ]

## THE RESPONSIBILITIES OF RULERSHIP

In the following essays Dong Zhongshu outlines the responsibilities of rulership. We see Dong synthesizing Daoist ideals that emphasized the quietude and passivity of the ruler with the more active orientation of the Confucian ideal. These essays also exemplify the tensions implicit in Dong's vision of imperial rulership. While he strove to limit and restrain the powers of the emperor by subordinating him to Heaven, he also endeavored to sanction and amplify the ruler's revered position as a "cosmic pivot" responsible for aligning the three realms of Heaven, Earth, and humanity.

### ESTABLISHING THE PRIMAL NUMEN[18]

### Section 2

He who rules the people is the foundation of the state. Now in administering the state, nothing is more important for transforming [the people] than reverence for the foundation. If the foundation is revered, the ruler will transform [the people] as if a spirit. If the foundation is not revered, the ruler will lack the means to unite the people. If he lacks the means to unite the people, even if he institutes strict punishments and heavy penalties, the people will not submit. This is called "throwing away the state." Is there a greater disaster than this? What do I mean by the foundation? Heaven, Earth, and humankind are the foundation of all living things. Heaven engenders all living things, Earth nourishes them, and humankind completes them. With filial and brotherly love, Heaven engenders them; with food and clothing, Earth nourishes them; and with rites and music, humankind completes them. These three assist one another just as the hands and feet join to complete the body. None can be dispensed with because without filial and brotherly love, people lack the means to live; without food and clothing, people lack the means to be nourished; and without rites and music, people lack the means to become complete. If all three are lost, people become like deer, each person following his own desires and each family practicing its own customs. Fathers will not be able to order their sons, and rulers will not be able to order their ministers. Although possessing inner and outer walls, [the ruler's city] will become known as "an empty settlement." Under such circumstances, the ruler will lie down with a clod of earth for his pillow. Although no one endangers him, he will naturally be endangered; although no one destroys him, he will naturally be destroyed. . . .

One who is an enlightened master and worthy ruler believes such things. For this reason he respectfully and carefully attends to the three foundations. He

---

18. The term *shen*, translated here as "numen," is translated elsewhere in this volume as "spirit."

reverently enacts the suburban sacrifice, dutifully serves his ancestors, manifests filial and brotherly love, encourages filial conduct, and serves the foundation of Heaven in this way. He takes up the plow handle to till the soil, plucks the mulberry leaves and nourishes the silkworms, reclaims the wilds, plants grain, opens new lands to provide sufficient food and clothing, and serves the foundation of Earth in this way. He establishes academies and schools in towns and villages to teach filial piety, brotherly love, reverence, and humility, enlightens [the people] with education, moves [them] with rites and music, and serves the foundation of humanity in this way.

[From *Chunqiu fanlu yizheng* 6:11a–16a; SQ]

## THE WAY OF THE KING PENETRATES THREE[19]

In ancient times those who created writing took three horizontal lines and connected them through the center to designate the king. The three horizontal lines represent Heaven, Earth, and humankind while the vertical line that connects them through the center represents comprehending the Way.[20] As for the one who appropriates the mean of Heaven, Earth, and humankind and takes this as the thread that joins and connects them, if it is not one who acts as a king then who can be equal to this [task]? Therefore one who acts as king is no more than Heaven's agent. He models himself on Heaven's seasons and brings them to completion. He models himself on Heaven's commands and causes the people to obey them. He models himself on Heaven's numerical categories and initiates affairs. He models himself on Heaven's Way and sends forth his standards. He models himself on Heaven's will and always returns to humaneness. The beauty of humaneness is found in Heaven. Heaven is humaneness. Heaven shelters and nourishes the myriad things. It transforms and generates them. It nourishes and completes them. Heaven's affairs and achievements are endless. They end and begin again, and all that Heaven raises up it returns to serve humankind. If you examine Heaven's will you will surely see that Heaven's humaneness is inexhaustible and limitless.

Since human beings receive their lives from Heaven, accordingly they appropriate Heaven's humaneness and are thereby humane. For this reason they possess reverence toward Heaven for receiving life; affection for their fathers, older brothers, sons, and younger brothers; minds-and-hearts that are loyal, trustworthy, and caring; actions that are right (*yi*) and yielding; and regulations that distinguish right from wrong and deviance from compliance. . . .

[From *Chunqiu fanlu yizheng* 11:9a–12a; SQ]

---

19. "Three" refers to Heaven, Earth, and humankind.

20. The Chinese character for *king* (*wang* 王) is written with three horizontal lines connected by a vertical line.

## DEFINING HUMAN NATURE

During the Han, as in earlier periods, scholars continued to discuss and debate the qualities inherent in human nature. Effecting a compromise between the theories identified with Mencius and Xunzi, Dong Zhongshu argued that human nature possessed the potential to become good, but it could not do so without the trans- forming influence of the ruler's instruction. In the essay that follows, we find one of the clearest expressions of the paternalism that characterized later Confucian politi- cal theory. This ideal, which held that the people are dependent upon the ruler for their moral guidance, greatly expanded both the authority and the responsibility of the ruler.

### AN IN-DEPTH EXAMINATION OF NAMES AND DESIGNATIONS

The term *person* (*shen*) is derived from Heaven (*tian*). Heaven has its dual operations of yin and yang, and one's person has its dual nature of greed and humanity. Heaven sometimes restricts yin. Likewise, a person sometimes weakens the emotions and desires, becoming one with the Way of Heaven. This is why when yin functions it cannot interfere with the spring and sum- mer, and the full moon is always overwhelmed by sunlight, so that at one moment it is full and at another it is not. If Heaven restricts yin in this way, how can a person not reduce his desires and suppress his emotions to respond to Heaven?

. . . We must acknowledge that if our Heavenly natures do not receive educa- tion, ultimately they will not be able to weaken the emotions and desires. If we examine the actuality and thereby consider the term [*nature*], how can nature be like this [that is, good] when it has not undergone education? . . .

. . . Now the nature of all people possesses a basic substance, but it has not yet been awakened, just as those with closed eyes await awakening. It must be educated before it can become good. Before it is awakened, we can say that it possesses a basic substance that is good, but we cannot yet say that it is good. . . .

. . . A person possesses the nature and emotions just as Heaven possesses yang and yin. To mention the basic substance of a human being with- out mentioning the emotions resembles mentioning the yang of Heaven without mentioning the yin. . . . Since Heaven has generated the people's nature, which possesses the basic substance of goodness but which is not yet capable of goodness, it sets up the king to make it good. . . . It is the duty of the king to obey Heaven's intent and to complete the people's nature. . . .

> [*Chunqiu fanlu* (SBCK) 10:1a–14a; adapted by SQ from Chan,
> *Source Book*, pp. 273–279]

## INTERPRETING OMENS

### HUMANENESS MUST PRECEDE WISDOM

The source of all portents and anomalies lies in faults that exist within the state. When faults have just begun to germinate, Heaven sends forth fearful portents to warn and inform the ruler of these faults. If after being warned and informed, the ruler fails to recognize the cause of these portents, then strange anomalies appear to frighten him. If after being frightened he still fails to recognize the cause of his fear, only then do misfortunes and calamities overtake him. From this we can see that Heaven's intent is humane and does not desire to entrap a person.

If one examines these portents and anomalies carefully, one will observe Heaven's intent. Heaven's intent desires certain things and does not desire other things. As for those things that Heaven desires and does not desire, if one examines oneself, one will surely find such warnings within oneself. If one observes affairs around oneself, one will surely find verification [of these warnings] in the state. Thus Heaven's intent is manifested in these portents and anomalies. . . .

[*Chunqiu fanlu yizheng* 8:23b–25b; adapted by SQ from BW]

## SELF-CULTIVATION

Dong Zhongshu believed that Confucius composed the *Spring and Autumn Annals* to set out a standard of rightness for all-under-Heaven. He held that each one of Confucius' Six Teachings excelled at developing a particular virtue, while, taken together, they provided the basis for ordering all aspects of human existence. According to Dong, the *Spring and Autumn Annals* rectified right and wrong and therefore excelled in ordering humaneness. The text embodied cosmic norms presented in light of the dynamic circumstances of human rule and the changing contexts of human relationships. The historical events that filled its pages, judged praiseworthy or blameworthy by Confucius, provided positive standards to be emulated and negative models to be avoided. The text possessed the power to transform the empire because it embodied a code of ethics to be followed by the ruler and the scholar-officials who served him.

### STANDARDS OF HUMANENESS AND RIGHTNESS

What the *Spring and Autumn Annals* regulates are others and the self. The means by which it regulates others and the self are humaneness and rightness. With humaneness it brings peace and security to others, and with rightness it rectifies the self. Therefore the term *humaneness* (*ren*) refers to "others" (*ren*), while the term *rightness* (*yi*) refers to the "self" (*wo*). . . . Generally speaking, it is because people are ignorant of the distinction between the other and the self, and they do not examine where humaneness and rightness properly apply. For this reason the *Spring and Autumn Annals* established standards (*fa*) of humaneness and rightness.[21] The standard of humaneness lies in loving others and not in loving the self. The standard of rightness lies in rectifying the self and not in rectifying others. . . . If you do not sincerely love others, extending your love from the people on down to the birds, beasts, and insects, so that there is nothing that is not an object of your love, then how can your love be sufficient to be called humaneness? *Humaneness* is the term that designates loving others. . . .

. . . One who loves only himself may be established in the position of Son of Heaven or Enfeoffed Lord, but being a solitary person he will lack the assistance of his ministers and his people. If the situation comes to this, although no one ruins him, he will ruin himself. . . .

Rightness does not refer to rectifying others but to rectifying the self. Even a reckless ruler living in a chaotic age desires to rectify others. How can this be called rightness! . . .

Rightness designates what is appropriate to the self. Only after what is appropriate relates to the self can one be called right. Thus the expression *rightness* combines the self (*wo*) and appropriate (*yi*) into one term. From this, one can grasp that rightness is for the purpose of designating the self. . . . Humaneness refers to what moves away from the self; rightness refers to what moves toward the self. Humaneness refers to what is distant; rightness refers to what is close. Love toward others is called humaneness, while appropriateness in the self is called rightness. Humaneness presides over others; rightness presides over the self. . . .

The *Spring and Autumn Annals* criticizes the ruler's faults and pities the people's hardships. When there were small evils beyond the state of Lu the *Spring and Autumn Annals* did not record them, but when they occurred within the person of the ruler the *Spring and Autumn Annals* recorded them and condemned them. In general, when it mentions such matters, it employs humaneness to regulate others and rightness to regulate the self; it is generous with criticisms of the self but sparing of them toward others. . . . If the ruler is not respectful in carrying forth propriety, his actions will be impeded, and the people will not respect him. If the ruler is not broadminded, his generosity will be impeded, and the people will not cherish him. If they do not feel affection for the ruler, they will not trust him. If they do not revere the ruler, they will not respect him. If the ruler defies these two principles of government and carries them forth in a biased way he will be condemned by the people below. Is it possible not to deliberate on the proper place of humaneness and rightness?

[From *Chunqiu fanlu yizheng* 8:16a–22a; SQ]

---

21. It is difficult to employ a single English term to capture the many connotations of the term *fa* used here. The *fa* of humaneness and rightness are at once standards of perfection, models of emulation, and methods of becoming humane and right.

## THE ISSUE OF MORAL AUTONOMY

Unlike Confucius, Mencius, or Xunzi, who served rulers of several of the contending feudal states of the late Zhou period, Dong Zhongshu served two powerful rulers of a unified Han empire. By contrast with his predecessors, Dong has sometimes been seen as rationalizing this enormous imperial power. Note, however, that in the preceding selections, Dong reveals a deep concern to impress upon the ruler both the extent of his power and its inevitable limitations. Playing as he does a crucial role in a highly interactive universe, the ruler must realize that he is both answerable to Heaven and responsible for the people.

Our final selection—along with considerable evidence from Dong's biography—suggests that Dong was not so much celebrating the imperial institution as he was seeking to reform it. Perhaps his most enduring contribution to an evolving Confucian tradition was to read into the *Spring and Autumn Annals* a model of sovereignty that, on the one hand, rejected the ruler's absolute and arbitrary exercise of power, his use of violence, and his primary reliance on impersonal laws and, on the other, emphasized his indebtedness to Heaven, his use of moral persuasion, and his reliance on the transforming influences of ritual and education.

Of particular importance to Dong in his reformist thinking was the fundamental Confucian concept of humaneness. Once, when confronted with a choice between humaneness and the duties involved in the five relationships—between ruler and subject, parent and child, husband and wife, elder and younger brother, friend and friend—Dong was unequivocal in choosing humaneness. "Faced with [an opportunity to practice] humaneness," he said, "do not yield to your commander." Here he was paraphrasing the *Analects* of Confucius,[22] yet the implications of this choice in the Han context were rather different, as the following passage from Dong's *Deciding Court Cases According to the Spring and Autumn Annals* suggests.

A prince was hunting and captured a fawn. He ordered his minister to take up the fawn and return with it. On the way home, the minister noticed that the fawn's mother was following him and whining. He was moved to release the fawn. [Upon discovering this] the ruler was angered. The [minister's] crime was under discussion and had not yet been determined when the ruler fell ill. Fearing that he would die, the ruler wished to entrust his young son [to someone's care]. He recalled the minister and exclaimed: "How humane is the minister! He encountered a fawn and treated it with compassion, how much more is this the case with regard to other human beings." He released the minister and entrusted his son to him. What opinion should be upheld? Dong Zhongshu stated: "The noble man does not take young animals or eggs. The minister did not protest when ordered to take the fawn home. This would have been contrary to rightness. Nevertheless, in the midst of carrying out his orders, he was moved by the fawn's

---

22. *Analects* 15:36.

mother and demonstrated his compassion. Although he disregarded his ruler's order, it is possible that he be transferred."[23]

[From *Chunqiu jueshi* 31:1b; SQ]

# THE CODIFYING OF THE CONFUCIAN CANON

## STATE ORTHODOXY

Gaozu, the founder of the Han, a commoner with no pretensions to learning, ridiculed pompous Confucian scholars, but he did not hesitate to make use of them and follow their advice when it helped his designs. Above all, he honestly accorded with the Confucian teaching that the emperor should act on the advice of his ministers, setting an important precedent that did much to check despotism among his successors.

Dong Zhongshu as teacher and government official during the reign of Emperor Wu, formulated doctrines and brought about the establishment of institutions that had a profound influence on later ages. It was his conviction that the Han should take constructive measures to change what remained of the old order inherited from the Qin. His recommendations to the emperor were presented in a series of answers to questions on government policy posed by the emperor himself. One of these advocated rejecting all but the Five Confucian Classics as the teaching of the state.

Emperor Wu eventually followed this suggestion, removing official support from the other teachings and endorsing Confucianism. Thus he promoted a unification of thought that the violent proscriptions of Qin had sought but failed to produce.

## STATE UNIVERSITY

Closely connected with this plan to give official support to Confucianism was Dong Zhongshu's suggestion to establish a government college for the training of officials in which Confucian ideas would be taught. He wrote:

Among the things paramount for the upbringing of scholars, none is more important than a state college. A college is intimately related to the fostering of virtuous scholars and is the foundation of education. . . . Your servant desires Your Majesty to erect a college and appoint illustrious teachers for it, for the upbringing of the empire's scholars.[24]

---

23. The harsher punishment usually associated with the crime of disregarding the ruler's command is reduced because of the minister's humaneness.

24. *Hanshu* 56:12b–13a.

In 124 B.C.E., by imperial order, a college was established near the capital in which government-appointed teachers gave instruction to students selected and sent to the capital by provincial authorities. The course of study was normally one year, and upon graduation all those shown to be capable were given positions in the bureaucracy. By the end of the first century B.C.E. there were some three thousand students enrolled in the college, and in the Latter Han the number grew to more than thirty thousand. Thus the bureaucracy became filled with men trained in the official Confucian learning.

## CIVIL SERVICE

As early as the reign of the first Han emperor, the government had sent out requests asking the provincial officials to recommend capable scholars and men of ability to serve the government. This idea, old in Confucian tradition, gradually increased in power and effectiveness. Dong Zhongshu himself was selected for an official career after having written outstanding answers, quoted above, to the examination questions set by the emperor. It was consistent with his plans for the shaping of a Confucian bureaucracy that he should exert his influence to encourage and develop what would later grow into the famous examination system. Thus he recommended that the emperor have

> the marquises, governors of commanderies, and officials of two thousand piculs salary all select those of worth among the officials and common people and once a year send to the capital two men each who will be housed there and taken care of. . . . In this way all will do their best in seeking out men of worth, and scholars of the empire can be obtained, given official posts, and used in the government.[25]

## THE RIVALRY BETWEEN LEGALISM
## AND CONFUCIANISM

In spite of these measures taken under his rule, Emperor Wu himself was far from a model Confucian ruler. His system of harsh and detailed laws, heavy taxes, extensive military expeditions, and government monopolies embodied specifically Legalist measures. He disregarded the precedent set by the founder of the dynasty, acting on his own initiative and often ignoring the counsel of his ministers. In private life he devoted much time and expense to pursuing the elixir of immortality, attempting to communicate with the spirits of the dead, and other occult practices. So averse was he to any criticism of his measures that under his reign an official was executed on the charge of "disapproval in the

---

25. Ibid., 56:9b.

heart," based on the evidence of a reported "subtle wry twist of his lips" when a new law was being discussed.[26] Nothing could be further from the Confucian insistence upon outspoken criticism and discussion of all administrative practices as the sacred duty of ministers and scholars.

It was not until the reign of Emperor Xuan's son, Emperor Yuan (r. 49–33 B.C.E.), that a ruler more fully in accord with Confucian ideals for the first time occupied the throne. Unfortunately, by this time the influence of the emperor's maternal relatives and the eunuchs had become so strong that the emperor, though well meaning, was largely ineffectual, and the decay of the dynasty was clearly foreshadowed.

## THE CONFUCIAN CANON

As Confucianism came to hold a dominant position as the official teaching of the Chinese state, the classic literature of this school came to be compiled into a canon of works known today as the Confucian Classics. As we have already seen, most of the Confucian Classics had their origins in the Zhou period. But it was during the Han that they were recovered and compiled in the form in which they would be transmitted to later generations.

As might be expected, however, scholars often could not agree upon authoritative texts, and so there existed side by side slightly different versions of the classical works, each with its own traditions, masters, and disciples. Some of these versions, reported by legend to have been found sealed in the wall of Confucius' home, came to be known as Old Text versions, so called because they were written in part not in the style of characters adopted by the Qin and used by the Han but in an archaic orthography used during the Zhou. Others, called New Texts, were identified with Dong Zhongshu and his followers, who made use of yin-yang theories in the interpretation of omens and portents. Another group of private scholars who adhered to the Old Texts was led by men from the area of Confucius' own state of Lu — one of the most famous, Kong Anguo (156?–74? B.C.E.), being himself a direct descendant of the sage. The first important official patron of the Old Texts was Liu Xin (46 B.C.E.–23 C.E.), an outstanding scholar whose reputation has suffered because of his association with Wang Mang whose short-lived Xin ("New") dynasty (9–23 C.E.) marked an interregnum between the Former Han and the Latter Han dynasties.[27] Emperor Guangwu (r. 25–57 C.E.), who restored the Han after Wang's execution, lent his support to the New Texts, abolishing the study of the Old Texts that had been established at the end of the Former Han. Despite this, the Old Texts gained acceptance from some important thinkers and scholars of the Latter Han. Much later, in the late nineteenth and early twentieth centuries, differences between these two textual traditions

---

26. *Shiji* (BNB) 30:13b–14a.
27. See chap. 11.

became construed as subjects of great political and scholastic controversy, but there is little evidence that these issues figured prominently in the Han itself.

In 53 B.C.E., Emperor Xuan called a conference of scholars to discuss varying interpretations of the classics, with the emperor himself attending and acting as final judge in the controversies. The conference continued for two years, and the results were published to form the official interpretation, though varying interpretations were not actually proscribed.

Some years later, during the reign of Emperor Cheng (r. 33–7 B.C.E.), a still more ambitious program was undertaken. Under the directorship of Liu Xiang (79–8 B.C.E.), a court official and eminent scholar, a group of scholars set to work collecting copies of all the existing literature of the day. For each work a copy of the table of sections and an abstract of its contents was made. When Liu Xiang died, his work was continued by his son, Liu Xin, who presented to the throne a bibliography in seven sections listing all the important books in the imperial library. This bibliography was incorporated into the *History of the Former Han Dynasty*, forming an invaluable aid to the study of ancient China and its literature.

After the troubled times of Wang Mang, a council of scholars was again held, modeled on that held under Emperor Xuan. The results, combined with those of the former council, were compiled and published in a work known as *Discourses in the White Tiger Hall (Bohu tong)*, representing an official interpretation of the Confucian Classics and Confucian teachings.

Thus the classics were established as the basis for all Confucian learning, and, in turn, for entrance into official position. With minor exceptions, this is the canon as it was known in later ages and as it has come down to us.

Toward the end of the dynasty, by imperial order, the complete texts of the Five Classics and the Confucian *Analects* were engraved on stone tablets and set up at the imperial college, a monument to the scholarly labors of the Han Confucians.

In addition to the canonical works included in this chapter, there was another "classic," not formally installed in the Confucian canon but with virtually that status as a standard text of female instruction: Ban Zhao's *Admonitions for Women*. The sister of the famous historian Ban Gu, Ban Zhao (48?–116? C.E.) upheld the scholarly tradition of her family and was honored at the Han court for her learning. On account of its enduring importance, her *Admonitions for Women* was later included in the Four Books for Women, selections from which are found in the section on "Women's Education" in chapter 23.

## THE FORMATION OF THE *CLASSIC OF CHANGES (YIJING)*

Much of the *Classic of Changes (Yijing)* derives from the Zhou period, and traditionally it, with its later overlay of Confucian interpretation, ranked as the primordial source of traditional wisdom and first of the Confucian classics.

Known also as the *Changes of Zhou* (*Zhouyi*), it was originally a divination manual, which later gradually acquired the status of a wisdom book. We include a discussion of this important work here because, while parts of the text derived from earlier sources, it was during the Han period that the *Changes* acquired this reputation and assumed its canonical form.

The *Classic of Changes* consists of sixty-four hexagrams (*gua*) and related texts. The hexagrams are formed by combinations of six unbroken (yang — ) and/or broken (yin – –) lines (*yao*), arranged one atop the other in vertical sequence. Though many questions surround the origin of the hexagrams, it was traditionally believed that they were developed by King Wen of Zhou out of the eight primary trigrams invented by the legendary culture hero and sage Fu Xi:

For one consulting the *Changes* as a divination manual, the relevant hexagrams were originally identified through a process of numerical manipulation of divining sticks—milfoil (*Achillea millefolium*) or yarrow stalks—and, later, by the casting of coins. In early times this process apparently resembled the kind of divination that had been practiced in the Shang period; over time, however, divination changed from a method of consulting and influencing ancestors—the "powerful dead"—to a method of penetrating moments of the cosmic process to learn how the Way is configured, what direction it takes at such moments, and what one's own place is—and should be—in the scheme of things. By developing the capacity to anticipate and accord with change, one could avert wrong decisions, avoid failure, escape misfortune, and, on the other hand, make right decisions, achieve success, and garner good fortune.

Each hexagram is accompanied by (1) a hexagram name (*guaming*), (2) a hexagram statement (*guaci*) or "Judgment" (*tuan*), and (3) line statements (*yaoci*) for each of the six lines. Again, the traditional Chinese belief was that King Wen composed the hexagram statements or Judgments, the line statements having been the contribution of the Duke of Zhou. The hexagram names suggest crucial life situations—for example, Birth Throes (3), Viewing (20), Suppression of the Light (36), Abundance (55). The hexagrams, hexagram statements or Judgments, and line statements, while no longer ascribed to sagely authorship, are still generally recognized as the oldest parts of the *Changes*, going back perhaps as far as the latter part of the ninth century B.C.E. and constituting the first layer in the text.

Another layer consists of two parts: (1) commentaries on the hexagram statements or Judgments called Commentaries on the Judgments (*Tuanzhuan*) and (2) commentaries on the abstract meanings or "Images" (*xiang*) of the Judgments and the line statements called Commentaries on the Images (*Xiangzhuan*). The Judgments have "Great Images" (*daxiang*)—the abstract meanings of hexagrams as whole entities—and the line statements have "Little Images" (*xiaoxiang*)—the abstract meanings of individual lines. These commentaries are the first of the exegetical materials in the *Changes* traditionally attributed to Confucius.

The traditional format of the *Changes* divides the Commentaries on the Judgments (*Tuanzhuan*) and the Commentaries on the Images (*Xiangzhuan*) each into two sections; they thus form the first four of the "Ten Wings" (*Shiyi*) of the exegetical material included in the classic. Of the Ten Wings, the most philosophically influential have been the sixth and seventh, formed by the two sections of the *Great Commentary* (*Dazhuan*), otherwise known as the *Commentary on the Appended Phrases* (*Xici zhuan*).

## THE COMMENTARY ON THE APPENDED PHRASES, PART 1

As the *Changes* is supposed to be a "paradigm of Heaven and Earth," the *Commentary on the Appended Phrases* has a great deal to say about the universal order that underlies the myriad phenomena. The universe may be mysterious, but, thanks to the *Changes* and to the sages who first created it and who forever after employ it as guide, its mysteries can be plumbed, the secrets of good fortune and misfortune can be known, and human beings, as individuals and in society, can learn how to live in accordance with the cosmic and moral Way.

1. As Heaven is high and noble and Earth is low and humble, so it is that *qian* [pure yang, Hexagram 1] and *kun* [pure yin, Hexagram 2] are defined. The high and the low being thereby set out, the exalted and the mean have their places accordingly. There are norms for action and repose, which are determined by whether hardness or softness is involved. Those with regular tendencies gather according to kind, and things divide up according to group; so it is that good fortune and misfortune occur. In Heaven this process creates images, and on Earth it creates physical forms; this is how change and transformation manifest themselves. In consequence of all this, as hard and soft stroke each other, the Eight Trigrams activate each other. It [the Way] arouses things with claps of thunder, moistens them with wind and rain. Sun and moon go through their cycles, so now it is cold, now hot. The Way of *qian* forms the male; the Way of *kun* forms the female. *Qian* has mastery over the great beginning of things, and *kun* acts to bring things to completion. *Qian* through ease provides mastery over things, and *kun* through simplicity provides capability. As the former is easy, it is easy to know, and as the latter is simple, it is easy to follow. If one is easy to know, he will have kindred spirits; and if one is easy to follow, he will have meritorious accomplishments. Once one has kindred spirits, he can endure, and once one has meritorious accomplishments, he can grow great. Being able to endure is inherent in a worthy man's virtue, and being able to grow great is inherent in the enterprise of the worthy man. It is through such ease and simplicity that the principles of the world obtain. As the principles of the world obtain in this way, they form positions here between them [Heaven and Earth].

2. The sages set down the hexagrams and observed the images. They appended phrases to the lines in order to clarify whether they signify good fortune or misfortune and let the hard and the soft lines displace each other so that change and transformation could appear. Therefore, good fortune and misfortune involve images of success or failure. Regret and remorse involve images of sorrow and worry. Change and transformation involve images of advance and withdrawal. The strong and the weak provide images of day and night. The respective functions of the six hexagram lines embody the Way of the Three Ultimates [Heaven, Earth, and the human]. Therefore, what allows the noble person to find himself anywhere and yet remain secure are the sequences presented by the *Changes*. . . .

4. . . . As [a sage] rejoices in Heaven and understands its decrees, he will be free from anxiety. As he is content in his land and is genuine about humaneness, he can be loving. He perfectly emulates the transformations of Heaven and Earth and so does not transgress them. He follows every twist and turn of the myriad things and so deals with them without omission. He has a thorough grasp of the Way of day-and-night and so is knowing. Thus, the numinous (*shen*)[28] is not restricted to place, and change is without substance.

5. The reciprocal process of yin and yang is called the Way. That which allows the Way to continue to operate is human goodness (*shan*), and that which allows it to bring things to completion is human nature (*xing*). The humane see it and call it humaneness, and the wise (*zhi*) see it and call it wisdom. It functions for the common folk on a daily basis, yet they are unaware of it. This is why the Way of the noble person is a rare thing! . . .

12. That which transforms things and regulates them is called change. By extending this to practical action one may be said to achieve complete success. To take up this [the Way of change] and integrate it into the lives of the common folk of the world is called the great task of life. . . . To plumb the mysteries of the world to the utmost is dependent on the hexagrams; to drum up people to action all over the world is dependent on the phrases; to transform things and regulate them is dependent on change; to start things going and carry them out is dependent on the free flow of change; to be aware of the numinous and bring it to light is dependent on the men involved; to accomplish things while remaining silent and to be trusted without speaking is something intrinsic to virtuous conduct.

[From *Yijing, Xici zhuan*, Part 1, *Shisanjing zhushu*; RJL]

## THE COMMENTARY ON THE APPENDED PHRASES, PART 2

1. Thanks to constancy, the Way of Heaven and Earth reveals itself. Thanks to constancy, the Way of the sun and the moon makes them bright. All the activity

---

28. Translated elsewhere in this volume as "spiritual."

that takes place in the world, thanks to constancy, is the expression of the One. *Qian* being unyielding shows us how easy it is; *kun* being yielding shows us how simple it is. The lines reproduce how particular things act, and the images provide likenesses of particular things. As the lines and images move within the hexagrams, so do good fortune and misfortune appear outside them. Meritorious undertakings are revealed in change, and the innate tendencies of the sages are revealed in the attached phrases. The great virtue of Heaven and Earth is called "generation." The great treasure of the sage is called his "position." The means by which such a one preserves this position we call "humaneness"; the means by which he gathers people to him we call "resources." The regulation of resources, the rectification of pronouncements, and his preventing the people from doing wrong we call "rightness." . . .

5. The Master said, "To understand incipience, is this not a matter of the numinous! The noble person is not fawning toward what is above and is not contemptuous of what is below. Is this not to understand incipience! As for incipience itself, it is the infinitesimally small beginning of action, the point at which the precognition of good fortune can occur. The noble person acts upon something as soon as he becomes aware of its incipience and does not wait for the day to run its course. . . ."

[From *Yijing, Xici zhuan*, Part 2, *Shisanjing zhushu*; RJL]

## HEAVEN, EARTH, AND THE HUMAN IN THE *CLASSIC OF FILIALITY* (*XIAOJING*)

Filial piety was an age-old concept and practice even before Confucius' time, but only toward the end of the Zhou period did it become the subject of a "classic" text emerging from the school of Confucius' disciple Zengzi, in what purported to be a dialogue between him and the Master. Its main point is that filiality, as the generic source of all virtue, serves as the basis of public morality, maintains the spiritual continuity between the living and the dead, and links together the creative powers of Heaven, Earth, and the Human order.

Some differentiation in the practice of filiality is recognized in separate sections addressed to the Son of Heaven, the enfeoffed nobility, the great officers, scholar-officials, and common people. While thus envisioning a structured, hierarchical society, the creators of the text also stress the universality of the filial relationship as the common moral denominator among people of all classes. Moreover, it co-implicates authority and responsibility, underscoring the ruler's responsibility to the people and the ministers' duty of forthright remonstration to keep the ruler from going astray—also a duty of the son to remonstrate with his father to keep him from wrong. Both illustrate the basic Confucian principle of reciprocity or mutual response.

As a text emerging from the family school of Confucius in the Han period, the *Classic of Filiality* maintained quasi-canonical status down into the twentieth century. The Tang emperor Xuanzong recognized it as one of the "Thirteen Classics." Versions of varying length, organization, and commentary fueled scholarly controversy down through the centuries. Zhu Xi, who had doubts about the text (though not about the importance of filiality) did not include it among the Four Books and Five Classics in the core of the Neo-Confucian curriculum. Still, this did not keep the *Classic of Filiality* from enjoying wide popularity throughout premodern East Asia. It became especially influential in Japanese thought of the Tokugawa period (1603–1868) and figured prominently in nationalistic ideologies of late nineteenth- and early twentieth-century Japan. Questions of authenticity did not impede its being widely accepted as a classic statement not only of the virtue of filial piety but of the Confucian values of self-preservation, reciprocity, reverence, moderation, diligence, service to others, and moral remonstration.

## THE *CLASSIC OF FILIALITY* (*XIAOJING*)

### 1. Introduction to Basic Principles

Confucius was at leisure, with Zengzi in attendance. He asked Zengzi, "Do you know by what surpassing virtue and essential way the early kings kept the world in order, the people in harmony both with their relatives and at large, and all, both high and low, uncomplaining?" Zengzi, rising from his seat, said, "Unenlightened as I am, how could I know that?" Confucius said, "Filiality is the root of virtue and the wellspring of instruction. Take your seat and I shall explain.

"Our body, skin, and hair are all received from our parents; we dare not injure them. This is the first priority in filial duty. To establish oneself in the world and practice the Way; to uphold one's good name for posterity and give glory to one's father and mother—this is the completion of filial duty. Thus filiality begins with service to parents, continues in service to the ruler, and ends with establishing oneself in the world [and becoming an exemplary person].

"As it is said in the *Daya* [of the *Classic of Odes*]: 'Forget not your forebears; cultivate the virtue received from them.' "[29]

*The following sections typically end with a similar, memorable quotation from the* Classic of Odes *or the* Classic of Documents, *which for brevity's sake we delete from this abridgement.*

### 2. The Son of Heaven

The Master said, "Loving one's parents, one dare not hate others. Revering one's parents, one dare not be contemptuous of others. When his love and reverence

---

29. Ode 235.

are perfected in service to parents, [the ruler's] moral influence is shed on all the people and his good example shines in all directions. . . ."

*Deleted here are similar maxims for the conduct of the enfeoffed nobility and high officers. Observance of these is a filial duty, but the conduct itself relates to the office, not to filiality.*

## 5. Scholar-Officials (*Shi*)

As one serves one's father, one serves one's mother, drawing on the same love. As one serves one's father, one serves one's prince, drawing on the same reverence. The mother draws upon one's love, the prince on one's reverence. Therefore, if one serves one's prince with the filiality one shows to one's father, it becomes the virtue of fidelity (loyalty). If one serves one's superiors with brotherly submission it becomes the virtue of obedience. Never failing in fidelity and obedience, this is how one serves superiors. Thus one may preserve one's rank and office and continue one's family sacrifices. This is the filiality of the scholar-official. . . .

## 6. Commoners

In keeping with Heaven's seasons and Earth's resources, by one's industry and frugality one supports one's father and mother. This is the filiality of the common people.

From the Son of Heaven down to the common people, if filiality is not followed from beginning to end, disaster is sure to follow.

*In some editions the previous paragraph is a separate section titled "Equality of Filiality." This means that although filial duties are differentiated according to particular stations, the filial obligation is shared by all—a common human denominator and the genetic basis of all moral relations.*

## 7. The Three Powers [Heaven, Earth, and the Human]

The Master said, "Filiality is the ordering principle of Heaven, the rightness of the Earth, and the norm of human conduct. This ordering of Heaven and Earth is what people should follow; illumined by the brightness of Heaven and benefited by the resources of the Earth, all-under-Heaven are thus harmonized. This is how the teachings [of the sage king] succeed without being stringent, and his rule achieves order without being severe. The early kings, seeing that instruction could transform the people, gave them an example of outspreading love so that people did not neglect their kin; promulgated virtue and rightness, which the people willingly emulated in practice; set an example of respect and deference, by which the people became non-contentious; led them by rites and music, by which the people became harmonious; distinguished between good and evil, whereby the people knew what was forbidden. . . ."

## 8. Governing by Filiality

The Master said, "The reason the illustrious kings of old governed all-under-Heaven by filiality was that, not daring to neglect the ministers even of small states (much less their own enfeoffed nobility), they sought to engender in the myriad states an eagerness to serve [sacrifice to] their predecessors. Heads of states, not daring to abuse widows and widowers (much less scholar-officials and commoners), instilled in all an eagerness to serve the princely ancestors. Heads of families, not daring to mistreat servants and concubines (much less their own wives and children), instilled in all an eagerness to serve their parents. Living, they were at peace; in death, content. Thus with all-under-Heaven at peace, no calamities occurred, no disasters or disorders arose. This is why the illustrious kings governed through filiality. . . ."

## 9. The Governance of the Sages

The Master said, ". . . In the virtue (*de*) of the sage is there anything that can surpass filiality?. . . The Way of parent and child is rooted in the Heavenly moral nature and engenders the [relation of] rightness between prince and minister. Parents give one life; no bond could be greater. . . . Therefore not to love one's parents but to love others is to act against one's moral nature (*de*). Not to respect one's parents but to respect others is to violate the ritual order. . . ."

## 12. The Essential Way, Further Expounded

The Master said, "For teaching people love and affection, nothing is better than filiality. For teaching people ritual restraint, nothing is better than fraternal love. For transforming manners and customs, nothing is better than music. For stability [of the throne] above and order [among the people] below, nothing is better than the rites. And ritual decorum [accordance with the rites] is essentially reverence. . . ."

## 15. Remonstrance

Zengzi said, "I have heard your instructions concerning affection and loving respect, comforting one's parents, and upholding one's good name. May I presume to ask, if a child follows all of his parents' commands, can this be called filiality?"

The Master replied, "What kind of talk is this! What kind of talk is this! Of old the Son of Heaven had seven counselors, so that even if he himself lost the Way, he still would not lose his sway over all-under-Heaven. . . . If a father had even one son to remonstrate with him, he still would not fall into evil ways. In the face of whatever is not right, the son cannot but remonstrate with his father, and the minister cannot but remonstrate with his prince. If it is not right, remonstrate! . . ."

## 18. Mourning One's Parents

The following passage is marked by the characteristic Confucian qualities of balance and moderation in all things, and of care of one's own body as the primary filial obligation to one's parents.

The Master said, "In mourning for his parents, the filial child weeps but does not wail, performs the rites without affectation, speaks without adorning his words, does without splendid raiment, hears music without taking any joy in it, and eats without relish—all these are feelings natural to one who grieves. After three days one again takes food, in order to show people that death should not be allowed to harm life and that destruction [of one's body] should not lead to the destruction of [another] life. These are how the sages regulated things. . . ."

[From *Songke xiaojing* 5–31; Kurihara, *Kōkyō*, 67–335; dB]

# THE *RECORD OF RITES (LIJI)* AND THE RITUAL TRADITION

Rites were at the heart of early Confucian thought and practice, as will have been evident in the selections from the *Analects* and *Xunzi* especially.[30] Rites represented a connection between the Confucian tradition and the earliest Chinese religious practices known to us, so that within the tradition was preserved something very ancient, together with a keen and appreciative consciousness of its antiquity. At the same time, ritual practice and the understanding of the purpose and significance of ritual also evolved over time along with the evolution of Confucianism itself. Among the noteworthy developments were a heightened sense of the moral significance of the rites and of their educative and disciplinary value within the life of an individual as well as in the life of the state and the empire. In fact, it was characteristic of the adherents of the tradition known as *ru*—the ritualists—to believe that it was through rites that individuals were best able to cultivate themselves, to exert positive influence over others, and ultimately to bring order to the family, the state, and the world at large.

---

30. See chaps. 3 and 6.

Here we offer a selection from two of the most important Confucian ritual texts, the *Great Learning* and the *Mean*. These two texts were chapters of a classic known as the *Record of Rites* (*Liji*), a work compiled at the end of the first century B.C.E. and the beginning of the first century C.E. on the basis of materials that were in many cases considerably older. Though the interest and importance of these works were noted already during the Han period, they were preserved for many centuries simply as part of this much larger compilation. In the Song period (960–1279) they would receive fresh attention when Zhu Xi (1130–1200), one of the leading scholars of the Song dynasty, selected them from the *Record of Rites*, assigning them an independent status, alongside the *Analects* and the *Mencius*, as two of the Four Books. From that time on these four—the *Great Learning*, the *Mean*, the *Analects*, and the *Mencius*—became the most important and formative texts deriving from the classical Confucian tradition and, as we shall see, a focus and point of reference for much of the tradition that would develop from the twelfth through the seventeenth centuries and that has been identified as Neo-Confucian.

## THE GREAT LEARNING (DAXUE)

For all its brevity, the *Great Learning* is one of the most seminal works in the Chinese tradition. Its Chinese title, *Daxue*, is usually understood to mean education for the adult, or higher education; its central theme is self-cultivation. Most famous in the *Great Learning* is the catena—known in Chinese as the "eight items"—setting forth a series of links connecting intellectual and moral cultivation on the part of the individual with the establishment of harmony in the family, order in the state, and peace in the world. The *Great Learning* has been variously attributed to Confucius' grandson Zisi (483?—402? B.C.E.), to Confucius' disciple Zengzi, and to one of his pupils. Some scholars, however, have dated it as late as the Former Han period (ca. 200 B.C.E.).

## The Text

The Way of the Great Learning lies in illuminating luminous virtue, treating the people with affection, and resting in perfect goodness. Knowing where to rest, one is able to be settled; having become settled, one is able to become tranquil; having become tranquil, one is able to be at peace; being at peace, one is able to reflect; through reflection one is able to attain understanding.

Things have their roots and their branches; affairs have their ends and their beginnings. Knowing what to put first and what to put last, one comes near to the Way.

Those in antiquity who wished to illuminate luminous virtue throughout the world would first govern their states; wishing to govern their states, they would first bring order to their families; wishing to bring order to their families, they would first cultivate their own persons; wishing to cultivate their own persons, they would first rectify their minds; wishing to rectify their minds, they would first make their thoughts sincere; wishing to make their thoughts sincere, they would first extend their knowledge. The extension of knowledge lies in the investigation of things.

It is only when things are investigated that knowledge is extended; when knowledge is extended that thoughts become sincere; when thoughts become sincere that the mind is rectified; when the mind is rectified that the person is cultivated; when the person is cultivated that order is brought to the family; when order is brought to the family that the state is well governed; when the state is well governed that peace is brought to the world.

From the Son of Heaven to ordinary people, all, without exception, should regard cultivating the person as the root. It can never happen that the root is disordered and the branches are ordered. It should never be that what is significant is regarded lightly and what is insignificant is regarded with gravity. This is called knowing the root; this is called the perfection of knowledge.

## From the Commentary to the Text

Chapter 6: What is meant by "making one's thoughts sincere" is this: One allows no self-deception, just as when one hates a hateful smell or loves a lovely color. This is called being content within oneself, and this is why the noble person must be watchful over himself in solitude. The petty person, when living alone, is quite without restraint in doing what is not good. As soon as he sees a noble person he moves to dissemble, concealing what is not good and making a display of what is good. The other sees right through him, as if seeing his lungs and liver. Of what use is his dissembling? This is a case of what is truly within being manifested without, and this is why the noble person must be watchful over himself in solitude. . . .

Chapter 7: What is meant by "cultivating the person depends upon correcting the mind" is this: Whenever one is influenced by anger and resentment, the mind will not attain correctness; whenever one is influenced by fear and dread, the mind will not attain correctness; whenever one is influenced by enjoyment and pleasure, the mind will not attain correctness; whenever one is influenced by sorrow and distress, the mind will not attain correctness. When the mind is not present, one looks but does not see; one listens but does not hear; one eats without knowing the flavors. This is what it means to say that "cultivating the person depends upon correcting the mind."

Chapter 8: What is meant by "bringing order to one's family depends on the cultivation of one's person" is this: A person is biased by the objects of his affection and love, biased by the objects of his derision and hate, biased by the objects of his awe and reverence, biased by the objects of his pity and compassion, and biased by the objects of his contempt and scorn. This is why there are so few in the world who, being fond of something, are yet aware of its faults and who, disliking something, are yet aware of its merits. Thus the adage has it that "a person never knows his son's faults, nor does he realize the fullness of the growing grain." This is what is meant by saying that unless one's person be cultivated, one cannot regulate the family.

Chapter 9: What is meant by "governing the state requires that one first bring order to one's family" is this: No one who is unable to teach his own family will be able to teach others. Therefore the ruler, without going beyond his own family, brings to completion his teachings throughout the state: filial devotion, which is the way to serve a ruler; brotherliness, which is the way to serve elders; and kindness, which is the way to treat the multitude. . . .

As the humaneness of one family evokes humaneness in an entire state, and the courtesy of one family evokes courtesy in an entire state, so covetousness and cruelty on the part of one man will bring chaos to the entire state.[31] . . .

Chapter 10: What is meant by "bringing peace to the world depends on governing the state" is this: When those above treat the old as the old should be treated, filial devotion will be evoked among the people. When those above treat elders as elders should be treated, brotherliness will be evoked among the people. When those above treat the orphaned with compassion, the people will not do otherwise. Therefore the ruler has the Way of the measuring square.

What one dislikes in those above, let him not employ in the treatment of those below; what one dislikes in those below, let him not employ in serving those above. . . .

Therefore the ruler is watchful first over his virtue. Having virtue, he will have the people; having the people, he will have the land; having the land, he will have its wealth; having its wealth, he will have its resources for expenditure.

Virtue is the root; wealth, the branch. But if the ruler regards the root as inconsequential, and the branch as consequential, he will contend with the people and teach them to plunder. Therefore by gathering wealth one causes the people to be dispersed, and by dispersing wealth, one causes the people to be gathered. . . . Never has it happened that the one above loves humaneness while those below do not love rightness. Nor has it happened that where the people love rightness, their work has not been brought to completion, nor that the wealth gathered in treasuries and granaries has ceased to exist.

[From *Liji zhengyi* 60:1a–b, 4b–6b; IB]

## THE MEAN (ZHONGYONG)

The Chinese title of the essay, *Zhongyong*, is composed of the elements "centrality" or "equilibrium" (*zhong*) and "normality" (*yong*). The translation of these two words as the *Mean* suggests the fundamental moral idea of moderation, balance, and suitable-

---

31. While potentially true of all families, this refers primarily to the ruling house and the ruler himself.

ness. But in this essay the concept is much deeper, denoting a basic norm of human action that, if comprehended and complied with, will bring human beings into harmony with the whole universe.

Another important concept in the *Mean* is that of *cheng*—sincerity or truth. Sincerity involves the moral integrity that enables an individual to become a fully developed person. One is to be "genuine" with others but also "genuinely" oneself, a true human being. But the *Mean* also seeks to relate what is most essential and real in human beings to the underlying reality or truth of the universe. Human virtue does not exist or act in a sphere all its own, an "ethical" sphere that might be understood to be distinct from the metaphysical order. Rather, sincerity puts us in touch with ourselves, with our fellow human beings, and with the universe as a whole. The moral order and the cosmic order are one, and, through ethical cultivation, the individual not only achieves human perfection but also becomes part of a unity with Heaven and Earth. In this way sincerity, as an active and dynamic force, works for the realization not only of human beings but also of all things. The *Mean*, in other words, expresses in psychological and metaphysical terms the same progression from the individual self to world order and unity that the *Great Learning* expresses in social and political terms.

The *Mean* has traditionally been ascribed to Zisi, the grandson of Confucius. Though some scholars have suggested that it may actually be a combination of two or more texts dating in part as late as the Qin or early Han, there is also support in recent scholarship for the view that the text does indeed have much earlier origins.

1. What Heaven has endowed is called the nature. Following the nature is called the Way. Cultivating the Way is called instruction.

The Way cannot be departed from for so much as an instant. If it were possible to depart from it, it would not be the Way. Therefore the noble person is cautious and watchful about what is unseen and fearful and apprehensive about what is unheard. There is nothing more visible than what is hidden, nothing more apparent than what is minute. Therefore the noble person is watchful over himself while alone.

Before pleasure, anger, sorrow, and joy have arisen, this is called centrality. After they have arisen and have attained their appropriate degree, this is called harmony. Equilibrium is the great root of the world, and harmony is the pervasive Way of the world. Once centrality and harmony are realized, Heaven and Earth take their proper places and all living things are nourished.

13. The Master said, "The Way is not far from human beings. If a human being takes as the Way something that distances him from others, it cannot be the Way. The Ode says,

> In hewing an ax handle,
> In hewing an ax handle,
> The pattern is not far off.[32] . . ."

---

32. Ode 158.

14. The noble person acts in accordance with his position and does not desire what goes beyond it. When his situation entails wealth and honor, he acts in a way consistent with wealth and honor. When his situation entails poverty and lowliness, he acts in a way consistent with poverty and lowliness. . . . There is no circumstance in which the noble person is not himself. When he is in a superior position, he does not look down on his inferiors; when he is in an inferior position he does not seek to ingratiate himself with his superiors. Rectifying himself, seeking nothing from others, he is free from resentment. Above, he finds no fault with Heaven; below, he bears no grudge against men. Therefore the noble person remains quiet, awaiting destiny;[33] the small person follows dangerous ways, anticipating good fortune. The Master said, "In archery there is something that resembles the Way of the noble person: when one misses the center of the target, one turns back and seeks the cause within oneself."

20. . . . The Master said, ". . . The universal Way of the world involves five relations, and practicing it involves three virtues. The five are the relations between ruler and minister, between parent and child, between husband and wife, between older and younger brother, and among friends. These five are the universal way of the world. The three—knowledge, humaneness, and courage—are the universal virtues of the world. And the means by which they are practiced is oneness. Some are born with knowledge of them; some attain knowledge of them through learning; and some acquire knowledge of them through painful exertion. But the knowledge having been achieved, it comes to the same thing. . . ."

Sincerity is Heaven's Way; achieving sincerity is the human Way. One who is sincere attains centrality without striving, apprehends without thinking. One who naturally and easily is centered in the Way is a sage. One who attains sincerity chooses what is good and holds to it firmly. This involves broad learning, extensive inquiry, careful thought, clear discrimination, and earnest practice. . . .

22. Only that one in the world who is most perfectly sincere is able to give full development to his nature. Being able to give full development to his nature, he is able to give full development to the nature of other human beings and, being able to give full development to the nature of other human beings, he is able to give full development to the natures of other living things. Being able to give full development to the natures of other living things, he can assist in the transforming and nourishing powers of Heaven and Earth; being able to assist in the transforming and nourishing powers of Heaven and Earth, he can form a triad with Heaven and Earth.

---

33. The Chinese term is *ming*, meaning what is ordained or endowed by Heaven (or, in other contexts, the Mandate of Heaven). It is the same word used in the opening line of the *Mean*, which refers to the nature as that which is *endowed* by Heaven.

25. Sincerity is completing oneself; the Way is to be followed for oneself. Sincerity is the end and the beginning of living things; without sincerity there is nothing. Therefore the noble person regards sincerity as precious. Sincerity is not only completing oneself but is also the means for completing other living things. Completing oneself is humaneness; completing other living things is understanding. These are the virtues of the nature and the way of uniting inner and outer. Therefore whenever one employs them one is right.

26. . . . The Way of Heaven and Earth can be fully expressed in one sentence: these things being without doubleness, their giving birth to living things is unfathomable. The Way of Heaven and Earth is broad, deep, lofty, bright, far-reaching, and long-lasting.

[From *Liji zhengyi* 52:1a–2b, 10a–12b; 53:1a–3b; IB]

## THE MEANING OF SACRIFICES (JIYI)

This chapter of the *Record of Rites* affords a moving insight into the psychology of the most fundamental of all ritual performances — the sacrifice for departed parents.

1. Rites should not be frequently repeated. Such frequency is indicative of importunateness, and importunateness is inconsistent with reverence. Nor should they be at distant intervals. Such infrequency is indicative of indifference; and indifference leads to forgetting them altogether. Therefore the noble person, in harmony with the course of Heaven, offers the sacrifices of spring and autumn. . . .

2. The most complete vigil is carried on inwardly, while a less intense vigil is maintained externally. During the days of such vigil, the mourner thinks of his departed, how and where they sat, how they smiled and spoke, what were their aims and views, what they delighted in, and what things they desired and enjoyed. On the third day of such exercise he will see those for whom it is employed.

5. The noble person, while [his parents] are still alive, reverently nourishes them; and when they are dead, he reverently sacrifices to them; his thought is how to the end of life not to disgrace them. The saying that the noble person mourns all his life for his parents has reference to the recurrence of the day of their death. That he does not do his ordinary work on that day does not mean that it would be unpropitious to do so; it means that on that day his thoughts are occupied with them, and he does not dare to occupy himself as on other days with his private and personal affairs.

8. At the autumnal sacrifice, when Zhongni[34] advanced, bearing the offerings, his general appearance was indicative of simple sincerity, but his steps were short and oft repeated. When the sacrifice was over, Zigong questioned him,

---

34. I.e., Confucius.

saying, "The Master said that sacrifice should be marked by dignity and intense absorption; now how is it that in the Master's sacrificing there is no such dignity and absorption?" The Master said, "Dignity is in the demeanor of one who is distant.[35] Absorption is in the demeanor of one who turns within.[36] . . .

14. A filial son, cherishing a deep love, will have a harmonious air; having a harmonious air, he will have a look of pleasure; having a look of pleasure, his demeanor will be mild and compliant. A filial son will move as if he were carrying jade, as if he were bearing a vessel. Grave, grave! rapt, rapt!—as if he could not bear them, as if he would lose them. A severe gravity and austere manner are not proper to the service of parents: this is the way of the mature man.

20. The rites observed by all-under-Heaven bring about a return to the beginning. They reach spiritual beings, effect harmonious use [of all resources], promote rightness, and encourage humility. Because they bring about a return to the beginning, there is honor for the source. Because they reach spiritual beings, there is respect for superiors. Because they effect harmonious use of things, regulations are established [for the well-being of] the people. Because they promote rightness there is no conflict between high and low. Because they encourage humility occasions of strife are eliminated. Let these five things be united through the rites for the regulation of all-under-heaven, and, though there may be those who are extravagant and perverse and are not kept in order, they will be few.

[*Liji zhengyi* 47:1a–7b; adapted by IB from Legge, *Li ki*]

## THE EVOLUTION OF RITES (*LIYUN*)

The following passage from the *Record of Rites*, one of the most celebrated in Confucian literature, has been traditionally taken as representing Confucius' highest ideal in the social order, the age of Grand Commonalty (*Datong*), in which the world was shared by all the people (*tianxia wei gong*). This ideal has been of special importance in modern China, and the latter motto was often inscribed on public buildings and monuments, such as the tomb of the Nationalist leader Sun Yat-sen. Following the age of Grand Commonalty came the rise of dynastic rule.

This excerpt depicts a primordial ideal state ordered by the spontaneous workings of natural human sentiments in a shared cooperative community—a loving society such as had been identified with the beneficent rule of Emperor Yao in the first chapter of the *Classic of Documents* (*Shujing*). This stage is succeeded by a less

---

35. I.e., distantly connected to the one to whom the sacrifice is directed.
36. Suggesting self-consciousness and concern on the part of the one sacrificing lest he should make any mistake.

perfect human order in which people pursue their own selfish interests and can only be restrained by leaders who civilize them by adopting institutions of government, ritual, and moral instruction. The heroic figures here are Confucian sage kings and worthy ministers who make the best of a less than ideal situation but who are also identified as founders and rulers of dynasties—in this respect not unlike the Han. Thus, responding to time and change, Confucian ideals are adjusted to realistic, historical circumstances.

## The Age of Grand Commonalty and the Rise of Dynastic Rule

[Confucius said,] "The practice of the Great Way, the illustrious men of the Three Dynasties—these I shall never know in person. And yet they inspire my ambition! When the Great Way was practiced, the world was shared by all alike. The worthy and the able were promoted to office and men practiced good faith and lived in affection. Therefore they did not regard as parents only their own parents, or as sons only their own sons. The aged found a fitting close to their lives, the robust their proper employment; the young were provided with an upbringing, and the widow and widower, the orphaned and the sick, with proper care. Men had their tasks and women their hearths. They hated to see goods lying about in waste, yet they did not hoard them for themselves; they disliked the thought that their energies were not fully used, yet they used them not for private ends. Therefore all evil plotting was prevented and thieves and rebels did not arise, so that people could leave their outer gates unbolted. This was the age of Grand Commonalty.

"Now the Great Way has become hid and the world is the possession of private families. Each regards as parents only his own parents, as sons only his own sons; goods and labor are employed for selfish ends. Hereditary offices and titles are granted by ritual law while walls and moats must provide security. . . . Therefore intrigue and plotting come about and men take up arms. Emperor Yu, Kings Tang, Wen, Wu, Cheng, and the Duke of Zhou achieved eminence for this reason: that all six rulers were constantly attentive to ritual, made manifest their rightness, and acted in complete faith. . . . This is the period of Lesser Prosperity."

[From *Liji zhengyi* 21:1a–3a; BW]

### THE RECORD OF MUSIC (YUEJI)

The Confucian rites recognize both the affective nature of man and the need for powerful human emotions to be directed into life-sustaining channels and life-ornamenting expression. The following passage describes how human desires arise in the natural course of things but need to be guided by civilized norms embodied in the rites.

## Human Desires and the Rites

What the ancient kings intended in instituting rites and music was not to satisfy fully the desires of the mouth and the stomach, the ears and the eyes, but to teach people to moderate their likes and dislikes and return to the proper human Way (*rendao*). Human beings are tranquil at birth; this is their nature as given by Heaven. As they are influenced by external things they become active; this is the nature as prompted by desire. With things arriving, and knowledge increasing, likes and dislikes take form in them. When these are not regulated from within, and knowledge misleads from without, they cannot return to themselves, and the principle of Heaven in them is extinguished.

. . . Then the strong coerce the weak; the many oppress the few; the knowing deceive the unknowing; the bold abuse the timid; the ill are not nurtured; the old and the young, the orphaned and the solitary are neglected: such is the way of great chaos. Therefore the ancient kings, in instituting the rites and music, regulated them according to human behavior.

[From *Liji zhengyi* 37:5a–6b; IB]

### BAN GU: *DISCOURSES IN THE WHITE TIGER HALL*

The *Discourses in the White Tiger Hall* (*Bohu tong*), from which this excerpt is taken, is a record by the historian Ban Gu (32–92 C.E.) of discussions on the classics and on Confucian themes held at the court of the Han Emperor Zhang (r. 75–88 C.E.) in 79 C.E. It is typical of the process by which Confucianism became codified through state patronage of classical scholarship linked to public morality. The formula of the "Three Mainstays" (the relationship of ruler/minister, parent/child, husband/wife), though mentioned by Dong Zhongshu, is not found in the Confucian classics, and in giving primacy to state over family loyalties, it stands in some contrast to the Five Moral Relations enunciated in *Mencius*, wherein the parent/child relation takes priority over ruler/minister. Presumably the Han imperial view of cosmic hierarchy, with the ruler in the center, is at work here.

In late imperial China official interpretations of the Three Mainstays (sometimes less literally rendered as the "Three Bonds," *San'gang*), tended to stress subordination of inferiors to superiors in a manner that buttressed hierarchical authority rather than emphasizing the complementarity of human relations. Yet in the *Discourses in the White Tiger Hall* there is a clear reaffirmation of the Confucian emphasis on complementarity, on the heavy moral responsibilities of the ruler, on the minister's duty to remonstrate with the ruler lest he go wrong (or leave his service if this is unavailing), and on the son's duty to remonstrate with his father, as well as the wife's to admonish her husband ("because they form one body and share glory and shame together").[37]

---

37. *Bohu tongde lun* 4:10a.

The *Classic of Filiality* is often quoted to the same effect. Moreover, these positions would be reiterated in the Song by the leading Neo-Confucian thinker, Zhu Xi. Nevertheless, in modern times the view of the Three Mainstays as enforcing a traditional authoritarianism was so strong that twentieth-century critics of Confucianism often singled out the "Three Bonds" for special attack.

## The Three Mainstays

Here *mainstays* (the main ropes of a net) and lesser *ties* (threads) represent the social network and moral fabric that sustain the human order.

What are the Three Mainstays? They are [the relations] of ruler and minister, parent and child, and husband and wife. The six [lesser] ties are those that link the father's brothers, elder and younger brothers, kinsmen, mother's brothers, teachers and elders, and friends. Thus the ruler is the mainstay of the minister, the parent the mainstay of the child, the husband the mainstay of the wife. . . .

What is meant by "mainstays" (*gang*) and "ties" (*ji*)? *Gang* means *zhang*, to extend or lengthen; *ji* means *li*, to order or regulate. The greater ones constitute the mainstays; the lesser ones the ties; thereby the higher and lower are linked and ordered, and the Way of humankind is regulated. All men cherish the instinct for the Five Constant Virtues and possess a loving mind-and-heart, which are developed through the network [of human moral relations], just as a net has mainstays and ties, spreading out into [the fine mesh of] a myriad minor ties.

Why is it that, though ruler and minister, parent and child, husband and wife are altogether six people, they are referred to as the "Three Mainstays"? [Because] the alternation of yin and yang constitutes one Way. The yang completes itself by obtaining the yin; the yin finds order in the yang; the firm and soft complement each other. Therefore, together, the six people make up Three Mainstays.

[From Ban Gu, *Bohu tongde lun*, 7:15a–16a; cf. Tjan,
*Po-hu t'ung*, pp. 467, 559–561; dB]

# HAN VIEWS OF THE UNIVERSAL ORDER

## THE CREATION OF THE UNIVERSE

### FROM THE *HUAINANZI*

The following account of the creation is taken from the *Huainanzi*. Though mainly Daoist in conception, it was adopted by Han Confucians to round out their cosmology, as seen in the previous selection, from the *Discourses in the White Tiger Hall*. This same account of the creation was also taken over by the Japanese and prefaced to their native mythology in the *Nihongi.*

Before Heaven and Earth had taken form all was vague and amorphous. Therefore it was called the Great Beginning. The Great Beginning produced emptiness, and emptiness produced the universe. The universe produced material-force,[38] which had limits. That which was clear and light drifted up to become Heaven, while that which was heavy and turbid solidified to become Earth. It was very easy for the pure, fine material to come together but extremely difficult for the heavy, turbid material to solidify. Therefore Heaven was completed first and Earth assumed shape after. The combined essences of Heaven and Earth became the yin and yang; the concentrated essences of the yin and yang became the four seasons; and the scattered essences of the four seasons became the myriad creatures of the world. After a long time the hot force of the accumulated yang produced fire, and the essence of the fire force became the sun; the cold force of the accumulated yin became water, and the essence of the water force became the moon. The essence of the excess force of the sun and moon became the stars, while Earth received water and soil. [3:1a]

When Heaven and Earth were joined in emptiness and all was unwrought simplicity, then, without having been created, things came into being. This was the Great Oneness. All things issued from this Oneness, but all became different, being divided into various species of fish, birds, and beasts. . . . Therefore while a thing moves it is called living, and when it dies it is said to be exhausted. All are creatures. They are not the uncreated creator of things, for the creator of things is not among things. If we examine the Great Beginning of antiquity we find that man was born out of nothing to assume form as something. Having form, he is governed by things. But he who can return to that from which he was born and become as though formless is called a "true man." The true man is one who has never become separated from the Great Oneness. [14:1a]

[From *Huainanzi* (SBCK) 3:1a, 14:1a; BW]

## THE FIVE PHASES

Similar in concept to the yin-yang theory is that of the Five Phases or Agents (*wuxing*) of fire, water, earth, wood, and metal. The Five Phases were quantitative

---

38. The word *qi*, translated in our readings as "vital force" or "material-force," in order to emphasize its dynamic character, plays an important part in Chinese cosmological and metaphysical thought. At times it means the spirit or breath of life in living creatures, at other times the air or ether filling the sky and surrounding the universe. In some contexts it denotes the basic substance of all creation.

## A Table of Correspondences for the Five-Phases System
### The Five Phases

| Five Phases or Agents | Wood | Fire | Earth | Metal | Water |
|---|---|---|---|---|---|
| *Correspondence* | | | | | |
| Seasons | Spring | Summer | | Autumn | Winter |
| Divine rulers | Tai Hao | Yan Di | Yellow Emperor | Shao Hao | Zhuan Xu |
| Attendant spirits | Gou Mang | Zhu Yong | Hou Tu | Ru Shou | Xuan Ming |
| Sacrifices | inner door | hearth | inner court | outer court | well |
| Animals | sheep | fowl | ox | dog | pig |
| Grains | wheat | beans | panicled millet | hemp | millet |
| Organs | spleen | lungs | heart | liver | kidneys |
| Numbers | eight | seven | five | nine | six |
| Stems | *jia/yi* | *bing/ding* | *mou/ji* | *geng/xin* | *ren/gui* |
| Colors | green | red | yellow | white | black |
| Five tones | *jue* | *zhi* | *gong* | *shang* | *yu* |
| Tastes | sour | bitter | sweet | acrid | salty |
| Smells | goatish | burning | fragrant | rank | rotten |
| Directions | East | South | center | West | North |
| Creatures | scaly | feathered | naked | hairy | shell-covered |
| Beasts of the directions | Green Dragon | Scarlet Bird | Yellow Dragon | White Tiger | Black Tortoise |
| Virtues | humaneness | wisdom | trust | rightness | ritual decorum |
| Planets | Jupiter | Mars | Saturn | Venus | Mercury |
| Officers | Minister of Agriculture | Minister of War | Minister of Works | Minister of Interior | Minister of Justice |

aspects of *qi*, which dominate or control processes in time or configurations in space in a fixed succession. For example, the Five Phases were thought to correlate spatially with the four directions plus the center and to correlate temporally with cyclical signs known as the ten heavenly stems and the twelve earthly branches,[39] as well as with the four seasons and twelve months.

Over time various theories were evolved to explain the cyclical relation among the Five Phases, the two most prominent among them being two major cycles of conquest and generation. According to the "conquest" series, fire is overcome by

---

39. See "The Concept and Marking of Time," pp. 192–93.

water, water by earth, earth by wood, and wood by metal, producing the series: fire—water—earth—wood—metal. The conquest cycle, with its correlated colors and dynasties, was the dominant court ideology of the Qin and Former Han dynasties until Wang Mang[40] replaced the Han with his Xin (or New) dynasty in 9 C.E. At this point the scholars Liu Xiang and Liu Xin, who were influential in laying an ideological foundation for Wang Mang's rule, proposed that the "generation" cycle of the Five Phases should replace the "conquest" cycle as the cosmological foundation for the imperial succession. The essentially Confucian idea of a "generation" cycle was based on the idea that the moral intention of Heaven was to prefer birth and nurturing and to dislike punishment and conquest. According to this "generation" cycle, wood produces fire, fire produces earth, earth produces metal, and metal produces water, yielding the series: wood—fire—earth—metal—water.

## THE RECONSTRUCTION OF CHINESE HISTORY

Important also is the application of this theory to history and the succession of dynasties. As each season is ruled by a phase or agent, so, it was believed, each dynasty ruled by virtue of a phase that it honored by adopting the color of that phase in its vestments and flags, and by similar ritual observances. The First Emperor of the Qin, for instance, believing that his dynasty ruled by the virtue or power of water, adopted black as his official color and even changed the name of the Yellow River to "Water of Power" (Deshui).

Because the Qin had claimed to rule by the power of water, it was urged by some scholars early in the Han that the Han dynasty should adopt earth, with the color yellow, as its phase, to signify that the Han had conquered the Qin, since, according to the "conquest" theory, earth conquers water.

Toward the end of the Former Han, however, there was, as we have noted above, a shift to the "generation" theory advanced by Liu Xiang and Liu Xin. Using this idea newly applied to the interpretation of history, Liu Xin and his school proceeded to reconstruct a history of past ages that would conform to the theory, assigning a ruling element to each ancient dynasty and inserting "intercalary reigns" of the element water where necessary to make it consistent. It is difficult to say exactly when each step of this new theory was set forth or accepted, but it was substantially completed by the time of Wang Mang, who made use of it in justifying his assumption of the throne.

Though with the downfall of Wang Mang many of his innovations and the doubtful texts used to support them were swept away, this account of the ancient past of China continued to be accepted. It is recorded in the *History of the Former Han Dynasty* (*Hanshu*) by Ban Gu,[41] who said he was following Liu

---

40. See chap. 12.
41. *Hanshu* 21B.

Xin, and it was generally accepted in China as historical fact until recent times. Thus, using a preconceived philosophical doctrine of historical evolution, the Chinese, with the best intentions and their customary love of order and system in all things, proceeded to rearrange and tailor their ancient legends and records to fit into a neat pattern that should be both immediately comprehensible in its past and infallibly predictable in its future development.

## THE CONCEPT AND MARKING OF TIME

The Chinese conception of history, as we have seen above, was cyclical. This is only natural, since history is no more than a counterpart in the human sphere of the similar cycles of Heaven and Earth, those of the planets and the seasons. For this reason Chinese historians, unlike their Japanese, Jewish, or Christian counterparts—but like the Greek philosophers—never attempted to assign a temporal beginning or end to the history of the world or the state. Since time is itself a series of cycles based upon the motions of the planets, it may be conceived as extending indefinitely into the past and future for as long as the planets themselves exist.

Dates in Chinese history are customarily recorded in terms of the years of the reigning monarch. But by Han times there was already in use an additional system of cyclical signs for designating years, days, and hours. The origin of these signs, one a set of ten known as the "ten heavenly stems," another of twelve called the "twelve earthly branches," remains today a mystery, though it is apparent that they are very ancient. It is probable that the ten stems were originally designations for the ten days of the ancient ten-day week, the twelve branches designations for the months. These signs and their associations are listed below:

| Five Phases | Ten Stems | Twelve Branches | Beasts | Directions | Hours |
|---|---|---|---|---|---|
| wood | jia | zi | rat | N | 11 P.M.–1 A.M. |
| | yi | chou | ox | NNE | 1–3 |
| fire | bing | yin | tiger | ENE | 3–5 |
| | ding | mao | hare | E | 5–7 |
| earth | mou | chen | dragon | ESE | 7–9 |
| | ji | si | snake | SSE | 9–11 |
| metal | geng | wu | horse | S | 11 A.M.–1 P.M. |
| | xin | wei | sheep | SSW | 1–3 |
| water | ren | shen | monkey | WSW | 3–5 |
| | gui | you | cock | W | 5–7 |
| | | xu | dog | WNW | 7–9 |
| | | hai | boar | NNW | 9–11 |

Sometime during the Zhou dynasty these two sets of signs were combined to form a cycle of sixty binomial terms used to designate a cycle of sixty days.

Again, this cycle of sixty binomial terms (A-I, B-II, etc.) was used to designate cycles of sixty years. The twelve branches, as indicated above, were used to designate thirty-degree divisions of the circle of the horizon. Observing the position of Jupiter in the sky for each year of its twelve-year cycle, the Chinese then employed the sign designating that portion of the sky for the year and combined these with the ten stems to form designations for a sexagenary cycle. This they used to reckon dates independent of the reigns of emperors. Finally, the twelve branches were used to designate twelve two-hour periods making up the day.

At least by Han times these twelve branches had become associated with twelve beasts, as indicated in the table. Because of this, the twelve hours of the day and the years of the sexagenary cycle were each associated with one of these beasts. This system of marking time was adopted by other countries in contact with China. Based on these various associations with the Five Phases and twelve beasts, a great deal of lore concerning lucky and unlucky times grew up about the various cycles. Yet, as we have seen, their basis is rational. They provided the Chinese with a convenient method of reckoning time as useful as Western time divisions, which replaced them only as a part of a thoroughgoing process of Westernization in the modern period.

*Chapter 11*

## THE ECONOMIC ORDER

Han moralists and philosophers, far from ignoring the mundane problems of the human struggle for livelihood, placed great stress on the material needs of the people. The importance of economic thought in the Han derives both from this basic recognition of the "facts of life" and from the appearance in Han times of acute agrarian crises such as have plagued China down through the centuries. The solutions proposed to these crises, as well as the actual measures taken by the government in the Han, tended to set a pattern for later times.

The wars and uprisings that marked the fall of the Qin led to extreme suffering and poverty among the people. Needed to effect a recovery, as the Han quickly realized, was a period of peace and security with a minimum of government expenditure and interference to allow the people to recoup their livelihood. Gaozu, the founder of the Han, therefore relaxed the harsh laws of Qin, reduced the land tax, which under the Qin was said to have been as high as two-thirds of the total produce, and kept court expenditures at a minimum. This policy of frugality and laissez-faire was continued more or less consistently by his successors during the early Han, with the result that the population increased and the nation recovered with remarkable success.

The government did, however, attempt to take steps to control the amassing of large fortunes by industrialists and traders. Gaozu passed sumptuary laws against merchants who had grown rich during the troubled times accompanying the founding of the dynasty, laws designed to turn people from trade—a subsidiary or "branch" activity—back to the fundamental occupation of farming. Though these laws were later relaxed, it was still forbidden for traders or their descendants to hold public office, thus preventing their rise in the social scale. This struggle to keep people in the more productive but less remunerative farming activities from seeking their fortunes in trade and manufacturing continued throughout the Han.

## CHAO CUO: MEMORIAL ON THE ENCOURAGEMENT OF AGRICULTURE

The following memorial, by the eminent Han statesman Chao Cuo, being dated 178 B.C.E., was one of a number of suggestions designed to alleviate the conditions of which he complains. The emperor approved Chao's suggestion, with the result that grain (according to this account) became plentiful and the government granaries were filled.

The reason people never suffered from cold or famine under the rule of the sage kings was not that these kings were capable of plowing to provide food or spinning to make clothes for them. It was that they opened up for the people the way to wealth. Therefore although emperors Yao and Yu encountered nine years of flood and King Tang seven years of drought, there were no derelicts or starving within the kingdom, because provisions had been stored up in plenty and all precaution taken beforehand.

Now all within the seas are united. The plenitude of land and people is not inferior to that of Tang and Yu, and in addition we have not suffered from natural calamities of flood or drought for several years. Why then are the stores of supplies so inferior? Because the land has benefits that have been overlooked and the people have untapped energies. There is still land suitable for growing grain that has not been brought under cultivation, resources of hills and lakes that have not been exploited, and vagrants who have not yet returned to agricultural pursuits. When the people are in poverty, then crime and evil-doing are born. Poverty is bred of insufficiency that is caused by lack of agriculture. If men do not farm, they will not be tied to the land; and if they are not tied to the land, they will desert their villages, neglect their families, and become like birds and beasts. Then although there be high walls and deep moats, strict laws and severe punishments, they still cannot be held in check.

. . . An enlightened ruler, realizing this, will encourage his people in agriculture and sericulture, lighten the poll tax and other levies, increase his store of supplies and fill his granaries in preparation for flood and drought. Thereby he can keep and care for his people. The people may then be led by the ruler, for they will follow after profit in any direction like water flowing downward.

Now pearls, jewels, gold, and silver can neither allay hunger nor keep out the cold, and yet the people all hold them dear because these are things used by the ruler. They are light and easy to store, and one who holds them in his grasp may roam the world and never fear hunger or cold. They cause ministers lightly to turn their backs upon their lords and the people easily to leave their villages; they provide an incentive for thieves and a light form of wealth for fugitives.

Grains and fibers, on the other hand, are produced from the land, nurtured through the seasons, and harvested with labor; they cannot be gotten in a day. Several measures of grain or cloth are too heavy for an average man to carry and so provide no reward for crime or evil. Yet if people go without them for one day they will face hunger and cold. Therefore an enlightened ruler esteems the five grains and despises gold and jewels.

At present in a farming family of five not fewer than two are required to perform labor service [for the state], while those who are left to work the farm are given no more than one hundred *mu* of land, the yield of which is not over one hundred *piculs*. . . . No matter how diligently they work nor what hardships they suffer, they still must face the calamities of flood and drought, emergency government measures, inordinate tax levies, and taxes collected out of season. Orders issued in the morning are changed before nightfall. Faced with such levies, the people must sell what they have at half price in order to pay, and those who have nothing must take money offered at 100 percent interest. Thus they are forced to sell their fields and houses, vend their children and grandchildren, to pay their debts.

Among the traders and merchants, on the other hand, the larger ones hoard goods and exact 100 percent profit, while the smaller ones sit lined up in the markets selling their wares. Those who deal in luxury goods daily disport themselves in the cities and market towns; taking advantage of the ruler's wants, they are able to sell at double price. Thus though their men neither plow nor weed, though their women neither tend silkworms nor spin, yet their clothes are brightly patterned and colored, and they eat only choice grain and meat. They have none of the hardships of the farmer, yet their grain is ten to one hundred-fold. With their wealth they may consort with nobles, and their power exceeds the authority of government officials. They use their profits to overthrow others. Over a thousand miles they wander at ease, their caps and cart covers filling the roads. They ride in fine carriages and drive fat horses, tread in silken shoes and trail white silk behind them. Thus it is that merchants encroach upon the farmers, and the farmers are driven from their homes and become vagrants.

At present, although the laws degrade the merchants, the merchants have become wealthy and honored, and although they honor the farmers, the farmers have grown poor and lowly. Thus what common practice honors the ruler degrades, and what the officials scorn the law exalts. With ruler and ruled thus at variance and their desires in conflict, it is impossible to hope that the nation will become rich and the law be upheld.

Under the present circumstances there is nothing more urgently needed than to make the people devote themselves to agriculture. To accomplish this one must enhance the value of grain. This may be done by making it possible for the people to use grain to obtain rewards and avoid punishments. If an order is sent out that all who send grain to the government shall obtain honorary rank or pardon from crimes, then wealthy men will acquire rank, the farmers will have money, and grain will circulate freely. . . . All men greatly desire to obtain high ranks and avoid penalties. If all are allowed to present grain for supplying the frontiers and thereby obtain rank or commutation of penalties, then in no more than three years there will be plenty of grain for the border areas.

[From *Hanshu* (*BNB*) 24A:9b–13a; BW]

### DONG ZHONGSHU: MEMORIAL ON LAND REFORM

In the latter years of his life the famous Confucian Dong Zhongshu[1] submitted a memorial to Emperor Wu advising limitation of land and slave ownership and other measures to relieve the rapidly developing agrarian crisis. Because of opposition from wealthy families and powerful officials, his suggestions and similar ones made later were never put into effect. It is noteworthy that Dong, while proclaiming the ancient "well-field" system of equal ownership as the ideal, did not go so far as to advocate its restoration. Not until Wang Mang came to power was this drastic step attempted to return to the ideal enshrined in Confucian tradition.

In ancient times the people were not taxed over one-tenth of their produce, a demand that they could easily meet. They were required to give no more than three days of labor a year, which they could easily spare. The people had wealth enough to take care of the aged and look after their parents, serve their superiors and pay their taxes, and support their wives and loved ones. Therefore they took delight in obeying their rulers.

But the Qin changed all this. It used the methods of Shang Yang (Legalism), altered the imperial institutions, did away with the well-field system, and allowed the people to buy and sell land. The rich bought up great connecting tracts of ground, and the poor were left without enough land to stick the point of an awl into. In addition, the rich had sole control of the resources of rivers and lakes and the riches of hills and forests. Their profligacy overstepped all restrictions and they outdid each other in extravagance. In the cities they commanded as much respect as the rulers, and in the villages their wealth equaled that of the nobles. How could the common people escape oppression? . . .

Since the Han began it has followed the ways of the Qin without change. Although it would be difficult to restore at once the ancient well-field system, it is proper that present usage be brought somewhat closer to the old ways. Ownership of land should be limited so that those who do not have enough may be relieved and the road to unlimited encroachment blocked. The rights to salt and iron should revert to the people. Slavery and the right to execute servants

---

1. See chap. 10.

on one's own authority should be abolished. Poll taxes and other levies should be reduced and labor services lightened so that the people will be less pressed. Only then can they be well governed.

[From *Hanshu* (BNB) 24A:14b–15b; BW]

## STATE CONTROL OF COMMERCE AND INDUSTRY

Ban Gu, principal author of the *History of the Former Han Dynasty*, saw the reign of Emperor Wu as the turning point from prosperity to eventual ruin of the dynasty. Though economic life recovered considerably after Wu's reign, the historian designated this period as the beginning of policies and trends that led to the downfall of the Han.

The non-Chinese tribes bordering China on the north and west had constituted a constant menace to the empire, frequently invading and pillaging as far as the capital itself. Emperor Wu set out upon a series of military conquests that extended Chinese hegemony far out to the northwest, placing the empire for the first time in close contact with the states of Central and Western Asia and indirectly with Rome. Following these conquests, he undertook vast programs of colonization of the newly acquired areas, as well as extensive canal and road building, repairing of dikes, and other government projects. Famous and glorious as these military conquests and other undertakings were, they may well have undermined the economic health of the nation. Because of the frugality of his predecessors and the prosperity of the empire, Wu was able to embark upon his grandiose plans. But he soon found it necessary to secure new revenues to sustain them.

The means that he took to acquire the needed funds were not really in the nature of a state-planned economy to benefit the nation as a whole, though this was claimed for them; they were merely attempts to fill the imperial coffers at any cost.

Perhaps most famous and widely discussed of his fiscal measures was the setting up of government monopolies in iron, salt, liquor, and coinage of money, as well as offices to engage in government trading. The iron and salt industries had formerly been the source of great wealth to private individuals or feudal lords who controlled them. By making them government monopolies the emperor sought to divert these profits to the imperial treasury. Moreover, he set up, under a bureau of "Equalization and Standardization," a system of government marketing offices that bought up goods at low prices or collected taxes in produce and sold them in other areas or, at other times, at an advantageous price. Though it was claimed that this measure, like the salt and iron monopolies, was designed to protect the people from exploitation by unscrupulous private traders, its main function was to secure government revenues.

Emperor Wu, though professing support of Confucian ideals, was, in fact, by establishing such government monopolies and controls, using traditional

Legalist methods such as the Qin had followed. Moreover, to ensure the success of his ventures, he appointed competent industrialists and financial experts to administer the government monopolies, pursuing Legalist policies.

In 81 B.C.E., shortly after the death of Emperor Wu, a debate was called at court between these Legalist officials, headed by the Lord Grand Secretary, and a group of Confucian literati representing the opposition. A record of this famous debate, the *Debate on Salt and Iron (Yantie lun)*, shows clearly the struggle of the Confucian scholars to reverse the policies of the Legalists installed by Emperor Wu.

## THE DEBATE ON SALT AND IRON

In this debate the government argued that its fiscal policies were necessary to maintain defensive warfare against the Xiongnu tribes (probably Huns) who threatened the empire; that the government by its disinterested control of vital industries was protecting the people from private exploitation; and, finally, that the trade opened up by the western expansion had brought to the empire heretofore unknown goods and luxuries such as horses, camels, furs, rugs, precious stones, exotic fruits, and so on.

To these arguments the Confucian literati stolidly replied that the Chinese had no business in the barbarian lands of Central Asia, that China should make peace with its neighbors and be content to remain safely within its traditional boundaries. The government, they claimed, was in actuality entering into competition with the people (private enterprise) in trade, an area outside its proper sphere of activity. On the question of increased foreign trade, they noted that the furs, precious stones, and exotic fruits bought with silk produced at great labor by the common people found their way only to the houses of the rich and noble. The debate was a lively affair, the government constantly taunting the scholars with their poverty, which, though claimed as evidence of their frugality and moral probity, was alleged by their critics to be proof of their incompetence in worldly affairs. The scholars replied that the government's pursuit of increased revenue was not, as claimed, serving the public interest but instead set a bad example of profiting at the people's expense, thereby undermining public morality by putting "profit" ahead of what was right. Many of these arguments were couched in terms of the doctrines of Mencius on governing through humaneness and rightness, maintaining the well-field system of equal landholding, and providing schools to educate the people.

The literati had some immediate success, but the government monopolies were not all abolished because of the need for revenue, and many of the same economic problems persisted.

In the sixth year of the era Shiyuan [81 B.C.E.], an imperial edict was issued directing the chancellor and the imperial secretaries to confer with the worthies and literati who had been recommended to the government and to inquire into the grievances and hardships of the people.

The literati responded: We have heard that the way to govern men is to prevent evil and error at their source, to broaden the beginnings of morality, to discourage secondary occupations, and open the way for the exercise of humaneness and rightness. Never should material profit appear as a motive of government. Only then can moral instruction succeed and the customs of the people be reformed. But now in the provinces the salt, iron, and liquor monopolies and the system of equitable marketing have been established to compete with the people for profit, dispelling rustic generosity and teaching the people greed. Therefore those who pursue primary occupations [farming] have grown few and those following secondary occupations [trading] numerous. As artifice increases, basic simplicity declines; and as the secondary occupations flourish, those that are primary suffer. When the secondary is practiced the people grow decadent, but when the primary is practiced they are simple and sincere. . . . We recommend that the salt, iron, and liquor monopolies and the system of equitable marketing be abolished so that primary pursuits may be advanced and secondary ones suppressed. This will have the advantage of increasing the profitableness of agriculture.

His Lordship [the Imperial Secretary Sang Hongyang] replied: The Xiongnu have frequently revolted against our sovereignty and pillaged our borders. If we are to defend ourselves, then it means the hardships of war for the soldiers of China, but if we do not defend ourselves properly, then their incursions cannot be stopped. . . . [sec. 1, 1:1a–2a]

His Lordship stated: In former times the peers residing in the provinces sent in their respective products as tribute, but there was much confusion and trouble in transporting them and the goods were often of such poor quality that they were not worth the cost of transportation. For this reason transportation offices have been set up in each district to handle delivery and shipping and to facilitate the presentation of tribute from outlying areas. Therefore the system is called "equitable marketing." Warehouses have been opened in the capital for the storing of goods, buying when prices are low and selling when they are high. Thereby the government suffers no loss and the merchants cannot speculate for profit. Therefore this is called the "balanced level" [stabilization]. With the balanced level the people are protected from unemployment, and with equitable marketing the burden of labor service is equalized. Thus these measures are designed to ensure an equal distribution of goods and to benefit the people and are not intended to open the way to profit or provide the people with a ladder to crime.

The literati replied: In ancient times taxes and levies took from the people what they were skilled in producing and did not demand what they were poor at. Thus the husbandmen sent in their harvests and the weaving women their goods. Nowadays the government disregards what people have and requires of them what they have not, so that they are forced to sell their goods at a cheap price in order to meet the demands from above. . . . The farmers suffer double hardships and the weaving women are taxed twice. We have not seen that this kind of marketing is "equitable." The government officials go about recklessly opening closed doors and buying everything at will so they can corner all the goods. With goods cornered prices soar, and when prices soar the merchants make their own deals for profit. The officials wink at powerful racketeers, and the rich merchants hoard commodities and wait for an emergency. With slick merchants and corrupt officials buying cheap and selling dear we have not seen that your level is "balanced." The system of equitable marketing of ancient times was designed to equalize the burden of labor upon the people and facilitate the transporting of tribute. It did not mean dealing in all kinds of commodities for the sake of profit. [sec. 1:5a–b]

### Confucian Literati Ridiculed

His Excellency spoke: . . . Now we have with us over sixty worthy men and literati who cherish the ways of the Six Confucian Arts, fleet in thought and exhaustive in argument. It is proper, gentlemen, that you should pour forth your light and dispel our ignorance. And yet you put all your faith in the past and turn your backs upon the present, tell us of antiquity and give no thought to the state of the times. Perhaps we are not capable of recognizing true scholars. Yet do you really presume with your fancy phrases and attacks upon men of ability to pervert the truth in this manner? [sec. 10, 2:10a–b]

See them [the Confucians] now present us with nothingness and consider it substance, with emptiness and call it plenty! In their coarse gowns and worn shoes they walk gravely along, sunk in meditation as though they had lost something. These are not men who can do great deeds and win fame. They do not even rise above the vulgar masses. [sec. 19, 4:10b]

[From *Yantie lun*, sec. 1, 1:1a–5b; sec. 10, 2:10a–b; sec. 19, 4:10b; BW]

# THE REFORMS OF WANG MANG

Though a brief period of prosperity followed the relaxation of Emperor Wu's fiscal policies, the economic health of the nation gradually worsened. Corruption spread through the government from top to bottom. In spite of frequent recommendations for the limitation of land and slave ownership, land and wealth became concentrated in the hands of large official or merchant families. As the peasants were deprived of their land or lost it because of natural disasters, they went into slavery or formed bands of robbers. Government-maintained dikes and waterworks fell into disrepair, increasing the menace of flood and drought. It was when conditions had reached a critical stage that Wang Mang managed to seize power and attempted to remedy the situation by a series of sweeping reforms.

## WANG MANG: EDICT ON LAND REFORM

In 9 C.E. Wang Mang ordered the establishment of an equal landholding system based on the ancient "well-field" ideal. This involved the nationalization of all land, abolition of private landholding and prohibition of the sale of land or slaves. The attempt proved a failure and was repealed three years later. Subsequent proposals for solution of the land problem, which was a chronic difficulty in later dynasties, tended to follow along the lines suggested by these Han reformers, i.e., either simple limitation on landholding or outright nationalization and redistribution. Note how Wang Mang's edict follows the wording of Dong Zhongshu's memorial above.

The ancients set up cottages and wells with eight families to a "well-unit" (900 *mu*). One husband and wife cultivated one hundred *mu* of land, remitting one-tenth of the produce as tax. Thus the state enjoyed plenty, the people were rich, and the sound of hymns of praise arose in the land. This was the way of Yao and Shun, and it was followed and continued by the Three Dynasties. But the Qin was without principle and increased the levies and taxes for its own use, exhausting the strength of the people with its inordinate desires. . . .

The House of Han lightened the tax on land to one-thirtieth of the produce. However, there were taxes for commutation of military service, which even the aged and ill had to pay. In addition, the powerful and rich families oppressed the people, allotting lands for cultivation to sharecroppers and plundering them by high rents for borrowed lands. Thus, though in name the tax was one-thirtieth, actually it amounted to one-half. Though father and son, husband and wife, year in and year out plowed and weeded, yet the produce left to them was not enough to support life. Therefore the rich, whose very horses and dogs had a surplus of meal and grain, grew arrogant and perpetrated evil deeds, while the poor, without even the dregs of grain to satisfy themselves with, were reduced to despair and turned to a life of crime. Both sank into wickedness, and punishments had to be used and could not be set aside.

Formerly, when I occupied the position of regent, it was my intention to nationalize all land and apportion it into "well-units" according to the population. At that time the empire enjoyed the portentous blessing of the double-headed grain, but because of the unfortunate occurrence of rebellions and banditry, I was forced temporarily to abandon my plans.

Now at this time let the term be altered and the land throughout the empire be designated "king's fields" and slaves be called "private retainers." Neither land nor slaves are to be bought or sold. Those families whose adult males do not number eight, but whose fields amount to more than one "well-unit," shall divide the surplus lands among their near relatives of the nine generations and the people of their townships and boroughs. Thus those who are without lands shall justly receive them according to this system. Anyone who shall dare to criticize the well-field system of the sages, or seek in defiance of the law to delude the populace, shall be cast out beyond the four borders to face demons and evil spirits.

[From Hanshu (BNB) 99B:9a–10a; BW]

Wang Mang revived all the monopolies of Emperor Wu on coinage, salt, iron, liquor, and natural resources; he also restored the system of government marketing. As formerly, this had the same effect: it forced up the prices of necessary commodities, lowered the quality, deprived many people of their livelihood, and imposed an additional tax burden upon the population. In addition he imposed taxes on artisans and professional men, forced the officials to take reductions in salary during bad years, and demanded voluntary contributions of four-fifths of their salary to support military expenses.

These activities of Wang's brief reign served to antagonize all classes of society, and his purported attempts to revive ancient practices cost him the backing of the Confucian bureaucracy that had earlier supported him. Without the confidence of his officials, his measures foundered on the administrative level because of noncooperation and corruption. He tried vainly to carry on alone, working day and night to handle all administrative matters personally. But as Ban Gu relates in the *Hanshu*, nothing availed to allay the disaffection:

> The people could not turn a hand without violating some prohibition. . . . The rich had no means to protect themselves and the poor no way to stay alive. They rose up and became thieves and bandits, infesting the hills and marshes, and the officials, being unable to seize them, contrived on the contrary to hide their presence so that they grew more prevalent day by day. . . . Famine and pestilence raged and people ate each other so that before Wang Mang was finally punished half the population of the empire had perished. . . . [In 25 C.E.] the founder of the Eastern Han received the Mandate of Heaven and, washing away their vexations and hardships, together with all people of the empire made a "new beginning."[2]

This "new beginning" carried the Han dynasty until its final fall in 220 C.E. The period that followed was one of relative peace and cultural attainment. Yet the same economic problems that marked the history of the Former Han repeated themselves with ineluctable persistence. Court intrigue, official corruption, the concentration of land in the hands of wealthy families, and the displacement of the people from their fields, which turned them to banditry—all of this bred warlordism and antidynastic revolution. The reign of Wang Mang, which itself involved a prolongation and aggravation of the agrarian crisis of the Former Han, had precipitated a peasant revolt known as the Red Eyebrows,

---

2. *Hanshu* 24B:25a–b. The Eastern Han is also known as the Latter Han.

originating in the eastern province of Shandong. The Latter Han fell victim to a similar revolt, which began, under Daoist influence, in Sichuan, led by a group known as the Yellow Turbans. This cycle of agrarian crisis and decay of the central government, climaxed by peasant revolts originating in the hinterland, formed a recurring pattern in later Chinese history.

## Chapter 12

### THE GREAT HAN HISTORIANS

The intellectual and literary glory of the Han found its highest expression in two great histories of the period, the *Records of the Grand Historian* (*Shiji*) and the *History of the Former Han* (*Hanshu*). Few works outside the classics themselves have been so much admired, studied, and often in part committed to memory by the Chinese. They set the pattern for all later Chinese histories, establishing a precedent that was responsible for giving to the Chinese the most complete and unbroken record of their past possessed by any people.

From very early times the Chinese seem to have possessed an extraordinary love and respect for history. According to tradition, even the earliest dynasties had their official historians, who were closely associated with astronomical affairs and divination. They were also responsible for acting as mentors to the rulers, instructing them in the lessons of the past, and recording their deeds for the judgment of posterity. Confucianism, with its humanistic emphasis, did much to encourage and develop this sense of history and feeling for the past. Two of the five Confucian Classics, the *Classic of Documents* and the *Spring and Autumn Annals*, traditionally believed to have been compiled and edited by Confucius, are historical works, and the appeal to past example has always been among the principle techniques of Confucian instruction and argumentation.

The *History of the Former Han Dynasty* says of these two historical classics: "The *Classic of Documents* broadens one's information and is the practice of wisdom; the *Spring and Autumn Annals* passes moral judgments on events and is the symbol of trustworthiness."[1]

The function of history, as seen in this statement, is twofold: to impart tradition and to provide edifying moral examples as embodied in the classics. These two traditions, one recording the words and deeds of history, the other illustrating moral principles through historical incidents, run through all Chinese historiography. In practice, the former tradition has dominated. The common method of the Chinese historian has been to transmit verbatim as nearly as possible what his sources tell him, adding only such background and connecting narrative as may be necessary. For example, the historian does not tell us that the emperor issued an edict to such and such an effect but reproduces the edict whole or in part so that we may read what he said for ourselves. Since the Chinese historian was often working in an official capacity, he had access to government files of memorials, edicts, court decisions, and other papers that made such a procedure possible. His own job, then, became one of selecting the most pertinent documents and arranging them in a way best calculated to demonstrate the cause and effect of events. If in addition he wished to inject his own personal opinion, he usually marked it clearly by some conventional literary device so that the reader could readily distinguish it.

The tradition of the *Spring and Autumn Annals*, the didactic function of history, was by no means forgotten. Only a sage might dare actually to record moral judgments in his writing, as Confucius was supposed to have done in the *Spring and Autumn Annals*. But all literate people were expected to study the histories of the past carefully and thoughtfully to deduce for themselves the moral lessons embodied there, to descry the pattern hidden beneath the succession of recorded events. For, like all the rest of creation, history was thought to manifest an underlying order and process. Han scholars, influenced by yin-yang and Five Phases theories, conceived of history as a cyclical succession of eras proceeding in a fixed order. Not only this succession but all of history was a manifestation of the universal process of birth, growth, decay, and rebirth, constantly coming to realization in the course of human events. Thus, for the Confucian scholar, the proper study of humankind is human life as revealed in the pages of history.

## THE *RECORDS OF THE GRAND HISTORIAN*

During the Zhou, numerous chronicles and works of history were compiled by the various states and schools of philosophy. But not until the Han, when the Chinese acquired a new sense of cultural unity, was there any evidence of

---

1. *Hanshu* 30:12b.

an attempt to produce a comprehensive history of the entire past. The *Records of the Grand Historian (Shiji)* was begun by Sima Tan (d. 110 B.C.E.), Grand Historian under Emperor Wu, and carried on and brought to completion by his son, Sima Qian (145?–86? B.C.E.), who succeeded to his father's position. Comprising 130 chapters, it covers the history of the Chinese people from the Yellow Emperor to the time of the historians.

Sima Qian divided his material into five sections: "Basic Annals," "Chronological Tables," "Treatises," "Hereditary Houses," and "Memoirs." This arrangement, with various modifications, has been followed by almost all later official historians. In later histories the section called "Basic Annals" might better be referred to as "Imperial Annals," since it deals only with acts of the officially reigning emperors. Sima Qian, however, did not so confine himself but included here the account of Xiang Yu, who, though not officially emperor, in actuality ruled the country for a time. The "Chronological Tables" needs little explanation, being tables of dates for important events. The "Treatises," one of the most valuable parts of the work, comprises essays devoted to the history and description of important institutional matters and topical subjects. Below are listed the eight Treatises of the *Shiji* together with those of the *Hanshu* that were based upon *Shiji* material.

| *Shiji Treatises* | *Hanshu Treatises* |
|---|---|
| Rites | The Calendar |
| Music | Rites and Music |
| The Pitch Pipes | Punishments and Laws |
| The Calendar | Food and Money (Economics) |
| Astronomy | State Sacrifices |
| Sacrifices of Feng and Shan[2] | Astronomy |
| The Yellow River and Canals | Five Phases (Portents) |
| Balance of Commerce (Economics) | Geography |
| | Land Drainage |
| | Literature |

"Hereditary Houses," being largely accounts of feudal families, was not usually included after the abolition of the enfeoffment system. The "Memoirs" section was generally devoted to the lives of famous persons—military leaders, politicians, philosophers, and so on. Some chapters deal with particular groups such as famous assassins, upright officials, tyrannical officials, wandering knights, imperial favorites, and merchants. Others treat non-Chinese lands and people,

---

2. The Feng and Shan were sacrifices of the greatest solemnity, performed by the emperor at the sacred Mount Tai and addressed to Heaven and Earth respectively.

including those of Korea, southeast China, and Ferghana. The concluding chapter is the biography of the historians themselves.

### SIMA QIAN: THE SACRED DUTY OF THE HISTORIAN

The following excerpt from the autobiography of Sima Qian relates the words of Sima Tan to his son as he lay dying.

The Grand Historian [Sima Tan] grasped my hand and said, weeping, "Our ancestors were Grand Historians for the House of Zhou. From the most ancient times they were eminent and renowned when in the days of Yu and Xia they were in charge of astronomical affairs. In later ages our family declined. Will this tradition end with me? If you in turn become Grand Historian, you must continue the work of our ancestors. . . . When you become Grand Historian, you must not forget what I have desired to expound and write. Now, filial piety begins with the serving of your parents; next, you must serve your sovereign; and, finally, you must make something of yourself, that your name may go down through the ages to the glory of your father and mother. This is the most important part of filial piety. Everyone praises the Duke of Zhou, saying that he was able to expound in word and song the virtues of King Wen and King Wu, publishing abroad the odes of Zhou and Shao; he set forth the thoughts and ideals of Taiwang and Wang Ji, extending his words back to King Liu and paying honor to Hou Ji [ancestors of the Zhou dynasty]. After the reigns of Yu and Li the way of the ancient kings fell into disuse and rites and music declined. Confucius revived the old ways and restored what had been abandoned, expounding the *Odes* and *Documents* and making the *Spring and Autumn Annals*. From that time until today men of learning have taken these as their models. It has now been over four hundred years since the capture of the unicorn [481 B.C.E.]. The various feudal states have merged together, and the old records and chronicles have become scattered and lost. Now the House of Han has arisen and all the world is united under one rule. I have been Grand Historian, and yet I have failed to make a record of all the enlightened rulers and wise lords, the faithful ministers and gentlemen who were ready to die for duty. I am fearful that the historical material will be neglected and lost. You must remember and think of this!"

I bowed my head and wept, saying, "I, your son, am ignorant and unworthy, but I shall endeavor to set forth in full the reports of antiquity that have come down from our ancestors. I dare not be remiss!" . . .

[From *Shiji* (BNB) 130:8a–b; BW]

In 98 B.C.E., because he dared to speak out in defense of a military leader whom Emperor Wu and the rest of the court believed had disgraced himself, Sima Qian was condemned to suffer the punishment of castration. The following excerpt is from a famous letter that the historian wrote to a friend relating the circumstances of his disgrace and explaining why it was he chose to suffer the ignominy of castration rather than commit suicide. He consoles himself with the memory of the great men of the past who, in the midst of misfortune, produced writings that have guaranteed their everlasting fame, as he believes his history will do for him.

My father had no great deeds that entitled him to receive territories or privileges from the emperor. He dealt with affairs of astronomy and the calendar, which are close to divination and the worship of the spirits. He was kept for the sport and amusement of the emperor, treated the same as the musicians and jesters, and made light of by the vulgar men of his day. If I fell before the law and were executed, it would make no more difference to most people than one hair off nine oxen, for I was nothing but a mere ant to them. The world would not rank me among those men who were able to die for their ideals, but would believe simply that my wisdom was exhausted and my crime great, that I had been unable to escape penalty and in the end had gone to my death. Why? Because all my past actions had brought this on me, they would say.

A man has only one death. That death may be as weighty as Mount Tai, or it may be as light as a goose feather. It all depends upon the way he uses it. . . . It is the nature of every man to love life and hate death, to think of his relatives and look after his wife and children. Only when a man is moved by higher principles is this not so. . . .

. . . I have gathered up and brought together the old traditions of the world that were scattered and lost. I have examined the deeds and events of the past and investigated the principles behind their success and failure, their rise and decay, in 130 chapters. I wished to examine into all that concerns Heaven and the human, to penetrate the changes of the past and present, completing all as the work of one family. But before I had finished my rough manuscript, I met with this calamity. It is because I regretted that it had not been completed that I submitted to the extreme penalty without rancor. When I have truly completed this work, I shall deposit it in some safe place. If it may be handed down to men who will appreciate it and penetrate to the villages and great cities, then, though I should suffer a thousand mutilations, what regret would I have?

[From *Hanshu* (BNB) 62:17b–21b; BW]

## THE WRITING OF THE FIRST DYNASTIC HISTORY

The historical labors of Sima Qian were admirably carried on by Ban Biao (3–54 C.E.) and his son Ban Gu (32–92 C.E.), principal authors of the *History of the Former Han Dynasty* [*Hanshu*]. The following extracts are from the biographies of Ban Biao and Ban Gu in the *History of the Latter Han Dynasty*. It was apparently Ban Biao's intention only to continue the writing of history from the point at which Sima Qian had stopped. But Ban Gu conceived the idea of one unified work covering the entire Former Han period. His *Hanshu*, covering the complete span of one dynasty, has been the model for all the later "dynastic histories" compiled to cover every reigning house from Ban Gu's time down to the founding of the Republic in 1911.

It is noteworthy that Ban Gu's daughters carried on the scholarly traditions of their family, and his sister Ban Zhao (48?–116? C.E.), recognized at court for her scholarship, wrote the *Admonitions for Women* excerpted in chapter 23.

Ban Biao had great talent and was fond of writing, devoting himself solely to histories and chronicles. At the time of Emperor Wu, Sima Qian wrote the *Records of the Grand Historian* [*Shiji*], but for the period from the Taichu era [104–101 B.C.E.] on, the volumes were lacking or had never been written. . . . Biao then took up this work, continuing and selecting material from earlier histories and supplementing it with various traditions, and composed a "Supplementary Chronicle" in several tens of chapters.

Ban Gu took the continuation of the former history that Ban Biao had written and, since it was incomplete, immersed himself in study and shaped its ideas, intending to bring it to completion. At this time, however, someone sent a letter to Emperor Xianzong informing him that Ban Gu was privately revising and writing a dynastic history. An order was issued to the prefecture for Gu's arrest, and he was bound and placed in prison in the capital and all his personal books were seized. . . . Gu's younger brother, Chao, fearing that in the prefectural inquiry Gu would not be able to make his case clear, hastened to the capital and sent a request to the emperor for an audience. There he explained in detail what Gu's intentions were in writing his work, and the prefecture also sent Gu's book. Emperor Xianzong was amazed at it and summoned Gu to the Department for the Editing of Books, where he was appointed one of the official historiographers of the Lantai. . . . The emperor charged him to complete the former history. . . . He ordered all events, imbued them with the spirit of the Five Classics, and penetrated into all things above and below, completing season-by-season "Annals," "Chronological Tables," "Treatises," and "Memoirs," one hundred chapters in all. . . . His own age greatly honored his work and among men of learning there were none who did not read and praise it.

[From *Hou Hanshu* (BNB) 40A:2b–3a, 11b–12b; BW]

# Chapter 13

## LEARNING OF THE MYSTERIOUS

For almost four centuries after the disintegration of the Han dynasty, China was to be without that unity and stability that had seemed for the previous four centuries to be one of its chief characteristics. Instead, during the period of the Three Kingdoms and the Northern and Southern dynasties (220–589 C.E.), China's division into numerous contending states and subjection to successive ruling houses brought her perilously close to a loss of cultural identity—or so it appeared to many who lived during these troubled times. Owing to the prevailing disunity and disruption, the situation was hardly favorable to the kind of scholarly enterprise that the imperial court had once encouraged; at the same time Confucianism was deprived of its importance as a state cult. The textual study of the classics that had absorbed many of the best minds during the Han shifted to a different plane now that classical scholarship served no vital function for state or society. It was under such circumstances that intellectual interest in Daoism revived and a foreign religion, Buddhism, first gained a foothold among both the masses and the educated class.

The "Learning of the Mysterious," or *xuanxue*, was a many-sided movement that found expression in the spheres of metaphysics, religion, literature, and aesthetics. It can be described as a revival of Daoism in the sense that it centered on the study of the *Laozi* or *Daodejing*,[1] the *Zhuangzi*,[2] and the *Classic of*

---

1. See chap. 5.
2. Ibid.

*Changes*[3]—the first two being core texts of the Daoist tradition, the third having become during the Han period a classic revered by Confucians and Daoists alike. The term *xuan*—meaning "deep, dark, abstruse, profound, or mysterious"—is very old, being found on oracle-bone inscriptions. But for those steeped in Daoist tradition, *xuan* would specifically have recalled the first chapter of the *Laozi*, which, in its closing lines, evokes a reality recognized as "mysterious (*xuan*) and still more mysterious, the gateway of all subtleties!"[4]

Among the major contributors to the Learning of the Mysterious were Wang Bi (226–249 C.E.) and He Yan (d. 249 C.E.), both admirers of the *Laozi* and authors of early commentaries on that text, and Guo Xiang (d. 312 C.E.), author of what is still the most famous commentary on the *Zhuangzi*.[5] Probing the metaphysical depths of Daoism, these commentators shared a common search for the source of unity or oneness in a world in which any semblance of unity had disappeared from the political and social realm. Yet their philosophical explorations went far beyond elaboration of the earlier Daoist tradition, and the spirit in which these explorations were carried on was anything but detached. In a climate that was conducive to escapism and abandonment of the public sphere—and that demonstrably prompted just such a response on the part of some of their contemporaries—all three of these leading figures of *xuanxue* were involved in government and served in official positions. Committed to the value of active involvement in the world, they may be said to have reinterpreted Daoism in the light of the social and moral philosophy of Confucianism. Thus, while the Learning of the Mysterious was philosophically innovative, it did not entail a complete redirection of Chinese thought. In spite of Confucianism's decline as the basis of the bureaucratic institution, its ideals and values would remain important, and in this period, as in so many others in Chinese history, there was a strong tendency toward syncretism.

## WANG BI

Wang Bi's philosophical accomplishments were remarkable, particularly when we consider the fact that he lived in such troubled times and died at the early age of twenty-four. In some respects his underlying concerns resembled those of his predecessors in the Han period. Like Dong Zhongshu, for example, Wang devoted himself to the relation between ontology and ethics—that is, to the connections between how things ultimately are and how virtue is to be attained. But, perhaps in part because unity in the political sphere was now so obviously lacking and an imperial government was no longer a fixed point of reference,

---

3. See chap. 10.

4. See chap. 5.

5. This commentary is sometimes known as the Xiang-Guo commentary because parts of it are thought to have been written by Xiang Xiu in the mid-third century.

Wang's approach was characterized by greater philosophical openness and subtlety. His legacy to later Chinese thought would include new ways of conceptualizing the nature of reality and the criteria for human action, along with a new philosophical vocabulary for articulating this complex understanding.

Wang wrote extensive commentaries on the *Classic of Changes* and the *Laozi*, as well as a partial commentary on the *Analects* called *Resolving Uncertainties in the Analects* (*Lunyu shiyi*). His *General Remarks on the Changes of the Zhou* (*Zhouyi lüeli*) is a seven-part introduction to his commentary on the *Changes* that explains in detail how he read the classic. In it, his interests range from the pragmatics of realpolitik to the metaphysics of the Way, from strategies of living to the meaning of life.

Wang's emphasis is on the fundamental concept of *li*, or principle. *Li* was a term that had been used in the earlier Chinese tradition to refer to the patterns in natural things—the markings in jade, for example, or the grain in wood. Here we find Wang Bi using it to designate the order to be discovered in the universe and the processes of nature.

## GENERAL REMARKS ON *THE* CHANGES OF THE ZHOU

### Principle

#### CLARIFYING THE JUDGMENTS (*MING TUAN*)

What is a Judgment?[6] It discusses the body or substance of a hexagram as a whole and clarifies what the controlling principle is from which it evolves. The many cannot govern the many; that which governs the many is the most solitary [the One]. Activity cannot govern activity; that which controls all activity that occurs in the world, thanks to constancy, is the One. Therefore, for all the many to manage to exist, their controlling principle must reach back to the One, and for all activities to manage to function, their source cannot but be the One.

No thing ever behaves haphazardly but necessarily follows its own principle. To unite things there is a fundamental regulator; to integrate them there is a primordial generator. Therefore things are complex but not chaotic, multitudinous but not confused. This is why when the six lines of a hexagram intermingle, one can pick out one of them and use it to clarify what is happening, and as the hard and the soft supersede one another, one can establish which one is the master and use it to determine how they are ordered. . . .

Now, although past and present differ and armies and states then and now appear dissimilar, the way these central principles function is such that nothing

---

6. For an explanation of the nature of the "Judgments" on the hexagrams of the *Classic of Changes*, see chap. 10.

can ever stray far from them. Although kinds and gradations of things exist in infinite variety, there is a chief controlling principle that inheres in all of them. Of things we esteem in a Judgment, it is this that is the most significant. [*Zhouyi lüeli*, 591–592]

## THE SAGE

Wang Bi is known not only for such searching discussions of principle, being and nothingness, naturalness, and the relation of symbols and language to reality, but for a new view of the sage.

A lively issue in the period from the third to the fifth centuries was whether or not a sage experienced ordinary human emotions, and on this matter Wang Bi and his contemporary He Yan evidently disagreed. An indication of what Wang thought about the capacity of the sage for responsiveness and sensitivity is recorded by Wang's biographer He Shao, who summarized the disagreement between He Yan and Wang as follows.

It was He Yan's opinion that the sage is free of pleasure, anger, sadness, or happiness, and his discussion of this issue was meticulously argued. People such as Zhong Hui (225–264) transmitted what he had to say, but Wang Bi took a different position from them and thought that what makes the sage superior to people in general is his intelligence (*shenming*) and that what makes him the same as people in general is his having the five emotions.[7] It is because his intelligence is superior that he can embody gentleness and amiability and, in so doing, identify with nothingness (*wu*). It is because he is the same as other people in having the five emotions that he is unable to respond to things free from either sadness or pleasure. Nevertheless, the emotions of the sage are such that he may respond to things but without becoming attached to them. Nowadays because the sage is considered free of such attachment, one immediately thinks it can be said that he no longer responds to things. How very often this error occurs!
[From *Wei zhi* (*Chronicles of Wei*), in *Sanguo zhi* (*Chronicles of the Three Kingdoms*) (*Wang Bi ji jiaoshi* ed.) 2:639–644; RJL]

## GUO XIANG: COMMENTARY ON THE *ZHUANGZI*

In the commentary on the *Zhuangzi* by Guo Xiang (who was probably building on the work of the mid-third-century commentator Xiang Xiu), a positive note is struck in the emphasis on naturalness and spontaneity in both the internal and the external life. Guo Xiang returns to Zhuangzi's themes of naturalness and

---

7. Happiness, anger, sadness, pleasure, and desire.

spontaneity, self-transformation, and contentment; in Guo's view, however, the sage moves in the realm of human affairs as well as in the transcendental world.

## Society and Rulership

In adapting Daoist nonassertion or "doing nothing" (*wuwei*) to Confucian principles, Guo Xiang, like many of his contemporaries, recognized such values as humaneness and rightness but stressed the need to adapt them to changing times and circumstances. This raised questions similar to those encountered in the adaptation later of Buddhist doctrines to Chinese social and political practice. Did a laissez-faire Daoist "nonassertion" (*wuwei*) and "naturalness" or spontaneity (*ziran*) really accord with Confucian conceptions of constant human values, or did they not lend themselves readily to an amoral pragmatism, so that in contrast to the morally prudent and carefully measured response to change in the *Yijing*, we now get an amoral expediency and opportunism? Note that Guo Xiang has little to say about the organization and conduct of government but dwells on only how the sage king conducts himself—that is, how one rules.

Although the sage is in the midst of government, his mind seems to be in the mountain forest. . . . His abode is in the myriad things, but this does not mean that he does not wander freely. [sec. 1; 1:6b; 1:8a]

Man in society cannot get away from his fellow beings. The changes in society vary from generation to generation according to different standards. Only those who have no minds of their own and do not use their own judgment can adapt themselves to changes and not be burdened by them. [sec. 4; 2:4a]

When a thousand people gather together with no one as their leader, they will be either unruly or disorganized. Therefore when there are many virtuous people, there should not be many rulers, but when there is no virtuous person, there cannot but be a ruler. This is the Way of Heaven and man and the most proper thing to do. [sec. 4; 2:9a]

When the king does not make himself useful in the various offices, the various officials will manage their own affairs. Those with clear vision will do the seeing, those with sharp ears will do the listening, those with knowledge will do the planning, and those with strength will provide protection. What need is there to take any action? Only profound silence, that is all. [sec. 4; 2:13b]

Events that took place in the past have disappeared with the past. Some may be transmitted to us [in writing], but can this make the past exist in the present? The past is not in the present, and the events of the present are soon changed. Therefore only when one abandons learning, lets one's nature take its own course, and changes with the times, can one be perfect. [sec. 13; 5:18b–19a]

Humaneness and rightness are principles of human nature. Human nature undergoes changes and is different past and present. If one takes a temporary abode in a thing and then moves on, one will intuit [the reality of things].

If, however, one stops and is confined to one place, one will develop prejudices. Prejudices will result in hypocrisy, and hypocrisy will result in many reproaches. [sec. 14; 5:24a]

The ceremonies of ancient kings were intended to meet the needs of the time. When the time has passed and the ceremonies are still not cast away, they will become an evil influence to the people and serve to hasten the start of affectations and imitation. [sec. 14; 5:22b]

[*Commentary on the Zhuangzi* (SBBY); adapted from WTC by IB]

# Chapter 14

## DAOIST RELIGION

The historical development of Daoism in the first half of the Han dynasty was marked by its influence on political syncretism via the Huang-Lao movement, named after Laozi and the Yellow Emperor, Huangdi. At the same time, the search for immortality and the cult of the immortals spread to all levels of society. The influence of Huang-Lao teachings at court had reached a high point just before the reign of Emperor Wu (r. 141–87 B.C.E.), declining sharply as a result of his decision to confer official patronage on the teaching of five Confucian classics, effectively installing Confucianism as the state ideology.[1] The emperor's personal interest in immortality and various occult arts, meanwhile, continued to be celebrated in fiction and mythology.

With the gradual decline of the dynasty's political fortunes, during the reign of Wang Mang and under the Latter Han, apocalyptic prophecy came to the foreground. The *Great Peace Scripture (Taiping jing)* is said to have been presented to the Han court amidst millenarian expectations of the imminent collapse of the world order, to be followed by the survival of an elect people under a reign of good government and great peace. The popular Yellow Turban uprising in 182 C.E. and the simultaneous establishment of an autonomous theocratic state by a group known as the Heavenly Masters in Sichuan pursued visions that may have been similar.

---

1. See chaps. 9 and 10.

The Heavenly Masters movement founded by Zhang Daoling constitutes the earliest form of Daoist liturgical organization for which a relatively detailed record is available. The authority vested in Zhang Daoling, the putative founder, and his successors by means of a covenant with the Newly Appeared Lord Lao (Laozi deified) has with few interruptions been the mainstay of the Daoist ordination system throughout China to this day. After his arrival in Sichuan from eastern China, Zhang Daoling appears to have founded his movement in opposition to existing shamanistic practices among the peoples of the southwest, some of which were nevertheless partly incorporated. In the same way, the Heavenly Masters and other Daoist movements provided a liturgical superstructure for a variety of local cults and indigenous religious practices throughout its history. The introduction of Buddhism to China around the same time supplied to popular religion new forms and practices. Much of the subsequent textual tradition of Daoism shows distinct traces of Buddhist influence, especially in the areas of morality, eschatology, and iconography.

The most important medieval additions to the Daoist textual canon were provided by the Shangqing and Lingbao revelations of the fourth and fifth centuries, subsequently systematized by Tao Hongjing (456–536) and Lu Xiu-jing (406–477), respectively. The Shangqing corpus of inspired scriptures and cosmological and hagiographic revelations from the Maoshan area in southern Jiangsu province incorporated elements of ancient shamanistic traditions of southeast China. Shamanistic ritual seems indeed to have been at the origin of these texts, which in turn developed meditative and visionary techniques, while their ecstatic poetry and inspired calligraphy exercised a major influence on Chinese art and letters. The Lingbao revelations served essentially to create links between the Daoist canon and the transmitted public liturgy. For the most part inspired by Buddhism, they included new hymns using "Brahman" psalmody in pseudo-Sanskrit language, and such practices as scriptural recitation with circumambulation. The fifth century also saw the first compilation of Daoist scripture into a canon structured according to Three Caverns or Receptacles (*Sandong*), formed around the Shangqing, Lingbao, and Sanhuang corpora.

However, the rapport of Daoism with local cults worked as a deterrent to full centralization and ecclesiastical organization. In the fifth and sixth centuries apocalyptic cults produced new scriptures, which were eventually also incorporated into the canon. The *Divine Incantations Scripture* introduced below is but one example. The Tang dynasty, a high point of both the Chinese schools of Buddhism and of Daoism as the official imperial cult, generated a wealth of Daoist scholastic and literary texts and works related to ritual, meditative, and physiological practices. The bulk of Tang Daoist scriptures, meanwhile, was composed in plain imitation of popular Buddhist *sūtras*. The most prominent systematizer and creative author of this period was the scholar and court Daoist Du Guangting (850–933), whose life straddled the end of the Tang (618–906) and the beginning of the Five Dynasties (907–960).

The Song (960–1279) once again stands out as a period of revelation. The modern Daoist canon contains many scriptures and liturgical manuals of numerous new schools that sprang up in this period. In the face of the growing threat of foreign invasions, Northern Song (960–1126) rulers also increasingly turned to Daoism as a religion of state.

## COMMANDMENTS OF LORD LAO

The *One Hundred and Eighty Commandments Pronounced by the Lord Lao* (*Laojun shuo yibaibashi jie*, third century C.E.?) is, as the title indicates, a set of rules for Daoists. In this case the rules are intended as a guide for the life of the Libationers (*jijiu*), the leaders of Daoist communities in the early middle ages. The preface indicates that Lord Lao, or the Old Lord (that is, the divine form of Laozi), revealed these rules in ancient times to the immortal Gan Ji, the legendary founder of Taiping Daoism. Although this is no more than a pious legend, it is a fact that the set of rules is one of the oldest texts on communal Daoism that has come down to us. This can be seen from the evidence that it served as the model for another set of rules that was written toward the end of the fourth century C.E. Internal evidence suggests that it originated in the peasant society sometime during the Latter Han or the Three Kingdoms (220–280) periods. Many of the rules are about the necessity of maintaining a frugal life and about the protection of the natural environment. Others are directed against the ancient sacrificial practices, against divination, against politics, warfare, court intrigues, etc. Here follow some of the rules; the number given at the end of each of them indicates its place in the sequence of the 180 commandments.

Do not retain numerous servants or concubines. (1)
Do not commit adultery. (2)
Do not steal. (3)
Do not injure or kill any living being. (4)
Do not unjustly accept from other people anything worth more than
  one copper coin. (5)
Do not throw edibles into the fire. (6)
Do not keep any pigs or sheep. (7)
Do not write notes addressed to others in cursive script. (11)
Do not write frequent letters. (12)
Do not practice abortion. (13)
Do not burn fields or mountain forests. (14)
Do not seek knowledge of military or political matters, nor practice
  divination to determine what is auspicious or not. (16)
Do not cut trees without good reason. (18)
Do not wantonly pick herbs or flowers. (19)
Do not frequent the emperor or his officials; do not engage in mari-
  tal or other family relationships with them. (20)

Do not eat alone. (26)

Do not buy or sell slaves. (27)

Do not speak about the private matters of others. (32)

Do not throw anything poisonous into sources, lakes, rivers, or
seas. (36)

Do not commit suicide. (39)

Do not dig out the nests and hiding places of insects in winter. (95)

Do not wantonly climb trees to rob birds' nests of their eggs, nor
break them. (97)

Do not deceive elderly people. (102)

Do not urinate on plants or in water that people may drink. (116)

Do not stand guarantee for transactions involving the sale of land or
slaves. (123)

Do not proffer ugly or harsh sounds; always remain gently
smiling. (126)

Do not seek to obtain books with secret stratagems, nor read
them. (128)

If people scold you, listen with diffidence; never answer. (167)

[From *Taishang Laojun jinglü* (DZ) 562, no. 786, 2a–12b; KS]


### THE DIVINE INCANTATIONS SCRIPTURE

Every Daoist movement believed in the imminent end of the world, or at least of
the great part of the human community that had not undertaken worship of the
Way. *The Divine Incantations Scripture* (*Taishang dongyuan shenzhou jing*) is the
oldest book that details the coming apocalypse. It emerged from a reform movement
inside the Heavenly Masters during the exceptionally chaotic political turmoil of the
Jin dynasty (265–419). The earliest parts of the book, almost certainly written at the
beginning of the fifth century, refer to events in the Jin dynasty between 380 and 400.
The book is composed of several accumulated strata; in the early tenth century, it was
supplemented, edited, and printed by Du Guangting.

In the original Heavenly Masters tradition, the faithful reached salvation through
a series of initiations, which gave them "registers" (*lu*) that enrolled them among the
immortals. But this book offers a new route to transcendence. The book itself (like
a Buddhist text such as the *Heart Sūtra*) becomes not only the message but the all-
powerful talisman that guarantees life amidst all too prevalent death.

For Daoists, of course, the gods of popular religion are subordinates of the true
divinities—the Way and its emanations—about which "the vulgar" know nothing.
The gods are, in a word, merely the officials of the celestial bureaucracy. Like yamen
runners,[2] they can make trouble as well as enforce order. This text is typical in playing

---

2. I.e., low-ranking assistants of local officials.

on that ambiguity. The same gods who are sent to punish the unbelievers are the ones who restore peace and normalcy; the Way gives the orders. The overall motion of the section is from dire threat to deliverance.

The Dao says: Sexagenary year 21 is about to arrive. The flood is not far off. Now, epidemic demons are killing people. The world abounds in vice and lacks goodness. The people do not recognize the truth. The Three Caverns (*Sandong*)[3] revelations have been spreading for a long time, but the people are benighted and fail to seek out and accept them. They bring suffering on themselves. What can be done? The people are to be pitied. I will now send eight units of palace guards to annihilate the epidemic ghosts and dispatch an order to banish [the epidemic ghosts]. Let Daoist priests convert people and make them accept the Three Caverns revelations.

The Dao says: From now on, for those who accept this *Divine Incantations Scripture*, thirty thousand celestial elite troops will protect you. Convert all the unenlightened day by day on behalf of all the living. If the unenlightened persist in their confusion and ridicule people who do good, Heaven will send epidemic ghosts to kill these people. Souls of such people will enter the three evil paths of rebirth, with no prospect of egress.

The Dao says: In sexagenary years 18 and 19, eighty million great ghosts will come to annihilate bad people. As for those with forked tongues, those who slander the law of the Dao, those who refer to their masters by their taboo-names, those who dispute the scriptures, those who have no faith in the Three Caverns revelations, and those who are unwilling to accept the Dao, the great ghost king will come and annihilate all of them.

The Dao says: From now on, if there is a place where Daoist priests obediently follow the Three Caverns revelations, practice the Dao, and teach the people, I will send a multitude of ninety billion great soldiers to come all at once and protect you. If there is one ghost that won't leave, the divine protectors of the ten regions will come down immediately to arrest it.

The Dao says: From now on, wherever there are Daoist priests who recite this scripture, Heaven will order four hundred ninety thousand divine protectors of the Three Caverns, eight hundred thousand divine protectors from the six-fold heaven and ninety billion from the thirty-six-fold heaven to come and in unison kill those epidemic ghosts. Heaven will allow those among the living who are ill and those with official entanglements to obtain release.

---

3. The Three Caverns (*Sandong*) are the three traditions of divine revelation that came together to produce the body of Daoist scriptures. The text writes further on of the "divine protectors of the Three Caverns," gods dedicated to enforcing the prescriptions of the sacred writings. For a detailed discussion, see Ōfuchi Ninji, "The Formation of the Daoist Canon," in *Facets of Daoism*, ed. Welch and Seidel, pp. 257–265.

Illnesses will lighten or remit. A pleasant disposition will be brought about in all the gods, and there will be household felicity. Within and without, god of the locality and god of the stove will be made clearly distinguishable [i.e., will not intrude upon one another's responsibilities]. They will not act against the rules and make trouble for the living. Those ghosts that do not belong to the household cult will be exiled forever to other places. If there are ghost troops who disobey my orders and do not depart, each and every one will be executed by the demon kings, without lenience. . . .

[From *DZ* 170–173, no. 335, pp. 2–4; NS]

*Chapter 15*

## THE INTRODUCTION OF BUDDHISM

The coming of Buddhism to China was an event of far-reaching importance in the development of Chinese thought and culture and of Buddhism itself. After a long and difficult period of assimilation, this new teaching managed to establish itself as a major system of thought, contributing greatly to the enrichment of Chinese philosophy, and also as a major system of religious practice, which had an enduring influence on Chinese popular religion. Indeed, it came to be spoken of along with the native traditions, Confucianism and Daoism, as one of the Three Teachings or Three Religions, thus achieving a status of virtual equality with these beliefs.

By the time Buddhism reached China (according to official tradition, in the first century C.E.), it had already undergone several centuries of development in regard to both its philosophical doctrines and its religious practices. This is not the place to attempt a summation of that historical development, but a brief statement of the major principles and concepts of Buddhism in India is essential to understanding the forms it took in China.

## BASIC TEACHINGS OF BUDDHISM

The fundamental truths on which Buddhism is founded are not metaphysical or theological but, rather, psychological. Basic is the doctrine of the "Four Noble Truths": (1) all life is inevitably sorrowful, (2) sorrow is due to craving,

(3) sorrow can only be stopped by the stopping of craving, and (4) this can be done by a course of carefully disciplined conduct, culminating in the life of concentration and meditation led by the Buddhist monk. These four truths, which are the common property of all schools of Buddhist thought, are part of the true Doctrine (Sanskrit, *dharma*), which reflects the fundamental law of the universe.[1]

All things are composite, and, as a corollary of this, all things are transient, for the composition of all aggregates is liable to change with time. Moreover, being essentially transient, they have no eternal Self or soul, no abiding individuality. And, as we have seen, they are inevitably liable to sorrow. This threefold characterization of the nature of the world and all that it contains—sorrowful, transient, and soulless—is frequently repeated in Buddhist literature; without fully grasping its truth no being has any chance of salvation, for until one thoroughly understands the three characteristics of the world one will inevitably crave for permanence in one form or another, and as this cannot, by the nature of things, be obtained, one will suffer, and probably make others suffer also.

All things in the universe may also be classified into five components or are composed of a mixture of them: form and matter (*rūpa*), sensations (*vedanā*), perceptions (*saṃjñā*), psychic dispositions or constructions (*saṃskāra*), and consciousness or conscious thought (*vijñāna*).

The first consists of the objects of sense and various other elements of less importance. Sensations are the actual feelings arising as a result of the exercise of the six senses (mind being the sixth) upon sense-objects, and perceptions are the cognitions of such sensations. The psychic constructions include all the various psychological emotions, propensities, faculties, and conditions of the individual, while the fifth component, conscious thought, arises from the interplay of the other psychic constituents. The individual is made up of a combination of the five components, which are never the same from one moment to the next, and therefore the individual's whole being is in a state of constant flux.

The process by which life continues and one thing leads to another is explained by the Chain of Causation or Dependent Origination. The root cause of the process of birth and death and rebirth is ignorance, the fundamental illusion that individuality and permanence exist, when, in fact, they do not. Hence there arise in the organism various psychic phenomena, including desire, followed by an attempt to appropriate things to itself—this is typified especially by sexual craving and sexual intercourse, which are the actual causes of the next links in the chain, which concludes with old age or death, only to be repeated again and again indefinitely. Rebirth takes place, therefore, according to laws of karma, which do not essentially differ from those of Hinduism, though they are explained rather differently.

---

1. The word *dharma* in Buddhism, besides meaning "Law" or "Doctrine," also represents phenomena in general, as well as the qualities and characteristics of phenomena.

As we have seen, no permanent entity transmigrates from body to body, and all things, including the individual, are in a state of constant flux. But each act, word, or thought leaves its traces on the collection of the five constituents that make up the phenomenal individual, and their character alters correspondingly. This process goes on throughout life, and when the material and immaterial parts of the being are separated in death, the immaterial constituents, which make up what in other systems would be called soul, carry over the consequential effects of the deeds of the past life and obtain another form in one of the ten realms of existence: namely, those of hell dwellers, hungry ghosts, animals, human beings, *asuras* (or spirits), heavenly beings, *śrāvakas* (or direct disciples of Buddha), *pratyeka-buddhas*,[2] bodhisattvas, or buddhas. Thus there is no permanent soul, but nevertheless room is found for the doctrine of transmigration. Though Buddhism rejects the existence of the soul, this makes little difference in practice, and the more popular literature of Buddhism, such as the *Birth Stories* (*Jātaka*), takes for granted the existence of a quasi-soul, at least, which endures indefinitely.

The process of rebirth can be stopped only by achieving *nirvāṇa*, first by adopting right views about the nature of existence, then by a carefully controlled system of conduct, and finally by concentration and meditation. The state of *nirvāṇa* cannot be described, but it can be hinted at or suggested metaphorically. The word literally means "blowing out," as of a lamp. In *nirvāṇa* all idea of an individual personality or ego ceases to exist and there is nothing to be reborn: as far as the individual is concerned *nirvāṇa* is annihilation. But it was not generally thought of by the early Buddhists in such negative terms. It was rather conceived of as a transcendent state, beyond the possibility of full comprehension by the ordinary being enmeshed in the illusion of selfhood but not fundamentally different from the state of supreme bliss as described in other non-theistic Indian systems.

These are the doctrines of the Theravāda or Hīnayāna school, and with few variations, they would be assented to by all other schools of Buddhism. But when Mahāyāna Buddhism arose in India, claiming to offer salvation for all, it styled itself *Mahāyāna*, the Greater Vehicle to salvation, as opposed to the older Buddhism, which it referred to disparagingly as *Hīnayāna*, or the Lesser Vehicle. The Mahāyāna scriptures also claimed to represent the final doctrines of the Buddha, revealed only to his most spiritually advanced followers, while the earlier doctrines were merely preliminary ones. Though Mahāyāna Buddhism, with its pantheon of heavenly buddhas and bodhisattvas and its idealistic metaphysics, was strikingly different in many respects from the Theravāda, it can be viewed as the development into finished systems of tendencies that had existed long before.

A tendency to revere the Buddha as a god had probably existed in his own lifetime. In Indian religion, divinity is not something completely transcendent,

---

2. Private buddhas who have attained enlightenment for themselves.

or far exalted above all mortal things, as it is for the Jew, Christian, or Muslim; neither is it something concentrated in a single unique omnipotent and omniscient personality. In Indian religions godhead manifests itself in so many forms as to be almost, if not quite, ubiquitous, and every great sage or religious teacher is looked on as a special manifestation of divinity, in some sense a god in human form. How much more divine was the Buddha, to whom even the great god Brahma himself did reverence, and who, in meditation, could far transcend the comparatively tawdry and transient heavens where the great gods dwelt, enter the world of formlessness, and pass thence to the ineffable *nirvāṇa* itself! From the Buddhist point of view, even the highest of the gods was liable to error, for Brahma imagined himself to be the creator, when in fact the world came into existence as a result of natural causes. The Buddha, on the other hand, was omniscient.

Yet, according to theory, the Buddha had passed completely away from the universe, had ceased in any sense to be a person, and no longer affected the world in any way. But the formula of the "Three Treasures" or "Jewels" — "I take refuge in the Buddha, the *dharma*, and the *saṅgha*" — became the Buddhist profession of faith very early and was used by monk and layman alike. As such, the Buddha was worshiped from very early times, and he is said to have himself declared that all who had faith in him and devotion to him would obtain rebirth in paradise.

A further development that encouraged the tendency to theism was the growth of interest in the bodhisattva. This term, meaning literally "Being of Wisdom," was first used in the sense of a previous incarnation of the Buddha. For many lives before his final birth as Siddhārtha Gautama, the Bodhisattva did mighty deeds of compassion and self-sacrifice, as he gradually perfected himself in wisdom and virtue. Stories of the Bodhisattva, known as *Birth Stories (Jātaka)* and often adapted from earlier legends and fables, were very popular with lay Buddhists, and numerous illustrations of them occur in early Buddhist art.

It is probable that even in the lifetime of the Buddha it was thought that he was only the last of a series of earlier buddhas. Later, perhaps through Zoroastrian influence, it came to be believed that other Buddhas were yet to come, and interest developed in Maitreya, the future Buddha, whose coming was said to have been prophesied by the historical Buddha and who, in years to come, would purify the world with his teaching. But if Maitreya was yet to come, the chain of being that would ultimately lead to his birth (or, in the terminology of other sects, his soul) must be already in existence. Somewhere in the universe, the being later to become Maitreya Buddha was already active for good. And if this one, how many more? Logically, the world must be full of bodhisattvas, all striving for the welfare of other beings.

The next step up in the development of the new form of Buddhism was the changing of the goal at which the believer aimed. According to Buddhist teaching there are three types of perfected beings — Buddhas, who perceived the truth for themselves and taught it to others; *pratyeka*-buddhas, "private Buddhas," who perceived it but kept it to themselves and did not teach it; and *arhats*, "worthies," who learned it from others but fully realized it for themselves. According to earlier schools, the earnest believer should aspire to become an *arhat*, a perfected being for whom there was no rebirth, who already enjoyed *nirvāṇa* and who would finally enter that state after death, all vestiges of his personality dissolved. The road to *nirvāṇa* was a hard one and could only be covered in many lives of virtue and self-sacrifice; even so, the goal began to be looked on as selfish. Surely a bodhisattva, after achieving such exalted compassion and altruism, and after reaching such a degree of perfection that he could render inestimable help to other striving beings, would not pass as quickly as possible to *nirvāṇa*, where he could be of no further use, but would deliberately choose to remain in the world, using his spiritual power to help others, until all had found salvation. Passages of Mahāyāna scriptures describing the self-sacrifice of the bodhisattva for the welfare of all things living are among the most passionately altruistic in the world's religious literature.

The replacement of the ideal of the *arhat* by that of the bodhisattva is the basic distinction between the old sects and the new Mahāyāna. Faith in the bodhisattvas and the help they afforded was thought to carry many beings along the road to bliss, while the older schools, which did not accept the bodhisattva ideal, could save only a few patient and strenuous souls.

The next stage in the evolution of the theology of the new Buddhism was the doctrine of the "Three Bodies" (*Trikāya*). If the true ideal was that of the bodhisattva, why did not Siddhārtha Gautama remain one, instead of becoming a Buddha and selfishly passing to *nirvāṇa*? This paradox was answered by a theory of docetic type, which, again, probably had its origin in popular ideas prevalent among lay Buddhists at a very early period. Gautama was not in fact an ordinary man, but the manifestation of a great spiritual being. The Buddha had three bodies—the Body of Essence (*Dharmakāya*), the Body of Bliss (*Sambhogakāya*), and the Body of Transformation (*Nirmāṇakāya*). It was the Body of Transformation that lived on earth as Siddhārtha Gautama, an emanation of the Body of Bliss, which dwelled forever in the Heavens as a sort of supreme god. But the Body of Bliss was in turn the emanation of the Body of Essence, the ultimate Buddha, who pervaded and underlay the whole universe. Subtle philosophies and metaphysical systems were developed parallel with these theological ideas, and the Body of Essence was identified with *nirvāṇa*. It was in fact the World Soul, the Brahman of the Upaniṣads in a new form. In the fully developed Mahāyānist cosmology there were many Bodies of Bliss, all of them emanations of the single Body of Essence, but the heavenly Buddha chiefly concerned with our world was *Amitābha* (Immeasurable Radiance), who dwelt in *Sukhāvatī*, the "Happy Land" (or "Pure Land," as it was known to the Chinese), the Paradise of the West. With him was associated the earthly Gautama Buddha and a very potent and compassionate bodhisattva, Avalokiteśvara (the Lord Who Looks Down).

The older Buddhism and the newer flourished side by side in India during the early centuries of the Christian era, and we read of Buddhist monasteries in which some of the monks were Mahāyānist and some Hīnayānist. But, in general, the Buddhists of northwestern India were either Mahāyānists or members of Hīnayāna sects much affected by Mahāyānist ideas. The more austere forms of Hīnayāna seem to have been strongest in parts of western and southern India, and in Sri Lanka. It was from northwestern India, under the rule of the great Kushāna empire (first to third centuries C.E.) that Buddhism spread throughout Central Asia to China; since it emanated from the northwest, it was chiefly of the Mahāyāna or near-Mahāyāna type.

## THE COMING OF BUDDHISM TO CHINA

As Buddhism spread from its homeland, it became the harbinger of civilization in many of the areas that it penetrated. Many of them had no system of writing before the advent of the new religion. One of the most notable exceptions to this statement, however, was China. By the time Buddhism was introduced, China boasted a civilization that was already very old, a classic canon, time-hallowed traditions, and the conviction that its society was the only truly civilized society in the world. Thus, while Buddhism was the vehicle for the introduction into Central Asia of many arts of civilization, the Buddhist missionaries found in China a country that possessed these things in an already highly developed state. Buddhism was obliged to compete with indigenous philosophical and religious systems to win the hearts of the Chinese, and the Chinese, for their own part, were hindered in their understanding of Buddhist philosophy by preconceptions based on indigenous philosophical systems.

No one can say when or in what fashion the Chinese first came into contact with Buddhism. It is to be presumed, from conjecture, and from what sparse documentation there is, that this contact was with Buddhist icons worshiped by Central Asians coming into China. The Chinese of the time adopted the Buddha into their scheme of things as a demigod on the order of their own mythical Yellow Emperor and the philosopher Laozi, who was believed to have attained immortality. But the dawn of history for Chinese Buddhism came with the rendition of Buddhist sacred texts into the Chinese language.

The Chinese were particularly desirous of knowing whether Buddhism could add to their knowledge of elixirs and practices that would contribute to longevity, levitation, and other superhuman achievements. As it happened, Buddhism (like many other Indian religions) prescribed a precise set of practices, varying from school to school, which was believed to enhance the intuitive faculties. The early Buddhist missionaries found that the scriptures containing these prescriptions were what the Chinese wanted most to read, and so they proceeded to translate them. This was the beginning of Buddhist literature in China.

As time went on, and as the interest of China's intellectuals veered toward metaphysical speculation, it became fashionable to seek in Buddhism those sublime truths that persons so inclined were seeking in some of China's own canonized classics. When, in 317 C.E., non-Chinese peoples forced the Chinese court out of North China, an educated elite was displaced to the south. A refined and sophisticated culture developed among them, with the dominant trend in southern Buddhism being toward abstruse philosophical discussion in salons that brought together the cream of secular society and the best wits from the great metropolitan monasteries. An often facile interpretation of Buddhism in terms of Daoism and the Learning of the Mysterious[3] prevailed, and Buddhism's Indian origins were somewhat effaced.

There were contrary trends, however. In the first place, not a few monks, in both North and South China, were earnestly concerned with the true meaning of Buddhism and of Buddhist salvation. The Chinese aversion to foreign languages being what it was, these persons showed their zeal principally in seeking out capable translators or in participating in translation projects themselves. Also, simultaneously with the philosophical salons and the great translation projects a trend developed, more pronounced in the north than in the south, toward a practical and devotional Buddhism, which consisted of an emphasis on contemplative practices as well as on adoration and good works. Temples and statuary were soon erected all over China.

### MOUZI: *DISPOSING OF ERROR*

Though the date and authorship of this work are not known, the general tone of the composition leads one to suspect that the work was written at a time when Buddhism had gained a sufficient foothold to cause many Chinese to fear its influence and to attempt to strike back. While the counterattack against Buddhism in the north took the form of official persecution or curtailment, under the Southern Dynasties (317–589 C.E.) it usually took the form of polemics. *Disposing of Error*, or *Lihuo lun*, as it is known in Chinese, appears to be an apologia for Buddhism, written in answer to such polemical writings.

## Why Do Buddhist Monks Do Injury to Their Bodies?

One of the greatest obstacles confronting early Chinese Buddhism was the aversion of Chinese society to the shaving of the head, which was required of all members of the Buddhist clergy. The Confucians held that the body is the gift of one's parents and that to harm it is to be disrespectful toward them.

The questioner said, "The *Classic of Filiality* says, 'Our body, limbs, hair, and skin are all received from our fathers and mothers. We dare not injure them.'

---

3. See chap. 13.

When Zengzi was about to die, he bared his hands and feet.[4] But now the monks shave their heads. How this violates the sayings of the sages and is out of keeping with the way of the filial!" . . .

Mouzi said . . . "Confucius has said, 'There are those with whom one can pursue the Way . . . but with whom one cannot weigh [decisions].'[5] This is what is meant by doing what is best at the time. Furthermore, the *Classic of Filiality* says, 'The early kings ruled by surpassing virtue and the essential Way.' Taibo cut his hair short and tattooed his body, thus following of his own accord the customs of Wu and Yue and going against the spirit of the 'body, limbs, hair, and skin' passage.[6] And yet Confucius praised him, saying that his might well be called the ultimate virtue."[7]

## Why Do Monks Not Marry?

Another of the great obstacles confronting the early Chinese Buddhist church was clerical celibacy. One of the most important features of indigenous Chinese religion is devotion to ancestors. If there are no descendants to make the offerings, then there will be no sacrifices. To this is added the natural desire for progeny. Traditionally, there could be no greater calamity for a Chinese than childlessness.

The questioner said, "Now of felicities there is none greater than the continuation of one's line, of unfilial conduct there is none worse than childlessness. The monks forsake wife and children, reject property and wealth. Some do not marry all their lives. How opposed this conduct is to felicity and filiality!" . . .

Mouzi said . . . "Wives, children, and property are the luxuries of the world, but simple living and doing nothing (*wuwei*) are the wonders of the Way. Laozi has said, 'Of reputation and life, which is dearer? Of life and property, which is worth more?'[8] . . . Xu You and Chaofu dwelt in a tree. Boyi and Shuqi starved in Shouyang, but Confucius praised their worth, saying, 'They sought to act in accordance with humanity and they succeeded in acting so.'[9] One does not hear of their being ill-spoken of because they were childless and propertyless. The monk practices the Way and substitutes that for the pleasures of disporting

---

4. To show he had preserved them intact from all harm. *Analects* 8:3.

5. *Analects* 9:29. The full quotation is "There are those with whom one can learn but with whom one cannot pursue the Way; there are those with whom one can pursue the Way but with whom one cannot take one's stand; there are those with whom one can take one's stand but with whom one cannot weigh [decisions]."

6. Uncle of King Wen of the Zhou who retired to the barbarian land of Wu and cut his hair and tattooed his body in barbarian fashion, thus yielding his claim to the throne to King Wen.

7. *Analects* 8:1.

8. *Daodejing* 44.

9. *Analects* 7:14.

himself in the world. He accumulates goodness and wisdom in exchange for the joys of wife and children."

## Does Buddhism Have No Recipe for Immortality?

Within the movement broadly known as Daoism there were several tendencies, one the quest for immortality, another an attitude of superiority to questions of life and death. The first Chinese who took to Buddhism did so out of a desire to achieve super-human qualities, among them immortality. The questioner is disappointed to learn that Buddhism does not provide this after all. Mouzi counters by saying that even in Daoism, if properly understood, there is no seeking after immortality.

The questioner said, "The Daoists say that Yao, Shun, the Duke of Zhou, and Confucius and his seventy-two disciples did not die, but became immortals. The Buddhists say that men must all die, and that none can escape. What does this mean?"

Mouzi said, "Talk of immortality is superstitious and unfounded; it is not the word of the sages. Laozi said, 'Even Heaven and Earth cannot last forever. How much less can human beings!'[10] Confucius said, 'The wise man leaves the world, but humaneness and filial piety last forever.' I have looked into the six arts and examined the commentaries and records. According to them, Yao died; Shun had his [place of burial at] Mount Cangwu; Yu has his tomb on Kuaiji; Boyi and Shuqi have their grave in Shouyang. King Wen died before he could chastise [the tyrant] Zhou; King Wu died without waiting for [his son] King Cheng to grow up. . . . And, of Yan Yuan, the Master said, 'Unfortunately, he was short-lived,'[11] likening him to a bud that never bloomed.[12] All of these things are clearly recorded in the Classics: they are the absolute words of the sages. I make the Classics and the commentaries my authority and find my proof in the world of men. To speak of immortality, is this not a great error?"

[*Hongming ji*, TD, no. 2102:1–7; adapted from LH by IB]

## HUIYUAN: "A MONK DOES NOT BOW DOWN BEFORE A KING"

When an Indian entered the Buddhist clergy, he left his clan, his caste, and all his worldly possessions. As one standing outside of ordinary society, he from then on paid no outward signs of veneration to secular potentates. In China, too, early Buddhist

---

10. *Daodejing* 23.
11. *Analects* 11:6.
12. *Analects* 9:21.

clerics, though they knelt in their religious ceremonies, displayed no signs of respect to laymen in positions of authority, not even to the emperor.

At first this constituted no great problem, since only the most eminent monks were ever likely to meet the emperor, and these were usually foreigners who were not expected to follow full Chinese etiquette. When native Chinese came to constitute the majority of Buddhist clerics, however, the problem became more serious. The question was brought under discussion at court during the Eastern Jin period, but no settlement was reached until 402 C.E. At that time the high minister Huan Xuan (369–404), who had temporarily usurped the throne, referred the problem to one of the outstanding monks of the day, Huiyuan (334–417), for a recommendation. Huiyuan replied with a letter stating that, though Buddhist laymen, like other laymen, were obliged by the customary etiquette to acknowledge their loyalty and respect for their sovereign, the Buddhist clergy, who by the nature of their life and aims were far removed from ordinary men, could not be expected to go through the outward signs of obeisance. Huan Xuan accepted Huiyuan's argument and decreed that monks need not bow before the emperor. Shortly after this, Huiyuan composed a treatise titled "A Monk Does Not Bow Down Before a King" ("Shamen bu jing wang zhe lun"), stating his argument in greater detail.

## Buddhism in the Household

If one examines the broad essentials of the teachings of the Buddha, one will see that they distinguish between those who leave the household life and those who remain in it. . . . Those who revere the Buddhist laws but remain in their homes are subjects who are obedient to the transforming powers [of temporal rulers]. Their feelings have not changed from the customary, and their course of conduct conforms to the secular world. Therefore this way of life includes the affection of natural kinship and the proprieties of obedience to authority. Decorum and reverence have their basis herein, and thus they form the basis of the doctrine. That on which they are based has its merit in the past. Thus, on the basis of intimacy it teaches love and causes the people to appreciate natural kindness; on the basis of austerity it teaches veneration and causes the people to understand natural respect. . . . Thus obedience is made the common rule, and the natural way is not changed. . . .

Hence one may not benefit by [the ruler's] virtue and neglect propriety, bask in his kindness and cast aside due respect. Therefore they who rejoice in the way of Śākya invariably first serve their parents and respect their lords. They who change their way of life and throw away their hair ornaments must always await [their parents'] command, then act accordingly. If their lords and parents have doubts, then they retire, inquire of their wishes, and wait until [the lords and parents] are enlightened. This, then, is how the teaching of Buddha honors life-giving and assists kingly transformation in the way of government.

## Buddhism Outside the Household

This second part sets forth the core of Huiyuan's argument as to why the monk should not make a display of respect for worldly potentates. The monk, so the argument goes, is not a disrespectful, much less an impious, person, but he stands completely outside of the framework of lay life; hence he should not abide by its regulations insofar as merely polite accomplishments are concerned.

He who has left the household life is a lodger beyond the earthly [secular] world, and his ways are cut off from those of other beings. The doctrine by which he lives enables him to understand that woes and impediments come from having a body, and that by not maintaining the body one terminates woe. . . .

If the termination of woe does not depend on the maintenance of the body, then he does not treasure the benefits that foster life. This is something in which the principle runs counter to physical form and the Way is opposed to common practice. Such men as these commence the fulfillment of their vows with the putting away of ornaments of the head [shaving the head] and realize the achievement of their ideal with the changing of their garb. . . . Since they have changed their way of life, their garb and distinguishing marks cannot conform to the secular pattern. . . . Afar they reach to the ford of the Three Vehicles,[13] broadly they open up the Way of Heaven and the human. If but one of them be allowed to fulfill his virtue, then the Way spreads to the six relations and beneficence flows out to the whole world. Although they do not occupy the positions of kings and princes, yet, fully in harmony with the imperial ultimate, they let the people be. Therefore, though inwardly they may run counter to the gravity of natural relationships, yet they do not violate filial piety; though outwardly they lack respect in serving the sovereign, yet they do not lose hold of reverence.

## He Who Seeks the First Principle Is Not Obedient to Change

In general, those who reside within the limits [of ordinary existence] receive life from the Great Change. . . . Life is fettered by physical form, and life depends upon change. When there is change and the feelings react, then the spirit is barred from its source and the intellect is blinded to its own illumination. If one is thus shut up as in a hard shell, then what is preserved is only the self, and what is traversed is only the state of flux. Thereupon the bridle of the spirit loses its driver, and the road to rebirth is reopened daily. One pursues lust in the long

---

13. That is, postponing enlightenment in order to bring others closer to salvation, attaining enlightenment by personal exertions in an age in which there is no Buddha, and attaining enlightenment by hearing the Buddha's preaching. These three are associated with the bodhisattva, the *pratyeka* or "private buddha," and the *śrāvaka* or "voice-hearer," respectively.

stream of time; is one thus affected only once? Therefore he who returns to the source and seeks the First Principle does not encumber his spirit with life. He who breaks out of the grimy shell does not encumber his life with feelings. If one does not encumber one's spirit with life, then one's spirit can be made subtle. The subtle spirit transcending sense-objects — this is what is meant by *nirvāṇa*. The name *nirvāṇa*, can it possibly be an empty appellation? I beg leave to extend this argument and so to prove its truth. Heaven and Earth, though they are great because they give life to living beings, cannot cause a living being not to die. Kings and princes, though they have the power of preserving existence, cannot cause a preserved creature to be without woe. Therefore in our previous discussion we have said, "[He who has left the household life] understands that woes and impediments come from having a body and that by not maintaining the body one terminates woe. He knows that continued life comes from undergoing change, and by not obeying this change he seeks the First Principle." Herein lay our meaning, herein lay our meaning. This is why the monk refuses homage to the Lord of the Myriad Chariots [i.e., the emperor] and keeps his own works sublime, why he is not ranked with kings or princes and yet basks in their kindness.

[From *Hongming ji*, *TD* 52, no. 2102:29–32; LH]

## ADMONITIONS OF THE *FANWANG SŪTRA*

The following admonitions represent the basic moral code to which many Mahāyāna monks in China subscribed when they took the bodhisattva vows or precepts. From what now appears to be an apocryphal text, never canonically sanctioned, these admonitions purport to come from the mouth of the Buddha. In effect they constitute a substantial reduction and modification of the disciplinary code for monks in the earlier, so-called Hīnayāna or Smaller Vehicle (seen as "smaller" because it was more restrictive, difficult to practice, and thus limited in its practicability for all). Here the unlimited expedient or adaptive means available through the later, Greater Vehicle enable it to overcome some of the Chinese objections to the Hīnayāna cited in the preceding Mouzi text.

Note in these admonitions the strong invocation of filiality as a basis for Buddhist discipline. This adaptation to the more life-affirming, family orientation of Confucianism contrasts with the earlier characterization of the Buddhist religious vocation as "leaving the family" (*chujia*). As a major concession to Chinese values, this new view of Buddhism as fulfilling the ends of filial piety became a marked feature of East Asian Buddhism in general.

Later even this simplified code was further minimized in the two main schools of Chinese Buddhist practice, Pure Land and Chan, which emphasized means other than adherence to the traditional disciplinary code for the attainment of salvation.

At that time, the Buddha Śākyamuni, seated under the Bo tree after having attained supreme enlightenment, first set up the Precepts (*Prātimokṣa*): to be filial to one's parents, teacher[s], members of the Buddhist community, and the Three Treasures. Filial obedience is the way by which one attains the Way. Filial piety is called the "admonitions"; it is also called the "prohibitions." Then the Buddha emanated infinite light from his mouth.

At that time, trillions of participants in the assembly, including all the bodhisattvas, eighteen Brahmin kings, the kings of the six heavens in the realm of desires, and sixteen great kings, etc., all joined their palms in front of their chests and listened to the Buddha reciting the Mahāyāna Admonitions of all the Buddhas.

The Buddha told all the bodhisattvas: "I now recite by myself every fortnight, the Admonitions of the Law. All of you bodhisattvas—bodhisattvas who have just aspired [for supreme enlightenment]—should also recite them; bodhisattvas who are in the ten stages of directional decision, the ten stages of the well-nourished heart, the ten stages of "diamond heart," and bodhisattvas who are in the ten stages before attaining Buddhahood, should also recite them. This is why the light of the Admonitions issues forth from my mouth. It has some conditions that make it possible, and it is not without a cause; hence the manifestation as light. [Yet] the light is neither green, nor yellow, nor red, nor white, nor black. It is neither material nor mental. It is neither being nor nonbeing. It is not causation. It is the source of all Buddhas and the root of all bodhisattva deeds. It is the root of all sons of the Buddha in this assembly. Therefore, all sons of the Buddha should receive it and hold to it. You should read, recite, and master it.

"All sons of the Buddha, listen carefully: those who wish to receive the Admonitions, be they kings, princes, ministers, prime ministers, monks, nuns, eighteen Brahmin kings, the six kings of Heaven's realm of desire, or sixteen great kings, commoners . . . male prostitutes, female prostitutes, male servants, female servants, the eight classes of supernatural beings, guardians, animals, even illusory beings, as long as they understand the language of the master [who gives the Admonitions], they are all able to receive the Admonitions and thereby be called 'most pure ones.'"

The Buddha proclaimed to all the sons of the Buddha, saying, "There are ten major precepts. Anyone who has received the Bodhisattva Admonitions and yet does not recite them is not a bodhisattva, nor is one the seed of a Buddha. I also recite them. All the [past] bodhisattvas have learned, all the [future] bodhisattvas will learn, and all the [present] bodhisattvas are learning them. Now that I have explained briefly the nature of the Bodhisattva Precepts, you should learn them and follow them with respect."

1. The Buddha said: "Sons of the Buddha, in the case of killing or urging others to kill; killing for expediency or condoning others who kill; or rejoicing at seeing others kill, or killing by means of a spell—whatever the causes of killing, the condition of killing, the method of killing, or the action of killing—the killing of any living being should not be done intentionally. A bodhisattva

should always give rise to a heart of compassion, a heart of filial piety, using all expedient means to save all sentient beings. If, on the contrary, one kills living beings as one pleases, one commits an unpardonable offense for a bodhisattva.

2. "In the case of a son of the Buddha stealing, urging others to steal, stealing for expediency, or stealing by means of spells—whatever the cause of stealing, the condition of stealing, the method of stealing, and the action of stealing—even things owned by gods and spirits—and whatever the goods—even a needle or a blade of grass—there should be no intentional stealing. A bodhisattva should give rise to the heart of filiality of the Buddha-nature, a heart of compassion, always helping all people to achieve felicity and happiness. If, on the contrary, one goes so far as to steal the property of others, one commits a most unpardonable offense for a bodhisattva.

3. "In the case of a son of the Buddha committing fornication, urging others to commit fornication, or committing fornication with any woman—there should be no intentional fornication, no matter what the cause, condition, method, or act of fornication, whether with female animals, female deities, or female spirits, or any such sexual misconduct. A bodhisattva should give rise to the heart of filiality, bring all sentient beings to salvation, and offer them pure truth. If, on the contrary, one commits any kind of fornication, whether with animals, one's own mother, sisters, and relatives, showing no compassion or restraint, one commits an unpardonable offense for a bodhisattva.

4. "In the case of a son of the Buddha lying, urging others to lie, or lying for expediency—whatever the cause . . . condition . . . method . . . or the act of lying—even if one says one sees something without actually seeing it, or says one did not see something when one has seen it—a bodhisattva should always give rise to correct speech and [help] all sentient beings to give rise to correct speech and correct views. If, on the contrary, one prompts sentient beings to evil speech or evil views, one commits a most unpardonable offense for a bodhisattva.

5. "In the case of a son of the Buddha dealing in alcoholic liquors, or urging others to deal in them—whatever the cause . . . the condition . . . the method . . . or the act of dealing in alcohol—one should do nothing of that kind. Alcoholic liquors are a cause and condition that give rise to wrongdoing, whereas a bodhisattva should give rise to the clear and thorough wisdom of all sentient beings. If, on the contrary, one causes confusion in the minds-and-hearts of all sentient beings, one commits an unpardonable offense for a bodhisattva.

6. "In the case of a son of the Buddha criticizing the transgressions of a bodhisattva who has renounced the world, a bodhisattva who is a householder, a *bhikṣu* monk or a *bhikṣunī* nun, or of someone urging others to criticize such people— whatever the cause . . . condition . . . method . . . or act of criticizing—or when a bodhisattva hears an evil person of a non-Buddhist sect or an evil person who is either a *śrāvaka* or a *pratyeka*-buddha criticizing any Buddhist's violations of law or discipline, if, instead of motivating such an evil person to adopt a positive Mahāyāna mind, the bodhisattva rather lends himself to such criticism, it is a transgression of the Buddha's law and a most unpardonable offense.

7. "In the case of a son of the Buddha himself praising or blaming others, or telling others to do so—whatever the cause . . . the condition . . . the method . . . or act of blaming—whereas the bodhisattva should take upon himself the blame or shame that attaches to all other living beings, whether for evil deeds to oneself or great deeds of others, if, instead, he praises his own merits and conceals others' good deeds, or lets others take the blame, it is a most unpardonable offense for a bodhisattva."

Similar formulations are given for three other offenses—stinginess, anger, and slander against the Three Treasures—which, with the preceding items, make up the ten major vices. These are then followed by a detailing of forty-eight minor violations or vices to be avoided by the bodhisattva, such as disrespect to one's master, drinking liquor, eating meat, eating five forbidden spices, and so on.

[From *Fanwang jing, TD* 24, no. 1484:1004–1005; THT]

*Chapter 16*

## SCHOOLS OF BUDDHIST DOCTRINE

Doctrinal Buddhism developed in China at least three hundred years after Buddhism's presence was first noted there in the first century. It arose not as a result of violent schisms or protestant revolts but as an outgrowth of tendencies already manifest in the earlier period of Buddhist thought.

## THE GENERAL CHARACTER
## OF DOCTRINAL BUDDHISM

The division of Chinese Buddhism into discrete schools had its origins in the tendency to concentrate on the study of one particular scripture or group of scriptures, as containing the most essential truths of.the religion. The Chinese knew almost nothing of the splintering of Buddhism into sects in India and Central Asia. They did not know to what extent the scriptures themselves were sectarian writings, nor did they properly understand the sectarian motivation that lay behind the selection by the various missionaries of the scriptural texts they translated. For them, any Buddhist text translated into Chinese was the word of the Buddha. And since all of the Buddha's pronouncements had to be true, it was necessary to find some way to reconcile the frequently glaring inconsistencies found in the scriptures. A suggestion on how to deal with this problem was furnished to them by the Mahāyāna scriptures themselves.

By the time of the emergence of the Mahāyāna, the so-called Hīnayāna scriptures had already been canonized, and anyone calling himself a Buddhist regarded them as the word of the Buddha. The Mahāyānists composed their own scriptures as they went along, and they found themselves obliged to justify their scriptures as the good coin of Buddhism to a religious community accustomed to reading religious writings of a vastly different tone. To deny the validity of the firmly entrenched Hīnayāna canon was impossible, and the Mahāyānists resorted to a more subtle device. They said that the Hīnayāna was not untrue but was merely a preparatory doctrine, preached by the Buddha to disciples whose minds were not yet receptive to the ultimate truth. When he had prepared them with the provisional doctrine, he then revealed to them his final truth. Thus the Hīnayāna and the Mahāyāna alike were the word of the Buddha, but the full significance of the former became apparent only with the later revelation.

The difficulty here, as far as the Chinese were concerned, was the fact that while the Hīnayāna scriptures, having been canonized by a series of ecclesiastical councils, were more or less homogeneous, the Mahāyāna scriptures had never been canonized or coordinated, and they frequently contradicted not only the Hīnayāna sacred writings but each other as well. To deal with this, the first distinct schools in Chinese Buddhism either concentrated on one scripture or set of scriptures in preference to all others or catalogued the entire canon in such a way as to make one particular scripture appear to contain the Buddha's ultimate teaching. The great Tiantai and Huayan schools did both.

Their doctrines, however, were of a kind that could never have much popular appeal. In addition, the religious practices prescribed by them for the attainment of salvation could be performed only by monks whose whole lives were devoted to religion. On both accounts these schools tended to be limited to the few who had the leisure and training that were required for the study and practice of such sophisticated teachings. Among the great masses of people, therefore, it was not doctrine of this type but rather salvationism of the type represented by the Pure Land school[1] that prevailed.

Furthermore, the view that all scriptures represented the word of the Buddha tended to blur, even for the learned, the doctrinal differences that might have distinguished one sect from another. In the latter half of the Tang dynasty, from about 750 to about 900, one frequently encounters an eminent Chinese monk going about from one center to another studying the precepts of all the schools, as if anything short of mastery of all of them was an imperfect knowledge of Buddhism. Some Chinese monks are claimed as patriarchs by as many as three or four different schools. Thus was confirmed in Chinese Buddhism a strong tendency toward syncretism, which had long been a feature of Chinese thought.

---

1. See chap. 17.

## SCHOOLS OF CHINESE BUDDHIST PHILOSOPHY

From the readings in chapter 15 it will be apparent that some of the most fundamental concepts of Buddhism were comprehended and assimilated by the Chinese with the greatest of difficulty, if at all. Moreover, as one takes up the writings of Buddhist philosophers, one is conscious of having entered another world—not just different from one's own but different even from the Chinese traditions that preceded it. For one thing, one is dealing with metaphysical and psychological questions to which earlier Chinese writers had given less attention than they had to the problems of the individual in society. Yet not only are these questions in their very nature extremely complex and elusive, but also, as discussed by Chinese writers, they presupposed some familiarity with a vast body of Buddhist doctrine from India possessed only by those who had some education (always a small minority in traditional China) and who had dedicated themselves to the pursuit of the religious life, most often in monasteries. Their audience was neither "the general public," nor the "congregation," nor anything resembling the general membership of a creedal church.

Buddhist philosophy first began to flourish in the fourth century C.E., when it was interpreted largely in Daoist terms, on the basis of which "six schools and seven branches" were formed, including Daoan's theory of Original Nonbeing or the Originally Undifferentiated; the same theory as modified by Fashen; Zhi Daolin's theory of Matter-as-Such; and Fawen's theory of No Mind or the Emptiness of Mind. These were simply the teachings of individual thinkers, not of sectarian leaders. As important Indian texts were introduced and translated, as Indian masters arrived, and as Chinese Buddhist scholars finally developed their own systems, differences in opinion appeared and schools came into being. In their zeal to defend their ideas, certain schools of thought denounced others as heretical and established a lineage to earlier masters in order to claim for themselves the authority of tradition. Yet as far as the ordinary Buddhist was concerned, these differences were academic.

Altogether there were ten principal schools, traditionally divided into two main categories, schools of Being and schools of Nonbeing, depending on whether they affirmed or denied the self-nature of the *dharmas* (here "elements of existence") and the ego. There was also the Disciplinary school, based on the Vinaya section of the Buddhist canon. Its doctrine was elaborated and completed by Daoxuan (596–667) in the South Mountain. The discipline for which it was known included 250 "prohibitive precepts" for monks and 348 for nuns. Nevertheless, this school hardly existed as an independent sect in China, and its precepts were largely superseded by the Ten Admonitions presented in chapter 15.

None of these schools exerted much influence or lasted very long. The same may be said of two Mahāyāna schools, the Three-Treatise or Emptiness school and the Consciousness-Only school. The concepts of Emptiness and of the Mind, however, were accepted as basic presuppositions of the remaining schools, and thus were important to what followed.

The common Chinese saying "The Tiantai and Huayan schools for doctrine; the Meditation and Pure Land schools for practice" accurately describes both the strong influence of these schools in particular and the syncretic nature of Chinese Buddhism in general. Of these, the Tiantai did not exist at all in India and the Pure Land, Huayan, and Meditation schools, while traceable to India, developed along characteristically Chinese lines, which enabled them to persist throughout Chinese history.

The remaining Mahāyāna school, the Esoteric school (*Zhenyan*, true word), believed that the universe consists of the "three mysteries" of action, speech, and thought. All phenomena represented by these categories of action, speech, and thought are manifestations of a cosmo-theism centered on the Great Sun Buddha. Through secret language, "mystical verse," "true words," and so on, the quintessential truth of the Buddha can be communicated to human beings. This doctrine was transmitted to China by several Indian monks and attained a considerable vogue in the eighth century but lost its separate identity thereafter. Its influence as a distinct school was felt mostly in Tibet and Japan, while in China its practice became widely diffused into indigenous popular religion.

## THE THREE-TREATISE SCHOOL

The Three-Treatise (*Sanlun*) school is the Chinese representative of the Indian Mādhyamika (Middle Doctrine) school of Nāgārjuna (ca. 100–200 C.E.). It was introduced into China by a half-Indian missionary named Kumārajīva (344–413), who translated into Chinese three Indian works systematizing the Middle Doctrine. Two of these by the Mādhyamika school taught that the phenomenal world has only a qualified reality, as opposed to those who maintained the ultimate reality of the chain of events or elements that make up the phenomenal being or object. According to the Mādhyamika view, a monk with defective eyesight may imagine that he sees flies in his begging bowl, and they have full reality for the perceiver. Though the flies are not real, the illusion of flies is. The Mādhyamika philosophers tried to prove that all our experience of the phenomenal world is like that of the shortsighted monk, that all beings labor under the constant illusion of perceiving things as real, whereas in fact they are only "empty." This pervasive Emptiness or Void (*Śūnyatā*) is the only true reality; hence the Mādhyamikas were sometimes also called *Śūnyavādins* (exponents of the doctrine of Emptiness). Although the phenomenal world is true pragmatically, and therefore has qualified reality for practical purposes, the whole chain of existence is seen as composed only of a series of transitory events, and these, being impermanent, cannot have reality in themselves. Emptiness, on the other hand, never changes. It is absolute truth and absolute being—in fact, it is the same as *nirvāṇa* and the Body of Essence, or *Dharma*-Body, of the Buddha.

Nāgārjuna's system, however, went farther than this. Nothing in the phenomenal world has full being, and all is ultimately unreal. Therefore every rational theory about the world is a theory about something unreal evolved by an unreal thinker with unreal thoughts. Yet, by the same process of reasoning, even the arguments of the Mādhyamika school in favor of the ultimate reality of Emptiness are unreal, and this argument against the Mādhyamika position is itself unreal, and so on in an infinite regression. Every logical argument can be reduced to absurdity by a process such as this.

The effect of Mādhyamika nihilism was not what might be expected. Skeptical philosophies in the West, such as that of existentialism, are generally strongly flavored with pessimism. The Mādhyamikas, however, were not pessimists. If the phenomenal world was ultimately unreal, Emptiness was real, for though every logical proof of its existence was vitiated by the flaw of unreality, it could be experienced in meditation with a directness and certainty that the phenomenal world did not possess. The ultimate Emptiness was here and now, everywhere and all-embracing, and there was, in fact, no difference between the great Emptiness and the phenomenal world (samsāra). Thus all beings were already participants in the Emptiness that was nirvāṇa; they were already Buddha if only they would realize it. This aspect of Mādhyamika philosophy was especially congenial to Chinese Buddhists, nurtured in the doctrine of the Dao, and it had much influence on the development of the special forms of Chinese and Japanese Buddhism, which often show a frank acceptance of the beauty of the world, and especially of the beauty of nature, as a vision of nirvāṇa here and now.

For an understanding of this doctrine as it is discussed in Chinese texts, familiarity with certain technical terms is necessary. One is the concept of *common truth* and *higher truth*. From the standpoint of common or worldly truth, that is, relatively or pragmatically, *dharmas* are said to exist. From the standpoint of higher truth, they are seen to be transitory and lacking in any substantiality or self-nature. Emptiness or the Void alone represents the changeless Reality. The dialectical process by which this ultimate truth is reached is known as the "Middle Path of Eightfold Negations," which systematically denies all antithetical assertions regarding things: "There is no production, no extinction, no annihilation, no permanence, no unity, no diversity, no coming in, no going out." Production, extinction, and so on are shown to be unreal by the use of the "Four Points of Argument"—that is, by refuting any concept of being, of nonbeing, of both being and nonbeing, and of neither being nor nonbeing. The belief in any of the four is an extreme and must be transcended by a higher synthesis through the dialectic method until the Ultimate Void is arrived at, which is the Absolute Middle.

The Middle Way was greatly elaborated and systematized by Jizang (540–623), who had a Parthian father and a Chinese mother. Jizang made the Three Treatises the center of his system of thought, and his influence extended to the eighth century. However, as a school it rapidly declined after the ninth century, while its method was assimilated into other teachings.

A large number of Jizang's writings survive, consisting principally of commentaries on Mahāyāna scriptures and treatises, and containing one of the earliest overall attempts at a systematization of Mahāyāna doctrine.

## JIZANG: THE PROFOUND MEANING OF THE THREE TREATISES

Having set forth his interpretation of the Three Treatises in detailed commentaries to each of them, Jizang arranges topically what he considers to be the essential doctrine of the treatises as a whole.

Of those who misunderstand the Twofold Truth[2] there are, in all, three kinds of men. First are the Abhidharmists, who insist upon the existence of a definite substance, who err in [taking as ultimate what is in fact no more than] dependent existence [that is, a thing coming into existence depending on causes and conditions] and who therefore lose [the true meaning of] Common Truth. They also do not know that dependent existence, just as it is, has no existence, and thus they also lose [the true meaning] of the One True Emptiness. Second are those who learn the Great Vehicle and who are called Men of the Extensive and Broad Way. They adhere to a belief in Emptiness and fail to recognize dependent existence, hence they lose the [true meaning of] Common Truth. Having adhered to the misunderstood Emptiness, they err with regard to the true Emptiness, and thus also lose the [true meaning of] Higher Truth. Third are those in this very age who, though knowing of the Twofold Truth, in some cases say that it is one substance, in some cases say that it is two substances. These theories are both untenable, hence they lose the [true meaning of both] Higher and Common Truth.

Question: "Higher and Common Truths are one substance." What error is there in this?

Answer: If Higher and Common Truths are one and the same in being true, then Higher Truth is true and Common Truth is also true. If Higher Truth and Common Truth are one and the same in being common, then Common Truth is common and Higher Truth is also common. If Higher Truth is true and Common Truth is not true, then Common Truth and Higher Truth are different. If Common Truth is common and Higher Truth is not common, then Higher Truth and Common Truth are different. Therefore both ways are blocked, and the two cannot be one.

Question: If it is an error to regard the two as one substance, then it should be blameless to regard them as different.

---

2. The Common Truth—that *dharmas* have a relative or dependent existence—and the Higher Truth—that they are ultimately unreal and that Emptiness or Voidness alone constitutes changeless reality.

Answer: The scriptures say, "Matter in and of itself is void; void in and of itself is matter." If you say that each has its own substance, then their mutual (shared) identity is destroyed. If they have mutual identity, then duality of substance cannot be established. Therefore there is no latitude [for argument] in any direction, and conflicting theories are all exhausted.

*Mahāyāna Truth is beyond all predication. It is neither one nor many, neither permanent nor impermanent. In other words, it is above all forms of differentiation or, as its adherents might say, it transcends both difference and identity. In order to make this point clear, the Three Treatises doctrine teaches that each thesis that may be proposed concerning the nature of Truth must be negated by its antithesis, the whole process advancing step by step until total negation has been achieved. Thus the idea of being, representing Common Truth, is negated by that of nonbeing, representing Higher Truth. In turn, the idea of nonbeing, now having become the Common Truth of a new pair, is negated by the idea of neither being nor nonbeing, and so forth, until everything that may be predicated about Truth has been negated.*

Objection: If there is neither affirmation nor negation, then there is also neither wrong nor right. Why, then, in the beginning section do you call it the "refutation of wrong" and the "demonstration of right"?

Answer: That there are negation and affirmation, we consider "wrong." That there is neither affirmation nor negation, we call "right." It is for this reason that we have explained it in this section in terms of the "Refutation of Wrong" and the "Demonstration of Right."

Objection: Once there are a wrong to be refuted and a right to be demonstrated, then the mind is exercising a choice. How can one say then that it "leans [depends] on nothing"?

Answer: In order to put an end to wrong, we force ourselves to speak of "right." Once wrong has been ended, then neither does right remain. Therefore the mind has nothing to which it adheres [or on which it depends].

[From *Sanlun xuanyi*, TD 45, no. 1852:1–11; LH]

## THE LOTUS SCHOOL: THE TIANTAI SYNTHESIS

From the philosophical standpoint, and in terms of its influence on other schools in China, Korea, and Japan, the Lotus or Tiantai teaching is of major importance. Moreover, it has distinctively Chinese features. Though its basic scripture is the *Lotus of the Wonderful Law (Saddharmapuṇḍarīka Sūtra)*, a work from North India or Central Asia, the school is founded upon the interpretation given this text by the great Chinese monk Zhiyi (538–597), and its other name indicates its place of geographical origin, the Tiantai (Heavenly Terrace) Mountain of Zhejiang province, where Zhiyi taught.

For this Grand Master of the Tiantai, the *Lotus*, one of the most popular of Mahāyāna *sūtras*, was not primarily a philosophical text but a guide to religious salvation through practice. Zhiyi lectured for years on its written text, minutely examining every detail of language and subtlety of meaning and giving special attention to the methods of religious practice embodied in the *Lotus*. His deliberations were recorded by his pupil Guanding and have come down to us as the "Three Great Works" of the school, namely, the *Words and Phrases of the Lotus* (*Fahua wenju*), the *Profound Meaning of the Lotus* (*Fahua xuanyi*), and the *Great Calming and Contemplation* (*Mohe zhiguan*).

In Zhiyi's time, Buddhist thought in South China was distinctly philosophical in character, while in the north Buddhists were developing a religion of faith and discipline. Himself a product of the southern Chinese gentry, but with a northerner, Huisi (514–577), as his teacher, Zhiyi came to the conclusion that the contemplative and philosophical approaches to religion were like the two wings of a bird. Consequently, the Tiantai school is characterized by a strong philosophical content and at the same time an even stronger emphasis on meditative practice.

The Tiantai doctrine centers around the principle of the Perfectly Harmonious Threefold Truth: (1) all things or *dharmas* are empty because they are produced through causes and conditions and therefore have no self-nature, but (2) they do have tentative or provisional existence, and (3) being both Empty and Tentative is the nature of *dharmas* and is the Mean. These three—Emptiness, Tentativeness, and the Mean—involve one another so that one is three and three are one, the conditional thus being correlated with the unconditional.

Furthermore, within this threefold scheme of Emptiness, Tentativeness, and the Mean an additional distinction may be made among ten realms of existence—those of the hell dwellers, hungry ghosts, animals, human beings, *asuras* (spirits), heavenly beings, *śrāvakas* ("voice-hearers" or direct disciples of the Buddha), *pratyeka*-buddhas ("private" buddhas or buddhas-for-themselves), bodhisattvas, and Buddhas.

Each of these ten realms shares the characteristics of the others, thus making one hundred realms. Each of these in turn is characterized by ten thusnesses or such-likenesses through which the true state is manifested in phenomena, namely, such-like character, such-like nature, such-like substance, such-like power, such-like activity, such-like causes, such-like conditions, such-like effects, such-like retributions, and such-like beginning-and-end-ultimately-alike. This makes one thousand realms of existence. In turn, each realm consists of the three divisions of living beings, of space, and of the aggregates that constitute *dharmas*, thus making a total of three thousand realms of existence, representing experienced reality in all its diversity.

These realms are so interwoven and interpenetrated that they may be considered "immanent in a single instant of thought." This does not mean that they are produced by the thought of man or Buddha, as taught in some Mahāyāna schools, but rather that in every thought-moment, all the possible worlds are involved. Accordingly, the great emphasis in this school is on calming and contemplation as a means of perceiving the ultimate truth embodied in such a thought-moment. In short, this teaching is crystallized in the celebrated saying that "Every color or fragrance is none other than the Middle Path." Every *dharma* is thus an embodiment of the real essence of the Ultimate Emptiness, or True Thusness. It follows that all beings have the Buddha-nature in them and can be saved. This is the great message of the *Lotus*, as explained by Zhiyi.

The school claims that the *Lotus* offers the most complete doctrine among all the Buddhist teachings. It classifies the teachings of the Buddha into five periods. The first four, represented by the literature of various schools, are regarded as provisional or tentative, whereas the teaching contained in the *Lotus* is considered final. Thus a qualified truth is seen in the teachings of other schools, which in certain respects are mutually contradictory, while the *Lotus* is seen as fulfilling and reconciling them in a final synthesis. It is an attempt to replace the Three Vehicles[3] by One Vehicle. In its all-inclusiveness, then, the Tiantai points again to the doctrine of universal salvation, the outstanding characteristic of the Mahāyāna movement.

### EXCERPTS FROM THE *LOTUS SŪTRA*

The *Lotus Sūtra* is by far the most popular and influential of Mahāyāna scriptures in East Asia. It claims to represent the culmination of Śākyamuni Buddha's teaching before his decease and final translation into *nirvāṇa*. The excerpts given here, taken from Kumārajīva's translation into Chinese of 406 C.E., illustrate the following main doctrines of the text: (1) the fulfillment of successive stages in the Buddha's teaching in the One Great Vehicle; (2) the principle of accommodation or expedient means and the parables used for this comprehension; (3) the revelation of Śākyamuni, the human Buddha, as identical with the ageless Eternal Buddha; (4) the *Lotus Sūtra* itself as embodying the Buddha's truth; (5) the salvation of women as personified by the Dragon King's daughter; and (6) the personification of infinite expedient means in the popular Bodhisattva of Compassion or Goddess of Mercy, Guanyin (Perceiver of the World's Sounds).

This is what I heard:

At one time the Buddha was in Rājagṛha, staying on Mount Gṛdhrakūṭa. Accompanying him were a multitude of leading monks numbering twelve thousand persons. All were *arhats* whose outflows had come to an end, who had no more earthly

---

3. Those of the *pratyeka*-buddhas, who attain to their personal enlightenment by their own exertions; the *śrāvakas*, who attain to their own salvation by hearing the Buddha's teaching; and the bodhisattvas, who postpone their translation into final *nirvāṇa* for the sake of helping all beings to be saved.

desires, who had attained what was to their advantage and had put an end to the bonds of existence, and whose minds had achieved a state of freedom. . . .

There were bodhisattvas and *mahāsattvas*, eighty thousand of them, none of them ever regressing in their search for supreme perfect enlightenment. All had gained *dhāraṇīs*, delighted in preaching, were eloquent, and turned the wheel of the Law that knows no regression. They had made offerings to immeasurable hundreds and thousands of Buddhas, in the presence of various Buddhas had planted numerous roots of virtue, had been constantly praised by the Buddhas, had trained themselves in compassion, were good at entering the Buddha wisdom, and had fully penetrated the great wisdom and reached the farther shore. Their fame had spread throughout immeasurable worlds and they were able to save countless hundreds of thousands of living beings. . . .

At that time the Buddha emitted a ray of light from the tuft of white hair between his eyebrows, one of his characteristic features, lighting up eighteen thousand worlds in the eastern direction. There was no place that the light did not penetrate, reaching downward as far as the Avīci hell and upward to the Akaniṣṭha heaven. . . .

At that time Bodhisattva Maitreya had this thought: Now the World-Honored One has manifested these miraculous signs. But what is the cause of these auspicious portents? . . .

At that time Bodhisattva Maitreya wished to settle his doubts concerning the matter. And in addition he could see what was in the minds of the four kinds of believers, the monks, nuns, laymen, and laywomen, as well as the heavenly beings, dragons, spirits, and the others who made up the assembly. So he questioned Mañjuśrī, saying, "What is the cause of these auspicious portents, these signs of transcendental powers, this emitting of a great beam of brightness that illumines the eighteen thousand lands in the eastern direction so we can see all the adornments of the Buddha worlds there?" . . .

## The Buddha Preaches the One Great Vehicle

At that time Mañjuśrī said to the bodhisattva and *mahāsattva* Maitreya and the other great men, "Good men, I suppose that the Buddha, the World-Honored One, wishes now to expound the great Law." . . .

At that time the World-Honored One calmly arose from his *samādhi* and addressed Śāriputra, saying, "The wisdom of the Buddhas is infinitely profound and immeasurable. The door to this wisdom is difficult to understand and difficult to enter. . . .

"Śāriputra, ever since I attained Buddhahood I have through various causes and various similes widely expounded my teachings and have used countless expedient means to guide living beings and cause them to renounce their attachments. Why is this? Because the Thus-Come One is fully possessed of both expedient means and the perfection of wisdom. . . .

"Śāriputra, to sum it up: the Buddha has fully realized the Law that is limitless, boundless, never attained before. . . .

"Śāriputra, the Buddhas preach the Law in accordance with what is appropriate, but the meaning is difficult to understand. Why is this? Because we employ countless expedient means, discussing causes and conditions and using words of simile and parable to expound the teachings. This Law is not something that can be understood through pondering or analysis. Only those who are Buddhas can understand it. . . .

"Śāriputra, I know that living beings have various desires, attachments that are deeply implanted in their minds. Taking cognizance of this basic nature of theirs, I will therefore use various causes and conditions, words of simile and parable, and the power of expedient means and expound the Law for them. Śāriputra, I do this so that all of them may attain the one Buddha vehicle and wisdom embracing all species. . . .

"Śāriputra, if any of my disciples should claim to be an *arhat* or a *pratyeka*-buddha and yet does not heed or understand that the Buddhas, the Thus-Come Ones, simply teach and convert the bodhisattvas, then he is no disciple of mine; he is no *arhat* or *pratyeka*-buddha.

"Again, Śāriputra, if there should be monks or nuns who claim that they have already attained the status of *arhat*, that this is their last incarnation, that they have reached the final *nirvāṇa*, and that therefore they have no further intention of seeking supreme perfect enlightenment, then you should understand that such as these are all persons of overbearing arrogance. Why do I say this? Because if there are monks who have truly attained the status of *arhat*, then it would be unthinkable that they should fail to believe this Law. . . . There is no other vehicle, there is only the one Buddha vehicle." . . .

## The Parable of the Burning House

"Moreover, Śāriputra, I too will now make use of similes and parables to further clarify this doctrine. For through similes and parables those who are wise can obtain understanding.

"Śāriputra, suppose that in a certain town in a certain country there was a very rich man. He was far along in years, and his wealth was beyond measure. He had many fields, houses, and menservants. His own house was big and rambling, but it had only one gate. A great many people—a hundred, two hundred, perhaps as many as five hundred—lived in the house. The halls and rooms were old and decaying, the walls crumbling, the pillars rotten at their base, and the beams and rafters crooked and aslant.

"At that time a fire suddenly broke out on all sides, spreading through the rooms of the house. The sons of the rich man—ten, twenty, perhaps thirty—were inside the house. When the rich man saw the huge flames leaping up on every side, he was greatly alarmed and fearful and thought to himself, 'I can escape to safety through the flaming gate, but my sons are inside the burning house enjoying themselves and playing games, unaware, unknowing, without alarm or fear. The fire is closing in on them, suffering and pain threaten them, yet their minds have no sense of loathing or peril and they do not think of trying to escape!'

"Śāriputra, this rich man thought to himself, 'I have strength in my body and arms. I can wrap them in a robe or place them on a bench and carry them out of the house.' And then again he thought, 'This house has only one gate, and moreover it is narrow and small.

"'My sons are very young, they have no understanding, and they love their games, being so engrossed in them that they are likely to be burned in the fire. I must explain to them why I am fearful and alarmed. The house is already in flames, and I must get them out quickly and not let them be burned up in the fire!'

"Having thought in this way, he followed his plan and called to all his sons, saying, 'You must come out at once!' But though the father was moved by pity and gave good words of instruction, the sons were absorbed in their games and unwilling to heed him. They had no alarm, no fright, and in the end no mind to leave the house. Moreover, they did not understand what the fire was, what the house was, what danger was. They merely raced about this way and that in play and looked at their father without heeding him.

"At that time the rich man had this thought: 'The house is already in flames from this huge fire. If I and my sons do not get out at once, we are certain to be burned. I must now invent some expedient means that will make it possible for the children to escape harm.'

"The father understood his sons and knew what various toys and curious objects each child customarily liked and what would delight them. And so he said to them, 'The kind of playthings you like are rare and hard to find. If you do not take them when you can, you will surely regret it later. For example, things like these goat-carts, deer-carts, and ox-carts. They are outside the gate now where you can play with them. So you must come out of this burning house at once. Then whatever ones you want, I will give them all to you!'

"At that time, when the sons heard their father telling them about these rare playthings, because such things were just what they had wanted, each felt emboldened in heart and, pushing and shoving one another, they all came wildly dashing out of the burning house.

"At this time the rich man, seeing that his sons had gotten out safely and all were seated on the open ground at the crossroads and were no longer in danger, was greatly relieved and his mind danced for joy. At that time each of the sons said to his father, 'The playthings you promised us earlier, the goat-carts and deer-carts and ox-carts—please give them to us now!'

"Śāriputra, at that time the rich man gave to each of his sons a large carriage of uniform size and quality. The carriages were tall and spacious and adorned with numerous jewels. A railing ran all around them and bells hung from all four sides. A canopy was stretched over the top, which was also decorated with an assortment of precious jewels. Ropes of jewels twined around, a fringe of flowers hung down, and layers of cushions were spread inside, on which were placed vermilion pillows. Each carriage was drawn by a white ox, pure and clean in hide, handsome in form and of great strength, capable of pulling the carriage smoothly and properly at a pace fast as the wind. In addition, there were many grooms and servants to attend and guard the carriage.

"What was the reason for this? This rich man's wealth was limitless, and he had many kinds of storehouses that were all filled and overflowing. And he thought to himself, 'There is no end to my possessions. It would not be right if I were to give my sons small carriages of inferior make. These little boys are all my sons and I love them without partiality. I have countless numbers of large carriages adorned with seven kinds of gems. I should be fair-minded and give one to each of my sons. I should not show any discrimination. Why? Because even if I distributed these possessions of mine to every person in the whole country I would still not exhaust them, much less could I do so by giving them to my sons!'

"At that time each of the sons mounted his large carriage, gaining something he had never had before, something he had originally never expected. Śāriputra, what do you think of this? When this rich man impartially handed out to his sons these big carriages adorned with rare jewels, was he guilty of falsehood or not?

"Śāriputra said, 'No, World-Honored One. This rich man simply made it possible for his sons to escape the peril of fire and preserve their lives. He did not commit a falsehood. Why do I say this? Because if they were able to preserve their lives, then they had already obtained a plaything of sorts. And how much more so when, through an expedient means, they are rescued from that burning house.'" . . .

## The Impoverished Son

At that time, the men of lifelong wisdom . . . gazing up in reverence at the face of the Honored One, said to the Buddha, "We stand at the head of the monks and are all of us old and decrepit. We believed that we had already attained *nirvāṇa* and that we were incapable of doing more, and so we never sought to attain supreme perfect enlightenment. . . .

"When we heard of this supreme perfect enlightenment, which the Buddha uses to teach and convert the bodhisattvas, our minds were not filled with any thought of joy or approval. But now in the presence of the Buddha we have heard this voice-hearer receive a prophecy that he will attain supreme perfect enlightenment, and our minds are greatly delighted. . . .

"World-Honored One, we would be pleased now to employ a parable to make clear our meaning. Suppose there was a man, still young in years, who abandoned his father, ran away, and lived for a long time in another land, for perhaps ten, twenty, or even fifty years. As he grew older, he found himself increasingly poor and in want. He hurried about in every direction, seeking for clothing and food, wandering farther and farther afield until by chance he turned his steps in the direction of his homeland.

"The father meanwhile had been searching for his son without success and had taken up residence in a certain city. The father's household was very wealthy, with immeasurable riches and treasures. . . .

"At this time the impoverished son wandered from village to village, passing through various lands and towns, till at last he came to the city where his father was residing. The father thought constantly of his son. . . . 'If I could find my son and entrust my wealth and possessions to him, then I could feel contented and easy in mind and would have no more worries.'

"World-Honored One, at that time the impoverished son drifted from one kind of employment to another until he came by chance to his father's house. He stood by the side of the gate, gazing far off at his father, who was seated on a lion throne, his legs supported by a jeweled footrest, while Brahmans, noblemen, and householders, uniformly deferential, surrounded him. . . .

"When the impoverished son saw how great was his father's power and authority, he was filled with fear and awe and regretted he had ever come to such a place. Secretly he thought to himself, 'This must be some king, or one who is equal to a king. This is not the sort of place where I can hire out my labor and gain a living. It would be better to go to some poor village where, if I work hard, I will find a place and can easily earn food and clothing. . . .' Having thought in this way, he raced from the spot.

"At that time the rich old man, seated on his lion throne, spied his son and recognized him immediately. . . .

"Thereupon he dispatched a bystander to go after the son as quickly as possible and bring him back. At that time the messenger raced swiftly after the son and laid hold of him. The impoverished son, alarmed and fearful, cried out in an angry voice, 'I have done nothing wrong! Why am I being seized?' But the messenger held on to him more tightly than ever and forcibly dragged him back. . . .

"The father, observing this from a distance, spoke to the messenger, saying, 'I have no need of this man. Don't force him to come here, but sprinkle cold water on his face so he will regain his senses. Then say nothing more to him!'

"Why did he do that? Because the father knew that his son was of humble outlook and ambition, and that his own rich and eminent position would be difficult for the son to accept. He knew very well that this was his son, but as a form of expedient means he refrained from saying to anyone, 'This is my son.' . . .

"At that time the rich man, hoping to entice his son back again, decided to employ expedient means and send two men as secret messengers, men who were lean and haggard and had no imposing appearance. 'Go seek out that poor man and approach him casually. Tell him you know a place where he can earn twice the regular wage. If he agrees to the arrangement, then bring him here and put him to work. If he asks what sort of work he will be put to, say that he will be employed to clear away excrement, and that the two of you will be working with him.' . . .

"Later he spoke to his son again, saying, 'Now then, young man! You must keep on at this work and not leave me anymore. I will increase your wages. . . . I have an old servant I can lend you when you need him. You may set your mind at ease. I will be like a father to you, so have no more worries. . . . From now on you will be like my own son.' And the rich man proceeded to select a name and assign it to the man as though he were his child.

"At this time the impoverished son, though he was delighted at such treatment, still thought of himself as a person of humble station who was in the employ of another. Therefore the rich man kept him clearing away excrement for the next twenty years. By the end of this time, the son felt that he was understood and trusted, and he could come and go at ease, but he continued to live in the same place as before. . . .

"After some time had passed, the father perceived that his son was bit by bit becoming more self-assured and magnanimous in outlook, that he was determined to accomplish great things and despised his former low opinion of himself. Realizing that his own end was approaching, he ordered his son to arrange a meeting with his relatives and the king of the country, the high ministers, and the noblemen and householders. When they were all gathered together, he proceeded to make this announcement: 'Gentlemen, you should know that this is my son, who was born to me. In such-and-such a city he abandoned me and ran away, and for over fifty years he wandered about suffering hardship. . . . Now everything that belongs to me, all my wealth and possessions, shall belong entirely to this son of mine. Matters of outlay and income that have occurred in the past this son of mine is familiar with.'

"World-Honored One, when the impoverished son heard these words of his father, he was filled with great joy, having gained what he had never had before, and he thought to himself, 'I originally had no mind to covet or seek such things. Yet now these stores of treasures have come of their own accord!'

"World-Honored One, this old man with his great riches is none other than the Thus-Come One, and we are all like the Buddha's sons. The Thus-Come One constantly tells us that we are his sons. But because of the three sufferings, World-Honored One, in the midst of birth and death we undergo burning anxieties, delusions, and ignorance, delighting in and clinging to lesser doctrines. But today the World-Honored One causes us to ponder carefully, to cast aside such doctrines, the filth of frivolous debate." . . .


## The Emergence of the Treasure Tower

At that time in the Buddha's presence there was a tower adorned with the seven treasures, five hundred *yojanas* in height and two hundred and fifty *yojanas* in width and depth, that rose up out of the earth and stood suspended in the air. Various kinds of precious objects adorned it. . . .

At that time a loud voice issued from the treasure tower, speaking words of praise: "Excellent, excellent! Śākyamuni, World-Honored One, that you can take the great wisdom of equality, a Law to instruct the bodhisattvas, guarded and kept in mind by the Buddhas, the *Lotus Sūtra of the Wonderful Law*, and preach it for the sake of the great assembly!" . . .

At that time there was a bodhisattva and *mahāsattva* named Great Joy of Preaching, who . . . said to the Buddha, "World-Honored One, for what reason has this treasure tower risen up out of the earth? And why does this voice issue from its midst?"

At that time the Buddha said, "Bodhisattva Great Joy of Preaching, in the treasure tower is the complete body of a Thus-Come One. Long ago, an immeasurable thousand, ten thousand, million *asaṅkhyeyas* of worlds to the east, in a land called Treasure Purity, there was a Buddha named Many Treasures. When this Buddha was originally carrying out the bodhisattva way, he made a great vow, saying, 'If, after I have become a Buddha and entered extinction, in the lands in the ten directions there is any place where the *Lotus Sūtra* is preached, then my funerary tower, in order that I may listen to the *sūtra*, will come forth and appear in that spot to testify to the *sūtra* and praise its excellence.'" . . .

## The Unity and Diversity of Buddhahood

At that time Śākyamuni Buddha saw the Buddhas that were his emanations all assembled, each sitting on a lion seat, and heard all these Buddhas say that they wished to participate in the opening of the treasure tower. . . .

Śākyamuni Buddha with the fingers of his right hand then opened the door of the tower of seven treasures. A loud sound issued from it, like the sound of a lock and crossbar being removed from a great city gate, and at once all the members of the assembly caught sight of Many Treasures Thus-Come One seated on a lion seat inside the treasure tower, his body whole and unimpaired, sitting as though engaged in meditation. And they heard him say, "Excellent, excellent, Śākyamuni Buddha! You have preached this *Lotus Sūtra* in a spirited manner. I have come here in order that I may hear this *sūtra*."

At that time the four kinds of believers, observing the Buddha who had passed into extinction immeasurable thousands, ten thousands, millions of *kalpas* in the past speaking in this way, marveled at what they had never known before and took the masses of heavenly jeweled flowers and scattered them over Many Treasures Buddha and Śākyamuni Buddha.

At that time Many Treasures Buddha offered half of his seat in the treasure tower to Śākyamuni Buddha, saying, "Śākyamuni Buddha, sit here!" Śākyamuni Buddha at once entered the tower and took half of the seat, seating himself in cross-legged position.

At that time the members of the great assembly, seeing the two Thus-Come Ones seated cross-legged on the lion seat in the tower of seven treasures, all thought to themselves, "These Buddhas are seated high up and far away! If only the Thus-Come Ones would employ their transcendental powers to enable all of us to join them there in the air!"

Immediately Śākyamuni Buddha used his transcendental powers to lift all the members of the great assembly up into the air. And in a loud voice he addressed all the four kinds of believers, saying, "Who is capable of broadly preaching the *Lotus Sūtra of the Wonderful Law* in this *sahā* world? Now is the time to do so, for before long the Thus-Come One will enter *nirvāṇa*. The Buddha wishes to entrust this *Lotus Sūtra of the Wonderful Law* to someone so that it may be preserved." . . .

## The Daughter of the Dragon King

Bodhisattva Wisdom Accumulated questioned Mañjuśrī, saying, "This *sūtra* is very profound, subtle, and wonderful, a treasure among *sūtras*, a rarity in the world. Are there perhaps any living beings who, by earnestly and diligently practicing this *sūtra*, have been able to attain Buddhahood quickly?"

Mañjuśrī replied, "There is the daughter of the dragon king Sāgara, who has just turned eight. Her wisdom has keen roots, and she is good at understanding the root activities and deeds of living beings. She has mastered the *dhāraṇīs*, has been able to accept and embrace all the storehouse of profound secrets preached by the Buddhas, has entered deep into meditation, thoroughly grasped the doctrines, and in the space of an instant conceived the desire for *bodhi* and reached the level of no regression. Her eloquence knows no hindrance, and she thinks of living beings with compassion as though they were her own children. She is fully endowed with blessings, and when it comes to conceiving in mind and expounding by mouth, she is subtle, wonderful, comprehensive, and great. Kind, compassionate, benevolent, yielding, she is gentle and refined in will, capable of attaining *bodhi*." . . .

At that time Śāriputra said to the dragon girl, "You suppose that in this short time you have been able to attain the unsurpassed way. But this is difficult to believe. Why? Because a woman's body is soiled and defiled, not a vessel for the Law. How could you attain the unsurpassed *bodhi*? The road to Buddhahood is long and far-stretching. Only after one has spent immeasurable *kalpas* pursuing austerities, accumulating deeds, practicing all kinds of *pāramitās*, can one finally achieve success. Moreover, a woman is subject to the five obstacles. First, she cannot become a Brahma heavenly king. Second, she cannot become the king Śakra. Third, she cannot become a devil king. Fourth, she cannot become a wheel-turning sage king. Fifth, she cannot become a Buddha. How then could a woman like you be able to attain Buddhahood so quickly?"

At that time the dragon girl had a precious jewel worth as much as the thousand-millionfold world, which she presented to the Buddha. The Buddha immediately accepted it. The dragon girl said to Bodhisattva Wisdom Accumulated and to the venerable one, Śāriputra, "I presented the precious jewel and the World-Honored One accepted it—was that not quickly done?"

They replied, "Very quickly!"

The girl said, "Employ your supernatural powers and watch me attain Buddhahood. It will be even quicker than that!"

At that time the members of the assembly all saw the dragon girl in the space of an instant change into a man and carry out all the practices of a bodhisattva, immediately proceeding to the Spotless World of the south, taking a seat on a jeweled lotus, and attaining impartial and correct enlightenment. With the thirty-two features and the eighty characteristics, he expounded the wonderful Law for all living beings everywhere in the ten directions. . . .

## The Bodhisattva Perceiver of the World's Sounds (Guanyin)

The following brief extracts are from chapter 25 of the *Lotus*, which became separately known and widely recited as the "Guanyin Sūtra." Note that whatever the expedient means or transformations employed by Guanyin (also popularly known as the Bodhisattva of Mercy), the primary function of the bodhisattva is to enlighten deluded, suffering beings. Under this aspect, Guanyin is portrayed iconographically as carrying the lamp of enlightenment.

At that time the bodhisattva Inexhaustible Intent immediately rose from his seat, bared his right shoulder, pressed his palms together, and, facing the Buddha, spoke these words: "World-Honored One, this Bodhisattva Perceiver of the World's Sounds—why is he called Perceiver of the World's Sounds?"

The Buddha said to Bodhisattva Inexhaustible Intent, "Good man, suppose there are immeasurable hundreds, thousands, ten thousands, millions of living beings who are undergoing various trials and suffering. If they hear of this bodhisattva Perceiver of the World's Sounds and single-mindedly call his name, then at once he will perceive the sound of their voices and they will all gain deliverance from their trials. . . .

"If there should be living beings beset by numerous lusts and cravings, let them think with constant reverence of Bodhisattva Perceiver of the World's Sounds, and then they can shed their desires. If they have great wrath and ire, let them think with constant reverence of Bodhisattva Perceiver of the World's Sounds, and then they can shed their ire. If they have great ignorance and stupidity, let them think with constant reverence of Bodhisattva Perceiver of the World's Sounds, and they can rid themselves of stupidity. . . .

"If they need a monk, a nun, a layman believer, or a laywoman believer to be saved, immediately he becomes a monk, a nun, a layman believer, or a laywoman believer and preaches the Law for them. . . .

"If they need a heavenly being, a dragon, a *yakṣa*, a *gandharva*, an *asura*, a *garuḍa*, a *kinnara*, a *mahoraga*, a human, or a nonhuman being to be saved, immediately he becomes all of these and preaches the Law for them. . . .

"Inexhaustible Intent, this Bodhisattva Perceiver of the World's Sounds has succeeded in acquiring benefits such as these and, taking on a variety of different forms, goes about among the lands saving living beings. . . ."

[From Watson, *The Lotus Sutra*, pp. 3–6, 23–24, 31–32, 56–58, 80–86, 170–176, 186–188, 298–304; trans. based on the *Myōhō-renge-kyō narabi ni kaiketsu*]

## HUISI: *THE METHOD OF CALMING AND CONTEMPLATION IN THE MAHĀYĀNA*

By calming is meant to know that all *dharmas*, originally having no self-nature of their own, are never created nor annihilated by themselves but come into being because they are caused by illusions and imagination, and exist without real existence. In those created *dharmas*, their existence is really non-existence. They are only the One Mind, whose substance admits of no differentiation. Those who hold this view can stop the flow of false ideas. This is called calming (or stopping).

By contemplation is meant that although we know that [things] are originally not created and at present not annihilated, nevertheless they were caused to arise out of the Mind's nature and hence are not without a worldly function of an illusory and imaginative nature. They are like illusions and dreams; they [seem to] exist but really do not. This is therefore contemplation.

As to the function of calming and contemplation: It means that because of the accomplishment of calming, the Pure Mind is merged through Principle with the Nature, which is without duality and is harmoniously united with all beings as a body of one single character. Thereupon the Three Treasures [the Buddha, the Law, and the Order] are combined without being three, and the Two Levels of Truth are fused without being two. How calm, still, and pure! How deep, stable, and quiet! How pure and clear the inner silence! It functions without the appearance of functioning, and acts without the appearance of acting. It is so because all *dharmas* are originally the same everywhere without differentiation, and the nature of the Mind is but *dharma*. This is the substance of the most profound *Dharma*-nature.

It also means that because of the accomplishment of contemplation, the substance of the Pure Mind and the functioning of the objective world are manifested without obstacle, spontaneously producing the capabilities of all pure and impure things. . . . Again, owing to the accomplishment of calming, one's mind is the same everywhere and one no longer dwells within the cycle of life and death; yet owing to the accomplishment of contemplation, one's attitudes and functions are results of causation and one does not enter *nirvāṇa*. Moreover, owing to the accomplishment of calming, one dwells in the great *nirvāṇa*, and yet, owing to the attainment of contemplation, one remains in the realm of life and death.

[From *Dacheng zhiguan famen*, TD 46, no. 1924:642–661; LH]

## THE FLOWER GARLAND (HUAYAN) SCHOOL

The basic scripture of the Flower Garland (*Huayan*) school is the *Flower Garland Sūtra* (*Huayan jing*), a lengthy work describing an enormously grand vision of the universe. The language of the *sūtra* is mythic and extravagant, so much so that it has acquired a reputation for being abstruse and impossible to comprehend. Widely regarded in the Mahāyāna tradition as being the first sermon preached by the Buddha, revealing the full content of his enlightenment, the *sūtra* was said to be too profound and lofty for human understanding. Thereafter, making concessions to human limitations, the Buddha preached other sūtras that were easier to understand.

Despite its reputation for complexity, the *Flower Garland Sūtra* teaches tenets similar to those developed in other schools, and contributes to a doctrinal common ground for Mahāyāna Buddhism in general. The terms *interdependence, interpenetration, simultaneous co-arising,* and *nonduality* express this basic notion of how the diverse elements of the universe are interdependent and interrelated with each other. This is not to say that everything is identical; quite to the contrary, the Huayan vision affirms diversity and attempts to explain an inherent and simultaneous interrelatedness of each thing with all things, and all things with each thing, without loss of individual identities.

The patriarchs of the Huayan school often enjoyed the patronage of rulers. Dushun (557–640), the founder of the school, was held in high esteem by Emperor Wen (r. 589–605) of the Sui dynasty; and Fazang (643–712), the third patriarch and great systematizer of Huayan teachings, was honored several times by Empress Wu (r. 684–704) of the Tang,[4] who supported a new Chinese translation of the *Flower Garland Sūtra* by Śikṣānanda.

### THE FLOWER GARLAND SŪTRA

The last section of the *Sūtra* tells of the pilgrimage of Sudhana, a youth who visits a wide variety of people, each of whom teaches him something about the Flower Garland universe. Maitreya welcomed Sudhana by showing him the great tower of Vairocana, the central Buddha of the *sūtra*. The tower was a place in which the interrelatedness of the universe could be seen.

In the Huayan view, a Buddhist state (*foguo*) would be one which lent itself to the support of this universal spiritual communion. However, as a universal principle underlying a universal state, the mutual fusion and permeability of all things, while acting as a solvent of all local loyalties and cultural particularism, also left questions as to the solid ground on which one might erect any social or political structure or ethic.

---

4. Actually, Empress Wu assumed the title of "Emperor" (the only woman in Chinese history to have done so) and adopted the dynastic name of Zhou, rather than Tang, during her ascendancy.

## Indra's Net

One of the most memorable metaphors in Huayan literature is that of Indra's Net, which describes a vision of all things in an interrelationship with each other without being blended into a single homogeneous entity. This characteristic metaphor is found at the end of *Calming and Contemplation in the Five Teachings of Huayan*, a work often, though perhaps inaccurately, attributed to Dushun.

The jeweled net of Śakra is also called Indra's Net, and is made up of jewels. The jewels are shiny and reflect each other successively, their images permeating each other over and over. In a single jewel they all appear at the same time, and this can be seen in each and every jewel. There is really no coming or going.

Now if we turn to the southwest direction and pick up one of the jewels to examine it, we will see that this one jewel can immediately reflect the images of all of the other jewels. Each of the other jewels will do the same. Each jewel will simultaneously reflect the images of all the jewels in this manner, as will all of the other jewels. The images are repeated and multiplied in each other in a manner that is unbounded. Within the boundaries of a single jewel are contained the unbounded repetition and profusion of the images of all the jewels. The reflections are exceedingly clear and are completely unhindered.

[From *Huayan wujiao zhiguan*, TD 45, no. 1867:513; GT]

## The Buddha-Kingdom of the *Flower Garland Sūtra*

A common refrain in Huayan Buddhism is the claim that the perfect realm of the Buddha (*li*) is interfused with the ordinary world (*shi*) without obstruction (*wu ai*), and that earthly rulers should manifest this universal harmony and order by "turning the wheel of the *dharma*" throughout the land. With its vivid descriptions of this unity of all parts within a whole, the *Flower Garland Sūtra* articulated a spiritual ideal that easily resonated with political objectives for unification and stability. In other East Asian countries as well, the Huayan ideal of harmony inspired the building of Bulguk-sa (Temple of the Kingdom of the Buddha), which commemorated the unified rule of the Korean kingdom of Silla; and the establishment of the Great Temple of the East (Tōdaiji) in Nara, which exemplified Emperor Shōmu's (r. 724–749) vision of centralized rule in Japan.

### CHAPTER ON THE EXQUISITE ADORNMENTS
### OF THE RULERS OF THE WORLD

All of the kingdoms in the ten directions
Will become purified and beautiful in a single moment

When rulers turn the wheel of the *dharma*
With the wondrous sounds of their voices
Reaching everywhere throughout their lands
With no place untouched.
The world of the Buddha is without bounds,
And his *dharma* realm inundates everything in an instant.
In every speck of dust the Buddha establishes a place of practice,
Where he enlightens every being and displays spiritual wonders.
The World-Honored One practiced all spiritual disciplines
While coursing through a past of a hundred thousand aeons,
Adorning all of the lands of the buddhas,
And manifesting himself without obstruction, as if in empty space.
The Buddha's divine powers are unbounded,
Filling endless aeons;
No one would tire of constantly watching him
Even for countless ages.
You should observe the realms of the Buddha's power
Purifying and adorning all of the countries in the ten directions.
In all these places he manifests himself in myriad forms,
Never the same from moment to moment.
Observe the Buddha for a hundred thousand countless aeons,
But you will not discern a single hair on his body,
For through the unhindered use of expedient means
It is his radiance that shines on inconceivably numerous worlds.
In past ages the Buddha was in the world
Serving in a boundless ocean of all the buddhas.
All beings therefore came to make offerings to the World-Honored One,
Just as rivers flow to the sea.
The Buddha appears everywhere in the ten directions,
And in the countless lands of every speck of dust
Wherein are infinite realism
The Buddha abides in all, infinitely unbounded.
The Buddha in the past cultivated an ocean
Of unbounded compassion for sentient beings,
Whom he instructed and purified
As they entered life and death.
The Buddha lives in the *dharma* realm complex of truth
Free of forms, signs, and all defilements.
When people contemplate and see his many different bodies,
All their troubles and sufferings disappear.

[*Huayan jing, TD* 10, no. 279:22; GT]

# BUDDHISM'S ASSIMILATION TO TANG
## POLITICAL CULTURE

Buddhism's early claim to exist beyond the authority of the state, as asserted by Huiyuan,[5] was radically transformed in Tang China when institutionally it became an arm of the state. The institution of "superintendent of the Buddhist clergy (saṅgha)," which first appeared under the Northern Wei in the mid-fifth century, marked the inception of this transformation. The superintendent headed a bureaucracy staffed by lay officials or nominal "monks," charged with oversight of monastic affairs. He was not the head of an autonomous religious organization but rather an appointee of the emperor and given tonsure by the emperor's hand.

The religious rationale for this government-run Buddhism was supplied by the first superintendent Faguo, who justified monks' service of the government by directly identifying the emperor as the Buddha. In contrast to Huiyuan's rigorous defense of clerical independence, Faguo said that "Taizu is enlightened and loves the Way. He is in his very person the Thus-Come One. Monks (śramaṇas) must and should pay him all homage. . . . He who propagates the teaching of the Buddha is the lord of men. I am not doing obeisance to the Emperor, I am merely worshiping the Buddha."[6] In response, the anonymous author of the *Perfect Wisdom Sūtra for Humane Kings Who Wish to Protect Their States* saw superintendency as a sure sign of the corruption of Buddhism in the last days or decadent End of the Teaching, saying, "If any of my disciples, *bhikṣu* and *bhikṣunī*, accept registration (of monks and nuns) and serve as officials, they are not my disciples."[7]

### THE HUMANE KING AS PROTECTOR OF BUDDHISM

As an alternative to Buddhism's serving the state, the *Sūtra for Humane Kings* proposes that the state and Buddhism serve each other. Using the vocabulary of Chinese monarchy, the scripture asserts that "humane" or "benevolent" kings (*renwang*) practice "outer protection" (*waihu*) and that this protection involves the patronage of an independent saṅgha who practice the "inner protection" (*neihu*) of the bodhisattva virtue of "forbearance" (*ren*). The pun on the term *ren*[8] is the basis of the scripture and the starting point of all of its commentaries. Thus, according to an early seventh-century *Commentary on the Sūtra for Humane Kings*, the ruler who protects Buddhism thereby protects the state.

Because the humane king (*renwang*) explicates the Teaching and disseminates virtue here below, he is called "humane." Because he has transformed

---

5. See chap. 15.

6. Hurvitz, *Wei Shou*, p. 53.

7. *TD* 8, no. 245:833.

8. *Ren*, meaning "humaneness," and *ren*, meaning "forbearance," are near homophones, but the words are written with different Chinese characters.

himself, he is called "king." The humane king's ability is to protect (*hu*). What is protected is the state. This is possible because the humane king uses the Teaching to order the state. Now if we consider the Highest Perfect Wisdom (*Prajñāpāramitā*), its ability is to protect. The humane king is he who is protected. Because he uses the Highest Perfect Wisdom, the humane king is tranquil and hidden. Thus, if he uses his ability to propagate the Teaching, the king is able to protect [the state], and it is the Highest Perfect Wisdom that is the [method of] protection. Moreover, one who is humane is forbearing [*renzhe ren ye*]⁹. Hearing of good he is not overjoyed; hearing of bad he is not angry. Because he is able to hold to forbearance in good and bad, therefore he is called forbearing (*ren*).

[*TD* 33, no. 1705:253; CO]

*Here the scripture's adroit use of language to reorder the relationship between religion and the state is coupled with Mahāyāna teachings of Perfect Wisdom. Amoghavajra's eighth-century recension of the text further accentuates these teachings through the addition of such passages as the following, based on the dialectics of negation.*

At that time the World-Honored One said to King Prasenajit, "By what signs do you contemplate the Thus-Come One?" King Prasenajit answered, "I contemplate his body's real signs; [I] contemplate the Buddha thus: without boundaries in front, behind, and in the middle; not residing in the three times and not transcending the three times; not residing in the five aggregates, not transcending the five aggregates; not abiding in the four great elements and not transcending the four great elements; not abiding in the six abodes of sensation and not transcending the six abodes of sensation; not residing in the three realms and not transcending the three realms; residing in no direction, transcending no direction; [neither] illumination [nor] ignorance, and so on. Not one, not different; not this, not that; not pure, not foul; not existent nor nonexistent; without signs of self or signs of another; without name, without signs; without strength, without weakness; without demonstration, without exposition; not magnanimous, not stingy; not prohibited, not transgressed; not forbearing, not hateful; not forward, not remiss; not fixed, not in disarray; not wise, not stupid; not coming, not going; not entering, not leaving; not a field of blessings, not a field of misfortune; without sign, without the lack of sign; not gathering, not dispersing; not great, not small; not seen, not heard; not perceived, not known. The mind, activities, and senses are extinguished, and the path of speech is cut off. It is identical with the edge of reality and equal to the [real] nature of things. I use these signs to contemplate the Thus-Come One."

[*TD* 8, no. 246:836; CO]

---

9. A punning inversion of *Mencius* 7B:16, "To be humane (*ren*) is what it means to be human (*ren*)," recalling also Confucius' pun on "humaneness" (*ren*) and "forbearance" (*ren*) in *Analects* 12:3.

*In the preceding passage the "unboundedness" of the Buddha's body and the principle of universal emptiness in the* Prajñāpāramitā *(expressed in the negation of all determinate views) could also be understood in the more affirmative terms of the Huayan philosophy, that is, the universal tolerance and mutual non-obstruction of all things (expressed as "nothing precludes or bars anything else," shishi wu ai, or, politically, anything goes if it serves the purposes of Buddhism). Both formulations underlay the practice of Amoghavajra's Esoteric Buddhism or Mystical Teaching, which was predicated on a view similar to Huayan's "True Emptiness [allows for] Mysterious or Wondrous Manifestations (zhen kong miaoyou)." Thus mystic rites and incantations could play a part in Esoteric Buddhism's consecrating and legitimating of imperial rule.*

*By the time of Amoghavajra's new recension of the* Sūtra *for Humane Kings, Chinese Buddhism was unquestionably an arm of the state. His recension deepened its theological component while softening and transforming objections to the monks' service of the government—a transformation motivated by Amoghavajra's role as* sangha *superintendent and by his Esoteric Buddhist ideology. Thus, he added a long incantation (dhāraṇī) to the text and produced three new commentaries that outlined esoteric rites for invoking the wrathful "Kings of Illumination" (ming wang, Sanskrit vidyārāja) for the defense of the state. In Amoghavajra's new recension of the* Sūtra *for Humane Kings, one of these Kings of Illumination says:*

Because of our original vows we have received the Buddha's spiritual power. If, in all the states of the worlds of the ten directions, there is a place where this scripture is received and held, read, recited, and expounded, then I and the others go there in an instant, to guard and protect the Correct Teaching or to establish the Correct Teaching. We will ensure that these states are devoid of all calamities and difficulties. Swords, troops, and epidemics all will be entirely eliminated.

World-Honored One! I possess a *dhāraṇī* that can afford wondrous protection. It is the speedy gate originally cultivated and practiced by all the Buddhas. Should a person manage to hear this single scripture, all his crimes and obstructions will be completely eliminated. How much more benefit will it produce if it is recited and practiced! By using the august power of the Teaching, one may cause states to be eternally without the host of difficulties. Then, before the Buddha and in unison, they pronounced this *dhāraṇī*:

Namo ratna-trayāya, nama ārya-vairocanāya tathāgatāyarhate saṃyaksambuddhāya, nama ārya-samanta-bhadrāya bodhisattvāya mahāsattvāya mahākāruṇikāya, tad yathā; jñāna-pradīpe aṣaya-kośe pratibhānavati sarva-buddhāvalokite yoga-pariniṣpanne gambhīra-duravagāhe try-adhva-pariniṣpanne bodhi-citta-saṃjānāni

[844a] sarvābhiṣekābhiṣikte *dharma*-sāgara-sambhūti amogha-śravane mahā-samanta-bhadra-bhūmi-niryāte vyākaraṇa-pariprāptāni sarva-siddha-namaskṛte sarva-bodhi-sattva-saṃjānāni bhagavati-buddhamāte araṇe akarane araṇakaraṇe mahā-prajñā-pāramite svāhā!

At that time the World-Honored One heard this pronouncement and praised Jingangshou and the other bodhisattvas, saying, "Excellent! Excellent! If there are those who recite and hold this *dhāraṇī*, I and all the Buddhas of the ten directions will always be supportive and protective [of them], and all of the evil demons and spirits will venerate them like Buddhas and in not a long time they should attain the highest perfect enlightenment."

[*TD* 8, no. 246:843–844; CO]

*Amoghavajra's new recension of the* Sūtra *for Humane Kings was part of a comprehensive relationship between the state and Esoteric Buddhism that flowered in the second half of the eighth century. Under three successive Tang emperors—Xuanzong (r. 713–756), Suzong (r. 756–762), and Daizong (r. 762–779)—Amoghavajra and his disciples developed a new vision of Buddhist-state polity that wedded the idioms of Buddhism to those of Chinese rulership. This new vision was nowhere more apparent than in the correspondence between Amoghavajra and the three emperors whom he served. It was not uncommon for Amoghavajra to address the emperor using the idiom of the loyal minister, while the emperor often addressed Amoghavajra in the Buddhist idiom of a disciple. Some exchanges are a skillful blend of Chinese and Buddhist rhetoric, a blend that indicates the assimilation of Buddhism to Chinese culture and politics. In the following memorial to Suzong, dated 17 March 758, Amoghavajra expressed his appreciation of a gift of incense in a way that simultaneously evokes his role as servant of the ruler and as the cosmocratic protector of the empire.*

The monk Amoghavajra says: Your Majesty gave me rare incense; through your messenger you bestow upon me great favor. I am speechless with delight. . . . I have dedicated my life to the Buddhist cause . . . I have prayed with the strength of the all-embracing [bodhisattva] vow that I would encounter the triumphant appearance of a world-ruler (*Cakravartin*). . . . [During the early part of the rebellion][10] your majesty's noble plans were carried out by you alone, yet the Teaching mysteriously contributed [toward victory]; the gang of bandits was fragmented and destroyed, and the imperial portents have returned to their normative state. . . . In the tenth month you cleansed the palace by setting up an assembly to drive out evil influences; when you rectified your rule by granting official titles, you went up to the altar (*bodhimaṇḍa*) for consecration (*abhiṣeka*). . . . Already you have showered me with gifts. When can I ever repay you? It is proper that I reverently bathe the statues at the appointed times and that I perform the immolation (*homa*) rites at the half moon in order that the thirty-seven divinities [of the Diamond world, *Vajradhātu maṇḍala*] may protect your earth, my brilliant king, and that the sixteen protectors [bodhisattvas of the *Vajradhātu maṇḍala*] might guard your majestic spirit, so that you may live as long as the southern mountain, eternally, without limit.

[*TD* 52, no. 2120:827–828; trans. adapted from Orlando,
"Life of Amoghavajra," pp. 45–49; CO]

---

10. The Rebellion of An Lushan, which began in 755.

## Chapter 17

### SCHOOLS OF BUDDHIST PRACTICE

In the preceding chapter, three of the major schools of Buddhist doctrine were presented. Here we introduce two of the most important schools of Buddhist religious practice. The first of them, the Pure Land sect, emphasized salvation by faith and became the most popular form of Buddhism in China. The second, the Meditation sect, though appealing to a more limited following, became the most influential form of Buddhism among artists and intellectuals, as well as monks. Together they may be taken to represent a general reaction against the scriptural and doctrinal approach to religion, but their growing ascendancy in later centuries should not be regarded as the superseding of older schools by newer ones. In fact, both the Pure Land and the Meditation schools existed along with the others, even antedating some, like the Tiantai, and their enduring popularity was only a matter of their surviving better the vicissitudes of religious and social change.

## THE PURE LAND SCHOOL

The "Pure Land" (Chinese *Jingtu*; Sanskrit *Sukhāvatī*) is the sphere believed by Mahāyāna Buddhists to be ruled over by the Buddha Amitābha (also known as Amitāyus and Amita). Indian Mahāyānists conceived of the universe as consisting of an infinite number of spheres and as going through an infinite number of cosmic periods. In the present period there is, according to this belief, a sphere

called the Pure Land, the beauties and excellences of which are described in
the most extravagant terms by certain of the Mahāyāna scriptures. Among its
advantages is the fact that it is free of the temptations and defilements (for example, the presence of women, thought to be impure) that characterize the world
inhabited by mortals.

A common belief among Mahāyāna Buddhists, and one supported by
scripture, was that the earthly dispensation of each Buddha's teaching termi-
nated with his final *nirvāṇa* and was followed by a gradual degeneration of the
teaching. The period immediately following the Buddha's demise, known as
the era of the True Law or Doctrine, is characterized by the continued vigor
of the religion in spite of his absence. That is followed in turn by the era of
Reflected Law, in which the outward forms of the religion are maintained but
the inner content perishes. Finally comes the era of the Final Degeneration of
the Law, in which both form and substance come to nought. The scriptures
dealing with the spiritual reign of Śākyamuni differ considerably as to the relative length of the three eras following his entry into *nirvāṇa*. But it was possible
for certain Chinese clerics during the Northern and Southern Dynasties period
(420–589) to find scriptural justification for their sense that the period in which
they themselves were living was the very era of Final Degeneration of the Law
that the sacred writings had predicted. The confused state of Buddhist doctrine
and the difficulty of any but a few to master it, either in the pursuit of scriptural studies or in the practice of monastic disciplines, helped to convince many
clerics and untold numbers of laymen that their only hope of salvation lay in
faith—faith in the saving power of the buddhas.

In the *Sūtra of the Buddha of Limitless Life* (*Sukhāvatīvyūha*), one of the
principal scriptural bases of Pure Land salvationism, Amita, while yet a bodhisattva under the name Dharmākara, took forty-eight vows that were instrumental in his attainment of buddhahood. The eighteenth of these, which came to be
considered the most important, was, "If, O Blessed One, when I have attained
enlightenment, whatever beings in other worlds, having conceived a desire for
right, perfect enlightenment, and having heard my name, with favorable intent
think upon me, if when the time and the moment of death are upon them,
I, surrounded by and at the head of my community of mendicants, do not stand
before them to keep them from frustration, may I not, on that account, attain to
unexcelled, right, perfect enlightenment." Since, according to believers in this
scripture, the bodhisattva Dharmākara *did* in fact become a Buddha (Amita),
the efficacy of his vows is proved, and anyone who meditates or calls upon his
name in good faith will be reborn in his Buddha-world.

Hence the simple invocation or ejaculation of Amita's name (*A-mi-tuo-fo*
in Chinese) became the most common of all religious practices in China and
the means by which millions sought release from the sufferings of this world.
Nor was it simply a sectarian devotion. The meditation upon Amita and his
Pure Land became a widespread practice in the temples and monasteries of
other sects as well. In religious painting and sculpture too, Amita, seated on a

lotus throne in his Western Paradise and flanked by his attendant bodhisattvas (e.g., Guanyin, the so-called Goddess of Mercy), was a favorite theme.

## DAOCHUO: *COMPENDIUM ON THE HAPPY LAND*

The compendium from which these extracts are taken was compiled by Daochuo (d. 645), a monk who was particularly devoted to the recitation of the Buddha's name and became one of the great patriarchs of Pure Land Buddhism.

## A Teaching Appropriate to the Times

If a particular teaching is appropriate to the times and suits the capacity of the particular individual, then it is easy to practice and easy to become enlightened. But if capacity, teaching, and age are out of harmony, then practice will be laborious and realization difficult to achieve. Thus the *Sūtra on Mindfulness of the True Dharma* says, "Practitioners in single-minded pursuit of the Path should carefully evaluate the situation at hand and the expedient means appropriate to it."[1] If the occasion is not right and there is no proper expedient, then it will be tantamount to failure and is not what we call benefit. . . .

Therefore the *Sūtra of the Bodhisattva Candragarbha* (*Daji yuezang jing*) says, "In the first five hundred years after I, the Buddha, have entered final extinction (*parinirvāṇa*), my followers will be able to achieve firm stability [in the Way] through the cultivation of wisdom (*prajñā*). During the second five hundred years they will become established in the Way [primarily] through the practice of *samādhi* [meditative concentration]. In the third five hundred years academic learning, reading, and recitation [of scripture] will be on a firm foundation. During the fourth five hundred years they will become established in the faith through the building of reliquaries [*stūpa*] and monasteries, as well as the cultivation of merits and repentance [of sins]. In the fifth five hundred years the pure *Dharma* will enter [final] eclipse, and there will appear considerable controversy and strife. Beings will be able to establish themselves through only the most meager deeds of virtue."[2]

Furthermore that same *sūtra* says, "When the Buddhas come forth in the world they have four types of *Dharma* by which they save living beings. What are the four? The first is preaching by word the twelve classes of scripture. This is known as delivering beings through the giving of the *Dharma*. The second is [the thirty-two major] marks and [eighty minor] excellent qualities as well

---

1. *Zhengfa nian[chu] jing* (TD 17, no. 721).
2. *Sūtra of the Bodhisattva Candragarbha* from the *Mahāsaṃnipāta* [Collection] (*Dajijing, Yuezang fen*) (TD 13, no. 397:363a–b).

as the infinite radiance possessed by all Buddhas. If beings can simply fix their minds on and discern these features they will all receive benefit. This is known as delivering beings through the activity of the body. Third, [the Buddhas] are endowed with all manner of supernatural powers and modes through which to manifest themselves that arise as a function of their infinite merits. This amounts to saving beings through supernatural powers. Fourth, the Buddha *Tathāgatas* have an infinite number of names: some are common epithets, some specific names. If beings fix their minds on and invoke (*chengnian*) these names, without fail they will eliminate impediments [to the Path], gain great benefit, and all be reborn in the presence of the Buddhas. This is known as delivering sentient beings through name."[3]

We calculate that sentient beings of the present age are in the period of the fourth five hundred years after the Buddha departed from the world. It is precisely the period to which repentance, cultivation of merits, and invocation of the Buddha's name are most suited. [As it states in the *Sūtra on the Contemplation of the Buddha of Limitless Life*], "If you invoke the name of Amitābha Buddha for even a single instant you will be able to expel sins accumulated over eighty million aeons [*kalpas*] of lifetimes."[4] If just one instant [of recitation has such power], how much more must it hold true for those who practice constant recollection and recitation (*nian*)! Indeed, this is a person who is constantly repenting.

[From *Anleji*, TD 47, no. 1958:4; DS]

## The Difficult Path and the Easy Path

Dwelling in the realm of the burning house, I harbor fear in my breast and look to the Three Vehicles. Yet . . . even if I should manage to return to the true and correct path [of the Mahāyāna] after following the [less difficult] course of the two vehicles, my progress would still be convoluted and roundabout. I could aspire directly to the One Great Cart [of the Buddha Vehicle]. But even though it may be one single path, I fear that my progress may still be steep and long, for I am yet at a stage of practice where I may easily backslide. Indeed, if one's meritorious powers are not yet sufficiently established it is very difficult to make steady progress [on one's own].

For this reason the Bodhisattva Nāgārjuna said, "There are two paths by which one may seek the stage of non-retrogression [in one's advance to Buddhahood]. One is by a path that is hard to tread; the other a path that is easy to tread."[5]

---

3. Ibid., TD 13, no. 397.

4. *Sūtra on the Contemplation of the Buddha of Limitless Life* (*Guan wuliangshou fo jing*) (TD 12, no. 366:346a).

5. *Avaivartika*, or "non-retrogression," refers to the stage on the bodhisattva path at which the bodhisattva is assured of future Buddhahood and is sufficiently established in wisdom and merits as to be beyond the danger of "falling back" into deluded paths.

Now, the "difficult path" refers to the fact that it is difficult to seek the stage of non-retrogression in an age when there is no Buddha present and the world is afflicted with the five turbidities. Actually the difficulties are quite numerous, but in essence we reduce them to five. What are they? The first is the fact that notions of relative good espoused by heterodox teachers intermingle with and confuse the bodhisattva teachings. Second is the fact that the aims of self-benefit espoused by the *śrāvakas* impede [development of] great kindness and compassion. Third is the fact that evil people who have no regard for others do their utmost to destroy the virtues of others. Fourth is the fact that goals falsely esteemed as good by gods and humans undermine the practice of the *brahmacarin* (i.e., renunciation and celibacy). Fifth is the fact that people advocate reliance only on self-power (*zili*) and so lack sustainment through other-power (*tali*). . . . Because it is analogous to traveling overland on foot, it is called "the path that is difficult to traverse."

The expression "path that is easy to traverse" refers to the vow to be reborn in the Pure Land through recourse to faith in the Buddha [Amitābha]. One puts forth the great determination [to achieve Buddhahood], establishes merits, and undertakes various practices. Then, through the power of the Buddha Amitābha's original vow one is born in the Pure Land. Sustained by the Buddha's power one enters the ranks of those properly assured [of Buddhahood], which is itself none other than the stage of non-retrogression. Because it is likened to traveling by boat down a river, it is called "the path that is easy to traverse."

[From *Anleji*, TD 47, no. 1958:8–11; DS]

## SHANDAO: THE PARABLE OF THE WHITE PATH

Shandao (613–681), a disciple of Daochuo, is another of the great patriarchs of the Pure Land faith. He is known especially for his *Guanjing shu*, a commentary on the *Amitāyur-dhyāna Sūtra*, in which appears this famous parable vividly delineating the existential crisis of man and his need for faith.

And to all those who wish to be reborn in the Pure Land, I now tell a parable for the sake of those who would practice the True Way, as a protection for their faith and a defense against the danger of heretical views. What is it? It is like a man who desires to travel a hundred thousand *li* to the West. Suddenly in the midst of his route he sees two rivers. One is a river of fire stretching south. The other is a river of water stretching north. Each of the two rivers is a hundred steps across and unfathomably deep. They stretch without end to the north and south. Right between the fire and water, however, is a white path barely four or five inches wide. Spanning the east and west banks, it is one hundred steps long. The waves of water surge and splash against the path on one side, while the flames of fire scorch it on the other. Ceaselessly, the fire and water come and go.

The man is out in the middle of a wasteland and none of his kind are to be seen. A horde of vicious ruffians and wild beasts see him there alone and vie with one another in rushing to kill him. Fearing death, he runs straightway to the west and then sees these great rivers. Praying, he says to himself: "To the north and south I see no end to these rivers. Between them I see a white path, which is extremely narrow. Although the two banks are not far apart, how am I to traverse from one to the other? Doubtless today I shall surely die. If I seek to turn back, the horde of vicious ruffians and wild beasts will come at me. If I run to the north or south, evil beasts and poisonous vermin will race toward me. If I seek to make my way to the west, I fear that I may fall into these rivers."

Thereupon he is seized with an inexpressible terror. He thinks to himself: "Turn back now and I die. Stay and I die. Go forward and I die. Since death must be faced in any case, I would rather follow this path before me and go ahead. With this path I can surely make it across." Just as he thinks this, he hears someone from the east bank call out and encourage him: "Friend, just follow this path resolutely and there will be no danger of death. To stay here is to die." And on the west bank there is someone calling out, "Come straight ahead, single-mindedly and with fixed purpose. I can protect you. Never fear falling into the fire or water!"

At the urging of the one and the calling of the other, the man straightens himself up in body and mind and resolves to go forward on this path, without any lingering doubts or hesitations. Hardly has he gone a step or two when from the east bank the horde of vicious ruffians calls out to him: "Friend, come back! That way is perilous and you will never get across. Without a doubt you are bound to die. None of us means to harm you." Though he hears them calling, the man still does not look back but single-mindedly and straightway proceeds on the path. In no time he is at the west bank, far from all troubles forever. He is greeted by his good friend, and there is no end of joy.

That is the parable and this is the meaning of it: what we speak of as the "east bank" is comparable to this world, a house in flames. What we speak of as the "west bank" is symbolic of the precious land of highest bliss. The ruffians, wild beasts, and seeming friends are comparable to the Six Sense Organs, Six Consciousnesses, Six Dusts, Five Components, and Four Elements [that constitute the "self"]. The lonely wasteland is the following of bad companions and not meeting with those who are truly good and wise. The two rivers of fire and water are comparable to human greed and affection, like water, and anger and hatred, like fire. The white path in the center, four or five inches wide, is comparable to the pure aspiration for rebirth in the Pure Land, which arises in the midst of the passions of greed and anger. Greed and anger are powerful, and thus are likened to fire and water; the good mind is infinitesimal and thus is likened to a white path [of a few inches in width]. The waves inundating the path are comparable to the constant arising of affectionate thoughts in the mind, which stain and pollute the good mind. And the flames that scorch the path are comparable to thoughts of anger and hatred, which burn up the treasures of *dharma* and virtue. The man proceeding on the path toward the west is comparable to one who directs all of his actions and practices toward the West[ern Paradise].

The hearing of voices from the east bank encouraging and exhorting him to pursue the path straight to the west is like Śākyamuni Buddha, who has already disappeared from the sight of men but whose teachings may still be pursued and are therefore likened to "voices." The calling out of the ruffians after he has taken a few steps is comparable to those of different teachings and practices and of evil views who wantonly spread their ideas to lead people astray and create disturbances, thus falling themselves into sin and losing their way. To speak of someone calling from the west bank is comparable to the vow of Amitābha. Reaching the west bank, being greeted by the good friend, and rejoicing there, are comparable to all those beings sunk long in the sea of birth and death, floundering and caught in their own delusions, without any means of deliverance, who accept Śākyamuni's testament directing them to the West and Amitābha's compassionate call, and obeying trustfully the will of the two Buddhas, while paying no heed to the rivers of fire and water, with devout concentration mount the road of Amitābha's promised power and when life is over attain the other Land, where they meet the Buddha and know unending bliss.

[From *Guanjing shu, TD* 37, no. 1753: 272–273; dB]

# THE MEDITATION SCHOOL

The Meditation School, called Chan in Chinese from the Sanskrit *dhyāna*, is best known in the West by the Japanese pronunciation, "Zen." As a religious practice, of course, meditation was not peculiar to Chan; it had been a standard fixture in all forms of Buddhism, whether Indian or Chinese, from earliest times. Indian texts on yoga practice and *dhyāna* were among the first works translated into Chinese, and they found an enthusiastic audience among the intelligentsia, many of whom were ardent followers of Daoism. Yet these Indian texts were obscure and at times almost unintelligible; thus the concept of *dhyāna* gradually went through a process of sinicization, whereby it was greatly simplified and altered. Before the emergence of Chan as an independent school, early Buddhist monks had arrived at a variety of interpretations, some highly scholastic and close to the Indian original, and others quite near to the later Chan version.

Little is known of the teaching methods and techniques used in early Chan. Great emphasis was undoubtedly placed on meditation practice as a means of attaining an intuitive realization of the Ultimate Truth or First Principle. In order to achieve this intuitive recognition, all conceptual thinking was to be set aside and external influences rejected. Emphasis was placed chiefly on the ability to meditate successfully. In fact, achievement in meditation was equated with intuitive wisdom.

As Chan developed in China, it came to style itself as "a separate transmission outside the scriptures, not dependent on words and phrases" and to describe its teachings as "transmitted from mind to mind." Here the Master played a dominant role; all practice and study was done under his direction. The monk was completely subservient to his will, and it was the Master who verified the degree of progress a monk had made; it was the Master again who acknowledged the understanding of his disciple and who, in the end, transmitted his teaching to him.

"To see into one's own nature and become Buddha" was the objective of all Chan practitioners, and it was to this end that all study was directed. Different Masters developed various techniques to bring the student to realization and awakening. In addition to meditation over a period of months and years, physical work, initially instituted for the purpose of supporting the community of monks, was stressed and eventually became an integral part of the Chan training program. The most commonly used method of instruction came to be the use of the *gongan* (*kōan* in Japanese). Originally a legal term meaning "public case," it came to refer to the brief stories, primarily questions and answers of an enigmatic or paradoxical nature, with which Chan literature abounds. Most likely the first *gongan* were used in public meetings before an assemblage of monks. On these occasions an encounter dialogue might take place; the Master would put forth a question or statement to which a member of the gathering might reply by stepping forward and offering a response. At another time a monk might step forward, pose his question, hear his answer, and retire to meditate upon its purport. For the more advanced practitioner, going on pilgrimage from one Master to another in order to test and mature one's understanding became standard practice in the school. Gradually these *gongan* came to be collected and written down, and to gain wide circulation. Instead of making *gongan* of their own, later Masters used the stories of famous old monks to teach their own disciples, until eventually a system evolved in which a series of *gongan* formed what might be called a planned program of instruction, in which the student would meditate until he satisfied his Master that he had come to an intuitive understanding of each *gongan*. Frequently these *gongan* could not be answered verbally, which accounts in part for the beatings, shouts, and gestures so often described in the stories. Often the Master would find his disciple's mind so sensitized and receptive, that a scream, a blow of the stick, or a blasphemous word would be the cause of his awakening to the Truth.

Traditionally, Chan traces its origin to Śākyamuni Buddha, who, holding a flower before the assembly, saw Kāśyapa smile and realized that he alone had understood. Thus the True Law was entrusted to Kāśyapa and from him it passed through twenty-eight generations in India until it came to Bodhidharma, a prince of southern India, who is said to have come to China in 520 C.E. and who became the First Patriarch there. From Bodhidharma the Law was passed to succeeding generations until Huineng (638–713), the Sixth Patriarch, inherited the teachings. This is the traditional version of early Chan. But it is so encrusted with legendary accretions that it is almost impossible to know what the true facts are. Recent research has established that a person known as Bodhidharma was indeed in China, but during the years 420 to 479. An ascetic, his teachings were based on the *Laṅkāvatāra Sūtra*, and he practiced an exceedingly simplified form of meditation. His disciples, of whom virtually nothing is known, carried on his teachings until they reached Hongren (600–674), the Fifth Patriarch, who resided at Dongshan, the East Mountain. Hongren had a large number of disciples who scattered throughout China, each teaching his own style of Chan. Some of these schools soon faded away; others prospered for a brief period; several of them composed histories, each of which championed its own lineage.

By the third decade of the eighth century two schools had attained a significant prosperity. One, which came to be called Northern Chan, was led by a distinguished Master, Shenxiu (606?–706), who was greatly honored by the Tang court. The other school, known as Southern Chan, claimed Huineng as its founder. Its cause was championed by an obscure monk, Shenhui (684–758), who had studied briefly with Huineng. In 732 Shenhui mounted a platform at his temple north of Loyang and opened a virulent attack on Puji (651–739), the heir of Shenxiu, who enjoyed the strong support of the imperial throne. Claiming his own teacher, Huineng, to be the true heir of the Fifth Patriarch, he condemned the meditation concepts of the Northern School, maintaining that the Southern enlightenment doctrine, which emphasized "absence of thought" and the "identity of meditation (*samādhi*) and intuitive wisdom (*prajñā*)" was the true teaching. His eloquence won the day; Southern Chan was accepted as the official teaching, and its popularity increased, not only in the cities but in outlying areas as well.

During the eighth century numerous Chan teachers, all tracing themselves to Huineng, spread their versions of the meditation doctrines, and many Chan works were composed: histories, treatises, biographies, all of which added to the legends and stories, until in the Song period the traditions concerning the early Masters became codified in very nearly the present form.

During the Tang dynasty all sects of Buddhism enjoyed the lavish patronage of the court and the elite, vast temples were erected and great fortunes amassed by the church. Chan remained aloof, to some extent, from this process, but during this period its temples were not clearly distinguishable from other monastic institutions. Nevertheless, when a persecution of Buddhism was instituted in 845, the anti-Buddhist measures may have wreaked greater havoc in urban areas than in the provinces. This was particularly so in northern China, where the military commanders, who were "barbarians" with little interest and fewer prospects in the Confucian environment of the cities, continued their enthusiastic support of Chan as lay believers. It was in the north that one of the greatest leaders, Yixuan (d. 867) of Linji, propagated his iconoclastic doctrines and individualistic teachings with great success.

The Linji school, established by his followers, came to dominate Chinese Buddhism in the succeeding centuries. During the Tang (618–906) and Five Dynasties (907–960) periods a variety of Chan sects developed, the so-called Five Schools and Seven Houses, but by the eleventh century the most significant were the Linji and the Caotong, which claimed Liangjie (807–869) as its founder and had been further developed by Benji (840–901) of Caoshan and other masters. By this time, Chan, which had had a strong lay following, had made significant inroads in elite society, and a considerable number of Chan masters of the Song exercised substantial influence among the intellectual and ruling circles of the capital. Chan, while priding itself on being a transmission that did not depend on words and phrases, continued to produce and see into print a vast body of literature: biographical histories, records of individual masters, poetry, *gongan* collections, prose literature, inscriptions, and other writings. Indeed, Chan has produced the greatest body of literature of any school of Buddhism.

The selections given below include excerpts from a basic Chan work attributed to Huineng; examples of two methods of Chan teaching, the sermon and the encounter dialogue (or question-and-answer session); a selection from a collection of *gongan* with detailed commentary; and materials related to temple discipline and the conduct of monks.

## THE PLATFORM SŪTRA OF THE SIXTH PATRIARCH

This brief work is said to represent a collection of a number of sermons and the autobiography of Huineng (638–713), as purportedly transcribed by an obscure disciple, Fahai. Recent scholarship attributes the work to a monk of the same name but of an unrelated school who, around the year 780, determined to write a record of Huineng, recognized by this time throughout Chan as the legitimate Sixth Patriarch. Our text, which was discovered in the Dunhuang caves in northwest China, is corrupt and contains numerous errors; it is probably a copy made by a semiliterate scribe. The continued popularity of this work in China, however, is attested to by the great number of versions that have appeared over the centuries. The traditional version, current today, which was printed some five hundred years after the present text, is greatly revised and expanded and is almost twice the size of the original.

Following are autobiographical passages and others that reflect the thought afterward developed by later Chan masters. Deleted, however, is a prefatory passage purporting to describe the precise circumstances in which the Sixth Patriarch's sermon was recorded. It is typical of Chan accounts that retrospectively conjure up an aura of historical verisimilitude for what is essentially a mythmaking process, serving in the absence of any other criteria of public certification or doctrinal orthodoxy to support claims to a legitimate lineage inheritance. (The section numbers follow those established by D. T. Suzuki in his edition of the Dunhuang text.)

2. The Master Huineng said, "Good friends, purify your minds and concentrate on the *Dharma* of the Great Perfection of Wisdom."

The Master stopped speaking and quieted his own mind. Then after a good while he said, "Good friends, listen quietly. Although my father was originally an official at Fanyang, he was dismissed from his post and banished as a commoner to Xinzhou in Lingnan. While I was still a child my father died, and my mother and I, a solitary child, moved to Nanhai. We suffered extreme poverty, and here I sold firewood in the marketplace. By chance a certain man bought some firewood and then took me with him to the lodging house for officials. He took the firewood and left. Having received my money and turning toward the front gate, I happened to see another man who was reciting the *Diamond Sūtra*.

"I asked him, 'Where do you come from that you have brought this *sūtra* with you?'

"He answered, 'I have made obeisance to the Fifth Patriarch Hongren at the East Mountain, Fengmu shan, in Huangmei *xian* in Qizhou. At present there are over a thousand disciples there. While I was there I heard the Master encourage the lay followers, saying that if they recited just the one volume, the *Diamond Sūtra*, they could see into their own natures and with direct apprehension become buddhas.'

"Hearing what he said, I realized that I was predestined to have heard him. Then I took leave of my mother and went to Fengmu shan in Huangmei and made obeisance to the Fifth Patriarch, the monk Hongren.

3. "The monk Hongren asked me, 'Where are you from that you come to this mountain to make obeisance to me? Just what is it that you are looking for from me?'

"I replied, 'I am from Lingnan, a commoner from Xinzhou. I have come this long distance only to make obeisance to you. I am seeking no particular thing, but only the Buddhadharma.'

"The Master then reproved me, saying, 'If you're from Lingnan, then you're a barbarian. How can you become a Buddha?'

"I replied, 'Although people from the south and people from the north differ, there is no north and south in Buddha nature. Although my barbarian's body and your body are not the same, what difference is there in our Buddha nature?'

"The Master wished to continue the discussion with me; however, seeing that there were other people nearby, he said no more. Then he sent me to work together with the assembly. Later a lay disciple had me go to the threshing room, where I spent over eight months treading the pestle.

4. "Unexpectedly one day the Fifth Patriarch called all his disciples to come, and when they had assembled, he said, 'Let me preach to you. For people in this world birth and death are vital matters. You disciples make offering all day long and seek only the field of blessings, but you do not seek to escape from the bitter sea of birth and death. Your own self-nature obscures the gateway to blessings; how can you be saved? All of you return to your rooms and look into yourselves. Men of wisdom will of themselves grasp the original nature of their *prajñā* intuition. Each of you write a verse and bring it to me. I will read your verses and if there is one who has awakened to the cardinal meaning, I will give him the robe and the *Dharma* and make him the Sixth Patriarch. Hurry, hurry!'

5. "The disciples received his instructions and returned each to his own room. They talked it over among themselves, saying, 'There's no point in our purifying our minds and making efforts to compose a verse to present to the priest. Shenxiu, the head monk, is our teacher. After he obtains the *Dharma* we can rely on him, so let's not compose verses.' They all then gave up trying and did not have the courage to present a verse.

"At that time there was a three-sectioned corridor in front of the Master's hall. On the walls were to be painted pictures of stories from the *Laṅkāvatāra Sūtra*, together with a picture in commemoration of the Fifth Patriarch transmitting the robe and *Dharma* in order to disseminate them to later generations. The artist, Lu Zhen, had examined the walls and was to start work the next day.

6. "The head monk, Shenxiu, thought, 'The others won't present a mind-verse; how can the Fifth Patriarch estimate the degree of understanding within my mind? If I offer my mind-verse to the Fifth Patriarch with the intention of gaining patriarchship, then it cannot be justified. Then it would be like a common man usurping the saintly position. But if I don't offer my mind, then I cannot learn the *Dharma*.' For a long time he thought about it and was very much perplexed.

"At midnight, without letting anyone see him, he went to write his mind-verse on the central section of the south corridor wall, hoping to gain the *Dharma*. 'If the Fifth Patriarch sees my verse [tomorrow and is pleased with it, then I shall come forward and say that I wrote it. If he tells me that it is not worthwhile, then I will know that][6] there is a weighty obstacle in my past karma, that I cannot gain the *Dharma* and shall have to give it up. The honorable patriarch's intention is difficult to fathom.'

"Then the head monk, Shenxiu, at midnight, holding a candle, wrote a verse on the wall of the central section of the south corridor, without anyone else knowing about it. The verse read:

> The body is the *bodhi* tree,
> The mind is like a clear mirror.
> At all times we must strive to polish it,
> And must not let the dust collect.

7. "After he had finished writing this verse, the head monk, Shenxiu, returned to his room and lay down. No one had seen him.

"At dawn the Fifth Patriarch called the painter Lu to draw illustrations from the *Laṅkāvatāra Sūtra* on the south corridor. The Fifth Patriarch suddenly saw this verse and, having read it, said to the painter, 'I will give you thirty thousand

---

6. There is a gap in the Dunhuang text at this point. The missing passage has been supplied from the Northern Song version (*Kōshōji* text).

cash. You have come a long distance to do this arduous work, but I have decided not to have the pictures painted after all. It is said in the *Diamond Sūtra*, "All forms everywhere are unreal and false." It would be best to leave this verse here and to have the deluded ones recite it. If they practice in accordance with it, they will not fall into the three evil ways. Those who practice by it will gain great benefit.'

"The Master then called all his disciples to come, and burned incense before the verse. The disciples came in to see and were all filled with admiration.

"[The Fifth Patriarch said], 'You should all recite this verse so that you will be able to see into your own natures.[7] With this practice you will not fall [into the three evil ways].'

"The disciples all recited it and, feeling great admiration, cried out, 'How excellent!'

"The Fifth Patriarch then called the head monk, Shenxiu, inside the hall and asked, 'Did you write this verse or not? If you wrote it, you are qualified to attain my *Dharma*.'[8]

"The head monk, Shenxiu, said, 'I am ashamed to say that I actually did write the verse, but I do not dare to seek the patriarchship. I beg you to be so compassionate as to tell me whether I have even a small amount of wisdom and discernment of the cardinal meaning or not.'

"The Fifth Patriarch said, 'This verse you wrote shows that you still have not reached true understanding. You have merely reached the front of the gate but have yet to be able to enter it. If common people practice according to your verse they will not fall. But in seeking the ultimate enlightenment (*bodhi*) one will not succeed with such an understanding. You must enter the gate and see your own original nature. Go and think about it for a day or two and then make another verse and present it to me. If you have been able to enter the gate and see your own original nature, then I will give you the robe and the *Dharma*.' The head monk, Shenxiu, left, but after several days he was still unable to write a verse.

8. "One day an acolyte passed by the threshing room reciting this verse. As soon as I heard it I knew that the person who had written it had yet to know his own nature and to discern the cardinal meaning. I asked the boy, 'What's the name of the verse you were reciting just now?'

"The boy answered me, saying, 'Don't you know? The Master said that birth and death are vital matters, and he told his disciples each to write a verse if they wanted to inherit the robe and the *Dharma*, and to bring it for him to see. He who was awakened to the cardinal meaning would be given the robe and the *Dharma* and be made the Sixth Patriarch. There is a head monk by the name of Shenxiu who happened to write a verse on formlessness on the wall of the south

---

7. This statement contradicts the story as it later develops. It represents, probably, an interpolation in the text.

8. A further contradiction; the text is corrupt here.

corridor. The Fifth Patriarch had all the disciples read the verse, [saying] that those who awakened to it would see into their own self-natures and that those who practiced according to it would attain emancipation.'

"I said, 'I've been treading the pestle for eight months but haven't been to the hall yet. I beg you to take me to the south corridor so that I can see the verse and make obeisance to it. I also want to recite it so that I can establish a causation for my next birth and be born in a Buddhaland.'

"The boy took me to the south corridor and I made obeisance before the verse. Because I was uneducated I asked someone to read it to me. As soon as I had heard it I understood the cardinal meaning. I made a verse and asked someone who was able to write to put it on the wall of the west corridor, so that I might offer my own original mind. If you do not know the original mind, studying the *Dharma* is to no avail. If you know the mind and see its true nature, you then awaken to the cardinal meaning.[9] My verse said:

> The *bodhi* tree is originally not a tree,
> The mirror also has no stand.
> Buddha-nature is always clean and pure;
> Where is there room for dust?

> Another verse said:
> The mind is the *bodhi* tree,
> The body is the mirror stand.
> The mirror is originally clean and pure;
> Where can it be stained by dust?

"The followers in the temple were all amazed when they saw my verse. Then I returned to the threshing room. The Fifth Patriarch realized that I had a splendid understanding of the cardinal meaning. Being afraid lest the assembly know this, he said to them, 'This is still not complete attainment.'

9. "At midnight the Fifth Patriarch called me into the hall and expounded the *Diamond Sūtra* to me. Hearing it but once, I was immediately awakened, and that night I received the *Dharma*. None of the others knew anything about it. Then he transmitted to me the *Dharma* of Sudden Enlightenment and the robe, saying, 'I make you the Sixth Patriarch. The robe is the proof and is to be handed down from generation to generation. My *Dharma* must be transmitted from mind to mind. You must make people awaken to themselves.'

"The Fifth Patriarch told me, 'From ancient times the transmission of the *Dharma* has been as tenuous as a dangling thread. If you stay here, there are people who will kill you. You must leave at once.'

---

9. These two sentences are out of context and represent a later interpolation.

10. "I set out at midnight with the robe and the *Dharma*. The Fifth Patriarch saw me off as far as Jiujiang Station. I was instantly enlightened. The Fifth Patriarch instructed me, 'Leave, work hard, take the *Dharma* with you to the south. For three years do not spread the teaching or else calamity will befall the *Dharma*. Later, work to convert people; you must guide deluded persons well. If you are able to awaken another's mind, he will be no different from me.'[10] After completing my leave-taking I set out for the south.

11. "After about two months I reached Dayuling. Unknown to me, several hundred men were following behind, wishing to try to kill me and to steal my robe and *Dharma*. By the time I had gone halfway up the mountain they had all turned back. But there was one monk of the family name of Zhen, whose personal name was Huiming. Formerly he had been a general of the third rank, and he was by nature and conduct coarse and evil. Reaching the top of the mountain, he caught up with me and threatened me. I handed over the *dharma*-robe, but he did not dare to take it.

"[He said], 'I have come this long distance just to seek the *Dharma*. I have no need for the robe.' Then, on top of the mountain, I transmitted the *Dharma* to Huiming, who when he heard it was at once enlightened. I then ordered him to return to the north and to convert people there.

13. "Good friends, my teaching of the *Dharma* takes meditation and wisdom as its basis. Never under any circumstances say that meditation and wisdom are different; they are one unity, not two things. Meditation itself is the substance of wisdom; wisdom itself is the function of meditation. Just when there is meditation, then wisdom exists in meditation. Good friends, this means that meditation and wisdom are alike. Students, be careful not to say that meditation first gives rise to wisdom, or that wisdom first gives rise to meditation, or that meditation and wisdom are different from each other. To hold this view implies that things have duality, and if good is spoken while the mind is not good, meditation and wisdom will not be alike. If mind and speech are both good, then the internal and the external are the same and meditation and wisdom are identical. The practice of self-awakening does not lie in verbal arguments. If you argue which comes first, meditation or wisdom, you are deluded people. You won't be able to settle the argument and instead will attach to objective things and will never escape from the four states of phenomena.[11]

14. "The *samādhi* of oneness is direct mind at all times, walking, staying, sitting, and lying. The *Vimalakīrti Sūtra* says, 'Direct mind is the place of practice; direct mind is the Pure Land.'[12] Do not with a dishonest mind speak of the

---

10. Following the Northern Song text.

11. Birth, being, change, and death.

12. *Jingming jing*, another name for the *Vimalakīrti Sūtra* (TD 14, no. 475:537–557). The quotation here does not appear as such in the *sūtra*; the first five characters are from the *Pusa pin* (p. 542c); the second from the *Foguo pin* (p. 538b).

directness of the *Dharma*. If while speaking of the *samādhi* of oneness, you fail to practice direct mind, you will not be disciples of the Buddha. Just practicing direct mind only, and in all things having no attachments whatsoever, is called the *samādhi* of oneness. The deluded man clings to the characteristics of things, adheres to the *samādhi* of oneness, [thinks] that the direct mind is sitting without moving and casting aside delusions without letting things arise in the mind. This he considers to be the *samādhi* of oneness. This kind of practice is the same as insentiency and is the cause of an obstruction to the Dao. Dao must be something that circulates freely; why should he impede it? If the mind does not abide in things, the Dao circulates freely; if the mind abides in things, it becomes entangled. If sitting in meditation without moving is good, why did Vimalakīrti scold Śāriputra for sitting in meditation in the forest?[13]

"Good friends, some people[14] teach men to sit viewing the mind and viewing purity, not moving and not activating [the mind], and to this they devote their efforts. Deluded people do not realize that this is wrong, attach to this doctrine, and become confused. There are many such people. Those who instruct in this way are from the outset greatly mistaken.

17. "Good friends, in this teaching of mine, from ancient times up to the present, all have set up no-thought as the main doctrine, non-form as the substance, and non-abiding as the basis. Non-form is to be separated from form even when associated with form. No-thought is not to think even when involved in thought. Non-abiding is the original nature of man.

"Successive thoughts do not stop; prior thoughts, present thoughts, and future thoughts follow one after the other without cessation. If one instant of thought is cut off, the *Dharma* body separates from the physical body, and in the midst of successive thoughts there will be no place for attachment to anything. If one instant of thought attaches, then successive thoughts attach; this is known as being fettered. If in all things successive thoughts do not attach, then you are unfettered. Therefore, non-abiding is made the basis."

> [From the photographic reproductions of the Dunhuang manuscript;
> section numbers as in D. T. Suzuki, ed; PY]

## THE LEGEND OF BAIZHANG, "FOUNDER"
## OF CHAN MONASTIC DISCIPLINE

A theme commonly found in modern as well as traditional writings on the history of Chan Buddhism is the idea that during the Tang dynasty (618–906) the Chan school developed a unique, independent system of monastic training that allowed it to exist apart from the mainstream of Chinese Buddhist institutions.

---

13. Reference is to a passage in the *Vimalakīrti Sūtra*.
14. Practitioners of Northern Zen.

According to the traditional account, this development was instigated by the Chan master Baizhang Huaihai (Dazhi, 720–814), who is credited with founding the first Chan monastery and authoring the first Chan monastic rules (known generically as "rules of purity" [*qinggui*]).

In point of fact, there is scant historical evidence to support the traditional account of the founding of a Chan institution in the Tang by Baizhang or anyone else. Tang accounts, including biographies and epigraphs memorializing Baizhang written closest to his lifetime, say nothing about independent Chan monasteries or rules. The first Chan monasteries on record actually appeared in the early decades of the Song dynasty (960–1279), when the imperial court decreed that the abbacies of certain large state monasteries were to be reserved for members of the Chan lineage. Shortly thereafter, the abbacies of other state monasteries similar in organization and operation were reserved for eminent monks in the Tiantai lineage, and others, in the thirteenth century, to members of the Nanshan Vinaya lineage.

The oldest depiction of Baizhang as the inventor of a Chan system of monastic discipline is found in a brief text known as the *Regulations of the Chan School* (*Chanmen guishi*), which first appeared in the late tenth century—just the time when major Buddhist monasteries were beginning to be designated as Chan abbacy establishments. The text circulated widely from the Song onward in several different redactions, was frequently quoted in other works, and became the basis for a cult of the "founder" Baizhang that was centered in the patriarch halls (shrines to ancient patriarchs in the lineage and former abbots) of Chan monasteries. Its account of Baizhang's role thus became widely accepted and its historicity went unquestioned down to modern times.

Although the *Regulations of the Chan School* is often said to represent "Baizhang's rules," or the oldest extant set of Chan rules, the text is actually not a set of monastic rules as such. It speaks in a voice that is historical and descriptive, not the imperative, prescriptive voice ("you must/must not do such-and-such") that is characteristic of the genre of texts known as "rules of purity." The oldest extant set of monastic rules associated with the Chan school is actually the *Rules of Purity for Chan Monasteries* (*Chanyuan qinggui*)[15] a work compiled in 1103.

The *Regulations of the Chan School* implies that the main features of monastery organization and training it describes were invented by Baizhang and unique to Chan institutions. Those features include: the key role played by the abbot as a spiritual teacher and object of veneration; communal life in a *sangha* hall, where the monks ate, slept, and sat in meditation; the establishment of separate administrative offices that ran the monastery and thus enabled the *sangha* hall monks to concentrate on spiritual training, communal manual

---

15. Editions of the *Chanyuan qinggui* (*Zennen shingi*) may be found in ZZ 2:16.5; *Sōtōshū zensho, Shingi*, pp. 867–934; *Kanazawa bunkoshi zensho, Zenseki hen*: for a critical edition and annotated Japanese translation, see Kagamishima Genryū, Satō Tetsugen and Kosaka Kiyū, eds. and trans., *Yakuchū zennen shingi* (Tokyo: Sōtōshū Shūmuchō, 1972).

labor, and procedures for expelling troublemakers and rule breakers. It is true that Chan monasteries in the Song and later were organized along these lines, but so too were the large state-sanctioned monasteries where monks in the Tiantai or Vinaya lineages served as abbots. The monastic discipline described in the *Regulations*, moreover, had precedents in earlier, non-Chan monastic rules.

In light of the apparent falsity of its historical claims, the *Regulations of the Chan School* is best interpreted today as a piece of religious mythology. By singling out features of monastic discipline that were in fact the common heritage of Chinese Buddhists at large and suggesting that they had been invented by the Chan patriarch Baizhang, the text articulated an idealized vision of monastic practice that Chan could claim as its own. It thus provided a justification for the unprecedented and essentially arbitrary designation of existing Buddhist establishments as Chan monasteries. At the same time, the installation of an image of the "founder" Baizhang in the patriarch halls of monasteries recently converted to Chan obscured the true history of their founding.

## REGULATIONS OF THE CHAN SCHOOL (CHANMEN GUISHI)

The following translation of the *Regulations of the Chan School* is based primarily on the redaction of the text appended to the biography of Baizhang in the *Jingde Era Record of the Transmission of the Lamp* (*Jingde chuandeng lu*), completed in 1004. It follows other redactions and pericopes of the text,[16] at some points where the *Record of the Transmission of the Lamp* is in error. Passages in the translation that are indented represent interlinear comments found in the text. These were added by one or more redactors subsequent to the work of the original author(s). The longest of these notes speaks to the problem of how the supposedly "wordless" Chan could deal with problems of organization and discipline without committing itself to words. Since the recording of "public cases" (*gongan*) and disciplinary rules arose together with the "organizing" of the tradition in the Song period, both reflect the compromise by which "wordless" Chan produced a great body of literature, while radical purists like Dahui railed against such perversions.

From the origination of the Chan lineage with Shaoshi [the first patriarch Bodhidharma] up until Caoqi [the Sixth Patriarch Huineng] and after, members of the lineage resided in Vinaya monasteries.[17] Even when they had

---

16. Other redactions and pericopes of the *Chanmen guishi* are found in: the *Song gaoseng zhuan* (TD 50, no. 2061:770–771), written in 988; the *Da Song sengshi lüe* (TD 54, no. 2126:240), written by Zanning (919–1001); the *Shishi yaolan* (TD 54, no. 2127:301), compiled in 1019; the *Chanyuan qinggui* (ZZ 2:16.5:465–469), written in 1103; the *Fozu lidai tongzai* (TD 49, no. 2036:619), compiled in 1333; and the *Chixiu Baizhang qinggui* (TD 48, no. 2025:1157–1158), completed in 1343.

17. "Vinaya monastery" here means a monastery regulated by the Buddhist monastic rules translated from Indic languages.

separate cloisters, they did not yet follow independent regulations pertaining to preaching the *dharma* and the appointment of abbots.

Chan Master Baizhang Dazhi was always filled with regret on account of this. He said, "It is my desire that the way of the patriarchs be widely propagated. If we wish to escape destruction in the future, why should we regard the teachings of the various *Āgamas* (*A-ji-mo*) as practices to be followed?"

*Formerly this Sanskrit term was transliterated as* A-han. *The new way of saying it is* A-shi-mo. *It means the Hīnayāna teachings.*

Someone said, "The *Yujia shidi lun* and the *Pusa yingluo benye jing* are texts containing the Mahāyāna precepts. Why not follow them?" Baizhang said, "What we hold as essential is not bound up in the Mahāyāna or Hīnayāna, nor is it completely different from them. We should select judiciously from a broad range [of earlier rules], arrange them into a set of regulations, and adopt them as our norms." Thereupon he conceived the idea of establishing a Chan monastery separately.

A spiritually perceptive and morally praiseworthy person was to be named as abbot, just as in India, where spiritually advanced senior monks were called Subhūti. When serving as chief instructor, the abbot was to occupy "ten-foot-square" quarters. It was to be a room like Vimalakīrti's,[18] not a private residence.

A buddha hall was not built, and only a *dharma* hall erected. That was because the current abbot, representing the buddhas and patriarchs in his very person, was to be regarded as the "honored one."[19]

Those belonging to the assembly of trainees, regardless of their numbers or status, all had to enter the *saṅgha* hall, where they were placed in rows in accordance with their seniority.

Platforms were constructed in the *saṅgha* hall, and a robe rack provided, where the trainees hung up their monkish implements.

When reclining, they had to place their pillows on the edge of the platform and sleep on their right sides in the auspicious posture.[20]

In order to sit in meditation for a long time, they took only a brief rest and then got up again. Thus they maintained the proper deportment at all four times [when standing, walking, sitting, or lying down].

The exception was entering the abbot's room to request instruction, which was left up to the diligence of the trainees. Neither seniors nor juniors were bound by any set of rules in this regard.

---

18. Vimalakīrti, the protagonist of a famous Buddhist *sūtra* by that name, was a lay bodhisattva who magically received and debated a huge audience of sages in his room despite the fact that it was only "ten-feet square" (*fangzhang*).

19. The "honored one" (*benzun*) is the central image on the altar in a buddha hall.

20. The posture in which the Buddha entered *nirvāṇa*.

The great assembly of the entire monastery convened in the morning and gathered in the evening when the abbot entered the *dharma* hall and mounted the lecture seat. The monastery officers and assembly of followers stood in ranks at the sides and listened. Questions and answers between guests and host stimulated the raising of essential points of doctrine, which showed how to dwell in accordance with the *dharma*.

Meals,[21] in accordance with what was proper, were served only twice a day and were distributed equally to all. Thus temperance was maintained and the joint revolving of the [wheels of] *dharma* and food was manifested.

The rule for the practice of communal labor was for seniors and juniors to do equal work.

Ten administrative departments were established. These were called offices. Each had one person as chief who supervised a number of other persons in managing [the office's] affairs. . . .

The Chan school's independent practice followed from Baizhang's initiative. At present I have briefly summarized the essential points and proclaimed them for all future generations of practitioners, so that they will not be forgetful of our patriarch [Baizhang]. His rules should be implemented in this monastery.

[From *TD* 51, no. 2076:250–251; TGF]

## THE CHANYUAN MONASTIC CODE (*CHÜN-FANG YÜ*)

This list of questions for monks to test the depth of their religious understanding is found in the *Chanyuan Code* cited earlier. We do not know if it was to be read aloud in an assembly, as was the *Prātimokṣa* at the semimonthly ceremony, in which case, as each question was asked aloud, the members of the congregation might have reflected on their own moral purity and spiritual maturity. There is no evidence, however, that this was actually done. More probably the text served instead for either classroom instruction or individual study and review, as a comprehensive outline of the key areas of moral and spiritual cultivation. The list of questions is also known to have been circulated as an independent book, separate from the *Chanyuan Code*, in order to facilitate its wider use.

The 120 questions cover a wide range of topics, which for purposes of discussion, may be divided into five areas: (1) morality common to Confucianism and Buddhism — filial piety, loyalty, respect, kindness, humility, and other virtues; (2) Buddhist precepts stressed in the *Vinaya*, particularly those of nonharming; (3) Mahāyāna ideals such as the six perfections and thought for enlightenment; (4) technical knowledge of Buddhist doctrine and philosophy, heavily Tiantai and Huayan; and (5) Chan, primarily knowledge of public cases [*gongan*]. Aside from these categories, Zongze asks learners to seek out good teachers, not to exploit their disciples, not to use their

---

21. Literally, "the forenoon meal and morning congee."

position to oppress others, to obey the law of the land, to make commitments to the Buddhist way of life, and to be diligent in the Buddhist practice of burning incense, worship, and cultivation. Warnings against befriending officials and criticism of the desire for fame and profit reflect concerns frequently expressed by contemporary Chan leaders. Finally, the call to treat "barbarians" the same as Chinese, although based in Mahāyāna universalism, bears the mark of Zongze's own forceful way of thinking.

## One Hundred and Twenty Questions

1. Do you respect the Buddha, the *Dharma*, and the *Saṅgha*?
2. Do you try to seek out good teachers?
3. Have you given rise to the thought for enlightenment?
4. Do you have faith that you can enter into Buddhahood?
5. Have you exhausted the feelings for the past and the present?
6. Are you securely settled without relapsing?
7. Can you stand on the edge of a cliff of a thousand feet without flinching?
8. Do you understand clearly the meaning of purifications and prohibitions?
9. Are your body and mind relaxed and tranquil?
10. Do you always delight in sitting meditation?
11. Have you become as pure and clear as the sky?
12. Have you attained the state of "one in all, all in one"?
13. Can you be unmoved confronting any circumstances?
14. Has *prajñā* [wisdom] appeared in front of you?
15. Can you cut off language and words?
16. Can you extinguish activities of the mind?
17. Can you regard any form you see as mind?
18. Can you regard any sound you hear as nature?
19. Can you be like Bodhidharma facing the wall?
20. Can you be like Master Longya hiding his body?[22]
21. Can you be like the Bodhisattva of One Thousand Arms and Eyes?
22. Do you understand the meaning of "old buddhas communing with the pillars"?[23]
23. Do you have no difficulties with the ultimate Way?
24. Can you raise up the mountain like level ground?[24]

---

22. Probably a *gongan*, but not yet identified.

23. This *gongan* is no. 83 in the *Blue Cliff Records* (*Biyanlu*) and no. 31 in Hongzhi Zhengjue's (1090–1157) *Record of Natural Ease* (*Congronglu*). "Yunmen spoke to his disciples and said, 'The old buddhas communed with the pillars; what dimension of activity is this?' He supplied the answer himself, saying, 'When clouds gather on the southern mountains, rain falls on the northern mountains.'"

24. An unidentified *gongan*.

25. Have you met Bodhidharma without realizing it?[25]
26. "As a resident within the retreat, can you be oblivious of events happening outside the retreat?"[26]
27. "When clouds gather on the southern mountain, will rain fall on the northern mountain?"[27]
28. Are you as fierce and energetic [in meditation] as a lion?
29. Do you teach others with compassion?
30. Can you sacrifice your body in order to protect the *Dharma*?
31. Is your mind illumined by ancient teachings?
32. Is your spirit calmed by the three contemplations of the empty, the Mean, and the unreal?
33. Can you freely go in and out of *samādhi*?
34. Has the "Universal Door" [Guanyin] been manifested to you?
35. Have you studied deeply the "six qualities" (*liu xiang*)?[28]
36. Have you understood thoroughly the "ten mysteries" (*shixuan*)?[29]
37. Have you harmonized the perfect causations for the "six stages" [of the Bodhisattva career]?[30]
38. Have you attained the ocean of fruition of the "ten bodies" of the Buddha (*shishen guohai*)?[31]
39. Do you have the faith of Mañjuśrī?
40. Can you follow the example of Samantabhadra [of returning to work for the sentient beings after his enlightenment]?
41. Is your deportment dignified?
42. Is your speech correct?

---

25. Ibid.

26. A *gongan* used by Song monks. For instance, a monk asked this *gongan* when he was with Xiatang Huiyuan (1102–1176).

27. See question 22 and the accompanying note.

28. The six qualities refer to generalness, specialness, similarity, diversity, integration, and disintegration. This is a basic concept in Huayan Buddhism.

29. The Huayan master Fazang (see chap. 16) explains another basic Huayan concept, the ten mysteries: (1) simultaneous completeness; (2) pure and mixed attributes of various storehouses; (3) mutual compatibility between the dissimilarities between the one and the many; (4) mutual freedom among things; (5) hidden-and-displayed correlation; (6) peaceful compatibility of the minute and abstruse; (7) the realm of Indra's net; (8) relying on phenomenal things in order to elucidate things; (9) the variable formation of the ten ages in sections; and (10) excellent achievement according to the evolutions of mind only.

30. The six stages of Bodhisattva development, according to the *Flower Garland Sūtra* (*Huayan jing*).

31. The ten perfect bodies of a Buddha are (1) *bodhi*-body in possession of complete enlightenment; (2) vow-body, i.e., the vow to be born in and from the Tuṣita Heaven; (3) *Nirmāṇakāya*; (4) Buddha who still occupies his relics or what he has left behind on earth and thus upholds the *Dharma*; (5) *Sambhogakāya*; (6) power-body embracing all with his heart of mercy; (7) at-will body, appearing according to wish or need; (8) *samādhi*-body or body of blessed virtue; (9) wisdom-body, whose nature embraces all wisdom, and (10) *Dharmakāya*.

43. Does your word accord with your thought?
44. Do you praise yourself but denigrate others?
45. Can you step back to let others advance?
46. Do you make known others' merits?
47. Can you refrain from speaking about others' mistakes?
48. Can you refrain from showing a dislike for difficult questions?
49. Can you not be fond of jests and jokes?
50. Do you always take delight in silence?
51. Can you be without self-deception even in a dark room?
52. Can you be as firm as a mountain in managing the community?
53. Do you always practice humility?
54. Are you peaceful and without argument?
55. Are you fair in handling affairs?
56. Are you glad to hear flattering words?
57. Do you not dislike to hear true words?
58. Can you bear suffering with patience and fortitude?
59. Can you endure harsh scolding?
60. Can you subdue thoughts of pleasure?
61. Can you stop butting into others' affairs?
62. Can you refrain from laziness and neglect in your religious practice?
63. Can you refrain from appropriating public property?
64. Can you refrain from using money and things of others?
65. Can you refrain from keeping gold, silk, and jewels?
66. Can you refrain from hoarding books, paintings, and antiques?
67. Can you refrain from borrowing from others?
68. Do you realize that, even though you do not practice sericulture, you nevertheless have clothes to wear?
69. Do you realize that, even though you do not farm, you nevertheless have food to eat?
70. Do you realize that, even though you do not fight in war, you nevertheless live in safety?
71. Can you be satisfied with your upkeep?
72. Can you moderate your eating and drinking?
73. Are you tireless in giving offerings?
74. Can you be without greed in receiving offerings?
75. Can you do without extra robes and begging bowls?
76. Do you give *dharma* talks without thought of profit?
77. Do you not seek others' admiration?
78. Do you not exploit your disciples?
79. Can you be without desire for fame?
80. Can you stay away from royalty and officials?
81. Can you refrain from oppressing others because of your position?
82. Can you refrain from interesting yourself in official affairs?
83. Do you fear and obey the law of the land?

84. Can you refrain from engaging in fortune-telling?
85. Can you refrain from becoming intimate with women?
86. Can you refrain from jealousy of the worthy and the able?
87. Can you refrain from envy of those who are superior to you?
88. Can you refrain from despising the poor and lowly?
89. Can you protect the minds of others [from distraction or temptation]?
90. Can you refrain from bothering and harming sentient beings?
91. Can you always carry out "releasing life" [saving the lives of animals, birds, etc.]?
92. Do you always think of protecting the living?
93. Do you respect the old and treat the young with kindness?
94. Do you take care of the sick?
95. Do you feel pity for those who are in prison?
96. Do you help the hungry and the cold?
97. Do you stay away from military battles?
98. Do you regard Chinese and barbarians the same way?
99. Have you repaid the kindness of the sovereign and officials?
100. Have you returned the kindness of your parents who bore you and nourished you?
101. Have you thanked your teachers and friends for their instruction?
102. Do you remember the kindness of patrons who provide your livelihood?
103. Do you cherish the aid your relatives and friends have rendered to you?
104. Do you notice the kindness with which the servants work for you?
105. Do you think about the protection provided by *nāgas* and *devas?*
106. Are you aware of your indebtedness to soldiers who guard the state?
107. Do you feel sorry for the decay of *devas?*
108. Do you feel pity for the eight distresses[32] found among human being?
109. Do you feel sad over the fighting among the *asuras?*
110. Do you lament the loneliness of the hungry ghosts?
111. Do you mourn the ignorance of animals?
112. Do you grieve for the beings in hell?
113. Do you treat the enemy the same way as loved ones?
114. Do you respect everyone as you respect the Buddha?
115. Do you love everyone as you love your parents?
116. Do you vow to save all sentient beings without exception?
117. Do you examine yourself at the three times [morning, noon, and evening]?
118. Have you finished doing what you were born to do?
119. Have you obtained great liberation?
120. Have you realized the great *nirvāṇa?*

[*Chanyuan qinggui* 8:461–462; CFY]

---

32. These are birth, age, sickness, death, parting with what one loves, meeting with what one hates, unattained aims, and all the ills of the five *skandhas*.

# BUDDHIST RITUALS
# AND DEVOTIONAL PRACTICES

## ZHONGFENG MINGBEN: *ADMONITION ON FILIALITY*

Ever since Buddhism was introduced into China, Buddhist monks have had to defend themselves against the charge of unfiliality because they had to leave the life of the householder and observe the precept of celibacy. This short essay by the Yuan Chan master Zhongfeng Mingben (1263–1323) is a well-known example of this genre of writing.

Mingben at first plays on the homophones of *xiao*, which can mean either filiality or imitation. Filiality is essentially imitation. Since our parents nurture and love us, we in turn should nurture and love them. But to nurture one's parents' physical body and to practice "love with form" is the filiality appropriate for a householder, while a monk shows his filial piety by nurturing the parents' *dharma*-nature and by practice of "formless love." The former, mundane type of filiality has a time limit, for we can love and serve our parents this way only when they are alive, whereas by leading a pure and disciplined life, by serious and sustained effort at meditation, and finally by achieving enlightenment, a monk can fulfill the requirements of filiality on the basis of the Buddhist principle of the "transference of merit," by which a son applies the merits of a sanctified life to benefit his parents spiritually, whether they are alive or dead.

All parents of this world nurture and love their children. Therefore sages and worthies teach us to be filial to our parents. Filiality (*xiao*) means imitating (*xiao*). Children imitate parental nurturing and repay their parents with nurturing. Children imitate parental love and repay their parents with love. Therefore, filiality cannot be exceeded by nurturing, but it reaches its utmost with love. However, there are two ways of nurturing and two ways of love. To serve parents with grain and meat and to clothe them with fur and linen is to nourish their physical bodies. To discipline oneself with purity and restraint and to cultivate blessedness and goodness for them is to nourish their *dharma*-nature. The nourishment of their physical bodies follows human relationships, but the nourishment of their *dharma*-nature conforms to heavenly principle. Even sages and worthies cannot perform both. That is because there is a difference between being a householder and being a monk. If one is a householder but fails to nourish the physical bodies of his parents, he is unfilial. If one is a monk but fails to nourish the *dharma*-nature of his parents, he is also unfilial. This is what I mean by the two ways of filiality.

To inquire after one's parents morning and evening and dare not leave them for any length of time is what I call love with form (*youxing zhi ai*). To engage in the effort of meditation whether walking or sitting, to vow to realize the Way within the span of this life, and, with this, to repay the kindness of parents is what I call formless love (*wuxing zhi ai*). Love with form is near and intimate, but love without form is distant and inaccessible. But if a person feels no love, he cannot even reach the near, not to mention the distant and inaccessible. One cannot fulfill both the easy and the difficult types of love. This is because there is a difference between remaining in the world and leaving the world. To remain in the world but not to carry out the love with form is unfilial. To leave the world but not to carry out the formless love is also unfilial. This is why I say that there are two ways of love.

Furthermore, the mundane type of nurturing and love has a time limit, but the otherworldly type of nurturing and love has no time limit. Why does the former have a time limit? Because we can only love our parents when they are alive. When they die, this love vanishes. Why does the latter have no time limit? Because my mind of studying the Way is not altered by the existence or death of my parents. Parents are the great foundation of my physical form. Yet is my physical form something I only have in this life? From innumerable *kalpas* until now, I have transmigrated in the three realms [of desire, form, and formlessness] and have received forms as numberless as the grains of sand. The so-called foundation of physical form fills the universe and pervades the cosmos. All that I see and hear could be the basis of my previous existences. There is no way to take account of my parents' labors and sufferings. That I should fail to repay their kindness may cause my parents to fall into other realms of rebirth and suffer the pain of transmigration. Thus the Way is no other than filial piety, and filial piety is no other than the Way. When a person does not know how to be filial but says that he wants to study the Way, that is like seeking water while turning his back on it.

If someone is unable to practice this but is only able to nourish the parents' physical bodies and to love them with form, can we call this filial piety? I would say this is the filial piety of a householder. The reason we monks cannot engage in worldly filial piety is because we have entered the gate of emptiness and silence and have put on the monastic robe. We may try to emulate the otherworldly filial piety of the Great Sage of the Snowy Mountain [Śākyamuni]. Suppose we should make a mistake in one single thought; we would then lose both benefits [of the worldly and otherworldly filial love]. This is the height of unfiliality.

[*Tianmu Mingben Chanshi zalu*, ZZ 2:27.4:366; CFY]

*Chapter 18*

## SOCIAL LIFE AND POLITICAL
## CULTURE IN THE TANG

The Tang (618–906) is known for the vitality and vibrancy of its culture—the dynamic and cosmopolitan cultural life of the capital city of Changan, a flourishing trade and cultural contact with Western Asia, the evolution of distinctively Chinese forms of Buddhism, the proliferation of Buddhist sculpture and painting, the early development of the short story and the fictional imagination, an unprecedented and dazzling efflorescence in the art of poetry. In government too there were remarkable developments that had a profound effect not only on Tang political culture but also on the course of later Chinese civilization—the revival of the civil service examination system as a basis for recruiting an effective bureaucracy based on the principle of merit, a far-reaching land reform designed to equalize landholding, the establishment of an administrative structure of the central government that would endure, with minor modifications, down to the twentieth century.

The Tang is also known for its vigorous empire-building—a familiar pattern seen under the Qin, the Han, and the Sui (589–617) dynasties—in which there was expansion in the early years of the dynasty, followed by contraction in later periods as the burdens of war took their toll. Early in the reign of the Tang emperor Taizong (r. 627–649) Chinese forces succeeded against the Turks in Central Asia and brought Tibet under Chinese control, while in subsequent reigns Chinese influence was established in Korea and in part of Vietnam. By the end of the seventh century China was the largest empire and the most powerful state in the world.

This empire was maintained until well into the eighth century, when several developments, including intense pressure from non-Chinese peoples in the north and northwest and the dynasty's loss of control of its own military organization, brought about irreversible changes in the Tang world. These developments are epitomized in the Rebellion of An Lushan of 755, which brought warfare, devastation, and famine into the Tang heartland.

## THE ROLE OF CONFUCIANISM IN THE TANG

If today Chinese civilization seems almost synonymous with Confucian culture, we need to be reminded of the long centuries during which Buddhism and Daoism exerted a powerful and formative influence. For nearly eight centuries, from the fall of the Han (220 C.E.) to the rise of the Song (960), Chinese culture was so closely identified with Buddhism that neighbors like the Japanese and the Koreans embraced the one with the other and thought of great Tang China, the cynosure of the civilized world, as perhaps more of a "Buddha-land" than the "land of Confucius." The famed centers of learning to which pilgrims came from afar were the great Buddhist temples, where some of the best Chinese minds were engaged in teaching and developing new schools of Buddhist philosophy. The great works of art and architecture, which impressed these same visitors with the splendor of China, were most often monuments to the Buddha. Until the close of this period few among the Confucians could dispute the preeminence of the Buddhist philosophers or slow the progress of the Daoist church, officially supported by the Tang imperial house.

Indeed, it may be said that during this period, though there were Confucian scholars, there were virtually no Confucians—that is, persons who adhered to the teachings of Confucius as a distinct doctrine that set them apart from others. The sense of orthodoxy came later and mostly to an educated elite. People followed Confucius in the home or in the office, but this did not prevent them, high or low, from turning to Buddhism or Daoism to find satisfaction of their spiritual needs.

Still, it is significant that, if Confucianism could not contend with its rivals in the religious sphere, neither were they able to displace it in the social or political sphere. Though in an attenuated and not very dynamic form, Confucianism remained the accepted code of ethics and the basis of the educational system. The family and the imperial bureaucracy kept Confucian teachings alive during these times until their validity and relevance to a wider sphere of thought could be reasserted by more vigorous minds. Even a patron of Buddhism like Emperor Wu of the Liang dynasty (464–549) saw to it that his sons studied the Five Classics, the *Analects*, and the *Classic of Filiality*.

The chief means by which Confucian teachings were perpetuated were the civil service examination system and the schools serving it. Revived by the Sui, based on a Han model, and continued under the Tang dynasty, this system became more highly organized and efficiently administered than ever before, and the basic subjects were still the Confucian classics. (Because the imperial house claimed descent from Laozi, there was also one type of examination based on a knowledge of Daoist texts.) Buddhists might from time to time win a monarch's favor, eliciting contributions to religious establishments or securing his participation in their special rites. Individual monks, too, might occasionally rise high in the government ranks. Buddhism itself, however, both as a philosophy and as a religion, sought to transcend politics and offered nothing in the way of either a political program or a set of basic principles that might have been incorporated into the examination system. Therefore the vast majority of those whose education conformed to the requirements of the civil service system, the great avenue to worldly success in China, submitted to a curriculum in which the position of the Confucian classics remained unchallenged. To many this study of the classics served only as a method for achieving a degree of mastery over the language. To others it provided also a treasury of historical lore and prudential maxims that might be drawn upon in the business of government.

The nature of Confucian scholarship in the Tang dynasty reflected the function that it served for the bureaucracy. Carrying on in the manner of the Han classicists, learned men devoted themselves to the kind of textual annotation and exegesis that would provide more definitive editions of the Confucian canon used in the examinations. From the scholarly point of view this work was important, and yet we find in it evidence more of painstaking study than creative thought. In the actual conduct of state affairs, however, we may see quite readily how Confucianism continued to influence thinking on the vital political and economic issues of the day.

The vast problems with which the Han had had to wrestle confronted the Tang as well, and the latter showed itself capable of strong action on a grand scale. At the inception of the dynasty, for instance, it embarked on a program of land nationalization and redistribution, upon which was based the whole system of taxation and military organization, the two most vital operations of the state. So impressive was this system that both the Japanese and the Koreans copied it almost to the last detail.

## HOUSE INSTRUCTIONS OF MR. YAN (YANSHI JIAXUN)

Following are extracts from the prime extant example of a genre of family instruction perennially important not only in China but elsewhere in East Asia down into the nineteenth century. Yan Zhitui (531–591) was from a leading family of scholar-officials known for their public service and literary accomplishments. In times of great military and political turmoil before the reunification of China under the Sui, Yan experienced hardships and poverty but served four successive, brief dynasties (with foreigners among them) while sustaining his family's commitment to Chinese cultural traditions. His life and work illustrate a more general long-term pattern in Chinese history: the persistence of Confucian social and scholarly values through periods dominated by foreign rulers, as well as by Buddhist or Daoist religious influences.

Yan's *Instructions* cover such matters as the conduct of family relations, social customs, the importance of education, dedication to high moral and cultural standards (rather than rank and wealth), proper bureaucratic practice, and various scholarly matters of concern to the literati. Predominantly Confucian in tone and subject matter, the *Instructions* are noteworthy also in this age of strong Buddhist influence for one chapter expressing respect for Buddhism, based on its doctrines of moral retribution, affirmation of a moral and spiritual order beyond the sensate and sensible, and respect for life, as shown in the nonkilling of living beings.

## Preface

Of books written by sages and worthies that teach men to be sincere and filial, to be careful in speech and circumspect in conduct, and to take one's proper place in society and be concerned for one's reputation, there are more than enough already. Since the Wei and Jin periods prudential writings have reiterated principles and repeated practices as if adding room upon room [to the household] or piling bed upon bed. In doing the same now myself, I do not presume to prescribe rules for others or set a pattern for the world, but only to order my own household and give guidance to my own posterity. . . .

The habits and teaching of our family have always been regular and punctilious. In my childhood I received good instruction from my parents. With my two elder brothers I went to greet our parents each morning and evening to ask in winter whether they were warm and in summer whether they were cool; we walked steadily with regular steps, talked calmly with good manners, and moved about with as much dignity and reverence as if we were visiting the awe-inspiring rulers at court. They gave us good advice, asked about our particular interests, criticized our defects and encouraged our good points—always zealous and sincere. When I was just nine years old, my father died. The family members were divided and scattered, every one of us living in dire straits. I was brought up by my loving brothers; we went through hardships and difficulties. They were kind but not exacting; their guidance and advice to me were not strict. Though I read the ritual texts, and was somewhat fond of composition, I tended to be influenced by common practices; I was uncontrolled in feelings, careless in speech, and slovenly in dress. When about eighteen or nineteen years old I learned to refine my conduct a little, but these bad habits had become second nature, and it was difficult to get rid of them entirely. After my thirtieth year gross faults were few, but still I have to be careful always, for in every instance my words are at odds with my mind, and my emotions struggle with my nature. Each evening I am conscious of the faults committed that morning, and today I regret the errors of yesterday. How pitiful that the lack of instruction has brought me to this condition! I would recall the experiences of my youth long ago, for they are engraved on my flesh and bone; these are not merely the admonitions of ancient books, but what has passed before my eyes and reached my ears. Therefore I leave these twenty chapters to serve as a warning to you boys.

## Instructing Children

Those of the highest intelligence will develop without being taught; those of great stupidity, even if taught, will amount to nothing; those of medium ability will be ignorant unless taught. The ancient sage kings had rules for prenatal training. Women when pregnant for three months moved from their living quarters to a detached palace where they would not see unwholesome sights nor hear reckless words, and where the tone of music and the flavor of food were controlled by the rules of decorum [rites]. These rules were written on jade tablets and kept in a golden box. After the child was born, imperial tutors firmly made clear filial piety, humaneness, the rites, and rightness to guide and train him.

The common people are indulgent and are unable to do this. But as soon as a baby can recognize facial expressions and understand approval and disapproval, training should be begun so that he will do what he is told to do and stop when so ordered. After a few years of this, punishment with the bamboo can be minimized, as parental strictness and dignity mingled with parental love will lead the boys and girls to a feeling of respect and caution and give rise to filial piety. I have noticed about me that where there is merely love without training this result is never achieved. Children eat, drink, speak, and act as they please. Instead of needed prohibitions they receive praise; instead of urgent reprimands they receive smiles. Even when children are old enough to learn, such treatment is still regarded as the proper method. Only after the child has formed proud and arrogant habits do they try to control him. But one may whip the child to death and he will still not be respectful, while the growing anger of the parents only increases his resentment. After he grows up, such a child becomes at last nothing but a scoundrel. Confucius was right in saying, "What is acquired in infancy is like original nature; what has been formed into habits is equal to instinct."[1] A common proverb says, "Train a wife from her first arrival; teach a son in his infancy." How true such sayings are!

Generally parents' inability to instruct their own children comes not from any inclination just to let them fall into evil ways but only from parents' being unable to endure the children's looks [of unhappiness] from repeated scoldings, or to bear beating them, lest it do damage to the children's physical being. We should, however, take illness by way of illustration: how can we not use drugs, medicines, acupuncture, or cautery to cure it? Should we then view strictness

---

1. Not in any of the Confucian classics but quoted by Jia Yi (201–168? B.C.E.) in *Jiazi xinshu* (*SBBY*) 5:3b and also in Jia Yi's biography in *Hanshu* 48.

of reproof and punishment as a form of cruelty to one's own kith and kin? Truly there is no other way to deal with it. . . .

As for maintaining proper respect between father and son, one cannot allow too much familiarity; in the love among kin, one cannot tolerate impoliteness. If there is impoliteness, then parental solicitude is not matched by filial respect; if there is too much familiarity, it gives rise to indifference and rudeness.

Someone has asked why Chen Kang [a disciple of Confucius] was pleased to hear that gentlemen kept their distance from their sons, and the answer is that this was indeed the case; gentlemen did not personally teach their children [because, as Yan goes on to show, there are passages in the classics of a sexual kind, which it would not be proper for a father to teach his sons.] . . .

In the love of parents for children, it is rare that one succeeds in treating them equally. From antiquity to the present there are many cases of this failing. It is only natural to love those who are wise and talented, but those who are wayward and dull also deserve sympathy. Partiality in treatment, even when done out of generous motives, turns out badly. . . .


## Family Governance

Beneficial influences are transmitted from superiors to inferiors and bequeathed by earlier to later generations. So if a father is not loving, the son will not be filial; if an elder brother is not friendly, the younger will not be respectful; if a husband is not just, the wife will not be obedient. When a father is kind but the son refractory, when an elder brother is friendly but the younger arrogant, when a husband is just but a wife overbearing, then indeed they are the bad people of the world; they must be controlled by punishments; teaching and guidance will not change them. If rod and wrath are not used in family discipline, the faults of the son will immediately appear. If punishments are not properly awarded, the people will not know how to act. The use of clemency and severity in governing a family is the same as in a state.

Confucius said, "Extravagance leads to insubordination, and parsimony to meanness. It is better to be mean than to be insubordinate."[2] Again he said, "Though a man has abilities as admirable as those of the Duke of Zhou, yet if he be proud or niggardly, those other things are really not worth being looked at."[3] That is to say, a man may be thrifty but should not be stingy. Thrift means being frugal and economic in carrying out the rites; stinginess means showing no pity for those in poverty and urgent need. Nowadays those who would give alms are extravagant, but in being thrifty are stingy. It would be proper to give alms without extravagance and be thrifty without being stingy. . . .

---

2. *Analects* 7:35.
3. *Analects* 8:11.

A wife in presiding over household supplies should use wine, food, and clothing only as the rites specify. Just as in the state, where women are not allowed to participate in setting policies, so in the family, they should not be permitted to assume responsibility for affairs. If they are wise, talented, and versed in the ancient and modern writings, they ought to help their husbands by supplementing the latter's deficiency. No hen should herald the dawn lest misfortune follow. . . .

The burden of daughters on the family is heavy indeed. Yet how else can Heaven give life to the teeming people and ancestors pass on their bodily existence to posterity? Many people today dislike having daughters and mistreat their own flesh and blood. How can they be like this and still hope for Heaven's blessing? . . .

It is common for women to dote on a son-in-law and to maltreat a daughter-in-law. Doting on a son-in-law gives rise to hatred from brothers; maltreating a daughter-in-law brings on slander from sisters. Thus when these women, whether they act or remain silent, draw criticism from the members of the family, it is the mother who is the real cause of it. . . .

A simple marriage arrangement irrespective of social position was the established rule of our ancestor Qing Hou.[4] Nowadays there are those who sell their daughters for money or buy a woman with a payment of silk. They compare the rank of fathers and grandfathers, and calculate in ounces and drams, demanding more and offering less, just as if bargaining in the market. Under such conditions a boorish son-in-law might appear in the family or an arrogant woman assume power in the household. Coveting honor and seeking for gain, on the contrary, incur shame and disgrace; how can one not be careful?

[*Yanshi jiaxun jijie* 19–64; trans. adapted and revised from Teng, *Family Instructions*, 1–20, and Lau, "Advice," 94–98; AD]

## THE GREAT TANG CODE

One of the great achievements of the Tang dynasty was its legal system, especially the criminal code (*Tanglü*), which, supplemented by civil statutes and regulations, became the basis for later dynastic codes not only in China but elsewhere in East Asia. The *Code* synthesizes the Legalist tradition, centered on the state, and Confucian traditions, focused more on family relations and conflict resolution in the local community. Both traditions are mediated in forms characteristic of Han dynasty thought and practice. Important among these is the holistic view expressed earlier by the Han Confucian scholar Dong Zhongshu, who saw the human and natural orders as so intimately linked that

---

4. Qing Hou was the posthumous name of Yan Zhitui's ninth-generation ancestor. His name was Yan Han.

actions in the former have an effect on the latter. Prime responsibility for linkage between the two falls on the emperor and his ministers, whose actions can exert either a beneficial or a harmful influence on both the human and the natural orders. Preserving overall balance is the key. An offense is regarded as a disruption of society that requires compensatory, corrective action by the ruler if the natural balance and harmony are to be restored.

To this end the *Code* embodies a blend of Legalist concern for universality, consistency, impartiality, and inexorability in the application of the law, along with a Confucian disposition to take into account particular statuses, qualitative (hierarchical) distinctions, and degrees of personal relationship. Reference is made to earlier law codes as well as to the Confucian ritual classics, but little overt credit is given to the Legalists.

Overall, the *Code* reflects an attempt by a centralized, bureaucratic, dynastic state (not the decentralized "feudal" state idealized by the Confucians) to assert its authority and protect its power over all of China. Yet the effective limits of that authority are acknowledged by the *Code*'s heavy reinforcement of Confucian ritual practice by which social order would normally be maintained through the family system, without recourse to law or the intervention of state power. Law was only the last resort after other, more consensual mechanisms failed.

## ZHANGSUN WUJI: THE TANG CODE

Although the names of several early Tang officials are associated with the *Code*, the preface and major portions are attributed to the brother-in-law of Tang Taizong, Zhangsun Wuji (d. 659), one of the most powerful statesmen of his time.

## Preface

Coming to the time of Yao and Shun, their influence was pervasive, so that offenses were few. They discussed the punishments in order to fix the penalties and had pictures drawn illustrating them in order to shame the people.[5] The articles and sections of their laws, even though numerous, were simple and concise. The period was long ago, however, and we cannot know those laws in detail. In the time of Yao and Shun, the officer who maintained order was called the *shi*. Gao Yao held this office.[6] The general outline of their laws has been preserved

---

5. This refers to displaying pictures of the punishments on the palace gates on the first day of the new year, which is described in "Dasikou," *Zhouli*; Biot, *Le Techou li*, 2:314.

6. "Canon of Shun," *Classic of Documents*; Legge, *The Chinese Classics*, 3:44–45.

and is often in good part visible. This is what the *Treatise on Customs* speaks of when it states: "Gao Yao advised Shun in making the statutes."[7]

A statute is similar to a measure or a model. The *Classic of Changes* states: "The regulation of resources, the rectification of pronouncements, and his [the sage's] preventing the people from doing wrong we call 'rightness.'"[8] Therefore the lawmaker must measure the gravity of offenses; he institutes statutes in accordance with rightness. The *Great Commentary* on the *Classic of Documents* speaks of vast Heaven's great statute.[9] The commentary explains: "We receive Heaven's great law (*fa*). Law is also statute (*lü*)."[10] Hence the use of the term *statute*.

## Article 6: The Ten Abominations

The following illustrates, in an abridged form, the contents of a single article of the *Code*. Some of the articles from numbers 160 to 174 refer to the particular land, tax, and labor service systems adopted in the early Tang but no longer viable in the late Tang.

*Subcommentary*: The ten abominations (*shie*) are the most serious of those offenses that come within the five punishments. They injure traditional norms and destroy ceremony. They are specially placed near the head of this chapter [14b] in order to serve as a clear warning. The number of extreme abominations being classified as ten is the reason why they are called the ten abominations. . . .

*Article*: The first is called plotting rebellion (*moufan*).

*Subcommentary*: The *Gongyang Commentary* states: "The ruler or parent has no harborers [of plots]. If he does have such harborers, he must put them to death."[11] This means that if there are those who harbor rebellious hearts that would harm the ruler or father, he must then put them to death. The *Zuo Commentary* (*Zuozhuan*) states: "When the seasons of Heaven are reversed, we have calamities . . . when the virtues of men are reversed, we have disorders."[12]

The king occupies the most honorable position and receives Heaven's precious decrees. Like Heaven and Earth,[13] he acts to shelter and support, thus serving as the father and mother of the masses. As his children, as his subjects, they must be loyal and filial. Should they dare to cherish wickedness and have

---

7. *Fengsu tongyi*, p. 101.

8. *Commentary on the Appended Phrases, Classic of Changes*, Part 2; Lynn, *The Classic of Changes*, p. 77.

9. *Shangshu dazhuan* (SBCK) 3:3a.

10. Ibid.

11. *Gongyang zhuan*, Zhuang 32.

12. *Zuozhuan*, Xuan 15; Legge, *The Chinese Classics*, 5:328.

13. A paraphrase of the *Mean* in the *Record of Rites*. See chap. 10.

rebellious hearts, however, they will run counter to Heaven's constancy and violate human principle. Therefore this is called plotting rebellion.

*Commentary*: Plotting rebellion means to plot to endanger the Altars of Soil and Grain [*sheji*, that is, the ruler and the state that he rules].

*Subcommentary*: *She* is the spirit of the five colors of soil [corresponding to the Five Phases]. *Ji* is the regulator of the fields, which uses the spirits' earthly virtue to control the harvest.[14] The ruler is the lord of these spirits of agriculture. The food that they ensure is as Heaven to the people. When their lord is in peace, these spirits are at rest. When the spirits are in repose, the seasons give a plentiful harvest.

However, ministers and subjects may plot and scheme to rebel against traditional norms and have minds that would discard their ruler. If the ruler's position is endangered, what will the spirits rely upon? Not daring to make direct allusion to the honored name of the ruler, we therefore use the phrase "Altars of Soil and Grain" to designate him. The *Rites of Zhou* states: "On the left the Temple of the Ancestors, on the right the Altar of the Soil."[15] These are what the ruler honors.

## Book 4: The Household and Marriage

Following is a listing, by title only, of the 46 articles that comprise the fourth division or book (Articles 150–195 out of a total of 502).

150. Omitting to File a Household Register
151. Village Headmen Who Do Not Know That a Household Register Has Not Been Filed or That Household Members Have Been Left Off of It
152. Prefects and County Magistrates Who Do Not Know That a Household Register Has Not Been Filed or That Household Members Have Been Left Off of It
153. Village Headmen or Officials Who Erroneously Do Not File a Household Register or Who Leave Household Members Off of It
154. Unauthorized Ordainment as a Buddhist or Daoist Priest
155. Sons and Grandsons in the Male Line Are Not Permitted to Have a Separate Household Register
156. Having a Child During the Period of Mourning for Parents
157. Adopted Sons Who Reject Their Adoptive Parents
158. Violation of the Law in Taking a Wife
159. Adoption of a General Bondsman as a Son or Grandson

---

14. Apparently a garbled version of "The Single Victim at the Border Sacrifices" ("Jiao tesheng"), *Record of Rites*; Legge, *Li ki*, 1:425.

15. "Jiangren," *Zhouli*, p. 643; Biot, *Le Techou li*, 2:556. The same idea is expressed in "The Meaning of Sacrifices," ("Jiyi"), *Record of Rites*; Legge, *Li ki*, 2:235.

160. Manumission of a Personal Retainer as a Commoner
161. Falsely Combining Households
162. Family Members of a Lower Generation or of the Same Generation but Younger than Other Family Members Who Improperly Make Use of Family Goods
163. Sale of Personal Share Land
164. Possession of More than the Permitted Amount of Land
165. Illegal Cultivation of Public or Private Land
166. Wrongfully Laying Claim to or Selling Public or Private Land
167. Officials Who Encroach Upon Private Land
168. Illegal Cultivation of Other Persons' Grave Plots
169. Drought, Flood, Frost, or Hail Within an Area
170. Land Classified as Uncultivatable Land or Waste Land Within an Area
171. Village Headmen's Allocation of Land and Plots for Mulberry Trees
172. Not Allowing Rightful Exemption from Taxes and Labor Services
173. Violation of the Law in Assessment of Taxes and Labor Services
174. Violation of the Time Limit in Remitting Articles for Taxes
175. Betrothal of a Daughter and Announcement of the Marriage Contract
176. Wrongful Substitution by the Bride's Family in a Marriage
177. Taking a Second Wife
178. Making the Wife a Concubine
179. Marriage During the Period of Mourning for Parents or Husband
180. Marriage While Parents Are in Prison
181. Acting as a Master of the Marriage During the Period of Mourning for Parents
182. Marriage by Those of the Same Surname
183. Taking a Wife Within the Sixth Degree of Mourning
184. Remarriage of a Widow While Mourning Her Husband
185. Marrying a Runaway Wife
186. Marriage of Officials with Women Within Their Area of Jurisdiction
187. Marrying Another Man's Wife by Consent
188. Family Members of a Higher Generation or of the Same Generation but Older than Other Family Members Making Engagements to Marry for Relatives of a Lower Generation or of the Same Generation but Younger than Themselves
189. Divorcing a Wife Who Has Not Given Any of the Seven Causes for Repudiation
190. Divorce
191. Slaves Who Take Commoners as Wives
192. General Bondsmen Are Not Permitted to Marry Commoners
193. Marriages that Violate the *Code*
194. Divorce and Correction of Status in Marriages that Violate the *Code*
195. Violation of the *Code* in Giving and Taking in Marriage

[Adapted from Johnson, *The T'ang Code*, pp. 49–82, 278–280]

# HAN YU AND THE CONFUCIAN "WAY"

Han Yu (768–824) is one of the most important figures in the history of Confucianism between the classical Zhou dynasty paragons of the formative period and the Neo-Confucians of the eleventh century. Like Confucius, he was both a reviver and a transmitter of earlier tradition and at the same time an innovative, even iconoclastic, commentator on contemporary issues. His self-stated task was to restore a Confucian social and political order to a society long acclimated to Buddhist and Daoist teachings. His arguments against these teachings in his most famous tract—"Essentials of the Moral Way"—are mostly economic, social, and moral rather than philosophical.

Han Yu had a respectable if stormy career as a Tang civil servant but is best known as a writer of both prose and poetry. He invented and advocated a literary style known as *guwen*, "the literature of antiquity," to give voice to his program for Confucian revival. Like this program, *guwen* traces its origins to the language of the Zhou dynasty Confucian classics, and Han Yu posited *guwen* as an alternative to the highly rigid "parallel prose" style that had links to the Buddhist culture of the Six Dynasties. All the texts by Han Yu in this section were written in *guwen*, an eclectic and supple style that in the eleventh century became the literary standard for Neo-Confucianism.

Like all true Confucians, Han Yu was a practical man of action who wanted his Confucian program put into contemporary practice. The political aspect of that program was support for a strong, centralized monarchy. In his "Poem on the Sagacious Virtue of Primal Harmony," written in 807, Han Yu expressed his hope that the new Emperor Xianzong (r. 806–820) would unify the Tang state and act as a model Confucian sovereign. Han Yu put great emotional commitment behind Xianzong's effort to restore Tang unity, and in 817 he personally participated in the campaigns against the independent military governors. But his realization that the emperor was more interested in the benefits of political unity than in serving as a Confucian model sparked in 819 the Memorial on the Bone of the Buddha, a text that betrayed his outrage and frustration over the obstacles that blocked realization of his Confucian program and earned him exile to southern China.

Yet Han Yu's opposition to Buddhism was not inflexible: he saw value in several practical aspects of Buddhism, especially Buddhist teaching practice that encouraged direct learning sessions between master and disciple. His "Discourse on Teachers," although it does not mention the Buddhist prototype, was probably written to adapt the Buddhist example to Confucian practice and to provide a Confucian justification and pedigree for this type of teaching. Han Yu himself imitated such teaching methods, taking large numbers of students into his own household for personal instruction in the classics and composition.

## ESSENTIALS OF THE MORAL WAY

Han Yu's "Essentials of the Moral Way" (Yuandao) is among the most important texts in the history of Chinese thought. It is nothing less than an attempt to define the distinguishing characteristics of Chinese civilization. In other words, it states the case for civilization versus countercultural conceptions of the Way. The first two sections are prologue: Han Yu defines terms and explains the historical trends that have led to the demise of Confucian teachings in his day. The third and fourth sections present the economic argument against Buddhist and Daoist monasticism: monks (the new fifth and sixth classes of society) are nonproductive and exist on the labor of others, thus creating economic and social dislocation.

The fifth section, with its opening quotation from the *Great Learning* (see chapter 10), is the crux of the text. Confucian spirituality, unlike that of the Buddhists and Daoists, links the private, moral life of the individual with the public welfare of the state. In antiquity a personal unity of thought and action made possible the political and social unity of the state. The sages of antiquity achieved this unity and laid the foundations of Chinese civilization. This new conception of sagehood as spiritual wisdom expressed through political action was to form the intellectual basis for the spiritual and political world of Neo-Confucianism.

1. To love largely[16] is called humaneness (*ren*); to act according to what should be done is called rightness (*yi*). To proceed from these principles is called the moral Way (*dao*); to be sufficient unto oneself without relying on externals is called inner power (*de*). The first two, *ren* and *yi*, are fixed concepts; but the latter two, *dao* and *de*, are relative terms. Thus there is the Way (*dao*) of the superior man and the way of the petty man; and inner power (*de*) can work either for good or for evil.[17]

Laozi belittled humaneness and rightness; he disparaged and spoke ill of them. Yet his view was limited. Just because one sits in a well and says the sky is small does not mean the sky is really small. For Laozi humaneness meant a small kindness and rightness meant a petty favor, so it was natural that he belittled them. Therefore, the moral way and the inner power that he spoke of and put into practice are not the same as what I mean by the Way and its Power. Whenever I use these terms, they encompass both humaneness and rightness — which is the common interpretation of the whole world. Laozi's use divorces

---

16. Han Yu's choice of the expression *bo ai* (lit., "to love largely, amply") sets his idea apart from the Mohist concept of *jian ai* ("universal love"). Consideration of the semantic range of the two graphs (*bo*, "vast, large, ample" versus *jian*, "combine, unite") suggests that for Han Yu *bo ai* emphasizes the idea of love given generously yet always to known individuals with specific social relationships to the donor. It thus allows for particularity and heterogeneity, while avoiding the Mohist implication of an indiscriminate, homogenized love addressed to humankind in general.

17. *De*, often translated in this volume as "virtue," is rendered here as "inner power" to accommodate Han Yu's sense of it as a power that can work for good or ill.

humaneness and rightness from the Way and from inner power (virtue); and this is the private interpretation of only one man.[18]

3. . . . In ancient times men confronted many dangers. But sages arose who taught them the way to live and to grow together. They served as rulers and as teachers. They drove out reptiles and wild beasts and had the people settle the central lands. The people were cold, and they clothed them; hungry, and they fed them. Because the people dwelt in trees and fell to the ground, dwelt in caves and became ill, the sages built houses for them.

They fashioned crafts so the people could provide themselves with implements. They made trade to link together those who had and those who had not and medicine to save them from premature death. They taught the people to bury and make sacrifices [to the dead] to enlarge their sense of gratitude and love. They gave rites to set order and precedence, music to vent melancholy, government to direct idleness, and punishments to weed out intransigence. When the people cheated each other, the sages invented tallies and seals, weights and measures to make them honest. When they attacked each other, they fashioned walls and towns, armor and weapons for them to defend themselves. So when dangers came, they prepared the people; and when calamity arose, they defended people.

But now the Daoists maintain:

> Till the sages are dead,
> theft will not end . . .
> so break the measures, smash the scales,
> and the people will not contend.[19]

These are thoughtless remarks indeed, for humankind would have died out long ago if there had been no sages in antiquity. Men have neither feathers nor fur, neither scales nor shells to ward off heat and cold, neither talons nor fangs to fight for food.

4. . . . But now the Buddhist doctrine maintains that one must reject the relationship between ruler and minister, do away with father and son and forbid the Way that enables us to live and to grow together—all this in order to seek what they call purity and *nirvāṇa*. It is fortunate for them that these doctrines emerged after the Xia, Shang, and Zhou dynasties and so were not discredited by the ancient sages and by Confucius. It is equally unfortunate for us that they did not emerge before that time and so could have been corrected by the same sage. . . .

---

18. This attack against Laozi is directed against *Daodejing* 18: "When the great Way declined, / There were humaneness and rightness" and 38: "Therefore after the Way was lost there was virtue, / After virtue was lost there was humaneness, / After humaneness was lost there was rightness, / And after rightness was lost there was ritual propriety." See chap. 5.

19. Han Yu here excerpts two couplets from a long passage in *Zhuangzi*, chap. 10; Watson, *Chuang Tzu*, pp. 109ff.

5. According to a traditional text, "Those in antiquity who wished to illuminate luminous virtue throughout the world would first govern their states; wishing to govern their states, they would first bring order to their families; wishing to bring order to their families, they would first cultivate their own persons; wishing to cultivate their own persons, they would first rectify their minds; wishing to rectify their minds, they would first make their thoughts sincere."[20] And so what the ancients called rectifying the mind and making thoughts sincere were things they actually put into practice.

Yet today those who would rectify their minds do so by rejecting the empire and the state and by abrogating the natural principles of human relations: although they are sons, they do not regard their fathers as fathers. Although ministers, they do not regard their ruler as ruler. Although subjects, they do not attend to their duties. . . .

6. What is the teaching of the former kings? To love largely is called a sense of humaneness; to act according to what should be done is called rightness. To proceed from these principles is called the moral Way; to be sufficient unto oneself without relying on externals is called inner power. Its texts are the *Odes*, the *Documents*, the *Changes*, and the *Spring and Autumn Annals*. Its methods are the rites, music, chastisement, and government. Its classes of people are scholars, peasants, craftsmen, and merchants. Its social relationships are ruler and minister, father and son, teacher and pupil, guest and host, older and younger brother, husband and wife. Its dress is hemp and silk; its dwellings are houses; its foods are rice and grains, fruits and vegetables, fish and meat. Its ways are easy to explain; its teachings are easy to execute. . . .

7. What Way is this? It is what I call the Way, not what the Daoists and Buddhists have called the Way. Yao passed it on to Shun, Shun to Yu, Yu to Tang, Tang to King Wen, King Wu, and the Duke of Zhou; then these passed it on to Confucius, who passed it on to Mencius. But after the death of Mencius it was not passed on. . . . This being so, what can be done? Block them or nothing will flow; stop them or nothing will move. Make humans of these people, burn their books, make homes of their dwellings, make clear the way of the former kings to guide them, and "the widowers, the widows, the orphans, the childless, and the diseased all shall have care." This can be done.[21]

[From *Changli xiansheng wenji* (SBCK) 11:1a–3b; CH]

---

20. The quotation is from the *Great Learning*. See chap. 10.

21. This final quotation is from "Evolution of Rites," *Record of Rites* (trans. in chap. 10), where Confucius characterizes the utopian age of Grand Commonalty (*Datong*) as one where even persons without family were cared for. The quotation implies that "this can be done" by following the "great moral Way" that Han Yu has outlined in his text. There may also be a more subtle implication. Buddhist monasteries managed most charitable works in the Tang and provided economic subsistence to those left without resources by the established social order. Han Yu argues that realization of the "Grand Commonalty" of ancient times will reform this social order so as to provide for the welfare of these people.

## MEMORIAL ON THE BONE OF BUDDHA

Your servant begs leave to say that Buddhism is no more than a cult of the barbarian peoples, which spread to China in the time of the Latter Han. It did not exist here in ancient times. . . . When Emperor Gaozu [first emperor of the Tang] received the throne from the House of Sui, he deliberated upon the suppression of Buddhism. But at that time the various officials, being of small worth and knowledge, were unable fully to comprehend the ways of the ancient kings and the exigencies of past and present, and so could not implement the wisdom of the emperor and rescue the age from corruption. Thus the matter came to naught, to your servant's constant regret. . . .

Now Buddha was a man of the barbarians who did not speak the language of China and wore clothes of a different fashion. His sayings did not concern the ways of our ancient kings, nor did his manner of dress conform to their laws. He understood neither the duties that bind sovereign and subject nor the affections of father and son. If he were still alive today and came to our court by order of his ruler, Your Majesty might condescend to receive him, but . . . he would then be escorted to the borders of the state, dismissed, and not allowed to delude the masses. How then, when he has long been dead, could his rotten bones, the foul and unlucky remains of his body, be rightly admitted to the palace? Confucius said, "Respect spiritual beings, while keeping at a distance from them."[22] So when the princes of ancient times went to pay their condolences at a funeral within the state, they sent exorcists in advance with peach wands to drive out evil, and only then would they advance. Now without reason Your Majesty has caused this loathsome thing to be brought in and would personally go to view it. No exorcists have been sent ahead, no peach wands employed. The host of officials have not spoken out against this wrong, and the censors have failed to note its impropriety. Your servant is deeply shamed and begs that this bone be given to the proper authorities to be cast into fire and water, that this evil may be rooted out, the world freed from its error, and later generations spared this delusion. Then may all men know how the acts of their wise sovereign transcend the commonplace a thousandfold. Would this not be glorious? Would it not be joyful?

Should the Buddha indeed have supernatural power to send down curses and calamities, may they fall only upon the person of your servant, who calls upon high Heaven to witness that he does not regret his words. With all gratitude and sincerity your servant presents this memorial for consideration, being filled with respect and awe.

[From *Changli xiansheng wenji* (SBCK) 39:2b–4b; BW]

---

22. *Analects* 6:20.

## EMPEROR WUZONG'S EDICT ON THE SUPPRESSION
## OF BUDDHISM

The subjection of Buddhism and other foreign faiths to severe persecution under the Emperor Wuzong (r. 841–846) owed nothing directly to the fulminations of a Han Yu or to any concerted movement on the part of Confucians. The emperor, desperately seeking the secret of immortality, was under the influence of Daoist priests who urged on him this repression of their rivals. Still, the justification for this move as set forth in the following edict is largely practical, rather than ideological, in nature. The obvious advantages to the state of confiscating Buddhist wealth and secularizing monks and nuns, so that they might serve the state as cultivators liable to land and labor taxes, had been pointed out long before at the inception of the dynasty. The edict itself was merely a last step in the process of suppression that Wuzong had been pursuing for some time.

This process did not result in the complete elimination of Buddhism from China, which would have taken a greater and more sustained effort by Wuzong's successors than it had, but it was a setback for the religion. Organizationally weakened, Buddhism could not maintain its institutional or doctrinal identity as it did in Japan, and it tended to become fused with a welter of popular cults. The edict also served to reassert with awesome finality a basic principle of the Chinese bureaucratic state: that a religion maintained its corporate existence only on sufferance of the state.

## Edict of the Eighth Month [845]

We have heard that up through the Three Dynasties the Buddha was never spoken of. It was only from the Han and Wei on that the religion of idols gradually came to prominence. So in this latter age it has transmitted its strange ways, instilling its infection with every opportunity, spreading like a luxuriant vine, until it has poisoned the customs of our nation; gradually, and before anyone was aware, it beguiled and confounded men's minds so that the multitude have been increasingly led astray. It has spread to the hills and plains of all the nine provinces and through the walls and towers of our two capitals. Each day finds its monks and followers growing more numerous and its temples more lofty. It wears out the strength of the people with constructions of earth and wood, pilfers their wealth for ornaments of gold and precious objects, causes men to abandon their lords and parents for the company of teachers, and severs man and wife with its monastic decrees. In destroying law and injuring mankind, indeed, nothing surpasses this doctrine!

Now if even one man fails to work the fields, someone must go hungry; if one woman does not tend her silkworms, someone will be cold. At present there are an inestimable number of monks and nuns in the empire, each of them waiting for the farmers to feed him and the silkworms to clothe him, while the public temples and private chapels have reached boundless numbers, all with soaring towers and elegant ornamentation sufficient to outshine the imperial palace itself. . . .

Having thoroughly examined all earlier reports and consulted public opinion on all sides, we no longer have the slightest doubt in Our mind that this evil should be eradicated. Loyal ministers of the court and provinces have lent their aid to Our high intentions, submitting most apt proposals that We have found worthy of being put into effect. Presented with an opportunity to suppress this source of age-old evil and fulfill the laws and institutions of the ancient kings, to aid mankind and bring profit to the multitude, how could We forbear to act?

The temples of the empire that have been demolished number more than 4,600; 260,500 monks and nuns have been returned to lay life and enrolled as subject to the Twice-a-Year Tax; more than 40,000 privately established temples have been destroyed, releasing 30 or 40 million *qing* of fertile, top-grade land and 150,000 male and female servants who will become subject to the Twice-a-Year Tax. Monks and nuns have been placed under the jurisdiction of the Director of Aliens to make it perfectly clear that this is a foreign religion. Finally, We have ordered more than 3,000 men of the Nestorian and Mazdean religions to return to lay life and to cease polluting the customs of China.

Alas, what had not been carried out in the past seemed to have been waiting for this opportunity. If Buddhism is completely abolished now, who will say that the action is not timely? Already more than 100,000 idle and unproductive Buddhist followers have been expelled, and countless of their gaudy, useless buildings destroyed. Henceforth We may guide the people in stillness and purity, cherish the principle of doing nothing [*wuwei*], order Our government with simplicity and ease, and achieve a unification of customs so that the multitudes of all realms will find their destination in Our august rule.

[From *Jiu Tang shu*, 18A:14b–15a; BW]

*Chapter 19*

## THE CONFUCIAN REVIVAL IN THE SONG

As dynasties go in China, the Song (960–1279) was not known for its power and stability. It struggled against great odds to bring back under Chinese rule all the lands once held by the Tang. During the earlier years of the dynasty there was almost constant fighting with "barbarian" tribes in the north and west; during the latter half of the period these invaders held North China, the ancient seat of Chinese civilization, firmly in their grasp until the Mongols swept down to reunify the empire under alien auspices. Even within the Song domains the nation was beset by chronic fiscal, agricultural, and administrative problems such as those that had plagued earlier regimes.

Yet in spite of all this, Chinese society showed remarkable vitality. Commerce was expanding, and with it a more diversified economy developed. Money, especially the new paper currency, was coming into greater use. As a natural concomitant of such growth there was an increase in the number and size of cities, which at this time attained the wealth, culture, and sheer magnificence reported in the accounts attributed to Marco Polo. In the arts of peace, if not in those of war, the Song distinguished itself. Printing, which had been developed during the Tang, for the first time provided the means for more widespread education. Academies, which were centers of higher education, sprang up around the more sizable collections of books, sometimes endowed by grants of land from the state or from private individuals. It was in institutions such as these that the new scholarship, so much an expression of the whole Song concern for cultural achievement as opposed to military aggrandizement, arose. Whereas for centuries the great Buddhist temples had been the intellectual centers of China, now academies presided over by one or another noted scholar began to attract students in great numbers. Under such circumstances the new scholarship grew and flowered into the new (or Neo-) Confucianism.

As an example of this new type of scholar and teacher, we may cite Hu Yuan (993–1059), who typifies the spirit of the Confucian revival and whose influence was felt among its most prominent leaders. Hu Yuan answered well to the need that Han Yu saw for genuine teachers in the tradition of Confucius and Mencius. He was above all a man who took seriously his duties as a moral preceptor of youth and stressed a close teacher-disciple relationship as essential to education. It was regarded as noteworthy in his time that Hu Yuan "adhered strictly to the traditional concept of the teacher-disciple relationship, treating his students as if they were sons or younger brothers and being trusted and loved by them as if he were their father or elder brother." One of his disciples later explained Hu Yuan's contribution in the following terms to the Emperor Shenzong:

> It is said that the Way has three aspects: substance [or basis, *ti*], function [*yong*], and literary expression [*wen*]. The bond between prince and minister and between father and son, humaneness, rightness, rites, and music—these are the things that do not change through the ages; they are its substance. The *Classics of Odes* and *Documents*, the dynastic histories, the writings of the philosophers—these perpetuate the right example down through the ages; they are its literary expression. To activate this substance and put it into practice throughout the empire, enriching the life of the people and ordering all things to imperial perfection—this is its function.
>
> Our dynasty has not through its successive reigns made substance and function the basis for the selection of officials. Instead we have prized the embellishments of conventional versification, and thus have corrupted the standards of contemporary scholarship. My teacher [Hu Yuan], from the Mingdao through the Baoyuan periods (1032–1040), was greatly distressed over this evil and expounded to his students the teaching that aims at clarifying the substance [of the Way] and carrying out its function. Tirelessly and with undaunted zeal, for more than twenty years he devoted himself wholly to school-teaching, first in the Suzhou region and finally at the Imperial Academy. Those who have come from his school number at least several thousand. The fact that today scholars recognize the basic importance to government and education of the substance and function of the Way of the sages is all due to the efforts of my master.[1]

This tribute to Hu Yuan suggests several characteristic features of the Confucian revival in the early Song. Hu Yuan is both a traditionalist and a reformer. He is more a moralist than a metaphysician, and his primary interest is in the

---

1. *Song Yuan xue'an* 1:17.

application of Confucian ethics to the problems of government and everyday life. Hu Yuan is also an independent scholar, one whose success came through years of private study and teaching, and who gained official recognition only late in life. Echoing criticism by late Tang writers of the literary examination system, he condemns it as a perverter of scholarship and as productive of a mediocre officialdom. Finally, in the threefold conception of the Way as substance, function, and literary expression, Hu Yuan adapts the terminology of Neo-Daoist Buddhist philosophy (and also of Tiantai metaphysics) to the exposition of the traditional Confucian Way and suggests the manner in which Confucian thought would be enriched and deepened in the process of encountering Buddhism and Daoism.

According to this view, the classics were to be studied as deposits of enduring truth rather than as antiquarian repositories, and the true aim of classical studies was to bring these enduring principles, valid for any place or time, to bear upon both the conduct of life and the solution of contemporary problems. Conversely, no attempt to solve such problems could hope to succeed unless it was grounded in these enduring principles and undertaken by people dedicated to them. Yet neither classical teaching nor a practical program of reform could be furthered except through the mastery of literature and writing—not the intricacies of form and style with which the literary examinations were concerned but literature as a medium for preserving and communicating the truth in all its forms.

With this in mind we can recognize the many-sided character of the Confucian revival in the Song. The broad current of political reform, culminating in the New Laws (or Measures) of Wang Anshi, and the work of the great Song historians are as much products of this revival as the metaphysical speculations now identified with Neo-Confucianism. Even the work of the great philosopher Zhu Xi (1130–1200) must be appreciated as an expression of the Song spirit in the fields of history and government as well as in classical scholarship and metaphysics. Such breadth and versatility, indeed, were not uncommon in the great intellectual giants of the Song: Wang Anshi, whose reputation as an outstanding writer and classicist in his day has been overshadowed by his fame as a statesman; Sima Guang, his chief political antagonist, who is better known today as one of China's great historians; and Su Dongpo, the celebrated poet and calligrapher, who was also a man of affairs and played a leading part in the political struggles of that memorable era. These men—to name just a few—are all beneficiaries of the creative and widespread energies of the Song revival.

Especially in its emphasis upon the practical application of Confucian principles to the problems of the day, Hu Yuan's teaching points to the fact that political, economic, and social thought was to be as integral a part of the Confucian revival as were classical studies and philosophical inquiry. Hu Yuan himself urged practical measures to improve the people's livelihood, to strengthen military defenses against the barbarian menace, to expand irrigation projects in order to increase agricultural production, and also to promote the study of mathematics and astronomy. In his school Hu Yuan set up two study halls, one for the classics and the other for practical studies, the latter including government, military affairs, water control, and mathematics. Hu warmly praised the special achievement in water conservation of one of his former students. Later this educational model, combining the humanities and practical sciences, was cited in two of Zhu Xi's most influential educational works, his *Elementary Learning* (*Xiaoxue*) and *Reflections on Things at Hand* (*Jinsi lu*). Thus, though Neo-Confucianism was strongly oriented toward the humanities, and less so to the natural or pure sciences, it was by no means averse to specialized, technological studies.

Hu Yuan remained a teacher and did not engage in the politics of the court. At court it was men like Fan Zhongyan and Ouyang Xiu who led the reform movement. The latter, a noted poet and historian, proved himself a mighty champion of Confucian orthodoxy who carried on Han Yu's struggle against the twin evils of Buddhist escapism and literary dilettantism. He insisted that "literary activity just benefits oneself, while political activity can affect the situation around us." In him also the Song school found a vigorous defender of the scholar's right to organize politically for the advancement of common principles.

## THE CONFUCIAN PROGRAM OF REFORM

The first steps in the government itself to implement a broad program of reform were taken by the statesman and general Fan Zhongyan (989–1052), who was among those defended by Ouyang Xiu when he submitted his memorial on political parties. Fan was an earnest student of the classics, as well as a man of practical affairs, who became known as a staunch upholder of the Confucian Way and a vigorous opponent of Buddhism. When a young man he adopted for himself the maxim "To be first in worrying about the world's worries and last in enjoying its pleasures,"[2] which expresses his high ideal of public service as a dedicated Confucian. During the reign of Renzong, Fan tried as prime minister to implement a ten-point program including administrative reforms to eliminate entrenched bureaucrats, official favoritism, and nepotism; examination reform; equalization of official landholdings to ensure a sufficient income for territorial officials and to lessen the temptation toward bribery and squeeze; land reclamation and dike repair to increase agricultural production and facilitate grain transport; creation of local militia to strengthen national defense; and reduction of the labor service required of the people by the state.

---

2. Amusement parks and ball fields in Japan have drawn on this celebrated motto by incorporating it in their names, such as "Later Enjoyment Park" (*Kōraku-en*).

There is nothing startling or revolutionary in this program, but many of the reforms proposed by Fan anticipate changes later made by Wang Anshi that aroused great controversy. To us they represent simply a reorganization of certain governmental activities or practices, and we may fail to appreciate that in a society so dominated by the state and so sensitive to its operations, even administrative changes of this sort could have a deep impact. As it turned out, however, these reforms dealing with education and the examination system had the most significant effect. In his memorial Fan called for the establishment of a national school system through which worthy men could be trained and recruited for the civil service. Though conceived, characteristically enough, more to meet the needs of the government for trained personnel than to make education available to one and all, this system nevertheless represented the first real attempt to provide public school education on a large scale in China. Since nothing on that scale had been set up before, it also represented a departure from the established order as embodied in dynastic tradition and precedent. Fan appealed therefore to an earlier and, from his point of view, more hallowed tradition, justifying the change as a return to the system set forth in the classics as obtaining under the humane rule of the early Zhou kings.

Fan also asked that in the examinations conducted at the capital for the *jinshi* degree (the highest in the regular system of advancement), more importance be attached to an understanding of the classics and of political problems than to the composition of poetry. One of his most revealing proposals was to abolish the pasting of a piece of paper over the candidate's name on an examination paper, a practice that had been designed to ensure impartial judgment by the examiner. The reasoning behind this suggestion follows from the importance that Fan attached in both teaching and politics to a man's personal integrity. It was just as vital to know the candidate's moral character as his literary and intellectual capacities, and character was impossible to judge except from personal knowledge.

Prompted by Fan's memorial, the emperor called for a general discussion of these questions at court. Fan's proposals were supported by Song Qi and others, who spoke out against the evils of the existing system and urged a "return" to the ancient ideal. As a result, a national school system was promulgated by Renzong in 1044, calling for the establishment of a school in each department and district, to be maintained and staffed by the local magistrate. At the same time the civil service system was reformed so that the examinations were divided into three parts, with priority given to problems of history and politics, then to interpretation of the classics, and last of all to composition of poetry. Subsequently, instruction in the Imperial Academy was also revamped by Hu Yuan, who had been brought to court by Fan Zhongyan, to conform to the methods Hu had used in his private academy.

Few of Fan's reforms survived when he fell from power as a result of bitter factional struggles. Nevertheless, the agitation for reform went on among some of the best minds of the age. One of these was Li Gou (1009–1059), a scholar who wrote extensively on the need for Confucians to pay more attention to military matters (advocating primary reliance on a soldier-farmer militia, rather than a large standing army), economy in administration, land redistribution, public granaries, and a more extensive school system. Many of his ideas, especially his strong emphasis on the *Rites of Zhou* as a recipe for achieving the early Song ideal of "Supreme Peace and Order" (*Taiping*), were taken up by the great reformer Wang Anshi. These included the need for administrative efficiency and economy, the orderly management of the court and imperial household, the proper expenditure of state revenues, and equitable collection of taxes—all in practical detail of a kind that Confucian scholars rarely dealt with. The selections that follow are meant to illustrate the types of reform most widely espoused in Confucian circles. To show that this ferment was not confined to persons whose interests and activities were mostly political, but instead pervaded the Song school in general, we have made selections from scholars later identified with Neo-Confucian orthodoxy and better known as philosophers than as officials. They are, moreover, thinkers whose intellectual antecedents are found among the progenitors of the Song school already mentioned (e.g., Hu Yuan) and whose political and scholarly affinities early linked them to Wang Anshi.

## THE WAY AS THE BASIS FOR GOVERNMENT POLICY

### CHENG YI: MEMORIAL TO EMPEROR RENZONG

This memorial was presented in 1050, a few years after the fall of Fan Zhongyan and his allies, when Cheng Yi (1033–1107) was still only seventeen years old. It is prefaced by a long appeal (abbreviated here) for acceptance of the Confucian Way as the basis of government policy. Only a full return to the ideal society of the sage kings will suffice to meet the needs of the day. To imitate the Han and Tang dynasties, great though these were in some respects, would mean succumbing eventually to the same weaknesses that brought them down. This is a recurrent theme of the reformers, who had to overcome widespread skepticism at court that ancient institutions, as well as Confucian moral precepts, could have any practical application in the very different social circumstances of the Song period. Cheng Yi then describes the prevailing economic and social evils that must be remedied, and like so many other reformers of the time, he concludes that the first step in solving them must be a change in the civil service system, so as to bring into the government men with the ability and the determination to rectify these conditions.

In the Three Dynasties the Way was always followed; after the Qin it declined and did not flourish. Dynasties like the Wei and Jin indeed departed far from it. The Han and Tang achieved a limited prosperity, but in practicing the Way they adulterated it. . . .

In the *Classic of Documents* it says: "The people are the foundation of the nation; when the foundation is solid the nation is at peace."[3] Your servant thinks that the way to make the foundation firm is to pacify the people, and that the way to pacify the people is to see that they have enough food and clothing. Nowadays the people's strength is exhausted and there is not enough food and clothing in the land. When spring cultivation has begun and the seed has been sown, they hold their breath in anxious expectation. If some year their hopes are disappointed, they have to run away [and abandon the land]. In view of these facts, the foundation can hardly be called firm. Your servant considers that Your Majesty is kind and benevolent, loves the people as his children, and certainly cannot bear to see them suffer like this. Your servant suspects that the men around Your Majesty have shielded these things from Your Majesty's discerning sight and prevented you from learning about them.

Now the government frequently has insufficient funds to meet its expenditures. Having an insufficiency, it turns to the fiscal intendants of the various circuits. But where are the fiscal intendants to get the money? They simply have to wring it from the people. Sometimes peace is disturbed in all directions at once, and so troops are called out just when the men should attend to the cultivation of their fields, causing still more grievous harm. As these pressing demands are put upon the people, their blood and fat become exhausted; frequently they are brought to financial ruin and their livelihood is lost, while the members of the family are separated and dispersed. Even ordinary men are pained at the sight of this. Surely Your Majesty, who is like a parent to the people, cannot help but take pity on them! The people have no savings and the government granaries are empty. Your servant observes that from the capital on out to the frontiers of the empire, there is no place that has a reserve sufficient to carry over two years. If suddenly there is a famine for more than one year, such as the one that occurred in the Mingdao period (1032–1033), I do not know how the government is going to deal with it.

The soldiers who do no work and yet must be fed number more than one million. Since there is no means to support them, the people will be heavily taxed. And yet the people have already scattered. If strong enemies seize the opportunity to attack from without, or wicked men aspire to power from within, then we may well be fearful of a situation that is deteriorating and threatens to collapse.

Your servant considers that humaneness is the foundation of the Kingly Way. He observes that the humaneness of Your Majesty is the humaneness of Yao and Shun; and yet the empire has not had good government. This is because Your Majesty has a humane heart but not a humane government. Therefore Mencius says, "Though he may have a humane heart and a reputation for humaneness, one from whom the people receive no benefits will not serve as a model for later generations because he does not practice the Way of the former kings."[4] . . . Good

---

3. "Songs of the Five Sons," *Classic of Documents*; Legge, *The Chinese Classics*, 3:158.
4. *Mencius* 4A:1.

government in the empire depends upon obtaining worthy men; misgovernment in the empire derives from a failure to obtain worthy men. The world does not lack worthy men; the problem is how to find them. . . .

In the selection of scholars for the civil service, though there are many categories under which men may qualify, yet there are only one or two persons who may be considered [under the category of] "wise, virtuous, square, and upright."[5] Instead, what the government obtains are scholars who possess no more than erudition and powerful memory. Those who qualify in [the examination on] understanding of the classics merely specialize in reciting from memory and do not understand their meaning. They are of little use in government. The most prized and sought after is the category of *jinshi*, which involves composition of verse in the *ci* and *fu* form according to the prescribed rules of tone and rhythm. In the *ci* and *fu* there is nothing about the way to govern the empire. Men learn them in order to pass the examination, and after the passage of a sufficient time, they finally attain to the posts of ministers and chancellors. How can they know anything of the bases of education and cultivation found in the Kingly Way? . . .

For two thousand years the Way has not been practiced. Foolish persons of recent times have all declared that times are different and things have changed, so that it can no longer be practiced. This only shows how deep their ignorance is, and yet time and again the rulers of men have been deceived by their talk. . . . But I see that Your Majesty's heart is filled with solicitude for the people; how can any difficulties stand in the way?

[From *Yichuan wenji* (SBBY) 1:14a–16b; dB]


## THE NEW LAWS OF WANG ANSHI

The reform movement that marked time after Fan Zhongyan's fall from power reached its greatest heights during the reign of the Emperor Shenzong (r. 1068–1085) under the leadership of Wang Anshi (1021–1086), one of China's most celebrated statesmen. With the sympathetic understanding and patient support of Shenzong, who was widely acclaimed for his conscientiousness as a ruler, Wang embarked on a most ambitious and systematic program of reform, designed to remedy the evils already described in the memorials and essays of his Confucian contemporaries. A brilliant scholar and a vigorous administrator, Wang had close ties both officially and intellectually to the leading figures in the Confucian revival, and he burned with a desire to achieve the restoration of the ancient order that they believed to be the only solution to China's ills. This came out in Wang's first interview with the emperor in 1068, when the latter asked what Wang thought of the famous founder of the Tang dynasty as a model

---

5. A title conferred on a limited number of candidates given a special imperial examination which was held at infrequent intervals.

for later rulers. Wang replied: "Your Majesty should take [the sage kings] Yao and Shun as your standard. The principles of Yao and Shun are very easy to put into practice. It is only because scholars of recent times do not really understand them that they think such standards of government are unattainable."

Wang, as a matter of fact, had no thought of completely revamping Chinese society and restoring the institutions described in the classical texts. As the first of the readings to follow makes clear, his aim was rather to adapt the general principles embodied in those institutions to his own situation, making due allowance for vastly changed circumstances. Furthermore, from the manner in which he set about his reforms, we can see that he was no social revolutionary or utopian theorist but, rather, a practical statesman whose first concern was always the interests of the Chinese state and only secondarily the welfare of the Chinese people. Thus his initial reforms were aimed at the reorganization of state finances, with a view to achieving greater economy and budgetary efficiency. And virtually all of the important economic changes later effected by Wang were proposed by a special "brain trust" assigned to the task of fiscal reorganization, with state revenue very much in the forefront of their minds. Nevertheless, it is to the credit of Wang that he saw what few Chinese statesmen or emperors were willing to consider: that in the long run the fiscal interests of the state were bound up with the general economic welfare of the people, and both with the promotion of a dynamic and expanding economy. Therefore, even though he did nothing so drastic as the reorganization of Chinese agriculture into well-fields, his approach was bold and visionary in the sense that he saw the problem of reform as reaching into virtually all spheres of Chinese life; and, though few of his measures were new or highly original, his program taken as a whole was broader in scope and more diversified in character than anything attempted before or after—until Communist rule.

The first of Wang's New Laws (or Measures) (xinfa) aimed at achieving greater flexibility and economy in the transportation of tax grain or tribute in kind to the capital. His basic principle was that officials be enabled to resell the goods collected and use funds at their disposal to procure at the most convenient time and place (and with the least transportation cost) the goods required by the government. This was later expanded greatly into a vast state marketing operation that extended to all basic commodities the type of price control and storage system traditionally associated with the "Ever-Normal Granary." In this way the state's assumption of a much more active role in the economy was justified by the common interest of the state and the people in reducing the cost of government and stabilizing prices.

So, too, with the second of Wang's measures, a system of crop loans to provide peasants in the spring with necessary seed, implements, and so on, which would be repaid at harvest time. It was designed, on the one hand, to help the peasant stay out of the clutches of usurers at a difficult time of the year, while on the other hand, it brought revenue to the government through the interest paid on the loans.

Besides the sphere that would be recognized as pertaining to government finance, there were two other activities of the state that vitally affected both the physical well-being of the people and the health of the state. These had to do with the time-honored "right" or "power" of the government to demand from the people both labor service and military service. In the Song, Chinese armies were maintained on a professional basis, with tax revenues providing the means for hiring constabulary and soldiery. To eliminate the great expense of such mercenaries, who were idle much of the time, Wang introduced a militia system whereby each locality would be organized for self-defense and self-policing, with families grouped pyramidally in units of ten, a hundred, and a thousand, taking a regular turn at providing such able-bodied service. This represented not only a system of collective security in each locality but one of collective responsibility as well, the various members of each group being held mutually responsible for the misconduct of any individual. Curiously enough, to achieve the same ends of economy and efficiency in the handling of local government services, Wang used precisely the reverse method. That is, the minor functions of government, which were sometimes menial and often burdensome, had always been performed on an unpaid, draft basis. Wang considered this a system that weighed too heavily on the individuals and households to whom the assignment fell. In place of the draft services, which were essentially a labor tax, he therefore substituted a money tax graduated to "soak the rich," and from the proceeds of that tax men were hired to perform these official services.

The same principle of equalization was applied to the land tax through a new system of land registration and assessment, which was designed to accomplish the same aim as the legendary "well-field" system without any actual redistribution of land or property. This was known as the "square-fields" system, because all taxable land was divided up into units one *li* square, upon which the taxes were graduated in accordance with the value of the land, so that those with less productive land paid proportionately less.

The foregoing examples will serve to indicate the general character and scope of the *New Laws* having an economic importance. In addition, Wang embarked on a fundamental overhauling of the civil service examination system, which in the early Song had come in for much criticism from Confucians who deplored the premium it placed on literary style and memorization of the classics at the expense of a genuine understanding of Confucian principles and their practical application. In place of the traditional forms of composition and memory testing, Wang substituted an essay on the "general meaning" of the classics. This raised problems, however, as to how traditional standards of objectivity and impartiality could be maintained in judging the performance of candidates with respect to the handling of ideas and interpretation. Wang solved this in his own way by promulgating a standard essay form and a revision of the classics with modernized commentary to serve as an authoritative guide for both candidates and judges.

Almost immediately controversy developed over Wang's interpretations of the classics, which were closely bound up with his whole political philosophy and governmental program. Whether or not Wang's policies were truly in keeping with the basic teachings of the Confucian tradition is a question that has been debated right down to modern times. There can be no doubt that the New Laws or systems that he adopted bore a strong resemblance to Legalist-inspired institutions that had vastly augmented the economic power of the state during the reign of Emperor Wu of Han. It is equally evident, however, that the benevolent paternalism ascribed by Confucians to the ancient sage kings could be easily construed, as it was by Wang, to justify a vigorous exercise of state power to promote the general welfare. Wang's memorials are replete with classical precedents for each of the actions he proposes to take. Perhaps nowhere is the close tie between Wang's reforms and classical authority better illustrated than in his use of the *Rites of Zhou*, which he revised under the title *New Interpretation of the Institutes of Zhou (Zhouguan xinyi)*. For this classical text Wang made the strongest claims in his personal preface:

> When moral principles are applied to the affairs of government . . . the form they take and the use they are put to depend upon laws, but their promotion and execution depend upon individuals. In the worthiness of its individual officials to discharge the duties of office, and in the effectiveness with which its institutions administered the law, no dynasty has surpassed the early Zhou. Likewise, in the suitability of its laws for perpetuation in later ages, and in the expression given them in literary form, no book is so perfect as the *Institutes of Zhou (Zhouguan)*.

So effectively did Wang use this book to justify his reforms that his edition of it became one of the most influential and controversial books in all Chinese literature. To deny Wang the support he derived from it, his opponents alleged that the *Institutes of Zhou* was itself a comparatively recent forgery. In later times writers commonly attributed the fall of the Northern Song dynasty to Wang's adoption of this text as a political guide.

Thus Wang's espousal of the *Institutes of Zhou* represents the culmination in the political sphere of the long debate in Confucian circles over the applicability of classical institutions, as described in the books of rites, to conditions obtaining in the Song dynasty. At the same time Wang's effort to reinterpret these texts—to discard the Han and Tang commentaries—and to use a modernized version as the basis for a reformed civil service examination system, stressing the general meaning of the classics instead of a literal knowledge of them, is a concrete expression of the Confucian urge to break with the scholarship of the Han and Tang dynasties, both in the field of classical scholarship and in the form of civil service examinations, in order to return to the essential purity of the classic order. In this respect Wang stands together with the Cheng brothers, Zhu Xi, and a host of other Song scholars in their determination to set aside accepted interpretations and find new meaning in their Confucian inheritance, just as subsequent scholars of a more critical temper would someday reject the Song interpretations and press anew their inquiry into the meaning and validity of the classics.

### WANG ANSHI: MEMORIAL TO EMPEROR RENZONG (1058)

This document, sometimes called the Ten Thousand Word Memorial, is famous as Wang's first important declaration of his political views. Those who look to it for a manifesto outlining his later program will be disappointed, for aside from his general philosophy it deals only with the problem of recruiting able officials. Those who recognize, however, that in China any reformer had to wrestle first of all with the intractable bureaucracy will appreciate why Wang, like many other Song reformers, should have given first priority to this question. Subsequent readings, including the protests of Wang's critics, will show that in the final analysis this remained the most crucial issue.

Note how Wang strikes a balance between the importance of laws and systems (the Legalist tendency) and the Confucian view that good government depends ultimately on men of character and ability, unhampered by legalistic restrictions. Observe also his final insistence that the accomplishment of needed reform may justify coercive measures.

Your servant observes that Your Majesty possesses the virtues of reverence and frugality and is endowed with wisdom and sagacity. Rising early in the morning and retiring late in the evening, Your Majesty does not relax for even a single day. Neither music, beautiful women, dogs, horses, sight-seeing, nor any of the other objects of pleasure distract or becloud your intelligence in the least. Your humanity toward men and love of all creatures pervade the land. Moreover, Your Majesty selects those whom the people of the empire would wish to have assisting Your Majesty, entrusts to them the affairs of state, and does not vacillate in the face of [opposition from] slanderous, wicked, traitorous, and cunning officials. Even the solicitude of the Two Emperors and Three Kings did not surpass this. We should expect, therefore, that the needs of every household and man would be filled and that the empire would enjoy a state of perfect order. And yet this result has not been attained. Within the empire the security of the state is a cause for some anxiety, and on our borders there is the constant threat of the barbarians. Day by day the resources of the nation become more depleted and exhausted, while the moral tone and habits of life among the people daily deteriorate. On all sides officials who have the interests of the state at heart are fearful that the peace of the empire may not last. What is the reason for this?

The cause of the distress is that we ignore the law. Now the government is strict in enforcing the law, and its statutes are complete to the last detail. Why then does your servant consider that there is an absence of law? It is because most of the present body of law does not accord with the government of the ancient kings. Mencius says, "Though he may have a humane heart and a reputation for humaneness, one from whom the people receive no benefits will not serve as a model for later generations because he does not practice the Way of the former kings."[6] The application of what Mencius said to our own failure in the present is obvious.

Now our own age is far removed from that of the ancient kings, and the changes and circumstances with which we are confronted are not the same. Even the most ignorant can see that it would be difficult to put into practice every single item in the government of the ancient kings. But when your servant says that our present failures arise from the fact that we do not adopt the governmental system of the ancient kings, he is merely suggesting that we should follow their general intent. . . . [1a–2a]

The most urgent need of the present time is to secure capable men. Only when we can produce a large number of capable men in the empire will it be possible to select a sufficient number of persons qualified to serve in the government. And only when we get capable men in the government will there be no difficulty in assessing what may be done, in view of the time and circumstances, and in consideration of the human distress that may be occasioned, gradually to change the decadent laws of the empire in order to approach the ideas of the ancient kings. . . . [3a]

In ancient times, the Son of Heaven and feudal lords had schools ranging from the capital down to the districts and villages. Officers of instruction were widely appointed, but selected with the greatest care. The affairs of the court, rites and music, punishment and correction were all subjects that found a place in the schools. What the students observed and learned were the sayings, the virtuous acts, and the ideas underlying the government of the empire and the states. Men not qualified to govern the empire and the states would not be given an education, while those who could be so used in government never failed to receive an education. This is the way to conduct the training of men. [4a]

What is the way to select officials? The ancient kings selected men only from the local villages and through the local schools. The people were asked to recommend those they considered virtuous and able, sending up their nominations to the court, which investigated each one. Only if the men recommended proved truly virtuous and able would they be appointed to official posts commensurate with their individual virtue and ability. . . . When we have investigated those whose conduct and ability are of the highest level, and have appointed them to high office, we should ask them in turn to select men of the same type, try them out for a time and test them, and then make recommendations to the ruler, whereupon ranks and salaries would be granted to them. This is the way to conduct the selection of officials. [5a–b]

---

6. *Mencius* 4A:1.

[In ancient times] officials were selected with great care, appointed to posts that suited their qualifications, and kept in office for a reasonable length of time. And once employed, they were given sufficient authority for the discharge of their duties. They were not hampered and bound by one regulation or another but were allowed to carry out their own ideas. It was by this method that Yao and Shun regulated the hundred offices of government and inspired the various officials. [6a–b]

Today, although we have schools in each prefecture and district, they amount to no more than school buildings. There are no officers of instruction and guidance; nothing is done to train and develop human talent. Only in the Imperial Academy are officers of instruction and guidance to be found, and even they are not selected with care. The affairs of the court, rites and music, punishment and correction have no place in the schools, and the students pay no attention to them, considering that rites and music, punishment and correction are the business of officials, not something they ought to know about. What is taught to the students consists merely of textual exegesis [of the classics].

. . . In recent years, teaching has been based on the essays required for the civil service examinations, but this kind of essay cannot be learned without resorting to extensive memorization and strenuous study, upon which students must spend their efforts the whole day long. Such proficiency as they attain is at best of no use in the government of the empire, and at most the empire can make no use of them. . . . [6b–7a]

[Of old] . . . those scholars who had learned the way of the ancient kings and whose behavior and character had won the approval of their village communities were the ones entrusted with the duty of guarding the frontiers and the palace in accordance with their respective abilities. . . . Today this most important responsibility in the empire . . . is given to those corrupt, ruthless, and unreliable men whose ability and behavior are not such that they can maintain themselves in their local villages. . . . But as long as military training is not given, and men of a higher type are not selected for military service, there is no wonder that scholars regard the carrying of weapons as a disgrace and that none of them is able to ride, or shoot, or has any familiarity with military maneuvers. This is because education is not conducted in the proper way. [8a–9b]

In the present system for selecting officials, those who memorize assiduously, recite extensively, and have some knowledge of literary composition are called "splendid talents of extraordinary accomplishment" or "men of virtue, wise, square, and upright." These are the categories from which the ministers of state are chosen. . . . [11b]

In addition, candidates are examined in such fields as the Nine Classics, the Five Classics, specialization [in one classic], and the study of law. The court has already become concerned over the uselessness of this type of knowledge and has stressed the need for an understanding of general principles [as set forth in the classics]. . . . When we consider the men selected through "understanding of the classics," however, it is still those who memorize, recite, and have some knowledge of literary composition who are able to pass the examination, while those who can apply them [the classics] to the government of the empire are not always brought in through this kind of selection. [12b]

Your servant also observes that in former times when the court thought of doing something and introducing some reforms, the advantages and disadvantages were considered carefully at the beginning. But whenever some vulgar opportunist took a dislike to the reform and opposed it, the court stopped short and dared not carry it out. . . . Since it was difficult to set up laws and institutions, and since the men seeking personal advantages were unwilling to accept these measures and comply with them, the ancients who intended to do something had to resort to punishment. Only then could their ideas be carried out. [17a]

Now the early kings, wishing to set up laws and institutions in order to change corrupt customs and obtain capable men, overcame their feeling of reluctance to mete out punishment, for they saw that there was no other way of carrying out their policy. [17b]

[From *Linchuan xiansheng wenji* (SBCK) 39:1a–19a; dB]

### WANG ANSHI: IN DEFENSE OF FIVE MAJOR POLICIES

In this memorial Wang reaffirms the correctness of his principal policies, while conceding that in three cases much will depend on the effectiveness with which the officials concerned administer them.

During the five years that Your Majesty has been on the throne, a great number of changes and reforms have been proposed. Many of them have been set forth in documents, enacted into law, and have produced great benefits. Yet among these measures there are five of the greatest importance, the results of which will only be felt in the course of time and which, nevertheless, have already occasioned a great deal of discussion and debate: (1) the pacification of the Rong [Tangut] barbarians, (2) the crop loans, (3) the local service exemption, (4) the collective security [militia], (5) the marketing controls.

Now the region of Jingtang and the Tiao River [in the northwest] extends more than three thousand *li* and the Rong tribes number two hundred thousand people. They have surrendered their territories and become submissive subjects of the empire. Thus our policy of pacifying the Rong barbarians has proved successful.

In former times the poor people paid interest on loans obtained from powerful persons. Now the poor get loans from the government at a lower rate of interest, and the people are thereby saved from poverty. Thus our policy on agricultural loans has worked in practice.

It is only with regard to the service exemption, the militia, and the marketing controls that a question exists as to whether great benefit or harm may be done. If we are able to secure the right type of man to administer these acts, great benefits will be obtained, but if they are administered by the wrong type of man, great harm will be done. Again, if we try to enforce them gradually, great benefits will be obtained, but if they are carried out in too great haste, great harm will be done.

The *Commentary* says, "Things not modeled after the ancient system have never been known to last for a generation." Of these three measures mentioned above, it may be said that they are all modeled after the ancient system. However, one can put the ancient system into practice only when he understands the Way of the ancients. This is what your servant means about great advantages and disadvantages.

The service exemption system is derived from the *Institutes of Zhou* [i.e., the *Rites of Zhou*], in which the *fu, shi, xu,* and *du* are mentioned. They are what the King's System [section of the *Record of Rites*] describes as "the common people who render services to the government."

However, the people of the nine provinces vary in wealth, and the customs of the various regions are not the same. The classifications used in the government registration [for local service] are not satisfactory for all. Now we want to change it forthwith, having officials examine every household so that they will be assessed on an equitable basis and requiring the people to pay for the hiring of men for all kinds of local services, so that the farmers can be released and return to their farms. If, however, we fail to secure the right kind of person for the administration of this measure, the classification of people into five grades [in proportion to their financial status] is bound to be unfair, and the hiring of men to perform services would not be executed in an equitable manner.

The militia act had its origin in the *qiujia*[7] system of the Three Dynasties, which was adopted by Guan Zhong in Qi, Zichan in Zheng, and Lord Shang in Qin, and was proposed by Zhong Zhangtong to the Han ruler. This is not just a recent innovation. For hundreds and thousands of years, however, the people of the empire have been free to live together or to disperse and go in all directions as they chose, not subject to any restriction. Now we want to change it forthwith, organizing the people into units of fives and tens and attaching one village to another. Unlawful activities would thus be kept under observation while humaneness would be manifested to all; the soldiers would be housed in their own homes and ready for any use. If, however, we fail to secure the right kind of person to administer this measure, the people will be alarmed by summonses and frightened by mobilization, and thus the people's confidence will be lost.

The marketing controls originated with the Supervision of the Market in the Zhou dynasty and the Price Stabilization and Equalization System of the Han dynasty. Now with a fund of one million cash we regulate the prices of commodities in order to facilitate the exchange of goods and also lend the people money on which they pay the government an interest of several tens of thousands of cash annually. We are, however, aware of the fact that commodities and

---

7. A system under which units of 128 families each provided men and weapons for military service.

money do not circulate very well in the empire. It is feared that officials eager for personal fame and rewards will seek to achieve speedy results within a year's time, and thus the system will be subverted.

Therefore, your servant considers that the above three measures, if administered by the right kind of person and put into effect with due deliberation, will bring great benefits, whereas, if administered by the wrong men and put into effect with too great haste, they may do great harm.

Thus, if we succeed in carrying out the Service Exemption Law, the seasonal agricultural work of the farmers will not be disturbed and the manpower requirements [of the state] will be borne equally by the people. If the Militia Law is carried out, the disturbances caused by bandits will be brought to an end and our military power will be strengthened. If we succeed in carrying out the Marketing Control Law, goods and money will be circulated and the financial needs of the state will be met.

[From *Linchuan xiansheng wenji* (SBCK) 41:4a–5a; dB]

## OPPOSITION TO THE NEW LAWS OF WANG ANSHI

### SIMA GUANG: A PETITION TO DO AWAY WITH THE MOST HARMFUL OF THE NEW LAWS

Sima Guang (1019–1086) was one of the giants among the scholar-statesmen of the Confucian revival in the eleventh century. He had already had a long and distinguished career in high office when he left the government in 1070 out of opposition to Wang Anshi's policies and subsequently devoted himself to writing his monumental general history of China. Following the death of Wang's patron, the Emperor Shenzong, Sima Guang served briefly as prime minister before his own death and was responsible for the abolition of many of Wang's reforms.

Your servant sees that the late emperor was sagacious and intelligent, did his utmost to govern well, and sought to employ an able man to assist him in achieving peace and order. This man was entrusted with the administration of government. His advice was acted upon, and his plans were followed. Nothing could ever come between them. . . . Unfortunately the one in whom he placed his trust was a man who largely failed to understand the feelings of men and the principles of things and who could not fulfill the expectations of his sage master. He was self-satisfied and opinionated, considering himself without equal among the men of the past and the present. He did not know how to select what was best in the laws and institutions of the imperial ancestors and to bring together the happiest proposals put forth throughout the empire, so as to guide the imperial intelligence and assist in accomplishing the great task. Instead he often adulterated the traditional regulations with his own ideas, which he termed "the New Laws (or Measures)." Whatever this man wanted to do could neither be held up by the ruler nor changed by the people. Those who agreed with him were given his help in rising to the sky, while those who differed with him were thrown out and cast down into the ditch. All he wanted was to satisfy his own ambitions, without regard to the best interests of the nation. . . .

The crop loans, the local service exemption, the marketing controls, the credit and loan system, and other measures were introduced. They aimed at the accumulation of wealth and pressed the people mercilessly. The distress they caused still makes for difficulties today. . . . Besides, officials who liked to create new schemes that they might take advantage of to advance themselves suggested setting up the collective security militia system (*baojia*), horse-raising system, and the horse-care system[8] as a means of providing for the military establishment. They changed the regulations governing the tea, salt, iron, and other monopolies and increased the taxes on family property, on [buildings] encroaching on the street,[9] on business and so forth, in order to meet military expenses. The result was to cause the people of the nine provinces to lose their livelihood and suffer extreme distress, as if they had been cast into hot water and fire. All this happened because the great body of officials were so eager to advance themselves. They misled the late emperor and saw to it that they themselves derived all the profit from these schemes while the emperor incurred all the resentment. . . .

Your servant has already pointed out that training and inspection of the militia involves a great expenditure of labor and money for both the government and the people, and yet the militia is of no real use in war. To pay money in lieu of local services is easy on the rich and hard on the poor, who must contribute to the support of idlers and vagrants [paid to perform these services]. It results in the peasantry losing their property and being reduced to utter misery, without recourse or appeal. The general commanderies now have absolute control over the army administration, while local civil officials have no authority whatever and no means of coping with emergencies. [47:9b]

The best plan now is to select and keep those New Laws that are of advantage to the people and of benefit to the state, while abolishing all those that are harmful to the people and hurtful to the state. This will let the people of the land know unmistakably that the court loves them with a paternal affection. . . . This worthy achievement will be crowned with glory, and there will be no end to the blessings it bestows. Would this not be splendid?

[From *Wenguo wenzheng Sima gong wenji* (SBCK) 46:5b–9b, 47:9b; dB]

---

8. These systems were designed to provide horses for the army after the old grazing lands had been occupied by hostile tribes. Under the horse-raising system (*huma*), people bought horses that, when raised, were sold to the government. Under the horse-care system (*baoma*), the government provided the horses or the funds to buy them, and the people were expected to take care of them for the militia. In either case, horses that died had to be replaced at the individual's expense.

9. A tax on roadside stalls, kiosks, etc.

# "THE LEARNING OF THE EMPERORS"
## AND THE CLASSICS MAT

The "Classics Mat" is an antique expression for a place where a scholar interpreted the contemporary significance of the classics (or, in Buddhism, a place from which senior monks lectured on the *sūtras*). Much promoted in the neoclassical Confucian revival of the Song, it stood for a privileged space at court wherein a learned Confucian could lecture and discuss with the emperor and his ministers how passages from the classics and histories bore on current issues. Cheng Yi, a leading philosopher in the new School of the Way, sought to make it nearly a full-time educational process for the heir apparent and young emperor Zhezong, thinking to elevate the Classics Mat lecturers into a role of almost constant companions and mentors to the emperor, equal in status to the prime minister. Thus, in a time of increasing centralization of power in the Song, reformist Confucians sought to convert the new importance of the scholar-official class as civil servants into a "constitutional" role at court, granting a certain immunity or freedom of speech to those who might criticize the ruler and his administration and thus balance to some degree the heightened power and authority of the supreme autocrat himself.

"The Learning of the Emperors" is an expression used for the content and method of Classics Mat discussions by which rulers might be educated to their responsibilities, based on the example of sage kings and worthy ministers from high antiquity to the present. It is also the title of a work by the eminent historian Fan Zuyu (1041–1098), an associate of the even more famous historian and statesman Sima Guang, who was, like Fan and others of their prominent contemporaries, a participant in the Classics Mat discussions.

Out of these discussions arose a literary genre recording the historical cases cited by these lecturers, along with the advice that went with them. Thereafter the collected works of leading Neo-Confucians included their Classics Mat lectures and accompanying memorials—scholars including Cheng Yi, Zhu Xi, Zhen Dexiu (1178–1235), and Xu Heng (1209–1281), who were leading proponents of the Neo-Confucian movement. Indeed, so influential was this advocacy that the institution, lectures, and writings identified with the Classics Mat became fixtures of Neo-Confucian discourse in later dynasties and were especially emphasized at the court of the Korean Yi dynasty.

A basic theme of this "Learning" was that the earliest rulers combined both sage wisdom and political authority, but when these two subsequently became disjoined, worthy rulers modestly relied on wise ministers for guidance, especially with regard to education. Close correlates of the "Learning" were the concepts of the Succession to the Way as the rejoining of humane wisdom and ruling authority, and the Message (or Method) of the Mind-and-Heart as the content and practice of the ruler's "rectification of his mind-and-heart." Concomitant with this came the rising importance of the *Great Learning* as the textual basis for this instruction.

## FAN ZUYU: *THE LEARNING OF THE EMPERORS*

Fan's work consists of quotations from the classics, histories, and philosophers, characterizing the rule of successive sage kings and emperors and evaluating their successes and failures in relation to the effort each made to learn and get good advice. The earliest of the sages exhibited an innate intelligence that enabled them to learn directly from the observation of the heavens and natural processes. Later sages, including Yao and Shun, had to learn from other human beings. Thus Fan quotes the "Canon of Shun" from the *Classic of Documents*:

"Examining into antiquity [we find] that Emperor Shun . . . was profound, wise, refined, and brilliant. He was completely gentle and courteous, genial and sincere. . . ."[10]

Mencius said, "The great Shun took great [delight in what was good]. He [regarded] virtue as a thing to be shared in common with all people, giving up his own way to follow that of others and taking delight in learning from others to practice what is good. From the time when he plowed and sowed, exercised the potter's art, and was a fisherman, to the time when he became emperor, he was continually learning from others. To take example from others to practice virtue is to help them in the same practice. . . ."[11]

Your subject Zuyu comments: The learning of the emperors is called the *Great Learning*. . . .

[There follow the opening lines of the *Great Learning* and the further comment by Fan:] The reason that learned individuals attached importance to the extension of knowledge, to making the intentions sincere, to the rectification of their hearts, to the cultivation of their persons, to the regulation of their families, to governing the state well, and to illuminating their bright virtue in the world is because that was the Way of Yao and Shun. "The Learning of the Emperors" is to be found in learning from Yao and Shun. . . .

Yang Xiong said, "Those who follow Yao, Shun, and King Wen all act to rectify the Way.[12] In later generations, the only one who was able to learn from Yao and Shun and reach their level was King Wen. That is why Confucius took Yao and Shun as his ancestors, modeled institutions on [those of] Wen and Wu, and put into practice [the teachings of] the Duke of Zhou. To do anything else is contrary to the Way."

[From *Dixue* 1:5a–6a, 12a–14b; MG]

---

10. "Canon of Shun," *Classic of Documents*; Legge, *The Chinese Classics*, 3:29.
11. *Mencius* 2A:8; Legge, *The Chinese Classics*, 2:205.
12. Yang Xiong, *Fayan* (SKQS) 3:2a (p. 290).

## CHENG YI: LETTER TO THE EMPRESS DOWAGER
### CONCERNING THE CLASSICS MAT

When Zhezong as a child of twelve acceded to the throne in 1086, the Empress Dowager was the power behind the throne. On being invited to serve as a Classics Mat lecturer, Cheng Yi had doubts about the Classics Mat being used merely as an adornment, whereby the prestige of Confucian scholarship would be lent to a regime that did not actually take Confucian principles seriously. Hence he addressed this letter to the Empress Dowager to emphasize how serious a matter was the education of the young emperor. Although conforming to the polite, self-deprecating conventions of the court, Cheng Yi was quite frank in his criticisms. He insisted, after the manner of Mencius, that he was unprepared to let himself be used improperly but rather meant to be quite forthright in speaking out on matters of principle. On the one hand, it was more important for him to preserve his own integrity than to pursue high office; on the other hand, if he were to serve at all, he should be treated with the proper dignity and respect.

An example of Cheng Yi's strong sense of self-respect is the episode involving his stipend as Classics Mat lecturer. The convention at court was that the lecturer should submit an application for his salary to the Board of Revenue. This Cheng Yi would not do, even though he had to borrow money to live on. When asked about this, he replied that to apply for his salary, as if for a favor, was demeaning, and especially so for the lecturer from the Classics Mat. "The trouble," he said, "is that today scholars and officials are accustomed to begging. They beg at every turn."

In my humble opinion, it is not a common occurrence for a Confucian scholar to have the opportunity to assist the ruler in his learning of the Way (*daoxue*). If I could choose any place I would like to be, no place would be better than this. Although I must decline appointment to the Classics Mat on the grounds that I am not talented enough, my mind to serve the state has nevertheless been aroused. . . .

Looking at antiquity, no one was better able to teach and nourish a young ruler than the Duke of Zhou.[13] What the Duke of Zhou did became the model for ten thousand generations. Your subject hopes that the emperor will extend the vision of the former dynasties, place his trust in the teachings of the sage [Confucius], carry out the way of the ancient kings, avoid following rigidly the advice of his own close entourage, and avoid becoming mired in confusion by popular sentiment. . . .

Broadly speaking, a ruler who has received the Mandate of Heaven [to found a dynasty] has a natural endowment that is exceptional. But a careful examination of history shows that the intelligence of most emperors and kings seldom surpasses that of other people. Why is it that rulers endowed with perfect virtue and possessing the Way are so rare? If those who are the emperor's teachers and nurturers have not gotten the Way themselves, then it is only natural that such a situation will occur. . . .

---

13. As regent to King Cheng, the successor to King Wu of the Zhou dynasty.

Since your subject has taken office, six officials-in-waiting have lectured from the Classics Mat, but it was observed that the gathered ministers all sat quietly with folded hands, and the lecturer, standing next to the imperial bench, explained a few lines and then withdrew. If things are conducted in such a fashion, even if the emperor were of mature age and accumulated experience, what benefit could he derive from such a lecture? This is completely different from the way the Duke of Zhou taught and nurtured King Cheng! And if the emperor is of a minor age and things are done like this, it shows that those responsible do not know the most fundamental things. . . .

Recently, the prime minister attends the lectures from the Classics Mat one day out of ten, and even so [his participation] stops at sitting silently and no more. . . . The Classics Mat is a place where questions can be raised and so it should be a place where people are at ease. When Your Majesty is about to begin his studies, his mind and body ought to be at ease so that it will be a pleasant [experience for him]. Now, however, facing the great officials, Your Majesty is made to feel anxious and uncomfortable. Standing nearby, the official historian calls out and perfunctorily writes things down. If Your Majesty wishes to let his thoughts flow, will he be able to? If he desires to speak, will he dare? This profoundly affects learning and must be corrected. . . .

Your Majesty has drawn me from out in the fields so that the emperor might read the words of the sage and hear the Way [of the sages]. Could your subject dare not to take what he has learned [in his lifetime] and report on it to the emperor? Your subject humbly suggests that the learning [of the sages] has not been transmitted for a long time. Fortunately, your subject has been able to obtain it from the classics that have been handed down, not because of any [intellectual capacity] of his own but because he took upon himself the responsibility for the Way. Although those who would ridicule this are many, in recent years those who follow the Way have grown more numerous. Now, your subject begs humbly to make use of what he has just spoken about in order to make learning manifest, with the ardent hope that this learning will be transmitted to later generations.

[From *He'nan Chengshi wenji* 6:541–546; MG]

## THE WRITING OF HISTORY

The Song Confucian revival brought with it a heightened interest in history. We have already noted how many of the leading Song figures were engaged in the writing of history—the statesmen Ouyang Xiu and Sima Guang, for instance, and the philosopher Zhu Xi. The breadth of their historical vision reflected the wide range of intellectual inquiry in the Song and found expression in a variety of literary forms and genres. Some of these were new to the Song; others went back to the Tang or earlier.

In the field of historiographical criticism, the Tang led the way. The *Understanding of History* (*Shitong*) of Liu Zhiji (661–721) discusses the origin, development, and relative merits of various forms of historical writing in detail unmatched in the Song, but he was concerned with substance as well as form. His insistence that the historian should employ a tight, disciplined style in which every word counts is just one indication of the seriousness with which he regarded the task of the historian.

Encyclopedias (*leishu*) were both a product of historical inquiry and an aid to it. This type of work, first attempted in the Northern and Southern Dynasties period (fourth to sixth centuries) consisted of compilations of references to given subjects culled from all possible written sources and arranged by topics. They were designed primarily as handy references for students, writers, and government officials. Such encyclopedias, which have continued to be compiled up to the present, have also preserved in quotation parts of many books that have otherwise been lost.

A similar genre was the political encyclopedia as exemplified by the *Comprehensive Institutions* (*Tongdian*) compiled by the Tang dynasty scholar Du You (735–812). This work in two hundred chapters contains historical essays on such subjects as economics, warfare, bureaucratic systems, laws, geography, and so on, tracing each from its beginnings in the dawn of Chinese history down to the time of the writer, for the word *tong* in the title of this and other works excerpted in this section signifies linkage through time. The *Records of the Grand Historian* (*Shiji*) and later histories modeled on it often included essays treating various topics historically, but Du You was the first to undertake such detailed and comprehensive coverage, producing a history centered not on the ups and downs of political power but on the long and unbroken development of institutions.

The basic organization of the encyclopedias was by topics, but there were other ways to write history. Continuing in the tradition of the dynastic histories of combining political chronology and topical treatises was Ouyang Xiu, whose *New History of the Tang Dynasty* and *New History of the Five Dynasties* went beyond the government records that constituted the principal sources for earlier historical works to include works of fiction, belles lettres, and historical anecdotes. An ardent advocate of the prose style known as *guwen* or ancient prose, which had developed in the late Tang, Ouyang employed that style exclusively in his historical writings, even going so far as to rewrite quotations from earlier sources written in a different style. He also followed the tradition associated with the *Spring and Autumn Annals* of conveying moral meanings by the precise use of terminology.

A champion of the value of history and the dynasty's most important and influential historian was Sima Guang (1019–1086), principal author of a chronological account of 1,362 years preceding the Song, with his own comments on events and principles inserted at various places. Compiled largely under official sponsorship, this work in 294 chapters was presented to the emperor, who conferred on it the title *Comprehensive Mirror in Aid of Governance* (*Zizhi tongjian*). As reflected in this title, history remained predominantly political history and was seen as having a political purpose. The image of history as a mirror is an old one in China, where it occurs in the *Classic of Odes*, in the sense that history reflects the past truthfully just as a mirror does not lie, and also in the sense that by looking into it the emperor and his minister could discover truths about themselves and the issues of their own day. These truths could be moral as well as political: the mirror would reveal beauty and ugliness, qualities seen as inherent and not just in the eyes of the beholder.

The *Comprehensive Mirror* inspired some historians to take the story back to the beginning of time. Most influential of all was the *Outline and Details of the Comprehensive Mirror (Tongjian gangmu)* planned by the philosopher Zhu Xi (1130–1200) and compiled by his disciples. This work followed the tradition of the *Spring and Autumn Annals* in selecting and reordering the materials in such a way that they would clearly convey the moral lessons of history.

Aside from formal works of history, the Song sense of the past found expression in many areas of intellectual life. There was an efflorescence of scholarly study of classic texts. Among what we may consider historical subgenres was the study of ancient bronzes and their inscriptions begun in the early Song and including among its practitioners Ouyang Xiu, author of the oldest extant work of this kind. Another new, essentially historical, form was the annalistic biography (*nianpu*) providing an account of a person's life year by year. From the very end of the dynasty comes China's first annalistic autobiography (self-written *nianpu*) composed by the Song loyalist Wen Tianxiang (1236–1283), a reminder that historical works were written to connect the present not only with the past but also with the future.

## SIMA GUANG: HISTORY AS MIRROR

From the Latter Han dynasty it had become the practice to have official historiographers at court taking notes on the emperor's words and actions as he attended to state business. These matters were then written up and preserved in the archives as the *Diaries of Action and Repose (Qijuzhu)* to provide source material for later historians. Meanwhile, they impressed on the emperor that everything he said or did would be recorded for posterity. During the Tang it was still the practice to keep the records out of the reach of the imperial glance in order to assure objectivity. This was no longer the case in the Song, but memorialists continued to appeal to emperors to act in a manner that would ensure their posthumous reputation.

The year 642, summer, fourth month. The Emperor Taizong spoke to the Imperial Censor Chu Suiliang, saying, "Since you, Sir, are in charge of the *Diaries of Action and Repose*, may I see what you have written?" Suiliang replied, "The historiographers record the words and deeds of the ruler of men, noting all that is good and bad, in hopes that the ruler will not dare to do evil. But it is unheard of that the ruler himself should see what is written." The emperor said,

"If I do something that is not good, do you then also record it?" Suiliang replied, "My office is to wield the brush. How could I dare not record it?" The Gentleman of the Yellow Gate Liu Ji added, "Even if Suiliang failed to record it, everyone else in the empire would"—to which the emperor replied, "True."

[*Zizhi tongjian* 196:642, no. 5; 3:6175; CS]

*Sima Guang's history was centered on emperors, and emperors needed to hear the truth about themselves face-to-face as well as having it recorded for posterity. The emperor in the following anecdote is Taizong, the de facto founder and second emperor of the Tang. Sima Guang's comment is clearly addressed to his own emperor.*

The emperor, troubled that many officials were taking bribes, secretly ordered his attendants to test some of them with bribes. When a registrar in the Board of Punishments took a roll of silk and the emperor wanted to have him executed, Minister of the Treasury Bei Zhu remonstrated, "An official taking a bribe should be punished by death, but Your Majesty entrapped this man by sending someone to give it to him. This, I fear, is not 'leading the people by virtue and restraining them by the rules of decorum.'"[14] Delighted, the emperor summoned all officials above the fifth rank and told them, "Bei Zhu was able to contest this case forcefully at court and did not pretend acquiescence. If every matter is handled this way, what cause will there be to worry about misgovernment?"

Your official Guang comments, The ancients had a saying that if the ruler is enlightened, the ministers will be honest. That Bei Zhu was given to flattery under the Sui dynasty but to loyalty under the Tang was not because his personality changed: a ruler who resents hearing of his faults turns loyalty into flattery, but one who is pleased by straight talk turns flattery into loyalty. Thus we know that the ruler is the gnomon [or post for measuring the height of the sun], the minister the shadow. When the gnomon moves, the shadow follows.

[*Zizhi tongjian* 192:626, no. 16; 3:6029; CS]

*Sima Guang has been much criticized for his defense of the "hegemons" (ba), leaders who during the Eastern Zhou were able to prevail for a time but none of whom succeeded in unifying China. Mencius had charged that these rulers, in contrast to genuine worthies, only pretended to virtue [7A:30] but Sima holds that they met the needs of their time. This, however, does not make him a historical relativist, for he stresses that there is only one Way.*

*Sima dates the following exchange, which he recapitulates as a basis for his own comment on the subject of the king and the hegemon, to 53 B.C.E. during the Former Han dynasty. The speakers are the heir apparent and future emperor Yuan (r. 49–33 B.C.E.) and his father, the reigning emperor, Xuan (r. 74–49 B.C.E.). The heir apparent appeals to his father to employ more Confucian scholars and fewer Legalists in his government.*

---

14. *Analects* 2:3.

The heir apparent was soft and humane. He liked scholars but observed that many legal officials employed by the emperor used punishments in order to control subordinates. Once at a banquet he let himself go and said, "Your Majesty relies too heavily on punishments. It would be appropriate to employ scholars." The emperor changed expression. "The House of Han has its own system based on mixing the way of the hegemon and that of the king. How could we possibly rely solely on moral instruction and employ Zhou governance? Moreover, ordinary scholars do not understand the needs of the day but like to affirm antiquity and deny the present, causing men to confuse name and reality so that they don't know what to hold on to. How can they be entrusted with the state?"[15]

Your official Guang comments, There are not different ways for king and hegemon. Of old when the Three Dynasties flourished and "rites, music, and punitive expeditions proceeded from the Son of Heaven"[16] [the ruler] was called "king." When the Son of Heaven became weak and was unable to control the lords, there appeared among them those who could lead allied states to punish false states, thereby honoring the royal house: these were called hegemons. Their conduct in both cases was based on humaneness and founded on rightness. They entrusted the worthy and employed the capable, rewarded the good and punished the evil, prohibited cruelty and executed the rebellious. Therefore, they differ in the honor or pettiness of their status, in the depth or shallowness of their virtue, in the greatness or insignificance of their achievements, in the breadth or narrowness of their governmental orders, but they do not contradict each other like white and black or sweet and bitter.

The reason why the Han could not return to the government of the Three Dynasties was because the rulers did not do it and not because the way of the former kings could not again be carried out in later ages. Among scholars there are superior and petty men. Ordinary scholars truly are not qualified to participate in government. But why could they not have sought for genuine scholars and employed them? Ji, Xie, Gao Yao, Boyi, Yi Yin,[17] the Duke of Zhou, and Confucius were all great scholars. Had the Han employed men such as these, the glory of its accomplishments would not have been as limited as it was.

[*Zizhi tongjian* 27:53 B.C.E., no. 3, 1:880–881; CS]

## ZHU XI: HISTORY AND PHILOSOPHY IN TANDEM

Zhu Xi, as a student of history and author of the well-considered historical works *Words and Deeds of Eminent Ministers of Eight Courts* (*Bazhao mingchen yanxing*)

---

15. The difference in outlook between these two Han rulers has already been discussed by Fan Zuyu.

16. *Analects* 16:2.

17. All exemplary and semi-legendary ministers.

and *Record of the Origins of the School of the Two Chengs* (*I Luo yuanyuan lu*), did not minimize the importance of history. At the same time that he gave priority to the study of enduring principles in the classics, his thinking about issues of his time was informed by a sense of history.

Zhu Xi's attitude toward history was more nuanced and complex than one would think if one read the following guidelines for the compilation of his *Outline and Details of the Comprehensive Mirror* only as an attempt to contain history in a moral straitjacket. The wide readership of the resulting work suggests that the effort to condense, simplify, and structure the record on the basis of defined criteria served an educational purpose for many.

The legitimate dynasties are Zhou, Qin, Han, Jin, Sui, and Tang. Feudal states are those that have been enfeoffed by legitimate dynasties. Usurpers are those who usurp the throne, interfere with the legitimate line of succession, and do not transmit their rule to their heirs. The periods in which there is no legitimate line occur between Zhou and Qin, Qin and Han, Han and Jin, Jin and Sui, Sui and Tang, and during the Five Dynasties period.

Rulers of legitimate dynasties: those of Zhou are called "kings," those of Qin, Han, and after are called "emperors." Rulers of feudal states: those of Zhou are referred to by state, feudal rank, and name. Those who unlawfully usurped the title of king are referred to as "so-and-so, the ruler of such-and-such a state"; from the Han on they are referred to as "so-and-so, the king of such-and-such." Those who usurped the title of emperor are referred to as "so-and-so, the lord of such-and-such." Those who revolted and usurped the throne of a legitimate dynasty are referred to by name only.

Ascending the throne, legitimate dynasties: when the Zhou kings passed their rule on to their heirs, write: "his son so-and-so was set up" and note that this person then became king so-and-so. When the succession is by natural heir, write: "so-and-so succeeded to the throne." When someone establishes a state and sets himself up as ruler, write: "so-and-so set himself up as king of such-and-such." If someone else sets him up, write: "so-and-so honored so-and-so with such-and-such a title." When someone usurps a state and begins to style himself emperor, write: "so-and-so (title, family, and personal name) styled himself emperor." When the rule of a state is transferred to a brother of the ruler, this is called "transmission;" when to someone else, it is called "cession."

[*Zhiyuan kaoding tongjian gangmu*, introduction; BW]

*In the following conversation Zhu Xi tells a disciple that the study of history requires much preparation, that to turn to history too soon is futile but never to turn to it misses the whole purpose of study.*

If people today who have not yet read many books, nor attained an integrated understanding of moral principles, go and read history in order to examine past and present, order and disorder, and to comprehend institutions and statutes, the situation will be like building a pond to irrigate fields. Only if you drain the pond after it is already full can the water flow and nourish the crops in the fields. If the pond holds only a foot of water and you drain it in order to irrigate the fields, it will not only fail to benefit the fields, but the foot of water will also be lost. If someone has already read many books, thoroughly understands moral principles with the details clear in his mind, does not read history, examine past and present, order and disorder, comprehend institutions and statutes, it is like a pond being full and failing to open it to irrigate the fields. But if one who has not read many books, nor attained an integrated understanding of moral principles, impulsively makes reading history his first priority, this is like draining a pond holding a foot of water in order to irrigate a field. It will dry up while you stand and wait.

[*Zhuzi yulei, juan* 11, 1:195; CS]

*Chapter 20*

# NEO-CONFUCIANISM: THE PHILOSOPHY OF HUMAN
# NATURE AND THE WAY OF THE SAGE

The Confucian revival in the Song was distinguished by its broad range of interests and intellectual vigor. But among the many fields of learning that it pursued, the philosophy of human nature, buttressed by a new metaphysics, was the one in which it achieved the widest and most enduring influence. Intense intellectual struggles might have been fought over political and social questions, on the outcome of which the very fate of China, threatened by foreign conquest, seemed to depend. Yet the passage of time quickly deprived these debates of their urgency and point, while the philosophical speculations emerging from the academies of the Song eventually won victories at home and abroad of which the statesman and soldier never dreamed.

When we speak of the new Confucian learning that emerged in the Song period as "Neo-Confucianism," we refer primarily to the Learning of the Way as synthesized by Zhu Xi (1130–1200). During the Song it was also known as the Learning of the Sage(s) and the Way to Sagehood, and subsequently as the Learning of Human Nature, of Principle, and of the Mind-and-Heart. Since Zhu Xi's view of it dominated Chinese (and later East Asian) tradition down into the nineteenth century, however, it is essentially his view of the Learning of the Way that we present here—not a fully representative account of Song intellectual history but a capsulized version, a conspectus of key figures and texts as Zhu Xi saw them contributing to the repossession and fuller exposition of the Confucian Way.

As seen by Zhu, this revival exhibited both elements of continuity and discontinuity. He followed Han Yu in depicting the Way as having lapsed after Mencius, and he believed that it had been two thousand years since it had been practiced. In the Song, he credited the Cheng brothers and Zhou Dunyi (at different times and in different connections) with having rediscovered the True Way after China had long been submerged under Daoism, Buddhism, and utilitarianism. Like Confucius, Zhu claimed no originality for himself in achieving a new synthesis but gave credit to key Song predecessors as major contributors to his own version of the Succession to the Way (*daotong*). These thinkers he anthologized in his *Reflections on Things at Hand (Jinsi lu)*, a collection of Song dynasty writings[1] that he saw as updating Confucian thought (*Jinsi lu* can be read as *Record of Recent Thinking* as well as *Reflections on Things at Hand*). Zhu's anthology quickly became a classic of the Neo-Confucian movement, along with his selection of the "Four Books,"[2] defining for centuries its key issues, doctrines, and players. The present chapter attempts to reproduce that Neo-Confucian story and worldview.

In formulating it, Song Confucians faced fundamental challenges on the philosophical level, paralleling those in the practical order already seen in the last chapter. One was the need for a more coherent and systematic cosmology on which to ground its central conception of human nature as moral, rational, and (following Mencius) fundamentally good. Another need, in defense of the Confucian belief in constant human values, was to meet the challenge of the Buddhist doctrines of impermanence, "Emptiness," and moral relativism. Implicit in these latter doctrines was a profound questioning of the existence of the "self" or "self-nature," which tended to undermine the Confucians' prime concern with the moral person and practical self-cultivation.

In response to these challenges the Neo-Confucians came up with a new doctrine of human nature as integrated with a cosmic infrastructure of principle (*li*) and material-force (*qi*), along with a reaffirmation of the morally responsible and socially responsive self. This culminated in a lofty spirituality of the sage, preserving a stability and serenity of mind even while acting on a social conscience in a troubled world.

Until this time Confucianism had focused on the Way of the sage kings or Way of the noble person as social and political leader. Now, aiming at education for all through universal schooling and a neoclassical curriculum — an aim furthered by the spread of printing and literacy — the Neo-Confucians aspired to a spiritual ideal of sagehood for everyone, achievable by methods of cultivation outlined by Zhou Dunyi, the Cheng brothers, and Zhang Zai, as anthologized in the *Reflections on Things at Hand (Jinsi lu)* and explained in Zhu Xi's Four Books. Herein one found the Neo-Confucian response to Mahāyāna Buddhism's

---

1. Coauthored with Lü Zuqian.
2. The *Great Learning*, the *Mean*, the *Analects*, and the *Mencius*.

conception of the universality of the Buddha-nature, as well as the latter's lay ideal of the compassionate bodhisattva.

Given the difficulties—military, political, and economic—in which Southern Song Neo-Confucians found themselves after the fall of Wang Anshi and the loss of the North to non-Chinese conquerors, they had much less confidence than Northern Song reformers in programmatic solutions that depended on the effectiveness of the central state. In these limiting circumstances they looked more to what individuals could do through self-discipline, personal initiative, and voluntary association on the local level. This depended in turn on restraint and unselfish serving of the common good. Thus the sagely ideal was meant to inspire heroic self-sacrifice on the part of all, but especially of the educated leadership class of scholar-officials and, above all, of the ruler. Yet this stress on the rigorous, demanding role of the cultural elite stood in some tension with the realities of life among the less advantaged common people. Much of the subsequent history of Neo-Confucianism involved the working out of such tensions between an elitist ideal and Neo-Confucianism's avowed aim to promote universal education and serve the general welfare.

A philosophy concerned very much with this world, at the center of which is always the human, Neo-Confucianism reasserted in an even more far-reaching manner what Confucius and his followers had always taught—that the human sense of order and value does not leave one alienated from the universe but is precisely what unites one to it. The world of human ethics, of social relations, of history and political endeavor is a real one, an unfolding growth process, and not just a passing dream or nightmare from which men must be awakened to the truth of Emptiness or Nothingness. It is this conviction that gave to Neo-Confucianism its abundant vitality and a degree of universality that recommended it strongly not only to the Chinese but also to many Mongols, Koreans, Japanese, and Vietnamese, who likewise sought assurance that their lives had meaning and value.

## ZHOU DUNYI: THE METAPHYSICS AND PRACTICE OF SAGEHOOD

Zhou Dunyi (or Zhou Lianxi, 1017–1073) occupies a position in the Chinese tradition based on a role assigned to him by Zhu Xi (1130–1200). According to one version of the Succession to the Way (Daotong) given by Zhu Xi,[3] Zhou was the first true Confucian sage since Mencius (385?–312? B.C.E.) and was a formative influence on Cheng Hao and Cheng Yi, from whom Zhu Xi drew

---

3. Another version credited Cheng Hao with this. See chap. 21, preface to the *Mean*.

significant parts of his system of thought and practice. Thus Zhou Dunyi came to be known as the "founding ancestor" of the Cheng-Zhu school, which dominated Chinese philosophy for more than seven hundred years. His "Explanation of the Diagram of the Supreme Polarity" ("Taijitu shuo"), as interpreted by Zhu, became the accepted foundation of Neo-Confucian cosmology.[4] Along with his other major work, *Penetrating the Classic of Changes (Tongshu)*, it established the "wings" or appendices to the *Classic of Changes* as basic textual sources of the Neo-Confucian revival of the Song dynasty. He was most remembered by his contemporaries for the quality of his personality and mind. He was known as a warm, humane man who felt a deep kinship with the natural world, a man with penetrating insight into the Way of Heaven, the natural-moral order. To later Confucians he personified the virtue of "authenticity" (*cheng*), the full realization of the innate goodness and wisdom of human nature.

## EXPLANATION OF THE DIAGRAM OF THE SUPREME POLARITY (*TAIJITU SHUO*)

Zhou's best-known contribution to the Neo-Confucian tradition was his brief "Explanation of the Diagram of the Supreme Polarity" and the diagram itself. The text has engendered controversy and debate ever since the twelfth century, when Zhu Xi and Lü Zuqian (1137–1181) placed it at the head of their Neo-Confucian anthology, *Reflections on Things at Hand (Jinsi lu)*, in 1175. It was controversial from a sectarian Confucian standpoint because the diagram explained by the text was attributed to a prominent Daoist master, Chen Tuan (Chen Xiyi, 906–989), and because the key terms of the text had well-known Daoist origins. Scholars to the present day have attempted to interpret what Zhou Dunyi meant by them.

The two key terms, which appear in the opening line, are *wuji* and *taiji*, translated here as "Non-Polar" and "Supreme Polarity."[5]

---

4. For a note on the translation of *taiji* as "Supreme Polarity," see the introduction to the "Taijitu shuo."

5. *Taiji* is usually translated as "Supreme Ultimate" and sometimes as "Supreme Pole," but neither of these terms conveys the meaning that both Zhou Dunyi and Zhu Xi seem to have intended. For example, in both texts translated here, Zhou identifies the yin-yang polarity as *taiji*. And Zhu Xi says: "Change is the alternation of yin and yang. *Taiji* is this principle (*li*)" (*Zhouyi benyi* 3:14b, comment on *Commentary on the Appended Phrases (Xici)*, Part 1, 11.5, quoted below). He also insists that *taiji* is not a thing (hence "Supreme Pole" will not do). Thus, for both Zhou and Zhu, *taiji* is the yin-yang principle of bipolarity, which is the most fundamental ordering principle, the cosmic "first principle." *Wuji* as "Non-Polar" follows from this. Both are also consistent with later Daoist usage of the terms (see below), with which Zhou must certainly have been familiar.

*Taiji* was found in several classical texts, mostly but not exclusively Daoist. For the Song Neo-Confucians, the *locus classicus* of *taiji* was the *Commentary on the Appended Remarks* (*Xici*), or *Great Treatise* (*Dazhuan*), one of the appendices of the *Classic of Changes* (*Yijing*): "In change there is the Supreme Polarity, which generates the Two Modes [yin and yang]." *Taiji* here is a generative principle of bipolarity.

But the term was much more prominent and nuanced in Daoism than in Confucianism. It was sometimes identified with Taiyi, the Supreme One (a Daoist divinity), and with the polestar of the Northern Dipper. It carried connotations of a turning point in a cycle, an end point before a reversal, and a pivot between bipolar processes. In effect, Zhou was co-opting Daoist terminology to show that the Confucian worldview was actually more inclusive than the Daoist: it could accept a primordial chaos while still affirming the reality of the differentiated, phenomenal world. For Zhu Xi and his school, the most important contribution of this text was its integration of metaphysics (*taiji*, which Zhu equated with *li*, the ultimate natural/moral order) and cosmology (yin and yang and the Five Phases).

Non-Polar (*wuji*) and yet Supreme Polarity (*taiji*)![6] The Supreme Polarity in activity generates yang; yet at the limit of activity it is still. In stillness it generates yin; yet at the limit of stillness it is also active. Activity and stillness alternate; each is the basis of the other. In distinguishing yin and yang, the Two Modes are thereby established.

The alternation and combination of yang and yin generate water, fire, wood, metal, and earth. With these Five [Phases of] *qi* harmoniously arranged, the Four Seasons proceed through them. The Five Phases are simply yin and yang; yin and yang are simply the Supreme Polarity; the Supreme Polarity is fundamentally Non-Polar. [Yet] in the generation of the Five Phases, each one has its nature.[7]

The germ of the Non-Polar and the essence of the Two [Modes] and Five [Phases] mysteriously combine and coalesce. "The Way of *qian* becomes the male; the Way of *kun* becomes the female";[8] the two *qi* stimulate each other,

---

6. The line reads simply, "*Wuji er taiji.*" Since *er* can mean "and also," "and yet," or "under these circumstances," the precise meaning of the line is far from clear. Another possible translation would be "The Supreme Polarity that is Non-Polar!" It seems to be an expression of awe and wonder at the paradoxical nature of the ultimate reality.

7. In other words, seen as a whole system, the Five Phases are based on the yin-yang polarity; the yin-yang polarity is the Supreme Polarity; and the Supreme Polarity is fundamentally Non-Polar. However, taken individually as temporal phases, each of the Five Phases has its own nature (as do yin and yang).

8. *Commentary on the Appended Phrases* (*Xici*), part 1:1, *Classic of Changes* (*Zhouyi benyi* 3:1b). *Qian* and *kun* are the first two hexagrams, symbolizing pure yang and pure yin, or Heaven and Earth, respectively.

## The Diagram of the Supreme Polarity

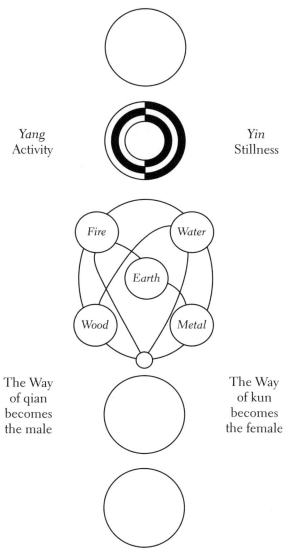

*Yang*
Activity

*Yin*
Stillness

*Fire*

*Water*

*Earth*

*Wood*

*Metal*

The Way
of qian
becomes
the male

The Way
of kun
becomes
the female

Transformation and generation of the myriad things

transforming and generating the myriad things.[9] The myriad things generate
and regenerate, alternating and transforming without end.[10]

---

9. Paraphrasing the *Tuan* commentary to hexagram 31 (*xian*), *Classic of Changes*: "The two *qi*
stimulate and respond in mutual influence, the male going beneath the female. . . . Heaven and
Earth are stimulated and the myriad things are transformed and generated" (*Zhouyi benyi* 2:1a–b).
    10. Cf. *Commentary of the Appended Phrases* (*Xici*), part 1, 5.6, "Generation and regeneration
are what is meant by *yi* (change)" (*Zhouyi benyi* 3:6a).

Only humans receive the finest and most spiritually efficacious [*qi*]. Once formed, they are born; when spirit (*shen*)[11] is manifested, they have intelligence; when their fivefold natures are stimulated into activity, good and evil are distinguished and the myriad affairs ensue.[12]

The sage settles these [affairs] with centrality, correctness, humaneness, and rightness (the Way of the Sage is simply humaneness, rightness, centrality, and correctness) and emphasizes stillness. (Without desire, [he is] therefore still.)[13] In so doing he establishes the ultimate of humanity. Thus the sage's "virtue equals that of Heaven and Earth; his clarity equals that of the sun and moon; his timeliness equals that of the four seasons; his good fortune and bad fortune equal those of ghosts and spirits."[14] The superior person (*junzi*) cultivates these and has good fortune. The inferior person rejects these and has bad fortune.

Therefore [the *Classic of Changes* says], "Establishing the Way of Heaven, [the sages] speak of yin and yang; establishing the Way of Earth they speak of yielding and firm [hexagram lines]; establishing the Way of Humanity they speak of humaneness and rightness."[15] It also says, "[The sage] investigates beginnings and follows them to their ends; therefore he understands death and birth."[16] Great indeed is [the *Classic of*] *Changes*! Herein lies its perfection.

[From "Taijitu" and "Taijitu shuo," in *Zhou Lianxi ji* 1:1b–2b; JA]

### PENETRATING THE CLASSIC OF CHANGES (*TONGSHU*)

The *Tongshu*, in forty sections, focuses on the sage as the model of humanity. Here Zhou Dunyi defines sagehood in terms of *authenticity* or *sincerity* (*cheng*), a term found prominently in the classical Confucian text, the *Mean* (*Zhongyong*). To be authentic is to be true to the innate goodness of one's nature; to actualize one's moral potential. Zhou defines authenticity in cosmological terms taken from the appendices to the *Classic of Changes* (*Yijing*). In this way he uses the concept of authenticity

---

11. The word *shen* can refer either to a deity or to the finest form of *qi* (psycho-physical energy), which is capable of penetrating and pervading things and accounts for human intelligence. See *Tongshu*, chaps. 3, 4, and 16.

12. The fivefold nature consists of the "Five Constant Virtues": humanity (*ren*), rightness (*yi*), ritual decorum (*li*), wisdom (*zhi*), and trustworthiness (*xin*). They correspond to the Five Phases. For incipient activity and the differentiation of good and evil, see *Tongshu*, sec. 3.

13. The two parenthetical notes are by Zhou; they are taken from *Tongshu*, sec. 6 and sec. 20. The terms "without desire" and "emphasizes stillness" were questionable to many Confucians, who usually preferred to speak of limiting desires (especially selfish desires) but not eliminating them. Both terms had Buddhist as well as Daoist connotations.

14. "Commentary on the Words of the Text" (*Wenyan*), under hexagram 1 (*qian*), *Classic of Changes* (*Zhouyi benyi* 1:8b).

15. "Explaining the Trigrams" (*Shuogua*) 2, *Classic of Changes* (*Zhouyi benyi* 4:1b).

16. *Commentary on the Appended Phrases* (*Xici*), part 1:4, *Classic of Changes* (*Zhouyi benyi* 3:4a–b).

to link cosmology and Confucian ethics. There is significant overlap between the *Tongshu* and the "Taijitu shuo," especially in their discussions of activity and stillness as the basic expressions of yang and yin. But the *Tongshu* is less metaphysical; the emphasis here is on the moral psychology of the sage.

## 1. Being Authentic (*cheng*), Part 1

Being authentic is the foundation of the sage. "Great indeed is the originating [power] of *qian*! The myriad things rely on it for their beginnings."[17] It is the source of being authentic. "The way of *qian* is transformation, with each [thing] receiving its correct nature and endowment."[18] . . . [5:2a–3b]

## 3. Authenticity, Incipience, and Virtue

In being authentic there is no deliberate action (*wuwei*). In incipience (*ji*) there is good and evil.[19] As for the [Five Constant] Virtues,[20] loving is called humaneness (*ren*), being right is called rightness (*yi*), being principled (*li*) is called ritual decorum (*li*), being penetrating is called wisdom (*zhi*), and preserving is called trustworthiness (*xin*). One who is by nature like this, at ease like this, is called a sage. . . . [5:11b–12a]

## 20. Learning to Be a Sage

[Someone asked:] "Can Sagehood be learned?" Reply: It can. "Are there essentials (*yao*)?" Reply: There are. "I beg to hear them." Reply: To be unified (*yi*)[21] is essential. To be unified is to have no desire.[22] Without desire one is vacuous when still and direct in activity. Being vacuous when still, one will be clear (*ming*); being clear one will be penetrating (*tong*). Being direct in activity one will be impartial (*gong*); being impartial one will be all-embracing (*pu*). Being clear and penetrating, impartial and all-embracing, one is almost [a sage]. [5:38b]

[From *Tongshu*, in *Zhou Lianxi ji* 5:2a–3b, 11b–12a, 38b; JA]

---

17. *Tuan* commentary on hexagram 1 (*qian*), *Classic of Changes* (*Zhouyi benyi* 1:3a).

18. Ibid (*Zhouyi benyi* 1:3b).

19. As explained below and in the previous section, the sage is authentically good without deliberate effort. "Incipience" is the first subtle stirring of activity, the first point at which good and evil can meaningfully be differentiated. The "Five Constant Virtues" are the full expression of the innately good nature.

20. See note 12.

21. I.e., to focus the mind on fundamentals.

22. See Zhou's parenthetical note in the "Explanation."

# ZHANG ZAI AND THE UNITY OF ALL CREATION

Zhang Zai (1020–1077), a native of the old capital region, Chang'an (Xi'an, in modern Shaanxi province), was a prominent scholar-official among the reformist protégés of Fan Zhongyan, one whom we have already encountered (Chapter 18) as a proponent of decentralization through a revival of the ancient enfeoffment and well-field systems and as a critic of Wang Anshi. A teacher of other leading Song school figures, including his nephews the Cheng brothers and the historian-statesman Sima Guang, Zhang Zai based his learning, like others of this movement, on the *Classic of Changes* and the *Mean* and came to be identified as the second leading figure in the "Succession to the Way" (*daotong*) as propounded by Zhu Xi.

Zhang's essay titled the "Western Inscription" (from having been inscribed on the west wall of his study), became celebrated as a concise and cogent statement of his ethical philosophy, based on his conception of the unity of all things in their shared psycho-physical substance of *qi* (material-force or matter-energy). According to this view, as further expounded in Zhang's larger work, *Correcting Youthful Ignorance* (*Zhengmeng*), the universe and all phenomena are not illusory products of the mind, or ephemeral manifestations of an all-pervading Emptiness, but productions of the primal life force emerging from the Supreme Ultimate or Polarity [the first principle of the *Changes*]. This primal force is in a constant process of change, understood as an ordered, natural growth process. *Qi*, a psycho-physical substance that includes both spirit and matter, manifests itself as a dynamic energy which integrates and consolidates to form all creatures, and then, in the natural course, disintegrates to return to the original undifferentiated state of primal vacuity. The task of human beings is to comprehend the processes of change and harmonize with them, not to try to transcend or overcome them.

## THE "WESTERN INSCRIPTION" (*XIMING*)

This essay is one of the most celebrated in all of Neo-Confucian literature, reproduced in all of its canonical anthologies and much discussed by later thinkers. As an eloquent statement of the human ideal in its integral relation to the cosmos, it often served as the basis for a critique of the established order. In it Zhang Zai expounds the ethical implications of his theory that all creation is formed of and united by this single underlying substance. In the terms of family relationships, so poignant and meaningful to Chinese readers, he relates how all human beings, all Heaven and Earth, must be joined together as though creatures of one flesh and blood and ruled, as appropriate to their kinship, by the principle of unselfish and humane love.

Perhaps nowhere else in all Neo-Confucian literature does lofty metaphysical theory combine so effectively with the basic warmth, compassion, and humanism of ancient Confucianism as in this short passage—a combination no less true of the language Zhang Zai uses here. For all its expansive Neo-Confucian idealism and cosmic spirit, this short essay is studded with allusions redolent of classic Confucian tradition.

Heaven is my father and Earth is my mother, and even such a small creature as I finds an intimate place in their midst.

Therefore that which extends throughout the universe I regard as my body and that which directs the universe I consider as my nature.

All people are my brothers and sisters, and all things are my companions.

The great ruler [the emperor] is the eldest son of my parents [Heaven and Earth], and the great ministers are his stewards. Respect the aged—this is the way to treat them as elders should be treated. Show affection toward the orphaned and the weak—this is the way to treat them as the young should be treated. The sage identifies his virtue with that of Heaven and Earth, and the worthy is the best [among the children of Heaven and Earth]. Even those who are tired and infirm, crippled or sick, those who have no brothers or children, wives or husbands, are all my brothers who are in distress and have no one to turn to.

When the time comes, to keep himself from harm—this is the care of a son. To rejoice in Heaven and have no anxiety—this is filiality at its purest.

One who disobeys [the principle of Heaven] violates virtue. One who destroys humanity (*ren*) is a robber. One who promotes evil lacks [moral] capacity. But one who puts his moral nature into practice and brings his physical existence to complete fulfillment can match [Heaven and Earth].

One who knows the principles of transformation will skillfully carry forward the undertakings [of Heaven and Earth], and one who penetrates spirit to the highest degree will skillfully carry out their will.

Do nothing shameful even in the recesses of your own home and thus bring dishonor to it. Preserve the mind and nourish the nature and thus [serve them] with untiring effort.

[From *Zhangzi quanshu* 1:1a–6b; WTC]

CORRECTING YOUTHFUL IGNORANCE

## Supreme Harmony (Chapter 1)

The Supreme Harmony (*taihe*) is called the Way (*dao*). It embraces the nature that underlies all counterprocesses of floating and sinking, rising and falling, and motion and rest. It is the origin of the process of fusion and intermingling, of overcoming and being overcome, and of expansion and contraction. At the commencement, these processes are incipient, subtle, obscure, easy, and simple, but at the end they are extensive, great, strong, and firm. It is *qian* (Heaven) that begins with the knowledge of change and *kun* (Earth) that models itself after simplicity. That which is dispersed, differentiated, and capable of assuming form becomes material-force (*qi*), and that which is pure, penetrating, and not capable of assuming form becomes spirit. Unless the whole universe is in the process of fusion and intermingling like fleeting forces moving in all directions, it may not be called the Supreme Harmony. . . .

The Supreme Vacuity (*taixu*) has no physical form. It is the original substance of material-force. Its integration and disintegration are but objectifications caused by change. Human nature at its source is absolutely tranquil and unaffected by externality. When it is affected by contact with the external world, consciousness and knowledge emerge. Only those who fully develop their nature can unify the state of formlessness and unaffectedness, and the state of objectification and affectedness.

Although material-force in the universe integrates and disintegrates, and attracts and repulses in a hundred ways, nevertheless the principle (*li*) according to which it operates has an order and is unerring. . . .

The Supreme Vacuity of necessity consists of material-force. Material-force of necessity integrates to become the myriad things. Things of necessity disintegrate and return to the Supreme Vacuity. Appearance and disappearance following this cycle are all a matter of necessity. When, in the midst [of this universal operation] the sage fulfills the Way to the utmost and identifies himself [with the universal processes of appearance and disappearance] without partiality, his spirit is preserved in the highest degree. . . .

When it is understood that Vacuity, Emptiness, is nothing but material-force, then something and nothing, the hidden and the manifest, spirit and external transformation, and human nature and destiny, are all one and not a duality. He who apprehends integration and disintegration, appearance and disappearance, form and absence of form, and can trace them to their source, penetrates the secret of change.

If it is argued that material-force is produced from Vacuity, then because the two are completely different, Vacuity being infinite while material-force is finite, the one being substance and the other function, such an argument would fall into the naturalism of Laozi, who claimed that something comes from nothing and failed to understand the eternal principle of the undifferentiated unity of something and nothing.[23] . . .

## Recorded Sayings

The great benefit of learning is to enable one to transform one's physical nature oneself. Otherwise one will have the defect of studying in order to impress others, in the end will attain no enlightenment, and cannot see the all-embracing depth of the sage. [12:3a]

The mind unites [or commands] human nature and feelings. [14:2a]

[*Zhangzi quanshu* 2:1b–5b, 12:3a; 14:2a; adapted from WTC]

-------

23. Or, being and non-being.

# THE CHENG BROTHERS: PRINCIPLE, HUMAN NATURE, AND THE LEARNING OF THE WAY

With the appearance of the Cheng brothers—Cheng Hao (1032–1085) and Cheng Yi (1033–1107)—Zhang Zai's concept of *qi* as the psycho-physical stuff of all things was joined to the concept of *li* as the inner structure or directive principle of things—something like a genetic coding, identified by the Cheng brothers with the creative life-principle (*shengsheng*) as expressed in the *Changes*. All things were seen by them as compounded of both this directive, normative principle and material-force or ether (*qi*). In humans, this principle was structured as human nature (*xing*), the moral nature (*dexing*) or Heavenly nature (*tianxing*), the perfection of which was humaneness or humanity (*ren*). Moreover, all things and affairs of the Way shared in some manner this genetic, magnetic, growth-principle of the Way. Thus the Chengs taught the "unity of principle and the diversity of its particularizations," in the sense that every existent thing or affair was rooted in a shared physical existence as well as in a moral nature, which, following Mencius, they saw as good.

Human fulfillment could be achieved by a combination of two approaches—investigation of the principles in things and introspection of principles in the mind—but the point was not to pursue separate lines of objective inquiry and judgment but to experience the convergence or unity of principle, rational and moral, in both thought and action. This experience was described in affective terms as "the humanity which forms one body with [i.e., feels for] Heaven-and-Earth and all things"—a holistic experience that allowed for the empathetic recognition of things in both their shared unity and their distinct particularity.

The Chengs had many followers, but their bold claim to speak authoritatively for the Way on the basis of strong personal conviction, arising from direct experience of the Way in oneself (*zide*), aroused strong opposition to and official condemnation of their "learning of the Way" (*daoxue*). The Cheng school became dispersed, and it is mainly in the form reconstituted by Zhu Xi that this "learning of the Way" survived.

## PRINCIPLE AND THE UNIVERSE

All things under Heaven can be understood by their principle. As there are things, there must be specific principles of their being. [As it is said in the *Classic of Odes*:] "Everything must have its principle."[24] [*Yishu* 18:9a]

Due to the interaction of the two material forces [yin and yang] and the Five Phases, things vary as weak and strong in thousands of ways. What the

---

24. Ode 260.

sage follows, however, is the one principle. People must return to their original nature [which is one with principle]. [6:2b]

The mind of each human being is one with the mind of Heaven and Earth. The principle of each thing is one with the principle of all things. The course of each day is one with the course of a year. [2A:1a]

There is only one principle in the world. You may extend it over the four seas and it is everywhere true. It is the unchangeable principle that "can be laid before Heaven and Earth" and is "tested by the experience of the three kings."[25] Therefore to be serious (reverent, *jing*) is to be serious with this principle. To be humane is to be humane according to this principle. And to be truthful is to be truthful to this principle. [2A:19a]

The Master said: The principle of Heaven generates and regenerates, continuously without ceasing. This is because it takes no conscious action. If it had acted by exhausting its knowledge and skill, it could never continue without cease. [*Cuiyan*, 2:4a]

[From *Er Cheng yishu* 2A:1a, 19a; 6:2b; 18:9a; and *Er Cheng cuiyan* 2:4a]

### HUMAN NATURE

The nature cannot be spoken of as internal or external. [*Er Cheng cuiyan* 3:4a]

The mind in itself is originally good. As it expresses itself in thoughts and ideas, it is sometimes evil. When the mind has been aroused, it should be described in terms of feelings, and not as the mind itself. For instance, water is water. But as it flows, some to the east and some to the west, it is called streams and branches. [*Er Cheng yishu* 18:17a]

The nature comes from Heaven, whereas capacity comes from material-force. When material-force is clear, capacity is clear. On the other hand, when material-force is turbid, capacity is turbid. Take, for instance, wood. Whether it is straight or crooked is due to its nature. But whether it can be used as a beam or as a truss is determined by its capacity. Capacity may be good or evil, but the nature [of man and things] is always good. [*Er Cheng yishu* 19:4b]

Human nature is universally good. In cases where there is evil it is because of one's capacity. The nature is the same as principle, and principle is the same whether in the sage emperors Yao and Shun or in the common man in the street. Material-force, which may be either clear or turbid, is the source of capacity. Men endowed with clear material-force are wise, while those endowed with turbid material-force are stupid.

[From *Er Cheng cuiyan* 3:4a and *Er Cheng yishu* 18:17a; 19:4b; adapted from WTC]

---

25. *Mean* 29.

### CHENG HAO'S REPLY TO ZHANG ZAI'S LETTER ON THE STABILIZING OF HUMAN NATURE

By stabilizing the nature we mean that the nature is stabilized whether it is in a state of activity or in a state of tranquillity. One does not lean forward or backward to accommodate things, nor does one make any distinction of the internal and external. To regard things outside the self as external, and drag oneself to conform to them, is to regard one's nature as divided into the internal and external. If one's nature is conceived to be following external things, then while it is outside what is it that is within the self? One may indeed have the intention of getting rid of external temptations, but one must realize that human nature itself does not possess the two aspects of internal and external. As long as one holds that things internal and things external form two different bases, how can one hastily speak of stabilizing [human nature]?

The constant principle of Heaven-and-Earth is that their mind is in all things, yet of themselves they have no mind; and the constant principle of the sage is that his feelings are in accord with all creation, yet of himself he has no feelings. Therefore, for the training of the gentleman there is nothing better than to become broad and open and to respond spontaneously to all things as they come. . . .

[From *Mingdao wenji* 3:1a–b; adapted from WTC]

### REVERENT SERIOUSNESS AND HUMANITY

*Jing*, usually understood as "reverence" in classical Confucianism, has, as a basic Neo-Confucian virtue, the sense of moral seriousness and attentiveness.

As to the meaning of the Principle of Heaven: To be sincere is to be sincere to this principle, and to be serious [or reverent] is to be serious about this principle. It is not that there is something called sincerity or seriousness by itself. [*Yishu* 2A:13b]

For moral cultivation, one must practice seriousness; for the advancement of learning, one must extend his knowledge to the utmost. [18:5b]

Further Question: Is reverent seriousness not tranquillity?

Answer: As soon as you speak of tranquillity, you fall into the doctrine of Buddhism. Only the word "reverent seriousness" (*jing*) should be used but never the word "tranquillity" (*jing*). As soon as you use the word "tranquillity," you imply that seriousness is deliberate forgetting. Mencius said, "Always be doing something, but without fixation, with a mind inclined neither to forget nor to help things grow."[26] "Always be doing something" means that the mind is active. "Neither to forget nor to help things grow" means not to try to force their growth. [18:6b]

---

26. *Mencius* 2A:2. See chap. 6.

Reverent seriousness means unselfishness. As soon as one lacks reverent seriousness, thousands of selfish desires arise to injure one's humanity. [15:9a]

[From *Er Cheng yishu* 2A:13b; 15:9a; 18:5b, 6b; WTC, dB]

## ON UNDERSTANDING THE NATURE OF HUMANITY

This essay by Cheng Hao is one of the most celebrated in Chinese literature.

The student must first of all understand the nature of humanity (*ren*). The humane man forms one body with all things comprehensively. Rightness, decorum, wisdom, and trustworthiness are all [expressions of] humanity. [One's duty] is to understand this principle and preserve humanity with sincerity (*cheng*) and reverent seriousness (*jing*), that is all. There is no need to avoid things or restrict oneself. Nor is there any need for exhaustive search. It is necessary to avoid things when one is mentally negligent, but if one is not negligent, what is the necessity for avoidance? Exhaustive search is necessary when one has not found the truth, but if one preserves humanity long enough, the truth will automatically dawn on him. Why should one have to wait for exhaustive search?

[From *Er Cheng yishu* 2A:3a–b; adapted from WTC]

## On Humaneness

The Master said, The humane person regards Heaven-and-Earth and all things as one body. There is nothing that is not part of one's self. Knowing that, where is the limit [of one's humanity]? If one does not possess [humanity as part of] oneself, one will be thousands of miles away from Heaven-and-Earth and the myriad things. [1:7b]

Essentially speaking, the way of humanity may be expressed in one word, namely, impartiality.[27] However, impartiality is but the principle of humanity; it should not be equated with humanity itself. When a person puts impartiality into practice, that is humaneness. Because of impartiality, one can accommodate both others and oneself. [15:8b]

[From *Er Cheng yishu* 1:7b; 15:8b]

## Investigation of Things

To investigate things in order to understand principle to the utmost does not require the investigation of all things in the world. One has only to investigate

---

27. *Gong* (sense of commonality, public-mindedness).

the principle in one thing or one event exhaustively. For example, when we talk about filiality, we must find out what constitutes filiality. If principle cannot be exhaustively understood in one event, investigate another. One may begin with either the easiest or the most difficult, depending on one's capacity. There are thousands of tracks and paths to the capital, yet one can enter it if he has found just one way. Principle can be exhaustively understood in this way because all things share the same principle. Even the most insignificant of things and events have principle.

[From *Er Cheng yishu* 15:11a; adapted from WTC]

## THE SYNTHESIS OF SONG NEO-CONFUCIANISM IN ZHU XI

Part of the greatness of Zhu Xi (1130–1200) lay in his remarkable capacity to adapt and enfold in one system of thought the individual contributions of his Song predecessors. For this task he was well equipped by his breadth and subtlety of mind, and by powers of analysis and synthesis that enabled him, while putting ideas together, to articulate each of them with greater clarity and coherence than their originators had done. In this way he defined more precisely such concepts as the Supreme Ultimate (Supreme Pole or Polarity, *taiji*), principle (*li*), material-force (*qi*), human nature (*xing*) and the mind-and-heart (*xin*). Of his predecessors it was Cheng Yi upon whose philosophy he mostly built. Consequently his school of thought is often identified as the Cheng-Zhu school, and the doctrine of principle (*li*) is the most characteristic feature of their common teaching.

Zhu Xi likened principle in things to a seed of grain, each seed having its own particularity but also manifesting generic, organic elements of structure, growth pattern, direction, and functional use, whereby each partakes of both unity (commonality) and diversity. Unlike the analogy of the Buddha-nature to the moon and its innumerable reflections in water (in which the latter are understood to be insubstantial, passing phenomena), principle for Zhu was real both in its substantial unity and in its functional diversity. Hence he called the study of principle in all things, under both aspects, "real," "solid," "substantial" learning (*shixue*).

In humankind this principle is one's moral nature, which is fundamentally good. The human mind, moreover, is in essence one with the mind of the universe, capable of entering into all things and understanding their principles. Zhu Xi believed in human perfectibility, in the overcoming of those limitations or weaknesses that arise from an imbalance in one's psycho-physical endowment. His method was the "investigation of things" as taught in the *Great Learning*—that is, the study of principles, and also self-cultivation to bring one's conduct into conformity with the principles that should govern it.

In this type of self-cultivation, broad learning went hand in hand with moral discipline. The "things" that Zhu Xi had in mind to investigate may be primarily understood as "affairs," including matters of conduct, human relations, and political problems. To understand them fully required of the individual both a knowledge of the literature in which such principles are revealed (the classics and histories) and an active ethical culture that could develop to the fullest the virtue of humaneness (ren). It is through humaneness that one overcomes all selfishness and partiality, enters into all things in such a way as to identify oneself fully with them, and thus unites oneself with the mind of the universe, which is love and creativity itself. Ren is the essence of being human, one's "humanity," but it is also the cosmic principle that produces and embraces all things.

At the same time Zhu spoke of this teaching as "real" or "practical" learning (shixue) because it was based in natural human sentiments and could be practiced in daily life through normal intellectual and moral faculties. These were to be developed through what Confucius, and now Zhu Xi, called "learning for one's self" (meaning for one's own self-development and self-fulfillment), a learning Zhu Xi urged on all, ruler and subject alike.

In contrast to Buddhism there is in Zhu Xi a kind of positivism that affirms the reality of things and the validity of objective study. His approach is plainly intellectual, reinforcing the traditional Confucian emphasis upon scholarship. Zhu Xi himself is probably the most stupendous example of such scholarly endeavor in the Chinese tradition. He wrote commentaries on almost all of the Confucian Classics, conceived and supervised the condensation of Sima Guang's monumental history of China, and interested himself in rites, governmental affairs, education, and agriculture. He was a dynamic teacher at the Academy of the White Deer Grotto and kept up an active correspondence on a wide variety of subjects. He had less interest, however, in pursuing his "investigation of things" into the realms of what we would call natural or social science. To the last his humanism manifested itself in a primary concern for human values and ends. The kind of objective investigation that set these aside or avoided the ultimate problems of human life would have seemed to him at best secondary and possibly dangerous. Nevertheless, his philosophy, which stressed the order and intelligibility of things, could in a general way be considered conducive to the growth of science in a larger sense.

Zhu's later influence was felt chiefly through his commentaries on the Four Books—the Great Learning, the Mean, the Analects, and the Mencius—which he first canonized as basic texts of the Confucian school. In subsequent dynasties these texts, with Zhu Xi's commentaries, became the basis of the civil service examinations and thus, in effect, the official orthodoxy of the empire from the fourteenth century down to the turn of the twentieth century. Though subsequent thinkers arose to dispute his metaphysics, few failed to share in his essential spirit of intellectual inquiry, which involved focusing upon the Classics and reinterpreting them to meet the needs of their own time. Moreover, in Japan and Korea his writings likewise became accepted as the most complete and authoritative exposition of Confucian teaching. As such, they exerted a significant influence on the entire cultural development of East Asia well into modern times.

## PRINCIPLE AND MATERIAL-FORCE

In the universe there has never been any material-force (*qi*) without principle (*li*) or principle without material-force.

Question: Which exists first, principle or material-force?

Answer: Principle has never been separated from material-force. However, principle is above the realm of corporeality, whereas material-force is within the realm of corporeality. Hence when spoken of as being above or within the realm of corporeality, is there not a difference of priority and posteriority? Principle has no corporeal form, but material-force is coarse and contains impurities. [49:1a–b]

Fundamentally, principle and material-force cannot be spoken of as prior or posterior. But if we must trace their origin, we are obliged to say that principle is prior. However, principle is not a separate entity. It exists right in material-force. Without material-force, principle would have nothing to adhere to. Material-force consists of the Five Phases of metal, wood, water, fire, and earth, while principle includes humaneness, rightness, ritual decorum, and wisdom. [49:1b]

Question about the relation between principle and material-force:

Answer: Cheng Yi[28] expressed it very well when he said that principle is one but its manifestations are many. When Heaven, Earth, and the myriad things are spoken of together, there is only one principle. As applied to human beings, however, there is in each individual a particular principle. [49:1b]

Question: What are the evidences that principle is in material-force?

Answer: For example, there is order in the complicated interfusion of yin and yang and the Five Phases. This is [an evidence of] principle [in material-force]. If material-force did not consolidate and integrate, principle would have nothing to attach itself to. [49:2b]

Question: May we say that before Heaven and Earth existed there was first of all principle?

Answer: Before Heaven and Earth existed, there was certainly only principle. As there is this principle, therefore there are Heaven and Earth. If there were no principle, there would also be no Heaven and Earth, no human beings, no things, and, in fact, no containing or sustaining [of things by Heaven and

---

28. Zhu Xi refers to predecessors by honorific titles, which have been converted in the following texts to their ordinary names.

Earth] to speak of. As there is principle, there is therefore material-force, which operates everywhere and nourishes and develops all things.

Question: Is it principle that nourishes and develops all things?

Answer: As there is this principle, therefore there is this material-force operating, nourishing, and developing. Principle itself has neither corporeal form nor body. [49:3a–b]

Question: "The Lord-on-High has conferred even on inferior people a moral sense."[29] "When Heaven intends to confer on a person a great responsibility . . . "[30] "Heaven, to protect the common people, made for them rulers."[31] "Heaven, in the production of things, is sure to be bountiful to them, according to their qualities."[32] "On the good-doer, the Lord-on-High sends down all blessings, and on the evil-doer, He sends down all miseries."[33] "When Heaven is about to send calamities to the world, it will usually produce abnormal people as a measure of their magnitude."[34] In passages like these, does it mean that there is really a master doing all this up in the blue sky or does it mean that Heaven has no personal consciousness and the passages are merely deductions from principle?

Answer: These passages have the same meaning. It is simply that principle operates this way. [49:4a]

Throughout the universe there are both principle and material-force. Principle refers to the Way, which is above the realm of corporeality and is the source from which all things are produced. Material-force refers to material objects, which are within the realm of corporeality: it is the instrument by which things are produced. Therefore in the production of man and things, they must be endowed with principle before they have their material-force, and they must be endowed with material-force before they have corporeal form. [49:5b]

There is principle before there can be material-force. But it is only when there is material-force that principle finds a place to settle. This is the process by which all things are produced, whether [as] large as Heaven-and-Earth or as small as ants. Fundamentally, principle cannot be interpreted in the sense of existence or nonexistence. Before Heaven-and-Earth came into being, it already was as it is. [49:6a]

The nature of man and things is nothing but principle and cannot be spoken of in terms of integration and disintegration. That which integrates to produce life and disintegrates to produce death is only material-force, and what we call the spirit, the soul (*hunpo*), and consciousness are all effects of material-force.

---

29. "Announcement of Tang," *Classic of Documents*; Legge, *The Chinese Classics*, 3:184–85.

30. *Mencius* 6B:15. "When Heaven intends to confer on a person a great responsibility it first visits his mind and will with suffering, toils his sinews and bones, subjects his body to hunger, exposes him to poverty, and confounds his projects."

31. "Great Declaration," 1, *Classic of Documents*; Legge, *The Chinese Classics*, 3:286.

32. *Mean* 17.

33. "Instruction of Yi," *Classic of Documents*; Legge, *The Chinese Classics*, 3:198.

34. Source unidentified.

Therefore when material-force is integrated, there are these effects. When it is disintegrated, they are no more. As to principle, fundamentally it does not exist or cease to exist because of such integration or disintegration. As there is a certain principle, there is the material-force corresponding to it, and as this material-force integrates in a particular instance, its principle is also endowed in that instance. [49:8a]

[From *Zhuzi quanshu* 49:1a–8a; WTC, dB]

## THE SUPREME ULTIMATE (POLARITY)

Question: The Supreme Ultimate (Polarity, *taiji*) is not a thing existing in a chaotic state before the formation of Heaven-and-Earth but a general name for the principles of Heaven-and-Earth and the myriad things. Is that correct?

Answer: The Supreme Ultimate is merely the principle of Heaven-and-Earth and the myriad things. With respect to the myriad things, there is the Supreme Ultimate in each and every one of them. Before Heaven-and-Earth existed, there was assuredly this principle. It is this principle that through movement generates the yang. It is also this principle that out of tranquillity generates the yin. [49:8b–9a]

Fundamentally, there is only one Supreme Ultimate, yet each of the myriad things has been endowed with it and each in itself possesses the Supreme Ultimate in its entirety. This is similar to the fact that there is only one moon in the sky, but when its light is scattered upon rivers and lakes, it can be seen everywhere. It cannot be said that the moon has been split. [49:10b–11a]

The Supreme Ultimate is not spatially conditioned; it has neither corporeal form nor body. There is no spot where it may be fixed. When it is considered in the state before activity begins, this state is nothing but tranquillity. Now activity, tranquillity, yin and yang are all within the realm of corporeality. However, activity is after all the activity of the Supreme Ultimate and tranquillity is also its tranquillity, although activity and tranquillity themselves are not the Supreme Ultimate. This is why Master Zhou Dunyi only spoke of that state as Non-finite (or Non-Polar) — the unconditioned.

The Supreme Ultimate is simply the principle of the highest good. Each and every person has in him the Supreme Ultimate, and each and every thing has in it the Supreme Ultimate. What Master Zhou called the Supreme Ultimate (or Supreme Polarity) is an appellation for all virtues and the utmost good in Heaven-and-Earth, human beings, and things. [49:11b]

The Supreme Ultimate is similar to the top of a house or the zenith of the sky, beyond which point there is no more. It is the ultimate of principle. Yang is active and yin is tranquil. In these it is not the Supreme Ultimate that acts or remains tranquil. It is simply that there are the principles of activity and tranquillity. Principle is not visible; it becomes visible through yin and yang. Principle attaches itself to yin and yang as a man sits astride a horse. As soon as yin and yang produce the Five Phases, they are confined and fixed by physical nature and are thus differentiated into individual things, each with its nature. But the Supreme Ultimate is in all of them. [49:13a]

[From *Zhuzi quanshu* 49:8b–13a; WTC]

## HUMAN NATURE, THE NATURE OF THINGS, AND THEIR DESTINY

[The *Classic of Odes* says], "Heaven produces the teeming multitude in such a way that inherent in every single thing there is the principle for its being."[35] This means that at the very time when a person is born, Heaven has already given him his nature. The nature is nothing but principle. It is called the nature because it is endowed in man. It is not a concrete entity by itself, to be destined as nature, and to exist without beginning and without end. As I once illustrated, destiny or mandate is like an appointment to office by the throne, and the nature is like the office retained by the officer. This is why Cheng Yi said that destiny is what is endowed by Heaven and the nature is what things receive.[36] The reason is very clear. Therefore when ancient sages and virtuous men spoke of the nature and destiny, they always spoke of them in relation to concrete affairs. For example, when they spoke of full development of human nature they meant the complete realization of the moral principles of the three mainstays [or bonds]: [between ruler and minister, father and son, and husband and wife] and the Five Constant Virtues [rightness on the part of the father, love on the part of the mother, brotherliness on the part of the elder brother, respect on the part of the younger brother, and filiality on the part of the child], covering the relationships between the ruler and ministers and between father and son. When they spoke of nourishing our nature, they meant that we should nourish these moral principles so as to keep them from injury.

[From *Zhuzi quanshu* 42:2b–5a; adapted from WTC]

## THE NATURE AS PRINCIPLE

Original nature is an all-pervading perfection not contrasted with evil. This is true of what Heaven has endowed in the self. But when it operates in human beings, there is the differentiation of good and evil. When humans act in accord with it, there is goodness. When humans act out of accord with it, there is evil. How can it be said that the good is not the original nature? It is in its operation in human beings that the distinction of good and evil arises, but conduct in accord

---

35. Ode 260.
36. *Er Cheng yishu* 18:17a.

with the original nature is due to the original nature. If, as they say, there is the original goodness and there is another goodness contrasted with evil, there must be two natures. Now what is received from Heaven is the same nature as that in accordance with which goodness ensues, except that as soon as good appears, evil, by implication, also appears, so that we necessarily speak of good and evil in contrast. But it is not true that there is originally an evil existing out there, waiting for the appearance of good to oppose it. We fall into evil only when our actions are not in accord with the original nature. [42:9b–10a]

In your letter you[37] say that you do not know whence comes human desire. This is a very important question. In my opinion, what is called human desire is the exact opposite of the Principle of Heaven [Nature]. It is permissible to say that human desire exists because of the Principle of Heaven, but it is wrong to say that human desire is the same as the Principle of Heaven, for in its original state the Principle of Heaven is free from human desire. It is from the deviation in the operation of the Principle of Heaven that human desire arises. Cheng Hao says, "Good and evil in the world are both the Principle of Heaven. What is called evil is not originally evil. It becomes evil only because of deviation from the Mean."[38] Your quotation, "Evil must also be interpreted as the nature," expresses the same idea. [42:14b–15a]

[From *Zhuzi quanshu* 42:6a–15a; adapted from WTC]

## THE PSYCHO-PHYSICAL NATURE

The nature is principle only. But, without the material-force and solid substance of the universe, principle would have nothing in which to inhere. When material-force is received in its clear state, there will be no obscurity or obstruction and principle will express itself freely. If there is obscurity or obstruction, then, in the operation of principle, the Principle of Heaven will dominate if the obstruction is small, and human selfish desire will dominate if the obstruction is great. From this we know that the original nature is perfectly good. However, it will be obstructed if the psycho-physical nature contains impurity. In our discussion of the nature, we must include the psycho-physical nature before the discussion can be complete. [43:2b–3a]

The nature is like water. If it flows in a clean channel, it is clear; if it flows in a dirty channel, it becomes turbid. When the nature is endowed with material substance that is clear and balanced, it will be preserved in its completeness. This is true of human beings. When the nature is endowed with material substance that is turbid and unbalanced, it will be obscured. This is true of animals. Material-force may be clear or turbid. That received by humans is clear and

---

37. He Shujing.
38. *Er Cheng yishu* 2A:1b.

that received by animals is turbid. Humans mostly have clear material-force and hence are different from animals. However, those whose material-force is turbid are not far removed from animals. [43:7a–b]

Someone asked about this inequality in the clearness of the material endowment. The teacher said: Differences in the material endowment are not limited to one kind and are not described only in terms of clearness and turbidity. There are human beings who are so bright that they know everything. Their material-force is clear, but what they do may not all be in accord with principle. The reason is that their material-force is not pure. There are others who are respectful, generous, loyal, and truthful. Their material-force is pure, but their knowledge is not clear. From this you can deduce the rest. [42:8a]

[From *Zhuzi quanshu* 42:8a, 43:2b–3a, 7a–b, 8a; WTC]


### THE MIND-AND-HEART


Here the Chinese word *xin* represents both the mind and the heart, intellect as well as feelings.

The principle of the mind is the Supreme Ultimate. The activity and tranquillity of the mind are the yin and yang. [44:1b]

Question: Is consciousness what it is because of the intelligence of the mind or is it because of the activity of material-force?

Answer: Not material-force alone. Before [material-force] existed, there was already the principle of consciousness. But principle at this stage does not give rise to consciousness. Only when it comes into union with material-force is consciousness possible. Take, for example, the flame of this candle. It is because it has received this rich fat that there is so much light.

Question: Mind is consciousness and the nature is principle. How do the mind and principle pervade each other and become one?

Answer: Without the mind, principle would have nothing in which to inhere. [44:2a]

Question: Mind as an entity embraces all principles. The good that emanates, of course, proceeds from the mind. But the evil that emanates is all due to physical endowment and selfish desires. Does it also proceed from the mind?

Answer: It is certainly not the original substance of the mind, but it also emanates from the mind.

Further Question: Is this what is called the human mind?[39]

---

39. The "human mind" is contrasted with the "moral mind," or the mind of the Way, in that the former is in a precarious position and liable to make mistakes, whereas the moral mind follows Heaven's principles. The terms derive from "Counsels of the Great Yu," *Classic of Documents*; Legge, *The Chinese Classics*, 3:61–62.

Answer: Yes.

In the passage [by Zhang Zai], "When the mind is enlarged, it can enter into all things in the universe,"[40] the expression "enter into" is like saying that humaneness enters into all events and is all-pervasive. It means that the operation of the principle of the mind penetrates all as blood circulates and reaches the entire [body]. If there is a single thing not yet entered, the reaching is not yet complete and there are still things not yet embraced. This shows that the mind still excludes something. For selfishness separates and obstructs, and consequently the external world and the self stand in opposition. This being the case, even those dearest to us may be excluded. "Therefore the mind that excludes is not qualified to be one with the mind of Heaven."[41] [44:12b]

Question: How can the mind by means of moral principle (Dao) penetrate all things without any limit?

Answer: The mind is not like a side door that can be enlarged by force. We must eliminate the obstructions of selfish desires, and then it will be pure and clear and able to know all. When the principles of things and events are investigated to the utmost, comprehension will come as a great release. Zhang Zai said, "Do not allow what is seen or heard to fetter the mind." "When the mind is enlarged, it can enter into all things in the universe." This means that if penetration is achieved through moral principles, there will be comprehension like a great release. If we confine [the mind] to what is heard and what is seen, naturally our understanding will be narrow. [44:13a–b]

Someone asked whether it is true that the Buddhists have a doctrine of observation of the mind.

Answer: The mind is that with which human beings rule their bodies. It is one and not a duality, is subject and not object, and controls the external world instead of being controlled by it. Therefore, if we observe external objects with the mind, their principles will be apprehended. Now, [in the Buddhist view], there is another thing to observe the mind. If this is true, then outside this mind there is another one which is capable of controlling it. But is what we call the mind a unity or a duality? Is it subject or object? Does it control the external world or is it controlled by the external world? We do not need to be taught to see the fallacy of the [Buddhist] doctrine.

Someone may say: In the light of what you have said, how are we to understand such expressions by sages and worthies as "discrimination and oneness of mind"[42] or "hold it fast and you preserve it—let it go and you lose it,"[43] "fully develop one's mind and know one's nature,"[44] "preserve one's mind and nourish one's nature"[45] . . .

---

40. *Zhangzi quanshu* 2:21a.
41. Ibid.
42. "Counsels of the Great Yu," *Classic of Documents*; Legge, *Chinese Classics*, 3:61.
43. *Mencius* 6A:8.
44. *Mencius* 7A:1.
45. *Mencius* 6A:8.

Answer: These expressions [and the Buddhist doctrine] sound similar but are different, just like the difference between seedling and weeds, or between vermilion and purple, and the student should clearly distinguish them. What is meant by the precariousness of the human mind is the budding of human selfish desires, and what is meant by the subtlety of the moral mind is the mysterious depth of the Principle of Heaven. The mind is one; it is simply called differently depending on whether or not it is rectified. The meaning of "be discriminating [in regard to the human mind] and be one [with the mind of the Way]" is to abide by what is right and discern what is wrong, and to discard the wrong and restore the right. If we can do this, we shall indeed "hold fast the Mean," and avoid the partiality of too much or too little. . . . "Holding it fast"[46] is another way of saying that we should not allow our conduct during the day to fetter and destroy our innate mind, which is characterized by humaneness and rightness. It does not mean that we should sit in a rigid posture to preserve the obviously idle consciousness and declare that "this is holding it fast and preserving it"! As to the full development of the mind, this is to investigate things and study their principles to the utmost, to arrive at broad penetration, and thus to be able fully to realize the principle embodied in the mind. By "preserving the mind" is meant "seriousness to straighten the internal life and rightness to square the external life,"[47] a way of cultivation similar to what has just been called discrimination, oneness, holding fast, and preserving. Therefore one who has fully developed his mind can know his nature and know Heaven because the reality of the mind is unclouded and he is equipped to search into principle in its natural state. One who has preserved the mind can nourish his nature and serve Heaven because the substance of the mind is not lost and he is equipped to follow principle in its natural state.

[*Zhuzi quanshu* 44:1b–13b, 28a–29b; adapted from WTC]

[Amending Cheng Yi's comment that "the human mind-and-heart is human desires":] The human mind cannot be taken simply as human desires. If the human mind were simply human desires, the sage [Shun] would not have spoken of it as "precarious." To say that it is "precarious" means only that it is in danger of running after human [selfish] desires.

[Quoting Lu Xiangshan:] "If Shun had meant to say that the human mind was entirely evil, then he would have stated that it was no good, so men would shun it. His referring to it instead as "precarious" means that it was unsafe and could not be relied upon [being liable to either good or evil]. When he spoke of the need for discrimination, he sought discriminating judgment so as not to allow the good to become mixed with the bad!"

[Zhu Xi's comment:] This is of course correct.

[*Zhuzi yulei* 78:27a (p. 3193); 62:9a (p. 2363); dB]

---

46. *Mencius* 6A:8.
47. *Hexagram 2 (kun), Classics of Changes.*

*Chapter 21*

## ZHU XI'S NEO-CONFUCIAN PROGRAM

Zhu Xi's philosophical views have already been recounted in the preceding chapter. These have long commanded the attention of scholars in East Asia and the West because they represent the most general and abstract formulation of his teachings, even though many of them are found not in purely philosophical treatises or discussions but in texts that Zhu Xi thought addressed educational needs. This chapter deals with his more practical concerns, especially with the close connection between his educational and social programs, which were well known to later scholars and many officials throughout East Asia.

The son of a Confucian scholar-official, Zhu Xi was a highly precocious youth who in his teens was attracted to Chan (Zen) Buddhism, while also preparing himself for the civil service examinations. Successful in passing the highest regular examination (*jinshi*) at the age of eighteen, he embarked on a career combining periods of official service with longer periods of teaching and writing. Both were marked by a remarkable consistency of philosophical reflection and practical activity in addressing the problem of the self (brought into fundamental question by Chan Buddhism) and its proper relation to society and the cosmos ("Heaven, Earth, and all things").

Zhu's actual service at court was brief, and much of it was limited to lectures and memorials conveying the most general sort of advice to the emperor. But he also spent considerable time in local administration, dealing with problems of a most mundane sort, including the improvement of agricultural methods, the establishment of charitable granaries, famine relief, community organizations, the administration of justice, and the reform of schools and rehabilitation of local academies. Modern philosophers have paid little attention to these quotidian aspects of Zhu's work, and even historians have tended either to overlook them altogether or to dismiss them as not comparing in importance with the great matters of state administered at the central court. Thus they have remained unaware of the great significance attached to these more political writings by generations of scholar-officials and local elite who had to deal in the provinces with many of the same problems that Zhu did, not only in China but elsewhere in East Asia as well.

In this chapter we give samples of Zhu's recommendations for the community granaries and community compacts. In addition, we focus on a range of social proposals that often became models for others later on. Since these are more readily understandable in terms of Zhu's general educational philosophy, we present first his prefaces to two of the Four Books, the *Great Learning* (*Daxue*) and the *Mean* (*Zhongyong*). Though the *Great Learning*, the *Mean*, and the *Mencius* are commonly identified today with the Confucian Classics, it is not often realized that these three of the Four Books, while drawn from the corpus of classical writings, had no separate canonical status before Zhu Xi (following up an earlier Song development) identified them, together with the *Analects*, as four texts that merited special attention alongside the already recognized "Five [or as they were sometimes counted, Six, Nine, or Thirteen] Classics" (*jing*). It should be added, however, that toward the end of his life, Zhu suffered serious political persecution. One consequence of this persecution was that, though his teachings quickly won wide acceptance among scholars, the canonical status of the Four Books would not be officially certified until some years later.

## PREFACE TO THE *GREAT LEARNING BY CHAPTER AND PHRASE*

Zhu Xi's commentary is not just another annotation of a classic text. The suffix "by Chapter and Phrase" actually indicates a significant rearrangement of the text, and Zhu's preface, brief and modest though it may seem, attempts in a concise and systematic way to justify not only the liberties he takes with the text but also its extraction from the original *Record of Rites* and elevation to prime status among the Four Books that he is now canonizing. As the first thing to be read by those educated in the new Neo-Confucian curriculum for the "greater" (i.e., higher) learning, the key doctrines compressed in this short preface were to have a powerful influence on generations of literate East Asians.

Zhu's initial premise is that all learning is predicated on the unity and universality of the human moral nature, the full development of which is a responsibility of the ruler but, even more, a prerequisite to sound government. For this purpose the sage kings of antiquity maintained a universal school system, Zhu says, one that could legitimately be called a public school system, since it was open to all and aimed at the general uplift of humankind, not just the recruitment of an elite into state service. Nor does Zhu Xi mean by this just some form of learning in the home or private tutoring. Rather, he has in mind the physical establishment of schools in every village, providing for all who are capable of it an education that is carefully structured and sequenced in order to bring the individual learning process to its full maturity in the "greater learning."

At this point a question naturally arises: "If the system was so great in ancient times, why didn't it last?" The trouble, says Zhu, lay not with the system but with the failure of later dynasties to implement it. The Way itself did not cease to hold true; only the power to practice it was lost to those, like Confucius, who still understood it but did not rule. Fragments of the original model survived in the *Great Learning*, but their true significance was not appreciated until much later, when the Cheng brothers rediscovered it. Now Zhu Xi, picking up the loose or tangled threads from the Cheng school, is attempting to reconstitute it.

In the end Zhu's justification for presuming to speak for this ideal from the prehistoric past, while disallowing the results of most subsequent historical experience, is based on his prophetic claim that only through such a universal school system and the regeneration of all humankind can society be properly reconstituted. Here Zhu's key expression, appearing first in his preface and commentary (not found in the classics or the writings of the Cheng brothers), is *xiuji zhiren*. This could be read simply as "cultivating self, governing others," referring to two distinct duties of the educated elite, except that Zhu is mindful of the former as a precondition of the latter, as in the *Mean* 20 (see chapter 10). But Zhu's whole argument goes beyond simply the cultivation of leaders ("noble men") to govern others, important though that is for rulers and the leadership (*shi*) class themselves to learn. He implies that universal self-cultivation and self-discipline are indispensable to human governance in general — in other words, that the true "governance of men" is not just the "governing of [some by] others" but an undertaking that involves everyone's assuming responsibility for his own self-discipline and self-governance.

The Book of the *Great Learning* comprises the method by which people were taught in the higher learning of antiquity. When Heaven gives birth to the people, it gives each one, without exception, a nature of humaneness, rightness, ritual decorum, and wisdom. They could not, however, be equal in their physical endowments, and thus they do not all have the capacity to know what that nature consists in or how to preserve it whole. Once someone appears among them who is most intelligent and wise, and able fully to develop his nature, Heaven is sure to commission him as ruler and teacher of the myriad peoples, so that, being governed and instructed, they may be able to recover their original nature. This is how Fu Xi, the Divine Farmer, the Yellow Emperor, and [the sage kings] Yao and Shun succeeded to [the work of] Heaven, establishing the norm [for all to follow], and how they came to set up the post of Minister of Education and the office of Director of Music.

In the flourishing days of the Three Dynasties [Xia, Shang, and Zhou] their institutions were steadily perfected until everyone, from the king's court and feudal capitals down to the smallest lane or alley, had schooling. At the age of eight all children of the king and dukes, on down to the common people, started their elementary learning, in which they were instructed in the [social] disciplines of sprinkling and sweeping, responding to others, and coming forward or withdrawing from [the presence of others] [as recorded in *Analects* 19:12], and in the polite arts of ritual, music, archery, charioteering, writing, and arithmetic. Then at the age of fifteen, starting with the heir apparent and other princes, and down through the legitimate sons of the dukes, chief ministers, grandees, and lower aristocracy to the talented sons of the common people—all started their higher learning, in which they were taught the way of self-cultivation and governance of men through the fathoming of principle and rectifying of the mind. This is also how the distinction was made in the gradations of elementary and higher instruction in schools.

Thus widely were schools established, and thus precisely defined was the art of instruction in the details of its sequence and itemized content! As to the reasons for providing this instruction, they followed naturally from the superabundance of the ruler's personal attention to the practice of virtue and did not need to go beyond the constant norms that govern the people's livelihood and everyday needs. This being the case, there was no one without learning in those times, and as to the learning itself, no one would be without an understanding of what was inherent in his individual nature or what was proper to the performance of his individual duties so that each could exert himself to the fullest extent of his energies. This is why, in the great days of high antiquity, good government prevailed on high and beautiful customs below, to a degree that later ages have not been able to attain.

[*Daxue zhangju*, preface; dB]

### THE *GREAT LEARNING BY CHAPTER AND PHRASE*, CHAPTER 1

The expression "by Chapter and Phrase" refers to Zhu Xi's rearrangement of the passages in the original text and his phrase-by-phrase interpretation of it. Zhu explains its antique and broadly suggestive wording in terms of his own philosophy of human nature. "Luminous virtue" is understood here as the moral nature or inherent principle [infrastructure], which in its original state is both radiant and transparent, rather than dark or mysterious, though subject to obscuration in the individual psychophysical condition. The Three Main Guidelines [*San gangling*] involve the clarifying and manifesting of this innate goodness and extending it to others, so that one's self-renewal naturally leads to the renewal of others and thus to the regeneration of all humankind, which brings order to the state and peace to all-under-Heaven.

The following is an abridged translation of the text and commentary.

[COMMENTARY] Master Cheng said, "The *Great Learning* is a surviving work of Confucius, and stands as the gate by which the beginner in learning enters on the path to virtue. Today it is only owing to the preservation of this text that we can see in what sequence the ancients took up the pursuit of learning. The *Analects* and *Mencius* come next. He who pursues learning must start his studies with this, and then he may not go far wrong."

[CLASSIC TEXT] The way of the *Great Learning* lies in clearly manifesting luminous virtue, renewing the people, and resting in the utmost good.

[COMMENTARY] Master Cheng [I] says *qin*, "to be kind," should be *xin*, "to renew."

The *Great Learning* (*Daxue*) is learning to become a great person. "Clearly manifesting" (*ming*) means clarifying. "Luminous virtue" (*mingde*) is what a person gets from Heaven. Open, spiritual, and unobscured, it is replete with all the principles by which one responds to the myriad things and affairs, but being hampered by the physical endowment and obstructed by human [selfish] desires, there are times when it becomes obscured. Nevertheless, the radiance of the original substance [nature] is never lost, and one who pursues learning need only keep to what emerges from it and clarify it, so as to restore it to its original condition.

"To renew" means to reform the old. It means that once one has clearly manifested his own clear and bright virtue, he should extend it to others so that they too can do away with the stain of earlier soiling.

"To rest" means to arrive at this point and stay there. The "utmost good" is the ultimate norm in the principled handling of affairs. It means that by clearly manifesting luminous virtue and renewing the people one should reach the point of the utmost good [in that context] and stay there. Thus one would be sure to have a way to fulfill the ultimate norm of Heaven's principle, without one iota of the selfishness of human desires.

These three together are the mainstays [guiding principles] of the *Great Learning*.

[CLASSIC TEXT] Knowing where to rest [stop], there is stability; with stability, one can have composure; with composure one can be at peace; at peace one can deliberate [reflect], and with reflection one can get there [understand].

*The following passage discusses the celebrated Eight Items or Steps in the process of self-cultivation and dealing with society. Zhu appreciates them for their specificity and their systematic, sequential order, so much in contrast to the Daoist and Buddhist predilection for the undefined and undetermined.*

*It is important to recognize the broad connotations of the word* zhi, *"to know," "to learn," "to understand." Here it refers to the mind's faculty or capacity for knowing, more than to knowledge as "what is known," but both readings are possible, which leaves open the question of how much emphasis is put on cognitive learning and moral evaluation (later an issue for Wang Yangming in the early sixteenth century). In terms of the Cheng-Zhu learning of principle, the investigation of things and extension of knowing involve a meeting or matching of the inner, directive principles (infrastructure) inherent in both the mind and things and affairs—a qualitative appreciation and empathetic identification with the objects of one's learning experience, not just an objective grasp of them.*

[CLASSIC TEXT] The ancients, wishing clearly to manifest luminous virtue to all-under-Heaven, first put in order their own states. Wishing to govern their states, they first regulated their families. Wishing to regulate their families, they first cultivated [disciplined] their own persons. Wishing to cultivate their persons, they first rectified their minds-and-hearts. Wishing to rectify their minds-and-hearts, they first made their intentions sincere. Wishing to make their intentions sincere, they first extended their knowing. The extension of knowing lies in investigating things and affairs.

[COMMENTARY] . . . "Clearly to manifest luminous virtue to all-under-Heaven" is to provide all persons the wherewithal for clearly manifesting their luminous virtue. The mind-and-heart is the master of one's person. "To make sincere" is to make real, to substantiate. "One's intention" is what emerges from the mind-and-heart. "To substantiate" what emerges from the mind-and-heart is to try to integrate with the good, free of any self-deception. "Extend" means to project to the limit [the ultimate]. "Knowing" is like recognizing, to project our knowing to the limit, hoping that our knowing [capacity] will be fully employed. "To investigate" is to reach. "Thing" is like "affair." Fathoming the principles of things and affairs, one hopes always to reach the ultimate point.

These eight items are the specific items in the *Great [Higher] Learning*.

[CLASSIC TEXT] Things being investigated, knowing can be extended; knowing being extended, the intentions can be made sincere; the intentions being made sincere, the mind can be rectified; the mind rectified, the person can be cultivated [self disciplined]; with the self disciplined, the family can be regulated; the family regulated, the state can be governed; the state governed, all-under-Heaven can be at peace.

[COMMENTARY] . . . "Things being investigated" means unfailingly to reach the ultimate point in the principles of things-and-affairs. "Knowing being extended" means that the knowing of our minds-and-hearts is fully utilized. Knowing having been fully utilized, one's intention can be substantiated. One's intentions substantiated, the mind-and-heart can be rectified.

All the items preceding the "cultivating of the person" [disciplining of the self] have to do with "manifesting luminous virtue" [manifesting the moral nature]. All that follows "the regulating of the family" has to do with "renewing the people." Things having been investigated and knowing where to rest, one's knowledge has "reached" [fulfillment]. All that follows "one's intentions being made sincere" represents the order of priorities in "coming to rest."

[CLASSIC TEXT] From the son of Heaven down to the common people, they all as one take cultivating the person to be the root.

*Editor's note: None of Zhu Xi's interventions into the text of the Great Learning was more important than the following special note on the "investigation of things and extension of knowing." It suggested that the gradual and progressive "fathoming of principle," as both an intellectual and a moral enterprise, would culminate in a state of mind wherein all sense of opposition between self and others was overcome and one experienced a consciousness of oneness with all things.*

[Zhu Xi's note] The preceding, the fifth chapter of commentary, explained the meaning of "to investigate things and extend one's knowing," which is now lost. (In the old text this chapter, which connected with the following passage, was erroneously placed after the classic text.) I have ventured to take Master Cheng's ideas to supplement it as follows: "The extension of knowing lies in the investigation of things" means that if we wish to extend our knowing, it consists in fathoming the principle of any thing or affair we come into contact with, for the intelligent [spiritual] human mind always has the capacity to know [learn], and the things of this world all have their principles, but if a principle remains unfathomed, one's knowing [learning] is not fully utilized. Hence the initial teaching of the Great Learning insists that the learner, as he comes upon the things of this world, must proceed from principles already known and further fathom them until he reaches the limit. After exerting himself for a long time, he will one day experience a breakthrough to integral comprehension. Then the qualities of all things, whether internal or external, refined or coarse, will all be apprehended and the mind, in its whole substance and great functioning, will all be clearly manifested. This is "things [having been] investigated." This is the utmost of knowing.

*Zhu's reference to a sudden "breakthrough to integral comprehension" carried with it a sense of self-realization and self-fulfillment akin to a mystical experience, and it is not surprising that some understood it as an enlightenment similar in certain respects but different in approach from Chan [Zen] Buddhism. Interpretation of this suggestive passage remained highly controversial among later Neo-Confucians. What seems clear is that Zhu Xi thought of this culmination neither as a comprehensive grasp of empirical knowledge (i.e., encyclopedic learning, "knowing everything") nor as a trans-rational, trans-moral gnosis ("knowing nothing"), but rather as a thorough empathetic understanding or enlargement of the spirit that overcomes any sense of self and other, inner and outer, subjective and objective.*

## Self-Watchfulness

The following passage provides the classic basis for the Neo-Confucian practice of self-examination, often abetted by the praxis of quiet-sitting. Many Neo-Confucians set great store by constant self-awareness and rigorous self-discipline, through which one's adherence to the Way would become, so to speak, second nature; that is, one's moral sense would be so heightened and one's conduct so disciplined, that one's response to good and evil would be as natural and immediate as the reactions of one's sense of sight or smell. Thus the moral nature was to be grounded in and integral to the affective nature. Such a view was strongly reinforced by the rigorism of Zhu Xi's message and method of the mind-and-heart (*xinfa*) as propounded in his preface to the *Mean* (the selection following this one).

[CLASSIC TEXT] What is called "making one's intentions sincere" allows for no self-deception, as with one's detesting bad smells and being attracted to things pleasing to the sight. This means satisfying one's self [one's own conscience]. Thus the noble person is watchful over himself when alone.

[COMMENTARY] . . . "Making one's intentions sincere" is the first thing in self-cultivation. . . . "Self-deception" means that, even though one knows the good to be done and the bad to be avoided, yet what issues from the mind-and-heart does not bear this out. . . . If one wishes to cultivate oneself, then, knowing the good to be done and the evil to be avoided, one devotes his efforts to accomplishing this, puts an end to self-deception, and sees to it that his detesting of evil is like his [immediate] detesting of bad odors and his attraction to the good is like his [immediate] attraction to what is pleasing to the sight. Resolving to do so and striving to achieve this, one finds inner satisfaction in it. . . .

[*Daxue zhangju* 1; dB]

## PREFACE TO THE *MEAN BY CHAPTER AND PHRASE*

Zhu Xi's preface to the *Mean* has an importance among his writings almost equal to that of his preface to the *Great Learning*. Among the reasons for this is, first, that Zhu used this preface to introduce key ideas of his own, which then could be followed up in his commentary; and second, while Zhu himself had said the *Mean* was deep and difficult to understand and therefore should be read only after the other three of the Four Books, as a much shorter work than the *Analects* or the *Mencius*, it was usually printed together with the briefer *Great Learning*, i.e., up front in most editions. Thus given special prominence were two key formulations in his preface not found in the original text: the Message (or Method) of the Mind-and-Heart (*xinfa*) and its transmission through the orthodox tradition or Succession to the Way (*daotong*). Both became often quoted and highly contested issues in later Neo-Confucian discourse.

The Message of the Mind (*xinfa*), also alluded to in the preface to the *Great Learning*, refers to the sixteen-word message coming down from the sage kings Yao and Shun concerning the human mind and the mind of the Way as the key to rulership. Here Zhu correlates it with the discussion of the Way, human nature, and instruction featured in the first chapter of the *Mean*, which was to become the basis of Neo-Confucian mind cultivation. It focused on the conflict in a human mind precariously balanced between selfish and unselfish tendencies—the former identified with what were called "human desires" (customarily used to mean "selfish desires") and the latter with the moral imperatives of the Way implanted in human nature as received from Heaven. A distinction is made between Heaven's principles and human desires in the *Record of Rites*, "Record of Music" (*Yueji*), where "human desires" are identified with various excesses harmful to others, and in the subcommentary with greed and lust, in contrast to the purity of the Heaven-endowed moral nature. The contested ground between them was the natural inclinations, affections, and appetites constitutive of one's individual psycho-physical makeup, which could readily be made to serve the common good [*gong*] when directed by the Mind of the Way and the Principles of Heaven, or else could be turned to selfish ends. The easy susceptibility to abuse of one's legitimate self-interest, one's fallibility, as well as one's proneness to self-deception, found expression for Zhu Xi in the terms of "the human mind is precarious, the mind of the Way is subtle [and difficult to perceive]." Thus careful self-examination was called for, consisting of "refined discrimination" as to what was fair and proper, even what was legitimately self-regarding (e.g., the proper care of one's person), in contrast to what was ulterior and selfish, i.e., prejudicial to others, to the common good and even to one's true selfhood. "Single-mindedness" meant adherence to the unity of principle in a shared humanity (*ren*); "holding to the Mean" referred to a mind properly balanced in this respect, and not given to partiality.

What is highlighted in the second concept, Succession to the Way (*daotong*), is not a continuous tradition, passed on from one master to another (as with the "mind-to-mind" transmission in Chan [Zen]), but the long breaks from the founders of the Zhou to Confucius, and from Mencius to the Cheng brothers, who were at least able to reconstitute the Way, rescuing an all too fragile and misunderstood tradition from near oblivion.[1] Later Zhou Dunyi would be added to Zhu's list of those highly perceptive individuals who were able to grasp the Way, as revealed in fragmentary texts, without receiving direct transmission from a teaching lineage. What is emphasized, then, is the special genius and prophetic insight of a few heroic individuals, who speak with authority concerning a Way that endures as an unchanging ideal because it is rooted in the inherent nature of humankind, even though it has not been practiced for millennia.

Corollary to this is the notion of a split in the Way, surviving after the Duke of Zhou only as a tradition of learning, since it has ceased to be practiced by rulers as a way of government (see Fan Zuyu's *The Learning of the Emperors* in chapter 19). Though this conception draws on ideas of Zhu Xi's predecessors and is a natural evolute from the Learning of the Way, which claimed direct, unmediated authority to

---

1. A comparable use of *tong* (or succession) in relation to dynastic legitimacy also allows for legitimate succession to occur with the reconstituting of a unified empire after a long period of disunity. (See chap. 19.)

speak for the Way, the term *daotong* itself is Zhu Xi's. It became a standard feature of later Neo-Confucian discourse and rhetoric: a prophetic role and stance often claimed for one's teacher or ruler, and sometimes, amidst much avowed self-depreciation, implicitly assumed by the writer himself.

Why was the *Mean* written? Master Zisi wrote it because he was worried lest the transmission of the Learning of the Way (*daoxue*) be lost. When the divine sages of highest antiquity had succeeded to the work of Heaven and established the Supreme Norm [of governance], the transmission of the Succession to the Way (*daotong*) had its inception. As may be discovered from the classics, "hold fast the Mean"[2] is what Yao transmitted to Shun. That "the human mind is precarious" and "the mind of the Way is barely perceptible," that one should be discriminating [with regard to the human mind], be one [with the mind of the Way], and should "hold fast the Mean" is what Shun transmitted to Yu.[3] Yao's one utterance is complete and perfect in itself, but Shun added three more in order to show that Yao's one utterance could only be carried out in this way. . . .

As I have maintained, the mind in its empty spirituality [pure intelligence and consciousness] is one and only one. But if we make a distinction between the human mind and the mind of the Way, it is because consciousness differs insofar as it may spring from the self-centeredness of one's individual physical form or may have its source in the correctness of one's innate nature and moral imperative. This being so, the one may be precarious and insecure, while the other may be subtle and barely perceptible. But humans all have physical form, so even the wisest do not lack this human mind; and all have the inborn nature, so even the most stupid do not lack the mind of the Way.

These two [tendencies] are mixed together in the square-inch of the mind-and-heart, and if one does not know how to order them, the precariousness becomes even more precarious, and the barely perceptible becomes even less perceptible, so that the sense of the common good [impartiality] of Heaven's principle [in the mind of the Way] is unable in the end to overcome the selfishness of human desires. "Be discriminating" means to distinguish between the two and not let them be confused. "Be one [with the mind of the Way]" means to preserve the correctness of the original mind and not become separated from it. If one applies oneself to this without any interruption, making sure that the mind of the Way is master of one's self and that the human mind always listens to its commands, then the precariousness and insecurity will yield to peace and security, and what is subtle and barely perceptible will become clearly manifest. Then, whether in action or repose, in whatever one says or does, one will not err by going too far or not far enough.

---

2. *Analects* 20:1.

3. "Counsels of the Great Yu," *Classic of Documents*; Legge, *The Chinese Classics*, 3:61.

Yao, Shun, and Yu were great sages among all-under-Heaven, and for them to pass on succession to [rulership of] the world was a major matter for all-under-Heaven. As great sages performing a major undertaking for all-under-Heaven, on such momentous occasions their repeated admonitions still consisted only of these few words. How then could anything more be added to this from among all the principles under Heaven?

Subsequently sage upon sage succeeded one another: Tang the Completer, Wen and Wu as rulers, Gao Yao, Yi Yin, Fu Yue, the Duke of Zhou, and Duke Shao as ministers, received and passed on the succession to the Way. As for our master Confucius, though he did not attain a position of authority, nevertheless his resuming the learning of the past sages and imparting it to later scholars was a contribution even more worthy than that of Yao and Shun. Still, in his own time those who recognized him were only [his disciples] Yan [Hui] and Zeng [Shen], who grasped and passed on his essential meaning.

Then in the next generation after Master Zeng, with Confucius's grandson Zisi [reputed author of the *Mean*], it was far removed in time from the sages, and divergent views had already arisen. Zisi, fearing that the more time passed the greater the danger of losing the truth, traced back these ideas transmitted from Yao and Shun, substantiated them from what he had heard his father and teacher say from day to day, and drawing upon one to explain the other, produced this book for the edification of later scholars. His concern being so deep, his words were thus penetrating; his cogitations being so farsighted, his language was thus carefully chosen. When [in the opening lines of the *Mean*] he spoke about "Heaven's ordinance" [being imparted as human nature] and "following one's nature" [being the Way] he was referring to the mind of the Way [the moral mind]. When he spoke [*Mean* 20] about "choosing the good and holding fast to it" he referred to "being discriminating and being one." And when he spoke [*Mean* 2] about the "noble person's timeliness in holding to the Mean," he was referring to "hold fast the Mean." He came more than a thousand years after the age [of Yao and Shun], but his words, differing in no way from theirs, rather tallied exactly with them! In selecting the writings of the former sages and setting forth main principles, as well as in bringing deep secrets to light, there has never been a work so lucid and thoroughgoing as this.

Thereafter the transmission was resumed by Mencius, who was able to interpret and clarify the meaning of this text [the *Mean*] and succeed to the tradition of the early sages; but upon his demise the tradition was finally lost. . . . Fortunately, however, this text was not lost, and when the Masters Cheng, two brothers, appeared [in the Song] they had something to study in order to pick up the threads of what had not been transmitted for a thousand years, and something to rely on in exposing the speciousness of the seeming truths of Buddhism and Daoism. Though the contribution of Zisi was great, had it not been for the Chengs we would not have grasped his meaning from his words alone. But alas, their explanations also became lost.

[From *Zhongyong zhangju*, preface; dB]

## THE *MEAN BY CHAPTER AND PHRASE* (*ZHONGYONG ZHANGJU*), CHAPTER 1

[Zhu Xi] *Zhong* means not inclining or leaning to one side; it is an expression for not falling short or going too far. *Yong* (the *Mean*) refers to normality.

Master Cheng says, "Not being one-sided is called centrality (*zhong*); to be unchanging is called normality (*yong*). Centrality is the correct course for all-under-Heaven; normality is the fixed principle for all-under-Heaven." This work contains the Message (or Method) of the Mind-and-Heart (*xinfa*) handed down in the Confucian school. [Confucius's grandson] Zisi, fearing lest errors arise with the passage of time, committed it to writing and passed it on to Mencius.

This book starts with one principle, then extends it to myriad things and affairs, and finally returns to embrace all in one principle again. Opened out, it reaches in every direction; rolled back, it lies wrapped in the subtlest of mysteries. Its savor is inexhaustible, [but] it is all solid learning. One who studies it well, exploring and assimilating it, will find that it serves one well as an inexhaustible resource throughout life.

[CLASSIC TEXT] What Heaven has ordained is called [human] "nature" (*xing*); to follow that nature is called the Way. To cultivate that Way is called "instruction."

[COMMENTARY] An "ordinance" is like a command. The "nature" is principle. Heaven's generating the myriad things through the interaction of yin and yang and the Five Phases, their becoming embodied with psycho-physical force and endowed with principle, is like Heaven's giving a command or commission. Thus human beings, each receiving their endowment of principle, are constituted with the Five Constant Virtues [humaneness, rightness, ritual decorum, wisdom, and trustworthiness], which are one's nature. "To follow" means to accord with. The Way is like a path. Human beings, each following in their daily life and activities what is natural to their own nature, have their own path for what they should do, which is what we call the Way. "Cultivation" involves the making of measured gradations. Although the Way of [the common] human nature is the same for all, their psycho-physical endowments may differ, so there cannot but be differences in going too far or not far enough. The sage takes into account these individual differences in what it may be expected of them to do, and makes appropriate gradations in setting the norms for all-under-Heaven — and this is what is called instruction. . . .

*In conclusion, Zhu Xi sums up the main points of the Mean's first chapter as follows:*

Zisi relates the ideas that have been handed down to him as the basis of his discourse. First he explains that the Way originally derives from Heaven and cannot be altered. Its substance inheres in the self and cannot be departed from.

Next he sets forth the essentials of preserving and nourishing this [substance in the mind] and of practicing self-examination. Finally, he expresses the ultimate achievement of sagely and spiritual persons in the transforming power of their virtue. In this Zisi wishes for the learner to look within and find it [the substance of the Way] in oneself.

[From *Zhongyong zhangju* 1:1a–3a; dB]

*From the foregoing it may be seen how Zhu Xi explains the* Mean *in terms of his philosophy of human nature and principle, focuses attention on rigorous self-examination and interior cultivation of the mind-and-heart, and equates this with the sixteen-word message of the mind (xinfa) coming down from Yao and Shun. While this message and method are the key to proper governance, and have the utmost importance for the ruler and the ruling elite, they are rooted in a human nature shared by all, wherefore the same essential method is applicable to all. Finally, in using the language of Mencius concerning the noble person's "wishing to find the Way in himself," Zhu returns to a main theme of his teaching as a whole: that the ultimate value is found in the self and that all human governance is ultimately grounded in the human moral nature, which is perfected through "learning for one's self." This, in turn, links up with Zhu's emphasis on "self-discipline for the governance of men" in his preface to the* Great Learning.

*From this close linking of the concepts of learning for one's self (weiji zhi xue), the sixteen-word Message and method of the Mind-and-Heart (xinfa), and the Succession to the Way (daotong), they became much discussed and highly controversial elements in subsequent Neo-Confucian discourse.*

### PERSONAL PROPOSALS FOR SCHOOLS AND OFFICIAL RECRUITMENT

Written in 1195, Zhu Xi's proposals contain his most important ideas for the reform of education, the examination system, and the Imperial College. While there is a strong emphasis on moral and intellectual self-cultivation, his proposals also aim to have students study what will be practical to society and to test useful knowledge and skills in the examination system. In other words, it has a core in the humanities but allows for some technical specialization. Broadly conceived, these proposals reflect a consistent set of values as well as Zhu's larger vision for a system of general public education, starting in the village and reaching up to the capital, so as to have the same values govern official recruitment as well. The comprehensiveness of Zhu's recommendations, as well as the problems in evaluating virtuous conduct [exemplary performance], would make them difficult to implement wholesale. Nevertheless, in subsequent debates at court, in imperial decrees of the Yuan and Ming, and in general scholarly discourse down into the Qing (in Korea as well as China) the issues raised by Zhu, as well as the language he used, became standard rhetoric, even if actual official practice was often only a pale reflection of, and often contrary to, the views expressed here.

It has been my view that if one wants to take advantage of the present opportunity to reform the current system so as gradually to restore the ancient order of the Three Kings and improve today's customs, one must implement the proposal Master Mingdao (Cheng Hao) presented in the Xining reign (1068–1077). Then one can significantly rectify the foundation and completely eradicate the ills created by the extreme degradation [of these institutions]. Yet if this is deemed too much [to hope for], the next best alternative is to adopt [the following steps]: to equalize the quotas for successful candidates in each prefecture so as to strengthen students' sense of purpose; to establish moral conduct as a category in the examinations so as to give students a firm foundation; to abolish the composition of *ci* and *fu* poetry in the examinations and instead to test on the classics, masters, histories, and current affairs in separate years so as to make students' learning complete. Moreover, students should be made to base themselves on a definite school of exegesis (*jiafa*) in dealing with the classics, and examiners should see that they follow the correct punctuation of the text, that in their replies students show a thorough understanding of the text, and that they expound the various commentaries one by one before concluding with their own personal views. Moreover, in schools persons of authentic moral character should be chosen diligently to teach and guide students and to attract scholars who are committed to solid learning.

Then, having changed the system, you will have genuine commitment and not a spirit of opportunism, real practical conduct and not just empty words, solid learning and unfailingly useful talent. . . .

[From *Zhuzi daquan, Wenji* 69:18a–26a; RGC, dB]

## ARTICLES OF THE WHITE DEER GROTTO ACADEMY

As prefect of Nangang, Jiangxi, Zhu Xi led an effort to revive the White Deer Grotto Academy, located at the foot of Mount Lu by the great bend of the Yangzi River, a scenic spot famous as the site of Buddhist temples and Daoist sanctuaries. It is significant that Zhu took a strong interest in both public schools and the "private" (i.e., quasi-independent) academies that were centers of scholarship and ritual for the educated elite in local settings. The latter became important media for the propagation of his teachings.

The articles translated here are a set of stated precepts, posted for all to see as the basis for the conduct of instruction in the academy when it was reopened in 1180. As was typical of Zhu's work, the articles or precepts consist mostly of quotations from the classics or other early writings (unattributed by him, since he assumed that his readers would recognize the source from memory). Zhu Xi's contribution was in putting them together in a definite order and sequence. Particularly to be noted is the balance that Zhu strikes between personal cultivation and social relations, as well as that between moral and intellectual development.

Affection between parent and child;
Rightness between ruler and minister;
Differentiation between husband and wife;
Precedence between elder and younger;
Trust between friends. [*Mencius* 3A:4]

The above are the items of the Five Teachings, that is, the very teachings that Yao and Shun commanded Xie reverently to propagate as Minister of Education. For those who engage in learning, these are all they need to learn. As to the proper procedure for study, there are also five items, as follows:

Study extensively, inquire carefully, ponder thoroughly, sift clearly, and practice earnestly. [*Mean* 20]

The above is the proper sequence for the pursuit of learning. Study, inquiry, pondering, and sifting are for fathoming principle to the utmost. As to earnest practice, there are also essential elements at each stage from personal cultivation to the handling of affairs and dealing with others, as listed separately below:

Be faithful and true to your words and firm and sincere in conduct. [*Analects* 15:5]
Curb your anger and restrain your lust; turn to the good and correct your errors. [*Yijing*, hexagrams 41, 42]
The foregoing are the essentials of personal cultivation.
Be true to moral principles and do not scheme for profit; illuminate [exemplify] the Way and do not calculate the advantages [for oneself]. [Dong Zhongshu, in *Hanshu* 56:12b]
The foregoing are the essentials for handling affairs.
Do not do to others what you would not want them to do to you. [*Analects* 12:2; 15:24]
When in your conduct you are unable to succeed, reflect and look [for the cause] within yourself. [*Mencius* 4A:4]
The foregoing are the essentials for dealing with others.

*To these precepts Zhu Xi added a postscript of his own, emphasizing important points that were not explicit in the quoted precepts, namely that learning should be both individual and social, with appropriation by oneself and discussion with others essential to both self-integration and the conduct of affairs. The same approach had been recommended in Zhu's memorials and lectures to the emperor: that he should first form his own opinion of things and then discuss his opinions with others before making up his mind.*

I [Zhu] have observed that the sages and worthies of antiquity taught people to pursue learning with one intention only, which is to make students understand the meaning of moral principle through discussion, so that they can cultivate their own persons and then extend it to others. The sages and worthies did not wish them merely to engage in memorizing texts or in composing poetry and essays as a means of gaining fame or seeking office. Students today obviously act contrary [to what the sages and worthies intended]. The methods that the sages and worthies employed in teaching people are all found in the classics. Dedicated scholars should by all means read them frequently, ponder them deeply, and then inquire into them and sift them.

*Zhu concludes this note by taking issue with what became a growing trend in the Song: the adopting of school rules (as also monastic rules in Buddhism, see chapter 17), which he considers demeaning to students, who should be mature enough to take responsibility for their own learning and conduct. Ironically, when these precepts were widely circulated in other Neo-Confucian academies of China, Korea, and Japan, despite what Zhu says here, they were often identified as school rules (xuegui).*

If one understands the necessity for principles and accepts the need to take responsibility oneself for seeing that they are so, then what need will there be for someone else to set up such contrivances as rules and prohibitions for one to follow? In recent times regulations have been instituted in schools, and students have been treated in a shallow manner. This method of making regulations does not at all conform with the intention of the ancients. Therefore I shall not now try to put them into effect in this lecture hall. Rather, I have specifically selected all the essential principles that the sages and the worthies have used in teaching people how to pursue learning; I have listed them, as above, one by one, and posted them on the crossbar over the gate. You, sirs, discuss them with one another, follow them, and take personal responsibility for their observance. Then in whatever a man should be cautious or careful about in thought, word, or deed, he will certainly be more demanding of himself than he would be the other way [of complying with regulations]. If you do otherwise or even reject what I have said, then the "regulations" others talk about will have to take over and in no way can they be dispensed with. You, sirs, please think this over.

[From Zhu, *Wenji* 74:18a, 18b–19a; dB]

## PREFACE TO THE *FAMILY RITUALS*

Although the main focus of Zhu Xi's work was the theory and practice of self-cultivation, the defining and shaping of the self always took place in a social context, and the study of rites remained a major concern of his, as it had been earlier for the Confucius of the *Analects*, in which humaneness and rites were twin themes. Throughout his lifetime, Zhu sustained a strong interest in the classical rites, the critical, historical study of which he recognized as of great importance, as well as in the question, already of concern to predecessors such as the Cheng brothers and Sima Guang, of how these might be adapted to his own times. This reflects Zhu's strong conviction that scholarly study of the ancient rites was not enough; one must somehow put them into practice.

As a practical matter for the local elite, Zhu gave family ritual priority over the royal and state rituals that occupied so much of the Zhou texts. Yet Zhu's preface reveals his keen awareness of how much the circumstances of the Song scholar-official class (*shi*) have changed from those of the ancient Zhou aristocracy; indeed he himself was much too poor to carry on the classic rites. Accordingly, he sought to make them simpler, less costly, and more practical for the average family. Thus he focused on the more common ones: capping (coming of age), weddings, funerals, and ancestral rites. (There was a separate "Pinning Ritual" for girls at the time of their engagement to be married.) Note the absence of a birth rite, while the "capping" remains as a vestige of ancient induction into the leadership class. Subsequently, Zhu's prescriptions became models for the cultural and social elite, adopted widely in premodern East Asia.

Ritual "has fundamental elements and elaborations" [articulated form].[4] From the perspective of how ritual is carried out at home, the fundamental elements are to preserve roles and responsibilities and give substantial form to love and respect; the elaborations are the ceremonies and specifications for capping, weddings, funerals, and ancestral rites. The fundamental elements are the daily courtesies of householders, the things they must not fail to perform for even a single day. The articulated forms serve further to regulate the beginning and ending of human affairs. Even though the forms are only performed at particular times and places, unless one discusses them clearly and practices them until they become familiar, when the need arises one will not be able to do what is right and fitting. Thus one must also daily discuss and practice the forms.

During the three ancient dynasties[5] the classical texts of the rituals were fully adequate, but in the texts that survive today, the regulations on dwellings, utensils, and clothes, and the instructions on matters like coming and going, rising and sitting are no longer suited to our age. Even when contemporary gentlemen (*junzi*) accommodate the changes from antiquity to the present to formulate a temporary system for today, they still may not attain the proper balance, with some parts too detailed and some too sketchy. It can reach the point where they omit the fundamental elements and concentrate on the secondary ones, showing indifference to the substance but concern about the articulated forms. Thus, even committed scholars who are dedicated to the rites may still fail to perform the essential parts. And those who suffer from poverty have the added worry that they will not have the means to fulfill the ritual.

In my ignorance, I have suffered from both [lack of clear guidance and lack of funds], so I once took on the task of reviewing the ancient and recent texts [on ritual]. I started by identifying the major structures that cannot be changed and made minor emendations, my purpose being to put together a manual for one school [of thought]. In general I paid careful attention to roles and responsibilities

---

4. "Rites in the Formation of Character," *Record of Rites* 23:2a; Legge, *Li Ki*, 1:394–395.
5. Xia, Shang, and Zhou, the periods described in the classics.

and gave a high place to love and respect, considering them to be the fundamental elements. As for the situations in which these values are put into practice, I have been sketchy on the details, concentrating on the fundamental substance.

In writing this book I presume to follow Confucius's idea of carrying on what came from our predecessors. I sincerely hope to be able to discuss these matters fully with some like-minded gentlemen and make every effort to put them into practice. That way we might possibly again see the way the ancients "cultivated themselves and regulated their families"[6] and the heart whose "attention to the departed continues until they are far away."[7] Moreover, this book might make a small contribution to the state's effort to transform and lead the people.

> [Zhuzi daquan, Wenji 75:16b–17a; trans. adapted from Ebrey,
> Chu Hsi's Family Rituals, pp. 3–4]

## PROPOSAL FOR COMMUNITY GRANARIES

This proposal is typical of many initiatives Zhu took as a government official to encourage local elites to deal with chronic problems more or less on their own. It is also indicative of the fact that, however much private or local initiative might be promoted, the problem remained one of how local groups could do so with the necessary official approval and oversight but without direct government interference. In this respect Zhu envisaged some kind of civil infrastructure, between the private or household level and the state administration (guan), that would serve local public functions through relatively autonomous, cooperative, not-for-profit organizations. In the proposal here one should note especially how interest repayment was used initially to build up a reserve for later operation of a system of interest-free loans. Note too that Zhu first demonstrated the practicality of his plan by a fourteen-year pilot program in one area before recommending it for general authorization by the central government.

In connection with other proposals reported in this chapter, Zhu's proposals for community granaries also serve as an expression of his belief (and Mencius' long before) that a strong economic (i.e., agricultural) base was needed to sustain any program of educational or cultural uplift. Some of Zhu's followers (Xu Heng in the Yuan and Wu Yubi in the Ming) believed a system of independent scholar-farmers was preferable to having a class of scholar-officials largely dependent on state funds or the ruler's largesse.

## Imperial Edict

On the 28th day of the twelfth month, in the eighth year of the Chunxi era (1181), the Secretariat forwarded a memorial to the emperor from the Ministry of

---

6. Allusion to "Great Learning," Record of Rites; Legge, Li Ki, 2:411. See chap. 10.
7. Analects 1:9, a statement attributed to Zengzi.

Revenue submitted by the Commissioner for Ever-Normal Granaries, Salt, and Iron in the Liangzhe Eastern District, Zhu Xi.

The memorial says:

There is a community granary in Kaiyao village in Chongan county, Jianning superior prefecture. It was founded in the fourth year of the Qiandao era (1168) because of a famine in the village. An appropriation of 600 *tan* of rice from the Ever-Normal Granary of the prefecture was to serve as the seed rice. I was entrusted with the responsibility for working with Liu Ruyu, a local scholar with the honorific title of "Gentleman for Court Service," to use the amount for lending to those in need of support. The rice was appropriated in the winter. The following summer the prefectural office instructed that the rice should continue to be lent out and those who borrowed should then pay back in the winter.

We consulted the prefectural office and decided that the interest should be two *dou* per *dan* of rice borrowed [i.e., 20 percent]. This rate was to be in force for the coming [several] years, although it was agreed that should any borrower have difficulty in repayment, the interest rate could be reduced by a half, or even in full in the case of serious famine.

The granary has been in operation for fourteen years and we have managed to build three warehouses and have accumulated 3,100 *dan* of interest rice after the initial amount of 600 *dan* had been paid back to the prefecture. The amount of the interest rice has been properly reported to the prefecture.

I further suggest that the lending should continue, although the borrowers should no longer have to pay interest. An administrative fee of three *sheng* (i.e., 3 percent) will be collected, and the [retired] officials residing in this village, together with the local literati and myself, will [continue to] manage the granary. During the lending season, we ask that a county official be present to supervise the process.

Because of this granary, the village, comprising an area of about 40 to 50 [square] *li*, has not suffered hunger even in bad years. I believe that this is a method that could be introduced to other areas. Because there is no legal precedent, and no one would take it upon himself to initiate the system on his own, I request that it be instituted in all circuits and prefectures by Imperial decree, and further that should local households wish to establish a granary, the prefectural or county office should allocate a suitable amount of rice from its Ever-Normal Granary and entrust it to the leading household in the area to manage the lending and borrowing. The interest should also be two *dou* of rice. I hope that the village leaders, resident retired officials, and respected local scholars would work with the county magistrate to manage the lending and collecting. Once the interest rice has accumulated to ten times the seed rice, then the seed rice should be returned to the government and the interest rice be used for future lending, at a fee of three *sheng* [but] without interest. If well-to-do families are willing to contribute rice for seed purposes, they should be encouraged to do so. Their contribution should be paid back in a similar manner. Moreover, if certain regions have different customs, they should follow what is convenient for them and devise their own regulations and submit them to the government for recognition. This granary system is designed for creating long-term benefit, and if any village decides that it does not wish to establish a granary, then the government should not apply any pressure or force them to establish it. . . .

The emperor ordered the Ministry of Revenue to consider the memorial and the following is its opinion:

The Secretariat, commenting on the opinion submitted by the Department of Revenue, says:

We think it desirable that this memorial be circulated to the circuits and various supervisory offices and the prefectural and county offices under them. It should be made known that any people wishing to do as the memorial specifies would be assisted to do so. Retired officials—either coming originally from the county or those retired to the county—if they have shown themselves to be morally upright, should be allowed to apply to the prefectural or county offices for establishing such a granary. The local government should then allocate an amount of rice from the government's own "righteous [charitable] granary" to serve as seed rice. The retired officials should work with local elders to manage the granary, while the prefectural and county offices should not intervene or seek to control things.

[*Wenji* 99:17b–19b; THCL]

## PROCLAMATION OF INSTRUCTIONS

This proclamation was issued when Zhu was prefect of Zhangzhou in 1190. It is perhaps the most important proclamation that Zhu Xi issued, the most representative of his efforts in popular education, and the most quoted in later times. There is a great consistency in the views on public morality and community life expressed here and those found in the community compact (next selection).

Particularly to be noted are (1) the elements of basic morality in article 1 (later incorporated in the Sacred Edicts of the Ming and Qing dynasties; (2) the emphasis on filiality (despite Zhu's reservations about the *Xiaojing* as a "Classic" of Filiality); and (3) the identifying of the marital relation as prime among all human relationships. It is also noteworthy that, although there is some functional differentiation, most of the injunctions here apply equally to all members of the community, both scholar-officials (*shi*) and common people (*min*).

Following are items of instructions to be observed:

1. Instructions to members of community units (*baowu*) on matters about which they should encourage and remind each other:

All members should encourage and remind each other to be filial to parents, respectful to elders, cordial to clansmen and relatives, and helpful to neighbors. Each should perform his assigned duty and engage in his primary occupation. None should commit vicious acts or thefts, or indulge in drinking or gambling. They should not fight with or sue each other.

If there are filial sons or grandsons, or righteous husbands and virtuous wives, and their deeds are noteworthy, they should be reported. The government, in accordance with provisions of the statutes, will reward them and honor them with banners. Those who do not follow instructions should be reported, examined, and punished in accordance with the law.

2. Injunctions to members of community units on matters of which they should mutually watch and investigate each other:

People should always be alert to save water, prevent fire, investigate thefts and robberies, and prevent infighting.[8] Do not sell salt that is privately produced,[9] or kill plow oxen. They should not gamble with their properties. Nor should they spread or practice demon religion (*mojiao*).[10] People in the same community unit should watch each other. Anyone who is aware of a crime but fails to report it will share in the punishment.

3. Instructions to gentlemen (*shi*) and commoners (*min*):

People should understand that our body originates from our parents and that brothers come from the same source. Thus, we are endowed by nature with a feeling of obligation to parents and brothers, most profound and grave. What makes us love our parents or respect our elder brothers is not forced but comes spontaneously from the original mind-and-heart. And this love is inexhaustible.

Now some people are unfilial to parents and disrespectful to brothers. They often violate their parents' instructions and commands and even fail to provide for them; they easily become angry and fight with their brothers and even refuse to help them out. They defy Heaven and violate all principles. I deeply lament and feel sorry for them. They should urgently reform their conduct, otherwise they will invite immediate disaster.

4. Instructions to gentlemen and commoners:

It should be understood that the marital relationship between husband and wife is chief among the human moral relationships.[11] The rites and laws regarding betrothal and engagements are very strict. However, the customs of this region include what is called "looking after [someone]," that is, living openly with a woman who is neither a wife nor a concubine. Another is called "elopement," when two people who are not betrothed seduce each other and flee in secrecy. No violating of the rites and breaking of the law is more serious. The offenders should urgently reform so as to avoid punishment.

---

8. The people of Zhangzhou were said to be much given to feuding.

9. Trading salt outside the salt monopoly was prohibited.

10. Although *mojiao* sometimes refers to Manichaeanism, it is more likely that the term here means "unorthodox, folk religion."

11. Refers to the *Classic of Changes*, "Providing the Sequence of the Hexagrams" ("Xu gua"): "When there are husband and wife, then there are parent and child. When there are parent and child, then there are ruler and minister"; *Zhouyi zhengyi* (*SBBY*) 9:7b.

5. Instructions to gentlemen and commoners:

People should be kind and cordial toward villagers, neighbors, clansmen, and relatives. If sometimes a minor quarrel occurs, both parties should reflect deeply and make every effort to negotiate and reach a reconciliation. They should not lightly bring suit. Even if one is right, one's property will become diminished and one's work and livelihood may be cut off. How much worse is it if one is not right? In that case one cannot avoid imprisonment and punishment. It will end in calamity. All should earnestly take this as a serious warning.[12]

6. Instructions to official households (*guanhu*):

Since these are known as "households of public servants," and they thus differ from the common people, they should be especially content with their status and obey the law. They should devote themselves to "controlling oneself" and benefiting others. Moreover, villagers and neighbors are, in fact, all relatives and friends. How can one rely on his strength to bully the weak, or his wealth to appropriate the property of the poor? Prosperity and decline come in cycles. This calls for deep reflection.

7. Instructions when there has been a death in the family:

There should be timely burial of the dead. It is not permissible to keep the coffin at home or in a temple. If coffins or ashes have been temporarily stored in a temple, they should be buried within one month. Never should one employ Buddhist monks to make offerings to the Buddha, nor engage in extravagant display at funerals. The ceremony should be on a scale in keeping with one's resources. What matters is only that the dead should be returned to the soil soon. Anyone violating this should be flogged a hundred strokes with a heavy rod in accordance with the law. In addition, officials [violating this] should not be eligible for appointment, nor should scholars be allowed to take the civil examinations. Villagers, relatives, and friends who come to console may assist by making contributions. They should not oblige the family to provide food and drink for them.

8. Instructions to men and women:

They should not establish hermitages on their own under the pretext of engaging in religious practice. If there are such people, they should be expected to marry before long.

9. Restrictions on temples and people:

They are prohibited from holding mixed gatherings of men and women during the day or evening under the pretext of worshiping the Buddha or transmitting the sutras.

---

12. Instructions 1, 2, and 5 contain admonitions that are similar to those in the Lü Family Community Compact, to be discussed in the following section.

10. Restrictions on town and village:

They are prohibited from collecting money or donations, or making and parading figurines under the pretext of averting disasters or gaining good fortune.[13]

With respect to the instructions above, I only wish that everyone understand what is right and be a good person. Everyone should realize that if he does not offend the authorities, there is no reason why he should be subject to punishment. All should earnestly follow these instructions so that peace and harmony will be with them. If anyone does not follow them and dares to be defiant, the law of the state is clear and officials must be impartial [in enforcing the law]. Everyone should deeply reflect on this so he will have no cause for regret later.

[*Wenji* 100:5b–7a, "Quanyu bang"; RGC]

## THE LÜ FAMILY COMMUNITY COMPACT, AMENDED AND EMENDED

Although Zhu Xi was remarkable for both his originality and his powers of high-level synthesis, he characteristically expressed himself by editing or commenting on some earlier work—not only the classics but often the work of recent predecessors, as if to build on the prior insights and experience of others who either represented a kind of local, indigenous tradition or have tried to deal with the same problems as he in circumstances not too different from his own. In not a few cases these works would have been lost had it not been for Zhu's initiative in reclaiming and preserving them.

Such is no doubt the case with the Lü Family Community Compact, originally composed by Lü Dajun (1031–1082), in the Northern Song, which represented an attempt by members of the cultural and social elite to lead in the organization of local associations that would embody in contemporary (eleventh century) form some of the communitarian values that Confucians identified with the ancient enfeoffment system. Reference is made to the same values, attributed to the Cheng brothers, in the "Systems and Institutions" chapter of Zhu's *Reflections on Things at Hand (Jinsi lu)*. The compact emphasized voluntary subscription to certain values and practices that would govern the common life, stressing moral relations, self-help, and cooperative assistance—all basic human needs and values shared by members of the community regardless of status. At the same time, Zhu recognized the importance of leadership in any group endeavor and was particularly concerned to specify the necessary hierarchy of authority, fix the functions and responsibilities attaching thereto, and embody them in community rituals.

Many variations of this basic pattern were attempted later in imperial China and Korea, but while local structures differed, the key elements were those classified under the four headings indicated at the beginning of the compact's text: (1) mutual

---

13. In describing this custom, Zhu Xi's disciple Chen Chun said that people dressed earthen figurines like generals and commanders and marched with them in a parade so as to demand money from spectators (*Beixi daquanji* 47:5b).

encouragement of virtue and meritorious deeds; (2) mutual correction of faults; (3) mutual association in rites and customs; and (4) mutual sympathy [aid] in calamities and difficulties. Other provisions specify the leadership, organization, and conduct of meetings of the members, described in precise detail but too extensive to be reported on here.

Although the excerpts included here may not fairly represent it, the compact as a whole expresses Zhu's conviction that education through joint participation in proper rites and community functions is far more effective for achieving social harmony and promoting the general welfare than attempts at forced indoctrination or punitive laws.

## Mutual Encouragement of Virtue and Meritorious Deeds

"Virtue" means being sure to act upon seeing the good and being sure to reform upon hearing of faults; to be able to govern oneself; to be able to govern one's family; to be able to serve father and elder brothers; to be able to instruct sons and younger brothers; to be able to manage servants; to be able to serve superiors; to be friendly with relatives and acquaintances; to be able to choose friends; to be able to maintain integrity; to be able to extend kindness; to be able to fulfill a trust; to be able to relieve distress; to be able to correct faults; to be able to plan things for men; to be able to accomplish things for the people; to be able to resolve conflicts; to be able to decide right and wrong; to be able to promote the beneficial and abolish the harmful; to be able to hold office and reinvigorate offices.

"Meritorious deeds" means, at home, serving one's father and elder brothers, instructing one's children and younger brothers, and managing one's wife and concubines. Outside, it means serving one's superiors, entertaining friends, instructing students, and managing servants. As to reading books, overseeing the fields, managing the household, helping creatures, and favoring the practice of rites, music, archery, charioteering, writing, and arithmetic—all are the kinds of things that should be done. To do anything not of that kind is of no benefit.

The foregoing virtuous deeds should be the subjects of individual emulation and mutual encouragement. At meetings of the compact members they should be cited as cause for mutual congratulation, and the names of those performing them should be recorded for the encouragement or admonition of others.

## Mutual Correction of Faults

"Faults" means six faults of violating right conduct, four faults of violating the compact, and five faults of unbecoming conduct.

The faults of violating right conduct:

1. Drunken quarreling, gambling, fighting, litigation.

Drunken quarreling means a brawling argument under the influence of wine.

Gambling means gambling for valuables.

Fighting means assaulting and reviling.

Litigation means accusing someone of a crime with the intention of harming him. If [however] it is a case of going so far that someone attacks and injures another and is accused of it, it [litigation] is not to be disallowed.

2. Excessiveness and abnormality in conduct.

The many evils of exceeding and deviating are all included.

3. Irreverent and unyielding conduct.

To be rude to those of virtue or age; to bully men and to impose on people by relying on one's superior strength; to know of a fault and not change; to hear remonstrance and do even worse.

4. Stating what is not true and not being trustworthy. . . .

5. Making up statements of false accusation and slander. . . .

6. Managing things to one's own undue advantage.

The faults of violating the compact:

1. Not mutually encouraging virtue and meritorious deeds.

2. Not mutually correcting faults.

3. Not mutually observing rites and customs.

4. Not mutually expressing sympathy for the distressed.

The faults of unbecoming conduct:

1. Mixing with men not of the right kind.

Not restricting oneself to the general class of people, but mixing with the wicked and loafing with bad actors who do not conform to ordinary humankind. If one consorts with them day and night, that is mixing with those not of one's own kind. If, [however,] one cannot avoid contact with them briefly, it is not to be faulted.

2. Rambling, playing around, and idling.

Rambling means coming and going without reason. It includes visiting people and stopping them from working or from doing what they ought to be doing.

Playing around means sporting and laughing without limit. It includes ridiculing in contempt and possibly such activities as racing horses and hitting balls without betting valuables. Idling means not practicing one's proper occupation or managing family affairs, not keeping one's gate and courtyard in order, and being sloppy.

3. Acting without proper manners.

Advancing and withdrawing rudely. This includes not being respectful, speaking when it is not fitting to speak, and not speaking when it is fitting to speak.

Dressing ostentatiously, not dressing neatly, and going into the street without proper clothing.

4. Not treating pressing matters with due care.

In directing affairs, to be wasteful and forgetful, late in keeping appointments, and careless about urgent matters.

5. Uneconomical expenditures.

Not reckoning the family's resources and exceeding them by extravagant expenditure. Not being able to accept poor circumstances, and not seeking to improve one's condition in a proper manner.

Those who have joined the compact should each examine themselves in regard to the foregoing faults and mutually admonish one another. If the fault is slight, confidential admonition is in order; if it is great, group admonition is called for. If the person charged will not listen, then at a general meeting the head of the compact, so informed, shall try to reason with him and if he agrees to reform, the matter shall simply be recorded in the register, but if he resists, will not submit, and proves incorrigible, all shall agree to his ejection from the compact. . . .

*Not included here are the norms for mutual participation in family, community, and seasonal rituals, prescriptions with regard to polite social correspondence, wedding gifts, help with funerals, proper mourning dress, and so on. Seven kinds of calamities calling for mutual aid are indicated, including fire and flood, catching robbers, illness, death, orphanhood, false accusation, and aid to the poor in times of distress. There is a general emphasis on sharing information and offering help to those in need, while setting reasonable standards as to what kind of help one might be expected to give.*

*Finally the compact concludes with detailed instructions by Zhu Xi on the holding of meetings of the compact members. For brevity's sake we reproduce here the shorter version in the original Lü text:*

Every month there shall be a meeting where a meal is served. Once every three months there shall be a gathering where wine and a meal are served. The person in charge each month shall be responsible for covering these expenses. At these meetings, good and bad deeds shall be entered in a register and rewards and penalties administered. Any troublesome matter should be dealt with on the basis of general discussion (*gongyi*).

[From *Zhuzi daquan, Wenji* 74:25a–32a; JM, dB]

## Chapter 22

### IDEOLOGICAL FOUNDATIONS
### OF LATE IMPERIAL CHINA

## XU HENG AND KHUBILAI KHAN

From 1127 to 1368 much of China and most of its ancient heartland fell under foreign rule by conquest dynasties from the north. A pattern developed of military control by a garrison state superimposed upon an agricultural society still largely managed through somewhat modified civil bureaucratic rule. Religious Daoism and Buddhism continued to thrive on the popular level, as did many forms of popular culture. Confucianism had greater difficulty regaining its political footing in the midst of marked dynastic instability, but in the traditional form of family ethics and rituals, its position was not seriously challenged, and eventually the Jurchen (Jin) and Mongol (Yuan) dynasties recognized the need for Confucian literati to maintain civil services and serve as an interface between the state and those who worked or managed the land.

Initially, however, things were different for adherents of the new Neo-Confucian Learning of the Way. Though Zhu Xi's teaching had spread rapidly in private academies during the late years of the Southern Song (early and mid-thirteenth century), hostilities and border controls tended to insulate the North from this new development. Only with the Mongol conquest of central and south China, largely completed by 1270, did China again become a unified political and cultural sphere, and did Khubilai (r. 1260–1294) establish a formal Chinese dynasty, the Yuan. At that time a leading exponent of Zhu Xi's teachings, who had already made converts among young scholars, set up an Academy of the Supreme Ultimate in Peking and introduced both Mongols and Chinese to Zhu's major works and the new Neo-Confucian curriculum.

One of the most influential of this new generation of scholars, Xu Heng (1209–1281), inspired by the possibility of regenerating society on the basis of Zhu Xi's teachings, was especially moved by what seemed to him the great educational practicability of Zhu's *Elementary Learning* and the moral/social vision of Zhu's Preface and Commentary on the *Great Learning*. He became "committed to the Learning of the Way as his personal responsibility (*yi daoxue ziren*) and was soon recognized as a prime leader among a group of scholarly activists, likewise converts to the Learning of the Way, who dedicated themselves to 'saving the day' or 'rescuing the times' (*jiushi*) by engaging in efforts of practical use in governing the world (*jingshi zhiyong*)." In memorials to Khubilai and debates at court they emphasized the need for basic laws and institutions of a traditional Han type. In the larger Confucian sense these institutions represented a kind of orderly, constitutional government, combining regular and systematic administration (to which the Mongols were generally unaccustomed) with strong education in public morality, especially through a proper school system. Xu Heng's proposals for reform of tax policies and strengthening of agriculture are a case in point, for Xu considered himself a peasant, not a scholar-official set apart from the common people. Indeed, he believed that Confucian scholars should have a dependable livelihood of their own—preferably agriculture or commerce—rather than be dependent on the largesse of the ruler or the outcome of a competitive struggle for office.

In his writings, Xu Heng sought to convey his basic teachings in simple, unadorned language. He did not strive for originality or stylistic effects but only to get the educational message across, to convert and enlist human talents in the service of the Way. As a self-identified farmer-teacher, with the rugged character of the peasant, Xu communicated his message to his imperial "students" and a new generation of scholar-officials with great earnestness. He was deeply dedicated to the teaching of Mongols, firmly convinced that a Neo-Confucian education was the best way to develop their native intelligence as well as to ensure the survival of the tradition. Yet, for all this, he was charged by some later Neo-Confucians with being a collaborationist who compromised the high principles of the Way.

### FIVE MEASURES REQUIRED BY THE TIMES

Xu Heng performed the role of mentor to the emperor both through his memorials and his services as adviser and tutor to the heir apparent. His five-point memorial is believed to have been prepared first as lectures from the Classics Mat, the importance of which had been stressed by Cheng Yi and Zhu Xi, and its opening lines adopt the same stance as they did vis-à-vis the ruler—the high seriousness of the minister's role as sharing responsibility for the governance of all-under-Heaven.

Thus Xu quotes the words of Confucius and Mencius (the latter having been made canonical in Zhu Xi's Four Books):

Mencius said, "Charging one's ruler with what is difficult is called showing respect for him. Exposing goodness while foreclosing on evil is called being reverent toward him. Saying that he is 'unable to do it' is called stealing from him."[1] And Confucius said, "[A great minister is one who] serves his ruler according to the Way, and, when he finds he cannot do so, withdraws [from his service]."[2] The larger purpose that your minister cherishes in his heart is nothing less than this. . . .

In both past and present, though the models and regulations on which the state was established varied from dynasty to dynasty, the most essential thing was to win the hearts of all-under-Heaven. To win the hearts of all-under-Heaven is nothing other than to manifest love and an impartial devotion to the common good. If one loves them, the people's hearts become compliant; if one is impartially devoted to the common good, the people's hearts become willing to serve. Compliance and willingness to serve are what makes for good government.

[From *Yuan wenlei* 13:1b–2a; dB]

*In the body of his memorial, Xu Heng stresses the urgent importance of governmental reform, telling Khubilai that China can be governed only through traditional Han Chinese institutions and methods, not Mongol ones. Much of his advice is organizational, practical, and prudential, having to do with the emperor's exercise of key leadership functions. Toward the end of the memorial, however, Xu dwells particularly on the need for proper management of agriculture and sericulture (which Mongols had little experience of and handled badly), as well as on the need for universal education, which he (like Mencius) sees as the foundation for all political and social order. In so doing, Xu draws on ideas previously set forth by Zhu Xi.*

If from the capital districts down to the local districts schools are set up so that, from the imperial princes on high to the sons of the common people below, the young can engage in study; if day by day the great moral relationships of parent and child, ruler and minister, are explained, along with the great Way that begins [in the home] with the [*Elementary Learning's*] "sweeping up and responding to questions" and extends to the [*Great Learning's*] pacifying of the world, then after ten years those above will know how to guide those below and those below will know how to serve those above. With those above harmonious and those below cooperative, it would be far better than what you have now.

If you can do these two things [i.e., provide for the people's livelihood and education], a myriad other things can be accomplished. If you cannot do these things, then nothing can be expected from any of the other things you try to do.

---

1. *Mencius* 4A:1. Mencius was here quoting an earlier saying.
2. *Analects* 11:23.

This Way is the Way of Yao and Shun. The Way of Yao and Shun fostered life
and promoted unselfishness. If you can do these things, they will foster life and
promote unselfishness. Mencius said, "Anything other than the Way of Yao and
Shun I would not dare propose to my king."[3]

[From "Nongsang xuexiao," *Yuan wenlei* 13:16b–18a; dB]

## THE EXAMINATION DEBATE UNDER KHUBILAI

In their concern for moral self-cultivation, the Neo-Confucian reformers did
not neglect consideration of the complex political and intellectual issues of the
day. Their record is replete with discussions of such questions. What prompted
their reassertion of the moral claims of Confucian humanism was the need to
cope with the pragmatic realism on the part of the Mongols and their fiscal
technicians, whose main aim was to maximize the conqueror's power and
resources.

In the background of the Neo-Confucian discussion of selfish interest versus
the commonweal lies the question of the employment of worthy, humane men
able to defend the long-term public interest against those who seek only immediate gains for the state. In 1267 a proposal was made by the Hanlin academician
Wang E (1190–1273), a leading scholar among the survivors from the Jin and
a *jinshi* degree winner in 1224, that the civil service examinations should be
reintroduced. Wang cited the precedents of earlier dynasties from the Zhou and
Han down through the Liao and Jin, as well as the example of Ögödei's (r. 1229–
1241) examinations in 1237. He argued that if such a system were not available,
there would be no ladder of advancement for able and ambitious men to follow.
In the absence of such they would be easily diverted into less worthy callings,
either becoming sub-officials whose expertise had not benefited from a classical
training, or attaching themselves to the service of local satraps, or perhaps even
using their talents as merchants and artisans rather than as officials at court or
in central administration.

When Khubilai sought other opinions on the matter, he may have been
surprised to find a difference of opinion between Confucian traditionalists like
Wang E, whose education had prepared them for the earlier Song-style examinations, and those committed to the new Learning of the Way, whose views
reflected the Neo-Confucian critique of the Song examinations as placing too
much emphasis on literary style and memorization and not enough on practical
affairs and the cultivation of moral character based on the teachings of the classics. A colleague of Xu Heng's, Dong Wenzhong (d. 1281), expressed it this way
to Khubilai, who suspected him of being one of the School of the Way because
he was always citing the Four Books:

---

3. *Mencius* 2B:2.

Your Majesty has often said that those who neglect the study of the classics and do not ponder deeply the Way of Confucius and Mencius, but rather engage in composition of *shi* and *fu* poetry, have no concern for self-cultivation and nothing of benefit to offer the governance of the state. Therefore, scholars throughout the land wish to engage in studies that are solid and practical (*shixue*). What I cite are the works of Confucius and Mencius; I make no claim to knowing about the School of the Way. But some scholars cling to the ways of fallen dynasties [i.e., the Song and Jin] and talk like this to mislead Your Majesty. I fear that this is not in accord with Your Majesty's intention of setting a proper model on high and maintaining self-discipline among those below.

[Yao Sui, "Shendaobei," in Su, *Shilüe* 61:5b–6a; dB]

Another associate of Xu, Yang Gongyi (d. 1294), told Khubilai he should discard the examinations based on *shi* and *fu* poetry and instead employ men recommended by officials for their personal character and understanding of the classics:

These men should then be examined both on their understanding of the larger significance and precise meaning of the Five Classics and Four Books and on their knowledge of history as it relates to contemporary problems. If this is done and they engage in studies of a practical sort (*shixue*), then the whole climate and style of scholarship will be improved, the people's customs will be enhanced, and the state will obtain men of talent who know how to govern.

[Su, *Shilüe* 13:9a; dB]

Hao Jing (1223–1275), also associated with Xu Heng, depreciated literary skills as opposed to moral character in the following terms:

What the world thinks of as Confucian scholarship is only letters. That is what is used for instruction by parents and teachers; it is what scholars occupy them-selves with and what official careers are determined by . . . but it does not cor-respond to what made a scholar a scholar in ancient times. Really letters are only the outer branches of scholarship; it is moral action and virtuous conduct (*dexing*) that constitute the root and core of scholarship.

[*Hao Wenzhong gong ji* 7:8b–9a; dB]

Whether because of this cleavage between old-style Confucians and the rising Neo-Confucians led by Xu Heng, or because of fears held by Mongols and their Central Asian collaborators that they would be at a disadvantage vis-à-vis Chi-nese competing in exams based on a knowledge of Chinese classics, nothing was actually done to reestablish the civil service examinations at this time. In the meantime, however, Khubilai appointed Xu Heng to the Directorate of Educa-tion with authority to implement a new curriculum based on the Four Books, Five Classics, and other texts either prepared by or sanctioned by Zhu Xi, in state schools from the Imperial College down to the prefectural and county level. Although this curriculum had already gained wide acceptance in private academies associated with the spread of Neo-Confucianism, Khubilai's action was a historic first step in establishing it as an official orthodoxy.

Subsequently, two other important steps were taken to implement Zhu Xi's educational program, at least in a qualified manner. After the appointment of Zhang Wenqian (1217–1282) a protégé of Xu, as minister of agriculture, in 1270 he ordered the establishment of village schooling (i.e., below the county level), which would bring education to people in the countryside in the manner recommended by Zhu Xi and Xu Heng. This was in line with Xu's dual emphasis on promoting agriculture and education together, as shown in his five-point memorial of 1266. There is evidence, however, that this measure, as carried out under the Court of Imperial Granaries, actually involved only part-time, off-season instruction for the moral uplift of farmers in local communities and differed from the full-time instruction in classical studies conducted under the Ministry of Rites in state schools (county and above) for prospective recruits in the bureaucracy. Such a bifurcation in schooling was not what Zhu Xi or Xu Heng had had in mind, but it kept alive, at least nominally, the ideal of universal education.

The next and even more historic step was taken in 1313 by another follower of Xu Heng, Cheng Jufu (1249–1318), a southerner who was highly successful in recruiting scholars for the Mongols who represented a generation educated in the new curriculum. He proposed a resumption of the civil service examination on a new basis but claimed the earlier endorsement of Khubilai:

In the matter of examinations Khubilai . . . repeatedly called for its implementation and his successors, Zhengzong and Wuzong, also shared this intention, but as of now nothing has come of it, apparently because of some obstructionists. Now the proper method for the recruitment of scholars is through classical studies that fulfill the Way of Self-discipline for the Governance of Men. The composition of *ci* and *fu* poetry is only artful display. Since the Sui and Tang dynasties there has been exclusive emphasis on the *ci* and *fu*. Therefore scholars have become accustomed to superficiality. Now what we propose . . . will emphasize virtuous conduct and an understanding of the classics. If scholars are chosen in this way, they will all be the right kind of men.

[*Yuanshi* 81:2018; dB]

Thereupon the Mongol emperor Renzong issued an edict drafted by Cheng Jufu:

After our founding emperor settled the world as if by divine power, Emperor Shizu [Khubilai] established organs of government, defined official functions, recruited Confucian scholars of great distinction, sanctioned schools for the training of men's abilities, and proposed examinations as a means of recruiting scholar-officials—thus setting an example of great breadth of vision and foresight. . . . Since the Three Dynasties each age has had an examination system with a definite order of priorities. In the recommendation of scholars virtuous conduct should be the first consideration and in the testing of skills proficiency in the classics should come first, with the composition of prose and poetry subordinated to that. The frivolous and fanciful we can do without. Therefore I command the Central Secretariat to deliberate over past and present practice and fix the details of the system.

[*Yuanshi* 81:2018; dB]

While thus paying lip service to the values espoused by Zhu Xi and Xu Heng, Cheng Jufu in the Central Secretariat set aside the Neo-Confucian preference for advancement through the schools and personal recommendations and made concessions to gain consensus in favor of an examination system that Neo-Confucians had previously criticized. The most important change was the installing of a Neo-Confucian curriculum, featuring the Four Books and Five Classics with commentaries by Zhu Xi or other Neo-Confucians. Tactical concessions included a less demanding examination format and quota provisions in favor of Mongols and Central Asians. The quotas, however, did not outlive Mongol rule, while the new curriculum, similar to Xu Heng's for the schools, survived into the early twentieth century.

In the Yuan period many (though by no means all) adherents of the Learning of the Way regarded the new system as a great triumph. In 1315, the year the new exams began, Cheng Duanli, a noted proponent of Zhu Xi's curriculum, was euphoric:

In the recruitment of scholars virtuous conduct is being put ahead of all else and study of the classics is being given precedence over literary composition. . . . In the interpretation of the classics the views of Master Zhu are the sole authority, uniting as one the philosophy of principle and study for the civil service examination, to the great advantage of scholars committed to the Way [as distinct from opportunistic candidates]. This is something the Han, Tang, and Song never achieved, and the greatest blessing that has come to scholars throughout the ages.

[Cheng Duanli, Preface 1, *Chengshi richeng* 1; *Song Yuan xuean* 87:65; dB]

Thus Cheng exudes the idealistic expectation that resurrecting the civil service examinations with this new curriculum will at last join the wisdom of Zhu Xi and his practical learning method to an official recruitment process that will transform state and society.

## SAGE KING AND SAGE MINISTER: OUYANG XUAN ON KHUBILAI AND XU HENG

The ideal of sagehood in Neo-Confucianism came to one culmination in the Learning of the Emperors and Kings, in which the Way of Governance and the

Learning of the Way would be brought together by a sage king and sage minister. From the foregoing accounts of historic developments in the Yuan period, for which the great prestige of both Khubilai and Xu Heng are often invoked, it is not hard to see why they should be eulogized as sage ruler and sage minister by the distinguished scholar Ouyang Xuan (1283–1357).

> With his heavenly endowment [Khubilai] resumed the lost teaching of the sage emperors and kings, while Xu Heng, with the gift of heavenly talents, was able to repossess the untransmitted teachings of the sages and worthies, connecting up with the tradition of the Duke of Zhou, Confucius, Zengzi, Zisi, Mencius, and the other noble men who came after them, to become a minister of unparalleled stature in those times. The aspirations of ruler and minister matched perfectly, and all that was enunciated in the emperor's name served to uphold the perfect norm of rulership, set up proper guidelines for the people, resume the lost teaching, and usher in an era of great peace—all as if myriad ages were fulfilled in one day.
>
> [*Guizhai wenji* (SBCK) 9:1a; dB]

This is not the last time that such an ideal blending of rulership and Confucian learning would be proposed or claimed, as aspiring scholars in almost every age attempted to ride the tiger of imperial power. Other Neo-Confucians of the time, like the distinguished scholar Wu Cheng (1248–1333) and the reclusive Liu Yin (1249–1293), disassociated themselves from such concessions as were made by Xu Heng and Cheng Jufu, either declining to serve or withdrawing from office out of higher allegiance to the purity and integrity of the Way. Both images of the Confucian scholar—of collaborationist ministers like Xu and of scholars heroically resisting the pretensions of sage rulers—recur in later history, as we shall see in the case of Fang Xiaoru in the early Ming.

## MING FOUNDATIONS OF LATE IMPERIAL CHINA

It was far from a foregone conclusion that the Yuan dynasty would have the Ming as its successor. Indeed, through many of the seventeen years of civil war (1351–1368), it was not clear that there would be any unifying successor at all, let alone the Ming. For many years, the chances of the future founder, former peasant and outlaw Zhu Yuanzhang (Ming Taizu, r. 1368–1398), appeared slim. Taizu lacked education; his resources were meager, and his geostrategical advantages slight. That he succeeded despite all the initial odds against him owes much to his openness to the advice offered him by some of the leading Confucian thinkers of his time. These men convinced Taizu that an equitable system of requisitions, coupled with the merciless suppression of corruption, would overcome his disadvantage of slender resources. They convinced him he could vanquish his better-placed rivals if his army and bureaucracy were more tightly centralized and disciplined than theirs were. These counsels worked.

Yet the builders of the Ming did not consider efficiency and discipline to be simply instrumental. They were ends in themselves, firmly grounded in Confucian ethics. Fiscal efficiency would result when the idea of impartial service of the common good was put into effect. Centralization was the result when everyone understood that to concede powers or to tolerate indiscipline among subordinates was to allow selfish evil to triumph over good. The Ming foundation soon became a national moral crusade. The founders of the Ming firmly believed that they possessed the Mandate of Heaven and that that mandate charged them with the task not just to reunify China politically but also to carry out the ethical remaking of its people in the light of the Confucian ideals of antiquity—taking the sage kings as their model, not the rule by accommodation or expediency of the Han, Tang, and Song.

Acting upon its sense of mission, the Ming dynasty laid much of the institutional and ideological framework for later imperial China. This included the concentration of all legitimate decision-making authority in the hands of the emperor, accomplished by abolishing the prime ministership and imposing centralized controls over the imperial bureaucracy. From the beginning of the Ming it seemed clear that the use of one or another form of the merit principle was the only acceptable way to recruit officials: first, Taizu reinstituted the Yuan examination system in 1370, dropped it, and then resumed it in 1382; it was implemented again under the Yongle emperor (r. 1402–1424) and continuously thereafter. There was also an assumption by the state of an obligation to "nurture" future scholar-officials by providing the students of China with a public school system, together with Confucian instructors and approved Confucian texts, as well as stipends and other personal benefits.

By 1368, Ming Taizu made himself literate enough to start composing what became a very large number of essays, colloquies, commentaries, Confucian moral exhortations, and political and social regulations, all in a peculiarly crabbed style of his own. He defined his own role as both ruler and teacher of China. He strove intensely to reach out directly to everyone in the realm, so as to explain to them in his own words what good behavior was and to warn them of the dire consequences of moral lapses. Although few of Taizu's successors in the Ming could sustain his vision of the good society, many of his ideas and enactments nonetheless remained influential through the Ming and Qing dynasties.

## MING TAIZU: AUGUST MING ANCESTRAL INSTRUCTION

As a commoner become emperor, Taizu thought of himself as a great communicator, conveying his own brand of imperial populism in slightly different form to different audiences: the common people, scholar-officials, his prospective dynastic successors, and so on. It is especially in his instructions to the last group that he reveals his larger vision of rulership and the dynastic constitution as well as many detailed regulations for the management of the palace and members of the imperial family. Here we present just a few (out of ninety-six in all), including his general preface.

Notice that in Taizu's preface he makes no attempt to ground the lawmaking function, as does the preamble to the Tang Code, in a cosmological theory of correspondences between man and nature, by which the ruler is called upon to redress imbalances between the two arising from human violations of the natural order. Rather he asserts it as the product of his own personal experience of life and the need for the ruler to take personal responsibility for carrying out the Way. Here we can see the danger that lies in the Neo-Confucian conception of the ruler's living up to the responsibilities of a sage king, directly intuiting the Way in his own mind-and-heart.

Preface: I have observed that since ancient times, when states established their laws it was always done by the ruler who first received the mandate. At that time the laws were fixed and the people observed them. Thus was the imperial benevolence and authority extended throughout the realm so that people could enjoy peace and security. This was because at the outset of the founding the ruler endured hardships, saw many men, and became experienced in handling affairs. In comparison with a ruler born and bred deep within the palace, unfamiliar with the world, or a hermit scholar living alone in the mountains or forests considering himself enlightened, how different it was for me. When I was young I was orphaned and poor and grew up amidst warfare. At the age of twenty-four I joined the ranks and was ordered about for three years. Then I gathered together able followers and studied the ways of training soldiers, planning to compete with the warlords. It was trying and worrisome. I was apprehensive and on guard for nearly twenty years until I was able to eliminate the powerful enemies and unite the empire. Of human deceit I have known plenty. Therefore, drawing on what I have seen and done, together with the officials, I have fixed the law of the land. This has eliminated the indulgent rule of the Yuan dynasty and those who defiled the old customs. The warlords were powerful and deceitful. They were hard to govern, but I have governed them. The people, encountering disorder, tried by all manner of evil means to pass through the unrest. They were hard to manage, but I have managed them. Now since the pacification of Wuzhang there was discussion about enacting the *Code* and the *Commandments*. The additions, deletions, and changes have been innumerable. Ten years have passed and we accomplished the task. They were promulgated and gradually the people came to know the prohibitions. In order to teach later generations the *Ancestral Instruction* was also created. It was set up as a family law. It was written in big characters in the Western Corridor and was read day and night to make the text perfect. From start to finish it has been six years. It went through seven drafts and is now done. How difficult! Many shallow scholars affirm the past and decry the present. Evil officials constantly twist words and bend the law. If I had not selected the able from the masses and made decisions resolutely, I would have been confused by them and unable to accomplish anything. Now I have ordered the Hanlin to compile this book and the Minister of Rites to print it and pass it on to eternity. All my progeny may adhere to my orders and not be crafty and confuse the laws that I have fixed forever. Not a single word may be changed. Not only will you not fail to live up to my intentions to pass on the law, but Heaven and Earth and the Ancestors will also bless and protect you without end. Ah! Heed this. . . .

*One of Taizu's most famous enactments was his abolition of the prime ministership after the exposure of an alleged plot by the existing prime minister to usurp the throne. Thenceforth all executive power was concentrated in the emperor, assisted by a secretariat, a system that persisted through the late imperial period.*

2. From ancient times policy was discussed among the three dukes (*sangong*), and the duties of government were divided among the six ministers, but a prime minister was never established. The Qin began the establishment of a prime minister and fell soon thereafter. The Han, Tang, and Song continued the practice. Although there were some virtuous prime ministers, many of them were evil men who monopolized power and confused administration. Now our dynasty has abolished the prime ministership and established such offices as the five chief commissions, the six ministries, the Censorate, the Office of Transmission, and the Grand Court of Revision to manage the affairs of the realm. They parallel one another and dare not seek to dominate each other. It is the court that provides overall control of government affairs. That is why there is stability. From now on, when my descendants become emperors, they absolutely shall not establish a prime minister. If there are officials who dare to memorialize requesting such establishment, civil and military officials shall immediately submit accusations. The offender shall be put to death by slicing and his whole family executed.

[From *Huang Ming zuxun*, in *Mingzhao kaiguo wenxian* 3:1579–1591; EF]

## EDUCATION AND EXAMINATIONS

As mentioned earlier, Taizu had a use for both education and trained scholars. Thus he was easily persuaded by his advisers to reestablish state school systems and civil service examinations set up by the Mongols. Taizu shared Khubilai's low esteem for literary refinement, while feeling no less a desire than the Mongols for a curriculum and examination system that would promote basic literacy and practical virtue rather than produce pundits. Instead of scrapping the simpler examinations for Mongols, he favored something much like them for the Chinese themselves, settling essentially for a curriculum of the Four Books and Zhu Xi's commentaries.

Ming Taizu's proclamation in 1370 reestablishing the examinations adopts essentially the same stance as Renzong and Cheng Jufu in the Yuan, using much the same language as they. To have some kind of definite system was the traditional practice, the proclamation says, though the system of each earlier dynasty had its own merits and demerits. Thus when Taizu proceeds to reinstitute the same system as the one established in the Yuan, he feels no need to acknowledge it. He will see to it personally that men are selected for their practical virtue and understanding of the classics, and he issues a stern warning, at the conclusion of the proclamation, against the pursuit of power and privilege by self-seeking individuals, who will meet with strong condemnation and heavy punishment. Actually, Taizu had second thoughts about the value of the system in turning out men of practical ability, and suspended it for more than ten years, but none of his doubts had to do with the content of the exams, which, after its resumption in 1384, was even more squarely focused on the Four Books and Zhu Xi.

When it came to schooling, however, the plebeian autocrat Taizu left no doubt that he conceived of it as training and indoctrination — not at all the voluntaristic process of learning for one's self that Zhu Xi had advocated. He provided Ming China with a universal, state-funded Confucian school system, down to the county level. A college in the capital, and schools in each of some thousand prefectural and county seats throughout China, served a student body of some 25,000 licentiates (*shengyuan*). In 1382 the emperor ordered the Ministry of Rites to have twelve rules for students cut into stone slabs and to have the slabs placed at the left of the Minglun tang (Hall for Clarifying Human Relationships) in each school. (In 1652, the Qing dynasty did exactly the same thing, although it revised and condensed Taizu's original rules.) The students were forbidden to argue with their teachers, discuss public issues, or serve as lawyers or advocates. They constituted a pool from which the best would eventually be selected by recommendation or examination for salaried positions in the bureaucracy.

## MING TAIZU: PLACARD FOR THE INSTRUCTION OF THE PEOPLE

This proclamation was promulgated in the last year of Taizu's reign and remained the basis for public guidance in the villages during the Ming (and one key part, article 19, even into the Qing). It was the last of Taizu's many efforts to reach below the county level of state administration and address the people directly. Many of its forty-one articles have to do with the maintenance of public order, village organization, conduct of family and community rituals, agriculture, water conservation, and so on. Its provisions were closely linked to Taizu's *lijia* system of local administration in groups of ten and a hundred households.

Note that the proclamation was issued through what is usually called the Ministry of Revenue (*hubu*). A more literal reading of the title would be "Ministry of Households," but the households referred to are commoners and most often farmers, and the more common rendering is indicative of the state's main interest in them as producers of revenue. It signified that instruction on this lower, local level was of a different order from that of the schools and examinations conducted under the Ministry of Rites at the county and prefectural level with a view to bureaucratic recruitment. Note especially how Taizu celebrates his own achievements, denigrates scholar-officials as often venal, and, while charging them with having corrupted and obstructed his own plans, invites the people to side with him against them.

In ancient times, rulers represented Heaven and managed human affairs by setting up various offices and delegating the various duties, so as to bring peace to the lives of the people. The worthies and the gentlemen of those times feared lest they not be employed by the rulers. After being employed, they exerted the utmost diligence to serve the rulers, thus bringing glory to their parents, honor to their wives and children, and establishing their reputations throughout the world. How could there have been any lawbreaking conduct? Therefore, the officials were competent for their posts and the people were content in their livelihoods. Since the world has been unified, I have set up the cardinal principles, promulgated laws, and established offices according to ancient rules: in the capital, the six ministries and the Censorate; in the provinces, the provincial administration commissions, the provincial surveillance commissions, prefectures, subprefectures, and districts. Although the titles are different from previous dynasties, the system of government is the same.

However, most of the appointed officials are from among the common people. For some time it has been very difficult to tell whether they were virtuous or wicked. The scholars are not real scholars, and the officials are all cunning ones. They often take bribes and break the law, turn humaneness and rightness upside down and injure the good people, so that the common people bring all of their complaints to the capital. So it has been for years without cease. Now this order is promulgated to declare to the people of the realm that all minor matters involving household and marriage, land, assault and battery, and disputes shall be judged by the elders and the *lijia* of their communities (*li*). Serious matters involving sexual crime, robbery, fraud, or homicide shall be reported to the officials. After this order is promulgated, any officials or functionaries who dare to violate it shall be sentenced to the death penalty. For those commoners who dare to violate it, their entire families shall be banished to the frontiers. These regulations have been declared before. You in the Ministry of Revenue shall once again proclaim them.

[From *Jiaomin bangwen*, in *Huang Ming zhishu* 3:1404–1407; EF]

## Article 19

This provision, disarming in its homely simplicity, actually proved the most enduring part of Taizu's proclamation, much of which lapsed with the breakdown of the *lijia* system of local organization. The core of its message of moral instruction, which became known as the "Six Maxims" or "Sacred Edict," is actually taken from an earlier proclamation of Zhu Xi (unacknowledged by Taizu and unnoticed by most modern commentators, but no doubt instigated by advisers familiar with Zhu Xi's works; see chapter 20).

In each village and *li* a bell with a wooden clapper shall be prepared. Old persons, disabled persons unable to function normally, or blind persons shall be selected and guided by children to walk through the *li* holding the bell. If there are no such persons in the *li*, then they shall be selected from other *li*. Let them shout loudly so that everyone can hear, urging people to do good and not violate the law. Their message is: "Be filial to your parents, respect elders and superiors, live in harmony with neighbors, instruct and discipline children and grandchildren, be content with your occupation, commit no wrongful acts." This shall be done six times each month. At the time of the autumn harvest the people of the village and *li* shall give food to the bell carriers in accordance with their ability to pay. If the residents of the village are scattered and remote, each *jia* unit shall prepare a bell, and it will be easy to deliver the message. The style of the bell: it shall be made of copper with a wooden clapper hanging in the middle.

[*Jiao min bangwen* 1419–1420; EF]

## Article 32

This article refers to the establishment of community schools in the Yuan period, then their reestablishment by Taizu early in his reign (acclaimed as a glorious achievement by Taizu's adviser, Song Lian, in language reminiscent of earlier Neo-Confucian rhetoric), and finally abandoned for reasons cited in this article as follows:

In the Yuan dynasty, many village children attended school. In the early years of the Hongwu period (1368–1398) villages everywhere were ordered to establish community schools (*shexue*) to instruct the children in good conduct. Incompetent officials and *lijia* took advantage of this to indulge in corrupt practices. The children of families with adult males obviously had the spare time to attend school, but the officials took bribes and excused them from attending school. Nevertheless, the children of families without adult males, who had no spare time to attend school, were forced to go to school. This caused hardship for the people. Therefore, the community schools were abolished. From now on, the children of the common people, regardless of their location and number, shall be instructed by virtuous persons. The schools shall open early in the tenth month and close at the end of the twelfth month each year. If families with many adult males have enough spare time, they may have their children continually engaged in study. Those officials, functionaries, and *lijia* who dare to interfere with them shall be punished severely.

[*Jiao min bangwen* 1433–1434; EF]

Note: This short article has at least three major significances: (1) it marked the effective privatization of schooling on the village level, with the consequence that only children of the well-to-do would engage in regular study that might prepare them for official schools and exams, while most commoners, engaged in agriculture and handicrafts, would get minimal off-season instruction, if any; (2) taken together with article 19, the regular moral instruction came mostly through the ritual recitation of the Six Instructions (Sacred Edict); (3) the effect of the foregoing was to create two different levels of education, one administered through the Ministry of Revenue on the local level and the other by the Ministry of Rites, leading up to official recruitment. Administratively, then, what had once been envisioned by Neo-Confucians as a single system of general education had become bifurcated into two: one below the county level, largely privatized but retaining a ritual of the Six Instructions for public moral uplift, and the other for the elite, oriented toward the civil service. Alongside this, of course, were the private academies, increasingly the focus of serious scholarly study and discussion but largely maintained by local support of the educated elite.

## Chapter 23

### NEO-CONFUCIAN EDUCATION

The basic pattern of schooling in late imperial China, which developed in response to new needs and challenges in the Song period, became codified in the Yuan (fourteenth century) and was confirmed in the early Ming. As will be seen from the curricular materials in this chapter, the core of this system, widely adopted by local academies, reflected the views of the Cheng-Zhu school of the Learning of the Way, which, with some variations and modifications, remained standard down into the nineteenth century. Although many new trends of thought and scholarship would emerge out of this basic educational system, the core curriculum itself remained stable and proved remarkably durable.

In the formative stage of this process, as we have seen, education had become a major issue in the Northern Song, partly stimulated by the expansion of the civil bureaucracy early in the life of the dynasty and by the demand thus created for persons with the requisite learning and skills. In addition, economic development and diversification, as well as rising affluence and increased leisure for the pursuit of cultural activities, created new opportunities outside of government for educated persons. Prime among these occupations was teaching, as economic expansion and technological advances created a wider popular interest in learning and led to an increase in the number of schools and academies. Over time the growth of local, semiprivate academies outpaced that of public schools. With this development, tensions arose, but not so much from rivalry between public and private endeavors as from either political pressures and literati involvement with them or resistance to state control and the distorting effects of the civil service examinations on education.

Schools, especially local academies (*shuyuan*), centered on teachers and collections of books. Hence the spread of printing was bound to have a significant impact on them, as on cultural activity in general. The effect has been concisely stated in reference to Feng Dao's printing of the Confucian Classics in 953:

> The printing of the Classics was one of the forces that restored Confucian literature and teaching to the place in national and popular regard that it had held before the advent of Buddhism, and a classical renaissance followed that can be compared only to the Renaissance that came in Europe after the rediscovery of its classical literature, and that there too was aided by the invention of printing. . . . Another result of the publication of the Classics was an era of large-scale printing, both public and private, that characterized the whole of the Song dynasty.[1]

A development of such epochal proportions confronted the literati with both new opportunities for the dissemination of knowledge and new problems about how this technological change would affect the learning process. Neo-Confucians became much occupied with the nature and significance of book learning. On a wider scale, the question became which of the traditional teachings would take advantage of the new printing technology. Buddhists earlier had been quick to do so,[2] but Chan Buddhism, the dominant form among artists and intellectuals, had declared its independence of the written word (*buli wenzi*) and was divided on the question, as we have seen in Dahui's opposition to the publication of *gongan* (*kōan*) (chapter 17). Two questions emerged: Which of these teachings would want to reach a larger public through the use of this medium? And how would they adapt teaching methods to it? Even among Neo-Confucians there was not one single answer, but most found themselves compelled to deal with such issues as the relative importance of reading, lecturing, and discussion. "How to read books" was much discussed in the Cheng-Zhu school, and Zhu Xi's "reading method" (*dushufa*) was widely disseminated.

These questions were only heightened by the emergence in the Southern Song of a literati class less oriented toward service in the central government and more directed toward involvement with local affairs—less with advancement to the top than with public morality and local leadership at ground level. Thus, underlying Zhu Xi's proposals were at least three major concerns: how to provide for competent leadership on both the higher and the lower levels; how to reconcile the need for both broad humanistic education and the increase in professional and technical specialization in the Song; and how

---

1. Carter and Goodrich, *The Invention of Printing in China*, p. 83.
2. Ibid., pp. 26–28, 38–51, 57–58, 63–65.

to deal with the problems of infrastructure (including costs) in providing expanded education.

In his *Reflections on Things at Hand* (*Jinsi lu*), Zhu cites the views of two of his predecessors on these matters. He notes that Hu Yuan, a model teacher of the Northern Song, allowed in his school for both broad classical learning and specialization in a particular field, such as political economy, military affairs, hydraulic engineering, or mathematics. He also notes the grand plan of Cheng Hao for a universal school system with government support of all teachers and students. Zhu then raises a pair of key questions: how feasible is this in terms of cost and where would the resources come from to support it? Having such doubts about the practicability of this ideal, Zhu apparently believed that on the local level schooling would have to be seasonal—available to all but with most students self-supporting, that is, continuing to be gainfully employed in the fields.[3]

Childhood education was a major interest of Song scholars, and this is reflected in the special attention that Zhu Xi gave to it in his *Elementary Learning* (*Xiaoxue*), which became a major text of the Neo-Confucian educational movement. Since some such training in the home or neighborhood school was presupposed by the more formal studies begun at age eight, we begin the presentation of basic texts here with reference to the *Elementary Learning* and the most famous of all Chinese primers, the *Three Character Classic*. Next comes the centerpiece: the syllabus of Cheng Duanli (1271–1345), including basic texts ancillary to the classic core of that syllabus, followed by excerpts from the *Four Books for Women*, as formulated in the Ming period.

## ZHU XI: PREFACE TO THE *ELEMENTARY LEARNING*

Formal schooling was considered to be preceded by the study of certain primers in the home, among them the *Elementary Learning* (*Xiaoxue*) and the *Three Character Classic* (*Sanzijing*). As we have seen in the case of Xu Heng in the Yuan period, the *Elementary Learning* was a most influential text in the early spread of the Neo-Confucian movement. In effect it expressed the fundamentals of its educational philosophy, starting not only "from the cradle" but even with prenatal influences in the womb.

The contents are divided into three main parts: (1) the "Setting Up of Instruction" (i.e., the basic importance of a defined, structured sequence of education); (2) the prime human/moral relations; and (3) the fundamental, as well as ultimate, value of self-respect ("reverencing the self"), that is, the need to take responsibility for, to define, and to shape one's self in the context of the foregoing environmental factors and relationships. Each section includes quotations from the classics and histories. For this reason, to read it required a fair knowledge of classical Chinese—unlikely to

---

3. Chan, *Reflections on Things at Hand*, p. 265.

be found among small children. Hence it was actually more a book *about* childhood education than it was suitable reading for beginners.

In the elementary learning of ancient times, instruction followed the steps of "sprinkling and sweeping, listening and responding, advancing and retiring [in the presence of others]," as well as the loving of parents, respecting of elders, honoring of teachers, and being intimate with friends. All of these constituted the basis for cultivating the self, regulating the family, ordering the state, and bringing peace to all-under-Heaven. Thus they were sure to be discussed and put into practice during the learner's younger years; in this way knowledge and discipline would grow together for the full development and transformation of the mind-and-heart, so that there would be no danger of conflict between nature and nurture.

Today, although there is no complete text extant, there are many fragments indicative of this [elementary learning] to be found mixed into other accounts. Still, those who encounter these in their reading, believing that there are too many differences in circumstances between past and present, do not put these into practice. They do not realize that in some things there is no difference between past and present and nothing that should ever keep one from practicing them. Therefore we have collected some of these pieces into a book, so that they may be imparted to the young, to serve as a resource for their study and practice, hoping that it might make some small contribution to the improvement of the mores of our times.

(Zhu) Huian, First day, third month, fourteenth year of Chunxi (1187)
[From Uno, *Shōgaku,* 5–6; dB]

## WANG YINGLIN: THE THREE CHARACTER CLASSIC (*SANZI JING*)

This "classic" of childhood education has traditionally been attributed to Wang Yinglin (1223–1296), a distinguished scholar, classicist, encyclopedic historian, and versatile exemplar of the broad learning and interest in popular education characteristic of the Zhu Xi school. Although its authorship has been disputed, the other likely candidates are from the same era, the thirteenth century, in which Neo-Confucians were actively spreading their teachings. The opening line, affirming the goodness of human nature, takes a position not established as "orthodox" before Zhu Xi's time.

To most readers or reciters of this most popular of all primers down into the twentieth century, questions of authorship would have been of little concern. The style is remarkable only for its amazing economy, balance, and simplicity, with three characters to a line, and each two-line couplet a statement unto itself. The regular rhythm, the use of common vocabulary and familiar characters, and the smooth flow of the diction all rendered the text highly readable, easy to recite, and most memorable.

If great popularity and durability were not enough to make this a "classic" of demonstrated appeal, it could also be said that the thirteenth century witnessed frequent loose usage of the term *jing* ("classic") for similar Neo-Confucian reformulations of classic teachings, as we have seen with Zhen Dexiu's *Heart Classic* and *Classic of Governance*.

The content, too, qualifies it as classic: it is basic, easily understood Confucian teaching, yet also neoclassical and Neo-Confucian in that its main points—the goodness of human nature, its perfectibility through individual effort at self-cultivation, the importance of learning and education, the priority of the family and essential human/moral relationships, the need to apply oneself to study, and the lessons of history in illustrating these [too numerous for many to be included here]—all are points reemphasized strongly by the Neo-Confucians.

In 1878 H. A. Giles, a leading British sinologue, published a metrical, rhymed translation, the Victorian style and elegance of which appealed to many scholars as conveying the flavor of the original "classic." Much later, in 1910, Giles published a revised version, more literal and prosaic, saying that the early work "passed muster at the time, but will not do now." In view of his disowning of it, we must forgo, regrettably, the majestic cadences of the metrical translation; we have instead followed the later one, with some adaptations to the style and usage of the present volume.

Human beings at birth / Are naturally good.
Their natures are much the same / [But] nurture takes them far apart.
If there is no teaching / The nature will deteriorate;
The right way in teaching / Is to value concentration.
To feed the body and not the mind / Would be the father's fault;
Instruction without discipline / Is sloth on the teacher's part.
If the child does not learn / This is not as it should be;
If he does not learn while young / When old what will he do?
. . .
Of old, Mencius' mother chose a [good] neighborhood / [For her son to grow up in], avoiding a cemetery and a market place [but near a school] . . .
A jade unwrought serves no useful purpose.
If one does not learn / One cannot know what is right.
For the child to become a man / When he is young [he must]
Attach himself to teachers and friends / Practice rites and ceremonial usage. . . .
To behave as the younger toward the older / Is one of the first things to learn.
First comes filial piety, then fraternal love / Next what is seen and heard;
Learn to count and then to read. . . .
The Three Powers are / Heaven, Earth, and the Human.
The Three Luminaries are / Sun, moon, and stars.
The Three Bonds are / Rightness between prince and minister,
Love between parent and child / Harmony between husband and wife. . . .
One speaks of humaneness and rightness / Ritual decorum, wisdom and
    trustworthiness;

These five constants / Admit of no laxity or confusion. . . .
One speaks of joy and anger / Of pity and of fear.
Of love, of hate, and of desire / These are the seven feelings. . . .
Great-great-grandfather, great-grandfather, and grandfather,
Father and self, self and son, son and grandson
From son and grandson / To great-grandson and great-great-grandson,
These are the nine agnates / Constituting the kinship relations. . . .
In the instruction of the young / There should be explanation and investigation;
Careful instruction in philology / Clarification of paragraphs and sentences.
One who would learn / Must know where to begin;
The *Elementary Learning* now finished, / One proceeds to the Four Books
In the *Analects'* twenty chapters, / The disciples record [Confucius'] fine words.
The *Mencius* / In seven chapters
Explains the Way and virtue; speaks of humaneness and rightness.
The writing of the *Mean* / Was from the pen of Zisi;
Centrality does not lean to one side / Normality is what does not change.
The Composer of the *Great Learning* / Was Master Zeng;
From self-cultivation and regulation of the family / It goes on to ordering the
     state and bringing peace to all-under-Heaven.
With [*The Classic of*] *Filiality* mastered / And the Four Books well digested,
Next the Six Classics / Are there to be read—
The *Odes, Documents, Changes* / The two *Rites* and *Spring and Autumn
     Annals.* . . .
When the classics are understood, / Then read the masters,
Pick out the important points in each / And take note of all the facts.
There are the Five Masters / Xunzi and Yang Xiong
     Wen Zhongzi[4] / And Laozi and Zhuangzi.
The classics and masters well understood, next the several histories should be
     read. . . .

*There follows a long conspectus of Chinese dynastic histories and the Veritable Records.*

Su Laoquan / [Only] at age twenty-seven
First bent his energies / To study the books and records.
Then, already old, / He repented his tardiness.
You little ones / Think of this early in time.
There was Liang Hao who / At the age of eighty-two,
In an interview at the palace / Distinguished himself among scholars.
Though a latecomer / All called him a prodigy.

---

4. Wen Zhongzi was the honorific title of Wang Tong (584–617), and the title was sometimes applied to the *Zhongshuo*, a work attributed to him. He was a classicist and teacher in the Sui period, and some of the statesmen who were his students later became prominent in the early Tang.

Thus you little ones / Should commit yourselves to learning. . . .
Xie Daoyun [famous poetess of the fourth century] / Was able to compose verses
Only a girl / Yet bright and sharp of mind.
You boys / Should take this as a challenge. . . .
If you do not study / How can you become a [true] human being. . . .
Learn while young / When grown up put it to practice
Influence the ruler above / Benefit the people below.
Make a name for yourself / Do honor to father and mother
Shed luster on your forebears / Enrich your posterity.
Men bequeath to their children / Coffers of gold.
What I teach the child / Is just this one book.
Diligence has its reward / Play yields no benefit;
Oh, be on your guard / And put forth all your strength.

[Adapted from Giles, *San-tzu ching*, pp. 7–150; dB]

# THE STANDARD SCHOOL CURRICULUM

Although government schools in late imperial China generally followed the civil service examination requirements, a standard curriculum had already become widely accepted in the semiautonomous "private academies" that had become the main vehicles for the spread of Neo-Confucianism even before the examinations were resumed in 1313–1315. In fact, the movement to establish a definite method and pattern for the conduct of education had already begun in Zhu Xi's school during his lifetime and spread quickly thereafter. It culminated in Cheng Duanli's (1271–1345) widely emulated "Daily Schedule of Study in the Cheng Family School, Graded According to Age," published in 1315, the same year the new examinations came into effect.

The significance of these new developments may be seen in the biography of Cheng Duanli in the *Yuan History*:

At the end of the Song, the Qing-Yuan area [near Ningbo in Eastern Zhejiang], all followed the school of Lu Xiangshan (Lu Jiuyuan) and the Zhu Xi school was not carried on. Cheng Duanli by himself took up with Shi Jing [i.e., Shi Mengqing (1247–1306)] in propagating Zhu Xi's doctrine of "clarifying the substance and applying it in practice" (*mingti shiyong*). Scholars came to his gate in great numbers. He wrote the "Working Schedule for Study of Books" (*Dushu gongcheng*), which the Directorate of Education then had distributed to officials in the local schools to serve as a model for students.[5]

---

5. Song Lian et al., *Yuan shi* 90:4343.

Note here the process of conversion from Lu Jiuyuan's (Xiangshan's) teaching to Zhu Xi's, drawing attention to the combination of principle and practice. A later historian had this to say concerning the significance of this development:

> In the late Song the Qing-Yuan area was all of the Lu school, and the Zhu Xi school was not transmitted there. With Shi Mengqing, however, there came a change. Following Yang Jian [1140–1125, disciple of Lu] most of the school went into Chan and pursued a form of learning without the reading of books. Departing from the source, they drifted apart. Thus, what they transmitted from Master Lu was the very thing that made them lose Master Lu. Having studied Cheng's Daily Reading Schedule, [I find that] there is nothing missing from root to branch and there is a sequential order in its method, from which one may proceed.[6]

Here a connection is suggested between the Lu school's lack of a reading method, reflecting Lu's own depreciation of textual study, the school's getting lost in Chan Buddhism, which "did not depend on the written word," and the contrasting growth of the Zhu Xi school linked to its definite program of study and reading.

In the published "Daily Schedule," prefixed to it were the following texts, which were considered preparatory or ancillary to it:

"Articles of the White Deer Grotto"

"School Code of Masters Cheng and Dong"

Zhen Dexiu's "Instructions for Children"

Zhu Xi's Reading Method in "Essentials of Reading"

Several other selected writings of Zhu Xi on aspects of learning and instruction.


### ZHEN DEXIU: "INSTRUCTIONS FOR CHILDREN"

In many early academies and in later collections of basic educational texts, this short work of Zhen Dexiu (1178–1235) had almost canonical status, along with Zhu Xi's "Articles of the White Deer Grotto Academy" and the "School Code of Masters Cheng and Dong." Zhen's stern rigorism accounts for the highly restrained behavior prescribed here and added an element of stiff formality and constraint to the School of the Way, which became a mark of its distinctive behavior. Other Neo-Confucians reacted against this as contrary to the naturalism and spontaneity that the teaching also encouraged. (In this connection one might also recall that Confucians of the Han period were likewise ridiculed for their stiff formalism and overseriousness.)

1. Learning the rites: To be [truly] human, one must know the Way and its principles and the different ritual prescriptions. At home one must serve parents;

---

6. *Song Yuan xuean* 87:54.

at the academy one must serve his teacher. They are entitled to equal respect and compliance. Follow their instructions. Listen to what they say; do what they prescribe. Do not be lazy, careless, or presumptuous.

2. Learning to sit: Settle yourself and sit straight; control your hands and feet; do not sit cross-legged or lean on anything; do not lie back or lean down.

3. Learning to walk: Hold your arms in and walk slowly; do not swing your arms or jump about.

4. Learning to stand: Fold your hands and straighten your body; do not lean to one side or slouch over.

5. Learning to speak: Be plain and honest in your speech; do not lie or boast; speak softly and circumspectly; do not yell or shout.

6. Learning to bow [in salute]: Lower the head and bend at the waist; speak without gesticulating; do not be flippant or rude.

7. Learning to recite: Look at the characters with undivided attention; read slowly, short passages at a time; clearly distinguish, character by character; do not look at anything else or let your hands fiddle with anything.

8. Learning to write: Grasp the brush with firm intent; the characters must be balanced, regular, and perfectly clear; there must be no carelessness or messiness.

[*Yangzheng yigui* (SBBY) A:13a–14a; RGC]

# WOMEN'S EDUCATION

Education in traditional China was always male-oriented, but women's roles in the households, especially those of the ruling elite and the imperial family, were of such importance that much attention was given to their training for family roles and responsibilities. Moreover, since women played a key role in the early education of the young, it was essential for mothers and their female surrogates (grandmothers, aunts, older sisters) to achieve a mastery of the classical texts and primers that they taught to the young males before the latter went off to school. Often great scholars and historical figures paid tribute, on this account, to the women whose educational influence had been crucial in their lives. Further, in the days when the transmission of classical learning was largely in the custody of particular families, there were spectacular cases of women in those families who ensured the perpetuation of the family tradition when no male was available or capable of carrying on. Thus education for women was strongly abetted by the centrality of the family and requirements of family life.

Women's education achieved a new level of importance with the rise of the Song learning and its Neo-Confucian extensions in the Ming, marked by the great spread of printing, literacy, and schooling. As we have seen, Zhu Xi's simplification and recodification of the classic Confucian canon had much to do with the propagation of the new culture, and it is not surprising that his Four Books (the *Great Learning*, the *Mean*, the *Analects*, and the *Mencius*) became the pretext for a similar compilation in the Ming of the Four Books for Women

(*Nü sishu*). These consisted of Ban Zhao's Han period work *Admonitions for Women* (*Nüjie*); two Tang texts, the *Classic of Filiality for Women* (*Nü xiaojing*) and Song Rozhao's *Analects for Women* (*Nü lunyu*); and the Ming Empress Xu's *Instructions for the Inner Quarters* (*Neixun*). Later, during the Kangxi period in the Qing, a certain Wang Xiang substituted an instructional text written by his mother, *A Handy Record of Rules for Women* (*Nüfan jielu*), for the *Nü xiaojing*, and it is his grouping that has come down to us in most editions.

The female authors of these texts, each in her own distinctive way, sought to advise other women on the Confucian Way for women, the *fudao*, or "wifely way." They accept the general assumption in Confucianism that all humans, male and female, operate in a highly contextual world of hierarchical relationships where behavior is dictated by detailed codes of ritual propriety. In addition, they accept the particular roles assigned to women according to the Confucian sense of their position in the cosmic and human orders. Like the earth, which occupies the inferior position below, women are to be subservient, passive, and yielding, while men are to be dominant, active, and strong like the superior force of Heaven. A woman's sphere of activity is the family, the family of her husband, and her duties in marriage are to assist her husband in serving his family in its broadest terms, that is, to honor the family's dead ancestors with periodic sacrifices, to obey and care for the husband's living parents, and to assist in the procreation of new life to keep the family's bloodline going.

Though the authors of these texts take the subservient but central role of women as their starting point, each has different aspects to emphasize and different ways of approaching the reader. The focus of this section will be on the content of these texts and the variety of articulations of the "wifely Way" found in them. Further work needs to be done on such matters as their historical context and readership. Suffice it to say for now that the texts are written in a fairly literary style with frequent allusions to classical texts, which would indicate that they were meant for women of elite, leisured, cultured families. Eventually, however, much of their content did filter down to a broader audience in such popular rhyming primers as the *Elementary Learning for Women* (*Nü xiaoxue*) and the *Three Character Classic for Girls* (*Nüer sanzijing*).

### BAN ZHAO: ADMONITIONS FOR WOMEN (NÜJIE)

This text was written during the Latter Han dynasty, when Confucianism became established state teaching and attempts were made to bring women into the mainstream of the tradition. One of the first such attempts was by the scholar Liu Xiang (79–8 B.C.E.), who compiled the *Biographies of Virtuous Women* (*Lienü zhuan*).[7] Ban Zhao's work represents a second.

---

7. An English translation of this text is available in Albert O'Hara, *The Position of Women in Early China* (Washington, D.C.: Catholic University Press, 1945).

Ban Zhao (48?–116? C.E.), author of *Admonitions for Women*, was a highly educated woman, publicly recognized for her scholarship and intellect. She was called to court to tutor the women of the imperial family and also was instrumental in completing the dynastic history of the Former Han, which her brother left unfinished upon his death. Indeed, the volume and variety of her writings are impressive and leave no doubt that she served as the mainstay of her family's tradition of learning. In the preface to her *Admonitions for Women*, excerpts of which follow, she explains the circumstances and her motive for writing them. Other excerpts from the text emphasize wifely virtues but also the need for women to be treated with respect according to the rites. Education should not be for males only.

## Preface

This lowly one is ignorant and by nature unclever. I was favored because of my ancestry and, relying on the teachings of governess and instructress, at fourteen I clutched dustbasket and broom [as a young wife] in the Cao household. Now more than forty years have passed . . . and at last I am released [from such duties]. . . .

Yet I am anxious for you, [my daughters] who are about to marry and have not been instructed over the course of time nor heard about proper behavior for wives. I dread that you will lose face [when you are living behind] another's gate and bring shame on our lineage. . . . Whenever I think of you like this, I am fearful and anxious and so have written these "Admonitions for Women" in seven sections. . . . Now that it is done, I urge you to study them. . . .

## Humility

On the third day after the birth of a girl, the ancients observed three customs: [first] for three days to place the baby below the bed; [second] to give her a spindle with which to play; and [third] to fast and announce her birth to her ancestors by an offering. Now to lay the baby below the bed plainly indicated that she was lowly and humble and should regard it as a prime duty to submit to others. To give her a spindle with which to play signified that she should accustom herself to labor and consider it a prime duty to be industrious. To announce her birth before her ancestors clearly meant that she ought to esteem it a prime duty to see to the continuation of the ancestral sacrifices.

These three ancient customs epitomize a woman's ordinary way of life and the teachings of the rites and regulations. Let a woman modestly yield to others; let her respect others; let her put others first, herself last. Should she do something good, let her not mention it; should she do something bad, let her not deny it. Let her bear contempt; let her even endure when others speak or do evil to her. Always let her seem to tremble and to fear. [When a woman follows such maxims as these] then she may be said to humble herself before others.

Let a woman retire late to bed, but rise early to her duties; let her not dread tasks by day or by night. Let her not refuse to perform domestic duties whether easy or difficult. That which must be done, let her finish completely, tidily, and systematically. [When a woman follows such rules as these] then she may be said to be industrious.

Let a woman be composed in demeanor and upright in bearing in the service of her husband. Let her live in purity and quietness [of spirit] and keep watch over herself. Let her not love gossip and silly laughter. Let her cleanse, purify, and arrange in order the wine and the food for the offerings to the ancestors. [Observing such principles as these] is what it means to continue the ancestral rites. . . .

## Husband and Wife

Note in the following passage that though the wife's role is clearly subordinate, the complementarity and mutual responsibility of the conjugal relationship are stressed; if the wife as the embodiment of softness is to be compliant, the husband as the embodiment of strength is obliged to be self-controlled and not beat his wife. Further, the indispensability of one to the other becomes the ground for Ban Zhao's question: Isn't education as necessary for women as for men?

The Way of husband and wife is intimately connected with yin and yang and relates the individual to gods and ancestors. Truly it confirms the great principle of Heaven and Earth and the great rule of human relationships. Therefore the *Rites* honor the interrelation of man and woman; and in the *Odes* the first Ode manifests the principle of marriage. For these reasons the relationship cannot but be an important one.

If a husband be unworthy, then he possesses nothing by which to control his wife. If a wife be unworthy, then she possesses nothing with which to serve her husband. If a husband does not control his wife, then he loses his authority. If a wife does not serve her husband, then right principles [the natural order] are neglected and destroyed. As a matter of fact, in practice these two [the controlling of women by men and the serving of men by women] work out in the same way.

Now examine the gentlemen of the present age. They only know that wives must be controlled and that the husband's authority must be maintained. They therefore teach their boys to read books and [study] histories. But they do not in the least understand how husbands and masters are to be served or how rites and right principles are to be maintained.

Yet only to teach men and not to teach women—is this not ignoring the reciprocal relation between them? According to the *Rites*, book learning begins at the age of eight, and at the age of fifteen one goes off to school. Why, however, should this principle not apply to girls as well as boys?

## Respect and Compliance

As yin and yang are not of the same nature, so man and woman differ in behavior. The virtue of yang is firmness; yin is manifested in yielding. Man is honored for strength; a woman is beautiful on account of her gentleness. Hence there arose the common saying, "A man born as a wolf may, it is feared, become a woman; a woman born as a mouse may, it is feared, become a tigress."

Now for self-cultivation there is nothing like respectfulness. To avert harshness there is nothing like compliance. Consequently it can be said that the Way of respect and compliance is for women the most important element in ritual decorum. . . .

[If a wife] does not restrain her contempt for her husband, then it will be followed by scolding and shouting [from him]. [If a husband] does not restrain his anger, then there is certain to be beating [of the wife]. The correct relationship between husband and wife is based upon harmony and intimacy, and [conjugal] love is grounded in proper union. If it comes to blows, how can the proper relationship be preserved? If sharp words are spoken, how can [conjugal] love exist? If love and proper relationship are both destroyed, then husband and wife are parted.

## Womanly Behavior

In womanly behavior there are four things [to be considered]: womanly virtue, womanly speech, womanly appearance, and womanly work. . . .

To guard carefully her chastity, to control circumspectly her behavior, in every motion to exhibit modesty, and to model each act on the best usage: this may be called womanly virtue.

To choose her words with care, to avoid vulgar language, to speak at appropriate times, and not to be offensive to others may be called womanly speech.

To wash and scrub dirt and grime, to keep clothes and ornaments fresh and clean, to wash the head and bathe the body regularly, and to keep the person free from disgraceful filth may be called womanly appearance.

With wholehearted devotion to sew and weave, not to love gossip and silly laughter, in cleanliness and order [to prepare] the wine and food for serving guests may be called womanly work.

[*Hou Hanshu*, 84, Chunghua ed., 2786–2789;
rev. from Swann, *Pan Chao*, pp. 82–86]

*Note that here, even though Ban Zhao preaches submission and dedication to her husband, the husband at least counts. Later, serving the husband himself becomes*

subordinate to caring for his parents. Also, for all the talk about submission to the husband, Ban Zhao has a greater sense of the complementary nature of marriage than later
writers in this genre, who tend to put greater stress on the hierarchical nature of the
relationship.

This text later became the prototype of other instructional texts for women, and Ban
Zhao became canonized as the archetypal female wisdom figure, so much so that the
authors of the two texts we examine next adopt Ban Zhao's voice rather than their own
as the principal speaker.

## MADAM CHENG: *CLASSIC OF FILIALITY FOR WOMEN* (*NÜ XIAOJING*)

In the Tang period the two most popular Confucian texts were the *Analects* and the
*Classic of Filiality* (*Xiaojing*); thus it is not surprising that the two female authors of
instructional texts for women written during this period would draw on these titles
for their works, the *Analects for Women* and the *Classic of Filiality for Women*.

The first of these was written by the wife of a Tang official, Chen Miao, whose own
family name was Cheng. She presented it to her niece upon her impending marriage
to a Tang prince.

The text opens with Ban Zhao sitting at leisure, attended by a group of women.
She asks them if they have heard about the greatness of filiality, especially as
exemplified by the two wives of Shun, and how its practice by women consists
of mastering the *fudao*, or "wifely way." The women confess their ignorance and
beg her to instruct them in these matters. In the instructions that follow, the most
striking feature is the extraordinary moral influence and leadership role attributed
to women in the domestic sphere, particularly with respect to their husbands.
Service to a husband goes beyond obedience and deference to him; it includes
responsibility for his moral character and the obligation of firm remonstrance lest
he go wrong—points already made in the *Classic of Filiality* and the formulas of
the *Three Mainstays*.

Her ladyship [Ban Zhao] said, "By studying [the classics] with thoroughness,
questioning with deep penetration, and 'hearing much and casting aside the
doubtful parts,'[8] one can serve as a standard for others. If you are willing to
heed such teachings and incorporate them into your behavior, I will set them
forth for you. Now filiality embraces Heaven and Earth and enriches all human
relationships. It moves ghosts and spirits and affects birds and animals. 'Show
respect according to the dictates of propriety';[9] 'think three times and then act.'[10]

---

8. *Analects* 2:18.
9. *Analects* 1:13.
10. *Analects* 5:19.

Do not relax your efforts, do not harm your goodness. Be affable and gentle, modest and deferential, humane and understanding, filial and affectionate. Then you will have perfectly embodied correct moral behavior and be without blame. . . ." [15a–b]

*The next several sections, deleted here, discuss the "wifely Way" for the empress, the wives of high officials, the wives of feudal lords, and those of common people—paralleling the original text of the* Classic of Filiality. *Also, in parallel to the latter, each set of precepts ends with a quotation from the* Odes, Record of Rites, *or some other classic—also not reproduced here.*

## Serving One's Parents-in-Law

In serving her parents-in-law, a woman gives the same respect [to her father-in-law that] she has shown her own father and the same love [to her mother-in-law that] she has shown her own mother. She keeps to this in accord with rightness and holds to it in accord with the rites. At cock-crow, she washes and dresses to start the morning off early. She makes sure her parents-in-law are cool in summer and warm in winter. She settles them in at night and checks on them first thing in the morning.[11] She uses "reverence to straighten the inner life and rightness to square the outer."[12] She establishes an order for the proper household rituals and then carries them out. . . . [17a]

## The Three Powers

Referring to men and women as counterparts of and co-respondents to Heaven and Earth.

Guard against idleness, hold fast to ritual decorum, and you will be able to make a successful marriage. Then, by your guiding of him with respect and love, your gentleman [husband] will not forget his sense of filiality to his parents. By your presenting him with a model of virtuous conduct, he will improve his behavior. By your guiding of him with a sense of modesty and deference, he will refrain from being contentious. By your leading him on with rites and music, he will become pleasant and easy to get along with. By your demonstrating the difference between good and evil, he will understand what conduct is not allowable. . . . [17a–b]

---

11. "Summary of the Rules of Propriety" ("Quli"), *Record of Rites* A:2; Legge, *Li ki,* 1:67.
12. *Classic of Changes,* hexagram 2, *kun.*

## Governing Through Filiality

Her ladyship said, "The virtuous women of ancient times used filiality to govern the nine degrees of familial relations. They never dared demean the younger wives; how much more solicitous were they about their sisters-in-law! Therefore, they won the hearts of the whole family, which made it possible for parents-in-law to be well served. In managing the household, they dared not mistreat the chickens and dogs; how much more careful were they about the servants! Therefore, they were able to please all, high and low, which made it possible for husbands to be better served. . . ." [17b–18a]

## Chaste Behavior

Her ladyship said, "What a woman must take seriously is her person, for it is the source of all her actions. One who is good at cultivating her person[13] will correct her thoughts, keep a careful watch over her motives, hold firmly to moral standards, and not allow one iota of selfishness to entangle her. She commits herself to correctness and composure, not erring even a little bit. She does not allow considerations of life and death to change her resolve, nor let the prospects of living in affluence or poverty affect her commitment to chastity. . . ."

## The Duty of Remonstrance

Note here how the duty of remonstrance takes precedence over obedience, as it does for the minister vis-à-vis the ruler.

The women said, ". . . We dare to ask whether if we follow all our husbands' commands, we could be called virtuous?"

Her ladyship answered, "What kind of talk is that! What kind of talk is that! Long ago, King Xuan of Zhou was late rising to attend his court, so his wife threw down her jewels in the public tribunal [to take the blame]. King Xuan because of this started getting up early again. Emperor Cheng of the Han ordered his concubine to ride out with him, but she refused, saying, 'I have heard that in the Three Dynasties, wise rulers took only their worthy officials by their side. I never heard of them taking their concubines.' Because of her, Emperor Cheng changed his manner. . . .

From these cases, we can see that 'if the Son of Heaven has ministers to advise him, even if he is neglectful of the Way, he won't lose his empire. If a

---

13. *Xiushen*, i.e., self-cultivation.

lord has remonstrating officials, then even if he is neglectful of the Way, he won't lose his state. If a great officer has someone to remonstrate with him, then even if he is neglectful of the Way, he won't lose his home domain. If a scholar has a remonstrating friend, then he can't be parted from his good name. If a father has a remonstrating son, then he won't fall prey to what is against moral standards.'[14] If a husband has a remonstrating wife, then he won't fall into evil ways. Therefore, if a husband transgresses against the Way, you must correct him. How could it be that to obey your husband in everything would make you a virtuous person?"

[From *Nü xiaojing, xia,* 15a–21b; TK]

### SONG RUOZHAO: *ANALECTS FOR WOMEN*

Song Ruozhao, author of the *Analects for Women,* was the second of five daughters of a high Tang official, Song Fen. According to her biography in the *Tang History,* her elder sister, Ruohua, actually wrote the text, but Ruozhao was the one who propagated it. She made it clear that she wished not to marry but rather to dedicate her life to the example of Ban Zhao in the work of instructing women. After an audience with the Emperor Dezong in the late eighth century, she was made a female scholar at court, assigned to instruct the royal princesses.

The importance of this text lies in its specificity of detail in spelling out the basic Confucian way of wifely perfection for those women needing more explicit guidance. By virtue of its practical approach, the *Analects for Women* was widely used and, along with Ban Zhao's *Admonitions for Women,* remained the most popular and influential instructional text for women in premodern times.

## Establishing Oneself as a Person

To be a woman, you must first learn how to establish yourself as a person. The way to do this is simply by working hard to establish one's purity and chastity. By purity, one keeps one's self undefiled; by chastity, one preserves one's honor.

When walking, don't turn your head; when talking, don't open your mouth wide; when sitting, don't move your knees; when standing, don't rustle your skirts; when happy, don't exult with loud laughter; when angry, don't raise your voice. The inner and outer quarters are each distinct; the sexes should be segregated. Don't peer over the outer wall or go beyond the outer courtyard. If you have to go outside, cover your face; if you peep outside, conceal yourself as much as possible. Do not

---

14. The preceding passage is quoted, though not verbatim, from the *Classic of Filiality* (*Xiaojing*). See chap. 10.

be on familiar terms with men outside the family; have nothing to do with women of bad character. Establish your proper self so as to become a [true] human being.

## Learning How to Work

To be a woman one must learn the details of women's work. Learn how to weave with hemp and ramie; don't mix fine and rough fibers. Don't run the shuttle of the loom so quickly that you make a mess. When you see the silkworms spinning their cocoons, you must attend to them day and night, picking mulberry leaves to feed them. . . . Learn how to cut out shoes and make socks. Learn how to cut fabric and sew it into garments. Learn how to embroider, mend, and darn. . . .

Do not learn the ways of lazy women who from an early age are silly and shiftless and who have a distaste for women's work. They don't plan ahead in making clothes to fit the needs of each season and hardly ever pick up a needle to sew. . . . Married, they bring shame upon their new family, who go around in ill-fitted, patched, and ragged clothing, so that meeting others they are pointed to as the laughingstock of the neighborhood. . . .

## Ritual Decorum: Learning Proper Etiquette

To be a woman one must learn the rules of ritual decorum. When you expect a female guest, carefully clean and arrange the furniture and tea implements. When she arrives, take time to adjust your clothing, and then, with light steps and your hands drawn up in your sleeves, walk slowly to the door and with lowered voice, invite her in. Ask after her health and how her family is doing. Be attentive to what she says. After chatting in a leisurely way, serve the tea. When she leaves, send her off in a proper manner. . . .

If you are invited to someone's house, understand your female duties and help with the preparation of the tea. After having talked for a time, rise to leave. Don't overstay your welcome. If your hostess presses you to stay longer to share a meal, conduct yourself with propriety. Don't drink so much that your face turns red and you get sloppy in the handling of your chopsticks. Take your leave before all the food is gone and before you forget your manners. . . .

## Rising Early [to Begin Household Work]

To be a woman one must learn to make it a regular practice, at the fifth watch when the cock crows, to rise and dress. After cleaning your face and teeth, fix your hair and makeup simply. Then go to the kitchen, light the fire, and start the morning meal. Scrub the pots and wash the pans; boil the tea water and cook the gruel. Plan your meals according to the resources of the family and the seasons of the year, making sure that they are fragrant and tasty, served in the appropriate dishes and in the proper manner at the table. If you start early, there is nothing you can't get done in a day!

Do not learn the ways of those lazy women who are thoughtless and do not plan ahead. The sun is already high in the sky before they manage to get themselves out of bed. Then they stagger to the kitchen, disheveled and unwashed, and throw a meal together, long past the hour. What is more, they are overly fond of eating and compete to get the tastiest morsels at each meal. If there is not enough of the best to go around, they steal some to eat later on the sly. Their inconsiderate manners are displayed to all their neighbors, to the humiliation of their parents-in-law. Talked about by everyone, how can they not be overcome with shame!

## Serving One's Parents-in-Law

Your father-in-law and mother-in-law are the heads of your husband's family. . . . You must care for them as your own father and mother. Respectfully serve your father-in-law. Do not look at him directly [when he speaks to you], do not follow him around, and do not engage him in conversation. If he has an order for you, listen and obey.

When your mother-in-law is sitting, you should stand. When she gives an order, you should carry it out right away. Rise early in the morning and open up the household, but don't make any noise that would disturb your mother-in-law's sleep. Sweep and mop the floors, wash and rinse the clothes. When your mother-in-law wakes up, present her with her toiletry articles, withdraw while she bathes until she beckons you. Greet her and then withdraw. Prepare tea and broth; set out spoons and chopsticks. As long known, the aged have poor teeth, so you should be especially careful in the preparation of food for them, so that they might enjoy their old age with all sorts of delicacies, cooked in a manner that allows them to be easily chewed and swallowed. At night before retiring, check to see if they are comfortably settled for the night. Bid them good night and then go to bed. . . .

## Serving a Husband

Women leave their families to marry, and the husband is the master of the household [they marry into]. . . . The husband is to be firm, the wife soft; conjugal affections follow from this. While at home, the two of you should treat each other with the formality and reserve of a guest. Listen carefully to and obey whatever your husband tells you. If he does something wrong, gently correct him. Don't be like those women who not only do not correct their husbands but actually lead them into indecent ways. . . . Don't imitate those shrewish wives who love to clash head on with their husbands all the time. Take care of your husband's clothing so that he is never cold in winter, and of his meals so that he never gets thin and sickly from not being fed enough. As a couple, you and your husband share the bitter and the sweet, poverty and riches. In life you share the same bed; in death the same grave. . . .

## Instructing Sons and Daughters

Most all families have sons and daughters. As they grow and develop, there should be a definite sequence and order in their education. But the authority/ responsibility to instruct them rests solely with the mother. When the sons go out to school, they seek instruction from a teacher who teaches them proper [ritual] form and etiquette, how to chant poetry, how to write essays. . . .

Daughters remain behind in the women's quarters and should not be allowed to go out very often. . . . Teach them sewing, cooking, and etiquette. . . . Don't allow them to be indulged, lest they throw tantrums to get their own way; don't allow them to defy authority, lest they become rude and haughty; don't allow them to sing songs, lest they become dissolute; and don't allow them to go on outings, lest some scandal spoil their good names.

Worthy of derision are those who don't take charge of their responsibility [in this area]. The sons of such women remain illiterate, they poke fun at their elders, they get into fights and drink too much, and they become addicted to singing and dancing. . . . The daughters of such women know nothing about ritual decorum, speak in an overbearing manner, can't distinguish between the honorable and the mean, and don't know how to serve or sew. They bring shame on their honorable relatives and disgrace on their father and mother. Mothers who fail to raise their children correctly are as if they had raised pigs and rats!

## Managing the Household

A woman who manages the household should be thrifty and diligent. If she is diligent, the household thrives; if lazy, it declines. If she is thrifty, the household becomes enriched; if extravagant, it becomes impoverished. . . . If your husband has money and rice, store and conserve them. If he has wine or foodstuffs, save and keep them for the use of guests when they come; do not take any to indulge your own desires. Great wealth is a matter of fate and fortune; a little wealth comes from persistent thrift. . . . Thus a couple may be blessed with riches and enjoy life.

## Entertaining Guests

Most families have guests. You should have hot water and clean bottles, and keep the table clean and neat, ready for guests. When a guest arrives, serve him tea and then retire to the rear of the hall and await your husband's orders about the meal. . . .

Don't learn the ways of the lazy woman who doesn't attend to household matters anyway, so that when a guest arrives, the place is in a mess and she is unprepared to offer him tea right away. She is so flustered that she loses her head. If her husband asks the guest to stay for a meal, she is annoyed and loses her temper. She has chopsticks but no soup spoons, soy sauce but no vinegar. She scolds and slaps the servants around, to her husband's great chagrin and the guest's embarrassment.

[From *Nü sishu, Nü lunyu* 2:1a–16b; TK]

### EMPRESS XU: *INSTRUCTIONS FOR THE INNER QUARTERS* (*NEIXUN*)

The title of this work is suggestive of the carefully defined and limited sphere of women's allowable activity. The author, however, was no ordinary woman. She was the Empress Xu, wife of the third Ming emperor, Chengzu (or Yongle, r. 1402–1424), and daughter of the famous general Xu Da, who served under the founder of the dynasty. A redoubtable figure in her own right, she is described in the dynastic annals as a strong character, and as such was accorded a place of her own in the *Dictionary of Ming Biography*, which called her "a strong-willed and colorful person, with some of her father's spirit."[15]

At a time when Neo-Confucian teachings were giving a vital impetus to education, Empress Xu became dissatisfied with the conventional literature available for the cultivation of women and aimed to produce a guide of her own, based on the personal instruction she had received from her mother-in-law, the Empress Ma,[16] wife of the dynasty's founder, Ming Taizu. In contrast to the stereotype of the arbitrary and abusive mother-in-law in China, Empress Ma was much admired by the later Empress Xu as a firm but humane and sympathetic mentor.

As a peasant woman married early to Taizu before his rise to power, the future Empress Ma was, like him, largely self-educated and eventually quite well read (not an altogether uncommon thing in traditional China, for many women did overcome the handicap imposed by a lack of formal schooling, just as Ming Taizu himself did). Moreover, as an empress, with several daughters-in-law under her charge, she conducted regular study groups on the classics for the women of the palace.

---

15. Biography by Chou Tao-chi and Ray Huang, in Goodrich and Fang, eds., *Dictionary of Ming Biography*, pp. 566–569.

16. *Mingshi* 128:3784–3788; biography by Chou Tao-chi, in ibid., pp. 1023–1026; and biography of Hsü Ta (Xu Da) by Edward L. Farmer, in ibid., p. 606.

Taizu himself, as we have seen, was well known for his despotic rule, his hot temper, his violence and cruelty, his bloody purges, and his suspiciousness and vindictiveness toward any who opposed him or whom he suspected of treason. Yet there are numerous stories about how Empress Ma remonstrated with and restrained him, saving the lives of many who were unjustly accused. Such was the case when Taizu turned against one of his foremost Neo-Confucian advisers, Song Lian (1310–1381),[17] and ordered his execution. Empress Ma defended Song and got his sentence reduced to exile. In another significant case, when Taizu complained about Empress Ma's interference in state affairs, she refused to back off, saying that just as he had responsibilities as Father of the country, so was she as its Mother entitled to be concerned about the welfare of her children. Thus she turned the family/state analogy into one that set paternal and maternal care nearly on a par, with the latter a definite counterweight to the former. Empress Ma died a natural death after many others in the emperor's service had suffered unnatural ones, and she was said to have been deeply mourned by Taizu, who did not replace her as empress (and earlier defended her strongly for not having bound feet).

Empress Ma's view of her larger social responsibilities seems to have taken deep root in the consciousness of Empress Xu and pervades virtually all of the *Instructions for the Inner Quarters*, at each successive stage of which the "inner" or restricted conception of a woman's role gives way to a more expansive one. For anyone with a sensitivity to its Neo-Confucian meanings, the *Neixun* may be recognized as far from a rehash of conventional views covering the place of women in the home. Indeed, the very structure and thematic development of the work are reminiscent of the Neo-Confucian genre of instruction to rulers and noble men as found in Zhu Xi's memorials and lectures to the emperor, his *Reflections on Things at Hand, Elementary Learning,* and *Commentary on the Great Learning* and Zhen Dexiu's lectures from the Classics Mat, as well as the latter's monumental *Extended Meaning of the Great Learning*.

The opening portion deals with women's self-cultivation. Yet instead of leading off with a gendered presentation of the strictly defined role of the woman (and most often of the wife in the home), the previous basis established here for any such role-playing or modeling is the making of a human self and the shaping of a human life, based on the Neo-Confucian principle of the shared moral nature in all human beings: "If you do not cultivate your own moral character, then your chances of managing your own family will be slim, how much less of your bringing order into the world" (3:7a). From this, the work goes on to many specific prescriptions on how this cultivation is to be accomplished in the woman's case, paralleling what is set forth for men in Zhu's *Elementary Learning*. Yet the thought that a woman should undertake this with the ultimate goal of "bringing order into the world" suggests how far beyond the confines of the home goes the aspiration for this Neo-Confucian education.

---

17. *Mingshi* 128:3784–3788; biography by F. W. Mote, in ibid., pp. 1225–1231.

Subsequent chapters cite historical examples of women who played major roles in assisting founders of dynasties and great rulers in governing well (much as Fan Ziyu's *Learning of the Emperors* credits great scholar-mentors in similar roles). The standout case is, of course, Empress Ma. With such models to emulate, it is not too much, says Empress Xu, for women to aspire even to sagehood. Contrary to a widespread view that only men could achieve this goal, Empress Xu argued that all humans, female as well as male, have the same innate Heavenly endowment of a moral nature, which represents the potential for sagehood. It is a gift not just to certain specially favored persons or just to men, but something anyone could hope to achieve through learning—echoing the assertion of Zhou Dunyi in his *Tongshu*, and prominently quoted in Zhu Xi's *Reflections on Things at Hand*, that sagehood can be learned and should be striven for by all.

Altogether, this is a thoroughly Neo-Confucian work. Taking full advantage of literary genres and concepts developed by Song Neo-Confucians and of their doctrines as synthesized by Zhu Xi, it argues the case for women's education and their participation in the *Great Learning*'s social program, which proceeds from self-cultivation to the managing of the family, the ordering of the state, and the bringing of peace to the world. This is not at all to say that, for the Empresses Ma and Xu, the way for women is the same as for men, but that women could and should play a major active role in pursuing Neo-Confucian goals and thereby achieving their own self-fulfillment in some approximation of sagehood.

Finally, it should be emphasized that this woman's "classic" illustrates for us some of the ironies and ambiguities of the Confucian social involvement in general. On the one hand, as one of the Four Books for Women, it has a claim to some of the same canonical status as Zhu Xi's Four Books, and one could take it—in the absence of any serious rivals—as probably the most authoritative statement of a Neo-Confucian education program for women. We know, too, that it had considerable currency in Korea and Japan as well. On the other hand, we recognize it as an ideal prescription that could not at all be taken as a reliable description of conduct prevailing among women. That is not the function of classics and canons; they do not imitate life so much as propose models to emulate; thus there is always a discrepancy or tension between the two.

## Preface

As a child, I was well instructed by my parents, reciting such classics as the *Classic of Odes* and the *Classic of Documents* and carrying out the details of women's work. On account of the accumulated goodness and blessings of our ancestors, I by chance was chosen to enter the imperial harem. Morning and night, I served at court. The Empress Ma instructed all the wives of her sons, especially in the area of proper decorum and ritual. I respectfully accepted and tried to carry out her orders. Every day I received instructions from her, respectfully obeyed them, not daring to transgress even one of her rules.

I have respectfully served the present [Yongle] Emperor for thirty-some years. In doing so, I have tried to carry out completely my predecessor's [Empress Ma's] wishes by putting into practice her teachings on governance of the inner palace. . . .

I often read accounts in the histories, searching for virtuous wives and chaste women of the past. Although they are all praised for the greatness of their [innate] moral nature, still none among them has succeeded without having had some instruction. With the ancients, education had to have some method to it. [According to the *Record of Rites*,] boys at the age of eight entered elementary school and girls at ten received instruction from a governess. But no textbooks for elementary learning were passed down until Zhu Xi compiled and edited a text for this level [the *Elementary Learning*]. It is only in the area of elementary education for girls that there still remains no comprehensive text. . . .

There has been a recent increase in publications of female instructions but . . . better than any of these are the words of our illustrious Empress Ma's instructions, which stand above anything written before and which are well worth being passed down to future generations. I listened to them avidly and stored them in my heart. . . .

For a person to master sagehood, nothing is more crucial than nourishing one's moral nature so that one is able to cultivate one's self. Therefore I begin the text with "The Moral Nature" followed by "Cultivation of the Self." . . .

## The Moral Nature

Being upright and modest, reserved and quiet, correct and dignified, sincere and honest: these constitute the moral nature of a woman. Being filial and respectful, humane and perspicacious, loving and warm, meek and gentle: these represent the complete development of the moral nature. The moral nature being innate in our endowment, it becomes transformed and fulfilled through practice. It is not something that comes from the outside but is actually rooted in our very selves.

Of old, upright women ordered their feelings and nature based on moral principle (*li*), kept control over the workings of their mind, and honored the Way and its virtue. Therefore they were able to complement their gentlemen [husbands] in fulfilling the teachings of the Way. This is the reason they took humaneness to be their abode, rightness as their path of action, wisdom as their guide, trustworthiness as their defense, and ritual decorum as the embodiment of it. . . .

The accumulation of small faults will mount up to great harm to one's virtue. Therefore a great house will topple over if the foundation is not solid. One's moral nature will have deficiencies if the self is not restrained.

Beautiful jade with no flaws can be made into a precious jewel. An upright woman of pure character can be made the wife of a great family. If you constantly examine your actions to see if they are correct, you can be a model mother. If you are hardworking and frugal without a trace of jealousy, you are fit to be an exemplar for the women's quarters. . . .

## Cultivation of the Self

. . . In the Way of the ancients, if the eye looks at evil sights, then one becomes confused inside; if the ear listens to lewd music, one disturbs one's innate virtue; if the mouth utters boastful talk, arrogance takes over the mind. These are all dangers to the self. Therefore, the wife, while at rest, will certainly be correct so as to guard against harm; and when active in household affairs, will show no partialities so that she can fulfill her moral character.

. . . Now if the self is not cultivated, then virtue will not be established. If one's virtue is not established, rarely can one be an influence for good in the family—how much less in the wider world. Therefore the wife is one who follows her husband. The way of husband and wife is the principle of the strong and the weak. In the past, the reason why enlightened monarchs were careful about establishing marriage was that they valued the way of procreation and perpetuation. The prosperity or decline of the family, the rise and fall of the state are intimately linked to this. . . .

## Diligence and Hard Work

Laziness and licentiousness are disasters to the self, while diligence and hard work without any letup are morally beneficial to the self. Therefore, farmers labor hard at their crops, scholars at their studies, and women at their work. . . .

The *Classic of Odes* says, "A woman shall have nothing to do with public affairs [yet] she discards her silkworms and weaving [for this]."[18] This is a defect that comes from laziness. For persons in low and mean positions, it is easy not to be lazy; it is persons of wealth, in high positions, who find it hard not to be lazy. You must exert yourself with respect to this difficulty. Do not be remiss in your ease.

## Frugality

. . . The *Zuozhuan* says, "Frugality is the precious jewel of the sage." It also says, "Frugality is the fullness of virtue. Extravagance is the greatest of evils."[19]

---

18. Ode 264, reading *she* (to discard) for *xiu* (to abide).
19. *Zuozhuan*, Duke Zhuang 24; Legge, *The Chinese Classics*, 5:107.

Each strand of silk comes from the labor of some working woman; each grain of rice comes from the hard work of a farmer. The efforts that went into the final product were not made easily. To use these without some sense of limits is to do violence to what comes from Heaven—there is no greater fault. . . . Now those above lead those below, the inner [quarters of the palace are] a gauge for the outer [world of other women]. Therefore, the empress must value frugality in order to lead the rest of the palace women. The wives of princes all the way down to those of scholars and commoners must honor the value of frugality in running their households. If this happens, then not one person will go cold or starve to death; rites and rightness will flourish; and the change [for the good] in people's behavior will merit being recorded [for posterity].

## Returning to the Good

Now the [principal] faults of women are none other than laziness, jealousy, and licentiousness. Laziness leads to arrogance and then filial respect vanishes. Jealousy leads to harsh treatment of others, whereupon cruelty and avarice take over. Licentiousness leads to self-indulgence and then one's chastity is ruined. These three are all impediments to one's virtue and injurious to the self. Even if you have only one of these, you should get rid of it as you would a grub and distance yourself from it as you would from hornets and wasps. If hornets and wasps are not kept at a distance, they will sting you; if grubs are not gotten rid of, they will eat your grain. If you don't correct your faults, they will compromise your virtue.

## Looking Up to Virtuous Exemplars [of the Past]

Those who aspire to be sages flourish; those who walk in evil ways perish. . . . If, in taking the ancients as models and trying to emulate them, you equal them, then you can be a sage. Short of this, you can be a worthy; and if you are not this [successful], you still will not have failed to follow what is good.

Pearls and jade are not what is precious [to a woman]; to emulate sageliness is. If your moral character is without any deficiency, you can order well your household. The Ode says, "The high mountain is to be looked up to. The great road is easy to be traveled on."[20] This is what I mean.

[From *Nü sishu, Neixun* 3:1a–19b; TK]

---

20. Ode 218.

*Chapter 24*

SELF AND SOCIETY IN THE MING

With Zhu Xi's curriculum established in most Ming schools and academies (albeit in much-abridged form), as well as in the civil service examination system, it is understandable why the editors of the Complete Library of the Four Treasuries should later have observed that the intellectual and moral formation of educated persons in the Ming was all based on Zhu Xi's version of the Four Books and also why scholarship in the Ming mostly developed along lines already set by Zhu Xi. Much of it was cast in the language, concepts, and structure of the *Great Learning* and Zhu's Commentary: it remained largely within the terms of Zhu Xi's discourse.

Although the pattern of schooling and examination was well established, this by no means prevented the further development of thought by individual teachers and scholars, some of whom maintained their independence of the state by refusing to serve in office, either out of dissatisfaction with the routinized learning of the examination system or out of unwillingness to be associated with the despotic actions of Ming rulers like Taizu and Chengzu. Thus, for all the limiting effects of Ming autocracy and bureaucracy, and contrary to the dominant early twentieth-century Western view (much influenced by Hegel and Marx) that late imperial China was stagnant and wholly unprogressive, there was actually much new intellectual and cultural activity in the Ming, stimulated by economic growth, social change, and the spread of education and literacy, encouraged by both Zhu Xi's works and the populist views of Ming Taizu, who, as we have seen, could be egalitarian and autocratic at once.

The main lines of new thought and scholarship pursued directions already implicit in Zhu Xi's broad view of "solid learning" (*shixue*)—that is, it combined both intense moral/spiritual cultivation and broad intellectual inquiry, ritual practice as well as public service, with the latter understood as service of the "common good" (*gong*) on several levels of society and in education, as well as in office. In this chapter it is not possible to represent all of these diverse trends adequately or to deal with all the tensions that arose among them. With the great expansion of scholarship, however, and the increasing demands for technical specialization (even in the specialized art of writing examination essays!), a prime problem arose for those who still held to the Neo-Confucian ideal of learning for one's self: how could one be heavily engaged with such a complex world and still achieve the self-integration of the sage?

## WANG YANGMING

### WANG YANGMING'S NEW LEARNING OF THE MIND-AND-HEART

There can be little doubt that among the new trends in the Ming it was the teachings and personal example of Wang Yangming that were to have the most explosive effect. His views on the mind-and-heart—quickly recognized as strikingly new—dynamized the conception of the self, sagehood, and the individual as nothing had before and came to dominate the intellectual scene during the sixteenth century almost as if they represented a new orthodoxy.

Wang Yangming himself thought of these new formulations as fully orthodox because he understood his own mission in the world against the background of Zhu Xi's concept of the repossession of the Way (*daotong*) and the deep sense of personal responsibility for the Way that was characteristic of the great man.

> Whenever I think of people's degeneration and difficulties I pity them and have a pain in my heart. I overlook my own unworthiness and wish to save them by this teaching. And I do not know the limits of my ability. When people see me trying to do this, they join one another in ridiculing, insulting, and cursing me, regarding me as insane. . . . Of course, there are cases when people see their fathers, sons, or brothers falling into a deep abyss and getting drowned. They cry, crawl, go naked and barefooted, stumble, and fall. They hang on to dangerous cliffs and go down to save them. Some gentlemen who see them behave like this . . . consider them insane because they cry, stumble, and fall as they do. Now to stand aside and make no attempt to save the drowning, while mocking those who do, is possible only for strangers who have no natural feelings of kinship, but even then they will be considered to have no sense of pity

and to be no longer human beings. In the case of a father, son, or brother, because of love he will surely feel an ache in his head and a pain in his heart, run desperately until he has lost his breath, and crawl to save them. He will even risk drowning himself. How much less will he worry about whether people believe him or not?[1]

The key, however, to Wang's near revolution in the sage learning that came down to him through the Cheng-Zhu school was his reformulation of the Learning of the Mind-and-Heart, especially as represented by the message and method of the mind-and-heart (*xinfa*), as shown in the following excerpts.

## MEMOIR ON THE RECONSTRUCTION OF SHANYIN PREFECTURAL SCHOOL

Notice here how Yangming takes the Cheng-Zhu "method of the mind-and-heart" and concentrates on the original unity of the mind with Heaven-and-Earth and all things, as expressed in the spontaneous affective response to things and affairs.

The sages' learning is the "Learning of the Mind-and-Heart." It is learning that seeks fully to employ the mind-and-heart. What Yao, Shun, and Yu passed on from one to the other was, "The human mind is precarious; the mind of the Way is subtle. Be discriminating, be one [with the mind of the Way]. Hold fast the Mean." The "mind of the Way" refers to what [in the *Mean*] "follows the nature. . . ." It is unmixed with the human, has no sound or smell, and is manifested with the utmost subtlety. It is the source of sincerity. The mind of man is mixed with the human and thus becomes prone to err. It has the potential for unnaturalness and insincerity. When one sees an infant about to fall into a well and feels a compassionate impulse [to rescue it], that is [an instance of] the Way guiding human nature. If that impulse becomes confused by thought of gaining the approbation of parents or a reputation in the community, that is the [self-regarding] human mind. . . .

To be unified is to be one with the mind of the Way; to be discriminating is to be concerned lest the mind of the Way should lose that oneness and possibly become separated from the human mind. Always to be centered on the Mean and to be unceasingly one with the mind of the Way is to "hold fast the Mean." If it is one with the mind of the Way, the mind will always be kept on center, and in its expressed state there will be no disharmony. Thus, following the mind of the Way, its expression in a parent-child relationship is always affectionate; as expressed in the ruler-minister relationship it is always right; as expressed in the relationship of husband-wife, senior-junior, friend and friend,

---

1. Adapted from Chan, *Instructions*, pp. 168–169.

it is always respectful of gender differences, always respectful of precedence, always respectful of fidelity to friends. . . .

Shun had Xie as minister of education see to instruction in these moral relationships and teach people the Universal Way.[2] At that time people were all noble men and could all be entrusted with the responsibilities of noble rank. There was no instruction but this instruction, and no learning but this learning. With the passing of the sages, however, the learning of the mind-and-heart became obscured, human conduct unnaturally strove for fame and profit; those who pursued the learning of textual exegesis, memorization and recitation, and literary embellishments arose together in confusion and profusion. Fragmentation and divisiveness flourished apace. Month by month and year by year, one scholar copied from another, each confirming the other's mistakes. Thus day by day the human mind became more swollen with self-importance and could no longer perceive the subtlety of the mind of the Way. . . .

How then is the learning of the mind-and-heart to be clarified? . . . In this learning there is no distinction between self and other, internal or external; the mind is one with Heaven-and-Earth and all things. Chan [Buddhist] learning, however, arises from self-interest and expediency and cannot avoid division into internal and external. This, then, is the reason for the difference between the two. Today those who pursue the learning of the mind and nature while not treating human relations as external to one or leaving out things and affairs, but who rather concentrate on preserving the mind and make it their business to nourish the nature, certainly represent the learning of discrimination and oneness in the sages' school.

[From *Wang Yangming quanshu, Wenlu* 4:215–217; dB]

## "QUESTIONS ON THE GREAT LEARNING"

In this memoir Wang sees the method of "discrimination and oneness" as a means of preserving the mind of the Way, originally and essentially one with Heaven, Earth, and all things. As something already complete within the mind, it requires nothing external to it but only unmixed, unobstructed expression of its human feelings—its natural empathy for all things. There is no place then for principles to be studied as if they were objects of investigation, no room for the nature, as Heaven's Principle in human beings, to be learned or assimilated from outside. All one needs in the learning of the mind is single-minded attention to the unity of the mind and principle, the oneness of humans with Heaven, Earth, and all things. For Wang this is a unity one starts with and expands upon, in contrast to Zhu Xi, who in his note on the investigation of things in the *Great Learning*, speaks of the gradual penetration of principles until finally one achieves a breakthrough to integral comprehension and coalescence.

---

2. "Canon of Shun," *Classic of History*; Legge, *The Chinese Classics* 3:44.

Wang's new interpretation of the Learning of the Mind-and-Heart, along with his revision of the Succession to the Way, immediately preceded his enunciation of the doctrine of innate knowing (*liangzhi*) and was followed in 1527 by his important "Questions on the *Great Learning*" ("Daxuewen").

As the title implies, this essay deals with central questions in the text of the *Great Learning*. It also presents the starting point and basic premises of Wang's teaching as drawn from both the *Mean* and the *Great Learning*. Zhu Xi had explained the *Great Learning*'s "manifesting luminous virtue" in terms of the original endowments of Heaven's nature (principle) in the mind, to be nourished and cultivated by methodical practice of intellectual inquiry, the refining of value distinctions, and the exercise of moral restraint—lest the human mind, precariously perched between selfish and unselfish desires, should stray from correct principles as represented by the mind of the Way. Wang's alternative view was that "luminous virtue," instead of being a mind of the Way at odds with the human mind, consisted essentially in the cardinal virtue of humaneness, as expressed in a feeling of oneness with Heaven-and-Earth and all things. Cultivation of this virtue, then, should consist essentially of encouraging the free and full expression of that empathetic feeling without the intervention of any ratiocination or calculation involving self/other or subject/object distinctions. In this, Wang placed a prime value on the feeling of love for, or oneness with, all creation and on the natural integrity of the mind, as opposed to a mind divided against itself by the counterposing of the human mind to the mind of the Way (i.e., the nature).

Wang's original given name was Shouren, meaning "to preserve humaneness"; his honorific name, Yangming, means "luminous and clear," which expresses the brilliant, charismatic appeal of both his outgoing, open personality and his simple, direct, inspirational message.

Question: The *Great Learning* was considered by the former scholar [Zhu Xi] as the learning of the great person. I venture to ask why the learning of the great person should consist in "clearly manifesting luminous virtue"?

Answer: The great person regards Heaven, Earth, and the myriad things as one body, the world as one family, and the state as one person. . . . Thus the learning of the great person consists entirely in getting rid of the obscuration of selfish desires by one's own efforts to make manifest one's luminous virtue, so as to restore the condition of forming one body with Heaven, Earth, and the myriad things. . . . To manifest luminous virtue [i.e., the moral nature (*mingde*)] is to bring about the substance of forming one body with Heaven, Earth, and the myriad things, whereas loving the people is to put into universal operation the function of forming one body. Hence manifesting luminous virtue consists in loving the people, and loving the people is the way to manifest luminous virtue.

People fail to realize that the highest good is in their minds and seek it outside. As they believe that everything or every event has its own definite principle, they search for the utmost good in individual things. Consequently, the mind becomes fragmented, isolated, broken into pieces. Mixed and confused, it has no definite direction. Once it is realized that the utmost good is in the mind and does not depend on any search outside, then the mind will have definite direction and there will be no danger of its becoming fragmented, isolated, broken into pieces, mixed, or confused.

Now the original substance of the mind is human nature. Human nature being universally good, the original substance of the mind is correct. How is it that any effort is required to rectify the mind? The reason is that, while the original substance of the mind is originally correct, incorrectness enters when one's thoughts and intentions are in operation. Therefore one who wishes to rectify one's mind must rectify it in connection with the operation of one's thoughts and intention. If, whenever a good thought arises, one really loves it as one loves beautiful colors, and whenever an evil thought arises, one really hates it as one hates bad odors, then one's intention will always be sincere and one's mind can be rectified. . . .

The extension of knowledge is not what later scholars understand as enriching and widening knowledge.[3] It is simply extending one's innate knowing to the utmost. This innate knowing is what Mencius meant when he said, "The sense of right and wrong is common to all human beings."[4] The sense of right and wrong requires no deliberation to know, nor does it depend on learning to function.[5] This is why it is called innate knowing. It is my nature endowed by Heaven, the original substance of my mind, naturally intelligent, shining, clear, and understanding.

Whenever a thought or a wish arises, my mind's faculty of innate knowing itself is always conscious of it. Whether it is good or evil, my mind's innate knowing faculty itself also knows it. It has nothing to do with others. Therefore, although an inferior person may have done all manner of evil, when he sees a superior man he will surely try to disguise this fact, concealing what is evil and displaying what is good in himself.[6] This shows that innate knowing does not permit any self-deception. Now the only way to distinguish good and evil in order to make the intention sincere is to extend to the utmost this innate knowing faculty.

*Wang identified the original pure mind with the "utmost good" of the* Great Learning, *regarding it not as a perfection beyond one, to be reached or achieved, but as an inherent perfection within, to be uncovered, released, and extended to others. He says:*

As the utmost good emanates and reveals itself, we will consider right as right and wrong as wrong. Things of greater or less importance and situations of grave or light character will be responded to as they act upon us. In all our changes and movements, we will stick to no particular point but possess in ourselves the Mean that is perfectly natural. This is the ultimate of the normal nature of

---

3. See Zhu Xi's commentary on the *Great Learning*, chap. 20.
4. *Mencius* 2A:6, 6A:6.
5. *Mencius* 7A:15.
6. Paraphrasing the *Great Learning*, chap. 6.

man and the principle of things. There can be no consideration of adding to or subtracting anything from it—such a suggestion reveals selfish ideas and shallow cunning and cannot be said to be the utmost good. Naturally, how can anyone who does not watch over himself carefully when alone, and who lacks refined discrimination and unity, attain to such a state of perfection? Later generations fail to realize that the utmost good is inherent in their own minds, but exercise their selfish ideas and cunning and grope for it outside their minds, believing that every event and every object has its own peculiar and definite principle.

*In this passage we see how Wang incorporates into his doctrine of the mind the language of the Cheng-Zhu method of the mind—the method of refined discrimination and one-ness and holding fast to the Mean—and focuses it on the unity of principle rather than on the diversity of principles in events and things. Thereby he sets a higher priority on primary intuition, or undifferentiated sensibility, than on acquired learning or second-ary rational and moral judgments. In the same way, Wang places a prime emphasis on the substantial unity of innate knowing, rather than on the different steps in the* Great Learning's *method of self-cultivation. He says:*

While the specification of tasks can be expressed in terms of a graded sequence of priorities, in substance they constitute a single unity and in reality there is no distinction of a graded sequence to be made; yet, while there is no such distinc-tion to be made, in respect to function (discrimination, *wei-wei*), these cannot be left wanting in the slightest degree. This is why the [*Great Learning's*] doctrine of investigation, extension, being sincere, and rectifying can be taken as a cor-rect exposition of the transmission from Yao and Shun and as evincing the mind of Confucius.

[From *Wang Yangming quanshu, Wenlu* 1:123; WTC, dB]

### THE IDENTIFICATION OF MIND AND PRINCIPLE

One basis for Wang's endorsement of Lu Xiangshan's approach to learning is his acceptance of the idea that the mind and principle are not only inseparable (which Zhu Xi himself had said) but identical.

What Zhu Xi meant by the investigation of things is "to investigate the principle in things to the utmost as we come into contact with them." To investigate the principle in things to the utmost, as we come into contact with them means to search in each individual thing for its so-called definite principle. It means further that the principle in each individual thing is to be sought with the mind, thus separating the mind and principle into two. To seek for principle in each individual thing is like looking for the principle of filiality in parents. If the prin-ciple of filiality is to be sought in parents, then is it actually in my own mind or is it in the person of my parents? If it is actually in the person of my parents, is it true that as soon as parents pass away the mind will then lack the principle of filiality? When I see a child about to fall into a well [and have a feeling of commiseration], there must be the principle of commiseration. Is this principle of commiseration actually in the person of the child or is it in the innate knowledge of my mind? Perhaps one cannot follow the child into the well [to rescue it]. Perhaps one can rescue it by seizing it with the hand. All this involves principle. Is it really in the person of the child or does it emanate from the innate knowledge in my mind? What is true here is true of all things and events. From this we know the mistake of separating the mind and principle into two.

[From *Chuanxilu*, in *Wang Yangming quanshu* (SBBY) 2:4b–5a; WTC]

## THE UNITY OF KNOWING AND ACTING

The following is recorded in *Instructions for Practical Living* by Wang's disciple Xu Ai.

I [Xu Ai] did not understand the Teacher's doctrine of the unity of knowing and acting and debated over it back and forth with Huang Zongxian and Gu Weixian without coming to any conclusion. Therefore I took the matter to the Teacher. The Teacher said, "Give an example and let me see." I said, "For example, there are people who know that parents should be served with filiality and elder brothers treated with respect, but they cannot put these things into practice. This shows that knowing and acting are clearly two different things."

The Teacher said, "The knowing and acting you refer to are already separated by selfish desires and are no longer knowing and acting in their original substance. There have never been people who know but do not act. Those who are supposed to know but do not act simply do not yet know. When sages and worthies taught people about knowing and acting, it was precisely because they wanted them to restore this original substance, and not just to have them behave like that and be satisfied."

[From *Chuanxilu*, in *Wang Yangming quanshu* (SBBY) 1:3a–b; WTC]

## THE COLLOQUY AT THE TIANQUAN BRIDGE

The two points of view represented in this famous colloquy are those that tended to polarize the school of Wang Yangming, one wing emphasizing the importance of moral cultivation and the other, intuitive spontaneity. The latter, with some leanings in the direction of Chan Buddhism, believed that the original reality or inner substance of the mind transcended good and evil and that natural spontaneity rather than conscious moral effort was the characteristic of the sage.

In the ninth month of the sixth year of Jiajing [1527] our Teacher had been called from retirement and appointed to subdue once more the rebellion in

Sien and Tianzhou.[7] As he was about to start Ruzhong [Wang Ji] and I [Qian Dehong] discussed learning. He repeated the words of the Teacher's instruction as follows:

"In the original substance of the mind there is no distinction of good and evil.

"When the intentions become active, however, such a distinction exists.

"The function of innate knowing is to know good and evil.

"The investigation [rectification] of things is to do good and remove evil."

I asked, "What do you think this means?"

Ruzhong said, "This is perhaps not the last word [i.e., there is more to it than this]. If we say that in the original substance of the mind there is no distinction between good and evil, then there must be no such distinction in the intentions, in knowing, or in things. If we say that there is a distinction between good and evil in the intentions, then in the final analysis there must also be such a distinction in the substance of the mind."

I said, "The substance of the mind is the nature endowed in us by Heaven, and is originally neither good nor evil. But because we have a mind dominated by habits, we see in our thoughts a distinction between good and evil. The work of investigating things, extending knowledge, making the intentions sincere, rectifying the mind, and cultivating the person is aimed precisely at recovering that original nature and substance. If there were no good or evil to start with, what would be the necessity for such effort?"

That evening we set ourselves down beside the Teacher at the Tianquan Bridge. Each stated his view and asked to be corrected. The Teacher said, "I am going to leave now. I wanted to have you come and talk this matter through. You two gentlemen complement one another very well and should not hold on to one side. Here I deal with two types of people. The man of sharp intelligence apprehends straight from the source. The original substance of the human mind is in fact crystal-clear without any impediment and is the equilibrium before the feelings are aroused. The man of sharp intelligence has already accomplished his task as soon as he apprehends the original substance, penetrating the self, other people, and things internal and things external all at the same time. On the other hand, there are inevitably those whose minds are dominated by habits so that the original substance of the mind is obstructed. I therefore teach them definitely and sincerely to do good and remove evil in their intention and thoughts. When they become expert at the task and the impurities of the mind are completely eliminated, the original substance of the mind will become wholly clear. I adopt Ruzhong's view in dealing with the man of sharp intelligence, and that of Dehong for the second type. If you two gentlemen use your views

---

7. Both were counties in Guangxi.

interchangeably, you will be able to lead all people—of the highest, average, and lowest intelligence—to the truth.

[*Chuanxilu*, in *Wang Yangming quanshu* (SBBY) 3:30b–31a; adapted from Chan, *Instructions*, pp. 243–244]

## SOCIAL AND POLITICAL MEASURES OF WANG YANGMING

Although Zhu Xi had by no means been uninvolved with government, Wang Yangming led an even more active life. His career as an official and general, though marked by both great successes and the conflicts and sharp reversals often experienced by conscientious officials, notably exemplified his doctrine of the unity of knowing and acting. For his followers, too, it exemplified the life of a martyred hero-sage. It is understandable that his personal example should have inspired new forms of activism in many directions, which serve as a reminder that Wang's approach, while somewhat more subjective than Zhu Xi's, was primarily directed at stimulating the inner springs of practical moral action, not at encouraging any form of quietism. In fact, Yangming abjured quiet-sitting for this reason.

It is not surprising that among these active concerns were matters already put high on the Neo-Confucian agenda by Zhu Xi: local schooling and community organization. Others included his recommendations for military policy and defense of the northwestern frontiers. The following selections demonstrate particularly the close connection between his thought and his official measures, as well as the continuity of basic ideas from Zhu Xi, along with the distinct emphasis given them by Wang.

### FUNDAMENTAL IDEAS ON ELEMENTARY EDUCATION

In April 1518, after leading a successful campaign to subdue rebels in Jiangxi, Wang adopted a policy of pacification through reeducation rather than through reprisals or repression. In this case he reemphasized the need for community schools (as had Zhu Xi) but put even greater stress on voluntarism and the active liberation of human beings' natural capacities. Note especially the appeal to the affective nature of man, rather than to cognitive learning, but note also his view of the practice of rites and music as stimulating, not stultifying, the natural affections.

In education the ancients taught the fundamental principles of human relations. As the habits of memorization, recitation, and the writing of flowery compositions of later generations arose, the teachings of ancient kings disappeared. In educating young boys today, the sole task should be to teach filiality, brotherly respect, loyalty, faithfulness, ritual decorum, rightness, integrity, and the sense of shame. The ways to raise and cultivate them are to lure them into singing so their will will be roused, to direct them to practice etiquette so their demeanor will be dignified, and to urge them to read so their intellectual horizon will be widened. Today, singing songs and practicing etiquette are often regarded as unrelated to present needs. This is the view of small and vulgar people of this degenerate modern age. . . .

Generally speaking, it is the nature of young boys to love to play and to dislike restriction. Like plants beginning to sprout, if they are allowed to grow freely, they will develop smoothly. If twisted and interfered with, they will wither and decline. In teaching young boys today, we must make them lean toward rousing themselves so that they will be happy and cheerful at heart, and then nothing can check their development. . . .

However, in recent generations the teachers of youngsters merely supervise them every day as they recite phrases and sentences and imitate civil service examination papers. They stress restraint and discipline instead of directing their pupils in the practice of the rites. They emphasize cognitive learning instead of nourishing goodness. They beat the pupils with a whip and tie them with ropes, treating them like prisoners. The youngsters look upon their school as a prison and refuse to enter. They regard their teachers as enemies and do not want to see them. They avoid this and conceal that in order to satisfy their desire for play and fun. They pretend, deceive, and cheat in order to indulge in mischief and meanness. They become negligent and inferior, and daily degenerate. Such education drives them to do evil. How can they be expected to do good?

In truth the following is my idea of education. . . . Every day, early in the morning, after the pupils have assembled and bowed, the teachers should ask all of them one by one whether at home they have been negligent and lacked sincerity and earnestness in their desire to love their parents and to respect their elders, whether they have overlooked or failed to carry out any details in caring for their parents in the summer or the winter, whether in walking along the streets their movements and etiquette have been disorderly or careless, and whether in all their words, acts, and thoughts they have been deceitful or depraved, and not loyal, faithful, sincere, and respectful. All boys must answer honestly. If they have made any mistake, they should correct it. If not, they should devote themselves to greater effort. . . .

In singing, let the pupils be tidy in appearance and calm in expression. Let their voices be clear and distinct. Let their rhythm be even and exact. Let them not be hasty or hurried. Let them not be reckless or disorderly. And let them not sound feeble or timid. In time their spirits will be free and their minds will be peaceful. . . .

In the practice of rites, let the pupils be clear in their minds and reverently serious in their thoughts. Let them be careful with details and correct in demeanor. Let them not be negligent or lazy. Let them not be low-spirited or disconcerted. And let them not be uncontrolled or rude. Let them be leisurely but not to the point of being dilatory and be serious but not to the point of being rigid. In time their appearance and behavior will be natural and their moral nature will be firmly established. . . .

In reading, the value does not lie in the amount read but in learning the material well. Reckoning the pupils' natural endowments, if one can handle two hundred words, teach him only one hundred so that he always has surplus energy and strength, and then he will not suffer or feel tired but will have the beauty of being at ease with himself.

[Adapted from Chan, *Instructions*, pp. 182–185]

### THE COMMUNITY COMPACT FOR SOUTHERN GANZHOU

In southern Jiangxi and Fujian, where he suppressed bandits and rebels, Wang, instead of following a punitive policy, stressed the need to convert the former disaffected peoples to take up a life as "new citizens." He turned to the model of Zhu Xi's Community Compact as a method of enlisting people's cooperation in the rehabilitation of former outlaws and for appealing to the better side of the latter's nature.

It should be noted that the movement to reform local government and reorganize village life arose with the breakdown of the *lijia* and village elder system instituted by Ming Taizu at the founding of the dynasty. Wang's is just one example among others of Confucian scholar-officials attempting to address these problems in the sixteenth century. It is significant that the compact had become accepted here as somewhat more an instrument of state policy than the kind of voluntary, grassroots organization originally envisaged by the Lü family and Zhu Xi in the Song. Nevertheless, collective, shared responsibility on the part of both "new citizens" and officials—in short, a spirit of mutuality and reciprocity—is a marked feature of Wang's proposal. Note also that in the second paragraph the essentials of public morality are largely defined in the same terms as Zhu Xi's compact, as Taizu had incorporated them in the "Six Precepts" of the village lecture system.

In the past, new citizens have often deserted their own clans, rebelled against their own community, and gone in all directions to do violence. Was this merely because their nature was different and they were criminals? It was also because, on our part, the government did not govern them properly or teach them in the right way, and on your part, all of you, both old and young, did not reach and regulate your families early enough or exert good influence on your fellow villagers regularly enough. You did not put inducement and encouragement into practice and had no sufficient arrangements for cooperation and coordination. . . .

Alas! Nothing can be done to change what has already gone by, but something can still be done in the future. Therefore a community compact is now specially prepared to unite and harmonize all of you. From now on, all of you who enter into this compact should be filial to your parents and respectful to your elders, teach your children, live in harmony with your fellow villagers, help one another when there is death in the family and assist one another in times of difficulty, encourage one another to do good and warn one another not to do evil, stop litigations and rivalry, cultivate faithfulness and promote harmony, and be sure to be good citizens so that together you may establish the custom of humanity and kindness. Alas! Although a man is most stupid, when it comes to criticizing others his mind is quite clear, and although a person is quite intelligent, when it comes to criticizing himself his mind is beclouded. All of you, both old and young, should not remember the former evil deeds of the new citizens and ignore their good deeds. As long as they have a single thought to do good, they are already good people. Do not be proud that you are good citizens and neglect to cultivate your personal life. As long as you have a single thought to do evil, you are already evil people. Whether people are good or evil depends on a single instant of thought. You should think over my words carefully. Don't forget.

Item: Elect from the compact membership an elderly and virtuous person respected by all to be the compact chief and two persons to be assistant chiefs, four persons who are impartial, just, and firm in judgment to be compact directors, four persons who are understanding and discriminating to be compact recorders, four persons who are energetic and scrupulous to be compact executives, and two persons who are well versed in ceremonies to be compact masters of ceremonies. Have three record books. One of these is to record the names of compact members and their daily movements and activities, and is to be in the charge of the compact executives. Of the remaining record books, one is for the purpose of displaying good deeds and the other for the purpose of reporting evil deeds, both to be in the charge of the compact chief.

Item: Each member shall contribute three cents (*fen*) at each banquet meeting to the compact executives, who will provide the food. Do not be extravagant. The point is that there shall be no thirst or hunger, that is all.

Item: The time of meeting shall be the fifteenth of each month. Those who because of illness or other business are unable to attend may send a messenger to inform a compact executive ahead of time. Those who fail to attend without reason will be recorded as having committed an evil deed and, in addition, fined one dollar (*liang*)[8] for the use of the group.

Item: Build a compact hall on level ground. Choose a spacious temple compound and build it there.

Item: To display good deeds, the language used must be clear and decisive, but in reporting mistakes, the language must be indirect and gentle. . . .

Item: . . . After the meal, the compact master of ceremonies shall sound the drum three times, and in a chanting voice announce the issuance of warning. All shall rise. The compact directors shall stand in the middle of the hall and say in a loud voice, "Oh! All members of the compact please listen distinctly to this warning. Who among men has no good in him, and who has no evil in him?

---

8. 100 *fen*.

Although our good deeds are not known to others, as they accumulate, in time this accumulation of good will no longer remain hidden. If we do evil deeds and do not reform, in time they will accumulate and reach the point where they can no longer be pardoned."

[Adapted from Chan, *Instructions*, pp. 298–306]

## THE WANG YANGMING SCHOOL

Wang's disciple Qian Dehong, in a comment on Wang's *Questions*, appropriates to the latter Zhu Xi's concept of the Succession to the Way, asserting that "the teaching of the *Great Learning* had, after Mencius, found no worthy transmitter for more than a thousand years, but with this exposition in terms of [Wang's] innate knowing (*liangzhi*) it was restored to full clarity of understanding as if one day had encompassed all of time past."[9] Qian thereby advances the claim that Wang's doctrine of innate knowing represents the authentic renewal of the tradition of the Way and succession to the mind of the sages.

This new learning, encapsulated in the doctrine of innate knowing and the "extension of innate knowing," transformed the sage learning from the "learning of past sages" to "the Learning of Sagehood" for all in the present time, rendering it accessible to Everyman to a degree that Zhu Xi's "Learning to Be a Sage" may have aspired to but in ways Zhu had not conceived. Wang thereby ushered in a kind of "popular" movement with a greater potential for the participation of ordinary people in the fulfillment of Neo-Confucian ideals.

It was possible so to popularize the notion of sagehood only because Wang had internalized or subjectivized it. "How can the signs of sagehood be recognized," he asks, and answers, "If one clearly perceives one's own innate knowing, then one recognizes that the signs of sagehood do not exist in the sage but in oneself."[10] And the way to achieve sagehood is not to set up some idealized image far beyond one, as many scholars have done, "seeking to know what they cannot know and do what they cannot do."[11] It is to stop relying on external standards, to become completely identified with the Principle of Heaven within oneself and thus become self-sustaining. This anyone can do with even a modicum of education.

It would be the mission of the Wang Yangming school to take this message far beyond the usual scholarly audience, now that erudition was no longer a prime qualification. Wang's holistic approach—so evident in the doctrine of "humaneness forming one body with Heaven, Earth, and all things"—stressed what was shared and common to all more than what was unique and different in each individual. Indeed, its common character was almost Wang's fundamental article of

---

9. *Wang Yangming quanshu* 1, *Wenlu* 1:123.
10. *Wang Yangming quanshu* 1, *Chuanxilu* 2:48.
11. Chan, *Instructions*, p. 69.

faith. Individual differences were important for him, but the uniqueness of the individual is not something Wang sets in opposition to common humanity, any more than one would, accepting the doctrine of the "unity of principle and diversity of its particularizations," see these two aspects as antithetical or mutually exclusive.

Wang's confidence in trusting one's own mind as the ultimate authority rests squarely on his faith that all human minds reflect and express a common standard of truth. Thus we recall him saying, "The Way is public and belongs to the whole world, and the doctrine is also public and belongs to the whole world. They are not the private properties of Master Zhu [Xi] or even Confucius. They are open to all and the only proper way to discuss them is to do so openly."[12]

There is perhaps no more striking example than this of Wang's basically Confucian—and we might even say Chinese—outlook: for all his emphasis on individual effort and personal intuition of truth, he retains a faith in the fundamental rationality of man; and for all his insistence on discovering right and wrong for oneself, it does not occur to him that there could be any essential conflict between subjective and objective morality, or that genuine introspection could lead to anything other than the affirmation of clear and common moral standards.

Here is the underlying reason why Wang Yangming's teaching could have had such a quickening effect on the thought of those times and such an explosive impact on all levels of Ming society and culture—its tremendous moral dynamism, its enormous confidence in human beings, and its faith that life could be dealt with by opening people up to one another from within.

Wang's strength as a teacher lay in his seemingly deliberate cultivation of ambiguities that could be explored by his own students and clarified by their own experience, as we have seen in the Colloquy at the Tianquan Bridge. Had he not allowed these ambiguities to stand, there might have been far less discussion and debate within his school, less room for individual and regional differentiation, and perhaps no such ranges of opinion as justify making distinctions between right, center, and left tendencies. Nor could we have found so many remarkable personalities, so many striking individuals, among his followers.

## WANG GEN: THE COMMON MAN AS SAGE

Among the influential followers of Wang Yangming was Wang Gen (1483–1541), who carried forward most vigorously the idea of the common man as sage. He began life as the son of a salt maker and never sought or attained the status of a Confucian scholar-official. A man of tremendous energy and vitality, he seemed to draw strength and self-confidence as if through a taproot striking deep into the soil of China.

---

12. Ibid., p. 164.

After only five years of instruction at the village school, economic necessity forced him, at the age of eleven, to leave it and assist his father in the family business. Later, on repeated business trips to Shandong province, he carried copies of the Four Books and the *Classic of Filiality* in his sleeve and discussed them with anyone he could find who might aid his understanding. His determination to become a sage was aroused, it is said, when he visited the shrine of Confucius at Qufu and realized that the immortal sage himself had been, after all, just a man.

By the age of twenty-one Gen had become established as an independent salt dealer and prospered enough that he could devote more time to self-study. He developed the practice of shutting himself up in a room for quiet-sitting, meditating in silence day and night for long periods of time. His spiritual awakening followed a dream in which he saw the heavens falling and people fleeing in panic. Answering their cries for help, he stood forth, pushed up the heavens, and restored order among the heavenly bodies. People were overjoyed and thanked him profusely. When Gen awoke, bathed in perspiration, he suddenly had his enlightenment, described in terms of an experience of being united with all things through his humanity (*ren*) and of finding the universe within himself.

From this experience arose Wang Gen's sense of mission, a vocation to become a teacher to humankind. But since he had had little formal education, his approach to learning was quite rudimentary, emphasizing personal spirituality and activity as opposed to scholarly study. The classics, he said (in language similar to Lu Xiangshan in the Song), were to be used simply to document one's own experience.

Not long before he met Wang Yangming, Wang Gen's reading of *Mencius* and his reflections on the true meaning of sagehood in one's daily life produced a startling thought. Referring to *Mencius* 6B:2, he said, "Can one speak the words of [the sage king] Yao, and perform the actions of Yao, and yet not wear the clothing of Yao?"[13] Whereupon, following some prescriptions found in the *Record of Rites*, he made himself a long cotton gown, a special hat and girdle to wear, and a ceremonial tablet to carry around with him. Above his door he inscribed the declaration "My teaching comes down through [the sages] Fu Xi, Shennong, the Yellow Emperor, Yao, Shun, the Great Yu, Kings Tang, Wen, and Wu, the Duke of Zhou, and Confucius. To anyone who earnestly seeks it, whether he be young or old, high or low, wise or ignorant, I shall pass it on." Many people laughed at this, but some were moved by Wang Gen's sense of active concern to make the ancient Way live in the present and, ignoring the ridicule of others, they took up the cause.

After meeting Yangming and becoming his disciple, Gen found that his active disposition still made him restless to carry the true Way to all human beings. He returned home, built himself a cart like the one Confucius was said to have used when he traveled to the courts of feudal princes, and went off to Peking. There his dress, his cart, and his somewhat piglike appearance attracted much

---

13. A permutation of the original Mencian saying.

attention, and great crowds came to hear him. Many people became convinced of his deep sincerity and were drawn to his ideas. In ruling circles, however, he was looked on either as a joke or as a potential troublemaker. Later he seems to have settled down to a less spectacular role while Yangming remained alive, but thereafter he resumed an active life as a teacher in his own school and had wide influence.

Wang Gen was not a social revolutionary, but his efforts, following up the implications of Zhu Xi's and Wang Yangming's teachings, probably did more to reach a larger public audience than anyone since Xu Heng in the Yuan had done. The Ming founder, it is true, had tried to promote universal schooling, but the close link between schooling and official recruitment tended to vitiate this effort by orienting education too much toward entry into the governing elite, while Wang Gen explicitly disavowed and personally renounced any such intention, emphasizing instead general education for the ordinary man. In this respect, he may well stand as the preeminent example of a Neo-Confucian who, spurning political power, believed that the main action lay in bringing the benefits of education to every man.

### THE HUAINAN INVESTIGATION OF THINGS

Before visiting Wang Yangming, Wang Gen had described his own teaching as "the investigation of things," but he recognized that his interpretation of it was similar to Yangming's "innate knowing." The similarity lies in the fact that "investigation of things" means for both essentially the "rectification of affairs." In other words, the starting point of all self-cultivation as formulated in the *Great Learning* should be an understanding of things, matters, actions, and events, so that these conform to one's own sense of right and wrong, shame and deference, etc., and thus become "rectified." In particular Wang Gen stressed the self as the active center of things. In his view self and society were one continuum, with the self as the trunk or base and society as the branch or superstructure (not unlike Xu Heng's version of the *Elementary Learning*).

The following is a typical expression of what became known as the "Huainan [method of] the investigation of things," so called because Huainan is the classical name for Wang Gen's home region. It rests on two cardinal Confucian principles: that reciprocity is the basis of all social relations and that higher forms of social organization depend on the self-cultivation of individuals in the lower forms and, ultimately, on the individual himself.

When the *Classic of Changes* speaks of the preservation of the state being dependent on the security of the individual it is speaking to the "gentleman" who is a member of the ruling class, if not the ruler himself. Wang Gen, however, is actualizing the theoretical potential in this principle, and broadening its significance to include the common individual as well as the traditional Confucian "gentleman" or "noble person."

If in one's conduct of life there is any shortcoming, one should look for the fault within oneself. To reflect on oneself is the fundamental method for the rectification of things. Therefore, the desire to regulate the family, order the state, and pacify the world [as in the *Great Learning*], rests upon making the self secure (*anshen*). The *Classic of Changes* says, "If the self is secure, then the empire and state can be preserved."[14] But if the self is not secure, the root is not established.

To make the self secure, one must love and respect the self, and one who does this cannot but love and respect others. If I can love and respect others, others will love and respect me. If a family can practice love and self-respect, then the family will be regulated. If a state can practice love and self-respect, then the state will be regulated, and if all-under-Heaven can practice love and self-respect, then all under Heaven will be at peace. Therefore, if others do not love me, I should realize that it is not particularly because of others' inhumanity but because of my own, and if others do not respect me, it is not particularly that others are disrespectful but that I am.

[From "Wang Gen zhuan," *Mingru xuean* 32:69–70; dB]

## "CLEAR WISDOM AND SELF-PRESERVATION"

Wang Gen's brief essay "Clear Wisdom and Self-Preservation" ("Mingzhe baoshen lun"),[15] from which the following passage is drawn, is expressed in a simple style and somewhat repetitious argumentation, which reflect both his own homespun character and his desire to communicate to the simplest people.

Clear wisdom is innate knowing. To clarify wisdom and preserve the self is innate knowing and innate ability. It is what is called "to know without deliberating and to know how without learning how."[16] All men possess these faculties. The sage and I are the same. Those who know how to preserve the self will love the self like a treasure. If I can love the self, I cannot but love other people; if I can love other people, they will surely love me; and if they love me, my self will be preserved. . . . If I respect my self, I dare not but respect other people; if I respect other people, they will surely respect me; and if they respect me, my self is preserved. If I respect my self, I dare not be rude to other people; if I am not rude to others, they will not be rude to me; and if they are not rude to me, then my self is preserved. . . . This is humaneness! This is the Way whereby all things become one body!

[From "Mingzhe baoshen lun," *Wang Xinzhai yiji* 1:12b–13a; dB]

---

14. *Classic of Changes, Commentary on the Appended Phrases*, part 2; Lynn, *Classic of Changes*, p. 83.

15. The title of Wang's essay involves an allusion to Ode 260, which speaks of a minister who has "clear wisdom" and "preserves his person."

16. *Mencius* 7A:15.

## LI ZHI: ARCH-INDIVIDUALIST

The tide of individualistic thought in the late Ming reached its height with Li Zhi (1527–1602), who has been both condemned and acclaimed as the greatest heretic and iconoclast in China's history. He is in any case one of the most brilliant and complex figures in Chinese thought and literature.

As a radical individualist who disavowed any school ties, Li does not fit exactly under the heading of the Wang Yangming school, but he did admire Yangming and was much influenced by several of the latter's followers, notably Wang Ji, so he serves as an example—and a particularly striking one—of new trends in that movement, especially the independent, critical temper generated by Wang's doctrine of innate knowing, which in the pursuit of learning for one's self led to a profound questioning of sagehood as both an elite and a popular ideal.

Li was born and raised in the port city of Quanzhou, Fujian province, which in earlier times had been a center of foreign trade, with a somewhat cosmopolitan character. Li's forebears had been active in this trade. The commercial atmosphere of Quanzhou is vividly recalled in Li's writing by his frequent use of the language of the marketplace and by his aggressive, hard-driving mentality. But Quanzhou's foreign trade had been largely cut off by the Ming seclusion policy; what survived was mostly illicit or severely regulated—trade of a kind that had the nefarious connotations of smuggling, the black market, official collusion, and squeeze. Its spirit could hardly have been that of the self-confident bourgeois, the expansive builder of a new world.

Li received a classical Confucian training but, as he said later, he was a skeptic from his youth, repelled by anything or anyone—Confucian, Buddhist, or Daoist—identified with an organized creed. He felt a great revulsion, too, against the kind of mechanical learning required for the examinations to enter an official career, and though he managed to overcome his scruples and pass the provincial examinations in 1552, he did not go on to the higher examinations at the capital. Such an attitude on Li's part fits into a recognizable pattern of alienation among members of the educated class in Ming and Qing China, typified by the sensitive, highly intelligent child of a well-to-do family on the decline, who feels a fundamental conflict between the integrity of the sagely ideal and what one must do to succeed in the world and discharge one's family responsibilities. Something of the same conflict, however, was widely felt in the sixteenth and seventeenth centuries by scholars of varying background and temperament.

After his qualifying examination Li spent almost thirty years in the status of an official, going from one routine assignment to another. Though a somewhat frustrating life, marked by frequent conflict with his superiors, it was not without considerable leisure, in which he could pursue his own studies. A profound spiritual unrest was at work within him, however. As he put it, he yearned to "hear the Way," borrowing the phrase from Confucius: "Hearing the Way in the morning, one could die content in the evening."[17] In other words, he was searching for something worth living and dying for.

Thus through five years at the Board of Rites in Peking, Li's mind was little occupied with official duties but rather was "sunk deep in the Way." In the course of these years, he formed close associations with members of the Wang Yangming school, who introduced him to the teachings of Wang Yangming, Wang Ji, and the Taizhou school. He had a strong aversion, however, to the lecture meetings promoted by that school for "learning by discussion" and did not take part in them. Later, drawn to a life of independent study and contemplation, he resigned from official service and took up residence in a Buddhist temple, sending his wife and children home to Fujian. When a few years later he took the Buddhist tonsure, it signified as much as anything else his determination to make a complete break with family cares and social obligations.

Li gave many different reasons for his decision to shave off his hair and become a monk, some of them perhaps only half serious and some apparently dubious rationalizations. The most plausible was simply that he wished to escape the control of others and achieve a degree of personal freedom not possible for the layman. There can be no doubt of his serious interest in Buddhism, but he was as individualistic in this respect as in all others. In fact, his desire "to be an individual" (*cheng yige ren*) is given by Li as intimately involved in his decision to become a "monk." Officially he was not a licensed monk, nor did he keep the monastic discipline. Instead he pursued even more intensively scholarly interests quite unusual for a monk.

Two years after becoming a "monk," in 1590, he published his *Fenshu* (*A Book to Burn*), the title of which acknowledged the dangerousness of its contents. It was a collection of letters, essays, prefaces, and poems expressing his repudiation of conventional morality, his belief in the essential identity of the Three Teachings, and his nonconforming views on history, literature, and a wide range of other subjects. He expected the book to be condemned as heresy and it was. But despite attacks upon it and mounting pressure against him, Li persisted in his course. He became even freer in his conduct and, though the charges of social and sexual misconduct made against him are undoubtedly exaggerated, he did not hesitate to relieve his intense scholarly efforts with pleasant diversions in and out of the temple. After the publication in 1600 of *Cangshu* (*A Book to Be Hidden Away*), which challenged many long-accepted Confucian views of history, a mob incited by local authorities burned down his residence at the temple, and he spent the remaining few years of his life taking refuge in the home of friend after friend in different places. Finally, in 1602, a memorial at the court in Peking charged him with a long list of offenses, and an edict was issued ordering his arrest and the burning of his books. In prison in Peking he made his last protest, committing suicide by slashing his throat.

---

17. *Analects* 4:8.

## THE CHILDLIKE MIND-AND-HEART

Basic assumptions for Li Zhi are, first, the cardinal Neo-Confucian doctrine of the essential goodness of the human mind and second, Wang Yangming's view that the manifesting of this inherent virtue comes through the direct, uninhibited expression of "good [innate, intuitive] knowing." Li contrasted this natural innocence and spontaneity to the glib professions of sagely morality all around him. These seemed to him the hypocritical mouthings of "scholars" whose learning and "virtue" were quite conventional, secondhand, and pretentious—uninformed by the searching self-scrutiny ("self-watchfulness") so emphasized in the *Great Learning* and the *Mean*.

The childlike mind, he says, is originally pure, but it can be lost if received opinions come in through the senses and are allowed to dominate it. The greatest harm results when moral doctrines are imposed upon it, and the mind loses its capacity to judge for itself. This comes mainly from reading books and learning "moral principles."

Once people's minds have been given over to received opinions and moral principles, what they have to say is all about these things, and not what would naturally come from their childlike minds. No matter how clever the words, what have they to do with oneself? What else can there be but phony men speaking phony words, doing phony things, writing phony writings? Once the men become phonies, everything becomes phony. Thereafter, if one speaks phony talk to the phonies, the phonies are pleased; if one does phony things as the phonies do, the phonies are pleased; and if one discourses with the phonies through phony writings, the phonies are pleased. Everything is phony, and everyone is pleased.

[*Fenshu* 3:97; dB]

### PHONY SAGES

In Li's scathing attacks on these "hypocrites" one can see what has become of the grand humanitarian slogans of Wang Yangming and Wang Gen among the "lecturers" who propagated their teachings.

If there is something to be gained by it and they want to take charge of public affairs, then the "lecturers" will cite the saying that "all things are one body" [and it is their duty to serve humankind]; if they stand to lose by it, however, and they wish to avoid blame and censure, then they invoke the saying "The clearest wisdom is self-preservation"[18] [in order to withdraw from threatening danger].

[Or again:] In ordinary times when there is peace, they only know how to bow and salute one another, or else they sit the day long in an upright posture

---

18. Alluding to Ode 260.

[practicing quiet-sitting] like a clay image, thinking that if they can suppress all stray thoughts they will become sages and worthies. The more cunning among them participate in the meetings to discuss innate knowledge, secretly hoping to gain some recognition and win high office. But when a crisis comes, they look at each other pale and speechless, try to shift the blame to one another and save themselves on the pretext that "the clearest wisdom is self-preservation." Consequently, if the state employs only this type of scholar, when an emergency arises it has no one of any use in the situation.

*Of their activities as teachers, he says the "lecturers" gather crowds of followers and take in students:*

to enhance their own name and fame and make themselves rich and honored, not realizing that Confucius never sought wealth or honors or to surround himself with disciples. . . . But the teachers of today—one day out of office and their disciples abandon them; one day without funds and their followers scatter.

[From *Xufenshu* 3:94; *Fenshu* 4:159, 2:61; dB]

*Again and again Li mocks the moralistic pretensions of those who preach the Way but have "their hearts set on high office and the acquisition of wealth." He compares them with a type of literary man whom he considers equally "phony"—the so-called mountainmen (shanren) who affect the independence and eccentricity of artists and poets who live alone in the midst of nature:*

Those who consider themselves sages today are no different from the mountain men—it is all a matter of luck. If it is a man's luck that he can compose poetry he calls himself a "mountain man"; if it is not and he cannot compose poetry and become a mountain man, he calls himself a "sage." If it is a man's luck that he can lecture on "innate knowledge," he calls himself a "sage," but if it is not and he is unable to lecture on innate knowledge, he gives up being a sage and calls himself a "mountain man." They turn around and reverse themselves in order to deceive the world and secure their own gain. They call themselves "mountain men," but their hearts are those of the merchants. Their lips are full of the Way and virtue, but their ambition is to become "thieves of virtue."[19]

Those who call themselves "mountain men," if considered as merchants, would not be worth one copper cash and without the protection of high officials would be despised among men. And how do I know that I am any better? Who knows but that I too have the heart of a merchant and have put on Buddhist robes just to deceive people and make use of the name?

[*Fenshu* 2:46; dB]

---

19. *Analects* 17:13.

## THE LEGITIMACY OF BEING SELF-INTERESTED

Having no self-deception, and being thoroughly honest with oneself, meant for Li Zhi recognizing the basic, legitimate self-interestedness in man, rather than pretending to a lofty disinterestedness. Here he takes issue with those hypocrites who profess a great unselfishness while rationalizing ulterior motives, not openly acknowledging their natural self-regarding interests. He is at particular pains to debunk the idea in Buddhism and Neo-Confucianism of the sage or bodhisattva as "having no mind [of his own (*wuxin*)]."

The learning of the sage does nothing and yet all is accomplished (*wuwei er cheng*). But those who talk about "doing nothing" today only speak of "not minding" [lit., "having no mind," *wuxin*]. However, once you start talking about the mind-and-heart, how can you speak about "having no mind"? And when you start talking about "doing," how can you "do something" without having a mind [to do it]? If a peasant did not "mind" [what he was about], his fields would surely go to weeds. If the artisan did not mind [what he was about], his tools would surely get ruined. If the scholar did not mind [what he was about], his task would certainly be left undone. How is it possible "not to mind"?

Some explain this "not minding" as meaning not that one literally has "no mind" but that one has no selfish mind or intentions. Now "self-interest" is "man's minding." Man must be self-interested if his mind is to be made known. If he were not self-interested, there would be no mind. It is like tending a field; there must first be some self-interest to obtain the autumn's harvest before one would go to the "effort of working the field." Or like the husbandman, there must first be the self-interest to gain by "storing things up" before one will go to the effort of husbandry. Or like the scholar, there must first be the desire for self-advancement before one will undertake to prepare for examinations.

Thus an officer who had no thought of gaining the emoluments of office would not be responsive to an invitation to serve. If he were to have no high rank, no amount of exhortation could persuade a man to come forth and serve. And even in the case of a sage like Confucius, if there were no office of minister of justice by which he shared in the business of governing, he certainly would not have found even a day of service in the state of Lu tolerable. This is a natural principle, to which practice must conform. One cannot just engage in airy talk and groundless speculation. . . .

Confucius said, "The humane person first faces the difficulties and only later thinks of the rewards."[20] He speaks of facing the difficulties first, after which one could expect some reward. He does not say there should be no seeking for reward at all, nothing aimed at, and all done thoughtlessly and without any consideration.

Thus if you wish to be true to moral principle, there must be some thought of gain. If there is no thought of gain, there can be no "being true." If the Way is to

---

20. *Analects* 6:20.

be made manifest, one's own success must thereby be accomplished. If there is no consideration of one's own success, how can the Way ever be made manifest? Now if someone says that in the learning of the Sage there is no self-interestedness, and thus no such aim could be allowed, how could anyone aim to achieve sagehood?

[From *Cangshu* 32:544; dB]

## LUO QINSHUN AND THE PHILOSOPHY OF *QI*

While much of the story of sixteenth-century Chinese thought can be told in terms of the charismatic figure of Wang Yangming and the creative innovation and popular appeal of his school, Wang's was not the only compelling voice to be heard in the mid-Ming period. Serious alternative views were espoused as well, some of them by thinkers associated with the Cheng-Zhu school and some as philosophically innovative as Wang's, if less susceptible to popularization.

Luo Qinshun (1465–1547) was a leading figure in the Cheng-Zhu school of the mid-Ming, a contemporary of Wang's, and one of his most effective and influential philosophical opponents. Like Wang, and at similar personal peril, Luo served in high official positions in the Ming government, including that of director of studies at the Imperial University in Nanking and as a minister in the Ministry of Personnel in Nanking and Peking. Also like Wang, Luo was actively involved in public life and concerned with practical issues of governance, land distribution, education, and the management of economic and military affairs. And he too regarded as fundamental the enduring Neo-Confucian idea that an ultimate goal of human life is "forming one body with Heaven, Earth, and all things."

Where Wang and Luo diverged most crucially was in their assessments of how such a goal of identification of the individual with all living things should be understood and how it could be realized—a disagreement over the nature of knowledge. Whereas Wang, developing his idea of "the extension of innate knowledge," came to redefine all significant knowledge as *moral* knowledge, dependent upon the creative projection of the individual's own moral mind, Luo, following the Cheng brothers and Zhu Xi, continued to insist on the importance of the acquisition of intellectual knowledge of the "external" world and on a carefully preserved balance between intellectual and moral cultivation.

While regarding himself as among the heirs of the Cheng-Zhu tradition of the Song, and retaining several of the most defining commitments of his predecessors, Lo was not merely rehearsing or recasting their views. He was at pains to explain that, as one who honored and trusted his predecessors, he was duty-bound to confront certain unresolved problems in their thought. For all of his devotion to the Neo-Confucian tradition and his conception of learning as a cumulative and ongoing enterprise, he was also a creative thinker who set forth metaphysical, psychological, and epistemological positions that were both new and, arguably, modern.

Among the innovative aspects of Luo's thought are his rejection of the Song dualism of principle (*li*) and material-force (*qi*) and development of a philosophical monism of *qi*, applied in an innovative metaphysics and in a philosophical psychology that rejected the Song dualism of a "nature ordained by Heaven" and a "physical nature," comprehending the nature as one and affirming the importance of both the emotions and sense knowledge.

Luo Qinshun's major work, *Knowledge Painfully Acquired* (*Kunzhiji*), is a work of the study, clearly composed in solitude. The tone is reflective; the choice of language is precise; issues are sharply defined. Luo is revealed in this collection of reading notes as a scholar of formidable erudition, given to meticulous accuracy in his textual research and rigorous development of his philosophical views.

## MONISM OF *QI*

Luo Qinshun was among the first of the Ming thinkers to put forward the argument that all reality, both physical and phenomenal, is *qi*, which is dynamic and constantly in process. The regularity that can be observed in an endless process of recurrence is *li* or principle. Luo explicitly rejected Zhu Xi's view that *li* represents a causal or determinative power distinct from *qi*, as expressed in Zhu's statement that "*li* attaches to *qi* and thus operates." *Li* is simply the pattern to be observed in the natural process rather than its origin or final cause. With *qi* being the fundamental reality of the universe, *li* is a designation (*ming*) for the "unregulated regularity" or spontaneous order to be discovered in *qi*. It is not, in itself, a "thing" (*wu*). It cannot be understood as ontologically prior to *qi*, or as superior to it, or as allied with *qi* but nonetheless metaphysically distinct from it. As energy, *qi* is originally one; as order or regularity, *li* is also one in the sense that it recurs in all the processes of nature.

When Confucius, in compiling the *Classic of Changes*, began with the words "probing principle to the utmost" (*qiong li*), what, in fact, did he mean by "principle" (*li*)? That which penetrates Heaven and Earth and connects past and present is nothing other than material-force (*qi*), which is unitary. This material-force, while originally one, revolves through endless cycles of movement and tranquillity, going and coming, opening and closing, rising and falling. Having become increasingly obscure, it then becomes manifest; having become manifest, it once again reverts to obscurity. It produces the warmth and coolness and the cold and heat of the four seasons, the birth, growth, gathering in, and storing of all living things, the constant moral relations of the people's daily life, the victory and defeat, gain and loss in human affairs. And amid all of this prolific variety and phenomenal diversity there is a detailed order and an elaborate coherence that cannot ultimately be disturbed, and that is so even without our knowing why it is so. This is what is called principle. Principle is not a separate entity that depends on material-force in order to exist or that "attaches to material force in order to operate."[21]

---

21. An explicit rejection of the language used by Zhu Xi in his statement (*Zhuzi quanshu* 49:4b): "Principle attaches to material-force and thus operates."

The phrase "there is in the changes the Supreme Ultimate"[22] has led some to suspect that there is a single entity that acts as a controlling power amid the transformations of yin and yang. But this is not the case. "Change" is a collective name for the two primary forces, the four secondary forms, and the eight trigrams. "The Supreme Ultimate" is a collective name for all principles taken together. To say that "there is in the changes the Supreme Ultimate" means that manifold diversity takes its origin from a single source.[23] This is then extended to the process of "production and reproduction"[24] to clarify that the dispersal of the single source produces manifold diversity. This is certainly the working of nature, its unregulated regularity, and not something that can be sought in the tangible realm.

It was only the elder Master Cheng [Cheng Hao] who described this most incisively. The views of the younger Master Cheng [Cheng Yi] and Master Zhu [Zhu Xi] seem to have been slightly different, and inasmuch as their theories all coexist, one must try to find a way to reconcile them and recover the ultimate unity.

[*Kunzhiji* 1, no. 11; Bloom, *Knowledge*, pp. 58–59; IB]

*Li* is only the *li* of *qi*. It must be observed in the phenomenon of revolving and turning of *qi*. Departing is followed by returning, and returning is followed by departing: this is the phenomenon of revolving and turning. And in the fact that departure must be followed by return, and return must be followed by departure, there is that which is so even without our knowing why it is so. It is as if there were a single entity acting as a regulating power within things and causing them to be as they are.[25] This is what we designate as *li* and what is referred to in the statement "There is in the changes the Supreme Ultimate."[26] If one gains a clear understanding of the phenomenon of revolving and turning, one will find that everything conforms to it.

Master Cheng said, "Within Heaven and Earth there is only the process of action and reaction. What else is there?"[27] Now, given the reaction of going, there is the action of coming, and given the action of coming, there is the reaction of going. Action and reaction follow in endless succession, and there is nowhere that principle does not pertain. It is the same in Heaven [or Nature, *tian*] and

---

22. *Classic of Changes, Commentary on the Appended Phrases*, Part 1; Lynn, *Classic of Changes*, p. 65.

23. *Mencius* 3A:5.

24. *Classic of Changes, Commentary on the Appended Phrases*, Part 1; Lynn, *Classic of Changes*, p. 54.

25. It should be noted that Luo says, "*as if there were* a single entity acting as a regulating power." In the preceding passage he has explicitly denied that this is *actually* the case.

26. *Classic of Changes, Commentary on the Appended Phrases*, Part 1; Lynn, *Classic of Changes*, p. 65.

27. Cheng Yi in *Yishu* 15:7b.

in humans. Because the Way of Heaven is what is common to all, action and reaction are constant and unerring. As the human emotions cannot be free of the encumbrance of selfish desires, action and reaction may be inconstant and liable to error.

What acts and reacts is *qi*, while the fact that a particular action involves a particular reaction without there being the slightest possibility of error is *li*. . . . The so-called "correct principle which is central and straight"[28] does not allow for an instant's deviation. It is what Heaven has ordained and also what constitutes the nature of human beings and things. I have therefore said that *li* must be identified as an aspect of *qi*, and yet to identify *qi* as *li* would be incorrect.

[*Kunzhiji xu* 3, no. 40; Bloom, *Knowledge*, pp. 173–174; IB]

## HUMAN NATURE

. . . I submit that the subtle truth of the nature (*xing*) and endowment (*ming*) is summarized in the formulation "Principle is one; its particularizations are diverse."[29] This is simple and yet complete, concise and yet utterly penetrating.

This [oneness of principle and diversity of its particularizations] owes nothing to compulsion or to contrivance, and by its nature it is utterly insusceptible to change. At the inception of life, when they are first endowed with *qi*, the principle of human beings and things is just one. After having attained physical form, their particularizations are diverse. That their particularizations are diverse is nothing but natural principle, for the oneness of their principle always exists within diverse particularizations. This is the explanation for the subtle truth of the nature and endowment. In terms of its oneness, "every human being can become a Yao or a Shun,"[30] and in terms of diversity, "only the very wisest and the very dullest do not change."[31]

[From *Kunzhiji* 1, no. 14; Bloom, *Knowledge*, p. 65; IB]

## DESIRES AND FEELINGS

One of the corollaries of Luo's denial of the notion of two natures, an original nature and a physical nature, was his rejection of the idea, basic to the psychological thought of most of the Song Neo-Confucians, that there was a fundamental antagonism between the Principle of Heaven (or Nature) and human desires. Selfish desires had often been thought to arise from the physical nature, to be counter to the original nature, and

---

28. Alludes to a statement of Cheng Hao's in *Yishu* 11:11a.
29. A statement of Cheng Yi's found in *Yichuan wenji* 5:12b, in *Er Cheng yishu*.
30. *Mencius* 6B:2.
31. *Analects* 17:3.

to demand either eradication or fairly rigorous curtailment. Human desires, in Luo's view, are, like the emotions, signs and expressions of human nature. They are natural and in conformity with principle. What requires control and regulation is the extremity of "selfishness" per se, the lack of awareness that one is fundamentally like others and has the same dispositions and needs.

The desire, love, and hate spoken of in the "Record of Music,"[32] together with the pleasure, sorrow, anger, and joy mentioned in the *Mean*,[33] are collectively termed the seven emotions. Their principles in each case are rooted in the nature. Among the seven emotions, desire is relatively important. Heaven [or Nature] produces people with desires. By following their desires people find pleasure. From the flouting of them they feel anger. In fulfilling them they feel joy. And in finding them thwarted they know sorrow. Therefore the "Record of Music" speaks only of "the desires arising from the nature."[34] The desires cannot be spoken of as evil. They may be good or evil depending solely on whether they are regulated.

[*Kunzhiji* 1, no. 17; Bloom, *Knowledge*, p. 68; IB]

## THE PRACTICAL LEARNING OF LÜ KUN

The late Ming witnessed a wide variety of intellectual developments, some stimulated by the challenge of Wang Yangming's philosophy, others reacting against it, and still others following through on the more practical side of Confucian and Neo-Confucian teaching. Lü Kun (1536–1618), a scholar-official of broad practical experience known for his integrity and forthrightness, spoke for a growing impatience in the late Ming with philosophical disputation ("empty talk") concerning the mind and human nature. In his refusal to be identified with any one doctrinal school (he insisted, "I am just me"), Lü, though less radical than Li Zhi, nevertheless typified the independent and individualistic spirit increasingly evident in late Ming thought.

Well reputed for his effectiveness as an administrator and outspokenness as a minister, Lü pictured himself as a "doctor to the people," approaching the problems of his society empirically and pragmatically, looking for practical solutions rather than adhering to bookish rules or established ways. Much concerned with education, like Zhu Xi and Wang Yangming before him, Lü reflected the growing populism of the Ming period in his efforts to spread learning beyond the elite to the common people and women. He promoted community schools on the local level, while commending literacy among women

---

32. "Record of Music," *Record of Rites*; Legge, *Li Ki*, 2:96.

33. *Mean* 1:4.

34. "Record of Music," *Record of Rites*; Legge, *Li Ki*, 2:96.

and emphasizing their moral equality and autonomy. To make his points he often wrote in the colloquial language, using popular rhyme schemes reset to simple tunes and colorful anecdotes. None of this was wholly unprecedented or unique to Lü, but he did it so well that his work was much used. His guidelines for local administration, published under the title "Records of Practical Administration" ("Shizheng lu"), became a model for administrative practice in the following Qing dynasty. His enduring fame is shown by the installation of his tablet in the Confucian temple (1826) and the respect with which his work was regarded by eighteenth- and nineteenth-century Japanese Confucian scholars.

## RESTORATION OF COMMUNITY SCHOOLS

The "restoration" called for here evokes the early advocacy of such schools by Zhu Xi, attempts in the fourteenth century under the Yuan dynasty to establish elementary schools, as well as the Ming founder's initial adoption and subsequent abolition of them in favor of private schools. Revival of the idea became a feature of sixteenth-century reform efforts (along with the community compacts advocated by Wang Yangming) to deal with the crisis in local governance after the decline of the early Ming *lijia* system of local administration. In this essay Lü's comments on the deterioration of education on the local level point to chronic ills: neglect of general, public education in official schools by teachers who emphasize only literary skills useful in civil service examinations, with a consequent aversion to this kind of study by a farming population, which sees in it no tangible benefit to compensate for the loss of able-bodied young men from work in the fields.

Lü emphasizes that learning should appeal to the emotions, especially through group singing, and also be directed at general moral uplift, not preparation for the civil service examinations.

—Ever since true education has deteriorated, the whole world has ceased to understand what book learning is all about. For more than two thousand years it has been misconceived, and right down to the present: what teachers have told their disciples and fathers have transmitted to their sons is only that they should come out first in the (*jinshi*) examinations as a stepping-stone to wealth and rank. Today, in selecting teachers for the community [schools], one should pick twenty or so scholars (*shi*) who are more than forty years old, whose pure hearts are intact, and whose purpose is upright—no matter whether they have already attended [state] schools or not. The official in charge should have them assemble at the Confucian Temple and give them daily grain rations. Instruction should begin with explanations of the *Elementary Learning* (*Xiaoxue*) and the *Classic of Filiality* (*Xiaojing*), as well as the study of characters and keys to pronunciation. After a year, if the students' recognition [of characters] is almost correct, their pronunciations accurate, the meaning of the texts roughly understood, and their explications are also correct, then the official in charge should pay a visit to the school to examine them and select the ones who are worthy of teaching others. Looking into where there are community schools, he should assign [the newly trained teachers] accordingly. . . .

—The best thing in the world is for young people to study—whether [they do so] for the lofty goals of achieving a reputation and accomplishing great deeds or for the modest aim of recognizing characters and understanding their meanings. There are some unenlightened parents who do not teach their sons to read; the sons end up becoming evil men, with depraved minds-and-hearts and untamed natures; they turn into thieves and break the laws—all because of this [failure in education]. Have you ever seen anyone who understands principles and recognizes characters willing to become a thief?

The official in charge should proclaim to the common people: Hereafter, students of an age to study are to be sent to community schools; even if they are poor and needed for work at home, they must attend school after the tenth month [harvest] and only return to their homes after the third month [for planting]. If after three years, their talents prove to be such that nothing more can be expected of them, then have them return to their usual occupations. . . .

—Whenever expounding on texts, one should instruct the children to apply [the contents] to their own personal experience [by asking]: "Are these words relevant to you? Can you learn from this passage or not?" One should also tell a couple of stories that provide models and warnings, so as to enlighten [the children]. If on some later day the [children] should commit transgressions, then reprimand them by using the stories already told to them, so that they might be improved in body and mind.

—Every day, whenever one encounters children feeling tired and lazy, chant one stanza of *shi* poetry. Select old and new [poems] that are very simple, that are trenchant, to the point, emotionally stirring, and germane, to be assembled into a book; have [the students] chant them, and give them explanations and require that the students learn them. . . . Sing one stanza each day. As for those who practice new tunes or provocative and seductive words: punish them as soon as they are found out.

—Those who have just entered the community schools, from the age of eight [*sui*] on, should first read the *Three Character Classic*[35] in order to practice identifying what they see and hear; *The Hundred Surnames*, which facilitates the knowledge of everyday things; and the *Thousand Character Essay*, which also contains moral principles. . . .

*There follow detailed instructions on calligraphy, reading method, care in the handling of books, writing compositions, and so on.*

---

35. See chap. 23.

—In studying, diligence is most important. Whether living nearby or far away, the children should all arrive at school at the crack of dawn. After reciting their texts from memory, they should study new texts. After eating, let them outside for a while to run freely for one or two quarters of an hour, after which they should read, write compositions, make copies, and then read some more. After lunch, let them again go outside to run about for one or two quarters of an hour and then study further. After sundown, divide them into rows facing one another. Take out one correct essay and one blemished essay, and then explain the corrections. After that, school should be dismissed. Because the young have weak stomachs, [the students] should not immediately use their mental energies after [the evening] meal, lest they get indigestion. . . .

—Community schools are not intended for the preparation of examination candidates. Their entire purpose is to set straight the habits of the young. If the curriculum fails to call for the practice of virtuous deeds and [instead] emphasizes the acquisition of literary skills, then the community school teachers, even if learned men, should be dismissed.

[From *Shizheng lu* 3:7a–12b; JHS]

# MORALITY BOOKS

In the sixteenth century the spread of Wang Yangming's thought gave a further stimulus to education among the lower classes and contributed to the increased demand for popular morality books (*shanshu*). This type of book, which had made its appearance in the Song period, became much more popular in the Yuan and Ming. Together with the encyclopedias for daily use, the morality books served a wide public, especially in the late Ming. By calling them "popular" we mean that these books served not only the lower levels of society but all types and classes of people, irrespective of social status, gender, economic position, and religious affiliation. In fact, so basic was their appeal to the common denominator in ethical thought that they were read and used even by some scholars identified with the main schools of learning.

The underlying idea of the morality books is that virtue is rewarded and vice punished. Besides identifying good deeds and their rewards, as well as bad deeds and their retributions, the morality books give homely tales drawn from the popular consciousness and imagination to illustrate them. Probably the best-known representative of this type is the *Treatise of the Most Exalted One on Moral Retribution (Taishang ganying pian)*, which was published for the first time in the Southern Song period and republished often thereafter. Much of its content was Confucian—that is, it represented Confucianism as practiced among the common people, supplemented and supported by religious notions drawn from Daoism and Buddhism.

## THE TREATISE OF THE MOST EXALTED ONE
## ON MORAL RETRIBUTION

This popular treatise was sometimes considered the work of Laozi, but it is probably a work of the twelfth century, authorship still uncertain. Millions of copies of this work, and of the *Silent Way of Recompense*, which follows here, have been distributed over the years by individuals and organizations of goodwill. They are standard texts in most popular cults and would probably be found in any rural village that possessed even a few books.

The Most Exalted One said, "Calamities and blessings do not come through any [fixed] gate; it is man himself that invites them." The reward of good and evil is like the shadow accompanying the body. Accordingly, there are in Heaven and Earth spiritual beings who record a man's evil deeds and, depending upon the lightness or gravity of his transgressions, reduce his term of life by units of three days. As units are taken away, his health becomes poor, and his spirit becomes wasted. He will often meet with sorrow and misery, and all other men will hate him. Punishments and calamities will pursue him; good luck and joy will shun him; evil stars will harm him. When the allotted units are exhausted, he will die.

Furthermore, there are the Three Ministers of the Northern Constellation residing above a man's head. They register his crimes and misconduct and take away from his term of life periods of three hundred or three days. There are also the Three Worm-Spirits residing inside man's body. Whenever the fifty-seventh day [of the sixty-day cycle, the day characterized by severity and change] comes around, they ascend to the court of Heaven and report man's misconduct and transgressions. On the last day of the month, the Kitchen God does the same. When a man's transgressions are great, three hundred days are taken away from his term of life. When they are small, three days are taken away. Great and small transgressions number in the hundreds. Those who seek long life on earth must first of all avoid them.

Go forward if your deed follows the Way (*dao*) but withdraw if it violates it. Do not tread evil paths. Do nothing shameful even in the recesses of your own house. Accumulate virtue and amass merits. Have a compassionate heart toward all creatures. Be loyal to your sovereign, filial to your parents, friendly to your younger brothers, and brotherly to your older brothers. Rectify yourself and so transform others. Be compassionate to orphans and sympathetic to widows. Respect the old and cherish the young. Even insects, grass, and trees you must not hurt. How much more should you grieve at the misfortune of others and rejoice in their good fortune! Assist those in need and save those in danger. Regard others' gain as your own gain and their loss as your own loss. Do not publicize their shortcomings nor boast of your own superiorities. Stop evil and promote good. Yield much but take little. Accept humiliation without complaint and favor with a sense of apprehension. Bestow kindness and seek no recompense. Give without regret.

He who is good is respected by all men. The way of Heaven helps him, happiness and wealth follow him, all evil things shun him, and spiritual beings protect him. Whatever he does will succeed. He may even hope to become an immortal.

He who seeks to become an immortal of Heaven should perform 1,200 good deeds. He who seeks to become an immortal of earth should perform 300.

But if he acts contrary to rightness or behaves improperly . . . [Here follows a long list of misconduct and crimes to be avoided, concluding with:] if he is insatiably covetous and greedy or takes oaths and swears to seek vindication; if he loves liquor and becomes rude and disorderly or is angry and quarrelsome with his relatives; if as a husband he is not faithful and good, or if as a wife she is not gentle and obedient; if the husband is not in harmony with his wife; if the wife is not respectful to her husband; if he is always fond of boasting and bragging; if she constantly acts out her jealousy and envy; if he behaves immorally toward his wife and children; if she behaves improperly toward her parents-in-law; if he treats with slight and disrespect the spirits of his ancestors or disobeys the commands of his superiors; if he occupies himself with what is not beneficial to others or cherishes a disloyal heart; if he curses himself and others or is partial in his love and hatred; if he steps over the well or hearth [which should be taken seriously because water and fire are indispensable to life] or leaps over food [served on the floor] or a person [lying on a floor mat]; if he kills babies or brings about abortion or does many actions of secret depravity; if he sings or dances on the last day of the month or year [when the ends should be sent off with sorrow] or bawls out or gets angry on the first day of the year or the month [when the beginning should be welcomed with joy]; if he weeps, spits, or urinates when facing north [the direction of the North Star and the emperor] or chants and laughs facing the hearth [which should be treated solemnly because the family depends on it for food]; and, moreover, if he lights incense with hearth fire [a sign of disrespect] or uses dirty fuel to cook food; if he shows his naked body when rising at night or executes punishment on the eight festivals of the year; if he spits at a shooting star or points at a rainbow; if he suddenly points to the three luminaries or gazes long at the sun and the moon; if in the spring months [when things are growing] he burns the thickets in hunting or angrily reviles others when he faces north; if without reason he kills tortoises or snakes [which are honored along with the Northern Constellation], if he commits these or similar crimes, the Arbiter of Human Destiny will, according to their lightness or gravity, take away from the culprit's term of life periods of three hundred or three days. When these units are exhausted, he will die. If at death there remains guilt unpunished, the evil luck will be transferred to his posterity.

Moreover, if one wrongly seizes another's property, his wife, children, and other members of his family are to be held responsible, the expiation to be proportionate up to punishment by death. If they do not die, there will be disasters from water, fire, thieves, loss of property, illness, quarrels, and the like to compensate for the wrong seizure.

Further, he who kills men unjustly puts a weapon into the hands of others who will turn on him and kill him. He who seizes property unrighteously is like one who relieves hunger with spoiled food or quenches thirst with poisoned wine. He will be full for the time being, but death will inevitably follow. If good thoughts arise in one's mind, even though the good deeds may not be performed, spirits of good fortune attend one. If evil thoughts arise in one's mind, even though the evil is not performed, the spirits of misfortune descend on him.

If one has already done an evil deed but later repents of his own accord and corrects his way, refrains from doing any evil, and earnestly practices many good deeds, in time he will surely obtain good fortune. This is what is called changing calamities into blessings.

Therefore the man of good fortune speaks good, sees good, and does good. Every day he performs three good deeds. At the end of three years Heaven will send down blessings on him. Why not make an effort to do good?

[From *Taishang ganying pian*, DZ 834–839, no. 1167; WTC]

THE *SILENT WAY OF RECOMPENSE* (*YINZHIWEN*)

The general purport of the text (popularly attributed to the Daoist deity Wenchang) is to encourage people to practice good deeds in secret. The "silent way" means that one should not look for others' approbation when carrying out good deeds. In fact, the implication of the "silent way" is that only good deeds done in secret accrue full merit. The concept of "hidden virtue" (another term for the "silent way") became an important feature of later morality books.

The Lord says, For seventeen generations I have been incarnated as a high official, and I have never oppressed the people or my subordinates. I have saved people from misfortune, helped people in need, shown pity to orphans, and forgiven people's mistakes. I have extensively practiced the Silent Way of Recompense and have penetrated Heaven above. If you can set your minds on things as I have set mine, Heaven will surely bestow blessings upon you. Therefore, I pronounce these instructions to humankind, saying . . .

Whoever wants to expand his field of happiness, let him rely on the ground of his mind-and-heart.

Do good work at all times and practice in secret meritorious deeds of all kinds.

Benefit living creatures and human beings. Cultivate goodness and happiness.

Be honest and straight and, on behalf of Heaven, promote moral reform.

Be compassionate and merciful and, for the sake of the country, save the people.

Be loyal to your ruler and filial to your parents.

Be respectful toward elders and truthful to friends.

Obey the purity [of Daoism] and worship the Northern Constellation; or revere the scriptures and recite the holy name of the Buddha.

Repay the four kindnesses [done to us by Heaven, Earth, the sovereign, and parents]. Extensively practice the three religions.

Help people in distress as you would help a fish in a dried-up rut. Free people from danger as you would free a sparrow from a fine net.

Be compassionate to orphans and kind to widows. Respect the aged and have pity on the poor.

Collect food and clothing and relieve those who are hungry and cold along the road. Give away coffins lest the dead of the poor be exposed.

If your own family is well provided for, extend a helping hand to your relatives. If the harvest fails, relieve and help your neighbors and friends.

Let measures and scales be accurate, and do not give less in selling or take more in buying. Treat your servants with generosity and consideration; why should you be severe in condemnation and harsh in your demands?

Write and publish holy scriptures and tracts. Build and repair temples and shrines.

Distribute medicine to alleviate the suffering of the sick. Offer tea and water to relieve the distress of the thirsty.

Buy captive creatures and set them free, or hold fast to vegetarianism and abstain from taking life.

Whenever taking a step, always watch for ants and insects. Prohibit the building of fires outside [lest insects be killed] and do not set mountain woods or forests ablaze.

Light lanterns at night to illuminate where people walk. Build riverboats to ferry people across.

Do not go into the mountain to catch birds in nets, nor to the water to poison fish and shrimps.

Do not butcher the ox that plows the field. Do not throw away paper with writing on it.

Do not scheme for others' property. Do not envy others' skill or ability.

Do not violate people's wives or daughters. Do not stir up litigation among others.

Do not injure others' reputation or interest. Do not destroy people's marriages.

Do not, on account of personal enmity, create disharmony between brothers.

Do not, for a small profit, cause father and son to quarrel.

Do not misuse your power to disgrace the good and the law-abiding. Do not presume upon your wealth to oppress the poor and needy.

Be close to and friendly with the good; this will improve your moral character in body and mind. Keep at a distance from the wicked; this will prevent imminent danger.

Always conceal people's vices but proclaim their virtue. Do not say "yes" with your mouth and "no" in your heart.

Cut brambles and thorns that obstruct the road. Remove bricks and stones that lie in the path.

Put in good condition roads that have been rough for several hundred years. Build bridges over which thousands and tens of thousands of people may travel.

Leave behind your moral instructions to correct people's faults. Donate money to bring to completion the good deeds of others.

Follow the Principle of Heaven in your work. Obey the dictates of the human heart in your words.

[Admire the ancient sages so much that you] see them while eating soup or looking at the wall. [Be so clear in conscience that] when you sleep alone, you are not ashamed before your bedding, and when you walk alone, you are not ashamed before your own shadow.

Refrain from doing any evil, but earnestly do all good deeds.

Then there will never be any influence of evil stars upon you, but you will always be protected by good and auspicious spirits.

Immediate rewards will come to your own person, and later rewards will reach your posterity.

A hundred blessings will come as if drawn by horses, and a thousand fortunes will gather about you like clouds.

Do not all these things come through the Silent Way of Recompense?

[From *Yinzhiwen guangyi*, Zhou Mengyan ed.; WTC]

## THE DONGLIN ACADEMY

The Donglin Academy has long been seen as of major historical importance in the late Ming and a focal point of controversy, for at least four main reasons. First, it represented a reaction, morally conservative and politically reformist, against libertarian tendencies in the Wang Yangming school identified particularly with Wang Ji and Li Zhi. Second, although it was heir to Neo-Confucian teachings concerning the philosophy of human nature, it emphasized practice more than theory, and especially socially relevant action. Third, though it represented a mainline consensus on certain basic principles, which could be called neo-orthodox, it included scholars of diverse views and encouraged the "discussion of learning" or "discursive learning" (*jiangxue*), which to some meant active, open intellectual and political discussion, but by others later was dismissed as empty, airy speculation or partisan polemics. Fourth, the academy represented a notable trend in the late Ming toward the formation of voluntary associations—social, cultural, and religious—that in the modern West might be identified with civil society or a public sphere.

The Donglin Academy was organized at Wuxi in the lower Yangtze Valley, as a private (i.e., unofficial) center for the discussion of philosophical questions. Its principal founder, Gu Xiancheng (1550–1612), had turned to this type of activity after being forced out of the government for his outspoken criticism of those in power around the throne. Other participants in the discussions of the academy were identified, like Gu, with the so-called Righteous Circles at court, considered the champions of legality and official integrity in the government. Nevertheless, the purpose of their discussions was not primarily to exert some kind of public pressure upon their political enemies. Rather, as convinced Confucians, they believed that their efforts should first be directed toward intellectual weaknesses that had corrupted the educated class and undermined public life. Their aim was nothing less than the aim of Confucius himself—the moral regeneration of the ruling class. In this respect, then, they thought of themselves not as breaking new ground or departing from tradition but as returning to the original spirit of Confucianism. Gu and other leading members of the group still regarded Zhu Xi as the soundest exponent of this tradition, and in fact the stated aims of the school were based on the stated principles of Zhu Xi's own academy. Others were more strongly influenced by the philosophy of Wang Yangming. While thus differing in their philosophical approach, however, they agreed in reaffirming the fundamentally ethical character of Confucianism and in condemning the more extreme wing of the Wang Yangming school, which leaned in the direction of Chan Buddhism.

The tendency of this latter group, as we have seen, was to interpret Wang's doctrine of innate knowledge as meaning that the original mind of man was endowed with a transcendental perfection, beyond all relative notions of good and evil. To manifest this perfection, man need only rid himself of arbitrary or conventional conceptions of morality, and respond freely to the promptings of this innate, originally pure mind. "Naturalness" and "spontaneity" were the ideals of this group. Conscious moral effort they considered at best a preparatory method for those who still were fettered by ordinary habits of mind.

Gu Xiancheng and his colleagues saw in this kind of freethinking the abandonment of the moral struggle that Confucius had put forward as the highest destiny of man. To it they attributed the moral laxity at court, the readiness of many officials to cooperate with corrupt ministers and powerful eunuchs, and the prevailing fuzziness about right and wrong. Against such opportunism, dignified by the appearance of broadmindedness and spontaneity, the Donglin upheld the human moral nature.

To its reformist struggle the Donglin brought all the fervor and intensity that characterized the bitter battles being waged at court. By their outspoken criticism of those in power, these men risked flogging, official degradation, and perhaps torture and death in the dungeons of the eunuch's secret police.

Though it was a policy of the Donglin to discuss political questions "outside of school," the distinction was actually difficult to draw. Many of the issues discussed centered upon personalities in the government, and the Donglin group engaged more in what was called "the judging of other men's characters" than in what we would consider the discussion of public issues or the advancement of a concrete political program.

GU XIANCHENG: COMPACT FOR MEETINGS
OF THE DONGLIN ACADEMY

This charter, prepared in 1604 by Gu Xiancheng and subscribed to by several leading scholars, served as an open invitation to meetings, the philosophical and procedural basis for which was set forth in the form of a voluntary compact or agreement. Its main point is to reaffirm the rational, moral nature of man, the value of study and intellectual inquiry, and the need for practical action to reform human society.

In form, the charter combines features of Zhu Xi's "Articles of the White Deer Grotto Academy," with procedural and ritual provisions similar to Zhu Xi's version of the community compact. Like Zhu Xi's works, too, it draws heavily on earlier texts and precedents, while Gu's important contributions are offered ostensibly as subcommentary.

The centerpiece is Zhu Xi's "Articles," which Gu extols for its clarity and logical sequence. This is preceded by quotations from the *Analects*, the *Great Learning*, and the *Mean*, and others from *Mencius* emphasizing the goodness of human nature and man's capacity for sagehood. Following Zhu's "Articles" and postscript, Gu proceeds with a lengthy discussion of Four Essentials, Two Misconceptions, Nine Benefits, and Nine Detriments, which point up the contemporary significance of the basic principles. They are presented here in abridged form.

## Four Essentials

1. Know what is fundamental.

What then is fundamental? What is fundamental is one's nature. One learns in order fully to develop one's nature. Developing one's nature starts with recognizing one's nature. If this is not recognized, one can hardly talk about fully developing one's nature, and if one's nature is not to be developed, one can hardly talk about learning. In my estimation, Zhu Xi's "Articles of the White Deer Grotto Academy" is the [true] learning of one's nature, which one cannot fail to ponder with care. Thus the intimate affection between parent and child, rightness between ruler and minister, differentiation between husband and wife, the order of priority between older and younger, trustworthiness between friends, as well as what in fact makes each of these what it is, what indeed is to be studied, inquired into, reflected upon, evaluated, and performed [as in the *Mean* and Zhu Xi's "Articles"]—all of these must be pondered with care. In the cultivation of one's self, can one's speech of itself be true and trustworthy [without careful judgment being exercised], can one's conduct of itself be reverential and exemplary [without careful judgment being exercised], can indignation restrain itself, can desires be controlled of themselves, good deeds be accomplished of themselves, evil deeds be reformed of themselves? In the management of affairs, is there such a thing as questions of right and wrong, merit and profit, being decided of themselves spontaneously [without reflection]; in dealings with others is there such a thing as not doing to others what one does not want for oneself, or being able to reflect upon oneself without having to consider these carefully? [4b–5a]

*There follows a lengthy discussion of the erroneous view that "the substance of the mind [the nature] is beyond good and evil"—the first of Wang Yangming's Four Dicta from the Colloquy at the Tianquan Bridge—which Gu identifies with Buddhism and Daoism and earlier with Gaozi's view of human nature as neither good nor evil. This view, he says, subverts the practice of the moral and intellectual virtues encouraged by Confucius, Mencius, and Zhu Xi.*

2. Establish a firm resolve.

What does it mean to speak of "firm resolve"? Firm resolve sets the direction the mind-and-heart goes in. It is what a person's whole life spirit converges on, what a person's whole life undertaking is rooted in, what one needs in order to stand on one's own feet. As Master Zhou [Dunyi] says, "The sage aspires to Heaven, the worthy aspires to sagehood, the scholar-official aspires to be worthy." . . . Master Zhang [Zai] says, "Establish one's mind-and-heart for the sake of Heaven and Earth; establish one's mission in life for the sake of the welfare of humankind; follow the sages in carrying on the oft-lapsed tradition for the sake of bringing peace to ten thousand generations. . . ." Scholars who would succeed to the mission inherited from the Song masters find that it all lies in this. Therefore it is essential for the gentleman to establish a firm resolve. [9b–10a]

3. Revere the Classics.

*In this section, not translated here, Gu argues for the importance of studying the Six Classics expounded by Confucius and the Four Books as commented on by Zhu Xi. These embody the constant and unvarying Way, which is to be made a part of oneself by careful reading of texts and assimilating of them to one's own experience, rather than following the self-delusory view of Lu Xiangshan, who claimed that the classics are no more than footnotes to oneself.*

4. Examine one's motives.

What does it mean to speak of examining one's motives? It is the distinguishing of sincerity and insincerity in the most minute sign of the incipient spring of one's actions. What has its source in the mind-and-heart is bound to show itself in one's person, and what has its source in one's person must become evident to others. Let there be no mistake! . . . Therefore it is essential for the gentleman to examine his motives at their very source.

[From Gu Xiancheng, *Donglin huiyue* 1, in *Donglin shuyuan zhi* 17:4b–12a; dB]

## Nine Benefits

For brevity's sake, the benefits of such discussions may be summarized as:

1. They promote the fundamental aim of learning to become a sage or worthy.
2. They make moral instruction available to all comers.
3. The solemnity of the proceedings lifts the mind to higher things.
4. An atmosphere suffused with moral instruction and ritual practice has a quiet, transforming influence on the self.
5. A collegial atmosphere of teachers and students is supportive of self-cultivation.
6. The collective experience and wisdom of a large gathering helps to broaden one's horizons and solve one's problems.
7. In such a setting one can get a new perspective on one's past and future life.
8. The ritual observances in the Confucian shrine inspire one to emulate the sages and worthies enshrined therein.
9. The meetings encourage one to keep one's mind set on the primary values of the Way rather than on ephemeral fame and fortune. [12b–14b]

## Procedural Rules for Donglin Meetings

Details are given here for the rituals, protocols, and formalities that should govern the proceedings, which are open to all but show special respect for seniority and for guests. Major meetings are held annually in fall or spring; minor meetings monthly in favorable seasons. Leading scholars preside in turn. The following excerpts explain the conduct of philosophical discussion at meetings:

For every meeting someone is to be chosen to make the main presentation on a chapter in the Four Books. If someone has a question, let him ask it; if one wants further discussion of a point, let it be discussed. During the meeting, let all listen with an open ("empty") mind. Even if one has a point to make, let him wait a little. After the lecture is over, one may in turn ask permission to speak, without disturbing the proceedings.

After prolonged sitting at the meetings, some verses from classic odes [*shi*] should be sung as a way of relaxing and restoring one's spirits. All should sing in unison and deeply savor the melody and meaning. After repeated singing, the mind-and-heart and voice become blended together, one's whole spirit enters into the singing, and the whole experience leaves a deep, lasting impression.

[18a–19a; trans. adapted from Busch, "Tung-lin," p. 38; dB]

*The first stipulation, focusing the discussion on the Cheng-Zhu Four Books, marks this as a Neo-Confucian, neo-orthodox movement. The last provision underscores the importance attached to engaging the spirit and emotions, as well as the intellect and moral sense, in these scholarly meetings. Thus the Donglin Academy continued the strong tradition of Neo-Confucian academies as religious, liturgical, and social centers for the educated classes.*

## LIU ZONGZHOU ON LIFE AND DEATH

Liu Zongzhou (1578–1645), who had close affinities with the Donglin school, was a leading thinker of the late Ming and the teacher of the eminent scholar and political theorist, Huang Zongxi, whom we will meet in chapter 58 (vol. 2). Though differing in some respects from the Donglin academicians, Liu shared their commitment to the Zhu Xi tradition of learning, their concerns with the moral regeneration of the ruling class, and their courage in speaking out against misgovernment. Like several of his contemporaries, he was unafraid to speak out against the notorious eunuch Wei Zhongxian in the 1620s or, as president of the Censorate,[36] to memorialize in favor of dynastic reform in the early 1640s. His criticisms offended the emperor, leading to Liu's dismissal from office. But, though he had personal experience of the failings of Ming despotism, Liu remained loyal to the Ming cause following the fall of Peking to the invading Manchus in 1644, and when he was reappointed to the Censorate in the Ming government after its retreat to Nanking, he continued his demands for reform. When Nanking fell in turn, and it was clear that the dynasty could not be revived, Liu demonstrated the depth of his convictions about service and sacrifice, committing suicide by fasting for twenty-one days. Liu represents a consummate example of courage, moral scrupulousness, and a typically Confucian kind of loyalty— a loyalty more to principle than to persons. We conclude this volume with his brief but moving "Teaching on Life and Death," which may recall his tribute to Fang Xiaoru (earlier in this chapter) and reevoke the affirmative spirit found in the "Western Inscription" composed centuries earlier by Zhang Zai, though, in this seventeenth-century context, the affirmation seems to be asserted against a sense of darkness and crisis.

### TEACHING ON LIFE AND DEATH (*SHENGSI SHUO*)

When they do not clearly understand the learning of the Sages, students often give rise to views based on the physical vessel [the body]. They see that, for the

---

36. The Censorate (*yushi tai*, lit., the "terrace or pavilion of imperial scribes") was, as Charles Hucker describes it, "an agency in the top echelon of the central government [from Han through Ming]. . . with the paramount and characteristic responsibility of maintaining disciplinary surveillance over the whole of officialdom, checking records and auditing accounts in government offices, accepting public complaints and impeaching officials who in their private or public lives violated the law or otherwise conducted themselves improperly" (*Dictionary of Official Titles*, p. 593, no. 8184).

body, the affair of life and death is the greatest of all, and they place the myriad things of Heaven and Earth on the outside of the barrier. They have already cut off the seeds of the constantly reborn living potential of this mind, and so in their work [of self-cultivation] they concentrate on reaching the road of birthlessness, so that all that remains undestroyed is an awareness that is still active. This enables them to become humans again. However, if they follow this way, they cannot escape the cycle of coveting life and fearing death.

Our Confucian learning takes forming one body with Heaven and Earth and the myriad things as the great body. The starting point of Heaven, Earth, and the myriad things is our own starting point, and the end point of Heaven, Earth, and the myriad things is our own end point. From beginning to end, from end to beginning, the cycle never ends. This is our teaching on life and death.

Actually, life and death are commonplace things. Master Cheng Hao said, "If a person can let go of this self and view all things within Heaven and Earth, great and small, in the same way—what joy this would be!"[37] I say that the teaching on life and death ought to be placed between Heaven and Earth, and great and small are all seen as equal. To realize this is at last the learning of fully fathoming the true principle, fully realizing our true nature, and thoroughly extending to Heaven's command. If we merely hold to the life and death of a single life-span in order to know life and death, then, knowing that life ends, we only know the life of coveting life, and knowing the finality of death, we only know the death of fearing death.

Someone asked: "So then, is it unnecessary to know the life and death of a single life-span?"

[The teacher] said, "How can we not know them? This is what Confucius meant when he said, 'If you hear of the Way in the morning, it is all right to die that evening.'[38] What is the hearing of the Way? . . . If there are no arising and no demise, then there are naturally no birth and no death.' " He also said, "If you exhaust the path of speech and silence, then you can exhaust the path of going away and coming back. If you exhaust the path of going away and coming back, then you can exhaust the path of birth and death. Birth and death are not great matters;[39] speech and silence and going away and coming back are not small matters. For those engaged in learning, the barrier of birth and death is often hard to pass through. If you acquire a penetrating understanding of this point, Heaven, Earth, and the myriad things are none other than this. And this at last is 'hearing of the Way.' "

[From "Shengsi shuo," in *Liuzi quanji* 2:378–81; TW]

---

37. Liu appears to have slightly adapted a statement by Cheng Hao in *Er Cheng yishu* (SBBY ed.) 2A:15b in *Er Cheng quanshu*.

38. *Analects* 4:8.

39. Buddhists were told to be constantly mindful of the "great matter" of life and death.

# GLOSSARY OF KEY TERMS

Following are key Chinese terms appearing in this volume, with renderings in order of (1) *pinyin* romanization; (2) alternate Wade-Giles romanization (if any); (3) the Chinese character; (4) standard or preferred English translation herein; (5) variant translations used in particular contexts (the Chinese character often connotes several such meanings at once).

*ben/pen* 本      root, trunk, base; (adj.) primary, fundamental, essential (often in combination with *mo*, branch, secondary, etc. [see *mo*])

*benxin/pen-hsin* 本心      original or essential mind/heart

*chen/ch'en* 臣      minister, subject

*cheng/ch'eng* 誠      sincerity, genuineness, integrity, authenticity

*dao/tao* 道      the Way, way, path

*de/te* 德      virtue, moral force, inner power

*fa* 法      law, system, measure, method (in Buddhism: law, doctrine, phenomenon)

*fengjian/feng-chien* 封建      enfeoffment, feudal

*gewu/ko-wu* 格物      investigation of things, rectification of affairs

*gong/kung* 公      common good, shared, public, fair to all

*guo/kuo* 國      state, dynastic state, nation

*jian ai/chien-ai* 兼愛      embracing love, universal love

*jing/ching* 敬      reverence, reverent seriousness

*jing/ching* 經      classic (Confucianism); scripture (Daoism); *sūtra* (Buddhism)

*jun/chün* 君      ruler, prince

| | |
|---|---|
| *junzi/chün-tzu* 君子 | noble person, gentleman, superior person |
| *li* 禮 | rites, ritual decorum |
| *li* 理 | principle, order, directive or guiding principle, numen, coding, infrastructure |
| *li* 利 | gain, profit, advantage, resources |
| *liang zhi/chih* 良知 | innate or good knowledge/knowing |
| *ming ming de/te* 明明德 | to clarify or manifest luminous virtue |
| *mingde/ming-te* 明德 | luminous virtue, clear virtue, the moral nature |
| *mo* 末 | branch, outgrowth; (adj.) secondary, derivative, degenerate |
| *qi/ch'i* 氣 | vital force, vital energy, material-force, ether; (adj.) psycho-physical |
| *qing/ch'ing* 情 | emotion, feeling |
| *ren/jen* 仁 | humaneness (as practical virtue); humanity (as perfection of all virtue); co-humanity (as shared virtue) |
| *ren/jen* 人 | humankind, human being, person, man |
| *renyu/jen-yü* 人欲 | human desires; selfish desires (i.e., when conflicting with the common good, especially in rulers and those entrusted with responsibility for others) |
| *ru/ju* 儒 | Confucian school or scholar |
| *sangang/san-kang* 三岡 | Three Mainstays or Three Bonds |
| *sangangling/san-kang-ling* 三岡領 | Three Main Guidelines |
| *shen* 神 | spirit, deity, numen, *anima*; (adj.) spiritual, numinous |
| *shen* 身 | self, person, body |
| *shi/shih* 事 | thing, affair, matter, fact, event, instantiation |
| *shi/shih* 實 | substantial, real, solid, practical |
| *shi/shih* 士 | scholar-official, literatus, man of service |
| *shu* 恕 | reciprocity, mutuality, empathy |
| *si/ssu* 私 | private or self-interest (as complementary to common good [*gong*]); selfishness (when in conflict with common or public good) |
| *taiji/t'ai-chi* 太極 | Supreme Ultimate, Pole, or Norm; Supreme Polarity |
| *ti/t'i* 體 | substance, body, essence |
| *tian/t'ien* 天 | Heaven, celestial; (adj.) natural |
| *tianming/t'ien-ming* 天命 | Heaven's Mandate, ordination, ordinance, charge, decree |
| *tianxia/t'ien-hsia* 天下 | All under Heaven, everyone, the world, realm |
| *tiyong/t'i-yung* 體用 | substance/function |
| *wen* 文 | culture, civil, writing, literature, pattern, decoration |
| *wu* 無 | nothing, nothingness, absence |
| *wuji/wu chi* 無極 | non-finite, nonpolar, indeterminate |
| *wuwei/wu-wei* 無為 | doing nothing, nonassertion, taking no deliberate action |
| *wuxing* 五行 | Five Phases |
| *xiao/hsiao* 孝 | filiality, filial piety or devotion |

| | |
|---|---|
| *xin/hsin* 心 | mind-and-heart, mind, heart |
| *xin/hsin* 信 | trustworthiness, trust, faith |
| *xing/hsing* 性 | human nature, *the* nature (not Nature) |
| *xiu/hsiu* 修 | cultivation, discipline |
| *xiushen/hsiu shen* 修身 | self-cultivation, self-discipline, cultivation of one's person |
| *xu/hsü* 虛 | empty, void, open, receptive |
| *xue/hsüeh* 學 | learning, study, school |
| *yi/i* 義 | rightness, what is right, concept, meaning; (adj.) moral |
| *yi/i* 意 | intention, thought |
| *yong/yung* 用 | function, use, operation |
| *yu/yü* 欲 | desire, appetite |
| *zhengxin/cheng-hsin* 正心 | correcting or rectifying the mind-and-heart |
| *zhi/chih* 知 | know, learn; knowledge, knowing, understanding |
| *zhi/chih* 智 | wisdom |
| *zhi/chih* 止 | stop, rest (Buddhism: calming, cessation) |
| *zhi/chih* 治 | order, governance, peaceful rule |
| *zhi/chih* 志 | will, resolve, commitment, set one's heart on |
| *zhizhi/chih-chih* 致知 | the extension of knowledge or of one's capacity to know (knowing) |
| *ziran/tzu-jan* 自然 | naturally, so-of-itself, self-, auto-spontaneous |

| Pinyin | Wade-Giles | Pinyin | Wade-Giles | Pinyin | Wade-Giles | Pinyin | Wade-Giles |
|---|---|---|---|---|---|---|---|
| a | a | cou | ts'ou | gu | ku | kong | k'ung |
| ai | ai | cu | ts'u | gua | kua | kou | k'ou |
| an | an | cuan | ts'uan | guai | kuai | ku | k'u |
| ang | ang | cui | ts'ui | guan | kuan | kua | k'ua |
| ao | ao | cun | ts'un | guang | kuang | kuai | k'uai |
| | | cuo | ts'o | gui | kuei | kuan | k'uan |
| ba | pa | | | gun | kun | kuang | k'uang |
| bai | pai | da | ta | guo | kuo | kui | k'uei |
| ban | pan | dai | tai | | | kun | k'un |
| bang | pang | dan | tan | ha | ha | kuo | k'uo |
| bao | pao | dang | tang | hai | hai | | |
| bei | pei | dao | tao | han | han | la | la |
| ben | pen | de | te | hang | hang | lai | lai |
| beng | peng | deng | teng | hao | hao | lan | lan |
| bi | pi | di | ti | he | ho | lang | lang |
| bian | pien | dian | tien | hei | hei | lao | lao |
| biao | piao | diao | tiao | hen | hen | le | le |
| bie | pieh | die | tieh | heng | heng | lei | lei |
| bin | pin | ding | ting | hong | hung | leng | leng |
| bing | ping | diu | tiu | hou | hou | li | li |
| bo | po | dong | tung | hu | hu | lia | lia |
| bou | pou | dou | tou | hua | hua | lian | lien |
| bu | pu | du | tu | huai | huai | liang | liang |
| | | duan | tuan | huan | huan | liao | liao |
| ca | ts'a | dui | tui | huang | huang | lie | lieh |
| cai | ts'ai | dun | tun | hui | hui | lin | lin |
| can | ts'an | duo | to | hun | hun | ling | ling |
| cang | ts'ang | | | huo | huo | liu | liu |
| cao | ts'ao | e | o | | | long | lung |
| ce | ts'e | en | en | ji | chi | lou | lou |
| cen | ts'en | er | erh | jia | chia | lu | lu |
| ceng | ts'eng | | | jian | chien | lü | lü |
| cha | ch'a | fa | fa | jiang | chiang | luan | luan |
| chai | ch'ai | fan | fan | jiao | chiao | lüan | lüan |
| chan | ch'an | fang | fang | jie | chieh | lüe | lüeh |
| chang | ch'ang | fei | fei | jin | chin | lun | lun |
| chao | ch'ao | fen | fen | jing | ching | luo | lo |
| che | ch'e | feng | feng | jiong | chiung | | |
| chen | ch'en | fo | fo | jiu | chiu | ma | ma |
| cheng | ch'eng | fou | fou | ju | chü | mai | mai |
| chi | ch'ih | fu | fu | juan | chüan | man | man |
| chong | ch'ung | | | jue | chüeh | mang | mang |
| chou | ch'ou | ga | ka | jun | chün | mao | mao |
| chu | ch'u | gai | kai | | | mei | mei |
| chua | ch'ua | gan | kan | ka | k'a | men | men |
| chuai | ch'uai | gang | kang | kai | k'ai | meng | meng |
| chuan | ch'uan | gao | kao | kan | k'an | mi | mi |
| chuang | ch'uang | ge | ke | kang | k'ang | mian | mien |
| chui | ch'ui | gei | kei | kao | k'ao | miao | miao |
| chun | ch'un | gen | ken | ke | k'o | mie | mieh |
| chuo | ch'o | geng | keng | kei | k'ei | min | min |
| ci | tz'u | gong | kung | ken | k'en | ming | ming |
| cong | ts'ung | gou | kou | keng | k'eng | miu | miu |

| Pinyin | Wade-Giles | Pinyin | Wade-Giles | Pinyin | Wade-Giles | Pinyin | Wade-Giles |
|---|---|---|---|---|---|---|---|
| mo | mo | qie | ch'ieh | song | sung | ya | ya |
| mou | mou | qin | ch'in | sou | sou | yai | yai |
| mu | mu | qing | ch'ing | su | su | yan | yen |
|  |  | qiong | ch'iung | suan | suan | yang | yang |
| na | na | qiu | ch'iu | sui | sui | yao | yao |
| nai | nai | qu | ch'ü | sun | sun | ye | yeh |
| nan | nan | quan | ch'üan | suo | so | yi | i |
| nang | nang | que | ch'üeh |  |  | yin | yin |
| nao | nao | qun | ch'ün | ta | t'a | ying | ying |
| nei | nei |  |  | tai | t'ai | yong | yung |
| nen | nen | ran | jan | tan | t'an | you | yu |
| neng | neng | rang | jang | tang | t'ang | yu | yü |
| ni | ni | rao | jao | tao | t'ao | yuan | yüan |
| nian | nien | re | je | te | t'e | yue | yüeh |
| niang | niang | ren | jen | teng | t'eng | yun | yün |
| niao | niao | reng | jeng | ti | t'i |  |  |
| nie | nieh | ri | jih | tian | t'ien | za | tsa |
| nin | nin | rong | jung | tiao | t'iao | zai | tsai |
| ning | ning | rou | jou | tie | t'ieh | zan | tsan |
| niu | niu | ru | ju | ting | t'ing | zang | tsang |
| nong | nung | ruan | juan | tong | t'ung | zao | tsao |
| nou | nou | rui | jui | tou | t'ou | ze | tse |
| nu | nu | run | jun | tu | t'u | zei | tsei |
| nü | nü | ruo | jo | tuan | t'uan | zen | tsen |
| nuan | nuan |  |  | tui | t'ui | zeng | tseng |
| nüe | nüeh | sa | sa | tun | t'un | zha | cha |
| nuo | no | sai | sai | tuo | t'o | zhai | chai |
|  |  | san | san |  |  | zhan | chan |
| ou | ou | sang | sang | wa | wa | zhang | chang |
|  |  | sao | sao | wai | wai | zhao | chao |
| pa | p'a | se | se | wan | wan | zhe | che |
| pai | p'ai | sen | sen | wang | wang | zhen | chen |
| pan | p'an | seng | seng | wei | wei | zheng | cheng |
| pang | p'ang | sha | sha | wen | wen | zhi | chih |
| pao | p'ao | shai | shai | weng | weng | zhong | chung |
| pei | p'ei | shan | shan | wo | wo | zhou | chou |
| pen | p'en | shang | shang | wu | wu | zhu | chu |
| peng | p'eng | shao | shao |  |  | zhua | chua |
| pi | p'i | she | she | xi | hsi | zhuai | chuai |
| pian | p'ien | shen | shen | xia | hsia | zhuan | chuan |
| piao | p'iao | sheng | sheng | xian | hsien | zhuang | chuang |
| pie | p'ieh | shi | shih | xiang | hsiang | zhui | chui |
| pin | p'in | shou | shou | xiao | hsiao | zhun | chun |
| ping | p'ing | shu | shu | xie | hsieh | zhuo | cho |
| po | p'o | shua | shua | xin | hsin | zi | tzu |
| pou | p'ou | shuai | shuai | xing | hsing | zong | tsung |
| pu | p'u | shuan | shuan | xiong | hsiung | zou | tsou |
|  |  | shuang | shuang | xiu | hsiu | zu | tsu |
| qi | ch'i | shui | shui | xu | hsü | zuan | tsuan |
| qia | ch'ia | shun | shun | xuan | hsüan | zui | tsui |
| qian | ch'ien | shuo | shuo | xue | hsüeh | zun | tsun |
| qiang | ch'iang | si | ssu | xun | hsün | zuo | tso |
| qiao | ch'iao |  |  |  |  |  |  |

*Source*: From *People's Republic of China: Administrative Atlas* (Washington, D.C.: Central Intelligence Agency, 1975), pp. 46–47.

PART II

*Traditional Korea*

*Edited by*
## Wm. Theodore de Bary

WITH THE COLLABORATION OF

*Yŏngho Ch'oe*
*Peter H. Lee*
*Hugh H. W. Kang*

# EXPLANATORY NOTE

The romanization of Korean names follows the McCune-Reischauer system and certain suggestions made in *Korean Studies* 4 (1980): 111–125. The apostrophe to mark two separate sounds (e.g., *han'gŭl*) has been omitted throughout. For Chinese, the pinyin system is used; for Japanese, Kenkyusha's *New Japanese-English Dictionary* (Tokyo: Kenkyusha, 1974).

Dates for rulers of China and Korea are reign dates without *r*. They are preceded by birth and death dates if required.

Names of places or suffixes (mountains, river, monastery) are translated whenever possible. We have, however, attempted to avoid such pleonasms as Pulguk-sa Monastery, except for such cases as Mount Muak.

For the translation of Buddhist terms we have consulted W. E. Soothill and Lewis Hodous, *A Dictionary of Chinese Buddhist Terms, with Sanskrit and English Equivalents and a Sanskrit-Pali Index* (London: Kegan Paul, 1937), and Mochizuki Shinkŏ, ed., *Bukkyō daijiten* (Tokyo: Sekai seiten kankō kyōkai, 1960–1963). For Sanskrit terms we have followed Sir Monier Monier-Williams, *A Sanskrit-English Dictionary Etymologically and Philologically Arranged with Special Reference to Cognate Indo-European Languages* (Oxford: Clarendon Press, 1899), and Franklin Edgerton, *Buddhist Hybrid Sanskrit Dictionary* (New Haven: Yale University Press, 1953). For Sanskrit titles of works in the Buddhist canonical collections, we have also consulted Hajime Nakamura, *Indian Buddhism: A Survey with Bibliographical Notes* (Delhi: Motilal Banarsidass, 1987).

The translation of Chinese institutional titles generally follows Charles O. Hucker, *A Dictionary of Official Titles in Imperial China* (Stanford: Stanford University Press, 1985). The translation of Korean institutional titles, together with Korean names of distance, area, and linear measure, generally follows Ki-baik Lee, *A New History of Korea*, trans. Edward W. Wagner with Edward J. Shultz (Cambridge: Harvard University Press, 1984).

We have avoided using brackets in the translations where possible for the sake of fluency. The sources, after the first mention of a person by his full name, subsequently identify him, not by the full name, but by the given name, polite name (*cha*), pen name (*ho*), posthumous epithet (*si*), or some other sobriquet. Believing that this practice could prove confusing to the modern reader unfamiliar with the texts (and with East Asian patterns of nomenclature), we have given the full names of people on subsequent mention but have omitted the brackets around them to avoid cluttering the text. Allusions to the Chinese canonical texts and histories are worked into the translations whenever possible, and sources are indicated in notes. Contentious points are also explained in notes.

Brackets are retained for interpolated dates in the translations. They are also used around the original term supplied along with its translation — for example, "The Wa marauders [*Woegu*] were utterly defeated." When so used, the brackets are italicized. In one or two selections, material missing from the original has been reconstructed by the translators; in these cases the reconstructed text is given in italic within roman (nonitalic) brackets, thus: "Thereupon [*having taken possession of*] fifty-eight towns and seven hundred villages. . . ." Editorial interpolations supplied for clarity or English idiom, however, are set roman within roman brackets.

Works frequently cited are abbreviated as follows:

HKC     *Haedong kosŭng chŏn* (T. 50, no. 2065)
HPC     *Hanguk pulgyo chŏnsŏ*
KRS     *Koryŏ sa* (Yŏnse taehakkyo, Tongbanghak yŏnguso edition)
KSGN    *Kŭmgang smmaegyŏng non* (T. 34, no. 1730)
KT      *Korean Tripiṭaka* (Koryŏ taejanggyŏng)
Legge   James Legge, *The Chinese Classics*, 5 vols.
SBBY    *Ssu-pu pei-yao*
SBCK    *Ssu-pu ts'ung-k'an*
SGSG    *Samguk sagi* (Yi Pyŏngdo edition)
SGSZ    *Sung kao-seng chuan* (T. 50, no. 2061)
SGYS    *Samguk yusa* (Ch'oe Namsŏn edition)
SKC     *Sourcebook of Korean Civilization*, vol. 1
T       *Taishō shinshū daizōkyō*
VS      *Vajrasamādhi sūtra* (T. 9, no. 273)
XGSZ    *Hsü kao-seng chuan* (T. 50, no. 2060)
XZJ     *Hsü Tsang-ching* (Hong Kong reprint of *Dai-Nihon zokuzōkyō*)

# CONTRIBUTORS

The translator's initials follow each selection.

ES      Edward J. Shultz, University of Hawaii at Manoa
HK    Hugh H. W. Kang, University of Hawaii at Manoa
JB      Jonathan W. Best, Wesleyan University
JD      John B. Duncan, University of California, Los Angeles
JW     Jinwol Lee, University of Hawaii at Manoa
MD    Martina Deuchler, University of London
MK    Michael Kalton, University of Washington at Tacoma
MR    Michael C. Rogers, University of California, Berkeley
PL     Peter H. Lee, University of California, Los Angeles
RB    Robert E. Buswell, Jr., University of California, Los Angeles
SP     Sungbae Park, State University of New York, Stony Brook
YC    Yŏngho Ch'oe, University of Hawaii at Manoa

# CHRONOLOGY

| | |
|---|---|
| 2333 B.C.E. (?) | Legendary Tangun |
| 1122 B.C.E. (?) | Kija |
| 2000–500 B.C.E. | Megaliths, rice, and Bronze Age |
| 400–300 B.C.E. | Iron Age |
| 109–8 B.C.E. | Chinese Commandery of Lolang (P'yŏngyang) |
| | Three Kingdoms |
| 57 B.C.E.–668 C.E. | Silla |
| | Buddhist Master Wŏnhyo (617–686) |
| 37 B.C.E.–668 C.E. | Koguryŏ |
| | King Kwanggaet'o (r. 391–413) |
| 18 B.C.E.–660 C.E. | Paekche |
| 668–935 | Unified Silla |
| 751 | State Temple of Bulguksa (Temple of the Buddha Land), founded near Kyŏngju |
| 918–1392 | Koryŏ dynasty, founded by Wang Kŏn (r. 918–943) |
| | Buddhist master Chinul (1158–1210) |

1231                    Mongol invasion
                        Neo-Confucianism introduced by An Hyang (1243–1306)
1392–1910               Chosŏn dynasty, founded by Yi Sŏnggye (r. 1392–1398)
                        Chŏng Tojŏn (d. 1398)
                        Kwŏn Kŭn (1352–1409)
                        King Sejong (1418–1450)
1443                    Hangŭl script (Korean letters) produced by royal commission
                        Yi Hwang (1501–1570)
                        Yi I (1536–1584)

*Chapter 25*

## ORIGINS OF KOREAN CULTURE

The history of human activity in Korea can be traced far into the ancient past. Some of the earliest archaeological finds include Paleolithic remains at Sŏkchang-ni (South Ch'ungch'ŏng), Kulp'ori (Unggi in North Hamgyŏng), Sangwŏn, Haesang-ni, Tŏkch'ŏn (South P'yŏngan), Chech'ŏn (North Ch'ungch'ŏng), and Chŏngok (Kyŏnggi). These finds include mammal bone fossils, scrapers, choppers, and chopping tools. Radiocarbon dating indicates that habitation began between 40,000 and 30,000 B.C. The oldest Neolithic artifacts are primitive pottery found in the lower layer of Tongsamdong in Pusan, and Unggi in North Hamgyŏng. The use of comb-pattern pottery emerged around 4,000 B.C. Both the Neolithic primitive pottery people and the comb-pattern pottery people seem to have been clan peoples engaged in gathering, hunting, and fishing.

They were followed by other clan peoples who farmed, used plain pottery, and lived side by side with fishing people. The influence of the former on the latter can be seen in the remains unearthed in Chit'am-ni, Hwanghae (middle of the comb-pattern pottery period), and Tongsamdong—cultivation and hunting are evidenced by carbonized millet at the first site and by the bones of animals at both sites. Finally, the fishing people seem to have been absorbed by the plain-pottery culture. For example, in Mirim-ri and Ch'ŏngho-ri, northeast of P'yŏngyang on opposite shores of the Taedong River, plain coarse pottery and stone axes and knives were unearthed at the former site and comb-pattern pottery and stone net sinkers at the latter. Judging from the coexistence of the fishing and farming people, there might have been some form of economic exchange. Conflicts arising from the process of exchange and the amalgamation of the clans into tribes called for some form of arbitration. Further change in this early Korean society came with the influx of metal culture from the Scytho-Siberian and the Han Chinese civilizations.

Farming techniques improved in the Bronze Age, and rich remains such as semilunar stone knives, stone hoes, and stone axes with grooves are found on the slopes overlooking fertile valleys and plains. People continued to use stone tools in the Bronze Age, while bronze itself was reserved for weapons, sacrificial vessels, and ornaments. This practice suggests the existence of a dual social structure in which peoples possessing superior bronze weaponry expropriated the agricultural production of Neolithic peoples. To distinguish themselves from their subordinates, the members of a superior tribe would proclaim themselves "sons of heaven" and build imposing dolmens to display their power. Amid such changes in social relationships, some form of political power began to grow in the peninsula.

## THE FOUNDATION MYTH

During the Neolithic period, the Tung-i (Eastern Barbarian) tribes, who lived in an area stretching from the Huai River, Shandong Peninsula, and southern Manchuria to the Gulf of Pohai and the Korean Peninsula, came under the influence of the Shang and Scytho-Siberian civilizations, the latter coming from Central Asia through northern China. The tribes' close ties with these civilizations helped them develop their own Bronze Age. In addition, those along the Huai and on the Shandong Peninsula were in contact with the civilization south of the Yangtze. Included among the Tung-i were the Yemaek and Han tribes that constituted the original nucleus of the Korean people. In their eastward migration, these tribes absorbed or pushed out societies distinguished by their production of comb-pattern pottery and became the core of the patternless-pottery society. Linguistically, they are said to be a branch of the Tungusic tribes and thus belong to the Altaic language family. With agriculture as their economic basis, they absorbed the red-pottery and black-pottery cultures, thus building a broad basis for their own civilization. With the fall of the Shang and the rise of the Zhou to the west, tribes migrated from along the Huai River and Shandong Peninsula to southern Manchuria and the Korean Peninsula. Those who reached the Taedong River basin merged with the inhabitants there and formed Old Chosŏn. The illustrations on the stone slabs in the Wu family shrine in Jiaxiang hsien in Shangdong built in 147, depict the content of the foundation myth—the Tangun legend—as it is recorded in Iryŏn's *Memorabilia of the Three Kingdoms* (*Samguk yusa*).

The superior bronze culture tribes of Old Chosŏn ruled over those who were still in the Neolithic stage and tried to assert the authority of their tradition and heritage. The natives' worship of the gods of the wind, rain, and cloud, together with their totemic belief in the bear and the tiger, gave way to the worship of the god of the sun. According to the Korean foundation myth, Hwanung came down to the world of man and married a she-bear who bore Tangun, the first ruler of the age of theocracy. The bear cult, the core of the Tangun legend, descends from the Paleolithic period and is still prevalent among the Ainu and some tribes in Siberia. The stone slabs in the Wu family shrine are proof that the legend was not formed at the time of the Mongol invasion of Korea, as has been suggested by some Japanese scholars. The Wu family may have been part of the tribe belonging to the Korean people or of a tribe close to the Northeast Asian people.

According to the version in the *Rhymed Record of Emperors and Kings* (*Chewang ungi*) by Yi Sŭnghyu (1224–1300), the great king Hwanung gave medicine to his granddaughter so that she would change into a human. She married a god of the sandalwood tree and bore Tangun, an indication that the Tangun legend originated in the north and was transmitted to the south, where it absorbed tree worship.

In Iryŏn's *Memorabilia of the Three Kingdoms*, the account of the legend was based on the *Wei shu* and *Old Record* (*Kogi*). While such Confucian historians as Kim Pusik (1075–1151) rejected the legend, Great Master Iryŏn's inclusion of it is evidence that Buddhism tried to absorb the autochthonous beliefs during its spread in the peninsula. But even Confucian scholars began to acknowledge the importance of their native tradition, as evinced by Paek Munbo (d. 1374), who pointed out that the year 3600 in the Tangun calendar (1267) marked a year of prosperity.

## TANGUN

The *Wei shu* tells us that two thousand years ago, at the time of Emperor Yao, Tangun Wanggŏm chose Asadal as his capital and founded the state of Chosŏn. The *Old Record* notes that in olden times Hwanin's son, Hwanung, wished to descend from Heaven and live in the world of human beings. Knowing his son's desire, Hwanin surveyed the three highest mountains and found Mount T'aebaek the most suitable place for his son to settle and help human beings. Therefore he gave Hwanung three heavenly seals and dispatched him to rule over the people. Hwanung descended with three thousand followers to a spot under a tree by the Holy Altar atop Mount T'aebaek, and he called this place the City of God. He was the Heavenly King Hwanung. Leading the Earl of Wind, the Master of Rain, and the Master of Clouds, he took charge of some three hundred and sixty areas of responsibility, including agriculture, allotted lifespans, illness, punishment, and good and evil, and brought culture to his people.

At that time a bear and a tiger living in the same cave prayed to Holy Hwanung to transform them into human beings. The king gave them a bundle of sacred mugworts and twenty cloves of garlic and said, "If you eat these and shun the sunlight for one hundred days, you will assume human form." Both animals ate the spices and avoided the sun. After twenty-one days the bear became a woman, but the tiger, unable to observe the taboo, remained a tiger. Unable to find a husband, the bear-woman prayed under the altar tree for a child. Hwanung metamorphosed himself, lay with her, and begot a son called Tangun Wanggŏm.

[From *Samguk yusa* 1:33–34; PL]

## KOREA IN THE CHINESE DYNASTIC HISTORIES

The *Records of the Historian* (*Shiji*; chap. 115) records the development of Old Chosŏn and its successor state, Wiman Chosŏn, as well as the establishment of the four Chinese commanderies in northern Korea. A similar account is in the *History of the Former Han* (*Hanshu*; chap. 95). The monograph on geography in the latter (chap. 28) describes the territory of the Han commanderies and tells how native customs changed under the Han administration. The iron culture introduced by the Han colonies resulted in considerable change in the peninsula. While the ruling class had monopolized bronze vessels in the Bronze Age, the iron culture spread rapidly, bringing about pervasive changes in society. The head of a family became the head of a clan; as the number of clans increased, it became more difficult to form a federation strong enough to oppose the ruling power. Since the policy of Han colonies was to obstruct the growth of a leading power in the peninsula, the state of Chin south of the Han River was dissolved, and even the indigenous society, only indirectly controlled by China through trade, could not grow into an independent force.

Thus the ancient Korean states had two aims: to free themselves from Chinese cultural forces and to remain intact in their struggles against other peoples outside the Great Wall. Internally, they had to build a base for uniting the power of clan chiefs and to find a footing for the establishment of a ruling system. The social conditions during this period of travail are best portrayed in the chapter on the Dongyi in the *History of the Later Han* (*Hou Hanshu*) and *History of the Three Kingdoms* (*Sanguo zhi*).

### ACCOUNTS OF THE EASTERN BARBARIANS

The *Book of Documents* says, "To the east they envelop the sea, to the west they encompass the drifting sands." One can indeed use such words to describe the system of the Nine Zones of Submission. But if one proceeds, relying on multiple translation of tongues, beyond the Desolate Region (the outermost zone), it isn't worth the trouble to mark on maps the places where cart tracks reach, nor is there anyone who knows about the strange forms of national customs to be found there.

Sometime later, when Koguryŏ became refractory and rebellious, Wei further sent an army detachment to visit chastisement upon them. The army went to the end of the earth in exhaustive pursuit and having trampled upon the encampments of the Suksin, they gazed eastwards upon the great sea.

As our elders tell it, there were people of strange faces, the product of proximity to the sun. Accordingly they surveyed the several states, noting their norms and customs and distinguishing small from great; each had its own name and could be described in detail. Even though there were the principalities of the I and the Ti, the shapes of ritual vessels were retained among them. It would seem that one can indeed have credence in the saying, "When the Middle Kingdom has lost the rites, seek them among the Four Barbarians." Therefore we have placed their states in appropriate order, and have set forth their similarities and differences, in order to supply what the previous histories have not provided.

## Koguryŏ

Koguryŏ lies a thousand *li* to the east of Liaodong, being contiguous with Chosŏn and Yemaek on the south, with Okchŏ on the east, and with Puyŏ on the north. They make their capital below Hwando. Their territory is perhaps two thousand *li* on a side, and their households number three myriads. They have many mountains and deep valleys and have no plains or marshes. Accommodating themselves to mountain and valley, the people make do with them for their dwellings and food. With their steep-banked rivers, they lack good fields; and though they plow and till energetically, their efforts are not enough to fill their bellies; their custom is to be sparing of food. They like to build palaces. To the left and right of their dwellings they erect large houses, where they offer sacrifices to ghosts and spirits. They also have rituals for numinous stars and for the spirits of the land and grain. By temperament the people are violent and take delight in brigandage.

As for their placement of officials: when there is a *taero* they do not install a *p'aeja*, and vice versa. In the case of the royal family, their Great *ka* are all called *koch'u ka*. Members of the Yŏnno clan originally were rulers of the state; although they are now no longer kings, their legitimate chieftain can still claim the title *koch'u ka* and can also erect an ancestral temple in which to offer sacrifices to the numinous stars and to the altars of the land and grain. The Chŏllo clan by hereditary custom intermarries with the royal clan and is vested with the title of *koch'u*. The several Great *ka* in like manner install their own *p'aeja* and *choŭi* and *sŏnin*; the latter's names are communicated to the king, like the house vassals of our great ministers. In the sessions of their assemblages, however, they are not permitted to line up on the same level with their counterparts of the royal house. Members of the great houses of their state do not till the fields, and those who thus eat the bread of idleness number more than a myriad. It is the lower households who keep them supplied, bearing rice, grain, fish, and salt from afar.

Their people delight in singing and dancing. In villages throughout the state, men and women gather in groups at nightfall for communal singing and games. They have no great storehouses, each family keeping its own small store, which they call a *pugyŏng*. They rejoice in cleanliness, and they are good at brewing beer. When they kneel to make obeisance, they extend one leg; in this they differ from the Puyŏ. In moving about on foot they all run. In the tenth month they sacrifice to Heaven in a great national assembly which they call *tongmaeng*. In their public gatherings they all wear colorfully brocaded clothing and adorn themselves with gold and silver. The Great *ka* and the *chubu* wear Ze caps on their heads that are similar to ours but have no additional crown. Their Small *ka* wear "wind-breakers" shaped like *pian* caps. To the east of their state there is a large cave called the Tunnel Cave. At the great national festival of the tenth month they welcome the Su spirit at its return to the east of the state and offer sacrifice to it, placing a Su spirit of wood on the spirit seat. They have no prisons; when a crime is committed the several *ka* deliberate together, then kill the guilty one and take his wife and children as slaves.

As for their marriage customs, after the words of the contract have been fixed, the girl's family builds a small house behind the big house, which they call "the son-in-law's house." In the evening the son-in-law comes to the outside of the girl's family gate and, naming himself, bows in obeisance, begging permission to approach the girl's room. After he has done this two or three times, the girl's parents allow him to approach the small house and spend the night there. He stores his money and valuables on one side, and after his offspring have grown up, he takes his wife and returns to his own house. Such is the lewdness of their customs. After a man and a woman have already been married, they then make some clothing for the burial of their parents. They bury their dead with full ceremony; their treasure of gold and silver is consumed in funeral expenses. They pile up stones to make grave mounds and plant pine and oak trees before them in rows.

[From *Sanguo zhi* 30:840–853; MR]

## Chapter 26

### THE RISE OF THE THREE KINGDOMS

From the third century, the Three Kingdoms were aware of the existence of the states of Wei, Shu, and Wu on the mainland. The successive rise and fall of such mainland states and dynasties was strongly felt in the Three Kingdoms, since they related to their own fortunes. Koguryŏ, the first to be aware of its place in international politics, was also the first to grow as a state, and it was politically and culturally superior to Paekche and Silla. When the Gongsun clan encouraged internal dissension in Koguryŏ during the reign of King Sansang, Koguryŏ obstructed the alliance between Liaodong and Xuantu. Thus Koguryŏ was able to withstand a Chinese policy aimed at its dissolution. When Silla and Tang were at odds, the Tang attempted a similar policy of fostering internal discord in Silla, as attested by diplomatic papers exchanged between the two. Koguryŏ alone was able to see through China's designs and to take advantage of political divisions on the Chinese mainland. The state's negotiations with peoples outside the Wall are another example of Koguryŏ's aggressive diplomacy. Through expansion Koguryŏ extended its sphere of influence to the Moho and Khitan tribes, and the state became the center of Northeast Asia and the leader in the struggle against China. After the fall of the Sui, the founder of the Tang wondered if Koguryŏ should be treated as a tributary state.[1]

Paekche and Silla, on the other hand, were able to send emigrants to Japan to establish political authority there but were unable to subjugate the Japanese. Their foreign policy was aimed at stopping the southward advance of Koguryŏ, and during the struggle among the Three Kingdoms, they turned to the Sui and Tang for help. The unification of China by the Sui and the rise of the Tuque Turks prompted Koguryŏ to ally itself with the latter to oppose the former. Then Koguryŏ's ally Paekche established ties with people residing in what later became Japan. The north-south pact among the Tuque, Koguryŏ, Paekche, and Japan was opposed by the alliance between Silla and the Sui. And as leaders of the two opposing forces, Koguryŏ and Sui came to war in 598 and again in 612–614. At this crucial moment in Koguryŏ's history, its foremost general was Ŭlchi Mundŏk.

When King Chinhŭng of Silla inspected the newly conquered territories, he erected monuments to mark his visit with such inscriptions as follows.

[PL]

### KING CHINHŬNG'S MONUMENT AT MAUN PASS

If a benevolent wind does not blow, the way of the world perverts truth. And if moral enlightenment is not set forth, evils will vie with one another. Therefore, emperors and kings established their reign titles, cultivated themselves to the utmost, and brought peace to their subjects. I, however, confronting destiny,

---

1. The biography Wen Yanbo in *Jiu Tang shu* 61:2360 reads:

Wen Yanbo was transferred to the post of vice-director of the Secretariat *[zhongshu shilang]* and enfeoffed as duke of Xiho Commandery. At that time Ko[gu]ryŏ sent an envoy with tribute of local products. The Eminent Founder [Taizu] said to his ministers: "Between name and fact, principle demands that there be perfect correspondence. Ko[gu]ryŏ declared its vassalage to Sui, but in the end fended off Emperor Yang: what kind of vassal have we here? In our respect for the myriad things we have no desire to be overbearing or lofty; but since we are in possession of the terrestrial vault, it is our task to bring all men together in harmony: why then must we let them declare their vassalage just to exalt and magnify themselves? Let a rescript be drawn up setting forth our concerns in this matter!" Yanbo stepped forward and said, "The territory east of the Liao was the state of Jizi [Kija] under the Zhou, and under the house of Han was Xuantu Commandery. Thus, prior to Wei and Jin it was nearby and inside the imperial domain: we should not now let it off without a declaration of vassalage. Besides, if we were to contend with Koguryŏ about rites, what would the barbarians of the four quarters have to look up to? Moreover, the Middle Kingdom's attitude toward the barbarians should be like that of the sun toward the planets. In the order of things our downward gaze should favor all the barbarians in equal measure, without any question of demeaning or exalting." The Eminent Founder thereupon rescinded his order.

[MR]

inherited the foundation of our progenitor and succeeded to the throne. Cautious and circumspect, I was fearful of going against the Way of Heaven. As I basked in Heaven's favor, good fortunes were manifested, the spirits of Heaven and earth responded, and every enterprise tallied with the norm. Hence, the four quarters entrusted their borders to us, and we gained extensively in territory and population. Neighboring countries pledged their trust, and envoys of peace were exchanged. The court sympathized with the people and nurtured both old and new subjects. The people now say, "The transforming process of the Way extends outward and its favor pervades everywhere."

Thereupon, in the eighth month, autumn, of this year, *muja* [568], I have inspected the territory under my jurisdiction and inquired into popular feelings. I intend to encourage by rewards the loyal and the trustworthy, the sincere and the talented, those who apprehend danger and those who fight with valor and serve with loyalty. They shall be rewarded with rank and title and honored for their loyal services.

[From *Samguk yusa*, Appendix 14; PL]

## POLITICAL THOUGHT

A major feature of the political life of the Three Kingdoms was the emergence of hereditary lines of kingship as the three entities evolved from loose tribal confederations into centralized monarchies. These royal lines had to achieve for themselves a position superior to the old aristocracy from which they had emerged. This effort was both shaped by and reflected in the political thought of the time, most notably in Confucianism.

In Silla, as shown in the monument at Maun Pass, royal authority was described in terms of the kingly way in the *Book of Documents* and Confucian political thought in the *Analects* in order to justify Silla's territorial expansion. In his request to the Sui for military aid, Great Master Wŏngwang also cited the kingly way to justify Silla's position. Moreover, reign titles, such as *kŏnwŏn* (Established Prime) for King Pŏphŭng as well as *kaeguk* (Opened State), *t'aech'ang* (Great Glories), and *hongje* (Vast Relief) for King Chinhŭng, were attempts to rationalize the development of a state by means of Confucian ideology.

The advocacy of kingly virtue was a means to curb autocratic rule. The fifth, seventh, and fourteenth rulers of Koguryŏ were deposed because of their cruelty. Minister Ch'ang Chori admonished the fourteenth king, Pongsang, for his extravagance and disregard for the welfare of the people. In his admonition, Ch'ang Chori invoked goodness and loyalty to underscore the importance of elements in the Confucian political system that had become popularly accepted. Likewise in Silla, Kim Hujik (fl. 579–631), the erstwhile minister of war, quoted passages from the *Book of Documents* and *The Way and Its Virtue*, an indication of the influence of Chinese political thought at that time.

[PL]

## CH'ANG CHORI

Ch'ang Chori, a man of Koguryŏ, became prime minister under King Pongsang [292–300]. At that time there were frequent border raids by Muyong Hui, and the king asked his ministers, "Muyong's force is strong and invades our territory. What shall we do?"

Ch'ang replied, "The *taehyŏng* of the Northern Enclave, Konoja, is wise and brave. If you wish to defend the country from foreign invasions and bring peace to the people, Konoja is the only person to employ." When the king made Konoja the governor of Sinsŏng, Muyong's forces did not come again.

In the eighth month of the ninth year [300], the king mobilized all adult males above the age of fifteen to repair the palace complex. Suffering from hunger and fatigue, many began to flee. Ch'ang admonished the king, "Because of repeated national disasters and bad crops, the people have lost their homes. The adult flee to the four directions while the old and the young die in ditches. This is the time to heed Heaven, to concern yourself about the people, to be apprehensive and fearful, and to examine yourself with a view to reform. Unmindful of all this, Your Majesty drives the hungry forth and plagues them with public works, contrary to your role as father to the people. Moreover, we have a strong enemy on our border. Should our enemy seize this opportunity to attack, what will become of our dynasty and our people? I beg Your Majesty to consider my words carefully."

The king retorted angrily, "The people must look up to their king. If the palace is not magnificent, we cannot show our majesty. Now you wish to slander me in order to win the praise of the people."

Ch'ang replied, "If the ruler does not relieve the sufferings of the people, he is not good. If a subject does not offer remonstrance, he is not loyal. Having succeeded to the post of prime minister, I cannot help but speak out. How could I have thought of my own reputation?"

Laughing, the king said, "Do you wish to die for the people? I beg you not to mention it again."

Knowing that the king would not mend his ways, Ch'ang withdrew and planned with other ministers to depose him. The king knew that death was inevitable and hanged himself.

[From *Samguk sagi* 49:448; PL]

# SOCIAL STRUCTURE

The organization of the ruling structure issuing from the federation of tribal chiefs took the form of the bone rank system. The system had eight classifications:

| Holy Bones | | |
|---|---|---|
| True Bones | royal clan | Ranks 1–5 |

| six | | | Rank 6 |
| five | } | aristocracy | Rank 10 |
| four | | | Ranks 12–17 |
| | | | |
| three | | | |
| two | } | commoners | no rank |
| one | | | |

This rigid system of social stratification appears to have taken its final form in the early sixth century, probably as a means of distinguishing the royal line while also protecting the aristocratic status and privileges of the various tribal leaders who were being incorporated into a centralized sociopolitical system. The bone rank system set the top two strata, the Holy Bones and the True Bones, far above the rest of society. Members of the Holy Bone class monopolized the throne until the reign of Queen Chindŏk; those of the True Bone class ruled from kings Muyŏl to Kyŏngsun. Members of both classes could reach the highest rank of *ibŏlch'an*, and only they could occupy the top four ranks. Members of the sixth through fourth head ranks (*tup'um*) could occupy the sixth to the last ranks, each with different privileges and restrictions. A special promotion system allowed them, within limits, to rise faster through the ranks. The bone rank system even dictated what kinds of clothes, carriages, daily utensils, and houses members could have.

As King Hŭngdŏk's edict of 834 shows, the state tried to enforce the system. Sŏl Kyedu, however, a member of the Sŏl clan belonging to the sixth head rank, disliked this rigid class system. In 621, he left Silla for China and took part in a war against Koguryŏ.

[PL]

## KING HŬNGDŎK'S EDICT ON CLOTHING, CARTS, AND HOUSING

There are superior and inferior people, and humble persons, in regard to social status. Names are not alike, for example, and garments too are different. The customs of this society have degenerated day by day owing to the competition among the people for luxuries and alien commodities, because they detest local products. Furthermore, rites have now fallen to a critical stage and customs have retrogressed to those of barbarians. The traditional codes will be revived in order to rectify the situation, and should anyone transgress the prohibition, he will be punished according to the law of the land.

[From *Samguk sagi* 33:320–326; PL]

## SŎL KYEDU

Sŏl Kyedu was a descendant of a Silla official. Once he went drinking with his four friends, each of whom revealed his wishes. Sŏl said, "In Silla the bone rank is the key to employment. If one is not of the nobility, no matter what his talents, he cannot achieve a high rank. I wish to travel west to China, display rare resources and perform meritorious deeds, and thereby open a path to glory and splendor so that I might wear the robes and sword of an official and serve close to the Son of Heaven."

In the fourth year, *sinsa*, of Wude [621], Sŏl stealthily boarded an oceangoing ship and went to Tang China.

[From *Samguk sagi*, 47:436; PL]

*Chapter 27*

THE INTRODUCTION OF BUDDHISM

Buddhism was transmitted to each of the Three Kingdoms during their transition from tribal federations to ancient states: to Koguryŏ in 372, to Paekche in 384, and to Silla in 527. During its dissemination Buddhism absorbed the myths, legends, and shamanist beliefs of the tribes and forged a more systematized religion and philosophy. By offering a way for the people to comprehend the conflicts and contradictions in society, it provided the social and spiritual basis for each of the Three Kingdoms to develop into a state.

The introduction of Buddhism meant the importation not only of the religion but also of an advanced Chinese culture because by nature Buddhism was neither closed nor exclusive. The inclusion of monks in the *hwarang* order in Silla indicates that Buddhism provided the social and spiritual basis for the development of Silla into a state.

From its inception Buddhism was allied with the royal authority. But this alliance was most conspicuous in Silla, which had the lowest standard of culture and was the last to develop as a state. In Silla, Buddhism became a force accelerating the growth of the state structure and of royal power. In order to strengthen kingly powers, the ruler was viewed as the wheel-turning emperor of the Kṣatriya caste. The twenty-third to twenty-eighth rulers adopted Buddhist names—for example, King Chinp'yŏng adopted the name of Śuddhodana, his queen became Māyā, and Queen Chindŏk became Śrīmālā.

Although Buddhism in Koguryŏ and Paekche also had a nationalist color, these states were more advanced in their cultural standards, were familiar with

Daoist literature, and distinguished the Buddhadharma from royal authority. Koguryŏ, which had contacts with the Chinese mainland and Central Asia, adopted the Buddhism that used the method of *geyi* (employing Daoist terms to elucidate Buddhist ideas). Likewise, Paekche had contacts with the Han commanderies and the southern dynasties, and the aristocracy was more powerful than the royal house. Thus the nobles were able to uphold the independence of the Buddhist church. Instead of holding Buddhist ceremonies to pray for the protection of the country, monks in Paekche and Koguryŏ specialized in the study of Buddhist doctrines or disciplinary texts (Vinaya)—in Paekche the *Nirvana Scripture* and the *Perfection of Wisdom Scripture* and in Koguryŏ the Three Treatise school. Active Koguryŏ monks include P'ayak, a disciple of Zhiyi, who transmitted the teachings of the Tiantai school in 596; Sŭngnang, who played a major role in China as a master of the Three Treatise school; and Hyegwan, who founded the same school in Japan.

In Paekche the study of the disciplinary texts flourished; it was founded by Kyŏmik, who had returned from India in 526; three Japanese nuns traveled to Paekche to study it. Studies in the *Nirvana Scripture* continued, judging from the request to the Liang during the reign of King Sŏng (523–554) for commentaries on the text; the Koguryŏ monk Podŏk, who sought refuge in Paekche, further stimulated the study of the same text. Other eminent monks include Hyehyŏn, who did not go to China but whose biography was included in the *Xu gaoseng zhuan* (*Further Lives of Eminent Monks*); Kwallŭk and Hyech'ong, who went to Japan as experts on the Three Treatise school; and Tojang, who founded the Tattvasiddhi (Jōjitsu) school in Japan.

Early Buddhism in Silla developed under the influence of Koguryŏ. Hyeryang, an exile from Koguryŏ, was made the national overseer of monks (*kukt'ong*), and Chajang, upon returning from the Tang, succeeded to the position as great national overseer (*taegukt'ong*). Both contributed to the institutional development of the church and the consolidation of Buddhist thought. Chajang also systematized the belief that Silla was the land of the Buddha—that in Silla, a land supposedly chosen and blessed by former buddhas, Buddhism was not a new religion.

[PL]

# PAEKCHE BUDDHISM

Paekche imported the Buddhism of the southern dynasties of China and focused its study on the Disciplinary (Vinaya) school. The key document shedding light on this aspect is the record of events of Mirŭk Pulgwang Monastery. According to this record, Paekche sent the monk Kyŏmik to India to bring back the Sanskrit texts of *Wufen lu* and translate and annotate them. This was under King Sŏng (523–554), who adopted the policy of restoring Paekche power and encouraged overseas trade. Kyŏmik entitled his translation, which took seventy-two rolls, *New Vinaya* to show that the Koreans had access to the same texts then current in China.

The Disciplinary school in Paekche enjoyed international authority. In 588, three Japanese nuns studied the rules of discipline for three years in Paekche and upon their return became the founders of the Disciplinary school in Japan. Hyech'ong, a Paekche monk, went to Japan in 590 and transmitted the rules to Soga no Umako. Within Paekche itself, a decree was issued in 599 to prohibit the killing of living beings; it was realized by setting free domestic birds and burning the implements used for hunting and fishing.

## KYŎMIK AND THE DISCIPLINARY SCHOOL

In the fourth year, *pyŏngo*, of King Sŏng of Paekche [526], the monk Kyŏmik resolved to seek the rules of discipline and sailed to central India. He studied Sanskrit for five years at Great Vinaya Monastery in Sanghāna [*this name and Vedatta, below, are unidentified reconstructions*] and acquired a sound knowledge of the language. He then studied the disciplinary texts thoroughly and solemnly embodied morality [*śīla*] in his heart. He returned together with an Indian monk, Tripiṭaka Master Vedatta, and brought with him the Sanskrit texts of the *Abhidharma Piṭaka* and five recensions of the Discipline. The king of Paekche welcomed the two at the outskirts of the capital with a plume-canopied carriage and drums and pipes and had them reside at Hŭngnyun Monastery. The king also summoned the country's twenty-eight famous monks and, together with Dharma Master Kyŏmik, had them translate seventy-two rolls of the rules of discipline. Thus Kyŏmik became the founder of the Disciplinary school in Paekche. Thereupon Dharma Masters Tamuk and Hyein wrote commentaries on the rules of discipline in thirty-six rolls and presented them to the king. The king composed a preface to the *Abhidharma* and this *New Vinaya*, treasured them in the T'aeyo Hall, and intended to have them carved on wood blocks for dissemination. The king died, however, before he could implement his plan.

[From *Chosŏn pulgyo t'ongsa* 1:33–34; PL]

## HYŎNGWANG AND THE *LOTUS SCRIPTURE*

Like Zhiyi (538–597), Hyŏngwang (fl. 539–575) was a disciple of Huisi (515–577). Biographies of eminent monks in China call Hyŏngwang a native of Silla, but his life included the period before the demise of Paekche and his activities were centered around Ungju in Paekche. Hence it is proper to consider him a Paekche national. The *Lives of Eminent Monks Compiled During the Song* (*Song gaoseng Zhuan*) portrays Hyŏngwang as having been praised by Huisi for his grasp of the *Lotus Scripture*. Upon returning home, Hyŏngwang resided on Mount Ong in Ungju, where he practiced the Dharma Blossom *samādhi*[1] and taught the people to believe in the Buddha as a manifestation of the eternal truth and universal salvation. Thus, after Hyŏngwang's return from China, the *Lotus Scripture* was studied and practiced in Paekche during the time of King Mu (600–641). The eminent monk Hyehyŏn made the chanting of the *Lotus* a central Buddhist activity.

[PL]

The monk Hyŏngwang was a native of Ungju in Korea. As a youth—and one of marked intelligence—he abruptly abandoned the secular life and determined to gain access to a religious teacher of high repute. Thereafter he devoted himself to a pure and celibate existence and when fully grown, he resolved to cross the ocean in order to seek training in the meditative methods of China.

Accordingly, he made a journey to the state of Chen where to his good fortune, he visited Mount Heng and met the Reverend Teacher Huisi, who opened his understanding to the transience of phenomena and brilliantly elucidated all the matters they discussed. Master Huisi comprehended Hyŏngwang's reasons for having come there and thoroughly instructed him in the "Method of Ease and Bliss" of the *Lotus Scripture*. Hyŏngwang's progress was like that of a supremely sharp awl that meets no impediment and does not deviate from its course; he was as unblemished as a freshly dyed length of cotton cloth. Having requested and received instruction in the method, he was assiduous and meticulous in his practice of it and achieved abrupt entrance into the Lotus Samādhi. When he requested confirmation of this attainment, Huisi verified his accomplishment, saying: "That which you have experienced is genuine and no delusion. Closely guard and sustain it, and your penetration of the dharma will become fuller and more profound. You should now return to your homeland and there establish this efficacious means. It is well 'to dislodge the *mingling* caterpillars from their nests so that they may all be transformed into sphex wasps.' "[2] Hyŏngwang, with tears flowing, did reverence to the master.

Following his return to Korea, Hyŏngwang settled on Mount Ong in Ungju, where initially only a simple hermitage was constructed, but in time this was developed into a full monastery. It is written that "notes of the same key respond to each other,"[3] and so it was that those who wished to attain to the dharma clustered at his gate and opened themselves to his instruction. The carefree and young, those solemnly resolved to adhere to the true Path, even those who

---

1. One of the sixteen *samādhi* mentioned in the chapter "The Bodhisattva Fine Sound," in Leon Hurvitz, trans., *Scripture of the Lotus Blossom of the Fine Dharma* (New York: Columbia University Press, 1976), p. 303.

2. It was believed that the sphex wasp carried away the young of the *mingling* and raised them as its own, and thus Hyŏngwang is urged to nurture others in the dharma (*Book of Odes* 196, Legge 3:334).

3. *Zhou i* (SBCK) 1:3a (Legge, *Yi King*, Sacred Books of the East 16 [Oxford: Clarendon, 1882], p. 411).

still craved the taste of flesh—they all, like ants in a line, sought him. Among these, there was one who ultimately ascended to a position of eminence and was designated as Hyŏngwang's successor. There was also one who achieved the "Fire Radiance Samādhi," two who achieved the "Water Radiance Samādhi," and even some who became proficient in both of these practices. Those who followed him and distinguished themselves were especially celebrated for their attainments in meditation. In fact, his disciples could be likened to the flocks of birds that haunt Mount Sumeru in that they all were of one color. While Hyŏngwang was yet living, he left Mount Ong and disappeared; where he went is not known.

When the patriarch of Nanyue built an image hall, Hyŏngwang's likeness was one of the portraits of twenty-eight honored masters displayed there. His likeness is also to be seen in the Patriarchs' Hall at Guoqing Monastery on Mount Tiantai.

[From *Song gaoseng zhuan* 18:820c–821a; JB]

# SILLA BUDDHISM

Masters Wŏngwang and Chajang devoted their lives to importing an advanced culture from the continent and establishing Buddhism as the state religion. Wŏngwang's close ties to the monarch and the country's expansionist policy may be seen in his simplified form of the bodhisattva ordination, in which he gave five—rather than ten—commandments to Silla warriors. They contain secular and religious injunctions not to retreat from a battlefield and not to take life indiscriminately. As great national overseer, Chajang set up Buddhist discipline and supervised the order. The nine-story stupa at Hwangnyong Monastery, built at his request, was constructed to unify the peninsula and to encourage the surrender of neighboring enemies. The plan was originally suggested by a guardian of the dharma, who appeared to Chajang during his study tour in China. As a symbol of national protection (and later as one of the three national treasures), the stupa became the focus of a belief in Silla as the land of the former as well as the present and future Buddha, an impregnable fortress designed to frustrate the territorial designs of enemies.

## PŎPKONG DECLARES BUDDHISM THE NATIONAL FAITH

The monk Pŏpkong was the twenty-third king of Silla, Pŏphŭng [514–540]. His secular name was Wŏnjong; he was the first son of King Chijŭng [500–514] and Lady Yŏnje. He was seven feet tall. Generous, he loved the people, and they in turn regarded him as a saint or a sage. Millions of people, therefore, placed confidence in him. In the third year [516] a dragon appeared in the Willow Well. In the fourth year [517] the Ministry of War was established, and in the seventh year

[520] laws and statutes were promulgated together with the official vestments. After his enthronement, whenever the king attempted to spread Buddhism, his ministers opposed him with much dispute. He felt frustrated, but remembering Ado's devout vow, he summoned all his officials and said to them: "Our august ancestor, King Mich'u, together with Ado, propagated Buddhism, but he died before great merits were accumulated. That the knowledge of the wonderful transformation of Śākyamuni should be prevented from spreading makes me very sad. We think we ought to erect monasteries and recast images to continue our ancestor's fervor. What do you think?" Minister Kongal and others remonstrated with the king, saying, "In recent years the crops have been scarce, and the people are restless. Besides, because of frequent border raids from the neighboring state, our soldiers are still engaged in battle. How can we exhort our people to erect a useless building at this time?" The king, depressed at the lack of faith among his subordinates, sighed, saying, "We, lacking moral power, are unworthy of succeeding to the throne. The yin and the yang are disharmonious and the people ill at ease; therefore you opposed my idea and did not want to follow. Who can enlighten the strayed people by the wonderful dharma?" For some time no one answered.

In the fourteenth year [527] the Grand Secretary Pak Yŏmch'ok (Ich'adon or Kŏch'adon), then twenty-six years old, was an upright man. With a heart that was sincere and deep, he advanced resolutely for the right cause. Out of willingness to help the king fulfill his noble vow, he secretly memorialized the throne: "If Your Majesty desires to establish Buddhism, may I ask Your Majesty to issue a false decree to this officer, stating that the king desires to initiate Buddhist activities. Once the ministers learn of this, they will undoubtedly remonstrate. Your Majesty, declaring that no such decree has been given, will then ask who has forged the royal order. They will ask Your Majesty to punish my crime, and if their request is granted, they will submit to Your Majesty's will."

The king said, "Since they are bigoted and haughty, we fear they will not be satisfied even with your execution." Yŏmch'ok replied, "Even the deities venerate the religion of the Great Sage. If an officer as unworthy as myself is killed for its cause, miracles must happen between heaven and earth. If so, who then will dare to remain bigoted and haughty?" The king answered, "Our basic wish is to further the advantageous and remove the disadvantageous. But now we have to injure a loyal subject. Is this not sorrowful?" Yŏmch'ok replied, "Sacrificing his life in order to accomplish goodness is the great principle of the official. Moreover, if it means the eternal brightness of the Buddha Sun and the perpetual solidarity of the kingdom, the day of my death will be the year of my birth." The king, greatly moved, praised Yŏmch'ok and said, "Though you are a commoner, your mind harbors thoughts worthy of brocaded and embroidered robes." Thereupon the king and Yŏmch'ok vowed to be true to each other.

Afterward a royal decree was issued, ordering the erection of a monastery in the Forest of the Heavenly Mirror, and officials in charge began construction. The court officials, as expected, denounced it and expostulated with the king.

The king remarked, "We did not issue such an order." Thereupon Yŏmch'ok spoke out, "Indeed, I did this purposely, for if we practice Buddhism the whole country will become prosperous and peaceful. As long as it is good for the administration of the realm, what wrong can there be in forging a decree?" Thereupon the king called a meeting and asked the opinion of the officials. All of them remarked, "These days monks bare their heads and wear strange garments. Their discourses are wrong and in violation of the Norm. If we unthinkingly follow their proposals, there may be cause for regret. We dare not obey Your Majesty's order, even if we are threatened with death." Yŏmch'ok spoke with indignation, saying, "All of you are wrong, for there must be an unusual personage before there can be an unusual undertaking. I have heard that the teaching of Buddhism is profound and arcane. We must practice it. How can a sparrow know the great ambition of a swan?" The king said, "The will of the majority is firm and unalterable. You are the only one who takes a different view. I cannot follow two recommendations at the same time." He then ordered the execution of Yŏmch'ok [15 September 527].

Yŏmch'ok then made an oath to Heaven: "I am about to die for the sake of the dharma. I pray that rightness and the benefit of the religion will spread. If the Buddha has a numen, a miracle should occur after my death." When he was decapitated, his head flew to Diamond Mountain, falling on its summit, and white milk gushed forth from the cut, soaring up several hundred feet. The sun darkened, wonderful flowers rained from heaven, and the earth trembled violently. The king, his officials, and the commoners, on the one hand terrified by these strange phenomena and on the other sorrowful for the death of the Grand Secretary who had sacrificed his life for the cause of the dharma, cried aloud and mourned. They buried his body on Diamond Mountain with due ceremony. At the time the king and his officials took an oath: "Hereafter we will worship the Buddha and revere the clergy. If we break this oath, may heaven strike us dead."

In the twenty-first year [534], trees in the Forest of the Heavenly Mirror were felled in order to build a monastery. When the ground was cleared, pillar bases, stone niches, and steps were discovered, proving the site to be that of an old monastery. Materials for beams and pillars came from the forest. The monastery being completed, the king abdicated and became a monk. He changed his name to Pŏpkong, mindful of the three garments and the begging bowl. He aspired to lofty conduct and had compassion for all. Accordingly, the monastery was named Taewang Hŭngnyun because it was the king's abode. This was the first monastery erected in Silla.

The queen, too, served Buddha by becoming a nun and residing at Yŏnghŭng Monastery. Since the king had patronized a great cause, he was given the posthumous epithet of Pŏphŭng (Promoter of Dharma), which is by no means idle flattery. Thereafter, at every anniversary of Yŏmch'ok's death, an assembly was held at Hŭngnyun Monastery to commemorate his martyrdom.

[From *Haedong kosŭng chŏn* 1A:1018c–1019b; PL]

# MAITREYA AND ESOTERIC BUDDHISM

The Maitreya cult in Silla was a product of a belief that Silla was the Buddha Land of Maitreya. This version of the Maitreya cult played an important role in Silla Buddhism. Not only was Maitreya (The Friendly One) the patron saint of the *hwarang*, but members of the *hwarang* class were thought to be reincarnations of Maitreya. Kim Yusin and his group were called "the band of the Dragon Flower tree," a reference to the bodhi tree of Maitreya. By adopting the Buddhist name Pŏbun (Dharma Cloud), King Chinhŭng sought to be a wheel-turning king (the ideal Buddhist ruler) in the land of Maitreya. The monk Chinja prayed before an image of Maitreya, asking that the celestial bodhisattva be reborn as a *hwarang* so that he, Chinja, could serve him. Chinja's prayer was answered. The discovery of stone statues of Maitreya at various places, and reincarnations of the dead youth in Silla, underscore the power of the cult over its devotees. In his poem "Song of Tuṣita Heaven," composed in 760, Master Wŏlmyŏng enjoins flowers to serve Maitreya. Chinp'yo received from Maitreya two special sticks to be used in divination ceremonies. The eighth and ninth sticks, two bones from Maitreya's fingers, represent the two Buddha natures: the innate Buddha nature and that realized through religious practices.

Two types of belief in Maitreya existed in Silla. One was a belief that Maitreya would come down to earth when the wheel-turning king ruled, as in the period before the unification. (The *hwarang* Miri was thought to be an incarnation of Maitreya, and Chinja was a member of the clergy who assisted the *hwarang* order.) The other was a belief in rebirth in the Tuṣita Heaven, a prevalent trend after the unification of the Three Kingdoms.

The esoteric teaching that cannot be revealed to the uninitiated was popular just before the unification. The monk Myŏngnang returned from the Tang in 635 and transmitted the secret incantation. In 671, he set up a secret platform to the south of Mount Nang and was reputedly able to sink the battleships of the invading Tang forces. The monk Milbon healed the illness of Queen Sŏndŏk (632–647) and Kim Yangdo (SGYS 5:211–212). Healing the sick, once the function of the shaman, was taken over by the Buddhist clergy.

[PL]

## MAITREYA'S INCARNATION AS A *HWARANG*

The surname of King Chinhŭng, the twenty-fourth monarch of Silla, was Kim. His given name was Sammaekchong, or Simmaekchong. He ascended the throne in the sixth year, *kyŏngsin*, of Datong [540]. In pursuance of the will of his uncle, King Pŏphŭng, he devotedly served the Buddha, erected monasteries, and issued certificates to monks and nuns. Endowed with grace, he respected the *hwarang* and made beautiful girls *wŏnhwa* [female leaders of the *hwarang*]. His purpose was to select persons of character and teach them filial piety, brotherly love, loyalty, and sincerity—the substance of governing the country.

After many years, he thought it best for the health of the country to establish the way of the *hwarang* and ordered a selection of virtuous youths from good families to be its members. At first, the knight Sŏrwŏn was made *hwarang [kuksŏn]*—that was the beginning of the *hwarang* institution. Thereafter a monument was erected in Myŏngju, and the king had the people refrain from evil and do good, respect their superiors, and be kind to their inferiors. Thus the five constant ways (humaneness, rightness, ritual decorum, wisdom, and trustworthiness), the six arts (etiquette, music, archery, chariot driving, calligraphy, and mathematics), the three teachers, and the six ministers came into use.

During the reign of Chinji [576–579], the monk Chinja (or Chŏngja) of Hŭngnyun Monastery would make this plea before the image of Maitreya: "O Maitreya, please incarnate yourself as a *hwarang* so that I might be near you and serve you!" His kind sincerity and the fervor of his prayers increased day by day. One night he had a dream in which a monk told him, "If you go to Suwŏn Monastery in Ungch'ŏn (now Kongju), you will behold Maitreya." The stunned Chinja set out, bowing at every step throughout the whole ten days of his journey. Outside the monastery gate a handsome youth welcomed him with a smile and led him through a small gate into a guest room. Chinja went up, bowed, and said, "You don't know me. Why do you treat me so warmly?"

"I too am from the capital. I saw you coming, Master, and merely wished to refresh you," replied the youth. Then he went out of the gate and vanished.

Chinja thought this a coincidence and did not marvel at it. He told the monks about his dream and the purpose of his trip, adding, "If you don't mind, I'd like to wait for Maitreya at the last seat." The monks realized that they were being fooled, but sensing Chinja's sincerity, they said, "Go south and you'll find Mount Ch'ŏn, the traditional abode of the wise, where there have been many responses from the invisible. Why don't you go there?"

So Chinja reached the foot of the mountain, where a mountain god changed into an old man and welcomed him.

"What would you do here?" asked the god.

"I wish to behold Maitreya," Chinja replied.

"You already saw one outside the gate of Suwŏn Monastery. Why do you seek further?"

The stunned Chinja hurriedly returned to the monastery.

After a month, King Chinji heard the story and asked for the facts: "The boy is reported to have said that he was from the capital—and the sage doesn't lie. How is it that he does not visit the city?"

With his followers, Chinja sought the youth in the village and soon caught sight of a handsome youth strolling and amusing himself under a tree northeast of Yŏngmyo Monastery. Chinja approached him and said, "You're Maitreya. Where is your home, and what is your name?"

"My name is Miri, but I don't know my surname, because I lost my parents as a child," the youth replied.

Chinja then conducted the youth to the palace in a palanquin. The King respected and loved him and made him *kuksŏn*. He maintained harmony with other youths, and his decorum and elegant teaching were uncommon. After seven years of a brilliant career, he vanished. Although Chinja was sunk in sorrow, he basked in Miri's favor. Continuing his pure transformation of the group, he cultivated the faith with sincerity. We do not know how he died.

Now, the people call the *hwarang* "Maitreya Sŏnhwa" and a mediator is called *miri*— these are all vestiges of Chinja.

[From *Samguk yusa* 3:153–155; PL]

## THE *HWARANG*

The origin of the *hwarang*, Silla's unique social group, may be traced to the "age set" organization of earlier times. Through that group's communal life and rites, young men learned the society's traditional values; through military arts, poetry, and music, they learned mutual understanding and friendship. Generally organized at the village or clan level, this basic social group maintained the fixed social structure. Beginning in the middle of the fourth century, however, as Silla accelerated its development toward statehood, the village- or clan-based group became harder to maintain. Starting in the early sixth century, Silla began to expand its territory, and a transformation of the youth group became inevitable. Under the new conditions, the *hwarang*, now a semiofficial body at the national level, came into being as an organization dedicated to the nurturing of talent.

A *hwarang* group, comprising several hundred young men, was headed by a youth from the True Bone aristocracy and several monks. For a fixed period, they lived together to learn military arts and cultivate virtue. They also toured famous mountains and rivers to nurture love of their country, and they learned the beauty of order and harmony through poetry and music. Together they prayed for the country's peace and development. Monks serving as chaplains were entrusted with their religious education and taught them universalistic Buddhism and loyalty to the king.

Wŏngwang's "Five Commandments for Laymen" best illustrate the content of the *hwarang's* education: serve the king with loyalty; tend parents with filial piety; treat friends with sincerity; never retreat from the battlefield; be discriminate about the taking of life (SGSG 45:425). Here courage required in the war for unification and the Buddhist concept of compassion were added to the Confucian virtues. Of these, loyalty and sincerity were considered fundamental. Some *hwarang* members went on to study the Confucian classics, the *Record of Rites*, and the *Zuo Commentary*.

Willing to lay down his life for the country, the *hwarang* member vowed to serve it in times of need. Such spirit continued to inspire the youth as he came of age and began his career as a politician or soldier. With the firm bases of national morality and spirit established, the *hwarang* became a prime source of Silla's success in wars against its enemies.

After the unification of the Three Kingdoms by Silla military power was accomplished, however, the *hwarang* as a military organization went into decline. With the ensuing peace, Silla's people no longer felt the threat of war, and the virile spirit once manifested by the *hwarang* disappeared. The *hwarang* subsequently came to be known more as a group specializing in poetry, music, and dance—not for moral cultivation but for enjoyment and "play."

[PL]

### ORIGINS OF THE *HWARANG*

The *wǒnhwa* ["original flower"; female leaders of the *hwarang*] were first presented at court in the thirty-seventh year [576] of King Chinhǔng. At first the king and his officials were perplexed by the problem of finding a way to discover talented people. They wished to have people disport themselves in groups so that they could observe their behavior and thus elevate the talented among them to positions of service. Therefore two beautiful girls, Nammo and Chunjǒng, were selected, and a group of some three hundred people gathered around them. But the two girls competed with one another. In the end, Chunjǒng enticed Nammo to her home and, plying her with wine till she was drunk, threw her into a river. Chunjǒng was put to death. The group became discordant and dispersed.

Afterward, handsome youths were chosen instead. Faces made up and beautifully dressed, they were respected as *hwarang*, and men of various sorts gathered around them like clouds. The youths instructed one another in the Way and in rightness, entertained one another with song and music, or went sightseeing to even the most distant mountains and rivers. Much can be learned of a man's character by watching him in these activities. Those who fared well were recommended to the court.

Kim Taemun, in his *Annals of the Hwarang [Hwarang segi]*, remarks: "Henceforth able ministers and loyal subjects shall be chosen from them, and good generals and brave soldiers shall be born therefrom."

[From *Samguk sagi* 4:40]

# Chapter 28

## CONSOLIDATION OF THE STATE

## UNIFICATION OF THE THREE KINGDOMS

As Koguryŏ pressed hard upon Paekche and Silla, its enemies in the south, Silla turned to China for an alliance. Silla's envoy Kim Ch'unch'u obtained China's agreement that in the event the Silla-Tang allied army won the war against Koguryŏ, the territory south of P'yŏngyang would belong to Silla. In 660, the combined Chinese and Silla forces destroyed Paekche. But after the conquest, the Tang ignored the earlier agreement and set up five commanderies in Paekche. When Silla opposed this policy and executed pro-Chinese elements inside Silla, conflicts arose with Tang China. But as long as Koguryŏ existed in the north, Silla avoided direct confrontation with the Chinese.

Although Koguryŏ repulsed the Tang invasions, the continuous warfare dissipated its energy. Moreover, the Khitan and Moho tribes under Koguryŏ's control submitted to the Chinese, Koguryŏ's defense line in Liaodong weakened, and the Tang navy began to haunt the Yalu. After the fall of Paekche, the navy led by Su Dingfan entered the Taedong River and laid siege to P'yŏngyang, but without success. At this critical juncture, the Koguryŏ prime minister, Yŏn Kaesomun, died, his two sons feuded with each other, and his younger brother surrendered to Silla. Taking advantage of this internal discord, the Tang army under Li Ji and the Silla army under Kim Inmun surrounded P'yŏngyang and reduced it in 668, after a fierce month-long battle.

With the fall of Koguryŏ, Silla and the Tang openly collided. In 670, after the main Chinese forces had left Korea, Silla joined with the loyal forces of Paekche and Koguryŏ and attacked the Chinese army. Although the Chinese mobilized the Khitan and Moho tribes and the navy, they were compelled to withdraw after a number of battles. Finally, Silla was able to control the territory south of the Taedong River and Wŏnsan Bay and to unify the peninsula.

There were three queens among Silla's fifty-five monarchs. Queen Sŏndŏk (632–647) came to power at a pivotal time in Silla's history. She and her cousin Queen Chindŏk were the last rulers to be of the prestigious Holy Bone (*sŏnggol*) lineage, Silla's highest social status. After these two queens all subsequent rulers were of the slightly lower True Bone (*chingol*) status. Furthermore, during Sŏndŏk's reign the foundations were laid for the ultimate unification of the Korean Peninsula. Culturally, Silla and Tang enjoyed frequent contacts, and the first record of Sŏn Buddhist practices in Korea dates from this reign.

Queen Sŏndŏk's reign also sheds light on the importance of women in Korean society. Besides fulfilling traditional roles, Korean women occupied the highest positions of power and enjoyed elite status. The selection given here also indicates that the queen was considered to possess unique spiritual powers that enabled her to perceive omens and predict the future. Early monarchs were believed to be both shamans and political leaders, and this passage suggests that the queen enjoyed such powers.

[PL]

### ACCOUNT OF THE SILLA-TANG WAR

In the second month of the fifteenth year of King Munmu [675], the Tang general Liu Rengui defeated the Silla army at the walled town of Ch'ilchung [Chŏksŏng] and returned home with his men. Then the emperor appointed Li Jinxing as Commissioner for Pacification of the East to govern the area. Thereafter the Silla king sent an envoy with tribute to beg for forgiveness, whereupon Emperor Gauzong forgave him and restored his office and title. Upon hearing the news on his way home from Tang China, Kim Inmun went back and was enfeoffed as duke of Lin-hai Commandery.

Silla, however, took Paekche's territory as far as the southern borders of Koguryŏ and established provinces and districts of Silla.

At the news of the invasion of the Tang army, together with Khitan and Moho soldiers, Silla mobilized its nine armies and waited. In the ninth month, using the beheading of Kim Chinju, the father of P'unghun, a Silla student and imperial guard in Tang China, as a pretext, the Tang general Xue Rengui with P'unghun as a guide, attacked the walled town of Paeksu. The Silla general Munhun and others met the attack and won the battle, beheading fourteen hundred of the enemy and taking forty war vessels. The Silla army also took a thousand war horses as Xue raised his siege and fled.

On the twenty-ninth day of the ninth month, Li Jinxing stationed two hundred thousand men in Maech'o Walled Town [Yangju], but the Silla forces again routed them, capturing 30,380 horses and weapons in the process. Silla built a garrison along the Anbuk River [north of Tŏgwŏn] and built the Ch'ŏlgwan wall [Tŏgwŏn].

The Moho attacked the walled town of Adal and plundered it; the Silla commander Sona was killed in action.

The Tang army, together with Khitan and Moho soldiers, besieged the walled town of Ch'ilchung, but could not take it. The Silla official Yudong died in battle.

The Moho again besieged and reduced the walled town of Chŏngmok; the magistrate T'algi led his people in a heroic resistance, but all of them died. Again, Tang troops took the walled town of Sŏkhyŏn after a siege. Magistrates Sŏnbaek and Silmo and others died in battle.

The Silla forces won all their eighteen engagements with the Tang, large and small alike, beheading 6,047 of the enemy troops and capturing 200 warhorses.

[From *Samguk sagi* 7:75–76; PL]

# CONFUCIAN POLITICAL THOUGHT

King Muyŏl, unifier of the Three Kingdoms, was not of the Holy Bone but of the True Bone class. He suppressed the revolts of Pidam and Alch'ŏn and emerged victorious. He took his wife not from the Pak clan, which had hitherto supplied queens, but from the Kim clan, of Kaya origin. He also abandoned Buddhist names and adopted Chinese-style nomenclature. Thus he inaugurated the middle period of Silla, during which the realm was ruled by his direct descendants until King Hyegong (765–779). This period was marked by the weakening of the aristocracy and the strengthening of royal authority. The *chipsabu* (state secretariat) became the principal administrative office, supplanting the *hwabaek* council. By the time of King Sinmun, the government consisted of six ministries. Local administration was also expanded to govern the conquered territory; King Sinmun set up nine prefectures and five subsidiary capitals. Likewise the army, consisting of nine banners (*sŏdang*) and ten garrisons (*chŏng*, stationed in the provinces), defended the country. With the central and local administration firmly in place, Silla felt a strong need for an ideology such as Confucian political thought to buttress the country's administrative structure.

[PL]

## KING SINMUN'S PROCLAMATION OF HIS ACCESSION

Sixteenth day [3 October 681]: The king issued a proclamation: "To honor the meritorious is a worthy admonition of the former sages; to punish the criminal is the law of the former kings. With my own insignificant body and negligible virtue I have inherited a great undertaking. I have gone without meals, risen early, retired late. Together with my ministers I have wished to bring peace to the country. How could I have imagined that while I was in mourning a rebellion would arise in the capital? The rebel leaders, Hŭmdol, Hŭngwŏn, and Chingong, had obtained their positions not through talent but by royal favor. Being incapable of prudence and thrift, they plotted to aggrandize themselves by their iniquities. They insulted the officials and deceived those in high position and low. Each day gave new proof of their insatiable ambition, as they perpetrated various outrages, invited the wicked to their board, and associated with the petty officials in the palace. Misfortune spread within and without, and the evildoers banded together and set the date for their revolt. Luckily, I have relied on the help of Heaven and earth from above and have received the help of my royal ancestors from below, and the plot of those who planned yet more grievous sins was brought to light. This indeed shows that they were abandoned by men and gods and were unacceptable to Heaven and earth. Never before have there been more blatant violations of justice or such injury to public good. Therefore I assembled the troops, intending to do away with the disloyal ones. Some of these fled to the mountain valleys, while others surrendered in the palace courtyard. We hunted down the stragglers and wiped them out. In three or four days, we were done with the criminals; there could have been no other outcome. I alarmed the officials because of this matter, and I cannot quiet my conscience morning or evening. Now that this evil band has been purged, no threat exists near or far. Quickly let the mustered soldiers and cavalry return and proclaim my wishes to the four quarters."

[From *Samguk sagi* 8:79–80; PL]

## CONFUCIAN LEARNING

When an ideology was needed to manage the society and politics of Silla, King Sinmun established the Royal Confucian Academy and had scholars teach Confucianism and the classics. The establishment of institutions had already inspired interest in Confucian political thought, as evinced by the "Five Commandments for Laymen" and the "Record of the Oath Made in the Year *Imsin*." Thus in 636, even before the foundation of the Royal Confucian Academy, Queen Chindŏk had appointed scholars to teach Chinese learning. With the establishment of the Royal Confucian Academy in 682, the core curriculum consisted of the *Analects* and the *Book of Filial Piety* and specialization in one of the following: the *Book of Odes*, the *Book of Changes*, the *Book of Documents*, the *Record of Rites*, the *Zuo Commentary*, or the *Anthology of Refined Literature* (*Wen xuan*). Students ranged in age from fifteen to thirty. In 788, a state examination system was instituted whereby students were classified into three classes. This system lasted only briefly, however, and never truly challenged the hereditary bone rank order.

## THE ROYAL CONFUCIAN ACADEMY

The Royal Confucian Academy belongs to the Ministry of Rites. Established in the second year of King Sinmun [682], the academy was called *Taehakkam* by King Kyŏngdŏk [742–765] but was again called *Kukhak* by King Hyegong [765–780]. There was one director, which King Kyŏngdŏk called *saŏp* but which King Hyegong renamed *kyŏng*. The director's rank was the same as that of other directors. Erudites *[paksa]* and instructors were appointed in 651 as well as two holding the rank of *taesa*, who were called *chubu* by King Kyŏngdŏk but were again called *taesa* by King Hyegong. The ranks ranged from *saji* to *naema*. There were two erudites of history, and two more were added by King Hyegong.

The curriculum included the *Book of Changes*, the *Book of Documents*, the *Book of Odes [Mao shi]*, the *Record of Rites [Li Ji]* the *Spring and Autumn Annals*, the *Zuo Commentary*, and the *Anthology of Refined Literature*. One erudite or instructor taught in each of the three areas of study: (1) the *Record of Rites*, the *Book of Odes*, the *Book of Changes*, the *Analects*, the *Book of Filial Piety*; (2) the *Spring and Autumn Annals*, the *Zuo Commentary*, the *Book of Odes*, the *Analects*, the *Book of Filial Piety*; (3) the *Book of Documents*, the *Analects*, the *Book of Filial Piety*, and the *Anthology of Refined Literature*.

Students graduated in three ranks. Those proficient in the *Spring and Autumn Annals, the Zuo Commentary, the Record of Rites*, and the *Anthology of Refined Literature*, as well as the *Analects* and the *Book of Filial Piety*, were assigned to the top rank. Those who had read the "Various Rites" *[Zhu li]* the *Analects*, and the *Book of Filial Piety* were middle-ranking students. Those who had read the "Various Rites" and the *Book of Filial Piety* were ranked lowest. A student who was versed in the Five Classics, the Three Histories, and the various schools of Chinese philosophy was elevated a rank for employment. One erudite or instructor of mathematics was made to teach the *Zhuijing*, the *Sankai*, the *Nine Chapters on the Art of Mathematics*, and the *Six Chapters on the Art of Mathematics*. The ranks of the students ranged from *taesa* to no rank, and their ages ranged from fifteen to thirty. The period of study was nine years. Simple, dull, and otherwise unpromising students were dismissed, but those who showed undoubted potential while still failing to complete the curriculum were allowed to remain beyond the standard nine-year period. Students were allowed to leave the academy only after attaining the rank of *taenaema* or *naema*.

[From *Samguk sagi* 38:366–367; PL]

## DAOISM

Records are scarce on the subject of Daoism in the Three Kingdoms, but it appears that the aristocracy was attracted to its tenets. In his heptasyllabic quatrain sent to Yu Zhonqwen Ŭlchi Mundŏk cites a line from the *Laozi*. The cult of immortality, as evinced in the murals of Koguryŏ tombs, merged with popular beliefs in prognostication. After the transfer of the capital to P'yŏngyang, Koguryŏ had close contacts with the Northern Wei and must have learned about Daoism. Upon entering diplomatic relations with Koguryŏ, Emperor Gaozu sent Daoist priests and images in 624, and in the following year Koguryŏ envoys were dispatched to China to study Buddhism and Daoism. In 643, at the request of Yŏn Kaesomun (d. 665), Taizong sent eight Daoist priests. Yŏn's promotion of Daoism was felt strongly by the Buddhist clergy: the monk Podŏk sought refuge in Paekche in 650.

We do not know when Daoism was first transmitted to Paekche, but it seems to have been quite early in the history of the kingdom. In its developmental stage, Paekche absorbed the civilization of Lolang and Daifang, the Chinese commanderies in the north, and later received the refined aristocratic culture of the southern dynasties in China. The earliest historical mention of Daoism in Paekche dates from the first year (214) of King Kŏngusu. When the Paekche army was about to pursue the fleeing army of Koguryŏ, General Makkohae admonished Kŭngusu, then heir apparent, with a quotation from the *Laozi* (chap. 46): "There is no disorder greater than not being content; there is no misfortune greater than being covetous. Hence in being content, one will always have enough." By the time of King Kŭngusu, the *Laozi* and *Zhuangzi* were widely read among the educated.

When a lake was dug in his palace, King Mu had an island built in the lake and called it Fangzhang (fairyland; a sacred mountain); the monk Kwallŭk, who went to Japan in 602, is said to have been a master of *dunjia* (a method of prognostication and making oneself invisible). The inscription of Sat'aek Chijŏk (654) presented here is another indication of the understanding of Daoist philosophy among the aristocracy.

We do not know when Daoism was transmitted to Silla, either, but Daoist texts were known among the educated during the Three Kingdoms period. In his admonition to King Chinp'yŏng, who loved to hunt, Kim Hujik cited a passage from the *Laozi* and the *Book of Documents*. Kim Inmun is said to have studied not only the Confucian classics but also the *Laozi*, the *Zhuangzi* and Buddhist scriptures. The official transmission of the *Laozi* is dated 738, when the Tang envoy Xing Dao presented King Hyosŏng with a copy, but inscriptions for the images at Kamsan Monastery (discovered in 1915), built by Kim Chisŏng (Kim Chijŏn in the inscription below) in 719, show the merging of Yogācāra philosophy and Daoism. Those who were disillusioned with the True Bone class, or had lost their struggles against it, lived in exile, voluntary or enforced, and espoused Daoist tenets. Kim Kagi died as a Daoist priest in Tang China.

[PL]

INSCRIPTION ON AN IMAGE AT KAMSAN MONASTERY (SILLA)

Among the sources indicating the spread of Daoism among the nobility are the inscriptions composed upon the completion of the images of the Bodhisattva Maitreya and Amitābha the Thus Come One in Kamsan Monastery. Upon his retirement, Kim Chisŏng (or Kim Chijŏn, died c. 720), who held the rank of vice-minister of state (*chipsabu sirang*), had these two images cast to aid the souls of his parents. Upon retirement, the inscription says, Kim read the *Compendium of Mahāyāna* (*Mahāyānasangraha*), the *Stages of Yoga Practice* (*Yogācārabhūmi*), the *Laozi*, and the "Free and Easy Wandering" chapter from the *Zhuangzi*. Of two inscriptions at Kamsan, one of them, written by Sŏl Ch'ong to mark the casting of the image of the Thus Come One of Infinite Life, is given here.

*Chungach'an* Kim Chijŏn was born in a blessed land and received the power of the stars. His nature was in harmony with the clouds and mist; his emotion befriended the mountains and waters. Equipped with outstanding ability, his name was known to his generation; carrying wise strategies in his heart, he assisted his time. He went to China as envoy, and the Son of Heaven bestowed on him the title of *shangshe fengyu* [chief steward in the palace administration]. Upon returning to Silla, he was granted the important post of minister of state [*chipsa sirang*]. At age sixty-seven he withdrew and, shunning the world, lived in seclusion. He emulated the lofty magnanimity of the Four White Heads, declined glory, and nourished his nature. Like brothers Shu Guang and his nephew Shu Shou[1] he retired at an opportune time.

Looking up with respect to the true teaching of Asanga [fourth century], he read the *Stages of Yoga Practice* from time to time. In addition, he loved the dark and mysterious way of *Zhuangzi* and read the "Free and Easy Wandering" chapter. He intended to repay his parents' love thereby, but it could not match the power of the Buddha. He wanted to repay the favor of his king, but it could not equal the primary cause of the Three Jewels: the Buddha, the Dharma, and the Order.

[From *Chōsen kinseki sōran* 1:36; PL]

---

1. *Han Shu* 71:3039–40. For the translation and commentary on Tao Qian's poem "In Praise of the Two Tutors Surnamed Shu," see James R. Hightower, *The Poetry of T'ao Ch'ien* (Oxford: Clarendon Press, 1970), pp. 215–219.

## Chapter 29

### THE RISE OF BUDDHISM

About the time of the unification of the Three Kingdoms, the learned Silla monks Wŏnhyo, Wŏnch'ŭk, and Ŭisang began to study Buddhist philosophy and popularize the faith. The epochal development of Silla Buddhism at this time, almost a century after its introduction, was made possible by political and ideological factors that facilitated the study and understanding of Buddhist thought. Although Silla received Buddhism from Koguryŏ and Paekche, it may have come into direct contact with Chinese Buddhism when the Liang monk Yuanbiao arrived as an envoy. Beginning with the time of King Chinhŭng (540–576), Silla monks studying abroad began to return home, bringing with them Buddhist images and scriptures. Thus toward the end of the seventh century, most scriptures translated into Chinese were known in Silla, as evinced by Wŏnhyo, who never went to China but was able to establish his own unique system of Buddhist philosophy based on translated scriptures.

Earlier Silla Buddhism may have leaned toward the *geyi* (matching the meaning) technique used by translators of the Prajñā scriptures, but the influx of Mahāyāna texts enabled Silla to better understand the Great Vehicle — that is, the vehicle of the bodhisattva leading to Buddhahood. Although the doctrines of the Three Treatise school (as propagated in Koguryŏ) and the Tiantai school (as propagated in Paekche) were little known, the efforts of Wŏngwang (d. 640) and Chajang (fl. 636–645) enabled Silla monks to understand the tenets of the *Compendium of Mahāyāna* of the Consciousness-Only school and, later, those of Flower Garland metaphysics.

The impetus for the development of Buddhist philosophy in Silla was the unification of the Three Kingdoms, which also entailed the absorption of Koguryŏ and Paekche Buddhism. Opposing the state's adoption of Daoism, the Koguryŏ monk Podŏk lectured on the *Nirvana Scripture* and finally moved to Wansan prefecture (now Chŏnju) in Paekche (650). His eleven disciples built monasteries and lectured on the *Nirvana Scripture*, and Wŏnhyo and Ŭisang are said to have attended Podŏk's lecture. Wŏnhyo wrote a commentary on the text, and other commentaries followed—an indication of Koguryŏ influence on the formation of the Nirvana school in Silla. Likewise, the transmission of the Three Treatise school may have helped make Silla monks aware of the doctrinal differences between Mādhyamika and Vijñānavāda (or Yogācāra).

In China, Zhiyi (538–597) established the Tiantai school, Xuanzang (c. 596–664) translated the texts of the Consciousness-Only school that he had brought from India, and Kuiji (632–682) founded the idealistic Fa-zang (dharma-characteristics) school. Thus the polemics between the Mādhyamika and Yogācāra schools were intensified—one upholding the truth of emptiness (*śūnyatā*) and the other expounding that everything exists in consciousness only. A new doctrinal system that could overcome these two opposing philosophies was Huayan (Flower Garland) metaphysics. As Silla pursued active diplomatic relations with the Sui and Tang, trends in doctrinal studies in China were introduced and became the subject of inquiry for Silla monks. Mutual stimulation and development in Tang and Silla testify to a close interaction between the two countries. Wŏnhyo, for example, wished to study and transmit the Consciousness-Only philosophy from Xuanzang but remained in Silla all his life to develop his own system of Buddhist philosophy. Indeed, by abandoning his studies abroad he became the most original and prolific Buddhist philosopher in Korea and East Asia at that time. Wŏnhyo's accomplishments were transmitted to Tang where they stimulated the development of Huayan metaphysics—for example, Wŏnhyo's commentary on the *Awakening of Faith* inspired a similar work by Fazang. Conversely, Tang developments in Consciousness-Only and Flower Garland philosophy influenced the formation of these schools in Silla, and Silla's contributions to the two schools were transmitted to Tang.

With the development of royal authority in Silla came an awareness of the limits and contradictions of a Buddhism established and legitimized as a bulwark of the state. In its effort to consolidate power within and without, Silla used Buddhism to enhance the privilege and status of the ruling house and to foster enthusiasm for unification. Until unification occurred, Buddhism was regarded primarily not as a religion but as a political-religious ideology that furthered the secular objectives of the state, and the faith was thereby deprived of its religious autonomy. With unification an accomplished fact, however, Silla Buddhism aspired to a new dimension: the abolition of conflict between the state's earthly objectives and the religion's otherworldly outlook, as well as the separation of church and state.

Meanwhile, in response to the consolidation of the administrative machinery after unification, Confucianism began to replace Buddhism as a political ideology. As Buddhism separated itself from politics, its political influence began to decline. The king was no longer considered a Buddha (as King Chinhŭng had been) but instead was accorded a Chinese-style posthumous epithet. Similarly, the state sought Buddhism's aid not through eminent monks but through the Buddhist community.

Such Confucian scholars as Kangsu and Sŏl Ch'ong emerged to play a major role in importing Chinese civilization, drafting diplomatic papers, and functioning as political advisers, roles hitherto reserved for eminent monks. They also began to criticize a Buddhism that had forgotten its primary religious function, as the remarks attributed to Kangsu show. King Munmu, who wished to adopt Confucian political thought, banned contributions of land and money to monasteries in 664. Aware of the contradiction inherent in upholding Buddhism with its magic and incantations as the state religion, he intended to curtail a drain on the kingdom's economic resources. In his attempts to point out a new direction for Buddhism, King Munmu ordered Ŭisang, who had just returned from China, to construct Pusŏk Monastery as the major place of worship for the Flower Garland school. In his will, he recommended Kyŏnghŭng, the master of the Consciousness-Only school, as national preceptor.

The outstanding questions around the time of unification, then, were the reconciliation of the tenets of the Mādhyamika and Yogācāra schools and a blending of the state's secular aims with the otherworldly goals of Buddhism. The solutions to these problems took the form of research into Buddhist doctrine and popularization of the faith.

[PL]

# WŎNHYO'S BUDDHIST PHILOSOPHY

Toward the end of the seventh century, Silla Buddhism made great strides in establishing a unique version of Buddhist philosophy through the efforts of Great Master Wŏnhyo (617–686). Posthumously honored as the "National Preceptor Who Harmonizes Disputes," he systematized different schools of Buddhism and established a basis on which the people of Silla might understand them. Wŏnhyo had no special teacher, nor did he travel to China. He read widely and interpreted every text he could find, regardless of its doctrinal affiliation. His works indicate the scope of his broad reading and acute comprehension of Mahāyāna texts.

Focusing on the *Flower Garland Scripture* and the *Awakening of Faith*, Wŏnhyo was able to establish his unique universalistic and syncretic Buddhist philosophy, a harmonization of nature and characteristics. He traced various texts to their origins and periods of formation. His *Treatise on Ten Approaches to the Reconciliation of Doctrinal Controversy* (*Simmun hwajaeng non*) offers a logical basis for overcoming doctrinal inconsistencies and differences. Thus while Zhiyi classified and rated the Buddha's teachings by periods, methods, and modes of doctrine, Wŏnhyo harmonized them and established their essential equality and unity.

Wŏnhyo's works were transmitted to China and Japan, where they exerted considerable influence. Known as the *Korean Commentary* (*Haedong so*), his commentary on the *Awakening of Faith*, which offers a theoretical system resolving the controversy between Mādhyamika and Yogācāra, is one of the three great commentaries on that text. His *Exposition of the "Adamantine Absorption Scripture,"* which presents the practical theory of his Buddhism, was elevated to the status of *non* (treatise), indicating that the author was a bodhisattva, not just a mortal man; his *Treatise on Ten Approaches*, together with the *Meaning of Two Obstructions* (*Ijangŭi*), influenced Fazang's *Wujiao zhang* and was said to have been carried to India to be translated into Sanskrit. Chinese masters who were influenced by Wŏnhyo include Fazang (643–712), Li Tongxuan (635–730 or 646–740), and Chengguan (738–839). The Japanese monks Gyōnen (1240–1321) of the Flower Garland school and Zenshu (723–797) and Jōtō (740–815) of the Faziang school were also influenced by him. Furthermore, Wŏnhyo visited Ŭisang at the Avalokiteśvara Cave on Mount Nak and discussed with him *Diagram of the Dharmadhātu* (*Ilsŭng pŏpkye to*; 668), an indication that he maintained close ties with Ŭisang after the latter's return from China. Unlike Ŭisang, however, Wŏnhyo had no intention of founding a school or nurturing disciples. Hence he failed to form a school of his own, was accorded less esteem in Silla than in China, and had fewer disciples than Ŭisang. Only Ŭich'ŏn (1055–1101) was able to appreciate Wŏnhyo's contribution. Wŏnhyo's works were quoted by Silla monks but received no serious study—in sharp contrast to a host of later studies on Ŭisang's diagram.

Wŏnhyo, perhaps the most seminal Buddhist thinker in Korea, contributed greatly to the development of a distinctively Korean style of Buddhist philosophy and practice. His range of scholarly endeavor spanned the whole of East Asian Buddhist materials, and some one hundred works are attributed to him. Wŏnhyo was a master of Chinese prose. The prefaces to his commentaries on various Mahāyāna scriptures are known for their concision and clarity, and he had a gift for summarizing the doctrine presented in various scriptures. Presented here are his introduction to *Exposition of the "Adamantine Absorption Scripture," Arouse Your Mind and Practice!*, and the beginning section of his commentary on the *Awakening of Faith*, which greatly influenced Fazang's commentary on the same text.

[PL]

INTRODUCTION TO EXPOSITION OF THE
"*ADAMANTINE ABSORPTION SCRIPTURE*"

Wŏnhyo's introduction to his *Exposition of the "Adamantine Absorption Scripture,"* portions of which are translated here, is one of the principal statements of his ecumenical approach to Buddhist thought and practice. The adamantine absorption (*vajrasamādhi*) is a special type of meditative concentration that is said to catalyze the final experience of enlightenment. Just as adamant, or diamond, shatters all other minerals, so too the adamantine absorption destroys all forms of clinging, initiating the radical nonattachment that is nirvana. In this treatise, Wŏnhyo seeks to treat the *vajrasamādhi* as not only consummating all the progressive stages of the Buddhist path of religious training but as in fact subsuming those stages. He therefore uses this absorption as a tool for effecting his syncretic vision, especially with respect to Buddhist practice. There is, briefly, a fourfold structure to the explication of this scripture: a narration of its principal ideas, an analysis of its theme, an explanation of its title, and an explication of the meaning of passages in the text.

## Narration of Its Principal Ideas

Now, the fountainhead of the one mind, which is distinct from existence and nonexistence, is independently pure. The sea of the three voidnesses[1] which amalgamates absolute and mundane, is calm and clear. Calm and clear, it amalgamates duality and yet is not unitary. Independently pure, it is far from the extremes and yet is not located at the middle. It is not located at the middle and yet is far from the extremes: hence, a phenomenon that does not exist does not just abide in nonexistence; a characteristic that does not nonexist does not just abide in existence. It is not unitary, and yet it amalgamates duality: hence, its nonabsolute dharmas have not once been mundane; its nonmundane principle has not once been absolute. It amalgamates duality and yet is not unitary: hence, there are none of its absolute or mundane natures that have never been established; there are none of its tainted or pure characteristics with which it has not been furnished. It is far from the extremes and yet is not located at the middle; hence, there are none of the existing or nonexisting dharmas that do not function; there are none of their positive or negative aspects with which it is not equipped. Accordingly, while nothing is negated, there is nothing not negated; while nothing is established, there is nothing not established. This can be called the ultimate principle that is free from principles, the great thusness that is not thus. These are said to be the principal ideas of this scripture.

---

1. Voidness of characteristics, voidness of voidness, and voidness of both.

## Analysis of the Theme

The thematic essentials of this scripture have an analytic and a synthetic aspect. From a synthetic standpoint, its essential point is the contemplation practice that has but a single taste. From an analytic standpoint, its fundamental doctrine involves ten types of approaches to dharma.

### SYNTHETIC STANDPOINT

In the approach to contemplation outlined in this scripture, there are six practices established—from initial resolute faith through equal enlightenment. When the six practices are completed, the ninth consciousness appears by way of an evolutionary process. The manifestation of this immaculate consciousness is the pure dharma realm. The other eight consciousnesses evolve into the four wisdoms.[2] Once these five dharmas are perfected, one is then furnished with the three bodies.[3] In this wise, cause and fruition are not separate from phenomenal objects and wisdom. Since phenomenal objects and wisdom are free from duality, there is only a single taste. Thus, the contemplation practice that has but a single taste is considered to be the theme of this scripture.

### ANALYTIC STANDPOINT

From an analytic standpoint, the themes of this scripture can be explained through ten approaches—that is to say, from an approach based on monads to an approach based on decades.

What is the approach based on monads? Within the one mind, one thought develops and conforms with the one reality. There is cultivation of one practice, entrance into the one vehicle, abiding in the one path, putting to use the one enlightenment, and awakening to the one taste.

What is the approach based on dyads? Not abiding on either of the two shores of samsara or nirvana, one accordingly abandons the two assemblies of ordinary people and Hīnayānists. Not grasping at the two kinds of selfhood, of person and dharmas, one accordingly leaves behind the two extremes of eternality and annihilationism. Penetrating to the twofold voidness of person and dharmas, one does not drop to the level of the two vehicles of śravākas and pratyekabuddhas. Assimilating both of the two truths, absolute and mundane, one does not turn away from the two accesses of principle and practice.

---

2. Fixed wisdom ( = integrative wisdom), unfixed wisdom ( = sublime-observation wisdom), nirvana wisdom ( = perfection in action wisdom), ultimate wisdom ( = great perfect mirror wisdom).

3. Of buddhahood: the fruition buddha who is endowed with all meritorious qualities ( = reward body); the *tathāgatagarbha* buddha ( = dharma body); and the form buddha ( = transformation body).

What is the approach based on triads? Taking refuge oneself with the three buddhas as above, one receives the three moral codes.[4] One conforms with the three great truths[5] and gains the three liberations,[6] the three levels of equal enlightenment,[7] and the three bodies of sublime enlightenment.[8] One accesses the three groups of voidness as above and annihilates the minds of the three existences.[9] What is the approach based on tetrads? One cultivates the four right efforts[10] and enters the four bases of supranormal powers.[11] Through the power of the four great conditions,[12] the four postures are constantly benefited. One transcends the four stages of meditative absorption and leaves far behind the four types of slander.[13] The four wisdoms flow out from its four vast grounds.

What is the approach based on pentads? With the arising of the five *skandhas*,[14] one comes into possession of fifty evils.[15] For this reason, while planting the five spiritual faculties[16] one can develop the five powers.[17]

---

4. The rules of conduct and deportment; the cultivation of all wholesome dharmas; aiding all sentient beings.

5. The path to enlightenment is all-embracing; enlightenment is attained by correct understanding; one enters enlightenment by not differentiating concentration from wisdom.

6. Empty-space liberation; adamantine liberation; *prajñā* liberation.

7. Abiding on the equal-enlightenment state for one hundred, one thousand, or ten thousand aeons.

8. The dharma, reward, and transformation bodies.

9. Existence in the realms of sense desire, subtle form, and formlessness.

10. To avoid unwholesome states that have not yet arisen; to overcome unwholesome states that have already arisen; to develop wholesome states that have not yet arisen; to maintain wholesome states that have already arisen.

11. Concentration of will, mind, effort, and investigation.

12. Wŏnhyo explains that these are four powers inherent in the mind's original enlightenment and act as the conditions for the observation of the three moral codes given above. The four powers are (1) the tranquil aspect of original enlightenment, which is distinct from all the defilements and acts as the condition for the perfection of the rules of conduct and deportment; (2) the wholesome aspect of original enlightenment, which conforms with all the wholesome faculties and acts as the condition for the cultivation of all whole some dharmas; (3) the compassionate aspect of original enlightenment, which does not abandon any sentient being and acts as the condition that prompts one to help all sentient beings; (4) the wisdom aspect of original enlightenment, which is separate from any mundane characteristic and acts as the condition for freeing the mind from any attachment to the phenomenal characteristics of the three types of moral conduct so that they will conform with thusness. VS, p. 370c25–28; KSGN 3:991a3–b14.

13. Of cause, effect, path, and extinction.

14. Form, feeling, perception; impulse, consciousness.

15. The fifty evils are another unusual listing found in VS. The consciousness aggregate (*vijñānaskandha*) includes eight evils—the eight consciousnesses—as do both the feeling and perception *skandhas*. The impulse *skandha* possesses nine evils: eight associated with mind and one dissociated from it. The form *skandha* possesses seventeen evils: the four primary elements and the thirteen derivative forms. These make a total of fifty evils. KSGN 2:981b25–c3.

16. Faith, exertion, mindfulness, concentration, wisdom.

17. The development of the five spiritual faculties into potent forces.

One wades through the sea of the five voidnesses,[18] topples the five levels,[19] gains the five pure dharmas, ferries across the beings of the five destinies,[20] and so on.

What are the approaches based on hextads, heptads, octads, enneads, and so forth? Perfecting the cultivation of the six perfections,[21] one forever abandons the six sense-bases.[22] Practicing the seven branches of enlightenment,[23] one annihilates the sevenfold matrix of meaning.[24] "Its sea of the eighth consciousness is limpid, and the flow of its ninth consciousness is pure." From the ten faiths up through the ten stages, the hundreds of practices are completely accomplished and the myriads of meritorious qualities are fully perfected. In this wise, all of these approaches are the themes of this scripture. They all appear in the text of the scripture and will be explained in the commentary to that particular passage in the text.

Nevertheless, these latter nine approaches are all included in the approach based on monads, and the approach based on monads contains all nine; none are distinct from the contemplation of the single taste. Therefore, even if they are explained analytically, they do not add to the one; even if they are explained synthetically, they do not take away from the ten. Neither increase nor decrease is this scripture's thematic essential.

[From *Taishō Tripiṭaka* 34:961a–963a; RB]

## AROUSE YOUR MIND AND PRACTICE!

In addition to his exegetical writings, Wŏnhyo made a profound personal commitment to disseminating Buddhism among the people of Silla Korea. His Korean biographer, Iryŏn, tells us that Wŏnhyo "composed a song that circulated throughout the land. He used to sing and dance his way through thousands of villages and myriads of hamlets, touring while proselytizing in song." Wŏnhyo's *Arouse Your Mind* probably dates from between 677 and 684. It is Wŏnhyo's most edifying work and one of the strongest

---

18. Voidness of—the three existences, the six destinies, the characteristics of dharmas, the characteristics of names, and mind and consciousness.

19. Faith, consideration, cultivation, practice, relinquishment.

20. Gods, humans, animals, hungry ghosts, and denizens of hell.

21. Giving, morality, patience, exertion, concentration, and wisdom.

22. Eye, ear, nose, tongue, body, mind.

23. Mindfulness, investigation of dharmas, exertion, joy, serenity, concentration, equanimity.

24. A peculiar classification unique to VS. The term appears in VS as "great matrix of meaning," which the sutra elucidates as follows: "great" means the four great elements of earth, air, fire, and water; "meaning" refers to such lists as the aggregates, elements, and senses; "matrix" means the original consciousness (*mūlavijñāna*) (VS, p. 372a21–23). Wŏnhyo interprets these as contemplations on the four gross phenomena (the four great elements), as well as the contemplation of three subtler categories of dharmas (the aggregates, and so forth), making a total of seven meanings. These contemplations lead to the destruction of the beginningless seeds of conceptual proliferation (*prapañca*) within the *mūlavijñāna* (KSGN 3:988a4–8, 998c2–11).

admonitions about the urgency of religious practice to be found in all of Buddhist literature. Even today it is among the first works read by Korean postulants who have just joined the Buddhist monastic community.

Now all the buddhas adorn the palace of tranquil extinction, nirvana, because they have renounced desires and practiced austerities on the sea of numerous kalpas. All sentient beings whirl through the door of the burning house of samsara because they have not renounced craving and sensuality during lifetimes without measure. Though the heavenly mansions are unobstructed, few are those who go there; for people take the three poisons (greed, hatred, and delusion) as their family wealth. Though no one entices others to evil destinies, many are those who go there; for people consider the four snakes and the five desires to be precious to their deluded minds.

Who among human beings would not wish to enter the mountains and cultivate the path? But fettered by lust and desires, no one proceeds. But even though people do not return to mountain fastnesses to cultivate the mind, as far as they are able they should not abandon wholesome practices. Those who can abandon their own sensual pleasures will be venerated like saints. Those who practice what is difficult to practice will be revered like buddhas. Those who covet things join Māra's entourage, while those who give with love and compassion are the children of the King of Dharma himself. . . .

Although talented and wise, if a person dwells in the village, all the buddhas feel pity and sadness for him. Though a person does not practice the path, if he dwells in a mountain hut, all the saints are happy with him. Though talented and learned, if a person does not observe the precepts, it is like being directed to a treasure trove but not even starting out. Though practicing diligently, if a person has no wisdom, it is like one who wishes to go east but instead turns toward the west. The way of the wise is to prepare rice by steaming rice grains; the way of the ignorant is to prepare rice by steaming sand.

Everyone knows that eating food soothes the pangs of hunger, but no one knows that studying the dharma corrects the delusions of the mind. Practice and understanding that are both complete are like the two wheels of a cart. Benefiting oneself and benefiting others are like the two wings of a bird. If a person chants prayers when receiving rice gruel but does not understand the meaning, should he not be ashamed before the donors? If one chants when receiving rice but does not tumble to its import, should one not be ashamed before the sages and saints? . . .

A broken cart cannot move; an old person cannot cultivate. Yet still we humans lie, lazy and indolent; still we humans sit, with minds distracted. How many lives have we not cultivated? Yet still we pass the day and night in vain. How many lives have we spent in our useless bodies? Yet still we do not cultivate in this lifetime either. This life must come to an end; but what of the next? Is this not urgent? Is this not urgent?

[From *Hanguk pulgyo chŏnsŏ* 1:841a–c; RB]

COMMENTARY ON THE *AWAKENING OF FAITH*

## On Revealing the Essence of the Doctrine

The essence of the Great Vehicle is described as being completely empty and very mysterious. But no matter how mysterious it may be, how could it be anywhere but in the world of myriad phenomena? No matter how empty it may be, it is still present in the conversation of the people. Because Bodhisattva Aśvaghoṣa had unconditioned great compassion, he was distressed over those people whose minds, moved by the wind of ignorance and delusion, are easily tossed about. He was grieved that the true nature of original enlightenment, which sleeps in a long dream, is difficult to awaken. Since Bodhisattva Aśvaghoṣa had the power of wisdom by which one regards others as his own body, he patiently wrote this treatise that expounds the deep meaning of the Thus Come One's profound scriptures. He wished to cause scholars who open this small treatise even for a moment to completely extract the meaning of *Tripiṭaka*; he wished to cause practitioners to permanently stop myriad illusory phenomena and finally return to the source of one mind. Although what is discussed in the treatise is vast, it may be summarized as follows. By revealing two aspects in one mind,[25] it comprehensively includes the 108 jewels of the Mahāyāna teaching.[26]

Such being the intent of this treatise, when unfolded, there are immeasurable and limitless meanings to be found in its doctrine; when sealed, the principle of two aspects in one mind is found to be its essence. Within the two aspects are included myriad meanings without confusion. These limitless meanings are identical with one mind and are completely amalgamated with it. The meaning of this treatise is so profound, however, that interpreters hitherto have seldom presented its doctrine completely. Indeed, stuce all of them were attached to what they had learned, they distorted the meaning of the sentences. Not able to abandon their preconceptions, still they sought the meaning. Therefore, their interpretations do not come close to the author's intent.

[From *Hsü Tsang-ching* 71:310a-311a; SP]

### DIAGRAM OF THE DHARMADHĀTU ACCORDING TO THE ONE VEHICLE

Based on the doctrinal essentials of the *Flower Garland Scripture* and the *Treatise on the Scripture Concerning the Ten Stages* (*Daśabhūmika sūtra śāstra*), this thirty-line heptasyllabic verse in two hundred and ten logographs begins with the logograph *pŏp* (dharma) at the center, goes through fifty-four meanderings, and ends at the logograph *pul* (Buddha).

---

25. The aspect of suchness in one mind and the aspect of arising and ceasing in one mind.
26. The number 108 is frequently used to indicate abundance.

First Ŭisang explains the meaning of the seal and analyzes its marks. The form of the seal expresses the idea that three worlds—the material world, the world of sentient beings, and the world of perfectly enlightened wisdom—contained in Śākyamuni's teaching are produced from the ocean-seal *samādhi*, and the three worlds contain and exhaust all dharmas. He then interprets the seal's marks in three sections: the marks of the sentences, the marks of the logographs, and the meaning of the text. The one path of the seal expresses the one sound of the Thus Come One, the wonderfully skillful expedient means. Many meanderings in his expedient means show the differences in the capacities and desires of sentient beings and stand for the teachings of the three vehicles [*triyana*]. The poem, however, has no beginning and end, because the Thus Come One's expedient means have no fixed method but correspond to the world of dharmas so that the ten worlds mutually correspond and are completely interfused. This is the round teaching of the one vehicle, the Flower Garland school. The four sides and four corners in the diagram manifest the four embracing virtues (almsgiving, kind words, conduct benefiting others, and adaptation to others) and the four immeasurables (benevolence; compassion, sympathetic joy, and impartiality). This shows the one vehicle by means of the three vehicles. The fact that the logographs at the center have a beginning and end shows that cause and effect are not equal from the standpoint of expedient means in practice. The unenlightened perceive a great distance between cause and effect; but from the standpoint of the dharma nature, cause and effect are simultaneous, and this is the essence of the Middle Path.

The dharma nature is perfectly interfused; it has no duality.
All dharmas are unmoving; by nature they are quiescent;
They have no names or characters; all distinctions are severed.
It is known through realization wisdom and not by any other means.
True nature is very profound and supremely fine.
It has no self-nature, but arises from causation.
It is the one in the all, the one in the many.
The one is the all, the many are the one.
A mote of dust contains the ten directions;
All the motes are thus.
The immeasurably distant cosmic age is the same as a single thought-moment,
A single thought-moment is the same as the immeasurably distant cosmic age.
Nine time periods and ten time periods are mutually identical;
They are not in confusion, but have been formed separately.
The first production of the thought of enlightenment is the same as true
    enlightenment.
Samsara and nirvana are always in harmony.
Noumenon and phenomenon are invisible and indistinct.
The ten Buddhas and Samantabhadra are the realm of great men.
Śākyamuni, in his ocean-seal meditation,
Constantly manifests inconceivable supernatural power—
A rain of jewels that benefits the living fills all space,
And all the living benefit according to their capacity.
Therefore the practitioner of conduct must return to the original source,

For he cannot attain it without ceasing from false thoughts.
By expedient, unconditional means, he attains complete freedom,
Returns home, and obtains food according to his capacity.
With the inexhaustible treasure of *dhāraṇī,*
He adorns the dharma realm—a true palace of jewels.
Finally, seated on the throne of the Middle Way of Ultimate Reality,
From times long past he has not moved—hence his name is Buddha.

[From *Taishō Tripiṭaka* 45:711a; PL]

## BELIEF IN THE PURE LAND

Early Buddhism in Silla, as noted earlier, was used by reigning monarchs as a political tool. The conversion effort by Wŏngwang and Chajang contributed to the establishment of unified Silla and a new moral system, but their audience was limited to the nobility in the capital. The sixteen-foot Śākyamunibuddha statue (574) and the nine-story stupa (645) in Hwangnyong Monastery (566–645) demonstrated the splendor of court Buddhism as a means of controlling society. The purpose of the Assembly of One Hundred Seats (Paekkojwa hoe) at Hwangnyong Monastery, where the *Scripture on Benevolent Kings* was recited and commented upon, was not so much to propagate the faith or convert the people as to pray for the Buddha's protection of the country and to enhance the ruler's prestige. Doctrinal development after the unification was too esoteric and abstract to serve the people as a guide to salvation. The form of Buddhism that fulfilled their needs was belief in the Pure Land and Avalokteśvara (He Who Observes the Sounds of the World).

Belief in the Pure Land of Maitreya was prevalent among the nobility during the Three Kingdoms period (some twenty images of Maitreya remain from this period), while belief in Amitāyus (Infinite Life) was prevalent about the time of unification. The worship of Amitāyus was intended for the people, as only faith and devotion were deemed necessary to ensure that one would be reborn in the Sukhāvatī (Happy Land), where Amitābha (Infinite Light), or Amitāyus (Amit'a is a short form), dwells. Thus its appeal lay in its promise of salvation to all people regardless of class, wealth, sex, or age. Viewing this world as a sea of sorrow, it sought rebirth in the future.

Belief in the Sound-Observer stressed that the bodhisattva's mercy would save people from suffering and calamity. The spread of Amitāyus worship fostered the worship of the Sound-Observer, as believers sought not only rewards in this world but also deliverance and enlightenment in the future. Stories of miracles performed by the Sound-Observer were joyfully transmitted from mouth to mouth. Faith in Amitāyus and the Sound-Observer was preached by monks who went among the people to proselytize. Unaided by the court or the nobility, they preached on the roadside or in the marketplace, making Buddhism a popular faith for the first time in Silla.

[PL]

UNGMYŎN

During the reign of King Kyŏngdŏk [742–765], a group of male devotees in Kangju set their minds on the Western Paradise, erected Amitābha Monastery on the border of Kangju, and prayed for ten thousand days. At that time a female slave, called Ungmyŏn, in the house of *Agan* Kwijin would follow her master to the middle courtyard and stand there chanting the name of Amitābha. Taking offense at this practice of Ungmyŏn, which was too exalted for her station, her master bade her pound two piculs of grain a night. She would finish her work in the early evening, go to the monastery, and call upon the name of Amitābha diligently day and night. She planted two poles, one to the left of the courtyard and one to the right, gouged holes in her hands, and passed a straw rope through them. This Ungmyŏn tied to the poles, and then moved her joined palms to the left and to the right in order to spur herself on.

Then a voice called to her, "Ungmyŏn, enter the main hall and invoke Amitābha." The worshipers then urged her to enter and devote herself to prayer as usual. Soon the sound of heavenly music was heard from the west, and the slave girl soared high through the roof beam and headed west to the outskirts of the town. There her mortal body fell away, and she changed into a true Buddha. Seated on a lotus and emitting brilliant rays of light, she slowly disappeared to the sound of music. The hole in the hall remains.

According to the lives of monks, the monk P'alchin, a reincarnation of the Sound-Observer, formed a society of one thousand, which was divided into two groups—one called "Labor" and the other "Spiritual Cultivation." A supervisor among the first could not fulfill the commandments and was reborn as a cow at Pusŏk Monastery. While carrying the scriptures, the cow, through the power of these scriptures, was reincarnated as Ungmyŏn, a slave in the household of Kwijin. One day she went on an errand to Mount Haga, where in a dream she was stirred to aspire to enlightenment. The house of Kwijin was near Amitābha Monastery, which had been erected by Dharma Master Hyesuk. Whenever Kwijin went there to pray, Ungmyŏn followed him and invoked the name of Amitābha. After nine years of devotion, on the twenty-first day of the first month of the fourteenth year, *ŭlmi* [8 February 755], during her worship she soared through the roof and reached Mount Sobaek, where she let fall one of her sandals. There she built Bodhi Monastery. Because she had shed her earthly form at the foot of the mountain, there she built the second Bodhi Monastery, calling the hall "Ungmyŏn's Ascension Hall." The hole in the roof is about ten arms' lengths wide, but a storm or thick snow could not wet the inside. Later, one of her followers covered the hole with a gilt stupa and recorded her miraculous deeds on it. Even today the tablet and stupa still stand.

[From *Samguk yusa* 5:217–219; PL]

*Chapter 30*

# LOCAL CLANS AND THE RISE OF
# THE MEDITATION SCHOOL

During the final years of Silla (780–935), the administration was tailored not to the state but to the True Bone aristocracy to prevent its disintegration and internal strife. The king's role shrank to that of protector of his own clan's power. When the bone rank system ceased to be functional, the True Bone class became divided, and powerful clans in the provinces rose to replace it. They built their economic base on international maritime trade or on the peasantry. In time, the course of history was determined by the composition and political character of such clans.

Silla Buddhism after the unification made great strides in the doctrinal studies pursued by Wŏnhyo, Ŭisang, and Wŏnch'ŭk. Wŏnhyo popularized Buddhism and spread it among the people. The more cultured circles, however, gradually distanced themselves from such studies. The Meditation school, with its emphasis on individual attainment of truth, was able to overcome both the ideological tendency of doctrinal schools and the superstitious Buddhism that resulted from the combination with native shamanism. By allying themselves with Meditation school adherents, provincial clans were able to oppose the central aristocracy.

Silla in its middle period was ruled by the direct descendants of King Muyŏl (654–661). By the time of King Kyŏngdŏk (742–765), the aristocracy had risen in revolt. To deal with the crisis, the king attempted to initiate a political reform, but without success. Under King Hyegong (765–780), revolts again broke out. Indeed, the king was assassinated by nobles who were his collateral relatives and who began to occupy the throne from the time of Sŏndŏk (780–785). One of the changes brought about by the aristocracy's revolt against the king's authoritarian rule was that the monarch no longer represented the aristocracy as a whole but only the group that installed him. With wealth of their own and private armies, members of the aristocracy now indulged in the struggle for power. Amid this warring among the aristocracy and provincial rebellions, members of the sixth head rank groped for a solution. But lacking local support and an economic base, they could not emerge as leaders. Such roles were reserved for powerful local clans. Denied participation in politics, some local chiefs had turned to international trade, weakening the economic position of the central nobility. The typical example is Chang Pogo, who built a naval garrison of ten thousand men on Wan Island in 828 and controlled the Yellow Sea. Silla settlements (*Silla bang*), administered by Silla nationals, emerged on the Shandong Peninsula and in the Kiangsu area. Chang also built the famous Dharma Blossom Cloister in Zhishang village in Shandong as described in Ennin's *Diary*.

Other strong leaders, originally village chiefs, allied themselves with the peasantry and had the power to collect taxes and mobilize soldiers. Heavy taxation and famine also drove many to banditry, and chiefs such as Yanggil were powerful enough to develop their own administrations. The power base of Kungye, a subordinate of Yanggil, was built by bandits. Exploiting the anti-Silla sentiments in an area that had once belonged to Koguryŏ, he founded Later Koguryŏ (T'aebong) but was unable to stop the plunder or to envision a better social structure. Indeed, he indulged in atrocities. By dealing a blow to Silla, however, Kungye helped to prepare Wang Kŏn's emergence as the founder of the Koryŏ dynasty. In the area of Paekche, Kyŏnhwŏn rose to found Later Paekche. Kyŏnhwŏn was a peasant-soldier who united the military, local clans, and pirates. Although he showed some skill in administration and diplomacy, he lacked any vision of a new society. By making a display of military might, he alienated the people and was destroyed. But by breaking down Silla's social iniquity, he too prepared the way for Wang Kŏn.

[PL]

## THE RISE OF LOCAL CHIEFS

Chang Pogo (d. 846) was a Korean adventurer and merchant prince whose name was once synonymous with the Korean maritime dominance in East Asia in the early ninth century. Son of a fisherman from Wan Island off the southwestern coast of the Korean Peninsula, Chang Pogo migrated to Tang China as a youth, and there he advanced to the position of captain in Xuzhou in the lower Huai River valley. Returning to Korea in 828, he alerted the throne to the danger of Chinese piracy in the Yellow Sea, whereupon the king appointed him commissioner of Ch'ŏnghaejin, the military headquarters of Wan Island. There Chang raised a private navy, at times numbering ten thousand men, by which he controlled the ocean commerce between China, Korea, and Japan.

The ships engaged in this international trade were owned and manned by Chang, and Korean trading communities flourished along the southern coast of the Shandong Peninsula and the lower reaches of the Huai. Some of these colonies, such as the famous Mount Chi community overlooking the sea route between China and Korea, enjoyed extraterritorial privileges. These colonies often served as intermediaries between Chinese authorities and Japanese visitors; indeed, the Japanese pilgrim Ennin once addressed a letter to Chang asking for his assistance and shelter.

In 836, Chang was involved in a royal succession struggle. From the end of the eighth century on, the Silla court had been beset by contention between the rising aristocracy and the authoritarian monarchy based on the bone rank system. Hence a claim to the throne, hitherto determined solely by bloodline, came to require political skill and military might. Often a contender, to bolster his claim, had to ally himself with local chiefs who were disillusioned nobles depending for their power on private soldiers recruited from serfs and vagrants. In 839 the son of the former king's rival ascended the throne as Sinmun.

History relates that Chang's downfall can be traced to his efforts to marry his daughter to the king. The marriage alliance had probably been promised by Sinmun during his protracted sojourn on Wan Island, but because of his untimely death Chang sought to force Sinmun's son to abide by the pledge. Chang's attempt in 845 to force the throne to adopt his daughter as royal consort irritated the central aristocracy, who frowned upon such an alliance as unsavory and potentially dangerous. Chang's death by assassination is traditionally placed in 846. In 851 Ch'ŏnghaejin was abolished as a military base. Thus ended the maritime kingdom of Chang Pogo and with it Silla's brief maritime dominance in East Asia.

## ESTABLISHMENT OF THE MEDITATION SCHOOL

The introduction of the Meditation school (Sŏn in Korean; Chan in Chinese; Zen in Japanese) to Silla is traced to Pŏmnang (c. 632–646), who returned to Silla in the latter half of the seventh century after studying with the Fourth Patriarch Daoxin (580–651). He transmitted the gradual teaching of the Northern school to his pupil Sinhaeng (d. 779). Robert Buswell suggests that Pŏmnang may have been the author of the *Adamantine Absorption Scripture*. Musang (680–762), a Silla monk, made seminal contributions to the school in China.

### THE LIFE OF MUSANG

Said to be the third son of King Sŏngdŏk of Silla, Musang went to Tang China in 728. There he was received by Emperor Xuancong and played an active part in the development of the Meditation school. In the area of Chengdu, he practiced the meditation of Chuji (648–734), a disciple of Zhishen (609–702), and became an abbot of Ching-chung Monastery. Musang was known for meditating on the name of Buddha and for his ascetic practices. He built a number of meditation centers and supervised the construction of Dashengzi Monastery in Chengdu by order of Emperor Xuancong. Musang became the monastery's abbot upon its completion. His disciples include Wuchu (714–774) and Mazu (709–788). The biographical account presented here comes from *Record of the Dharma Jewel in Successive Generations.*

The secular surname of Dhyāna Master Musang of Jingquan Monastery in Chengdu, Jiannan, was Kim; he was of the royal family. For generations his family lived in Korea. While he was still in his native country, his young sister, upon hearing that she was about to be given in marriage, cut her own face and vowed to become a nun. Upon seeing this, Musang said, "A woman is gentle and weak, but she has such a lofty determination. How can a man who is robust and strong be without aspiration?" At last he had his hair shaved and bade his parents farewell.

He sailed west and reached Tang China. There, in order to search for a teacher and seek the Path, he made a tour of the country. He arrived at Deshun Monastery in Zizhou and sought to pay his respects to Master Tang [Chuji]. The master was ill, however, and would not see Musang. Then Musang let his finger burn as a lamp and offered it to the master. Perceiving that Musang was an extraordinary person, the master allowed him to remain for two years. Then Musang lived on Mount Tiangu. Master Tang sent one of his followers, Wang Huang, and secretly transmitted his cassock to Musang. "This robe was transmitted from the patriarch Bodhidharma; Empress Wu bestowed it on Master Zhishen, who transmitted it to me. Today I entrust it to you." Thus Musang received the dharma succession and the robe. . . .

In the twelfth and first month of every year, Musang, together with millions of mendicant monks and nuns, lay brothers and sisters, set up the Platform of the Path and preached the dharma from the pulpit. "First, softly invoke the name of the Buddha. With all your breath meditate on the Buddha. Then stop the voice and stop thinking," he taught them. "The absence of memory, the absence of thought, and the absence of delusion: the first is *Śīla* [morality]; the second, *samādhi* [concentration]; and the third, *prajñā* [wisdom]. These three phrases furnish absolute control over good and evil passions and influences." Musang said again: "With the absence of thought, the mind is like a bright mirror that reflects all phenomena. The rise of thought is like the back of a mirror that cannot reflect anything."

He also said, "To know clearly birth and death—and to know them without interruption—is to see the Buddha. It is like a story of two men who went together to another country. Their father sent them a letter with instructions. One son obtained the letter, finished it, and followed his father's teachings without breaking the discipline. Another did the same, but he went against his father's teachings and committed many evil deeds. All living beings are like this.

One who relies on the absence of thought is like an obedient son. One who is set on words is like a disobedient son. To use another parable, when one man was drunk and lying about, his mother went and called him, 'Let's go home.' But the drunken son was bewildered and railed against his own mother. Likewise, all living beings, drunk with ignorance, do not believe that by looking into their own nature they can become buddhas."

[From *Lidai fabao ji: T.* 51:184c–185a; PL]

## TOŬI: QUESTIONS AND ANSWERS WITH CHIEF OF CLERICS CHIWŎN

Toŭi (d. 825) played an important role in transmitting the Meditation school to Silla. The *Collection from the Hall of Patriarchs* (*Zutang ji*) quotes the inscription on the monument erected in his honor at Chinjŏn Monastery, but the monument itself has been lost. Toŭi went to Tang in 784 and received the doctrinal transmission from Zhizang (735–814) at Kaiyuan Monastery in Hongzhou, Jiangsi. Then he sought Huaihai (720–814) and returned home in 821.

Toŭi's return marked a turning point in Silla Buddhism. Indeed, the Meditation school that Toŭi transmitted shook the foundations of the Doctrinal school. As contemporary Silla Buddhism either emphasized study of the scriptures or espoused a superstitious form of Buddhism mixed with native shamanism, the Meditation school, which questioned the true existence of man, could not be tolerated. Toŭi's teaching was denounced as devilish or fantastic, and he had to withdraw to Chinjŏn Monastery on Snow Mountain in Yangyang.

According to the *Record of Seven Generations in Korea* (*Headong Ch'iltae rok*) quoted in the *Sŏnmun pojang nok* (1293), complied by Ch'ŏnch'aek, Toŭi attempted to teach the "absence of thought and the absence of cultivation" and encouraged questions and answers that would lead to sudden awakening. Thus he adopted the tactics of the Southern school of Hongzhou and challenged the Flower Garland school, which represented the scholastic Buddhism of the day.

Chief of Clerics Chiwŏn asked National Preceptor Toŭi, "What other dharma realm is there besides the four dharma realms of the Flower Garland school? What other approach to dharma is there besides this progressive approach taught by fifty-five good friends? Except for the doctrine of this school, is there a separate path of meditation preached by the patriarch?"

Toŭi answered, "The four dharma realms you mention are the essence of the principle the school of patriarchs has brought up straightaway, and they dissolve like melting ice. Inside the fist of the True Principle the signs of the dharma realm cannot be found. One cannot see the signs of Mañjuśrī and Samantabhadra in the meditation of the patriarch's mind where originally there are no practice and wisdom. And the dharma gates of the fifty-five good friends are like foam on water. Such paths as the four forms of wisdom and enlightenment are like ore containing gold. Since it is mixed in indiscriminately, one cannot find it in the scriptural teachings. Therefore, when asked what is elucidated in the *Great Scripture Store [Tripiṭaka]* Master Kuizong of Tang merely raised his fist."

Chiwŏn asked again, "What is the purpose, then, of the principle and practice of the Doctrinal school, such as faith, understanding, practice, and realization? And what fruit of Buddhahood can one attain thereby?"

Toŭi answered, "Without thought and without cultivation, we understand the principle and nature by faith, understanding, practice, and realization. When the patriarch showed the dharma, he said, 'Buddhas and living beings cannot obtain it; the true nature of the Path can only be manifested straight-away.' Hence, in addition to the five doctrines, there is another transmission of the dharma, namely the patriarch's mind-seal transmission. The reason for the manifestation of the forms of the buddhas is for those who have difficulty in understanding the patriarch's True Principle. This is an expedient device of manifesting the body. Even if you desire to realize the transmission of the mind seal by reading scriptures for many years, you would not be able to do so even after many cosmic ages have passed."

Chiwŏn rose, bowed, and said, "Until now, I had only heard the Buddha's ornate teachings. The Buddha's mind-seal method cannot be obtained by a side-ways glance." He then respectfully gave himself to Toŭi and had an audience with him.

[From *Sŏnmun pojang nok* 2, in *Xu Zangjing* 113:499a–b; PL]

# Chapter 31

## EARLY KORYŎ POLITICAL STRUCTURE

This chapter focuses on Koryŏ's political development through the early twelfth century, especially on the political foundations of the dynasty. King T'aejo (918–943) relied on both indigenous institutions and borrowed systems from China as he cautiously formed his new government. This structure was further strengthened by reforms launched by his successors, Kwangjong (949–975) and Sŏngjong (981–997) in particular. It was in the latter reign that Koryŏ's state organization clearly emerged through the efforts of Confucianized officials such as Ch'oe Sŭngno (927–989). Reform-minded officials like Ch'oe urged the implementation of Confucian practices that stressed proper moral conduct while trying to curtail Buddhist practices considered corrupting influences. Throughout the eleventh century, the political institutions were further refined as Koryŏ modified the dynastic structure through the successful transplantation of major Song organizational forms.

While working on internal political stability, the dynasty also endeavored to normalize ties with the continental powers in the north. In response to shifting power, as first the Song and then the Liao and Jin states emerged in succession, Koryŏ pursued a realistic foreign policy that sought a peaceful settlement of disputes through diplomacy while not shirking from military confrontation when necessary. The northern orientation thus set remained the basic direction of foreign relations for the rest of the Koryŏ period.

[HK]

# FOUNDING OF KORYŎ

Wang Kŏn, Koryŏ's dynastic founder, came from a locally prominent family in central Korea that joined the new leader of the region, Kim Kungye, in rebelling against Silla's supremacy in the final days of the ninth century. Wang Kŏn rose quickly in Kungye's state of T'aebong, but as Kungye became more and more despotic in his rule, Wang Kŏn led disgruntled followers in a revolt, and they founded Koryŏ in 918.

It was not until 936, however, that Wang Kŏn was able to gain full control of the peninsula, and until this was done, legitimacy was the foremost issue confronting him. When Silla's last king, Kim Pu (927–935), transferred his mandate to rule in 935, Wang Kŏn achieved the status and respectability necessary for his kingdom to gain dynastic legitimacy.

Wang Kŏn, also known by his posthumous title, T'aejo, spent the rest of his life consolidating political power in his reunified kingdom. The examples of his proclamations presented here attempt to justify his usurpation of the throne. They are cautious, reassuring statements promising that as the new ruler he will look for honest and able officials. He also declares that he will seek consensus by using the best traditions of both Silla and T'aebong (which first appeared as Later Koguryŏ).

Besides gaining acceptance for his leadership, Wang Kŏn wanted to assure his subjects of a well-managed government. In the edict he issued while visiting Yesan-jin in western central Korea, he poignantly displayed his concern about the capricious and unscrupulous way local leaders exercised power in his new kingdom and urged them to be disciplined and compassionate. The edict also reveals how hard he had labored to secure fair and just authority.

In the "Ten Injunctions," Wang Kŏn left his descendants clear instructions at the end of his reign to assure the success and continuation of the dynasty. This important document exerted a powerful influence throughout the remainder of the Koryŏ period. It was significant not only as Wang Kŏn's final statement, but also because of its wide-ranging advice covering Buddhism, geomancy, potential threats to dynastic security, and royal succession. The "Ten Injunctions" provide another view of early Koryŏ's intellectual climate.

Wang Kŏn's genealogy, which glorifies both his family inheritance and the forces that were to secure the dynasty, reaffirms the dynastic legitimacy. The earliest known publication of this genealogy dates from the twelfth century, and there is no reason to take literally his family's alleged aristocratic origins, links with Tang China's imperial family, and sociopolitical prominence in central Koryŏ. The genealogy, rich in Buddhist, shamanistic, and geomantic references, is also revealing of certain mythological ideas prevailing in early Koryŏ.

## FORMATION OF GOVERNMENT

On the twentieth day of the sixth month of T'aejo's first year [918], the king issued a proclamation that stated:

> In establishing government offices and assigning functions, it is most important to appoint men of ability. In making conventions beneficial and the people peaceful, the most urgent task is choosing the wise. Truly if there is no negligence, how could the government be out of control? I recall that, having undeservedly received the Heavenly Mandate and being about to manage the affairs of government, I was not at ease in accepting the responsibilities of the throne. I remember my fear of appointing the mediocre and pretentious. My greatest fear still is that I might not know clearly who the right people are, and therefore there may be many oversights in appointing them to appropriate offices. This leads me to worry that I may omit the wise, profoundly violating the process of selecting the right scholars. I worry about this all the time. If all officials of the central and local governments perform their duties properly, it will not only help in governing today but will be commended by later ages. Everyone in the country should know that I intend to be fair and just in giving fitting employment to the local gentry and in continuously testing and carefully selecting all officials.

> [From *Koryŏ sa* 1:9b–11a; HK, ES]


### WANG KŎN: TEN INJUNCTIONS

In the fourth month, summer, of T'aejo's twenty-sixth year [943], the king went to the inner court, summoned *Taegwang* Pak Surhŭi, and personally gave him the injunctions, saying:

> I have heard that when great Shun was cultivating at Lishan he inherited the throne from Yao.[1] Emperor Gaozu of China rose from humble origins and founded the Han. I too have risen from humble origins and received undeserved support for the throne. In summer I did not shun the heat and in winter did not avoid the cold. After toiling, body and mind, for nineteen years, I united the Three Han [Later Three Kingdoms] and have held the throne for twenty-five years. Now I am old. I only fear that my successors will give way to their passions and greed and destroy the principle of government. That would be truly worrisome. I therefore

---

1. Yao and Shun are two mythical Chinese leaders who exemplified the classical ideal of the model ruler.

wrote these injunctions to be passed on to later ages. They should be read morning and night and forever used as a mirror for reflection.

His injunctions were as follows:[2]

1. The success of every great undertaking of our state depends upon the favor and protection of Buddha. Therefore, the temples of both the Meditation and Doctrinal schools should be built and monks should be sent out to those temples to minister to Buddha. Later on, if villainous courtiers attain power and come to be influenced by the entreaties of bonzes, the temples of various schools will quarrel and struggle among themselves for gain. This ought to be prevented.

3. In matters of royal succession, succession by the eldest legitimate royal issue should be the rule. But Yao of ancient China let Shun succeed him because his own son was unworthy. That was indeed putting the interests of the state ahead of one's personal feelings. Therefore, if the eldest son is not worthy of the crown, let the second eldest succeed to the throne. If the second eldest, too, is unworthy, choose the brother the people consider the best qualified for the throne.

4. In the past we have always had a deep attachment for the ways of China and all of our institutions have been modeled upon those of Tang. But our country occupies a different geographical location and our people's character is different from that of the Chinese. Hence, there is no reason to strain ourselves unreasonably to copy the Chinese way. Khitan is a nation of savage beasts, and its language and customs are also different. Its dress and institutions should never be copied.

7. It is very difficult for the king to win over the people. For this reason, give heed to sincere criticism and banish those with slanderous tongues. If sincere criticisms are accepted, there will be virtuous and sagacious kings. Though sweet as honey, slanderous words should not be believed; then they will cease of their own accord. Make use of the people's labor with their convenience in mind; lighten the burden of corvée and taxation; learn the difficulties of agricultural production. Then it will be possible to win the hearts of the people and to bring peace and prosperity to the land. . . .

9. The salaries and allowances for the aristocracy and the bureaucracy have been set according to the needs of the state. They should not be increased or diminished. The classics say that salaries and allowances should be determined by the merits of those who receive them and should not be wasted for private gain. . . .

[From *Koryŏ sa* 2:14b–17a; HK]

---

2. The remainder of this translation is from Hahm Pyong-Choon, *The Korean Political Tradition and Law: Essays in Korean Law and Legal History* (Seoul: Hollym, 1967), pp. 47–51, with minor changes.

# DEVELOPMENT OF CONFUCIAN POLITY

Ch'oe Sŭngno (927–989), the son of a Silla aristocrat, met King T'aejo at the age of twelve and so impressed the king that the latter gave Ch'oe an academic appointment. Ch'oe Sŭngno remained aligned with the court, and by the time Sŏngjong (981–997) became king, Ch'oe was one of the kingdom's leading statesmen.

### CH'OE SŬNGNO: ON CURRENT AFFAIRS

Although I am not bright, I unworthily hold an important position in the government. I therefore desire to memorialize the throne with no thought of avoiding my duty. . . .

It has been forty-seven years since our country united the Later Three Kingdoms. Our soldiers have yet to see peace, however, and military provisions are still in excessive demand. This is all because to the northwest there are many places to defend, as we border on barbarians. I hope Your Majesty will keep this fact in mind. Generally it was King T'aejo's intention to make Mahŏl Rapids a border, whereas it was the Chinese decision to make the stone wall on the banks of the Yalu River a border. I beg that between these two places Your Majesty in the future choose a more strategic location and establish a border for our territory. Then choose from among the local people those who are good at archery and riding and assign them to defend the area. . . .

The king, in governing the people, cannot visit them at home daily, and so he sends out magistrates to look into their welfare. After our T'aejo unified the country, he wished to set up provincial governments, but as it was still the formative age, many conditions were too unsettled for this. As I observe it now, the powerful local strongmen, under the pretext of public works, extort the people to the point that they can no longer endure it. I request that you establish provincial governments. And even if you cannot fill every office at once, first establish one provincial government for about ten *chu* and *hyŏn* and place two or three officials in each government to nourish and attend to the people. . . .

Although Chinese systems are good to follow, as the customs of each area have their own characteristics, it would be difficult to change every custom. As for the teachings of the classics on rites, music, poetry, and documents, as well as the ways of the ruler and subject and the father and son, we must fittingly follow China and reform our vulgar ways. In the rest of the systems, however, such as transport and clothing, we should follow our native traditions so that the ostentatious and frugal will be balanced. We need not be like China in everything. . . .

The laws governing the free and the lowborn in our country have existed for a long time. When King T'aejo first founded the country, except for those officials who had originally had slaves, all other officials who became slave owners had acquired them while in the army, either by obtaining prisoners of war or through purchase. T'aejo once wanted to free the slaves to be commoners, but being concerned about agitating the feelings of the meritorious subjects, he followed a course of expediency. Since then, for the last sixty years, no one has ever made an appeal. . . .

. . . I hope that Your Majesty will carefully reflect on this and not allow the lowborn to put the noble to shame, but will follow the Golden Mean by separating slaves and masters. Generally people who hold high office are reasonable and few commit illegalities. How can people of low status, when they have insufficient wisdom and gloss over their wrongdoings, be made commoners? . . .

[From *Koryŏ sa* 93:12a–b, 19b–22a; HK, ES]

### CH'OE SŬNGNO: ON BUDDHISM

I have heard that Your Majesty, in order to hold Buddhist rites to accumulate merit, at times personally grinds tea and barley. Your Majesty's diligent labor troubles me deeply. Such practices started from Kwangjong's reign. Believing slanderous defamations, he had many innocent people killed. Misled by the Buddhist theory of just retribution and wishing to remove the consequences of past sins, he exacted provisions from the peasants to hold Buddhist services. He established Vairocana confessional rituals, held Buddhist maigre feasts on the polo fields, and set up Buddhist Festivals of Equal Bestowal of Wealth and Law on Land and Sea in Kwibŏp Monastery.

The offerings at the Buddhist services were invariably provisions exacted from the people. At that time, children turned against their parents and slaves against their masters, and all sorts of criminals disguised as monks, many actually mingling with real monks, wandered about begging and came together to hold Buddhist services. What good would this do? . . .

Although the worship of Buddhism is not bad, the merits of pious acts performed by kings, officials, and commoners are in fact not the same. Since what the commoner toils on comes from his own labor and what he spends comes from his own wealth, harm comes to no others. In the case of a king, however, it comes from the toil of the peasants and it spends the wealth of the people.

Moreover, the Three Teachings [Buddhism, Confucianism, and Daoism] all have their own special qualities, and those who follow them should not get confused but keep them separate. Practitioners of Buddhism take spiritual cultivation as the basic principle. Practitioners of Confucianism take governing the state as the basic principle. Spiritual cultivation is valuable for the afterlife, but governing the country is the task of the present. The present is here and the afterlife is extremely distant. How could it not be wrong to sacrifice the present for the distant?

[From *Koryŏ sa* 93:15b–19b; HK, ES]

## Chapter 32

### MILITARY RULE AND LATE KORYŎ REFORM

The military coup of 1170 brought important political and social changes to Koryŏ. After rebellious officers seized power, military rule remained unstable until the rise of General Ch'oe Ch'unghŏn (1149–1219) in 1196. Under General Ch'oe and his immediate successor, there was a concerted effort to resolve the major social and political issues then confronting Koryŏ society. To strengthen control over the kingdom, the military leaders devised new institutional mechanisms to administer authority and recruit personnel as well as to support military force. They also continued to rely on civilian scholars to manage the government bureaucracy. Nevertheless, the start of the military period was accompanied by considerable domestic unrest as monks, peasants, and slaves rebelled, hoping to use the political instability triggered by the military revolt to redress their own grievances and to further their own interests. The power of the Ch'oe house rose as it demonstrated its mastery by quickly suppressing these uprisings.

By the middle of the thirteenth century, with the invasion of the Mongols, Koryŏ's military leaders faced a new challenge to their power. Although the military regime first met defeat by the Mongols in 1231, they continued resistance until 1259, when the Koryŏ court finally sued for peace, following the fall of the Ch'oe house. Despite the peace, relations with the Mongols frequently remained adversarial as Koryŏ officials and monarchs sought to sustain Koryŏ's independent identity. As Mongol power waned, Koryŏ leaders pursued anti-Mongol policies with greater vigor, and in the last decades of the dynasty, Neo-Confucian reformers came forward with sweeping reform proposals. Buddhism, which had closely associated itself with the old order, now came under attack as the reformers sought in their ideology a new framework for governance.

[HK]

## ESTABLISHMENT OF MILITARY RULE

The 1170 military coup d'état brought a distinct change to the Koryŏ kingdom as military officers vaulted into positions of power, crushing the traditional civilian leadership. Chŏng Chungbu (d. 1178), the mastermind of the coup, was a member of an old military family that had produced generals in preceding reigns. Unable any longer to stomach the insulting injustices being heaped upon military officials, he led a revolt. Joined by his subordinates, Yi Ŭibang and Yi Ko, in overthrowing the king, he attacked in particular those powerful officials and eunuchs who had belittled the military and discriminated against it. In the purge that followed, Chŏng and his men did not kill all high-ranking civilians, as has often been claimed— indeed, they executed some military officials unsupportive of their cause, as well. Employing both civil and military officials who were not antagonistic toward the new leadership, Chŏng and his associates attempted to build a new order.

With the military takeover, however, political and social conditions rapidly deteriorated as generals contended among themselves for power. This situation did not begin to improve until 1196, when another general, Ch'oe Ch'unghŏn, successfully revolted and established a new order through which he dominated the kingdom until his death.

Ch'oe Ch'unghŏn endeavored to build a strong and effective government. Shortly after seizing power, he presented a memorial (the first selection) delineating the fundamental faults of the previous rule and proposing ways to rectify the wrongs of the past. The memorial is a Confucian document chastising the king for allowing treacherous men to rule and for not being diligent in searching for honest officials. In it, Ch'oe also points out that abuses perpetrated by the Buddhist establishment and great families were the causes of the dynasty's woes. Through this call for reform and subsequent actions, he sought to revitalize the dynasty and its institutions with the goal of building a new, lasting order centered on Ch'oe authority.

The Ch'oe house inaugurated the privatization of government power through the construction of its own political and military machines. It never denied the court's nominal authority; it simply overshadowed the court. The two principal organizations through which the Ch'oes handled government affairs were the Directorate General of Policy Formation (Kyojŏng togam) and the Personnel Authority (Chŏngbang). The Directorate General coordinated the enactment of decrees for the Ch'oe house. The Personnel Authority, described in the second selection, specifically concerned itself with civil personnel matters in the government under Ch'oe control.

## CH'OE CH'UNGHŎN: THE TEN INJUNCTIONS

Ch'oe Ch'unghŏn and Ch'oe Ch'ungsu submitted a sealed memorial to the throne saying:

> We humbly submit that the treacherous outlaw Yi Ŭimin's character was treasonous. He slighted his superiors, belittled those below him, and plotted against the throne. As a result, disaster prevailed, causing calamity for the people. Relying on Your Majesty's august power, we took to arms to exterminate him. We wish Your Majesty to reform the failures of the past and plan the future, emulating the just rules of King T'aejo [Wang Kŏn] so as to brighten and restore the state. . . .
>
> Under the system set up by the former king, all land except "public" land was granted to officials and people according to rank. Those in office, however, have become very greedy and have snatched both "public" and "private" land and held them indiscriminately. A single family's holdings of fertile land may extend across districts, and that causes the state's taxes to decline and the military to wither. Your Majesty should instruct the agencies concerned to check official records and see that all illegally seized property is returned to its original owners.
>
> Rents from "public" and "private" land all come from the people. If the people are destitute, how can sufficient rent be collected? The local officials are sometimes dishonest and corrupt; they only seek profits, thereby injuring the people. The slaves of powerful houses fight to collect land rents, making the people groan in anxiety and pain. Your Majesty should select good and able officials and appoint them to the provinces to prevent the powerful families from destroying the people's property.
>
> The state dispatches officials to govern the two frontier districts and examine the five circuits, wishing merely to control local officials' treachery and alleviate the people's suffering. Now, although the various circuit commissioners ought to investigate conditions in the provinces, they do not. Rather they demand exactions, and on the pretense of presenting them to the king, they burden public facilities with transporting them. Sometimes they even appropriate them for personal expenses. Your Majesty should forbid the various circuit officials to present tributes, and make inspections their only duty.
>
> Now few monks are mountain dwellers. Most loiter around the royal palace and even enter the royal sleeping quarters. Your Majesty, being enticed by Buddhism, has on each occasion willingly allowed them to do this. The monks already abuse Your Majesty's good graces and through their activities often tarnish Your Majesty's virtue. But Your Majesty has aided them by commanding the palace attendants to take charge of the Three Jewels—Buddha, Dharma, and Sangha—and to use grain as loans to collect interest from the people. The evils of this policy are not trivial.

Your Majesty should expel the monks and keep them away from the palace and refuse interest on grain lent to the people. . . .

Today court officials are neither frugal nor thrifty. They repair their homes and decorate their clothes and playthings with precious materials, thereby worshiping the exotic. Their customs have degenerated, and they soon will be in disarray. Your Majesty should admonish the bureaucracy by forbidding ostentation and luxury, and promoting frugality. . . .

The officials of the Chancellery and the censorate have the duty to remonstrate. If Your Majesty has any shortcomings, they should admonish regardless of the danger to themselves. Now everybody only thinks of flattering even with self-abasement and blindly agrees without discretion. Your Majesty should select the right men and have them speak out in court even to the point of subjecting Your Majesty to severe admonishment.

[From *Koryŏ sa* 129:4b–6b; HK, ES]

## ESTABLISHMENT OF THE PERSONNEL AUTHORITY

The Ministry of Civil Personnel handled the appointment of civilian officials, while the Ministry of Military Personnel was in charge of selecting military officials. They prepared the personnel files, recording personal information like the date of entrance into the government service and degree of hardship of positions held, merits and demerits, and appraising ability. The Royal Secretariat drew up a list of who was to be promoted and demoted, and reported it to the king for approval. The Chancellery received royal decisions and implemented them. This was the law of the country, and it generally coincided with Chinese practices.

When Ch'oe Ch'unghŏn arbitrarily exercised power, deposing and installing kings at will, he resided in the government compounds and with his subordinates controlled the personnel files, deciding on appointment. Through his partisan royal transmitters, he presented the list of his choices to the king for approval.

[From *Yŏgong p'aesŏl* 1A:8b–9a; HK, ES]

## PRIVATE ARMIES

At this time they were about to send troops to defend against the Khitans. The bravest soldiers were all Ch'oe Ch'unghŏn's and Ch'oe U's retainers. Those in the government army were all thin and weak and useless.

Ch'oe Ch'unghŏn reviewed his private troops: From Chwagyŏng-ri to Ugyŏng-ri they formed several lines stretching two or three *ri*. Their lances held three or four silver vases to display to the people of the kingdom in order to recruit more soldiers. His son U's troops, stretching from Sŏni Bridge to Sungin

Gate, hoisted banners and beat drums as they trained for battle. Anyone among his retainers who asked to join the government army to defend against the Khitans was at once banished to a distant island.

[From *Koryŏ sa* 129:23a–b; HK, ES]

## RELATIONS WITH THE MONGOLS

Koryŏ first encountered Mongol troops in the middle of Ch'oe Ch'unghŏn's rule. Wary from the beginning, Koryŏ soon learned of the terrifying power of this new enemy. After almost forty years of resistance, and with the kingdom in ruins, Koryŏ negotiated peace. The Mongols, taking the Chinese dynastic name of Yuan, dominated both Korea and China for nearly one hundred years and forced Koryŏ into a subordinate position.

Koryŏ experienced a gradual Mongolization of its aristocratic culture. The royal house, although still descendants of Wang Kŏn, was forced to inter-marry with the Yuan imperial household, and Koryŏ princes spent much of their youth in the Yuan capital. The Eastern Expedition Field Headquarters (Chŏngdong haengsŏng), which the Mongols established in 1280 to subjugate Japan, became their major instrument for dominating Koryŏ.

When the Mongols first attacked Koryŏ in 1231, the Ch'oe leadership quickly met the challenge and stymied Mongol advances. Soon, however, Mongol attacks became much more threatening, throwing Koryŏ's leadership into crisis. The question was whether to surrender or to resist by fleeing to offshore islands. Yu Sŭngdan (1168–1232), realizing that it was the peasantry who paid the price of resistance, advised a negotiated peace. The Ch'oe leadership, in the hands of Ch'oe I (d. 1249), rejected this appeal and called for the evacuation of the Koryŏ capital, Kaesŏng, to Kanghwa Island.

Resistance to the Mongol invasion was energetic. Peasants across the coun-try retreated to forts and fought. One of the greatest battles took place at Kuju in northern Korea, where a beleaguered town withstood months of Mongol attempts to destroy it. Under the leadership of Pak Sŏ, every Mongol siege tactic was effectively checked. Indeed, the people of Koryŏ resisted the Mongol war machine for as long and as effectively as any power in the world could. Slaves also helped in the struggle, but tensions existed within Koryŏ towns and malcon-tents used the Mongol attacks to redress domestic grievances.

The Mongol invasions finally ended with the Koryŏ court's capitulation. The dispute over the question of surrender ultimately brought about the fall of the Ch'oe house in 1258, leading to a restoration of the court's political authority. Mindful of the destruction inflicted by the Mongols, the civil leaders sued for peace in 1259, but they could not return to the capital until 1270, because of disaf-fected military leaders who resisted this move. The diehard Sam Pyŏlch'o troops carried their resistance from Kanghwa Island south to the islands of Chin and Cheju. The Sam Pyŏlch'o were destroyed in 1273, but their legacy of resistance to the Mongols has conferred on them a mantle of honor in the minds of Koreans.

Under Mongol domination, Koryŏ leaders were forced to spend years at the Yuan court and to explain every Koryŏ move. They endured Mongol rule but were anxious to avoid entangling their dynasty with Yuan ploys. The Mongols' grand design was the conquest of Japan, and they expected Korea to pay the bulk of the costs, both in manpower and provisions. Yi Changyong (1201–1272), the Koryŏ envoy to the Yuan court, repeatedly tried to blunt Mongol demands, placing Koryŏ interests above all other concerns.

By the middle of the fourteenth century, Mongol power was eroding, and in 1368 the Ming dynasty rose in China. Korea responded to these events by increasing resistance to Mongol demands. Yi Chehyŏn (1287–1367), one of the period's major writers, used many means to circumvent Mongol policy, while King Kongmin (1351–1374) led the struggle to eliminate Yuan interference.

[HK]

### YI CHEHYŎN: OPPOSITION TO YUAN POLICIES

I humbly submit that my country, from its founding by the Wang clan, has lasted more than four hundred years. We have submitted to Yuan sending tribute every year. Since this has continued for more than one hundred years, our people have benefited profoundly, just as our contributions to Yuan have been plentiful. . . .

When Emperor Shizu [Kublai Khan, 1260–1294] returned from his conquest of South China, our King Wŏnjong, realizing that the Mongols had the Mandate of Heaven and popular support, traveled more than five thousand *ri* to have an audience with the emperor in the distant land of Liangchu. . . . At the time of the Mongol conquest of Japan, he not only did everything to supply weapons but was in the vanguard of the army. . . .

Now I have heard that the imperial court intends to make Korea into a Yuan province by establishing a provincial government there. If this is true, even if we disregard Koryŏ's earlier contributions, what has become of Emperor Shizu's rescript? . . . Now for no reason, Korea, a small country that has existed for more than four hundred years, will be extinguished one morning. Its state shrines will have no spirits to enshrine; its royal tombs will no longer have sacrifices. This certainly is not reasonable. . . .

I humbly wish your excellency, keeping in mind how Emperor Shizu remembered our merit and what the instructions in the *Doctrine of the Mean* said, will allow the state to be as a state should be and allow the people to be as they should be. By fostering their government and tax system, you will make Koryŏ your defender. This will sustain boundless happiness for us, and accordingly not only will the people of Koryŏ congratulate each other and praise your virtue, but the spirits of the dynastic ancestral tombs and the state shrines will cry in gratitude, though invisibly.

[From *Koryŏ sa* 110:23b–25b; HK, ES]

# LATE KORYŎ REFORMS

Koryŏ leaders were divided among themselves on policy toward China in the waning days of the Yuan dynasty. Those who advocated a sharp break with Yuan eventually grew more vocal in their criticism of the Koryŏ order itself and ultimately moved to found a new dynasty, Chosŏn. Although these leaders were themselves products of the Koryŏ social order, their desire to reform society led them to the eventual overthrow of the dynasty. Ironically, King Kongmin (1351–1374), one of the first to understand his society's need for reform, was also instrumental in inaugurating the liberation from Mongol influence. As shown in the excerpt from the biography of Sin Ton (d. 1371), the king, with the help of his monk-adviser, launched a series of reforms that ultimately broke the control of the Mongol-backed elite. Although the reforms may have been necessary, they evoked harsh criticism from contemporaries and later Confucian historians, as seen in this biography (which, at least in parts, need not be taken literally), written by later Chosŏn court historians.

In the next two selections, Yi Chehyŏn and Yi Saek (1328–1396), leading intellectuals of the period, present their strong arguments for urgent reforms. Both men entered the central bureaucracy through the civil service examination and distinguished themselves as able officials and scholars active not only in Koryŏ but also in Yuan. As forerunners of the Neo-Confucian reformers of late Koryŏ, they addressed themselves to the most serious economic and military issues facing the government.

[HK]

## YI CHEHYŎN: REFORM PROPOSALS

Now Your Majesty, complying with the Yuan emperor's clear commands, has inherited the dynastic accomplishments of your ancestors at an age at which a crown prince customarily would enter school. Ascending in the wake of the former king's failures, how could you not be very careful, if only out of reverence and prudence?[1] As for the substance of reverence and prudence, there is nothing like cultivating virtue.

The important point in cultivating virtue is desiring to approach learning. Now as Master of Sacrifice Chŏn Sungmong has already been named royal tutor, select two wise Confucian scholars to lecture, together with Chŏn Sungmong, on the *Book of Filial Piety*, the *Analects*, *Mencius*, the *Great Learning*, and the *Mean*. Learn the way of attaining knowledge through the investigation of affairs and things and rectifying the heart through a sincere mind. From among the children

---

1. In 1343, Yuan removed and exiled King Ch'unghye (1330–1332 and 1339–1344) because of his licentious and cruel behavior. He died in 1344 while en route to exile.

of officials, select ten who are honest, genuinely attentive, and fond of learning and propriety to assist Your Majesty as scholars-in-waiting. After mastering the Four Books, study in sequence the Six Classics so that arrogance, extravagance, lewdness, indolence, music, women, and venal officials will not reach your eyes and ears. When you achieve this and it becomes second nature, you will effortlessly realize virtue. That should be the most urgent priority at this time.

Since the correct relationship between ruler and subject is that they be as one, how could they not be closely bound to each other? At present the state councillors only get together when they have banquets, and without a special summons they do not have an audience. What kind of principle is that? Fittingly I request that when Your Majesty sits in your rest hall daily, you discuss state affairs with the state councillors. Even if you have to divide your days to meet them, and even when there are no urgent matters, do not forgo this practice. Otherwise, I fear the great ministers will daily become distant, the eunuchs will daily get closer to you, and you will not be informed on the conditions of the people and the security of the dynasty.

If you get the right people in the posts of prefect and magistrate, then the people will reap benefits. If you do not get the right men, then the people will be harmed. . . . I request that, as in the ancient system, those officials who have yet to reach the court ranks [third to sixth grade] first be appointed as district magistrates. On reaching fourth grade, as in the regulation, they should be appointed provincial governors and have the royal inspectors evaluate their records before according them rewards and punishments. If unavoidable, give the so-called high officials, the aged, and those rural gentry who were recruited through a requested audience capital appointments but do not give them responsibilities close to the people in the provinces. If Your Majesty carries out this policy for twenty years, those who abandoned the land will all return and tax revenues will not be insufficient.

Gold, silver, and brocaded silks are not produced in our country. In the past, court officials used only plain satin, silks, and cotton for clothing, and for utensils they only used brass and earthenware. One can see that the country has been able to last more than four hundred years and preserve its dynastic state shrines only because we respected the virtue of frugality. Recently, extremely extravagant customs have brought hardship to the peasants' life and exhausted the state treasury. I request that the state councillors from now on use no brocaded silk for clothing or gold and jade for utensils. And those who ride horses in fine clothes should have no escort to follow. If each task is done frugally, remonstrating those above and inspiring those below, the customs will return to their former state of decency.

It has been nearly fifty years since the land in the capital province, except *choŏp* and *kubun*,[2] was all reallocated as land for official salaries. Recently,

---

2. The *choŏp* (ancestral occupation) and *kubun* (pension) land, though originally granted by the state, became hereditary, whereas most other state land grants did not.

as most of the land has been seized and occupied by powerful families, the government in the meantime has often discussed radical reform. But because of frightening words deceptively used in reporting to Your Majesty, in the end this was never carried out. That is also why the ministers did not insist on the reform. If we carry out the reform, many people will rejoice, while in the end only a few dozen powerful families will not share this joy. . . .

[From *Koryŏ sa* 110:34a–37b; HK, ES]

### YI SAEK: MEMORIAL ON CURRENT AFFAIRS

Your Majesty's subject Saek [1328–1396], on mourning leave, here offers some ideas.

I have learned that the demarcation of boundaries and the equalization of landholdings are the first tasks of governing people. Broadly speaking, the systems created and the regulations maintained by our dynastic ancestors left nothing uncovered, but after more than four hundred years have elapsed, how could there be no problems? This is especially so in the land system. The demarcation of boundaries is unjust, as powerful families compete to amalgamate small landholdings, much like eagles nesting in pigeon coops. . . .

I humbly implore you to use the principles established in the land and tax laws of the year *kabin* [1314] as your basis. By referring to the corrected official documents, rectify those lands forcibly seized and survey newly reclaimed land. If you tax newly reclaimed land and reduce excessive land grants, state revenues will increase. If you adjudicate land that has been forcibly seized and pacify people who cultivate the land, then the people will obey with happiness. The happy obedience of the people and increases in tax collections are aims greatly sought by rulers. Your Majesty, why would you hesitate to pursue these goals? Some say, "It is difficult to seize a rich man's land abruptly, and after succeeding years of abuse, it is difficult to reform suddenly." That is true of an incapable ruler, but not what we would hope for from Your Majesty. The questions of how to implement the reform and how to refine it are things that advising ministers must certainly deliberate on, and a newcomer like me dare not discuss this. But whether to carry it out or not depends only on Your Majesty's will. . . .

. . . As for the strategy of fighting on sea, our country is surrounded on three sides by water, and no fewer than one million people live on offshore islands. I believe handling boats and swimming are their special skills. These people do not farm but make their living from fishing and gathering salt. Recently, because of pirates, they have left their homes and lost their livelihood. Compared to the people living on the land, they hate the pirates ten times more. If you speedily send a detailed plan and summon those living by the water, offering them rewards, then you can get several thousand people in no time. If you use their great skills and have them fight against those whom they hate, how can they not be victorious? Moreover, if they kill the enemy and are rewarded, how can it not be more profitable than fishing and gathering salt? If you put them under the command of the police commissioner and have them always in boats at the ready, the local areas will benefit and the pirates can be defeated. These are the two main strategies to resist the invaders. If we simply guard the land and do not fight at sea, they will consider us cowards, and we will have no way to anticipate their raids. If we fight at sea but fail to guard the land, the enemy may come ashore at an unanticipated spot, causing considerable harm. Therefore, we defend the land to protect ourselves and fight at sea to overpower the enemy. If we follow this strategy, will we not accomplish both aims?

[From *Koryŏ sa* 115:1a–4b; HK, ES]

*Chapter 33*

BUDDHISM: THE CH'ŎNT'AE AND CHOGYE SCHOOLS

Buddhism, which first entered Korea in the Three Kingdoms period, remained a major religious and intellectual force in Koryŏ. It flourished at the start of the dynasty and then underwent several stages of reform in the middle period of the kingdom. Throughout the dynasty, Buddhism had close ties with the court as monarchs frequently allowed a son to enter the priesthood and sought advice on both political and religious problems from learned monks. Two major schools, Kyo (Doctrinal) and Sŏn (Meditation), dominated Buddhist thought, although in the late eleventh century the royal monk Ŭich'ŏn (1055–1101) tried to fuse the practices of the two schools into the Ch'ŏnt'ae (Tiantai) school. Apart from its intellectual vigor, Buddhism thrived economically through its monasteries, some of which, like T'ongdo, held vast tracts of land. Like many other powerful institutions, Buddhism became inevitably tainted by corruption and misuse of power, abuses that sometimes led to criticism of the monastic establishment.

Shortly after the rise of the military, Buddhism underwent a significant reform with the growth of the meditation-inspired Chogye school. The monk Chinul (1128–1210)—one of Koryŏ's most prolific Buddhist writers and profound thinkers—played an especially important role in this effort, calling for a new emphasis on the practice of meditation along with the study of texts. Ŭich'ŏn, writing a century earlier, had sought to compile the comments and interpretations of other Buddhist thinkers into a comprehensive compendium. This tradition of respect for printed scriptures was again dramatically demonstrated at the height of the Mongol invasions, when the Koryŏ court, in its search for the Buddha's divine protection, supervised the recarving of more than eighty thousand woodblocks that were needed to publish the complete Buddhist canon, the *Tripiṭaka*.

[HK]

# RESURGENCE OF BUDDHISM

The military coup of 1170 signaled the beginning of a new order. The great aristocratic lineages lost their preeminence and ability to dictate all state matters, a sign of a decline in their political and social power. The coup led to equally significant changes in Koryŏ's religious order as the Chogye sect of the Meditation school gradually emerged as the dominant spiritual voice in the kingdom.

During early Koryŏ, Kyo (Doctrinal) beliefs rather than Sŏn (Meditation) prescripts captured the imagination of the elite. By the start of the twelfth century, however, government officials and scholars alike, unhappy with the Doctrinal school's approach, had reinvigorated the Meditation school. And by the end of the twelfth century, the highest military and civil authorities were patronizing Meditation monks and monasteries.

Yi Kyubo (1168–1241) described Ch'oe Ch'unghŏn's active support of Meditation in his "On a Trip to Ch'angbok Monastery." The military leader Ch'oe Ch'unghŏn not only rebuilt many Meditation monasteries but also sought out Meditation monks and sponsored religious meetings to propagate the faith. The Meditation school's simple spiritual message of finding truth and spirituality within the self undoubtedly appealed to Ch'oe Ch'unghŏn and other military leaders, but the Ch'oe house's patronage of Meditation practices was also a reaction to the earlier opposition to Ch'oe rule by monks of the Doctrinal school. Since the Doctrinal monasteries had been closely aligned with the former aristocratic forces before the military rose to power, they felt threatened by the new military leadership. And as the passage describing the clash between the monks and military rulers shows, the monasteries were dealt a crippling blow by Ch'oe Ch'unghŏn's well-organized and well-equipped forces.

Chinul (1158–1210), one of the leading masters of Meditation of this period, was mostly responsible for the Meditation school's phenomenal rise under military rule. A devotee of Meditation practices from his youth, Chinul, also known as the National Preceptor Pojo, called for the individual to empty the mind and free the self from the world of the senses. The final passage offered here was issued in 1190 upon the formal establishment of Chinul's Samādhi and Prajñā Community. The community sought to achieve enlightenment through worship, scriptural recitation, common work, and meditation. In this composition, Chinul explains the development of the Meditation community at Kŏjo Monastery and then its move to the Chogye region in southwestern Korea. The work served as both the compact of the community members and a call to others to develop the practices Chinul considered crucial to a successful Buddhist vocation.

[HK]

## CHINUL: THE COMPACT OF THE SAMĀDHI AND PRAJÑĀ COMMUNITY

Reverently, I have heard:

A person who falls to the ground gets back up by using that very same ground. To try to get up without relying on that ground would be impossible.[1]

Sentient beings are those who are deluded in regard to the one mind and give rise to boundless defilements. Buddhas are those who have awakened to the one mind and have given rise to boundless sublime functions. Although there is a difference between delusion and awakening, essentially these both derive from the one mind. Hence to seek Buddhahood apart from the mind is impossible.

Since my youth, I have cast myself into the domain of the patriarchs of the Meditation school and have visited meditation halls everywhere. After investigating the teachings the Buddha and the patriarchs so compassionately bestowed on beings, I have found that they are primarily designed to make us bring to rest all conditioning, empty the mind, and then remain centered there quietly, without looking for anything outside. As it is stated in the *Flower Garland Scripture*, "If a person wants to comprehend the state of Buddhahood, he should purify his mind until it is just like empty space." Whatever we see, hear, recite, or cultivate, we should recognize how difficult it is to come into contact with such things; examining these things using our own wisdom, we should practice according to what has been expounded. Then it can be said that we are cultivating the Buddha mind ourselves, are destined to complete the path to Buddhahood ourselves, and are sure to requite personally the Buddha's kindness. . . .

In the first month of *imin* [1182], I traveled to Poje Monastery in the capital for a convocation called to discuss meditation. One day I made a pact with more than ten fellow cultivators saying: "After the close of this convocation we will renounce fame and profit and stay in seclusion in the mountain forests. There we will form a community designed to foster the constant training in *samādhi* [concentration] and *prajñā* [wisdom]. Through worship of the Buddha, recitation of scriptures, and even through common work, we will each discharge

---

1. Adapted from a verse attributed to the Fourth Chan Patriarch Upagupta.

the duties to which we are assigned and nourish the self-nature in all situations. We vow to pass our whole lives free of entanglements and to follow the higher pursuits of accomplished and true men. Wouldn't this be wonderful?". . .

I humbly hope that men of high moral standards who have grown tired of world affairs—regardless of whether they are adherents of Meditation, the Doctrinal school, Confucianism, or Daoism—will abandon the dusty domain of this world, roam high above all things, and devote themselves earnestly to the path of inner cultivation, which is commensurate with this aim.

[From *Hanguk pulgyo chŏnsŏ* 4:698a–b, 707a–c; RB]

## CHINUL AND THE CHOGYE SCHOOL

Chinul spent much of his life explaining and discussing both Meditation and Flower Garland beliefs. His extensive writings show him to be one of Korea's greatest Buddhist thinkers. The selection in this section is Chinul's abridgement of an important commentary to the *Flower Garland Scripture* by the Chinese exegete Li Tongxuan (635–730). Chinul's own success in developing a synthesis between scholarship and meditation in Buddhism was to a large extent inspired by Li's innovative, practice-oriented interpretations of Buddhist doctrinal teachings. In his preface to these excerpts, Chinul provides an extensive autobiographical account of his own quandary concerning the connection between doctrine and practice. Scholars of the *Flower Garland Scripture* whom Chinul consulted claimed that the Meditation school focus on "seeing the nature of the mind" produced only introspective awareness, not the consummate, holistic knowledge of the "unimpeded interfusion of all phenomena" that they presumed to be the quintessence of Buddhism. This claim prompted Chinul to undertake a three-year study of the Buddhist canon to discover scriptural passages that would vindicate Meditation. He believed that he found such vindication in the *Flower Garland Scripture* and Li's commentary on that text. His reading suggested to him that the words of the Buddha were what matured into the doctrinal teachings of Buddhism, while the mind of the Buddha was what evolved into Meditation. Just as the words of the Buddha reflected what was in his mind, so too the doctrinal teachings of Buddhism reflected the mystical knowledge engendered through meditation. Hence Chinul discovered a basis for synthesizing the Flower Garland and Meditation schools into a comprehensive system of Buddhist thought and practice, one that would inspire all future generations of Korean Buddhists.

Fundamental to Chinul's syncretic vision was the basic unity he perceived between the descriptions of truth presented in Buddhist doctrine and the experience of that truth that occurs through meditation. Through a series of questions and answers in "Straight Talk on the True Mind," Chinul sought to prove that the variant accounts of the absolute in both Doctrinal and Meditation records can all be traced to a single concept: the true mind. The true mind for Chinul meant Buddhahood itself; but it also referred to that quality of sentience that is basic to all ordinary "sentient" beings as well. The true mind, therefore, serves as the matrix between the conventional reality of the ordinary world and the absolute truth of the dharma realm. In order to gain access to absolute truth, and thus enlightenment, Buddhist practitioners need only recognize the enlightenment inherent in their own minds. Faith—the wholehearted acceptance of the fact of their innate enlightenment—is the soteriological attribute that will allow students to relinquish their delusion that they are unenlightened. It is this peculiar kind of faith in Meditation—what Chinul termed "right faith in the patriarchal school"—that will reveal to all persons that they are originally buddhas.

In "Secrets on Cultivating the Mind," the most accessible of his accounts of the process of Meditation training, Chinul offers a summation of his key ideas and reiterates his lament that people "do not recognize that their own natures are the true buddhas." Chinul demands that practice begin with a sudden awakening, which reveals to the student that he is innately enlightened. This initial awakening occurs through tracing the light emanating from the fountainhead of his mind back to its enlightened source. But simply because the student understands that he is a buddha does not mean that he will be able to act like one, any more than a clever infant will be able to act like an intelligent adult. Even after awakening, the student must continue to control the full range of old habits, to which he will still be subject, as well as to cultivate the host of wholesome qualities that will enable him to express his understanding to others. Finally, when the student's understanding and conduct work in perfect unison, he will become a buddha in fact as well as principle. Chinul's soteriological program of sudden awakening–gradual cultivation was unique among the mature Buddhist schools of East Asia and helped to define the indigenous Korean tradition of Meditation.

[RB]

## CHINUL: EXCERPTS FROM THE *EXPOSITION OF THE "FLOWER GARLAND SCRIPTURE"*: PREFACE

In the autumn months of Dading, *ŭlsa* [1185], as I began living in retreat on Mount Haga, I reflected constantly on the Meditation adage "Mind is Buddha."[2] I felt that if a person were not fortunate enough to meet with this approach, he would end up wasting many aeons in vain and would never reach the domain of sanctity.

I had always had doubts about the approach to entering into awakening of the Flower Garland teachings: what, finally, did it involve? Accordingly, I decided to question a lecturer on the *Flower Garland Scripture*. He replied: "You must contemplate the unimpeded interpenetration of all phenomena." He entreated me further: "If you merely contemplate your own mind and do not contemplate

---

2. This phrase is commonly attributed to Ma-tsu Tao-i (709–788).

the unimpeded interfusion of all phenomena, you will never gain the perfect qualities of the fruition of Buddhahood."

I did not answer, but thought silently to myself: "If you use the mind to contemplate phenomena, those phenomena will become impediments, and you will have needlessly disturbed your own mind; when then would there be a resolution of this situation? But if the mind is brightened and your wisdom purified, then one hair and all the universe will be interfused, for there is, perforce, nothing that is outside the mind." I then retired into the mountains and sat reading through the *Tripiṭaka* in search of a passage that would confirm the mind doctrine of the Meditation school.

Three winters and summers passed before I came upon the figure about "one dust mote containing thousands of volumes of scriptures" in the "Appearance of the Thus Come Ones" [*Rulai chuxian pin* chapter] of the *Flower Garland Scripture.* Later in the same passage the summation said: "The wisdom of the Thus Come Ones is just like this: it is complete in the bodies of all sentient beings. It is merely all these ordinary, foolish people who are not aware of it and do not recognize it." I put the scripture volume on my head in reverence and, unwittingly, began to weep.

As I was still unclear about the initial access to faith that was appropriate for ordinary people of today, however, I reread the explanation of the Elder Li Tongxuan [635–730] of the first level of the ten faiths in his *Exposition of the "Flower Garland Scripture"* [*Xin Huayan jing lun*]. It said: "Chief of Enlightenment Bodhisattva has three realizations. First, he realizes that his own body and mind are originally the dharma realm because they are immaculate, pure, and untainted. Second, he realizes that the discriminative nature of his own body and mind is originally free from the subject-object dichotomy and is originally the Buddha of Unmoving Wisdom. Third, he realizes that his own mind's sublime wisdom, which can distinguish the genuine from the distorted, is Mañjuśrī. He realizes these three things at the first level of faith and comes to be known as Chief of Enlightenment."

It says elsewhere: "The difficulties a person encounters in entering into the ten faiths from the ordinary state are due to the fact that he completely accepts that he is an ordinary man; he is unwilling to accept that his own mind is the Buddha of Unmoving Wisdom."

It also says: "The body is the reflection of wisdom. This world is the same. When wisdom is pure and its reflection clear, large and small merge with one another as in the realm of Indra's net."

Thereupon, I set aside the volume and, breathing a long sigh, said: "What the World-Honored One said with his mouth are the teachings. What the patriarchs transmitted with their minds is Meditation. The mouth of the Buddha and the minds of the patriarchs can certainly not be contradictory. How can students of both Meditation and Doctrinal schools not plumb the fundamental source but instead, complacent in their own training, wrongly foment disputes and waste their time?" From that time on, I have continued to build my mind of faith and have cultivated diligently without indolence; a number of years have already passed.

I say to men who are cultivating the mind that first, through the path of the patriarchs, they should know the original sublimity of their own minds and should not be bound by words and letters. Next, through the text of Li Tongxuan's *Exposition*, they should ascertain that the essence and function of the mind are identical to the nature and characteristics of the dharma realm. Then the quality of the unimpeded interpenetration among all phenomena and the merit of the wisdom and compassion that have the same essence as that of all the buddhas will not be beyond their capacity.

[From *Hanguk pulgyo chŏnsŏ* 4:767a–768b; RB]

## PUBLICATION OF THE *TRIPITAKA*

The first orally redacted Buddhist canons are presumed to have been compiled in India shortly after the Buddha's death. The Chinese compiled their own manuscript canons early in the history of their own Buddhist tradition, and such canons were soon introduced into Korea. With the invention of xylographic printing techniques, a complete woodblock canon was carved in China during the tenth century, and the first Koryŏ canon, a similar project, was begun in 1011.

The Buddhist canons of East Asia were open collections, which permitted dramatic expansions in coverage when compared to their Indian counterparts. The monk Ŭich'ŏn (1055–1101) had the most liberal outlook toward the canon. Earlier Chinese Buddhist bibliographic cataloguers considered canonical chiefly translations of Indian materials. But Ŭich'ŏn believed that East Asian exegetes and authors also had made seminal contributions to Buddhist thought that warranted inclusion in the canon. Ŭich'ŏn feared that unless the canon were opened to such indigenous works, they would be doomed to drop from circulation and would be lost to posterity.

To prevent such a fate, Ŭich'ŏn sent agents throughout East Asia to procure Buddhist texts by native authors. In 1090, he published his catalog of this collection, which listed some 1,010 titles in 4,740 rolls. Woodblocks for each of these texts were carved, and the collection was termed a *Supplement to the Canon* (*Sokchanggyŏng*). Unfortunately, the woodblocks of the first Koryŏ canon and its supplement were burned during the Mongol invasion in 1231. While the main canon was recarved between 1236 and 1251, the *Supplement* was not. As Ŭich'ŏn had feared, most of the texts collected in his *Supplement* were lost to history; only his catalog of that collection has survived.

The Koryŏ government actively supported Buddhism, and the most dramatic expression of state-sponsored Buddhist activities was the printing of the *Tripitaka*, the Buddhist canon. Centuries earlier, Buddhist devotion and advances in printing had already been linked. With the recent discovery of a copy of a *dhāranī* scripture dating from before 751, Silla claims the oldest extant example of woodblock printing in the world.

A printing of the *Tripiṭaka* in woodblocks was undertaken on two separate occasions. The first blocks were started in 1011 in the midst of Khitan attacks, Koreans believed that the publication of the *Tripiṭaka* would invoke the divine protection of the Buddha, sparing Koryŏ from further attacks. This project lasted nearly seventy years. When the Mongols invaded in the thirteenth century, Koryŏ once again turned to aid from the Buddha with the second manufacture of the *Tripiṭaka* in woodblocks. The eighty-one thousand separate blocks completed at this time can still be seen at Haein Monastery in south central Korea.

This last production of the *Tripiṭaka*, in the middle of the Mongol invasions, attracted considerable attention. In the selection presented here, Yi Kyubo, reflecting on the significance of this project, believes that publishing the *Tripiṭaka* will guarantee the safety of the nation. The publication of the *Tripiṭaka* demonstrated the faith of the Koreans and their belief in the power of the Buddha to afford them divine protection. It is also another clear example of the technological sophistication of a people who could carry out such a mammoth project while fighting a terrible war.

[RB, HK]

### YI KYUBO: ROYAL PRAYER ON THE OCCASION OF THE PRODUCTION OF THE *TRIPIṬAKA*

I, King Kojong [1213–1259], together with the crown prince, dukes, lords, counts, state councillors, and civil and military officials, have respectfully cleansed our bodies and souls and pray to all the buddhas and bodhisattvas and the Sakradevanam Indra everywhere in the infinite void as well as to all the spirit-officials who protect the dharma in the thirty-three heavens.

Severe indeed is the calamity caused by the Tartars. The nature of their cruelty and vindictiveness is beyond description. With foolishness and stupidity greater than that of beasts, how could they know what is respected in this world and what is called the Buddhadharma? Because of this ignorance there was not a Buddhist image or Buddhist writing that they did not entirely destroy. Moreover, as a state that worships the Buddhadharma when we do not have this great treasure we certainly cannot be content with its loss. How can we hesitate over its reproduction on account of the magnitude of such an undertaking.

As we are truly sincere in our prayer, we have nothing to be ashamed of before our ancestors. Therefore, we humbly pray that the various buddhas and sages in the thirty-three heavens receive our earnest prayers, extend to us divine power, cause the stubborn and vile barbarians to flee far away, and never again let them enter our territory. When the fighting ceases and peace prevails all over, may the queen dowager and crown prince enjoy long life forever and may Korea's good fortune last ten thousand years.

[From *Tongguk Yi sangguk chip* 25:18b–20a; HK, ES]

# Chapter 34

## NEO-CONFUCIANISM

Confucianism remained an important ideology of the state throughout the Koryŏ dynasty, but in the closing years of Koryŏ new interest grew in Neo-Confucianism, which had developed earlier in Song and Yuan China.

An Hyang (1243–1306) is traditionally credited with introducing Neo-Confucianism to Korea. An's first exposure to the ideas of Neo-Confucianism came in 1286 when he read the *Complete Works of Zhu Xi* (*Zhuzi quanshu*) while staying in the Yuan capital as a member of a Koryŏ embassy to the Mongol court. Impressed by the ideas of Zhu Xi (1130–1200), An made a copy of the *Complete Works* and brought it back to Koryŏ. He subsequently devoted himself to reviving Confucian studies in Korea. An's major contribution to the development of Neo-Confucianism in Korea came not from the originality of his thought but rather from his efforts to promote Confucian education and propagate the ideas of Zhu Xi. Nonetheless, it is important to note that when he cites social ethics in his discussion of Confucius's legacy, An introduces one of the major recurring themes of fourteenth-century Korean Neo-Confucianism. Within a century after its introduction by An Hyang, Neo-Confucianism spread rapidly among the ranks of the officialdom and became the major focus of the curriculum in the highest academic institution. This is illustrated in the first selection, from the biography of Yi Saek (1328–1396), one of the most prominent Neo-Confucianists of the fourteenth century.

Chŏng Tojŏn (d. 1398) was a central political figure in the change of dynasties between Koryŏ and Chosŏn; he was a major scholar of statecraft who did much to shape the institutions of the new dynasty, and at the same time also a seminal thinker of the Nature and Principle philosophy who began to develop a new philosophical dimension in Korean Neo-Confucianism through his rebuttals of Buddhism and Daoism. One of Chŏng's most significant writings was the three-part work *Mind, Material Force, and Principle (Simgi ip'yŏn)*. In the first two parts of this work, mind (for Buddhism) and material force (for Daoism) criticize each other, leading to the crucial third part, where principle, representing Nature and Principle Neo-Confucianism, exposes (in Chŏng's view) the falseness in the underlying assumptions of both Buddhism and Daoism and presents Neo-Confucian principle as the only way that comprehends both mind and material force. It is this third part, entitled "Principle Admonishes Mind and Material Force," that is reproduced in part in the second selection, along with annotations by Kwŏn Kŭn (1352–1409), Chŏng Tojŏn's contemporary.

[HK]

## YI SAEK: THE SPREAD OF NEO-CONFUCIANISM

In the sixteenth year [1367] of King Kongmin, the Royal Confucian Academy [Sŏnggyungwan] was rebuilt, and Yi Saek [1328–1396] was appointed concurrently to be superintendent of the Capital District and supervisor of sacrificial rites in the Royal Academy. The number of classics licentiates *[saengwŏn]* was increased. Kim Kuyong [1338–1384], Chŏng Mongju [1337–1392], Pak Sangch'ung [1332–1375], Pak Ŭijung, and Yi Sungin [1349–1392], all scholars skilled in the classics, were given concurrent appointments as instructors in addition to the offices they held. Prior to this time, the number of students at the academy had been no more than a few dozen. But Yi Saek revised academic procedures and sat daily in Myŏngnyun Hall, where he divided the students [into sections] on different Confucian classics and taught them. When the lecture was over, the students debated among themselves, forgetting their fatigue. Scholars gathered to share their perceptions and feelings. Thus began the rise of the Cheng-Zhu school of Neo-Confucianism in Korea.

[From *Koryŏ sa* 115:10b–11a; JD, HK]

## CHŎNG TOJŎN: PHILOSOPHICAL REBUTTAL OF BUDDHISM AND DAOISM

The principle of Heaven resides in humankind to become human nature while the material force of earth resides in humankind to become physical form. The mind combines principle and material force to become master of the body. Thus principle exists prior to heaven and earth, and material force comes into being from principle, which is also received by the mind and becomes virtue. A human being is different from beasts because he has a sense of right.

If a human being has no rightness, then his consciousness is no more than emotion, desire, and the selfishness of worldly gain, while his activity is like a mass of squirming insects. Even though he may be called human, how far removed can he be from the birds and beasts? That is why when examining his mind and cultivating his material force, the Confucianist necessarily emphasizes rightness.

The learning of Buddha and Laozi worships purity and annihilation. Thus they necessarily strive to close off and eradicate even the greatness of moral duty and the beauty of ritual and music. The person who has no desire in his heart may be different from people who pursue worldly gain, but he does not know how to emphasize the commonality of the principle of Heaven so as to control the selfishness of desire. Therefore, in his daily speech and conduct, he always becomes trapped in worldly gain but does not himself know it. . . .

Mencius said: "Now when people suddenly see a young child about to fall in a well, they all have feelings of fear and pity."[1] He continued to say: "The feeling of commiseration is the beginning of humaneness." This means that the feeling of compassion is inherent in our minds and reveals the error of the Buddhist elimination of thought and forgetting of emotion. As for humans being born with the life-creating mind of heaven and earth, this is what is called humaneness. This principle is truly embodied in our minds. Therefore, that feeling of pity when we see a young child crawling into a well arises of itself and cannot be blocked. If one pursues this mind and expands it, his humaneness will be inexhaustible, and he will be able to join and succor the whole world. Thus the Confucianist does not fear the rise of concern but only follows the natural manifestation of the principle of Heaven. How could he be like the Buddhist, who fears the rise of feeling and concern and strives forcibly to eliminate them in order to return to annihilation?

The Analects says: "The determined scholar and the humane man will not seek life at the expense of their humaneness; they will sacrifice their bodies to achieve humaneness."[2] This means that rightness is important and life is unimportant, and it reveals the error of the Daoists' lusting after life by nurturing material [vital] force. Generally the superior man, having seen and acquired the genuine principle, cannot bear to save his life for even one day once it is rightly the time to die. Is his life or death important, or is his rightness important? Therefore, when the Confucian must come to the aid of his lord or his father, he will sacrifice his body and his life racing to them. This is not like the Daoists, who devote themselves to self-cultivation in their lust after life.

The Daoists do not know that material force is based in principle, and they use material force as their Way. The Buddhists do not know that principle is embodied in the mind, and they use mind as their religion. Both the Daoists

---

1. *Mencius* 2A:6 (Legge 2:202).
2. *Analects* 15:8 (Legge 1:297).

and the Buddhists think of themselves as the ultimate in abstraction, but they do not know what incorporeality is and speak only in reference to that which is corporeal. They ensnare themselves in the shallow and common, the crooked and the skewed, but they do not know it.

[From *Sambong chip* 10:5b–9a; JD]

# HISTORY

Korea's oldest extant history is the *Historical Record of the Three Kingdoms* (*Samguk sagi*), which was compiled by Kim Pusik (1075–1151) and others during Injong's reign (1122–1146). The *Historical Record of the Three Kingdoms* is an official court-sponsored history that reflects the Confucian values of its compilers. It was assembled to provide Koreans with a greater understanding of their own history and heritage; yet it is obvious that its compilers did not include all the facts and legends then known, particularly those that went against their own view of history. For this omission they have often been criticized by modern historians.

Koryŏ's other great historical work is the *Memorabilia of the Three Kingdoms* (*Samguk yusa*). Written by the monk Iryŏn (1206–1289) during the devastating Mongol invasions, it presents many traditions and tales that were not included in the *Historical Record of the Three Kingdoms*. Reflecting its author's religious beliefs, the *Memorabilia* is replete with Buddhist themes. It is also interesting to note that Korea's mythical founder, Tangun, is described for the first time in this work.

[HK]

## KIM PUSIK: ON PRESENTING THE *HISTORICAL RECORD OF THE THREE KINGDOMS* TO THE KING

Your subject, Kim Pusik, wishes to report. All the states of the past established official historians to record events. Accordingly, Mencius said: "Such were *Sheng*, the annals of Jin; *Taowu*, the annals of Zhu; and the *Spring and Autumn Annals* of Lu."[3] The histories of Korea's Three Kingdoms are long, and their events should be set forth in an official record. Therefore, Your Majesty has ordered your subject to compile this book.

In your leisure Your Majesty has read widely in histories of earlier ages and said: "Of today's scholars and high-ranking officials, there are those who are well versed and can discuss in detail the Five Classics and other philosophical treatises as well as the histories of Qin and Han, but as to the events of our country, they

---

3. *Mencius* 4B:21 (Legge 2:327).

are utterly ignorant from beginning to end. This is truly lamentable. Moreover, because Silla, Koguryŏ, and Paekche were able to have formal relations with China from their beginnings to the unification wars [660–668], they were discussed in the biographical sections of Fan Ye's *History of the Later Han* and Song Qi's *History of the Tang* but these books are detailed on internal Chinese affairs and terse about foreign matters and did not record everything of historical significance. As for the ancient records of the Three Kingdoms, the writing is unrefined, and the recording of historical events is deficient. Accordingly, they do not always expose whether the ruler is good or evil, the subjects are loyal or treasonous, the country is at peace or in crisis, the people are orderly or rebellious. To create a history that can serve as a guide, I ought to have a person who has three talents—intelligence, scholarship, and wisdom. This will lead to a work of outstanding quality to be handed down for eternity, shining like the sun and stars."

Your subject basically lacks these talents as well as profound knowledge. Although his scholarship is shallow and the history of the earlier ages is vague, by exhausting his spirit and energy, your subject has barely been able to complete this volume. Although it may not be good enough to be stored on a sacred mountain, may it not be set aside as merely a useless thing. Your subject's foolish thought is to have Heaven's light shine down on it.

[From *Tong munsŏn* 44:12b–13b; HK, ES]

## Chapter 35

### POLITICAL THOUGHT IN EARLY CHOSŎN

## RULING THE NEW DYNASTY

Kwŏn Kŭn (1352–1409) was one of the spiritual founders of Chosŏn Korea. In his treatises and commentaries on the Chinese classics he laid out the basic concepts of Neo-Confucianism and illuminated their relevance for the political as well as the social life of the new dynasty. He emphasized the importance of Confucian learning for activating people's moral nature, a process of self-realization that was to culminate in the development of the proper human relationships between ruler and subject, father and son, elder and younger. One of Kwŏn Kŭn's favorite texts was the *Great Learning*, in which he found an outline for social and political action.

The following memorial (1401) was written after a fire in Such'ang Palace, the royal home of the last Koryŏ kings, in which Yi Sŏnggye had held his enthronement ceremony. Because this fire was interpreted as a warning of Heaven to King T'aejong's young rule (1400–1418), Kwŏn Kŭn pointed out six matters to which the king should pay special attention: loyalty to King T'aejo (1392–1398), administration of state affairs, treatment of officials, attendance at royal lectures, rewarding of loyalty, and performance of state rituals. Kwŏn Kŭn advocated in particular the rehabilitation of his teacher, Chŏng Mongju (1337–1392), who had died as a Koryŏ loyalist.

[MD]

## On Treating Court Officials

Although the distinction of ruler and minister is ceremonially strict, their relationship must be emotionally intimate. In olden times, the ruler was intimate and close to his high ministers, and he met face to face with his court officials.

Rulers of later generations lived hidden in their palaces, and the ministers they received at court bowed perfunctorily and then retired. Since the feelings of ruler and ministers did not at all match, the wicked and the false deceived their ruler and took pleasure in concealing from him the gains and losses outside the palace and the interests and urgent concerns of the people.

Your servant wishes that from now on Your Majesty would regularly sit in court and receive your ministers in audience all through the day. You should grant an audience to all officials who depart and take leave or come from outside the court, regardless of their rank. If you use warm words to console them and clear questions to draw them out, all your officials will have grateful hearts, and you will learn all about the affairs of the people.

## On Attending Royal Lectures

The way of emperors and kings is made bright through scholarship, and the rule of emperors and kings is extensive because of scholarship. From antiquity, those kings who were good even established royal lectures in order to investigate the learning of the sages.

Your servant respectfully wishes that, regardless of the brilliance of your natural talents or the inadequacy of the Confucian scholars, Your Majesty would daily attend the royal lectures and, with unprejudiced mind and humble determination, diligently pursue the studies.

[From *T'aejong sillok* 1:4b–7b; MD]

# NEW GOVERNMENT

With his broad erudition and energetic character, Chŏng Tojŏn was a prime mover in the founding process of the new dynasty. In his philosophical works he outlined the Confucian point of view and aggressively turned against Buddhism. He put an end to the Confucians' traditional tolerance of the Buddhist creed and advanced philosophical arguments against it. He also paid close attention to renewing and tightening the governmental structure. Inspired by the *Rites of Zhou* (*Zhou li*), Chŏng Tojŏn wrote the *Administrative Codes of Chosŏn* (*Chosŏn kyŏngguk chŏn*), in which he drafted the constitutional outline of the new dynasty. Although he emphasized the ruler's pivotal position in the governing process, he equally envisaged a strong standing for the *ch'ongjae* (prime minister), whose major task was to assist the king at the head of a well-organized administration. He also recognized the importance of the censorial agencies for checking the king as well as for supervising the officialdom. Chŏng Tojŏn's major concern, however, was the building of a government that would function through benevolence rather than force. In this sense he followed the Mencian tradition that eschewed coercion and espoused virtue as the sole means for winning the people's hearts. Chŏng Tojŏn's ideas exerted a lasting influence on the legislative process during the dynasty's first century.

[MD]

### CHŎNG TOJŎN: ON THE PRIME MINISTER

The administrative department is the domain of the prime minister. As the functionaries, et cetera, are all subject to the prime minister, administering the educational department also is one of the prime minister's duties. If the prime minister gets the right men, the Six Ministries are well run, and the hundred offices are well regulated. Therefore it is said: "The ruler's task consists in settling for one chief minister." This points to the prime minister.

Above, he assists the king; below, he guides the officials and controls all the people. His task is indeed great! Furthermore, the abilities of rulers differ: some are dull, and some bright; some are strong, and some weak. The prime minister goes along with the ruler's goodness, but corrects his badness; he presents him with the feasible, but withholds from him the wrong. By so doing, he enables the ruler to enter the realm of the Great Mean. Therefore he is called "assistant"; this means that he supports and assists.

All the officials have different tasks, and the people have different occupations. The prime minister treats them fairly so that each does not lose what is proper for him; he treats them impartially so that all gain their proper place. Therefore he is called "chief minister"; this means that he rules and directs.

Only the prime minister knows about the services of the royal consorts and concubines, the duties of the eunuchs, the enjoyments of carriages and horses, of dress and ornaments, the provision of food and drink within the confines of the royal palace. He is an important minister. He is the one the ruler faces with ritual decorum, yet he personally attends to the minutest matters. Is this not trivial? No! The royal consorts, the concubines, and the eunuchs are actually ready for the royal summons. But if the prime minister does not watch over them, they might deceive the king with wickedness and flattery. The carriages and horses, the dress and ornaments, the food and drink are actually for the provision of the royal person. But if the prime minister does not economize, there might be luxurious and lavish expenditures. Therefore the earlier kings established laws and entrusted them all to the prime minister, who uses them for regulating and restraining. Their concern was far-reaching!

The great Confucian of the Song, Zhen Dexiu [1178–1235], discussed the task of the prime minister and said: "He corrects himself and rectifies the ruler; he knows the people and tends to the affairs." How excellent are these words! In my opinion, the perfection of self and the rectification of the ruler are the foundation of politics, and knowing the people and administering the affairs are the mechanism of politics. Therefore I have discussed this topic here.

[From *Sambong chip* 7:5a–6a; MD]

## THE WAY OF PRINCIPLE

At the end of the dynasty's first century, the founders' Confucian vision of a perfect government under a virtuous ruler still remained unfulfilled. Indeed, the century had witnessed Sejo's (1455–1468) usurpation of the throne and Yŏnsangun's (1494–1506) contemptuous and arbitrary rule. The Confucian officialdom itself had lost much of its initial enthusiasm and was bogged down in sterile book learning. Only a relatively small number of scholar-officials continued to pursue the Neo-Confucian dream. Collectively, they became known as the Neo-Confucian literati (*sarim*). One of them was Cho Kwangjo (1482–1519), who became the recognized leader of an ideological and political restoration movement that centered on the embodiment of the Way (*to*) in government. Emphasizing the value of scholarship for an enlightened rule, Cho had as one of his principal concerns the cultivation of personal virtue as the mainspring of a ruler's transforming influence (*hwa*). Ruler and scholar were therefore interdependent, and only the ruler's judicious use of the scholar-officials could result in the re-creation of government on the pattern of Yao and Shun, the idealized legendary rulers in China. Cho Kwangjo and his followers espoused these views from the vantage point of the censorial agencies, but, as it had before, such ideological pressure in the end proved counterproductive. Cho Kwangjo became the most prominent victim of the literati purge of 1519. His legacy, however, endured throughout the sixteenth century.

[MD]

### CHO KWANGJO: ON PROBLEMS OF THE TIME

In our country at the time of King Sejong [1418–1450], rites, music, literature, institutions, and implementations were similar to those of the Zhou period. But in the first years of the deposed Yŏnsangun [1494–1506], King Sŏngjong's [1469–1494] coffin had not been long in the memorial chamber when matters in the palace were already deplorable and not one person was able to preserve its integrity. Therefore the scholar-officials all lost their determination and finally were bewildered and confused, but nobody came to their rescue. Because the virtue and benevolence of the dynastic founders were abundant and rich and had penetrated the people's minds, after Your Majesty ascended the throne the people's minds were about to turn toward goodness. Old habits and corrupt customs, however, are difficult to reform all at once. If at this very moment the scholars' mores are not rectified, the people's livelihood is not enriched, and an indestructible basis for many future generations is not established, what will the royal descendants take as a model? Why is it that from ancient times the one who wished to rule was not able to rule well? It is because there were inferior men who took pleasure in slandering others and starting trouble. Your servant says that if Your Majesty's learning is daily progressing toward higher knowledge and brighter insights and you treat your high ministers with greater sincerity, they will not dare make wild statements in front of you and will certainly devote themselves completely to the affairs of the state. If the affairs of the state are not handled by Your Majesty's high ministers, high and low will oppose each other and not find harmony, and good rule will not be achieved.

[From *Chŏngam chip* 3:12b–14b; MD]

### CHO KWANGJO: ON THE SUPERIOR MAN AND THE INFERIOR MAN

The ruler's entire mind must be brilliantly clear before he is able to recognize the wicked and the upright among men. Since even among inferior men there are some who resemble superior men, there are certain to be inferior men among the officials. If one observes their words and actions, one naturally recognizes whether they are worthy or not. If the ruler, however, does not make an effort to investigate matters and extend his knowledge, he may take a superior man for an inferior man or an inferior man for a superior man. Furthermore, when an inferior man attacks a superior man, he may point at him and call him an inferior man. Or someone may say that a man's words and actions are incongruous, or that he is fishing for fame. A ruler cannot but closely observe such cliquish scholars. Now the ruler should clearly differentiate their kind. If there are wicked men who speak up, he should call them wicked. He should evaluate them and call them either right or wrong. If the judgment of right and wrong emanates from the ruler, the scholars' mores will naturally turn toward what is correct.

[From *Chungjong sillok* 32:66a–b; MD]

## ON SAGE LEARNING

Yi Hwang (1501–1570) did not have a brilliant political career in the central government, but his influence on the political thinking at court, exercised from deep in the countryside, was nevertheless considerable. In 1568, during his last sojourn in the capital before his death, he submitted the *Memorial on Six Points Presented in 1568 (Mujin yukcho so)* to King Sŏnjo (1567–1608). This document is one of the most powerful political statements of the Chosŏn dynasty.

After reading it, Sŏnjo exclaimed: "These six points are indeed the wise legacy of antiquity, but equally the most urgent matters of our days."

The first two points deal with problems that had become acute because Sŏnjo, at the age of fifteen, had been chosen to succeed his uncle Myŏngjong (1545–1567), who had died without leaving an heir. They include correct continuation of the royal line, close relations with the two dowager-regents, and guarding against slander. The theme of the third point, here translated in large part, is Sage Learning (sŏnghak) as the basis of good rule. It adheres closely to the teachings of Zhu Xi in the *Great Learning* and the *Mean*. The fourth point elucidates the development of the Way (to) from antiquity to early Chosŏn, warns against heterodox teachings (Buddhism), and entreats the young king to give the Way a permanent abode in Korea. In the fifth point Yi Hwang emphasizes the importance of trustworthy high officials and the censorial agencies. The last point shows the close connection between recognizing the will of Heaven and the kingly way.

Yi I (1536–1584), who with his older contemporary Yi Hwang dominated the field of Neo-Confucian philosophy in the sixteenth century, did not exhaust his efforts in speculative thinking. He paid equally close attention to the practical problems of his time, and his pronouncements on political, economic, and social issues were widely respected. He did not tire of repeating his fundamental insight, according to which the health and stability of the state rested solely on the peasantry, and he therefore termed the strengthening of the peasants' livelihood the most urgent task of his time.

The *Memorial in Ten Thousand Words* (1574), of which some key passages are translated here, is only one of several important political documents Yi I submitted to King Sŏnjo. It combines Neo-Confucian instruction on kingly rule and popular indoctrination with practical advice on economic, military, and administrative matters. Most significantly, Yi I called for flexibility in policy planning and legislation, and thus distinctly distanced himself from timeworn legal conservatism. For him, too, the basic program of internal cultivation and its application to politics, outlined in Zhu Xi's commentary on the *Great Learning*, remained the foundation of all moral and, by extension, political action.

[MD]

### YI HWANG: *MEMORIAL ON SIX POINTS*

## Third: By Esteeming Sage Learning, the Basis of Good Rule Is Built

Your servant has heard that the essential method of the mind, which is part of the learning of the emperors and kings, originated from the Great Shun's order to Yu that said: "The mind of man is precarious. The mind of the Way is barely perceptible. Be discriminating, be single-minded. Hold fast to the Mean."[1]

---

1. *Shang shu* 2:4a–b (Legge 3:61–62, with minor changes).

Shun entrusted the world to Yu with the wish that he should pacify it. Among the words with which he addressed him, none were more urgent than those on government. But Shun's injunctions and admonitions to Yu did not go beyond these words, because he realized that learning and perfect virtue constitute the great foundation of ruling, while discrimination and single-mindedness are the great law of scholarship. If the great foundation of ruling is established with the great law of scholarship, all the governances of the world will emanate from this. Because the plans of the sages of antiquity are like this, even your ignorant servant understands that Sage Learning is the basis of perfect rule and presumptuously addresses Your Majesty on this subject.

Even so, Shun's words only spoke of precariousness and subtlety without giving the reason for them; they only instructed the ruler to be discriminating and single-minded without indicating the method of being discriminating and single-minded. It was very difficult for men of later generations who wanted, on the basis of these words, to know the method exactly and put it into practice. Therefore several sages followed one upon the other, and with Confucius the method became well established. This was the *Great Learning's* "investigation of things" and "extending of one's of knowledge [understanding]," "being sincere in one's intentions," and "rectifying the mind-and-heart"; and the *Mean's* manifesting goodness and being sincere with oneself. Thereafter various Confucians successively emerged until Zhu Xi. His theories, which were indeed brilliant, were embodied in his commentaries and questions on the *Great Learning* and the *Mean*. If we now concentrate on these two books and pursue the learning of true knowledge and practice, it is like seeing the sun in the sky upon opening one's eyes, or like walking on the wide path simply by placing one's foot on it.

Regrettably, however, there are few rulers in this world who aspire to this learning. And among those who do aspire to it and are able to make a beginning, few reach the end. Ah! That is the reason why this learning has not been transmitted and government is not like that of old. Yet there is hope that it will become like this!

From the nearness of our own nature and appearance and daily applied human relationships to the myriad things of heaven and earth and the vicissitudes of past and present, everything has in itself the principle of what is and the norm of what must be. This is what is called the Mean of what exists by itself through nature. Therefore, learning must be broad, inquiry accurate, thinking careful, and judgment enlightened. These are the four elements of the extension of knowledge, and among them careful thinking is the most important. What is thinking? It means to search for it in the mind and to obtain it through experience. If one can experience it in the mind and clearly differentiate its principle, if one wishes the inner workings of good and bad and the judgment of rightness and profit, of right and wrong, to be completely exact and free of error, then it is possible to know truly and without doubt the reason for what are called "precariousness" and "subtlety" and the method of being discriminating and single-minded.

Because Your Majesty has already made a beginning in the study of these four elements and set out on this course, your servant hopes that, on the basis of this beginning, you will make an even more sustained effort. The procedure and the items of your study should be based on the details pointed out in Zhu Xi's queries. You should make reverent seriousness your priority and investigate all matters in terms of the reason for their existence and the norm of what they should be. You should ponder this deeply, turn it over in your mind, thoroughly internalize it, and finally reach the ultimate limits of these four elements. If you make such great efforts over a long period of time, one morning, without your realizing it, all problems will dissipate and be solved and there will be a sudden breakthrough to integral comprehension. Then at last you will understand the meaning of the statement that "substance and functions have one source, and there is no gap between the manifest and the hidden."[2] Neither confused by precariousness and subtlety nor bewildered by discrimination and single-mindedness, you will hold fast to the Mean: this is what is called true knowledge.

Your servant wishes also to speak about earnest action. To be sincere in one's intentions is to investigate thoroughly the subtle, even the reality of a single hair. To rectify one's mind is to investigate action and quiescence, even the correctness of one single matter. Cultivating your personal life, don't get trapped in partiality. Regulating the family, don't err in one-sidedness. Be alert and fearful; be watchful when alone. Strengthen your determination without resting. These are the elements of earnest action, and among them mind and intention are the most important. The mind is the heavenly ruler, and the will comes forth from it. If one first makes sincere what comes forth, this sincerity will be sufficient to stop the ten thousand errors. If one rectifies the heavenly ruler, that is, the mind, the whole body will follow its orders, and its movements will all have reality.

Your Majesty has already made a beginning and a start in regard to these various efforts. Your servant hopes that, on the basis of this start, you will make an even more sincere effort. For rules and guidance you should follow the instructions that these two books, *Great Learning* and the *Mean*, hand down, and make reverent seriousness your priority. If at all times and everywhere, in all your thoughts, you are guided by them and remain cautious in all your affairs, the manifold desires will be washed away from the mind, and the Five Relations and all actions will be polished to their very best.

Someone may say: "The learning of emperors and kings is not the same as the learning of scholars and students." But this difference only applies to textual exegesis and laboring over compilation. If one makes reverent seriousness the basis, investigates the principles of all things in order to extend knowledge, and examines oneself in order to practice it—are these not the essentials for making the method of mind subtle and transmitting

---

2. This is a quotation from Cheng Yi's preface to the *Commentary to the "Book of Changes."*

the learning of the Way? And is there in this respect any difference between emperors and kings and ordinary men?

If you pay attention to this, it will indeed be fortunate!

[From *T'oegye chŏnsŏ* 6:42a–46b; MD]

### YI I: *MEMORIAL IN TEN THOUSAND WORDS*

What is called timeliness means being flexible in accordance with time to establish laws and to save the people. Master Cheng, when discussing the *Book of Changes*, said that to know time and to recognize the timely circumstances are the great method of learning the *Book of Changes*. He also said: "Change according to time is the constant rule." In general, laws are established according to a particular time; as times change, the laws do not remain the same. Shun followed upon Yao, and appropriately everything remained unchanged, yet he divided the nine provinces into twelve Yu followed upon Shun, and appropriately everything remained unchanged, yet he changed the twelve provinces back to nine. Was this because sages like to make changes? They did so only in accordance with their time. In general, what can be changed in accordance with a particular time are the laws and institutions. Unchangeable, however, in ancient as well as in present times, are the kingly way, humane government, the three bonds that exist between ruler and minister, father and son, and husband and wife, and the five constants of humaneness, rightness, ritual decorum, wisdom, and trustworthiness. In later generations, when skilled mastery of the Way was no longer to be found, the unchangeable was at times changed, and the changeable was at times adhered to. For this reason the days of political order were generally few, whereas the days of disorder were generally numerous.

Speaking of our eastern region, Korea, there is no textual evidence of Jizi's Eight Rules,[3] and when at the time of the Three Kingdoms, disturbances broke out, the government policies were obliterated. The five hundred years of the former dynasty, Koryŏ, were darkened by the wind and rain of political crises. Arriving at our dynasty, King T'aejo started the dynastic fortunes. King Sejong preserved and advanced them and first used the *Six Codes of Governance* (*Kyŏngje yukchŏn*). Under King Sŏngjong the *State Code* [1485] was published, and thereafter, in accordance with time, laws were established and called the *Supplementary Code*. Because sage-king followed upon sage-king, there was appropriately nothing that was not the same; the one used the *Six Codes of Governance*, the other the *State Code*. That these were augmented by the *Supplementary Code* was but an adjustment to the time.

---

3. According to the *Book of Documents*, Jizi refused to acknowledge the sovereignty of King Wu, the founder of Zhou (Legge 3:320). Jizi (Kija) thus became the second legendary founder of Korea and made his "Eight Rules" the basis of his rule.

At the beginning of the dynasty, the officials were free to submit their opinions. Institutions were created, but people did not regard them as strange nor was the execution of law interrupted. The people were thus able to rest easy. In contrast, Yŏnsangun was wild and unruly and his expenditures lavish. He changed the tribute laws of the dynastic founders and was daily intent on harming the people and benefiting the royal house. When King Chungjong brought about a restoration, the government should have been made as before, but during the first years those in charge of the state were only ignorant meritorious subjects. Thereupon the worthies of the year *kimyo* [1519] wanted action, but they were falsely accused and destroyed. This was followed by the purge of the year *ŭlsa* [1545], which was even more cruel than the one of [1519]. From then on the Neo-Confucian literati lost heart and regarded an unobtrusive life as good luck. Since they did not dare speak up on state affairs, cunning and powerful groups acted according to their own will and without scruples. What was profitable to them they preserved as old laws; what stood in their way they abolished with new laws. They were solely intent on fleecing the people and fattening themselves. They went so far that the state was daily more hard pressed and the national foundation daily more weakened. Was there anyone who thought about this matter, even if only for an instant?

There are five principles for pacifying the people: first, to open one's sincere mind in order to obtain the sympathy of all subordinates; second, to revise the tribute plan in order to abolish the hardship of coercion and extortion; third, to uphold frugality in order to reverse the trend of extravagance; fourth, to change the selection of slaves for service in the capital in order to relieve the unhappy lot of the public and private slaves; fifth, to revise the military administration in order to strengthen internal as well as external security.

Now I see that Your Majesty's qualifications are impressive: your humanity sufficient to protect the people, your intelligence sufficient to discern cunning, your resoluteness sufficient to decide on sanctions. But Your Majesty's aspiration to become a sage is not firm, and your sincerity to seek right rule is not genuine. Assuming that you cannot reach the level of earlier kings, you withdraw and refer to your own smallness, giving no thought to advancement and development. I do not know what you have experienced to make you like this. If you make a genuine effort toward self-cultivation and put your sincere mind to pacifying the people, you will be able to find worthies and rule with them, you will be able to correct the abuses and salvage the situation.

[From *Yulgok chŏnsŏ* 5:13b–15b; 24b–25b; MD]

*Chapter 36*

CULTURE

Once the dynastic foundation was consolidated, the Chosŏn state attained brilliant achievements in many fields. Respect for education and scholarship was a hallmark of the dynasty. There were many incentives for talented young men to pursue careers in scholarship and government service, since scholars and officials were accorded the highest prestige in Chosŏn society. In 1420, King Sejong organized the Hall of Worthies, where selected scholar-officials were assigned to devote their time to scholarly research. From these studies came a number of important publications on the classics, history, geography, linguistics, law, music, agriculture, astronomy, and medicine. Most important, however, was the invention of the Korean alphabet in 1443.

The early phase of the Chosŏn dynasty was also characterized by brilliant achievements in science and technology. A number of scientific instruments—sundials, clepsydras, armillary spheres, rain gauges—were invented and refined. Moreover, a strong emphasis on the practical application of knowledge to the needs of daily life led to the publication of several manuals for farming as well as medical treatises and compendia of herbal remedies for various diseases. The highly sophisticated advances in book printing developed in Korea at this time easily accommodated these publications.

[YC]

# INVENTION OF THE KOREAN ALPHABET

The invention of the Korean alphabet, called *chŏngŭm* (Correct Sounds), is the crowning achievement of the Chosŏn dynasty. Prior to devising its own writing system, Korea had used Chinese graphs for transcription. But because the Korean language is totally different from Chinese, there were many problems in the use of Chinese graphs in a Korean setting. It was to amend this situation that King Sejong (1418–1450) assembled a group of scholars to devise scripts suitable for the Korean language. Under the personal leadership of the king, after many years of painstaking studies, a phonetic alphabet was finally created in 1443. To ensure the practicability and wide use of the newly devised alphabet, King Sejong published a eulogy cycle called *Songs of Flying Dragons* (*Yongbi ŏch'ŏn ka*) and the translation of a Chinese classic, among other works, using the new script before it was formally proclaimed in 1446.

When the new writing system was officially published, it was called *Correct Sounds to Instruct the People* (*Hunmin chŏngŭm*). Consisting of twenty-eight letters—seventeen consonants and eleven vowels—the Korean alphabet is wholly phonetic and capable of transcribing almost any sound. Hailed by modern linguists as one of the most scientific writing systems in the world, the script is extremely simple and very easy to learn. In the twentieth century, this alphabet has been called *hangŭl* (Great Letters).

In publishing the *Correct Sounds to Instruct the People* in 1446, King Sejong wrote a preface explaining his motivation for devising the new writing system, which was followed by a detailed explanation of how the alphabet worked. Chŏng Inji, an official who assisted the king in the invention of the alphabet, then wrote a postscript. The first two selections that follow are King Sejong's preface and parts of Chŏng Inji's postscript.

Although the invention of the Korean alphabet was hailed as a great achievement of the sagely rule of King Sejong, there was a group of scholar-officials, led by Ch'oe Malli (fl. 1419–1444), who strongly opposed the use of Korea's own script. They believed that Korea had long emulated Chinese ideas and institutions and that the adoption of Korea's own writing system would make it impossible to identify Korean civilization with that of China. The third selection is the memorial submitted by Ch'oe Malli offering his reasons against the use of the Korean alphabet.

[YC]

## KING SEJONG: PREFACE TO *CORRECT SOUNDS TO INSTRUCT THE PEOPLE*

The sounds of our language differ from those of Chinese and are not easily communicated by using Chinese graphs. Many among the ignorant, therefore, though they wish to express their sentiments in writing, have been unable to communicate. Considering this situation with compassion, I have newly devised twenty-eight letters. I wish only that the people will learn them easily and use them conveniently in their daily life.

[From *Hunmin chŏngŭm* 1a; YC]

### CHŎNG INJI: POSTSCRIPT TO *CORRECT SOUNDS TO INSTRUCT THE PEOPLE*

In general, the languages of different countries have their own enunciations but lack their own letters, so they borrowed the Chinese graphs to communicate their needs. That is, however, like trying to fit a square handle into a round hole. How could it possibly achieve its objective satisfactorily? How could there not be difficulties? It is, therefore, important that each region should follow the practices that are convenient to its people and that no one should be compelled to follow one writing system alone.

In the winter of the year *kyehae* [1443], His Majesty, the king, created twenty-eight letters of the Correct Sounds and provided examples in outline demonstrating their meanings. His Majesty then named these letters *Hunmin chŏngŭm*. Resembling pictographs, these letters imitate the shapes of the old seal characters. Based on enunciation, their sounds correspond to the Seven Modes in music. These letters embrace the principles of heaven, earth, and men as well as the mysteries of yin and yang, and there is nothing they cannot express. With these twenty-eight letters, infinite turns and changes may be explained; they are simple and yet contain all the essence; they are refined and yet easily communicable. Therefore, a clever man can learn them in one morning, though a dull man may take ten days to study them. If we use these letters to explain books, it will be easier to comprehend their meanings. If we use these letters in administering litigations, it will be easier to ascertain the facts of a case. As for rhymes, one can easily distinguish voiced and voiceless consonants; as for music and songs, twelve semitones can be easily blended. They can be used whatever and wherever the occasion may be.

[From *Hunmin chŏngŭm haerye* 26b–29b; YC]

### CH'OE MALLI: OPPOSITION TO THE KOREAN ALPHABET

Twentieth day of the second month of the year [1444]. Ch'oe Malli, first counselor in the Hall of Worthies, and his associates offered the following memorial: We humbly believe that the invention of the Korean script is a work of divine creation unparalleled in history. There are, however, some questionable issues we wish to raise for Your Majesty's consideration.

Ever since the founding of the dynasty, our court has pursued the policy of respecting the senior state with utmost sincerity and has consistently tried to follow the Chinese system of government. As we share with China at present the same writing and the same institutions, we are startled to learn of the invention of the Korean script.

Only such peoples as the Mongolians, Tanguts, Jurchens, Japanese, and Tibetans have their own writings. But this is a matter that involves the barbarians and is unworthy of our concern. It has been said that the barbarians are transformed only by means of adopting Chinese ways; we have never heard of Chinese ways being transformed by the barbarians.

[From *Sejong sillok* 103:19b–22a; YC]

## EDUCATION AND SCHOLARSHIP

Education was one of the principal areas emphasized by the Chosŏn dynasty. Indeed, the Neo-Confucian state of Chosŏn held an almost religious belief that the ideals of Neo-Confucianism could be realized only through education. Thus, from its very beginning, the Chosŏn dynasty set up a well-planned nationwide school system to offer the Confucian education to qualified students. In the capital city of Seoul, a district school was organized in four of the five districts; local schools called *hyanggyo* were established in every county throughout the country; for higher education, the Royal Academy (Sŏnggyungwan) was organized in the capital. Usually well endowed by the state, these schools became centers for training future leaders of the government, since all the candidates for the state civil service examinations were drawn from them.

From the mid-sixteenth century on, moreover, private academies, called *sŏwŏn*, were organized in the countryside at the initiative of local scholars and in time became important centers of Confucian scholarship in Korea. The private academies were usually richly endowed through private donations, and they also received a royal charter from the king in the form of a name plaque along with generous grants of books, land, and servants from the government.

The Office of Special Advisers (Hongmungwan) was a unique institution in Korea. Originally organized in 1420 by King Sejong as a royal research institute called Chiphyŏnjŏn (Hall of Worthies), it was reorganized by King Sejo into the Hongmungwan in 1463. Assigned to provide advisory services on all matters dealing with the Confucian classics and literature, this office maintained a library within the palace and offered the royal lecture (*kyŏngyŏn*) for the king. Thus, its officials had the highest prestige and honor.

The *Administrative Code of Chosŏn* (*Chosŏn kyŏngguk chŏn*) by Chŏng Tojŏn served as the basic code for the Chosŏn dynasty since its foundation in 1392. The article dealing with the establishment of schools, translated here, describes the structure of the national educational system as envisioned by the dynasty's foremost architect. The description of the Royal Academy is taken from the *Revised and Augmented Gazetteer of Korea* (*Sinjŭng Tongguk yŏji sŭngnam*), which was published in 1530. The White Cloud Grotto Academy, organized in 1543 by Chu

Sebung, was Korea's first private academy. Fashioned after the renowned White Deer Grotto Academy of Song China, this academy, later renamed the Sosu Academy, became the model for the hundreds of private academies that subsequently sprang up throughout the country. The description of its foundation is taken from an account given in the *Veritable Records of King Myŏngjong* (*Myŏngjong sillok*).

[YC]

### CHŎNG TOJŎN: ESTABLISHMENT OF SCHOOLS

Schools are the center of teaching and transformation, where the cardinal principles of human relations are further illustrated and men of talent receive training. At the times of the Three Dynasties in ancient China, the laws regarding schools were well prepared. Since the Qin and the Han dynasties, despite certain shortcomings in the educational system, there have been few who did not see that schooling was important and that the vigor or decline of the schools was the key to the success or failure of the government. All these characteristics are applicable to the present situation also. Our state has established the Royal Confucian Academy to teach the sons and brothers of the nobility and the officials as well as men of superior talent among the people. The state has also established district schools in the capital city, where instructors are assigned to teach young students. Extending this law to districts, towns, big counties, and counties, the state has organized local schools, where teachers have been assigned to instruct students. In addition, schools for military affairs, law, mathematics, medicine, and foreign languages have been established, and appropriate instructors have been assigned to teach the students enrolled there. In these ways, our educational system has achieved great success.

[From *Chosŏn kyŏngguk chŏn*, in *Sambong chip* 7:30b; YC]

### ROYAL CONFUCIAN ACADEMY

The Royal Confucian Academy, located in the eastern section of Sunggyo district of the capital, is charged with the mission of instructing the Confucian students. The Hall of Illustrating the Cardinal Principles stands north of the Confucian Shrine; to the east of the shrine is the library, and to the north is the Office of Sacrificial Offerings.

Sŏng Kan (1427–1456) wrote the following essay of eulogy for the Hall of Illustrating the Cardinal Principles:

At daybreak each morning, with the beating of a drum, the headmaster and the instructors of the academy assemble the students in the courtyard. After making a bow to the instructors, the students enter the hall, where lectures and discussions on the classics take place. They study, deliberate, and counsel and assist one another to reach a full understanding of the relationships between ruler and minister, father and son, husband and wife, elder brother and younger brother, and friend and friend. For days and months, they work and rest together as one body to train themselves until they become new men. It is from these students that the future loyal ministers and the future filial sons are produced in prolific number to serve the state and their families. Indeed, never before in the history of our country have we witnessed such a splendid success in nurturing loyal officials and filial sons as we see now. Some people object that since the sage's teachings are many, there is no reason why this hall alone should be called the Hall of Illustrating the Cardinal Principles. To them I say: The relationships between ruler and minister, father and son, husband and wife, elder brother and younger brother, and friend and friend are rooted in the heavenly principle, and hence they are unchanging and everlasting. How can there be any teaching more important than this?

[From *Sinjŭng Tongguk yŏji sŭngnam* 2:10a–b; YC]

## WHITE CLOUD GROTTO ACADEMY

White Cloud Grotto Academy in P'unggi was founded by the incumbent governor of Hwanghae, Chu Sebung, when he was serving as the magistrate of P'unggi [1543]. All the rules and regulations governing the academy have been modeled after those of the White Deer Grotto Academy of the Great Master Zhu Xi. The academic setup, the library, and the land and food and other supplies have all been richly endowed so that men of talent can further cultivate their potential. Yi Hwang [1501–1570] petitioned the king to grant a charter in the form of a name plaque as well as books, land, and servants. The king granted the charter with the name plaque, books, and two or three additional items, and these grants have encouraged Confucian scholars in the countryside to pursue their scholarship with greater zeal. As for land, the endowment arranged by Chu Sebung is sufficient for the academy to sustain itself, and there are adequate numbers of servants. In order for the Confucian scholars to pursue their scholarship, it is essential that they do so in surroundings of peace and quiet. If the provincial governor or the county magistrate, wishing to exalt their study, prescribes restrictive rules for these scholars, it will deprive them of their freedom and divert them from the proper way of cultivation. There should be no interference from outside.

[From *Myŏngjong sillok* 10:6a–b; YC]

# THE RECRUITMENT EXAMINATIONS

The Chosŏn dynasty relied mainly on recruitment examinations to select officials to serve in the government. There were three types of examinations—the civil, the military, and the technical—and of these the civil examination was the most important and carried the highest prestige. The civil examination in turn consisted of the lower civil examination, which awarded the graduates either the *saengwŏn* degree for the classics or the *chinsa* degree for literary writings, and the higher civil examination for the *munkwa* degree, which qualified the holder to serve in the government as an official. Normally, all candidates in the civil examinations had to go through three stages of rigorous testing—demonstrating their knowledge in the classics, history, and literature—before the successful candidates were finally selected. For ambitious young men, to become a successful candidate in the higher civil examination was the most coveted honor, and many devoted considerable time and energy in preparing themselves to qualify for such an honor.

The account of the examination scene given here, by Sŏng Hyŏn (1439–1504), describes how the examination was conducted.

[YC]

### SŎNG HYŎN: ON THE CIVIL SERVICE EXAMINATION

The recruitment examination under the previous dynasty was conducted under the supervision of only two men, the chief examination officer and the deputy examination officer. Because these officials had been appointed in advance, prior to the examination, there were deficiencies in the way it was conducted, leading to the criticism that the successful candidates tended to have been drawn from influential families or from immature scholars. Although the present dynasty continued these deficiencies at the beginning, King Sejong introduced drastic reforms in the examination system.

According to the new system, the Ministry of Personnel at first makes a list of the qualified examiners and presents it to the king, who will in turn select and appoint the examination officers from the list just before the examination. Once appointed, the examination officers go to their respective examination sites. The officials of the Three Offices in charge of registrations assemble all the candidates, and at daybreak each candidate's name is called, one after another, and they are led into the fenced-in examination ground. The inspection officers, standing at the entrance, search each candidate's clothes and writing brush container. If anyone is caught carrying books or notes, he is handed over to arresting officers. If he is arrested before entering the examination site, he is barred for one triennial examination; if he is arrested inside the examination site, he is suspended for two triennial examinations.

Just before sunrise, the examination officers appear on the large platform and take seats under torchlight. Their august appearances resemble those of immortals. The officials of the Three Offices then enter the examination ground, arrange the proper seating of the candidates, and leave. At sunrise, the examination questions are posted. At noon, the examination papers are collected and stamped and then returned to the candidates for further work. As the sun begins to set, with the beating of a drum, the candidates present their papers to the collection officers, who in turn hand them over to the registration officers. These officers then record the matching numbers on both ends of the examination papers and cut them apart—one part has the name of the candidate, now concealed, and the other contains the candidate's answers to the examination questions. The officials responsible for concealing the candidates' identities retire to a separate room carrying with them the portions of the papers with the concealed names. To prevent recognition of candidates' handwriting, the recording officials have the copyists rewrite the candidates' answers in red ink. When the rewriting is finished, the collating officer reads the originals to the assistant collating officer, who checks the copied version to make sure it is accurate. When all these things have been done, the copied versions of the examination papers are given to the readers. Only after these papers have been graded and their rankings decided upon are the officials responsible for concealing the names of candidates allowed to identify the authors of the examination papers.

Moreover, the candidates must go through the oral examination on the classics in three different stages—the preliminary, the middle, and the final. At the end, the points scored at each stage are added up. All the examination processes are supervised not just by one man but by many, and the evaluation of the candidates is conducted not just by one man but by many. Indeed, there is nothing in the state system that is more judicious than the recruitment examination.

[From *Yongjae ch'onghwa* (Koryŏ taehakkyo ed., 1963), pp. 391–392; YC]

## PRINTING BOOKS

The invention of movable metallic type can be regarded as one of Korea's most significant contributions to world civilization. Having learned from China the technique of book printing by means of woodblocks, Korea became the first country in the world to develop movable metallic type, as early as the beginning of the thirteenth century. Continuing this tradition, the Chosŏn dynasty frequently undertook book printing projects, constantly improving and refining the technique of typesetting. A recent study has verified the casting of as many as twenty-one different species of type during the fifteenth century alone. The various types cast in Korea are usually identified by the year in which they were cast. For the Confucian state of Chosŏn, book printing was important not only for promoting scholarship but also for striving to realize the ideals of good government. The account translated here indicates the extent of painstaking effort the early Chosŏn state expended in the matter of book printing.

[YC]

SŎNG HYŎN: ON PRINTING

In the third year, *kyemi* [1403], King T'aejong remarked to the courtiers around him: "If the country is to be governed well, it is essential that books be read widely. But because our country is located east of China beyond the sea, not many books from China are readily available. Moreover, woodblock prints are easily defaced, and it is impossible to print all the books in the world by using woodblock prints. It is my desire to cast copper type so that we can print as many books as possible and have them made available widely. This will truly bring infinite benefit to us." In the end, the king was successful in having copper type cast with the graphs modeled after those of the *Old Commentary on the Book of Odes* and the *Zuo Commentary*, and that is how the typecasting foundry became established in our country.

*Sŏng proceeds with a discussion of different kinds of type and processes of typecasting in different reigns, omitted here.*

[From *Yongjae ch'onghwa* (Koryŏ taehakkyo ed., 1963), pp. 456–457]

## Chapter 37

### SOCIAL LIFE

The establishment of the new dynasty in 1392 ushered in an era of social reform that led to a fundamental restructuring of Korean society. Champions of the Confucian way and vigorous opponents of Buddhism, the scholar-officials surrounding the dynastic founders envisaged a new sociopolitical order rooted in Confucian moral principles. Theirs was an idealistic program that favored the formation of a controlled political elite. Inspired by the models they found in Chinese classical literature, the Confucian legislators laid the groundwork from which the highly structured patrilineal descent groups characteristic of Chosŏn society eventually emerged. New standards of ritual behavior and thinking were to provide the elite with values relevant to private as well as to public life. Their platform of ritual action was the *Family Rites of Zhu Xi* (*Zhuzi jiali*), the most authoritative ritual manual of the Chosŏn period.

The reforms, although propagated through moral incentives as well as legal sanctions, were slow in taking root, and the dynasty's first two centuries were a distinct transition period. Traditional institutions and beliefs resisted change and were therefore not reformed "in one morning." The acculturation process went through several stages. The first is illustrated by the documents that are presented here.

[MD]

# THE ROLE OF RITES

In their effort to transform Korean society into a Confucian society, the Confucians never tired of pointing out the fundamental role of the four rites (*sarye*)—capping, wedding, funeral, and ancestor worship—in this transformatory process. To the Confucian, rites were not an imposition upon human nature. Rather, they activated what was good in a person and thus formed the human mind. If properly observed, they determined the relationships within the domestic sphere and stabilized the social foundation of the public realm. The peace and prosperity of a state were thus guaranteed in proportion to the purity of its ritual life.

[MD]

## SŎNG HYŎN: THE FUNDAMENTAL ROLE OF RITES

Rites must be cultivated. If they are not cultivated, the human mind is unstable, laws and orders are numerous, and the way of good rule cannot emerge. It is comparable to curing a man's sickness: if one tried to remedy it hastily in one morning with poisonous medicine, would his constitution not also be harmed? One should first provide the taste of the five grains; thereafter the body naturally regains vitality, and the sickness disappears.

If a man lives idly and does not have instruction, he is insolent and disorderly and differs but slightly from wild animals. Therefore the sages have made the rites as guidelines so that the one who overshoots them retrenches and adapts himself, and the one who falls short desires to reach them. When a man grows up and is capped, he reaches adulthood. The sages, fearing it might look hasty and ill-prepared, have made the rite of divining the date and the names of the guests, the rite of adding the three things,[1] and the rite of the libation; hereby they cultivated the proper rites. The wedding is the great desire of men; it is the match by which two surnames are joined. Fearing that it might look intimate and be lacking the proper separation of the sexes, the sages have made the rites of betrothal [*napch'ae*], of asking the name of the bride's mother [*munmyŏng*], of divining the bride's qualities [*napkil*], and of sending the wedding gifts [*napp'ye*]; hereby they cultivated the proper rites. The funeral is the final act by which a man is sent off, and a son devotes all his mind to it. Fearing that he might be negligent and incomplete, the sages have made for the son the rites of drinking water and eating gruel, of weeping and mourning; hereby they cultivated the proper rites. Ancestor worship is the communication with the spirit of the deceased. It is the means by which the son pays his gratitude to his parents. Fearing that

---

1. The three things are the topknot (*sangt'u*), the headband (*manggŏn*), and the hat (*kat*).

there might be distance and forgetfulness, the sages have made the rites of presenting offerings and libations to the soul of the deceased; hereby they cultivated the proper rites. People communicate with each other, and visitors come. Therefore the sages have made the rites of entertaining the guests and presenting gifts; hereby they cultivated the proper rites. People get together and feast. Therefore the sages have made the rites of bowing and yielding and exchanging the wine cups.

[From *Hŏbaektang chip* 10:12a–13b; MD]

### YI CHI: ON THE ESTABLISHMENT OF DOMESTIC SHRINES

Inspector-General Yi Chi [d. 1414] and others memorialize [in 1401]:

In recent years the state has been concerned about the daily deterioration of customs, and every time Your Majesty issued an edict, you gave priority to the order to establish domestic shrines, wishing the people's virtue to return to wholesomeness. That nobody has yet willingly complied is due to the strength and persistence of the Buddhists' false theories, and there may also be some who do not yet know how to establish domestic shrines.

In our opinion the royal capital is the source of the civilizing influence and the mainstay of good government. If the scholar-officials are ordered to establish shrines first, and the order reaches the rest of society later, would there be noncompliance? Moreover, quarters are cramped within the city walls, and thus it may be difficult to establish shrines. Instead, for convenience, a wooden box may be used to store the spirit tablets in a clean room. Outside the capital, a domestic shrine should provisionally be built at the east side of the government office in each prefecture and district. If those appointed magistrates are eldest sons, they should take the spirit tablets to the place of their appointment; if they are not eldest sons, they should use paper tablets in the district shrines and perform the rites. Whether inside or outside the capital, those in charge of the rites in the domestic shrine should rise at dawn daily, burn incense, and bow twice, and when they go in or out of the house, they should announce this in the domestic shrine. If the ancestral rites follow the *Family Rites* completely in order to give an example to those below, this influence will naturally reach the people without special encouragement.

[From *T'aejong sillok* 2:21b–22a; MD]

## THE POSITION OF WOMEN

The Confucians' emphasis on the patrilineal descent line had serious consequences for women's relations to men and their position in society. In Koryŏ, it had not been uncommon for an upper-class man to have several wives who were not subject to any social ranking order. In the patrilineal society the Confucians envisioned, however, only one woman, the primary wife, could qualify to become the mother of her husband's lineal heir. Any other women the husband might have were therefore of lesser importance, and the differentiation between main wives and concubines (*ch'ŏch'ŏp*) became one of the sharpest social dividing lines, and the most tragic one, in Korean society.

The union between husband and wife was regarded as the foundation of human morality and the mainspring of the socialization process that extended from the relation between father and son to that between ruler and subject. The main wife was in charge of the domestic sphere (*nae*), while the husband's domain was the public sphere (*oe*). The peace and stability of the family were a precondition for the peace and prosperity of the state. Women, although inferior members of society, nevertheless bore the responsibility of providing the government with loyal and capable men.

[MD]

## ON DIFFERENTIATING BETWEEN MAIN WIFE AND CONCUBINE

The Office of the Inspector-General memorializes [in 1413] as follows:

Husband and wife are the mainstay of human morality, and the differentiation between main wife and concubine may not be blurred. Embodying the great principles of the one hundred kings of the Spring and Autumn period, King T'aejo accentuated the boundary between main wife and concubine [devised by] the scholar-officials and instituted the law of conferring ranks and land on main wives. The distinction between main wife and concubine has thus become clear and the root of human morality straight.

At the end of the former dynasty, the influence of ritual decorum and morality was not pervasive, and the relationship between husband and wife deteriorated. The members of the officialdom followed their own desires and inclinations: some who had a wife married a second wife; others made their concubine their main wife. This has consequently become the source of today's disputes between main wives and concubines.

We have carefully examined the Ming code, which reads: "The one who makes a concubine his main wife while the latter is alive is to be punished with ninety strokes of the heavy bamboo, and the situation must be rectified. Someone who already has a main wife and still gets another one is also to be punished with ninety strokes, and they must separate."

[From *T'aejong sillok* 25:13a–b; MD]

## ON TREATING THE MAIN WIFE

[In 1425] the Office of the Inspector-General demands the punishment of Yi Chungwi, who maltreated his wife.

The king says: "If we leave such a case untreated, there will be no warning for the future, and this will certainly lead people to throw off all restraint. Each of you should state how he would settle such a matter."

Inspector-General Ko Yakhae [1377–1443] says: "If there is a ranking order of main wife and concubine, the domestic way is straight. If it gets lost, the domestic way is in disorder. If somebody treats his concubine preferentially and does not look after his main wife, he should be punished according to the law."

Minister of Personnel Hŏ Cho [1369–1439] says: "The woman manages the interior of the house; the man manages the exterior. If someone allows his concubine to become the mistress of his household and to dominate his house, not only does the social ranking break down but this also leads to discord among the brothers and estrangement among the slaves. How is it possible to manage a house under such circumstances? It is absolutely necessary to punish the crime of such fellows."

Royal Secretary Kwak Chonjung says: "If someone loves his concubine and estranges his main wife, his property is generally transferred entirely to the concubine's house, leaving the main wife poor and destitute and causing mutual resentment. It is proper to punish such a man severely."

The king agrees and orders to proceed according to the law, so that it is made known.

[From *Sejong sillok* 30:20a–b; MD]


### PROHIBITION AGAINST REMARRIAGE OF WOMEN

Marriage was largely an affair between "two surnames," and, as far as the wife was concerned, it lasted beyond her husband's death. Confucian ideology stressed the woman's devotion to one husband, and this emphasis on the exclusive nature of the marital relationship provided Confucian legislators with the arguments they needed to prohibit the remarriage of women, a custom prevalent during Koryŏ. The lost version of the *State Code* of 1469 apparently barred the sons and grandsons of thrice-married women from advancing into the higher officialdom. The debate of 1477 makes it clear that the majority of the discussants, here represented by Kim Yŏngyu (1418–1494), were in favor of keeping the restriction to third and not extending it to second marriages. King Sŏngjong (1469–1494), who was especially concerned with improving upper-class mores, sided with the minority opinion, here represented by Im Wŏnjun (1423–1500). How sensitive the issue was is documented by the fact that the *State Code* of 1485 did not directly outlaw remarriage but provided that the sons and grandsons of remarried women would not be eligible for civil or military office and would be barred from taking the lower and higher civil service examinations. The ideological and legal implications thus, in fact, made remarriage for a woman impossible.

[MD]


[In 1477] the king orders the members of the highest officialdom to discuss the prohibition against the remarriage of women.

Inspector-General Kim Yŏngyu and others say:

"Now, according to the *State Code* [1469], thrice-married women are listed together with licentious women, and their sons and grandsons are barred from the examinations and cannot receive posts in the censorial and administrative offices. Twice-married women are not mentioned. Generally, statutes are based on fundamental law, and ritual decorum is connected with human feelings. For a woman of a poor and lowly house who on neither side has supportive relatives, it is difficult to keep her chastity when she becomes widowed in early years. If her parents or relatives decide that she should marry for a second time, that does not harm ritual decorum. We think that the law of the *State Code* according to which the sons and grandsons of thrice-married women do not receive high office should be strictly enforced."

Sixth State Councillor Im Wŏnjun and others argue: "A state without strict prohibitions will cause the sons and grandsons of those who lost their integrity to hold important office. Such a practice will then turn into a custom that nobody will consider strange. Under such circumstances there will be women who, even without a master of ceremonies, will obtain a husband on their own initiative. If this is not prohibited, where will it lead? From now on remarriage must be strictly prohibited."

Royal edict to the Ministry of Rites: "The *Record of Rites* says: 'Faithfulness is the virtue of a wife. Once married to her husband, she does not change it during her lifetime.'

From now on, in order to correct the customs, the sons and grandsons of twice-married women will no longer be listed as members of the upper class."

[From *Sŏngjong sillok* 82:9b–20a; MD]

## SIN SUKCHU: HOUSE RULES

Confucian society functioned through the proper observance of the rites (*ye*). Their practice started with the cultivation of the moral potential of the individual and extended to those with whom the individual interacted most closely: his family and relatives. House rules (*kahun*) were aimed at smoothing the relationships within a kin group and spreading a civilizing influence even into the domestic sphere of the house, the women's quarters. They constituted an idealized code of conduct based on the assumption that people have to be constantly encouraged to strive for moral perfection. If the principal members of the family were to observe the rules of proper conduct, it was reasoned, even the domestic slaves could be persuaded to lead moral lives. Prepared by Sin Sukchu (1417–1475) in 1468, "House Rules" preached moral integrity and economic austerity and linked the harmony in the domestic sphere directly to peace and stability in the public realm. These "House Rules," then, contained the essence of the moral capabilities of the Confucian society, which, if properly developed, were the mainstay of the Confucian state.

[MD]

## Rule One: Make the Mind Discerning

Man's mind does not have constancy. If it is trained, it exists; if it is neglected, it vanishes. If the mind does not exist, one looks but does not see; one listens but does not hear. How much more is it like this in the discernment of right and wrong? The mind is the prime minister of the body. In the eye's relationship to color, it is the mind that sees. In the ear's relationship to sound, it is the mind that hears. All the members of the body depend on the mind for functioning. That is why it is the prime minister of the whole body. Therefore, if one wishes to straighten out the members of the body, one should straighten out the mind first.

## Rule Two: Be Circumspect in Behavior

If the body is not trained, it is not possible to regulate the house. Why do I say this? If in serving my father I do not exert myself to be filial, my son will do to me as I have done to my father. If in serving my elder brother I am not respectful, my younger brother will do to me as I have done to my elder brother. Therefore, only if I make myself stand on faultless ground will everyone among father and son, elder brother and younger brother, husband and wife, be equally correct. This can be extended to the relationship between ruler and subject and between friends.

## Rule Three: Be Studious

One who has narrow ears and eyes can never have a wide mind. For widening eyes and ears nothing is better than reading books. The ways of the sages and worthies are laid out in books. If, once the determination is firm, one progresses step by step and with great care, in the course of time one naturally gets results. The essential of learning lies in gathering up the dissipated mind. If the mind is concentrated, it is naturally brilliant and circumspect, and its understanding is more than sufficient. It is not possible to advance in scholarship without a settled mind. The essence of gathering up one's mind lies solely in seriousness.

For a human being, not to study is exactly like facing a wall. If what has been studied is not vigorously practiced, it is of no use to read even ten thousand volumes. Therefore, when reading the books of sages and worthies, one should search for their minds and incorporate them one by one in oneself.

## Rule Four: On Managing a Household

Under present customs father and son and brothers rarely live under one roof. As they establish their own households, each keeps his own slaves, and gradually they become estranged from each other and are no longer on friendly terms.

As father and elder brother, one should be patient and forbearing, generous and humane, and not petty and small. As son and younger brother, one should leave the unimportant and think of the important, advance sincerity and be mutually sympathetic, filial, and friendly.

The harm of extravagance is greater than a natural disaster. If a house declines, it is usually because of overspending. Therefore frugality is the first principle in managing a household. This does not mean one should be stingy and avaricious. If the needs of the house are met—the living fed and the dead sent off properly, the needy supported, and emergencies relieved—is this not enough of prosperity?

We and our relatives derive from the same source and split up into branches. Seen by our ancestors, we are all alike. If we are able to establish households thanks to the accumulated good and the extra blessings of our ancestors, we have to be mindful of aiding the poor and sympathizing with the orphans in order to counterbalance the blessings of our ancestors.

## Rule Five: On Holding Office

As a high official, one cannot rule independently; one must rely on one's subordinates. The way to treat a subordinate is to extend sincerity in order to employ him. In case of doubt, don't employ him. If employed, don't doubt him. If a man knows that he is doubted, he certainly does not dare to do his best. A high official thus should not have doubts about his subordinates. Once he has a doubtful mind, he cannot but be a bad administrator.

## Rule Six: On Instructing Women

The wife is the mate of the master of the house and has the domestic management in her hands. The rise and fall of a house depends on her. Usually people know how to instruct their sons, but do not know how to instruct their daughters. This is misguided.

A wife is loyal and pure, self-controlled, flexible and obedient, and serving others. She minds the domestic realm exclusively and does not concern herself with public affairs.

Above, she serves her parents-in-law; if she is not sincere and respectful, she cannot fulfill her filial loyalty. Below, she treats the slave servants well; if she is not kind and benevolent, she is not able to win their hearts. Only if she is sincere and respectful in serving her superiors and kind and benevolent in treating her subordinates is there complete affection between husband and wife.

Generally, she should also be accomplished in female tasks. If she herself is not diligent, she lacks the capacity to lead her subordinates.

[From *Pohanjae chip* 13:1a–4b; MD]

*Chapter 38*

ECONOMY

Like most preindustrial societies, the Chosŏn dynasty was predominantly an agrarian state, and land was its main source of wealth and revenue. Thus, the primary emphasis of the state economy was on agriculture. After the drastic land reform of 1390, based on the principle of an equitable redistribution, a great deal of effort was put into increasing the land's productivity. Advanced agrarian methods were introduced from China, and various experiments were conducted, leading to the publication of several manuals of farming. With the use of improved seeds, fertilizer, and irrigation, there was a significant increase in food production in early Chosŏn.

While the Neo-Confucian state of Chosŏn regarded agriculture as the root of all wealth, it treated commerce as an unproductive branch that existed at the expense of farming. Initially, commerce was limited strictly to licensed merchants; but the need to exchange goods for daily life gave rise to periodic markets in rural areas. The government's attempts to circulate paper currency early in the Chosŏn period were not successful, as people continued to use cloth as a medium of exchange. (The use of coins was not accepted widely until after the seventeenth century.) Believing the resources of wealth to be limited, Chosŏn society placed a great deal of emphasis on frugality in expenditure by both the state and individuals.

[YC]

# THE LAND SYSTEM

An equitable distribution of land to all tillers was the ideal of good government in traditional Korea. The disintegration of the land system in the latter period of the Koryŏ dynasty (918–1392) was a main contributing factor to its demise. As the state control over land weakened, the land system in late Koryŏ became chaotic. Ownership of land became concentrated in the hands of powerful families and Buddhist temples and monasteries. This concentration forced more and more people to leave the land, and they were thus reduced to desperate straits. It was in this situation in 1390 that General Yi Sŏnggye, after dramatically burning all the existing land registration records, carried out a drastic land reform. A member of Yi Sŏnggye's brain trust in founding the new Chosŏn dynasty, Chŏng Tojŏn was one of the masterminds of the 1390 land reform. In the essay translated here, Chŏng Tojŏn depicts the chaotic land system of late Koryŏ (at least partly to justify the reform he helped institute) and offers some basic ideas shaping the new land system, which the Chosŏn dynasty continued to maintain.

[YC]

## CHŎNG TOJŎN: ON LAND

In ancient times, all the land belonged to the state, and the state then granted land to the people; thus, all the land that the people cultivated had been given them by the state. There was no one who did not receive land, and there was no one who did not cultivate land. Therefore, there was no excessive differentiation between the rich and the poor and between the strong and the weak. Because all the produce from the land went to the state, the state was prosperous. But as the land system began to disintegrate, powerful individuals acquired more and more land. While the land of the rich extended far and wide, the poor had no land even to stand on. The poor thus were forced to lease land from the rich to till. Even though they worked hard and diligently all year round, they still did not have enough to eat. The rich, however, did not cultivate their land and remained idle. Instead, they hired men to work their land and collected more than half of the yield.

His Majesty King T'aejo had personally witnessed the evil effects of this chaotic land situation while he was still a private person and was determined, as one of his future missions, to abolish the private land system. He believed that all the land in the country should revert to the state and should then be given to the people on the basis of a careful account, in order to revive the rectified land system of ancient times. But the old families and the powerful lineage groups, realizing that His Majesty's plan would work against their interests, slandered and obstructed the plan with all the power at their command. His Majesty, however, together with two or three like-minded ministers, investigated the laws of the former dynasties, deliberated about what would be good for the present situation, and surveyed and measured all the land in the country in terms of *kyŏl*.[1] [His Majesty then instituted the land reform in the year 1390.] He established court land, military provision land for state use, and office land for civil and military officials. In addition, off-duty military men residing in the capital as guards for the royal court, widows remaining faithful to their deceased husbands, government workers in the local magistracies, postal station workers, and river ferry workers, as well as commoners and artisans performing public duties, have all been granted land. Although the distribution of land to the people may not have reached the standard set by the ancient sages, the new land law has restored equity and balance. Compared to the evil system of the former dynasty, the new land reform has brought infinite improvement.

[From *Sambong chip* 13:14b–16a; YC]

## PROMOTION OF AGRICULTURE

Fifteenth-century Korea witnessed a dramatic increase in food production as a result of technological advances in agriculture. First, the fallow system, whereby certain portions of land are periodically kept uncultivated, was gradually replaced by a new system of continuous cultivation. This more intensive use of land was made possible largely by the introduction of improved organic fertilizers developed in post-Song southern China. The second change involved shifting from dry farming to wet farming in rice cultivation. Wet farming at this time involved direct seeding of rice in wet land. The transplantation system that is currently used in Korea was gradually adopted in the three southern provinces during the fifteenth and sixteenth centuries. For this kind of wet farming, it is essential to secure sufficient water. Largely to meet the demands of these changes, King Sejong ordered the compilation of a farm manual, *Straight Talk on Farming* (*Nongsa chiksŏl*), which was printed for wide distribution in 1429. Designed to increase productivity, the manual emphasizes four points: the appropriate timing of sowing, the effective use of fertilizers, the need for weeding, and the autumn plowing. As stated in the preface to the manual, the information contained in the book was obtained from actual experimentation carried out by veteran farmers in various regions as well as from various manuals published in Korea and China. The manual provided the practical information and ideas that were suitable to local climate and soil conditions.

In addition to his brilliant achievements in language, literature, science, and technology, King Sejong vigorously promoted agriculture throughout his thirty-two-year reign. In 1444, the king issued the Edict for the Promotion of Agriculture. As the direct responsibility for overseeing the farmers was in the

---

1. *Kyŏl* is a unit of land measurement based on acreage as well as soil fertility.

hands of magistrates, the edict was addressed largely to these officials, outlining what the king expected of them in their dealings with farmers. Noteworthy is King Sejong's strong belief that the effects of natural disaster, such as those caused by drought, could be averted by human effort.

As the eldest son of King Sejong, King Munjong had received a good education and training for Confucian rulership before he succeeded his father in 1450. He remained on the throne for only a little over two years, however, as he died in 1452 at the age of thirty-eight. As the fifth monarch of the Chosŏn dynasty, Munjong continued the brilliant achievements of his father. The progress in agriculture during the fifteenth century necessitated a greater and more efficient use of water. Since the ancient period, reservoirs had been constructed at higher elevations by damming water from mountains and hills, thus allowing a controlled flow of water to farmland below. These reservoirs alone, however, were not sufficient to meet the increasing demands of fifteenth-century agriculture. Thus, there were a number of attempts to devise new methods of irrigation. Both Kings T'aejong and Sejong attempted a wider use of water mills, for example, borrowing ideas from China and Japan, but water mills proved ill suited to Korea's terrain and soil conditions. A new method, however, was more successful and eventually became widely used throughout the country. This method involved drawing water from a river by constructing embankments. For land at higher elevations, the embankment was made at an upper river flow; for lower land, the embankment was constructed along the river to divert small channels of the flow. This irrigation method later came to be called *po*. Although the southern provinces had developed an efficient system of irrigation, the northwestern regions lagged behind. So when a drought struck the two northwestern provinces of Hwanghae and P'yŏngan in 1451, King Munjong issued an edict emphasizing that human effort can avert natural disasters.

[YC]

## KING SEJONG: EDICT FOR THE PROMOTION OF AGRICULTURE

The people are the root of the state, and food is an indispensable necessity of the people. Because all food and clothing are produced by the farmers, our government must give them foremost priority. When King T'aejo, responding to the call of destiny, inaugurated our dynasty, he first rectified the land system to relieve the people of misery and allow them to enjoy the benefits of agriculture. The ways by which he tried to promote agriculture have been incorporated into laws. King T'aejong, continuing the task, redoubled the efforts to promote agriculture. Apprehensive that the people might not be well informed about the proper ways of sowing and reaping, King T'aejong ordered his officials to translate the books on farming into the vernacular script and to publish and transmit them widely.

I sincerely wish to continue the works of our forefathers. I believe that agricultural matters should be entrusted to those officials who are in intimate contact with the people.

As I examined the sagacious magistrates of the past, I found they were able to achieve good works and bring benefit to the people only through diligence and hard work. In general, men need to be aroused to work hard; when not aroused, they tend to be indolent.

In general, farm families who start early also harvest early, and those who put in more effort reap more. Therefore, the key to agrarian administration lies in not missing the appropriate time and in not depriving the people of their energies. As a man has only one body, his energy cannot be divided; if the government takes people's labor away, how can we exhort them to work hard on the land? Our recent experiment in the year *chŏngsa* [1437], conducted on land behind the palace, has shown that we can avert disaster from drought by means of the maximum use of manpower, as the land produced an abundant crop in spite of bad weather. This experiment has proved clearly that natural misfortune can be overcome by human effort. . . .

All the officials in my government . . . should emulate the rules practiced by the former sage officials for promoting agriculture, should investigate widely what may be good for the climate and soil of the region, and should consult the agrarian manual to prepare in advance so as not to be either too early for sowing or too late. Moreover, no one should impose corvée duties upon the farmers that will deprive them of their time. Instead, everyone should devote his mind and effort to guiding the people into attending to agriculture.

[From *Sejong sillok* 105:25a–26b; YC]

*Chapter 39*

THOUGHT

Neo-Confucianism is the name given by Western scholars to a Confucian revival movement that began about A.D. 1000 in China. After centuries of Buddhist and Daoist predominance, a new Confucian movement creatively synthesized traditional Confucian social and moral concerns with a new metaphysics and spirituality that rivaled the sophistication of the Buddhists and Daoists. Neo-Confucianism subsequently became the predominant intellectual and spiritual tradition throughout East Asia. The first and "orthodox" school of Neo-Confucian thought was that of the great synthesizer Zhu Xi (1130–1200); the second major school was that of Wang Yang-ming (1472–1529), which at times overshadowed Zhu Xi's school in China and Japan. One of the distinctive characteristics of Korea was its consistent and almost exclusive development of the Zhu Xi tradition.

Introduced to the Korean Peninsula toward the end of the Koryŏ dynasty, Neo-Confucianism played a central role in the political, intellectual, and spiritual life of the subsequent Chosŏn dynasty. The selections that follow are taken from the works of outstanding Neo-Confucians of the first half of the Chosŏn dynasty.

[MK]

## YI HWANG AND THE SAGE LEARNING

Yi Hwang (1501–1570), better known by his pen name T'oegye, was born of a modest *yangban* lineage and lived for most of his life near Andong. His father died when he was still an infant, but his mother eked out a meager living for seven sons and a daughter through agriculture and sericulture. With the help of an uncle, Yi Hwang received an education, and showed promise enough to enter the Royal Confucian Academy in Seoul in 1523. After passing the two lower-level exams for the civil service in 1527 and 1528 and the final examinations in 1534, he spent fifteen years in routine official service before, on his retirement in 1549, he could pursue his scholarly interests, attract many students, and win fame as the leading Korean proponent of Zhu Xi's teaching.

Among many important writings that would gain Yi Hwang not only a large following among generations of Koreans but the high respect of Confucian scholars in Tokugawa period Japan and warm tributes later from Chinese scholars in the twentieth century, are his *Essentials of Zhu Xi's Correspondence* and his *Comprehensive Record of Song, Yuan, and Ming Neo-Confucianism*, both demonstrating his capacity for scholarly research and astute criticism, as well as his *Record of Self-Reflection*, manifesting his efforts at intense moral and spiritual self-cultivation.

Worthy of special note is Yi Hwang's involvement in the most celebrated controversy in Korean Neo-Confucian history, the Four-Seven Debate, which he carried on in correspondence with a younger colleague. In it Yi Hwang broke new ground in the metaphysically based psychological theory of the Cheng-Zhu school, which set the Korean intellectual agenda for generations to come. Highly technical and philosophically sophisticated, it does not lend itself to summary treatment here.

*The Ten Diagrams* is Yi Hwang's last great work, as well as his best known and most popular writing. Generations of students have appreciated the clarity and brevity with which it presents the essential framework of, and linkages among, Neo-Confucian metaphysics, psychological theory, moral conduct, and spiritual discipline.

In content it focuses on the central theme of Neo-Confucian teaching: Sage Learning as a theory of human nature and practice of self-cultivation. In form it carries on the tradition of lectures to the ruler (or heir apparent) by Cheng Yi, Zhu Xi, and Zhen Dexiu known as the "Learning of the Emperors and Kings" or "Classics Mat Lectures," which were adopted by the Chosŏn dynasty court. When Yi Hwang retired from this function in 1568, he left this concise summation of his teachings for King Sŏnjo.

[MK]


### TEN DIAGRAMS ON SAGE LEARNING

The basic format is a diagram accompanied by a text from one or more of the Neo-Confucian masters with additional commentary by Yi Hwang. Here space considerations compel further abridgement of Yi Hwang's already concise exposition; only two of the actual diagrams, and only some of the text and commentary, are reproduced— yet enough, we hope, to make each of the topics comprehensible.

## Section 1: *Diagram of the Supreme Ultimate*

This chapter presents Zhou Dunyi's *Diagram of the Supreme Ultimate* and his *Explanation of the Diagram of the Supreme Ultimate*. These works, as interpreted by Zhu Xi, became the cornerstone of Neo-Confucian metaphysical thought; here we find the essential framework for understanding both man's place in the universe and the process by which he achieves his ultimate perfection and fulfillment— matters which are taken up at length in the remainder of this work. Two of the most

### 1. *Diagram of the Supreme Ultimate*

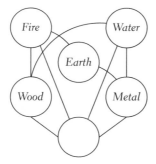

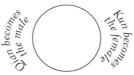

*The production and transformation of all creatures*

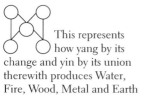

⃝ This represents the Supreme Ultimate and the Indeteminate. That is [it gives ries to] yin and yang, but this indicates that in its fundamental substance there is no admixture of yin and yang

◎ This represents how ⃝ moves and produces yang, quiesces and produces yin. The ⃝ in the center repre- sents their fundamental substance. ☽ is the root of ☾ ; ☽ is the root of ☽.

This represents how yang by its change and yin by its union therewith produces Water, Fire, Wood, Metal and Earth

☳ represents how the Indeterminate and yin and yang and the Five Agents wonderously unite and are without separation

⃝ This represents how by the transformations of material forces. Qian becomes the male and Kun becomes the female.

Male and female each have their own natures, but are the one Supreme Ultimate.

⃝ This represents how all things evolve and are produced by transforma- tions of form.

Each thing has its own nature but all are the one Supreme Ultimate.

important Chinese compilations of Neo-Confucian thought, the *Jinsilu* and the *Xingli da chuan*, begin with the same work. Yi Hwang abridges Zhu Xi's analysis of the graphics of the *Diagram of the Supreme Ultimate* and incorporates it as a gloss into the diagram itself.

### YI HWANG'S COMMENTS

This diagram has been placed at the very beginning of this work for the same reason that its explanation was placed at the beginning of [Zhu Xi's] *Reflections on Things at Hand*. That is, one who would learn to be a sage should seek the beginning here in this [diagram] and apply his efforts to the practice of [what is presented in] such works as the *Elementary Learning* and the *Great Learning*.

Master Zhu in discussing the Indeterminate and yet the Supreme Ultimate says: "If one does not say 'Indeterminate,' then the Supreme Ultimate would become the same as a single thing and would not suffice as the root of the ten thousand transformations; if one does not say 'Supreme Ultimate' then the Indeterminate would be confused with a quiescent emptiness and would not be able to serve as the root of the ten thousand transformations." Ah! Ah! This saying can be said to perfectly encompass the matter in every respect.

[From *T'oegye chŏnsŏ* 1:16:04b; MK]

## Section 2: Diagram of the *Western Inscription*

The *Western Inscription* is the work of Zhang Zai (1020–1077), and it stands with the *Diagram of the Supreme Ultimate* as one of the most fundamental documents of the Neo-Confucian tradition. It puts flesh and blood on the bare bones of metaphysics, reflects on Heaven and Earth as the common parents of all creatures; stemming from a single common origin, all of creation is therefore a single body, and all people form a single great family.

### ZHANG ZAI'S WESTERN INSCRIPTION

*Qian* [Heaven] is called the father and *Kun* [Earth] is called the mother. I, this tiny being, am commingled in their midst; therefore what fills all between Heaven and Earth is my body, and that which directs Heaven and Earth is my nature.

All people are from the same womb as I, all creatures are my companions. The Great Ruler is the eldest son of my parents, and his great ministers are the household retainers of the eldest son. By honoring those who are advanced in years, I carry out the respect for age which is due my aged, and by kindness to the solitary and weak, I carry out the tender care for the young which should be paid to my young. The Sage is at one with the character [of Heaven and Earth], and the wise man is of their finest [stuff]. All persons in the world who are exhausted, decrepit, worn out, or ill, or who are brotherless, childless, widowers, or widowed, are my own brothers who have become helpless and have none to whom they can appeal.

To maintain [our awe of Heaven] at the proper time is to show the respect of a son; to feel joy [in what Heaven allots] without anxiety is to exemplify filial piety in its purity. Deviation from [the will of Heaven] is called a perverse disposition; doing injury to humanity [ren] is called villainous. One who promotes evil is lacking in [moral] capacity; he who fulfills his bodily design [by doing good] resembles [his parents, Heaven and Earth]. Understanding the transformations [of the universe] is being skillful in carrying forward [one's parents'] activities; exhaustively plumbing the spiritual is being good at perpetuating their intentions. He who even in the recesses of his house does nothing shameful will bring no shame; he who is mindful and fosters his nature will not be negligent.

Wealth, honor, good fortune, and abundance have as their aim the enrichment of our lives. Poverty, meanness, grief, and sorrow serve to discipline us so as to make us complete. In life I shall serve [my parents, Heaven and Earth] compliantly and in death I shall be at peace.

## YI HWANG'S COMMENTS

. . . The learning of the sages consists in the seeking of humanity. It is necessary to deeply inculcate in oneself the intention [of becoming humane], and then understand that one makes up a single body with Heaven and Earth and the myriad creatures. To truly and actually live this way is what is involved in becoming humane. One must personally get a taste [of this experience]; then he will be rid of the problem [of thinking that] it is something so vast as to be unobtainable and also will be free from the mistaken notion that other things are identical with himself, and the inner dispositions of his mind-and-heart will thus become perfect and complete. Thus Master Cheng says, "The meaning of the *Western Inscription* is exceedingly perfect and complete; it is the substance of humanity." And again, "When one has fully attained to this, he will be a sage."

[Zhang Zai] employs the terms people use to refer to their own persons; all who read this work should neither consider these ten [first-person pronouns] as references to the self of Hengqu, nor put them off as referring to the self of others: they must all be seen as indications of one's personal responsibility for what is one's own affair. Only then will one be able to grasp how the *Western Inscription* is fundamentally a formulation of the substance of humanity. Hengqu also regards humanity as something that, although [it means] being as one body with Heaven and Earth and all creatures, must nevertheless first come from the self as its fundamental source and master; one must attain a personal realization of the interrelatedness of the self and others in the unity of principle. . . .

[From *T'oegye chŏnsŏ* 1:7:50a–b; MK]

## Section 3: Diagram of the *Elementary Learning*

The *Elementary Learning* is a compilation of 386 passages, a little more than half of which are drawn from the classics and the remainder from the writings of outstanding Confucians of the postclassical period, including a liberal selection from the early Song dynasty Confucians. Its purpose was to present the most fundamental teachings and values of the Confucian tradition for the instruction of the young; it includes extensive materials dealing with the Five Relations, which constitute the core of traditional Confucian ethical teaching.

This work became the gateway to serious study for generation upon generation of Confucian scholars. In Korea it was considered virtually one of the classics, and from the first decades of the Chosŏn dynasty its memorization became a prerequisite for admittance to the lowest level of the civil service examinations.

### YI HWANG'S COMMENTS

. . . [T]he Confucian way of learning is that in order to ascend to lofty heights one must begin with the lowly, to travel afar one must begin with what is near. Indeed, to begin from the lowly and near certainly is a slow process. But apart from it, whence comes the lofty and distant? In applying one's efforts to gradual advancement one attains what is lofty and distant without parting from what is lowly and near; it is in this that it is different from Buddhist and Daoist learning.

[From *T'oegye chŏnsŏ* 1:19:26b; MK]

## Section 4: Diagram of the *Great Learning*

### COMMENTS FROM ZHU XI'S *QUESTIONS AND ANSWERS ON THE "GREAT LEARNING"*

Someone asked: "How does one apply himself to the practice of mindfulness [reverent seriousness]?"

Master Zhu said: "Cheng Yi spoke of it as 'concentrating on units and not departing [from it],' and again in terms of being 'well-ordered and even-minded, grave and quiet.'"

*Establishing Instruction*

Establishing instruction in womb nurture, fostering and rearing

Establishing instruction: the Small and the Great the beginning and the end

Establishing instruction: the "three matters" and the "four skills"

Establishing instruction: master and disciple giving and receiving

*Clarifying Relationships*

Clarifying affection between father and son

Clarifying righteousness between ruler and minister

Clarifying distinction between husband and wife

Clarifying order between elder and younger

Clarifying intercourse between friends

*Making One's Person Mindful*

Clarifying the essential skills of dealing with inner dispositions

Clarifying the norms of proper decorum and dignity

Clarifying regulations regarding clothing

Clarifying proper moderation in food and drink

*Examining Ancient Examples*

ESTABLISHING INSTRUCTION

CLARIFYING RELATIONSHIPS

MAKING ONE'S PERSON MINDFUL

*Fine Sayings*

Expanding on establishing instruction

Expanding on clarifying relationships

Expanding on making one's person mindful

*Fine Deeds*

Actual practice of establishing instruction

Actual practice of clarifying relationships

Actual practice of making one's person mindful

Once the mind is established in this condition, one may proceed with this state of mind to pursue the investigation of things and the extension of knowledge, and thereby exhaustively comprehend principle as it is present in things and affairs; that is what is meant by "honoring the good inborn qualities of one's nature and following the path of inquiry and study." One may proceed with this state of mind to make his intentions sincere and rectify his mind, and thereby cultivate his person; that is what is meant by "first establish that which is greater, and the lesser will not be able to take it away." One may proceed in this state of mind to regulate the family, and properly order the state, and thereby attain even to making the whole world tranquil; that is what is meant by "Cultivate your own person in order to give ease to the people; make much of reverence [in your own person] and the world will enjoy tranquillity." All of this shows that one cannot absent himself from the practice of mindfulness for a single day. That being the case, how can the one word, "mindfulness," but be the essence of both the beginning and the completion of sage learning?

### YI HWANG'S COMMENTS

In what one investigates, sometimes one meets with complexities and intricacies that using all one's strength one cannot get through, or sometimes one's nature happens to have a blind spot on the matter and it is difficult to force illumination and break it open. Then one ought to set the matter aside and approach another and investigate it. In this way, investigating one way and then another, there is an accumulation which deepens and ripens; the mind naturally gradually clears, and the actuality of moral principle gradually becomes manifest to one's eye. Then if one again takes up what one formerly could not successfully investigate and reflects on it, combining it for consideration and comparison with what one has already successfully investigated, while one hardly is aware of what is happening, they will interact at the same time to produce enlightenment and understanding regarding what had not been investigated [successfully]. This is the flexible approach to the investigation of principle; it does not mean that when an investigation is not successful one just puts it aside [for good].

[From T'oegye chŏnsŏ 1:14:21a; MK]

## Section 7: Diagram of the Explanation of Humaneness

### YI HWANG'S COMMENTS

I venture to say that the great virtue of Heaven and Earth is to produce and give life. Between Heaven and Earth there is a dense multitude of living creatures; whether they be animals or plants, large or small, they are all compassionately covered and loved by Heaven. How much more is this the case when it comes to the likes of us humans, who are the most spiritual and are as the mind of Heaven and Earth! Although Heaven has this mind it is not able itself to manifest it, but must especially favor the most sagacious, wise, and excellent, one whose virtue can unite spirits and men, and make him ruler, entrusting him with the duty of looking after [the people] in order to put its humane and loving governance into practice.

[From *T'oegye chŏnsŏ* 1:6:34a; MK]

## Section 8: Diagram of the Study of the Mind

From Yi Hwang's youth Zhen Dexiu's *Classic of the Mind-and-Heart* was one of the most important and formative influences on him. Yi Hwang's constant emphasis upon the centrality of mindfulness is a faithful reflection of Zhu Xi, but it is also an unmistakable reflection of the influence of Zhen's *Classic*.

### YI HWANG'S COMMENTS

The human mind is the foundation of [selfish] human desires. Human desires are the flow of the human mind; they arise from the mind as physically conditioned. The sage likewise cannot but have [the human mind]; therefore one can only call it the human mind and cannot directly consider it as human desire. Nevertheless human desires in fact proceed from it; therefore I say it is the foundation of human desires. The mind ensnared by greed is the condition of the ordinary man who acts contrary to Heaven; therefore it is termed "human desire" and called something other than "human mind." This leads one to understand that such is not the original condition of the human mind; therefore I say it is the "flow" of the human mind. Thus the human mind is prior and [selfish] human desire come later; the former is correct and the latter is evil.

In general, although the study of the mind-and-heart is complex, one can sum up its essence as nothing other than blocking [selfish] human desires and preserving the principle of Heaven, just these two and that is all. All the matters that are involved in blocking human desires should be categorized on the side of the human mind, and all that pertain to preserving the principle of Heaven should be categorized on the side of the Dao Mind.

[From *T'oegye chŏnsŏ* 1:40:9b–10a; 1:37:28b; MK]

# YI I

Yi I (Yulgok; 1536–1584) rivals Yi Hwang for the position of foremost philosopher of the Chosŏn dynasty. He was a great statesman and theorist of government as well as a metaphysical thinker of rare perceptiveness and clarity. In the decade after Yi Hwang's death, Yi I resurrected the position finally abandoned by

Ki Taesŭng in the Four-Seven Debate and further developed it in debate with his friend Sŏng Hon (1535–1598).

Yi Hwang and Ki Taesŭng had argued the question in terms of two sets of feelings: the purely good Four Beginnings and the sometimes good and sometimes evil Seven Feelings. In this selection Yi I refers instead to the "Dao Mind" and the "Human Mind," classical terms that likewise referred to normative and good inclinations versus those of a more dubious sort. The basic question—whether or not this differentiation is founded upon different modal relationships of principle and material force—remains the same, however.

[MK]

## LETTER TO SŎNG HON

There is a single thread running through both the explanation of principle and material force and the explanation of the Human Mind and the Dao Mind. If one has not comprehended the meaning of the Human Mind and the Dao Mind, it amounts to not comprehending principle and material force. If one has already clearly understood the inseparability of principle and material force, then one can extend that to an understanding of the fact that the Human Mind and Dao Mind do not have a twofold origin. Only if there is something not yet comprehended about the relationship between principle and material force might one perhaps regard them as separate, with each occupying its own distinct place. And thus one might also then question whether in the case of the Human Mind and the Dao Mind there might be two distinct origins.

Principle is above forms; material force is on the level of form. The two cannot be separated from each other. If they cannot be separated, then their issuance as function is single and one cannot speak of them as mutually possessing issuing functions. If one says they mutually possess issuing functions, that would mean that when principle issues as function, material force at times might not be right with it, or that when material force issues as function, there might be times when principle is not right with it. In that case the relation of principle and material force would admit of both separation and conjunction and prior and posterior. Activity and tranquillity would have a commencement; yin and yang would have a beginning. The error in all this is indeed anything but small!

But principle is nonactive; rather it is material force that has concrete activity. Therefore in the case of feelings that emerge from the original nature and are not disrupted by our physical constitution, they are classed on the side of principle. Those that, although at the beginning emerging from the original nature, are then disrupted by the physical constitution are classed on the side of material force. One cannot get by without such propositions. That which accounts for the original goodness of man's nature is principle; but if it were not for material force, principle, being nonactive, would have no issuance. Then as for the Human Mind and the Dao Mind, are they not indeed both rooted in principle? It is not a matter of the outgrowth of the Human Mind already standing in contrast to principle in the mind-and-heart in the state before it is aroused. The wellspring is single but its outpouring is dual; how could Master Zhu not have understood this? It's just that the kinds of expression used to clarify the matter for others all have their own particular focus. . . .

As for developing the terminology of "Human Mind" and "Dao Mind,"[1] how did the sage have any alternative? Principle in its original condition is definitely perfectly good, but it mounts material force to issue as function, and this is where good and evil diverge. If one only sees that it mounts material force and involves both good and evil and does not understand principle in its original condition, then that amounts to not knowing the Great Foundation. If one only sees principle's original condition and does not understand its mounting on material force to issue as function—a condition that may develop into evil—then that is like mistaking the bandit for a son. Therefore the sage was concerned about this matter and categorized the feelings that directly follow from our normative nature in its original conditions as the "Dao Mind" in order to get people to preserve, nurture, and develop it to the fullest extent. The feelings that are disrupted by the effects of our physical constitution and are unable to be the direct consequence of our normative nature in its original condition he categorized as the "Human Mind" in order to get people to examine the excess or deficiency involved in such feelings and moderate them accordingly.

That which moderates them is the Dao Mind. Indeed, concrete form is a part of the nature with which we are endowed by Heaven. As for the Human Mind, how is it likewise not good? But its negative connotation is from its involving excess or deficiency and devolving into evil, that is all. If one is able to develop the Dao Mind to its fullest extent and moderate the Human Mind, making the proclivities that attend our physical constitution each follow its proper norm, then whether in activity or tranquillity, speech or deeds, there will be nothing that is not of our normative nature in its original condition.

[From *Yulgok chŏnsŏ* 10:11a–18a; MK]

---

1. The terms originated in the *Book of Documents* (Legge 3:61, with minor changes), a famous passage that reads: "The mind of man is precarious. The mind of the Way is subtle. Be discriminating, be single-minded. Hold fast to the Mean!"

*Chapter 40*

BUDDHISM

One of the most important changes from the Koryŏ to the Chosŏn dynasty was the shift from sponsoring Buddhism to the Confucianization of the state through the adoption of Neo-Confucianism, based in particular on the writings of Zhu Xi. Generally, Confucian rulers, except King Sejo (1455–1468) and Queen Dowager Munjŏng (1501–1565), who acted as a regent to the young King Myŏngjong from 1545 until her death, attempted to suppress all beliefs and practices other than those of Zhu Xi regarding the nature and patterns of government, society, and people. Thus, as Confucianism enjoyed unreserved governmental patronage, Buddhism was continuously suppressed and even persecuted. Eminent Buddhist monks made efforts to defend Buddhism against attacks from the Confucian view and to find ways to reconcile and integrate their views with Confucianism. The most famous of these thinkers are Kihwa (1376–1433), Pou (1515–1565), and Hyujŏng (1520–1604).

[JW]

## KIHWA

Kihwa (1376–1433) was one of the eminent Meditation masters who advocated reconciliation among religions in the early Chosŏn dynasty. The *Treatise on*

*Manifesting Rightness* (*Hyŏnjŏng non*), excerpted here, compares Buddhist principles and their function in the world with Confucianism.

[JW]

### TREATISE ON MANIFESTING RIGHTNESS

[H]uman beings receive their birth from their parents and owe their survival to the state. Filial piety at home and loyalty to the state are proper duties for a subject and a son. Marriage and memorial services for ancestors are also the great principles of men's cardinal relationships. Without marriage, the principle of reproduction may be annihilated; without memorial services, the tradition of ancestor worship may be extinguished. But to fulfill completely the duties of loyalty and filial piety as a subject and as a son is difficult. To remain married while maintaining rightness till the end of one's life, to perform ancestor worship with heart and soul, and to abide in perfect purity are also difficult. If one scrupulously keeps his office while at the same time remaining totally dedicated to loyalty and filial piety, and if one continuously upholds rightness and abides in perfect purity until his death, he will not only not lose his good name while he is alive but will also gain rebirth as a human being after death. This is a result of adhering to the unchangeable way of the principle.

Most people attempt to obtain fame only; very few try to restrain themselves from passion. Most people only want rebirth as a human being and find it difficult to free themselves from endless transmigration. Passion is the root cause of transmigration; lust is the immediate cause of birth. For those people who are no longer in a position to avoid ties to their wives and children, can they possibly cut themselves off from passion? If they cannot remove themselves from passion, can they possibly free themselves from transmigration? If one wants to be free from transmigration, one should first eliminate passion; if one wants to eliminate passion, one should first leave one's wife and children; if one wants to leave one's wife and children, one must abandon the mundane world. If one does not abandon the mundane world, one cannot leave one's wife and children, nor can one eliminate passion and be free from transmigration. . . .

Moreover, monks never neglect their prayers for the king and the state at the daily ritual services in the morning and evening. How could this not be called loyalty? Whereas the rulers promote virtue by conferring honors and emoluments and prohibit evil by punishing crimes, we Buddhists instruct people that good deeds bring happiness and evil deeds bring disaster. Therefore those who learn Buddhism will naturally withdraw from evil thoughts and develop good intentions. Although the Buddhists do not confer honors as rewards or awe the people with punishment, our Buddha's teachings cause the people to be transformed. Is this not assisting the king and the state?

[From *Hanguk pulgyo chŏnsŏ* 7:217a–225b; JW, YC]

# KIM SISŬP

Kim Sisŭp (1435–1493) is renowned for syncretizing Buddhism and Confucianism. In *On No-Thought* (*Musa*), Kim, writing under his pen name of Ch'ŏnghanja, comments on Buddhist practices of his time, criticizes those idle Meditation practitioners who were not sincere in their meditation while pretending to be transcendent, and insists on a syncretic approach to Buddhist practices within a secular life of Confucian perspective.

[JW]

## ON NO-THOUGHT

Ch'ŏnghanja said: "That which has no thought or anxiety is the essence of the Way. To be anxious with great care and not to be idle are the essentials of its practice. We see all the time in our worldly affairs that neglecting to be anxious leads to the destruction of myriad things. If such is the case, how can one attain the true Way of no delusion through idleness? Therefore, Jiwen of the state of Lu thought over three times before acting.[1] Confucius set up the 'Nine Items of Thoughtful Consideration.'[2] Zengzi kept a reminder: 'One attains only through anxiety.' Confucius had a precept for profound anxiety. Unless one is an innately intelligent person who does not need to exert himself, how can it be possible for one not to think? The dispositions of men are not the same; some are stupid and ignorant, and some are bright and intelligent. If one is not diligent and steadfast, how can one become equal to superior sages? One must think and be anxious studiously and meticulously, and one must train daily and discipline oneself monthly until one attains the realm of enlightenment by oneself. Only thereafter can one say that, in the Way, there is no thought and anxiety."

[From *Maewŏltang chip* 16:1a–2b; JW, YC]

# HYUJŎNG

Hyujŏng (1520–1604) is generally regarded as the greatest monk of the Chosŏn dynasty. Most of the eminent masters of modern Korean Buddhism trace their dharma lineage back to him. Although he studied the Confucian classics at the Royal Academy in Seoul, he became a Buddhist monk at the age of nineteen. Having passed the monk examination in 1552, he was appointed director of the Doctrinal school and then director of the Meditation school in 1555. In 1557 he retired to the mountains until 1592, when Japan invaded

---

1. *Analects* 5:19 (Legge 1:180).
2. *Analects* 16:10 (Legge 1:314).

Korea. Despite his religious beliefs and age—he was then seventy-two—he organized and led a militia, largely composed of Buddhist monks, to repel the invaders. Because of his successful military exploits, he has become a legendary folk hero even to this day.

In the *Mirror of Three Religions (Samga kwigam)*, Hyujŏng attempted to show that the three religions, Confucianism, Daoism and Buddhism, were ultimately not divergent in transmitting the truth and that the ultimate messages they convey are basically the same.

[JW]

## SECRETS OF MEDITATION AND DOCTRINE

. . . Nowadays, among those who erroneously transmit the goal of meditation, some consider the gate of "sudden and gradual" enlightenment the correct lineage; some take the teaching of "complete and sudden" enlightenment to be the essential vehicle; some cite non-Buddhist scriptures to explain the secret meaning of meditation; some frivolously play with karmic consciousness as being the fundamental dimension of meditation; some regard mental light and shadow as the real self; and some even commit unrestrained actions, like the blind wielding a stick and the deaf shouting without remorse or shame. What is their true mind? How can I dare talk about these transgressions of slander against the dharma?

I say that what is transmitted outside the doctrine cannot be known by studying nor be grasped by thinking. Only after thoroughly devoting one's mind to the extent that its way is totally cut off can it be known. Only after the realization is reached willingly can it be obtained. Can it be obtained by thinking? Can it be obtained by deliberation? It is, it can be said, like a mosquito trying to bite the back of an iron ox.

We are now in the last days of the world, and many practitioners are ill equipped for the special transmission outside the doctrine. Therefore, they only value the "complete and sudden approach" to make people see, listen, believe, and understand the use of the Way to produce seeing, hearing, belief, and understanding. They do not value the shortcut approach that has no principles, no meanings, no mind, no words, no taste, and no pattern for searching out a foundation. . . .

But if students of meditation believe the dharma of the shortcut approach, then even though they may yet have to achieve enlightenment in this life, they will not be taken to bad places by evil karma upon their death; instead, they will immediately enter the correct path toward enlightenment.

In the past, Mazu's one shout caused the deafness of Bozhang and enabled Huang-bo's tongue to spill out. This is the origin of the Lin-zhi tradition. You must select the orthodox lineage of meditation. . . . If you fail to live up to this elderly monk's expectations, you fail to meet a great obligation owed to the buddhas and patriarchs. Think carefully; think carefully.

[From *Hanguk pulgyo chŏnsŏ* 7:657b–658a; JW, YC]

PART III

# Traditional Japan

*Edited by*
# Wm. Theodore de Bary

WITH THE COLLABORATION OF

*Donald Keene*
*George Tanabe*
*H. Paul Varley*

# EXPLANATORY NOTE

The consonants of Japanese words or names are read as in English (with "g" always hard) and the vowels as in Italian. There are no silent letters. The name Abe, for instance, is pronounced "Ah-bay." The long vowels "ō" and "ū" are indicated except in the names of cities already well known in the West, such as Tokyo and Kyoto. All romanized terms have been standardized according to the Hepburn system for Japanese, pin-yin for Chinese, and the McCune-Reischauer for Korean. Chinese philosophical terms used in Japanese texts are given in their Japanese readings (e.g., *ri* instead of *li* for "principle," "reason") except where attention is specifically drawn to the Chinese original. Sanskrit words appearing in italics follow the standard system of transliteration found in Louis Renou's *Grammaire sanskrite* (Paris 1930), pp. xi–xiii. Sanskrit terms and names appearing in roman letters follow *Webster's New International Dictionary*, second edition unabridged, except that a macron is used to indicate long vowels and the Sanskrit symbols for ś (ç) are uniformly transcribed as "sh" in the text itself. Personal names also are spelled in this manner except when they occur in the titles of works.

Japanese names are given in their Japanese order, with the family name first and the personal name last. The dates given after personal names are those of birth and death except in the case of rulers, whose reign dates are preceded by "r." Generally, the name by which a person was most commonly known in Japanese tradition is the one used in the text. Since this book is intended for general readers rather than specialists, we have not burdened the text with a list of the alternative names or titles that usually accompany biographical references to a scholar in Chinese or Japanese historical works. For the same reason, the sources of translations given at the end of each selection are as concise as possible. There is a complete bibliography at the end of the book.

Contributors are identified with their work in the table of contents; unattributed chapters are the responsibility of the editors. Unless otherwise indicated, in the reference at the end of each selection, the author of the book is the writer whose name precedes the selection. The initials following the source citation are those of the translator or the compiler of the section. Excerpts from existing translations have often been adapted and edited to suit our purposes. In particular, we have removed unnecessary brackets and footnotes and have inserted essential commentary in the text whenever possible rather than add a footnote. Those interested in the full text and annotations may, of course, refer to the original translation cited with each such excerpt. As sources for our own translations, we have tried to use standard editions that would be available to other scholars.

Titles of collections frequently cited are abbreviated as follows:

*BD*　　*Bukkyō daijiten.* Ed. Mochizuki Shinkō. 10 vols., rev. ed. Kyoto: Sekai seiten kankō kyōkai, 1955–1963.

*NKBT*　*Nihon koten bungaku taikei.* 100 vols. Tokyo: Iwanami shoten, 1958–1968.

*NST*　　*Nihon shisō taikei.* 67 vols. Tokyo: Iwanami shoten, 1970–1982.

*TD*　　*Taishō shinshū daizōkyō.* Ed. Takakusu Junjirō and Watanabe Kaigyoku. 85 vols. Tokyo: Taishō issaikyō kankōkai, 1924–1932.

# CONTRIBUTORS

The translators' initials follow each selection.

AG    Allan Grapard, University of California, Santa Barbara
dB    Wm. Theodore de Bary, Columbia University
GT    George Tanabe, University of Hawaii, Manoa
JPL   Jeroen Pieter Lamers, Royal Dutch Ministry of Economic Affairs
JSAE  Jurgis S. A. Elisonas, Indiana University
PV    Paul Varley, University of Hawaii, Manoa
WB    William Bodiford, University of California, Los Angeles

# CHRONOLOGY

| | |
|---|---|
| First century B.C.E. | First reference to Japan (called land of Wa) in Chinese dynastic histories. |
| C.E. 57 | Envoy from country of Nu in land of Wa makes tributary visit to Han court. First exact date concerning Wa in dynastic histories. |
| 239 | Envoy sent by Queen Himiko of Yamatai in land of Wa to Wei court. |
| 538 | Recognized as date for formal introduction of Buddhism to Japan. |
| 562 | Kingdom of Silla destroys Mimana, Japanese enclave at tip of Korean Peninsula (present-day Korean scholars disclaim existence of such an enclave). |
| 592–628 | Reign of Empress Suiko. Prince Shōtoku serves as regent. |
| 600 | First Japanese embassy to Sui Court. |
| 604 | Prince Shōtoku's Seventeen-Article Constitution. First official use in Japan of Chinese calendar. |
| 630 | First Japanese embassy to Tang court. |
| 645 | Taika reform. |
| 668 | Tenchi becomes emperor, Silla unifies Korea. |
| 672 | Tenmu becomes emperor after armed succession dispute (Jinshin War). |
| 702 | Promulgation of Taihō Code. |

*Nara Period*

| | |
|---|---|
| 710 | Establishment of first permanent capital at Nara. |
| 712 | *Records of Ancient Matters* (*Kojiki*). |
| 720 | *Chronicles of Japan* (*Nihongi* or *Nihon shoki*). |
| 741 | Copies of *Golden Light Sūtra* distributed to all provinces. |
| 751 | *Kaifūsō* (*Fond Recollections of Poetry*), first collection of Chinese verse by Japanese poets. |
| 752 | Dedication of Great Buddha (*Daibutsu*) at Tōdaiji Temple in Nara. |
| 754 | Chinese monk Ganjin arrives in Japan and establishes ordination center at Tōdaiji. |
| c. 759 | Compilation of *Man'yōshū* (*Collection of a Myriad Generations*), oldest anthology of *waka* (or *tanka*) poetry. |
| 764 | Empress Kōken reascends throne as Empress Shōtoku; appoints priest Dōkyō as prime minister. |
| 770 | Death of Empress Shōtoku and fall of Dōkyō from power. |
| 781 | Kanmu becomes emperor. |
| 788 | Saichō founds Enryakuji Temple on Mount Hiei. |

*Heian Period*

| | |
|---|---|
| 794 | Court moves capital to Heian (Kyoto). |
| 805 | Saichō returns from study in China. |
| 806 | Kūkai returns from study in China. |
| 815 | *New Compilation of the Register of Families* (*Shinsen shōjiroku*). |
| 816 | Kōyasan Monastery founded by Kūkai. |
| 817 | Saichō codifies regulations for monks at Enryakuji Temple on Mount Hiei. |
| 838 | Last official mission to Tang China. |
| 847 | Ennin returns from China to found Tendai esotericism in Japan. |
| 858 | Beginning of Fujiwara regency at court. Enchin returns from China and founds study center at Miidera Temple. |
| 905 | *Kokinshū* (*Collection of Ancient and Modern Poems*), first imperially authorized anthology of *waka* (or *tanka*) poetry. |
| 972 | Death of Kūya, early popularizer of devotion to Amida Buddha. |
| c. 990–1020 | Classical age of Japanese court prose: *Tale of Genji, Pillow Book, Izumi Shikibu Diary, Honchō monzui* (Chinese prose by Japanese). |
| 1017 | Death of Genshin, author of *Essentials of Salvation*. |

| 1068 | Accession of Emperor Go-Sanjō and beginning of attempt to curb power of Fujiwara regents. |
| 1086 | Abdication of Emperor Shirakawa and commencement of age of ascendancy of senior retired emperors at court (1086–1156). |
| 1132 | Death of Ryōnin, early popularizer of Pure Land Buddhism. |
| 1156 | Beginning of rise to power at court of Taira warrior family under Kiyomori. |
| 1180–1185 | Minamoto-Taira (*Genpei*) War. Victory of Minamoto. |

*Kamakura Period*

| 1185 | *De facto* founding of Kamakura Shogunate by Minamoto Yoritomo. |
| 1191 | Eisai (Yōsai), founder of Rinzai branch of Zen sect, returns from second trip to China; introduces tea to Japan. |
| 1192 | Yoritomo receives title of shogun. |
| 1205 | Beginning of rise to power of Hōjō as shogunal regents. |
| 1212 | Death of Hōnen. |
| 1220 | *Gukanshō* by Jien. |
| 1223 | Dōgen, founder of Sōtō branch of Zen sect, goes to China. |
| 1232 | *Jōei shikimoku* (basic law code of Kamakura Shogunate). |
| 1260 | Nichiren first predicts a foreign invasion. |
| 1262 | Death of Shinran, founder of True Pure Land sect. |
| 1268 | Nichiren warns of impending Mongol invasion. |
| 1271 | Nichiren sentenced to death, escapes, and is banished. |
| 1274 | First Mongol invasion. |
| 1281 | Second Mongol invasion. |
| 1289 | Death of Ippen, popularizer of Amida cult. |
| 1325 | At suggestion of Zen master Musō Soseki, Emperor Go-Daigo sends first official embassy to China since Tang dynasty. |
| c. 1331 | *Essays in Idleness* (*Tsurezuregusa*). |
| 1333 | Overthrow of Kamakura Shogunate. Beginning of Kenmu Restoration (1333–1336). |

*Muromachi (Ashikaga) Period*

| 1336 | *De facto* founding of Muromachi Shogunate in Kyoto by Ashikaga Takauji. Beginning of period of War Between Northern and Southern Courts (1336–1392). |
| 1338 | Takauji receives title of shogun. |
| 1339 | *Chronicle of the Direct Succession of Divine Sovereigns* (*Jinnō shōtōki*) by Kitabatake Chikafusa. |

| 1368 | Ashikaga Yoshimitsu becomes shogun; fosters diplomatic and trade relations with China. |
| 1384 | Death of Kan'ami, early master of Nō drama. |
| 1443 | Death of Zeami, greatest master of Nō drama. |
| 1467–1477 | Ōnin War. Much of Kyoto destroyed. |
| 1478 | Commencement of Age of War in Provinces (*Sengoku*, 1478–1568). |
| 1488 | Death of Nisshin, evangelizer of Nichiren sect. |
| 1499 | Death of Rennyo, leader of True Pure Land sect. |
| 1511 | Death of Yoshida Kanetomo of the "Primal Shinto" movement. |
| 1543 | Portuguese merchants land on Tanegashima—first Europeans to visit Japan. Introduce European guns (harquebuses). |
| 1549 | St. Francis Xavier arrives in Japan and founds Jesuit mission. |
| 1568 | Oda Nobunaga enters Kyoto and begins process of military unification of Japan. |
| 1571 | Nobunaga's army destroys Enryakuji Temple on Mount Hiei. |
| 1582 | Nobunaga assassinated; Toyotomi Hideyoshi succeeds him as unifier. |
| 1591 | Death of Sen no Rikyū, greatest of tea masters. |
| 1592 | Hideyoshi's first invasion of Korea. |
| 1597 | Hideyoshi's second invasion of Korea. |
| 1598 | Death of Hideyoshi. |
| 1600 | Battle of Sekigahara and founding of Tokugawa Shogunate by Ieyasu. |
| 1603 | Ieyasu receives title of shogun. |

## Chapter 41

### THE EARLIEST RECORDS OF JAPAN

The oldest extant annals in Japanese are the *Records of Ancient Matters* (*Kojiki*, 712 C.E.) and the *Chronicles of Japan* (*Nihon shoki* or *Nihongi*, 720). The *Records* opens with chapters on the mythological Age of the Gods and continues the story of Japan to about 500 C.E.[1] Although this book reveals early Japanese ways of thinking and patterns of behavior, it contains little that can be taken as historical fact. The *Chronicles*, a much longer work, covers the same story from the Age of the Gods to 500 but continues for some two hundred years more until the end of the seventh century (697). The *Chronicles* becomes increasingly reliable as history after about the late sixth century. Indeed, the bestowal of the posthumous name of Suiko, meaning "conjecture the past," on an empress who reigned from 592 to 628 seems to suggest that it was around this time that the Japanese, no doubt under Chinese influence, first began the serious writing of history, albeit often in the interests of the ruling house that the historians served.

An important source of written information about Japan before the sixth century is the Chinese dynastic histories. By the time Japan first came into the Chinese purview, about the first century B.C.E., the writing of history had left far behind the foundation myths of the *Classic of Documents*, and Chinese historians were compiling generally reliable records of the past. In the first century B.C.E.,

---

1. The *Records of Ancient Matters* also provides genealogical data for the sovereigns of the sixth and early seventh centuries.

Japan was called Wa by the Chinese[2] and was described as a land comprising more than a hundred tribal communities. As late as the Chinese Three Kingdoms period (220–265), according to the dynastic accounts, Wa was still divided into some thirty communities (although we know from the archaeological record in Japan that the country was then evolving into its first centralized state).

The Chinese histories do not tell us how the people now known as the Japanese first found their way to the islands. Without conclusive evidence on this subject, modern scholars have expounded various theories based on linguistics, archaeology, architecture, and a great many criteria, with some contending that the Japanese originally came from Southeast Asia and others insisting that they were a northern people. The Japanese probably had diverse origins, with various peoples entering from different directions. The mainstream of cultural influence came from the continent by way of Korea. When the first Qin emperor (247–210 B.C.E.) unified China and built the Great Wall to prevent the northern barbarians from making incursions on the fertile plains of the Yellow River, it seems likely that his actions helped direct the migrations of different peoples eastward or westward along the wall. Disturbances resulting from the movement of tribes were sometimes so severe that Emperor Wu (r. 140–87 B.C.E.) of the Han dynasty was compelled to send expeditionary forces to restore order. An outpost of the Han empire thus was established in northern Korea and served as a model of organized government to the surrounding tribes, possibly including the Japanese.

It may seem surprising that Japanese were in Korea in the first century C.E., but there appears to have been no fixed boundary at the time between the territory of the Koreans and that of the Japanese. Very likely there was a fairly steady eastward migration from north of China to the Korean peninsula and thence to the Japanese archipelago. During the third century, the Chinese withdrew from Korea, and the country was divided into three states, Koguryŏ, Paekche, and Silla, and beginning in the fourth century, Japanese periodically fought in Korea, usually siding with Paekche against Koguryŏ and Silla. Japanese historians claim that Japan established a territorial enclave at the tip of the Korean Peninsula called Mimana sometime during the fourth century, although nationalistic Korean historians vigorously deny that such an enclave ever existed. Whatever interests the Japanese may have had in Korea were finally destroyed in 562. During the seventh century, Silla, with Chinese aid, subjugated the rival kingdoms of Koguryŏ and Paekche and unified the peninsula. These successes of the combined forces of Silla and Tang China drove the Japanese from the continent into the relative isolation of their islands, an event that may have helped bring about the birth of the historical Japanese state. That is, the rise of powerful dynasties in China and Korea impelled Japan to achieve a unified government in order not to be overwhelmed.

To understand some of the important influences on Japanese thought since earliest times, we turn next to the islands' geographical features. The Chinese

---

2. Wa is the Japanese pronunciation. In Chinese, it is Wo.

account of Japan in the *History of the Latter Han Dynasty* opens with the words "The people of Wa live on mountainous islands in the ocean," and in fact, the two elements of water and mountains, together with a kind of sun worship, have always been very close to the Japanese. Although we are likely to find in any country's religious beliefs a worship of noticeable or beneficial aspects of nature, the combination of these three elements is especially characteristic of Japan. The numerous clear streams and the ever-present ocean have always delighted the Japanese, as we can tell from their earliest poetry. To their love of water the Japanese joined a passion for lustration and cleanliness and, in our own day, for swimming. The Japanese love of mountains is not surprising in a country renowned for its numerous peaks, especially the incomparable Mount Fuji, and the worship of the sun is not unnatural in a country blessed with a temperate climate. Today we can still appreciate what an awe-inspiring experience it must have been for the Japanese of any age to stand on the summit of Mount Fuji and greet the sun as it rose from the waters of the Pacific. Other characteristics of the Japanese recorded in the early Chinese accounts that are still noticeable today include honesty, politeness, gentleness in peace and bravery in war, a love of liquor, and religious rites of purification and divination.

The Japanese accounts of the birth of the gods and of the foundation of their country belong, of course, to the realm of mythology rather than history, but they afford us a glimpse of Japanese attitudes toward the world and nature. Also, since later Japanese attached importance to these legends, some knowledge of them is indispensable to understanding Japanese thought.

## JAPAN IN THE CHINESE DYNASTIC HISTORIES

The following extracts are from the official histories of successive Chinese dynasties, beginning with the Latter Han (25–220 C.E.), although the first of these accounts was written for the Kingdom of Wei (220–265) and compiled about 297 C.E.

These accounts are contained in a section devoted to the barbarian neighbors of China at the end of each history. Thus they do not occupy a prominent place in these works, being more in the nature of an afterthought or footnote. Particularly in the earlier accounts, the information is apt to be scattered and disconnected and, not surprisingly, is presented by official chroniclers who viewed Japanese affairs with an eye to Chinese interests and prestige.

Nevertheless, we can discern some of the main outlines of Japan's development in these early centuries. In the first accounts, Japan appears to be a heterogeneous group of communities in contact with China, with one ruling house bidding for Chinese recognition of its supremacy over the others. In one case, the influence of the Chinese ambassador is said to have been the decisive factor in settling a dispute over the succession to the Yamato throne. The kings of Wa, as the Yamato rulers were known, also made strong claims to military supremacy in Korea, which were at times acknowledged by the Chinese court. In the later accounts, the unification of Japan has progressed noticeably. The sovereignty of the Yamato house has been asserted over hitherto autonomous regions, and its government displays many of the trappings of the Chinese imperial structure. On occasion, the Japanese court is rebuked for its pretensions to equality with the Chinese and even for its hinted superiority, as when the Japanese ruler addressed the Chinese, "The Child[3] of Heaven in the land where the sun rises addresses a letter to the Child of Heaven in the land where the sun sets."

## ACCOUNTS OF THE EASTERN BARBARIANS

### HISTORY OF THE KINGDOM OF WEI (WEI ZHI, CA. 297 C.E.)

The people of Wa [Japan] dwell in the middle of the ocean on the mountainous islands southeast of [the prefecture of] Daifang. They formerly comprised more than one hundred communities. During the Han dynasty, [Wa] envoys appeared at the court; today, thirty of their communities maintain intercourse with us through envoys and scribes. . . .

The land of Wa is warm and mild. In winter as in summer the people live on raw vegetables and go about barefooted. They have [or live in] houses; father and mother, elder and younger, sleep separately. They smear their bodies with pink and scarlet, just as the Chinese use powder. They serve food on bamboo and wooden trays, helping themselves with their fingers. When a person dies, they prepare a single coffin, without an outer one. They cover the graves with earth to make a mound. When death occurs, mourning is observed for more than ten days, during which period they do not eat meat. The head mourners wail and lament, while friends sing, dance and drink liquor. When the funeral is over, all members of the family go into the water to cleanse themselves in a bath of purification.

When they go on voyages across the sea to visit China, they always select a man who does not comb his hair, does not rid himself of fleas, lets his clothing get as dirty as it will, does not eat meat, and does not lie with women. This man behaves like a mourner and is known as the "mourning keeper." When the voyage meets with good fortune, they all lavish on him slaves and other valuables. In case there is disease or mishap, they kill him, saying that he was not scrupulous in observing the taboos. . . .

Whenever they undertake an enterprise or a journey and discussion arises, they bake bones and divine in order to tell whether fortune will be good or bad. First they announce the object of divination, using the same manner of speech

---

3. The term *tenshi*, usually rendered as "Son of Heaven," is actually gender neutral; here, in the Japanese case, it refers to Empress Suiko.

as in tortoise shell divination; then they examine the cracks made by fire and tell what is to come to pass.

In their meetings and in their deportment, there is no distinction between father and son or between men and women. They are fond of liquor. In their worship, men of importance simply clap their hands instead of kneeling or bowing. The people live long, some to one hundred and others to eighty or ninety years. Ordinarily, men of importance have four or five wives; the lesser ones, two or three. Women are not loose in morals or jealous. There is no theft, and litigation is infrequent. In case of violations of the law, the light offender loses his wife and children by confiscation; as for the grave offender, the members of his household and also his kinsmen are exterminated. There are class distinctions among the people, and some men are vassals of others. Taxes are collected. There are granaries as well as markets in each province, where necessaries are exchanged under the supervision of the Wa officials. . . .

When the lowly meet men of importance on the road, they stop and withdraw to the roadside. In conveying messages to them or addressing them, they either squat or kneel, with both hands on the ground. This is the way they show respect. When responding, they say "ah," which corresponds to the affirmative "yes."

The country formerly had a man as ruler. For some seventy or eighty years after that there were disturbances and warfare. Thereupon the people agreed upon a woman for their ruler. Her name was Pimiko. She occupied herself with magic and sorcery, bewitching the people. Though mature in age, she remained unmarried. She had a younger brother who assisted her in ruling the country. After she became the ruler, there were few who saw her. She had one thousand women as attendants, but only one man. He served her food and drink and acted as a medium of communication. She resided in a palace surrounded by towers and stockades, with armed guards in a state of constant vigilance. . . .

In the sixth month of the second year of Jingchu [238 C.E.], the Queen of Wa sent the grandee Nashonmi and others to visit the prefecture [of Daifang], where they requested permission to proceed to the Emperor's court with tribute. The Governor, Liu Xia, dispatched an officer to accompany the party to the capital. In answer to the Queen of Wa, an edict of the Emperor, issued in the twelfth month of the same year, said as follows:

> Herein we address Pimiko, Queen of Wa, whom we now officially call a friend of Wei. The Governor of Daifang, Liu Xia, has sent a messenger to accompany your vassal, Nashonmi, and his lieutenant, Tsushi Gori. They have arrived here with your tribute, consisting of four male slaves and six female slaves, together with two pieces of cloth with designs, each twenty feet in length. You live very far away across the sea; yet you have sent an embassy with tribute. Your loyalty and filial piety we appreciate exceedingly. We confer upon you, therefore, the title "Queen of Wa Friendly to Wei," together with the decoration of the gold seal with purple ribbon.

The latter, properly encased, is to be sent to you through the Governor. We expect you, O Queen, to rule your people in peace and to endeavor to be devoted and obedient. . . .

When Pimiko passed away, a great mound was raised, more than a hundred paces in diameter. Over a hundred male and female attendants followed her to the grave. Then a king was placed on the throne, but the people would not obey him. Assassination and murder followed; more than one thousand were thus slain.

A relative of Pimiko named Iyo, a girl of thirteen, was [then] made queen and order was restored. Zheng [the Chinese ambassador] issued a proclamation to the effect that Iyo was the ruler. Then Iyo sent a delegation of twenty under the grandee Yazaku, General of the Imperial Guard, to accompany Zheng home [to China]. The delegation visited the capital and presented thirty male and female slaves. It also offered to the court five thousand white gems and two pieces of carved jade, as well as twenty pieces of brocade with variegated designs.

[Adapted from Tsunoda and Goodrich, *Japan in the Chinese Dynastic Histories*, pp. 8–16]

## HISTORY OF THE SUI DYNASTY (*SUI SHU*, CA. 630 C.E.)

During the twenty years of the Kaihuang era (581–600), the King of Wa, whose family name was Ame and personal name Tarishihoko, and who bore the title of Ahakomi, sent an envoy to visit the court. The Emperor ordered the appropriate official to make inquiries about the manners and customs [of the Wa people]. The envoy reported thus: "The King of Wa deems Heaven to be his elder brother and the sun, his younger.[4] Before break of dawn he attends the court, and, sitting cross-legged, listens to appeals. Just as soon as the sun rises, he ceases these duties, saying that he hands them over to his brother." Our just Emperor said that such things were extremely senseless,[5] and he admonished [the King of Wa] to alter [his ways].

[According to the envoy's report], the King's spouse is called Kemi. Several hundred women are kept in the inner chambers of the court. The heir apparent is known as Rikamitahori. There is no special palace. There are twelve grades of court officials. . . .

There are about one hundred thousand households. It is customary to punish murder, arson and adultery with death. Thieves are made to make restitution in accordance with the value of the goods stolen. If the thief has no property with

---

4. At variance with the later claim of the imperial line to be descended from the Sun Goddess.

5. According to Chinese tradition, a virtuous ruler showed his conscientiousness by attending to matters of state the first thing in the morning. Apparently the Japanese emperor was carrying this to a ridiculous extreme by disposing of state business before dawn.

which to make payment, he is taken to be a slave. Other offenses are punished according to their nature—sometimes by banishment and sometimes by flogging. In the prosecution of offenses by the court, the knees of those who plead not guilty are pressed together by placing them between pieces of wood, or their heads are sawed with the stretched string of a strong bow. Sometimes pebbles are put in boiling water and both parties to a dispute made to pick them out. The hand of the guilty one is said to become inflamed. Sometimes a snake is kept in a jar, and the accused ordered to catch it. If he is guilty, his hand will be bitten. The people are gentle and peaceful. Litigation is infrequent and theft seldom occurs.

As for musical instruments, they have five-stringed lyres and flutes. Both men and women paint marks on their arms and spots on their faces and have their bodies tattooed. They catch fish by diving into the water. They have no written characters and understand only the use of notched sticks and knotted ropes. They revere Buddha and obtained Buddhist scriptures from Paekche. This was the first time that they came into possession of written characters. They are familiar with divination and have profound faith in shamans, both male and female. . . .

Both Silla and Paekche consider Wa to be a great country, replete with precious things, and they pay her homage. Envoys go back and forth from time to time.

In the third year of Daye [607], King Tarishihoko sent an envoy to the court with tribute. The envoy said: "The King[6] has heard that to the west of the ocean a Bodhisattva of the Sovereign reveres and promotes Buddhism. For that reason he has sent an embassy to pay his respects. Accompanying the embassy are several tens of monks who have come to study Buddhism." [The envoy brought] an official message which read: "The Child of Heaven in the land where the sun rises addresses a letter to the Child of Heaven in the land where the sun sets. We hope you are in good health." When the Emperor saw this letter, he was displeased[7] and told the official in charge of foreign affairs that this letter from the barbarians was discourteous, and that such a letter should not again be brought to his attention.

[Tsunoda and Goodrich, *Japan in the Chinese Dynastic Histories*, pp. 229–232]

## THE EARLIEST JAPANESE CHRONICLES

The great native chronicles of early Japan, the *Records of Ancient Matters* (*Kojiki*) and the *Chronicles of Japan* (*Nihongi*), were completed as late as the first decades of the eighth century C.E., when Japanese writers were already strongly influenced by Chinese traditions. It is therefore difficult to distinguish any pure native traditions in these works, nor are they fully reliable as accounts

---

6. Actually, in 607, Empress Suiko.

7. Because of the presumptuousness of the Japanese ruler in claiming the title of Child of Heaven, to be on a par with the Chinese emperor.

of Japan's early history. Many of the events described are anachronistic, and many of the legends are selected with a view to confirming the religious or political claims of the ruling dynasty. The emphasis on ancestry is already quite apparent, although other evidence indicates that family genealogies were in a very confused state before the introduction of writing and the Chinese practice of compiling genealogical records (chap. 44).

The following excerpt from Aston's translation of the *nihongi* was selected to show what seem to be the most unsystematic and unsophisticated of legends dealing with the age of the gods and the creation of the land. In contrast to the founding myths of the Confucian *Classic of Documents* (*Shujing*), which focus on the sage-kings as the founders of civilization and culture heroes, the focus of attention here is on the creative role of numerous gods in the formation of many islands. Again in contrast to the Chinese classic account, which is unicentered and projects a single moral and political authority, the Japanese mythic world is polytheistic, polycentric, nature oriented, and alive with an almost ungovernable spiritual élan, riotous creativity, and irrepressible fertility.

### BIRTH OF THE LAND

Before the land was created, there were twelve deities, whose "forms were not visible." Izanami and Izanagi were the last of these, not the first, but they were directed by the other deities in concert to solidify the drifting flotsam and jetsam on the sea to shape the land. In the subsequent profusion of creativity, many islands and regions were formed, each reflecting the Japanese people's strong sense of place and pluralism.

Izanagi and Izanami stood on the floating bridge of Heaven and held counsel together, saying, "Is there not a country beneath?" Thereupon they thrust down the jewel-spear of Heaven[8] and, groping about therewith, found the ocean. The brine which dripped from the point of the spear coagulated and became an island which received the name of Ono-goro-jima.

The two deities thereupon descended and dwelt in this island. Accordingly they wished to become husband and wife together, and to produce countries.

So they made Ono-goro-jima the pillar of the center of the land.

Now the male deity turning by the left and the female deity by the right, they went round the pillar of the land separately. When they met together on one side, the female deity spoke first and said, "How delightful! I have met with a lovely youth." The male deity was displeased and said, "I am a man, and by right should have spoken first. How is it that on the contrary thou, a woman, shouldst have been the first to speak? This was unlucky. Let us go round again." Upon this the two deities went back, and having met anew,

---

8. Considered by some commentators to resemble a phallus. Compare Aston, *Nihongi*, vol. 1, p. 10.

this time the male deity spoke first and said, "How delightful! I have met a lovely maiden."

Then he inquired of the female deity, saying, "In the body is there aught formed?"

She answered and said, "In my body there is a place which is the source of femininity." The male deity said, "In my body again there is a place which is the source of masculinity. I wish to unite this source-place of my body to the source-place of thy body." Hereupon the male and female first became united as husband and wife.

Now when the time of birth arrived, first of all the island of Ahaji was reckoned as the placenta, and their minds took no pleasure in it. Therefore it received the name of Ahaji no Shima.[9]

Next there was produced the island of Ō-yamato no Toyo-aki-tsu-shima.[10] (Here and elsewhere [the characters for Nippon] are to be read Yamato.)[11]

Next they produced the island of Iyo no futa-na[12] and next the island of Tsukushi.[13] Next the islands of Oki and Sado were born as twins. This is the prototype of the twin-births which sometimes take place among mankind.

Next was born the island of Koshi,[14] then the island of Ō-shima, then the island of Kibi no Ko.[15]

Hence first arose the designation of the Great Eight-Island Country.

Then the islands of Tsushima and Iki, with the small islands in various parts, were produced by the coagulation of the foam of the salt-water.

[Adapted from Aston, *Nihongi*, vol. 1, pp. 10–14]

---

9. "The island which will not meet"; that is, it is unsatisfactory. Ahaji may also be interpreted as "my shame." The characters with which this name is written in the text mean "foam-road." Perhaps the true derivation is "millet-land."

10. Rich-harvest (or autumn) island of Yamato.

11. Yamato probably means "mountain gate." It is the genuine ancient name for the province containing Nara and many of the other early capitals of Japan, and it was also used for the whole country. Several emperors called themselves *yamato-neko*, and it is mentioned by the historian of the Later Han dynasty of China (23–220 B.C.E.) as the seat of rule in Japan at that time.

12. Now called Shikoku.

13. Now called Kyushu.

14. Koshi is not an island but comprises the present provinces of Etchū, Echigo, and Echizen.

15. These two are not clear. Kibi is now Bingo, Bizen, and Bitchū. Ko, "child" or "small," perhaps refers to the small islands of the Inland Sea.

*Chapter 42*

## EARLY SHINTO

From the early days of the opening of Japan, Western scholars, intrigued by what they imagined to be the indigenous nature of Shinto, have devoted considerable attention to this religion. By the turn of the twentieth century, scholars from many Western nations were studying what has been termed the "national faith of Japan" in the hope of discovering in it an explanation of Japanese characteristics long obscured to foreigners by the country's self-imposed isolation. Strictly speaking, however, Shinto is not a purely indigenous religion, for it shares continental features and absorbed foreign elements from earliest times. Thus it is both native and hybrid. Shamanistic and animistic practices similar to those of Shinto, which seem to spring from some earlier common religious ground, have been found throughout northeast Asia, especially Korea.

Shinto had diverse origins and remained an aggregate of heterogeneous cults well into historical times. Its failure to develop into a unified religion can be largely attributed to Japan's natural features and the people's strong sense of regionalism. That is, the numerous tribal communities living in the river basins held to their own beliefs even after the unified control of the central government began to be felt early in the seventh century.

The objects of worship in all Shinto cultures were known as *kami*, a term for which it is difficult to find a translation. A famous student of Shinto, Motoori Norinaga (1730–1801), wrote:

> I do not yet understand the meaning of the term *kami*. Speaking in
> general, however, it may be said that *kami* signifies, in the first place, the

deities of heaven and earth that appear in the ancient records and also the spirits of the shrines where they are worshiped.

It is hardly necessary to say that it includes human beings. It also includes such objects as birds, beasts, trees, plants, seas, mountains and so forth. In ancient usage, anything whatsoever which was outside the ordinary, which possessed superior power, or which was awe-inspiring was called *kami*. Eminence here does not refer merely to the superiority of nobility, goodness or meritorious deeds. Evil and mysterious things, if they are extraordinary and dreadful, are called *kami*. It is needless to say that among human beings who are called *kami* the successive generations of sacred emperors are all included. The fact that emperors are also called "distant *kami*" is because, from the standpoint of common people, they are far-separated, majestic and worthy of reverence. In a lesser degree we find, in the present as well as in ancient times, human beings who are *kami*. Although they may not be accepted throughout the whole country, yet in each province, each village and each family there are human beings who are *kami*, each one according to his own proper position. The *kami* of the divine age were for the most part human beings of that time and, because the people of that time were all *kami*, it is called the Age of the Gods (*kami*).[1]

Primitive Shinto embraced cults of diverse origins, including animism, shamanism, fertility cults, and the worship of nature, ancestors, and heroes. Over time, the distinctions among these various cults gradually disappeared. The Sun Goddess, for instance, became the chief deity not only of nature worshipers but of ancestor worshipers as well. She was also considered to be the dispenser of fertility and of the fortunes of the nation. Similarly, an object of animistic worship could assume the role of a fertility god or shamanistic deity or even pose as the ancestor of the land on which a community lived. Before Shinto could become the "national faith" of Japan, however, it had to be successively bolstered by the philosophical and religious concepts of Han Confucianism, Esoteric Buddhism, Neo-Confucianism, and, finally, Christianity. The forms of these influences will be discussed in later chapters. In the early period with which we are concerned here, Shinto was still a primitive and almost inarticulate group of cults.

The oldest center of Shinto worship was the Izumo Shrine on the Japan Sea coast, which was close to the Korean Peninsula and by way of which continental civilization reached Japan. The Kashima and Katori Shrines in the Tone River basin to the north for a long time marked the frontier between the lands of the Japanese and those of less civilized inhabitants. The shrine at Ise, that of the Sun Goddess, came to be the most important, and it was there that various symbols of the imperial power were displayed.

---

1. Holtom, *The National Faith of Japan*, pp. 23–24.

The buildings of the shrines were architecturally very simple, generally consisting of a single room (which was sometimes partitioned) raised off the ground and entered by steps at the side or front. The building was invariably made of wood, with whole tree trunks used for beams. A mirror, sword, or other form of "god embodiment" (*shintai*) might be enshrined within, but often the building served merely as a place where the *kami*, visible or invisible, could be worshiped.

Outside the shrine's main building, two other architectural features usually are found, a gateway called a *torii* and a water basin where worshipers could wash their mouth and hands. Indeed, the characteristic Japanese insistence on cleanliness finds its expression in many forms, and two important acts of worship at Shinto shrines, the *harai* and the *misogi*, reflect this tendency. The former apparently originated in the airing of the cave or pit dwellings of prehistoric times and came to refer to both the sweeping out of a house and the special rites of chasing out evil spirits. The latter refers to the washing of the body, an act of increasingly spiritual significance. In addition to these formal acts of religion, formulas, prayers, and ritual practices were associated with almost all human activities (but especially the arts and crafts), whereby divine power was invoked to ensure success.

Worship at a Shinto shrine consisted of "attendance" and "offering." Attendance meant not only being present and giving one's attention to the object of worship but often also performing ceremonial dances or joining in processions, which have always been an important part of Shinto ritual. The offerings usually consisted of the firstborn of a household, the first fruits of the season, or the first catch from the water but might also include booty of war, such as the heads of enemies. The shrine was in the charge of a medium who transmitted messages from both the *kami* and the political rulers. The mediums were assisted by "supplicators"— the general term for officers of the shrine—and ablutioners. Some of the texts of the prayers and rituals of this early time have been preserved and often are beautiful, with a simplicity characteristic of Shinto.

## LEGENDS CONCERNING SHINTO DEITIES

There is virtually no documentary evidence to indicate the original character of Shinto belief. Before the introduction of Chinese writing and Chinese ideas, the Japanese were unable to record their religious beliefs, and there is little reason to believe that they had produced an articulate body of doctrine or dogma. The legends in the *Kojiki* and *Nihongi*, often cited as containing the original deposit of Shinto folklore, are late compilations in which political considerations and specifically Chinese conceptions intrude themselves almost everywhere. This intrusion was recognized by the great Neo-Shinto scholars of the eighteenth and nineteenth centuries who tried almost in vain to find in these texts any evidence of pure Japanese beliefs. Elements of Chinese cosmology are most apparent in rationalistic passages explaining the origin of the world in terms of the yin and yang principles, which seem to come directly from Chinese works such as the *Huainanzi*. The prevalence of paired male and female deities such as Izanagi and Izanami may also be the result of conscious selection with the yin and yang principles in mind. Also, the frequency of numerical sets of deities, such as the Five Heavenly Deities of the *Kojiki* and the Seven Generations of Heavenly Deities of the *Nihongi*, may represent an attempt at selection and organization in terms of a Chinese cosmological series, in this case the Five Elements and the Seven Heavenly Luminaries.

Chapter 41 showed us the strong sense of place in early myth and the special preoccupation with the creation of the Japanese islands. Since the first histories were produced in an era when the Yamato house was asserting its hegemony over other communities, the historians, writing at their ruler's direction, naturally were concerned with establishing the dynasty's bid for sovereignty, which they based on genealogy, claiming descent from the gods. Because we have little besides these official accounts to go by, it is easy to understand how these dynastic myths came to dominate the scene. However, even passages meant to assert dynastic supremacy or that became systematized along this line betray the existence of diverse and competing cults or inadvertently reveal traditional attitudes and practices taken for granted by all. Note, too, in the following excerpts that the names of deities and semidivine beings are composed of vivid images from nature and that often their activities suggest a concern with fertility, ritual purification, ancestor or hero worship, and animism.

## BIRTH OF THE SUN GODDESS

In this account from the *Nihongi*, the Sun Goddess, Amaterasu, is identified not as the first of the gods or the creator of the world but simply as the Sun Maiden or Sun Princess, one among the many offspring of the primal pair Izanagi and Izanami.

Izanagi no Mikoto and Izanami no Mikoto consulted together saying, "We have now produced the great-eight-island country, with the mountains, rivers, herbs, and trees. Why should we not produce someone who shall be lord of the universe?" They then together produced the Sun Goddess, who was called Ō-hiru-me no muchi.[2]

(Called in one writing Amaterasu no Ō-hiru-me no muchi.)[3]

(In one writing she is called Amaterasu-ō-hiru-me no Mikoto.)[4]

---

2. Great-noon-[sun] maiden-of-possessor.

3. Heaven-illumine-of-great-noon-maiden-deity.

4. Heaven-illumine-great-noon-maiden-of-augustness.

The resplendent luster of this child shone throughout all the six quarters.[5] Therefore the two deities rejoiced saying, "We have had many children, but none of them have been equal to this wondrous infant. She ought not to be kept long in this land, but we ought of our own accord to send her at once to Heaven and entrust to her the affairs of Heaven."

At this time Heaven and Earth were still not far separated, and therefore they sent her up to Heaven by the ladder of Heaven.

They next produced the Moon-god.

(Called in one writing Tsuki-yumi[6] no Mikoto or Tsuki-yomi no Mikoto.)

His radiance was next to that of the Sun in splendor. This god was to be the consort of the Sun Goddess and to share in her government. They therefore sent him also to Heaven.

Next they produced the leech child, which even at the age of three years could not stand upright. They therefore placed it in the rock-camphor-wood boat of Heaven and abandoned it to the winds.

Their next child was Susa-no-o no Mikoto.[7]

(Called in one writing Kami Susa-no-o no Mikoto or Haya Susa-no-o no Mikoto.)[8]

This god had a fierce temper and was given to cruel acts. Moreover he made a practice of continually weeping and wailing. So he brought many of the people of the land to an untimely end. Again he caused green mountains to become withered. Therefore the two gods, his parents, addressed Susa-no-o no Mikoto, saying, "Thou art exceedingly wicked, and it is not meet that thou shouldst reign over the world. Certainly thou must depart far away to the Nether-land." So they at length expelled him.

[Adapted from Aston, *Nihongi*, vol. 1, pp. 18–20]

## DESCENT OF THE DIVINE GRANDSON WITH THE THREE IMPERIAL REGALIA

In this account, the Sun Goddess commissions the Divine Grandson to rule the land, bearing the so-called Three Imperial Regalia — a mirror, a sword, and a curved jewel — as symbols of divine authority. Actually the bronze mirror, long sword, and curved jewel are of continental origin (found earlier in north China and Korea), so originally they represented not native tradition but prestigious items of a higher civilization, of which the dynasty was the proud bearer among culturally less advanced tribes.

---

5. North, south, east, west, above, below.

6. *Yumi* means "bow"; *yomi*, "darkness." Neither is inappropriate as applied to the moon.

7. Better known as Susa-no-o, a god particularly associated with the Izumo people, who was probably relegated to a subordinate role when these people were displaced or eclipsed in power by the Yamato group.

8. *Kami*, "deity"; *haya*, "quick."

Note also that the legitimacy of the ruling house is shared with its supporting clans and service corporations, whose primal ancestors likewise received their charge from the Sun Goddess. These include the Nakatomi, from whom the Fujiwara derived their own claim to share in imperial rule. No such pluralistic arrangement was attached to Chinese conceptions of dynastic sovereignty.

"All the Central Land of Reed-Plains is now completely tranquilized." Now the Heaven-Shining-Deity gave command, saying: "If that be so, I will send down my child." She was about to do so when in the meantime an August Grandchild was born whose name was called Ama-tsu-hiko-hiko-ho-no-ninigi no Mikoto. Her son represented to her that he wished the August Grandchild to be sent down in his stead. Therefore the Heaven-Shining-Deity gave to Ama-tsu-hiko-hiko-ho-no-ninigi no Mikoto the Three Treasures, viz. the curved jewel of Yasaka gem, the eight-hand mirror, and the sword Kusanagi and joined to him as his attendants Ame no Koyane no Mikoto, the first ancestor of the Nakatomi; Futo-dama no Mikoto, the first ancestor of the Imbe; Ame no Uzume no Mikoto, the first ancestor of the Sarume; Ishi-kori-dome no Mikoto, the first ancestor of the mirror makers; and Tamaya no Mikoto, the first ancestor of the jewel makers; in all gods of five *be*.[9] Then she commanded her August Grandchild, saying: "This Reed-plain-1500-autumns-fair-rice-ear Land is the region which my descendants shall be lords of. Do thou, my August Grandchild, proceed thither and govern it. Go! and may prosperity attend thy dynasty, and may it, like Heaven and Earth, endure for ever."

[Adapted from Aston, *Nihongi*, vol. 1, pp. 76–77]

## SHINTO PRAYERS (NORITO)

The *norito* are prayers or mantras uttered on ritual occasions or festivals. Those presented here are mostly preserved in the *Engi-shiki* of 927 C.E., a compilation of the Heian court that reflects the codification of Shinto practice in relation to the unification and bureaucratization of the state but that also records many aspects of Japanese religion long antedating the process of state building.

Most of the *norito* thus preserved are highly formulaic, ritualized, and repetitive. Typically they consist of an invocation of a god or gods; a recollection of the founding of the shrine, which is the site of the ceremony; an identification of the recitant and his status; a list of offerings; a petition for certain benefits or blessings; a promise of recompense to be made in return; and a final salutation. Along with this generalized formality, there is great specificity in regard to particular deities, places, and details of local history and myth. Here, however, the main focus is on the imperial house and its Grand Shrine at Ise.

---

9. *Be*, hereditary guilds or corporations of craftsmen.

## NORITO FOR THE FESTIVAL OF THE SIXTH MONTH

This prayer was offered in the sixth month by a priest of the Nakatomi clan to pray for the well-being of the emperor and imperial house. It is similar to one offered at Ise for the success of the grain-growing season. Although much of it is addressed to the Sovereign Deities in general, the following excerpts focus on a prayer to Amaterasu on behalf of the reigning emperor, spoken of here as the Sovereign Grandchild.

Hear me, all of you assembled priests (*kamu-nushi*) and exorcists (*hafuri*). Thus I speak.

> I humbly speak before you,
> > The Sovereign Deities whose praises are fulfilled as
> > > Heavenly Shrines and Earthly Shrines
> > By the command of the Sovereign Ancestral Gods and Goddesses
> > > Who divinely remain in the High Heavenly Plain. . . .

> I humbly speak with special words in the solemn presence
> > Of the deity Ama-terasu-oho-mi-kami,
> > > Who dwells at Ise:
> The lands of the four quarters, upon which you gaze out,
> > As far as the heavens stand as partitions,
> > As far as the land extends in the distance,
> > As far as the bluish clouds trail across the sky,
> > As far as the white clouds hang down on the horizon:

> On the blue ocean
> > As far as the prows of the ships can reach,
> > Without stopping to dry their oars,
> > On the great ocean the ships teem continuously;
> On the roads by land
> > As far as the horses' hooves can penetrate,
> > The ropes of the [tribute] packages tightly tied,
> > Treading over the rocks and roots of trees,
> > They move over the long roads without pause, continuously;
> The narrow land is made wide,
> > The steep land is made level;
> And you entrust the distant lands [to the Sovereign Grandchild]
> > As if casting myriad ropes about them and drawing them hither.
> [If you vouchsafe to do all this], then in your presence
> > The first fruits of the tribute will be piled up
> > Like a long mountain range,
> > And of the rest [the Sovereign Grandchild] will partake tranquilly.
> Also because you bless the reign of the Sovereign Grandchild

As a long reign, eternal and unmoving,
And prosper it as an abundant reign,
As my Sovereign Ancestral Gods and Goddesses,
Like a cormorant bending my neck low,
I present to you the noble offerings of the Sovereign Grandchild
And fulfill your praises. Thus I speak.

[Adapted from Philippi, *Norito*, pp. 36–39]

### THE GREAT EXORCISM OF THE LAST DAY OF THE SIXTH MONTH

This *norito* is of special interest because it details the sins to be exorcised, some of them in the nature of moral faults but others simply baneful occurrences—misfortunes or things that have just gone wrong and need to be remedied. Notice again that the gods act in concert; also notice the means of purification that they use: washing away, blowing away, and "losing" them (keeping away).

By the command of the Sovereign Ancestral Gods and Goddesses,
Who divinely remain in the High Heavenly Plain,
The eight myriad deities were convoked in a divine convocation.
Consulted in a divine consultation,
And spoke these words of entrusting:
"Our Sovereign Grandchild is to rule
"The Land of the Plentiful Reed Plains of the Fresh Ears of Grain
"Tranquilly as a peaceful land."
Having thus entrusted the land,
They inquired with a divine inquiry
Of the unruly deities in the land,
And expelled them with a divine expulsion. . . .
The lands of the four quarters thus entrusted,
Great Yamato, the Land of the Sun-Seen-on-High,
Was pacified and made a peaceful land;
The palace posts were firmly planted in the bed-rock below,
The cross-beams soaring high towards the High Heavenly plain,
And the noble palace of the Sovereign Grandchild constructed,
Where, as a heavenly shelter, as a sun-shelter, he dwells hidden,
And rules [the kingdom] tranquilly as a peaceful land.

The various sins perpetrated and committed
By the heavenly ever-increasing people to come into existence
In this land which he is to rule tranquilly as a peaceful land.
First, the heavenly sins:
Breaking down the ridges,

Covering up the ditches,
Releasing the irrigation sluices,
Double planting,
Setting up stakes,
Skinning alive, skinning backwards,
Defecation—
Many sins [such as these] are distinguished and called the heavenly sins.
The earthly sins:
Cutting living flesh, cutting dead flesh,
White leprosy, skin excrescences,
The sin of violating one's own mother,
The sin of violating one's own child,
The sin of violating a mother and her child,
The sin of violating a child and her mother,
The sin of transgression with animals,
Woes from creeping insects,
Woes from the deities on high,
Woes from the birds on high,
Killing animals, the sin of witchcraft—
Many sins [such as these] shall appear.

When they thus appear,
By the heavenly shrine usage. . . .
Pronounce the heavenly ritual, the solemn ritual words.
When he thus pronounces them. . . . the heavenly deities
Will hear and receive [these words].

When they thus hear and receive,
Then, beginning with the court of the Sovereign Grandchild,
In the lands of the four quarters under the heavens,
Each and every sin will be gone.
As the gusty wind blows apart the myriad layers of heavenly clouds;
As the morning mist, the evening mist is blown away by the
morning wind, the evening wind; . . . .
As a result of the exorcism and the purification,
There will be no sins left.
They will be taken into the great ocean
By the goddess called Se-ori-tsu-hime,
Who dwells in the rapids of the rapid-running rivers
Which fall surging perpendicular
From the summits of the high mountains and the summits of the low
mountains.

When she thus takes them,
> They will be swallowed with a gulp
>> By the goddess called Haya-aki-tsu-hime. . . .

When she thus swallows them with a gulp,
> The deity called Ibuki-do-nushi,
>> Who dwells in the Ibuki-do,[10]
> Will blow them away with his breath to the land of Hades, the
> under-world.

When she thus loses them,
> Beginning with the many officials serving in the Emperor's court,
> In the four quarters under the heavens,
> Beginning from today,
> Each and every sin will be gone.

[Philippi, *Norito*, pp. 45–48]

---

10. Literally, "breath-blowing entrance."

## Chapter 43

### PRINCE SHŌTOKU AND HIS CONSTITUTION

The reign of Empress Suiko (592–628 C.E.) was one of the most remarkable periods in Japanese history. A crisis had developed in Japan toward the end of the sixth century as a result of the loss of Japanese domains on the Korean peninsula and the defeat of its ally, the kingdom of Paekche. Within the country, there also was serious contention among the powerful clans, partly on account of developments in Korea. The large numbers of Korean refugees who fled to Japan from the turmoil of the peninsula added to the authorities' difficulties. Besides political and economic problems, the arrival of Buddhism some fifty years earlier had caused bitter controversies. Some of the important clans, representing traditional Shinto views, were violently opposed to what they considered a foreign and harmful religion. Above all was the fact that a unified and expanding China under the Sui and a unifying Korea under Silla were now facing a weak and decentralized Japan. Apart from whatever threat to their security that the Japanese felt to lie in the changing situation on the continent, they also, of course, wanted to emulate the superior achievements of the rising Chinese and Korean dynasties.

Accordingly, the Yamato court attempted to enhance its power and prestige in the eyes of foreigners and domestic rivals alike by adopting many features of the superior Chinese civilization and especially its political institutions. The first measures included a reorganization of court ranks and etiquette in accordance with Chinese models, the adoption of the Chinese calendar, the opening of formal diplomatic relations with China, the creation of a system of highways, the erection of many Buddhist temples, and the compilation of official chronicles. Most important, perhaps, was the proclamation of a "constitution"—a set of principles of government in seventeen articles, this number probably having been derived from the combination of eight, the largest yin number, and nine, the largest yang number.

The chief architect of this project was Prince Shōtoku (573–621), who served as "regent" during much of the reign of his aunt, Empress Suiko. The veneration of Prince Shōtoku after his death may be inferred from his name itself, which might be translated as "sage virtue" or "sovereign moral power." Shōtoku, although a member of the imperial family, was also a member of the powerful Soga family, which had been the main support of Buddhism during its early days in Japan, and he always showed a deep interest in the religion and appears to have been well read in Confucian literature. Shōtoku's military achievements were less conspicuous than his civil ones, but at one time he had under his control in Kyushu a considerable army whose function was to have been the reassertion of Japanese influence in Korea.

Although Shōtoku was a devout Buddhist, it was to Confucian models that he turned for guidance when faced with the enormous task of state building. His most crucial problem, the establishment of the court as the central authority, was well met by the teachings of Confucianism as it had developed during the great Han empire. According to these teachings, the universe consisted of three realms, Heaven, Earth, and Man, with man playing a key creative role between the other two. The basis of all authority and order lay in Heaven and was manifested to Earth by the stately progress of the sun, moon, and planets across the firmament. It was the duty of the ruler to make sure that his country was governed in accordance with the pattern established by Heaven. This is the reason for the importance of the calendar in countries dominated by Confucian thought; that is, unless the "time" was correct, the government on Earth would be out of step with the movements of Heaven.

A regular, determined system of government was exactly what was needed in Japan during Shōtoku's time. The statement of the Han Confucian ideal of government itself is found in article III of his constitution: "The lord is Heaven; the vassal, Earth. Heaven overspreads; Earth upbears. When this is so, the four seasons follow their due course, and the powers of Nature develop their efficiency." Hints of Legalist and other non-Confucian ideas may be detected elsewhere. Buddhism recognized no unvarying universal order except the law of constant change and adaptability—in this case, to the Han state system. Thus Buddhism and Confucianism were able to exist side by side in Japan for a thousand years without any serious conflict, but both had to adapt to Japanese ways.

Shōtoku's policy of internal reforms was complemented by his attitude toward China. He realized how much Japan had to learn from China and wanted to cultivate good relations with that country. To that end, Japanese students (though possibly of Chinese or Korean ancestry) were sent to Sui China to study both Confucianism and Buddhism. Shōtoku's own respect for

Chinese learning is obvious from his constitution, which makes no mention of traditional Japanese religious practices or the Japanese principle of a hereditary line of emperors. Many Japanese historians, however, have professed to discover an assertion of equality with China in the letters that Shōtoku sent to the Sui court. One of them, as we saw in the excerpts from the Chinese dynastic histories, bore the superscription "The Child of Heaven in the Land of the Rising Sun to the Child of Heaven in the Land of the Setting Sun," and another, "The Eastern Emperor Greets the Western Emperor." Whether these letters represented serious attempts by Shōtoku to assert Japan's parity with China or merely reflected an ignorance of Chinese protocol and sensibilities is difficult to ascertain. In any case it is recorded that the Sui emperor was highly displeased.

# THE REIGN OF SUIKO AND RULE OF SHŌTOKU

From the many entries in the *Chronicles of Japan* for Suiko's reign, we have selected a few to show how greatly this empress and Prince Shōtoku came to be revered for the accomplishments of their joint rule. Particularly noteworthy is Shōtoku's reputation as a profound student of Buddhism, such that he could expound some of the great sūtras at a time when few Japanese could read any Chinese. In addition to this prince's legendary feats are recorded the building of many temples, the adoption of Chinese court ceremonial in the form of cap ranks, the sending of embassies (including students) to China, and the first project to write an official history of Japan comparable to the great Chinese histories.

### THE EMPRESS SUIKO

The Empress Toyo-mike Kashikiya-hime (592–628)[1] was the second daughter of the Emperor Ame-kuni oshi-hiraki hiro-niha[2] and a younger sister by the same mother of the Emperor Tachibana no toyo-hi.[3] In her childhood she was called the Princess Nukada-be. Her appearance was beautiful, and her conduct was marked by propriety. At the age of eighteen, she was appointed empress consort of the Emperor Nunakura futo-dama-shiki.[4] When she was thirty-four years of age, in the 5th year and the 11th month of the reign of the Emperor Hatsuse-be,[5] the emperor was murdered by the Great Imperial Chieftain Mumako no

---

1. *Toyo*, "abundant"; *mi*, "august"; *ke*, "food"; *Kashikiya*, "cook house"; *hime*, "princess."
2. Kinmei.
3. Yōmei.
4. Bidatsu.
5. Sujun.

Sukune, and the succession to the Dignity being vacant, the ministers besought the empress consort of the Emperor Nunakura futo-dama-shiki, viz. the Princess Nukada-be, to ascend the throne. The empress refused, but the public functionaries urged her in memorials three times until she consented,[6] and they accordingly delivered to her the imperial seal. . . .

1st year [593 C.E.], Summer, 4th month, 10th day. The Imperial Prince Mumayado no Toyotomimi [Shōtoku] was appointed Prince Imperial. He had general control of the government and was entrusted with all the details of administration. He was the second child of the Emperor Tachibana no Toyo-hi. . . . He was able to speak as soon as he was born and was so wise when he grew up that he could attend to the suits of ten men at once and decide them all without error. He knew beforehand what was going to happen. Moreover he learned the Inner Doctrine[7] from a Koryo priest named Hye-cha and studied the Outer Classics[8] with a doctor called Kak-ka. In both of these branches of study he became thoroughly proficient. The emperor his father loved him and made him occupy the Upper Hall South of the Palace. Therefore he was styled the Senior Prince Kami-tsu-miya,[9] Muma-ya-do Toyotomimi. [pp. 121–123]

. . .

11th year [604], 12th month, 5th day. Cap-ranks[10] were first instituted in all twelve grades:

| | | |
|---|---|---|
| Dai-toku: | . . . | greater virtue |
| Shō-toku: | . . . | lesser virtue |
| Dai-nin: | . . . | greater humanity |
| Shō-nin: | . . . | lesser humanity |
| Dai-rei: | . . . | greater decorum |
| Shō-rei: | . . . | lesser decorum |
| Dai-shin: | . . . | greater trust |
| Shō-shin: | . . . | lesser trust |
| Dai-gi: | . . . | greater rightness |
| Shō-gi: | . . . | lesser rightness |
| Dai-chi: | . . . | greater wisdom |
| Shō-chi: | . . . | lesser wisdom |

---

6. It was the Chinese custom to decline such an honor twice and accept it only when offered it a third time.

7. That is, Buddhism.

8. That is, the Chinese Classics. Inner and Outer have here something of the force of our words "sacred" and "secular."

9. Kami-tsu-miya means "upper palace."

10. The Chinese custom, transmitted through Korea, of distinguishing rank by the form and materials of the official cap.

Each cap was made of sarcenet of a special color.[11] They were gathered up on the crown in the shape of a bag and had a border attached. Only on the first day of the year were hair flowers[12] worn.

*In this year also, a Chinese-style calendar was officially adopted for the first time.*[13] [pp. 127–128]

. . .

14th year [606], 5th month, 5th day. The imperial commands were given to Kuratsukuri no Tori, saying: "It being my desire to encourage the Inner Doctrines, I was about to erect a Buddhist temple, and for this purpose sought for relics. Then thy grandfather, Shiba Tattō, offered me relics. Moreover, there were no monks or nuns in the land. Thereupon thy father, Tasuna, for the sake of the Emperor Tachibana no Toyohi, took priestly orders and reverenced the Buddhist law. Also thine aunt Shimame was the first to leave her home and, becoming the forerunner of all nuns, to practice the religion of Shākya. Now, we desired to make a sixteen-foot Buddha and, to that end, sought for a good image of Buddha. Thou didst provide a model which met our wishes. Moreover, when the image of Buddha was completed, it could not be brought into the hall, and none of the workmen could suggest a plan of doing so. They were, therefore, on the point of breaking down the doorway when thou didst manage to admit it without breaking down the doorway. For all these services of thine, we grant thee the rank of Dainin, and we also bestow on thee twenty *chō* of paddy fields in the district of Sakata in the province of Afumi." With the revenue derived from this land, Tori built for the empress the temple of Kongō-ji,[14] now known as the nunnery of Sakata in Minabuchi.

Autumn, 7th month. The empress requested the Prince Imperial to lecture on the Sūtra of Queen Śrīmālā.[15] He completed his explanation of it in three days.

In this year the Prince Imperial also lectured on the Lotus Sūtra[16] in the Palace of Okamoto. The empress was greatly pleased and bestowed on the Prince Imperial one hundred *chō* of paddy fields in the province of Harima. They were therefore added to the temple of Ikaruga. [pp. 134–135]

. . .

---

11. In imitation of China's contemporary Sui dynasty, purple was for officials of the fifth rank and upward. *Nin* was green, *rei* red, *shin* yellow, *gi* white, and *chi* black. Princes and chief ministers wore the cap of the highest rank, namely, *toku*.

12. Hair ornaments of gold or silver in the shape of flowers. Specimens are preserved in the Nara Museum.

13. Compare Reischauer, *Early Japanese History*, A, p. 140.

14. Diamond temple.

15. Skt: Shrīmālādevīsimhanāda; J: Shōmangyō.

16. The Saddharmapuṇḍarīka Sūtra; J: Hokke-kyō.

16th year [608], Autumn, 9th month. At this time there were sent to the land of Tang[17] the students Fukuin [and others], together with student priests Nichibun [and others], in all eight persons.

In this year many persons from Silla came to settle in Japan. [p. 139]

. . .

22nd year [614], 6th month, 13th day. Mitasuki, lord of Inugami, and Yatabe no Miyakko were sent to the land of Great Tang. [p. 145]

. . .

28th year [620]. This year, the Prince Imperial, in concert with the Great Imperial Chieftain Soga, drew up a history of the emperors, a history of the country and the original record of the imperial chieftains, deity chieftains, court chieftains, local chieftains, the one hundred eighty hereditary corporations and the common people.[18] [p. 148]

. . .

29th year [621], Spring, 2nd month, 5th day. In the middle of the night the Imperial Prince Mumayado no Toyotomimi no Mikoto died in the palace of Ikaruga. At this time all the princes and imperial chieftains, as well as the people of the empire, the old, as if they had lost a dear child, had no taste for salt and vinegar[19] in their mouths; the young, as if they had lost a beloved parent, filled the ways with the sound of their lamenting. The farmer ceased from his plow, and the pounding woman laid down her pestle. They all said: "The sun and moon have lost their brightness; heaven and earth have crumbled to ruin: henceforward, in whom shall we put our trust?"

In this month the Prince Imperial Kamitsumiya[20] was buried in the Shinaga Misasagi.

At this time Hye-cha, the Buddhist priest of Koguryō, heard of the death of the Prince Imperial Kamitsumiya and was greatly grieved thereat. He invited the priests and, in honor of the Prince Imperial, gave them a meal and explained the sacred books in person. On this day he prayed, saying: "In the land of Nippon there is a sage, by name the Imperial Prince Kamitsumiya Toyotomimi. Certainly Heaven has freely endowed him with the virtues of a sage.[21] Born in the land of Nippon, he thoroughly possessed the three fundamental principles,[22] he continued the great plans of the former sages. He reverenced the Three Treasures[23] and assisted the people in their distress. He was truly a great sage. And now the Prince Imperial is dead. I, although a foreigner, was in heart

---

17. When this occurred, China was ruled by the Sui dynasty, but at the time of this writing, it was ruled by the Tang dynasty.

18. Almost all of this work was burned during disturbances in 645, and the remainder is no longer extant.

19. To be understood generally of well-flavored food.

20. Prince Shōtoku.

21. According to the Confucian conception.

22. Heaven, Earth, and Man. The meaning is that he was a philosopher.

23. Of Buddhism.

closely united to him. Now what avails it that I alone should survive? I have determined to die on the 5th day of the 2nd month of next year.[24] So shall I meet the Prince Imperial Kamitsumiya in the Pure Land and together with him pass through the metempsychosis of all living creatures." Now when the appointed day came, Hye-cha died, and all the people that day said one to another: "Prince Kamitsumiya is not the only sage, Hye-cha is also a sage." [pp. 148–149]

. . .

30th year [622], Autumn, 7th month. . . . At this time the Buddhist priests E-sai and E-kō, with the physicians E-jitsu and Fuku-in, students of the learning of the Great Tang, arrived in company with . . . others. Now E-jitsu and the rest together made representation to the empress, saying: "Those who have resided in Tang to study have all completed their courses and ought to be sent for. Moreover, the land of Great Tang is an admirable country, whose laws are complete and fixed. Constant communication should be kept up with it." [p. 150]

[Aston, *Nihongi*, vol. 2, pp. 121–150]

## THE SEVENTEEN-ARTICLE CONSTITUTION
## OF PRINCE SHŌTOKU

The influence of Confucian ethical and political doctrines is apparent in this set of basic principles of government, a key document in the process of state building led by Shōtoku. The fact that most of these principles are stated in very general terms reflects the characteristic outlook of Confucianism: the ruler should offer his people moral guidance and instruction, not burden them with detailed laws involving compulsion rather than eliciting cooperation. Therefore this constitution exhorts the people to lay aside partisan differences and accept imperial rule in order to achieve social harmony. Ministers and officials are urged to be diligent and considerate, prompt and just in the settlement of complaints or charges, careful in the selection of assistants and wary of flatterers, conscientious in the performance of their duties while not overreaching their authority, and ever mindful of the desires of the people so that public good is put above private interest. Articles XII and XV alone refer to the imperial government's specific functions or prerogatives: the power to raise taxes and the seasons in which forced labor is to be exacted, likewise an aspect of the power to tax. Both of these represent practical measures indispensable to the establishment of the imperial authority over a hitherto uncentralized society, no doubt with a view to achieving the uniformity and centralization that the Chinese empire exemplified.

12th year [604], Summer, 4th month, 3rd day. The Prince Imperial in person prepared for the first time laws. There were seventeen clauses, as follows:

---

24. The anniversary of the prince's death.

I. Harmony is to be valued,[25] and contentiousness avoided. All men are inclined to partisanship and few are truly discerning. Hence there are some who disobey their lords and fathers or who maintain feuds with the neighboring villages. But when those above are harmonious and those below are conciliatory and there is concord in the discussion of all matters, the disposition of affairs comes about naturally. Then what is there that cannot be accomplished?

II. Sincerely reverence the Three Treasures. The Buddha, the Law, and the religious orders are the final refuge of all beings and the supreme objects of reverence in all countries. It is a law honored by all, no matter what the age or who the person. Few men are utterly bad; with instruction they can follow it. But if they do not betake themselves to the Three Treasures, how can their crookedness be made straight?

III. When you receive the imperial commands, fail not scrupulously to obey them. The lord is Heaven, the vassal is Earth. Heaven overspreads, and Earth upbears. When this is so, the four seasons follow their due course, and the powers of Nature obtain their efficacy. If the Earth attempted to overspread, Heaven would simply fall in ruin. Therefore is it that when the lord speaks, the vassal listens; when the superior acts, the inferior yields compliance. Consequently when you receive the imperial commands, fail not to carry them out scrupulously. Let there be a want of care in this matter, and ruin is the natural consequence.

IV. The ministers and functionaries should make ritual decorum their leading principle, for the leading principle in governing the people consists in ritual decorum. If the superiors do not behave with decorum, the inferiors are disorderly; if inferiors are wanting in proper behavior, there must necessarily be offenses. Therefore it is that when lord and vassal behave with decorum, the distinctions of rank are not confused; when the people behave with decorum, the governance of the state proceeds of itself.

V. Ceasing from gluttony and abandoning covetous desires, deal impartially with the suits which are submitted to you. Of complaints brought by the people, there are a thousand in one day. If in one day there are so many, how many will there be in a series of years? If the man who is to decide suits at law makes gain his ordinary motive and hears cases with a view to receiving bribes, then will the suits of the rich man be like a stone flung into water,[26] while the plaints of the poor will resemble water cast upon a stone. Under these circumstances the poor man will not know whither to betake himself. Here too there is deficiency in the duty of the minister.

VI. Chastise that which is evil and encourage that which is good. This was the excellent rule of antiquity. Conceal not, therefore, the good qualities of others, and fail not to correct that which is wrong when you see it. Flatterers and

---

25. From the *Analects* of Confucius, 1:12.
26. That is, they meet with no resistance.

deceivers are a sharp weapon for the overthrow of the state, and a pointed sword for the destruction of the people. Sycophants are also fond, when they meet, of dilating to their superiors on the errors of their inferiors; to their inferiors, they censure the faults of their superiors. Men of this kind are all wanting in fidelity to their lord, and in benevolence towards the people. From such an origin great civil disturbances arise.

VII. Let every man have his own charge, and let not the spheres of duty be confused. When wise men are entrusted with office, the sound of praise arises. If unprincipled men hold office, disasters and tumults multiply. In this world, few are born with knowledge; wisdom is the product of earnest meditation. In all things, whether great or small, find the right man, and they will surely be well managed; on all occasions, be they urgent or the reverse, meet but with a wise man, and they will of themselves be amenable. In this way will the state be lasting and the temples of the Earth and of grain will be free from danger. Therefore did the wise sovereigns of antiquity seek the man to fill the office, and not the office for the sake of the man.

VIII. Let the ministers and functionaries attend the court early in the morning, and retire late. The business of the state does not admit of remissness, and the whole day is hardly enough for its accomplishment. If, therefore, the attendance at court is late, emergencies cannot be met; if officials retire soon, the work cannot be completed.

IX. Trustworthiness is the foundation of right. In everything let there be trustworthiness, for in this there surely consists the good and the bad, success and failure. If the lord and the vassal trust one another, what is there which cannot be accomplished? If the lord and the vassal do not trust one another, everything without exception ends in failure.

X. Let us cease from wrath, and refrain from angry looks. Nor let us be resentful when others differ from us. For all men have hearts, and each heart has its own leanings. Their right is our wrong, and our right is their wrong. We are not unquestionably sages, nor are they unquestionably fools. Both of us are simply ordinary men. How can any one lay down a rule by which to distinguish right from wrong? For we are all, one with another, wise and foolish, like a ring which has no end. Therefore, although others give way to anger, let us on the contrary dread our own faults, and though we alone may be in the right, let us follow the multitude and act like them.

XI. Give clear appreciation to merit and demerit, and deal out to each its sure reward or punishment. In these days, reward does not attend upon merit, nor punishment upon crime. Ye high functionaries who have charge of public affairs, let it be your task to make clear rewards and punishments.

XII. Let not the provincial authorities or the Kuni no Miyatsuko[27] levy exaction on the people. In a country there are not two lords; the people have not

---

27. The Kuni no Miyatsuko were the old local nobles whose power was at this time giving way to that of the central government.

two masters. The sovereign is the master of the people of the whole country. The officials to whom he gives charge are all his vassals. How can they, as well as the government, presume to levy taxes on the people?

XIII. Let all persons entrusted with office attend equally to their functions. Owing to their illness or to their being sent on missions, their work may sometimes be neglected. But whenever they become able to attend to business, let them be as accommodating as if they had had cognizance of it from before and not hinder public affairs on the score of their not having had to do with them.

XIV. Ye ministers and functionaries! Be not envious. For if we envy others, they in turn will envy us. The evils of envy know no limit. If others excel us in intelligence, it gives us no pleasure; if they surpass us in ability, we are envious. Therefore it is not until after a lapse of five hundred years that we at last meet with a wise man, and even in a thousand years we hardly welcome one sage. But if we do not find wise men and sages, wherewithal shall the country be governed?

XV. To turn away from that which is private, and to set our faces towards that which is public—this is the path of a minister. Now if a man is influenced by private motives, he will assuredly fail to act harmoniously with others. If he fails to act harmoniously with others, he will assuredly sacrifice the public interest to his private feelings. When resentment arises, it interferes with order, and is subversive of law. Therefore in the first clause it was said that superiors and inferiors should agree together. The purport is the same as this.

XVI. Let the people be employed [in forced labor] at seasonable times. This is an ancient and excellent rule. Let them be employed, therefore, in the winter months, when they are at leisure. But from Spring to Autumn, when they are engaged in agriculture or with the mulberry trees, the people should not be so employed. For if they do not attend to agriculture, what will they have to eat? If they do not attend to the mulberry trees, what will they do for clothing?

XVII. Matters should not be decided by one person alone. They should be discussed with many others. In small matters, of less consequence, many others need not be consulted. It is only in considering weighty matters, where there is a suspicion that they might miscarry, that many others should be involved in debate and discussion so as to arrive at a reasonable conclusion.

[Ienaga, *Shōtoku taishi shū*, NST, 2:128–133; trans. adapted from Aston, *Nihongi*, vol. 2, pp. 128–133; dB]

Questions have long been asked about the actual authorship and dating of this document, but even if not everything in the Seventeen Articles is by Shōtoku's own hand, few scholars have doubted that the contents are generally representative of his thinking. Since the text appears in the *Nihon shoki* (720 C.E.), it must in any case reflect views current in the early state-building period, and as recorded in that early chronicle, it became canonical as one of the founding myths of

Japan. More than that, however, there are signs of a singular intelligence at work in its composition.[28]

Besides their importance as a political document, Shōtoku's Seventeen Articles are significant as a remarkable synthesis of Confucian and Buddhist thought with native Japanese tradition. In the first article, the Confucian ideal of social harmony is set forth, and in the seventh article, the Confucian idea of having the "right man" or "wise man" (the sage) is said to be indispensable to attaining this ideal. However, in the tenth article, serious doubts are raised about the possibility of knowing right from wrong, no doubt reflecting Shōtoku's own awareness of Buddhist skepticism in this regard, as taught by the Emptiness (Three Treatise) school. Moreover in Article XIV, the extreme difficulty of finding a wise man—and, even more, the rarity of a sage—is emphasized. How then, without them, can one hope to achieve "harmony"? The answer is found in the concluding article: not by relying on one person to decide things, but by engaging in general consultation. If we recall how often in early myths the gods themselves met in council and consulted together, we can see how Shōtoku's reference to concord in the discussion of affairs (in the first article) and consultation (in the last) evokes a native tradition of consensus formation that is characteristic also of the Japanese inclination, down to the present, for informal, consensual decision-making processes as a way of handling affairs. Note also that the Japanese emperor or empress is nowhere directly cited. He or she remains on a mystical plane or behind the scenes, symbolizing an ultimate authority whose mysterious power is in proportion to its not being directly used but only ritually exercised. Suiko reigns while Shōtoku rules and lays down the law.

In Shōtoku's case, we know that his promotion of constitutional law (kenpō) was only one aspect of an age marked by its promotion of spiritual as well as secular law. Whether or not Shōtoku is accepted as the author of all three of the sūtra commentaries attributed to him, the Lotus, Vimalakīrti, and Shrīmālā Sūtras are known to have traveled together through China and Korea and to have achieved great prominence in Japan at this time. The Lotus itself, as its title "The Lotus of the Wondrous Law" suggests, preached a universal law on a spiritual plane, which could be easily reconciled, through the principle of Emptiness and adaptive means, to the Chinese secular law and institutions that furnished the main content of the Seventeen Articles. Indeed, it was the principle of accommodation that enabled these two conceptions of law, religious and

---

28. Konishi, *A History of Japanese Literature*, vol. 1, p. 311, concludes his weighing of the evidence, pro and con, with: "The Constitution may well be Shōtoku's work, but Korean immigrant intellectuals in his entourage must have also made major contributions. I would like to think that the solicitation of cooperation from these intellects, and the consolidation of a composition of such speculative force, could only have been effected if Prince Shōtoku himself was the author of the work." In any case, says Konishi, "we may conclude that the extant Constitution remains essentially a work of Suiko Tennō's time."

secular, to coexist in seventh-century Japan. The religious conception, with its lofty spiritual aspiration, took wings in the pagodas of temples like Shōtoku's own Hōryūji, "Temple of the Ascendancy of the Law," and numerous other temple structures that rose over the Yamato plain with the Law of Buddhism written into their names: Hōkōji, Hōrinji, Hokkiji, Hokkeji, and so on. In due time, alongside these embodiments of the religious law came the successive codifications of the secular law that gave more precise definition, at least in writing, to Shōtoku's "exemplary law" (*kenpō*).

## THE LOTUS SŪTRA

The Lotus Sūtra, the chief text of the Buddhism sponsored by Shōtoku, was also one of the most influential and popular sūtras among Mahāyāna Buddhists in East Asia. Although its authorship and date are obscure, the Lotus was first translated from Sanskrit into Chinese during the third century C.E. In vivid language arousing the imagination, it relates what it claims to be the most profound teaching of Shākyamuni. More than any other sūtra, the Lotus is revered not only for its profound message but also because the text itself is sacred, with each Chinese character regarded as the embodiment of the Buddha. Nichiren Buddhists, who subsequently identified the Lotus Sūtra as their chief text, have treated the book itself as an object of worship, just as buddhas and bodhisattvas are worshiped by others.

Chinese and Japanese commentators have traditionally summarized the message of the Lotus Sūtra in three lessons. The first is that Shākyamuni was both a mortal being and a manifestation of the Eternal Buddha. As such, the questions of his demise are settled decisively in favor of his being present forever. That is, the Buddha does not die. Just as the Buddha's presence is extended throughout time, so the salvation of the Buddha extends to all beings. The second lesson is that salvation is universal and includes even women, who were regarded in other sūtras as being incapable of becoming buddhas. Third, the Lotus Sūtra encompasses all approaches to salvation in the One Vehicle, which is sometimes equated with Mahāyāna Buddhism; at other times the One Vehicle is limited to the Lotus Sūtra itself. Together these three lessons comprise a message that is eternal, universal, and comprehensive.

## Preaching the One Great Vehicle [*Mahāyāna*]

At that time the World-Honored One calmly arose from his samādhi and addressed Shāriputra, saying: "The wisdom of the Buddhas is infinitely profound and immeasurable. The door to this wisdom is difficult to understand and difficult to enter. . . .

Shāriputra, ever since I attained Buddhahood I have through various causes and similes widely expounded my teachings and have used countless expedient means to guide living beings and cause them to renounce their attachments.

Why is this? Because the Thus-Come One is fully possessed of both expedient means and the perfection of wisdom. . . .

Shāriputra, to sum it up: the Buddha has fully realized the Law that is limitless, boundless, never attained before. . . .

Shāriputra, the Buddhas preach the Law in accordance with what is appropriate, but the meaning is difficult to understand. Why is this? Because we employ countless expedient means, discussing causes and conditions and using words of simile and parable to expound the teachings. This Law is not something that can be understood through pondering or analysis. Only those who are Buddhas can understand it. . . .

Shāriputra, I know that living beings have various desires, attachments that are deeply implanted in their minds. Taking cognizance of this basic nature of theirs, I will therefore use various causes and conditions, words of simile and parable, and the power of expedient means and expound the Law for them. Shāriputra, I do this so that all of them may attain the one Buddha vehicle and wisdom embracing all species." . . .

[Adapted from Watson, *The Lotus Sūtra*, pp. 23–31]

### THE VIMALAKĪRTI SŪTRA (*YUIMA-KYŌ*)

The Vimalakīrti Sūtra eulogizes Buddha's lay disciple, Vimalakīrti, who lives as a householder and yet achieves a wisdom unmatched even by those following a monastic discipline. At the Japanese court, this ideal of the Buddhist layman found favor among men active in state affairs, and later under Fujiwara auspices, a date was reserved on the court calendar for reading and expounding on this sūtra. An extant commentary on the Vimalakīrti text has been traditionally ascribed to Prince Shōtoku. Although some modern scholarship has questioned this attribution, there can be little doubt that the sūtra itself and its teaching of Emptiness and Expedient Means were influential in seventh-century Japan.

At the time in the great city of Vaishali there was a rich man named Vimalakīrti. Already in the past he had offered alms to immeasurable numbers of Buddhas, had deeply planted the roots of goodness and had grasped the truth of birthlessness. Unhindered in his eloquence, able to disport himself with transcendental powers, he commanded full retention of the teachings and had attained the state of fearlessness. He had overcome the torments and ill will of the devil and entered deeply into the doctrine of the Law, proficient in the perfection of wisdom and a master in the employing of expedient means. He had successfully fulfilled his great vow and could clearly discern how the minds of others were tending. Moreover, he could distinguish whether their capacities were keen or obtuse. His mind was cleansed and purified through long practice of the Buddha Way, firm in its grasp of the Great Vehicle, and all his actions were well thought and planned. He maintained the dignity and authority of a Buddha, and his mind was vast as the sea. All the Buddhas sighed with admiration, and he commanded the respect of the disciples, of Indra, Brahma and the Four Heavenly Kings.

Desiring to save others, he employed the excellent expedient of residing in Vaishali. His immeasurable riches he used to relieve the poor, his faultless observation of the precepts served as a reproach to those who would violate prohibitions. Through his restraint and forbearance he warned others against rage and anger, and his great assiduousness discouraged all thought of sloth and indolence. Concentrating his single mind in quiet meditation, he suppressed disordered thoughts; through firm and unwavering wisdom he overcame all that was not wise. . . .

He frequented the busy crossroads in order to bring benefit to others, entered the government offices and courts of law so as to aid and rescue all those he could. He visited the places of debate in order to guide others to the Great Vehicle, visited the schools and study halls to further the instruction of the pupils. He entered houses of ill fame to teach the folly of fleshly desire, entered wine shops in order to encourage those with a will to quit them. . . .

The common people honored him as first among them because he helped them to gain wealth and power. The Brahma deities honored him as first among them because he revealed the superiority of wisdom. The Indras honored him as first among them because he demonstrated the truth of impermanence. The Four Heavenly Kings, guardians of the world, honored him as foremost because he guarded all living beings.

In this way the rich man Vimalakīrti employed immeasurable numbers of expedient means in order to bring benefit to others.

Using these expedient means, he made it appear that his body had fallen prey to illness. Because of his illness, the king of the country, the great ministers, rich men, lay believers and Brahmans, as well as the princes and lesser officials, numbering countless thousands, all went to see him and inquire about his illness.

Vimalakīrti then used this bodily illness to expound the Law to them in broad terms: "Good people, this body is impermanent, without durability, without strength, without firmness, a thing that decays in a moment, not to be relied on. It suffers, it is tormented, a meeting place of manifold ills.

"Good people, no person of enlightened wisdom could depend on a thing like this body. This body is like a cluster of foam, nothing you can grasp or handle. This body is like a bubble that cannot continue for long. This body is like a flame born of longing and desire. This body is like the plantain that has no firmness in its trunk. This body is like a phantom, the product of error and confusion. This body is like a shadow, appearing through karma causes. This body is like an echo, tied to causes and conditions. This body is like a drifting cloud, changing and vanishing in an instant. This body is like lightning, barely lasting from moment to moment.

"This body is like earth that has no subjective being. This body is like fire, devoid of ego. This body is like wind that has no set life span. This body is like water, devoid of individuality. . . .

This body is impure, crammed with defilement and evil. This body is empty and unreal; though for a time you may bathe and cleanse, clothe and feed it, in the end it must crumble and fade. This body is plague-ridden, beset by a hundred and one ills and anxieties. This body is like the abandoned well on the hillside, old age pressing in on it. This body has no fixity, but is destined for certain death. This body is like poisonous snakes, vengeful bandits or an empty village, a mere coming together of components, realms and sense-fields.

"Good people, a thing like this is irksome and hateful and therefore you should seek the Buddha body. Why? Because the Buddha is the Dharma body. It is born from immeasurable merits and wisdom. It is born from precepts, meditation, wisdom, emancipation and the insight of emancipation. It is born from pity, compassion, joy and indifference. . . .

The body of the Thus-Come One is born of immeasurable numbers of pure and spotless things such as these.

"Good people, if you wish to gain the Buddha body and do away with the ills that afflict all living beings, then you must set your minds on attaining supreme perfect enlightenment."

In this manner the rich man Vimalakīrti used the occasion to preach the Law to those who came to inquire about his illness. As a result, numberless thousands of persons were all moved to set their minds on the attainment of supreme perfect enlightenment. [pp. 32–36]


## Entering the Gate of Nondualism

In the following passage, the sūtra deals with the question of how one enters "the gate of nondualism," that is, the entrance to "supreme perfect enlightenment."

At the time Vimalakīrti said to the various bodhisattvas, "Sirs, how does the bodhisattva go about entering the gate of nondualism? Let each explain as he understands it."

One of the bodhisattvas in the assembly, whose name was Dharma Freedom, spoke these words: "Sirs, birth and extinction form a dualism. But since all dharmas are not born to begin with, they must now be without extinction. By grasping and learning to accept this truth of birthlessness, one may enter the gate of nondualism." . . . .

The bodhisattva Delight in Truth said, "The true and the not true form a dualism. But one who sees truly cannot even see the true, so how can he see the untrue? Why? Because they cannot be seen by the physical eye; only the eye of wisdom can see them. But for this eye of wisdom there is no seeing and no not seeing. In this way one may enter the gate of nondualism."

When the various bodhisattvas had finished one by one giving their explanations, they asked Manjushri, "How then does the bodhisattva enter the gate of nondualism?"

Manjushri replied, "To my way of thinking, all dharmas are without words, without explanations, without purport, without cognition, removed from all questions and answers. In this way one may enter the gate of nondualism."

At that time Vimalakīrti remained silent and did not speak a word.

Manjushri sighed and said, "Excellent, excellent! Not a word, not a syllable; this truly is to enter the gate of nondualism."

[Adapted from Watson, *The Vimalakirti Sūtra*, pp. 32–36, 104, 110–111]

## Chapter 44

### CHINESE THOUGHT AND INSTITUTIONS
### IN EARLY JAPAN

At this point a chapter devoted especially to Chinese influences in early Japan may seem needless, for in every topic discussed so far this influence has been quite conspicuous. As the Yamato people consolidated their position in central Japan and their rulers attempted to win undisputed supremacy over other clans of the confederacy, it was to the Chinese example that they turned more and more for political guidance and cultural direction. In Prince Shōtoku we have already seen the embodiment of this tendency to adopt and adapt all that China might contribute to the unification and pacification of a restless, turbulent people.

The most striking examples of this trend are to be found in the series of imperial edicts issued during the period of Great Reform (Taika), which began in 645. Proceeding from the theory enunciated in Shōtoku's constitution that "in a country there are not two lords; the people have not two masters," these reforms asserted the doctrine that "under the heavens there is no land which is not the king's land. Among holders of land there is none who is not the king's vassal." On this ground an ambitious program was launched to curb the powers of the clan leaders, who had frequently jeopardized the throne itself in their struggles for power. In place of the old political organization based on clan units was to be the systematic territorial administration of the Chinese, with local governors designated by the court, centrally directed and executing a uniform law to represent the paramount authority of the emperor. In keeping with this, the central administration itself was overhauled so as to provide a close replica of the great Tang empire's vast, symmetrical bureaucracy. A new aristocracy was thereby created of those who held office and court rank conferred by the throne. Thus the old and complex class structure, along with the clan hierarchy based on birth and blood, was to be replaced by a simpler division of society into two main classes, the rulers and the common people, characteristic of imperial China.

The reformers did not limit their actions to the political sphere. Indeed, implicit in the erection of this state machinery was the need for economic changes that would channel the wealth of the country toward the center of political power. Thus it was recognized from the first that the Tang tax system was indispensable to the functioning of the Tang-type administration. The Tang tax system, moreover, presupposed a system of land nationalization and redistribution such as that instituted during the early years of that dynasty by the famous monarch Taizong. Accordingly, the Japanese reformers attempted to abolish "private" property, nationalize the land, redistribute it on the basis of family size, and adopt the Chinese system of triple taxation on land, labor, and produce. In fact, so meticulously was the Chinese example followed that land and tax registers for this period, preserved in the imperial repository at Nara, are almost identical in form and terminology to contemporary Chinese registers discovered at the western outpost of the Chinese empire, Dunhuang. Furthermore, by their assertion of the imperial right to universal labor and military service, the reformers went far toward achieving for the ruling house the control over all the elements of power characteristic of the greatest Chinese dynasties. But with this wholesale imitation of China came likewise the chronic difficulties experienced by these dynasties, which tended to undermine the new state almost from the start.

In these early years, however, China exerted an influence more profound and lasting than the political changes inaugurated in the seventh century. This was the vast system of coordinated knowledge and belief of which the Chinese imperial structure was indeed the most imposing terrestrial symbol but that stretched out into realms of thought and action both transcending and penetrating the immediate political order. Like the imperial pattern itself, this far-reaching syncretism was a product of the Han dynasties (202 B.C.E.–220 C.E.), in which parallel tendencies unified and organized both the political and intellectual lives of China. In the realm of thought, this development was most apparent in the adoption of Confucianism as the state creed and cult, expounded in the imperial university, incorporated into the civil service examinations, and systematized by scholars working for the throne who tried to arrive at a definitive version of the Confucian classics.

The Confucianism of the Han dynasties, introduced to Japan at the latest by the sixth and seventh centuries C.E., represented more than the essential ethical teachings of Confucius and his early followers. Although these teachings were there, at the base of the new intellectual edifice, they had become overlaid and, to some extent, obscured by the great weight of correlative learning and doctrine that had since accumulated. This was not necessarily because many popular beliefs sought to gain respectability by associating with doctrines having the sanction of tradition and the state. Rather, Confucianism itself had to battle with other potent philosophies for official favor, and in the process its fundamental rationalism penetrated realms of thought that it had previously not explored fully. By so doing, it absorbed much from other traditions, such as the Daoist and Five Phases or Elements (or yin-yang) schools, to fill out its own lean frame.

Modern minds may find a great deal here that seems to have been poorly digested. Yet we must recognize that in terms of the knowledge then available, this synthesis is remarkable for its order and coherence, and in the hands of an articulate spokesman such as Dong Zhongshu, it served well to reinforce some of the fundamental political doctrines of the Confucian school, persuading absolute monarchs to use their power wisely and with restraint. At the heart of all such Confucian speculation is the doctrine, which Confucianism shared with other influential schools of thought, that the universe is a harmonious whole in which humankind and nature constantly interact with each other in all aspects of life. From this doctrine it was concluded that human actions, particularly those of rulers, affect the natural order, which is sensitive above all to the ethical quality of their acts. If people fail to fulfill their proper functions, nature will act or operate to restore the total balance or harmony. For this reason, it was believed that natural occurrences, especially spectacular aberrations, would reveal—when properly interpreted—the extent to which a person or ruler had lapsed from his duty or his proper course of conduct.

The importance in China of divination and other early arts or sciences is evident when we consider that the earliest Chinese writing now preserved is found on oracle bones, recording the questions and responses that the diviners obtained by scrutinizing the cracks made when the bones were heated. In later times we find that astrologers were called "historians" (*shi*) and combined the functions of both diviners and compilers of records. Their influence is apparent in the Chinese view of history as the expression of the processes and decrees of Heaven. For the early Chinese, a noteworthy event was not merely a fact to be recorded—it was to be interpreted as either a bad omen or a sign of Heaven's approval. Eclipses and comets were evident attempts of Heaven to express its desires, but the sight of an unusually shaped cloud was also sometimes considered important enough to warrant changing the name by which a part of an emperor's reign was known. The close connection between the diviner and the historian is revealed in the statement in the preface to the *True Records of Three Japanese Reigns* (901 C.E.), in which the compilers declare their intent of fully recording the "auspicious signs with which Heaven favors the Lord of Men and the portents with which Heaven admonishes the Lord of Men." The application of this method is already fully evident in such an early history as the *Chronicles of Japan* (*Nihongi*).

Behind such a statement lay the belief in the necessary correspondences between the worlds of Heaven and earth. When the astronomers reported that the heavenly bodies had reached their spring positions, the rites suitable to spring had to be performed on earth. Or if a lucky cloud indicated that some favorable change had been decreed by Heaven, a corresponding change, such as in the reign name, had to be made on earth. A failure to observe the changes in Heaven might lead to disasters on earth. If, for example, a rite suitable to winter were performed in the spring because of a faulty calendar, the crops would be destroyed in the bud by wintry weather. The proper rites, on the other hand, could ensure such blessings as seasonal rainfall. The Han philosopher Dong Zhongshu described various ways of making sure that rain fell when it was needed; one of them was to have the government employees and other subjects cohabit with their wives on a day chosen by yin-yang methods.

Different sciences were evolved to deal with events in the Three Realms of Heaven, Earth, and Humankind. These were, respectively, astrology, geomancy, and the art of "avoiding calamities." Astrology enabled people to discover what the fate of a kingdom or an individual was to be. The twelve divisions of the heavens (based on the twelve-year cycle of the planet Jupiter) had corresponding divisions on earth, so when, for example, Jupiter was in the division of the heavens "controlling" a particular country, that country was safe from invasion. By learning from the stars what Heaven decreed, one could predict events on earth. Conversely, by means of geomancy and the art of "avoiding calamities," people could cooperate with Heaven if this was in their interest. Thus, when the site of Kyoto was chosen because it possessed the "proper" number of rivers and mountains, it represented an attempt to secure by means of geomancy the most auspicious surroundings for the new capital. Heaven—understood here as Nature—had designed such a place for a capital, and humans could benefit by it. The art of "avoiding calamities" may have been especially congenial to the Japanese because, as earlier recorded in the Chinese dynastic histories, they favored the arts of prognostication.

In 602 C.E., the Korean monk Kwallŭk brought to Japan some books on geomancy and "avoiding calamities." Several members of the court were selected to study with Kwallŭk, and some of the extraordinary changes that took place in the next few years may be attributed to the influence of the new learning. In 604, a year whose astrological signs marked it for "avoiding calamities" as a "revolutionary year," Prince Shōtoku's Seventeen-Article Constitution was proclaimed. In the same year also appeared the first Japanese calendar, an event of immense importance to both the writing of history and the development of the rites of state.

Perhaps the chief purpose of the compilation of the *Records of Ancient Matters* (*Kojiki*) was to establish the legitimacy of the claim of Emperor Tenmu and his descendants to the throne. This was done in terms of both genealogy and virtue or accomplishment. For instance, it was declared of Tenmu that, among other things, "he held the mean between the Two Essences [yin and yang], and regulated the order of the Five Phases." We can see, then, how intimately yin-yang thinking was connected with early Japanese historiography.

Mention of the five phases brings us to the center of the art of "avoiding calamities." An elaborate system of correspondences among the planets, the elements, the directions, the seasons, the signs of the zodiac, and various other categories was created, as follows:

| Planet | Element | Direction | Season | Signs of the Zodiac |
|--------|---------|-----------|--------|---------------------|
| Jupiter | wood | east | spring | tiger, hare |
| Mars | fire | south | summer | serpent, horse |
| Saturn | earth | center | solstices[1] | dog, ox, dragon, sheep |
| Venus | metal | west | autumn | monkey, cock |
| Mercury | water | north | winter | boar, rat |

According to the theory of the five phases or elements, the two elements bordering any particular element were beneficial to it, whereas the two separated elements were harmful. Thus both wood and earth were beneficial to fire, but metal and water were harmful. Likewise, a person born under the sign of Mars would make a suitable spouse for one born under Jupiter and Saturn, but not for one born under Venus or Mercury. It was possible to "avoid calamity" by preventing a marriage or partnership between people born under conflicting elements.

In Japan, life came to be ruled largely by such beliefs. When we read novels of the Heian period (794–1186), we cannot help but notice the frequent mention of "unlucky directions" or "unlucky days." Depending on the planet governing a person, different directions were auspicious or inauspicious on a certain day. Diaries giving the astrological conditions of each day of the year were popular with the great men of the state, who made their plans according to the prevailing heavenly influences. To advise the government on all matters of yin-yang lore, a department of yin-yang (Onyōryō) was established as early as 675 C.E., and detailed provisions for its organization were given in the Taihō Code of 701–702.

The yin-yang attempt to explain both the physical and spiritual phenomena of the universe in terms of the five phases was increasingly successful and met little serious opposition. Some Buddhists appear to have been hostile at first to fortune-telling on the basis of the five phases but later attempted to do much the same with phases of their own choosing. By and large, however, the yin-yang teachings were widely accepted and remained unchallenged until modern times. Up to 1861, for example, the reign names continued to change regularly when one of the "revolutionary years" turned up in the cycle. The yin-yang system has been used on many occasions even in recent decades; lucky days are still chosen by yin-yang methods; and the zodiacal sign under which a person was born was rarely ignored when arranging marriages.

---

1. Summer and winter intervals between the seasons.

Yin-yang was not the only variety of Chinese thought familiar to the Japanese court of the Nara and Heian periods. The classics of Confucianism and Daoism were relatively well known, as is evinced by the poetry of the *Manyōshū*, an anthology completed in the eighth century. Here we find frequent echoes of Chinese thought in a form indicating their familiarity even at that early date. Outright imitations of Chinese thought and literature can be found in the *Kaifūsō*, a collection of poetry written in Chinese dating from 751 C.E. It was not only in literary works that Japanese writers showed their indebtedness to Chinese style and sentiments. When, for example, the commentary on the legal code of 833 C.E. was submitted to the throne, it was accompanied by a memorial that is a tissue of allusions to Chinese literature. Thus, Japan borrowed the legal institutions of the Tang dynasty not only for its own purposes but also for the flowery phraseology in which the Chinese were accustomed to give their reasons for the existence of laws. The use of such language undoubtedly had a great influence on the development of thought in Japan, and specimens of it can be found in innumerable prefaces and memorials.

The lasting remains of the introduction of Chinese thought to early Japan are apparent in every field, but especially in the concept of imperial rule, sometimes called Tennōism. In modern times, Tennōism has been identified with the claims made for the divine ancestry of the imperial house, its unbroken succession from the Sun Goddess, and the commission of the Divine Grandson's imperial descendants to rule the land. The formulation of this idea and the title itself, however, reflect a convergence of the state-building process on the Chinese model (what might be called Han imperial absolutism) and its fusion of Chinese religious and cosmological notions with native Japanese traditions.

We mentioned earlier that when the Japanese addressed the Sui court, speaking for the "Child of Heaven in the Land of the Rising Sun" to "the Child of Heaven in the Land of the Setting Sun," the Chinese court was incensed by Japan's temerity in making this claim to parity, if not superiority. Diplomatic niceties aside, the Japanese themselves could have had some difficulty with the Chinese concept of the child or son of Heaven to which attached the Confucian idea that the emperor, out of filial respect, should conform to Heaven's mandate, that is, conduct his rule in accordance with the moral, rational, and generally human principles identified with Heaven and its mandate. Chinese emperors were thus theoretically subject to the criteria of merit, and rulers or dynasties could forfeit the mandate to rule if they did not live up to them. Japanese rule (and Japanese social life generally), however, was governed by the hereditary principle, not the merit principle, and those who represented the Japanese dynasty must have been somewhat uneasy with the language of the "Child of Heaven" and its implied basis of legitimacy in moral accountability.

For their purposes, a more convenient non-Confucian Chinese term existed in the expression (Ch: *tien-huang*, J: *tennō*) "Heavenly Emperor," which in Chinese religious cosmology (often thought of as Daoist) was identified with the North Star as patron deity of the northern quarter of the imperial capital.

Moreover, since the Imperial Palace (both in China and, by now, in Nara-period Japan) was located in the northern quarter according to this cosmological scheme, imperial rule was considered to be under the aegis of this god, which conveniently bore no moral connotations.

The final step in this process linked the *tennō* concept with the claim of the imperial house to be descended from the Sun Goddess. She was not, however, first among the gods in time, generation, or seniority. As we have seen, some of the early accounts referred to her diminutively as the Sun Princess or Sun Maiden (Ōhirume), and she was the younger sister of Susa no wo. But by referring to her as Amaterasu no Ōmikami (Great Heaven Shining Deity, her name as written in Chinese characters, *tien* or *ten* for "Ama"), the authority of Heaven as expressed by a prime Japanese religious symbol, the sun, could be invoked to legitimize imperial rule without incurring any responsibility for answering to moral, rational criteria. Such Confucian qualities might be attributed to individual rulers personally without subjecting the imperial line itself to any such accountability.

The successive steps taken toward establishing a strong central government reflect Japanese adherence to the Chinese concept of the sovereign as the sole possessor of Heaven's sanction. Prince Shōtoku's constitution, the Taika reforms, and the adoption of Chinese legal and bureaucratic institutions all were intended to strengthen the emperor's claim to be a true polar star about whom the lesser celestial luminaries turned. Symbolic of this trend is the choice of posthumous titles for the two great rulers of the late seventh century, Tenchi (or Tenji) (Heavenly Wisdom) and Tenmu (Heavenly Might).

The establishment of a more permanent capital at Nara in 710 also was necessary for the prestige of the emperor in the eyes of his people as well as in those of such Chinese or Korean emissaries as might visit the country. The capitals at Nara and then Kyoto were built in imitation of Changan, closely following yin-yang theories. Kyoto was divided by eight streets and nine avenues. The palace, situated in the north in accordance with yin-yang, was surrounded by ninefold walls. The emperor was served by a bureaucracy organized into nine departments of state, with eight ranks of officials. And as if to protect the capital from baleful influences coming from the northeast, the unlucky quarter, a Buddhist monastery was built as a spiritual bastion on Mount Hiei, which lay in that direction. But before this event, Buddhism itself had become a force to be reckoned with by the government, and to this development we shall turn in the next chapter.

## CHINESE-STYLE HISTORY AND THE IMPERIAL CONCEPT

The following excerpts should be read with those from the *Chronicles of Japan* (*Nihongi*), in chapters 41 and 42, which trace the legendary beginnings of the Japanese people and ruling house. The selections here, while related to the same subject, are intended to show especially how, in the writing of history on

Chinese models, the imperial line is clothed with all the attributes of the ideal Chinese ruler and how the Chinese concept of sovereignty has been adapted to the Japanese situation so as to strengthen the claims of the Yamato kings.

## FROM THE PREFACE TO *RECORDS OF ANCIENT MATTERS* (*KOJIKI*)

The following excerpt, written as a preface to the *Records of Ancient Matters*, the first extant book, expresses a more sober, rational, and critical attitude, reflecting the difficulty of providing a coherent and credible account from legendary sources that are quite unsystematic, diverse, and uncritically naive in their native simplicity. Nevertheless, the author does his best to measure up to the standards and forms of Chinese historiography.

Hereupon, regretting the errors in the old words and wishing to correct the misstatements in the former chronicles, [Empress Genmyō], on the eighteenth day of the ninth moon of the fourth year of Wadō [November 3, 711], commanded me, Yasumaro, to select and record the old words, learned by heart by Hieda no Are according to the imperial decree, and dutifully to lift them up to her.

In reverent obedience to the contents of the decree, I have made a careful choice. But in high antiquity, both speech and thought were so simple that it would be difficult to arrange phrases and compose periods in the characters.[2] To relate everything in an ideographic transcription would entail an inadequate expression of the meaning; to write altogether according to the phonetic method would make the story of events unduly lengthy.[3] For this reason have I sometimes in the same sentence used the phonic and ideographic systems conjointly and have sometimes in one matter used the ideographic record exclusively. Moreover, where the drift of the words was obscure, I have by comments elucidated their signification, but need it be said that I have nowhere commented on what was easy? . . . All together, the things recorded commence with the separation of Heaven and Earth and conclude with the august reign at Oharida.[4] So from the Deity Master-of-the-August-Center-of-Heaven down to His Augustness Prince-Wave-Limit-Brave-Cormorant-Thatch-Meeting-Incompletely makes the first

---

2. That is, the simplicity of speech and thought in early Japan renders it too hard a task to rearrange the old documents committed to memory by Are in such a manner as to make them conform to the rules of Chinese style.

3. That is, if I adopted in its entirety the Chinese ideographic method of writing, I should often fail to give a true impression of the nature of the original documents. But if I consistently used the Chinese characters, syllable by syllable, as phonetic symbols for Japanese sounds, this work would reach inordinate proportions, on account of the great length of the polysyllabic Japanese as compared with the monosyllabic Chinese.

4. That is, commence with the creation and end with the death of Empress Suiko (628 C.E.), who resided at Oharida.

volume; from the Heavenly Sovereign Kamu-Yamato-Ihare-Biko down to the august reign of Homuda makes the second volume; from the Emperor Ō-Sazaki down to the great palace of Oharida makes the third volume.[5] All together, I have written three volumes, which I reverently and respectfully present. I, Yasumaro, with true trembling and true fear, bow my head, bow my head.

Reverently presented by the Court Noble Futo No Yasumaro, an officer of the upper division of the first class of the fifth rank and of the fifth order of merit, on the 28th day of the first moon of the fifth year of Wadō [March 10, 712].

[Adapted from Chamberlain, Ko-ji-ki, pp. 11–13]

## EMPEROR JINMU

The following extract from the *Chronicles of Japan* deals with the reign of Emperor Jinmu, who reputedly founded the earthly domain of the imperial line. It is clear that the concept of sovereignty and pretensions to universal rule advanced here (and made much of in the emperor-centered nationalism of modern times) are based on Han Chinese models. Hence the incongruities that appear when the historian—obviously with one eye on the claims of imperial China to being the Central Kingdom of the world—makes similar claims for this remote island kingdom.

The Emperor Kami Yamato Ihare-biko's personal name was Hiko-hoho-demi. He was the fourth child of Hiko-nagisa-take-u-gaya-fuki-aezu no Mikoto. His mother's name was Tama-yori-hime, daughter of the sea god. From his birth, this emperor was of clear intelligence and resolute will. At the age of fifteen he was heir to the throne. When he grew up, he married Ahira-tsu-hime, of the district of Ata in the province of Hyūga, and made her his consort. By her he had Tagishi-mimi no Mikoto and Kisu-mimi no Mikoto.

When he reached the age of forty-five, he addressed his elder brothers and his children, saying: "Of old, Our Heavenly Deities Taka-mi-musubi no Mikoto and Ō-hiru-me no Mikoto, pointing to this land of fair rice-ears of the fertile reed-plain, gave it to Our Heavenly ancestor, Hiko-ho no ninigi no Mikoto. Thereupon Hiko-ho no ninigi no Mikoto, throwing open the barrier of Heaven and clearing a cloud path, urged on his superhuman course until he came to rest. At this time the world was given over to widespread desolation. It was an age of darkness and disorder. In this gloom, therefore, he fostered justice and so governed this western border.[6] Our imperial ancestors and imperial parent, like gods, like sages, accumulated happiness and amassed glory. Many years elapsed.

---

5. Kamu-Yamato-Ihare-Biko is the proper native Japanese name of the emperor commonly known by the Chinese "canonical name" of Jinmu. Homuda is part of the native Japanese name of Emperor Ōjin. Ō-Sazaki is the native Japanese name of Emperor Nintoku.

6. That is, Kyushu.

From the date when Our Heavenly ancestor descended until now it is over 1,792,470 years.[7] But the remote regions do not yet enjoy the blessings of imperial rule. Every town has always been allowed to have its lord, and every village its chief, who, each one for himself, makes division of territory and practices mutual aggression and conflict.

"Now I have heard from the Ancient of the Sea[8] that in the east there is a fair land encircled on all sides by blue mountains. Moreover, there is there one who flew down riding in a Heavenly Rock-boat. I think that this land will undoubtedly be suitable for the extension of the Heavenly task,[9] so that its glory should fill the universe. It is, doubtless, the center of the world.[10] The person who flew down was, I believe, Nigi-haya-hi.[11] Why should we not proceed thither, and make it the capital?"

All the imperial princes answered and said: "The truth of this is manifest. This thought is constantly present to our minds also. Let us go thither quickly." This was the year Kinoe Tora [fifty-first] of the Great Year.[12] [pp. 109–111]

The year Tsuchinoto Hitsuji, Spring, 3rd month, 7th day. The emperor made an order[13] saying: "During the six years that our expedition against the east has lasted, owing to my reliance on the Majesty of Imperial Heaven, the wicked bands have met death. It is true that the frontier lands are still unpurified and that a remnant of evil is still refractory. But in the region of the Central Land,[14] there is no more wind and dust. Truly we should make a vast and spacious capital and plan it great and strong.

"At present things are in a crude and obscure condition, and the people's minds are unsophisticated. They roost in nests or dwell in caves.[15] Their manners are simply what is customary. Now if a great man were to establish laws, justice could not fail to flourish. And even if some gain should accrue to the people, in what way would this interfere with the Sage's[16] action? Moreover, it

---

7. This is in imitation of the great number of years ascribed to the reigns of the early Chinese monarchs.

8. Shiho tsutsu no oji.

9. That is, for the further development of the imperial power.

10. The world is here the six quarters north, south, east, west, zenith, and nadir. This is, of course, Chinese, as indeed is this whole speech.

11. *Nigi-haya-hi* means "soft-swift-sun."

12. The great year is the Chinese cycle of sixty years. It is needless to add that such dates are, in this part of the *Nihongi*, purely fictitious.

13. This whole speech is thoroughly Chinese in every respect, and it is preposterous to put it in the mouth of an emperor who is supposed to have lived more than a thousand years before the introduction of Chinese learning into Japan.

14. Claiming for Japan the name always used for China: "Central Kingdom."

15. The reader must not take this as any evidence of the manners and customs of the ancient Japanese. It is simply a phrase suggested by the author's Chinese studies.

16. Meaning the emperor's action, because in Chinese tradition the early rulers were "sage-kings."

will be well to open up and clear the mountains and forests, and to construct a palace. Then I may reverently assume the Precious Dignity and so give peace to my good subjects. Above, I should then respond to the kindness of the Heavenly Powers in granting me the kingdom, and below, I should extend the line of the imperial descendants and foster rightmindedness. Thereafter the capital may be extended so as to embrace all the six cardinal points, and the eight cords may be covered so as to form a roof.[17] Will this not be well?

When I observe the Kashiwa-bara plain, which lies southwest of Mount Unebi, it seems the center of the land. I must set it in order."

Accordingly he in this month commanded officers to set about the construction of an imperial residence. [pp. 131–132]

[Aston, *Nihongi*, vol. 1, pp. 109–132]

# THE REFORM ERA

The way was cleared for the inauguration of the Taika reforms in 645 by the overthrow of the powerful Soga clan. Before this, the *Nihongi* records many strange occurrences and calamities, as if Heaven were showing its displeasure over the Soga usurpation of imperial power. Then Fujiwara no Kamatari and the future emperor, Tenchi, appeared on the scene as the leaders of a "restoration." Kamatari, from the Nakatomi clan traditionally charged with Shinto priestly functions, is said to have declined several times the post of superintendent of the Shinto religion. After his successful coup, the emperor that Kamatari installed on the throne is likewise identified in the *Nihongi* as one who "despised the Way of the Gods (Shinto)." Kamatari devoted himself to Chinese learning and is cast by the historian in the role of the duke of Zhou, the statesman instrumental in founding the Zhou dynasty in China and in establishing what was regarded by Confucians as the ideal social order.

## INAUGURATION OF THE GREAT REFORM ERA

After the assassination of the Soga leaders, the reigning empress abdicated and a new government was formed with the future Tenchi as crown prince and Kamatari as chief minister actually directing affairs. A new reign and era title was therefore announced, Taika, meaning "Great Transformation."

4th year of Kōkyoku (645), 6th month, 19th day. The emperor, the empress dowager, and the prince imperial summoned together the ministers under the great tsuki tree and made an oath appealing to the gods of Heaven and Earth, and saying:

---

17. The character for "roof" also means the "universe." The eight cords or measuring tapes simply mean "everywhere."

"Heaven covers us: Earth upbears us: the imperial way is but one. But in this last degenerate age, the order of lord and vassal was destroyed, until Supreme Heaven by our hands put to death the traitors. Now, from this time forward, both parties shedding their heart's blood, the lord will eschew double methods of government, and the vassal will avoid duplicity in his service of the sovereign! On him who breaks this oath, Heaven will send a curse and earth a plague, demons will slay them, and men will smite them. This is as manifest as the sun and moon."[18]

The style 4th year of the Empress Ame-toyo-takara ikashi-hi tarashihime was altered to Taika, 1st year.

[Aston, *Nihongi*, vol. 2, pp. 197–198]

### REFORM EDICTS

Only a few of the most important reform edicts are included here, outlining the major steps taken by the court to extend its political and fiscal control over the country. These steps were aimed at establishing a Chinese type of centralized administration over areas that previously had enjoyed considerable autonomy under hereditary clan chieftains.

1st year of Taika [645], 8th month, 5th day. Governors of the eastern provinces were appointed. Then the governors were addressed as follows: "In accordance with the charge entrusted to us by the gods of Heaven, We propose at present for the first time to regulate the myriad provinces.

"When you proceed to your posts, prepare registers of all the free subjects of the state and of the people under the control of others, whether great or small. Take account also of the acreage of cultivated land. As to the profits arising from the gardens and ponds, the water and land, deal with them in common with the people. Moreover it is not competent for the provincial governors while in their provinces to decide criminal cases, nor are they permitted by accepting bribes to bring the people to poverty and misery. When they come up to the capital, they must not bring large numbers of the people in their train. They are only allowed to bring with them the local chieftains and the district officials. But when they travel on public business, they may ride the horses of their department and eat the food of their department. From the rank of Suke[19] upwards, those who obey this law will surely be rewarded while those who disobey it shall be liable to be reduced in cap rank. On all, from the rank of Hangan[20] downwards, who accept bribes a fine shall be imposed of double the amount, and they shall eventually be punished criminally according to the greater or less heinousness of the case. Nine men are allowed as attendants on a chief governor, seven on an assistant,

---

18. Note that there is nothing Buddhist or Shinto in this vow. It is pure Chinese. Furthermore, it is not exactly an oath according to our ideas but an imprecation on rebellion.

19. Assistant to a governor.

20. Assistant district chief.

and five on a secretary. If this limit is exceeded, and they are accompanied by a greater number, both chief and followers shall be punished criminally." . . .

2nd year [646], Spring, 1st month, 1st day. As soon as the ceremonies of the new year's congratulations were over, the emperor promulgated an edict of reform, as follows:

"I. Let the people established by the ancient emperors, etc., as representatives of children be abolished, also the Miyake of various places and the people owned as serfs by the Wake, the imperial chieftains, and the village headmen. Let the farm-steads[21] in various places be abolished." Consequently fiefs[22] were granted for their sustenance to those of the rank of Daibu and upwards on a descending scale. Presents of cloth and silk stuffs were given to the officials and people, varying in value.

"Further we say. It is the business of the Daibu to govern the people. If they discharge this duty thoroughly, the people have trust in them, and an increase of their revenue is therefore for the good of the people.

"II. The capital is for the first time to be regulated, and governors appointed for the home provinces and districts. Let barriers, outposts, guards and post horses, both special and ordinary, be provided, bell tokens[23] made, and mountains and rivers regulated.[24]

"For each ward in the capital let there be appointed one alderman, and for four wards one chief alderman, who shall be charged with the superintendence of the population and the examination of criminal matters. For appointment as chief alderman of wards let men be taken belonging to the wards, of unblemished character, firm and upright, so that they may fitly sustain the duties of the time. . . .

"III. Let there now be provided for the first time registers of population, books of account and a system of the receipt and regranting of distribution land.[25]

"Let every fifty houses be reckoned a township, and in every township let there be one alderman who shall be charged with the superintendence of the population,[26] the direction of the sowing of crops and the cultivation of mulberry trees, the prevention and examination of offenses, and the enforcement of the payment of taxes and of forced labor. . . .

---

21. Of serfs.

22. Not a true feudal domain but office lands from which these officials could draw the tax proceeds as a form of salary.

23. Signs of rank indicating the number of horses to which an official was entitled—a Chinese practice.

24. The regulation of mountains and rivers means the provision of guards at ferries and mountain passes serving as boundaries between different provinces.

25. The Denryō (Land Regulations) says, "In granting Kō-bun-den [land shared in proportion to population] men shall have two *tan*, women a third less and children under five years of age none. Lands are granted for a term of six years."

26. That is, of the registers of population.

"IV. The old taxes and forced labor are abolished, and a system of commuted taxes instituted. These shall consist of fine silks, coarse silks, raw silk, and floss silk, all in accordance with what is produced in the locality. . . ."

[Aston, *Nihongi*, vol. 2, pp. 200–206]

## THE COMMENTARY ON THE LEGAL CODE (*RYŌ NO GIGE*)

One of the principal Chinese influences on the thought of early Japan was the legal codes of Tang China. As early as the reign of Emperor Tenchi (668–671), a Japanese code appears to have been compiled, but almost nothing of it remains. The Taihō Code of 701–702, however, continued to be the basic law of Japan until after the Meiji Restoration of 1868. This code directly adopted many Chinese institutions in spite of their unsuitability for the far less developed society of Japan, and an elaborate bureaucracy was organized based on the merit system. But the Taihō Code was not a mere copy of Tang precedents, as new provisions were made for the Shinto priesthood and other peculiarly Japanese institutions.

### REGULATIONS FOR FITNESS REPORTS

A merit system of recruitment and promotion was the heart of the imperial bureaucracy in China, and in the following, the Japanese attempt to duplicate it. Eventually, their inability to overcome by these means the strong native tradition of hereditary rank and officeholding completely vitiated the civil service system and, with it, the whole bureaucratic structure.

Fitness reports must be submitted annually by the chief of every department for all civil and military officers under his command in the court or in the provinces. The merits, demerits, conduct, and abilities of all persons for whom reports are made should be recorded in detail so that they may be consulted in classifying the officers into nine grades of merit. The reports must be completed by the thirtieth day of the eighth moon. Reports on officers stationed in the capital or the provinces of the Inner Circuit should be submitted to the Great Council of State by the first day of the tenth moon; reports for officers in other provinces should be submitted not later than the first day of the eleventh moon through the imperial inspectors. Acts of merit or demerit performed after the submission of reports should be entered in the records of the following year. In case a department is without a chief, the fitness reports should be made by a vice chief. . . .

[*Kokushi taikei*, vol. 22, p. 149]

## NEW COMPILATION OF THE REGISTER OF FAMILIES

The importance of genealogy in determining claims to sovereignty was demonstrated by the *Records of Ancient Matters* (712 C.E.). The Japanese, who thus stressed the divine descent of the imperial family, were confirmed in this by the Han view of the Mandate of Heaven as conferred not on individuals but on dynasties, which themselves had been provided with genealogies going back to the sage-kings. However, the genre of genealogy, like most forms of early written literature, came from China, in which during the late Six Dynasties period and into the Tang, membership in well-established aristocratic descent groups was an important determinant of social status, marriage alliances, and eligibility for office. For his part, the founder of the Tang dynasty, trying to curb the power of the old aristocracy and strengthen central control, had ordered the compilation of a comprehensive register of genealogies that would define and limit the powers of the old elite. Now, as a similar state-building effort was mounted in Japan and the ruling house attempted, with difficulty, to assert its dominion over the old clans, it too felt the need to order and control genealogical claims.

### PREFACE IN THE FORM OF A MEMORIAL TO EMPEROR SAGA

They say that the Divine Dynasty had its inception when the Grandson of Heaven descended to the land of So[27] and extended his influence in the West,[28] but no written records are preserved of these events. In the years when Jinmu assumed command of the state and undertook his campaign to the east, conditions grew steadily more confused, and some tribal leaders rose in revolt. When, however, the Heaven-sent sword appeared and the Golden Kite flew to earth,[29] the chieftains surrendered in great numbers and the rebels vanished like mist. Jinmu, accepting the mandate of Heaven, erected a palace in the central province and administered justice. Peace reigned throughout the country. Land was allotted to men who were deemed virtuous in accordance with their merits. Heads of clans were granted such titles as local chieftain [*kuni-no-miyatsuko*] and district chieftain [*agata-nushi*] for the first time.

Suinin cultivated good fortune by his ever-renewed benevolent favors. Through such acts the Golden Mean was attained. [At this time] clans and families were gradually distinguished one from the other. Moreover, Imna came under our influence and Silla brought tribute. Later, barbarians from other

---

27. An ancient name for the southern part of the island of Kyushu and the location of Mount Takachiho where Ninigi, the Grandson of Heaven, made his descent.

28. That is, in Kyushu.

29. Signs confirming Jinmu's divine right to imperial dominion (see Aston, *Nihongi*, vol. 1, pp. 115, 126).

countries, in due reverence for his virtue, all wished to come to Japan. Out of solicitude for these aliens, he bestowed family names on them. This was an outstanding feature of the time.

During the reign of Ingyō,[30] however, family relationships were in great confusion. An edict was accordingly issued, ordering that oaths be tested by the trial of boiling water. Those whose oaths were true remained unscathed, while the perjurers were harmed. From this time onwards the clans and families were established and there were no impostors. Rivers ran in their proper courses.

While Kōgyoku held the Regalia,[31] however, the provincial records were all burned, and the young and defenseless had no means of proving their antecedents. . . .

During the latter part of the Tempyō Hōji era (757–765) controversies about these matters grew all the more numerous. A number of eminent scholars were thereafter summoned to compile a register of families. Before their work was half completed, however, the government became involved in certain difficulties. The scholars were disbanded and the compilation was not resumed. . . .

Our present sovereign,[32] of glorious fame, desired that the work be resumed at the point where it was abandoned. . . . We, his loyal subjects, in obedience to his edicts, have performed our task with reverence and assiduity. We have collected all the information so as to be able to sift the gold from the pebbles. . . . The names of 1,182 families are included in this work, which is in thirty volumes. It is entitled the "New Compilation of the Register of Families." It is not intended for pleasure reading, and the style is far from polished. Since, however, it is concerned with the key to human relationships, it is an essential instrument in the hands of the nation.

[*Kōgaku sōsho*, vol. 4, pp. 123–124]

---

30. Traditional dates: 411–453 C.E.
31. 642–645 C.E.
32. Saga (809–823).

# Chapter 45

## NARA BUDDHISM

In the forms it took, Nara Buddhism was an extension of that of Tang China and Silla. For example, it is in the Nara period that we first hear of Buddhist sects in Japan, and it is customary to speak of the "six schools" then introduced from China. Some of them, particularly the two Hīnayāna sects, appear never to have been independent, having served primarily as forms of religious discipline for monks. The three main philosophical features of Nara Buddhism were the dialectics of negation (the Sanron or "Three-Treatises" sect, associated with the great Indian scholar Nāgārjuna and transmitted by Kumārajīva), the doctrine of the attainment of enlightenment through the powers of the mind (the Hossō or "Dharma-Character" sect, associated with Vasubandhu and Xuanzang), and the metaphysics of the harmonious whole (taught by the Kegon, or "Flower Garland," sect). The metaphysics of Kegon had been worked out and elaborated by gifted philosophers in China and Korea and was known by the time of its introduction to Japan as a philosophy so intricate and complex that it could never be realized in actual practice. It was not until the revival of Nara Buddhism during the early Kamakura period that practitioners like Myōe Shōnin (1173–1232) successfully took up the challenge of transforming the Kegon metaphysics of the interrelatedness of all things into a religion that could be practiced by lay persons as well as monks.

The sixth sect (the Ritsu, or Precepts, school) was based on the rules of discipline governing the lives of monks and nuns. A person could be initiated into this discipline (called "receiving the precepts") only by a qualified master of the precepts, and in 754 the intrepid Chinese priest Jianzhen (Ganjin) finally arrived in Nara after five earlier attempts that had ended in shipwrecks. With his legitimate transmission of the precepts to Japan and the establishment of the ordination platform at Tōdaiji, Buddhists could finally be ordained as authentic clergy. As it is with most rules, however, the precepts became a legalistic matter of formal obedience rather than the principles by which a Buddhist lived and sought enlightenment. Like the metaphysics of Kegon, the precepts in time became watered down and had to be infused with new life and philosophical meaning in the Kamakura period by monks like Myōe and Gedatsu Shōnin (1155–1213).

Common to these seemingly disparate views was the basic Buddhist doctrine of impermanence, of non-ego (the absence of any enduring, substantial self), and of the need for liberation from illusion and suffering by the attainment of Nirvana or Buddhahood. Buddhism insisted on the need to free oneself from relying on externals so changeable that they can only deceive. Therefore, these must be negated exhaustively until all the usual distinctions of becoming, which arise from incomplete knowledge, are denied and perfect knowledge can be attained. Such was the teaching of Nāgārjuna. For the followers of the Hossō sect, the school of the great Chinese pilgrim Xuanzang, the outer world did not exist at all but was a creation of the mind. How could someone turn to the motions of the stars for guidance when they were illusory and without permanent reality? Even in the Kegon school, which preached a cosmological harmony governed by Lochana Buddha—who sits on a lotus throne of a thousand petals, each of which is a universe containing millions of worlds like ours—it is the mutable nature of this system and not its permanence (like the Confucian Heaven) that is emphasized. Within the great harmony of the Kegon (or Flower Garland), all beings are related and capable of mutual interaction until they attain a fundamental communion with Buddha and, through him, with all other beings.

We do not know how much of these abstruse doctrines was understood by Japanese Buddhists of the Nara period, but expressions of religious fervor generally assumed a tangible form. The court's patronage of Buddhism led to the building of Nara's magnificent temples and monasteries, some of which still survive. Certain court ceremonies such as the open confession of sins (*keka*) show how the strong desire to lead a religious life permeated ruling circles. Buddhist influence led also to the making of highways and bridges, to the use of irrigation, and to the exploration of distant parts of the country by itinerant monks (who drew the earliest Japanese maps). Even such features of Japanese life as the public bath and cremation also date from the Buddhist inspiration of this time.

For the small number of monks and scholars of the Nara period who were well versed in Buddhist literature, four sūtras were of special importance: the Sūtra of Past and Present, Cause and Effect; the Sūtra of the Golden Light; the Sūtra of the Humane Kings; and the Kegon, or Flower Garland Sūtra. The first of these sūtras is a biography of Buddha that declares his extraordinary attainments to have been the cumulative merit of his meritorious deeds from the infinitely distant past to the present. This concept contrasts with the Han Confucian doctrine of kingly rule based on moral virtue in conformity with the Way of Heaven, or the theory of the *Record of Ancient Matters* (*Kojiki*), where we find genealogy to be essential to the legitimation of rulership.

The ruler's responsibilities—and indeed the entire question of the relationship between the state and Buddhism—were discussed most completely in the Sūtra of the Golden Light. This major work of Buddhist literature played a more important role than any other text in establishing Buddhism as the state religion of Japan, and its influence continued undiminished for centuries. It opens with an eloquent proclamation of the eternity of Buddha's life and declares that he exists not only as a historical figure with a human form but also in the cosmos as the ultimate law or Truth, and in the life hereafter as the savior possessed of an all-embracing love. Since Buddha is omnipresent, everything that exists is subject to his eternal vigilance of boundless compassion. The sūtra declares further that the gates of the paradise of the Lotus where Buddha dwells are always open to all of humanity, for anyone can become a Buddha. The methods the sūtra especially recommends for bringing about this change for the better are expiation and self-sacrifice, and accordingly, the climax of the entire narration is the parable of Buddha giving himself up to feed a hungry tiger.

The central theme of the sūtra is the life of wisdom—*prajñā*, which distinguishes good from evil and right from wrong. Everyone, from the king to his lowliest subject, must obey the dictates of the inner light of reason. The religious life starts with an awareness of one's sins and the need to atone for them. It is wisdom that enables people to surmount their failings, and the highest expression of the triumph of wisdom is an act of self-sacrifice. Wisdom is also associated with healing; Buddha is supremely possessed of wisdom and is the great healer as well. It was this aspect of Buddha that appealed most to Japanese of the Nara period, as witnessed by the predominant role of Yakushi, the Healing Buddha, in both temples specifically dedicated to him and in most centers of worship. The Sūtra of the Golden Light contains a chapter entirely devoted to medicine and healing, illustrating the close connection between religious belief and medicine. (Buddhist monks introduced many medicines from China during the Nara period.)

The political aspects of the sūtra are most clearly stated in the chapter on kingly law (Ōbōshō-ron), which declares that government and religion are united by the Buddhist Law (or dharma). The law of men must be universal but not final, always subject to change, with peace as its ultimate end. Any king who violates the Law will be punished, but as long as he is faithful to it, Buddha will see to it that he enjoys immeasurable blessings. Japanese monarchs during the Nara period held this sūtra in such reverence that they attempted to make it an instrument of state ideology. Copies of the sūtra were distributed in all the provinces in 741 C.E. by order of Emperor Shōmu, one of Japan's most devout rulers. At about the same time, Shōmu ordered each province to build a seven-story pagoda and to establish a Guardian Temple of the Province and an Atonement Nunnery of the Province.

Shōmu also was responsible for building the Great Image of Lochana Buddha, the most famous monument of the Nara period. Just as Lochana Buddha is the central figure of the cosmogony of the Kegon Sūtra, the Great Image and its temple were intended as the center of the provincial temples and nunneries. The Kegon Sūtra is said to have been the teaching delivered by Buddha immediately after attaining enlightenment, when he made no attempt to simplify the complexities of his doctrines for the benefit of the less capable. Its difficulty kept it from attaining the popularity of the Sūtra of the Golden Light, but its importance is evident from the efforts devoted to completing the Great Image (more than fifty feet high). In 749, when gold was discovered in Japan for the first time, it was regarded as an auspicious sign for completion of the monument. Emperor Shōmu declared:

> This is the Word of the Sovereign who is the Servant of the Three Treasures, that he humbly speaks before the Image of Lochana.
>
> In this land of Yamato since the beginning of Heaven and Earth, Gold, though it has been brought as an offering from other countries, was thought not to exist. But in the East of the land which We rule . . . Gold has been found.
>
> Hearing this We were astonished and rejoiced, and feeling that this is a Gift bestowed upon Us by the love and blessing of Lochana Buddha, We have received it with reverence and humbly accepted it, and have brought with Us all Our officials to worship and give thanks.
>
> This We say reverently, reverently, in the Great Presence of the Three Treasures whose name is to be spoken with awe.[1]

We cannot help but be struck by the humility of the terms that Shōmu uses. For him to claim to be a "servant" of the Three Treasures marks an astonishing departure from the previously held ideas of kingship in Japan. There seemingly remained only one more step to be taken to make Japan into a true Buddha land: to have a sovereign who was ordained as a minister to Buddha's Law so that the country could be governed in perfect consonance with these teachings. And during the reign of Shōmu's daughter, rule was nearly transferred to a Buddhist monk.

In 764 C.E., Empress Kōtoku, who had previously abdicated to enter the religious life, suddenly decided to resume her rule despite the Buddhist vows she had taken. Adopting a new reign title, Shōtoku, she appointed Dōkyō, a master of the Hossō sect, to be her chief minister. Dōkyō steadily rose in power. In 766 he was appointed "king of the law" (*hōō*), and several years later the empress, acting on a false oracle, was on the point of abdicating the throne in his favor. However, powerful conservative forces at the court blocked this move, and Japan

---

1. Sansom, "The Imperial Edicts in the Shoku-Nihongi," p. 26.

never again came so close to becoming a Buddha land. Empress Shōtoku died in 770; Dōkyō was disgraced; and later new rulers turned from Nara to Kyoto, where new forms of Buddhism were to dominate the scene.

### THE SŪTRA OF THE GOLDEN LIGHT

The full title of this work, Sūtra of the Sovereign Kings of the Golden Light Ray (Konkō myō saishō ōgyō), refers to the Deva Kings who came to pay homage to the Buddha. The sūtra is credited with inspiring the first temple built by the court, the Shitennōji (or Temple of the Four Deva Kings). When Tenmu seized the throne in 672, this sūtra appears to have influenced his decision to promote Buddhism in the interest of the new regime. His predecessor, Tenchi (Tenji), had been clearly associated with the Confucian political order, and as we have seen, Tenchi's assumption of power was justified by numerous portents indicating that he had received the Mandate of Heaven. Tenmu found a similar justification in the Golden Light Sūtra, which set forth a doctrine of kingship based on merit—merit achieved in former existences and through the wholehearted support of Buddhism. It thus strongly implied that kings rule by a kind of "divine right" not based on any hereditary claim but, rather, on the ruler's religious merit. In Tenmu's case, his realm would enjoy peace and harmony from the beneficial influence of Buddhist teachings on public morality, and even the cosmic order would respond to his virtue and bestow blessings on him and his people. Here, then, is a Buddhist claim to religious legitimacy overriding any customary right of dynastic inheritance. It is no wonder that Tenmu held this sūtra in particular honor and fostered the growth of Buddhism by ordering every family to have a Buddhist shrine in its house.

## The Protection of the Country by the Four Deva Kings

Then the Four Deva Kings, their right shoulders bared from their robes in respect, arose from their seats and, with their right knees touching the ground and their palms joined in humility, thus addressed Buddha:

"Most Revered One! When, in some future time, this Sūtra of the Golden Light is transmitted to every part of a kingdom—to its cities, towns, and villages, its mountains, forests, and fields—if the king of the land listens with his whole heart to these writings, praises them, and makes offerings on their behalf, and if moreover he supplies this sūtra to the four classes of believers, protects them, and keeps them from all harm, we Deva Kings, in recognition of his deeds, will protect the king and his people, give them peace and freedom from suffering, prolong their lives, and fill them with glory. Most Revered One! If when the king sees that the four classes of believers receive the sūtra, he respects and protects them as he would his own parents, we Four Kings will so protect him always that whatever he wishes will come about, and all sentient beings will respect him." . . .

Then Buddha declared to the Four Deva Kings:

"Fitting is it indeed that you Four Kings should thus defend the holy writings. In the past I practiced bitter austerities of every kind for 100,000 kalpas [eons]. Then, when I attained supreme enlightenment and realized in myself universal wisdom, I taught this law. If a king upholds this sūtra and makes offerings in its behalf, I will purify him of suffering and illness and bring him peace of mind. I will protect his cities, towns, and villages and scatter his enemies. I will make all strife among the rulers of men to cease forever.

"Know ye, Deva Kings, that the 84,000 rulers of the 84,000 cities, towns, and villages of the world shall each enjoy happiness of every sort in his own land; that they shall all possess freedom of action and obtain all manner of precious things in abundance; that they shall never again invade each other's territories; that they shall receive recompense in accordance with their deeds of previous existences; that they shall no longer yield to the evil desire of taking the lands of others; that they shall learn that the smaller their desires the greater the blessing; and that they shall emancipate themselves from the suffering of warfare and bondage. The people of their lands shall be joyous, and upper and lower classes will blend as smoothly as milk and water. They shall appreciate each other's feelings, join happily in diversions together, and, with all compassion and modesty, increase the sources of goodness.

"In this way the nations of the world shall live in peace and prosperity, the peoples shall flourish, the earth shall be fertile, the climate temperate, and the seasons shall follow in the proper order. The sun, moon, and the constellations of stars shall continue their regular progress unhindered. The wind and rain shall come in good season. All treasures shall be abundant. No meanness shall be found in human hearts, but all shall practice almsgiving and cultivate the ten good works. When the end of life comes, many shall be born in Heaven and increase the celestial multitudes."

[Tsuji, *Nihon bukkyō shi*, jōsei-hen, pp. 194–195]

## BUDDHISM AND THE STATE IN NARA JAPAN

### PROCLAMATION OF THE EMPEROR SHŌMU ON THE ERECTION OF THE GREAT BUDDHA IMAGE

Having respectfully succeeded to the throne through no virtue of our own, out of a constant solicitude for all men, We have been ever intent on aiding them to reach the shore of the Buddha land. Already even the distant seacoasts of this land have been made to feel the influence of our benevolence and regard for others, and yet not everywhere in this land do men enjoy the grace of Buddha's law. Our fervent desire is that under the aegis of the Three Treasures, the benefits of peace may be brought to all in heaven and earth, even animals and plants sharing in its fruits, for all time to come.

Therefore on the fifteenth day of the tenth month of the fifteenth year of the Tempyō reign [743], which is the year of the goat and water junior,[2] We take this occasion to proclaim our great vow of erecting an image of Lochana Buddha in gold and copper. We wish to make the utmost use of the nation's resources of metal in the casting of this image, and also to level off the high hill on which the great edifice is to be raised, so that the entire land may be joined with us in the fellowship of Buddhism and enjoy in common the advantages which this undertaking affords to the attainment of Buddhahood.

It is we who possess the wealth of the land; it is we who possess all power in the land. With this wealth and power at our command, we have resolved to create this venerable object of worship. The task would appear to be an easy one, and yet a lack of sufficient forethought on our part might result in the people's being put to great trouble in vain, for the Buddha's heart would never be touched if, in the process, calumny and bitterness were provoked which led unwittingly to crime and sin.

Therefore all who join in the fellowship of this undertaking must be sincerely pious in order to obtain its great blessings, and they must daily pay homage to Lochana Buddha, so that with constant devotion each may proceed to the creation of Lochana Buddha.[3] If there are some desirous of helping in the construction of this image, though they have no more to offer than a twig or handful of dirt, they should be permitted to do so. The provincial and county authorities are not to disturb and harass the people by making arbitrary demands on them in the name of this project. This is to be proclaimed far and wide so that all may understand our intentions in this matter.

[From *Shoku Nihongi*, in *Rikkokushi*, vol. 3, pp. 320–321]

## THE BODHISATTVA GYŌGI

Gyōgi (670?–749), a major figure in the Buddhism of the Nara period, gained great renown as a popular teacher and practitioner of good works—establishing hospitals, orphanages, old people's homes, rest houses, and the like and performing public works such as the construction of bridges, harbors, and canals for navigation and irrigation. At these sites, he established practice halls (*dōjō*) that also served as seminaries for those serving on these projects. Although early on, the court looked askance at Gyōgi's unconventional and unauthorized activities, in time, as he became popularly revered as a bodhisattva incarnate, the court sought to appropriate his popularity and prestige for itself, at which point Emperor Shōmu conferred on him high ecclesiastical rank (*daisōjō*) in recognition of his standing among the people.

---

2. Year designation according to the Chinese sexagenary cycle (chap. 44).

3. Although it might seem impious to think that the Cosmic Buddha himself could be so created, in the Kegon philosophy the particular and the universal are one and inseparable, so that an image properly conceived with a devout realization of the Buddha's true nature might stand for the Buddha himself.

The following is taken from a collection of hagiographical writings compiled by the Tendai monk Chingen around 1040, containing miracle stories ostensibly connected with the Lotus Sūtra. It shows how a charismatic figure like Gyōgi quickly became the stuff of legend and how the popularization of Buddhism attended the state-building process in the Nara period.

Bodhisattva Gyōgi was a man from the Ōtori District of Izumi Province. Koshi was his secular clan name.

When born, he was wrapped in a caul. His parents placed him on a tree branch as a method of decontaminating him. After one night, the parents found that their baby was out of the skin and already spoke well. They took him home and reared him. . . .

Later Gyōgi took the tonsure and became a monk of Yakushiji Temple. He read the commentaries including the *Yugayuishikiron*[4] and perceived the deep significance in these writings.

Gyōgi traveled widely in cities and in rural areas, cultivating the people. Nearly one thousand people followed him, wishing to be taught. . . .

Gyōgi visited various dangerous and yet important places. He constructed bridges and roads. He investigated the irrigation and cultivation of rice fields and he dug ponds for reservoirs and built dikes. Those who heard of his projects all gathered and helped him. So the construction was finished in a short time. Since then, farmers and peasants have greatly benefited. . . .

When the emperor built the Tōdaiji Temple,[5] he ordered Gyōgi to offer a dedication service for the temple as lecturer. Gyōgi replied that he would not be able to serve as a lecturer at such a great meeting, but that a holy man from a foreign country would come to offer the service.

When the day arrived, Gyōgi said that they should welcome the holy man. With an imperial order, Gyōgi led ninety-nine priests and the officials from three offices including those for aristocrats, for priests and nuns, and for music. He went to the port of Naniwa and waited there with music.

Holding a set of *argha*[6] (Buddhist utensils for offerings), with arranged flowers and burning incense, Gyōgi took the hundredth place among the priests and boarded a boat. . . .

After a while . . . they saw a small boat approaching. As it arrived at the shore, an Indian stepped on the beach. Seeing this, Gyōgi raised a hand, smiled at the Indian priest, and recited a poem,

> The truth of the words
> Vowed before Shākyamuni

---

4. A major text of the Dharma Character (Hossō) school translated by Xuanzang.

5. The Indian Bodhisena (704–760) came to Japan in 736 and, on Gyōgi's recommendation, presided at the Eye-Opening Ceremony of the Great Buddha of the Tōdaiji Temple in 752.

6. A set of special containers are used for the *aka* or the water offered to the Buddha.

At Vulture Peak
Did not die and
We have met again.

The holy man from the foreign country responded by reciting his poem,

As promised to each other
At Kapilavastu,
I can now see
The face of Mañjushrī.

Gyōgi said to the monks and laymen in his presence that the holy man was Bodhisena, a monk from South India. The people gathered at the place now knew that Gyōgi was an incarnation of Mañjushrī. There is no more space to itemize other miraculous happenings.

Gyōgi, at the age of eighty, passed away on the fourth day of the second month of the first year of Tenpyōshōhō (749).

[Trans. adapted from Dykstra, *Miraculous Tales*, pp. 27–29]

## REGULATION OF THE BUDDHIST ORDERS
## BY THE COURT

Not all those who embraced Buddhism, "left the world," and joined monastic orders did so with a full realization of what would be required of them in the religious life. Consequently, it was not long after the first establishment of monasteries and nunneries in Japan that charges were made of flagrant violations of Buddhist vows in regard to the taking of life, sexual incontinence, and drunkenness. Since the throne had taken a prominent part in establishing Buddhist institutions, it was expected that the court would likewise assert its control over them, as indicated by the measures taken by Suiko as early as 623 C.E. Such external controls proved largely ineffective, however, for serious violations were common throughout the seventh and eighth centuries, and it remained for reformers such as Ganjin and Saichō (chap. 46) to attempt to tighten discipline from within.

31st year [623], Spring, 4th month, 3rd day. There was a Buddhist monk who took an axe and smote therewith his paternal grandfather. Now the empress, hearing of this, sent for the Great Imperial Chieftain Soga, and gave command, saying: "The man who has entered religion should be devoted to the Three Treasures and should cherish devoutly the prohibitions of the Buddhist Law. How can he without compunction be readily guilty of crime? We now hear that there is a monk who has struck his grandfather. Therefore, let all the monks and nuns of the various temples be assembled, and investigation made. Let severe punishment be inflicted on any who are convicted of offenses." Hereupon the monks and nuns were all assembled, and an examination held. The wicked monks and nuns were all about to be punished, when Kwallŭk, a Buddhist monk of Paekche, presented a memorial, as follows: "The Law of Buddha came from the Western country to Han.[7] Three hundred years later it was handed on to Paekche, since which time barely one hundred years had elapsed, when our king, hearing that the emperor of Nippon was a wise man, sent him tribute of an image of Buddha and of Buddhist sūtras. Since that time, less than one hundred years have passed, and consequently the monks and nuns have not yet learned the Buddhist laws and readily commit wickedness. On this account all the monks and nuns are afraid and do not know what to do. I humbly pray that with the exception of the wicked [monk who struck his grandfather], all the other monks and nuns be pardoned and not punished. That would be a work of great merit."

Accordingly the empress granted [his petition].

13th day. A decree was made as follows: "If even the monks continue to offend against the Law, wherewithal shall the laymen be admonished? Therefore from this time forward we appoint a Sōjō and a Sōzu for the superintendence of the monks and nuns."

Autumn, 9th month, 3rd day. There was an inspection of the temples and of the monks and nuns, and an accurate record made of the circumstances of the building of the temples, and also of the circumstances under which the monks and nuns embraced religion, with the year, month, and day of their taking orders. There were at this time 46 temples, 816 monks, and 569 nuns—in all, 1,385 persons.

32nd year [624], Spring, 1st month, 7th day. The king of Koryŏ sent tribute of a Buddhist monk, named Hyegwan. He was appointed Sōjō [superintendent of monks and nuns].[8]

[Adapted from Aston, *Nihongi*, vol. 2, pp. 1522–1554]

## EDICTS OF THE EMPRESS SHŌTOKU CONCERNING DŌKYŌ

These edicts, one making the priest Dōkyō the chief minister of the court and the other naming him the king of the Law, preceded Empress Shōtoku's attempt to abdicate the imperial throne in his favor.

### EDICT OF OCTOBER 19, 764

It has been represented to us, in view of the master's constant attendance on us, that he has ambitions of rising to high office like his ancestors before him,

---

7. The Chinese dynasty of that name.
8. The Japanese were still such novices in Buddhism that Korean monks were generally selected as religious authorities.

and we have been petitioned to dismiss him from our court. However, We have observed his conduct and found it to be immaculate. Out of a desire to transmit and promote Buddha's Law, he has extended to us his guidance and protection. How could we lightly dismiss such a teacher?

Although our head has been shaven and we wear Buddhist robes, we feel obliged to conduct the government of the nation. As Buddha declared in the [Bonmō, Brahmajāla] Sūtra, "Kings, ye who take up thrones, receive the ordination of the bodhisattvas!" These words prove that there can be no objection even for one who has taken holy orders in administering the government. We deem it proper therefore, since the reigning monarch is ordained, that the chief minister should also be an ordained monk. Hearken, all ye people, to our words: We confer on the Master Dōkyō the title of chief minister and master, though the title is not of his seeking. [pp. 93–94]

### EDICT OF NOVEMBER 26, 766

We do affirm in this edict our belief that when the Law of Buddha, the Supreme One, is worshiped and revered with perfect sincerity of heart, he is certain to vouchsafe some unusual sign. The sacred bone of the Tathāgata which has now been manifested, of perfect shape and unusually large, is brighter and more beautiful of color than ever we have seen; the mind cannot encompass its splendor. Thus it is that night and day alike we pay it humble reverence with our unwavering attention. Indeed, it appears to us that when the Transformation Body of the Buddha extends its guidance to salvation in accordance with circumstances, his compassionate aid is manifested with no delay. Nevertheless, the Law depends on men for the continuation and spread of its prosperity. Thus, it has been due to acts of leadership and guidance in consonance with the Law performed by our chief minister and master, who stands at the head of all priests, that this rare and holy Sign has been vouchsafed us. How could so holy and joyous a thing delight us alone? Hearken, all ye people, to your sovereign's will: We bestow on our teacher, the chief minister, the title of king of the Law.[9] We declare again that such worldly titles have never been of his seeking; his mind is set, with no other aspiration, on performing the acts of a bodhisattva and leading all men to salvation. Hearken, all ye people, to your sovereign's will: We confer this position on him as an act of reverence and gratitude. [pp. 140–141]

[From *Shoku Nihongi*, in *Rikkokushi*, vol. 6, pp. 93–141]

---

9. Sometimes translated as "pope."

# THE MERGER OF BUDDHIST AND
# SHINTO DEITIES

It is difficult to trace the early stages of the important process by which Buddhism was made compatible with Shinto and thus became more easily acceptable to the Japanese. The first clear indication of this appears in the middle of the Nara period—more than two hundred years after the official introduction of Buddhism to Japan—in a biography of Fujiwara Muchimaro. The author was obviously a Buddhist himself, and he portrayed a Shinto deity seeking refuge in the power of Buddhism. The mutual relationship of Buddhism with Shinto later developed in complex ways and by the Kamakura period resulted in detailed explanations of the Shinto gods as the concrete manifestations of Buddhist deities. This Buddhist argument was widely accepted and contributed significantly to the doctrinal, ritual, and institutional blending of both religions. Muchimaro's biography marks the textual beginning of this merger and tells how a Shinto deity, still in command of its own powers, made a spiritual request that had an institutional answer.

In the year 715, Fujiwara Muchimaro had a dream in which a strange man appeared and said, "Since you revere the teachings of the Buddha, please build a temple for my sake. I beg of you to fulfill my request and save me, for my past karma has caused me to be a Shinto deity for a long time. Now I place my trust in the way of the Buddha, and I wish to perform meritorious acts for my happiness. Thus far, I have not been able to obtain the proper causes and conditions for this, and therefore I have come to speak with you."

Muchimaro was suspicious and thought that the man might be the Kibi deity. He wanted to say something in reply but found himself unable to speak. Then he woke up from his dream. He offered a prayer, saying, "The ways of the gods and men are different. What is obvious to the one is obscure for the other. Who was that strange man appearing in my dream last night? If he should prove himself to be a deity by showing me a sign, then I shall surely build a temple for him." At that point, the deity picked up a monk named Kume Katsuashi and placed him at the very top of a tall tree. That, he said, was the sign. Muchimaro then realized the truth and built a temple, which is now a part of a Buddhist-Shinto shrine complex in Echizen Province.

[Tsuji, *Nihon bukkyō shi*, vol. 1, p. 440; GT]

# Chapter 46

## SAICHŌ AND MOUNT HIEI

One day in the seventh moon of 788, a young monk made his way up the side of Mount Hiei repeating this song of prayer he had composed:

> O Buddhas
> Of unexcelled complete enlightenment
> Bestow your invisible aid
> Upon this hut I open
> On the mountain top.[1]

The monk was Saichō (767–822), and the little temple he founded developed into a center of learning and culture for the entire nation until, by order of a ruthless military leader, the complex of three thousand temple buildings on Mount Hiei was razed in 1571. Saichō's temple would almost certainly never have attained such a remarkable position had it not been for the decision of Emperor Kanmu (r. 781–806) to move the capital away from Nara, the stronghold of the established sects of Buddhism. Kanmu was a Confucian by training and, as such, was opposed to the encroachment into political power by the Buddhist clergy. The attempt to establish Dōkyō as the ruler of Japan represented the

---

1. *Dengyō Daishi zenshū*, vol. 4, p. 756 (1912 ed.).

closest the monks came to success in creating a "Buddha land," but even when this failed, they were by no means reduced to a purely religious status. It was in order to restore to the sovereign his full prerogatives that Kanmu determined to move the seat of government. In this decision he had the support of the Fujiwara and certain important families traditionally opposed to Buddhism, as well as that of the descendants of such Chinese immigrant families as the Hata, who are credited with having introduced sericulture to Japan. Saichō himself was of Chinese descent. Another outstanding figure of the period, General Sakanoue no Tamuramaro, who extended the imperial domains to the northern end of the main island of Japan, was of Korean descent.

Although Kanmu's dislike of the monks' secular ambitions and his impatience with their interminable wrangling had made him somewhat distrustful of them, he realized that he needed Buddhist support for the reforms he intended to effect. These included steps to enforce Buddhist discipline, to secularize those monks and nuns who violated the laws of celibacy, to limit the economic activities and acquisition of land by temples and monasteries, and to tighten the restrictions on the establishment or maintenance of private temples outside the authorized system of provincial monasteries and nunneries. Saichō suited Kanmu's purposes. He had originally left Nara because of his dissatisfaction with the worldliness and, he believed, the decadence of the monks there. He became convinced that only in an entirely different environment could a true moral purge and ethical awakening take place. When he first established his little temple, the area around Mount Hiei was mainly uncultivated marshland, but six years later, in 794, it was chosen as the site of the capital. Saichō may have been instrumental in adopting this site, but in any case, once the capital had been moved there, he enjoyed the patronage of Emperor Kanmu. Saichō was sent to China in 804, chiefly to gain spiritual sanction for the new Buddhist foundation on Mount Hiei. China was considered the "fatherland" of Japanese Buddhism, and without some Chinese credentials, Saichō's monastery would have no standing alongside those of the powerful sects in Nara.

Saichō did not originally intend to found a new sect but, rather, an ecumenical center for the combined study of the teachings separately established in Nara. When Saichō's first temple opened, the Healing Buddha was enshrined there, just as it was in so many of the Nara temples. Moreover Saichō's initial inclinations, no doubt in reaction to the intense sectarian rivalries in Nara, were to try to reconcile competing claims in an eclectic, ecumenical movement. In his early religious training, Saichō had learned about Zhiyi's commentaries on the Lotus Sūtra that had been brought to Japan by Ganjin, a disciplinary master invited from Tang China to help reform Nara Buddhism. Zhiyi's comprehensive synthesis of Mahāyāna Buddhist doctrine and practice—a religious accompaniment to the unification process in late-sixth-century China— also fitted Emperor Kanmu's efforts to build the new capital of Heian (Kyoto) and strengthen the state's control over many aspects of Japanese life, including religious institutions.

Thus when Saichō was designated by the court to visit China and learn the latest developments in Tang Buddhism, he made an effort to acquaint himself with several current trends, receiving initiation in forms of Esoteric Buddhism and Zen as well as Zhiyi's Tendai (Ch: Tiantai) teachings and practices then undergoing something of a revival in late-eighth- and early-ninth-century China. In the short year of his stay, however, Saichō devoted his attention mostly to Zhiyi's grand synthesis of Exoteric[2] Buddhism in scripture, philosophy, and meditation and less to the other two schools, which emphasized practice. By contrast, Kūkai, who accompanied Saichō on this mission, went on to the Tang capital and, during a much longer stay, acquired a greater mastery of Esoteric texts, mandalas, and practices.

On his return to Japan, Saichō was authorized to conduct a training program at his center on Mount Hiei, which was dedicated to the "One Way" (of the Mahāyāna) and the Tendai form of meditative praxis known as the "calming" (lit., "cessation") and "contemplation" (*shikan*). Thus Saichō's initial aim was clearly to promote the Tendai Lotus school, as it was known, but not to the exclusion of other schools. His program of study included the Esoteric discipline identified with the Vairochana Sūtra, as well as the study of Confucian Classics, and the students authorized to participate in the program included representatives of the Nara sects in an ecumenical company.

If, however, Saichō's hope was to promote an inclusive religious movement in keeping with Zhiyi's own synthetic philosophy and Kanmu's aim to overcome the divisive rivalries of the Nara temples, events turned in an opposite direction. Cooperation with other sects failed, and Saichō was compelled to press his own primary aims in a more single-minded way, almost, one might say, as a loner.

One of Saichō's disappointments was the deterioration of his relationship with Kūkai, whose superior knowledge of Esoteric rituals he had hoped to use. Saichō was much impressed with the splendid Esoteric rituals, and senior though he was to Kūkai, he humbly requested and received from him initiation into one of the most important of these rites. Also, he frequently borrowed texts from Kūkai's extensive library. Saichō even sent Taihan, one of his favorite disciples, to study with Kūkai. But these deferential relations only glossed over important differences in the interpretation of how Esoteric Buddhism was related to the Lotus, since Saichō believed in the essential harmony of the two, whereas Kūkai asserted the former's superiority over the latter. Relations between Saichō and Kūkai came to an abrupt end when Kūkai, writing on Taihan's behalf, refused Saichō's request that Taihan return to Mount Hiei. Then, when Saichō asked to borrow a certain Esoteric sūtra, Kūkai this time replied that if he wished to study the Truth, it was everywhere apparent in the cosmos, but if he wished to

---

2. That is, doctrines openly stated in rational, discursive terms rather than profound mysteries only hinted at or pointed to by subtle signs, symbols, and gestures (Esoteric Buddhism).

learn about Esoteric Buddhism, he would have to become a regular student. The tone of Kūkai's letter was condescending, and we cannot be surprised that Saichō was offended by it.

At the same time, Saichō's relations with the Nara temples worsened. Like Kanmu, he had hoped not to alienate the established sects but found himself increasingly embroiled with them (especially the dominant Hossō sect) over his proposals on behalf of the Tendai Lotus teaching and Zhiyi's system of practice as the culmination of the Mahāyāna. Defending himself from these criticisms, Saichō argued that with the exception of the Kegon, the Nara schools had derived authority for their doctrines from secondary sources—the commentaries—instead of from the sūtras themselves. Saichō denounced this feature of Nara Buddhism in pointing out the superiority of the Lotus's teachings based (as he supposed) on Buddha's own words.

Among the contentious issues between Hiei and Nara was Saichō's relaxation of the traditional disciplinary rules or precepts that the Nara monks accepted when they were inducted into the full Hīnayāna ordination. Hiei monks were allowed to take a simpler set of Mahāyāna or Bodhisattva vows less tied to the traditional monastic discipline and more adapted to the life of a lay bodhisattva. The latter "precepts" (actually more like injunctions) featured ten major and forty-eight minor rules of conduct, simpler and more general than the exacting 250 rules of the earlier monastic regimen directed toward strict disciplinary observance and meditative praxis. Ganjin's reform movement in the Nara period reinforced this strict discipline, but Saichō's featured a more generalized ethic, as found in the *Fanwang jing* (J:. *Bonmō kyō*), a Chinese text purporting to be the words of the Buddha in India. This text had come to be widely accepted in China, though disagreement remained over whether the *Fanwang* precepts alone were sufficient for the ordination of monks. Despite uncertainty over its authorship, Saichō believed that the *Fanwang* precepts were more in keeping with the Lotus's teaching of the universality of the Buddha nature and the accessibility of salvation for all, whereas the so-called Hīnayāna path—assuming that Nirvana was more difficult to attain and, practically speaking, achievable in this life only by a few—insisted on the need for monks to make a more rigorous and protracted effort to fulfill the traditional Noble Eightfold Path.

More was involved here, however, than simply issues of discipline. In opposing Saichō, the Nara temples were not only defending their vested interests—including a monopoly of the ordination process as established in the old capital, as well as their key role in the system of state superintendence over Buddhist institutions—but were also standing firm for what they believed to be authentic Buddhist tradition. Saichō found himself at odds with them on both counts.

Although the court-approved system of accredited students registered at Mount Hiei provided for a substantial representation of monks from the Nara denominations, records kept by Saichō himself indicate that many of them were not in residence on Mount Hiei but had drifted away, several back to their home temples, no doubt because they were more concerned with their own ordination and certification in Nara than with satisfying Saichō's curriculum.

Disappointed at this outcome but still undeterred, Saichō asked Kanmu's successor, Emperor Heizei, to approve a new set of regulations for Mount Hiei that would sequester the students on the mountain for a full twelve years. These regulations would also provide for an ordination platform to be established there that would free the monks from being held hostage to Nara and liberate Saichō's Enryakuji Temple from supervision by the Nara monks. Saichō's ordination, called the "Bodhisattva or Mahāyāna ordination," was based on the simpler rules of the *Fanwang jing*, which, being more generally adaptable to the roles of the Bodhisattva, also would serve his aim of training monks for service to state and society.

Thus on the one hand, Saichō's new regimen was more relaxed in relation to the earlier, more numerous and detailed disciplinary rules identified with the so-called Hīnayāna ("narrow or smaller vehicle"), but on the other hand, it imposed a new strictness insofar as it emphasized seclusion on the mountain to concentrate on an intensive program of study, known as the "Buddhist discipline (or regulations) of the mountain school" (*sanga buppō* or *sanga shiki*). In this way the demands of the training became associated not with the old *vinaya* but with the rigors of life for those identified as "monks confined to the mountain" (*rōzan bikku*) engaged in "mountain training and mountain learning" (*sanshū, sangaku*).

Yet for all this confinement and constraint, Saichō's program reflected his attempt to prepare the Bodhisattva monks for broad service to society. In this respect, the program incorporated some of the public, charitable activities earlier associated with Gyōgi (chap. 45) in Shōmu's time and also the secular roles traditionally identified with the Confucian "noble person" (Ch: *junzi*, J: *kunshi*). This breadth of scope and balance of learning was represented by the three roles that Saichō had in mind for his monks: those who were gifted in both speech and action, who would be called "treasures of the nation" (*kokuhō*) and would be kept at the mountain headquarters to serve as religious leaders; those gifted in speech but perhaps not in action, who would be "teachers of the nation" (*kokushi*) who would spread the teaching in the country at large; and those primarily adept at practical activities who would be known as "of service to the nation" (*kokuyō*), performing useful public works in construction, engineering, and charitable projects.

At the height of the state-building phase in early Japan, the word rendered here as "nation" had strong connotations of the dynastic state, and Saichō thought of his efforts as serving the aim of mutual support and protection between Buddhism and the imperial state, known as "Buddhism protective of the state" (*gokoku bukkyō*). Indeed, his monastic establishment—standing as a moral and spiritual bastion to the northeast of the capital (as protection against evil spirits from that direction)—was known as the "Protector of the Nation" (*Chingo kokka*). Hence Saichō, both dependent on Kanmu's support and intensely devoted to him, emphasized loyalty to the ruler and also, in his emphasis on service to the people and on making religious salvation more accessible to them, gave a certain populist, if not nationalist, tone to his concept of the state or nation (*koku*). In an age often obsessed with the pessimistic view that Buddhism had entered a state of decline (in the latter degenerate stage of the Law, *mappō*), Saichō seemed almost optimistic with regard to the Japanese people's capacity for fulfilling the Lotus's promise of universal salvation.

Saichō's last years were difficult ones personally. When his political fortunes were reversed after the death of his great patron Kanmu in 806, Saichō's petition to establish an independent ordination platform for his Bodhisattva monks and to be free of the state superintendency dominated by the Nara sects was strongly opposed by the latter, which held steadfastly to traditional Buddhist practices. Accusations between Nara and Mount Hiei became more and more acrimonious.

Thus, contrary to Saichō's original, rather generous, ecumenical impulses in the context of continuing sectarian rivalry, even his efforts to project and implement a vision of the Greater Vehicle as a broad-based religious movement were beset by sectarian defensiveness and a siege mentality. It was only after Saichō's death in 822, following years of unremitting and unrewarding struggle, that the court gave its belated approval, as a kind of posthumous tribute, to his proposals for an independent center at Mount Hiei.

The groundwork done and the broad religious base established by Saichō for this mountain monastery proved remarkably durable. The Tendai Lotus school and his Enryakuji Temple continued to serve as a major headquarters of Japanese Buddhism and as a fountainhead for many of the most vital religious currents of succeeding ages.

## THE TENDAI LOTUS TEACHING

### SAICHŌ: VOW OF UNINTERRUPTED STUDY OF THE LOTUS SŪTRA

This vow taken by monks on Mount Hiei expresses Saichō's (and their own) commitment to the Lotus teaching as expounded by Zhiyi and practiced according to his prescriptions for the calming and contemplation discipline. It also invokes the Imperial authority of Kanmu as the great patron and supporter of Saichō's project and, by its reference to the Golden Light Sūtra, reaffirms the monastery's role as protector of the state.

The disciple of Buddha and student of the One Vehicle [name and court rank to be filled in] this day respectfully affirms before the Three Treasures that the saintly Emperor Kanmu, on behalf of Japan and as a manifestation of his unconditional compassion, established the Lotus sect and had the Lotus Sūtra, its commentary, and the essays on "Calming and Contemplation" copied and bound together with hundreds of other volumes and installed them in the seven great temples. Constantly did he promote the Single and Only Vehicle, and he united all the people so that they might ride together in the ox cart of Mahāyāna[3] to the ultimate destination, enlightenment. Every year assemblies[4] on the Golden Light Sūtra were held to protect the state. He selected twelve students and established a seminary on top of Mount Hiei where the Tripiṭaka, the ritual implements, and the sacred images were enshrined. These treasures he considered the guardian of the Law and its champion during the great night of ignorance.

It is for this reason that on the fifteenth day of the second moon of 809, Saichō, with a few members of the same faith, established the uninterrupted study of the sūtra of the Lotus of the Wondrous Law.

I vow that, as long as heaven endures and earth lasts, to the most distant term of the future, this study will continue without the intermission of a single day, at the rate of one volume every two days. Thus the doctrine of universal enlightenment will be preserved forever and spread throughout Japan to the farthest confines. May all attain Buddhahood!

[*Dengyō Daishi zenshū* vol. 4, p. 749 (1912 ed.)]


### REGULATIONS FOR STUDENTS OF THE MOUNTAIN SCHOOL IN SIX ARTICLES I

Saichō's new regulations set forth his threefold conception of the vocation of bodhisattva monks who will both propagate the Mahāyāna teaching and engage in socially beneficial activities. These rules are intended specifically for monks authorized to pursue the Tendai Lotus teaching, but in addition to this exoteric (public) doctrine, they are to be versed in some esoteric mysteries, as well as with the standard texts associated with "Buddhism as the protector of the state." This broad program is to occupy them during their twelve-year confinement on the mountains, whose rigors supplant the strict observance of *vinaya* discipline.

The original version of these regulations, drawn up in 818, is in three sections, of which the first two are translated here. The first two paragraphs are often cited at Mount Hiei as a kind of charter for the school.


What is the treasure of the nation? The religious nature is a treasure, and he who possesses this nature is the treasure of the nation. That is why it was said of old that ten pearls big as pigeon's eggs do not constitute the treasure of a nation, but only when a person casts his light over a part of the country can one speak of a

---

3. The three vehicles are described in the Lotus Sūtra; of them the oxcart stands for Mahāyāna.

4. These assemblies, often called *gosaie* ("imperial vegetarian entertainments" of monks), were held during the first moon of the Imperial Palace from 802, when Kanmu founded them, until 1467 (see De Visser, *Ancient Buddhism in Japan*, pp. 471–479). The text studied was the Golden Light Sūtra.

treasure of the nation. A philosopher of old[5] once said that he who is capable in action but not in speech should be of service to the nation; but he who is capable both in action and speech is the treasure of the nation. Apart from these three groups, there are those who are capable neither of speech nor action: these are the betrayers[6] of the nation.

Buddhists who possess the religious nature are called in the west bodhisattvas; in the east they are known as superior men.[7] They hold themselves responsible for all bad things while they credit others with all good things. Forgetful of themselves, they benefit others. This represents the summit of compassion.

Among Buddha's followers there are two kinds of monks, Hīnayāna and Mahāyāna; Buddhists possessing a religious nature belong to the later persuasion. However, in our eastern land only Hīnayāna is revered[8] and not the Mahāyāna. The Great Teaching is not yet spread; great men have not been able to rise. I fervently pray that in accordance with the wishes of the Emperor,[9] all Tendai students annually appointed will be trained in the Mahāyāna doctrines and become bodhisattva monks.[10]

## Regulations for the Two Students Annually Appointed by the Court

1. All annually appointed Tendai Lotus students, from this year 818 to all eternity, shall be of the Mahāyāna persuasion. They shall be granted Buddhist names without, however, having their own family names removed from the register. They shall be initiated into the Perfect Ten Good Precepts of Tendai when they become novices and, when they are ordained government seals will be requested for their certificates.

2. All Mahāyāna students, immediately after their ordination, shall be administered the vows of Sons of Buddha and thus become bodhisattva monks. A government seal will be requested for the certificates of oaths. Those who take the Precepts will be required to remain on Mount Hiei for twelve years without ever leaving the monastery. They shall study both disciplines.

---

5. Mouzi, a late Han philosopher, who attempted to synthesize Buddhism, Confucianism, and Daoism, according to Buddhism, which had the highest position. (Saichō quotes from *Mouzi*, p. 13b, Bing-jin-guan cong-shu ed.)

6. This word seems far too strong for the offense, and it may be a corruption in the text in which Mouzi calls these people "mean" (or "lowly").

7. Or "gentlemen"—the name given by Confucius to people who followed his code.

8. Even though Nara Buddhism was predominantly Mahāyāna, Saichō deprecated its continued adherence to vestiges of the so-called Hīnayāna.

9. Emperor Kanmu issued this order shortly before his death in 806.

10. That is, Mahāyāna monks, for the bodhisattva was held up by Mahāyāna Buddhism as the ideal to be followed.

3. All monks studying the Calming and Contemplation (*shikan*) discipline shall be required every day of the year to engage in constant study and discussion of the Lotus, Golden Light, Sūtra of the Humane Kings, Protector, and other Mahāyāna sūtras for safeguarding the nation.[11]

4. All monks who study the Vairochana discipline shall be required every day of the year to recite the True Words (*mantra*) of the Vairochana, the Peacock, the Rope [of salvation], the Wise King, and other sūtras for safeguarding the nation.[12]

5. Students of both disciplines shall be appointed to positions in keeping with their achievements after twelve years' training and study. Those who are capable in both action and speech shall remain permanently on the mountain as leaders of the order: these are the treasures of the nation. Those who are capable in speech but not in action shall be teachers of the nation, and those capable in action but not in speech shall be of service to the nation.

6. Teachers and functionaries of the nation shall be appointed with official licenses as transmitters of doctrine and national lecturers. The national lecturers shall be paid during their tenure of office the expenses of the annual summer retreat and provided with their robes. Funds for these expenses shall be deposited in the provincial offices where they will be supervised jointly by provincial and district governors.

They shall also serve in undertakings which benefit the nation and the people, such as the repair of ponds and canals, the reclamation of uncultivated land, the reparation of landslides, the construction of bridges and ships, the planting of trees and ramie[13] bushes, the sowing of hemp and grasses, and the digging of wells and irrigation ditches. They shall also study the sūtras and cultivate their minds but shall not engage in private agriculture or trading.

If these provisions are followed, men possessing the religious nature will spring up one after another throughout the country, and the Way of the Superior Man shall never die.

Overcome by profound awe, I offer these articles of Tendai and respectfully request the imperial assent.

Saichō, the Monk who formerly sought the Law in China [June 19, 818].

[*Dengyō Daishi zenshū* vol. 1, pp. 11–13 (1989 ed.)]

## REGULATIONS FOR STUDENTS OF THE MOUNTAIN SCHOOL II

The following regulations provide more specific provisions governing the life of the monastery and the content of the curriculum. Scripture studies have priority over

---

11. Japanese names for the sūtras: *Hokkekyō, Konkōkyō, Ninnōkyō,* and *Shugokyō.*

12. Japanese names for the sūtras: *Dainichi-kyō, Kujaku-kyō, Fukū Kensaku Kannon-gyō,* and *Ichiji Chōrinnō-gyō.* These represent the Esoteric discipline.

13. A plant whose fibers are similar to those of hemp in their properties and uses.

meditative practice during the first six years, but the order is reversed in the last six. Confucian classics constitute one-third of the monks' textual studies, as if to acknowledge that a public philosophy and political ethos are not provided by the sūtras avowing loyalty to the state and that the latter needs to be supplemented if substantive service to the state and society is to be realized. Details are lacking, however, on the classics to be read or on how strictly the regulations were followed.

1. Twelve regular students of the Tendai sect will be appointed for terms of six years each. Each year as two places fall vacant, they are to be replaced by two new students.

The method of examining students will be as follows. All Tendai teachers will assemble in the Seminary Hall and there examine candidates on their recitations of the Lotus and Golden Light Sūtras. When a student passes the examinations, his family name and the date of the examination will be reported to the government.

Students who have completed six years of study will be examined in the above manner. Students who fail to complete the course will not be examined. If any students withdraw, their names, together with those of the candidates for their places, should be reported to the government.

2. Regular students must provide their own clothing and board. Students who possess the proper mental ability and whose conduct is excellent but who cannot provide their own clothing and board shall be furnished by the monastery with a document authorizing them to seek alms throughout the county for their expenses.

3. If a regular student's character does not accord with the monastic discipline and he does not obey the regulations, a report will be made to the government requesting his replacement in accordance with the regulations.

4. Regular students are required to receive the Mahāyāna initiation during the year of their ordination. After the ceremony, they shall remain for twelve years within the gates of the monastery engaged in study and practice. During the first six years, the study of the sūtras under a master will be their major occupation, with meditation and the observance of discipline their secondary pursuits. Two-thirds of their time will be devoted to Buddhism and the remaining third to the Chinese classics. An extensive study of the sūtras will be their duty, and teaching others about Buddhism, their work. During the second six years in residence, meditation and the observance of discipline will be their chief occupation, and the study of the sūtras their secondary pursuit. In the practice of Calming and Contemplation (*shikan*) students will be required to observe the four forms of meditation and in the esoteric practice will be required to recite the three sūtras.[14]

5. The names of Tendai students at the Ichijō Shikan Monastery[15] on Mount Hiei, whether students with annual grants or privately enrolled, should not be

---

14. The three basic sūtras of Esoteric Buddhism: the *Dainichi-kyō*, the *Kongōchō-gyō*, and the *Soshichi-kyō*.

15. The temple's name may be translated literally as "of the one Vehicle for Calming and Contemplation."

removed from the rolls of temples with which they were originally affiliated. For the purposes of receiving provisions, they should nevertheless be assigned to one of the wealthy temples in Ōmi.[16] In keeping with Mahāyāna practice, alms will be sought throughout the country to provide them with summer and winter robes. With the material needs of their bodies thus taken care of, they will be able to continue their studies without interruption. Once admitted to the monastery, it will be a fast rule for these students that a thatched hut will serve as their quarters and bamboo leaves as their seats.[17] They will value but slightly their own lives, reverencing the Law. They will strive to perpetuate the Law eternally and to safeguard the nation.

6. If ordained monks who belong to other sects and are not recipients of annual appointments wish of their own free will to spend twelve years on the mountain in order to study the two courses [of study or practice], their original temple affiliation and the name of their master, together with documents from this monastery, must be deposited in the government office. When they have completed twelve years of study, they will be granted the title of master of the Law as in the case of the annual appointees of the Tendai sect. If they should fail to live up to the regulations, they are to be returned to the temple with which they were originally affiliated.

7. The request will be made that the court bestow the title of great master of the Law on students who have remained twelve years on the mountain and have studied and observed the disciplines in strict adherence to the regulations. The request will be made that the court bestow the title master of the Law on students who, although they may not be accomplished in their studies, have spent twelve years on the mountain without ever having left it.

If any members of the sect fail to observe the regulations and do not remain on the mountain or if, in spite of their having remained on the mountain, they have been guilty of numerous infractions of the Law or have failed to remain the full period, they will be removed permanently from the official register of the Tendai sect and returned to the temple with which they were originally affiliated.

8. Two lay attendants will be appointed to this Tendai monastery to supervise it alternately and to keep out robbers, liquor, and women. Thus the Buddhist Law will be upheld and the nation safeguarded.

The above eight articles are for the maintenance of the Buddhist Law and the benefit of the nation. They should serve the way of goodness.

The imperial assent is respectfully requested.

Saichō, the Monk who formerly sought the Law in China [September 30, 818].

[*Dengyō Daishi zenshū* vol. 1, pp. 13–16 (1989 ed.)]

---

16. The region near Lake Biwa, where many rich immigrants, often of Chinese extraction, were domiciled.

17. That is, they will lead a life of poverty.

# SUBSEQUENT HISTORY OF TENDAI
# AND MOUNT HIEI

At the time of Saichō's death, the Tendai school consisted of only a few underfunded monks on Mount Hiei, a site that must have seemed cold and inhospitable compared with life in the monasteries of Nara and Kyoto. Saichō's attempts to master Esoteric Buddhism had been eclipsed by those of Kūkai's Shingon school, so much so that some of Saichō's students attempted to study with Kūkai even after relations between Saichō and Kūkai had worsened. Despite these inauspicious beginnings, within 150 years the Tendai institution on Mount Hiei became the most powerful religious institution in Japan. Some of the reasons for its success are surveyed next. The Japanese nobility were much more interested in Esoteric Buddhism than in the details of Chinese Tiantai doctrine or in complex systems of meditation. Whereas Kūkai had given the Shingon school a system of Esoteric doctrine that would seem to require little modification for several centuries, the Tendai school's incomplete system demanded additions. As a result, Ennin (794–864) and Enchin (814–891) traveled to China to bring back supplementary teachings and rituals. Tendai Esoteric teachings were then systematized by Annen (841–897?). The result was a body of Esoteric ritual and doctrine that rivaled and even surpassed that of the Shingon school.

By the tenth century, Tendai monks had forged close ties with factions of the nobility by performing rituals, often Esoteric, that were designed to help the lay patrons prosper and defeat their enemies. The purposes of Esoteric rituals performed by Ryōgen (912–985), the cleric who helped make Tendai power prominent in medieval Japan, serve as a good example. These rituals were directed at ensuring the repose of the regent Fujiwara no Tadahira (880–949), ensuring that Tadahira's son Morosuke (908–960) would succeed in his plans to control the throne, protect Morosuke's wives in childbirth as they gave birth to future emperors, and then protect those emperors against the angry ghosts of Morosuke's competitors, as well as healing various illnesses and bringing good fortune. In return for their services, the Tendai establishment received land in the form of manors (*shōen*). In addition, some of the younger sons of the nobility became monks so that they could oversee the manors and rituals, thereby cementing the ties between the monastic factions and their secular patrons.

The Tendai school's success was also ensured by the development of an impressive system for educating monks. Young monks were taught to read scriptures and then tested in a series of examinations that began at the local level and ended at the monasteries on Mount Hiei. The examinations often consisted of a question drawn at random. The student was then required to recite the relevant passages from scripture concerning the topic, discuss and reconcile passages that seemed to be contradictory, and then sum up his argument. Specially chosen older monks questioned him as he went through the process. A monk who successfully completed these would be a skilled lecturer and intellectually agile enough to compete with Tendai rivals, particularly the Hossō monks. The process of taking passages out of context sometimes gave Tendai scholars the freedom to develop doctrinal positions remote from those of their Chinese Tiantai antecedents.

A severe persecution of Chinese Buddhism in 845 had resulted in the loss of most Tiantai texts on the Chinese mainland. Accordingly, Japanese Tendai monks rarely consulted their Chinese counterparts about Tiantai doctrine and instead developed teachings in their own ways. When Japanese nobles became monks, they often maintained control over the lands they brought to the school, and so only certain monks could be appointed as high-ranking monastic officials in many Tendai temples. This system of favoritism, along with the alliances between certain temples and certain cliques of nobles, increased the factionalism within the school. By the early eleventh century, monks from Enchin's lineage were being expelled from the main complex on Mount Hiei by monks from Ennin's lineage and retreated to Onjōji near Lake Biwa. In the ensuing centuries, the monks from the two factions fought, sometimes burning each other's monasteries and killing each other.

One of the main components of Tendai doctrine during the middle ages was called *hongaku*, translated by such terms as "primordial" and "original enlightenment." This teaching, derived from Mahāyāna teachings on the Buddha nature, maintained that people already were enlightened but had lost sight of this truth. This insight was interpreted in a variety of ways. In its most extreme form, monks might argue that people, just as they were, were already Buddhas. Thus little or no religious practice was required. But the same teachings also could be interpreted as requiring a variety of degrees of religious practice. *Hongaku* teachings were often given verbally in secret transmissions that strengthened lineages.

Although the medieval Tendai school was often criticized for its involvement in politics, some Tendai monks were noted for their desire to withdraw from society. Ryōgen's student Genshin (942–1017) is typical of a number of Tendai monks who refused to become involved in politics. His work, *Essentials of Rebirth*, played a major role in popularizing Pure Land Buddhism in Japan. Shōshin (1136–1220 or 1131–1215) was famous for his classical learning, criticisms of *hongaku* interpretations, and attempts to promote the classical Chinese Tiantai works by Zhiyi. Although most of the Tendai school did not return to the Chinese interpretation of Zhiyi's texts, the return to the study of those texts remains a potent force in the modern Tendai school. Still other monks called for renewed emphasis on the disciplinary precepts. Among them were Shunjō (1166–1227), who traveled to China to bring back traditional "Hīnayāna" ordinations, and Kōen (1263–1317), who attempted to revive Saichō's system of being in retreat on Mount Hiei for twelve years and strictly observing the precepts. Such a wide range of teachings, practices, and interpretations indicates the Tendai school's success in creating a broad synthesis under the rubric of the Lotus Sūtra's teaching of the One-Vehicle.

The Tendai school's power came to an end when Oda Nobunaga burned down the Tendai establishment on Mount Hiei in 1571. However, the Tendai prelate Tenkai (1536–1643) managed to revive the Tendai's fortunes somewhat by establishing a mausoleum for Tokugawa Ieyasu at Nikkō. Today the Tendai school is one of the smaller Buddhist schools, although it still controls many historically significant temples.

## Chapter 47

### KŪKAI AND ESOTERIC BUDDHISM

Outstanding among the Buddhist leaders of the Heian period was Kūkai (774–835), a man whose genius has well been described: "His memory lives all over the country, his name is a household word in the remotest places, not only as a saint, but as a preacher, a scholar, a poet, a sculptor, a painter, an inventor, an explorer, and—sure passport to fame—a great calligrapher."[1] Indeed, his reputation was so great that Shingon Buddhism, the sect of Buddhism that he founded, is centered as much on the worship of Kūkai the saint as it is on the teachings of Esoteric Buddhism, the larger tradition to which Shingon belongs. From the ninth century to this day, faithful Shingon believers have revered Kūkai as a living savior who still sits in eternal meditation on Mount Kōya ready to respond to those who call on him for help. The divinization of Kūkai is the product of an imagination inspired by faith, and it is also based on the memory of a real person of extraordinary accomplishments.

Kūkai came from one of Japan's great aristocratic families. As a boy, he showed exceptional ability in his studies, and at the age of fifteen, he was taken by his uncle, a Confucian scholar and imperial tutor, to the capital for further education. In 791 the eighteen-year-old Kūkai entered the Confucian college that had been established to train young men to serve in official government positions, and there he read widely in the Confucian classics. By this time, his

---

1. Sansom, *Japan, a Short Cultural History*, p. 230.

family's political fortunes had waned, and his relatives expected him to use his talents and training to help restore their position. But Kūkai abruptly withdrew from college and left the capital to become a wandering mendicant in the forests.

The reasons for this sudden change are given in the preface to his first major work, *Indications of the Goals of the Three Teachings*, which he wrote in 797 at the age of twenty-four. He describes his meeting a Buddhist monk while he was a student at the university and learning a mantra for increasing his memory and understanding of Buddhist scriptures. "Believing what the Buddha says to be true," Kūkai threw himself into this practice in the mountains and by the seashore and had such a deeply moving experience that he decided to enter the Buddhist order against his family's wishes. In arguing for the superiority of Buddhism over Confucianism and Daoism, Kūkai wrote the *Indications* to justify his decision to take up the religious life and to explain why such a seemingly rash action was not really at odds with loyalty, filial piety, and morality.

Having discovered a copy of the Mahāvairocana Sūtra, one of the basic scriptures of Esoteric Buddhism, Kūkai was determined to learn more of its teachings and rituals. A rare opportunity was afforded him when he was selected to accompany an official diplomatic mission to China in 804. The ship on which he was traveling with the ambassador of the mission ran into severe weather and drifted far to the south, landing near the city of Fuzhou. Another ship carried the vice ambassador and the monk Saichō, the founder of Tendai Buddhism in Japan, and managed to arrive at Mingzhou to the south of the Yangtze River. Unlike Saichō, who studied different forms of Buddhism for less than a year before returning to Japan, Kūkai traveled far inland to the capital of Changan, where he stayed for two and a half years studying Sanskrit and Esoteric Buddhism with Indian and Chinese masters at the Ximing Temple, one of the major centers of Buddhist studies.

The international character of Buddhism was very much in evidence in Changan, one of the world's great cities at that time. Chinese, Japanese, Korean, and Southeast Asian students studied with learned teachers from India, Central Asia, and China and joined together to translate Sanskrit and Central Asian texts into Chinese. They also wrote commentaries, compiled dictionaries and concordances, wrote language textbooks, discussed doctrinal issues, debated sectarian differences, and engaged in the life of practice and rituals. Kūkai thrived in this rich atmosphere of learning and concentrated on studying Sanskrit with an Indian teacher and Esoteric Buddhism under the tutelage of Huiguo (746–805), the Chinese heir to the Esoteric tradition developed by Indian and Central Asian masters. He returned to Japan as the eighth—and first Japanese—patriarch of the Shingon school.

As used to describe the kind of Buddhism Kūkai learned in China, the term Esoteric has several meanings. In terms of *practice*, Esoteric Buddhism is characterized by—though it has no monopoly over—the use of *mantras* (formulaic chants), *mandalas* (diagrams of deities and the ritual universe), *mudras* (ritual hand gestures), and graphic forms of meditation that use the sensory faculties to allow the practitioner to be immersed in the world of the buddhas and bodhisattvas. In a strict *sectarian* sense, Esoteric Buddhism is identified primarily with the Shingon school, although it later included Tendai (technically a form of Exoteric Buddhism) after Saichō's successors adopted Shingon ideas and practices. In its style of *transmission*, Esoteric Buddhism is thought of as abstruse and secret and therefore can be passed on from a master only to qualified and worthy disciples who will maintain the confidentiality of the knowledge they receive. Kūkai related how Huiguo waited almost until his death before he found in his Japanese student an adequate receptacle of knowledge.

Shingon Buddhism was readily received by Heian aristocrats and later by commoners as well. The basis of its appeal lay in its bold reinterpretation of the basic Mahāyāna idea that the ordinary world is identical with the world of the buddhas. While Kūkai still affirmed that the world of the buddhas resists articulation and expression, he was optimistic in championing the teachings and rituals of Esoteric Buddhism as a means for overcoming that resistance. For instance, whereas in Exoteric teachings the dharma body (*dharmakāya*) of the Buddha was said to be beyond the reach of words and ideas, Kūkai asserted that the Dharmakāya Buddha preaches, has form, and therefore can be expressed in words and objects. In a society that valued literature and art so highly, Heian aristocrats found Shingon Buddhism aesthetically accessible. Kūkai brought back a trove of texts and ritual objects, and in his memorial to the emperor which lists and explains each item, he wrote:

> The law [dharma] has no speech, but without speech it cannot be expressed. Eternal truth [*tathatā*] transcends color, but only by means of color can it be understood. Mistakes will be made in the effort to point at the truth, for there is no clearly defined method of teaching, but even when art does not excite admiration by its unusual quality, it is a treasure which protects the country and benefits the people.
>
> In truth, the Esoteric doctrines are so profound as to defy their enunciation in writing. With the help of painting, however, their obscurities can be understood. The various attitudes and mudras of the holy images all have their source in Buddha's love, and one may attain Buddhahood at sight of them. Thus the secrets of the sutras and commentaries can be depicted in art, and the essential truths of the Esoteric teaching are all set forth therein. Neither teachers nor students can dispense with it. Art is what reveals to us the state of perfection. Shingon painting and sculpture utilize rich colors and elaborate motifs, all of which are filled with symbolic meanings communicated through the forms themselves and can be discussed with extensive elaboration.[2]

---

2. Kūkai, *Memorial on the Presentation of the List of Newly Imported Sutras*, quoted in Moriyama, ed., *Kōbō Daishi den*, p. 249.

Probably the Shingon school's most important use of painting was in the two mandalas, representations of the cosmos under the two aspects of potential entity and dynamic manifestations. The indestructible potential aspect of the cosmos is depicted in the Diamond (Vajra) Mandala. In the center, Mahāvairocana Buddha is shown in contemplation, seated on a white lotus and encircled by a white halo. Around him are various buddhas and sacred implements. The dynamic aspect of the cosmos is depicted in the Womb (Garbha) Mandala, "wherein the manifold groups of deities and other beings are arrayed according to the kinds of the powers and intentions they embody. In the center there is a red lotus flower, with its seed-pod and eight petals, which symbolizes the heart of the universe." [3] Mahāvairocana Buddha is seated on the seedpod of the lotus, and the petals are occupied by other buddhas.

The mandalas were used to represent the life and being of Mahāvairocana Buddha and also served to evoke mysterious powers, much in the way that the mudras were performed. One important ceremony in which the mandalas figured was that in which an acolyte was required to throw a flower on the mandalas. The Buddha on which his flower alighted was the one he was to worship and emulate particularly. It is recorded that Kūkai's flower fell on Mahāvairocana Buddha in both the Diamond and Womb Mandalas. His master was amazed at this divine indication of the great destiny in store for the young Japanese.

The special relationship between Kūkai and Mahāvairocana is symbolic of the central Shingon teaching of the Three Mysteries of the body, mouth, and mind by which even ordinary people can gain intimacy with the world of the Buddha. Through the use of mudras, which are prescribed gestures formed with the hands, a kind of ritual sign language is made possible by which one can both communicate with Mahāvairocana Buddha, the dharmakāya who speaks, and also be bodily identified with this central figure of the Shingon pantheon. With one's mouth, mantras can be recited, and in the proper ritual context, verbal communication and identity can be established. The mind is the means of meditation, and through it, one can think right thoughts and visualize the buddhas and the worlds they live in. Human faculties are thus capable of understanding and experiencing a good part, if not the entirety, of what it means to be enlightened, and it is this optimistic affirmation of the ability to become a buddha in this bodily existence that found ready appeal. Later in the Kamakura period, doubts about and a loss of confidence in this claim gave rise to Pure Land Buddhist movements that proposed rebirth in the Pure Land as an alternative to achieving enlightenment.

---

3. Anesaki, *History of Japanese Religion*, pp. 126–127.

Despite its inherent appeal, the Shingon Buddhism of Kūkai still represented a new sect and thus posed an institutional challenge to the Buddhism established in Nara. Saichō's Tendai Buddhism also faced the same difficulty of gaining acceptance, but unlike Saichō, who chose to oppose the Nara establishment and press for the independent right to ordain his own priests, Kūkai adopted a cooperative approach. He established good relations with major Buddhist leaders and even gained ecclesiastical appointments to important temples. These appointments were made by the government, and throughout his life after his return from China, he held a variety of positions in temples other than those of his own Shingon sect. In 810, for instance, Kūkai was made the administrative head of Tōdaiji, the most important institution of the Nara establishment, and in 827 he held the government post of senior director of monastic officials (*daisōzu*).

Kūkai held these and other positions all the while he worked to establish his own Shingon institution. In 816, at the age of forty-three, he received permission from the court to build a monastic center on Mount Kōya, a site he selected in the remote mountains far to the south of Nara and even farther from the new capital in Kyoto. He chose this location precisely because of its remoteness, believing that natural wilderness was most conducive to religious discipline and practice. Since his official duties kept him away from Mount Kōya most of the time, his disciples assumed the responsibility of developing the monastery as the headquarters of his growing sect. After Kūkai died on Mount Kōya at the age of sixty-two in 835, they propagated the legend that he really did not die but was still alive sitting in eternal meditation in his mausoleum. Mount Kōya is still the destination of many pilgrims who worship him as a living savior and call him by his posthumous name, Kōbō Daishi, the Great Master of the Extensive Dharma.

# KŪKAI AND HIS MASTER

### THE TRANSMISSION OF ESOTERIC BUDDHISM

This passage is taken from A *Memorial Presenting a List of Newly Imported Sutras and Other Items*, which Kūkai wrote to the emperor upon his return from studying in China. In addition to listing the many religious articles that he brought back with him, Kūkai reports on the results of his studies and extols the doctrines into which he was initiated. Among the points that he especially emphasizes are (1) his personal success in gaining acceptance by the greatest Buddhist teacher of the day in China; (2) the authenticity of this teaching in a direct line of succession from the Buddha; (3) the great favor in which this teaching was held by the recent emperors of the Tang dynasty, to the extent that it represented the best and most influential doctrine current in the Chinese capital; and (4) the fact that this teaching offers the easiest and quickest means of obtaining Buddhahood, probably an important recommendation for it in the eyes of a busy monarch.

The sea of dharma is of one flavor but has deep and shallow aspects in accordance with the capacity of the believer. Five Vehicles[4] can be distinguished, sudden and gradual according to the vessel. Among the teachings of sudden enlightenment, some are Exoteric and some, Esoteric. In Esoteric Buddhism itself, some aspects represent the source, others, the tributary. The teachers of the dharma of former times swam in the waters of the tributary and hung on to the leaves, but the teaching transmitted to me now uproots the stump which blocks the source and penetrates it through and through. Why?

In ancient times Vajrasattva personally received the teaching from Mahāvairocana. Several centuries later it was transmitted to the Bodhisattva Nāgārjuna, who transmitted it to the Acharya Vajrabodhi (670–741), the Tripiṭaka master, who for the first time taught the fivefold Esoteric Buddhist doctrine[5] in China during the Kaiyuan era (713–741). Although the emperor himself revered the doctrine, Vajrabodhi could not spread it widely. Only through my spiritual grandfather [Bukung], the Acharya of Broad Wisdom, did it become popular. Bukung first received the transmission from Vajrabodhi, the Tripiṭaka master, and moreover visited the Acharya Nāgabodhi in southern India and acquired completely the Vajraśekhara Sūtra comprising eighteen divisions. After having studied thoroughly the Esoteric Buddhist teachings consisting of the doctrines of the Matrix, etc., he returned to China during the Tianbao era (742–756). At this time Emperor Xuanzong first received *abhiṣeka* from him; the emperor revered him as his teacher. Since then Emperors Suzong (r. 756–762) and Daizong (r. 763–779) have received the Dharma. The Shenlong Monastery was built within the imperial palace, and everywhere in the capital the altars for *abhiṣeka* were set up. The emperor and the government officials went to the altars to receive *abhiṣeka*; the four classes of believers and the populace reverently learned the Esoteric Buddhist teachings. This was the period when the Esoteric Buddhist school began to flourish, and from this time on the practice of *abhiṣeka* was widely adopted.

According to Exoteric Buddhist doctrines, one must spend three eons to attain enlightenment, but according to the Esoteric doctrines, one can expect sixteen great spiritual rebirths [within this life].[6] In speed and in excellence, the two doctrines differ as much as one endowed with supernatural power differs from a lame donkey.

[Adapted from Hakeda, *Kūkai: Major Works*, pp. 143–144]

---

4. Vehicle (*yāna*) means the teachings that carry sentient beings to their respective goals. There are vehicles for common men, celestial beings, shrāvakas, pratyeka-buddhas, and bodhisattvas.

5. The fivefold Esoteric Buddhist doctrine means the teachings given in the Vajraśekhara Sūtra in which the buddhas, bodhisattvas, and others are classified under the five divisions—Buddha, Vajra, Ratna (jewel), padma (lotus), and karma (action). Vajrabodhi, who came from India to China in 720, first introduced the Esoteric Buddhist teachings belonging to the Diamond Realm.

6. To experience the samādhi of sixteen Bodhisattvas in the mandala of the Diamond Realm.

# ENLIGHTENMENT IN THIS BODILY EXISTENCE

Throughout the history of Buddhism, the central debate regarding enlightenment has been whether it can be realized in this existence or only after many lifetimes. Kūkai's position, which is characteristic of Esoteric Buddhism as a whole, is that it can be realized immediately, and he wrote a treatise, *Attaining Buddhahood in This Bodily Existence* (*Sokushin jōbutsu gi*), to explain and prove his point. After establishing that the idea is attested to in the scriptures, Kūkai presses his point forward with some standard Mahāyāna ideas such as harmony and the notion of the interpenetration of things with all other things, which is exemplified in the image of Indra's Net. He also uses Esoteric Buddhist ideas, in particular the teaching of the Three Mysteries and *kaji*, or grace. It is important to note—as Kūkai himself reiterates—that these ideas are to be experienced in meditation and ritual practice, for it is only in this context that the practitioner's three mysteries of body, mouth, and mind will be interfused with the Three Mysteries of Mahāvairocana. A similar harmony can be reached in the experience of *kaji*, which is linked with the practice of prayer. *Ka* is the bestowal or adding of grace by Mahāvairocana, and *ji* is the receiving and retaining of it by the practitioner. The idea of enlightenment in this existence was continually debated by those who accepted it as a practical goal and those who rejected it as an impossibility, and as such, it exerted an enormous influence on Buddhist thought in Japan.

> QUESTION: In sūtras and shastras it is explained that after three eons, one can attain enlightenment. Is there evidence for the assertion that one can attain enlightenment in this very existence?
>
> ANSWER: The Tathāgata has explained it in the Esoteric Buddhist texts.
>
> QUESTION: How is it explained?
>
> ANSWER: It is said in the Vajraśekhara Sūtra that "he who practices this samādhi can immediately realize the enlightenment of the Buddha." Also: "If the sentient beings who have come across this teaching practice it diligently four times day and night, they will realize the stage of joy in this life and perfect enlightenment in their subsequent sixteen lives."
>
> REMARKS: "This teaching" in the foregoing quotation refers to the king of teachings, the teaching of samādhi realized by the Dharmakāya Buddha himself. "The stage of joy" is not the first stage of Bodhisattvahood as defined in the Exoteric Buddhist teachings but the first stage of Buddhahood of our Buddha Vehicle, the details of which are explained in the chapter discussing stages.[7] By "sixteen lives" is meant that one is

---

7. Kūkai seems to be referring to the discussion of the ten stages of the development of the religious mind in the first chapter of the Mahāvairocana Sūtra (see pp. 706–708).

to realize the attainments of the sixteen great Bodhisattvas,[8] the details of which are also explained in the chapter discussing the stages. Again it is said: "If a man disciplines himself according to this superior doctrine, he will be able to attain in this life unsurpassed enlightenment." Furthermore: "It should be known that he himself turns into the Diamond Realm; since he becomes identical with the Diamond, he is firm and indestructible. An awareness will emerge that he is of the Diamond Body." The Mahāvairocana Sūtra states: "Without forsaking his body, he obtains supernatural power, wanders on the ground of great space, and perfects the Mystery of Body." Also: "If he wishes to gain the perfection of religious discipline in his lifetime, he must select a certain method of meditation that suits his inclinations and concentrate on it. For this, he must personally receive instruction in mantra recitation from an authentic master. If he observes the mantras and masters yoga, he will gain perfection."

. . .

QUESTION: How do you analyze the meaning of the words [attaining enlightenment in this bodily existence] given in these sūtras and shastras?

A summary in verse:

The Six Great Elements are interfused and are in a state of eternal harmony;
The Four Mandalas are inseparably related to one another:
When the grace of the Three Mysteries is retained,
[our inborn three mysteries will] quickly be manifested.
Infinitely interrelated like the meshes of Indra's net are what we call existences.

There is the One who is naturally equipped with all-embracing wisdom.
More numerous than particles of sand are those who have the King of Mind
    and the consciousnesses;
Each of them is endowed with the Fivefold Wisdom, with infinite wisdom.
All beings can truly attain enlightenment because of the force of mirrorlike
    wisdom.

. . .

These Esoteric Buddhist texts explain the methods of the samādhi of swift effect and suprarational action. If there is a man who wholeheartedly disciplines himself day and night according to the prescribed methods of discipline, he will obtain in his corporeal existence the Five Supernatural Powers.[9] And if he keeps

---

8. Kūkai interprets "sixteen lives" as realizing the samādhi of the sixteen Bodhisattvas surrounding the Four Buddhas in the inner circle of the Diamond Mandala, not as repeating the cycle of birth and death sixteen times.

9. Supernatural action, vision, hearing, ability to read the minds of others, and knowledge of former states of existences.

training himself, he will, without abandoning his body, advance to the stage of the Buddha. The details are as explained in the sūtras. For this reason it is said, "When the grace of the Three Mysteries is retained, [our inborn three mysteries will] quickly be manifested." The expression "the grace . . . is retained (*kaji*)" indicates great compassion on the part of the Tathāgata and faith (*shinjin*) on the part of sentient beings. The compassion of the Buddha pouring forth on the heart of sentient beings, like the rays of the sun on water, is called *ka* [adding], and the heart of sentient beings which keeps hold of the compassion of the Buddha, as water retains the rays of the sun, is called *ji* [retaining]. If the devotee understands this principle thoroughly and devotes himself to the practice of samādhi, his three mysteries will be united with the Three Mysteries, and therefore in his present existence, he will quickly manifest his inherent three mysteries. This is the meaning of the words, "[our inborn three mysteries will] quickly be manifested."

"Infinitely interrelated like the meshes of Indra's net are what we call existences." This line explains in simile the state of perfect interfusion and interpenetration of the infinite Three Mysteries of the manifestations [of Mahāvairocana]. Existence is my existence, the existences of the Buddhas, and the existences of all sentient beings. Also designated by this word is the Mahāvairocana Buddha in Four Forms, which represent his absolute state, his state of bliss, his manifesting bodies, and his emanating bodies. The three kinds of symbol—letters, signs, and images—are also included in this category. All of these existences are interrelated horizontally and vertically without end, like images in mirrors, or like the rays of lamps. This existence is in that one, and that one is in this. The Existence of the Buddha [Mahāvairocana] is the existences of the sentient beings and vice versa. They are not identical but are nevertheless identical; they are not different but are nevertheless different.

[Adapted from Hakeda, *Kūkai: Major Works*, pp. 225–232]

## *THE* TEN STAGES OF RELIGIOUS CONSCIOUSNESS

The realization of the nondual identity between Mahāvairocana and all forms of existence represents the highest level of consciousness that is not immediately apparent. This insight is attained by making progress through levels of understanding, which can be associated with the teachings of various religions and schools. The immediate occasion for Kūkai's *Ten Stages of Religious Consciousness*, in which Shingon is treated as a separate philosophy, was a decree issued in 830 by Emperor Junna ordering the six existing Buddhist sects to submit in writing the essentials of their beliefs. Of the works submitted at this time, Kūkai's *Ten Stages* was by far the most important in both quality and magnitude. Each of its ten chapters presents a successive stage upward of religious consciousness. The work was written entirely in Chinese, not merely good Chinese for a Japanese writer, but with an ornate poetical style somewhat reminiscent of Pope's attempt in his *Essay on Man* to present philosophical ideas in rhymed couplets. The following is Kūkai's own summary of his long and detailed essay on the ten stages.

### RECAPITULATION OF THE TEN STAGES
### OF RELIGIOUS CONSCIOUSNESS

1. The mind animal-like and goatish in its desires.

   The ordinary man in his madness realizes not his faults.

   He thinks but of his lusts and hungers like a butting goat.

2. The mind ignorant and infantile yet abstemious.

   Influenced by external causes, the mind awakens to temperance in eating.

   The will to do kindnesses sprouts, like a seed in good soil. [Confucianism.]

3. The mind infantile and without fears.

   The non-Buddhist hopes for rebirth in heaven, there for a while to know peace.

   He is like an infant, like a calf that follows its mother. [Brahmanism or popular Daoism.]

4. The mind recognizing only the objects perceived, not the ego.

   The mind understands only that there are Elements, the ego it completely denies.

   The Tripiṭaka of the Goat Cart is summed up by this verse [Shrāvaka vehicle of Hīnayāna Buddhism].

5. The mind freed from the causes and seeds of karma.

   Having mastered the twelve-divisioned cycle of causation and beginning, the mind extirpates the seeds of blindness.

   When karma birth has been ended, the ineffable fruits of nirvana are won. [Pratyeka Buddha vehicle of Hīnayāna Buddhism.]

6. The Mahāyāna mind bringing about the salvation of others.

   When compassion is aroused without condition, the Great Compassion first appears.

   It views distinctions between "you" and "me" as imaginary; recognizing only consciousness, it denies the external world [the Hossō school].

7. The mind aware of the negation of birth.

   Through eightfold negations, foolishness is ended; with one thought the truth of absolute Voidness becomes apparent.

   The mind becomes empty and still; it knows peace and happiness that cannot be defined [the Sanron school].

8. The mind which follows the one way of Truth.

   The universe is by nature pure; in it knowledge and its objects fuse together.

   He who knows this state of reality has a cosmic mind [the Tendai school].

9. The mind completely lacking characteristics of its own.

   Water lacks a nature of its own; when met by winds, it becomes waves.

   The universe has no determined form but, at the slightest stimulus, immediately moves forward [the Kegon school].

10.    The mind filled with the mystic splendor of the cosmic Buddha.

When the medicine of Exoteric teachings has cleared away the dust, the True Words open the Treasury.

When the secret treasures are suddenly displayed, all virtues are apparent [the Shingon school].

[*Kōbō Daishi zenshū*, vol. 1, p. 420; adapted from Hakeda,
*Kūkai: Major Works*, pp. 163–164]

## A SCHOOL OF ARTS AND SCIENCES

Kūkai's proposal to establish a "school of arts and sciences (*shūgei shūchi-in*)" reveals two important tendencies in his thought. First is the universalistic and egalitarian character of Mahāyāna Buddhism. Citing the teachings of the Lotus Sūtra, which stress the essential oneness of all being, Kūkai asks support for a school that would be open to all, regardless of social status or economic means. The second reflects Kūkai's catholic outlook, affirming the value of both religious and secular studies and also of combining the Three Teachings (Confucianism, Daoism, and Buddhism) in the school's curriculum.

Generally, in Japan as in China, religious and secular studies represented two separate ways of life. Recall that Saichō wished his monks to combine a religious and secular vocation, but classical Confucian studies had a very subordinate role in the training of Mount Hiei's monks, for whom he conceived social action and public service in very practical terms.

In Kūkai's time, secular education was closely linked to official recruitment and training and largely restricted to the ruling classes. Though ostensibly Confucian, it failed to measure up to Confucius's ideals of brotherhood, as Kūkai points out. Indeed, the aristocratic character of Japanese society strongly resisted the potentially egalitarian elements in Buddhism and Confucianism. In this case, even though a Fujiwara nobleman donated an attractive site for the school, Kūkai had difficulty obtaining continuing support for his work, and the school was forced to close ten years after his death, in 845. In recent times, however, it has been revived and is now an active four-year college supported by the Shingon sect.

Emperors have built state temples; their subjects have constructed private temples; in this way they have made efforts to spread the Way [Buddhism]. But those who wear robes in the temples study Buddhist scriptures, while scholars and students at the government college study non-Buddhist texts. Thus they are all stuck when it comes to books representing the Three Teachings and Five Sciences [as a whole]. Now I shall build a school of arts and sciences, offering instruction in the Three Teachings, and invite capable persons to join. With the aid of these teachings, which can be compared to the sun [Buddhism], the moon [Daoism], and the stars [Confucianism], my sincere desire is to enlighten those who are wandering in the dark down the wrong path, and lead them to the garden of enlightenment mounted on the Five Vehicles. . . .

It may be objected, however: "The government maintains a state college where the arts and sciences are encouraged and taught. What good is a mosquito's cry [a private school] compared to rumbling thunder [a government school]?"

My reply is: "In the capital of China, a school is set up in each ward to teach the young boys. In each prefecture a school is maintained in order widely to educate promising young students. Because of this, the capital is filled with talented young men and the nation is crowded with masters of the arts. In the capital of our country, however, there is only one government college and no local schools. As a result, sons of the poor have no opportunity to seek knowledge. Those who like to study but live a great distance from the college encounter great difficulty traveling to and fro. Would it not be good, then, to establish this school to assist the uneducated?" . . .

Although I am not of much ability, I am determined to pursue the plan under way; I will not give up this task, no matter how difficult it may be. Thus I may requite my vast obligations to the emperors, my parents, the people, and the Three Treasures and also make this a means of realizing Ultimate Truth, achieving the Highest Wisdom, and winning final deliverance.

[*Kōbō Daishi zenshū*, vol. 3, pp. 535–539]

## THE SPREAD OF ESOTERIC BUDDHISM

Students of the history of Japanese Buddhism may get the impression that the various schools were not only succeeded but also superseded by other sects as the religion developed. They may thus suppose that the schools of the Nara period gave way to Tendai and Shingon Buddhism, which in turn were replaced by one after another of the popular sects of the medieval period. Instead of following a regular sequence of rise, flourishing, decline, and extinction, however, most of the sects continued to exist long after their periods of glory and within their general patterns of growth, and were sometimes capable of unexpected revivals. This was certainly true of the Nara sects, some of which not only preserved their identity throughout the Heian and medieval periods but still exist today. Similarly, Esoteric Buddhism—by which is meant here both Tendai and Shingon—continued to be influential long after Kūkai's time. Esoteric Buddhism set the predominant tone of religious life in the Heian period, and its influence extended to all the other schools. Even the popular sects that turned away from its emphasis on ritual drew much of their inspiration from ideas and practices from the vast storehouse of Esoteric Buddhism. Its syncretism readily combined with other beliefs, whether the Buddhism of other sects, Shinto, or even disparate teachings like yin-yang. And a place for some new god could always be found in its spacious pantheon.

When, however, the hundreds of deities who populated the mandalas proved too much even for the polytheistic Japanese, their number was gradually reduced to thirteen preferred objects of worship: Fudō, Shaka, Monju, Fugen, Jizō, Miroku, Yakushi, Kannon, Seishi, Amida, Ashiku, Dainichi, and Kokūzō. Of these thirteen, the most exalted were considered to be Dainichi (Vairochana), Ashiku (Akshobhya), Amida (Amitābha), Miroku (Maitreya), and Shaka (Shākyamuni). Dainichi occupied the center of Esoteric Buddhism's pantheon. To the east of him sat Ashiku, the source of life, and, to the west, Amida, the dispenser of infinite love. Miroku, the Buddha of the future, and Shaka, the historical Buddha, completed this group of Tathāgatas.

Each of the thirteen deities had claims to the worshipers' attention, but by the late Heian period, three of them came to occupy a special place in the religious life of Japan: Kannon (Avalokiteshvara), one of the Bodhisattva attendants of Amida, who came to be worshiped as a goddess of mercy (although a male deity in India); Fudō (Achala), a fierce god apparently of Indian origin, although neither a Buddha nor a Bodhisattva; and Jizō (Ch: Dicang), whose cult took many forms identified with compassion and redemption. Statues of Kannon were erected at thirty-three sites of remarkable beauty in Japan, and pilgrimages to the different shrines were popular with all classes, from the imperial family downward. The famous temple of the "33,333 Kannons," in Kyoto, each with a "thousand hands" for dispensing mercy, was built in the twelfth century and serves as an indication of the great popularity of this deity during the late Heian period. In contrast to the merciful Kannon, Fudō was represented as a "terrible figure, livid in color and of a ferocious expression. He is surrounded by flames and carries a sword and a rope to smite and bind evil. He is generally explained as typifying the fierce aspect assumed by Vairochana when resenting wrong doing."[10] If Kannon represented the female (or Garbha mandala), Fudō stood for the male (or *vajra*) and, as such, was popular with the rising warrior class, who—as the guardians of the state in the face of disorder— may have likened themselves to the powerful Fudō. Accordingly, the cult of Fudō spread to regions where nature presented its severest face—rocky crags and seashores. Illustrations of Jizō's widespread cult are given in the following reading.

Probably the most important event in the history of Esoteric Buddhism after the death of Kūkai (who established the teachings in Japan) was its triumph on Mount Hiei, the stronghold of Tendai. Saichō himself had studied Esoteric learning with Kūkai, but it remained for his disciple and successor Ennin (794–864) to found Tendai esotericism (Taimitsu). Ennin had led a rather colorless life as a priest and teacher and was already in his forties when he was sent to China for study in 838. At first unable to obtain the necessary authorization to visit either Wutai or Tiantai shan, the two most important Buddhist centers,

---

10. Eliot, *Japanese Buddhism*, pp. 348–349.

Ennin managed with great difficulty to be set ashore on the Chinese coast and was later fortunate enough to meet a general who secured permission for him to visit Wutai shan and other holy sites. Ennin finally returned to Japan in 857 after extensive study with the masters of each of the Tendai disciplines. Upon his return to Mount Hiei, he organized study of the two mandalas, instituted Esoteric initiation, and promoted other branches of Esoteric learning. Ennin also introduced to Japan the invocation of Amida Buddha's name (*nembutsu*), which he had heard at Wutai shan, and had a special hall built for this purpose. For some people, the *nembutsu* became an all-sufficient means of gaining salvation, but for Ennin it was only one among many means of achieving Buddhahood.

Common to both Tendai and Shingon esotericism was the idea that all people could attain Buddhahood in this very life and body through the infinite variety of means and practices represented symbolically in the different forms of the mandala. These could range from the simplest forms of religious practice to the most sophisticated—from the rugged practices and severe austerities of mountain religion to the highly cultivated arts of court society. In this respect, the mysteries of the Esoteric religion, seen as emerging from the timeless bliss of the law body of the Buddha, could take any number of forms, including the secret transmission from master to monk, the aesthetic refinements that induced an emotional rapture among courtiers and court ladies alike, or the mantras, hand signs (*mudras*), and incantations that, for the ordinary believer, were a palpable expression of numinous mysteries.

In affirming this universality of means and ends, the esoteric teachings spoke of a simple gate to salvation that was the equivalent of all other gates, *ichimon fumon*, with a gate open to everyone corresponding to one's own personal makeup or level of religious consciousness, but all leading to Buddhahood. Through this gate, one entered into the reality of the Cosmic Buddha and the Buddha entered into oneself by a process of reciprocal response and interpenetration as the grace and power of the Buddha was "added" to one's own effort (*kaji*). In this way, Esoteric Buddhism could appeal to both the most refined sensibilities and the simplest or even crudest emotions. Functioning as both a court religion and a popular cult, it could exemplify the universalism of Mahāyāna salvation as well as the particularisms of an aristocratic, hierarchical society. What it did not attempt to provide or define was a universal political code, or a social ethic—no doubt reflecting the ambivalence of Kegon philosophy in these matters (chap. 45). The Kegon philosophy tended to turn to Confucianism, as Saichō and Kūkai had done.

Nevertheless, in the infinite variety of its adaptive means, Esotericism served as the dynamic source of new religious practices and movements that emerged in the medieval period, responding to conditions greatly changed from the relative peace and stability of the Heian period. The competitions and, indeed, conflict that often ensued in the darker, more dangerous medieval age, however, already had their antecedents in the rivalry among Mount Hiei and other religious centers in the late Heian period.

The rise of "warrior-monks" was a prominent feature of the late Heian period and medieval Buddhism. Their lawlessness grew during the reigns of Emperor Shirakawa (1082–1086) and his immediate successors. Whenever the monks had a demand, they would march in force on the capital, bearing with them the palanquins of the Shinto god Sannō, the guardian deity of Mount Hiei. The first such descent took place in 1095, and in almost every one of the next thirty or forty years, either the Tendai warrior-monks or those of the Hossō sect from the Kōfukuji in Nara, brandishing the sacred tree of the Kasuga (Shinto) Shrine, stormed into the capital. Frequent battles between the Tendai and the Hossō monks disturbed the peace in the capital for about a century starting with Shirakawa's reign. In 1165, the Hiei monks burned the Kiyomizudera, the stronghold of the Hossō sect in Kyoto, and the Hossō monks attempted unsuccessfully to burn the Enryakuji.

As time went on, various heresies gained currency that tended to discredit Esoteric Buddhism. The most notorious was the so-called Tachikawa school, founded in the early twelfth century by a Shingon believer with the aid of a yin-yang teacher whom he met while in exile. They evolved a doctrine teaching that "the Way of man and woman, yin and yang, is the secret of becoming a Buddha in this life. No other way exists but this one to attain Buddhahood and gain the Way."[11] As authority for this statement, the Vajra and Garbha Mandalas were declared to be symbols of the male and female principles, and other elaborate yin-yang correspondences were drawn as well. The Tachikawa school appears to have indulged in the sexual rites practiced by the somewhat similar Shāktist sects of Tibet. In 1335, as the result of a memorial submitted by the Mount Kōya monks against the Tachikawa school, its leader was exiled and books expounding its principles were ordered to be burned. Traces of its doctrines still survive, however, in existing Buddhist sects.

## SEX AND BUDDHAHOOD: A SHINGON HERESY

### SELECTIONS FROM THE PRECIOUS MIRROR (HŌKYŌSHŌ)

This short work written by the Shingon monk Yūkai (1345–1416) is of interest in tracing certain developments in the later history of Esoteric Buddhism. In its emphasis on the pedigree of the Shingon teachings, it was no more than echoing Kūkai's words of six hundred years before, but in the meantime the orthodox tradition suffered greatly from the numerous heresies that developed out of the religion's Tantric aspects. In the

---

11. Statement in the *Hōkyōsho*, an anti-Tachikawa work that is one of our chief sources of information about the school.

excerpts given here, Yūkai attacks one of the most notorious heresies, the so-called Tachikawa school, and in other parts of his essay, he mentions that Shingon's name had been lent to magical arts that bore little relation to the doctrines taught by Kūkai, including the art of discovering buried treasure and the art of flying about at will. Even the most outlandish heresy was capable of producing scriptural evidence for the validity of its view, for the Buddhist canon as transmitted to Japan contained an incredible variety of texts, some of them little more than formulas for magical rites. The Tachikawa school was almost extinct by Yūkai's day, as he himself states, but other bizarre heresies continued to dominate Esoteric Buddhism.

Shingon Esotericism is the secret doctrine taught by Vairochana, the King of Enlightenment, and transmitted by the Eight Founders. It is called the Supreme Highest Vehicle of the Buddha and bears the title of the Realm Surpassing All Sects. Indeed, only through this teaching can one exterminate the extremely heavy burdens of karma or save the living creatures difficult of conversion or quickly realize the Buddhist knowledge. That is why in ancient times eight wise philosophers who went to China to seek the Law received instruction in Shingon. The Eastern Temple [Shingon] had five transmitters of the teachings: Kūkai, Shūei, Eun, Engyō, and Jōgyō.[12] The other school [Tendai] had three transmitters: Saichō, Ennin, and Enchin. . . . Among the teachings received from China, those obtained by Kūkai are the senior ones because they were passed down from one heir to the traditions to the next, from the Great Founder Vairochana to Huiguo, the abbot of the Green Dragon Temple in China. I cannot enter into details here, but although Huiguo transmitted the Law to many people . . . only Kūkai and Yiming were instructed in the two mandalas, and Yiming was not fully instructed. He died without transmitting the Law to anyone. Only Kūkai was the true heir of Huiguo. . . . Kūkai in turn transmitted the teachings to many disciples. [Genealogical tables are omitted.]

Someone asked, "It is indeed true that the Shingon teachings are the highest of all the schools and are the direct road for attaining Buddhahood. However, in late years the false and the true have become confused. To enter a false path and to violate the true way of becoming a Buddha is like saying East is West, and the point of view becomes topsy-turvy. How then can one attain the goal of becoming a Buddha? I crave your instruction on this matter."

I replied, "It is difficult to distinguish jade and stone; it is easy to be misled by worthless things and difficult to establish the difference between the false and the true. For example, among the disciples of the Daigo-Sambō-in, there was a man called the *ajari* Ninkan. On account of some crime of which he was found guilty, he was exiled to the province of Izu, and there he earned his living by

---

12. Shūei (808–884), Eun (798–869), Engyō (799–852), and Jōgyō (d. 866)—together with the more famous Kūkai, Saichō, Ennin, and Enchin—are often spoken of as the eight monks who sought the Law in China.

teaching Shingon to married laity and to meat-eating, defiled people, whom he made his disciples. A yin-yang teacher from a place called Tachikawa in the province of Musashi studied Shingon with Ninkan and combined it with his yin-yang doctrines. The false and the true were thus confounded; the inner and the outer learning were indiscriminately mixed. He called it the Tachikawa school and expounded it as a branch of Shingon. This was the origin of the heresy. . . .

The principle of this sect was to consider the way of men and women, yin and yang, to be the secret art of obtaining Buddhahood in this flesh and the only means of obtaining Buddhahood and gaining the Way. They made outrageous assertions that the Buddha had previously taught their doctrines, a diabolic invention deserving of eternal punishment in hell. Ignorant people, not realizing this, upheld it as the most profound and secret Law. How can one say that they possessed true views and genuine knowledge? The Shūrangama Sūtra declares, "Those who secretly desire to perform acts of greed and lust are fond of saying that the eyes, ears, nose and tongue are all 'pure land' and that the male and female organs are the true places of perfect knowledge [bodhi] and nirvāna. The ignorant people believe these foul words. They are to be called poisoners, hinderers, and demons. When they die, they become devils who afflict and unsettle people in this world, causing them to become confused and unwittingly to fall into the hell of eternal punishment." How can people belonging to that hell be called Shingon believers? . . .

This Tachikawa school later spread to the province of Etchū. In successive generations, two teachers, Kakumei and Kakuin, lived on Mount Kōya [and taught Tachikawa doctrine there]. At this time, many secret manuals and texts of this heretical school were in circulation, often called "oral transmission of the secrets of esoteric doctrine." To this day, there are ignorant people who study such works and believe them to possess the loftiest thoughts. In truth, they are neither exoteric nor esoteric but merely so many stones wrapped in jade. . . . Many people studied these teachings, but they did not meet with divine favor, and for the most part, both the teachings and the men have perished. A few are left, but I do not know how many.

[From *TD* 77, no. 2456:847–849]

## ANNEN: "MAXIMS FOR THE YOUNG" (DŌJIKYŌ)

Annen (841–889) was a major figure in the promotion of Tendai esotericism at Mount Hiei after Saichō's time. "Esoteric," which basically means "mysterious," can be understood as "secret" or even "exclusive" in a particularistic sense but in its more universalistic aspect can represent the wondrous workings of the Three Mysteries (body, speech, and mind) in all humankind. It is in this sense that Annen's "Maxims for the Young" should be taken as an accommodation of Mahāyāna's adaptive means to the common person, often in a quite conventional and prosaic manner.

Many of these instructions for the young are drawn from the Chinese, and especially Confucian, canonical literature, syncretized with Indian and Buddhist views. Indeed, they often seem to express a proverbial wisdom or etiquette common to many cultures. But Annen makes it clear that Buddhism represents the highest wisdom, that worship of the native Japanese gods comes next in the hierarchy of values, and that Confucian morality stands on a lower level. Similarly, although filial piety is encouraged, loyalty to parents and lay teachers cannot compare with that to religious teachers, whose redemptive function goes far beyond this life. Given the religious goal toward which these instructions lead, it may not be surprising that instead of providing a guide for schooling or systematic education, the following excerpts often refer to matters of adult life and society that the young might find relevant only later in life.

In the presence of a superior, do not suddenly stand up.
If you meet [such a person] on the road, kneel and then pass on.
Should he summon you, comply respectfully
with hands clasped to your breast, face him directly.
Speak only if spoken to; if he addresses you, listen attentively.

Make threefold obeisance to the Three Treasures [of Buddhism],
twofold obeisance to the [Shinto] gods.
In the presence of others, bow once
But show the highest respect to your teacher or lord.

When passing a graveyard, be reverent;
When passing a [Shinto] shrine, descend [from horse or carriage],
In front of a [Buddhist] temple or pagoda, do nothing to defile it [such as
    defecation or urination].
When the writings of the [Confucian] sages are being read, do nothing
    indecorous.

In all human relations there are appropriate forms of ritual respect
At court there must be laws and regulations;
If men [in authority] contravene ritual respect, transgressions will follow
    among the masses.

In dealing with the people, say no more than is needed;
your business done, move on quickly.
In the conduct of business, let there be no breach of trust;
In your speech, keep to your word.

When words are many, they are worth little . . .
The man who is bold inevitably falls into danger . . .
The guileless man commits no transgressions . . .

The walls have ears; keep to yourself whatever might be taken in slander.
Even the heavens have eyes; commit no wrongdoing even in secret . . .
A three-inch tongue can do untold harm to a five-foot body;
The mouth is the gate of much misfortune; the tongue is the root of many
   mishaps . . .

Natural disasters can be averted; from disasters of one's own making, there
   is no escape.
Pile up good deeds and a house will have no end of blessings;
Indulge in evil deeds and it will have no end of calamities.

Good deeds done in secret/are bound to reap rewards in the open.
Good conduct performed unseen/will make one's good name shine . . .

Hearts, like faces, differ from one another; like water, they take the shape
   of the container.
Do not try to bend another man's bow or ride another's horse.

Seeing the cart ahead overturned should be a warning to the cart behind.
Not to forget what happened before is to learn a lesson for the future . . .
When the gods punish fools, it is not to slay but to chasten them,
A teacher strikes the student not from malice but for the student's own
   improvement.

Birth confers no honor on one; it is the practice of self-cultivation that
   endows one with wisdom and virtue.
The man of worth may not enjoy riches; the one who is rich may not be
   worthy of honor.
If one, though rich, still has many desires, he may be called poor.
If one, though poor, is contented, he may be called rich.

A teacher who fails to admonish his disciple, may be called a breaker of the
   commandments.
A teacher who admonishes his disciple may be called an upholder of the
   commandments.

When one keeps a bad disciple, both teacher and disciple will fall into Hell;
When one nourishes a good disciple, both teacher and disciple will attain
   Buddhahood. . . .

Leaving one's kin and cleaving to a strange teacher, one may achieve
   [the three forms of Buddhist learning]: Discipline, Concentration, and
   Compassion.

Even though one may be dull by nature, one can surely attain the learning
  of Buddhahood.

One character learned each day amounts to 360 in a year.
Each character learned is worth a thousand pieces of gold.
One stroke of the brush may save many lives.

One should not neglect a teacher who has taught you even for the length
  of one day; how much less a teacher who has taught you for years.

To a Buddhist teacher, you are indebted for three generations (past,
  present, and future, that is, for all time).
To a parent you are only indebted for one lifetime . . .
A disciple must walk seven feet behind his teacher, and not tread on his
  shadow. . . .

On a winter's night, dressed lightly, endure the cold as you recite the whole
  night through;
On a summer day with little to eat, repel hunger as you persist in learning
  till the day is done. . . .
Great though the vices of the wise man be, he will not fall into Hell;
Slight though the vices of the foolish man be, he will assuredly fall
  into Hell.
The fool clings to sorrow like a prisoner clasped in jail.
The wise man ever enjoys happiness, like one resplendent with Heaven's
  light. . . .

Each morning in the hills and fields, one kills other creatures to feed
  one's own;
Each night in the rivers and seas, one fishes to support one's life;
To support life day and night, day and night one creates evil karma.
To satisfy one's tastes for the span of a day, one falls into Hell for eons. . . .

The cycle of birth and death is unceasing; seek nirvana now.
The life of the body is impure, befouled by the passions; seek enlighten-
  ment straight away.
Even in the halls of Indra's palace, there is the grief of unceasing
  change.
Even in Brahmā's heaven, the pain of fire and sword awaits.

Compassion shown to one person is worth a sea of merit;
What is done for many but with selfish intent gains only a poppy seed's
  reward. . . .

Piling up sand to make a stupa will earn a golden body,
An offering of flowers to the Buddha will merit a lotus seat. . . .

For the guidance of the young, I have explained the doctrine of retribution.
What is drawn from the Inner and Outer [Buddhist and Confucian] canons,
let no reader despise or ridicule.

[*Annen Oshō no kenkyū*, pp. 2–32; dB]

## Chapter 48

# AMIDA, THE PURE LAND, AND THE RESPONSE
# OF THE OLD BUDDHISM TO THE NEW

By the end of the Heian period in the twelfth century, Buddhism was firmly established in the institutions and teachings of the Nara schools and Esoteric Buddhism, which by that time included both Tendai and Shingon. Taken as a whole, this Buddhist establishment was richly diverse, and even though each sect could claim to have its own unique characteristics, together they also had much in common. One of these common elements was the belief in gaining rebirth in one of the many Pure Lands that were part of the Buddhist cosmology. Each Pure Land was presided over by a buddha or bodhisattva and represented a perfect existence for those fortunate enough to be reborn there rather than in some lower level of transmigration. Rebirth in a Pure Land was as much desired as descent into one of many hells was feared.

Whether one was to be reborn in a Pure Land or in hell depended on one's karmic record, and accumulating merit through good works was thus of critical importance. This could be accomplished through actions ranging from ordinary moral behavior to ritual performances such as chanting sūtras, copying sūtras, sponsoring rituals, or giving alms. Popular among lay persons because of its simplicity was recitation of the name of Amida Buddha, who presided over a Pure Land known as the Western Paradise. The chant was the repetition of the phrase *namu Amida Butsu*, which simply means "praise be to Amida Buddha." Popular in China as well, this practice was known as the *nembutsu*, a term that originally meant meditating on Amida but later was understood primarily as reciting his name. Promoted by all schools of Buddhism, especially Tendai, the *nembutsu* was thought to be more efficacious with greater numbers of recitations, and exaggerated accounts tell of pious lay persons seeking maximum merit reciting the *nembutsu* up to a million times a day. With enough merit accumulated, one could be assured of being reborn in Amida's Pure Land; the only final condition needing to be fulfilled was death.

Even though the final reward of rebirth in paradise would come only after death, this objective was much easier to hold to than was the ideal goal of enlightenment or, as Kūkai put it, becoming a buddha in this existence. Becoming a buddha required serious practice and meditation informed by complex doctrines difficult to master. Chinese Pure Land Buddhists had already distinguished between the difficult path of the sages seeking enlightenment and the easy path of the Pure Land believers seeking rebirth in paradise. In noting the contrast between the easy and difficult paths, however, the Chinese masters did not see them as mutually exclusive or entirely contradictory: the recitation of the *nembutsu* was an excellent aid to meditation, not a rejection of it. Pure Land thought also emphasized reliance on the saving power of the Buddha rather than on individual effort, but as has already been seen in Kūkai's explanation of *kaji* (divine grace humanly received), the relationship between the two is complementary rather than contradictory.

This traditional understanding of Pure Land Buddhism had effective proponents such as Kūya (903–972), Genshin (942–1017), and Ryōnin (1072–1132), all monks of the Tendai school. Stressing the simplicity of reciting the *nembutsu*, Kūya propagated it in the streets and marketplaces. Dancing through the city streets with a tinkling bell hanging from his neck, Kūya called out the name of Amida and sang simple ditties of his own composition, such as

| | |
|---|---|
| *Hito tabi mo* | He never fails |
| *Namu Amida bu to* | To reach the Lotus Land of Bliss |
| *Yū hito no* | Who calls, |
| *Hasu utena ni* | If only once, |
| *Noboranu wa nashi.* | The name of Amida. |

And

| | |
|---|---|
| *Gokuraku wa* | A far, far distant land |
| *Harukeki hodo to* | Is Paradise, |
| *Kikishi kado* | I've heard them say; |
| *Tsutomete itaru* | But those who want to go |
| *Tokoro narikeri.* | Can reach there in a day. |

In the marketplaces, all kinds of people joined Kūya in his dance and sang out the invocation to Amida, *namu Amida Butsu*. Then, when a great epidemic struck the capital, Kūya proposed that these same people join him in building an image of Amida in a public square, saying that common folk could equal the achievement of their rulers, who had built the Great Buddha of Nara, if they cared to try. In country districts, he built bridges and dug wells for the people where these were needed, and to show that no one was to be excluded from the blessings of Paradise, he traveled into regions inhabited by the Ainu and, for the first time, brought to many of them the evangel of Buddhism.

Just as Kūya came to be called "the saint of the streets" for his dancing, so another Tendai monk, Ryōnin (1072–1132), later became known for his propagation of the *nembutsu* through popular songs. Ryōnin's great success in this medium reflected his own vocal talents and his mastery of traditional liturgical music. At the same time, his advocacy of the *nembutsu* chant reflected the influence on him of Tendai and Kegon doctrine. From the former philosophy, he drew the idea that "one act is all acts, and all acts are one act." From the Flower Garland (Kegon) Sūtra, he took the doctrine of the interrelation and interdependence of all things: "one man is all men, and all men are one man." Joining these to faith in Amida, Ryōnin produced the "circulating *nembutsu*" or "*nembutsu* in communion" (*yūzū nembutsu*). That is, if one person calls the name of Amida, it will benefit all persons; one person may share in the invocations of all others. Spreading this simple but all-embracing idea in a musical form, Ryōnin became an evangelist on a vast scale. Among his early converts were court ladies, and Emperor Toba was so deeply impressed that he gave Ryōnin a bell made from one of his own mirrors. With this, Ryōnin traveled the length and breadth of the land, inviting everyone to join him in the "circulating *nembutsu*" and asking them to sign their names in a roster of participants. According to tradition, the entries accumulated during a lifetime of evangelizing added up to the modest figure of 3,282.

In the early thirteenth century, shortly after the founding of the Kamakura shogunate, there appeared a Tendai monk, Hōnen, who rejected traditional Pure Land Buddhism in favor of a bold, new interpretation that became the basis of his new school of Pure Land Buddhism (Jōdo-shū). Although Hōnen (1133–1212) was a learned monk trained at Mount Hiei, because this was a time at which it was widely believed that Buddhist teaching and practice had entered an age of decline (*mappō*), he no longer thought that full enlightenment was a practical possibility, and he explicitly rejected even the aspiration toward enlightenment (*bodaishin*), which had long been regarded as the essential first step toward Buddhist liberation. Hōnen's rejection of traditional practice was sweeping, and he declared that except for the *nembutsu*, all other practices were useless.

Hōnen was keenly aware of how radical his teaching was and therefore kept it a closely guarded secret. Publicly, he presented himself as a traditional monk; privately, he had concluded that traditional Buddhism was no longer valid for the conditions of his time. For more than twenty years, he led this double life until finally in 1198, he committed his thoughts to writing. The result was *Choosing the Recitation of the Buddha's Name According to the Original Vow* (*Senchaku hongan nembutsu shū*), a book that he insisted on circulating only within his small band of disciples. Although word of it leaked out, causing a group of traditional monks to petition the imperial court to ban his teachings, *Choosing the Original Vow* was for the most part kept a secret and did not become widely available until 1212, the year that Hōnen died.

The publication of *Choosing the Original Vow* caused a great uproar. Hōnen's secret was now in the public domain for all to read, and many were surprised to learn that the monk whom they thought quite traditional was really quite radical. Hōnen's teaching was indeed revolutionary, and *Choosing the Original Vow* states his manifesto in no uncertain terms: throw out all traditional practices except for one, the recitation of the name of Amida Buddha. With a clear awareness of the long history of Buddhism, Hōnen argued that the historical Buddha was long gone and that his enlightenment was impossible to attain. In such a situation, it was useless to meditate, to follow the monastic rules, to chant the sūtras, to make images and statues, and to make a vow to become enlightened. Only one practice was effective in these terrible times, and that was reciting the name of Amida: "praise be to Amida Buddha."

Hōnen's argument is quite simple, but his rhetoric is complex and subtle. Since innovation in a religious tradition that valued transmission of past truths was an invitation to the charge of heresy, Hōnen had to show that his new interpretation really was an old doctrine, that is, that it had already been articulated by past masters. The problem, of course, was that Hōnen's message was in fact new and thus could not be found in the writings of earlier teachers. How, then, was he to collect passages from previous writers and make them support his teaching? He did this by taking passages maintaining that the recitation of Amida's name was the *best* practice and arguing that this meant it was the *only* practice. If something is the best of the lot, then why not throw out the rest? There was a certain persuasiveness to his argument, and many people accepted his claim that the exclusive practice of reciting Amida's name had the sanction of past tradition.

Hōnen's argument did not pass without vigorous debate, however. His most vociferous critic was Myōe (1173–1232), a monk whose thought and practice crossed sectarian boundaries. Myōe attacked *Choosing the Original Vow* by writing *Smashing the Evil Chariot (Zaijarin)*, in which he charged Hōnen with betraying the Pure Land tradition itself and also with no longer being a Buddhist. As a traditional Buddhist committed to a wide variety of religious disciplines, Myōe was shocked to read in *Choosing the Original Vow* of Hōnen's rejection of all practices except for the recitation of Amida's name. Against Hōnen's claim that traditional practices were taught in order to be discarded, Myōe contended that instead, these practices, especially the vow to attain enlightenment, were an integral part of practices for rebirth into the Pure Land, of which recitation was but one method. Against Hōnen's advocacy of the exclusive *nembutsu*, Myōe defended a pluralism of practices.

Although he was conservative, Myōe also saw the need to create simpler forms of practice. His own innovation was a simple chant, much like the *nembutsu*, that sang the praises of the Three Treasures (the Buddha, the dharma, and the sangha) and the aspiration toward enlightenment. Simplification, he was convinced, need not require rejecting traditional practices and, in fact, should be centered on them. Because other monks from the older sects were likewise active in the revival of traditional Buddhism, we should not let the remarkable developments in Pure Land, Nichiren, and Zen thought and practice obscure the activities and achievements of the Tendai, Shingon, and Nara schools. As a sect, Shingon, for instance, underwent its greatest expansion during the Kamakura period and was far from being effete or eclipsed by newer movements. Just as historians now recognize that court and bakufu, aristocrats and warriors, and Kyoto and Kamakura were equally influential in political circles, we should remember that many monks from the old establishment were just as active as the founders of new schools. In addition to Myōe, who worked to revive Kegon, the Tendai monk Jien (1155–1225) wrote the *Gukanshō*, an innovative history of Japan; the Hossō school's Jōkei (1155–1213) revived the disciplinary precepts; the Shingon monk Kakukai (1142–1223) argued that the Pure Land could be realized in this life; and another Shingon monk, Eizon (1201–1290), simplified the precepts for lay persons and carried out many social welfare projects.

As radical as Hōnen was in his innovations, it was Shinran (1173–1262) and Ippen (1239–1289), two of his spiritual descendants, who pushed the issue of simplicity even beyond Hōnen's position. Although they never disputed Hōnen's teachings openly, their interpretations differed from his understanding of the *nembutsu* as a means to rebirth that required human initiative and effort. While studying at Mount Hiei as a young monk, Shinran underwent a spiritual crisis in which he came to doubt the efficacy of his own efforts to gain perfection. Morality was of limited effect, as were ritual actions; nothing, it seemed, could eradicate the deep-seated imperfection of being human. When Shinran left Mount Hiei and the path of the sages, he turned to Hōnen's new teaching of the exclusive *nembutsu*, but he came to see that even chanting Amida's name was a matter of individual effort and therefore of limited effect in gaining full salvation. His dilemma was resolved when he realized that salvation was not won through human effort but was granted by Amida Buddha, the compassionate one who vowed to save all people, regardless of their moral standing or religious achievements. By rejecting all practices performed through one's own effort (*jiriki*), Shinran went even further than his teacher by suggesting that chanting the *nembutsu* should not result from deliberative effort but from the saving action granted by Amida. Monastic discipline and other religious rituals were no longer necessary, and while in exile with Hōnen, who had been banished to the northern province of Echigo for his heterodox teaching, Shinran openly married a woman and later had children by her. "If even good people can be reborn in the Pure Land," he said, "how much more the wicked man."

Despite his sweeping rejection of human effort, Shinran still retained the religious virtue of faith (*shinjin*). Instead of enlightenment, and even more than rebirth in the Pure Land, the objective in Shinran's religion was to have faith in Amida's power and compassion to save one despite oneself. The ideal believer was not characterized by doctrinal learning or religious discipline but by complete trust in Amida's vow. Although Shinran understood that his ideal of pure faith was actually more difficult to hold to than it would be to perform some kind of practice, it still was a goal easily understood and propagated. In his own lifetime, Shinran did not attempt to organize a new sect, but he did establish numerous religious communities bound together by loyalty to him and his teachings.

Ippen studied in Kyoto under one of Hōnen's leading disciples and later returned to his home in Shikoku, where he married and carried out his duties as both a monk and a head of a household. In 1263, at the age of twenty-five, he came to doubt the spiritual quality of his householder's life and, thinking that he should go to the mountains to practice asceticism, set out on a pilgrimage that took him to Zenkōji, a popular destination for pilgrims in what is now Nagano City. He returned home still imbued with the idea of becoming a recluse and thereafter set out on several more pilgrimages, mostly to mountainous areas. During his travels, he devised a means of propagating the *nembutsu* by asking people to recite the *nembutsu* just "once" (*ippen*) and, when they did so, giving them a *fuda*, a paper talisman on which was written the Chinese characters for "na-mu A-mi-da Butsu." Like Ryōnin before him, Ippen sought to propagate the *nembutsu* to as many people as possible, and the names in his registry numbered several hundred thousand.

The talismans distributed by Ippen signified assurance that the recipient was sure to be born in the Pure Land. Ippen's standard appeal was to ask each person to accept the talisman, awaken one moment of faith, and utter the *nembutsu*. While at the Kumano Shrine on one of his many travels, Ippen made his appeal to a monk, but the monk surprised Ippen by refusing the offer on the grounds that he did not feel the arising of faith. Ippen insisted that the monk accept the talisman even if he lacked faith, and the monk obliged, but Ippen wondered whether what he had done was effective and legitimate. That night, the Kumano deity appeared to him and told him that rebirth was not determined by his act of propagation or the faith of the recipients but by the decisive power of Amida. Thereafter, Ippen distributed his talismans without regard for whether people had faith. Ippen thus represents the furthest point of development among the Pure Land innovators: Hōnen rejected all practices but the *nembutsu*; Shinran rejected the *nembutsu* of self-power but retained the importance of faith in Amida's other-power; and Ippen, in a supreme act of faith, dispensed with faith as a spiritual requirement. During the last days of his life, Ippen burned the *sūtras* that he possessed and declared that all of the Buddha's teachings were epitomized in the *nembutsu*.

The tendency to reduce Pure Land Buddhism to its barest essentials challenged those who tried to institutionalize paths that rejected organized rituals and practices. Ippen's heirs successfully developed his Time (Ji) sect of Pure Land Buddhism through a strict system of loyalty to the head of the school, who was regarded as the incarnation of Amida and therefore could grant—or deny—salvation. As Amida, he also was the object of faith and gratitude. Of Shinran's lineal descendants who organized the True Pure Land Sect (Jōdo Shinshū), the most important was Rennyo (1415–1499), who, in an age torn by conflicting feudal loyalties, attracted adherents with his clear explanation of Shinran's teachings, specific rules to live by, and loyalty. Shinran had urged his followers to make every act an act of thanksgiving to Amida, and now this sense of obligation was redirected to Shinran's heirs, who were not, however, seen as incarnations of Amida.

Blessed with the charisma of a good preacher and effective leader, Rennyo also won the respect and allegiance of many for his common touch characterized by a personal openness and skill at explaining things clearly. His teaching emphasized an egalitarianism that recognized no fundamental difference between men and women, young and old, upper and lower classes, and good and evil. Even hunters and fishermen, who, according to Genshin's *Essentials of Salvation*, were condemned to hell for taking life, were saved by Amida's universal compassion. Rennyo held true to Shinran's teaching that reciting the *nembutsu* was not a means for gaining salvation and emphasized that it was an expression of gratitude for the salvation already granted by Amida despite one's faults and through no merit of one's own. But unlike Hōnen and Shinran, who felt that the *nembutsu* and faith were exclusively sufficient, Rennyo's reliance on Amida's broadly applicable compassion allowed him to tolerate social and religious conventions that his predecessors did not think necessary. *Rennyo's Rules* codified this tolerance and simplicity for his followers and laid a practical foundation for what is today the largest institutional system of temples in Japan.

## TRADITIONAL PURE LAND BUDDHISM

### GENSHIN: *THE ESSENTIALS OF SALVATION* (*ŌJŌYŌSHŪ*)

A monk of the Tendai school, Genshin promoted the practice of the *nembutsu* as an appropriate means for those who are not learned or wise enough to gain rebirth in the Pure Land. His *Essentials of Salvation* became popular for its graphic descriptions of the glories of the Pure Land and the torments of hell. The following excerpts are from the initial chapters in the first two divisions of the ten cited by the author. The scriptural authorities cited by Genshin are deleted from the text.

The teaching and practice which leads to birth in Paradise is the most important thing in this impure world during these degenerate times.[1] Monks and laymen, men of high or low station, who will not turn to it? But the literature of the exoteric and the esoteric teachings of Buddha are not one in text, and the practices of one's work in this life in its ritualistic and philosophic aspects are many. These are not difficult for men of keen wisdom and great diligence, but how can a stupid

---

1. A reference to *mappō*, the last of the three periods of Buddhist Law, that of degeneration and destruction of the Law that extends for countless years. The first period, *shōbō*, the period of the true Law, lasted for one thousand years. The second period, *zōbō*, the period of the simulated doctrine, endured for five hundred years.

person such as I achieve this knowledge? Because of this I have chosen the one gate of the *nembutsu* to salvation. I have made selections from the important sūtras and shāstras and have set them forth so that they may be readily understood and their disciplines easily practiced. In all there are ten divisions, divided into three volumes. The first is the corrupt life which one must shun, the second is the Pure Land for which one should seek, the third is the proof of the existence of the Pure Land, the fourth is the correct practice of *nembutsu*, the fifth is the helpful means of practicing the *nembutsu*, the sixth is the practice of *nembutsu* on special occasions, the seventh is the benefit resulting from *nembutsu*, the eighth is the proof of the benefit accruing from *nembutsu* alone, the ninth is the conduct leading to birth in Paradise, and the tenth comprises questions and answers to selected problems. These I place to the right of where I sit lest I forget them.

The first division, the corrupt land which one must shun, comprises the three realms[2] in which there is no peace. Now, in order to make clear the external appearances of this land, it is divided into seven parts: (1) hell; (2) hungry demons; (3) beasts; (4) fighting demons; (5) man; (6) Deva; and (7) a conclusion. The first of these, hell, is further divided into eight parts: (1) the hell of repeated misery; (2) the hell of the black chains; (3) the hell of mass suffering; (4) the hell of wailing; (5) the hell of great wailing; (6) the hell of searing heat; (7) the hell of great searing heat, and (8) the hell of incessant suffering.

The hell of repeated misery is one thousand *yojanas*[3] beneath the Southern Continent[4] and is ten thousand *yojanas* in length and breadth. Sinners here are always possessed of the desire to do each other harm. Should they by chance see each other, they behave as does the hunter when he encounters a deer. With iron claws they slash each other's bodies until blood and flesh are dissipated and the bones alone remain. . . .

Outside the four gates of this hell are sixteen separate places which are associated with this hell. The first is called the place of excrement. Here, it is said, there is intensely hot dung of the bitterest of taste, filled with maggots with snouts of indestructible hardness. The sinner here eats of the dung and all the assembled maggots swarm at once for food. They destroy the sinner's skin, devour his flesh and suck the marrow from his bones. People who at one time in the past killed birds or deer fall into this hell. . . .

The second division is the Pure Land towards which one must aspire. The rewards of Paradise are of endless merit. Should one speak of them for a hundred *kalpas* or even for a thousand *kalpas*, one would not finish describing them; should one count them or give examples of them, there would still be no way to know of them. At present, ten pleasures in praise of the Pure Land will be explained, and they are as but a single hair floating upon the great sea.

---

2. Past, present, and future.
3. The distance that an army can march in one day.
4. India and adjoining regions.

First is the pleasure of being welcomed by many saints. Second is the pleasure of the first opening of the lotus.[5] Third is the pleasure of obtaining in one's own body the ubiquitous supernatural powers of a Buddha. Fourth is the pleasure of the realm of the five wonders. Fifth is the pleasure of everlasting enjoyment. Sixth is the pleasure of influencing others and introducing them to Buddhism. Seventh is the pleasure of assembling with the holy family. Eighth is the pleasure of beholding the Buddha and hearing the Law. Ninth is the pleasure of serving the Buddha according to the dictates of one's own heart. Tenth is the pleasure of progressing in the way of Buddhahood.

[Yampolsky, "The Essentials of Salvation," pp. 10–16, 90–94]

## INNOVATORS OF THE NEW PURE LAND BUDDHISM

### HŌNEN: THE ONE-PAGE TESTAMENT

Written by Hōnen, two days before he died, for a disciple who asked that he "write me something with your own hand that you think will be good for me, so that I may keep it as a memento." After Hōnen's death, this note was honored as his final testament and as a complete credo for the faithful.

The method of final salvation that I have propounded is neither a sort of meditation, such as has been practiced by many scholars in China and Japan, nor is it a repetition of the Buddha's name by those who have studied and understood the deep meaning of it. It is nothing but the mere repetition of the "*Namu Amida Butsu*," without a doubt of His mercy, whereby one may be born into the Land of Perfect Bliss. The mere repetition with firm faith includes all the practical details, such as the three-fold preparation of mind and the four practical rules. If I as an individual had any doctrine more profound than this, I should miss the mercy of the two Honorable Ones, Amida and Shāka, and be left out of the Vow of the Amida Buddha. Those who believe this, though they clearly understand all the teachings Shāka taught throughout his whole life, should behave themselves like simple-minded folk, who know not a single letter, or like ignorant nuns or monks whose faith is implicitly simple. Thus without pedantic airs, they should fervently practice the repetition of the name of Amida, and that alone.

[Coates and Ishizuka, *Hōnen*, pp. 728–729]

---

5. The pleasure of being first born in this land.

## SHINRAN: *THE LAMENTATION AND SELF-REFLECTION OF GUTOKU SHINRAN*

Keenly aware of the personal flaws that make it impossible to save himself through the accumulation of merit, Shinran called himself Gutoku, the "Foolish Bald-headed One." This self-awareness of imperfection is at the heart of Shinran's religion of salvation by Amida's compassionate vow, and is understood to be part of the human condition shared by monks and commoners alike, who are criticized by Shinran not only for their moral failings but for worshipping Shinto deities as well.

> Although I have entered the Pure Land path,
> I remain incapable of true and genuine thoughts and feelings.
> My very existence is pervaded by vanity and falsehood;
> There is nothing at all of any purity of mind.

> Towards others we each may seek to conduct ourselves
> With the appearance of wisdom, virtue, and steadfastness,
> But within us desire, rage, and deviousness are rife,
> So that deceit in myriad forms permeates our existence.

> We cannot put a stop to our evil nature;
> Our own minds are like vipers and scorpions.
> Even the good we may do is poisoned;
> As practice, it must be called hollow and vain.

> Being unrepentant and lacking in shame,
> I have no mind of truth and sincerity.
> And yet, because the Name has been given by Amida Buddha,
> The universe is suffused with its virtues.

> As one lacking even small love and small compassion,
> I give not a thought to the good of others.
> If not for the ship of Amida's Vow,
> How could such a person cross beyond this ocean of pain?

> With minds of malicious deceit, minds like vipers and scorpions,
> There is no accomplishing good acts through self-power.
> Unless we entrust ourselves to Amida's giving of virtue,
> We will die having never known true shame or repentance.
> [Translated by Dennis Hirota from *Shōzōmatsu wasan*, in *Shinshū shōgyō zensho* (Kyoto: Ōyagi Kōbundō, 1941), vol. 2, pp. 527–529]

SHINRAN: A RECORD IN LAMENT OF DIVERGENCIES (TANNISHŌ)

This collection of sayings by Shinran is attributed to his disciple Yuienbō, who was concerned about the confusion and divergent understandings developing among Shinran's followers. Stating that rebirth in the Pure Land takes place "immediately" at the moment of faith in Amida's vow rather than after death, Shinran reiterates the possibility of salvation in this life for the evil as well as the good.

"Saved by the inconceivable working of Amida's Vow, I shall realize birth in the Pure Land": the moment you entrust yourself thus to the Vow, so that the mind set upon saying the Name (*nembutsu*) arises within you, you are brought to share in the benefit of being grasped by Amida, never to be abandoned.

Know that the Primal Vow of Amida makes no distinction between people young or old, good or evil; only the entrusting of yourself to it is essential. For it was made to save the person whose karmic evil is deep-rooted and whose blind passions abound.

Thus, entrusting yourself to the Primal Vow requires no performance for good, for no act can hold greater virtue than saying the Name. Nor is there need to despair of the evil you commit, for no act is so evil that it obstructs the working of Amida's Primal Vow.

Thus were his words. . . .

> Even a good person can attain birth in the Pure Land,
> so it goes without saying that an evil person will.

Though such is the truth, people commonly say, "Even an evil person attains birth, so naturally a good person will." This statement may seem well founded at first, but it runs counter to the meaning of the Other Power established through the Primal Vow. This is because a person who relies on the good that he does through self-power fails to entrust himself wholeheartedly to Other Power and therefore is not in accord with Amida's Primal Vow, but when he abandons his attachment to self-power and entrusts himself totally to Other Power, he will realize birth in the Pure land.

It is impossible for us, filled as we are with blind passions, to free ourselves from birth and death through any practice whatever. Sorrowing at this, Amida made the Vow, the essential intent of which is the attainment of Buddhahood by the person who is evil. Hence the evil person who entrusts himself to Other Power is precisely the one who possesses the true cause for birth.

Accordingly he said, "Even the virtuous man is born in the Pure Land, so without question is the man who is evil."

[Hirota, *Tannishō*, pp. 22–24]

## RENNYO: *RENNYO'S RULES*

As the True Pure Land (Shinshū) movement spread through the creation of local congregations, each group developed rules of conduct to define proper belief and behavior. In 1473, Rennyo composed the following rules, which became the standard for all Shinshū communities to follow in their relationships with the rest of society. Whereas his predecessors framed their teachings in somewhat exclusive terms, Rennyo is noteworthy for his tolerant and compromising attitude, especially in regard to the Shinto deities and practices.

## Items to Be Prohibited Among True Pure Land Adherents

1. Do not denigrate the various *kami* or the Buddhas and Bodhisattvas.

2. Never slander the various teachings or the various schools.

3. Do not attack other schools by comparing them to the practices of our own school.

4. Though taboos (*monoimi*) are not something to be adhered to by Buddhists, observe them scrupulously before public officials and [members of] other schools.

5. Do not proclaim the Buddhist teachings while arbitrarily adding alongside them words that have not been handed down in our school.

6. As *nembutsu* adherents, do not denigrate the provincial governor (*shugo*) or the steward (*jitō*).

7. In a state of ignorance, do not display your own ideas to other schools or proclaim the teachings of your own school without any sense of discretion.

8. If you yourself are not yet established in faith (*anjin ketsujō*), do not proclaim the teachings of faith (*shinjin*) using words you have heard from other people.

9. Do not eat fish or fowl when you meet for *nembutsu* services.

10. On the day that you assemble for *nembutsu* services, do not drink liquor and lose your senses.

11. Among *nembutsu* adherents, indulgence in gambling is prohibited.

Concerning these eleven items, you should expel from your assembly any people who turn their backs on these regulations.

[Dobbins, *Jōdo Shinshū*, pp. 141–142]

## *Nembutsu* as Gratitude

In his many letters to his followers, Rennyo repeated the theme of the *nembutsu* as an expression of gratitude to Amida. Since salvation, which is affirmed through faith, is a gift of Amida, the only necessary response is thankfulness.

If we have deep faith in the principal vow of the Tathāgata Amida, if we rely with single and undivided heart on the compassionate vow of the one Buddha Amida, and if our faith is true at the very moment that we think of him to please save us, then we will definitely be received into the salvation of the Tathāgata. Over and above this, what should we take to be the meaning of reciting the *nembutsu*? It is a response coming from one's indebtedness [to the Buddha] (*goon hōsha*), thanking him that one is saved through birth in [the] Pure Land by the power of faith in the present. As long as we have life in us, we should say the *nembutsu*, thinking of it as a response of thankfulness. It should be said by the person of faith (*shinjin*) who is established in the faith (*anjin*) of our tradition.

[Dobbins, *Jōdo Shinshū*, p. 145]

### IPPEN: SELECTIONS FROM *A HUNDRED SAYINGS*

Despite his conviction that Amida's compassion and the power of the *nembutsu* made religious practices and even faith unnecessary, Ippen was a prolific writer of aphorisms, sayings, and precepts that defined proper conduct for ordinary people. The tension between restrictive prescriptions and unrestrained freedom is a common theme for those whom Buddhist liberation still demands moral responsibility. Ippen's *Hundred Sayings* speaks to the side of an untrammeled freedom reminiscent of some types of Zen and Daoist emancipation.

> To reach the borders of the unconditioned
> Just let go! This is the real repayment of your debt of gratitude.
> Make an offering of your *nembutsu* chant
> To living beings everywhere.
> This is your eternal home;
> With no abode fixed in any place
> Your houses are many
> And keep you from being soaked by rain.
>
> . . .
>
> A single straw mat laid down
> Is not thought to be small.

The rising sound of the *nembutsu*
Is a dwelling where wicked thoughts do not arise.
I have no use for practice halls;
Walking, standing, lying, or sitting
Are all I need for reciting *namu Amida Butsu*,
The central object of my devotion.
Having no mind for profit or desire
I am not a monk soliciting donations.
Though I am not free from the four impurities of preaching,[6]
I promise not to teach the dharma.

. . .

Were it not for the sake of all living beings
There is no point to traveling about the world.
On a pilgrimage to Kumano one year
I worshiped at the Hall of Confirming Truth
And received a revelation in my dream.
Trusting in it I pass my days
Not relying on it for my next life
But for the equal benefit of all.

[Ōhashi et al., eds., *Ippen Shonin goroku*, pp. 294–296; GT]

# THE REVIVAL OF EARLIER BUDDHISM

## MYŌE: SMASHING THE EVIL CHARIOT

The new interpretations of Buddhism by Hōnen and other remarkable leaders of the Kamakura period were so unprecedented that they comprise what scholars call the New Buddhisms. Their challenge to the older Buddhisms of the Shingon, Tendai, and other schools did not, however, go unanswered, and the result was a renewed flaring of controversies and debates. When Hōnen died in 1212 and his *Choosing the Original Vow for the Recitation of the Buddha's Name* was made public, the reaction was swift. Myōe's primary criticism of Hōnen was that he rejected the aspiration or vow to gain enlightenment (*bodaishin*). Hōnen's *Choosing the Original Vow* was an "evil chariot" that had to be "smashed" because a religion without enlightenment as its goal could no longer be called Buddhism. In Myōe's view, Hōnen's understanding of the *nembutsu* was at odds with not only traditional Pure Land teachings but also Buddhism itself.

---

6. Including the claim to complete knowledge, deviating from the sūtras, doubting the teachers according to personal opinions, and preaching for personal gain.

In the fifth section of this work, I will give my interpretation and detailed explanation of the passage from the *Commentary to the Sūtra on Meditation* in which the Chinese Pure Land master Shandao says that although the benefits of both meditation and moral actions have been taught since ancient times, the intention of the Buddha according to his original vow was to make people recite the name of Amida Buddha with single-minded devotion. At this point, let me speak in general terms and point out that the meditation of mindfulness on the Buddha is not taught solely in the *Sūtra on Meditation* but is widely praised in many other doctrinal writings. This meditative practice of the *nembutsu* is nothing short of being the most direct cause of rebirth into the Pure Land. The meaning of the term for meditation is as I have already dealt with earlier. Moral acts such as the three services of caring for others, following the precepts, and engaging in practices leading to enlightenment are not the same as the meditative practices. The meditation on the sun as taught in the *Sūtra on Meditation*, for instance, is a companion to the meditation of mindfulness on the Buddha.

Now one of the methods of practicing this meditation of mindfulness on the Buddha is to call on the name of Amida single-mindedly. This is as it is explained in the writings on the wisdom of Mañjushrī. This is also explained in terms of all methods which are useful aids. What is mentioned here as single-minded recitation, however, is a practice that succeeds only by means of making the vow to attain enlightenment (*bodaishin*). If you separate single-minded recitation from the vow for enlightenment, then it will become entirely meaningless. Therefore all of the sections of the *Sūtra of Infinite Life*, which explain the single-minded recitation for the three classes of people, specify that the vow for enlightenment is fundamental. This is what is said in the sūtra. Concerning the superior class, it says, "Make the vow for enlightenment and recite the name of Amida with single-minded devotion." For the mediocre class, it says, "You must have a mind for the unsurpassed enlightenment and recite the name of the Buddha of Infinite Life with single-minded devotion." For the inferior class, it says, "You should have a mind for the unsurpassed enlightenment and recite the name of the Buddha of Infinite Life with single-minded devotion ten times."

My explanation of this is that the vow to become enlightened is the primary cause for attaining the way of the Buddha and is like the subject of a sentence. Calling on Amida single-mindedly is a separate practice for gaining rebirth and is like the direct object in a sentence. For you [Hōnen] to discard the subject and keep the object is like looking for smoke where there is no fire. What a joke! What a joke!

You should know that these interpretations in the commentaries sometimes leave aside the vow to attain enlightenment without discussing it and simply elaborate on all of the practices that arise from the vow. Why do you say that all of the other practices such as the vow to attain enlightenment are not found in Amida's original vows? The nineteenth vow says, "Make the vow to attain enlightenment and put all virtues into practice." Is this not the original vow? The phrase "make the vow to attain enlightenment" appears in many places, not just one. But even if the phrase "vow to become enlightened" is not to be found in Amida's forty-eight vows, it still is the primary cause for attaining the Buddha's way and therefore does not have to be explained for the first time in the vows. There are other words for referring to the vow to become enlightened. Ah, what a sad case you are! . . .

On this basis, we can say that those who make their own sincere vows can be regarded as practitioners of the vow to gain the great enlightenment. You should understand clearly that the words "sincere mind and joy in faith" mean that priority should be given to making the vow to gain the great enlightenment. The fact that the vow to become enlightened is the fundamental cause for all of the three classes of people in the Sūtra of Infinite Life to be reborn in the Pure Land is made explicitly clear in these interpretations. This being the case, it is entirely incorrect for you, Hōnen, to hold up the names of all the other practices apart from the recitation of Amida's name and say that they are not in the original vow.

Next, you argue that the recitation of Amida's name is the primary practice and is that which is assisted, while the vow to become enlightened is a secondary practice and is that which assists. There is no support for this. If it pleases you to set up this distinction between primary and secondary and between that which is assisted and that which assists, then I must tell you that you have it backwards. I say to you that the vow to become enlightened is primary and is that which is assisted, while recitation is secondary and that which assists. I say to you that the vow to become enlightened is the foundation for the practices for rebirth into the Pure Land. Therefore, in order to nurture single-mindedly the vow to become enlightened, you should renounce the life of a householder, become a disciple, and concentrate on calling on the name of Amida Buddha. I say to you that the vow to become enlightened is the very basis of all acts of morality and is the respected director of all actions. This is the reason why in all of the sūtras and commentaries of Exoteric and Esoteric Buddhism, the vow to become enlightened is praised as the genesis of Buddhism. The textual proofs for this are as profuse as clouds and dew, as plentiful as thick hair. . . .

In your *Choosing the Original Vow*, you say, "The recitation of Amida's name is a practice to be carried out over a long time period [of many rebirths] without losing any progress that has already been made, while the vow to become enlightened is a temporary, initial act that obstructs and destroys recitation." What in the world are you saying in this passage? First of all, what you call the practice of recitation is really meditation on the Buddha. In the five traditional kinds of meditations on the Buddha, there is no distinction made between them and the vow to become enlightened. If you take the practice of recitation and say that it is a practice to be carried out over a long period of time without losing any progress that has already been made, you are really making recitation into an expedient device for producing meditative visions. Once such expedient devices achieve their basic objectives, they can be abandoned. For instance, when you count your breaths while meditating, this technique is but an expedient device for entering into deep meditation. Once that state of meditation is achieved, you can stop counting your breaths.

Furthermore, recitation is significant only up to the end of your present life. Shandao explains what is important in our lives before we die in terms of those who go through the trouble of making initial vows and reciting Amida's name. This being the case, once we die and are reborn in the Pure Land and spiritually progress until the final stage of becoming a buddha, why would we want to make a point of clutching our rosaries and reciting Amida's name?

The vow to attain enlightenment, on the other hand, continues from the beginning until the final objective of becoming a buddha is reached. All virtuous deeds result in nothing if they are divorced from the vow to attain enlightenment. This vow is fundamental all the way up to the final stage. This is what is said in the *Essay on the Lack of Distinctions in the World of the Buddha's Truth*: "Because the vow to attain enlightenment is the supreme means for not losing any progress that has already been made, every act of virtue can be perfected and will result in achieving the final stage, which is nothing other than the world of nirvana."

Fazang, the Chinese master of the Flower Garland (Huayan) school, explained this by saying, "Not losing any progress that has already been made is not only the supreme basis for the final end of becoming a buddha but is also the reason why the progress made through practices one engages in along the way to that end will not be lost." This is because progress made with all practices will be lost if they are divorced from the vow to attain enlightenment. In the Flower Garland school, it is said that the practice of all good deeds apart from the vow to attain enlightenment is to be considered the work of the devil. . . .

This being the case, the practice of reciting Amida's name should also be perfected through the vow to be enlightened. But, you, Hōnen, say that the vow obstructs the recitation of Amida's name. Are you crazy? This is not the teaching of the Buddha. This is what the devil preaches!

> [Kamata and Tanaka, eds., *Kamakura kyū Bukkyō*, NST,
> vol. 15, pp. 80–89; GT]

## JŌKEI: GEDATSU SHŌNIN'S PETITION FOR REVIVING THE PRECEPTS

Like Myōe, Jōkei (1155–1213), also known as Gedatsu Shōnin, was a critic of the innovators. He, too, affirmed the efficacy of meditation and called for a revival of the precepts as the primary means for living the life that Shākyamuni had lived. The precepts, in other words, were a set of regulations and prohibitions, a guide for achieving the kind of spiritual intimacy with Shākyamuni that others claimed was no longer possible. In the pan-Buddhist spirit of his friend Myōe, Jōkei, a Hossō monk, regarded the precepts as the common property of all Buddhists, including the Precepts school. What was important about the precepts was not slavish obedience but the understanding that it defined the teachings of the Buddha as well as the lifestyle of a Buddhist.

The age was surely degenerate—the innovators and the indolent proved to Myōe and Jōkei that spiritual corruption was widespread—but it afforded an opportunity to practice what had always been valued: right mindfulness and correct living.

Since the death of Shākyamuni, our master is the precepts. Is there anyone among lay people, clergy, or the seven classes of disciples who does not revere them? *The Ten Recitations of the Precepts* says, "The World Honored One often rebuked the monks who simply recited the scriptures and the doctrines without studying the precepts. It is because of the existence of the precepts that the Buddha's teaching exists in the world." Little do we know how many other passages there are like this.

It is, however, an inevitable truth that a slow decline sets in with the passage of time. I, too, am in the dark; other people are also in the dark. We neither study nor practice the precepts. . . .

Now the Buddhist teaching in this degenerate age is not free from those who pursue fame and profit. If there is to be a foundation for the precepts, it must be found in courageous effort. In ancient times, the performance of rituals prescribed by the precepts was the condition for residence in all of the temples. Successful participation in the Grand Ceremony on the Vimalakīrti Sūtra set the stage for ecclesiastical advancement. Both of these activities have been discontinued. What are we to make of this? . . .

The administration of the precepts in Nara was carried out in all of the seven great temples and was the particular responsibility of the ten preceptors of the eastern and western halls of Kōfukuji. They carried out the rituals according to imperial decrees, and the ceremonies there were exceedingly dignified. Three officiating monks and seven witnessing monks were required for receiving the precepts. Even if the monks were impure or the rituals were not carried out in the prescribed manner, as long as there were one or two monks who knew the teachings, the conditions for the ceremony were excellent and sufficient. How can it be null and void? If there is no one to continue the precepts in our time, what will be done in the future? This is not a matter of the decline of only one sect but would be a tragedy for all monks, nuns, and novices. Although some expedient means might be used as a temporary remedy, the elder monks of the eastern and western halls must still put an end to their tiresome complaints and lay out some plans for making progress. Even one book of the precepts will serve as a constant foundation for younger monks; even one section of a doctrinal outline should be recommended for reading and recitation. It is most urgent that they take the time to teach them, make them understand, and give to the world this immense benefit. . . .

[Kamata and Tanaka, eds., *Kamakura kyū Bukkyō*, NST, vol. 15, pp. 10–11; GT]

# Chapter 49

## NEW VIEWS OF HISTORY

The Japanese learned from the Chinese how to write history sometime during the seventh and eighth centuries. In addition, the calendar that they imported taught them how to keep track of the passage of time in an orderly manner, and the great classics of Chinese history, including the *Spring and Autumn Annals* (*Chunqiu*), *Commentary on the Spring and Autumn Annals* (*Zuozhuan*), *Records of the Historian* (*Shiji*), *History of the Former Han Dynasty* (*Han shu*), and *History of the Latter Han Dynasty* (*Hou Han shu*), provided models for organizing records of the past. Prince Shōtoku (574–622) is said to have compiled or co-compiled two histories, *Chronicle of Emperors* (*Tennō-ki*) and *Chronicle of the Country* (*Kokki*), but neither has survived. The oldest extant history of Japan by the Japanese is the *Chronicles of Japan* (*Nihongi* or *Nihon shoki*).[1]

The *Chronicles of Japan*, completed in 720, was a product of a historiographical project inaugurated by Emperor Tenmu (r. 673–686) in the late seventh century. Written in Chinese, it begins with an account of the creation of the world (conceived primarily as Japan) and the "age of the gods." This is followed by annals of the reigns of Japan's emperors and empresses starting with Jinmu, who was believed to have founded the Japanese state in 660 B.C., to Jitō (r. 686–697), Tenmu's wife and successor. The first half of the *Nihongi*, covering up to about

---

1. The *Kojiki*, whose narrative ends in the late fifth century, is a work mainly of mythology and hence is not regarded as history for the purpose of this survey of history writing in ancient and medieval Japan.

the late sixth century, is essentially myth. But as it progresses, the second half becomes increasingly reliable as history. Thus when we speak of the *Nihongi* as Japan's first history, we refer to the work's second half, covering the period of about a century or so from the late sixth century until the *Nihongi*'s termination date of 697. Apart from scattered accounts of relations with Japan in Chinese and Korean records, the *Nihongi* is our sole written source of knowledge about Japan during this crucial age of the late sixth and seventh centuries when, as a result of extensive borrowing from the continent, it became a land of advanced civilization within the China-centered cultural sphere of East Asia.

Of the two principal Chinese models of history writing, the "chronicle" model (J: *hennen-tai*) and the "annals and biographies" model (J: *kiden-tai*), the *Nihongi* is primarily a chronicle, that is, a narrative arranged in chronological order with precise (although not always accurate) dating throughout. But the *Nihongi* also partakes of the annals and biographies model because, as just noted, it is divided from the time of Jinmu into the chronology of the passing years and also the reigns of emperors and empresses. This division of the *Nihongi* after the age of the gods into imperial reigns is, in fact, one of the work's most distinguishing features.

The annals and biographies model of history, originated by Sima Qian in *Records of the Grand Historian* (*Shiji*), was used in China primarily for compiling dynastic histories, that is, histories arranged according to the division of time into dynastic periods or cycles of history generated by the founding, flourishing, and fall of successive ruling dynasties. Each dynasty, it was believed, began when it received the Mandate of Heaven and fell when Heaven, judging the dynasty no longer worthy, withdrew the mandate. Although there are occasional references to the Mandate of Heaven in Japan's early writings about emperorship, the Japanese never adopted this Chinese idea as a theory for imperial succession. On the contrary, they firmly grounded the succession to their emperorship in another mandate: the one that the Sun Goddess bestowed on her grandson Ninigi when she sent him from Heaven to rule the land of Japan. As related in the *Nihongi*, the mandate was: "Do thou, my August Grandchild, proceed thither and govern it. Go! and may prosperity attend thy dynasty, and may it, like Heaven and Earth, endure for ever."[2] To the Japanese of later times, this mandate was the basis for the idea of *bansei ikkei*, "one dynasty [to rule] a myriad generations." Imperial rule in Japan was not to be governed by moral laws or cyclical forces; instead, the founding dynasty would rule forever.

After the *Nihongi*, the court compiled five more histories, also in Chinese, that cover the period from 697 through the reign of Emperor Kōkō (r. 884–887) and are known as the "Five National Histories" (*gokokushi*). Combined with the *Nihongi*, they are called the "Six National Histories" (*rikkokushi*). The Five National Histories are, however, works quite different from the *Nihongi*.

---

2. Aston, *Nihongi*, vol. 1, p. 77.

First, whereas the *Nihongi* extensively uses myths, oral stories, and foreign (Chinese and Korean) records, the *gokokushi* are compilations based entirely on Japanese government documents. In this sense, they are better, more reliable histories than the *Nihongi*. They also are examples of "objective" history, although one may question the value of that. In contrast to the *Nihongi*, which is lively, imaginative, and readable, the Five National Histories are dry-as-dust, bare-bones chronologies of court events—coronations, marriages, the changing of calendrical eras (*nengō*), the appointment of ministers, the promulgation of decrees, reports of omens, and so forth.

One distinctive feature of Chinese history writing that is almost entirely missing from the Five National Histories is the personal evaluations (J: *ronsan*) of the emperors made at the ends of their reigns and those of other important people in their biographies. These evaluations were a crucial means by which Chinese historians performed the Confucian function of judging morality or the lack of it in emperors and others. Neglect of the *ronsan* by the *gokokushi* authors appears to reflect a general disinterest by the Japanese at this early stage of their history in the force of individual morality in government and society.

## MEDIEVAL USES OF THE PAST

The shogunate's founding in 1185 did not mean that warrior rule immediately and completely supplanted courtier rule (for purposes of this discussion, the imperial family is included with the courtiers). Instead, the shogunate was a new, separate government that never entirely displaced the court. What emerged was a dyarchy of court (Kyoto) and camp (Kamakura), and only gradually did Kamakura assume all of the court's traditional ruling powers. Even when this was accomplished by the late Kamakura period (1185–1333), the courtiers as a class remained an economic force to be reckoned with by virtue of their continued possession of vast wealth in revenue-producing agricultural estates (*shōen*).

Because the court remained at least potentially a viable government, some of its members periodically dreamed of regaining actual ruling powers by either overthrowing the shogunate and carrying out an "imperial restoration" or seeking a more intimate accommodation with the military. It was in the context of such dreaming that the two most important histories of the medieval age were written, *Gukanshō* by Jien (1155–1225) and *Jinnō shōtōki* (*Chronicle of the Direct Succession of Gods and Sovereigns*) by Kitabatake Chikafusa (1293–1354). In composing these works, Jien and Chikafusa, both of whom came from high-ranking court families, opened new avenues of inquiry into the study of Japanese history. They stand apart from earlier historians of Japan in at least two important respects:

1. Unlike the earlier historians, who were content to narrate events of the past more or less on a straight continuum of time with little attempt to discern larger

processes of cause and effect or long-term change, Jien and Chikafusa divided Japanese history into periods and were at pains to analyze and explain the reasons for the transitions from one period to another.

2. Although their histories have been labeled, in the case of one (*Gukanshō*), a "Buddhist" history and, in the case of the other (*Jinnō shōtōki*), a "Shinto" history, Jien and Chikafusa appear to have been inspired to take up their brushes primarily to argue politics. Viewing the past in terms of the central issues of the times in which they lived and the interests of the class to which they belonged, as well as their personal political allegiances, they sought to interpret and use the past with the express aim of influencing and directing the course of the country in the present and future.

# JIEN

Jien was born into the Kujō branch of the Fujiwara family in 1155. A year later, 1156, armed conflict erupted in Kyoto for the first time in three and a half centuries. Known after the calendrical era as the Hōgen conflict, it centered on a factional dispute involving an emperor, a retired emperor, and leading Fujiwara ministers and was fought by members of the Taira and Minamoto warrior families. To Jien, writing in *Gukanshō*, the Hōgen conflict marked the start of the "age of warriors." In 1159, another, similar conflict in Kyoto (the Heiji conflict) broke out. This time, however, the Taira and Minamoto were more clearly pitted against each other in the fighting, and when the Taira emerged victorious, they began, under their leader Kiyomori (1118–1181), a dramatic rise to power at court. By the late 1170s, Kiyomori, who married his daughter into the imperial family and installed his infant grandson as emperor, had become a virtual dictator in Kyoto. But Kiyomori and the Taira were not to remain at this pinnacle of power for long. Beginning in 1180, chieftains of the Minamoto rose in rebellion in the provinces and provoked a five-year war (the Minamoto-Taira, or Genpei, War) that ended in the complete destruction of the Taira (Kiyomori himself died in 1181) and the establishment in 1185 of the Kamakura shogunate by Minamoto no Yoritomo (1147–1199).

Backed by Yoritomo, Jien's older brother Kujō no Kanezane (1149–1207) was appointed imperial regent at court in 1186, and in 1192 Jien, who had entered Buddhist orders, became head abbot of the Tendai temple of Enryakuji on Mount Hiei (thus embarking on the first of four terms as the head of the Enryakuji). With Kanezane serving as ranking minister at court and Jien occupying one of the highest positions in the Buddhist ecclesiastical world, the Kujō family flourished during these years. But in 1196 Kanezane, embroiled in political battle at court and no longer enjoying Yoritomo's strong support, was dismissed as regent, and at the same time, Jien was ousted as the abbot of Enryakuji. For the next thirteen years, the Kujō were, for the most part, outshone at court by the rival Konoe branch of the Fujiwara family.

Then in 1219, two developments gave rise to what Jien hoped would be a great revival of Kujō fortunes. First, it seemed that the Kujō would soon regain the office of regent, and second, Jien's two-year-old great grandnephew Yoritsune (1218–56) was adopted into the warrior family of Minamoto in order to become the shogun. This adoption was engineered by the Hōjō family, which during the years after Yoritomo's death in 1199 had emerged as the new power holders in the shogunate. Wielding their power through the office of shogunal regent (*shikken*), the Hōjō sought in Yoritsune a figurehead leader who would bring a fresh aura of legitimacy to the shogunate by virtue of his Kujō (Fujiwara) family origins. Jien, however, saw the pending appointment of Yoritsune as shogun in a very different light. He professed to believe that the appointment was the work of the "Great Hachiman Bodhisattva," who intended that once Yoritsune had attained his majority, he would become a ruler in fact as well as name. Jien was convinced that Yoritsune was destined to bring together court and camp to form a new, truly national government.

It is doubtful that many others at the time shared Jien's grandiose expectations for Yoritsune, least of all the retired emperor Go-Toba (1180–1239), who even then was plotting to overthrow the Kamakura shogunate. To Jien, such plotting was reckless adventurism that might jeopardize Yoritsune's chances to become the unifier of the country in the future. It was primarily to dissuade Go-Toba from pursuing the collision course on which he appeared to be set that Jien took up his brush in 1219 to write *Gukanshō*. But Jien's effort came to naught. In 1221 Go-Toba launched his "rebellion" against the Kamakura regime, which responded by dispatching a huge army westward that speedily and thoroughly defeated the ragtag force that Go-Toba had assembled to oppose it. As a result of this brief conflict, known as the Jōkyū War, Go-Toba was sent into exile, and the Kyoto court was left far weaker and more firmly under Kamakura's control than before. Yoritsune did become shogun, although not until 1226. He held the office for nearly twenty years (until 1244) but never became more than the figurehead the Hōjō intended him to be.

## GUKANSHŌ

*Gukanshō* has two parts: a history of Japan from the first emperor, Jinmu, until 1219, and a detailed chronology of names, dates, titles, court appointments, and the like for the same period.[3] The first part, the history, is divided approximately in half at 1156, the year of the Hōgen conflict. Thus, fully half of *Gukanshō* is devoted to Jien's own lifetime, which he identifies as the "military age."

---

3. The chronology actually precedes the history, but this discussion follows the order in Brown and Ishida's *The Future and the Past*.

Although Jien follows the chronology of historical events, dividing Japanese history into seven periods (the first four go to 1156 and the last three go from 1156 to 1219), his presentation of these events is not always orderly, and he is frequently repetitious. But even more daunting for the reader is that in seeking to explain why certain key events occurred and how and why history moved from one period to another, Jien relies heavily on a single concept: *dōri*, "principle." In effect, he attempts to analyze the course of Japanese history in terms of a great variety of principles, some of which he does not clearly or convincingly explain. At times, indeed, his discussion of principles collapses into confusion, as in the following passage dealing with his third period of Japanese history (571–1027, from the introduction of Buddhism to Japan through the age of Fujiwara no Michinaga):

> [This was the] period of the principle by which people of the visible world did not act in accord with the will of invisible beings, although everyone felt that what he was doing was actually a requirement of a principle [created by invisible beings]. This was a situation in which something that was thought to be good would certainly be regretted later on. In this period people who thought of something as a requirement of principle came to realize, later on and upon reflection, [that it was not in accord with the will of invisible beings].[4]

We can discern in *Gukanshō*, however, two general types of principles whose characteristics and interactions with each other tell us a great deal about the thinking of intellectuals in Jien's day. The first type is destructive principles, derived from the *mappō* ("end of the [Buddhist] Law") thought discussed earlier. *Gukanshō* is based on the belief that history is a process of long-term decline or deterioration in accordance with the Mahāyāna Buddhist notion of its passing through three downward-moving stages from the time of the death of the historic Buddha, Gautama. The third and final stage, *mappō*, by Japanese calculation, began in 1052.[5] The *mappō* interpretation of history provided the principal means by which Jien, who was not a trained or professional historian, became the first writer of Japanese history to interpret Japan's past in terms of cause and effect and to periodize it accordingly. This interpretation also gave rise to the popular conception of *Gukanshō* as a "Buddhist" history. But the second type of principles described in *Gukanshō*, constructive principles, derives from both Buddhism and Shinto, and indeed, those of Shinto often appear to be the more important. For this reason, we might well describe *Gukanshō* as *both* a Buddhist and a Shinto history. Then too, the Song Neo-Confucian concept of "principle" in human affairs may also be at work here, though not in systematic ways.

---

4. Brown and Ishida, *The Future and the Past*, pp. 206–207.

5. For a discussion of the various stages in the decline of the Buddhist Law and how the Japanese arrived at the date 1052 for the commencement of the age of *mappō*, see Ishida, "Structure and Formation of *Gukanshō* Thought," in ibid., pp. 423–425.

Constructive principles can bring about historical "improvement" or upward movement. Nothing can ultimately prevent long-term deterioration from running its course, but there can be occasional and partial reversals of that course. The introduction of Buddhism to Japan in the late sixth century, for example, caused such a reversal and brought temporary improvement when the Buddhist Law (*buppō*) became the protector of the Imperial Law (*ōhō*). But the constructive principle that interests Jien most in *Gukanshō* is that the Sun Goddess, Amaterasu, and the Great Hachiman Bodhisattva ordained that the Fujiwara family should assist emperors in ruling. Although Hachiman, with the designation Bodhisattva, is identified here as both a Shinto and a Buddhist deity, the principle to which Jien refers is clearly Shintoist, since its locus classicus is in the age of the gods section of the mythology. When the Sun Goddess sent her grandson, Ninigi, to Japan with the mandate to rule it forever, she had Ame no Koyane no Mikoto, the ancestral *kami* of the Fujiwara family, accompany him, ordering the *kami* to assist Ninigi in his rule.[6] The order to Ame no Koyane became the scriptural basis, so to speak, for the establishment of the Fujiwara regency.

Let us return to Jien's periodization of Japanese history in *Gukanshō*. We have noted that he divided it into seven periods. But more important, he also conceived of it in terms of three broad ages: ancient (*jōko*), medieval (*chūko*), and modern (*kindai*). In this he was not entirely original, for by the late Heian period, courtiers in general had come to think of Japanese history as progressing through such ages. Jien does not try to pinpoint the transition from the ancient age to the medieval age, but like other late-Heian courtiers who referred to it in their writings, he believed the transition occurred about the time when the Fujiwara consolidated their power as regents at court in the early tenth century. In regard to the transition to the modern age, however, Jien is precise: it occurred in 1156, the year of the Hōgen conflict, which, as we noted, he also calls the starting date of the age of warriors. In his thinking, "modern age" and "age of warriors" (or "military age") were synonymous.

Of the three ages, ancient, medieval, and modern, the medieval represented the ideal to Jien. In the ancient age, emperors (and some empresses) had been able to rule unaided. But by the medieval age, as history continued on its inexorable course of decline, it became necessary to enforce the Sun Goddess's order that the descendants of Ame no Koyane—the Fujiwara—help the emperors rule. The result was what Jien regarded as a brilliant, albeit temporary, revival of history, especially during the time of the greatest regent, Michinaga, in the late tenth and early eleventh centuries. Jien hoped that the spirit of the medieval

---

6. The Sun Goddess also ordered the ancestral *kami* of the Imbe family to assist Ninigi (Aston, *Nihongi*, vol. 1, p. 83). But the Imbe lost out politically to the Fujiwara during the early Heian period and declined into insignificance at court, thus enabling the Fujiwara to claim that they alone had been mandated by the Sun Goddess to be imperial assistants.

age might be revived in the early Kamakura period with the appointment of his great-grandnephew, Kujō no Yoritsune, as ruler of the Kamakura shogunate.

### ONE HUNDRED KINGS

In addition to the *mappō* theory of historical decline, Jien also subscribed to the belief that Japan would be ruled by only one hundred kings (or emperors; *hyakuō*). An idea received from China, "one hundred kings" seems originally to have meant simply many or an indefinite number of kings. But by the late Heian period, courtiers like Jien, under the influence of *mappō* thought, came to interpret "one hundred kings" literally as exactly one hundred. As Jien points out, only sixteen kingly reigns remained at the time he wrote *Gukanshō*. He tells us nothing about what would happen after the one-hundredth reign.

I have become keenly aware of principles that have been changing since ancient times. I do not know how it was in the Age of the Gods but I hear that after the beginning of the age of man and the enthronement of Emperor Jinmu, Japan is to have only one hundred reigns. Now that we are in the 84th reign not many more are left. . . .

Even [Prince Shōtoku's] Seventeen Article Constitution has become ineffective during these final reigns because the "principles of things" exist only faintly and unfamiliarly in the hearts of men. Persons of high position have no sympathy for those below, and those below have no respect for those above. Turning against the civil and penal codes (and their supplements) compiled long ago—with the Seventeen Article Constitution as their source—the state is simply going to ruin. It is sad to be thinking only about what can be done about such deterioration. All that can be done until the 100th reign is to rely upon the blessings of the Gods worshipped at the Imperial shrines of Ise and Iwashimizu, and Kashima and Kasuga, and upon the divine grace of the Three Buddhist Treasures and deities of the various Heavens.

[Adapted from Brown and Ishida, *The Future and the Past*, pp. 19, 82–83; PV]

### HELPING EMPERORS RULE

In the following passages, Jien refers to the Sun Goddess's directive to the descendants of Ame no Koyane to help emperors rule. He also alludes to what was apparently a second, similar order issued by the Sun Goddess and the Great Hachiman Bodhisattva.

It is desirable to have an Emperor whose behavior as an Emperor is good, but Japan is a country that has had the tradition, since the Age of the Gods, that no person should become Emperor who is not in the Imperial line of descent. It is also the tradition of the country to want an Emperor from that line who will be a good Emperor. But since it has necessarily become difficult for an Emperor to govern the state well by himself, it was established that a Great Imperial Chieftain [i.e., regent] would be appointed and used as Imperial guardian, and that the state would be governed in consultation with this minister. . . .

An instruction from the Sun Goddess and the Great Hachiman Bodhisattva created an arrangement . . . by which it would be deemed improper for an Emperor to be the least bit estranged from his guardian. Whether the empire is governed well or becomes chaotic depends on whether that instruction is respected. Long ago, the Sun Goddess made a divine agreement with Ame no Koyane no Mikoto [the ancestral God of the Fujiwara clan] that the latter was to reside in, and guard, the Imperial Palace. The descendants of Ame no Koyane no Mikoto grasped the implications of this Principle, which was not to be violated one iota. . . .

But nothing was amiss in governmental affairs during this Medieval Age, because the abilities of Fujiwara regents were superb and because they assisted Imperial rule and had the state governed well. . . . The reason why governmental affairs came to be handled in this way was that in the Age of the Gods the Sun Goddess had said to the ancestral Gods of the Fujiwara clan: "You will guard the Imperial Palace well." She did so because she realized that Emperors in the Medieval Age would not be like sovereigns in the Ancient Age. Therefore one descendant of the ancestral Gods of the Fujiwara clan after another was born with appropriate ability. . . . [The principle that Emperors would not be able to rule unassisted and the principle that the descendants of the ancestral Gods of the Fujiwara were to assist Emperors] were created together.

[Adapted from Brown and Ishida, *The Future and the Past*, pp. 210–211, 213; PV]

AN APPEAL TO RETIRED EMPEROR GO-TOBA

In this appeal, Jien refers to the retired emperor Go-Toba as both "sovereign" and "His Majesty." The purpose of the appeal is to dissuade Go-Toba from plotting against the Kamakura shogunate because of the possibilities for peace and national unity enabled by the adoption of Jien's great-grandnephew, Kujō no Yoritsune, into the Minamoto in order to become shogun. Jien suggests that Yoritsune will—or at least should—also be made imperial regent in the future in order to preside administratively over both the court and the shogunate. There is no evidence, however, that the court ever considered Yoritsune for the position of regent.

Under the conditions of this Age, the [mistakes] of people will not be rectified unless an honest Shogun emerges. But such a Shogun *has* emerged, because the Great Hachiman Bodhisattva planned to produce a person from the regental house who would protect the state and guard the sovereign with the prestige and power of both learning and military might. And yet the sovereign does not understand that Yoritsune was born for the benefit of state, man, and the sovereign.

A very serious matter indeed! It was definitely a divine decision that it would be good for the sovereign to have the same person serve as Shogun and Regent. The ancestral Gods decided to provide the sovereign with a guardian who would also be powerful and prestigious. It would be best if His Majesty understood that Yoritsune's birth and appointment were brought about in this way. . . . By rejecting the plan for Yoritsune to be both Shogun and Regent, the sovereign will be acting contrary to the will of the Sun Goddess and Hachiman. But by accepting it, he will become enlightened. . . .

It has come to my attention that the sovereign is making short-sighted plans [to oppose the shogunate] because he does not understand either the principle of deterioration alternating with improvement from the beginning to the end of the present small kalpa, nor the principle—granted by the ancestral Gods of the Imperial House and of the Fujiwara and Minamoto clans—for this Final Age, a principle that has come down to us from the ancient past. The principles of things, and the history of our country, will surely be stabilized if the sovereign acts according to these principles.

[Brown and Ishida, *The Future and the Past*, pp. 210–211, 213, 225–226; PV]

# KITABATAKE CHIKAFUSA AND
# THE SOUTHERN COURT

The Kamakura shogunate was overthrown in 1333 by warrior forces that rallied to the loyalist cause of Emperor Go-Daigo (r. 1318–1339). Go-Daigo interpreted the shogunate's overthrow as a mandate to revive what he believed had been government by direct imperial rule before the rise, from about the mid-Heian period, of, first, the Fujiwara regents, second, politically powerful retired emperors, and, third, the military (the Kamakura shogunate). This "imperial restoration," known as the Kenmu Restoration, lasted until 1336.

Japan at the time of the Kenmu Restoration was entering a turbulent new age of regionalism in which warrior chieftains throughout the country contended against one another for land and power. The restoration government, whatever its good intentions, was unable to deal either promptly or satisfactorily with the multitude of problems and demands presented to it by contentious warriors. It was bedeviled in particular by a personal struggle for power between Nitta Yoshisada (1301–1338) and Ashikaga Takauji (1305–1358), leaders of the main branches of the Minamoto. In 1335, fighting broke out between these two leaders in which Yoshisada championed the restoration government and Takauji and his army were stigmatized as rebels. In 1336, Takauji defeated Yoshisada in a key battle and captured Kyoto. Go-Daigo, unwilling to accept Takauji as the new military hegemon, fled to Yoshino in the mountainous region to the south. He proclaimed Yoshino the new seat of the court and himself still the rightful sovereign. Takauji, meanwhile, had a member of another branch of the imperial family chosen as emperor in Kyoto, creating a situation in which, for the first time in Japanese history, there were two emperors. Takauji also established a new shogunate, known in history as the Ashikaga or Muromachi shogunate (1336–1573), with its headquarters in Kyoto. During the first half-century of its existence, 1336 to 1392, the shogunate was embroiled in conflict with forces of the Yoshino regime in what came to be called the War Between the Northern (Kyoto) and Southern (Yoshino) Courts.

Kitabatake Chikafusa, scion of a high-ranking noble family (the Murakami Genji or Minamoto) and formerly a prominent minister at court, did not play a significant role in the Kenmu Restoration. He may have assisted in the arrangements made for Go-Daigo's flight to Yoshino in 1336, but the records remain largely silent about his activities until 1338. In that year, he joined a group that went by sea to the Kantō region in an effort to rally support among eastern warriors for the Southern Court. While in the Kantō, Chikafusa made a particularly intense effort to recruit the chieftain Yūki Chikatomo to the Southern Court's side. The nearly seventy remaining letters from Chikafusa to Chikatomo constitute the largest correspondence from one person to another still extant from the medieval age. In the end, however, Chikafusa was unsuccessful, for in 1343 Chikatomo joined the side of the Ashikaga and the Northern Court. Early the following year, 1344, Chikafusa returned to Yoshino. From then until his death in 1354, he served as one of the Southern Court's leading ministers under Emperor Go-Murakami (r. 1339–1368), the successor to his father, Go-Daigo, who died in 1339.

## DIRECT SUCCESSION OF GODS AND SOVEREIGNS (JINNŌ SHŌTŌKI)

Chikafusa began writing his *Direct Succession (Jinnō shōtōki)* in 1339 in the Kantō, using, we are told, an imperial genealogy as his only reference. He revised it in 1343. Chikafusa appears to have written the *Direct Succession* at this time as part of his effort to attract Yūki Chikatomo and other eastern warriors to the cause of the Southern Court. The work, like *Gukanshō*, is both a history and a political tract.

As a history, the *Direct Succession* was a product of a Shinto revival that began in the Kamakura period. One premise of this revival was that the gods of Shinto were the true protectors of the country, not the deities of Buddhism who had been thought to perform that function since at least the late seventh century. The effectiveness of the gods' protection appeared to be confirmed when the *kamikaze*, "divine winds," arose to annihilate the enemy fleets during the two Mongol invasions of Japan in 1274 and 1281. In the words of Chikafusa, "the gods, revealing their awesome authority and manifesting their form, drove the invaders away. Thus a great wind suddenly arose and the several hundreds of thousands [*sic*] of enemy ships were all blown over and demolished. Although people speak of this as a degenerate later age, the righteous power displayed by the gods [of Shinto] at this time was truly beyond human comprehension."[7]

Belief that the gods of Shinto held primacy as protectors of the country derived from the concept of Japan as a divine land or "land of the gods" (*shinkoku*), which was first expressed in the mythology as found in the *Kojiki* and the *Nihongi*. Used by Chikafusa as a key concept in his interpretation of Japanese history, *shinkoku* first appears in the *Jinnō shōtōki* in its famous opening lines: "Great Japan is the divine land. The heavenly progenitor founded it, and the Sun Goddess bequeathed it to her descendants to rule eternally. Only in our country is this true; there are no similar examples in other countries. This is why our country is called the divine land."[8] Whereas belief in the gods as the true protectors of the country was emphasized in divine-land thought during the late thirteenth century when the Mongols threatened Japan, by Chikafusa's time — or more precisely, because of Chikafusa — the emphasis, as succinctly but powerfully articulated in the preceding lines, was shifted to faith in the mandate of the Sun Goddess that the imperial dynasty would rule forever.

In writing *Gukanshō*, Jien began with the reign of the first emperor, Jinmu. But Chikafusa, in his *Direct Succession*, partly reflecting a revival of interest during the middle and late medieval age in the age of the gods before Jinmu, starts with the story of the creation of the land (Japan) and then describes the reigns of five godly rulers before entering into his main narrative of "human sovereigns," spanning the reigns from Jinmu through Go-Daigo and Go-Murakami.

In their overall views of Japanese history, Jien and Chikafusa differed markedly. Whereas Jien believed that history was following a fundamentally unalterable path of decline and deterioration that might possibly end in the destruction of the world (or at least Japan, as in the theory of one hundred kings), Chikafusa asserted that the Sun Goddess's mandate guaranteed that Japan and its ruling family would continue forever. To Chikafusa, the course of Japanese history was essentially a straight, "direct," and correct (*shō*) line. There might be periodic deviations, but these would always be rectified by a return to the direct line. Chikafusa also discerned a direct line within the imperial succession. Although in fact there had been occasional shifts away from the succession's direct line, all were straightened out with the passage of time. It was precisely the succession's capacity to return invariably to its direct course that guaranteed its legitimacy and ensured its eternal continuance, setting Japan apart from — and making it superior to — countries like India and China: "In our country alone, the imperial succession has followed in an unbroken line from the time when heaven and earth were divided until the present age. Although, as is inevitable within a single family, the succession has at times

---

7. Varley, *A Chronicle of Gods and Sovereigns*, p. 234.
8. Ibid., p. 49.

been transmitted collaterally, the principle has prevailed that it will invariably return to the direct line."[9]

Jien's and Chikafusa's views of history from the perspective of what might be called the short term, on the other hand, were quite similar. Both, for example, regarded history—especially recent history—from the same class perspective, that of the upper echelon of courtiers. Jien, of course, was one of the bluest of the blue-blooded courtiers by virtue of his birth into the regental branch of the Fujiwara. But Chikafusa was not far behind: he came from a ministerial family descended from Murakami (r. 946–967), one of the most illustrious emperors, that had rivaled the Fujiwara for ministerial power from at least the early years of the Kamakura period. Both Jien and Chikafusa were also imperial restorationists. But their idea of imperial restoration focused more on the return of actual governing power from the military to the hands of the Fujiwara and Murakami Genji in the service of "restored" emperors than to the emperors themselves. As Chikafusa put it: "First [in undertaking decisive administration], there is the selection and appointment of people to the offices of central government. Once the ruler has appointed the proper people to these offices, he need interfere no further in their activities."[10]

The *Direct Succession* is often believed to be a tract arguing the legitimacy of the Southern over the Northern Court, as suggested in the translation of its title into English as the "Chronicle of the Legitimate Succession of Divine Sovereigns (or Gods and Sovereigns)."[11] But Chikafusa has little to say directly about imperial legitimacy in the *Jinnō shōtōki*. He tacitly accepts the legitimacy of all the recognized sovereigns from Jinmu through Go-Daigo, including those from the branch of the imperial family that later provided emperors for the Northern Court. He does claim that Go-Daigo never willingly relinquished the emperorship in 1336, and hence the Northern Court, founded at that time with Ashikaga backing, was illegitimate. But Chikafusa does this in a way suggesting the point did not require arguing. And indeed, other records from the period make clear that the Ashikaga themselves privately believed that Takauji had acted improperly in establishing the Northern Court. Throughout the half century of the War Between the Northern and Southern Courts, the Ashikaga consistently sought not to destroy the Southern Court but to persuade its emperor to return to Kyoto in order to remove the stain of "illegitimacy" from the Northern Court.[12]

---

9. Ibid., pp. 60–61.

10. Ibid., p. 251.

11. "Divine Sovereigns" and "Gods and Sovereigns" mean the same thing, since the former phrase includes the five godly rulers who preceded the first human sovereign, Jinmu.

12. In 1392, when the Southern Court had lost most of its capacity to continue fighting, the Ashikaga finally persuaded its emperor to return to Kyoto with the promise that his line would be allowed to provide emperors alternately with the line of the Northern Court. But this promise was never honored, and the Southern Court line sank into historical oblivion.

## FUJIWARA AND MURAKAMI GENJI AS ASSISTANTS
## TO EMPERORS

Chikafusa here discusses the historical rise of the Fujiwara as assistants to emperors, based on the Sun Goddess's mandate to the family's godly forebear, Ame no Koyane (or Ama no Koyane). He then lays claim to a similar "right to assist the throne" for the Murakami Genji because of their descent from Emperor Murakami and the outstanding and virtuous service of many Murakami Genji ministers over the years. Chikafusa also recalls the selection of men in the remote past to serve as both army commanders and ministers at court, combining the functions of the civil (*bun*) and the military (*bu*). He himself became such a minister-commander during the War Between the Courts, and his son Akiie (1318–1338), qualified by birth to be a minister, gave his life fighting as a general in the service of Go-Daigo and the Southern Court.

The imperial family certainly stands apart from other families, yet in our country there has been a mandate since the Age of the Gods stating that while the sovereign, as a descendant of the Sun Goddess, rules over the land, those subjects in the line of Ame-no-Koyane are also mandated to assist the sovereign in his administration of affairs. The [Murakami] Genji are subjects who have recently branched off from the imperial family. Should they, without virtue or merit, rise to high offices and lord it over people, they will surely be visited with punishment by the two great deities, the Sun Goddess and Ame-no-Koyane.

In the ancient age many princes and other royal descendants were given official positions in the provinces and were even appointed as generalissimos. The first to assign such generalissimos [shoguns] was Emperor Sujin who, in the tenth year of his reign, appointed four, all of whom were members of the imperial family, and sent them to the four circuits. Emperor Keikō, in the fifty-first year of his reign, inaugurated the practice of designating a chief among his ministers. The person he selected was Takeuchi-no-Sukune. In the third year of Emperor Seimu's reign, Takeuchi was further advanced to the position of *ō-omi*. (This marked the beginning of the office of *ō-omi* or *daijin* [great minister] in our country.) A great-grandson of Emperor Kōgen, Takeuchi served as an administrator of government during six reigns.

Things changed, however, when Fujiwara no Kamatari revitalized his clan and Yoshifusa ultimately established an imperial regency. For this marked a return to the arrangement decided upon in the age of the gods whereby the descendants of Ame-no-Koyane were to serve as assistants to the throne. Fuyutsugu also contributed much to this reassertion of the divinely mandated rights of the Fujiwara. Lamenting the decline of his clan, Fuyutsugu not only engaged ceaselessly in good works and accumulated great merit, but also prayed to the gods and devoted himself to Buddhism.

Prince Tomohira was indeed a man of great ability and virtue. His son Morofusa, who received the [Murakami] Genji surname and joined the ranks of subjects, also possessed talent in no way inferior to the noted officials of ancient times and achieved fame that spread throughout the land. Morofusa was appointed counselor at the age of seventeen. Devoting himself over a period of decades to the study of ancient court precedent and ceremonial, he rose to the positions of great minister and general of the inner palace guards and served the court until the age of seventy. . . .

From Morofusa's time, the Murakami Genji have devoted themselves to both Chinese and Japanese learning and have been dedicated with total sincerity to loyal service to the state. Perhaps it is because of this that only the Morofusa line of Genji ministers has continued to thrive over many generations. Although within the line there have been some ministers of doubtful achievement and questionable virtue, their branch families have inevitably declined and died out. Genji in the future should carefully reflect upon the fate of such families as these.

Even though the intent of this book is mainly to record the affairs of sovereigns, I have also spoken several times about the origins of the Fujiwara clan. Moreover, in view of the longevity of the Murakami Genji line, I have wished to record something of the direct succession of ministers to which they are the inheritors. Emperor Murakami's line of sovereigns has continued through seventeen generations, and we note with great admiration and reverence that, thanks to Murakami's enduring virtue, the subject line of Murakami Genji, which he spawned, has continued to serve at court throughout this same sequence of reigns.

[Varley, *A Chronicle of Gods and Sovereigns*, pp. 188–189; PV]

## ON IMPERIAL RESTORATION

In this very revealing passage, Chikafusa sharply criticizes retired emperor Go-Toba for trying to overthrow the Kamakura shogunate in the Jōkyū War of 1221 when the time for doing it "had not yet arrived." In his analysis of the course of recent Japanese history, Chikafusa acknowledges the inevitability of the rise of the military and even praises Minamoto no Yoritomo and the early Hōjō for restoring and maintaining order when the court could not do so. But ultimately, he believes, there had to be a return to "direct" imperial rule. Ever the formalistic conservative in his social thinking, Chikafusa sees disorder occurring in the country when "those who are socially inferior seek to prevail over their superiors." His idea of the ideal military ruler is Hōjō no Yasutoki (1183–1242), who not only "knew his place" and did not himself take high (court) rank or office but also impressed on "the other members of his family and the warrior class in general" not to seek them. Although the *Direct Succession*, as noted, is often labeled a "Shinto history," Chikafusa in fact has a great deal to say also about both Buddhism and Confucianism. In this passage, as in many others, the Confucian tone is particularly strong, as Chikafusa repeatedly refers to virtuous rule and the welfare and contentment of the people.

In reflecting upon the disturbance of the Jōkyū era, one's mind is indeed apt to be bewildered about the course and meaning of events in this later age. One thing discernible is the beginning of a pattern of behavior whereby those who are socially inferior seek to prevail over their superiors.[13] It is essential, therefore, to assess the events of this time as carefully as possible. Minamoto no Yoritomo's achievements were beyond compare with anything since earliest times in history; yet we can understand why, as Yoritomo sought to gather all the power of the country into his own hands, the imperial family felt uneasy. It is even more understandable why, after Yoritomo's line came to an end and his widow (the nun [Hōjō no] Masako) and the rear vassal [Hōjō no] Yoshitoki took control of the country, Go-Toba should wish to do away with the Bakufu [shogunate] and rule directly himself.

Since the age of Shirakawa and Toba, the ancient way of government had declined steadily,[14] and in Go-Shirakawa's time armed rebellions occurred and treacherous subjects threw the country into disorder. The people of the land fell into almost total misery. Minamoto no Yoritomo restored order by his own force of arms; and, although the imperial house was not returned to its former state, the fighting in the capital was quelled and the burdens of the people were eased. High and low were once again at peace, and people everywhere submitted to Yoritomo's virtue. Apparently it was because of this submission that no one rebelled against the Bakufu, even at the time of Sanetomo's assassination. How then could the Kyoto court expect so readily to overthrow the Bakufu, if it did not have an administration of merit equal to that of Kamakura? Let us suppose the Bakufu had been destroyed. If the people were not thereby made content, Heaven would surely not assent to such a change in governance to the country. The sovereign's army chastises only those who have committed offenses, not the blameless.

It was strictly by means of the royal directives of retired monk-emperor Go-Shirakawa that Yoritomo rose to high offices and received appointment as constable-general of the country. One can scarcely say that he selfishly seized these offices for himself.

After Yoritomo's death, Masako took charge of affairs at Kamakura, and later Yoshitoki wielded power for a long while. But since Masako and Yoshitoki did not go against the hopes of the people, they committed no transgressions as subjects "from below." We may indeed say that the attempt by Go-Toba to overthrow the Kamakura Bakufu for insufficient reason was a transgression "from above."

---

13. This is the concept of *gekokujō* (those below overthrow those above) that was so aptly used to characterize social upheaval at various levels during the medieval age.

14. The ancient (and proper) way of government was, in Chikafusa's mind, that prevailing during the heyday of the Fujiwara regents: rule by the sovereign assisted by a small group of his highest ministers at court. The assumption of power by Shirakawa and Toba as retired emperors was a perversion of such government.

The Jōkyū incident cannot be likened to a conflict in which enemies of the throne rise in rebellion and are victorious. Since the time for opposing the Kamakura regime had not yet arrived, Heaven clearly would not permit Go-Toba's action to succeed. Nevertheless, it is the greatest of offenses for social inferiors to exceed their superiors, and ultimately the day must come when all people submit to the imperial sway. Until that time it is essential to understand that the proper course for the court is to begin by establishing a truly virtuous government and asserting its royal authority. Only then can those subjects who do not submit be overthrown. And even at that point the state of order or disorder in the country must be carefully assessed and the final decision to take up arms or set them aside must be based not on personal desire but on the will of Heaven and the hope of the people.

Eventually the imperial succession did return to the direct line, and in the time of Go-Toba's descendant, Go-Daigo, unity was restored to the country under direct imperial rule. Go-Toba's wish was thus ultimately fulfilled. But how regrettable it is that even for a brief while the throne was visited with such misfortune. . . .

Yoshitoki was succeeded by Yasutoki, who conducted government virtuously and codified strict laws. Not only did he know his own place, Yasutoki admonished the other members of his family and the warrior class in general, so that there was none among them who coveted high office and rank. Later, when Hōjō rule gradually declined and finally was destroyed, it was because the family's stock in Heaven's fate ran out. The Hōjō, however, had little to complain of, since the residue of Yasutoki's virtue had sustained their rule for as long as seven generations.

[Varley, *A Chronicle of Gods and Sovereigns*, pp. 224–226, 229; PV]

*Chapter 50*

THE WAY OF THE WARRIOR

Sometime in the late seventh century, as part of its long-term effort to construct a centralized, bureaucratic state on the Chinese model, the Japanese court developed a countrywide military system by establishing militia units in the provinces under the command of the provincial governors. These units, known as *gundan*, were made up of (1) foot soldiers conscripted from the peasantry as part of the corvée labor tax imposed under the Taika reform's equal-field system of landholding and (2) horse-mounted officers drawn from locally powerful families.

The origins of fighting on horseback in Japan are obscure, although it is possible that this form of combat was either introduced or greatly advanced by the importation of military technology, weapons, and equipment from the Asian continent—especially Korea—during the late fourth and fifth centuries. Terra cotta figurines (*haniwa*) of armor-clad, mounted warriors and their battle-ready mounts found on the surfaces of tombs from the fifth century suggest that by that time, if not earlier, a class of formidable equestrian warriors, armed with bows and swords, had evolved in Japan. The bow was the primary weapon, a fact reflected in the later description of the way of the warrior as the "way of the bow and horse" (*kyūba no michi*).

In addition to establishing *gundan* in the various provinces (usually one to a province), the court placed extra units in northern Kyushu to defend against possible invasion from the continent. Soldiers from some units were also assigned to perform guard duty in the capital, which from 710 on was Nara. When necessary, larger armies could be organized by mobilizing troops from two or more *gundan*. During such mobilizations, commanders favored men from the eastern provinces of the Kantō, which from earliest times was regarded as the home of Japan's best equestrian fighters. Kantō men had ready access to the finest horses, which were bred in the Kantō and in Mutsu Province just to the north, and these fighters were trained from infancy in riding, archery, and the other military skills.

The real test of the *gundan's* effectiveness came during the campaigns that the court conducted against the Emishi in northern Honshu during the last decades of the eighth century and the opening years of the ninth. In 801, the redoubtable commander Sakanoue no Tamuramaro (758–811) succeeded in conquering the Emishi and incorporating their land, which comprised Mutsu and Dewa Provinces, into the Japanese state. For this, Tamuramaro, who was the first to hold the title of *sei-i tai-shōgun* or "great general for subduing the eastern barbarians," has also been celebrated as the first great warrior chief in Japanese history. Thus we read in an eleventh-century war tale:

> Our court in ancient times often sent forth great armies. Although these armies destroyed many barbarians within the provinces [of Mutsu and Dewa], they never completely defeated them. Then Sakanoue no Tamuramaro was called upon to go down to Mutsu-Dewa, and he bequeathed his fame to myriad generations by conquering the barbarians throughout the six districts. He was like an incarnation of the god of the northern heavens, a general of distinction rarely to be seen.[1]

Although the Emishi were finally defeated, it took a long time and a number of campaigns. Whereas the Emishi were excellent horsemen and tough fighters, specializing in hit-and-run guerrilla tactics, the Japanese armies proved cumbersome and were often outwitted and embarrassed. The peasant foot soldiers, organized along Chinese lines and relying on the crossbow as their principal weapon, were largely ineffective fighters. Because of this and also because the conscription system as a whole had proved excessively burdensome to the peasantry, in 792—nearly a decade before Tamuramaro's great campaign—the court abandoned conscription. Although foot soldiers continued to be used in armies in the ninth and even tenth centuries, they were gradually eliminated, and warfare became almost exclusively the preserve of mounted warriors from locally powerful families. By the tenth century, a distinct warrior class drawn from these families had emerged in the provinces.

Much of our knowledge about the warrior class during its early centuries of evolution comes from a genre of writing called "war tales" (*gunki-mono*). The first of these tales, *The Chronicle of Masakado* (*Shōmonki*), which deals with the rebellion of Taira no Masakado (d. 940) in the Kantō in 939–940, was

---

1. *Mutsu wakī*, in Hanawa, comp., *Gunsho ruijū*, vol. 20, p. 32.

probably written in the late tenth century. Although war tales continued to be composed from this time until the seventeenth century, the finest of them recount the fighting that accompanied (1) the transition from the ancient age to the medieval age (or from the Heian period to the Kamakura period) in the late twelfth century and (2) the overthrow of the Kamakura shogunate and the ensuing War Between the Courts (1336–1392) in the fourteenth century.

Focused primarily on warriors and warfare, the war tales are based on historical events but have been embellished to various degrees. Hence they are mixtures of history and fiction. Little is known about the authorship of any of the tales, although in some cases, such as the two most important tales, *The Tale of the Heike* (*Heike monogatari*) and *Taiheiki*, they clearly are the products of more than one author. As the principal repositories of information about warriors, their values, behavior, and exploits for at least the tenth through the fourteenth centuries, the war tales are indispensable sources for historians investigating the early stages in the evolution of a warrior ethos in Japan. But historians also must be cautious, for when studying the tales, they constantly need to judge between fact and fiction.

Beginning with *The Chronicle of Masakado*, the early war tales were written in Chinese and therefore lack some of the flavor of the later tales (i.e., those from about the twelfth century), which were composed in a Japanese vernacular rich in the special vocabulary and lingo of the warriors. But even in *Masakado* and the other early tales in Chinese, we can see the essential character and style of the provincial warrior who was to dominate fighting in Japan for centuries to come. He was a man on horseback who specialized in archery and fought in a highly individualistic manner. When armies of warriors clashed, those on each side sought out opponents of equal or higher status on the other side with whom to engage in one-to-one combat. *The Chronicle of Masakado* tells us little about the relationships among the warriors of the same side or army, but in tales from the eleventh century we learn that they were bound by superior-inferior ties as lords and vassals and that the armies themselves were made up of bands of warriors, each consisting of a lord and his vassals.

The lord-vassal relationship, which became the central feature of what we call feudalism, is idealized in the war tales as a reciprocal compact bound by the highest degree of loyalty on the part of the vassal and by parent-like, loving care by the lord. Thus we read in *A Tale of Mutsu* (*Mutsu waki*), the story of a war fought in Mutsu Province in northern Honshu in 1056–1062, that because the chieftain Minamoto no Yoriyoshi (998–1075) "cared for [his vassals] and saw to their needs, more than half of the men of bow and horse east of Osaka became his followers." And after a particular battle in the Mutsu war, Yoriyoshi is said to have

> fed his soldiers and put their equipment in order. He personally went around the camp, tending to the wounded. The soldiers were deeply moved and all said: "We will repay our obligations (*on*) with our bodies.

We consider our lives as nothing compared to loyalty [or honor, *gi*]. If it is for the general, we do not in the least regret dying now.[2]

As portrayed in the war tales, the vassal warrior is typically motivated by great loyalty for his lord, but he is also highly sensitive to his personal honor and to the honor of his house. In this regard, warrior society in this age — and indeed throughout the premodern centuries — can aptly be described as a "shame" society, inasmuch as the maintenance of honor required that the warrior avoid shame above all or, if he has been shamed, that he avenge the insult and redeem his honor. And therein lay a problem, for the demands made on the warrior by loyalty to his lord on the one hand and personal honor on the other could easily lead to a clash of interests in which the warrior was obliged to choose between the two — that is, between loyalty (lord) and honor (self). Although the loyalty-honor clash is not, in fact, a theme found often in the war tales, it was always a potentially powerful issue among warriors. Thus, for example, in the tumultuous years of the Sengoku age (Age of the Country at War, 1478–1568), territorial chiefs known as *daimyō* staked their capacities to administer and maintain their domains largely on their success in preventing or stamping out the personal feuds over honor among their almost paranoically "face"-conscious vassals.

The war tales are celebrations of the warrior's way and life, and much of their focus is on the portrayal of great warrior heroes. In some cases, these heroes are historically authentic fighters or chieftains of note; in other cases, they are fictional creations of the tales' authors. In virtually all cases, however, the great heroes of the war tales have been inflated into larger-than-life — sometimes superhuman — champions. One of the earliest examples of such a champion is Minamoto no Yoshiie (1041–1108), the son of the aforementioned Yoriyoshi, who was in fact an eminent chief and probably also a very good combat warrior but who is described in *A Tale of Mutsu* in the following implausibly hyperbolic terms:

[Yoriyoshi's] oldest son, Yoshiie, was a warrior of peerless valor. He rode and shot arrows like a god. Defying naked blades, he broke through the rebel's encirclements, appearing first on their left and then on their right. With his large-headed arrows, he shot the rebel chieftains in rapid succession. He never wasted an arrow, but mortally wounded all those he attacked. Known throughout the land for his godly martial ways, Yoshiie rode like thunder and flew like the wind. The barbarians scattered and fled before Yoshiie, not one willing to confront him. The barbarians called . . . him Hachiman Tarō, the firstborn son of the war god Hachiman.[3]

---

2. Ibid., p. 29.
3. Ibid., p. 25.

An example of a fictional champion or superhero in the war tales is Minamoto no Tametomo (1139–1177), who appears in *The Tale of Hōgen* (*Hōgen monogatari*), the story of a clash of arms in Kyoto in 1156. There was, in fact, a real Minamoto no Tametomo, but almost nothing is known about him. In *The Tale of Hōgen*, however, Tametomo almost single-handedly holds off an entire army during a nighttime attack. His credentials for doing this are stated in the *Hōgen* in these words:

> More than seven feet tall, Tametomo exceeded the ordinary man's height by two or three feet. Born to archery, he had a bow arm that was some six inches longer than the arm with which he held his horse's reins. . . . [He used] a bow that was more than eight and a half feet in length.[4]

Elsewhere in the *Hōgen*, Tametomo is described as "unlike a human being" and "a demon or monster."

## TAIRA AND MINAMOTO

As warrior bands took shape in the provinces in the middle and late Heian period, they drew their leadership largely from the great Taira (or Heike) and Minamoto (or Genji) clans. Taira and Minamoto were the surnames of former imperial princes who, beginning in the ninth century, had taken up posts in the provincial governments, become warriors, and established positions of power in the regions where they served. By the time of the revolt by Taira no Masakado in the mid-tenth century, many branches of both Taira and Minamoto were scattered throughout the Kantō and elsewhere. One reason that these clans branched out so rapidly and widely was that many men not related by blood joined them in order to call themselves Taira and Minamoto and share in the high prestige of these names.

In the late eleventh century, one branch of the Minamoto gained great fame through their participation in two wars in the Mutsu-Dewa region of northern Honshu. The first of these wars, fought from 1056 to 1062 and known as the Former Nine-Years War (although the fighting spanned only six years), pitted the Minamoto under Yoriyoshi against the Abe, independent-minded local officials who had flouted the orders of the Kyoto court. In the second war, the Later Three Years War, which actually lasted for only two years, 1086 to 1087, Yoriyoshi's son Yoshiie, who helped his father defeat the Abe (in the process of which he was dubbed, according to *A Tale of Mutsu*, the "Firstborn Son of Hachiman" because of his fighting prowess), intervened in his capacity as governor of Mutsu in a dispute within the Kiyowara family. Although Yoshiie

---

4. Nagazumi and Shimada, eds., *Hōgen monogatari*, p. 81.

was able, under harsh climatic conditions and with great difficulty, to achieve victory for the Kiyowara chief he backed, he gained nothing personally from the Later Three Years War except enhanced status as a military commander. This, however, proved to be considerable: from this time on, Yoshiie was widely recognized as the first among warriors in the land.

Not long after Yoshiie gained renown in warfare in Mutsu-Dewa in the late eleventh century, members of a branch of the Taira family from Ise Province came into prominence in the service of senior retired emperors in Kyoto. During the twelfth century, both the Ise Taira and Yoshiie's line of the Minamoto became increasingly involved in court politics, the Taira as agents of the retired emperors and the Minamoto as armed guards or "claws and teeth" of the Fujiwara regents. In 1156, a factional dispute broke out between Emperor Go-Shirakawa (1127–1192) and Retired Emperor Sutoku (1119–1164), Go-Shirakawa's older brother. Fujiwara ministers lined up on both sides, as did Taira and Minamoto (some Taira and some Minamoto on each side). This dispute soon escalated into the first clash of arms in Kyoto since the early ninth century. Known in history as the Hōgen conflict, it lasted only one night and was won by Go-Shirakawa's side. Although brief, the Hōgen conflict was important because, in the words of a contemporary historian, it ushered in the "age of warriors."

## THE TALE OF HŌGEN (HŌGEN MONOGATARI)

On the night of the Hōgen conflict, Retired Emperor Sutoku and the courtiers and warriors who backed him gathered in the Shirakawa Palace in Kyoto, while Emperor Go-Shirakawa and his followers established themselves in the nearby Takamatsu Palace. In the following passage, the Sutoku side listens first to Minamoto no Tametomo on how to conduct the coming battle. Tametomo recommends that they attack the Takamatsu Palace and burn it. But Minister of the Left Fujiwara no Yorinaga (1120–1156), the ranking minister present, haughtily dismisses this advice as youthful impulsiveness and not at all appropriate to a situation in which men are fighting for an emperor and a retired emperor. Even assuming that this exchange between Tametomo and Yorinaga is apocryphal, it nicely contrasts the thinking of representatives of two ages: a courtier of the fast-vanishing ancient age, who looks with disdain on warriors as a lesser breed and does not hesitate to chide one for suggesting a breach of what he regards as the proper conduct of war, and a warrior chief from the provinces who, exemplifying the spirit of the advancing medieval age, cares nothing for "proper conduct" but thinks only of what must be done to win. His advice rejected, Tametomo grumbles as he withdraws from the audience with the retired emperor that surely his older brother Yoshitomo (1123–1160), one of the chiefs on Emperor Go-Shirakawa's side, will seize the opportunity to attack and burn *their* palace, the Shirakawa Palace. And in the central irony of *The Tale of Hōgen*, that is exactly what Yoshitomo does.

Retired Emperor Sutoku and all the people with him gathered to see the celebrated Minamoto no Tametomo. When the Great Minister of the left, Fujiwara no Yorinaga, then ordered, "State your plan as to the conduct of battle," Tametomo replied respectfully: "Tametomo has lived long in the Chinzei [Kyushu], and he has engaged in I do not know how many battles, great and small, in bringing under subjection the people of the Nine Provinces [of Kyushu]. Among them more than twenty required special effort. Whether to break strong positions though surrounded by enemy, or to destroy the enemy when attacking a fortified place, in any case there is nothing equal to night attack to achieve victory. Therefore if we bear down on the Takamatsu Palace immediately, set fire to it on three sides and hold them in check on the fourth side, those who escape the fire cannot escape the arrows, and those who fear the arrows cannot escape the fire. The warriors on the emperor's side are not awfully good. But only let my brother Yoshitomo and his kind try to rush out, I'll shoot them through the middle. All the more so with weak shots like Taira no Kiyomori. They are not likely to count for much; I'll sweep them away with my armor sleeve or kick them away. If the Emperor moves to another place, if it is clear that, begging his pardon, the people with him are going to get shot up a little, it is certain that the bearers will abandon the palanquin and try to escape. At that time Tametomo will come up and conduct the Emperor to this palace; putting our sovereign, Retired Emperor Sutoku, on the Throne should be like turning over my hand. Meeting and receiving the Emperor being only a matter of Tametomo letting off two or three arrows, what doubt can there be of settling the issue before dawn?"

When Tametomo had spoken thus freely, the Great Minister of the Left thereupon said: "What Tametomo proposes is a crude scheme which is quite out of the question. Perhaps it is something one does when one is young—a thing like a night attack is a private matter in a fight among you warriors, which involves only ten or twenty. In a struggle for the realm befitting the Emperor and Retired Emperor, when the issue is to be decided with every member of the Taira and Minamoto on one side or the other, it is completely out of the question. Besides, the Retired Emperor has summoned the soldier-monks from Nara. . . . We must wait for them, effect our joint arrangement of troops, and then engage the enemy.". . .

Tametomo gave in to superior authority, but leaving the audience he grumbled to himself: "Since this is a matter in no way resembling either previous precedents in Japan or China, or the traditional rules for conduct of Court ceremonial, he ought to leave the conduct of fighting to fighting men, but since he doesn't, what can one do about this senseless scheme? Since Yoshitomo is a man well versed in the stratagems of war, he must certainly intend to come at us tonight. If he postpones until tomorrow, the lay-monks from Yoshino and the soldier-monks from Nara will join us. If he advances now and sets fires upwind of us how can we possibly win, even if we fight? If the enemy follows up his advantage, not one of us is likely to escape."

[Wilson, Hōgen monogatari, pp. 26–28; PV]

## THE TALE OF THE HEIKE (HEIKE MONOGATARI)

Victory in the Hōgen conflict set the stage for the rise of Taira no Kiyomori and the Ise Taira at court. Although warriors, the Taira now devoted themselves primarily to court politics and advancement within courtier society. Kiyomori, in particular, acquired steadily higher court ranks and offices, finally becoming chancellor (*daijō daijin*), the court's highest appointive position. Having married his daughter into the imperial family, Kiyomori in 1180 capped his rise to supremacy at court by crowning his infant grandson as Emperor Antoku (1178–1185).

The rapid, and sometimes ruthless, advance of the Ise Taira incurred the resentment of many in Kyoto, including the retired emperor Go-Shirakawa, Kiyomori's chief rival for power at court. In 1177, Kiyomori suppressed a plot against him to which Goshirakawa was privy. Three years later, in 1180, a prince who had been passed over in the imperial succession to make way for Antoku dispatched an edict to Minamoto chieftains in the provinces, calling on them to take up arms and overthrow Kiyomori and the Ise Taira. Among those who responded to the edict was Minamoto no Yoritomo (1147–1199), who had been exiled as a youth to the Kantō twenty years earlier in the wake of the Minamoto defeat in the Heiji conflict. In the five-year war (Genpei War, 1180–1185) that was sparked by the prince's edict, Yoritomo gradually emerged as the supreme Minamoto commander, and it was under his orders that the Minamoto forces finally defeated and annihilated the Ise Taira at the naval battle of Dannoura in the straits between Honshu and Kyushu in 1185. Yoritomo himself remained at his headquarters at Kamakura in the Kantō throughout the Genpei War, simultaneously directing the Minamoto in battle from afar and establishing the offices of what became Japan's first warrior government, the Kamakura shogunate.

### "THE MIGHTY FALL AT LAST, THEY ARE DUST BEFORE THE WIND"

Like *The Tale of Hōgen* and *The Tale of Heiji*, *The Tale of the Heike* was first written in the early thirteenth century and subsequently underwent a long process of embellishment, primarily by guilds of blind monks who traveled the country telling its stories to the accompaniment of a lute-like instrument called a *biwa*. The most widely disseminated version of the *Heike* was completed in 1371, nearly two hundred years after the events it covers.

More than any other war tale, the *Heike* is a work unified throughout by a single theme, the rise and fall of the Ise Taira. This theme is dramatically enunciated in the *Heike*'s opening lines, in which we learn that the Ise Taira, full of arrogance and hubris, have risen to dizzying heights at court and in courtier society but, because of their very success, are in for a great fall. The Taira are led by Kiyomori, whom the *Heike* ranks among the most heinous villains of Chinese and Japanese history. This demonization of Kiyomori—and, by association, the entire Taira clan—provides the main "reason" that the Taira will surely fall, but in the larger scheme of things, the fall of the Taira symbolizes the inevitable decline of the world as a whole in the dark and disastrous age of *mappō*, the "end of the Buddhist Law."

The sound of the Gion Shōja bells echoes the impermanence of all things; the color of the *sala* flowers reveals the truth that the prosperous must decline. The proud do not endure, they are like a dream on a spring night; the mighty fall at last, they are dust before the wind.

In a distant land [China], there are examples set by Zhao Gao of Qin, Wang Mang of Han, Zhu Yi of Liang and Lushan of Tang, all of them men who prospered after refusing to be governed by their former lords and sovereigns, but who met swift destruction because they disregarded admonitions, failed to recognize approaching turmoil, and ignored the nation's distress. Closer to home [Japan], there have been Masakado of Shōhei, Sumitomo of Tengyō, Yoshichika of Kōwa and Nobuyori of Heiji, every one of them proud and mighty. But closest of all, and utterly beyond the power of mind to comprehend or tongue to relate, is the tale of Taira no Ason Kiyomori, the Rokuhara Buddhist Novice and Former Chancellor.

[McCullough, *The Tale of the Heike*, p. 23; PV]

EASTERN WARRIORS

We have noted that from early times, the warriors of the eastern provinces of the Kantō were regarded as the best fighters in Japan. In the Genpei War, as narrated in the *Heike*, the eastern warriors (the Minamoto) are portrayed as so superior to the western warriors (the Taira) in martial ability that there is never any doubt about the war's outcome. We are made aware of this discrepancy in fighting ability at the very beginning of the war when the commander of a Taira army sent to chastise the rebel Yoritomo in the east asks one of the warriors in his army, Saitō no Sanemori, who is from the east and was previously a follower of the Minamoto, "How many men in the Eight Provinces [of the Kantō] can wield a strong bow as well as you do?"

Sanemori uttered a derisive laugh. "Do you think I use long arrows? They barely measure thirteen fists.[5] Any number of warriors in the east can equal that: nobody is called a long-arrow man there unless he draws a fifteen-fist shaft. A strong bow is

---

5. Arrows were measured by units determined by the width of a fist.

held to be one that requires six stout men for the stringing. One of those powerful archers can easily penetrate two or three suits of armor when he shoots.

"Every big landholder commands at least five hundred horsemen. Once a rider mounts, he never loses his seat; however rugged the terrain he gallops over, his horse never falls. If he sees his father or son cut down in battle, he rides over the dead body and keeps on fighting. In west-country battles, a man who loses a father leaves the field and is seen no more until he has made offerings and completed a mourning period; someone who loses a son is too overwhelmed with grief to resume the fight at all. When westerners run out of commissariat rice, they stop fighting until after the fields are planted and harvested. They think summertime is too hot for battle, and wintertime too cold. Easterners are entirely different."

[McCullough, *The Tale of the Heike*, pp. 188–189; PV]

### THE TAIRA AS COURTIER-WARRIORS

A major phenomenon in the history of the samurai was the merging of the *bu* (the military) and the *bun* (the courtly)—that is, the assumption of courtly tastes and the adoption of courtly ways by warriors. This phenomenon was especially marked during times when samurai leaders and their followers lived in Kyoto in proximity to the court, for example, during the Ise Taira's residence there in the decades leading up to the Genpei War and during the entire Ashikaga or Muromachi period (1336–1573), when the Ashikaga shogunate was situated in the imperial capital. In the *Heike*, the Taira are portrayed as no match militarily for the Minamoto, in part because they have lived so long in Kyoto, enjoying the elegance of court life and becoming soft and "courtly." There are countless scenes in the *Heike* that portray the Taira as what can be described as courtier warriors. Probably the most famous such scene is "The Death of Atsumori," in which, after killing the young Taira commander Atsumori, a Minamoto adherent, Kumagai no Naozane, is astonished to find a flute in a bag at Atsumori's waist. Observing that no one in the Minamoto army would think of bringing such a thing as a flute into battle, Naozane observes, "These court nobles are refined men!" In his sense of awe and admiration for the socially and culturally superior, Naozane goes so far as to refer to the Taira as court nobles.

Kumagai no Jirō Naozane walked his horse toward the beach after the defeat of the Heike. "The Taira nobles will be fleeing to the water's edge in the hope of boarding rescue vessels," he thought. "Ah, how I would like to grapple with a high-ranking Commander-in-Chief!" Just then, he saw a lone rider splash into the sea, headed toward a vessel in the offing. The other was attired in crane-embroidered *nerinuki* silk *hitatare*, a suit of armor with shaded green lacing, and a horned helmet. At his waist, he wore a sword with gilt bronze fittings; on his back, there rode a quiver containing arrows fledged with black-banded white eagle feathers. He grasped a rattan-wrapped bow and bestrode a white-dappled reddish horse with a gold-edged saddle. When his mount had swum out about a hundred and fifty or two hundred feet, Naozane beckoned with his fan.

"I see that you are a Commander-in-Chief. It is dishonorable to show your back to an enemy. Return!"

The warrior came back. As he was leaving the water, Naozane rode up alongside him, gripped him with all his strength, crashed with him to the ground, held him motionless and pushed aside his helmet to cut off his head. He was sixteen or seventeen years old, with a lightly powdered face and blackened teeth—a boy just the age of Naozane's own son Kojirō Naoie, and so handsome that Naozane could not find a place to strike.

"Who are you? Announce your name. I will spare you," Naozane said.

"Who are you?" the youth asked.

"Nobody of any importance: Kumagae no Jirō Naozane, a resident of Musashi Province."

"Then it is unnecessary to give you my name. I am a desirable opponent for you. Ask about me after you take my head. Someone will recognize me, even if I don't tell you."

"Indeed, he must be a Commander-in-Chief," Naozane thought. "Killing this one person will not change defeat into victory, nor will sparing him change victory into defeat. When I think of how I grieved when Kojirō suffered a minor wound, it is easy to imagine the sorrow of this young lord's father if he were to hear that the boy had been slain. Ah, I would like to spare him!" Casting a swift glance to the rear, he discovered Sanehira and Kagetoki coming along behind him with fifty riders.

"I would like to spare you," he said, restraining his tears, "but there are Genji warriors everywhere. You cannot possibly escape. It will be better if I kill you than if someone else does, because I will offer prayers on your behalf."

"Just take my head and be quick about it."

Overwhelmed by compassion, Naozane could not find a place to strike. His senses reeled, his wits forsook him and he was scarcely conscious of his surroundings. But matters could not go on like that forever; in tears, he took the head.

"Alas! No lot is as hard as a warrior's. I would never have suffered such a dreadful experience if I had not been born into a military house. How cruel I was to kill him." He pressed his sleeve to his face and shed floods of tears.

Presently, since matters could not go on like that forever, he started to remove the youth's armor *hitatare* so that he might wrap it around the head. A brocade bag containing a flute was tucked in at the waist. "Ah, how pitiful! He must have been one of the people I heard making music inside the stronghold just before dawn. There are tens of thousands of riders in our eastern armies, but I am sure none of them has brought a flute to the battlefield. Those court nobles are refined men!"

When Naozane's trophies were presented for Yoshitsune's inspection, they drew tears from the eyes of all the beholders. It was learned later that the slain youth was Tayū Atsumori, aged seventeen, a son of Tsunemori, the Master of the Palace Repairs Office.

After that, Naozane thought increasingly of becoming a monk.

The flute in question is said to have been given by Retired Emperor Toba to Atsumori's grandfather, Tadamori, who was a skilled musician. I believe I have heard that Tsunemori, who inherited it, turned it over to Atsumori because of his son's proficiency as a flautist. Saeda [Little Branch] was its name. It is deeply moving that music, a profane entertainment, should have led a warrior to the religious life.

[McCullough, *The Tale of the Heike*, pp. 315–317; PV]

## CHRONICLE OF GREAT PEACE (*TAIHEIKI*): THE LOYALIST HEROES

The Kamakura shogunate was overthrown in 1333 by "loyalist" forces supporting Emperor Go-Daigo (1288–1339). Triumphant over the shogunate, Go-Daigo proclaimed the "restoration" of governing power to the imperial court in Kyoto. But Go-Daigo's restoration, known as the Kenmu Restoration, lasted a brief three years, until 1336. Ashikaga Takauji (1305–1358), a leading chieftain of the great Minamoto clan who had earlier helped Go-Daigo to power, turned against him and forced him to flee to Yoshino in the mountainous region south of the capital. There Go-Daigo, still claiming to be the rightful sovereign, founded the Yoshino, or Southern Court. Meanwhile, Takauji installed a member of another branch of the imperial family as emperor in Kyoto and, at the same time, founded a new military government, the Ashikaga or Muromachi shogunate (1336–1573), in the same city. The first half century of the Muromachi period (1336–1392), is also known as the age of War Between the Northern (Kyoto) and Southern (Yoshino) Courts.

The protracted War Between the Northern and Southern Courts resulted from the only major dynastic schism in the history of the Japanese imperial family. In a way not seen in earlier or later conflicts during premodern times, imperial legitimacy was a central issue. The principal war tale that narrates the fighting between, first, the supporters of Go-Daigo and of the Kamakura shogunate and, later, after the failure of the Kenmu Restoration, those of the Northern and Southern Courts is the *Taiheiki* (*Chronicle of Great Peace*). The *Taiheiki* is often thought to be a tract whose anonymous author or authors argue that the Southern, and not the Northern, Court was the legitimate seat of imperial authority between 1336 and 1392. But the *Taiheiki* does not explicitly declare the Southern Court to be legitimate; rather, it portrays a group of warrior heroes whose loyalty to Go-Daigo and, subsequently, the Southern Court was of such a superbly self-sacrificing, admirable character that later generations of Japanese believed the Southern Court was legitimate in large part because they could not believe that such heroes could have fought and died for an "illegitimate" cause. Foremost among the *Taiheiki*'s loyalist heroes—and indeed, the man regarded as Japan's greatest hero until at least the end of World War II—was Kusunoki Masashige (d. 1336).

In the following passage from the *Taiheiki*, we read how Masashige appeared almost magically to become the guiding spirit of Go-Daigo's loyalist movement in the early days of the emperor's opposition to the Kamakura shogunate. A consummate fighter in the new style of guerrilla warfare that had developed in the central and western provinces by the fourteenth century, Masashige speaks to Go-Daigo of using a "carefully devised strategy" to overcome the superior strength of the Kamakura shogunate's armies. He also tells the emperor, in words that were to become famous in Japanese history, that as long as he, Masashige, lived, the emperor's cause would prevail.

On the twenty-seventh day of the eighth month of Genkō,[6] Emperor Go-Daigo went to Kasagi Temple and made the temple's main hall his temporary palace. For several days, not a single person came to support His Majesty, because all feared the military might of Kamakura. But upon learning that an army from Rokuhara[7] had been defeated in battle at Higashi-Sakamoto at the foot of Mount Hiei, the monks of Kasagi and warriors from nearby provinces rode in from all directions. Even so, not a single noted fighter or great chieftain (*daimyō*) at the head of a force of one or two hundred riders had yet appeared. The emperor feared that the contingent that had gathered might be insufficient even to guard his temporary palace.

Dozing off, the emperor had a dream. The place of the dream appeared to be the garden in front of the Shishinden,[8] within which stood a giant evergreen tree whose branches grew densely. Those spreading southward were especially luxuriant. Beneath the tree, the three great ministers of state and all the other ministers were seated in rows according to their ranks. But the main seat, piled high with cushions, remained unoccupied. The dreaming emperor thought wonderingly, "For whom has this seat been prepared?" As he stood there, two youths with their hair parted in the middle and tied on each side, suddenly appeared. Kneeling before the emperor and drenching their sleeves with tears, the youths said, "There is no place in the land where Your Majesty can hide, even for a moment. But in the shade of that tree is a south-facing seat. It has been prepared as a throne for you, so please sit there awhile." So saying, the youths seemed to ascend high into Heaven. Soon the emperor awoke from his dream.

---

6. 1331.

7. Rokuhara was in the southeastern section of Kyoto. The deputies of the Kamakura shogunate who administered Kyoto had their offices there.

8. One of the halls at the imperial palace in Kyoto.

The emperor believed that the dream was a message to him from Heaven. Considering the written characters for what he had seen, he observed that, by placing the character for "south" next to that for "tree," together they formed a third character, *kusunoki*, or camphor tree. Hopeful, the emperor interpreted his dream this way: "The instructions of the youths to sit in the south-facing seat in the tree's shade meant that I will once again rule with sovereignly virtue and will draw the warriors of the land into the service of the court. This has been divinely revealed by the bodhisattvas Nikkō and Gekkō." When dawn broke, the emperor summoned Jōjubō, a priest of the temple.

The emperor asked Jōjubō, "Is there a warrior in these parts called Kusunoki?" The priest replied, "I have not heard of anyone with that name around here. But west of Mount Kongō in Kawachi Province is a man renowned as a wielder of bow and arrow named Kusunoki Tamon[9] Hyōe Masashige. Although he is said to be a descendant of the Ide Minister of the Left, Lord Tachibana no Moroe (himself a descendant in the fourth generation from Emperor Bidatsu), Masashige has long lived in the provinces. I hear that his mother, when young, worshiped Bishamon on Mount Shigi for one hundred days and gave birth to a child after receiving an oracle in a dream. She named the child Tamon." The emperor, regarding this as confirmation of the oracle he had received in his dream the night before, ordered, "Summon Kusunoki Masashige immediately." Lord Madenokōji Chūnagon Fujifusa, upon receiving the imperial edict, promptly summoned Masashige.

The imperial messenger, bearing the emperor's wishes, proceeded to the Kusunoki residence and explained everything to Masashige. Believing there was no greater honor for a man of bow and arrow, Masashige, without any hesitation, went secretly to Mount Kasagi. The emperor, speaking through Lord Fujifusa, said to Masashige, "When I dispatched an imperial messenger to call upon you to subjugate the eastern barbarians,[10] you rode here immediately. I am most pleased. So, what plans do you have to undertake unification of the country? How can you win a decisive victory and bring peace to the four seas? Speak your thoughts freely, without omitting anything."

Masashige respectfully replied, "The eastern barbarians, in their recent treasonous behavior, have drawn the censure of Heaven. If we take advantage of their weakness, resulting from the decline and disorder they have caused, what difficulty should we have in inflicting Heaven's punishment upon them? But the goal of unifying the country must be carried out by means of both military tactics and carefully devised strategy. Even if we fight them force against force and although we recruit warriors throughout the more than sixty provinces of Japan to confront the men of the two provinces of Musashi and Sagami,[11] we will

---

9. Another name for the Buddhist guardian deity Bishamon.

10. The men of the Kamakura shogunate.

11. These two provinces of the Kantō constituted the principal base of the Hōjō regents, who were the main power holders in the Kamakura shogunate.

be hard-pressed to win. But if we fight with clever scheming, the military force of the eastern barbarians will be capable of no more than breaking sharp swords and crushing hard helmets. It will be easy to deceive them, and there will be nothing to fear. Since the aim of warfare is ultimate victory, Your Majesty should pay no heed to whether we win or lose in a single battle. So long as you hear that Masashige alone is alive, know that your imperial destiny will in the end be attained." After delivering these earnest words, Masashige returned to Kawachi.

[Gotō and Kamada, eds., *Taiheiki*, vol. 1, pp. 96–98; PV]

In narrating the warfare that resulted in the overthrow of the Kamakura shogunate in 1333, the *Taiheiki* describes Kusunoki Masashige's innovative and brilliant methods for defending fortresses against attacks and sieges by huge shogunate armies. Indeed, the *Taiheiki* attributes much of the ultimate success of Go-Daigo's loyalist movement to the failure of the shogunate to deal promptly and effectively with Masashige. He kept the fires of antishogunate revolt burning until larger forces under Ashikaga Takauji and Nitta Yoshisada (1301–1338) could finally destroy the Kamakura regime.

After failure of the Kenmu Restoration in 1336, Go-Daigo, as we see in the first passage, rejects Masashige's advice about strategy and insists that he and Nitta Yoshisada, the leading loyalist general, meet in a showdown battle with Ashikaga Takauji at Minatogawa in Hyōgo. Masashige obeys with the knowledge that he will die in this battle, and symbolically, so also will Go-Daigo's cause.

The second passage relates the suicide of Masashige and his brother at Minatogawa after the battle has been lost.

As Lords Takauji and Tadayoshi headed toward the capital in command of a great army, Yoshisada sent a messenger on a fleet horse to the palace to report that he was pulling back to Hyōgo in order to establish a position from which to defend against the Ashikaga. The emperor, greatly alarmed, sent for Kusunoki Masashige. "Go quickly to Hyōgo to join forces with Yoshisada and do battle," he ordered.

Respectfully, Masashige replied, "Since Lord Takauji is already on his way up to the capital in command of an army from the nine provinces of Kyushu, his might will surely be as vast as clouds and mist. I fear that if a small, tired force like ours were to engage such a giant enemy army in high spirits, it would, by fighting in the conventional manner, undoubtedly be defeated. I recommend that Your Majesty recall Lord Yoshisada to Kyoto and have him accompany you again to Mount Hiei. I will go down to Kawachi and, with a contingent from the central provinces, defend Kawajiri. If we press Kyoto from two directions, north and south, and force the Ashikaga to exhaust their supplies, they will gradually tire and their numbers will dwindle. Meanwhile, our side will increase in strength day by day. Then, if Lord Yoshisada advances down from Mount Hiei and Masashige attacks from the rear, we can destroy the enemies of the court in a single battle. Lord Yoshisada undoubtedly agrees with me. But he is ashamed by the thought that he will be seen as cowardly if he avoids a battle while in the field. Hence he has decided to take a stand at Hyōgo. What matters most in war is who wins the final battle. I urge the court to make its decision after the most careful deliberation.

"Truly, war should be entrusted to warriors," the courtiers agreed. But Bōmon no Saishō Kiyotada again spoke out: "What Masashige says is not without merit. Yet to have His Majesty abandon the capital and proceed for a second time in the same year to Mount Hiei before an army, commissioned to pacify the country, has even fought one battle is tantamount to demeaning the imperial position. It also goes against the way of an imperial army. Although Takauji is advancing toward the capital in command of a Kyushu army, it surely does not exceed the force he brought to Kyoto last year after conquering the eight eastern provinces. At that time, our side, although small, never failed to prevail over the larger enemy in each battle, from the start of fighting until the final victory. This had nothing to do with superior military strategy but was thanks entirely to the imperial destiny. Therefore, if you engage the enemy in decisive battle away from the capital, what difficulty should there be in emerging victorious? Masashige must go at once to Hyōgo."

"I have no further objections," said Masashige. On the sixteenth day of the fifth month, he left the capital and, with five hundred riders, went down to Hyōgo.

Because he knew that this would be his final battle, Masashige stopped, as he had planned, at Sakurai Station to send his oldest son, Masatsura, age eleven this year, who had been accompanying him, back home to Kawachi. As he bid farewell to Masatsura, Masashige gave these instructions to him, "It is said that three days after the lioness gives birth to a cub, she throws it off a stone wall several thousand *jō* high.[12] But because the cub has a lion's nature, it is able, without having been taught, to right itself in midair and avoid being killed. The moral of this story applies even more to you, a young man who has passed his tenth birthday. You must heed my words and never disobey the advice I give you. The coming battle will decide the fate of the country. I fear this is the last time I will see your face in this life. If you hear that Masashige has died in battle, you will know with certainty that the country has fallen into the hands of the shogun, Takauji. But you must never surrender, and thus forsake years of unswerving loyalty by our family to the emperor, merely to preserve your transient life. So long as even one of the young men of our family survives, he must fortify himself in the vicinity of Mount Kongō and, if the enemy attacks, be prepared to expose himself to the arrows of Yang Yu[13] and fight with a devotion

---

12. The source of this story is not known. But "several thousand *jō*" is an implausibly great height.

13. Yang Yu was a famous archer of the Spring and Autumn period of early Chinese history.

comparable to the loyalty of Ji Xin.[14] This will be your most important filial duty to me." After Masashige had tearfully delivered these words, father and son parted, one going east and the other west.

Long ago, when Mu Gong attacked the state of Jin, Bai Lixi, realizing that defeat was inevitable, went to his son, General Meng Mingshi, and sadly bid him a final farewell.[15] In this age, Kusunoki Masashige, upon hearing that the enemy army was approaching the capital from the west and realizing, with great regret, that the country would surely be overthrown, left his son Masatsura behind with the admonition that he remain loyal to the emperor until his own death. Bai Lixi was a splendid subject of another land, and Masashige was a loyal subject of our country. Although separated in time by a thousand years, they were as one in their sageliness both in this life and the next. They were wise men rarely to be found.

When Masashige arrived in Hyōgo, Nitta Yoshisada immediately came to inquire about what the emperor had said. After Masashige explained in detail both his own thinking and the decision of the emperor, Yoshisada said, "Indeed, a small army that has suffered defeat cannot hope to win against a great army full of spirit. But ever since losing the battle for the Kantō last year and then failing to hold the line against the enemy on the way back up to the capital, I have been unable to avoid the derision of people. On top of that, I was not able to reduce a single enemy fortification when I was recently sent down to the western provinces. If now, upon learning that the enemy has a great army, I should withdraw to Kyoto without fighting even one battle, it would be a humiliation I could not bear. Victory or defeat do not concern me. I wish only to display my loyalty in the coming battle."

Masashige replied, "It has been said, 'Listen not to the biased views of the many who are fools, but heed the opinion of one wise man.'[16] Do not pay attention to the slander of those who do not know the way of war. The superior commander advances only when he judges the situation right for battle and retreats when he knows it is not. Thus Confucius admonished Zilu with these words, 'Do not follow the lead of one who would fight tigers with his bare hands and ford great rivers on foot, regretting not that he might be killed.'[17] Although it is said that destroying Hōjō Takatoki's violent rule at one stroke at the beginning of Genkō and forcing Takauji and the other rebels to retreat to Kyushu this spring were due to the imperial destiny, in fact they were entirely because of your outstanding strategy. In the way of war, who is there to deride you? Especially now,

---

14. Ji Xin was a loyal follower of Emperor Han Gaozu who, on one occasion, took the emperor's place during an attack in order to enable him to escape.

15. This is a story found in Watson, trans., *The Records of the Grand Historian (Shiji)*, vol. 1, *Qin Dynasty*, pp. 14–15.

16. Words similar to these can be found in several ancient Chinese texts, including *Shiji*.

17. "I would not take with me anyone who would try to fight a tiger with his bare hands or to walk across the River and die in the process without regrets"(*Analects* 7:11).

in returning to the capital region from the western provinces, your actions have been exemplary at each and every stage." At this, Yoshisada's face brightened. Throughout the night he and Masashige talked, raising their sake cups many times. Thinking about it later, Yoshisada was saddened to realize that this was his final meeting with Masashige. [pp. 149–152]

Kusunoki Masashige, facing his younger brother Masasue, said: "The enemy is blocking us, front and rear, and has cut us off from our allies. There seems no way to escape now. I suggest that we first attack those in the front, drive them away, then take on those in the rear." "That's fine!" said Masasue approvingly.

Aligning their force of seven hundred riders, the brothers drove into the center of the great enemy host. Ashikaga Tadayoshi's men, seeing the Chrysanthemum and Water standard[18] and realizing that the attackers were worthy foes, sought to surround and smash them. But Masashige and Masasue struck the Ashikaga from east to west and drove them from north to south. Whenever they saw worthy foes, they rode up, grappled with them, and took their heads. When they encountered foes they considered unworthy, they drove them away with their swords. During the course of battle, Masasue and Masashige met up seven times, and seven times they were separated. Their only thought was to reach Tadayoshi, grapple with him, and kill him. At length, however, Tadayoshi's force of five hundred thousand drove the Kusunoki seven hundred back, forcing them to retreat again toward Ueno in Suma.

The horse Tadayoshi was riding stopped, having picked up an arrowhead in its hoof. As it stood there lamely, favoring its right leg, the Kusunoki drove forward. Tadayoshi, it seemed, was about to be killed. But just then a single horseman, Yakushiji Jūrōjirō slashed the chests of the oncoming horses, felling one after another. In all, he cut down seven or eight riders. Tadayoshi, meanwhile, had changed mounts and fled far from the scene.

The shogun, Takauji, observing Tadayoshi's retreat in the face of the Kusunoki attack, issued an order: "Bring in fresh troops, and make sure Tadayoshi is not killed." Whereupon some six thousand riders of the Kira, Ishitō, Kō, and Uesugi galloped to the east of Minatogawa and surrounded the Kusunoki in order to cut them off from retreat. Turning back, Masashige and Masasue charged into the encircling horde, clashing with them, grappling them down, and killing them. During six hours they fought sixteen times but gradually their force was diminished until only seventy-three remained. Even then, if they had tried to break through the enemy and escape, they could have. But Masashige had decided when he left the capital that this would mark the end of his time in this world. So the Kusunoki fought without retreating a step, until their energy was exhausted. They then went north of Minatogawa and rushed into a house in one of the villages.

---

18. The standard of the Kusunoki family.

Masashige stripped off his armor in order to cut his belly. Examining himself, he found that he had suffered sword wounds in eleven places. Among the other seventy-two men, not one had fewer than three to five wounds.

The thirteen members of the Kusunoki family and their sixty retainers aligned themselves in two rows in the six-bay reception hall. Reciting the *nembutsu* ten times in unison, they cut their bellies as one. Masashige, occupying the seat of honor, turned to his brother Masasue. "Well now, it is said that one's last thoughts in this life determine the goodness or evil of one's next incarnation. Into which of the nine realms of existence would you like to be reborn?" Laughing loudly, Masasue replied: "It is my wish to be reborn again and again for seven lives into this same existence in order to destroy the enemies of the court!" Masashige was greatly pleased. "Although it is deeply sinful, it is also my wish. Let us therefore be born again into this life to fulfill our cherished dream!" Stabbing each other, the brothers fell down on the same pillow.

Sixteen men from prominent families, including Hashimoto Hachirō Masa-kazu, the governor of Kawachi, Usami Masayasu, Jingūji Tarō Masamoro, and Wada Gorō Masataka, along with fifty of their followers, lined up in a row, each in his own way, and cut their bellies.

Kikuchi Shichirō Taketomo had come as the emissary of his older brother, the governor of Hizen, to observe the fighting at Suma-guchi and happened upon Masashige's *seppuku*. How, he thought, could he shamelessly forsake Masashige and return home? And so he too committed suicide and fell into the flames.[19]

From the Genkō era, tens of millions of people graciously came forth in response to His Majesty's call, served loyally, and distinguished themselves in battle. But since this rebellion erupted, people ignorant of the way of benevolence have flouted the imperial favor and joined the enemy. Feckless individuals, hoping to escape death, have surrendered and, contrary to their expectations, have been executed. Other ignorant people, not comprehending the trend of the times, have gone against the Way. In the midst of this, Masashige, a man combining the three virtues of wisdom, benevolence, and courage, whose fidelity is unequaled by anyone from ancient times to the present, has chosen death as the proper way. His and his brother's deaths by suicide are omens that a sagely sovereign has again lost the country and trai-torous subjects are running amok. [pp. 158–160]

[Gotō and Kamada, eds., *Taiheiki*, vol. 2, pp. 149–152, 158–160; PV]

---

19. This is the first mention of fire or flames.

## Chapter 51

### NICHIREN: THE SUN AND THE LOTUS

The story of Nichiren (1222–1282) is that, to use his own words, of "a son of the shūdras (lowest caste)" on the seacoast of Japan, who was destined to become "the pillar of Japan, the eye of the nation and the vessel of the country." Like most of the great religious leaders of that age, this son of a humble fisherman spent years in study and training at the great monastic center of Mount Hiei. Unlike many others, however, he found new faith not by turning away from the teachings of its Tendai founder, Saichō, but by turning back to them. In doing so, he was forced to depart from Mount Hiei itself, which had long since become a stronghold of Esoteric Buddhism, and to embark on a preaching career of unceasing hardship, conflict, and persecution. But through it all, he became ever more convinced of his mission to save his country and Buddhism.

For Nichiren, the Lotus Sūtra, on which the Tendai teaching was based, was the key to everything. It is the final and supreme teaching of the Buddha Shākyamuni, revealing the one and only way of salvation. In this sūtra, the three forms of the Buddha—his Universal or Law Body (Dharmakāya), Body of Bliss (Sambhogakāya), and Transformation Body (Nirmānakāya)—are seen as one and inseparable, and the prevailing schools of Buddhism emphasized one form at the expense of the others. Esoteric Buddhism stressed the Universal Buddha, Vairochana, or Dainichi; and Amidism worshiped the Body of Bliss, Amitābha. By thus dispensing with the historical Buddha, Shākyamuni (the Transformation Body), they committed the inexcusable crime of mutilating Buddha's perfect body. Conversely, Zen Buddhism and the Vinaya school, which was undergoing something of a revival at that time, ignored the universal and eternal aspect of the Buddha in favor of the historical or actual Buddha. That is, the Lotus Sūtra alone upholds the truth of the triune Buddha, and only in this trinity is the salvation of all assured.

So it is the name of the Lotus Sūtra, not the name of Amida Buddha, which should be on the lips of every Buddhist. "All praise to the Lotus Sūtra of the Wondrous Law" (*namu myōhō rengekyō*) is the Buddha's pledge of salvation, which Nichiren often called out to the beat of a drum—"dondon dondoko dondon." Like Shinran, Nichiren was a man of no slight intelligence, and he spent his years of exile or enforced seclusion in an intensive study of scripture and doctrine. But this erudition served only to adorn a simple conviction, arrived at early in life and held to with single-minded devotion throughout his stormy career, that faith in the Lotus of the Wondrous Law was all that one needed for salvation.

Unlike Shinran, Nichiren stressed the importance of one's own efforts and became ever more deeply convinced that he himself was destined to fulfill a unique mission in the world. A man of active temperament who commanded attention because of his forceful and magnetic personality, Nichiren thought the Lotus Sūtra should be "read by the body" and not just with the eyes. To him, among its most significant passages were those describing the saints destined to uphold and spread abroad the truths of the Lotus. One of these was the Bodhisattva of Superb Action,[1] who was to be a stalwart pioneer in propagating the Perfect Truth. Another was the Bodhisattva Ever-Abused,[2] who suffered continual insults from others because he insisted on saluting everyone as a buddha-to-be, convinced that every man was ultimately destined to be such. The Lotus's account of these two saints he regarded as prefiguring his own mission, and often he referred to himself as a reincarnation of them, especially of the Bodhisattva of Superb Action. Nichiren also found special meaning in the vows taken by Buddha's disciples when his eternal aspect was revealed to them at the climax of the Lotus Sūtra. In these vows, they promised to proclaim the supreme scripture in evil times and to endure all the injury and abuse that were certain to descend on them. In this, too, Nichiren saw a prophecy of his own sufferings.

The immediate cause of his sufferings was Nichiren's unrelenting attack on the established sects and his outspoken criticism of Japan's rulers for patronizing these heretics. The repeated calamities suffered by the country at large and the threat of foreign invasion, which he hinted at ten years before the Mongol fleet appeared in Japanese waters, he regarded as the inevitable retribution for the false faith of the nation's leaders, both ecclesiastical and political. Contrasted to this sad state of affairs was Nichiren's vision of Japan as the land in which the true teaching of the Buddha was to be revived and from which it was to spread throughout the world. The name Nichiren, which he adopted,

---

1. Vishishtachārita (Viśistacāritra).
2. Sadāparibhūta.

symbolizes this exalted mission and his own key role in its fulfillment. *Nichi*, "the sun," represents both the Light of Truth and the Land of the Rising Sun, and *ren* stands for the Lotus.

To accomplish this aim, Nichiren urged all his followers to imitate the bodhisattva ideal of perseverance and self-sacrifice. In an age of utter decadence, as understood in terms of the theory concerning the Latter Day of the Law (*mappō*), everyone must be a man of Superb Action, ready to give his life if necessary for the cause. Nichiren himself was sentenced to death for his bold censure of the Hōjō regency in Kamakura and was saved only by miraculous intervention, according to his followers, when lightning struck the executioner's blade. Banished then to a lonely island in the Sea of Japan, Nichiren wrote, "Birds cry but shed no tears. Nichiren does not cry, but his tears are never dry." Ever after his narrow escape at the execution ground, Nichiren regarded himself as one who had risen from the dead, who had been reborn in the faith. "Tatsunokuchi is the place where Nichiren renounced his life. The place is therefore comparable to a paradise; because all has taken place for the sake of the Lotus of Truth. . . . Indeed every place where Nichiren encounters perils is Buddha's land."[3] In this way, Nichiren made suffering into a glorious thing and set an example for his disciples that did more to confirm their faith in the Lotus than could volumes of scripture.

## "RECTIFICATION FOR THE PEACE OF THE NATION" (*RISSHŌ ANKOKU RON*)

In this famous tract, which led to his banishment from Kamakura for his attacks on the shogun's authority, Nichiren speaks as a prophet condemning the faithlessness of Japan's rulers and people in abandoning the true teaching of the Lotus, to which they must return if the peace and security of the state and nation (*ankoku*) are to be restored. Later, it was this theme of "rectification"—that is, restoration of religious orthodoxy as a means of protecting the state and nation—that led to Nichiren's being honored by the Taishō Emperor in 1922 as "great teacher of rectification" (*risshō daishi*).

In the following, Nichiren reasserts what had earlier been Saichō's two main aims for Mount Hiei: Buddhism as protector of the state and nation, and the Lotus Sūtra as central to Mahāyāna Buddhism. The main focus of Nichiren's attack on false teachings is Hōnen's *Choosing the Original Vow* (*Senchakushū*), which set aside all other Buddhist scriptures and practices in favor of exclusive devotion to Amida. Other principal targets are Zen and Shingon.

The original text is in dialogue form, abbreviated here to focus on Nichiren's main argument, which starts with a lament for the disorders and disasters besetting Japan.

---

3. Anesaki, *Nichiren*, pp. 58–59.

Readers should be aware that such editorial abbreviation necessarily omits much of Nichiren's lengthy argument based on Buddhist scriptures, which he says the Pure Land and Zen sects have abandoned.

Once there was a traveler who spoke these words in sorrow to his host:

In recent years, there are unusual disturbances in the heavens, strange occurrences on earth, famine and pestilence, all affecting every corner of the empire and spreading throughout the land. Oxen and horses lie dead in the streets, the bones of the stricken crowd the highways. Over half the population has already been carried off by death, and in every family someone grieves. [p. 13]

All the while some put their whole faith in the "sharp sword"[4] of the Buddha Amida and intone this name of the lord of the Western Paradise. . . . There are also those who follow the secret teachings of the Shingon sect and conduct esoteric rituals, while others devote themselves entirely to Zen-type meditation and perceive the emptiness of all phenomena as clearly as the moon. . . .

Yet despite these efforts, they merely exhaust themselves in vain. Famine and disease rage more fiercely than ever, beggars are everywhere in sight and scenes of death fill our eyes. Cadavers pile up in mounds like observation platforms, dead bodies lie side by side like planks on a bridge. . . .

The host then spoke: I have been brooding alone upon this matter, indignant in my heart, but now that you have come, we can lament together. . . . I have pondered the matter carefully with what limited resources I possess, and have searched rather widely in the scriptures for an answer. The people of today all turn their backs upon what is right; to a man, they give their allegiance to evil. This is the reason that the benevolent deities have abandoned the nation, that sages leave and do not return. And in their stead come devils and demons, disasters and calamities that arise one after another. I cannot keep silent on this matter. I cannot suppress my fears. . . . [p. 14]

*Nichiren proceeds to invoke the Sūtra of the Golden Light (chap. 45) and the Sūtra of the Humane Kings on the important role of Buddhism as "protector of the nation."*

The Sūtra of the Humane Kings (Ninnō-kyō) states: "When a nation becomes disordered, it is the spirits which first show signs of rampancy. Because these spirits become rampant, all the people of the nation become disordered. Invaders come to plunder the country and the common people face annihilation. The ruler, the high ministers, the heir apparent, and the other princes and government officials all quarrel with each other over right and wrong. Heaven and earth manifest prodigies and strange occurrences; the twenty-eight constellations, the stars, the sun and the moon appear at irregular times and in irregular positions, and numerous outlaws rise up." . . . [p. 20]

---

4. A sword that would cut off earthly desires, karma, and suffering.

In the reign of Emperor Gotoba there was a monk named Hōnen who wrote a work entitled *Choosing the Original Vow (Senchakushū)*.[5] He contradicted the sacred teachings of Shākyamuni and brought confusion to people in every direction. The *Senchakushū* states: "The Chinese priest Daochuo[6] distinguished between the Shōdō or Sacred Way teachings and the Jōdo or Pure Land teachings and urged men to abandon the former and immediately embrace the latter. . . . We may assume that the esoteric Mahāyāna doctrines of Shingon and the true Mahāyāna teachings of the Lotus Sūtra are both included in the Sacred Way. If that is so, then the present-day sects of Shingon, Zen, Tendai, Kegon, Sanron, Hossō, Jiron, and Shōron—all these eight schools are included in the Sacred Way that is to be abandoned [according to Hōnen]." . . . [p. 22]

Hōnen also says: "The Chinese monk Shandao distinguished between correct and sundry practices and urged men to embrace the former and abandon the latter. Concerning the first of the sundry practices, that of reading and reciting sūtras, he states that, with the exception of the recitation of the Contemplation of Limitless Life Sūtra (Kammuryōju-kyō) and the other Pure Land sūtras, the embracing and recitation of all sūtras, whether Mahāyāna or Hīnayāna, exoteric or esoteric, is to be regarded as a sundry practice." . . .

Finally, in a concluding passage, Hōnen says: "If one wishes to escape quickly from the sufferings of birth and death, one should confront these two superior teachings and then proceed to put aside the teachings of the Sacred Way and choose those of the Pure Land. And if one wishes to follow the teachings of the Pure Land, one should confront the correct and sundry practices and then proceed to abandon all those that are incorrect and devote one's entire attention to those that are correct." . . . [p. 23]

And on top of that, he groups together all the sage monks of the three countries of India, China, and Japan as well as the students of Buddhism of the ten directions, and calls them a "band of robbers," causing the people to insult them! . . .

But because of this book written by Hōnen, this *Senchakushū*, the Lord Buddha Shākyamuni is forgotten and all honor is paid to Amida, the Buddha of the Western Land. The Lord Buddha's transmission of the Law is ignored and Yakushi, the Buddha of the Eastern Region, is neglected. All attention is paid to the three works in four volumes of the Pure Land scriptures, and all other wonderful teachings that Shākyamuni proclaimed throughout the five periods of his preaching life are cast aside. . . . As a result, the halls of the Buddha fall into ruin, scarcely a wisp of smoke rises above their mossy tiles; and the monks' quarters stand empty and dilapidated, the dew deep on the grasses in their courtyards. And in spite of such conditions, no one gives a thought to protecting the Law or to restoring the temples. . . . If people favor perverse doctrines and forget

---

5. See chap. 48.

6. Daochuo (562–645) is traditionally held to be the second patriarch of the Pure Land school in China.

what is correct, can the benevolent deities be anything but angry? If people cast aside doctrines that are all-encompassing and take up those that are incomplete, can the world escape the plots of demons? Rather than offering up ten thousand prayers for remedy, it would be better simply to outlaw this one evil doctrine that is the source of all the trouble! . . . [p. 25]

Though I may be a person of little ability, I have reverently given myself to the study of the Mahāyāna. A blue fly, if it clings to the tail of a thoroughbred horse, can travel ten thousand miles, and the green ivy that twines around the tall pine can grow to a thousand feet. I was born as the son of the one Buddha, Shākyamuni, and I serve the king of scriptures, the Lotus Sūtra. How could I observe the decline of the Buddhist Law and not be filled with emotions of pity and distress? . . . [p. 29]

The Lotus Sūtra says: "One who refuses to take faith in this sūtra and instead slanders it immediately destroys the seeds for becoming a Buddha in this world. . . . After he dies, he will fall into the hell of incessant suffering." . . .

If we accept the words of the Lotus Sūtra, then we must understand that slandering the Mahāyāna scriptures is more serious than committing the five cardinal sins. Therefore one who does so will be confined in the great fortress of the hell of incessant suffering and cannot hope for release for countless kalpas. . . .

The Lotus and the Nirvāna sūtras represent the very heart of the doctrines that Shākyamuni preached during the five periods of his teaching life. Their warnings must be viewed with the utmost gravity. Who would fail to heed them? And yet those people who forget about the Correct Way and slander the Law put more trust than ever in Hōnen's *Senchakushū* and grow blinder than ever in their stupidity. . . . [p. 35]

*In conclusion, Nichiren's opposite number in this dialogue concedes to him but, even more, is moved to take up the cause of warning and converting others to the correct teaching. Thus the prophetic warning prompts active proselytization among the people (in contrast to meditative praxis or esoteric rituals).*

The guest said: Now when I examine the passages you have cited from the sūtras and see exactly what the Buddha has said, I realize that slandering is a very grave offense indeed, that violating the Law is in truth a terrible sin. I have put all my faith in one Buddha alone, Amida, and rejected all the other Buddhas. I have honored the three Pure Land sūtras and set aside the other sūtras. . . . [p. 41]

But now I realize that to do so means to exhaust oneself in futile efforts in this life, and to fall into the hell of incessant suffering in the life to come. The texts you have cited are perfectly clear on this point and their arguments are detailed—they leave no room for doubt. . . . But it is not enough that I alone should accept and have faith in your words—we must see to it that others as well are warned of their errors.

[Yampolsky, ed., *Selected Writings of Nichiren*, pp. 13–41]

## THE EYE-OPENER (*KAIMOKU SHŌ*)

The following excerpts from *The Eye-Opener* were written in 1272 when Nichiren was in exile on the forbidding island of Sado on Japan's northwest coast. Experiencing great physical suffering and alarmed that his followers back in Kamakura were abandoning their faith under persecution, he wrote this work to encourage his disciples as if it were a last will and testament.

Nichiren begins this essay with the words "There are three categories of people that all men and women should respect. They are the sovereign, the teacher, and the parent." These three categories are equated with the three virtues that are the attributes of the sovereign, teacher, and parent and in turn are the qualifications of a Buddha. The virtue of the sovereign is the ability to protect all living beings; the virtue of the teacher is the ability to lead all to enlightenment; and the virtue of the parent is the possession of a compassion that will nurture and maintain them. These three virtues constitute a theme that runs throughout this essay and concludes the second volume of this work. Nichiren declares: "I, Nichiren, am sovereign, teacher, father, and mother to all the people of Japan."

At the conclusion of this treatise, Nichiren explains that there are two ways to propagate the Lotus Sūtra: *shōju*, gentle arguments, and *shakubuku*, strong refutation. Here Nichiren argues that both methods should be used because there are two kinds of countries, those whose people are ignorant and those whose people deliberately go against the Law. Japan, as a nation that slanders the Lotus Sūtra, requires the strong method.

Already over two hundred years have passed since the world entered the Latter Day of the Law. I was born in a remote land far from India, a person of low station and a monk of humble learning. During my past lifetimes through the six paths, I have perhaps at times been born as a great ruler in the human or heavenly worlds, and have bent the multitudes to my will as a great wind bends the branches of the small trees. And yet at such times I was not able to become a Buddha. . . . [p. 78]

Over a period of countless lifetimes, men are deceived more often than there are sands in the Ganges, until they [abandon their faith in the Lotus Sūtra and] descend to the teachings of the provisional Mahāyāna sūtras, abandon these and descend to the teachings of the Hīnayāna sūtras, and eventually abandon even these and descend to the teachings and scriptures of the non-Buddhist doctrines. I understand all too well how, in the end, men have come in this way to fall into the evil states of existence. . . . [p. 79]

I, Nichiren, am the only person in all Japan who understands this. But if I utter so much as a word concerning it, then parents, brothers, and teachers will surely criticize me and the government authorities will take steps against me. On the other hand, I am fully aware that if I do not speak out, I will be lacking in compassion. I have considered which course to take in the light of the teachings of the Lotus and Nirvana sūtras. If I remain silent, I may escape harm in this lifetime, but in my next life I will most certainly fall into the hell of incessant suffering. If I speak out, I am fully aware that I will have to contend with the three obstacles and the four devils. But of these two courses, surely the latter is the one to choose. . . .

The Buddha decided the time [when the votary of the Lotus Sūtra should appear], describing it as a "fearful and evil age," "a latter age," "a latter age when the Law will disappear," and "the final five hundred years," as attested by both [of] the Chinese versions of the Lotus Sūtra, Shō-hokke-kyō and Myōhō-renge-kyō. At such a time, if the three powerful enemies predicted in the Lotus Sūtra did not appear, then who would have faith in the words of the Buddha? If it were not for Nichiren, who could fulfill the Buddha's prophecies concerning the votary of the Lotus Sūtra? . . . [p. 84]

Prince Shōtoku of Japan was the son of Emperor Yōmei, the thirty-second sovereign of Japan. When he was six years old, elderly men came to Japan from the states of Paekche and Koguryŏ in Korea and from the land of China. The six-year-old prince thereupon exclaimed, "There are my disciples!" and the old men in turn pressed their palms together in reverence and said, "You are our teacher!" This was a strange happening indeed. . . . [p. 100]

The Great Teacher Dengyō[7] was the patriarch of both esoteric and exoteric Buddhism in Japan. In his *Exemplary Passages from the Lotus (Hokke Shūke)* he writes: "The sūtras that the other sects are based upon give expression in certain measure to the mother-like nature of the Buddha. But they convey only a sense of love and are lacking in a sense of fatherly sternness. It is only the Tendai sect, based upon the Lotus Sūtra, that combines a sense of both love and stern-ness. The sūtra is a father to all the worthy men, sages, those in the stages of learning and beyond learning, and those who have awakened in themselves the mind of the bodhisattva.". . . [p. 106]

In view of these facts, I believe that the devotees and followers of the various [provisional] sūtras such as the Flower Garland Sūtra (Kegon-kyō), Contem-plation of Limitless Life Sūtra (Kammuryōju-kyō), and Vairochana Sūtra (Dainichi-kyō) will undoubtedly be protected by the Buddhas, bodhisattvas, and heavenly beings of the respective sūtras that they uphold. But if the votaries of the Vairochana, Contemplation of Limitless Life, and other sūtras should set themselves up as the enemies of the votary of the Lotus Sūtra, then the Buddhas, bodhisattvas, and heavenly beings will abandon them and will pro-tect the votary of the Lotus Sūtra. It is like the case of the filial son whose father opposes the ruler of the kingdom. The son will abandon his father and support the ruler, for to do so is the height of filial piety. . . . [p. 109]

I, Nichiren, am the richest man in all of present-day Japan. I have dedicated my life to the Lotus Sūtra, and my name will be handed down in ages to come. If one is lord of the great ocean, then all the gods of the various rivers will

---

7. That is, Saichō.

obey him. If one is king of Mount Sumeru, then the gods of the various other mountains cannot help but serve him. . . .

Moreover, the Great Teacher Dengyō of Mt. Hiei is honored by monks throughout Japan as master of ordination into the priesthood. How could any monks turn their hearts toward a person like Hōnen, who is possessed by the Devil of the Sixth Heaven, and reject the Great Teacher Dengyō, who established the very ordination ceremonies that these monks themselves underwent? . . . [p. 120]

In volume five of the *Great Calming and Contemplation* (*Maka shikan*) Tiantai [Zhiyi] says: "There is a type called Zen men, but their leaders and disciples are blind [to the truth] and lame [in practice], and both leaders and disciples will fall into hell." In the seventh volume, we read: "[I have set forth ten ways of meditation.]" But the ninth way has nothing in common with the ordinary monks of the world who concentrate on the written word, nor does it have anything in common with the Zen masters who concentrate on practice. Some Zen masters give all their attention to meditation alone. But their meditation is shallow and false, totally lacking in the rest of the ten ways. . . . [p. 131]

We are living in an evil country and an evil age. I have discussed all this in detail in my work entitled *Rectification for the Peace of the Nation* (*Risshō ankoku ron*). This I will state. Let the gods forsake me. Let all persecutions assail me. Still I will give my life for the sake of the Law. . . . [p. 137]

Whether tempted by good or threatened by evil, if one casts aside the Lotus Sūtra, he destines himself for hell. Here I will make a great vow. Though I might be offered the rulership of Japan if I will only abandon the Lotus Sūtra, accept the teachings of the [Amidist] Sūtra of Limitless Life (Kammuryōju-kyō, and look forward to rebirth in the Western Pure Land, though I might be told that my father and mother will have their heads cut off if I do not recite the Nembutsu—whatever obstacles I might encounter, so long as men of wisdom do not prove my teachings to be false, I will never yield! All other troubles are no more to me than dust before the wind.

I will be the Pillar of Japan. I will be the Eyes of Japan. I will be the Great Ship of Japan. This is my vow, I will never forsake it! . . . [p. 138]

I, Nichiren, am sovereign, teacher, father, and mother to all the people of Japan. But the men of the Tendai sect [who do not refute the heretical sects] are all great enemies of the people. As Zhangan has noted, "He who makes it possible for an offender to rid himself of evil is acting like a parent to him."[8] [p. 147]

[Yampolsky, ed., *Selected Writings of Nichiren*, pp. 52–147]

---

8. From a commentary on the Nirvana Sūtra, *TD*(?), 38, 80b.

*Chapter 52*

## ZEN BUDDHISM

While most schools of Buddhism cite particular scriptures in support of their own special form of Buddhist practice, the Zen school, in contrast, rejects claims of scriptural authority and embraces many different practices. Its legitimacy rests on claims to an exclusive ancestral lineage that has been passed from teacher to disciple in an unbroken succession from Shākyamuni, the historical Buddha, down to the present day.

Zen legend says that one day on Vulture Peak, Shākyamuni Buddha preached a sermon not with words but by holding up a flower. Mahā Kāshyapa was the only one of Shākyamuni's many disciples who grasped the true significance of this wordless teaching, which he expressed by a slight smile. Mahā Kāshyapa thereby inherited Shākyamuni's robe and lineage as the second Zen ancestor. The Zen lineage was faithfully transmitted in India through twenty-eight generations until Bodhidharma (J: Daruma) brought it to China sometime in the sixth century. According to Zen teachers, certification in this lineage ensured that Zen monastics and their disciples practiced Buddhism correctly as living embodiments of the Buddha's awakened wisdom. Thus, regardless of whatever types of Buddhist practices Zen monks performed, they always would have more religious power than the exact same practices engaged in by other monks not affiliated with Zen. Because Zen orthodoxy rests on the teacher-disciple lineage alone, instead of issues of doctrine or practice, Zen clerics have historically enjoyed great flexibility in adapting a wide variety of activities, from tantric (esoteric) rituals to Pure Land chanting, to their Zen practice.

The development of the Zen lineage is difficult to determine on the basis of the extant historical evidence. During the Tang Dynasty (618–907), several competing Zen (Ch: Chan) lineages emerged, each with distinct unilinear genealogical claims and each seeming to advocate a different approach to Buddhist practice. Regardless of the relative importance any particular lineage afforded meditation exercise (the literal meaning of *zen* or *chan*), scriptural study, or other monastic routines, each insisted that all of their ancestors and teachers had attained full awakening to the wisdom of the Buddha Mind. Some of these Tang-dynasty lineages were transmitted to Japan, most notably by Saichō (767–822), the founder of the Tendai establishment on Mount Hiei. But in Heian-period Japan, when any accomplished practitioner of meditation or esoteric rituals could be called "Zen master" (*zenji*), teacher-disciple Zen lineages were not maintained.

During the Song dynasty (960–1279), a more comprehensive vision of the Zen lineage became dominant, a multibranched one encompassing five or more family lines to which almost any ordained cleric could find affiliation. Hagiographical compendiums, known as "flame records" (*tōroku*),[1] compiled during the Song dynasty, depicted the Zen ancestors of all lines as expressing the activity of Buddha awakening in novel ways, with shouts or gestures and strikes and with enigmatic and sometimes impious language. Collections of these individual episodes, known as *kōan* (Ch: *gongan*),[2] were compiled so that they could be studied as guidelines for Buddhist practice. Song-dynasty records explained the significance of these seemingly bizarre stories in a pithy verse, attributed to Bodhidharma, which summarizes the Zen message: "A special transmission outside the scriptures, not relying on words or letters; pointing directly to the human mind, seeing true nature is becoming a Buddha."

It is important to note that this emphasis on going outside the orthodox scriptures did not displace the traditional Buddhist monastic practices of chanting, meditation, and scriptural study. Rather, it revitalized them and charged them with increased soteriological significance by insisting that they must be performed as meaningful expressions of individual awakening realized in the here and now. The effectiveness of Zen rhetoric in promoting strict monastic practice was recognized by the Song government when it officially designated most state-recognized monasteries (i.e., public institutions, open to any legally ordained monk, that offer prayers for the long life of the emperor) as being Chan (Zen) cloisters. These temples housed the monastic elites, the monks with the best education (in both Buddhist scriptures and Confucian classics), the most sincere religious motivation, the strictest discipline, and the strongest ties

---

1. The term *tōroku* is commonly rendered as referring to the "transmission of the lamp," but the basic metaphor is one in which the flame of wisdom burning in one lamp is used to ignite other lamps. It is the flame that is transmitted, not the lamps.

2. Literally, "public cases" but better understood as "test cases."

to powerful political patrons. It was natural, therefore, that Japanese monks who traveled to Song-dynasty China in search of a new model of Buddhist vitality, as well as Chinese émigré monks who subsequently came to Japan, would identify themselves with the Zen lineage.

## ZEN IN JAPAN

Japanese Zen tradition customarily cites Eisai (aka Yōsai, 1141–1215) and Dōgen (1200–1253) as the first teachers of Song-dynasty Zen in Japan and as the founders of the Rinzai (Ch: Linji) and Sōtō (Ch: Caodong) Zen lineages, respectively. Certainly Eisai and Dōgen were important Zen pioneers who laid the foundation for subsequent developments, but their Zen teachings had little immediate impact. Even the wave of Chinese émigré Zen teachers who fled to Japan from the advancing Mongol armies and found new patrons among the military rulers of Kamakura immediately before and after the first Mongol invasion attempt of 1274 remained largely isolated from cultural currents. These Chinese monks provided the Hōjō regents and the new military government with a cosmopolitan aura otherwise lacking in the provincial town of Kamakura. But overall, the Kamakura warlords continued to sponsor established Buddhist schools and to join Pure Land and Nichiren movements as well. It was not until the second- and third-generation Japanese disciples of this first wave of Zen pioneers found new patrons among rival warlords and among members of the royal family that Zen became prominent in Japan.

Eisai was a Tendai monk who traveled to China twice (in 1168 and from 1187 to 1197). He was especially impressed by the resolute discipline of Chinese monasteries, which contrasted markedly with the moral laxity so common among Japanese clerics. Eisai believed that Zen would breathe new life into Japanese Tendai by reviving strict observance of the Buddhist precepts and the norms of monastic decorum. But Eisai's agenda was opposed by the Tendai establishment on Mount Hiei. He also had to contend with competition from the Darumashū, a rival Zen group founded by another Tendai monk named Nōnin, who never went to China but who had received mail-order certification in a Chinese Zen lineage. The Darumashū (named after Bodhidharma) promoted ideas completely opposite from Eisai's goals. They taught that no monastic discipline was required, since Buddha awakening could be expressed in any activity. In 1194, the court in Kyoto banned the Zen teachings of Eisai and the Darumashū. Eisai's most important work, the *Propagation of Zen for the Protection of the State* (*Kōzen gokokuron*, 1198), is an eloquent defense of Chinese Zen training that shows how it differs from normative Japanese Tendai and Darumashū practices.

Dōgen also began his monastic career in Tendai but soon switched to Zen under the guidance of one of Eisai's disciples. Dōgen spent four years in China (1223–1227), but unlike Eisai he was not edified by what he saw as political corruption in Song monasticism. Upon returning to Japan, he did not try to reform Tendai or promote Zen among the ruling elite. Instead, he established a small Zen temple on the outskirts of Kyoto. After a group of former Darumashū monks joined his community, Dōgen moved deep into the wilderness of Echizen (Fukui Prefecture), where his potential audience was even smaller. Although Dōgen died in relative obscurity, in modern times his writings have achieved wide recognition as works of religious and philosophical genius. His *How to Practice Buddhism* (*Bendōwa*, 1231) remains to this day a widely studied primer for Zen practice. And his *True Dharma Eye Treasury* (*Shōbōgenzō*, unfinished) is celebrated for the novel ways in which it analyzes *kōan* stories to express the wordless truth of Zen awakening in language.

Eisai's and Dōgen's very limited success at propagating Zen illustrates a crucial issue in our understanding of medieval Japanese religion. The religious life of the age often has been explained almost exclusively in terms of the so-called New Buddhism of the Pure Land, Nichiren, and Zen traditions that first appeared during the Kamakura period and remain the dominant forms of Japanese Buddhism to this day. Recent scholarship has emphasized, however, that these new schools for a long while remained relatively marginal movements with little political power or cultural influence compared with the orthodox mainstream of mixed exoteric and tantric (*kenmitsu*) Buddhism represented by the major landholding monasteries of Nara, Kyoto, and Mount Hiei. This Esoteric Buddhism was a dominant force in all aspects of medieval Japanese culture: politics, economics, literature, arts, and religion, including the worship of local gods (i.e., the *honji suijaku* forms of Shintō). To survive, the new forms of Kamakura Buddhism either had to move into the countryside beyond the reach of Esoteric Buddhist control or compromise with the preexisting Buddhist power structure or both.

Japanese Zen developed along both lines. Zen found a home in the state-recognized Buddhist establishment in the form of the Five Mountain (Gozan) temple networks of Kamakura and Kyoto. Although the title "Five Mountain" had been awarded to some Zen temples by the Hōjō regents, initially it was just an honorary designation. Through the political machinations of, first, Emperor Go-Daigo (1288–1339) and, subsequently, the Ashikaga military rulers, the Five Mountain system eventually consisted of some three hundred Zen monasteries, ranked into three tiers, that provided crucial income to the royal family and the military rulers. At the top tier were the large urban monasteries in Kyoto that performed tantric rites for the benefit of the state, sponsored foreign trade with China, managed the military government's estates, and, most of all, promoted the latest styles of Chinese culture. Five Mountain temples became centers of learning for the study of Neo-Confucian metaphysics, Chinese poetry, painting, calligraphy, and material arts such as printing, architecture, garden design, and ceramics. The role of Five Mountain Zen temples in introducing new styles of Chinese arts into medieval Japan has helped foster an indelible association between Zen and medieval forms of artistic expression.

At the center of the development of the Five Mountain system stood Musō Soseki (1275–1351), probably the most famous monk of his time, who achieved the unique distinction of receiving the title of "national teacher" (*kokushi*) from seven different emperors. Musō's career illustrates the precarious political waters that Zen abbots of his day had to navigate. He first rose to prominence under the sponsorship of the Hōjō regents, but when they finally selected him to become abbot of a Zen monastery in Kamakura, he refused to accept the post. In 1325, however, when Go-Daigo appointed him abbot of a Zen monastery in Kyoto, he accepted. But Musō resigned the following year and returned to Kamakura, where he finally served as abbot of Hōjō-sponsored Zen temples. Then, after forces loyal to Go-Daigo overthrew the Hōjō regents in 1333, Musō returned to Kyoto, where Go-Daigo again appointed him abbot. Musō nurtured close ties as well to the warrior Ashikaga Takauji (1305–1358), who, in 1336, removed Go-Daigo from power and established a new military government in Kyoto. At the time of Go-Daigo's death in 1339, Musō persuaded Takauji to sponsor the establishment of a new Zen monastery, Tenryūji, in order to pray for the late emperor's salvation. Naturally, Musō himself was appointed abbot. This event signaled the apex of the new Zen institution's identification with the ruling powers. Musō's sermon "Reflections on the Enmity Between Go-Daigo and the Shogun, Ashikaga Takauji" speaks volumes not only about church-state relations in medieval Japan but also about how little prestige Go-Daigo then commanded.

The other main branch of Zen in medieval Japan was the Rinka (literally, "forest") monasteries found primarily in the countryside. In contrast to the emphasis on Chinese learning found in the Five Mountain Zen temples, the Rinka generally housed less-educated monks who devoted more of their energies to the practices of "sitting Zen" (*zazen*) meditation and *kōan* study than to the writing of Chinese poetry. Rinka temples flourished among nouveau riche merchants of emerging trading centers and among the lower-ranked landed warriors and peasants, whose economic wealth and military power increased throughout the medieval period. For these merchants, warriors, and peasants, Rinka Zen monks performed simplified rites for worldly benefits, lay precept ordinations, and funerals and exorcized evil spirits and ghosts. When the Ashikaga shogunate declined in power, especially following the devastation of the Ōnin War (1467–1477), the Five Mountain system also declined in prestige and lost control of its lands, the source of its wealth. At this time, the Rinka temples' lack of political connections to the governing elites, which initially had left them less wealthy than the Five Mountains, proved to be a blessing in disguise. Many of the new warrior leaders who rose to power during the sixteenth century came from rural families who supported Rinka temples. The present-day Sōtō and Rinzai lineages also emerged from Rinka Zen.

Japanese Zen establishments, both the Five Mountain and the Rinka, owed much of their success to the strict discipline of their monks and to their teaching of traditional virtues, especially loyalty to one's lord. Warriors, court officials, and merchants alike patronized Zen monks for their stern moralizing sermons. As demonstrated by figures such as Nōnin or Ikkyū, however, Zen also has antinomian tendencies. The liberated lifestyle and free literary expression still had its serious side as a means of manifesting deeper insight or protesting abuses in institutionalized Zen and, in this, can be seen the interactions between two dominant themes in Zen: discipline and liberation.

## EISAI: PROPAGATION OF ZEN FOR THE PROTECTION OF THE STATE (KŌZEN GOKOKURON)

Eisai compiled this anthology in 1198, four years after the court had prohibited the establishment of independent Zen institutions in an attempt to persuade the court not merely to lift its ban but also to promote Zen in order to revitalize Japanese Buddhism. Since Eisai's chief adversaries at the Kyoto court were the monks of Mount Hiei monastery, which Saichō had founded, Eisai selected quotations primarily from scriptures and commentaries favored in the Tendai school to argue that Zen is the essence of true Buddhism. He points out that Saichō himself belonged to a Zen lineage and asserts that if Zen is illegitimate, then Saichō and the Tendai school he founded must also be illegitimate. In the following excerpts, Eisai equates Zen with the essence of mind, whose clarification is the goal of Buddhist practice. He asserts that mind is understood only by members of the special Zen lineage and emphasizes that the master-to-disciple transmission of the Zen lineage preserves the correct forms of monastic discipline as well as strict adherence to the precepts. He further attacks the Darumashū as false Zen, defends Zen's rejection of language, and attempts to show how Zen practice will reform wayward Japanese Buddhist monasticism.

## Preface

So great is Mind! Heaven's height is immeasurable, but Mind goes above it. Earth's depth is unfathomable, but Mind extends beneath it. The light of the sun and moon cannot be outdistanced, yet Mind reaches beyond them. Galaxies are as infinite as grains of sand, yet Mind spreads outside them. How great is the empty space! How primal is the ether! Still Mind encompasses all space and generates the ethereal. Because of it, Heaven and Earth treat us with their coverage and support. The sun and moon treat us with their circuits, and the four seasons treat us with their transformations. The myriad things treat us with their fecundity. Great indeed is Mind! Of necessity we assign it names: the Supreme Vehicle, the Prime Meaning, the True Aspect of Transcendental Wisdom [Prajñā], the Single Dharma Realm of Truth, the Unsurpassed Awakened Wisdom [Bodhi], the Heroic Concentration [Shūrangama samādhi], the True Dharma Eye Matrix, the Marvelous Mind of Nirvāna. All scriptures of the Three Turnings of the Dharma Wheel and eight canons, as well as all the doctrines of the Four Shāla Trees and Five Vehicles fit neatly within it.[3]

The Great Hero Shākyamuni's having conveyed this Mind Dharma to his disciple the golden ascetic Mahā Kāshyapa is known as the special transmission outside the scriptures. From their facing one another on Vulture Peak to Mahā Kāshyapa's smile in Cockleg Cave, the raised flower produced thousands of shoots; from this one fountainhead sprang ten thousand streams. In India the proper succession was maintained. In China the dharma generations were tightly linked. Thus has the true dharma as propagated by the Buddhas of old been handed down along with the dharma robe. Thus have the correct ritual forms of Buddhist ascetic training been made manifest. The substance of the dharma is kept whole through master-disciple relationships, and confusion over correct and incorrect monastic decorum is eliminated. In fact, after Bodhidharma, the great master who came from the West, sailed across the South Seas and planted his staff on the banks of the East River in China, the Dharma-eye Zen lineage of Fayan Wenyi was transmitted to Korea and the Ox-head Zen lineage of Niudou Farong was brought to Japan. Studying Zen, one rides all vehicles of Buddhism; practicing Zen, one attains awakening in a single lifetime. Outwardly promoting the moral discipline of the Nirvāna Scripture while inwardly embodying the wisdom and compassion of the Great Perfection of Wisdom Scripture is the essence of Zen.

In our kingdom the sovereign shines in splendor and his honor extends far and wide. Emissaries from distant fabled lands pay their respects to his court. Ministers conduct the affairs of the realm while monastics propagate the path of renunciation. Even the dharma of the Four Hindu Vedas finds use. Why then discard the five family lineages of Zen? Nonetheless, many malign this teaching, calling it the Zen of blind trance. Others doubt it, calling it the evil of clinging to emptiness. Still others consider it ill-suited to this latter age of dharma decline, saying that it is not needed in our land. Or they disparage my capacity, saying that I lack sufficient power. They belittle my spiritual ability, saying that it is impossible for me to revive what was already abandoned. Whoever attempts to uphold the Dharma Jewel in such a way destroys the Dharma Jewel. Not being me, how can they know my mind? Not only do they block the gateway through the Zen barriers, but they also defy the legacy of Saichō, the founder of Mount Hiei. Alas, how sad, how distressing. Which of us is right? Which of us is wrong?

---

3. The Three Turnings of the Dharma Wheel correspond to the Flower Garland Scripture (Buddhāvatamsaka), the provisional scriptures, and the Lotus Scripture (Saddharma pundarīka). The "eight canons" is a catchall term for all genres of Buddhist scripture. The Four Shāla Trees, a reference to the four trees among which Shākyamuni passed away into nirvāna, symbolize impermanence. The Five Vehicles refer to Buddhist practices that lead to human rebirth, heaven, or the spiritual attainments of the *arhat*, solitary Buddha, or bodhisattva (i.e., full Buddha realization).

I have compiled an anthology of the Buddhist scriptures that record the essential teachings of our lineage for consideration by today's pundits and for the benefit of posterity. This anthology is in three fascicles consisting of ten chapters, and it is entitled *Propagation of Zen for the Protection of the State* in accordance with the basic idea of the Sutra for Humane Kings. As my humble fictive words accord with reality, I ignore the catcalls of ministers and monastics. Remembering that the Zen of Linji benefits his later generations, I am not embarrassed by their written slanders. I merely hope that the flame of wisdom transmitted in Zen verse will not be extinguished until the arrival of Maitreya and that the fountain of Zen will flow unimpeded until the future eon of the Thousand Buddhas.

[Ichikawa et al., eds., *Chūsei zenke*, pp. 8–9; WB]

## Zen and Precepts

QUESTION: Some criticize you, asking what makes you think this new Zen lineage will cause Buddhism to flourish forever?

ANSWER: Moral precepts and monastic discipline cause Buddhism to flourish forever. Moral precepts and monastic discipline are the essence of Zen. Therefore, Zen causes Buddhism to flourish forever. Zhiyi's *Calming and Contemplation* states: "Worldly desires of ordinary people are denounced by all the holy ones. Evil is destroyed by pure wisdom. Pure wisdom arises from pure Zen. Pure Zen arises from pure precepts."

[Ichikawa et al., eds., *Chūsei zenke*, pp. 35–36; WB]

## Language

"Scriptures," or "Zen" are merely names. "Investigate," or "study" likewise are merely provisional designations. "Self," "other," "living beings," "*bodhi*," "nirvāna," and so forth are just words, without any real existence. Similarly, because the dharma preached by the Buddha is just such words, in reality nothing was preached.

For this reason Zen lies beyond the details of words and letters, outside mental conditions, in the inconceivable, in what ultimately cannot be grasped. "So-called Buddha dharma consists of the dharma that cannot be preached." So-called Zen is exactly the same. If anyone says the Buddha's Zen exists in words, letters, or speech, then that person slanders the Buddha and slanders the dharma. For this reason our ancestral teachers did not rely on words and letters, pointed directly at the human mind, saw nature, and became Buddhas. Such is Zen practice. Whoever clings to words loses the dharma, whoever clings to appearances becomes topsy-turvy. Fundamentally inactive, without a thing to grasp, is seeing the Buddha dharma. The Buddha dharma consists of merely walking, standing, sitting, and lying down. Adding even a single fine hair to it is impossible. Subtracting even a single fine hair from it is impossible. Once one attains this understanding, then expend not even the least effort. With even the slightest attempt at being clever, one has already missed it. Therefore, activity gives rise to *samsāra* while quietude leaves one in a drunken stupor, and avoiding both activity and quietude displays ignorance of Buddha nature. If one does none of the above, then what? This point lies outside clarification of doctrine. It cannot be fathomed through words. Look ahead and see! Get up and go! Once the arrow leaves the bow, there is no art that can bring it back. Even the thousand Buddhas could not grab it. As long as it has not hit the ground, no matter how much one might rue the crooked shot, one merely seizes air. Even if one tried until the last days of one's life, there is no grasping it.

[Ichikawa et al., eds., *Chūsei zenke*, pp. 62–63; WB]

## Ten Facilities for Zen Monasticism

Facilities for Zen Monasticism consist of ten items, which I describe in accordance with the *Pure Rules for Zen Cloisters* and other Chinese standards.

First, the monastery: Monasteries can be large or small, but all should conform to the layout of the Buddha's Jetavana Vihāra (Gion Shōja) in India. Along the four sides there are walls without side gates. There is only one main gate, which the gatekeeper shuts at dusk and opens at dawn. Nuns, women, and inauspicious people must not be allowed to stay the night. The decline of the Buddha dharma always results from women.

Second, ordinations: The distinction between Hīnayāna precepts and Mahāyāna precepts exists only in the hearts of men. Because one must merely embody sentiments of great compassion for the benefit of others, Zen does not choose between Mahāyāna or Hīnayāna precepts but merely focuses on living a pure life.

Third, observing the precepts: After ordination, if one violates the precepts, it would be the same as obtaining a precious jewel only in order to smash it. Therefore one must strictly observe the two hundred fifty *bhikshu* [monk] precepts, as well as the bodhisattva's three groups of pure precepts, ten major precepts, and forty-eight minor precepts. Twice each month during the *uposatha* ceremony, these precepts must be reviewed as explained in the precept scriptures. Anyone who violates the precepts must be kicked out. Such a one can be likened to a corpse cast into the ocean.

Fourth, academic study: Learning that spans the entire Buddhist canon and conduct that accords with the Mahāyāna and Hīnayāna precepts as well as proper monastic decorum constitute being a field of merit for gods and men. Inwardly embodying the great compassion of the bodhisattvas constitutes being a benevolent father to all living beings. In this way we become a valued jewel to the sovereign and a good physician to the country. To these goals we must aspire.

Fifth, ritual conduct: monastics observe dietary restrictions, practice chastity, and obey the Buddha's words. The schedule for each night and day are as follows: At dusk all monks assemble in the Buddha Hall to offer incense and worship. At evening they practice sitting Zen (*zazen*). During the third watch of the night (about 2:00 A.M.) they sleep. During the fourth watch they sleep. At the fifth watch they practice sitting Zen. At cockcrow they assemble in the Buddha Hall to offer incense and worship. At dawn they eat morning gruel. At the hour of the dragon (about 8:00 A.M.) they chant scriptures, study, or attend elder monks. At midmorning they practice sitting Zen. At noon they eat their daily meal. Afterwards they bathe or wash. During midafternoon they practice sitting Zen. Late afternoons are free time. The four periods of sitting Zen must be diligently practiced. Each moment of sitting Zen repays one's debts to the state; each act commemorates the sovereign's long life. These rituals truly cause the imperial reign to long prosper and the dharma flame to shine forever.

Sixth, monastic decorum: Old and young must always wear full robes. When they encounter one another, they must first place the palms of their hands together and then bow their heads to the ground in harmonious expressions of respect. Also, all meals, all walking exercises, all sitting Zen, all academic study, all chanting, and all sleeping must be performed as a group. Even if a hundred thousand monks are together inside one hall, each of them must observe correct monastic decorum. If someone is absent, the group leader (*inō*) must investigate and must not forgive even the slightest transgression.

Seventh, robes: Both inner and outer wear should conform to Chinese designs. These imply circumspection. One must be prudent in all affairs.

Eighth, disciples: Those who embody morality and wisdom without lapse should be admitted to the assembly. They must possess both mental and physical ability.

Ninth, economic income: As they say, "Do not cultivate the fields, since sitting Zen leaves no time for it; Do not hoard treasures, since the Buddha's words alone suffice." Aside from one cooked meal each day, eliminate all other needs. The dharma of monks consists of being satisfied with as little as possible.

Tenth, summer and winter retreats: The summer retreat begins on the fifteenth day of the fourth moon and ends on the fifteenth day of the seventh moon. The winter retreat begins on the fifteenth day of the tenth moon and ends on the fifteenth day of the first moon. Both of these two retreats were established by the Buddhas. Do not doubt it. In our land these retreats have not been practiced for a long time. In the great land of Song-dynasty China, however, not a single monk fails to participate in the two retreats. From the standpoint of the Buddha dharma, the Japanese practice of calculating one's monastic seniority in terms of the retreats without actually participating in them is laughable.

[Ichikawa et al., eds., *Chūsei zenke*, pp. 80–83; WB]

## DŌGEN: *HOW TO PRACTICE BUDDHISM* (*BENDŌWA*)

Dōgen wrote this treatise in 1231 at the beginning of his ministry as a basic introduction to Zen Buddhism. In the following excerpts, Dōgen argues that true Buddhism has been preserved only by members of the Zen lineage and can be learned only by studying under a fully initiated Zen teacher. True Buddhism consists of practicing sitting Zen (*zazen*), which Dōgen identifies as self-actualizing *samādhi* or, in other words, the concentration that transforms both self and the world experienced by self into its original state of awakened Buddha activity. According to Dōgen, other Buddhist practices lack this kind of spiritual efficacy.

After arousing dharma-seeking mind, I traveled throughout our kingdom searching for a good teacher. Finally I met Master Myōzen at Kenninji monastery. I followed him for nine swift years as I heard about the Rinzai family lineage. Master Myōzen was the foremost disciple of ancestor Eisai, from whom he alone received correct transmission of the supreme Buddha dharma. No one else compared to Myōzen.

Later I journeyed to the Great Song-dynasty China and visited various good teachers along both sides of the Qiantang River, where I learned the ways of the five family lineages of Zen. Finally, I met Zen Master Rujing on the Great White Peak of Mount Tiandong and completed the great goal of my lifelong study. Thereafter, I returned home in 1227 to save living beings by propagating the dharma. I felt as if I shouldered a heavy responsibility.

Yet I put aside my burden, and waiting for a favorable opportunity, I moved about like a cloud or tumbleweed, all the while wanting to teach in the style of my former mentor. I thought there must be a few student monks unconcerned with fame and fortune who consider the Buddha Way of first importance in their sincere study. What if they were led astray by false teachers who obscure correct understanding and thereby became self-deluded or sunk in *samsāra*? When would they ever sprout the true seeds of Prajñā [awakened wisdom] and attain the Way? As long as I move about like a cloud or tumbleweed, how can they cross the mountains or rivers to visit me? Out of concern for these monks, I have written about the practices that I saw and heard in the Zen monasteries of Great Song-dynasty China and about the abstruse import that my good teacher [Rujing] taught me. I dedicate this treatise to all students devoted to the Way so that they may know the true dharma. Here is the genuine initiation.

We teach: The Great Master, Lord Shākyamuni, atop Vulture Peak in India transmitted the dharma to Mahā Kāshyapa. Correctly transmitted from ancestor to ancestor, it subsequently reached the venerable Bodhidharma. Venerable Bodhidharma traveled to China and transmitted the dharma to Master Huike. Thus was the Buddha dharma first transmitted to China.

In this same manner the dharma was directly transmitted to Huineng, the sixth ancestor, also known as Great Mirror Zen Master. From him the authentic

Buddha dharma spread throughout China without divisions. He produced two fabulous disciples: Nanyue Huairang and Qingyuan Xing-si. Both of them transmitted and preserved the Buddha-mind Seal (*mudra*), and both were teachers of gods and men. From these two disciples, five family lineages emerged: the Fayan line, the Guiyang line, the Caodong line, the Yunmen line, and the Linji line. Today in Song-dynasty China only the Linji lineage is widespread. Although the five family lineages differ, there is just one Buddha-mind Seal.

In China, since the Later Han dynasty [first century], various Buddhist scriptures had been translated repeatedly, but no one could separate the grain from the chaff. When Bodhidharma came from the West, he cut through the confusion, and since then the single pure Buddha dharma spread everywhere. We must try to do the same in our land.

We teach: For all the Buddha dharma–preserving Zen ancestors and Buddhas, sitting upright in the practice of self-actualizing (*jijuyū*) *samādhi* [concentration] is the true path of awakening. Both in India and in China, all who have attained awakening did so in this way. Because in every generation each teacher and each disciple intimately and correctly transmitted this marvelous art, I learned the genuine initiation.

In the correctly transmitted Zen lineage we teach: This directly transmitted, authoritative Buddha dharma is the best of the best. Once you start studying under a good teacher, there is no need for lighting incense, worshipful prostrations, recalling the Buddha (*nembutsu*), repentance, or chanting scripture. Just sit (*shikan taza*) and slough off body-mind (*shinjin datsuraku*).

If you, for however short a while, imprint all your activities with the Buddha-mind Seal by sitting upright in *samādhi*, then all things in the entire dharma realm become imprinted with the Buddha-mind Seal, and the entire cosmos becomes awakening. Thereupon all Buddhas and Tathāgatas increase their fundamental essence of dharma joy, and the adornments of the way of awakening are revitalized. Moreover, at this very moment all living beings in the six courses of rebirth throughout all dharma realms of the ten directions simultaneously purify their body-minds, realize great liberation, and discover their original faces. All things realize complete awakening, all creatures access Buddha bodies, transcend the boundaries of awakening, sit as Buddhas at the base of the tree of awakening, and simultaneously turn the incomparable Dharma Wheel that expresses deep, ultimate, unconditioned Prajñā.

Because the Fully Awakened Ones [Buddhas] provide mysterious assistance, when you practice sitting Zen, you will definitely slough off body-mind, eliminate habitually defiled thought patterns, and realize divinely genuine Buddha dharma. You will aid all Buddha activity in all Buddha wayfaring sites as infinite as atoms. You will encourage the aptitude for practicing beyond Buddha and promote the dharma beyond Buddha. At that moment all lands, plants, fences, and roof tiles throughout the dharma realms of the ten directions also engage in Buddha activity, causing everyone to obtain the Buddha's inconceivable mysterious assistance in attaining awakening as easily as they receive natural blessings like wind and water.

Just as everyone makes use of water and fire, so too you will circulate the innate realization of Buddha deliverance so that everyone living or talking with you will all embody inexhaustible Buddha-virtue. As it unfolds and widens without end, without break, the inconceivable, infinite Buddha dharma will flow throughout the entire cosmos and beyond. The fact that the one who practices sitting Zen is unaware of the Buddha's mysterious assistance is because it is direct realization of nondeliberative quiescence. If, as ordinary people suppose, cultivation and realization are two separate processes, then it would be possible to be aware of each in isolation. But what interacts with our awareness cannot be fundamental realization because fundamental realization is beyond deluded human thoughts.

Moreover, although both subject and object disappear and reappear during the practice of quiescent realization, because it is the realm of self-actualizing *samādhi*, they become expansive Buddha activity and profound, miraculous Buddha deliverance without moving a single speck of dust or blemishing a single image. All the lands and plants reached by this path of Buddha deliverance radiate great brilliance and preach the profound, wondrous dharma endlessly. Plants and fences sermonize for humans, for Buddhas, and for all living beings. Humans, Buddhas, and all living beings expound the dharma for the sake of plants and fences. Because this realm of self-awakening and awakening others is permeated with the quality of universal Buddha realization, fundamental realization occurs ceaselessly.

Therefore, whenever you practice sitting Zen, for however short a while, you mysteriously merge with all existence, you completely permeate all time, and throughout the infinite dharma realm, you eternally perform past, present, and future Buddha deliverance. Each and every one equally performs the same cultivation and the same realization. It is so not just during seated cultivation. Echoes of emptiness sound during the intervals both before and after the temple bell is struck because it continues to vibrate due to its marvelous resonance. In this same manner, the original cultivation of original face possessed by each one of the infinite individual beings reverberates beyond all measurable calculation.

Know that even if all the Buddhas as infinite as grains of sand used all their Buddha wisdom in an attempt to sum up the amount of merit generated by just one person practicing sitting Zen, they could never reach the end of it.

[Ichikawa et al., eds., *Chusei zenke*, pp. 80–83; WB]

## "THE FULLY APPARENT CASE" (GENJŌ KŌAN)

The term *kōan* originally referred to case law or legal precedents that provided guidelines for subsequent affairs. In Zen, *kōan* record the sometimes enigmatic sayings or actions of Zen ancestors that should be studied as guidelines for Buddhist practice. A fully apparent (*genjō*) *kōan* is one that we might call an open-and-shut case, a matter whose settlement (or meaning) should be perfectly obvious. For Dōgen, it does not imply that something hidden becomes obvious but refers to the actualization of each moment of reality on its own terms, in the here and now, without the distortion of human biases. The fascicle entitled "Genjō kōan" is the first essay in Dōgen's *True Dharma Eye Treasury* (*Shōbōgenzō*) because it defines the agenda, namely, self-realization through Zen practice, for the entire work. The essay begins with the fundamental issue of life and death, the inescapable *kōan* of human life. Dōgen's seemingly paradoxical use of language rests on a logic of affirmation in which any single aspect of reality is completely true in the totality of itself, even though its exact opposite must also be completely true in its own totality.

In the synchronicity of all things as Buddha dharma, there is delusion and awakening, there is religious cultivation, there is birth, there is death, there is Buddhahood, and there is humanity. In the synchronicity of all existence unconnected to yourself, there is no delusion, no awakening, no Buddhahood, no humanity, no birth, and no death.

Because the Buddha Way ultimately transcends all surplus or dearth, the Buddha Way is both birth and death, both delusion and awakening, both humanity and Buddhahood. Even as the Buddha Way is thus, nonetheless flowers wilt and die in spite of our attraction while weeds sprout and live in spite of our rejection.

The individual self striving to realize all things is delusion; all things striving to realize the individual self is awakening.

Those who awaken to delusion are Buddhas, while those who are deluded about awakening are humanity. Furthermore, others attain awakening beyond awakening, and delusion deludes others.

When Buddhahood is truly Buddhahood, there is no individual self aware of Buddhahood. Nonetheless Buddhahood is realized as each activity is Buddha realization.

If you see sights with your whole body-mind, if you hear sounds with your whole body-mind [if you perceive objects with your whole body-mind], then you will comprehend them intimately, not in the way a mirror harbors a reflection [of an object outside itself], not in the way the moon appears in water. Illuminating one side obscures the other side.

To study the Buddha way is to study the individual self. To study the individual self is to forget the individual self. To forget the individual self is to be realized by all things. To be realized by all things is both the individual self's body-mind and the other selves' body-mind sloughing off.

[When body-mind sloughs off,] the afterglow of awakening fades away and this faded-away afterglow of awakening fades and fades away forever.

[Nishio, *Shōbōgenzō*, vol. 1, pp. 101–102; WB]

## BUDDHA NATURE (BUSSHŌ)

Buddha nature is sometimes explained as the spiritual potential to become a Buddha that is possessed by some or all living beings. In this treatise, Dōgen rejects any substantive conception of Buddha nature as a permanent innate characteristic or metaphysical reality. Dōgen emphasizes that Buddha nature is the "no-ness" (i.e., emptiness, void, or nonsubstantiality) of all things, which is realized only through the true practice of Buddhism (what he calls "doing Buddha"). The following excerpt is characteristic of Dōgen's style of *kōan* study in which he reads his own interpretations into the texts of *kōan*, often by ignoring the rules of Chinese grammar in favor of an overly literal, word-by-word translation.

Hui-neng, the sixth Zen ancestor of China, also known as Great Mirror Zen Master of Mount Caochi, began his study of Buddhism by going to the monastery on Mount Huangmei. When he arrived there, Hongren, the fifth Zen ancestor, asked him: "You came here from where?"

The sixth ancestor replied: "I am a Lingnan person from the south."

The fifth ancestor asked: "You came here seeking to do what?"

The sixth ancestor replied: "I seek to do Buddha."

The fifth ancestor said: "Lingnan People No Buddha Nature. How Can Do Buddha?"

This utterance "Lingnan People No Buddha Nature" does not say that people in Lingnan lack Buddha nature nor does it say that they possess Buddha nature. It says, "Lingnan People No Buddha Nature" [i.e., the emptiness of Buddha nature]. The utterance "How Can Do Buddha" means what kind of Doing Buddha will you do?

Overall only a few spiritual guides have clarified the truth of Buddha nature. Teachers of the *āgama* scriptures and of the Mahāyāna scriptures do not know it. Only descendants in the lineage of the Buddhas and Zen ancestors have transmitted this knowledge. The truth of Buddha nature is that it is not something we are endowed with before becoming a Buddha. We are endowed with it only after becoming a Buddha. Buddha nature and becoming a Buddha necessarily co-participate. Investigate and struggle with this truth well. If necessary, study and struggle with it for twenty or thirty years. Even holy celestial bodhisattvas have not clarified this truth. This truth is expressed by saying "Living Beings Exist Buddha Nature" and "Living Beings No Buddha Nature." The correct object of study is the truth that Buddha Nature is what we are endowed with since becoming Buddhas. If you do not study in this way, then you are not studying the Buddha dharma. Without this kind of study, Buddhism would not have survived until the present. If you do not clarify this truth, then you will not clarify becoming a Buddha, you will not even hear of it. This is why the fifth ancestor faced the sixth ancestor and said: "Lingnan People No Buddha Nature." When you first meet a Buddha and hear him preach the dharma, the most difficult words to understand are "Living Beings No Buddha Nature." Whether learning from a good teacher or learning from the scriptures, however, the most joyous words to hear are "Living Beings No Buddha Nature." If you do not fully embody the knowledge of seeing and hearing "Living Beings No Buddha Nature," then you have not yet seen nor heard of Buddha nature. For the sixth ancestor to attain Doing Buddha and for the fifth ancestor to help the sixth ancestor attain Doing Buddha, there was nothing else to say, no other method could have been as skillful. The only thing he could say is "Lingnan People No Buddha Nature." Know that the saying and the hearing of "No Buddha Nature" is itself the direct path of Doing Buddha. In other words, that very moment of No Buddha Nature is Doing Buddha. If you have not yet seen or heard No Buddha Nature, if you have not yet said No Buddha Nature, then you have not yet practiced Doing Buddha.

The sixth ancestor said: "People Exist North and South, but Buddha Nature No North or South." Let's take this utterance and struggle with its inner meaning. The words "north and south" seem quite innocent. The sixth ancestor's words, however, convey vital religious significance. That is to say, they imply the position that while people can practice Doing Buddha, Buddha nature cannot practice Doing Buddha. Did the sixth ancestor know this or not?

[Nishio, *Shōbōgenzō*, vol. 3, pp. 118–119; WB]

## MUSŌ SOSEKI: SERMON AT THE DEDICATION OF TENRYŪJI DHARMA HALL

The following sermon was delivered at the dedication of the Dharma Preaching Hall when Musō became the founding abbot of Tenryūji monastery, founded in memory of Go-Daigo. The dedication coincided with the anniversary of the Buddha's birthday. Musō used this occasion to remind his audience that the truth preached by the Buddha, the truth proclaimed by the Zen ancestors, and the truth taught by Musō were all the very same truth. Thus, Shākyamuni's message of salvation is not ancient history but must be realized in this present moment at this very spot.

(In the tenth month of the second year of the Rekiō period [1339] a court decree ordered the conversion of the detached palace of Kameyama *tennō* [emperor] into a monastery dedicated to the memory of Go-Daigo *tennō* and also nominated Musō to be its founding abbot. In the fourth year of Kōei [1345], fourth month, eighth day, the Dharma Preaching Hall was opened for the first time, with their lordships Shogun Ashikaga Takauji and Vice-Shogun Tadayoshi in attendance. Musō first performed the ceremony celebrating the Buddha's birth and then proceeded to say:)

The appearance in this world of all Buddhas, past, present, and future, is solely for the purpose of preaching the dharma that saves living beings. The Buddha used the arts of oratory and eight types of eloquence as the standards for his preaching the dharma, and the Deer Park and Vulture Peak both served as his halls of salvation. Our lineage of the Zen ancestors stresses the method of individual instruction directed toward the essential endowment, thus distinguishing itself from doctrinal schools. But examination of our aims reveals that we too focus solely on transmitting the dharma that saves the deluded. Thus all the ancestors, from the twenty-eight in India through the first six in China, each signaled his succession to the lineage with a dharma-transmission verse. The Great Master Bodhidharma said, "I came to China in order to transmit the dharma that saves deluded people." So it is clear that Huike's cutting off his arm in the snow and the conferring of the robe at midnight upon Huineng were both meant to signify the transmission of the marvelous dharma.[4] In all kinds of circumstances, whether under a tree, upon a rock, in the darkness of a cave, or deep in a glen, there is no place where the dharma banner has not been erected and no place where the Mind Seal has not been transmitted to whoever possessed the spiritual capacity. Ever since Baizhang Huaihai founded the first Zen cloister, China and Japan have seen numerous grand Zen monasteries erected. All of them, whether large or small, have included a Dharma Preaching Hall for proclaiming the message of salvation. . . .

As for this mountain monk appearing before you today on this platform, I have nothing special to offer as my own interpretation of the dharma. I merely join with my true master, Shākyamuni Buddha, and with all others throughout infinite empty space, all Buddhas, bodhisattvas, holy ones, assembled clerics, patrons, and officials, the very eaves and columns of this hall, lanterns, and posts, as well as all the people, animals, plants, and seeds in the boundless ocean of existence to turn in unison the great Dharma Wheel. At this very moment, what is happening?

(Musō raised his staff high into the air.)

Look! Look! Shākyamuni is here right now on top of my staff. He takes seven steps, points to heaven and to earth, announcing to all of you:

> Today I am born again here with the completion of this new Dharma Preaching Hall. All the holy ones are assembled here; people and gods mingle together. Every single person here is precious in himself, and everything here — plaques, paintings, square eaves and round pillars — every single thing is preaching the dharma. Wonderful, wonderful it is, that the true dharma lives and never dies. At Vulture Peak, indeed, this dharma was transmitted to the right man!

It is thus that Lord Shākyamuni, the most venerable, instructs us here. It is the teaching that comes down to men in response to their needs. But perhaps, gentlemen, you wish to know the state of things before Shākyamuni ever entered his mother's womb.

(Musō tapped his staff on the floor.)

Listen, Listen!

[*Musō kokushi goroku*, TD 80, no. 2555; 460c–461a; WB]

---

4. According to Zen legends, Huike, the second Zen ancestor of China, gained Bodhidharma's attention by cutting off his own arm as a gesture of his sincerity, and Huineng, the sixth Zen ancestor of China, visited his teacher in secret at midnight so as to avoid incurring the wrath of a jealous monk senior to him.

REFLECTIONS ON THE ENMITY BETWEEN GO-DAIGO AND THE
SHOGUN, ASHIKAGA TAKAUJI

This extract is from a sermon delivered by Musō upon resuming the office of abbot
of Tenryūji in 1351, in which he reflects on the reasons for dedicating this monastery
to the memory of Go-Daigo and analyzes the causes of the rupture between the latter and Ashikaga Takauji, his erstwhile supporter. He attributes the break to jealousy,
which blinded Go-Daigo and estranged him from his obedient servant. Musō's frank
censure of the deceased sovereign shows both how low the prestige of the imperial
house had fallen and how little awed by it was this Zen prelate, who considered it a
purely human institution and not divine.

In the realm of True Purity, there is no such thing as self or other. How much
less can friend or foe be found there! But the slightest confusion of mind brings
innumerable differences and complications. Peace and disorder in the world,
the distinction between friend and foe in human relationships, follow upon one
another as illusion begets delusion. A person of spiritual luminosity will immediately recognize false thought and eliminate it, but the shallow-minded person
will be enslaved by his own delusion so that he cannot put an end to it. In such
cases one's true friend may seem a foe and one's implacable enemy may appear
a friend. Enmity and friendship have no permanent character; both of them are
illusions.

During the disorders of the Genkō period [1331–1334] the shogun, acting
promptly on the court's order, swiftly subdued the foes [the Hōjō regents] of the
state, as a result of which he rose higher in court rank day by day and his growing
prestige brought a change in the attitude of others toward him. Ere long, slander
and defamation sprang up with the violence of a tiger, and this unavoidably
drew upon him the royal displeasure. Consider now the reasons for this turn
of events. It was because he performed a meritorious task with such dispatch
and to the entire satisfaction of his sovereign. There is an old saying that intimacy invites enmity. That is what it was. Thereupon, the auspicious clouds of
goodwill were scattered to the winds, and the august dragon [Go-Daigo] had to
take refuge in the mountains to the south, where the music of the court was no
longer heard and whence his royal phoenix palanquin could never again return
to the northern court.

With a great sigh the military leader [Takauji] lamented, "Alas, due to slander
and flattery by court ministers, I am consigned to the fate of an ignominious
rebel without any chance to explain my innocence." Indeed his grief was no per-
functory display, but without nurturing any bitterness in his heart, he devoutly
gave himself over to spiritual reflection and pious works, fervently praying for
the Buddhahood of Go-Daigo and subsequently constructing [in Go-Daigo's
memory] this grand monastery for the practice of great Buddha activity. . . .

The virtuous rule of Go-Daigo *tennō* accorded with Heaven's will and his
holy wisdom equaled that of the ancient sage-kings of China. Therefore the

royal family's fortunes rose high as reign and military power were unified. The phoenix reign inaugurated a new period of magnificence and splendor. Barbarians beyond the four borders were submissive and all within the borders were earnest. People compared his Yao-like reign to the wind, which always blows without end.[5] Who, then, would have thought that his Shun-like sun would appear for only a moment and then immediately disappear behind the clouds? And what are we to make of it—was it merely a random turn of events? No, the fact that Go-Daigo expended all his karmic connections to this defiled world and straightaway joined the happy assembly of the Pure Land was not because his august reign lacked luck. It was because he caused the people so much suffering and distress. As a result, from the time of his passing right up to the present there has been no peace, clergy and laity alike have been displaced, and there is no end to the complaints of the people.

What I have expounded above is all a dream within a dream. Even though it actually happened, there is no use finding fault with what is past and done—how much less with what has happened in a dream! We must realize that a Wheel-Turning Monarch (*cakravartin*), the highest position among humans, is itself but something cherished in a dream. Even Brahmā, the highest king of the gods, knows only the pleasure of a dream. This is why Shākyamuni forsook the option of becoming a Wheel-Turning Monarch and entered the mountains to practice austerities. What was his purpose? To teach all people that the King of Awakening [Buddha] far surpasses the highest rank of human society. Although the four social classes differ, each member of them is like every other in being a disciple of the Buddha, and should behave accordingly.

I pray therefore that our late sovereign will instantly transform his defiled capacity, escape from the bondage of delusion, bid farewell to his karma-producing consciousness, and realize luminous wisdom. May he pass beyond the distinctions of friend and foe and attain the luminous region wherein delusion and awakening are one. May he not forget that the dharma transmission of Vulture Peak lives on and extend his protection to this monastery, so that without ever leaving this spot his blessings may extend to all living beings.

This is indeed the wish of the military leader [Takauji]. He bears no grudge toward Go-Daigo but merely wishes for him to develop favorable karmic causes, which is no trifling affair. The Buddhas in their great compassion will surely respond by bestowing mysterious blessings. In this way may the warfare come to an end, all the land within the four seas enjoy true peace, and all the people rest secure from disturbances and calamities. May [Takauji's] military success pass on to his heirs, generation after generation. Our earnest prayer is that it should wash over all opposition.

[*Musō kokushi goroku*, TD 80, no. 2555; 463c–464b; WB]

---

5. Yao is remembered as a sage ruler in ancient China who chose Shun as his successor.

## Chapter 53

### SHINTO IN MEDIEVAL JAPAN

The introduction of Buddhism and its subsequent acceptance by the Japanese court resulted in the submergence of Shinto, the native religion, for many years. It was said of Emperor Kōtoku (who reigned at the time of the Great Reform of 645) that he "honored the religion of Buddha and despised the Way of the Gods."[1] Other sovereigns generally had more respect for Shinto, although the brilliant Buddhist ceremonies that marked the Nara and Heian periods occupied the court far more than did the simple observances of the native religion. The ethical values of the indigenous tradition—later the subject of much attention by scholars of the native learning—were seldom articulated in early Japan. Except for a few prayers (*norito*), Shinto did not produce religious writings, and anything resembling a theology had to be inferred from myths and legends.

But Shinto was not entirely absent from the scene in early Japan. The gods had their functions and rituals, chiefly concerned with particular localities and natural phenomena—rain, drought, earthquakes, and the like. This meant that among the peasants (and, in general, most people living away from the capital in the provinces), the local cults of Shinto continued to be the prevailing religion even when Buddhism was triumphant at the court. But even the court recognized the importance of the gods. Over and over in the *Chronicles of Japan*, we find such entries as the following (for 599 C.E.): "There was an earthquake

---

1. Aston, *Nihongi*, vol. 2, p. 195.

which destroyed all the houses. So orders were given to all quarters to sacrifice to the God of Earthquakes."[2] An entry for 689 contains the first mention of a state "department of Shinto," and in the eleventh month of 691 we are told that "the festival of first-fruits was held. Ōshima, Nakatomi no Ason, Minister of the Department of the Shinto religion, recited the prayers invoking the blessing of the Heavenly Deities."[3]

By the early tenth century, when the Institutes of the Engi Era were completed, more than six thousand Shinto shrines were enumerated where annual offerings were to be made by the court or the provincial governments. This official recognition of Shinto represented a great landmark in the systematization of the native cults, which until then had tended to remain loosely connected local shrines. In this attempt to systematize Shinto, we can detect the influence of Chinese-style administration and Buddhist practices. Indeed, already in the late Nara period (in 765), Buddhist monks and nuns had participated in the Great Thanksgiving Festival, one of the most sacred Shinto celebrations, and Empress Shōtoku declared on that occasion that she considered it her duty (having returned to the throne as a nun), "first to serve the Three Treasures, then to worship the Gods, and next to cherish the people."[4] The union of the two religions was further promoted in 768 when a Buddhist temple was erected next to the Ise Shrine, the holiest imperial shrine and Shinto sanctuary, and from this time on, many Shinto shrines included temples and Buddhist priests who served both religions.

The idea of fusing Buddhism with another religion did not originate in Japan. In India, Buddha himself had recognized the popular gods, the *devas*, as deities possessing powers far less considerable than his own but superior to those of ordinary men. The early texts frequently refer to the conversion of the Indian gods (*devas*) to Buddhism after they heard Buddha preach. In later Buddhist writings, Brahmā and the lesser deities were described as avatārs of Buddha and the bodhisattvas who had appeared on earth to save humankind. This concept was later adopted by the Mahāyāna sects. It is found in such works as the *Saddharma Puṇḍarīka*, the Vimalakīrti, and Vairochana Sūtras, and the Shingon mandalas.

In China, Buddhists sometimes claimed that Confucius, Laozi, and other famous philosophers were sent by Buddha to help humankind. By the middle of the Tang dynasty, we find the first mention of the phrase "manifest traces of the original substance" (*honji suijaku*) that figured so prominently in Japan. In an explanation of the Vairochana Sūtra, a commentator stated that the spirits and gods were avatārs of Vairochana—traces on earth of the original substance of divinity.

---

2. Ibid., p. 124.

3. Sansom, *Japan, a Short Cultural History*, p. 135.

4. Aston, *Nihongi*, vol. 2, p. 404. The Nakatomi family, later renamed Fujiwara, was one of the chief supporters of Shinto.

Although Buddhism had also joined the native religions in both India and China, it was in Japan that this fusion assumed its most significant form. Kūkai is often mentioned as the originator of *honji suijaku*, but despite the numerous forged works on the subject attributed to him, nothing indicates that the *honji suijaku* formula was known in his time. Later supporters tended to invoke Kūkai's name to lend greater authority to *honji suijaku*, a fact that may also explain the tales of how Kūkai taught Emperor Saga about the mysteries of Shinto or such supposed quotations as "Unless one studies Shinto, one will not understand the profundities of my school of Buddhism." Whether or not we believe such stories, it is certain that both Saichō and Kūkai did pay considerable attention to the gods. When he built his temple on Mount Kōya, which had been known as the seat of various gods, Kūkai called out to them:

> All evil spirits and gods, who may be to the east, south, west, above, or below this monastery: you hinderers and destroyers of the True Law, hie you seven leagues hence from my altar! If however there be any good spirits and gods who are beneficial to the Buddhist Law and protect it, you may dwell as you choose in this monastery and protect the Buddhist Law.[5]

The first clear evidence of *honji suijaku* thought in Japan seems to date from 937, when two gods were declared to be manifestations of bodhisattvas. In time, every god was established as a manifestation of one or another Buddha or bodhisattva. Most of the "original substances" of the different gods proved to be the thirteen Buddhas of Shingon, a fact indicative of the special affinity between this sect and Shinto. Shinto adopted the incantations, ritual fire ceremonies, charms, signs, and methods of instruction of Shingon, and these alien features soon became so much a part of Shinto that even purists later considered them to be part of the religion in its pristine form. The most important form of union between Buddhism and Shinto was called "Dual Shinto" (Ryōbu Shintō), a term derived from the equation between the two mandalas of Shingon Buddhism and the Inner and Outer Shrines at Ise. The Tendai monasteries of Mount Hiei and Miidera, which had become strongholds of Esoteric Buddhism, consummated their union with Shinto by adopting local tutelary deities, as had the Shingon center of Mount Kōya.[6] But Shingon was considered by most Shinto scholars to be the Buddhist sect closest to the native religion. Kitabatake Chikafusa declared that the "traditions from the age of the gods tally most closely with the teachings of this sect [Shingon]. That is probably why, though it [Shingon] enjoyed only brief popularity in China, it has persisted in Japan."

---

5. *Kōbō Daishi zenshū*, vol. 3, *Shōryōshū*, pp. 530–531.

6. At Mount Kōya, it was either the deity Nifu Myōjin (or Tanjō) or Kōya Myōjin who allegedly turned the mountain over to Kūkai; at Mount Hiei it was the mountain god Sannō; and at Miidera, the Korean goddess Shiragi Myōjin (Korean influence was pervasive in this region).

In medieval Japan, the fusion of Buddhist and Shinto ceremonies became almost invariable. Many of the nation's shrines were controlled by Buddhists. Within the shrines themselves, Buddhist images were worshiped as representations of the gods, and Buddhist implements (principally Shingon) were used alongside the traditional paper streamers and ropes of Shinto. The pantheism of Tendai and the cosmotheism of Shingon easily incorporated Shinto beliefs and legends, and even in the remote regions of Japan, where the Way of the Gods remained strongest, the two religions regularly intertwined. Although it is true that monks were not allowed to enter the Inner Shrine at Ise and certain Buddhist sects failed to show much interest in Shinto, by and large the union of Buddhism and Shinto, usually stated in *honji suijaku* terms, became a general feature of Japanese religious life and remained such at least until the Meiji Restoration of 1868.

At first, Shinto's part in the combined religion was relatively minor, but with the downfall of the court aristocracy at the end of the Heian period, the men from the outlying provinces brought to power retained a strong attachment to Shinto. Thus, the Taira clan proclaimed its loyalty to the goddess Itsukushima, and the Minamoto clan worshiped Hachiman, sometimes spoken of as the god of war. As early as the year 750, Hachiman is reported to have paid his respects to the Great Statue of the Buddha in Nara, and it was not many years afterward that he acquired the title of "great Bodhisattva." Later, the Minamoto shoguns adopted Hachiman at their headquarters in Kamakura, just as the imperial house had established his worship in Nara and Kyoto. Hachiman was considered a manifestation of Amida Buddha, while Itsukushima (at Miyajima) was the "manifested trace" of Kannon (Avalokiteshvara), further examples of *honji suijaku*.

The Mongol invasions of 1274 and 1281 aroused in the Japanese a strong national consciousness. The "divine winds" (*kamikaze*) that drove off the invaders were interpreted as signs of the protection afforded to Japan by the native gods (the Sun Goddess and Hachiman). Less than fifty years afterward Chikafusa wrote his *Chronicle of the Direct Succession of Gods and Sovereigns*, in which he proclaimed the supremacy of Japan over China and India because of Japan's single line of emperors descended from the gods. Chikafusa's work was primarily political, but at about the same time (or somewhat earlier), the Five Classics of Shinto appeared, forgeries purporting to have been composed in remote antiquity. The Five Classics are concerned mainly with the history of the Ise Shrine and attempt to set forth a Shinto philosophy and ethics. Whatever philosophical or ethical significance these books possess was borrowed from Buddhism, but the adherents of the "Prime Shinto" (Yuiitsu Shintō) school of the fifteenth century and later referred to the Five Classics as a treasury of pure Shinto teachings.

The chief figure in the Prime Shinto school was Yoshida Kanetomo (1435–1511). Kanetomo did not attempt, as did certain later Shinto scholars, to discredit Buddhism; instead, he tried to shift the emphasis in the combined religion from Buddhism to Shinto while maintaining the union. He interpreted *honji suijaku* as meaning that the Japanese gods were the original substance and Buddha and the bodhisattvas were the manifest traces. (This is comparable to a similar switch in India, where Hindus came to consider Buddha as the ninth avatār of Vishnu, or in China, where the Daoists thought of Buddha as an avatār of Laozi.) Kanetomo relied heavily on the forged Five Classics, and when they were insufficient to meet his needs, he appears not to have been above forgery of his own. In one of Kanetomo's works, we find his most famous statement, attributed to Prince Shōtoku, that Japan was the root of all civilization, China its branches and leaves, and India its flowers and fruit; thus all foreign doctrines were offshoots of Shintō. In this way, Kanetomo boldly attempted to turn the tables on Buddhism and Confucianism and assert the primacy of Shinto after centuries of subservience.

Kanetomo revealed his indebtedness to Buddhism, particularly Esoteric Buddhism, at every point in his exposition of Shinto principles; indeed, it often appears as if he has merely substituted a Shinto word in an otherwise Buddhist context:

> *Kami* or Deity is spirit, without form, unknowable, transcending both cosmic principles, the yin and the yang . . . changeless, eternal, existing from the very beginning of Heaven and Earth up to the present, unfathomable, infinite, itself with neither beginning nor end, so that the so-called "Divine Age" is not only in the past but also in the present. It is, indeed, the eternal now.[7]

This is an enunciation of the Shingon doctrine of *aji hompushō* (the eternity of creation) decked out in Shinto garments, and in the following passage we find Shingon cosmotheism expressed in the characteristic three aspects:

> With reference to the universe we call it *kami*, with reference to the interactions of nature we call it spirit (*rei*), in man we call it soul (*kokoro*). Therefore, *kami* is the source of the universe. He is the spiritual essence of created things. *Kami* is soul (*kokoro*) and soul is *kami*. All the infinite variety of change in nature, all the objects and events of the universe are rooted in the activity of *kami*. All the laws of nature are made one in the activity of *kami*.[8]

The most significant result of Kanetomo's teachings was that by his time the long period of Shinto apprenticeship to alien ideologies had ended; the Shinto spokesmen not only knew the intricacies of Buddhism and other foreign doctrines but also were adept at rewriting them in Shinto terms with ease and vigor. Kanetomo was a member of the Urabe family, one of the oldest and most

---

7. Kanetomo, *Shindaishō*, trans. in Holtom, *The National Faith of Japan*, pp. 39–40.
8. Adapted from ibid., p. 40.

important Shinto families of diviners. For centuries, this family had experienced all the tribulations that had befallen Shinto during its period of subservience to Buddhism, but when Kanetomo appeared, Shinto once more came into its own, and the Urabe family's persistent devotion was justified.

## YOSHIDA KANETOMO: *ESSENTIALS OF PRIME SHINTO (YUIITSU SHINTŌ MYŌBŌ YŌSHŪ)*

The following excerpts are taken from Yoshida Kanetomo's *Essentials of Prime Shinto*, written about 1485 and expounding in catechistical style what Kanetomo considered the key terms and teachings of Prime Shinto. These passages deal with the three main forms or divisions of Shinto and their relation to Buddhism; the scriptural bases for each; key terms, texts and rituals; the three Imperial Regalia; the divine origins and spiritual lineage of Prime Shinto; and the basic regulations governing the transmission and practice of the teachings. Much of Kanetomo's exposition is couched in the then widely current language of Esoteric Buddhism as if to establish that the real meaning of the latter derives from a primordial Shinto, which should now be followed to the exclusion of all "foreign" excrescences.

Q: What is the form of Shinto called "Original and Fundamental"?

A: The term *gen* designates the origin of origins predating the appearance of yin and yang. The term *hon* designates the state predating the appearance of thought processes. Hence the following verse:

Taking the Origin as such, one penetrates the origin of origins;
Taking the Original State as such, one sees the heart-mind.

Q: What do the terms *sō* and *gen* mean?

A: The term *sō* designates the original spirit predating the diversification of energy. All phenomena return to that single origin. The term *gen* designates the divine function referred to as "mingling with the dust and softening one's radiance."[9] This provides the basis of benefit for all living beings. . . .

Q: On what scriptural evidence is this claim founded?

A: Three Primordial Texts form the basis of the Exoteric Doctrine, and Three Divine Scriptures form the basis of the Esoteric Doctrine. Yuiitsu-Shinto is made up of those two doctrines.

Q: What are the Three Primordial Texts?

---

9. The term *wakō*, originally taken from the Daodejing, came to qualify in Japan the use of expedient means (Skt: *upāya*, J: *hōben*) on the part of those buddhas and bodhisattvas who would have manifested themselves in the form of *kami*. It is rendered as "soften the glare," as in Lau, trans., *Lao Tzu*, pp. 60, 117.

A: They are *Tendai-kuji-hongi*, compiled by Shōtoku Taishi;[10] *Kojiki*, compiled by Ō no Yasumaro;[11] and *Nihon shoki*, compiled by Toneri Shinnō upon imperial order.[12]

Q: What are the Three Divine Texts?

A: They are the Subtle Sacred Scripture of the Divine Metamorphoses of the Heavenly Foundation, the Subtle Sacred Scripture of the Divine Supernatural Powers of the Earthly Foundation, and the Subtle Sacred Scripture of the Divine Powers of the Human Foundation.[13]

Q: Were those Scriptures revealed by the kami or authored by wise men?

A: They were revealed by [the kami] Ame-no-koyane-no-mikoto. In later generations they were translated into Chinese by the True Lord of the Polar Star. Thus did they come to be called the Three Divine Scriptures. . . .

Q: What are the Three Imperial Regalia?

A: First is the divine mirror kept in the Onmeiden [Hall] of the imperial palace. Second is the Grass-cutting sacred sword. Third is the sacred seal of Yasakani.

Q: Is there a difference between these three kinds and the ten kinds?

A: These three kinds are different. Thus one reads in the fifth book of *Nihon shoki*:

> Then Amaterasu-ō-Kami gave to Ninigi-no-mikoto the curved stone of Yasakani, the Yata mirror, and the Kusanagi sword.

. . .

Q: What is the meaning of the term "Shinto"?

A: The term *shin* denotes the foundation of the ten thousand things in Heaven and Earth. Therefore, it is also qualified as unfathomable yin and yang. The term *tō* denotes the rationale of all activities. Therefore it is said, "The Way is not the constant way."[14] As a consequence there is nothing in the material world, nor in the worlds of life, of animate and inanimate beings, of beings with energy and without energy, that does not partake of this Shinto. Hence the verse:

> *Shin* is the heart-mind of all beings,
> *Tō* is the source of all activities.
> All animate and inanimate beings of the triple world are
>   ultimately nothing but Shinto only.

. . .

---

10. *Tendai kuji hongi* is found in vol. 8 of *Shintō taikei*.
11. See chap. 42.
12. Ibid.
13. Kanetomo wrote these three short texts.
14. The first line of the *Laozi* (chap. 5).

Q: Since when did the people of our sacred nation revere the law of the Buddha, and why are they searching for foreign doctrines?

A: An infinity of time after the creation of our sacred nation, the venerable Shākyamuni appeared in that other nation [India]. One must emphasize that the transmission of his doctrine to our nation occurred only in the recent past, in the reign of the thirtieth emperor, Kimmei, and already five hundred years after the Buddha had died. Buddhism was transmitted to our nation only after four hundred and some years of development within China. But the people of our nation did not originally believe in that new doctrine. During the reign of the thirty-fourth ruler of our nation [Empress Suiko], Shōtoku Taishi made to her the following secret declaration:

Japan produced the seed, China produced the branches and leaves, India produced the flowers and fruit. Buddhism is the fruit, Confucianism is the leaves, and Shinto is the trunk and the roots. Buddhism and Confucianism are only secondary products of Shinto. Leaves and fruit merely indicate the presence of the trunk and roots; flowers and fruit fall and return to the roots. Buddhism came east only to reveal clearly that our nation is the trunk and roots of these three nations.[15]

. . .

Q: Are there any more details about this term "Yuiitsu"?

A: There are three types of interpretation of this term. First, there is only one doctrine and not two. Second, there is only one lineage and not two. And third is the demonstration that it is One-and-Only in Heaven.

Q: What is meant by "there is only one doctrine and not two"?

A: This Shinto is a most subtle and obscure transmission that has taken place between Kuni-no-tokotachi-no-mikoto, who is the origin of the incommensurable yin and yang, and Amaterasu-ō-kami. This kami then transmitted it to Ame-no-koyane-no-mikoto. Since that time all the way down to this degenerate age of decadence, this Shinto has drawn on the primeval water of chaos and has not even once been corrupted by a single drop of the Three Teachings [Confucianism, Daoism, Buddhism]. That is why it is said that there is only one doctrine and not two.

## The Lineage of Yuiitsu-Shinto

Q: What is meant by the demonstration that it is One-and-Only in Heaven?

A: This country is a Sacred Land (*shinkoku*). Its way is the kami Way (*shintō*). The ruler of this country is the Sacred Emperor (*jinnō*). The Great Ancestor is Amaterasu-ō-kami. The awesome light of this one kami

---

15. This statement, attributed to Shōtoku Taishi by Japanese tradition since Jihen, is an adaptation of an earlier Chinese concoction.

pervades billions of worlds, and its will shall forever be transmitted along an imperial way laden with ten thousand chariots. Just as there are not two suns in heaven, there are not two rulers in a country. That is why, when the sun is in the sky, the light of the stars and planets cannot be seen. Such is the demonstration that it is One-and-Only in Heaven. . . .

## Regulations of Yuiitsu-Shinto

Caution shall be exercised when transmitting the doctrine.

Concerning the above. If within the true lineage of the Urabe one finds an adequate recipient of the doctrine, he shall be trained from a young age and with particular care. If it is someone from another lineage, it must be ensured that his capabilities are in accordance with the demands of the duty, and the degree to which he shares our purpose must be evaluated before he be accepted as a disciple.

It is absolutely forbidden to transmit the doctrine to priests of other shrines.

[Ōsumi, *Chusei Shintō ron*, pp. 209–251; trans. and adapted from Grapard, "Yuiitsu Shintō," pp. 137–161; AG]

# KITABATAKE CHIKAFUSA: *CHRONICLE OF THE DIRECT SUCCESSION OF GODS AND SOVEREIGNS (JINNŌ SHŌTŌKI)*

As noted in chapter 49, Kitabatake Chikafusa's *Direct Succession* is both a history of Japan from the creation of the country by the gods to the reign of Emperor Gomurakami, who succeeded Go-daigo in 1339, and a political tract intended primarily to draw supporters to the Southern Court during the fourteenth-century War Between the Courts. *Jinnō shōtōki* is also one of the most important documents of the Shinto revival of the medieval age. Thus in its opening lines (quoted in chap. 49), Chikafusa proclaims Japan to be a "divine land" (*shinkoku*), different from and superior to all other lands, because it has always been ruled by an unbroken line of emperors descended from the Sun Goddess.

In these first three passages from the *Direct Succession*, Chikafusa discusses the various names that have been used for Japan, its position in the universe according to Buddhist geographical concepts, and the differing Indian, Chinese, and Japanese accounts of the creation of the universe and its evolution. Chikafusa's preoccupation in the first passage with names and their etymologies is characteristic of writers on Shinto, who have never wearied of tracing the origins of names and words, such as Yamato and *kami*.

In the second and third passages, Chikafusa displays his familiarity with Indian (Buddhist) and Chinese writings. He does not reject them but attempts to show that they are incomplete—if not misleading—because they do not reveal the highest and most important truth: the uniquely divine character of Japan based on its unbroken line of sovereigns.

In the fourth passage, Chikafusa discusses the imperial regalia of mirror, sword, and jewel, seeking to show that they are symbols of both the Sun Goddess's mandate that one line descended from her will rule Japan forever and the morality with which that rule is invested.

Japan is the divine country. The heavenly ancestor it was who first laid its foundations, and the Sun Goddess left her descendants to reign over it forever and ever. This is true only of our country, and nothing similar may be found in foreign lands. That is why it is called the divine country.

### The Names of Japan

In the age of the gods, Japan was known as the "ever-fruitful land of reed-covered plains and luxuriant ricefields."[16] This name has existed since the creation of Heaven and Earth. It appeared in the command given by the heavenly ancestor Kunitokotachi to the Male Deity and the Female Deity.[17] Again, when the Great Goddess Amaterasu bequeathed the land to her grandchild, that name was used; it may thus be considered the prime name of Japan. It is also called the country of the great eight islands. This name was given because eight islands were produced when the Male Deity and the Female Deity begot Japan. It is also called Yamato, which is the name of the central part of the eight islands. The eighth offspring of the deities was the god Heavenly-August-Sky-Luxuriant-Dragonfly-Lord-Youth [and the land he incarnated] was called Ō-yamato, Luxuriant-Dragonfly-Island. It is now divided into forty-eight provinces. Besides being the central island, Yamato has been the site of the capital through all the ages since Jinmu's conquest of the east. That must be why the other seven islands are called Yamato. The same is true of China, where All-Under-Heaven was at one time called Zhou because the dynasty had its origins in the state of Zhou, and where All-Within-the-Seas was called Han when the dynasty arose in the territory of Han.

The word Yamato means "footprints on the mountain." Of old, when Heaven and Earth were divided, the soil was still muddy and not yet dry, and people passing back and forth over the mountains left many footprints; thus it was called Yama-to—"mountain footprint." Some say that in ancient Japanese *to* meant "dwelling" and that because people dwelt in the mountains, the country was known as Yama-to—"mountain dwelling."

In writing the name of the country, the Chinese characters Dai-Nippon and Dai-Wa have both been used. The reason is that when Chinese writing was introduced to this country, the characters for Dai-Nippon were chosen

---

16. Toyoshihara no Chiihoaki no Mizuho no Kuni. Translations of ancient names of places and deities are only approximate.

17. The Male Deity (Izanagi) and the Female Deity (Izanami) were ordered to descend to Earth and produce the terrestrial world.

to represent the name of the country, but they were pronounced as "Yamato." This choice may have been guided by the fact that Japan is the land of the Sun Goddess, or it may have thus been called because it is near the place where the sun rises. . . .

## Japan's Position Geographically

According to Buddhist scriptures, there is a mountain called Sumeru which is surrounded by seven gold mountains. In between them is the Sea of Fragrant Waters, and beyond the gold mountains stretch four oceans which contain the four continents. Each continent is in turn composed of two smaller sections. The southern continent is called Jambu (it is also known as Jambudvīpa, another form of the same name) from the name of the jambu tree. In the center of the southern continent is a mountain called Anavatapta, at the summit of which is a lake. A jambu tree grows beside this lake, seven yojanas in circumference and one hundred yojanas in height. (One yojana equals forty *li*; one *li* equals 2,160 feet.) The tallest of these trees grows in the center of the continent and gives it its name. To the south of Anavatapta are the Himālayas, and to the north are the Pamirs. North of the Pamirs is Tartary; south of the Himālayas is India. To the northeast is China, and to the northwest, Persia. The continent of Jambu is seven thousand yojanas long and broad; that is, 280,000 *li*. However big China may seem, when compared with India it is only a remote, minor country. Japan is in the ocean, removed from China. Gomyō Sōjō of Nara and Saichō of Hiei designated it as the Middle Country, but should not that name refer to the island of Chāmara, which lies between the northern and southern continents? When, in the Kegon Sūtra, it states that there is a mountain called Kongō [diamond], it refers to the Kongō Mountain in modern Japan, or so it is believed. Thus, since Japan is a separate continent, distinct from both India and China and lying in a great ocean, it is the country where the divine illustrious imperial line has been transmitted.

## Japan's Position Chronologically

The creation of Heaven and Earth must everywhere have been the same, for it occurred within the same universe, but the Indian, Chinese, and Japanese traditions are each different. According to the Indian version, the beginning of the world is called the "inception of the kalpas." (A kalpa has four stages—growth, settlement, decline, and extinction—each with twenty rises and falls. One rise and fall is called a minor kalpa; twenty minor kalpas constitute a middle kalpa, and four middle kalpas constitute a major kalpa.) . . .

In China, nothing positive is stated concerning the creation of the world, even though China is a country which accords special importance to the keeping of records. In the Confucian books nothing antedates King Fuxi.[18] In other works they speak of Heaven, Earth, and man as having begun in an unformed, undivided state, much as in the accounts of our age of the gods. There is also the legend of King Pangu,[19] whose eyes were said to have turned into the sun and the moon and whose hair turned into grasses and trees. There were afterward sovereigns of Heaven, sovereigns of Earth, and sovereigns of Man, and the Five Dragons, followed by many kings over a period of ten thousand years.

The beginnings of Japan in some ways resemble the Indian descriptions, telling as it does of the world's creation from the seed of the heavenly gods. However, whereas in our country the succession to the throne has followed a single undeviating line since the first divine ancestor, nothing of the kind has existed in India. After their first ruler, King People's Lord, had been chosen and raised to power by the populace, his dynasty succeeded, but in later times most of his descendants perished, and men of inferior genealogy who had powerful forces became the rulers, some of them even controlling the whole of India. China is also a country of notorious disorders. Even in ancient times, when life was simple and conduct was proper, the throne was offered to wise men,[20] and no single lineage was established. Later, in times of disorder, men fought for control of the country. Thus some of the rulers rose from the ranks of the plebeians, and there were even some of barbarian origin who usurped power. Or some families after generations of service as ministers surpassed their princes and eventually supplanted them. There have already been thirty-six changes of dynasty since Fuxi, and unspeakable disorders have occurred.

Only in our country has the succession remained inviolate from the beginning of Heaven and Earth to the present. It has been maintained within a single lineage, and even when, as inevitably has happened, the succession has been transmitted collaterally, it has returned to the true line. This is due to the ever-renewed Divine Oath and makes Japan unlike all other countries.

It is true that the Way of the Gods should not be revealed without circumspection, but it may happen that ignorance of the origins of things may result in disorder. In order to prevent that disaster, I have recorded something of the facts, confining myself to a description of how the succession has legitimately been transmitted from the age of the gods. I have not included information known to everyone. I have given the book the title of *The Chronicle of the Direct Succession of Gods and Sovereigns.* . . .

---

18. Fuxi was the legendary founder of Chinese culture, being credited, among other things, with establishing the laws of marriage, inventing writing, and preparing the first instruction in hunting and fishing.

19. The legend of Pangu was apparently of Central Asiatic origin and was not "naturalized" by the Chinese until post-Han times.

20. This refers to the decisions of the legendary emperors Yao and Shun to hand over the throne to wise men rather than to their own sons.

## The Imperial Regalia

Then the Great Sun Goddess conferred with Takami-musubi and sent her grandchild to the world below. Eighty million deities obeyed the divine decree to accompany and serve him. Among them were thirty-two principal deities, including the gods of the Five Guilds—Ame no Koyane (the first ancestor of the Nakatomi family), Ame no Futodama (the first ancestor of the Imbe family), Ishikoridome (the first ancestor of the mirror makers), and Tamaya (the first ancestor of the jewel makers). Two of these deities, those of the Nakatomi and the Imbe, which received a divine decree specially instructing them to aid and protect the divine grandchild, uttered these words of command, "The reed-plain-of-one-thousand-five-hundred-autumns-fair-rice-ear land is where my descendants shall reign. Thou, my illustrious grandchild, proceed thither and govern the land. Go, and may prosperity attend thy dynasty, and may it, like Heaven and Earth, endure forever."

Then the Great Goddess, taking in her own hand the precious mirror, gave it to her grandchild, saying, "When thou, my grandchild, lookst on this mirror, it will be as though thou lookst at myself. Keep it with thee, in the same bed, under the same roof, as thy holy mirror." She then added the curved jewel of increasing prosperity and the sword of gathered clouds, thus completing the three regalia. She again spoke, "Illumine all the world with brightness like this mirror. Reign over the world with the wonderful sway of this jewel. Subdue those who will not obey thee by brandishing this divine sword." It may indeed be understood from these commands why Japan is a divine country and has been ruled by a single imperial line following in legitimate succession. The Imperial Regalia have been transmitted [within Japan] just as the sun, moon, and stars remain in the heavens. The mirror has the form of the sun; the jewel contains the essence of the moon; and the sword has the substance of the stars. There must be a profound significance attached to them.

The precious mirror is the mirror made by him for the Great Goddess Ishikoridome, as is above recorded. The jewel is the curved bead of increasing prosperity made by him to the Great Goddess. The goddess's commands on the Three Regalia must indicate the proper methods of governing the country. The mirror does not possess anything of its own but, without selfish desires, reflects all things, showing their true qualities. Its virtue lies in its response to these qualities and, as such, represents the source of all honesty. The virtue of the jewel lies in its gentleness and submissiveness; it is the source of compassion. The virtue of the sword lies in its strength and resolution; it is the source of wisdom. Unless these three[21] are joined in a ruler, he will find it difficult indeed to govern

---

21. Compare the *Classic of Documents* (*Hongfan*); Legge, *Shoo-King*, in *The Chinese Classics*, p. 333: "The three virtues: The first is correctness and straightforwardness; the second, strong rule; and the third, mild rule."

the country. The divine commands are clear; their words are concise, but their import is far-reaching. Is it not an awe-inspiring thing that they are embodied in the Imperial Regalia?

The mirror stands first in importance among the regalia and is revered as the true substance of ancestor worship. The mirror has brightness as its form: the enlightened mind possesses both compassion and decision. As it also gives a true reflection of the Great Goddess, she must have given her profound care to the mirror. There is nothing brighter in Heaven than the sun and the moon. That is why, when the Chinese characters were devised, the symbols for the sun and for the moon were joined to express the idea of brightness. Because our Great Goddess is the spirit of the sun, she illuminates with a bright virtue which is incomprehensible in all its aspects but dependable alike in the realm of the visible and invisible. All sovereigns and ministers have inherited the bright seeds of the divine light, or they are descendants of the deities who received personal instruction from the Great Goddess. Who would not stand in reverence before this fact? The highest object of all teachings, Buddhist and Confucian included, consists in realizing this fact and obeying in perfect consonance its principles. It has been the power of the dissemination of the Buddhist and Confucian texts which has spread these principles.[22] It is just the same as the fact that a single mesh of a net suffices to catch a fish, but you cannot catch one unless the net has many meshes. Since the reign of the Emperor Ōjin, the Confucian writings have been disseminated, and since Prince Shōtoku's time Buddhism has flourished in Japan. Both these men were sages incarnate, and it must have been their intention to spread a knowledge of the way of our country, in accordance with the wishes of the Great Sun Goddess.

[From *Jinnō shōtō-ki*, pp. 1–22]

---

22. That is, Buddhist and Confucian texts have helped spread a knowledge of Shinto because they contain the same essential principles.

## Chapter 54

## THE VOCABULARY OF JAPANESE AESTHETICS

## THE WAY OF TEA

Tea was introduced to Japan sometime during the early Heian period, probably by monks such as Saichō (767–822) and Kūkai (774–835) returning from study in China. Tea drinking had become widespread in China by at least the seventh or eighth century and was brought to Japan in the wave of cultural borrowing from the continent that spanned the late sixth through early ninth centuries. In 815, Emperor Saga (r. 809–823) ordered that tea be grown in various provinces around Kyoto and that some of the annual harvest in leaves be presented as tribute to the court.

Tea drinking appealed primarily to two elite groups in Japan: nobles at the emperor's court, who, in emulation of their Chinese counterparts, drank tea and composed poetry (in Chinese) extolling the tea's taste and the elegant ways in which it could be prepared and served; and monks in Buddhist temples, who esteemed tea mainly for its medicinal value. But tea drinking at court declined from the late ninth century, when the Japanese ceased sending missions to China and lost at least some of their enthusiasm for Chinese culture. Although tea continued to be consumed at Buddhist temples and also Shinto shrines, there is no indication that people outside these establishments adopted it as a beverage during the remainder of the Heian period.

Tea was reintroduced to Japan from China in the late twelfth century (the early Kamakura period) by the monk Yōsai (aka Eisai, 1141–1215), who in

*Kissa yōjōki* analyzes and describes tea's medicinal efficacy. The kind of tea that Yōsai brought to Japan was unfermented, powdered green tea (called *matcha* in Japanese). During the Song period—mid-Heian times in Japan—the Chinese invented the tea whisk, which they used to dissolve powdered tea in hot water. Later, the Chinese abandoned the whisk and returned to their earlier practice of steeping or infusing tea (i.e., flavoring hot water by placing or dipping tea leaves into it). Most people today, including the Japanese in their everyday lives, drink infused tea, whether fermented (black tea), partially fermented (oolong tea), or unfermented (green tea). But the tea ceremony, *chanoyu*, which evolved in Japan in the late fourteenth through sixteenth centuries, has always used powdered green tea and the whisk.

Some of Yōsai's tea was planted at Toganoō, located in the mountains to the northwest of Kyoto. As the popularity of tea drinking spread among all classes during the thirteenth and fourteenth centuries, Toganoō tea came to be regarded as the finest in Japan. In tea-tasting contests held at Kyoto social functions of the new warrior elite of the Muromachi period, Toganoō tea was called "real tea" (*honcha*) and the products of other places "non-tea" (*hicha*). In later times, the tea of Uji, some ten miles south of Kyoto, became especially favored and remains today the preferred—and most expensive—of Japanese teas.

Tea-tasting contests were a form of *monoawase*, "comparisons of things," popular among the Japanese from at least the Heian period. The *Tale of Genji* and the *Pillow Book*, for example, refer to a variety of *monoawase* among courtiers involving the comparing or judging of things such as seashells, flowers, incense, perfume, poetry, and pictures. During the Muromachi period, many of these *monoawase*, which were essentially games, were transformed into serious pursuits described as the "way of flowers," the "way of incense," and so forth. Drawing on Buddhism, the devotees of these ways (*michi*) even regarded them as paths to religious enlightenment.

When it took form in about the late fourteenth or early fifteenth century, the tea ceremony had four principal components: rules, setting (the tea room), behavior (among host and guests), and aesthetic taste. All these components either derived from or were strongly influenced by Zen or the Zen establishment of Muromachi Japan.

The tea ceremony was born when rules were adopted to govern the preparation, serving, and drinking of tea, rules that distinguished the "ceremony" of tea drinking from the casual, everyday consumption of the beverage. The inspiration for the tea ceremony's rules were the monastic rules (J: *shingi*) that had been compiled in China to govern the daily lives of monks in Zen temples. Zen places great emphasis on mundane, quotidian acts such as scrubbing floors, cleaning latrines, or preparing tea as ways of pointing to or achieving enlightenment, and the procedures for carrying out these acts were described in detail in the *shingi* brought to Japan by Chinese Zen monks during the Kamakura period.

The tea room evolved as a variant of the *shoin*-style room, which took shape during the fifteenth and sixteenth centuries and was itself derived from the libraries (*shoin*) used by monks in Zen temples. The *shoin* became the prototypical Japanese room, having *tatami* matting, *shōji* and *fusuma* sliding doors, an alcove, asymmetrical shelves, and a low built-in desk. Among the special features that set a tea room apart from the regular *shoin* is the "crawling-in entrance" (*nijiriguchi*) and the hearth, a recessed space in the floor designed to accommodate a kettle in winter.

Behavior among the participants in the tea ceremony as it evolved in the medieval age was based on the spirit of Buddhism and especially Zen. By the late sixteenth century, when the tea ceremony reached the height of its development, tea masters were wont to say that "tea and Zen have the same flavor" (*cha-Zen ichimi*). The tea ceremony may also have been influenced at this time by the rituals of the Christian mass that were brought to Japan by European missionaries. Later, during the Tokugawa period, some tea masters based their practice of the tea ceremony on the ritual principles of Confucianism. Throughout its long history, the tea ceremony has been associated mainly with Buddhism, but many of its practices, such as those stressing simplicity, purity, and purification (e.g., the constant cleaning of utensils by the host and his or her careful selection and handling of water), derive from Shinto. Thus as a synthesis of native tastes and foreign influences, the tea ceremony evolved as a quintessentially Japanese art and ritual.

Aesthetic taste in the tea ceremony comes into play in both the construction of the tea room and the selection, handling, and display of utensils and other articles, such as scrolls and flowers, during tea gatherings. In the first form of the tea ceremony, which emerged in the Higashiyama cultural epoch of the late fifteenth century, the tea ceremony employed only "Chinese things" (*karamono*): objects of art and craft imported from China, including tea bowls and caddies, flower vases, incense burners, Song-style monochrome ink paintings (to be displayed in alcoves), and the portable stands known as *daisu* that were used to hold utensils. *Karamono* had been imported from the early medieval age, many of them by Zen monks who journeyed to China.

While the tea ceremony based on the aesthetics of *karamono* was maturing during the Higashiyama epoch, a new variation, *wabicha*, or *chanoyu* inspired by the *wabi* aesthetic, began to evolve. The person regarded as the founder of *wabicha* was Murata Shukō (or Jukō, d. 1502), who in his "Letter of the Heart" (*Kokoro no fumi*) wrote: "In pursuing this way of tea, great care should be taken to harmonize Japanese and Chinese tastes." By Japanese taste, Shukō meant taste for "Japanese things" (*wamono*), that is, for tea utensils made by Japanese artisans, especially ceramicware, that, in contrast to technically perfect Chinese things, were often crude, rough, and misshapen. These qualities did not reflect the incompetence of Japanese artisans. Rather, they were deliberately sought to satisfy the *wabi* aesthetic that, during the sixteenth century, was elevated to the highest level of taste in the tea ceremony.

Professor Haga Kōshirō has defined *wabi* as three kinds of beauty: a simple, unpretentious beauty; an imperfect, irregular beauty; and an austere, stark beauty.

According to *Nanpōroku*, Takeno Jōō (1502–1555) selected the following poem by Fujiwara no Teika to convey the *wabi* spirit in the tea ceremony:

> *Miwataseba*  Looking about
> *Hana mo momiji mo*  Neither flowers
> *Nakarikeri*  Nor scarlet leaves.
> *Ura no tomaya no*  A bayside reed hovel
> *Aki no yūgure.*  In the autumn dusk.

Jōō's student Sen no Rikyū (1522–1591), who became the greatest of all the tea masters, chose this poem by Fujiwara no Ietaka to illustrate his sense of *wabi*:

> *Hana o nomi*  To those who wait
> *Matsuran hito ni*  Only for flowers
> *Yamazato no*  Show them a spring
> *Yukima no kusa mo*  Of grass amid the snow
> *Haru o misebaya.*  In a mountain village.[1]

Professor Haga analyzes this last poem and surmises Rikyū's reasons for selecting it:

> We can imagine a mountain village in the depths of winter when the seven wild grasses of autumn have withered and the brilliant scarlet leaves have scattered. It is a lonely, cold, and desolate world, a world that is even more deeply steeped in the emptiness of non-being than that of "a bayside reed hovel in the autumn dusk." At first glance this may seem like a cold, withered world at the very extremity of *yin*. It is not, of course, simply a world of death. As proof, we have these lines: "When spring comes it turns to brightness and amid the snow fresh grass sprouts, here two, there three blades at a time." This is truly "the merest tinge of *yang* at the extremity of *yin*." Ietaka expressed this notion as a "spring of grass amid the snow." And Rikyū found in it the perfect image of *wabi*. Thus Rikyū's *wabi*, viewed externally, is impoverished, cold, and withered. At the same time, internally, it has a beauty which brims with vitality. While it may appear to be the faded beauty of the passive recluse, or the remnant beauty of old age, it has within it the beauty of non-being, latent with unlimited energy and change."[2]

*Wabicha* was created mainly by members of the wealthy merchant class of the three cities of Kyoto, Nara, and Sakai in the central provinces. Merchant tea

---

1. Varley and Kumakura, eds., *Tea in Japan*, pp. 199–200.
2. Haga Kōshirō, "The Wabi Aesthetic," in Varley and Kumakura, eds., *Tea in Japan*, p. 200.

masters from Sakai, including Jōō and Rikyū, played especially important roles during the sixteenth century in molding this form of the tea ceremony. Although *wabicha* was spiritually based on the rejection of materialism, a serious pursuit of it in fact required a great deal of money, primarily because of the enormous cost of the best tea articles. In pursuing the tea ceremony in general and *wabicha* in particular, Sakai tea masters had the double advantage of personal wealth and ready access to Chinese articles (*karamono*), since Sakai played a leading role in the trade with China during the sixteenth century. It was said that a person of this age could not be considered a true tea master (*meijin*) unless he owned at least one "famous [tea] article" (*meibutsu*)—that is, a tea article, whether Chinese or Japanese, that was judged to be of superior quality. With their wealth and connections, Sakai tea masters could compete even with the daimyo, the military lords of the country, in the acquisition of "famous articles."

When Oda Nobunaga (1534–1582) entered Kyoto in 1568 and began the military campaigning that unified Japan before the end of the century, he used the tea ceremony as one means to ritually legitimize his rule. Conducting a "hunt for famous tea articles" (*meibutsu gari*), he amassed, through both purchase and confiscation, the largest collection of tea articles in the land. In addition, he took into his employ the three leading tea masters of Sakai, the youngest of whom was Sen no Rikyū. By displaying his vast collection of "famous articles" and his Sakai tea masters, Nobunaga sought to confirm his right to rule in cultural (*bun*) as well as military (*bu*) terms.

When Nobunaga was assassinated in 1582, the job of unification was completed by his former lieutenant, Toyotomi Hideyoshi (1536–1598). Displaying even greater enthusiasm for the tea ceremony than Nobunaga had, Hideyoshi took possession of both his predecessor's *meibutsu* collection and his tea masters, and it was in the service of Hideyoshi that Rikyū rose to become Japan's foremost arbiter of taste and man of culture. Rikyū also became a confidant of Hideyoshi and came to exercise great political influence. Indeed, his involvement in the affairs of Hideyoshi's government may have contributed to his downfall. Although historians still dispute the reason or reasons, Hideyoshi ordered Rikyu to commit suicide in 1591. Later apotheosized as a god of the tea ceremony, Sen no Rikyū had brought the way of tea to its highest development.

In cultural history, Rikyū's age is known as the Momoyama epoch. It was a heroic time, witnessing the rise of the great warlords who strode across the country trying to unify it. Grandeur and show, including the erection of lofty castles and the mass display of tea articles, were the hallmarks of the epoch. In contrast to the monochromatic and quietistic art of the medieval age, Momoyama painting was dynamic and bursting with brilliant colors, especially gold. Hideyoshi, the parvenu hegemon and consummate showman of the age, had a portable, gilded tea room constructed for his use, and he furnished it with gold-plated utensils.

But Hideyoshi also had a rustic tea room, fashioned like a hut in a mountain village (*yamazato*), in which he practiced the subtleties of *wabicha* with Rikyū. Hideyoshi's two tea rooms, the rustic and the golden, symbolized the extremes of Momoyama taste, one epitomizing the highest spiritual and aesthetic values of the medieval age and the other heralding what scholars call the early modern age. It was an exciting time in Japanese history, and the tea ceremony and its masters, led by Sen no Rikyū, played central roles in the cultural—and also political—events that determined the direction that the country would take.

### DRINK TEA AND PROLONG LIFE

From its earliest use in China, tea was appreciated probably above all for its medicinal value, and the tradition of tea as good "medicine" accompanied the beverage on its transmission to Japan in the early Heian period (although, as noted, the Heian courtiers also very much esteemed tea as a feature of Chinese higher culture). When the Zen monk Yōsai reintroduced tea to Japan in the late twelfth century, at the beginning of the medieval age, he did so primarily to promote good health. Referring to "these degenerate times" (i.e., the age of *mappō*), Yōsai observed that "man has gradually declined and grown weaker, so that his four bodily components and five organs have degenerated." Of the five organs, the heart is "sovereign": its condition determines the well-being of all the organs. And because the heart craves the bitter taste found in tea, drinking it will "put the heart in order and dispel all illness." Drinking tea, a stimulant, was also an excellent means for Zen monks and others to fight drowsiness during meditation. Still another use for tea was as a cure for hangover, as Yōsai publicly demonstrated during a visit to Kamakura, when he provided relief for the shogun Sanetomo the morning after one of Sanetomo's frequent drinking bouts.

Tea is the most wonderful medicine for nourishing one's health; it is the secret of long life. On the hillsides it grows up as the spirit of the soil. Those who pick and use it are certain to attain a great age. India and China both value it highly, and in the past our country too once showed a great liking for tea. Now as then it possesses the same rare qualities, and we should make wider use of it.

In the past, it is said, man was coeval with Heaven, but in recent times man has gradually declined and grown weaker, so that his four bodily components and five organs have degenerated. For this reason even when acupuncture and moxa cautery are resorted to, the results are often fatal, and treatment at hot springs fails to have any effect. So those who are given to these methods of treatment will become steadily weaker until death overtakes them, a prospect which can only be dreaded. If these traditional methods of healing are employed without any modification on patients today, scarcely any relief can be expected.

Of all the things which Heaven has created, man is the most noble. To preserve one's life so as to make the most of one's allotted span is prudent and proper [considering the high value of human life]. The basis of preserving life is the cultivation of health, and the secret of health lies in the well-being of the five organs. Among these five the heart is sovereign, and to build up the heart the drinking of tea is the finest method. . . .

In regard to the Five Tastes: acid foods include oranges, lemons, and other citrus fruits; pungent foods include onions, garlic, and peppers; sweets include sugar, etc. (all foods are sweet by nature); bitter foods include tea, herb teas, etc.; salty foods include salt, etc.

The heart is the sovereign of the five organs, tea is the chief of bitter foods, and bitter is the chief of the tastes. For this reason the heart loves bitter things, and when it is doing well all the other organs are properly regulated. If one has eye trouble, something is wrong with the liver, and acid medicine will cure it. If one has ear trouble, something is wrong with the kidney, and salty medicine will cure it. [And so forth, running through the preceding table of correspondences.] When, however, the whole body feels weak, devitalized, and depressed, it is a sign that the heart is ailing. Drink lots of tea, and one's energy and spirits will be restored to full strength.

[*Kissa yōjōki*, pp. 899–901; PV]

### MURATA SHUKŌ: "LETTER OF THE HEART"

Murata Shukō (or Jukō), the late-fifteenth-century tea master from the merchant class of Nara, occupies a lofty position in tea history as the putative founder of the *wabicha* form of the tea ceremony. Yet we know little about Shukō. On the basis of the records that have come down to us, his reputation is based almost entirely on the brief "Letter of the Heart" (*Kokoro no fumi*), which he wrote to a disciple, the petty daimyo Furuichi Chōin. Terse and in places difficult to interpret, the letter is especially remembered, as noted, for its injunction "to harmonize Japanese and Chinese tastes"—that is, to develop an aesthetic appreciation for "Japanese things" (*wamono*) as well as "Chinese things" (*karamono*). To illustrate Japanese taste, Shukō speaks of the "cold," "withered," and "emaciated," using terms from the aesthetic vocabulary of the medieval age that appear to have been introduced to the tea ceremony (especially *wabicha*) from linked verse (*renga*) poetry. Shukō is concerned that people inexperienced in the tea ceremony will become so enamored of these qualities, which are the hallmarks of Bizen and Shigaraki ceramicware, that they will ignore others and thus fail to *harmonize* Japanese and Chinese tastes. Reflecting the influence of Buddhism on the tea ceremony, Shukō also speaks of the dangers of egotistical self-assertion and attachment. Warning practitioners of the tea ceremony to avoid these "faults," he enjoins them to pursue mastery of the way of tea with humility and sensitive awareness of their own limitations.

The worst faults in this way of tea are self-assertion and attachment. To envy the skilled and look down upon those seeking to learn is reprehensible in the extreme. You should approach the skilled to learn from them, conscious of your own limitations, and do your best to nurture those who are just beginning.

In pursuing this way of tea, great care should be taken to harmonize Japanese and Chinese tastes. Mark these words carefully and do not be negligent.

Nowadays those who are inexperienced speak of the "cold" and "withered" and covet Bizen and Shigaraki ware. Though lacking the recognition of others, they assume airs of being knowledgeable and experienced. This is unspeakably bad. "Withered" means to possess good utensils and understand their qualities thoroughly, and thus to attain knowledge and experience within the core of one's heart. What one does thereafter will manifest the "cold" and "emaciated," and will have the power to move. (One not in a position to appraise and acquire fine utensils should not vie with others in collecting them, but should use what one has.)

However cultivated one's manner, a painful self-awareness of one's shortcomings is crucial. Remember that self-assertion and attachment are obstructions. Yet the way is also unattainable if there is no self-esteem at all. A dictum of the Way states: "Become heart's master, not heart mastered"—the words of an ancient.

[Adapted from Hirota, *Wind in the Pines*, p. 198; PV]

THE SPIRITUAL BASIS OF THE TEA CEREMONY

In these passages, Rikyū speaks of the tea ceremony as an almost purely spiritual exercise. Material values are ignored, if not rejected, and the path to Buddhist enlightenment seems to be opened by the simple, mundane acts of preparing, serving, and drinking tea. These passages, and others in *Nanpōroku*, express an ideal of tea sought especially in the practice of *wabicha*. But most of *Nanpōroku* is a detailed analysis of the complexities of the tea ceremony, with more than a little attention given to the quest for and employment of fine tea articles. In reality, the tea ceremony has almost always been strongly governed by the tension between art and aesthetics (having and using fine articles), on the one hand, and the religious rejection of materialism, on the other.

Once when Rikyū had been speaking of the tea ceremony at Shūun-an,[3] I asked, "You often remark that, although the tea ceremony has its roots in the formal tea employing the *daisu* stand, when considering the deeper attainment of its spirit, nothing surpasses the informal tea held in a small room. Why should this be so?"

Rikyū responded: "The tea ceremony of the small room is above all a matter of performing practice and attaining realization in accord with the Buddhist path. To delight in the refined splendor of a dwelling or the taste of delicacies belongs to worldly life. There is shelter enough when the roof does not leak,

---

3. A hermitage at Nanshūji Temple in Sakai.

food enough when it staves off hunger. This is the Buddhist teaching and the fundamental meaning of the tea ceremony. We draw water, gather firewood, boil the water, and make tea. We then offer it to the Buddha, serve it to others, and drink ourselves. We arrange flowers and burn incense. In all of this, we model ourselves after acts of the Buddha and the past masters. Beyond this, you must come to your own understanding." . . .

Someone once asked Rikyū to explain the hearth and the brazier, revealing the proper bearing of the spirit and the crucial points in performing tea in summer and winter. Rikyū replied: "In summer, impart a sense of deep coolness, in winter, a feeling of warmth; lay the charcoal so that it heats the water, prepare the tea so that it is pleasing—these are all the secrets." Dissatisfied with this answer, the man remarked, "That is something everyone knows." Then Rikyū said, "If so, try performing in accord with what I have stated. I will be your guest, and perhaps become your student."

[*Nanpōroku*, in Hirota, *Wind in the Pines*, pp. 217, 223; PV]

## Chapter 55

### WOMEN'S EDUCATION

In the formal sense of the term "education" as schooling through a defined curriculum such as existed in the Confucian College in Nara or the kind of instruction designed by Saichō for his monks on Mount Hiei or by Kūkai for his Academy of Arts and Sciences, there was no formal education for women in early Japan. Nevertheless, women clearly did learn enough to take a prominent part in the life of the country, and especially in its cultural life. Great writers like Murasaki Shikibu and Sei Shōnagon were highly literate, and the court life of Nara and Heian Japan, in which literary culture figured so prominently, could not have been so brilliant had it not been for the participation of women at the highest levels.

Women obviously had access to learning in the home and at court, just as women did in Han and Tang China, even though they were somewhat disadvantaged in its pursuit. Especially among the upper classes with the leisure to devote to the cultural refinements they so prized, women had available not only a considerable body of classical literature but also some of the same primers and texts as the Han and Tang Chinese: the *Classic of Filiality* (Ch: *Xiao jing*) and the *Admonitions for Women* (Ch: *Nüjie*) of Ban Zhao, the *Household Instructions of the Yan Family* (Ch: *Yan-shi jiaxun*), the *Analects for Women* (Ch: *Nü lunyu*), and *The Learning Quest* (Ch: *Meng qiu*).[1]

---

1. See chaps. 18 and 23.

In this section we present two early Japanese texts for the edification of women in Buddhism. They were specifically intended for a female audience and spoke to the situation and condition in which women found themselves. Nevertheless, instead of emphasizing the social roles of women or addressing their specific problems or potentialities, these works propose a way of spirituality common to men and women (the one exception being the reference to the particular moral and spiritual failings of women as seen in traditional Buddhism). The fundamental spiritual problems addressed in these writings are those of all humankind, and most of the guidance offered would apply equally well to men.

## KEISEI: *A COMPANION IN SOLITUDE* (*KANKYO NO TOMO*)

A *Companion in Solitude* is believed to have been written in 1222 by the monk Keisei (1189–1268), of the Fujiwara Kujō branch, whose religious associations were with Tendai esotericism and who was a friend of the Kegon monk Myōe (chap. 48). The *Companion* is a collection of stories written for a high-ranking court lady for her spiritual edification, moving from accounts of prominent monks to ones of ordinary monks and laymen and then, down the scale, to women.

The stories excerpted here reveal the ambivalence of Mahāyāna Buddhism and Japanese religiosity with regard to the life of the senses and human emotions. In the first story, such attachments are seen as at once sinful and compelling in their emotional appeal, reflecting the same ambivalence in Heian literature. From this point of view, even the impurities traditionally attached to womanhood can be seen, in the light of the equation of Nirvana and Samsara, as instruments of salvation.

## About the Religious Awakening of the Nun Who Lived in the Mountains of Tsu Province

Long ago there was a nun who built herself a rough straw hut in the depths of the mountains in Tsu province. She abstained from eating the five cereals, and would pluck the seeds from a yew tree and use them for making her food. . . . The nun had a pale complexion and her appearance had declined to such an extent that it would be impossible to know whether she was good-looking or ugly.

A certain person met her by chance and asked her why she was living in such a place. She replied, "When I was at the height of my youth, I lost my husband. After completing the religious services of the forty-ninth day,[2] I shaved my head and entered the mountains. I have never returned to my village since.

---

2. The period after death and before rebirth in a new life, believed to last for forty-nine days, was known as *chūin*, or the intermediate state between death and the next life.

I loved my husband deeply, but when he died so suddenly I realized that the relationship between man and wife is but ephemeral, and so I became what I am today. I have several children. I owned a great deal of land and other possessions. Realizing, however, that all these are merely companions of one's dreams, I cast them all away." . . .

A woman's nature is such that whether of high rank or low birth, she pins her hopes on all sorts of things, but in the end is unable to realize her expectations. The depth of this lady's heart that made her decide to receive the tonsure was, by contrast, truly profound.

In truth we hear of many instances of couples who want to grow old together, pledging that they would be buried in the same grave and praying that they may be together again in the next world. Their acts are full of expectations for the future, but in fact these constitute a deep crime.[3] . . .

Throughout their lives people constantly think about love. Comparing their love to the flames of Mt. Fuji,[4] they display a heart that is tortured by love. How they must suffer during their lives! The sorrow of those who are endowed with great sensitivity must become greater and deeper, depending on the time and situation they are in. . . .

Then again there was the case of the person who compared his life with the ephemeral dew and said that he would gladly exchange it for one meeting with his lover. The bond that tied these lovers must have been truly hard to bear. These relationships are at once pitiable and shamelessly unmindful of the Buddha's Dharma.

[Pandey, "Women, Sexuality, and Enlightenment," pp. 335–337]

### MUJŪ ICHIEN: *MIRROR FOR WOMEN*

*Mirror for Women* was written in 1300 by Mujū Ichien (1226–1312), a monk with broad theoretical interests who ultimately allied himself with Rinzai Zen's Enni Ben'en (Shōichi, 1202–1280), founder of the Tōfukuji in Kyoto. In 1262, he restored the Chōboji in Miya (now Nagoya), where he lived until his death a half century later. Here he wrote a noteworthy collection of Buddhist "tales" (*setsuwa*), *Sand and Pebbles* (*Shasekishū*, 1279–1283), the *Mirror for Women, Collection of Sacred Assets* (*Shōzaishū*, 1299), and *Casual Digressions* (*Zōtanshū*, 1305). The prominent role of women in the early days of the Chōboji and their continuing support during Mujū's tenure there may help explain his concern for women's salvation.

Nevertheless, although Mujū often refers to the types of religious devotionalism popular among women (especially Amida and the Pure Land), for the most part his

---

3. *Tsumi fukaku*, or deeply sinful, as a violation of Buddhist precepts.
4. The fire and smoke that rose from Mount Fuji were popular symbols of the ardor and passion of a person in love.

argument is addressed to the human condition in general, not in ways that are gender specific. He quickly relativizes all moral, social, and cultural values, which become insignificant in comparison to the fundamental need to detach oneself from all worldly, even human, concerns and apply oneself to the "one great life and death matter": to rise beyond suffering and illusion to realize one's inherent Buddha-nature.

We say that a man is wise who takes care of himself, looks after others, visits his parents' birthplace, and acts to requite the benefits which have accrued to him over several lifetimes. The household of a man who accumulates good deeds prospers, while the family of one who cultivates wickedness is destroyed. When a man has committed no evil, why should he worry? They tell of men who spend a considerable portion of their wealth performing acts of merit in the discharge of filial obligations toward parents, teachers, and superiors. Nevertheless, only a seventh part of the merit redounds to the advantage of the deceased, while six-sevenths benefits the doer of the action. A man may neglect the Buddha's Law himself from the mistaken notion that he has descendants who will pray for his deliverance. But not to seek the Way of the Buddha oneself is foolishness indeed. . . .

Our actions may be of such merit as to help the blessed spirits of parents, teachers, and superiors, the objects of our solicitude. But although we may transform their grave crimes into minor ones or change a life of misfortune to happiness, our own actions cannot become the infallible road to birth in the Pure Land for either donor or recipient. . . .

Thus one's own practice of the *nembutsu* results in one's own birth in the Pure Land rather than another's. Nor are we to imagine that having another person call upon the name of Buddha or recite the scriptures can be a direct cause of our own birth in the Pure Land and attainment of Buddhahood. . . .

The mind of the sage is completely untroubled by the problem of good and bad Karma, nor is he vexed by the cleanness or impurity of the water in the great ocean [i.e., he is tolerant of all men and conditions]. It is as though he does not mind the impurity of the land. Within the general defilement, he employs delusion to attain what is of primary importance. . . .

Many serious instances of the sins of women, among the unregenerate who are all deluded, are cited in sacred scriptures and commentaries. Because of their abundance, there is no time to discuss these sins in detail. The Preceptor Daoxuan[5] said, "Basically these are the seven grave vices of women. First of all, like the myriad rivulets flowing into the sea, they have no compunction about arousing sexual desire in men. Secondly, when we observe women in a house,

---

5. Daoxuan (J: Dōsen, 596–667) is noted for his codification of monastic rules. Mujū's Japanese rendering of these seven grave vices is from *Rules to Purify Mind and Maintain Insight* (*Jing xin jie guan fa*, TD 45, no. 1893:1893).

we see that their jealous disposition is never idle. Friendly in speech, in their hearts is malice; with no thoughts for others, they are concerned only with their own affairs. Thirdly, on account of a disposition prone to deceit, they smile at a man even before he has said anything. In their speech, they say that they empathize, while in their hearts they are distant and cherish thoughts of envy. A person who faces you but whose thoughts look the other way is said to be prone to deceit. Fourthly, neglecting their religious practices and concentrating on how they may deck themselves with fine clothes, they think of nothing but their appearance and desire for the sensual attentions of others. Their hearts are attached to desire without regard to whether the object of their attention is closely related or distant. Fifthly, they take deceit as their guide and their honest words are few. They often vow to bring evil to others without fearing that they are piling up sins for themselves. Sixthly, burning themselves in the fires of desire, they have no shame toward others. Their hearts deluded, they fear not the tip of the sword; as though drunk, they know no shame. Seventh, their bodies are forever unclean, with frequent menstrual discharges. Seeing that both pregnancy and childbirth are both foul and the afterbirth unclean, the evil demons vie for possession while the good deities depart. The foolish find these things attractive, but the wise are repelled." . . .

The *Calming and Contemplation*[6] says: "The Great Sages in their wanderings all sought the Law without respect to the source. The youth of the Himalayas[7] took half a verse from an *asura*, and Indra venerated an animal, taking it as his teacher." Just as their resolve to practice the Buddha's teachings was so great, we too should take advantage of our youth and not neglect religious practice. It will do us no good to regret having ignored the One Great Matter and to have vainly passed our span of life in the karma of transmigration. To place the obsessions of the deluded mind before all else is not to know how to distinguish jewels from seaweed.

I do not care about the laughter of those who will come later and read this. Nor does it benefit me at all that I have collected together these leaves of words like free-floating grasses, diverting myself with a water-soaked reed which traces my thoughts as they ripple through my mind. But should a woman make these precepts her constant companion [as she would a mirror], she will show herself to be a person of sensibility, a follower of the Way. And so I give this work the title, *Mirror for Women*.

[Morrell, "Mirror for Women," pp. 51–75]

---

6. *Maka shikan*, chap. 4B.
7. That is, Gautama.

## Chapter 56

# LAW AND PRECEPTS FOR THE WARRIOR HOUSES

The Kamakura shogunate is perhaps best remembered in history as a regime of law and justice, although for most of its first half century it had no law of its own with which to dispense justice. When the regime was founded in 1185, it was administered autocratically by its leader, Minamoto Yoritomo, the lord of Kamakura, who made no significant effort to establish new laws for warrior society but, rather, accepted in general the jurisdiction of the country's two existing bodies of law: the law of the imperial court of Kyoto and the customary law compiled by the independent estates (*shōen*) that by this time controlled most of Japan's agricultural lands.

As noted in earlier chapters, after Yoritomo's death in 1199, a power struggle lasting several decades ensued in Kamakura that was finally won by the Hōjō, who were related to Yoritomo by marriage. By establishing the office of shogunal regent (*shikken*), the Hōjō became the real rulers of the young warrior government under figurehead shoguns (first Fujiwara and, later, imperial princes). In 1221 in a brief clash of arms, the Hōjō put down an attempt by the retired emperor Go-Toba to overthrow the shogunate (discussed in chap. 49). Victorious in this clash, which was known as the Jōkyū war, the Hōjō were able to assert Kamakura rule over the country far more extensively than before.

In 1224, the Hōjō established the Council of State (Hyōjōshū), which under their leadership became the shogunate's principal decision-making body. Through this council, assembly rule superseded the one-man governance of Yoritomo, the shogunate's founder. In 1232, Hōjō Yasutoki (1193–1242), generally regarded as the finest of the shogunal regents, issued a document known as the Jōei Code,[1] comprising fifty-one articles, that was intended as a guide for the conduct of the Council of State but that also became the starting point for the development of warrior law, distinct from both court law and estate law. The Jōei Code is not a formal set of laws. Rather, it establishes certain rules, identifies categories of legal concern, and provides standards for warrior behavior. Yasutoki clearly intended the code to be only a starting point for the creation of warrior law, stating that if anything were found to be missing from it, the code should be amended through the addition of supplementary articles (*tsuikahō*).

## THE JŌEI CODE

The fifty-one articles of the Jōei Code deal with a broad range of topics, including the granting and holding of land, the duties of shogunate officials, the bestowal and receipt of estate property, the rights of inheritance, and the apprehension and punishment of criminals. The following is a sampling of these articles, chosen to illustrate some of the distinctive features of the new warrior law promulgated by the Kamakura shogunate. Among the distinctive features are the limitations placed on the duties and rights of the shogunate's own principal officers in the provinces and estates, that is, the constables and stewards (articles 3 and 5); the recognition of the continuing, independent jurisdictions of both court-appointed officials (governors) and estate holders (article 6); and the granting and holding of land and adoption of heirs by women (articles 18, 21, and 23). The articles dealing with women are particularly interesting because they show that women enjoyed considerable rights of ownership and privileges of family membership in Kamakura warrior society based on the practice of divided inheritance, that is, the division of estate property to all offspring, female as well as male. But within a century or so, most of these rights and privileges were lost, as warrior society shifted to the practice of single inheritance or the exclusive inheritance of both economic wealth and political authority by the male successor to a family's headship.

Article 1. The shrines of the gods must be kept in repair; and their worship performed with the greatest attention. . . .

Article 2. Temples and pagodas must be kept in repair and the Buddhist services diligently celebrated. . . .

---

1. Jōei was a period that lasted only one year (1232). The formal name of the Jōei Code is Goseibai shikimoku (Formulary of Adjudications).

Article 3. Concerning the duties of the constables (*shugo*) in the provinces. It was decided in the time of Lord Yoritomo[2] that these duties should be: 1. providing for guard duty at the imperial capital [Kyoto]; 2. suppressing rebellions; and 3. tracking down and apprehending murderers. But of late, deputies (*daikan*) of the constables have been dispatched to districts and towns (*gunkō*), where they have imposed levies. Although not provincial governors (*kokushi*), they have interfered in the provinces' administration. Although not stewards (*jitō*), they have coveted profits from the land. Such behavior is utterly unprincipled. . . .

Article 5. Concerning the withholding by a steward (*jitō*) of the assessed amount of the annual rent (*nengu*). If a complaint is submitted to the central proprietor (*honjo*) of an estate that the annual rent has been withheld by a steward, an accounting will be made at once and the complainant will receive a certificate specifying the balance that may be due him. . . .

Article 6. Governors of the provinces and estate holders (*ryōke*) may continue to exercise their usual jurisdiction without reference to the Kantō [i.e., the Kamakura shogunate]. . . .

Article 11. Whether, because of a husband's crime, the landholding of a wife should be confiscated or not. In the case of serious crimes, such as rebellion and murder, as well as banditry, piracy, night attacks and burglary, the husband's guilt will extend also to the wife. But if, as the result of a sudden dispute, the husband wounds or kills someone, the wife will not be held responsible. . . .

Article 18. Whether or not parents, having given a daughter a holding in land, may reclaim it because of a later falling out with the daughter. Legal scholars have held that, although sons and daughters differ in gender, they are equal in terms of the benefits bestowed upon them by their parents. Hence, a gift to a daughter should be as irrevocable as one to a son. But if a gift to a daughter were irrevocable, she might rely upon that fact and not scruple to go against her filial duties. Parents therefore must, when thinking of bestowing a gift of land on a daughter, consider whether or not there might later occur a dispute between them and the daughter. . . .

Article 21. Whether or not a wife,[3] having received a grant of land from her husband, can retain that grant after divorce. If the wife has been rejected because of a serious transgression, she will not be allowed to retain the grant even if she possesses written documentation for it from an earlier time. But if the wife has been virtuous and innocent of any fault and was discarded by the husband in favor of something new, then the grant given her cannot be revoked. . . .

---

2. Here and elsewhere in the Jōei Code, Yoritomo is referred to as "Great General of the Right (*utaishō*)," which is an abbreviation of the highest court title he held, *ukon'e taishō*.

3. It states here "wife or concubine," but the remainder of the article refers only to "wife."

Article 23. Concerning the adoption of heirs by women. The intent of earlier law was not to allow adoption by women. But from the time of Lord Yoritomo to the present day it has been a fixed rule to allow a childless woman to bequeath her land to an adopted child. . . .

[Adapted from Hall, "Japanese Feudal Law," pp. 37–45; PV]

## THE LAW OF THE MUROMACHI SHOGUNATE

When Ashikaga Takauji overthrew the government of Emperor Go-Daigo's Kenmu Restoration in 1336 and established the Muromachi shogunate (chap. 50), he faced formidable problems. Go-Daigo himself fled to Yoshino in the mountainous region south of Kyoto, proclaimed that he was still the rightful emperor, and founded what came to be known in history as the Southern Court. Takauji and his followers were accordingly obliged to contend not only with the disorder and dislocations caused by the recent fighting against the Restoration government but also with a new, rival regime in the Southern Court whose warrior supporters launched a war against them that lasted for more than half a century (until 1392).

One of Takauji's first concerns was where to place the seat of his shogunate. Although he finally decided on Kyoto because of the geographical advantages it offered in fighting the Southern Court, he apparently passed over Kamakura, the capital of the previous military regime, only with great reluctance. As observed by Nikaidō Ze'en, head of a group of legal scholars and others whom Takauji consulted about policies and principles of governance, Kamakura had been a site of both glory and disgrace for the country's military. It was a site of glory when Yoritomo established the first shogunate there and when Hōjō Yoshitoki "seized the empire during the Jōkyōū era" (i.e., foiled the former emperor Go-Toba's "rebellion" against the Kamakura shogunate in 1221), but it was a site of disgrace when the later Hōjō regents "accumulated evil unceasingly by their arrogance and selfish desires" and the shogunate had to be destroyed. In Ze'en's thinking, what mattered most was how a government was run and not the location of its seat; therefore Kyoto would serve as well as Kamakura. In his words, "The rise and fall of a capital . . . depends on the quality of a government. . . . [M]an's misfortune is not to be found in the bad luck of his dwelling place."[4]

Ze'en and seven others presented to Takauji the Kenmu Code (Kenmu *shiki-moku*), a document in seventeen articles that Ze'en called an "opinion" to guide the shogun in rule. The decision to have the code divided into seventeen articles was clearly made with Prince Shōtoku's famous Seventeen-Article Constitution in mind, and indeed, the Kenmu Code bears some similarity to that constitution. Both are sets of maxims or principles for proper rule; but whereas the

---

4. Grossberg and Kanamoto, trans. and eds., *The Laws of the Muromachi Bakufu*, p. 15.

constitution, which is derived almost entirely from Confucian thought, offers very general, universalistic principles, the Kenmu Code is much more specific in applying these or similar principles to the particular problems of the disordered and dangerous time in which it was composed. Thus, for example, article 1 of the code calls for "the need for enforcing frugality" (whereas article V of the constitution speaks about "ceasing from gluttony and abandoning covetous desires") and then refers immediately to specific "extravagance[s] and excess[es]" that have recently become fashionable, such as "the wearing of twill damask and brocade, ornamental silver swords and elegant attire to dazzle the eyes."

The Kenmu Code served the same historical role for Muromachi warrior law that the Jōei Code served for Kamakura warrior law, becoming the starting point for the creation of new laws through "supplementary articles." Thus, as during Kamakura times, the judgments or decisions made in cases brought before the courts of the Muromachi shogunate became laws and were added as supplements to the Kenmu Code.[5] There are more than five hundred of these supplementary articles.

### THE KENMU CODE

A number of the articles in the Kenmu Code seem to address the particular problems of Kyoto in 1336 as the city swelled in size with the influx of warriors and others that accompanied the founding of the Muromachi shogunate. This appears clearly to be the case, for example, in articles 1 through 3, which call for the control of "extravagance and excess," "drinking in crowds and carousing," "gambling and sporting with women," and general lawlessness, including "breaking into buildings in broad daylight, burglary at night, [and] murder." No doubt these problems could also be found elsewhere in Japan, but we know from other records of the time that, as described in the Kenmu Code, they were primarily the problems of Kyoto, now the seat of both the imperial court and the shogunate.

Prince Shōtoku's Seventeen-Article Constitution is echoed in several articles of the Kenmu Code (e.g., articles 1 and 13, which discuss frugality and decorum), and article 15 about "hearing suits brought by poor and weak vassals" reminds us of Hōjō Yasutoki's wish, expressed in a letter to his brother as the Jōei Code was being compiled, to prevent the powerful and the socially elite from winning cases against those of lesser social standing through bribery, favoritism, and the like.

Two other points of note in the code are the calls to (1) select men of political ability to be constables (article 7) and (2) reward those who are upright and loyal (article 14). We may wonder whether much heed was actually paid to selecting constables from among men of ability, since the constable positions continued to be held

---

5. See ibid., p. 8, for a discussion of how suits were handled, according to category, by various organs of the Muromachi shogunate.

almost exclusively by men on the basis of birth into powerful families. But the call to reward warriors who are upright and loyal is worth noting because the Kenmu Code's precursor, the Jōei Code—which decrees what warriors should or should not do—says almost nothing about ethical behavior per se. In the late fifteenth and sixteenth centuries, as we will see, loyalty in particular becomes a central issue in the laws and precepts of that age's warrior chieftains.

Article 1. The need for enforcing frugality. Recently, fashion has been used as an excuse to indulge in extravagance and excess, such as the wearing of twill damask and brocade, ornamental silver swords and elegant attire to dazzle the eyes. This has become a mania. While the rich swell with pride, the poor are ashamed because they cannot match them. This is the major reason for the poverty of the population, and it must be severely suppressed.

Article 2. The need for suppressing drinking in crowds and carousing. As stated in the imperial supplementary laws, these must be strictly controlled. This also applies to gambling and to excessive sporting with women. In addition, large wagers are made at tea parties and linked-verse meetings, and incalculable sums of money are lost in this way.

Article 3. The need for suppressing lawlessness. Breaking into buildings in broad daylight, burglary at night, murder and highway robbery cause the cry for help to be heard incessantly. The shogun must take strenuous measures against these crimes.

Article 4. The need for prohibiting the commandeering of private houses [by warriors].

Article 5. The need for returning vacant lots in Kyoto to their former owners. . . .

Article 6. The need for reviving mutual financing associations and moneylenders. . . .

Article 7. The need for selecting men of political ability to fill the posts of constable (*shugo*) in the provinces. Constables are presently appointed on the basis of accumulated military service, and award lands are granted to them from among the estates (*shōen*). The office of constable is equivalent to the old office of provincial governor, and since the peace of the provinces depends on this office, stable rule for the people will be realized if the most able men are appointed.

Article 8. The need for preventing powerful courtiers, as well as women and Zen priests, from meddling [in government].

Article 9. The need for admonishing official negligence, and for selecting officials carefully. . . .

Article 10. The need for firmly prohibiting bribery. . . .

Article 11. The need for returning gifts which have been presented to the shogun and members of his court.

Article 12. The need for selecting the shogun's personal bodyguard. . . .

Article 13. The need for emphasizing decorum. An overriding concern for etiquette and decorum is most important for ruling the country. The lord must observe his own proper conduct and his vassal his own. High and low must each bear in mind their proper station, and strenuously observe decorum in both speech and conduct.

Article 14. The need for granting special rewards to those who have reputations for uprightness and loyalty. This is the way of advancing men of quality and removing those who are harmful. The shogun must bestow special praise in such cases.

Article 15. The need for hearing suits brought by poor and weak vassals. The government of Yao and Shun considered this very important. As it is written [in the *Classic of Documents*], ordinary people treat such petitions lightly, but sages treat them as important. The shogun must pay special attention to this, and show compassion for his poor vassals. His most important duty is to listen to their petitions.

Article 16. The need for listening to or rejecting suits presented by temples and shrines, depending on the merits of the cases. . . .

Article 17. The need for establishing fixed days and hours for judging suits. There is nothing which people complain of more than delays [in processing their suits]. But one must not neglect searching for the truth simply in order to speed up the procedure. The shogun must hand down his decision so that there is no cause for complaint either with respect to speed or thoroughness of the investigation.

> [Adapted from Grossberg and Kanamoto, trans. and eds., *The Laws of the Muromachi Bakufu*, pp. 16–21; PV]

# THE LAW OF THE WARRIOR HOUSES IN THE AGE OF WAR IN THE PROVINCES

Even at its peak in the late fourteenth and early fifteenth centuries, the Muromachi shogunate presided over only a loose territorial hegemony based on a balance of power between the shogun and those chieftains who held appointment to the office of constable. (One constable was appointed to each province, but some chieftains held more than one constableship.) The hegemony, moreover, did not extend over the entire country. Northern Honshu and the island of Kyushu, for example, were largely beyond the shogunate's effective control, and even the eastern provinces of the Kantō, administered by a rival branch of the Ashikaga family, frequently resisted shogunate rule.

The shogunate's hegemony weakened steadily from about the fifth decade of the fifteenth century as some leading constable families floundered and the shogunate itself suffered from weak leadership and internal conflict. In 1467, a succession dispute within the Ashikaga family provoked a decade-long war (the Ōnin War, 1467–1477), fought largely in Kyoto, that not only destroyed most of that venerable city but also shattered the shogunate's hegemony and plunged the country into a century of war and disorder known as the Age of War in the Provinces (Sengoku, 1478–1568).

Almost all the pre–Ōnin War constable families were overthrown or declined during and in the aftermath of the war, and the shogunate itself was reduced to near impotence as a central government. Beginning about the end of the fifteenth century, a new class of territorial rulers emerged in the provinces whom historians call Sengoku lords (daimyo). Many of these daimyo held the title of constable, although it was not essential to their rulership. For the most part, they were military commanders who carved out and defended their domains by their own military might and administered the domains as totally independent entities.

Living in a brutal age when "might made right," the Sengoku daimyo assembled armies of vastly greater size—up to fifty thousand or more—than any seen before in Japanese history. Although concerned first and foremost with military power, the daimyo also pursued policies—such as the encouragement of greater agricultural yields, the development of commerce, and the exploitation of mining resources—that were part of their overall endeavors to enrich their domains in every way possible.

Among the most important steps taken by the Sengoku daimyo to formalize control over their domains and enhance their personal rule was the compilation of legal formularies or house codes (kahō). Although they were called "house" codes, the kahō, ten of which have come down to us,[6] are not simply sets of rules for the daimyo's own houses. Rather, they prescribe law for all the warrior houses and for the general populace as well. Their articles deal with a wide range of matters, including relations between the daimyo and his vassals and among vassals, land disputes, judicial procedures, the payment and nonpayment of taxes, borrowing and lending, crime and the punishment of criminals, intercourse with other domains, and drinking and gambling. The great majority of the articles in the house codes, however, concern relations between the daimyo and his vassals, and it is to these that we turn next.

As far as relations with his vassals were concerned, a daimyo's main purpose in promulgating a house code was to assert his authority over them. As noted, the Sengoku daimyo were far more powerful and independent territorial rulers than the pre–Ōnin War constables. But they lived in a precarious and harsh age, and they could be—and not infrequently were—overthrown either in war with rival daimyo or through internal treachery and rebellion by vassals and even kin. Yet despite these dangers, the daimyo display through their house codes an unusually forceful authoritarianism toward their vassals that at least some may in fact have had difficulty enforcing. A possible explanation for this authoritarianism is that the daimyo were, in a sense, gamblers. The strict control of vassals was a matter of life and death for them; hence, they either

---

6. The ten are the codes of the Sagara, Ōuchi, Imagawa, Date, Takeda, Yūki, Rokkaku, Miyoshi, Chōsokabe, and Kikkawa houses.

enforced strong rules for vassals or, if unable to do so, probably did not long survive as daimyo.

At the heart of the problem of controlling vassals was the nature of honor in warrior society. The war tales, discussed in chapter 50, contain countless examples of vassals motivated by a self-abnegating loyalty that leads them to forfeit their lives without hesitation in the service of their lords. Such loyalty, however, was an ideal to which probably few actually subscribed. But if the loyalty of some, if not most, warriors toward their lords had its limitation, all seem to have been committed without reservation to maintaining their personal honor. Indeed, the records strongly suggest that it was honor rather than loyalty that served as the warrior's chief ethical guide. Any loss of face, including that incurred by a lord's poor performance or any slight or offense that might cause shame and stain his honor, was intolerable to the warrior and demanded reprisal or revenge.

This warrior society's preoccupation with honor was accompanied by the belief that warriors possessed a fundamental right of self-redress (*jiriki kyūsai*) and that such self-redress, which permitted reprisal for even the most trifling offense, was part of what Sengoku writers called "the manly way" (*otokodō*). But the exercise of self-redress by a vassal not only might go against the loyalty he owed his daimyo, it might also threaten the very order the daimyo was trying to maintain in his domain. Not surprisingly, therefore, the daimyo took steps to restrain their vassals from pursuing self-redress. Chief among these steps was the inclusion in their house codes of articles—known as *kenka ryō-seibai*, or articles "dealing with both/all parties to a fight" (henceforth referred to as simply as *kenka* articles)—that threatened punishment, without regard for who might be right or wrong, of any vassals who entered into a dispute or fight.

A classic example of a *kenka* article can be found in the house code of the Imagawa: "If any warriors [i.e., vassals] engage in fighting, both parties will be executed regardless of who may be right or wrong."[7] Not all daimyo prescribed such severe punishment for fighting as execution, but all *kenka* articles were military enactments designed to demonstrate the daimyo's authority to summarily mete out punishment to their vassals without any reference to such principles as reasonableness (*dōri*) and justice, which had been fundamental guides to warrior law from the time of the Jōei Code in the Kamakura period.

### THE YŪKI HOUSE CODE[8]

The authoritarianism of Sengoku law is clearly observed in the following articles from the house code of the Yūki family of Shimōsa Province in the Kantō. Articles 3 and 4

---

7. Satō et al., eds., *Chūsei hōsei shiryō shū*, vol. 3, p. 117.

8. The formal name of the Yūki Code is Yūki-shi shin-hatto. It contains 104 articles and 2 supplementary (*tsuika*) articles.

are, for example, typical *kenka* laws (although the revocation of family names is not a typical form of punishment found in the house codes as a whole). Strict authoritarianism also informs article 22, prescribing execution for disloyal vassals and their families; article 23, disallowing vassal marriages without the Yūki's permission; and article 72, prohibiting vassals from "making plans" without first consulting the Yūki daimyo.

The articles dealing with warriors setting out for battle (articles 26, 67, and 68) appear to be efforts by the Yūki to break the habit of their vassals, typical of warriors from earliest times, of fighting one against one. One of the notable developments in Sengoku warfare was the gathering of warriors (as officers) and peasant soldiers (as "men") into disciplined armies whose success did not allow the kind of one-against-one fighting tactics and individual heroics so common in pre-Sengoku battling.

Article 3. If a fight (*kenka*) or quarrel should arise, for whatever reason, and the participants should call upon relatives and associates to come together with them and form bands, those who form those bands will be punished without regard for the reason or reasons that provoked the fight or dispute. Be attentive to this. . . .

Article 22. Hereafter, those who are disloyal to the Yūki will be executed along with their families. They will also have their names revoked and their lands confiscated and assigned to others. . . .

Article 23. Henceforth, there will be no marriages without Yūki permission. This applies not only to marriages with people from other houses but also from one's own house. . . .

Article 26. Wherever it may be to, you must not gallop forth as a lone rider without receiving orders from the Yūki. But when summoned by the Yūki, you must not be tardy. If you have business that must be attended to or are sick, send a replacement. . . .

Article 28. No matter how distinguished his family background may be in terms of loyalty to the Yūki, a person who is indiscreet and neglects his duty as a warrior will have his family name revoked and his lands confiscated. . . . No matter how loyal his family has been, a person who is disloyal will be punished without leniency. . . .

Article 51. In a dispute between a parent and child, the child will be considered to have acted without justification. . . . But if a parent alienates his oldest son and heir and replaces him with a younger son and, in the process, is himself disloyal and induces the younger son to be disloyal too, then the parent is in the wrong. . . .

Article 53. No matter how many times a child may serve the Yūki loyally while both his parents are alive, if he should die the parents are not to interfere. The successor to his family will be decided from here by the Yūki. . . .

Article 65. There is a great deal of talking these days. You must not speak badly of people of this house or other houses while on the verandah of the Yūki fort. Slander among men of the Yūki is also strictly forbidden. . . .

Article 66. The warrior who works land worth five *kan* will report to camp wearing armor and helmet. He will be provided with an outfitted horse. The warrior possessing land worth ten *kan* will report to camp with a suit of armor and a horse. Warriors with land worth fifteen *kan* or more will report to camp with retainers.

Article 67. To gallop forth heedlessly and without thought because you hear the sound of the conch shell from the main fort that signals taking to the field is quite unpardonable. If the shell sounds, you should go to a village and quickly dispatch some underling or servant to the main fort and have him inquire into where you should go. Only then should you gallop forth. . . .

Article 68. No matter what the emergency, you should not dash off to a battle-field without your armor. Regardless of how brave and prompt you may be, you should not ride out as a lone rider. Wait, form a unit, and then proceed to the battlefield.

Article 69. To undertake surveillance without orders is to act like someone not involved in a battle. In leaving your force to undertake surveillance, you are not acting loyally, no matter what you achieve. . . .

Article 72. Men of the horse units (*umamawari*)[9] should obviously not join an outside group, nor should they join a different group within the Yūki house. No matter how well they may perform, it will not be acceptable and they will lose face. The horse units should always act in conjunction with ten or twenty other riders and not mingle with other groups.

Article 73. Even though it may be for my [the Yūki daimyo's] benefit, vassals are not to make plans without informing me. . . .

[Satō et al., eds., *Chūsei hōsei shiryō shū*, vol. 3, pp. 229–246; PV]

## PRECEPTS OF THE WARRIOR HOUSES

The house precepts (*kakun*) are documents—sometimes referred to as "testaments"— that were written by the heads or patriarchs of houses as guides for the deportment, behavior, and cultural (including religious) training of younger family members of both present and future generations. The idea for such precepts was originally received from China, probably during the seventh century. In the eighth century, Kibi no Makibi (693–775), a high-ranking official and leading scholar of the Nara court who had studied in China, wrote a treatise on a famous set of Chinese precepts

---

9. *Umamawari* were mounted horse guards whose duty was to protect the daimyo.

entitled "Family Instructions for the Yan Clan" (*Yan-shi jiaxun*); and during the Heian period, a number of courtiers wrote precepts for their families. The best known of the Heian *kakun* is Fujiwara no Morosuke's "The Testament of Lord Kujō" (*Kujō-dono go-ikai*).

The first two sets of warrior precepts came from the brush of Hōjō Shigetoki (1198–1261), younger brother of Yasutoki who served as Kyoto or Rokuhara deputy (Rokuhara *tandai*)[10] for the Kamakura shogunate and, later, as "cosigner" (*rensho*) or cochairman of the shogunate's Council of State.[11] Shigetoki wrote his first *kakun* sometime between 1237 and 1247, during his term as Rokuhara deputy. Often called the "Letter to Nagatoki," it was prepared for the edification and training of his son Nagatoki (1230–1264), who was preparing to succeed his father in the Kyoto deputyship.

Comprising a preamble and forty-three precepts, the Letter to Nagatoki is primarily a collection of practical advice on how Nagatoki should comport himself and how he should deal with others, including social inferiors, both while he was deputy and afterward.

1. Fear the Buddhas, the Gods, your feudal lord, and your father . . . act with imperturbable courage . . . [and] never be considered a coward . . . constantly train in bow and arrow . . . try to be charming; when facing others, see to it that they come to think well of you. . . .

3. However profitable an undertaking might be, desist from it, though the gain be huge, if your reputation is at stake; stick to your respectability. . . .

5. When otherwise well-behaving retainers or foot-soldiers commit some minor fault, calm down and let them off with a scolding, but do not be so strict as to punish them.

6. Never think big of yourself. You should always consider, "What do others think of the things I do?" Deliberately take a low posture. Be polite even to persons of no consequence. . . .

12. Never drink *sake*, even a single jar, alone. . . .

22. Let no person of discernment—not even a servant—ever see you with loosened topknot or in your underwear. . . .

[Steenstrup, *Hōjō Shigetoki*, pp. 143–151; PV]

---

10. There were two *tandai* or deputies, and they were known as Rokuhara deputies because their offices were located in the Rokuhara section of southeastern Kyoto. The deputies were the shogunate's representatives in Kyoto.

11. The *rensho* (literally, "cosigner") served with the shogunal regent as cochairman of the Council of State and ranked just below the regent in the shogunate's hierarchy of offices.

## HOUSE PRECEPTS IN THE SENGOKU AGE

One of the most striking features of Hōjō Shigetoki's letters, especially when compared to most of the warrior house precepts of the Sengoku age, is the paucity of references to military matters. The Letter to Nagatoki contains several precepts that refer to horses (although not in regard to how they should be used in battle), another that encourages Nagatoki to be courageous and "constantly train in bow and arrow" (precept 1), and still another that cautions him not to let his "short sword get rusty" (precept 30). Otherwise, the Nagatoki letter says nothing about military or martial behavior. And another letter, which is more than twice the length of Nagatoki's, is totally silent on these matters.

The Sengoku house precepts, on the other hand, are full of martial references, as we can see, for example, in these precepts from the "Ninety-Nine Article Testament" (*Iken kyū-jū-kyū-ka-jō*) of Takeda Nobushige, younger brother of the famous Sengoku daimyo Takeda Shingen (1521–1573):

> 2. You must not show the slightest cowardice on the battlefield.
> 4. You must devote yourself to military training and to the cultivation of a martial spirit.
> 39. Do not neglect to keep your weapons prepared.
> 44. When you are victorious in battle, do not hesitate [and allow the enemy to recoup]. Attack him again.

Although Nobushige's testament deals with many other matters, including etiquette, learning, and moral cultivation, many of its precepts concern the art of war and the proper conduct of a warrior.

The Sengoku age was, of course, a time of constant conflict, and hence we should not be surprised to find the authors of house precepts preoccupied with military matters. Such matters, as we have seen, are also the main focus of the Sengoku house codes, especially in regard to the relationship between the lord (the Sengoku daimyo) and his vassals. There is, however, a significant difference between how the house codes and the house precepts approach the lord-vassal relationship. Whereas the daimyo in their house codes, as noted, seek to assert their authority by summarily demanding that vassals be obedient and loyal, the authors of the house precepts (some of whom were daimyo) attempt to promote and sustain vassal loyalty primarily through persuasion. The principal form of persuasion advocated by the precepts is strong leadership. Thus a number of Sengoku house precepts devote much of their attention to instructing daimyo and other warrior chiefs how to behave as great leaders, especially wartime leaders, who will inspire their vassals to brave—and loyal—deeds in their service.

The testament of Asakura Sōteki, son of the daimyo of Echizen province and a leading battle commander of his family, is probably the richest source of precepts aimed at promoting great leadership. Here are some of the precepts:

3. When it comes to military matters, the commander must never say that anything is impossible. He will reveal his inner weakness.

9. When fighting a major battle or managing a difficult retreat, the commander's warriors will test him by observing his conduct with particular care. The commander must not show the slightest weakness at these times, and should not speak.

10. Call the warrior a dog, call him a beast: winning is his business.

53. For a person who aspires to be a commander, it is essential to earn a reputation as a man of bow and arrow inferior to none.

[Hanawa, ed., *Zoku zoku gunsho ruijū*, vol. 10, pp. 1–9; PV]

## "SEVENTEEN-ARTICLE TESTAMENT OF ASAKURA TOSHIKAGE" (*ASAKURA TOSHIKAGE JŪ-SHICHI-KA-JŌ*)

Asakura Toshikage was a leading vassal of the Shiba, a collateral family of the Ashikaga that held constable appointments to several provinces. Taking advantage of a great succession dispute that fractured the Shiba in the mid-fifteenth century and plunged it into the turmoil of the Ōnin War, the Asakura under Toshikage seized control of one of the Shiba provinces, Echizen. Appointed the new constable of Echizen by the shogunate in 1471, Toshikage became one of the first Sengoku daimyo and the founder of a family dynasty that ruled Echizen for a century.

Toshikage's testament, which contains seventeen precepts (in imitation, perhaps, of the seventeen articles of Prince Shōtoku's constitution), is often considered to be a house code. In content, however, it is much more like a set of house precepts. In the first two precepts, Toshikage presents one of the earliest and most forceful assertions that, in the Sengoku age, warriors should be judged more on ability than status. Yet, although he thus places ability ahead of status, Toshikage seems to be ambivalent when choosing between ability and loyalty. In precept 9, for example, he says that those warriors "who are unskilled and lack ability, but are steadfast in spirit [that is, are loyal], deserve special attention." But the most distinguishing characteristic of Toshikage's testament is its overall rationality. The highlighting of ability in the first two articles is itself an example of this, as is the advice to heirs and followers in precept 4 that they should not covet famous—and expensive—weapons. A sword worth a thousand *hiki*, he observes, is no match for a hundred spears worth one hundred *hiki* each.

Most impressive of all from the standpoint of rationality is Toshikage's criticism of the commander who, in his preparation for and conduct of battle, wastes time worrying about auspicious days and favorable directions (precept 13). Other records of the Sengoku age attest that many if not most commanders did, in fact, waste much of their time worrying about such things as auspicious days and favorable directions.

Some Sengoku daimyo even hired special advisers, called *"gunpai* men" because they carried a fanlike object called a *gunpai*,[12] whose jobs included making decisions about days and directions, judging the workings of the yin and the yang, and consulting the *Classic of Changes (Yijing)*.

1. In the Asakura domain you must not appoint people on the basis of seniority. They should be chosen for ability and loyalty.

2. You must not assign people without ability to lands or positions just because they have served the Asakura family for generations.

3. Even though the country may be at peace, station spies in domains far and near and always keep abreast of conditions in them.

4. You should not covet famous swords and dirks. The reason for this, to use an example, is that a single sword worth one thousand *hiki* cannot win out against a force of a hundred men supplied with spears costing one hundred *hiki* each. . . .

5. We should not eagerly invite troops of the four schools of *sarugaku*[13] down from Kyoto for the pleasure of viewing them. With the money saved, we could select talented people from our domain, send them to Kyoto for dance training, and take pleasure in them ever after.

6. There will be no performances of *nō* at night within the fort precincts.

7. There will be no dispatching of agents to Date and Shirakawa for fine horses, falcons, and the like on the grounds that they are for the use of samurai. . . .

8. At the time of the first attendance of the year, all who are in the service of the domains, beginning with those bearing the Asakura surname, should wear coats made of wadded cotton; and all coats, without exception, should bear the Asakura crest. If some, claiming consideration of status, should wear elegant clothing, lesser samurai of the domain will be reluctant to attend those occasions that are given to show and display. If these lesser samurai, falsely citing illness, should fail to appear for a year or two, the number of samurai attending upon the Asakura will decrease to a small number.

9. Among the men who serve the Asakura house: those fellows who are unskilled and lack ability but are steadfast in spirit deserve special attention. But this does not apply to those who, although of splendid appearance and manner, are weak-spirited. . . .

10. If you treat one who has neglected his duty and one who has served faithfully the same way, how can you expect the one who has served faithfully to maintain his spirit?

---

12. The *gunpai* were also sometimes carried by daimyo and other chiefs as symbols of command in battle. Today, *gunpai* are wielded by the referees in sumō matches.

13. Sarugaku is a theatrical form from which nō is derived. As used here, *sarugaku* may mean nō.

11. Make every effort not to employ *rōnin* and similar types from other provinces as secretaries.

12. No one skilled in an art, whether clergy or lay person, should be sent to another domain. However, a person who relies solely on his ability and neglects duty is of no use.

13. It is extremely regrettable if a commander, when fighting a battle that can be won or laying siege to a castle that can be taken, should change his time schedule after choosing an auspicious day and considering which directions are good and which are bad. But if a commander, disregarding auspicious days and favorable directions, assesses in detail the realities of the military situation, lays detailed plans for attacking, responds flexibly to circumstances as they present themselves, and maintains his basic strategy, he is sure to be victorious.

14. About three times each year you should direct three vassals, known for their ability and honesty, to travel around the domain and inquire into the views of the four classes of people. . . .

15. Other than the Asakura fort at Ichijōnotani, no other fortifications are to be constructed in the domain. All major vassals, without exception, are to move to Ichijōnotani.

16. When traveling around to visit shrines and temples or markets, stop your horse occasionally and offer some praise for an unusual place or express a few words of sympathy for one that is run down.

17. When you receive direct reports, you should not permit the slightest discrepancy in regard to truth or falsehood. If you hear that some functionary is seeking to enrich himself, you should firmly impose suitable punishment.

[Satō et al., eds., *Chūsei hōsei shiryō shō*, vol. 3, pp. 339–343; PV]

*Chapter 57*

## THE REGIME OF THE UNIFIERS

Midway into the sixteenth century, the traditional Japanese state was in crisis and approaching collapse. Its structure had been shaken to the foundations by decades of social upheaval. The two main pillars of its edifice of authority, the imperial institution and the shogunate, had been undermined and weakened, apparently beyond repair. The tide of *gekokujō*, the overthrow of superiors by subordinates, seemed to be irresistible. By the end of the century, however, that tide had been reversed, and a new order had emerged.

One of the architects of Japan's political and social reconstruction, Toyotomi Hideyoshi (1537–1598), stressed in a document included in this chapter that for many years before his advent, "the country was divided, the polity disturbed, civility abandoned, and the realm unresponsive to imperial rule." He was presumptuous to take sole credit for the country's unification, as his predecessor, Oda Nobunaga (1534–1582), had cleared the ground for it, but his descriptive phrases certainly express the historical truth. Not for nothing is the period between 1467 and 1568 called Sengoku, "the country at war." The nation broke up into innumerable fragments, each of them a small-scale polity. At every level, society was divided. Great warlords, called *daimyō*, fought over provincial domains; petty barons (*kokujin*) contended not only with one another but also with the daimyo for territory; the rural gentry (*jizamurai*) resisted being submerged from the top or washed away from the bottom; and farmers defended the newly gained independence of their villages by forming leagues (*ikki*) to protect their interests against their supposed betters. Country folk violently pressed their demands on townspeople, and religious institutions maintained military forces and engaged in attacks on secular lords or on one another.

Conditions being so, great determination, tactical skill, and strategic vision — not to speak of the military wherewithal — were required on the part of a leader who set out to pacify the country and stabilize society. Oda Nobunaga, the daimyo of Owari and Mino, demonstrated this ambition and showed that he had the capacity to pursue those goals.

By 1567, a seal bearing the device *tenka fubu*, "the realm subjected to the military," started appearing on documents issued by him. In Confucian terms, the word *tenka* signified humankind living under the moral aegis of Heaven. In conventional sixteenth-century Japanese, two meanings of that word were current: the nominal Japanese empire and, in a more limited geographical sense, the region of the capital city (i.e., Kyoto and the Kinai area), the heartland of Japan. Nobunaga later appropriated this term for the realm that he built and governed, a polity he identified with himself.

This provincial warlord attained national prominence by embracing the cause of the political fugitive Ashikaga Yoshiaki and marching on Kyoto, where he installed his protégé as shogun in the autumn of 1568. From the beginning, the relationship between the two was uneasy. As far as he was concerned, however, there was no doubt that he, the man of power, took precedence over Shogun Yoshiaki, who was only nominally the pillar of the military (*buke no tōryō*). Not only did Nobunaga preserve his independence, but he also presumed to dictate rules of behavior to the shogun. Nobunaga was to be the boss and Yoshiaki merely the figurehead in their unequal condominium. This time, in March 1573, Nobunaga decided that their partnership had outlived its usefulness and chased Yoshiaki into exile. Legally, the Ashikaga shogunate continued to exist until 1588, when Yoshiaki, a wanderer through the provinces, finally renounced his office. But in fact, the shogunate had been demolished in 1573.

Nobunaga sought to dominate the imperial court, too, but found Emperor Ōgimachi more difficult to intimidate than Shogun Yoshiaki. Until 1578, Nobunaga continued to accept imperial titles and ranks, rising to the position of minister of the right (*udaijin*), the third highest office in the court hierarchy. That year, however, he resigned his imperial appointments, stating that the pacification of the country demanded his full attention. In 1582, when he conquered the great eastern domain of the Takeda, Nobunaga appeared to be well on his way to achieving that goal. On his return from that campaign to Azuchi Castle, in May of that year, the court therefore decided to send him an embassy and offer him "any rank at all" in recognition of his latest triumph. Nobunaga arrived in Kyoto on June 19, 1582, on his way to a campaign against the great western domain of the Mōri. Two days later, he was killed there by a treacherous vassal, Akechi Mitsuhide. The court's proposal was thus left unanswered and the question of Nobunaga's preferred type of rulership unresolved.

Both Japanese and Jesuit sources contain ample evidence of Nobunaga's disdain for traditional religious forms and institutions. The most persistently invoked example of his sacrilegious destructiveness is the sack of the Enryakuji in 1571. That temple of the Tendai sect traced its origins to the year 785 and was the very symbol of orthodox Buddhism's entrenched power. Not surprisingly, its destruction was one of the most notorious acts of Nobunaga's violent career. In this regard, Nobunaga outdid himself by far on a number of other occasions when he took the field against combative adherents of the Honganji; he butchered them by the tens of thousands.

The principle that religion must be kept under state control was only one part of the legacy bequeathed by Nobunaga to his successor, Hideyoshi, and to the third of the great unifiers, Tokugawa Ieyasu (1543–1616). Some of Hideyoshi's most famous national policies—the transfers of daimyo from one domain to another, the demolition of provincial forts, the land survey, and even the sword hunt—were in fact initiated on a provincial or even regional scale in Nobunaga's realm. Hideyoshi's career owed its start to Nobunaga in more senses than one.

Hideyoshi's origins are obscure. After ascending to de facto power over Japan, he tried to exalt his pedigree literally to the skies, by describing his conception as a miraculous one brought about by the wheel of the sun. He is known to have used five family names, none properly his own. The first, Kinoshita, probably did not belong to his father, who was most likely too lowly to have a family name; instead, it appears to have been borrowed by Hideyoshi from his wife's genealogy. The fifth, Toyotomi, means "Bountiful Minister" and is self-descriptive; it was commissioned by Hideyoshi from the imperial court, which created the name of a new "aristocratic" house for the parvenu after his appointment as imperial regent (*kanpaku*) in 1585. Unlike Nobunaga, whose father was a daimyo of some significance (though the Oda were, astonishingly enough, of priestly stock), Hideyoshi had no traceable provenance at all. Legitimizing himself and his regime was therefore a problem that he appreciated keenly, and he resolved it ingeniously. Unlike Nobunaga, who refused to be entangled in the designs of the shogunate or the court, Hideyoshi avidly sought access to the imperial institution, the most hallowed if mummified vessel of authority in Japan. In the event, he found the ideal way to make himself the emperor's master and snatch away whatever prerogatives the court had left. The upstart appropriated the cultural capital of the elite. He had himself appointed to offices for which only members of the "Nine Ministerial Families" were qualified, insinuated himself by a forced adoption into the "Regency" lineage, translated his military liege men into the imperial aristocracy—and Kyoto was his oyster. In the process, he managed to revivify the imperial order of government. By holding its offices, he infused it with his actual power. The title of *kanpaku*—for a long time meaningless except in the court's inner circle—became synonymous with national public authority under Hideyoshi.

For all that dignity and splendor, we must not forget that Hideyoshi began his career under Nobunaga as a menial attendant. He rose in Nobunaga's service to the status of a daimyo and the function of a general charged with conducting important campaigns. After Nobunaga's violent death in 1582, Hideyoshi avenged his lord by destroying his assassin, Akechi Mitsuhide, in battle near Kyoto. Having seized the main chance, he established himself as the lead player on the central stage of Nobunaga's realm, and he confirmed his role as Nobunaga's heir by ordering a funeral for the fallen hegemon to be held with great pomp and circumstance later that year. In 1583, Hideyoshi destroyed those of Oda's paladins who resisted what they considered his unjustifiable assumption of power, in particular the daimyo of Echizen, Shibata Katsuie, and Nobunaga's son, Oda Nobutaka. Hideyoshi marched from one victory to another until he was stopped by Tokugawa Ieyasu in the inconclusive Komaki-Nagakute campaign of 1584. In January of the next year, the two reached an accommodation, and Hideyoshi's march of conquest resumed. In 1585, he subjected the island of Shikoku to the realm of unification; in 1587, he subdued Kyushu; in the summer of 1590, he and a great army of his vassal daimyo destroyed the last great independent power of the Kantō region, the Hōjō of Odawara, and extended the realm across the core area of eastern Japan.

There followed the last act of the drama of unification—the pacification of the vast provinces Dewa and Mutsu, Japan's Far North. Uprisings broke out in the northern provinces as soon as Hideyoshi's occupation army was withdrawn toward the end of 1590. According to one daimyo's plea for help to Hideyoshi, "all the samurai and peasants in the entire district hate the Kyoto rule," which was depriving them of their accustomed freedoms. By the autumn of 1591, however, the local leagues (*ikki*) had been wiped out with the assistance of another intervention force. Japan was unified. It was time to plan external exploits on the Asian mainland.

Hideyoshi's mission in invading the mainland, he stated, was to spread Japanese culture to China. For Korea, the country in between, his pretensions had tragic consequences. Hideyoshi's armies invaded that country in 1592 and devastated it all the way to the Yalu and Tumen rivers. But by the spring of the following year, they had been chased back south by the Chinese, stalemated, and forced to take up a garrison existence in a string of fortresses along the southern edge of the peninsula. In 1597, Hideyoshi decided to take the offensive again. Again, his armies ravaged the countryside; again, they were forced to withdraw to a string of forts along the sea; again, Hideyoshi stubbornly kept them there, refusing to admit failure until he died on September 18, 1598. His Five Great Elders, the executors of his heritage, brought the Japanese troops back from the earth they had scorched. Hideyoshi's attack on Korea—the tragic overseas export of his drive to mobilize and dominate the daimyo of Japan—proved to be the climacteric of this man of power.

Hideyoshi died imploring the grandees and the chief administrators of his state "again and again" to safeguard the interests of his five-year-old son, Hideyori, and to ensure his succession. Two years later, in 1600, the greatest of the Five Elders, Tokugawa Ieyasu, wrested the hegemony for himself. In 1603 he gave form to the new order in Japan by founding the Tokugawa shogunate. Hideyori had been reduced to the status of one of many daimyo, but he still occupied what was considered Japan's most formidable fortress, the castle his father had erected in Osaka.

In 1615, however, Ieyasu stormed Osaka Castle. Hideyori died in its defense, and the house of Toyotomi did not survive the fall of its mighty citadel. In one sense, however, strong traces of Hideyoshi's heritage did survive, as the foundations of the Tokugawa peace, a stable edifice that lasted for two and a half centuries, were built from the blueprint of his—and, more distantly, Nobunaga's—policies.

## ODA NOBUNAGA

### *THE ASSAULT ON MOUNT HIEI AND THE BLESSINGS OF NOBUNAGA*

As this extract from *The Chronicle of Lord Nobunaga* (*Shinchō-Kō ki*) seeks to demonstrate, Nobunaga's assault on the Enryakuji was not so much a wanton act of sacrilege as retaliation against a military adversary. The temple had permitted the strategic position it occupied on Mount Hiei between Kyoto and Lake Biwa to be used by the armies of the daimyo Asakura Yoshikage and Azai Nagamasa, enemies who had fallen on Nobunaga's rear and forced him to abandon a campaign in the area of Osaka in 1570. Sakamoto, the Enryakuji's rich municipality on Lake Biwa, became one of their bases, and they were given succor by the monks when Nobunaga counterattacked. In short, Nobunaga had ample justification when he took his revenge on the Enryakuji in September 1571.

The author of *The Chronicle of Lord Nobunaga* (*Shinchō-Kō ki*), Nobunaga's old vassal Ōta Gyūichi (1527–after 1610), went on to serve Hideyoshi in important administrative capacities and after Hideyoshi's death entered the service of his son Hideyori.

Ōta and other sixteenth- and seventeenth-century writers frequently refer to Tentō, the Way of Heaven, in seeking to explain history. Their notion of Tentō conveys the sense of a governing natural order that is impersonal yet exerts a moral force, guiding the endeavors of the virtuous to success while ensuring the downfall of the wicked. The Jesuit missionaries found the term to be related to their own concept of Heavenly Providence and used it as a synonym for God while stressing that pagans meant something else by it.

(5) On the 12th of the Ninth Month [September 30, 1571], Nobunaga attacked Mount Hiei. . . .

. . . Mount Hiei was the guardian of the imperial capital. Nevertheless, the monks who lived on the mountain and at its foot cared nothing for penances, ascetic exercises, and religious customs and felt no shame at the derision of the realm. Heedless of the Way of Heaven (Tentō) and its terrors, they gave themselves over to lewdness, ate fish and fowl, and became habituated to bribes in gold or silver. They took the side of the Azai and Asakura, and while they did as they pleased, Nobunaga restrained himself and let them be for the moment, because he was wont to adjust himself to the times and the circumstances. To Nobunaga's regret, he had to withdraw his army. In order to dispel his resentment, this day, the 12th of the Ninth Month, he invested Mount Hiei. Surging round in swarms, Nobunaga's troops in a flash set fire to a multitude of holy Buddhas, shrines, monks' quarters, and sūtra scrolls; they spared nothing, from the Central Hall and the Twenty-One Shrines of the Mountain King on down. How miserable it was to see it all reduced to ashes! At the foot of the mountain, men and women, young and old ran about panic-stricken. In feverish haste, barefooted, they all fled up Mount Hachiōji, seeking refuge in the precincts of the inner Hie Shrine. Soldiers shouting battle cries advanced up the mountain from all sides. One by one they cut off the heads of monks and laymen, children, wise men and holy men alike. They presented the heads to Lord Nobunaga, saying: "Here is an exalted prelate, a princely abbot, a learned doctor, all the men of renown at the top of Mount Hiei." Moreover, they captured countless beautiful women and young boys and led them before Nobunaga. "We don't care about the evil monks," they shrieked, "but spare us!" Nobunaga, however, absolutely refused to reprieve them. One by one, they had their heads chopped off, a scene horrible to behold. . . .

(6) The imperial palace had long gone to ruin and nothing was left of its former splendor. Thinking that it would bring blessings, Nobunaga had in a previous year appointed Nichijō Shōnin and Murai Sadakatsu as superintendents of a project to repair it. At length, after three years' work, the Shishiiden, the Seiryōden, the Naishidokoro, the Shōyōsha, and various other palace quarters were all finished. Lord Nobunaga moreover thought of a plan that would unfailingly provide for the imperial court's income for all times to come. He gave out a loan in rice to the townsmen of Kyoto and ordered that the interest be presented to the court every month. At the same time, Nobunaga also brought the maintenance of impoverished nobles in order, amply securing their family succession. The satisfaction of all the people of the realm could not have been greater. . . .

[Ōta, *Shinchō-Kō ki*, bk. 4, sec. 5–6, pp. 126–129; JPL]

## NOBUNAGA IN ECHIZEN

### LETTERS FROM THE BATTLEGROUND

Nobunaga shows his true face in these letters to Murai Sadakatsu, an old and valued vassal whom he had made governor of Kyoto (*tenka shoshidai*) upon Shogun Yoshiaki's expulsion from the capital. Rather than a military campaign, the conquest of Echizen is made to appear like a ruthless head-hunting expedition.

Your letter of the 15th arrived this morning, the 17th, and I have read it.

[1]. News about this front: I arrived at camp in Tsuruga on the 14th inst. and on the 15th distributed the troops for the advance, some by the Kinome approach and others along the seaside or by other routes. But first I attacked and destroyed two forts on the seaside, Sasanoo and Suizu, took many heads, and amused myself thoroughly.

[2]. . . . In the town of Fuchū itself we took as many as one and a half thousand heads, and in the environs we took in all two thousand more. . . . In short, I pacified the province in two days. The town of Fuchū is nothing but corpses, with not a clear spot anywhere around; I'd like to show it to you! Today I shall search every mountain and every valley, and I shall kill them all.

. . .

Your letter of the 20th arrived in Fuchū today, the 22nd, and I have read it.

[1]. After smashing the enemy defenses at Kinome and Hachibuse and decapitating Saikōji, Shimotsuma Izumi Hokkyō, and Wakabayashi as well as Toyohara Saihōin, Asakura Saburō and their ilk, I divided the troops into four contingents and had them search every mountain and every valley without exception, cutting heads. On the 17th, more than two thousand heads were delivered; seventy or eighty were taken alive, so their heads were cut off. On the 18th, five or six hundred heads at a time arrived from various places, quite impossible to tell how many in all. . . . Shibata Shuri no Suke and Korezumi Gorōzaemon no Jō attacked and destroyed the stronghold held by Asakura Yozō. They killed more than six hundred men of standing; more than a hundred were taken alive, so their heads were cut off. On the 20th I sent [Sakuma] Kuemon no Jō, Maeda Matazaemon, as well as men of the Horse Guards to a mountain called Hinagatake, where they cut down more than a thousand. More than a hundred were taken alive, so their heads, too, were chopped off. . . .

[Okuno, *Zōtei Oda Nobunaga monjo no kenkyū*, vol. 2,
pp. 61–64, no. 533, pp. 66–70, no. 535; JSAE]

## NOBUNAGA IN AZUCHI

### THE PROUD TOWER

At the end of 1575, the year of his conquest of Echizen, Nobunaga made a show of turning over the affairs of the house of Oda to his eldest son, Nobutada, whom he installed as the daimyo of Mino and Owari Provinces in Gifu Castle, his own headquarters since 1567. At the beginning of 1576, Nobunaga ordered the construction of a new fortress for himself at Azuchi in Ōmi Province, and he moved to the site in March. These actions underlined his claim to being more than a regional ruler. Azuchi Castle was to be the visible sign of his supremacy as the lord of the Tenka, the realm subjected by his military might and governed by virtue of his prowess.

Although Nobunaga is lord of Miyako and of the Tenka (for that is how the Japanese call the monarchy of Japan), he nonetheless resides ordinarily in the kingdom of Ōmi, in the town of Azuchiyama, which is located fourteen leagues from Miyako. . . . There Nobunaga built a new town [with] a fortress—a town that is now the most imposing sight in Japan, excelling all others in its site, its pleasant air, the nobility of its residents, and the opulence of its buildings. . . .

At its foot was built the township for the common people [and artisans] to reside, adorned by very broad and straight streets. By now it will have five or six thousand inhabitants. Elsewhere at the foot of the mountain, in a place separated by an arm of the lake from the township, Nobunaga ordered the lords and noblemen to build their houses. As all were eager to comply with his wishes, the lords of the kingdoms subject to him at once built very noble and rich edifices there. All their houses are encircled by graceful, high stone walls, topped by parapets, in such a manner that each in itself is a fine fortress. Thus the houses clamber up the mountain, surrounding the highest of the three hills on all sides.

[Coelho, in *Cartas*, pt. 2, ff. 35v–36; also Fróis, *Historia*, vol. 3, pp. 256–258; JSAE]

## THE FREE MARKET OF AZUCHI

To ensure that the town he called into being below his castle would prosper, Nobunaga made it a free market (*rakuichi*), safeguarding it from restraints on trade exercised by guilds—monopolistic organizations of merchants and transporters—and granting its residents various immunities. To be sure, the patent of privileges he conferred on Azuchi was not the first such decree issued by a daimyo. As early as 1549, the Rokkaku, masters of southern Ōmi until Nobunaga destroyed them in 1568, had proclaimed a free market at Ishidera beneath their mountain fort Kannonji, just a few kilometers from Azuchi. In 1567 Nobunaga himself had declared Kanō, the settlement below newly conquered Gifu Castle, to be a free marketplace, and the next year he also specified that the place was free from guilds (*rakuza*). But no similar decree issued previously was as detailed, comprehensive, or innovative as the following "Regulations."

## Regulations for the Township Below Mount Azuchi

[1]. This place is decreed to be a free market. Accordingly, it is immune from all guilds (*za*), duties (*yoku*), and taxes (*buji*).

[2]. The Upper Highway is closed to traveling merchants. Whether heading in the direction of the capital city or away from it, they shall take lodging in this township. However: In the case of goods being forwarded, this will be left up to the consignor.

[3]. Immunity from construction duties. However: A contribution shall be made when His Lordship leaves on a campaign, must be absent in Kyoto, or is otherwise called away unavoidably.

[4]. Immunity from remount duties.

[5]. Regarding fires: In case of arson, the householder will not be held liable. In case of an accidental fire, he is to be banished, on completion of an inquiry. However: Depending on the circumstances, the degree of severity may vary.

[6]. Regarding criminal offenders: Even if a tenant or someone living in the same house commits a crime, if the householder was unaware of the particulars and not in a position to intervene, then the householder will not be blamed for it. The perpetrator shall be brought to justice for his offense on completion of an inquiry.

[7]. Regarding the purchase of various goods: Even if they are stolen goods, the purchaser will not be held culpable if he was unaware of that. But if a judicial confrontation is thereupon held with the thief, then the purloined goods shall be returned [to their rightful owner] in accordance with the ancient law.

[8]. Even if a cancellation of debts (*tobusei*) is put into effect throughout the subject provinces, this place shall be exempted.

[9]. Those who come from other provinces or other localities to settle in this place shall be treated the same as long-standing residents. No objections will be raised to their being the retainers of anyone whatsoever. No one claiming to be an enfeoffed recipient will be permitted to levy extraordinary imposts on them.

[10]. Fights and quarrels, as well as coercion to stand surety for debtors from the same province or the same locality, forced sales, forced purchases, forced rents, and the like are all prohibited.

[11]. Regarding debt collectors and other intruders into the township: The matter shall be reported to Fukutomi Heizaemon no Jō and Kimura Jirōzaemon no Jō, an inquiry conducted, and the appropriate measures ordered.

[12]. Those living in the residential quarters, whether they be in service or artisans, are exempted from duties ordinarily imposed on each household. Add: Except for those residents who are under His Lordship's orders and receive his stipend, as well as artisans in his employ.

[13]. Regarding horse traders: The horse trade of this province shall be conducted entirely in this place.

Any violator of the above articles shall be swiftly brought to justice for his grave offense.

*Tenshō 5.VI.*[1]                    BLACK SEAL *[Nobunaga; on reverse]*

[Okuno, *Zōtei Oda Nobunaga monjo no kenkyū*, vol. 2, pp. 300–304, no. 722; JSAE]

---

1. The Sixth Month of Tenshō corresponds to June 16 to July 15, 1577, according to the Julian calendar.

# TOYOTOMI HIDEYOSHI

## *DOMESTIC POLICIES*

### THE DISARMAMENT OF THE POPULACE

It is no accident that the following two documents were promulgated on the same date, which corresponds to August 29, 1588, in the Gregorian calendar. They both address the same fundamental aims of the unifiers' regime: to deprive the common populace of the means to armed resistance and to guarantee that arms bearing became the exclusive preserve and privilege of the samurai class. The target of the "Decree" is the maritime population of fishermen and traders who occasionally metamorphosed into pirates. The "Articles" are directed at farmers. Commonly known as Hideyoshi's Sword Hunt Edict, this is arguably the most famous document issued on his orders. To be sure, the sword hunt was not his original idea. A well-known Japanese precedent is the sweep for weapons conducted in Echizen by Shibata Katsuie in 1576, the year after Nobunaga assigned him to govern that province. Under Hideyoshi, however, the disarmament of the populace was to be carried out as a nationwide policy.

The unstated purport of the "Articles" is that the samurai are to have a monopoly on the means to exercise violence. In exchange, the populace is promised peace and prosperity, security and happiness. Hideyoshi has the temerity to make the additional offer of rewards in the life to come: The "useless instruments" of mayhem collected from the farmers are to be put to a pious use, their scrap metal earning them a meritorious bond with the Buddha whose colossal image is to be erected in a temple complex being built in southeast Kyoto. (The foundation stone of the Kyoto Daibutsu project had been laid not quite three months earlier, on Tenshō 16.V.15, or June 8, 1588.) The Confucian vision of a well-ordered realm is also invoked by Hideyoshi, who does not hesitate to put himself on a level with Yao, one of the greatest culture heroes in all of Chinese myth.

Note that *seibai*, a word often seen in the documents of the unifiers' regime and translated here as "to punish," frequently but not always means "to put to death" and is indeed defined in the authoritative Japanese-Portuguese dictionary published in Nagasaki by the Jesuit mission in 1603 only as "to kill or to execute" and "to kill in the exercise of justice." Ambiguity is the spice of sixteenth-century Japanese documentary style, but there is little doubt what is meant to happen, for instance, to unregenerate pirates under the following "Decree."

## Decree

[1]. His Highness has banned pirate vessels from the seas of the various provinces with the utmost rigor. Nevertheless, sea robbers have recently been reported on Itsuki Island, between the provinces of Bingo and Iyo. Their activity has come to the attention of His Highness, who considers it miscreant.

[2]. The sea captains and fishermen of the provinces and the seashores, all those who go in ships to the sea, shall immediately be investigated by the local land steward or administrative deputy [of the lord's demesne; *daikan*] and made to subscribe jointly to written oaths, forswearing the slightest piratical activity henceforward. The provincial lords shall collect these pledges and forward them to His Highness.

[3]. From now on and hereafter, should the enfeoffed recipient of a domain prove so negligent that pirates are found [under his jurisdiction], the pirates shall be punished (*seibai*) and the fief containing the miscreant locality confiscated with its goods and chattels in all perpetuity.

These articles shall be enforced rigorously. Any transgressor shall swiftly be brought to justice for his offense.

*Tenshō 16.VII. 8*                    VERMILION SEAL [*Hideyoshi*]

## Articles

[1]. The farmers of the various provinces are strictly forbidden by His Highness to have swords, daggers, bows, spears, firearms, or other kinds of weapons in their possession. The reason is as follows: Those who stockpile useless implements, evade the payment of rents and dues, plot to band together in leagues (*ikki*), and commit criminal actions against the recipients of fiefs must of course be punished. As a consequence, however, the fields lie fallow and the fief goes to waste. Hence the provincial lords, recipients of fiefs, and administrative deputies shall collect all such weapons and forward them to His Highness.

[2]. The swords and daggers thus to be collected will not go to waste. They are to be made into nails and cramp irons for the Great Buddha building project recently begun by His Highness. Consequently, the farmers will benefit not only in this world but even unto the world to come.

[3]. As long as farmers have agricultural tools and devote themselves exclusively to tilling the fields, they and the generations of their children and children's children will prosper. It is out of compassion with the farmers that His Highness has issued these orders. This is truly the foundation of the country's security and the people's happiness. It is said that in deepest antiquity, when Yao, the lord of Tang, pacified all under Heaven, treasured swords and sharp blades were turned into farm tools, but that was in a foreign land. In our empire there can surely be no precedent. Let all who enforce these orders fully realize their purport and farmers put all their energies into agriculture and sericulture.

The aforesaid implements shall be collected and forwarded immediately.

*Tenshō 16.VII. 8*                    VERMILION SEAL [*Hideyoshi*]

[*Dai Nihon komonjo, iewake* 11: *Kobayakawa-ke monjo*, vol. 1, pp. 478–481, nos. 502–503; JSAE]

## RESTRICTIONS ON CHANGE OF STATUS

This decree is the unification regime's fundamental determination regarding social status. It fixes the positions of four orders of society—samurai, farmers, merchants, and artisans—and may therefore be considered the blueprint of the Tokugawa period's rigid class system. The samurai class is defined broadly to include everyone in military service down to miscellaneous attendants or varlets (*komono*) and men engaged in rough, nonmilitary duties (*arashiko*). Membership in that class is frozen as of the date of the brief expedition that Hideyoshi undertook to Mutsu, Japan's northernmost province, after defeating the powerful Hōjō family of Odawara, that is, conquering the Kantō region, in the summer of 1590. That expedition turned into a triumphal progress as the northern barons bent before Hideyoshi, submitted to his rearrangement of their territorial holdings, sent hostages to Kyoto, and began implementing the land survey, the sword hunt, and his other policies in the domains with which he had invested the lucky ones among them (a significant number of them were dispossessed). With the conquest of the Kantō and the subjugation of the north, the unification of Japan could be considered complete. Actually, revolts started breaking out throughout the north country, particularly in those areas confiscated by Hideyoshi, within weeks of his departure from the scene. A huge army was still engaged in their suppression even as this decree was issued. Nevertheless, 1590 remains the epochal date. With the formal integration of the eastern and northern provinces into his realm in August and September that year, the decrees ordained by Hideyoshi became the law throughout Japan.

Not only are samurai restrained from leaving their status group, they are prevented by a draconian rule from changing affiliations within it. The vassal bands of the daimyo houses are kept closed and intact. Farmers are tied to their fields. Townspeople are confined to their townships. Social mobility is virtually negated. Collective responsibility is the mechanism used to coerce the populace into compliance.

## Decree

[1]. Servicemen (*hōkōnin*), samurai, grooms, varlets, on down to ancillaries on fatigue duty, all those who may have newly turned themselves into townsmen or farmers since His Highness's expedition to Mutsu Province in the seventh month of last year shall be rooted out by the residents of the township or village concerned. None shall be permitted to remain. Should any be harbored in secret, the entire township or village shall be punished.

[2]. Any country farmer who abandons his fields and takes up either trade (*akinai*) or paid employment (*chin shigoto*, i.e., artisanship) shall of course be punished and, with him, also his community. Add: Those who neither are in service nor farm the fields shall be rigorously rooted out by the administrative

deputies or the recipients of fiefs and shall not be permitted to remain. Should any recipient fail to take the proper measures in this regard, the locality in question shall be confiscated from him for his negligence. Should townspeople or farmers secretly harbor such persons, the entire village and the entire township shall be considered miscreant.

[*Dai Nihon komonjo, iewake* 11: *Kobayakawa-ke monjo*, vol. 1,
pp. 481–482, no. 504; JSAE]

## THE LAWS AND REGULATIONS OF THE TAIKŌ

In February 1592 Hideyoshi passed on the office of imperial regent (*kanpaku*) to his nephew and adopted son Hidetsugu, seeking to demonstrate that the ruling power over Japan would thereafter be held by successive members of the Toyotomi family. In August 1593, however, Hideyoshi's natural son Hideyori was born, and Hideyoshi faced the quandary of how to regulate the succession in his favor. In the event, he decided to extirpate Hidetsugu's progeny. Hidetsugu himself was forced to commit suicide on August 20, 1595, and more than thirty members of his family were executed the day before these "Regulations" and their "Supplement" were issued. The post of *kanpaku* was left open, but Hideyoshi continued to rule under the title of Taikō, which applies to an imperial regent who has handed over his charge to his son.

Immediately upon Hidetsugu's suicide, Hideyoshi exacted oaths of loyalty to Hideyori and adherence to "the laws and regulations of the Taikō" from the leading daimyo. The most notable of these were Maeda Toshiie, appointed Hideyori's guardian; Ukita Hideie, who was to assist Maeda in that all-important task; Tokugawa Ieyasu, entrusted with enforcing Hideyoshi's laws and regulations in the east; Mōri Terumoto and Kobayakawa Takakage (d. 1597), charged with keeping the peace in the west; and Uesugi Kagekatsu, the daimyo of the great Echigo domain on the coast of the Sea of Japan. The issuance of these documents over their names in Hideyoshi's behalf signals the emergence of the group popularly known as the Five Great Elders (*gotairō*), a council that acted as the top executive organ of Hideyoshi's regime toward the end of his life.

First and foremost, these decrees seek to deprive the daimyo of the capability to form coalitions; even the freedom to select a marriage partner is taken from them. Hideyoshi is to be the ultimate arbiter of quarrels among them, and they are admonished regarding various aspects of their private behavior. But the daimyo and their samurai retainers are not the only social category being addressed. Indeed, comprehensiveness is these documents' most conspicuous and significant feature. They inform the imperial aristocracy that the pursuit of the arts is to be their principal mission in life, tell priests to be faithful to their calling, and remind the farmers that 67 percent is the basic tax rate on the harvest under Hideyoshi. The Taikō's regime lays down the law to all without exception, prefiguring the Tokugawa shogunate's arrogation of power to dictate to all orders of society.

## His Highness's Regulations

[1]. Daimyo shall contract marriages only upon obtaining His Highness's permission and in conformity with his directions.

[2]. It is strictly forbidden by His Highness for daimyo great or small to enter into solemn agreements, exchange written compacts, and the like.

[3]. In case of an accidental fight or quarrel, forbearance shall be exercised and reason made to prevail.

[4]. Should anyone claim that a false accusation has been made against him, both parties shall be summoned and a strict investigation conducted by His Highness.

[5]. Those privileged by His Highness to ride in a litter are Ieyasu, Toshiie, Kagekatsu, Terumoto, and Takakage, as well as members of the old imperial aristocracy, high prelates, and ranking abbots. Apart from these, the young shall ride on horseback, even if they are daimyo. Those aged fifty or older will be permitted to ride in a palanquin if the distance is one league or more. Those who are sick will also be permitted the use of a palanquin during their illness.

Any transgressor of the above articles shall be swiftly brought to justice for his grave offense.

*Bunroku 4.VIII.3 (6 September 1595)*

## Supplement to His Highness's Regulations

[1]. Members of the imperial aristocracy and heads of imperial abbacies shall apply themselves to the pursuit of the Ways (*michi*) fostered by their respective houses and shall devote themselves wholeheartedly to serving the public authority (*kōgi*, i.e., Hideyoshi).

[2]. Buddhist temples and Shinto shrines shall observe their temple rules and shrine rules in accordance with precedent, shall keep their buildings in good repair, and shall never be remiss in their pursuit of learning and their devotion to religious practice.

[3]. In fiefs of the realm, dues shall be collected on the basis of an inspection of the harvest: two-thirds for the steward, one-third for the farmers. In all events, dispositions shall be taken that fields do not lie fallow.

[4]. In addition to his wife, one who is of low rank may keep one housemaid in his service. However: He may not set up a separate household. Even one of high rank is not permitted more than one or two concubines.

[*Dai Nihon komonjo, iewake 2: Asano-ke monjo*, pp. 477–480,
nos. 265–266; JSAE]

## THE KOREAN WAR

### LETTER TO THE KING OF KOREA

On Tenshō 18.XI.7 (December 3, 1590), some two months after returning to Kyoto from his expedition to subjugate the Kantō region and the northern provinces, Hideyoshi received there a Korean embassy that presented him with a letter of state congratulating him on having unified Japan. This was his response.

*Hideyoshi, the Imperial Regent of Japan, sends this letter to His Excellency the King of Korea.*

I read your epistle from afar with pleasure, opening and closing the scroll again and again to savor the aroma of your distinguished presence.

Now, then: This empire is composed of more than sixty provinces, but for years the country was divided, the polity disturbed, civility abandoned, and the realm unresponsive to imperial rule. Unable to stifle my indignation at this, I subjugated the rebels and struck down the bandits within the span of three or four years. As far away as foreign regions and distant islands, all is now in my grasp.

As I privately consider the facts of my background, I recognize it to be that of a rustic and unrefined minor retainer. Nevertheless: As I was about to be conceived, my dear mother dreamt that the wheel of the sun had entered her womb. The diviner declared, "As far as the sun shines, so will the brilliance of his rule extend. When he reaches his prime, the Eight Directions will be enlightened through his benevolence and the Four Seas replete with the glory of his name. How could anyone doubt this!" As a result of this miracle, anyone who turned against me was automatically crushed. Whomever I fought, I never failed to win; wherever I attacked, I never failed to conquer. Now that the realm has been thoroughly pacified, I caress and nourish the people, solacing the orphaned and the desolate. Hence my subjects live in plenty and the revenue produced by the land has increased ten-thousand-fold over the past. Since this empire originated, never has the imperial court seen such prosperity or the capital city such grandeur as now.

Man born on this earth, though he live to a ripe old age, will as a rule not reach a hundred years. Why should I rest, then, grumbling in frustration, where I am? Disregarding the distance of the sea and mountain reaches that lie in between, I shall in one fell swoop invade Great Ming. I have in mind to introduce Japanese customs and values to the four hundred and more provinces of that country and bestow upon it the benefits of imperial rule and culture for the coming hundred million years.

... When the day comes for my invasion of Great Ming and I lead my troops to the staging area, that will be the time to make our neighborly relations flourish all the more. I have no other desire but to spread my fame throughout the Three Countries, this and no more.

I have received your regional products as itemized. Stay healthy and take care.

*Tenshō 18.XI.*

*Hideyoshi*
*Imperial Regent of Japan*

[*Zoku zenrin kokuhō ki*, XXX, in *Zoku gunsho ruijū*, demivol. 1, fasc. 881, 404; JSAE]

## KEINEN: "KOREA DAY BY DAY"

Keinen (1534?–1611), the author of *Chōsen hinikki* ("Korea Day by Day"), was a priest of the True Pure Land sect in Usuki, a castle town in Kyushu. In the summer of 1597, he was ordered to accompany the daimyo of Usuki, Ōta Hida no Kami Kazuyoshi, to Korea as his personal chaplain and physician. Hida no Kami (or Lord Hishū, as he is called here) was one of the inspectors-general (*yokome bugyō*) of the Japanese field armies during Hideyoshi's second campaign in that country. Keinen was an innocent abroad in this company, an unwilling eyewitness aghast at what he saw.

The vast majority of the writers who produced the voluminous Japanese literature of Hideyoshi's invasion of Korea gloried in the war of aggression. Keinen is the striking exception. No trace of bombast is found in his record of "Korea Day by Day," which is instead a remarkable outpouring of human compassion from what the author called the arena of demonic violence and described through the metaphor of hell. Keinen's memoir is a conscious literary product, written in the time-honored form of a poetic diary (*uta nikki*).

The excerpt translated here deals with the three and a half weeks from the disembarkation of Japanese troops in Chŏlla Province, called here by its Japanese code name "Red Country" (Akaguni), to their receipt of orders to invade the "Blue Country" (Aoguni), that is, Ch'ŭngch'ŏng Province.

Eighth Month, 4th day (September 15, 1597). Everyone is trying to be the first off the ship; no one wants to lag behind. They fall over each other in trying to get at the plunder, to kill people. It is a sight I cannot bear to see.

| | |
|---|---|
| *toga mo naki* | A hubbub rises |
| *hito no zaihō* | as from roiling clouds and mist |
| *toran tote* | where they swarm about |
| *unka no gotoku* | in their rage for the plunder |
| *tachisawagu tei* | of innocent people's goods. |

VIII.5. They are burning the houses. As I watched them go up in smoke, I thought that my own existence was like this and was seized by sympathy.

| | |
|---|---|
| *Akaguni to* | The "Red Country" is |
| *iedomo yakete* | what they call it, but black is |
| *tatsu keburi* | the smoke that rises |
| *kuroku noboru wa* | from the burning houses |
| *homura to zo miru* | where you see flames flying high. |

VIII.6. The very fields and hillsides have been put to the fire, not to speak of the forts. People are put to the sword, or they are shackled with chains and bamboo tubes choking the neck. Parents sobbing for their children, children searching for their parents—never before have I seen such a pitiable sight.

| | |
|---|---|
| *no mo yama mo* | The hills are ablaze |
| *yakitate ni you* | with the cries of soldiers |
| *musha no koe* | intoxicated |
| *sanagara shura no* | with their pyrolatry— |
| *chimata narikeri* | the battleground of demons. |

VIII.18. We displace camp deeper into the interior. As I looked at the surroundings of the fortress at daybreak, I saw corpses numberless as grains of sand scattered along the roadsides. It was a sight I could not bear to see.

| | |
|---|---|
| *Nanmon no* | Leaving behind the |
| *shiro o tachiide* | fortress of Namwŏn, |
| *mite are wa* | I look about me, |
| *me mo aterarenu* | and I witness a sight that |
| *fuzei narikeri* | my eyes cannot bear to see. |

VIII. 19. This place, too, appears to have been built as a fort, but everyone has fled to the hills and the moors.

| | |
|---|---|
| *kyō wa mata* | Once again today |
| *shiranu tokoro no* | I lie down in a strange place |
| *akiie ni* | in an empty house |
| *hitoyo o akasu* | to spend the night in sadness |
| *koto oshi zo omou* | at the transience of it all. |

[Keinen, *Chōsen nichinichi ki*, in *Chōsen gakūhō*, 35:69–75; JSAE]

# BIBLIOGRAPHY

## TRADITIONAL CHINA

*Analects (Lunyu)*. In Ruan Yuan, *Shisan jing zhushu*, or Legge, *The Chinese Classics*, vol. 1.

*Anleji. See* Daochuo.

Ban Gu. *Hanshu*. BNB ed.

Ban Zhao. *Nüjie. See Nü sishu.*

*Beixi daquanji. See* Chen Chun.

Biot, Edouard. *Le Tcheou li (Rites des Tcheou)*. 2 vols. Paris: Imprimerie Nationale, 1851.

Bloom, Irene, ed. and trans. *Knowledge Painfully Acquired: The K'un chih chi by Lo Ch'in-shun*. New York: Columbia University Press, 1987.

*Bohu tong de lun*. Hanwei congshu ed. Shanghai: Hanfen lou, 1925.

*Book of Odes, The*. Ed. and trans. B. Karlgren. Stockholm: Museum of Far Eastern Antiquities, 1950.

Busch, Heinrich. "The Tung-lin Shu-yüan and Its Political and Philosophical Significance." *Monumenta Serica* 14 (1949–1955). Tokyo: SVD Research Institute, 1955.

*Cangshu. See* Li Zhi.

Carter, Thomas, and L. Carrington Goodrich. *The Invention of Printing in China and Its Spread Westward*. New York: Ronald Press, 1955.

*Chan men guishi*. Appended to biography of Baizhang. *Jingde chuandeng lu*. TD 51, no. 2076.

Chan, Wing-tsit, ed. and trans. *Instructions for Practical Living and Other Neo Confucian Writings by Wang Yang-ming*. New York: Columbia University Press, 1963.

——. *Reflections on Things at Hand: The Neo-Confucian Anthology Compiled by Chu Hsi and Lü Tsu-ch'ien*. New York: Columbia University Press, 1967.

——. *Source Book in Chinese Philosophy*. Princeton: Princeton University Press, 1963.

*Changli xiansheng wenji*. See Han Yu.

*Chanyuan qinggui*. See Zongze.

Chen Chung. *Beixi daquanji*. Xiyin xuan ed., 1840.

Cheng Duanli. *Chengshi richeng*. CSJC ed.

Cheng Yi. *Henan Chengshi wenji*. In *Er Cheng ji*. Beijing: Zhonghua shuju, 1981.

*Chengshi richeng*. See Cheng Duanli.

*Chunqiu fanlu yizheng*. See Dong Zhongshu.

*Dacheng zhiguan famen*. TD 46, no. 1924.

Daochuo. *Anleji*, in TD 47, no. 1958.

*Dixue*. See Fan Ziyu.

Dong Zhongshu. *Chunqiu fanlu yizheng*. With commentary by Lu Yu and preface by Wang Xianqian. 1914. Reprint. Taibei: Heluo tushu chubanshe, 1974.

Duyvendak, J. J. L., ed. and trans. *The Book of Lord Shang*. London: Probsthain, 1928.

Fan Zuyu. *Dixue*. SKQS ed.

*Fanwang jing*. TD 24, no. 1484.

*Fenshu*. See Li Zhi.

Giles, Herbert. *San-tzu ching*. 2d ed. rev. 1910. Reprint. Taibei: Literature House, 1964.

Goodrich, L. Carrington, and Chaoying Fang, eds. *Dictionary of Ming Biography, 1368–1644*. New York: Columbia University Press, 1976.

Graham, A. C., ed. and trans. *Chuang-tzu: The Seven Inner Chapters and Other Writings from the Book Chuang-tzu*. London: George Allen and Unwin, 1981. Excerpts reprinted here with the permission of the literary estate of A. C. Graham and of Dawn and Der Pao Graham.

*Great Learning (Daxue)*. *Liji*. SBBY ed. Legge, *The Chinese Classics*, vol. 1.

Gu Xiancheng. *Gu Duanwen gong yishu*. Guangxu 3 (1877). Reprint of Wanli zongzi Library edition.

*Guanzi*. GXJC ed. Shanghai: Commercial Press, 1934.

*Guizhai wenji*. See Ouyang Xuan.

Guo Xiang. *Commentary on Zhuangzi*. In *Nanhua zhenjing*, SBCK ed.

*Han Feizi*. SBCK ed.

*Hanshu*. See Ban Gu.

Hao Jing. *Hao wenzhong gong ji*. In *Qiankun zhengqi ji*, 1848 ed.

*Hao wenzhong gong ji*. See Hao Jing.

*Henan Chengshi wenji*. See Cheng Yi.

*Hongming ji*. TD 52, no. 2102.

*Hou Hanshu*. BNB ed.

*Hou Hanshu*. Beijing: Zhonghua shuju, 1966.

*Huainanzi*. Ed. D. C. Lau. Chinese University of Hong Kong, Institute of Chinese Studies, Ancient Chinese Text Concordance Series. Hong Kong: Commercial Press, 1992.

*Huang Ming zhishu*. 6 vols. Taibei: Chengwen, 1969.

Huang Zongxi. *Mingru xuean*. Wanyu wenku ed. Taibei: Commercial Press, 1965.

*Huangdi sijing jinzhu jinyi*. Chen Guying, ed. Taibei: Commerical Press, 1995.

*Huayan jing*. TD 10, no. 279.

*Huayan wujiao zhiguan*. TD 45, no. 1867.

Hucker, Charles O. *A Dictionary of Official Titles in Imperial China*. Stanford: Stanford

University Press, 1985.

Hurvitz, Leon. *Wei Shou: Treatise on Buddhism and Daoism.* Kyoto, 1956.

Jia Yi. *Xinshu.* 10 *juan.* SBCK ed.; also ZZMJ ed. Reprint of Wang Tingjian ed. Taibei, 1977.

*Jiu Tangshu.* BNB ed.

Johnson, Wallace, ed. and trans. *The T'ang Code,* Vol. 1. Princeton: Princeton University Press, 1979.

Knoblock, John, ed. and trans. *Xunzi: A Translation and Study of the Complete Works.* 3 vols. Stanford: Stanford University Press, 1988–1994.

Kurihara Keisuke. *Kōkyō.* Tokyo: Meiji shoin, 1986.

*Laozi.* SBBY ed.

*Laozi weizhi lilüe. See* Wang Bi.

Lau, D. C., trans. "Advice to My Sons," by Yen Chih-t'ui. *Renditions* 1 (1973): 94–98, and "Yen's Family Instructions." *Renditions* 33 (1990): 58–62.

——, ed. *A Concordance to the Huai-nan Tzu.* Chinese University of Hong Kong, Institute of Chinese Studies, Ancient Chinese Text Concordance Series. Hong Kong: Commercial Press, 1992.

——, ed. *A Concordance to the Lüshi chunqiu.* Chinese University of Hong Kong ICS Ancient Chinese Text Concordance Series. Hong Kong: Commercial Press, 1994.

Legge, James. *The Chinese Classics.* 5 vols. Oxford: Clarendon Press, 1893–1895. Reprint. Hong Kong: Hong Kong University Press, 1979.

——. *Li ki (Li-chi). Book of Rites.* 2 vols. New York: University Books, 1967. Reprint of Oxford 1885 Sacred Books of the East ed.

*Li Zhi. Cangshu.* Beijing: Zhonghua shuju, 1959.

——. *Fenshu.* Beijing: Zhonghua shuju, 1961.

*Liexian zhuan. See* Liu Xiang.

*Liji.* 20 *juan.* SBBY ed.

*Liji.* In Ruan Yuan, *Shisan jing zhushu.* Reprint. Taibei: Yiwen yinshu guan, 1958.

*Linchuan xiansheng wenji. See* Wang Anshi.

Liu Zongzhou. *Liuzi quanshu,* vol. 2, ed. Dai Lianzhang, Wu Guang, and Zhong Caijun. Taibei: Zhongyang yenjiu yuan, Zhongguo wenzhe yanjiusuo, 1996.

*Liuzi quanshu. See* Liu Zongzhou.

*Lotus Sūtra. See Miaofa lianhua jing;* Watson, Burton. *The Lotus Sūtra.*

Lu Jia. *Xinyu.* 1592 ed., collated by Fan Dachong. Reprint. ZZMJ ed. Taibei, 1977.

*Lunyu.* In Ruan Yuan, *Shisan jing zhushu;* Legge, *The Chinese Classics,* vol. 1.

Luo Qinshun. *Knowledge Painfully Acquired—The K'un-chih chi by Lo Ch'in-shun.* Ed. and trans. Irene Bloom. New York: Columbia University Press, 1976.

*Lü Family Community Compact. See Lüshi xiangyue.*

Lü Kun. *Shizheng lu.* In *Lüzi yishu.*

*Lüshi chunqiu jiao shi.* Ed. Chen Qiyou. Shanghai: Xuelin chubanshe, 1984.

Lynn, Richard John, ed. and trans. *The Classic of Changes—A New Translation of the I Ching as Interpreted by Wang Bi.* New York: Columbia University Press, 1994.

*Mawangdui Hanmu boshu.* Beijing: Wenwu chubanshe, 1980.

[The] *Mean (Zhongyong).* In Ruan Yuan, *Shisan jing zhushu,* or Legge, *The Chinese Classics,* vol. 1.

*Mean (Zhongyong). Liji,* SBBY ed.

*Mencius (Mengzi).* In Ruan Yuan, *Shisan jing zhushu,* or Legge, *The Chinese Classics,* vol. 2.

*Mengzi*. See Mencius.

*Miaofa lianhua jing* (Lotus Sūtra), *TD* 9, no. 262.

*Mingru xuean*. See Huang Zongxi.

*Mingzhao kaiguo wenxian*. N.d. Reprint. 4 vols. Taibei: Xuesheng shuju, 1966.

*Mozi jiangu*. ed. Sun Yirang. Shanghai: Zhonghua shuju, 1954.

*Mozi*. 16 *juan*. *SBBY* ed.

*Mozi*. *SBCK* ed.

*Myōhō-renge-kyō narabi ni kaiketsu*. Tokyo: Soka Gakkai, 1961.

*Nüjie*. See Ban Zhao.

*Nü lunyu*. See Song Ruozhao.

*Nü sishu*. 1854 Japanese ed. Preserved in the Naikaku Bunko, Tokyo.

Orlando, Raffaello. "A Study of Chinese Documents Concerning the Life of the Tantric Buddhist Patriarch Amoghavajra (A.D. 705–774)." Ph.D. diss., Princeton University, 1981.

Ouyang Xuan. *Guizhai wenji*. *SBCK* ed.

*Platform Sutra of the Sixth Patriarch*. Ed. and trans. Philip B. Yampolsky. New York: Columbia University Press, 1963.

*Platform Sūtra of the Sixth Patriarch*. From the photographic reproductions of the Dunhuang manuscript housed in the Stein Collection (S5475) at the British Museum. Section numbers as in the D. T. Suzuki ed.

Rickett, W. Allyn. *Guanzi*. Vol. 1. Princeton: Princeton University Press, 1985.

*Sanlun xuan yi*. TD 45, no. 1852.

Shang Yang. *The Book of Lord Shang*. Ed. and trans. J. J. L. Duyvendak. London: Probsthain, 1928.

———. *Shangzi*. *SBCK* ed.

*Shangshu dazhuan*. *SBCK* ed.

*Shangzi*. See Shang Yang.

Shao Yong. *Huangji jingshi shu*. *SBBY* ed.

*Shiji*. See Sima Qian.

*Shijing*. Xuesheng guoxue congshu ed. Shanghai: Commercial Press, 1926. *See also* Karlgren, *The Book of Odes*, and Legge, *The Chinese Classics*, vol. 4.

*Shisan jing zhushu*. Nan Chang fuxue ed. Reprint. Taibei: Yiwen yinshu guan, n.d.

*Shizheng lu*. See Lü Kun.

*Shujing*. "Jin teng," in Legge, *The Chinese Classics*, vol. 3.

*Shujing* (*Shangshu jinguwen zhusu*). GXJC ed. See also Legge, *The Chinese Classics*, vol. 3.

Sima Guang. *Zizhi tong jian*. 4 vols. Beijing: Zhonghua shuju, 1956.

———. *Wenguo wenzheng gong wenji*. *SBCK* ed.

Sima Qian. *Shiji*. BNB ed.

Song Lian et al., eds. *Yuan shi*. Beijing: Zhonghua shuju, 1976.

Song Ruozhao. *Nü Lunyu*. See *Nü sishu*.

*Song Yuan xuean*. Comp. Huang Zongxi and Quan Zuwang. Beijing: Zhonghua shuju, 1986.

*Songke xiaojing*. Tianjin: Tianjin shi guji shudian, 1987.

*Sunzi huijian*. Ed. Yang Bingan. Henan: Zhongzhou guji chubanshe, 1986.

Swann, Nancy Lee. *Pan Chao: Foremost Woman Scholar of China*. New York: Century, 1932.

*Taishang ganying pian.* DZ 834–839, no. 1167.

*Taishang Laojun jinglü.* DZ 562, no. 786.

Teng Ssu-yü. *Family Instructions for the Yen Clan,* by Yen Chih-t'ui. Leiden: Brill, 1968.

Tjan Tjoe Som, trans. *Po-hu t'ung: The Comprehensive Discussions in the White Tiger Hall.* Leiden: Brill, 1952.

Uno Seiichi. *Shōgaku.* Tokyo: Meiji shoin, 1965.

Wang Anshi. *Linchuan xiansheng wenji.* SBCK ed.

Wang Bi. *Laozi weizhi lilüe.* In *Wang Bi ji jiaoshi.* 2 vols. Ed. Lou Yulie. Beijing: Zhoughua shuju, 1980.

Wang Gen. *Mingru Wang Xinzhai xiansheng yiji.* Beijing, 1911.

Wang Yangming. *Wang Yangming quanji.* Shanghai: Datong 1935.

——. *Wang Yangming quanshu.* Taibei: Zhengzhong shuju, 1953.

*Wang Yangming quanji. See* Wang Yangming.

*Wang Yangming quanshu. See* Wang Yangming.

Watson, Burton, ed. and trans. *Chuang Tzu: Complete Writings.* New York: Columbia University Press, 1963.

——, trans. *Han Fei Tzu: Basic Writings.* New York: Columbia University Press, 1964.

——, ed. and trans. *The Lotus Sutra.* New York: Columbia University Press, 1993.

——, trans. *Mo Tzu: Basic Writings.* New York: Columbia University Press, 1963.

——, trans. *The Tso chuan: Selections from China's Oldest Narrative History.* New York: Columbia University Press, 1989.

Welch, Holmes, and Anna Seidel. *Facets of Taoism.* New Haven: Yale University Press, 1979.

*Wenguo wenzheng gong wenji. See* Sima Guang.

*Xiaoxue. See* Zhu Xi.

*Xinshu. See* Jia Yi.

*Xinyu. See* Lu Jia.

*Xunzi.* HYISIS, supplement 22. Reprint. Taipei: Chinese Materials and Research Aids Service Center, 1966.

*Xunzi. The Works of Hsüntze.* Ed. and trans. Homer H. Dubs. London: Probsthain, 1928.

Yan Zhitui. *Yanshi jiaxun jijie.* Shanghai: Guji chubanshe, 1980.

*Yangzheng yigui. See* Chen Hongmou.

*Yanshi jiaxun jijie. See* Yan Zhitui.

*Yantie lun.* SBCK ed.

*Yijing.* In Ruan Yuan, *Shisan jing zhushu.* Reprint. Taibei: Yiwen yinshu guan, 1955.

*Yinzhi wen guangyi.* Ed. Zhou Mengyan. Yangzhou cangjing yuan ed. 1881.

*Yiquan wenji. See* Shao Yong.

*Yuan [Guochao] wenlei.* Comp. Su Tianjue. SKQS ed.

*Yuan shi. See* Song Lian.

Zhang Zai. *Zhangzi quanshu.* SBBY ed.

*Zhangzi quanshu. See* Zhang Zai.

*Zhongyong. See* Mean.

*Zhongyong zhangju. See* Zhu Xi.

*Zhouyi benyi. See* Zhu Xi.

*Zhouyi lüeli.* In *Wang Biji jiaoshi.*

Zhu Xi. *Daxue zhangju.* In *Sishu jizhu,* ZZMJ ed.

——. *Zhongyong zhangju.* In *Sishu jizhu, Zhongguo zixue mingju jicheng* ed. Taibei, 1978.

——. Zhouyi benyi. 1177. Reprint. Taibei: Hualian, 1978.

——. Zhuzi daquan (Zhuzi wenji). SBBY ed.

——. Zhuzi quanshu. 1714 ed.

——. Zhuzi wenji. In Zhuzi daquan, SBBY ed.

——. Zhuzi yulei. Beijing: Zhonghua shuju, 1986.

——. Zhuzi yulei. Zhengzhong ed. Taibei, 1970.

Zhu Xi, ed. Xiaoxue. In bilingual Chinese/Japanese edition of Uno Seichi, ed. and trans., Shōgaku. Tokyo: Meiji shoin, 1965.

Zhuangzi. Chuang Tzu: Complete Writings. Ed. and trans. Burton Watson. New York: Columbia University Press, 1963.

Zhuangzi. HYISIS, supplement no. 20.

Zhuangzi. SBBY ed.

Zhuangzi. SBCK ed.

Zhuzi daquan. See Zhu Xi.

Zhuzi quanshu. See Zhu Xi.

Zhuzi wenji. See Zhu Xi.

Zhuzi yulei. See Zhu Xi.

Zizhi tongjian. See Sima Guang.

Zongze. Chanyuan qinggui. Trans. adapted from Bielefeldt, Dōgen's Manuals of Zen Meditation, pp. 175–187.

## TRADITIONAL KOREA

Beal, Samuel. Buddhist Records of the Western World. London: Truebner, 1884. Reprint, New York: Paragon, 1968.

Best, Jonathan W. "Tales of Three Paekche Monks Who Traveled Afar in Search of the Law." Harvard Journal of Asiatic Studies 51, no. 1 (1991): 139–197.

Buswell, Robert E., Jr. The Formation of Ch'an Ideology in China and Korea: The Vajrasamādhi-Sūtra—A Buddhist Apocryphon. Princeton: Princeton University Press, 1989.

——. The Korean Approach to Zen: The Collected Works of Chinul. Honolulu University of Hawaii Press, 1983.

Chan, Wing-tsit, trans. Reflections on Things at Hand: The Neo-Confucian Anthology Compiled by Chu Hsi and Lu Tsu-ch'ien. New York: Columbia University Press, 1967.

Chang, Garma C. C. The Buddhist Teaching of Totality: The Philosophy of Hwa Yen Buddhism. University Park: Pennsylvania State University Press, 1971.

Edgerton, Franklin. Buddhist Hybrid Sanskrit Dictionary. New Haven: Yale University Press, 1953.

Fung, Yu-lan. A History of Chinese Philosophy. Trans. Derk Bodde. Princeton: Princeton University Press, 1953.

Guenther, Herbert V. Philosophy and Psychology in the Abhidharma. Berkeley: Shambhala, 1976.

Hahm Pyong-Choon. The Korean Political Tradition and Law. Seoul Hollym, 1967.

Henthorn, William. Korea: The Mongol Invasions. Leiden: Brill, 1963.

Hurvitz, Leon. "Chih-i (538–597): An Introduction to the Life and Ideas of a Chinese Buddhist Monk." *Mélanges chinois et bouddhiques* 12 (1962).

——. *Scripture of the Lotus Blossom of the Fine Dharma*. New York: Columbia University Press, 1976.

Inaba Shōju. "On Chos-grub's Translation of the *Chieh-shen-mi-ching-shu*." In *Buddhist Thought and Asian Civilization: Essays in Honor of Herbert V. Guenther on His Sixtieth Birthday*, ed. Leslie S. Kawamura and Keith Scott, 105–113. Emeryville, Calif.: Dharma Publishing, 1977.

Jan, Yüan-hua. "Tsung-mi: His Analysis of Ch'an Buddhism." *T'oung Pao* 58 (1972): 1–50.

Karlgren, Bernhard. *The Book of Odes*. Stockholm: Museum of Far Eastern Antiquities, 1950.

——. "Legends and Cults in Ancient China," *Bulletin of the Museum of Far Eastern Antiquities* 18 (1946): 206–344.

Lai, Whalen. "*The Chan-ch'a ching*: Religion and Magic in Medieval China." In *Chinese Buddhist Apocrypha*, ed. Robert E. Buswell, Jr., 175–206. Honolulu: University of Hawaii Press, 1990.

Lau, D. C. *Lao Tzu: Tao Te Ching*. Harmondsworth: Penguin, 1963.

Lee, Ki-baik. *A New History of Korea*. Trans. Edward W. Wagner with Edward J. Shultz. Cambridge: Harvard University Press, 1984.

Lee, Peter H. et al., ed. *Sourcebook of Korean Civilization*. Vol. 1. New York: Columbia University Press, 1993.

Legge, James. *The Chinese Classics*. 5 vols. Hong Kong: Hong Kong University Press, 1960.

——. *Li Ki*. 2 vols. Sacred Books of the East 27–28. Oxford: Oxford University Press, 1885.

——. *Yi King*. Sacred Books of the East 16. Oxford: Clarendon Press, 1882.

Liao, W. K., trans. *Complete Works of Han Fei Tzu*. London: Probsthain, 1959.

MacDonell, Arthur A. *Brhad-devata*. Harvard Oriental Series 5–6. Cambridge: Harvard University Press, 1904–1905.

Makra, Mary Lelia, trans. *The Hsiao Ching*. New York: St. John's University Press, 1961.

Needham, Joseph et al. *The Hall of Heavenly Records: Korean Astronomical Instruments and Clocks, 1380–1780*. Cambridge: Cambridge University Press, 1986.

Schafer, Edward H. *The Golden Peaches of Samarkand: A Study of T'ang Exotics*. Berkeley: University of California Press, 1963.

Seo, Kyung-bo. *A Study of Korean Zen Buddhism Approached Through the Chodang-jip*. Seoul: Poryŏngak, 1973.

Takakusu, Junjirō. *Amitayurdhyana sūtra*. Sacred Books of the East 49. Oxford: Clarendon Press, 1894.

——. *The Essentials of Buddhist Philosophy*. Honolulu: University of Hawaii Press, 1949.

Thurman, Robert. *The Holy Teaching of Vimalakīrti*. University Park: University of Maryland Press, 1976.

Vaidya, P. L., ed. *Gandavyuha sutra*. Buddhist Sanskrit Texts No. 5. Darbhanga: Mithila Institute, 1960.

Waley, Arthur. *The Analects of Confucius*, London: Allen & Unwin, 1949.

——. *The Book of Songs*. London: Allen & Unwin, 1954.

———. *The Way and Its Power: A Study of the Tao Te Ching and Its Place in Chinese Thought.* New York: Grove Press, 1958.

Watson, Burton. *The Complete Works of Chuang Tzu.* New York: Columbia University Press, 1968.

———. *Records of the Grand Historian.* 2 vols. New York: Columbia University Press, 1961; rev. ed. in 3 vols., 1993.

Watters, Thomas. *On Yuan Chwang's Travels in India, 620–645* A.D. 2 vols. London: Royal Asiatic Society, 1904.

Wayman, Alex, and Hideko Wayman. *The Lion's Roar of Queen Śrīmālā.* New York: Columbia University Press, 1974.

Weinstein, Stanley. "A Biographical Study of Tz'u-en." *Monumenta Nipponica* 15 (1959–1960): 119–149.

Yampolsky, Philip B. *The Platform Sutra of the Sixth Patriarch.* New York: Columbia University Press, 1967.

Yi T'aejin. "The Socio-Economic Background of Neo-Confucianism in Korea of the Fifteenth and Sixteenth Centuries." *Seoul Journal of Korean Studies* 2 (1989): 39–63.

## TRADITIONAL JAPAN

Anesaki, Masaharu. *History of Japanese Religion; with Special Reference to the Social and Moral Life of the Nation.* London: Kegan Paul, Trench, and Trübner, 1930.

———. *Nichiren, the Buddhist Prophet.* Cambridge: Harvard University Press. 1916.

*Annen Oshō no kenkyū.* Comp. Eizan gakkai. Kyoto: Dōmeisha, 1979.

Aston, W. G., trans. *Nihongi. Chronicles of Japan from the Earliest Times to* A.D. 697. 2 vols. Transactions and Proceedings of the Japan Society, supp. 1. London: Kegan Paul, Trench and Trübner, 1896.

Brown, Delmer, and Ichirō Ishida. *The Future and the Past: A Translation and Study of the Gukanshō, an Interpretive History of Japan Written in 1219.* Berkeley: University of California Press, 1979.

Chamberlain, Basil Hall, trans. *Ko-ji-ki or Records of Ancient Matters.* Transactions of the Asiatic Society of Japan, supp. to vol. 10. Yokohama, 1882.

Coates, Havelock Harper, and Ryugaku Ishizuka. *Hōnen, the Buddhist Saint.* Kyoto: Chionin, 1925.

Coelho, Gaspar, SJ, to General SJ, Nagasaki, February 15, 1582. *Cartas qve os Padres e Irmãos da Companhia de Iesus escreuerão dos Reynos de Iapã & China.* Evora, 1598.

*Dai Nihon komonjo,* iewake 11: *Kobayakawa-ke monjo,* vol. 1. Ed. Tōkyō daigaku shiryō hensanjo. Tokyo: Tōkyō daigaku shuppankai, 1979.

De Visser, M. W. *Ancient Buddhism in Japan.* Paris: P. Geuthner, 1928–1935.

*Dengyō Daishi zenshū.* 4 vols. Tokyo: Tendai-shū shūten kankō-kai, 1912.

*Dengyō Daishi zenshū.* 5 vols. Tokyo: Sekai seiten kankō kyōkai, 1989.

Dobbins, James. *Jōdo Shinshū: Shin Buddhism in Medieval Japan.* Bloomington: Indiana University Press, 1989.

Dobson, W. A. C. H., trans. *Mencius.* Toronto: University of Toronto Press, 1963.

Dykstra, Yoshiko Kurata. "Jizō, the Most Merciful: Tales from *Jizō Bosatsu Reigenki.*" *Monumenta Nipponica* 33, no. 2 (1978): 179–200.

——, trans. *Miraculous Tales of the Lotus Sūtra from Ancient Japan: The* Dainihonkoku hokekyōkenki *of Priest Chingen*. Hirakata City, Japan: Intercultural Research Institute, 1983.

Eliot, Sir Charles. *Japanese Buddhism*. London: Arnold, 1935.

Fróis, Luís SJ. *Historia de Japam*. Ed. José Wicki, SJ. Vol. 3. Lisbon: Presidencia do conselho de ministros, secretaria de estado da cultura, direccao-geral do patrimonio cultural, Biblioteca nacional de Lisboa, 1976–1984.

Gotō Tanji and Kamada Kisaburō, eds. *Taiheiki*, 6 vols. Tokyo: Asahi shinbunsha, 1961.

Grapard, Allan G. "The Shinto of Yoshida Kanetomo." *Monumenta Nipponica* 47, no. 1 (Spring 1992): 27–58.

——, trans. "Yuiitsu Shintō Myōbō Yōshū." *Monumenta Nipponica* 47, no. 2 (Summer 1992): 137–161.

Grossberg, Kenneth, and Kanamoto Nobuhisa, trans. and eds. *The Laws of the Muromachi Bakufu*. Tokyo: Monumenta Nipponica, 1981.

Hakeda, Yoshito S., trans. *Kūkai: Major Works*. New York: Columbia University Press, 1972.

Hall, J. C. "Japanese Feudal Law (*Go Seibai Shikimoku*)." Transactions of the Asiatic Society of Japan, 1st ser., no. 34 (1907): 1–44.

Hanawa Hokiichi, comp. *Gunsho ruijū*. 21 vols. Tokyo: Nagai shoseki, 1928–1932.

——, comp. *Zoku gunsho ruijū*. 33 vols. Tokyo: Zoku gunsho ruijū kansei-kai, 1923–1928.

——, ed. *Zoku zoku gunsho ruijū*. Vol. 10. Tokyo: Kokusho kankō kai, 1907.

Hirota, Dennis, trans. *Tannishō: A Primer*. Kyoto: Ryūkoku University, 1982.

——. *Wind in the Pines*. Fremont, Calif.: Asian Humanities Press, 1995.

Holtom, D. C. *The National Faith of Japan*. New York: Dutton, 1938.

Ichikawa Hakugen, Iriye Yoshitaka, and Yanagida Seizan, eds. *Chūsei zenke no shisō*. Vol. 16 of *NST*. Tokyo: Iwanami shoten, 1972.

Ishii Kyōdō, ed. *Shōwa shinshū Hōnen Shōnin zenshū*. Kyoto: Heirakuji shoten, 1974.

*Jinnō shōtō-ki*. Dokushi yoron, Sanyō shiron. Yūhō-dō bunko. Tokyo: Yūhō-dō shoten, 1927.

Kamata Shigeo and Tanaka Hisao, eds. *Kamakura kyū Bukkyō*. Vol. 15 of *NST*. Tokyo: Iwanami shoten, 1971.

Keinen. *Chōsen nichinichi ki*. Comp. Naitō Shunpo. In *Chōsen gakuhō* 35 (May 1965): 55–167.

*Kissa yōjōki*. In Hanawa Hokiichi, comp., *Gunsho ruijū*. 21 vols. Tokyo: Nagai shoseki, 1928–1932.

*Kōbō Daishi zenshū*. Ed. Sofū sen'yō-kai. 5 vols. Tokyo: Yoshikawa kōbunkan and Kyoto: Rokudai shimpō-sha, 1910.

[Shinshū] *Kōgaku sōsho*. Ed. Mozumi Takami. 12 vols. Tokyo: Kō-bunko kankōkai, 1927–1931.

[Shintei zōho] *Kokushi taikei*. Ed. Kuroita Katsumi. 60 vols. Tokyo: Kokushi taikei kankō-kai, 1935.

Lau, D. C., trans. *Lao Tzu: Tao Te Ching*. Baltimore: Penguin Books, 1963.

Legge, James, trans. *The Chinese Classics*. 5 vols. Hong Kong: Hong Kong University Press, 1960.

McCullough, Helen Craig, trans. *The Tale of the Heike*. Stanford: Stanford University Press, 1988.

Moriyama Shōshin, ed. *Bunkashijō yori mitaru Kōbō Daishi den*. Tokyo: Buzanha shūmusho, 1931.

Morrell, Robert E. "Mirror for Women: Mujū Ichien's *Tsuma Kagami*." *Monumenta Nipponica* 35, no. 1 (Spring 1980): 45–75.

*Mouzi*. Ed. Bing-jin guan cong-shu. Wuxian, Suzhou: Privately published, 1885.

*Musō kokushi goroku*. TD 80, no. 2555.

Nagazumi Yasuaki and Shimada Isao, eds. *Hōgen monogatari*. Vol. 31 of *Nihon koten bungaku taikei*. Tokyo: Iwanami shoten, 1961.

Nishio Minoru. *Shōbōgenzō zuimonki*. In *Nihon koten bungaku taikei*, vol. 8. Tokyo: Iwanami shoten, 1968.

Ōhashi Shunnō et al., eds. *Ippen Shōnin goroku*. In *Hōnen—Ippen*, vol. 10. Tokyo: Iwanami shoten, 1971.

Okuno Takahiro. *Zōtei Oda Nobunaga monjo no kenkyū*, vol. 1. Tokyo: Yoshikawa kōbunkan, 1994.

Ōta Gyūichi. *Shinchō-Kō ki*. Ed. Okuno Takahiro and Iwasawa Yoshihiko, *Kadokawa bunko*, vol. 254. Tokyo: Kadokawa shoten, 1970.

Pandey, Rajyashree. "Women, Sexuality, and Enlightenment: *Kankyo no tomo*." *Monumenta Nipponica* 50, no. 3 (Fall 1995): 325–356.

Philippi, Donald L. *Norito: A New Translation of the Ancient Japanese Ritual Prayers*. Tokyo: Institute for Japanese Culture and Classics, Kokugakuin University, 1959.

Reischauer, Robert Karl. *Early Japanese History (ca. 40 B.C.–A.D. 1167)*, pt. A. Princeton: Princeton University Press, 1937.

Sansom, G. B. "The Imperial Edicts in the *Shoku-Nihongi*." Transactions of the Asiatic Society of Japan, 2d ser., vol. 1 (1923–1924): 5–39.

——. *Japan, a Short Cultural History*. London: Cresset, 1946.

Satō Shin'ichi et al., eds. *Chūsei hōsei shiryō shū*. Vols. 1 and 3. Tokyo: Iwanami shoten, 1955–1965.

*Shoku Nihongi*. In Saeki Ariyoshi, *Rikkokushi*. 12 vols. Tokyo: Asahi shimbun-sha, 1940.

Steenstrup, Carl. *Hōjō Shigetoki (1198–1261)*. Scandinavian Institute of Asian Studies monograph series, no. 41. London: Curzon Press, 1979.

*Tendai kuji hongi*. In Shintō taikei hensankai, ed., *Shintō taikei*, vol. 8. Tokyo: Seikosha, 1984.

Tsuji Zennosuke, ed. *Nihon bukkyō shi*. 10 vols. Tokyo: Iwanami shoten, 1944–1955.

Tsunoda Ryusaku, and L. Carrington Goodrich. *Japan in the Chinese Dynastic Histories*. Perkins Asiatic Monograph no. 2. South Pasadena, Calif.: P. D. and Ione Perkins, 1951.

Varley, Paul, trans. *A Chronicle of Gods and Sovereigns: Jinnō shōtōki of Kitabatake Chikafusa*. New York: Columbia University Press, 1980.

Varley, Paul, and Isao Kumakura, eds. *Tea in Japan: Essays on the History of Chanoyu*. Honolulu: University of Hawaii Press, 1989.

Watson, Burton, trans. *The Lotus Sūtra*. New York: Columbia University Press, 1993.

——. *Records of the Grand Historian*. 3 vols. New York: Columbia University Press, 1992.

——. *The Vimalakirti Sūtra*. New York: Columbia University Press, 1997.

Wilson, William R., trans. *Hōgen monogatari: Tale of the Disorder in Hōgen*. Tokyo: Sophia University Press, 1971.

Yampolsky, Philip. "The Essentials of Salvation." Master's thesis, Columbia University, 1948.

——, ed. *Selected Writings of Nichiren*. Trans. Burton Watson et al. New York: Columbia University Press, 1996.

*Zoku zenrin kokuhō ki*. In *Zoku gunsho ruijū*, vol. 30. Tokyo: Zoku gunsho ruijū kanseikai, 1925.

# INDEX